T0309324

TRAUMA TO TRIUMPH
RISING FROM THE ASHES OF
THE ASIAN FINANCIAL CRISIS

TRAUMA TO TRIUMPH
RISING FROM THE ASHES OF THE ASIAN FINANCIAL CRISIS

Edited by

Hoe Ee Khor
Diwa C. Guinigundo
Masahiro Kawai

 World Scientific

Published by

World Scientific Publishing Co. Pte. Ltd.

5 Toh Tuck Link, Singapore 596224

USA office: 27 Warren Street, Suite 401-402, Hackensack, NJ 07601

UK office: 57 Shelton Street, Covent Garden, London WC2H 9HE

and

ASEAN+3 Macroeconomic Research Office (AMRO)

10 Shenton Way

#15-08 MAS Building

Singapore 079117

British Library Cataloguing-in-Publication Data
A catalogue record for this book is available from the British Library.

TRAUMA TO TRIUMPH
Rising from the Ashes of the Asian Financial Crisis

Copyright © 2022 by ASEAN+3 Macroeconomic Research Office (AMRO)

ISBN 978-981-125-325-6 (hardcover)
ISBN 978-981-125-356-0 (ebook for institutions)
ISBN 978-981-125-357-7 (ebook for individuals)

For any available supplementary material, please visit
https://www.worldscientific.com/worldscibooks/10.1142/12753#t=suppl

"AMRO has produced at the 25th anniversary of the Asian Financial Crisis an invaluable text for students, policymakers and stakeholders how Asian economies not only weathered the storm, but also made the ASEAN+3 region more resilient and embedded in the global economy. Truly commended to read, learn and not forget."

Andrew Sheng
Chairman of George Town Institute of Open and Advanced Studies
and former Chairman, Hong Kong Securities and Futures Commission

"The COVID-19 pandemic has reminded us of the importance of enhancing resilience and preserving policy space that can be deployed swiftly. This book, published in the midst of the pandemic, shares the history and the lessons of past crises and showcases best practice economic policy responses in difficult times."

Changyong Rhee
Director of the Asia and Pacific Department, International Monetary Fund

"This book provides unique insights into the Asian Financial Crisis from the perspective of its major players, offering lessons on how a crisis prevention and management mechanism can become more effective, thus better shaping future crises responses."

Klaus Regling
Managing Director of European Stability Mechanism

"This book offers the first comprehensive insights of those who taught us the fundamental ambition that ASEAN+3 economies need to solidify regional cooperation and institutionalize their financial safety net system. We should continue to work together to prevent financial stability risks and address the challenges we face."

Masatsugu Asakawa
President of Asian Development Bank

"It gives me great pleasure in participating in this book as one of the interviewees who battled at the front lines during the Asian Financial Crisis. I hope our narratives will provide some first-hand references to help readers gain some insights that would be useful in preventing and dealing with another financial crisis."

Norman T. L. Chan
Former Chief Executive of the Hong Kong Monetary Authority,
Honorary Professor of The Chinese University of Hong Kong Business School

"The entire world was plunged into an unprecedented crisis after the COVID-19 pandemic, creating global financial market panic and a wave of economic recessions sweeping across the globe. This book opens our eyes and reminds us of how Asian economies tackled the past crises in an efficient and sustainable way."

Perry Warjiyo
Governor of Bank Indonesia

"The Asian Financial Crisis was a defining moment in the macroeconomic evolution of the ASEAN+3 region. It was a rude shock and the painful lessons learnt from that crisis have served the region well in overcoming subsequent episodes of volatility and turmoil. This book provides an insightful account of that journey — of how the region navigated the Asian Financial Crisis and moved on to build sound macroeconomic fundamentals, strong surveillance capabilities, and effective financial safety nets."

Ravi Menon
Managing Director, Monetary Authority of Singapore

"The current global crisis stemming from COVID-19 has served as a wake-up call to all of us to improve our global economic resilience. It is critically important to learn from the past to address the challenging situation at this juncture."

Sri Mulyani Indrawati
Minister of Finance, Indonesia

Foreword by AMRO Director

The publication of this book holds extra meaning as it coincides with our institution's 10-year anniversary. The publication also could not have been more timely, as today, the region is gradually emerging from the coronavirus disease (COVID-19) pandemic which has put regional economies to the most stringent test they have faced in the last 25 years.

Thanks to the lessons learnt from the Asian financial crisis, regional economies had built up policy buffers and reserves to protect against unforeseen external shocks. In addition to allowing greater exchange rate flexibility, they worked hard to balance their current accounts, strengthen foreign exchange reserves, and adopted prudent financial, fiscal, and monetary policies.

When the COVID-19 pandemic struck in 2020, economies in the region were able to move swiftly to prevent the spread of infection and mitigate the shock. Besides strict containment measures, extraordinary measures were deployed to support households, businesses, and the financial systems.

Equally important, the regional economies have been able to draw support from the strong regional financial cooperation framework. Since the Asian financial crisis, the ASEAN+3 economies, comprising the ten members of the Association of Southeast Asian Nations (Brunei Darussalam, Cambodia, Indonesia, Lao People's Democratic Republic, Malaysia, Myanmar, the Philippines, Singapore, Thailand, and Vietnam), plus China;

Hong Kong, China; Japan; and Korea, have been working closely to enhance their regional policy dialogue and financial safety net to secure macroeconomic and financial stability in the region.

The ASEAN+3 economies decided in 2000 to establish the Chiang Mai Initiative (CMI), a network of bilateral swaps among central banks to provide liquidity support to one another. In March 2010, following the global financial crisis, the CMI evolved into the Chiang Mai Initiative Multilateralisation (CMIM) Agreement. With a financing power of US$240 billion, the CMIM is aimed at enhancing the region's financial stability and reducing its vulnerability to short-term external shocks such as sudden reversal of capital flows.

AMRO was established the following year, in 2011, to conduct regional macroeconomic surveillance and support the implementation of the CMIM.

Over the past decade, AMRO has performed the duty of a capable and trusted advisor to our members with great pride and commitment. As the international organization responsible for macroeconomic surveillance across the ASEAN+3 economies, AMRO's mandate to contribute to the region's economic and financial growth and stability is even more critical in today's environment of great change and uncertainty.

We have adopted a blueprint in the form of our medium-term work plan, which clearly lays out our strategic priorities. In a rapidly-evolving environment, we have been able to nimbly put forward new priorities and initiatives to cater to our members' needs, while staying close to our vision and mandate. A solid foundation has been laid to support the growth in AMRO's role in the next ten years and beyond.

Today, as we enter into a post-pandemic world, it is timely for us to chronicle our unique experiences and policy responses since the Asian financial crisis, and shed important insights on how the ASEAN+3 members reinforced the fundamentals of their economies, allowing them to weather the COVID-19 pandemic from a position of strength.

The documentation of our shared history and lessons learnt will hopefully inspire current and future leaders and policymakers as they battle the COVID-19 pandemic and continue the journey of building our resilience to future shocks and challenges.

Putting this book together was a mammoth task, made more challenging by COVID-19 restrictions. I would like to acknowledge, with gratitude, the steering committee members, contributors, interviewees, member authorities, and in particular, the secretariat — there are so many of you that I am unable to name everyone — for delivering this history book, so rich in knowledge and wisdom.

Enjoy reading!

Toshinori Doi
AMRO Director

Foreword by 2021 ASEAN+3 Co-Chairs

The 1997 Asian financial crisis, then the most devastating economic crisis for the region, had necessitated the strengthening of policy dialogue, coordination, and collaboration on the financial, monetary, and fiscal issues of common interest amongst the ASEAN+3 countries. Today, as the region continues to face the coronavirus disease (COVID-19) pandemic, the ASEAN+ 3 financial cooperation continues to be of paramount importance to support the regional economies overcoming COVID-19 and preparing for the post pandemic era.

We therefore welcome the publication of this important book, which archives the experience of past crises and guides us to reflect on optimal ways to sail through the pandemic and strengthen the regional economy, as well as prepare for the post-pandemic era. The book examines in detail what happened during the Asian financial crisis, which caused significant decline of GDP in the crisis-affected economies and plunged millions of people into economic hardship. The crisis was also devastating, as it left deep scars in the labor markets and corporate sectors of many ASEAN+3 economies that enjoying robust economic growth for years before the crisis. How could the crisis have happened despite the strong economic performance? How did the contagion spread so rapidly to neighboring ASEAN+3 economies?

Although many books have been published to answer these questions, we found that this book is unique in that it has not only compiled in-depth analyses by renowned scholars on the subject, but also provides a "real-time" narrative of the crisis based on extensive oral interviews with policymakers who were present during the Asian financial crisis period. This approach, which combines the academic analyses with oral interviews of the key players, has allowed the book to present a more comprehensive, balanced, and compelling views on the causes of the crisis, the policy responses, and its long-lasting legacies in the region.

As the book explains well, the sudden and massive capital outflows during the Asian financial crisis had prompted the ASEAN+3 authorities to respond to the problem of the so-called "original sin" of currency and maturity mismatches, by launching the Asian Bond Markets Initiatives (ABMI) to develop local-currency bond markets and the Chiang Mai Initiative which established bilateral swap arrangements among the central banks to provide foreign exchange liquidity. In 2010, the latter initiative subsequently evolved into the Chiang Mai Initiative Multilateralisation (CMIM) Agreement, as the regional financial safety net that is supported by AMRO, the surveillance arm of the CMIM, established in 2011 to help the ASEAN+3 member authorities maintain macroeconomic and financial stability in the region.

The book also shows how the regional economies have become more resilient and dynamic since the Asian financial crisis, through sound macroeconomic policies as well as economic reforms in their financial and corporate systems. The regional authorities also strengthened their external balance by building up foreign reserves as buffers against capital flow volatility shocks. In retrospect, all the policy and institutional reforms that were implemented after the Asian financial crisis at the national and regional levels have strengthened the regional economies and allowed them to weather the global crisis in 2008 relatively well.

That said, while the global economy is still struggling with the COVID-19 pandemic, it is important for the authorities in the region to work together in responding to the challenges ahead in the post-pandemic new normal. In this regard, we are pleased that the ASEAN+3 Members agreed this year to explore new areas of cooperation, for instance, in the areas of infrastructure financing; macro-structural instruments; the strengthening of financial resilience against natural disasters; and enhancing policy coordination for technological advancement.

We congratulate AMRO again for the publication of this important book that brings together the collective knowledge and experience of Asian policymakers. Armed with the lessons of the past, we can move forward with greater confidence in managing shocks and averting another financial crisis.

Suraya Jaidin
Permanent Secretary
(Performance and Corporate)
Ministry of Finance and Economy
Brunei Darussalam

Tae Sik Yoon
Deputy Minister for International Affairs
Ministry of Economy and Finance
Republic of Korea

Noorrafidah Sulaiman
Deputy Managing Director
Brunei Darussalam Central Bank
Brunei Darussalam

Jwahong Min
Deputy Governor
Bank of Korea
Republic of Korea

Preface

The year 2021 marks the 10th anniversary of the ASEAN+3 Macroeconomic Research Office (AMRO) since its establishment in 2011 as the surveillance arm of the Chiang Mai Initiative Multilateralisation (CMIM), and this book was planned to commemorate the anniversary and recollect the origin of the organization and developments so far in historical context.

Furthermore, the publication of this book has been undertaken as a joint research collaboration between the AMRO and the Asian Development Bank (ADB) on regional financial cooperation. This book will serve as the first volume of the joint project, focusing on macroeconomic aspects of the Asian financial crisis (AFC) and its consequences in retrospect. The subsequent volume led by ADB will discuss the future of regional financial cooperation in ASEAN+3, focusing on policy issues to strengthen micro-structures of the region's financial system from a forward-looking perspective. In this regard, both volumes would complement each other to help readers grasp key developments and main challenges toward strengthening regional financial cooperation.

The major theme of this book is to take stock of the stories and insights on the causes and impacts of the AFC, which is closely related to the creation of AMRO. The AFC served as an awakening call to the ASEAN+3 region and presented an opportunity to rethink the path toward regional economic growth and integration, leading to the establishment and strengthening of the ASEAN+3 Regional Financial Cooperation framework, and the creation of AMRO. Although the crisis took place more than 20 years ago, its legacy lingers and affects today's economic and policy thinking.

This book brings together a large group of policymakers and academics. We interviewed 29 key policymakers and officials, who were in the frontline fighting the crisis, taking us back to the scenes and providing us with a feel of the challenges each economy faced during the crisis. The interviewees include current and former high-level officials from member authorities, especially those which were most affected by the crisis, and some former senior staff at the International Monetary Fund (IMF) and World Bank. In addition, three prominent players from the private sector were interviewed to provide an industry perspective. We also invited 20 renowned economists who have profound knowledge of their economies to share their analyses and views on the causes, impact, and policy response of the individual economies and the region and reflect on the lessons learned from the crisis. We are confident that policymakers, academics, and readers alike will find these in-depth recollections and studies valuable and thought-provoking.

The AFC highlighted the imperative for stronger regional financial cooperation in economic surveillance, policymaking, and crisis management. Since then, ASEAN+3 economies have taken a leap forward in deepening regional financial cooperation through strengthening the region's financial safety net, enhancing economic and financial surveillance, and fostering local currency bond market developments.

Today, despite the massive shock from the coronavirus disease (COVID-19) pandemic, the ASEAN+3 economies have remained resilient and are responding to the shock and bouncing back relatively unscathed, thanks to the enhanced financial soundness, sizable policy cushions, and elevated foreign exchange reserves, as well as prudent policymaking over the past two and a half decades. Looking ahead, the crisis calls for ASEAN+3 economies to "hold hands" not only to continue navigating the unprecedented global health crisis but also to build up a stronger and more resilient regional economy in the post-pandemic era.

Over the past decade, AMRO has strengthened its ability to act as an effective and trusted regional surveillance organization. By adopting a systematic surveillance framework, developing a suite of analytical tools, and enhancing the outreach to peers and markets, AMRO has gradually gained respect and credibility to its current position as the premier regional surveillance organization to safeguard ASEAN+3's macroeconomic and financial stability. That said, there are challenges ahead. Continuing efforts are needed to enhance its functional and sectoral surveillance, expand its scope of surveillance toward more long-term and structural issues, and build up its expertise on program design for future economic and financial crises.

The book is a product of the collaboration and great teamwork of many people over the past two years. The three co-editors of the book, Hoe Ee Khor, Diwa C. Guinigundo, and Masahiro Kawai, have provided guidance and insights throughout the book's production process as the Steering Committee members of the book project. AMRO's History Book Project Team, led by Jae Young Lee, initiated the work plan and coordinated among the Steering Committee, interviewees, chapter authors, historians, the publisher, and other stakeholders to ensure a smooth and timely publication. Two historians, Freddy Orchard and Guanie Lim, dedicated a significant amount of their time to conduct the interviews and to provide an interesting and balanced account of events during the AFC for each economy.

The discerning recollections by prominent policymakers and analysts brought us back to the AFC moment. This would not have been possible without the candid sharing of reflections and insights from policymakers and major players during the AFC. Here, we thank the following: from *Thailand*, M.R. Chatu Mongol Sonakul (former Governor of the Bank of Thailand (BOT)), Thanong Bidaya (former Minister of Finance), Bandid Nijathaworn (former Deputy Governor of BOT), and Supavud Saicheua (then Head of Economic Research at Phatra Securities); from *Indonesia*, Ginandjar Kartasasmita (former Coordinating Minister of the Economy, Finance and Industry), and J. Soedradjad Djiwandono (former Governor of Bank Indonesia); from *Malaysia*, Nor Shamsiah (Governor of Bank Negara Malaysia (BNM)), Ooi Sang Kuang (former Deputy Governor of BNM), and Lin See-Yan (former Deputy Governor of BNM); from *Korea*, Chang-yuel Lim (former Deputy Prime Minister and Minister of Finance and Economy), Duck-koo Chung (former Minister of Commerce, Industry and Energy), Yang-ho Byeon (former Director General of Financial Policy, Ministry of Finance and Economy) Kyung-wook Hur (former Vice Minister of Strategy and Finance), and Joong-Kyung Choi (former Minister of Knowledge Economy); from the *Philippines*, Amando M. Tetangco, Jr. (former Governor of Bangko Sentral ng Pilipinas (BSP)), Diwa C. Guinigundo (former Deputy Governor of BSP), Gil S. Beltran (former Undersecretary of Finance), and Roberto F. de Ocampo (former Secretary of Finance); from *Hong Kong*,

China, Norman T. L. Chan (former Chief Executive of Hong Kong Monetary Authority (HKMA)) and Andrew Sheng (former Deputy Chief Executive of HKMA); from *Singapore*, Teh Kok Peng (former Deputy Managing Director of Monetary Authority of Singapore (MAS)), Kishore Mahbubani (former Permanent Secretary at the Ministry of Foreign Affairs), and Hoe Ee Khor (former Assistant Managing Director of MAS and the current Chief Economist of AMRO); from *China*, Wei Benhua (former Deputy Administrator of the State Administration of Foreign Exchange and former Director of AMRO) and Zhu Guangyao (former Vice Minister of Finance); from *Japan*, Eisuke Sakakibara (former Vice Minister of Finance), Haruhiko Kuroda (former Vice Minister of Finance), and Hiroshi Watanabe (former Vice Minister of Finance); and from *international organizations and others*, Hubert Neiss (former Director of Asia-Pacific Department at the IMF), Dennis de Tray (former Country Director of Indonesia Resident Unit at the World Bank), Anoop Singh (former Director of Asia-Pacific Department at the IMF), and Jim Walker (former Chief Economist of Credit Lyonnais Securities Asia (CLSA)).

The book also presents thought-provoking new studies and insights into the causes, impacts, and lessons of the AFC for an economy and the region as a whole. We were fortunate to have outstanding researchers and specialists to join us in this project, and to whom we are grateful: Chalongphob Sussangkarn; Diwa C. Guinigundo; Haihong Gao; Hans Genberg; Iwan J. Azis; Jayant Menon; Joon-Ho Hahm; Hyeon-Wook Kim; Masahiro Kawai; Lam San Ling; Satoru Yamadera; Soyoung Kim; Hyungji Kim; Shinji Takagi; Sukudhew Singh; Wilhelmina C. Mañalac; Yoichi Nemoto; and Hoe Ee Khor, Beomhee Han, Jinho Choi, Kimi Xu Jiang, and Faith Pang Qiying.

Throughout the project, we have received great support and collaboration from many people and organizations. We would like to thank the ASEAN+3 authorities for their strong support and useful suggestions during the interim updates, and, in particular, the authorities of China, Japan, and Korea for their generous financial support for this project. We are grateful to the colleagues of Regional Cooperation and Integration Division, Economic Research and Regional Cooperation Department at the ADB for their excellent coordination and kind provision of the book cover design. The team at World Scientific, consisting of Chua Hong Koon, Yolande Koh, Nicole Ong, and Lai Ann, provided superb editing and publishing services. Last but not the least, AMRO's Senior Management team and staff deserve our special thanks for initiating and embracing this book project, and providing their guidance and support along the way.

AMRO History Book Project Team
Jae Young Lee
Jinho Choi
Kimi Xu Jiang
Zhenyu Yuan
Kazuo Kobayashi
Masato Matsutani
Jing Luo

Contents

Part I

Introduction and Overview

Chapter 1

Introduction and Overview[1]

**Hoe Ee Khor, Diwa C. Guinigundo, Masahiro Kawai,
and Kimi Xu Jiang**

"A crisis is an opportunity riding the dangerous wind."
— Chinese proverb

Purpose and Methodology of This Volume

The Asian financial crisis (AFC) is considered one of the most significant
and devastating economic and financial crises in recent history. It is also
arguably the first global emerging market crisis as it spread across the world
affecting several other emerging market economies and a major United States
(US) hedge fund. Characterized by massive capital outflows and plunging
currencies, the AFC hit hard the economies across the region leading to
widespread corporate bankruptcies and retrenchment, financial sector
difficulties, high unemployment, and severe economic recessions. The crisis
broke out in Thailand in early July 1997, when the Thai baht's peg to the
US dollar was abandoned and the currency was devalued sharply. Within a
few months and to the surprise of many, the Thai crisis spread to several of
the major Association of Southeast Asian Nations (ASEAN)+3 economies,
threatening to wipe out the "economic miracle" this region had managed to
achieve over the previous three decades.

Unlike earlier financial crises, the AFC was unique in terms of its
dynamics. Triggered by speculative attacks and a loss of investor confidence,
it became a self-fulfilling spiral of market contagion affecting even economies
with seemingly sound macroeconomic fundamentals. The crisis was arguably ascribed to volatile capital flows induced by financial globalization, an
expanding corporate sector with weak balance sheets and governance, and

---

[1] Regarding the naming convention in this book, we refer to the full name of interviewees and authors for
analytical chapters as per his or her country's practice. After the first appearance, his or her preferred
name is mentioned. For well-known personalities, we use their commonly cited names, for example,
Kim Dae-jung, Lee Kuan Yew, and Zhu Rongji. Elsewhere, naming is provided by the chapter author(s).

a growing domestic financial sector characterized by inadequate regulatory oversight. Although capital account liberalization can attract capital inflows to domestic businesses and financial institutions to finance economic growth, it can also lead to a buildup in financial vulnerabilities such as credit boom, asset bubble, or maturity mismatch, especially when the inflows are short-term, denominated in foreign currencies, and unhedged. Lured by cheap funding, Asian economies overinvested in many large projects including several megaprojects and properties, relying directly or indirectly on funding denominated in foreign currencies with short maturities. This exposed domestic corporate and financial institutions to abrupt shifts in market sentiments and capital flows.

The strong regional recovery in 1999 was equally remarkable as the outbreak of the crisis in 1997. Thailand, Indonesia, Korea, and Malaysia, the highly-affected economies during the AFC, rebounded strongly, beating the market and official forecasts. Notably, the actual gross domestic product (GDP) growth rate of the four economies in 1999 was 4.6%, 0.8%, 11.5%, and 6.1%, compared to the International Monetary Fund's (IMF) forecasts of 1.0%, −4.0%, 2.0%, and 2.0%, respectively, published in May of the same year. The "V-shape" rebound from the AFC laid a good foundation for the strengthening of the macroeconomic fundamentals, repair of the balance sheets of the corporate and financial institutions, and the enhancement of regional cooperation in the subsequent years.

In comparison to the AFC, the global financial crisis (GFC), which originated in the US, can be regarded as an external shock to the region and ASEAN+3 economies were much less affected. Although these economies saw their exports slashed as a result of weak external demand, they managed to avert the worst of financial and economic instability experienced in the AFC, thanks to their stronger economic fundamentals, improved financial sector health, and enhanced regional economic linkages.

Crises, albeit detrimental to the economy and society, provide opportunities for deeper reflections of the past. Although the two crises elicited varied and arguably divergent responses, both the AFC and the GFC sped up regional cooperation and integration among the ASEAN+3 economies. Enhanced regional cooperation resulted in the creation of the Chiang Mai Initiative (CMI), which evolved into the Chiang Mai Initiative Multilateralisation (CMIM) facility as a regional safety net, the establishment of the ASEAN+3 Macroeconomic Research Office (AMRO) as a full-fledged regional surveillance arm, and the rapid development of local currency bond markets.

To mark the 10th anniversary of AMRO, the ASEAN+3 Regional Financial Cooperation Book Project, entitled *Trauma to Triumph — Rising from the Ashes of the Asian Financial Crisis*, aims to take stock of and analyze the events during the AFC and subsequent developments, including the GFC, that led to the establishment and strengthening of the ASEAN+3 Regional Financial Cooperation Framework. Thus, this book will cover the period before the AFC up to the post-GFC years when AMRO was established, became an international organization, and began to play a leading role in regional economic surveillance. The book will provide a narration of key events, supplemented by the personal views of policymakers and experts who participated in those events, which led to the establishment of a regional framework for macroeconomic and financial stability in the region.

Part II, "What Happened During the Asian Financial Crisis and the Global Financial Crisis," draws on the recollections of policymakers and analysts during the AFC as the basis for country-level narratives on the causes and developments of the crisis, and measures that led to recovery. Part III, "The Asian Financial Crisis and Global Financial Crisis: Experiences from the ASEAN+3 Economies," presents an analytical and deeper examination of country experiences during both crises. Part IV, "Assessments of the Crises, and the Development of Regional Financial Cooperation in Asia," blends analyses and assessments of the AFC and GFC, the management of the crises, and financial sector restructuring and reforms in the regional economies. This part will also cover the lessons learned from the crises, particularly with a focus on the development of regional financial cooperation.

Part V, "Conclusion and Challenges Ahead," concludes the volume with reflections on what has been achieved thus far and what the remaining gaps and challenges are, with the aim of catalyzing further discussions on the direction of the region's financial cooperation going forward.

The Asian Financial Crisis

Derailing of the East Asian Miracle

The severity of the AFC took many by surprise as it took place in a period of economic exuberance and bullish market sentiment in Asia. Asian economies were experiencing a broad-based and impressive development, many of which reached middle-income industrialized emerging markets status. Rapid economic growth contributed to poverty reduction, as well as to an improvement in literacy and health. The achievements were recognized by international organizations. The World Bank published a report in 1993 with the title "The East Asian Miracle: Economic Growth and Public Policy." The report sought to uncover the role that government policies played in the dramatic economic growth, improved human welfare, and more equitable income distribution in Hong Kong, China; Indonesia; Japan; Malaysia; Korea; Singapore; Taiwan Province of China; and Thailand. Moreover, in May 1997, the IMF labeled Hong Kong, Korea, Singapore, and Taiwan Province of China as "advanced economies."

In the run-up to the crisis, Asian economies were characterized by strong growth, booming investments, fiscal surpluses or small deficits, and low to moderate inflation. Market sentiments leaned more toward the view that currencies in this region might be undervalued rather than overvalued, given the strong economic performance, sizable international capital inflows, and the rapid accumulation of foreign exchange reserves across the ASEAN+3 region. Investors were rushing into the region and foreign banks were offering cheap loans to local banks, corporates, and governments in the region. Therefore, it was a period of optimism about Asian economies and a crisis was considered a remote possibility. With such optimism, the macroeconomic and financial surveillance framework for risk prevention and detection was still under development. It had yet to consider the vast changes in the global financial landscape. For instance, the IMF had not thought of compiling Special Data Dissemination Standard indicators until 1996. Moreover, early warning systems, while already being studied and developed, were not considered useful or relevant at that time because the last major crisis had taken place only a few years ago in 1994, when Mexico had to be bailed out by the US and the IMF with a USD 48.8 billion financial package. Therefore, the crisis took everyone by surprise, especially its severity, speed, and contagion.

The severity of the AFC was felt first in the financial markets. Currencies that had been stable for many years depreciated sharply. Thailand's usable foreign exchange reserves were quickly depleted in a desperate attempt to defend its currency, leading to its floating on July 2, 1997. Its experience indicated that reserves alone may not be sufficient to fend off speculative attacks in a world of free capital movement and large macro hedge funds. The then Malaysian Prime Minister Mahathir Mohamad blamed "evil" hedge funds that were willing to sacrifice emerging economies in the pursuit of profits. During the AFC, some hedge funds mobilized massive amounts of resources to attack a country's currency, often amplifying market volatilities and capital flows. A case in point is Hong Kong, where hedge funds reportedly used a strategy of "double shorts" — shorting its currency and equities at the same time to try to break the currency peg. In the wake of the crisis, markets panicked and the fear spread over to other emerging markets in the region. During the second half of 1997, the currencies of Thailand, Malaysia, Indonesia, Korea, and the Philippines lost about half of their value against the US dollar. Thailand sought an IMF program in August 1997, followed by Indonesia and Korea in October and December of the same year, respectively.

The sharp tightening of financial conditions induced by capital outflows and IMF austerity programs led to economic devastation across the region. The magnitude of negative impact on each economy differed depending on its specific structural and policy conditions, such as the structure of its debt, the strength of the domestic financial sector, the exchange rate and reserve policy, political situations, and the structural characteristics of its economy (Woo, Sachs, and Schwab 2000). For example, in Thailand, aggregate investment fell sharply and the economy contracted by more than 7% in 1998. In Malaysia and Korea, GDP fell by 7.3% and 5.1%, respectively, in 1998. More dramatically, in Indonesia, output fell by more than 13% in the same year, the largest fall among the AFC-hit economies.

The economic crisis was exacerbated in some economies because it was accompanied by a political crisis. Severe economic distress was likely to decrease political support for those in authority (Haggard 2000). In Thailand, the Chavalit government collapsed and a new Prime Minister, Chuan Leekpai, took office. In Indonesia, the economic crisis ended the three decades of the Suharto Presidency. In Korea, the crisis broke out less than one month before the presidential election and the citizens elected long-time dissident Kim Dae Jung as President. An uncertain political environment would heighten concerns over the political willingness to commit to corrective economic policies under an IMF program and, indeed in the case of Indonesia, exacerbated the economic and financial loss, triggering further capital flight by investors and residents.

Causes of the AFC — Macroeconomic Imbalances and Volatile Capital Flows

Although the AFC is a complex phenomenon with many causes, the underlying economic causes of the AFC derived from the confluence of growing macroeconomic imbalances in the affected economies and trends in the global financial markets. The volatilities in the global financial markets further amplified the macroeconomic imbalances. The imbalances in the external, banking, and monetary sectors were building up over the years, spurred by large capital inflows in the lead-up to the crisis in 1997. The crisis was triggered by speculative attacks, but what distinguished the AFC from the past crises was the sudden stop in lending and the quick reversal of capital inflows reflecting the high mobility of capital in international financial markets. Arguably, such quick withdrawal of foreign portfolio investment and bank loans across the region magnified the overall economic and financial impact of the preexisting imbalances.

With hindsight, there was a consensus among observers that Asian economies had suffered from some structural economic weaknesses before the AFC. Some argued that such weak fundamentals could largely explain the crisis. Corsetti, Pesenti, and Roubini (1999), for instance, emphasized the terms of trade shock, lending booms, and the maturity and currency mismatches of the financial and corporate sectors as the main factors. The macroeconomic weaknesses can be summarized by the following three aspects:

1. High external borrowing: To maintain a high level of economic growth, corporates and businesses overinvested despite visibly declining marginal returns. Excessive investments were supported by cheap external funding channeled through domestic financial institutions.

2. Pegged exchange rate policy: To spur export-driven economic growth, Asian economies typically resorted to some forms of currency peg, from a soft peg to the US dollar or a basket of currencies in most economies, to a hard peg to the US dollar in Hong Kong.

3. Weak financial institutions and regulatory oversight: Domestic bank credits grew rapidly, but were far from a market-based efficient allocation and partly financed by short-term international funds. Banks' capital was also inadequate to provide sufficient buffers. However, financial regulatory bodies at the time were complacent and were not fully aware

of the risks building up in the domestic banking system. This contributed to a buildup of vulnerabilities in financial sectors whose most visible manifestation was eventually a growing share of nonperforming loans (NPLs) (Goldstein 1998).

However, weaknesses in the macroeconomic fundamentals alone cannot fully explain the sudden and rapid collapse of the entire financial system. The AFC highlights another new type of crisis in which capital flows and market confidence played a greater role than in previous crises. The AFC put the spotlight on capital account liberalization, and the risks posed by short-term cross-border flows, Soyoung Kim and Hyungji Kim argued in their analytical chapter (Chapter 24). This view is widely shared by policymakers who were interviewed and authors who drafted the country chapters. As a reference, Chalongphob Sussangkarn (Chapter 14), former Finance Minister of Thailand, explained, "The most important lesson was probably related to the risks from financial globalization." According to Sukudhew Singh (Chapter 16), former Deputy Governor of Bank Negara Malaysia (BNM), "Portfolio investment flow was a source of vulnerability, and policymakers in Malaysia were challenged in dealing with the size and volatility of these flows."

Increased capital account openness brought about a surge in net capital inflows from the mid-1980s to 1996. The net flows were reversed and investors started to flee from the affected economies when the crisis hit them. Such capital flow dynamics led to boom-bust cycles and severe crises across the ASEAN+3 region. The devastating effects of capital flow reversals during the AFC can be ascribed to various sources. According to Soyoung Kim and Hyungji Kim, the AFC economies liberalized their capital account without enough preparation against volatile international capital flows. Therefore, massive reversals in capital inflows in bank loans and portfolio investments led to instability in the financial systems and caused financial crises. Moreover, the insufficiency of foreign exchange reserves also contributed to crises. Therefore, combined with the lack of restrictions on capital outflows, crisis-hit economies found themselves in an extremely difficult position to counteract the large negative effects of capital flow reversals.

As a result of the crisis, the economic performance of ASEAN+3 economies deteriorated sharply in 1998. Average real GDP growth rate of the region was about 0% in 1998, with real consumption dropping by 3%

and real investment declining by 17%. Moreover, deterioration in economic performance was much more severe among AFC-hit economies than other ASEAN+3 economies.

Policy Responses to the AFC

As the crisis unfolded and affected economies came to realize that their foreign reserves were insufficient to defend their currencies, the IMF, as the international "lender of last resort" for sovereigns, was called in to help deal with the problem and restore market confidence. However, views on the effectiveness of IMF's policies are divided.

The IMF recommended a general tightening of monetary policy by raising the policy rates to defend the currencies and reduce the size of capital outflows at the onset of the crisis. The move has remained controversial until today. On one hand, the IMF argued that this should quickly and effectively stabilize the currency. The key concern was that should currencies continue a free fall, the debts denominated in foreign currencies of the domestic banks and businesses would rise further in domestic currency value. This could lead to more bankruptcies and cause even larger scarring effects in the aftermath of the crisis. Ex-ante, the advice seemed to be reasonable as the IMF had prescribed this policy response for the Latin American crises in the 1980s and early 1990s. However, the higher interest rates failed to turn around the market sell-off and currencies continued to depreciate. Critics of such tightening monetary policy claim that high interest rates caused systemic bankruptcies of highly indebted corporates and the resulting surge in NPLs of banks. This contributed to a huge output loss that the program economies experienced during the AFC. In effect, the resulting corporate distress further undermined market confidence and triggered further capital outflows.

Moreover, while the fiscal position was not a concern in the run-up to the AFC, the IMF's approach involved a tighter fiscal stance to reduce domestic demand and improve the current account balance. The IMF argued that an improvement of the current account balance would restore market confidence in crisis-hit economies and currencies. Critics argued that in times of crisis, the fiscal stance should be countercyclical and thus expansionary, to support economic recovery, as lower government spending would cause crisis-hit economies to contract even more. As policymakers came to realize the depth of the crisis, the IMF changed course and relaxed the fiscal stance.

Another controversy lies in the requirement by the IMF to close down insolvent banks during the crisis, which many considered to be the key reason for the massive runs by depositors to healthy banks, particularly in Indonesia. Apart from the contagion issue, critics argued that bank closures without adequate protection of deposits during the crisis led to deposit and capital flight and a freeze in bank lending, which is contrary to what was urgently needed during the economic downturn. However, while Indonesia experienced contagious runs to healthy banks, this did not occur in Thailand or Korea. Corsetti, Pesenti, and Roubini (1999) pointed out that the difference between Indonesia and the other two program countries could be ascribed to the lack of an incentive-compatible deposit insurance scheme in Indonesia and the failure of Suharto's government to enact committed reforms in return for the USD 40 billion in IMF financial assistance.

Emerging from the AFC

Positive macroeconomic developments, such as improved current account balances, rising foreign reserves, and the beginning of exchange rate stability (and appreciation), achieved by the first half of 1998, led to a rapid recovery of confidence among investors and a progressive improvement in economic prospects of Asia (Corsetti, Pesenti, and Roubini 1999). Specifically, economic adjustments, including bank restructuring, easing of monetary and fiscal policies, structural reforms, and enhanced political commitment to pursue good governance, contributed to the sharp rebound of crisis-affected economies that was also beyond expectations of the IMF and others.

However, the pace of economic recovery was uneven across AFC-affected economies. Figure 1.1 shows that Korea recovered quickly after experiencing a 5% contraction of real GDP in 1998. In Thailand, even though foreign reserves were restored fairly quickly, recovery of the real economy took longer, almost 5 years before output recovered its pre-crisis peak. With a slow recovery in production, there was excess capacity in the economy, strong pressure on corporate deleveraging, and little incentive for new investment. In Indonesia, even with the low base level due to the crisis, GDP growth rate in the early post-AFC years never reached the pre-AFC level and was far lower than the rate needed to absorb the growing labor force (Azis 2008).

ASEAN+3 economies succeeded to restore financial health through a deep deleveraging process after the AFC. Figure 1.2 shows there was a sharp rise in credit-to-GDP gap, the difference between actual and trend [HP filtered] credit-to-GDP ratios, for Thailand, Malaysia, and Indonesia before and during the AFC. The gap was more than 30% of GDP for Thailand and Malaysia in the pre-AFC period, while it rose sharply to 60% for Indonesia during the AFC. Following the AFC, crisis-hit countries were forced to go through a long period of deleveraging. Figure 1.2 also indicates that for Thailand, the deleveraging took more than 10 years, followed by Malaysia. The deleveraging process for Indonesia was also deep but its duration was not as long as in Thailand or Malaysia. Korea was able to complete its deleveraging somewhat earlier.

As a result of aggressive financial and corporate sector restructuring, banking sector health was restored. Figure 1.3 shows that the NPL ratios, which had risen to close to 50% in Indonesia and 43% in Thailand during the AFC, began to decline due to bank restructuring efforts. The NPL ratios declined to less than 10% for all crisis-hit countries in the mid-2000s and less than 5% toward the end of the 2000s.

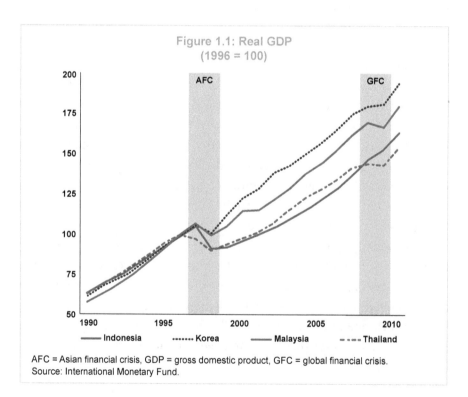

Figure 1.1: Real GDP
(1996 = 100)

AFC = Asian financial crisis, GDP = gross domestic product, GFC = global financial crisis.
Source: International Monetary Fund.

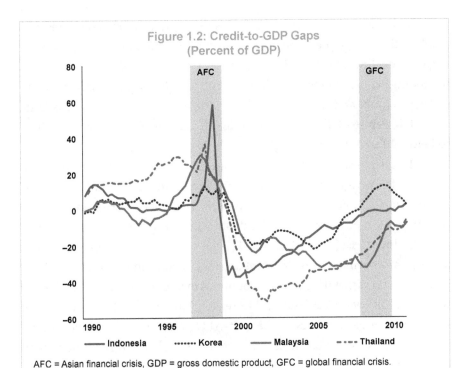

Figure 1.2: Credit-to-GDP Gaps
(Percent of GDP)

AFC = Asian financial crisis, GDP = gross domestic product, GFC = global financial crisis.
Source: Bank for International Settlements.

Figure 1.3: Bank NPL Ratios
(Percent of total bank loans)

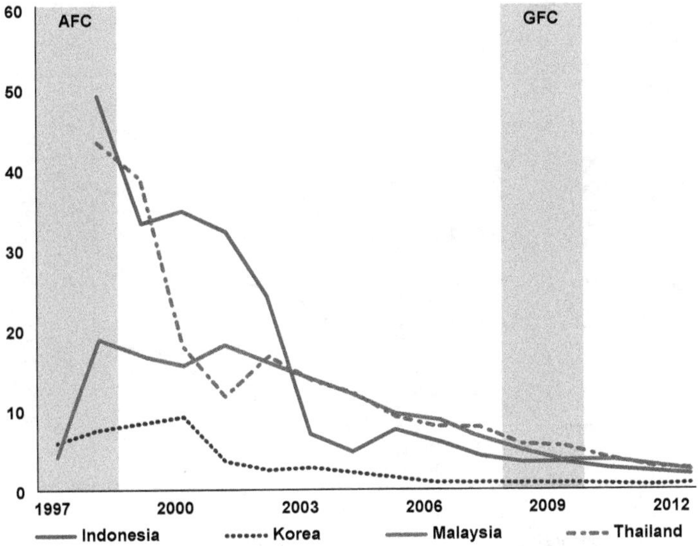

AFC = Asian financial crisis, GDP = gross domestic product, GFC = global financial crisis,
NPL = nonperforming loan
Source: World Bank.

Public sector debt, which also rose sharply in a few countries as a result of the effects of exchange rate devaluation and bank recapitalization, began to decline after the AFC (Figure 1.4). The public debt-to-GDP ratio for Indonesia, which reached close to 90% in 2000, began to decline in an orderly manner and was close to 25% by the end of the 2000s. In Thailand, the public debt-to-GDP ratio rose to close to 60% in 2000 and then declined to below 40% in the second half of the 2000s.

The crisis also generated some long-term adverse effects on investment activities in AFC-affected economies, according to Barro (2001). The AFC led to a massive collapse of investment in all crisis-hit countries, and over the next 10 years, the investment-to-GDP ratio never recovered its pre-AFC level, except in Indonesia (Figure 1.5). The flip side of the collapse of investment was a sharp improvement of the current account balance in crisis-hit countries. Figure 1.6 shows that the current account was in large deficit in Thailand (close to 8% of GDP), Malaysia (5%), and Korea (5%) in the pre-AFC period, which turned into large surpluses in the post-AFC period due to significant rises in savings-investment balances. The investment collapse turned the current account into a large surplus, and the current account surplus became the

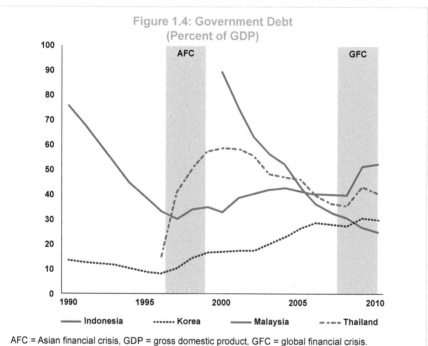

Figure 1.4: Government Debt (Percent of GDP)

AFC = Asian financial crisis, GDP = gross domestic product, GFC = global financial crisis.
Source: International Monetary Fund.

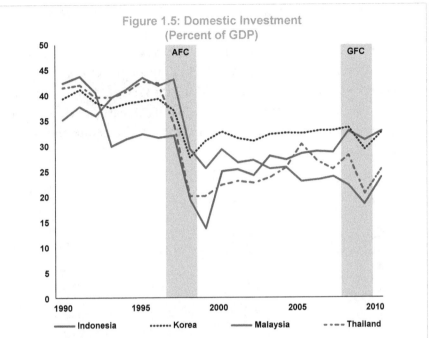

Figure 1.5: Domestic Investment (Percent of GDP)

AFC = Asian financial crisis, GDP = gross domestic product, GFC = global financial crisis.
Source: International Monetary Fund.

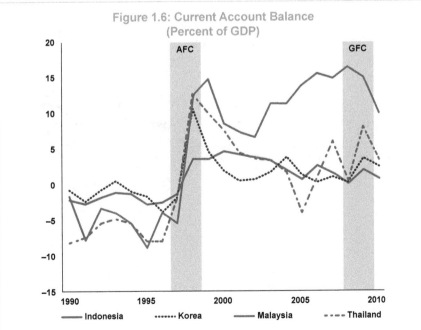

Figure 1.6: Current Account Balance (Percent of GDP)

AFC = Asian financial crisis, GDP = gross domestic product, GFC = global financial crisis.
Source: International Monetary Fund.

norm in the post-AFC period. Malaysia in particular registered large current account surpluses of more than 10% of GDP.

Figure 1.7 shows that short-term external debt as a ratio of foreign exchange reserves was larger than 100% in Korea, Indonesia, and Thailand in the pre-AFC period. The ratio fell during the AFC, and over the next 10 years, the ratio remained at a level way below 100%, partly as a result of the reduction in short-term external debt and a sharp rise in foreign exchange reserves (Figure 1.8).

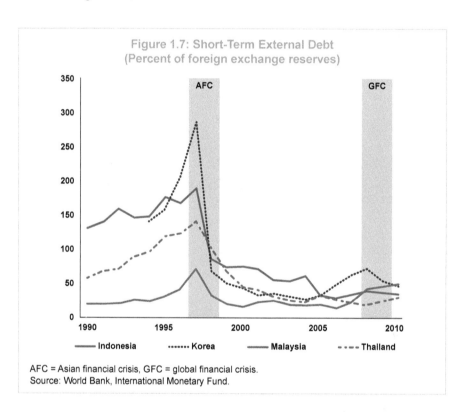

Figure 1.7: Short-Term External Debt
(Percent of foreign exchange reserves)

AFC = Asian financial crisis, GFC = global financial crisis.
Source: World Bank, International Monetary Fund.

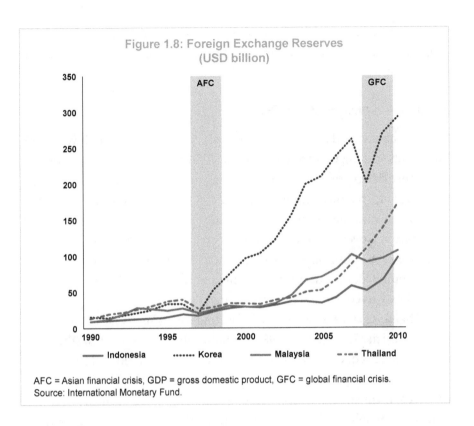

Figure 1.8: Foreign Exchange Reserves (USD billion)

AFC = Asian financial crisis, GDP = gross domestic product, GFC = global financial crisis.
Source: International Monetary Fund.

Weathering the Storm — Insiders and Experts' Perspectives

Asian economies were not equally affected during the AFC. While Thailand, Indonesia, and Korea ended up having an IMF program, Malaysia was able to get through the crisis without it. The Philippines had a precautionary measure to enable access to IMF funds, but the funding provision was eventually not invoked. Hong Kong and Singapore were relatively less affected because they had little external debt and strong fiscal and balance of payment positions. Hong Kong, though, came under the cross hairs of speculators. China and Japan were largely insulated from the crisis, as China had capital controls in place and Japan was a major creditor country even though it was experiencing its own domestic banking crisis.

We invited policymakers who were in the frontline fighting the crisis and economists with profound knowledge of their economies to share their ringside stories and insights. These oral interviews go into the causes and developments of the crisis, and measures to overcome it. The section write-ups by renowned economists provide an analysis of the origin, eruption, mitigation, and resolution of the AFC and reflect on the lessons learned from the crisis.

Thailand — Origin of the Crisis

Thailand abandoned its peg of the Thai baht to the US dollar on July 2, 1997. The events leading to it were recalled by Thanong Bidaya, former Minister of Finance. He revealed that what alarmed him was that "net reserves were about USD 1.5 billion as against total external debt of about USD 100 billion." Thanong saw no choice other than floating the baht. As the crisis mounted, the Chavalit Government was forced to formally request for IMF assistance when feelers to China and Japan for financial assistance were unsuccessful. Total funding for the Thai crisis amounted to about USD 17 billion, of which about 60% was contributions from regional economies.

Thai financial and economic indicators were still dismal some months into the crisis. In January 1998, the baht fell to a record low, the stock market collapsed, GDP was expected to fall 11%, and retrenchments were rife. It was a lethal combination for businesses. As an example, Supavud Saicheua, former Head of Economic Research at Phatra Securities, recalled that his firm sold half of its business to an American brokerage, and his research staff were reduced from about 60 to less than 10: "It had to be huge downsizing everywhere." It was also a difficult time for the government, M.R. Chatu Mongol Sonakul, former Governor of the Bank of Thailand (BOT), observed. He revealed the high public disaffection with BOT then: "Even the taxi drivers were so mad with the central bank. They would not even carry passengers to the central bank."

The crisis led to significant reforms in several areas. The BOT adopted the monetary policy framework centered on inflation targeting by introducing the modalities of open communication that would make for good monetary policy. The banking sector was strengthened. Banks were better capitalized. Banking supervision and prudential standards were raised to conform to international standards set by the Bank for International Settlements (BIS). Fiscal policy would be subject to a Fiscal Sustainability Framework that would set guidelines on government borrowing. Corporate governance standards were also strengthened and monitored.

Looking back, Chalongphob (Chapter 14) thought that the role of the IMF in the Thai crisis in the late 1990s was highly controversial. As an example, Bandid Nijathaworn, former BOT Deputy Governor, emphasized that the IMF's insistence on cutting the budget to reduce the current account deficit was misguided as the issue was mainly liquidity and confidence rather than overspending by the government. In addition to the harsh conditionality imposed on Thailand, Chalongphob also questioned why the IMF did not foresee a crisis or gave sufficient warning to the Thai authorities. On the other hand, IMF staff publicly stated that warnings were given about potential problems (on the high current account deficits and signs of asset price bubbles), but they could not get the Thai authorities to pay serious attention to them. On crisis mitigation, Chalongphob argued that when a country has to deal with very large capital inflows (or outflows), capital control measures should not be ruled out per se, as they can provide an additional instrument for the authorities to maintain economic stability. However, it would be very dangerous to simply copy measures that may have worked for some countries at some point in the past.

Indonesia — An Economic and Political Crisis

Unlike Thailand, Indonesia did not show signs of an imminent crisis. Despite downward pressure on the rupiah and stock market, most of the vital economic figures indicated sound fundamentals when the baht was devalued in July 1997. According to Ginandjar Kartasasmita, former Coordinating Minister of the Economy, Finance and Industry, "Real GDP growth averaged 8% per annum between 1989 and 1996, spurred by strong investment. The overall fiscal balance was in surplus after 1992, and public debt to GDP fell as the government used privatization proceeds to repay large amounts of foreign debt. Inflation, which hovered around 10%, was a little higher than that in other East Asian economies, but was still low among developing countries."

Faced with speculative attacks, Bank Indonesia (BI) took preemptive measures. It first widened the intervention margins of the crawling peg regime in the middle of July 1997, before free-floating the rupiah on August 14, 1997. However, these measures were not enough to curb rupiah depreciation and restore market confidence. J. Soedradjad Djiwandono, former BI Governor, revealed that Indonesian policymakers saw the need to convince the market that the IMF would be behind Indonesia. A formal approach to the IMF was thus made at the beginning of October 1997.

However, both the IMF and the Indonesian government misjudged the depth and nature of the crisis. Dennis N. De Tray, former World Bank Representative at its Indonesian Office, argued that Indonesia suffered from a private debt crisis, rather than a public debt crisis. Encouraged by a booming economy, Indonesian firms had borrowed in US dollar for years, even though their income streams were in rupiah. Jim Walker, former Chief Economist of Credit Lyonnais Securities Asia (CSLA), echoed this view and noted that large amounts of syndicated loans were coming in, mostly from Japanese banks but with some also coming from European and American banks. However, these capital flows were not properly captured in the official statistics.

Iwan J. Azis (Chapter 15) argued that as policy packages failed to restore confidence, capital outflows accelerated, the currency depreciated, and economic conditions worsened. As a result, what began as a vulnerable condition hit by a contagion quickly turned into a severe economic distress. As sociopolitical conditions deteriorated, the crisis rapidly turned into a socioeconomic and political crisis, which would in turn exacerbate financial instability.

For Ginandjar, the crisis underlined the need for "soft" infrastructure like good institutions, and law and order, as a country developed and exhausted gains from the "hard" infrastructure created in the earlier years. This view was shared by De Tray, who added that there was also a need to think seriously about political transition, especially in long-ruling administrations.

Malaysia — Unorthodox Use of Capital Controls as Part of Crisis Management

Malaysia's economic performance was not much different from the most affected economies in the run-up to the crisis. Pre-crisis, both the Malaysian government and the IMF considered the country's economic fundamentals fairly sound. However, as the crisis hit, several structural imbalances, which were being addressed, became the catalysts of weakness.

"Unlike Mexico and other countries, Malaysia's problem emanated from the private sector and the government was not the real source of the problem," said Lin See-Yan, former Deputy Governor of BNM. "Credit growth had been fast and meanwhile NPLs began to creep up. But fortunately, foreign currency debts were low."

As the crisis evolved, Malaysia was faced with the volatile movements of short-term capital flows and stock market turbulence. Nor Shamsiah, currently Governor of BNM, attributed the unprecedented plunge in stocks and currency to speculation and to "investors perceiving the region as a homogenous asset class": "I can still remember it distinctly given the severity and speed in which the crisis spread across the region." Ooi Sang Kuang, former BNM Deputy Governor, opined that the offshore ringgit and stock market facilitated capital flight, increasing the susceptibility of Malaysian financial markets to speculative activities.

Malaysia's initial policy responses to the crisis followed conventional IMF prescriptions by tightening its monetary and fiscal policy. Shamsiah, however, commented, "The combination of tight monetary policy and fiscal restraint was doing more harm than good to the economy. The measures had instead worsened businesses' cash flows. As a result, private sector activity contracted significantly."

Malaysia then charted an unorthodox course, eschewing the IMF and its one-size-fits-all approach, according to former BNM Deputy Governor Sukudhew Singh (Chapter 16). "The existing camp in BNM was quite orthodox, so Mahathir did not find them very helpful. Short-term capital flows and offshore ringgit were something we could not control. When both swung wildly, the only way left for us was capital controls. We really had no choice," Lin recalled. In Sukudhew's view, Malaysia's experiences showed that the selective use of capital controls can be applied appropriately. The measures enabled policymakers to pursue expansionary fiscal and monetary policies, and implement reforms to strengthen the banking and corporate sectors.

Looking ahead, Sukudhew argued that persisting with the regional and global economic and financial integration is a necessity for the continued growth of Malaysia's economy given its small domestic market. However, he also cautioned against the associated risks as experienced during the AFC and GFC. In this respect, he believed that ASEAN+3 economies have made efforts and benefited from regional cooperation in the post-AFC era to mitigate those risks.

Korea — Pulling Down the Curtain on its Economic Miracle

Kyung-wook Hur, former Vice Minister of Strategy and Finance, thought the crisis was "a great shock to Korea." The country was one of the "four

Asian tigers" and was part of the success stories of the World Bank's "The East Asian Miracle" report. The strong macroeconomic fundamentals made the authorities and the IMF complacent about the structural vulnerabilities as evidenced by excessive leverage of the corporate sector, hidden overseas liabilities, and double mismatches, namely, maturity and currency mismatches, of its external debts.

Joon-Ho Hahm and Hyeon-Wook Kim (Chapter 17) argued that the asymmetric information view explained particularly well the nature of the Korean crisis, although the crisis shared both features emphasized by the bad equilibrium (panic) view and the weak fundamentals view. The asymmetric information view emphasized internal balance sheet vulnerabilities and nonlinear disruptions with worsening information problems. This is largely in line with the diagnosis from Yang-ho Byeon, former Director General at Ministry of Finance and Economy, who argued, "The Korean crisis was due to lax corporate management because the banking sector, the government, and the politicians did not punish the non-competitive companies and just kept them operating until the crisis erupted."

As the crisis unfolded, Korea found itself short of foreign exchange reserves. The Korean won depreciated, the stock market melted down, corporations went bankrupt, and unemployment spiked. Chang-yuel Lim, former Deputy Prime Minister and Minister of Finance and Economy, revealed, "I came to realize that the excessive short-term foreign debt was the most pressing problem. The short-term foreign debt was USD 100 billion." while foreign exchange reserves were merely less than USD 30 billion." As a consequence, Korea had to resort to the IMF for help, which Hur recalled, "When we began to work with the IMF delegation, it was really humiliating."

However, Hahm and Kim opined that the IMF's tight macroeconomic policies were controversial as the high interest rates would have destabilizing effects by damaging corporate net worth whereas an expansionary fiscal policy would not have had any negative implications on foreign currency liquidity given the fiscal soundness of Korea. Critically, the external debt rescheduling policy provided the critical momentum in mitigating the liquidity crisis. Duck-koo Chung, former Vice Minister of Finance and Economy, noted that despite strong protests, they "had to implement high interest rates of 30% or higher for about 100 days. The government tried hard to solve the problems caused by higher interest rates from the outset in November 1997, but it was not that easy."

The role of the IMF in the crisis continues to evoke divergent views. Joong-Kyung Choi, former Minister of Knowledge Economy, recalled, "The massive displacement of workers caused by widespread bankruptcy of business firms brought about many cases of broken families. The IMF should apologize to the Korean people officially for its serious mistake." In contrast, Byeon believed, "Under the IMF's program, domestic reforms, especially in the financial sector, and restructuring were strongly implemented and followed by tight fiscal policy, slightly excessive monetary tightening, and capital market opening. I still believe that it should have gone like this after all." Similarly, in Lim's view, "When it comes to the IMF program, I think the positive effects outweighed the negative ones," despite some disagreement on how to manage interest rates and to handle banking capitals during the crisis.

The Philippines — Past Crisis Lessons and Laggard Economy Cushioned Crisis Impact

Roberto F. de Ocampo, then Secretary of Finance, commented, "The Philippines was better insulated from the AFC than its neighbors partly because it was a laggard economy of Southeast Asia." Through the 1980s, international investors and lenders largely saw the country as still being haunted by the political uncertainties and the debt crisis of the previous two decades. Consequently, "we were only able to go back to the international capital markets in the early 1990s," recalled Amando M. Tetangco, Jr., former Governor at Bangko Sentral ng Pilipinas (BSP). Thus, inadvertently, the limited capital inflows did the Philippines a good turn as its asset markets were less bubbly than in other regional economies and the Philippines was spared the massive outflows of capital that beset the more affected countries. Moreover, Wilhelmina C. Mañalac (Chapter 18) argued that the Philippine economy was able to exhibit greater resiliency vis-à-vis its peers arising from the lessons learned from the earlier crises and the policy responses it generated.

As the crisis mounted, de Ocampo said, "Our first reaction to the Thai crisis was that we were not likely to be affected. Our economy was pretty strong, our reserves position was good, and our exchange rate was stable and relatively strong." BSP's first reaction during the crisis was to intervene in the currency market and to raise interest rates, but the intervention did not quell capital outflows. Diwa C. Guinigundo (Chapter 28), former BSP Deputy Governor himself, recalled that despite the intervention and tightening of monetary policy, the peso depreciated very sharply: "The bloodbath in Asia was unprecedented and reverberated even through the goods market and the real estate industry." After a few days, BSP decided that intervention would not be effective as the problem was negative market sentiment and loss of confidence in Asian markets. It ceased foreign exchange market intervention to support the peso, allowing it to trade within a wider band. In subsequent years, BSP embraced flexible inflation targeting as its monetary policy framework and stepped up the adoption of international standards for effective banking regulation and supervision. The exchange rate was established on an independent float.

"As the fiscal policy was tightened, authorities decided to introduce price control to avert the risk of possible hoarding and, in turn, the impact of price increases on the poorer segment of Philippine society," Gil S. Beltran, former Undersecretary of Finance, explained.

Mañalac commented that instead of throwing the Philippine economy off course, the challenging conditions it encountered before the AFC enabled the authorities to recognize systemic frailties and adopt appropriate corrective measures. It became an opportunity not only for employing effective crisis management but for further strengthening the economy, ensuring that its growth prospects could be sustained for the long haul. She also highlighted that the AFC underscored the widespread effect and virulent nature of contagion, and therefore the establishment of a regional group that could offer financial support was considered appropriate. Looking back, participation in regional financial cooperation has benefited the country in responding to crises.

Hong Kong — Countering the Speculative Attacks

Hans Genberg (Chapter 19) argued that Hong Kong ended up having to face a severe exchange rate crisis in the AFC because of speculative attacks on the Hong Kong dollar (HKD). Similar to some other economies in the region, the rapid and significant market spillover had caught Hong Kong authorities by surprise. Norman T. L. Chan, former Chief Executive at the Hong Kong Monetary Authority (HKMA), recalled, "We thought that as Hong Kong has a much more mature and robust financial system, the AFC should not affect us that much, and even if it did, Hong Kong would be able to withstand the shockwaves." In addition, the HKMA had braced itself for market dislocations beforehand. Andrew Sheng, former Deputy Chief Executive of the HKMA, recalled, "The HKMA stress tested every market and wanted to make sure that the brokers didn't fail and the banks didn't fail because of liquidity issues."

The first target by speculators was the HKD exchange rate which is linked to the US dollar through a currency board system (CBS). The attacks began in August 1997 culminating in the week of October 20 with concerted and intense selling. This triggered the CBS' automatic defense mechanism where essentially the shorting of the HKD led to a contraction of the monetary base, which pushed up interbank rates. As a result, the cost of shorting the currency increased and the attacks fizzled out. In August 1998, the attacks resumed but with a twist. It was a double-play strategy of shorting both the HKD and stocks. The scheme was to sell both the HKD and stocks in the forward market. This would cause interest rates to automatically rise, which would cause stock prices to decline. The speculators would then buy back the stocks at a low price to square their forward position and make a profit. It seemed a sure-win proposition: they would win if the currency peg held and win even more if it broke.

Genberg highlighted, "The Hong Kong authorities reacted in very unorthodox ways to preserve the fixed exchange rate system by intervening directly in spot and forward markets for both foreign exchange and equities." The unprecedented action can be viewed as "probably one of the most brilliant pieces of policymaking during the Asian crisis," Walker opined. Chan, who was in charge of the operations, met the chief executive officers (CEOs) of the three largest brokers in Hong Kong to open stock and futures trading accounts to enable the HKMA to start trading. However, these actions drew sharp criticism globally. Alan Greenspan, former Chair of the US Federal Reserve, for instance, commented, "Hong Kong had abandoned its free-market principles." In response, Hong Kong officials subsequently traveled overseas to explain the policy actions and was able to turn international opinion around.

The Hong Kong economy did eventually recover. The underlying strengths of the economy enabled it to ride out the storm of the intense speculative attacks. These included "a highly flexible economy, especially its labor and product markets that could adapt to internal or external shocks," Chan stressed.

Singapore — Flexibility and Preemptive Measures Stave off Speculative Attacks

Similar to Hong Kong, Singapore adhered to its exchange rate regime — managing the exchange rate flexibly against a basket of currencies within an adjustable band — and was less affected by the market contagion throughout the AFC period. Hoe Ee Khor, former Assistant Managing Director at the Monetary Authority of Singapore (MAS) and currently Chief Economist at AMRO, recalled, "We widened the exchange rate target band but we did not want the exchange rate to move too much. We wanted to keep the exchange rate strong because we were a financial center, and we wanted to maintain investor confidence in the Singapore dollar." Teh Kok Peng, former Deputy Managing Director of MAS, clarified, "I don't think there were attempts to speculate against the Singapore dollar at that time." Singapore had enough reserves and did not have the problem of over-borrowing in the financial sector. So, "it was clearly a downturn induced by the neighbors."

During the AFC, Singapore was valued as a sounding post for regional developments and prospective solutions, and also participated in the financial assistance packages for Thailand and Indonesia. Khor recalled, "We were involved in terms of talking to the IMF missions and also the US Treasury officials, who would stop over in Singapore to seek the views of the Senior Minister and the Prime Minister, about the situation in the region." When Indonesia was under severe stress, "Singapore was of course very concerned about things getting bad there," said Kishore Mahbubani, former Permanent Secretary at the Singapore Ministry of Foreign Affairs. "There were packages coming out for Indonesia and we said we will contribute."

Lam San Ling (Chapter 20) opined that the MAS' cautious stance on the internationalization of the Singapore dollar likely helped to avert massive speculative attacks as it was harder to short the Singapore dollar in the offshore market. She also noted that compared to other economies in the region, Singapore adopted measures to cool down the overheated property market in the run-up to the AFC. She believed that if similar measures had been implemented in other crisis-hit economies, credit and overinvestment in property projects would have been curtailed, and thus the adverse impact of the AFC could have been mitigated.

However, keeping a stable and strong currency came at a price. In Khor's view, "The longer-term impact was actually quite significant because as a result of the crisis, our exchange rate became uncompetitive." Consequentially, labor-intensive industries were relocated outside Singapore and there was little growth until 2005 compared to other economies in the region.

In the wake of the AFC, Singapore started to reinvent itself and work on a new economic model. "We needed to move up the value chain if we were going to be competitive," Khor pointed out. That was when Singapore decided to open up the hospitality sector and attract a whole new group of manufacturing industries. Meanwhile, financial reforms were pursued vigorously to facilitate the development of new financial services including the asset management industry. The MAS shifted its regulatory approach to focus more on the oversight of banks' risk management systems. Monetary policy became more transparent and accountable.

BCLMV[2] — Low Financial Integration, Tiny Ripple Effects

Jayant Menon (Chapter 21) argued that "BCLMV economies were only indirectly affected by the AFC, as the financial systems of the BCLMV countries were fairly underdeveloped and not well-linked to global financial markets." They did not experience the rapid and disruptive flight of volatile and short-term capital that crippled other Asian countries because the amount of portfolio capital in these countries was small (Okonjo-Iweala et al. 1999). Moreover, a large agricultural sector provided a buffer during external crises because demand for the output was generally inelastic and a significant share of its demand was domestic.

"However, although trade and foreign direct investment did not contract as much as in the original ASEAN member countries, it was sufficient to reduce growth in all the BCLMV members in 1998, exposing and magnifying existing vulnerabilities in their macroeconomy and nascent financial sectors," Menon pointed out. He further argued that the real economic impact was aggravated by a weak capacity to implement countercyclical macro-economic policy. On the monetary side, varying degrees of dollarization and the multiple currency arrangements compromised the ability of the monetary authorities to implement a discretionary monetary policy. On the fiscal side, the authorities had limited fiscal headroom due mainly to weak tax collection capacity. There was also limited ability to implement countercyclical

[2] BCLMV represents Brunei, Cambodia, Lao PDR, Myanmar, and Vietnam.

stabilization policies using conventional instruments of spending, tax cut, and transfer policy. Of course, the countries' relative insularity and large agricultural sectors also meant less need for such policies.

The AFC highlighted the need to increase economic and financial cooperation in the ASEAN+3 region. In particular, BCLMV countries are vulnerable to internal and external shocks, and their capacity to identify and respond to shocks remains relatively low. The creation of the economic review and policy dialogue (ERPD), CMIM, and the ASEAN+3 Asian Bond Markets Initiative (ABMI) has been of limited value to BCLMV so far. Menon highlighted that "critics lament the peer review process as a beauty contest, the regional financial safety net remaining inoperable, and local currency bond market development not reaching BCLMV in any significant way. It would benefit BCLMV a great deal if the CMIM could be more 'user friendly' since alternative sources of liquidity are limited." Hence, until the CMIM becomes truly operational, BCLMV members would have to rely on the ASEAN Swap Arrangement (ASA) and bilateral support within the ASEAN+3 region if they want an alternative to the IMF as global lender of last resort.

China — Maintaining Yuan Stability as an Anchor of Regional Currency Stability

Haihong Gao (Chapter 22) argued that the impact of the AFC on China was relatively mild compared with other crisis-hit economies in the region, thanks to its strict capital control and limited external exposure. The AFC in 1997–1998 came at a time when China was still in the initial phase of economic reform and opening up since 1978. Nevertheless, the AFC was a wake-up call for China to draw lessons from other countries, particularly in the areas of conditions for capital account liberalization and soundness of the domestic financial system.

Gao opined that China's initial "mute" response to Japan's proposal of an Asian Monetary Fund (AMF) put forward immediately after the crisis reflected China's concerns about possible minimization of the role of the IMF in the region (Bowies and MacLean 2017). Moreover, Wei Benhua, former Director of AMRO, did not think "the preparatory process by Japan was adequate at that time. For such an important proposal, you need a lot of time to prepare, to talk with different economies, and with their support then you could make such a proposal."

However, overall, China's attitude toward a regional approach was positive. Wei recalled that during his time as the Executive Director for China at the IMF, "China always extended its strong support to Thailand, Indonesia, and Korea whenever they applied for financial assistance from the IMF and we also supported national policies proposed by those countries." China, as well as other Asian countries, realized that regional financial stability was a public good that required regional cooperation. In the wake of the crisis, Zhu Guangyao, former Vice Minister of Finance, highlighted, "We overcame the difficulties to set up the CMI framework."

China also learned from the AFC that its exchange rate policy could have a regional spillover effect. Zhu recalled that during the crisis time, "China's key policy was maintaining renminbi stability and no devaluation." "If we had devalued our exchange rate, then we would have had a direct impact on the region," Wei argued. Nevertheless, this came with a trade-off. "If we keep to the no devaluation policy, China's market share in the region particularly, or in the world, would decline," Zhu said.

Thanks to China's fast growth and continuous economic and financial liberalization, China has become a major trading partner and the hub of global value chains in Asia. The Chinese currency has also gained importance in the region because of the rise of China as the largest economy and trading nation in the region. However, Gao warned about the risks arising from nationalism and trade tensions among the major economies that could be detrimental to global multilateral cooperation in trade and financing. The outbreak of the coronavirus disease (COVID-19) crisis has further aggravated uncertainties about policy reactions and economic consequences. Perhaps the most pressing downside effect of the pandemic for China would be the pressure of economic decoupling and interruption of globalization.

Japan — Providing Significant Financial and Promoting Regional Cooperation

Even though Japan was suffering from a domestic banking crisis at around the same time as the AFC, its main role in the AFC was providing significant support for the AFC-affected countries and acting as a forceful promoter of ASEAN+3 financial cooperation, Masahiro Kawai and Shinji Takagi (Chapter 23) argued. "Even though there were some losses for Japanese banks from their operations in Thailand and Indonesia, they did not have so big an impact as to cause a domestic financial crisis in Japan," Hiroshi Watanabe, former Vice Minister of Finance, stated.

During the AFC, Japan actively supported both AFC-hit countries, with IMF programs (Thailand, Indonesia, and Korea) and those without (Malaysia). Soon after the financial crisis in Thailand erupted, the Japanese government hosted a meeting among the "Friends of Thailand" to reach an agreement to put together a financial package to support the IMF financial program for the country. Kawai and Takagi noted that "focusing on the immediate crisis period (through the end of 1998), Japan pledged approximately USD 44 billion in financial assistance for the AFC-hit countries" and argued that "Japan's commitment to provide substantial financial resources, particularly under the New Miyazawa Initiative (NMI), undoubtedly helped stabilize regional markets and economies, thereby facilitating the recovery process."

The crisis indicated that "some sort of standing facility within the region may be necessary," Haruhiko Kuroda, former Vice Minister of Finance, stated. Eisuke Sakakibara, former Vice Minister of Finance, shared a similar view: "We were very critical of the IMF's handling of the AFC and so we wanted to establish some institution." In September 1997, following the success of the "Friends of Thailand" meeting, Japan proposed to establish an AMF to supplement IMF resources, reportedly with the size of as much as USD 100 billion. The AMF would aim to pool foreign exchange reserves held by regional central banks and monetary authorities, both to deter currency speculation and, if a currency crisis were to occur, to contain the crisis and the resulting contagion in the region.

"ASEAN countries decided that they would support establishing the AMF. The major possible participants, China and Australia, took a somewhat neutral position during our meeting in Hong Kong. However, the IMF and the US opposed," Kuroda recalled. The IMF and the US shared the view that countries in the region affected by a currency crisis would bypass the tough conditionality of the IMF and receive easy money from the proposed AMF, thereby creating the potential for moral hazard. Overall, Kawai and Takagi noted that while the proposal of an AMF was welcomed by crisis-hit countries, Japan eventually shelved the idea because of the lack of clear support from China.

Kawai and Takagi noted that as an alternative to the AMF, in May 2000, Japan forcefully promoted ASEAN+3's other joint initiatives to strengthen the three pillars of a regional financial architecture: an economic and financial surveillance mechanism led by the ERPD process of the ASEAN+3 finance group, a liquidity support facility called the CMI, and an Asian bond market initiative. The hallmark liquidity support facility was the CMI (launched in May 2000 as an informal network of bilateral swap arrangements (BSAs) and multilateralized into the CMIM in 2010, which was designed to address short-term liquidity needs in the event of a crisis or contagion and to supplement the existing IMF financial arrangements. An important motivation for Japan's regional cooperation efforts is the recognition of ASEAN+3 as a key production base and as an expanding consumer market for Japanese multinational corporations, and the awareness that financial stability in the region is therefore vital to the Japanese economy.

IMF — Challenges, Controversies, and Reflections

To support the crisis-affected countries, almost USD 120 billion was pledged in IMF-led official rescue packages during the AFC. However, the IMF programs for Thailand, Indonesia, and Korea were controversial and the IMF's credibility was damaged during the AFC. The prescriptions by the IMF failed to restore market confidence or mitigate the devastating macroeconomic impact of the crisis. Most policies, such as tighter fiscal policies, higher interest rates, and quick closure of financial institutions, did not work as intended and required renegotiation as the crisis deepened. This reflected the inadequacy of traditional program design in dealing with the AFC.

A crisis in Thailand was not unexpected. Hubert Neiss, former Director of the IMF's Asia and Pacific Department, for instance, disclosed that Thailand "was the only country where we (the IMF) saw difficulties emerging at an early stage." He put Thailand on the list of "problem countries" in January 1997. "There were ample warnings, but looking back, I think everybody underestimated the magnitude of the financial crisis that was coming," Neiss added.

Shinji Takagi (Chapter 24) shared Neiss' view that "the problem with the IMF's pre-crisis surveillance was not one of ignorance, but largely of underestimation of the adverse impact of the identified weaknesses and vulnerabilities on investor confidence." The problem appeared to be that the Fund's staff tended to be weak at forecasting macroeconomic developments in the face of volatile capital movements (Boorman et al. 2000). In the case of the AFC, this reflected large errors in forecasting market reactions via exchange rates and capital movements.

"The problem was simply that there wasn't the governance from the IMF side or the Thai side on the supervision of the financial sector," Anoop Singh, former Director of the IMF's Asia and Pacific Department, argued. "I would say the problem was not the devaluation of the Thai baht. The problem was that they should have started acting on the corporate side and the financial side 12 months before that." Moreover, another non-negligible factor that prevented the authorities from adopting effective policies before the crisis was the political reluctance to cooperate. Singh recalled, "There were several major concerns. Firstly, there was no data transparency. Secondly, there might be data manipulation at work. Thirdly, there was a lack of cooperation with the IMF. Fourthly, there were no clear efforts at preventing a possible crisis. Lastly, there was a resistance to surveillance. Therefore, Thailand's crisis was not totally unexpected."

The Thai financial crisis quickly spread to Indonesia and Korea and caught many by surprise. Walker commented, "When one falls over, the next thing that investors do is to look for the next candidate." Neiss explained, "Indonesia was quite susceptible to contagion as there were, especially in the late period of the Suharto regime, great distortions in the market. The unraveling of the good economic times brought these elements more into the fore and contributed to the loss of confidence." Similar to those in Thailand, the causes of the Korean crisis were "apparent weaknesses of banks which led to the loss of confidence and capital flight."

Takagi took the view that the AFC represented a new type of crisis driven by capital flows rather than trade flows. Market expectation was the key factor in this new type of crisis. Nevertheless, the IMF programs during that time focused on raising interest rates to prevent capital from further fleeing and tightening fiscal stance at the onset of the crisis. This playbook — which worked well in fending off speculators in the 1980s and early 1990s — did not restore investors' trust. The doubt on the efficacy of high interest rate policy remained unsettled. The interest rate defense of a falling currency had been a standard practice in many contexts and had been successful in some cases. On fiscal policy, Furman and Stiglitz (1998) and Ito (2007), among others, argued that fiscal tightening as initially programmed was unwarranted not only because of a prospective deceleration of growth but also because fiscal profligacy was not a cause of the crisis.

Additionally, the IMF was criticized by many because "some of the measures in the programs were irrelevant to the current problems of the short-term crisis," Neiss recalled. Walker opined, "The IMF had a playbook and did not have very much in the way of flexibility in their toolkit." However, Neiss argued, "The IMF position was that we wanted to work for a recovery that had a lasting basis and that could be sustained. And for that reason, long-standing damage in the economic system would have to be repaired, and this was the occasion to do it."

Takagi further highlighted that "the use of capital controls was the elephant in the room that nobody either saw or wanted to see." Notably, this was a period when the international community, led by the majority of industrial countries, was about to agree to amend the IMF Articles of Agreement, giving the Fund a mandate to promote capital account liberalization. With capital controls, the economic contraction would have been limited because of the avoidance of sharp currency depreciation and significant increase in the domestic currency value of foreign currency debt, and the needed official financing would have been smaller in magnitude. A sudden imposition of capital controls, of course, would have created a myriad of legal issues, but the cost of legal work would have been small in comparison to the large official financing needed in the absence of capital controls.

Learning from the AFC, "the Fund has changed hugely," in Singh's view. "Number one, because of the AFC, the Fund created a financial sector assessment program (FSAP), which examines the financial sector of major economies every 1 to 3 years. Number two, our work on Basel III has helped in protecting banks. We have a better idea now to get a more structurally robust macroeconomic setting. Number three is transparency. Almost everything the Fund does now is transparent." He also called for regional institutions, such as AMRO, to do a lot more to contribute to regional cooperation and stability.

In a similar vein, Takagi concurred that with the lessons learned, the IMF's surveillance has become increasingly more focused on financial sector issues. Its crisis programs have become more realistic about macroeconomic assumptions and conditionality, informed by a better understanding of the nature of financial crisis driven by capital flow reversal. Structural conditionality has become more streamlined and focused on the IMF's core areas of competence. The IMF has become more transparent in its engagement with official partners and private investors. It has become more accommodative of the use of capital controls to stem capital outflows. By its very nature, a new crisis will inevitably happen from causes not sufficiently understood or anticipated. Attempts to improve surveillance and to strengthen crisis management capacity must be an ongoing process.

The Global Financial Crisis

Ten years after the AFC, the GFC, as if establishing a 10-year cyclical interval, broke out. Unlike past crises, the GFC originated in the US. The crisis rapidly spread from the housing sector to the financial sector. In March 2008, Bear Stearns, a major US global investment bank and securities brokerage, teetered on the verge of bankruptcy and was sold to JPMorgan Chase supported by a US Federal Reserves' guarantee. However, the collapse of Bear Stearns led to the cascading financial chaos that ensued. Half a year later, Lehman Brothers, a global financial services firm, unable to secure US government or the Federal Reserve's assistance, declared bankruptcy. It then quickly deepened into a global financial crisis through the interconnectedness of global banks and financial institutions, whose innovative financial products, such as collateralized debt obligations, were not fully understood at the time. Ex-post, policymakers realized that such financial products concealed risks underlying many subprime and low-rated mortgage loans and mortgage-backed securities.

Four major contributing causes of the GFC have been identified: excessively easy monetary policy; regulatory failures, both at the microprudential and macroprudential levels; the buildup of the global balance of payments imbalances; and weaknesses in the international financial architecture (Kawai, Lamberte, and Park 2012). However, there was no consensus on the relative importance of these factors.

Unlike during the AFC, the ASEAN+3 region was affected only moderately by contagion and spillover effects during the GFC. The contagion primarily worked through the outflow of portfolio funds as a result of risk aversion and flight to US dollar liquidity. However, both the extent of the portfolio outflows and the downturn in the stock market were of a smaller magnitude and ASEAN+3 economies were spared the worst experiences of the AFC. The economic impact, mainly through the channels of trade and investment, was also less severe, although that was partly due to the adoption of expansionary fiscal and monetary policies by many economies. As an example, Sussangkarn noted that "luckily for Thailand, the decline in world trade only lasted for four quarters starting from the fourth quarter (Q4) of 2008. Once the shortages of US dollar liquidity that led to declines in trade finance were addressed, global trade bounced back, and Thai exports grew quite rapidly." Similarly, the Malaysian economy rebounded sharply by 7.5% in 2010 after a 1.5% decline in 2009, driven by the recovery of private consumption and investments.

Ample monetary and fiscal space built-up in the aftermath of the AFC allowed ASEAN+3 authorities to adopt expansionary stimulus programs during the GFC. Moreover, the region's economic fundamentals had strengthened as a consequence of acting on the lessons learned from the AFC. Current account balances were in surplus and foreign exchange reserves were accumulated for precautionary purposes. In addition, the financial regulatory frameworks were strengthened and commercial banks built up higher capital buffers and better risk management capability.

One notable example of policy response was the Chinese government's massive CNY 4 trillion fiscal stimulus package that mainly targeted domestic infrastructure investment. The fiscal stimulus package was also aided by considerable credit expansion to the state-owned enterprises (SOEs). As a result, the Chinese economy avoided a deep downturn during the GFC but the stimulus policies sowed the seeds of imbalances, including overcapacity and overleverage in the economy, in the years to come.

For the ASEAN+3 region, the long-term effects of the GFC are perhaps more significant than the short-term ones, according to Kawai, Lamberte, and Park (2012). Although the GFC affected the region relatively less as compared to the AFC, the contagion, capital outflows, and US dollar liquidity crunch served as another rude wake up call, which prompted policymakers to further strengthen their resolve to enhance international and regional cooperation. Globally, many reforms were rolled out, including regulatory tightening with a focus on macroprudential regulation, reconsideration of capital flow liberalization issues such as the IMF's proposal on capital flow management, and the general quota increase at the IMF to enhance its role as a global crisis manager. The GFC also gave rise to the Group of Twenty (G20) Leaders' Summit to improve coordination among the heads of states and governments on global issues. Regionally, the decade in the aftermath of the GFC saw a faster buildup of foreign exchange reserves in the ASEAN+3 region, especially in China, as the ultra-easy monetary policies in the US and Europe led to massive inflows of liquidity into regional emerging markets. In addition, regional policymakers set up regional policy forums, enhanced swap arrangements, and further developed local currency bond markets.

Lessons from the Past Crises

Henry Paulson, former US Secretary of the Treasury, said, "I believe that the root cause of every financial crisis is the flawed government policies." The AFC in 1997–1998 and the GFC in 2007–2009 have shaped the trajectory of economic growth, as well as policymakers' perspectives on crisis management at both individual country and regional level. In particular, the AFC revealed the dramatic changes that had taken place in global financial markets since the breakdown of the Bretton Woods system in 1971, and the imperative for a revisit of IMF policies and for structural reforms by Asian economies.

According to Henning (2011), crises can potentially provide the necessary conditions that trigger a shift to a new and durable equilibrium, which in turn can lead to the creation of new regional institutions and arrangements. For ASEAN+3 economies, although the two crises elicited varied and arguably divergent responses, both have resulted in accelerating the development and institutionalization of the region's financial cooperation over the past two decades, particularly in three key areas — (i) financial safety net, (ii) economic and financial surveillance, and (iii) financial market development (Kawai and Morgan 2014; Morgan 2018).

Financial Safety Net

The regional financial safety net has been strengthened. Although Japan's early proposal of creating an AMF was not realized in 1997, the idea was revived in 2000 in the form of the CMI under the ASEAN+3 Finance Process, and its subsequent expansion into the CMIM Agreement in 2010.

Beomhee Han (Chapter 26) opined that the IMF's approach in handling the AFC had led to "IMF stigma" (European Central Bank 2018), which has prevented several regional governments from going to an IMF program for fear of being discredited by the electorate (political stigma) or financial markets (financial market stigma). The IMF, assuming the role of the global crisis manager, could not provide swift and large-scale liquidity support to contain and resolve the AFC. The scope and timing of IMF policy conditionality were based on a standard set of "structural performance criteria" following its experience with the crisis management of the 1980s, which was seen as "intrusive in national affairs" and undermined the national ownership of the IMF program. In fact, there is a view that even if structural reforms are relevant, it is not appropriate to implement them during a crisis.

As a result, according to Han, particularly since the GFC, global policymakers have shifted their focus to creating a strong global financial safety net. This is also expected to reduce reserve accumulation and lower sovereign risk premiums, which in turn would help reallocate capital to where it might be most productive. Therefore, the desire and endeavor to have a strong liquidity support mechanism in the region are natural. Against this backdrop, the CMI was launched at the ASEAN+3 Finance Ministers' Meeting in May 2000 and was further upgraded by consolidating individual CMI bilateral swap arrangements into one single multilateralized arrangement, the CMIM, in May 2007.

In recent years, ASEAN+3 members have continued to enhance the CMIM — particularly by increasing the IMF de-linked portion to 40%, and adopting the CMIM conditionality framework and the ERPD matrix for assessing eligibility by members to CMIM facilities. In doing so, members have paid particular attention to striking a balance between the concern over moral hazard and the need for a quick-disbursing self-help mechanism.

Economic and Financial Surveillance

Economic and financial surveillance capacities have been upgraded. ASEAN+3 members have been engaged in multiple regional cooperation forums and organizations for information exchange, economic monitoring, research and training, and policy dialogue for better policymaking. Among the various forums and initiatives with overlapping memberships are the Executives' Meeting of East Asia-Pacific Central Banks (EMEAP) and AMRO.

EMEAP comprises central banks and monetary authorities from Australia, China, Hong Kong, Indonesia, Japan, Korea, Malaysia, New Zealand, the Philippines, Singapore, and Thailand. Diwa C. Guinigundo (Chapter 28) pointed out that past crises have provided the impetus for a stronger regional identity and cooperation which in turn led to the enhancement of regional cooperation mechanisms such as EMEAP. Since its establishment in 1991, EMEAP has been perceived as the first successful regional forum in the region (Hamanaka, 2011). It has significantly contributed to fostering economic and financial cooperation in the region. Its efforts and initiatives to deepen regional bond markets and regional macro-financial surveillance, information sharing, and capacity-building activities have contributed to greater macroeconomic and financial stability in the region. Guinigundo reviewed the key developments of this initiative:

- The first EMEAP Governors' Meeting was held in July 1996 in Tokyo, Japan, and the Governors reviewed economic and financial developments in the region and discussed means to enhance cooperation to strengthen financial stability and foster market developments.

- During the third Governors' Meeting held on July 14, 1998, EMEAP Governors affirmed the importance of EMEAP activities in promoting information exchange and developing mutual trust among the economies in the region.

- In the run-up toward the GFC in 2007, EMEAP established the Monetary and Financial Stability Committee (MFSC). The GFC in 2008 underscored the importance of stepping up regional cooperation and surveillance efforts to jointly monitor the developments of the GFC and assess its impact on regional economies and its implications for EMEAP central banks (EMEAP 2008).

- At present, EMEAP is a multitiered forum without a dedicated secretariat. EMEAP depends on the capacities of member countries and its activities include meetings, committees, and working groups at various levels.

Notwithstanding EMEAP's significant contributions, Guinigundo opined that there would be scope to further advance the cause of regional cooperation. In the area of bond market development, more work remains in the area of developing corporate bonds. In addition, EMEAP has the potential to develop a regional scheme for the macro-prudential policies of its members. Furthermore, there could be scope to strengthen communication between AMRO and EMEAP to enhance early warning systems in the region and improve the crisis management framework. Lastly, observers suggest that EMEAP can benefit from greater openness in its current programs and initiatives.

AMRO, a macroeconomic surveillance organization focused on securing economic and financial stability and supporting the CMIM, is the fruit of the regional financial cooperation process over the past two decades. In May 2009, ASEAN+3 finance ministers reiterated their commitment to the establishment of an independent regional surveillance unit to monitor and analyze regional economies and support CMIM decision-making. AMRO was initially established as a company limited by guarantee in Singapore in April 2011 and was converted and officially designated as an international organization in February 2016.

Since then, AMRO has expanded and developed further in terms of organizational structure and capacity. An external assessment by Grimes and Kring (2020) noted AMRO's rapid progress in strengthening its surveillance and program design capabilities. However, given the lack of experience in managing a regional currency crisis, the study concluded that it is too early to judge AMRO's capability to fulfill its mission as a crisis manager.

Yoichi Nemoto and Faith Pang Qiying (Chapter 27) opined that despite the progress made over the past decade, there is further scope for AMRO to enhance its effectiveness and support members in the future. To achieve this, they noted that AMRO must persist with its efforts to build expertise on crisis management, program designs, and policy recommendations. The need to enhance the coverage, frequency, and quality of data and statistics will continue to be a long-term agenda for AMRO. Finally, there is a need for ASEAN+3 members to consider AMRO's status with regard to its role in supporting the CMIM. To ensure a smoother activation process of the CMIM, it is also worthwhile for ASEAN+3 members to consider legally upgrading the CMIM and to pool together a portion of the CMIM's total resources into a separate paid-in fund to ensure the swift disbursement of funds.

Nemoto and Pang further pointed out that "we must make hay while the sun shines." The ASEAN+3 region has built a strong foundation and sound macroeconomic fundamentals and strengthened the various layers of the regional financial safety net to create strong self-help buffers. They argued that it might be a good time now for policymakers to consider further enhancing and integrating regional facilities so that AMRO/CMIM can become a credible regional monetary fund and play a greater role in the provision of global financial safety net.

Financial Market Development

The AFC's adverse impact on some ASEAN+3 economies due to their high dependence on foreign borrowings and the "double mismatches" in maturity and currency led to the developments of local currency (LCY) bond markets in the region. Satoru Yamadera (Chapter 29) highlighted that the AFC demonstrated that a well-functioning domestic bond market would be helpful to minimize the currency and maturity mismatches that had made the region vulnerable to the sudden reversal of capital flows. Policymakers in ASEAN+3 recognized such needs and decided to launch the ABMI at the ASEAN+3 Finance Deputies Meeting in Chiang Mai, Thailand in December 2002 to mitigate the risks.

According to Yamadera, the main targets of regional cooperation among ASEAN+3 economies are to prevent market contagion in the short-term and to facilitate a more stable financing in the long run. In his view, the CMIM could address the issue of market contagion, whereas the ABMI could promote stable financing from local currency bond markets. The ABMI has demonstrated a role for regional cooperation that can address the problem of coordination failure and lack of knowledge and experience. Furthermore, it has pushed member economies to achieve more through peer pressure. Shared knowledge and experience have supported the identification of problems and provided appropriate policy advice.

Yamadera pointed out that during the initial phase of the ABMI (2002–2007), ASEAN+3 policymakers focused on establishing basic market infrastructures and regulations for LCY bond markets. The expansion of LCY bond markets showed that ASEAN+3 member economies made a great deal of progress in mitigating the "original sin" problem. Since the establishment of ABMI, the total size of LCY bond markets in ASEAN+2[3] has climbed to USD 18.7 trillion at the end of September 2020 (Asian Development Bank 2020), comparable in size to the markets for US Treasury bonds or euro-denominated bonds issued by the residents of the Euro Area. He further stressed that the ABMI has supported not only the growth of market size but also the functioning of LCY bond markets. Increased issuance and improved market liquidity have strengthened the yield curves' role as a benchmark for other assets. In addition, a wider range of benchmark issues has also allowed the creation of benchmark indexes across many regional markets. In terms of bond types, there is a wider range of bonds issued in the region, including inflation-linked bonds, green bonds, asset-backed securities, and Sukuk (Islamic bonds).

---

[3] ASEAN+2 includes the ASEAN countries, China, and Korea.

Yamadera emphasized that to overcome the remaining challenges of ABMI and deepen regional market integration, the scope of the regional initiative needs to be expanded beyond bond markets. The region would need to introduce more useable and cheaper hedging tools to mitigate foreign exchange risk, to promote more LCY to LCY transactions by expanding access to local currency liquidity, to consider using the increasing amount of high-quality liquid assets as cross-border collateral, and lastly to strengthen market confidence and reduce frictions to facilitate cross-border movement of capital flows. Therefore, ASEAN+3 economies must continue their efforts to improve the financial market and economic fundamentals.

Challenges and Outlook

We have revisited how the AFC and GFC erupted and spread across the region, analyzed their causes and consequences, and drawn lessons from both crises. Today, ASEAN+3 members remain highly diverse in terms of their economic, social, and cultural features and developments. From the viewpoint of economic development, the region is unique with its members ranging from developing to developed economies, with some resource-rich economies, manufacturing industrial economies, and global financial centers. That said, such diversity can actually provide opportunities for trade, investment and financial exchanges, and collaboration in economic policies. At the same time, the region also shares many common interests, and therefore, it can leverage such common interests to drive regional financial cooperation to an even higher level of development.

The outbreak of the COVID-19 pandemic has highlighted the need for ASEAN+3 economies to "hold hands" and work together in the spirit of regional cooperation, not only to navigate the unprecedented global health crisis but also to build up resilient economic systems in the post-pandemic era. Although ASEAN+3 economies are still quite distant from realizing the full potential of economic and financial integration, regional economic integration has taken a step forward recently with the signing of the Regional Comprehensive Economic Partnership (RCEP) Agreement. Further regional financial integration would demand greater cooperation among regional authorities, such as finance ministers, central banks, and financial regulatory bodies, to work toward a more integrated financial system while ensuring that such a system is under sound supervision.

References

Asian Development Bank. November 2020. *Asia Bond Monitor*. Manila.

Azis, Iwan J. 2002. "Indonesia's Slow Recovery after Meltdown." *Asian Economic Papers*, Vol. 6. MIT Press.

Barro, Robert J. 2001. "Economic Growth in East Asia Before and After the Financial Crisis." NBER Working Paper No. 8330.

Boorman, Jack, Timothy D. Lane, Marianne Schulze-Ghattas, and Ales Bulir. 2000. "Managing Financial Crises: The Experience in East Asia." IMF Working Paper 00/107.

Bowies, Paul, and Brian K. MacLean. 2017. "China and Asian Financial Cooperation." http://web.isanet.org/Web/Conferences/HKU2017-s/Archive/89f87f58-6374-4886-a029-9c6051197468.pdf.

Corsetti, Giancarlo, Paolo Pesenti, and Nouriel Roubini. 1999. "What Caused the Asian Currency and Financial Crisis?" *Japan and the World Economy* 11 (3): 305–373.

European Central Bank. 2018. "Stigma? What Stigma? A Contribution to the Debate on Financial Market Effects of IMF Lending." Working Paper Series No. 2198.

Executives Meeting of Asia-Pacific Central Banks. 2008. "Statement of the MFSC," October 30. http://www.emeap.org/wp-content/uploads/2015/04/EMEAPJointStatement2008-10-30.pdf.

Furman, Jason and Joseph Stiglitz. 1998. "Economic Crises: Evidence and Insights from East Asia." *Brookings Paper on Economic Activity* 2: 1–135.

Goldstein, Morris. 1998. "The Asian Financial Crisis: Causes, Cures and Systemic Implications." *Policy Analysis in International Economics*, Vol. 55. Washington, D.C.: Institute for International Economics.

Grimes, William W., and William N. Kring. 2020. "Institutionalising Financial Cooperation in East Asia: AMRO and the Future of the Chiang Mai Initiative Multilateralization." *Global Governance* 26: 428–448.

Haggard, Stephan. 2000. "The Political Economy of the Asian Financial Crisis." *Policy Analysis in International Economics*. Washington, D.C.: Institute for International Economics.

Hamanaka, S. 2011. "Asian Financial Cooperation in the 1990: The Politics of Membership." *Journal of East Asian Studies* 11 (1): 75–103.

Henning, C. Randall. June 2011. "Economic Crisis and Institutions for Regional Cooperation." ADB Working Paper Series on Regional Economic Integration, Vol. 81.

Ito, Takatoshi. 2007. "Asian Currency Crisis and the International Monetary Fund, 10 Years Later: Overview." *Asian Economic Policy Review* 2: 16–49.

Kawai, Masahiro, and Peter Morgan. 2014. "Regional Financial Regulation in Asia." ADBI Working Paper No. 460, Tokyo, Asian Development Bank Institute.

Kawai, Masahiro, Mario B. Lamberte, and Yung Chul Park. 2012. *The Global Financial Crisis and Asia-Implications and Challenges*. Oxford University Press.

Morgan, Peter J. May 2018. "Regional Financial Regulation in Asia." In *Global Shocks and the New Global and Regional Financial Architecture*, edited by Naoyuki Yoshino, Peter J. Morgan, and Pradumna B. Rana. Asian Development Bank Institute and S. Rajaratnam School of International Studies (RSIS).

Okonjo-Iweala, Ngozi, Victoria Kwakwa, Andrea Beckwith, and Zafar Ahmed. September 1999. Impact of Asia's Financial Crisis on Cambodia and the Lao PDR. *Finance & Development*, Vol. 36. Washington, D.C.: International Monetary Fund.

Woo, Wing Thye, Jeffrey Sachs, and Klaus Schwab. 2000. *The Asian Financial Crisis: Lessons for a Resilient Asia*. MIT Press.

Part II

What Happened During the Asian Financial Crisis and the Global Financial Crisis

Freddy Orchard and Guanie Lim

Chapter 2

Introduction

The narratives in this Part II are based on interviews arranged in conjunction with the publication of this volume. The interviews revolved around the theme of what happened during the Asian financial crisis (AFC). In essence, therefore, the following chapters can be taken as an oral history collection of this historical, momentous event in the region.

A total of 32 interviews were completed, involving interviewees from nine economies throughout the region and from the International Monetary Fund (IMF) and the World Bank. Five of the interviews were in written format, the rest were oral. The interview process coincided with, but was not derailed by, the coronavirus disease (COVID-19), which imposed restrictions on travel. Except for two face-to-face sessions in Singapore, the rest of the oral interviews were virtual.

Interviewees occupied leadership positions in the vital organizations engaged in responding to the crisis. These included the relevant ministries, central banks, international organizations, and investment firms. Through them, we are thus able to enrich the narratives with frontline, insider accounts of events as they unfolded, of the reasons for critical decisions and their repercussions — in short, for how and why the crisis evolved as it did in the different regional economies as well as the progress achieved in regional financial cooperation.

The nine economies covered can be grouped as follows:

(i) Thailand, Indonesia, and Korea had important commonalities: they were the most affected countries, going through the most severe economic contractions; problematic private sector external debt; an over-exposed banking system; depletion of reserves; and the consequent resort to IMF assistance. The role of politics was also most pronounced in these countries. The interviews shed light on the impact of these issues. Thus, the role of the IMF comes across as controversial. Politics played a most important role in Thailand. Its change of government saw more decisive policies. In Indonesia, regime change, initially destabilizing, led to sustainable recovery and to Indonesia becoming a democracy. And in Korea, a new president was hailed by one interviewee as Korea's equivalent of a Nelson Mandela in the way he put his shoulders to the wheel of reforms.

(ii) Malaysia is a stand-alone. While its economic growth was as affected by the AFC as Thailand, Indonesia, and Korea, it stands unique for its unorthodox response to the crisis: the use of selective capital controls. The policy was much criticized then, though Eisuke Sakakibara, then Vice Minister of the Japanese Ministry of Finance, revealed that Japan supported Malaysia's approach. When asked about Malaysia, other interviewees recalled then Prime Minister Mahathir Mohamad's repugnance to calling in the IMF, why he settled on the use of capital controls, the additional measures he took to reinforce them, and the extent to which Malaysia's approach was successful.

(iii) The Philippines also stands on its own. It was, as articulated in an interview, "a latecomer to the Asian party" and the only country that had an ongoing IMF program in the pre-crisis years. Hence, it was spared the excessive external borrowings and volatile capital flows that triggered crises elsewhere. But the interviews also emphasized that reforms in the 1980s–1990s helped shield the country from the worse of the AFC.

(iv) Hong Kong and Singapore share important characteristics. They are city-states and international financial centers, and had impeccable fundamentals such as strong banking systems, little external debt, and ample reserves. Yet, both were affected by the AFC, though in different ways.

Hong Kong was the quintessential case of a sound financial system that bore the brunt of the machinations of speculators. The interviews showed how these machinations reared their heads and were then beaten by ingenious policy response. But the speculative attacks caused property prices to tumble and slower gross domestic product (GDP) growth for several years.

Singapore was by-passed by speculators. However, its policy to keep the Singapore dollar stable led to a hollowing out of labor-intensive industries and a period of lower growth relative to the regional economies.

For both Hong Kong and Singapore, interviewees referred to the positive outcomes from their AFC experiences: for Hong Kong, these were the financial windfall from beating the speculators and the stock-exchange listing of a long-term investment product for residents; for Singapore, it was a revised long-term financial and economic strategy that led to the rapid development of the financial sector and economic boom in the second half of 2010s.

(v) Japan and China have two important commonalities. First, both were relatively insulated from the regional crisis. For Japan, it was more a case of the bursting of the Japanese asset bubble causing Japanese banks to withdraw funding from Asia rather than the AFC having a significant impact on Japanese banks. In China's case, it was insulated largely due to a closed capital account and little external debt.

Second, both countries were stabilizing influences for the region as well as instrumental in furthering regional financial cooperation. China's decision to keep the renminbi stable removed a major uncertainty for regional currencies. The interviews revealed what went into the decision.

Japan actively supported the crisis-hit countries from the start. The Japanese interviews indicated that Japan felt it was necessary to do so not only because of large Japanese investments in the region but also because of perceived shortcomings in the IMF's approach. Japan also floated the idea of an Asian Monetary Fund. It fell through mainly because of the United States (US) and IMF objections. More broadly, the Japanese interviews also went into the differences between Japan and the US on the causes of, and solutions for, the AFC.

Finally, Chinese interviews told of a breakthrough in China, Japan, and Korea relations that enabled regional financial cooperation to advance. This was a little-known meeting among Chinese, Japanese, and Korean officials that paved the way for the inception of the Chiang Mai Initiative and the other arrangements that followed.

Two other chapters follow the country chapters. One features excerpts from the transcripts of the two IMF officials interviewed. These excerpts elaborate on the IMF approach, how its view on the AFC evolved, and the pressure that teams undergo in negotiations with their counterparts on the other side of the table. A final chapter comprises quotations from our interviewees on their main takeaways and lessons from the AFC experiences.

Although close to 25 years have passed since the AFC, it is remarkable how clearly most interviewees could still recall events prevailing then. This speaks of the deep impression the AFC had cast on them, of recollections about how the crisis began, in many cases seemingly improbable; of the financial and economic stress that ensued; and finally of the success in surmounting the crisis and implementing reforms that made their economies more resilient.

Chapter 3

Thailand

This chapter draws on the interviews of seven persons: Bandid Nijathaworn, M.R.Chatu Mongol Sonakul, Supavud Saicheua, Thanong Bidaya, Hubert Neiss, Anoop Singh, and Haruhiko Kuroda. During the 1997 Asian financial crisis, Bandid served as the Director of the Banking and Foreign Departments, Bank of Thailand. Chatu Mongol was the Permanent Secretary at the Thai Ministry of Finance before taking over as Bank of Thailand Governor. Supavud was the then Executive Vice President and Head of Economic Research at Phatra Securities. Thanong became the Minister of Finance in June 1997, taking over from Amnuay Viravan. Neiss was the then Director of the Asia Pacific Department at the International Monetary Fund. Singh was then Deputy Director of the Asia Pacific Department at the International Monetary Fund. Kuroda was then Director General of the International Bureau at the Japanese Ministry of Finance.

On July 2, 1997, the Bank of Thailand (BOT) abandoned its long-standing policy to peg the baht to the United States (US) dollar at a fixed rate and floated the currency. The decision triggered the crisis in Thailand, which in turn was the precursor to a wider regional crisis. Observers like Haruhiko Kuroda took the view that the Asian financial crisis (AFC) would not have happened if there had been no Thai crisis. The Thai crisis, in other words, exposed the vulnerabilities and the policy blind spots that would be the underlying causes of the financial contagion that would sweep through the region.

Signs of Financial Stress

Signs of financial stress in Thailand had become acute by 1996. These included the collapse of the Bangkok Bank of Commerce; a bond default by Somprasong Land; the forced merger of Finance One, a high-profile finance company, with a bank; and the suspension of trading on bank and finance company stocks. Current account deficits of around 8.5% of gross domestic product (GDP) in 1995 and 1996 were also concerning. An outbreak of financial distress in Thailand was hence not unexpected.

Hubert Neiss recalled that Thailand was the only country where he and his colleagues saw difficulties emerging at an early stage. He elaborated:

"Since the beginning of 1997, I regularly reported to the Executive Board on Thailand in their meetings on 'problem countries,' in particular on speculative episodes against the baht in the foreign exchange market, and the overheating of the construction boom. Privately, Management urged the Thai authorities to give more flexibility to the exchange rate and to tighten macroeconomic policy in order to restore market confidence."

Kuroda opined that Thailand's dollar-pegged system had become unsustainable by 1997:

"I became Director General of the International Finance Bureau in July 1997; that was the time the Thai currency crisis erupted. Actually in February 1997, when I was Head of the Research Institute at the Ministry of Finance (MOF), before I went to Bangkok to participate in an international conference, I had just read the International Monetary Fund (IMF) consultation paper on Thailand and I found that Thailand had 8% of GDP equivalent current account deficit with a dollar-pegged exchange rate system. I got the impression that it was unsustainable."

Supavud Saicheua also thought the pegged exchange rate system was a problem:

"It was clear to me that the fixed exchange rate that the BOT had maintained was a very vulnerable point for Thailand. Especially as we were implementing the strategy in Thailand to become a financial center for the region, accumulating foreign debts at an accelerated pace, accompanied by the still large current account deficits. It was a lethal combination which I thought was unsustainable. So in 1996, you recall that there were periodic speculations against the baht, and it was those things that alarmed me."

A New Type of Crisis

Observers who warned of financial sector problems, however, would admit to two notable "blind spots" in their analysis. One was to misdiagnose the crisis, to perceive it as a conventional case of excess aggregate demand rather than financial market imbalance. Instead, it was, as Bandid Nijathaworn observed, a different type of crisis:

> "The AFC of 1997, which started in Thailand, was the first of its kind: meaning that it was the first financial market-driven crisis in the era of globalization, driven by international capital movement and triggered by sudden loss of confidence that leads to abrupt capital outflows in such a way that, you know, it affected the confidence of investors, led to the change of the exchange rate system, and so on."

Reflecting on his experience as a member of the IMF team working on Thailand, Anoop Singh also admitted:

> "It took us time to understand that this was not a normal crisis. It was a financial crisis which we were late in recognizing. There was the initial view that this was more a case of excess government spending; it was not. The problem was simply that there wasn't governance from the IMF side or from the Thai side on the supervision of the financial sector."

Misdiagnosing the crisis as a garden variety type also led to another blind spot; very few expected the crisis to be as severe as it turned out to be. As Neiss observed:

> "So there were ample warnings, but, looking back, I think everybody underestimated the magnitude of the financial crisis that was coming."

Both misperceptions would have profound consequences as they would shape the initial policy responses to the crisis and how the crisis would develop.

Vulnerabilities

Macroeconomic policy inconsistency and a weak banking system were the major reasons for the vulnerabilities in the Thai financial system. A fully liberalized capital account, domestic lending rates higher than US interest rates, and a fixed exchange rate incentivized Thai entities to borrow in foreign currencies, mainly US dollars. These loans were intermediated by domestic banks. Thus, the solvency of borrowers, as Bandid observed, "were ultimately levered to the banking sector."

The massive inflow of capital led to a spike in credit. Banks were not the only lenders. The number of finance companies, another source of easy credit because of lax governance, rose sharply. The results were an exuberant investment environment, a construction boom and unviable projects, and the buildup of private sector external debt.

Thanong Bidaya, who became Finance Minister, gave further explanation for the rise in private external debt:

> "It was all private. The Finance Ministry was very strong and disciplined. With a booming economy, it could collect a lot of taxes. That's why the economic position seemed very strong. But, the underlying position was not very strong because of the private external debt. Just why did the debt rise so quickly? Previously, there was a policy — Bangkok International Banking Facilities — to allow the private sector to import foreign exchange. The rationale was to stimulate growth rate. I believe the government's policy was to maintain an 8% growth for the next economic plan, and it was difficult to attain that rate if you relied purely on domestic savings.

> However, there was a fault in the policy. The foreign exchange rate was not relaxed, so the system favored importers. The private sector, especially those that engaged in non-tradable activities, took advantage of this and brought in a massive amount of foreign exchange debt, which grew rapidly. By 1996, the central bank started to sense that there was a bubble forming, so it jacked up interest rates. Domestic interest rates were raised to almost 10–12% and the deposit rate became about 8–10%."

As Thanong mentioned, the BOT tried to cool inflation and overheated property markets by raising rates. This, however, proved counterproductive, as noted by Supavud:

> "Paradoxically, that led to even more companies, more banks borrowing abroad because the arbitrage opportunities were there, and suddenly, you have lots of companies borrowing for the sake of borrowing dollars. And so, unfortunately, that exacerbated this borrowing of money that wasn't used properly because it was so cheap. For all those reasons, the investment, the money that came in, was not productively used. In just 3 years, private sector foreign debt went from very little to double the size of foreign reserves."

This meant that, by then, Thailand's current account deficit was largely financed by short-term external debt.

Thanong, who was a banker, observed that international banks had become wary of Thailand's current account deficits.

> "On the other hand, the lenders, i.e. the international bankers, started to realize that the Thai trade deficit had been rising for more than a decade. Without any adjustment of the exchange rate or the fundamentals of the economy, the fixed exchange rate might not be sustainable. So, the lenders started calling back their US dollar-denominated loans. That's why we saw the rapid reduction of foreign exchange reserves from USD 40 billion to about USD 25.5 billion in June 1997."

Then, questions about the sustainability of the baht rate attracted the attention of hedge funds. They began periodically attacking the baht. A Moody's downgrade on Thai debt in April 1997 sparked renewed attacks against the baht. The BOT intervened to support the currency to little effect except to expend its reserves.

Attacks on the baht escalated when Amnuay Viravan resigned as Finance Minister on June 21. He was succeeded by Thanong. The ministerial change was symptomatic of the unsettled political situation then, another factor that soured market sentiments. Expectations rose of an imminent baht devaluation and more baht selling ensued.

Floating the Baht

Thanong accepted the post as a call to duty. The pressure he would face would exceed his qualms about taking the job:

> "The Prime Minister (PM) asked me to become Finance Minister in June 1997 and I had to accept it. So, I was appointed and certainly I was not aware of the real financial difficulties of the country. I did not realize how deep it was until I looked into the real situation. The IMF had started to warn us, even before I entered office. It sent a letter to warn us about the weakening of the financial markets and similar situations in the past. The Mexican crisis started in 1994, so we were warned of a recurrence. The IMF also recommended the possibility of relaxing the foreign exchange fixed rate policy. But somehow, the previous governments did not do it."

Soon after his appointment, Thanong came to know of how precarious the BOT's reserves position was:

"I went to the BOT and had a secret meeting. That's when I learned about the real position of the central bank. There were three numbers that really frightened me. The first one relates to swap facilities. It was still hanging around USD 30 billion. The second number was the dwindling foreign exchange reserves. It shrank from almost USD 40 billion to USD 25.5 billion from the end of 1996 to June 1997. Out of this, not all of the reserves were legally usable because some were used to back up Thai baht issuance, etc. Effectively, only USD 1.5 billion was left for normal trade. This meant that we had close to nothing in the foreign exchange reserves to utilize. The third number is the total external debt. Thailand had more than USD 100 billion of external debt."

Thanong then sought the BOT's recommendation on a suitable exchange rate policy:

"In Thailand, the law stipulates that for any modification on foreign exchange policy, you need the consent of two parties: the BOT and the Ministry of Finance. The central bank will have to recommend the exchange rate policy and the Finance Minister will have to approve that. After that, the proposal is to be forwarded to the PM for endorsement. Without instructions from the Finance Minister, the BOT cannot do anything. Likewise, without the BOT's recommendation, the Finance Minister cannot do anything."

In fact, the separation of responsibilities between the BOT and the MOF had led to an impasse between them on exchange rate policy:

"When Amnuay resigned from the position of Finance Minister, I went to visit him on the Sunday before I became Finance Minister. He mentioned that there was an impasse between his side and the BOT on foreign exchange policy. He claimed that the BOT still felt that it didn't want to do anything. It wanted to maintain a basket of currencies approach. However, the Permanent Secretary at the MOF recommended that the currency be floated."

Various reasons have been given for the BOT's reluctance to move to a managed float system, which in the circumstances of the day would have meant a devaluation of the baht. Thanong's explanation was that the BOT did not realize the intensity of speculative attacks it had to intervene against until it was too late:

> "I think the BOT still felt that it could beat back the attack on the baht because it did prevail in the first two attacks. But the third attack was so huge, about USD 40 billion. I remember in May 1997, when I was still a banker, the then Finance Minister called us for dinner, informing us that Thailand was able to defeat the speculators in the same month. He also wanted us to not support the speculative motion by lending out baht for the purpose of foreign exchange manipulation. We complied with him by not lending any foreign exchange to manipulate the baht. That's how we sensed something was coming."

Supavud also makes the point that the BOT underestimated the speed of the buildup of short-term external loans and waited too late to adjust the exchange rate:

> "That's a really good question to this day. I would suspect that the speed with which Thailand accumulated foreign debts surprised everyone, and I think they would have been willing to let the baht be flexible and allowed the baht to gradually depreciate, if they had time to think about it. I think by the time they thought about it, it was too late. The foreign debt accumulation was too high, and they could not change the game."

Realizing the urgency, Thanong raised the exchange rate issue with the BOT again:

> "When I learned about the weak situation we were in, I asked the central bank governor what policies were available — do we float the baht, or do we widen the band? I also told him that I would support the BOT's decision. Over the weekend, the governor called me and said that widening the band would not work because there were not enough facilities to back up the baht's position against further speculative attacks. So, we decided to switch to a managed float system."

Thanong approved the BOT's recommendation. He then discussed with the BOT on the timing of the announcement:

> "The governor said the bank was ready to do it, but the earliest date to roll it out was June 30. However, June 30 is normally the closing of the

second quarter of the corporates. I was afraid that announcing it on June 30 would shock the banking sector. So, we decided to postpone it to July 2 as July 1 was a public holiday."

And so the BOT announced the shift to a managed float of the baht at 7.30 a.m. on July 2. The baht fell by about 18% on the first day of its float. It subsequently was to fall even more. A lower baht would improve the current account. Its more dramatic and immediate impact, however, was to raise the debt burden, in baht terms, of Thai foreign currency borrowers. This realization would shock the markets.

Supavud elaborated on how market perceptions changed from viewing the baht devaluation as a positive to a negative development. In fact, the devaluation would trigger a bigger crisis:

"I must admit that personally, I also made a huge analytical mistake. When the BOT declared that they would float the baht on the July 2, 1997, I had thought that, well, we've unlocked these constraints. The baht will depreciate by about 10–15%, and then the current account deficit will improve, and all will be well because you would have corrected the major distortion, the major disequilibrium economy by allowing the baht to depreciate.

What I had not thought about was the fact that we were thinking, focusing too much on the flow variables. Trade is a flow variable but the market eventually decided to look at the huge impact of the stock variable, which is the stock of foreign debt that the Thais had borrowed, and then we were told later on that the stock of debt that the Thais had borrowed was much bigger than we initially thought. I clearly thought we borrowed something like USD 40–50 billion, but it ended up apparently as much as about USD 80 billion or so. And we thought that the bank had some reserves left. Apparently, they had nothing left. So, with that huge stock of debt, it was the huge leverage that I had underestimated. It was the leverage that the market focused on, not the flow. And the market thought that Thailand could not repay that debt, so everyone exited Thai assets."

Bandid described how delinquent external debt affected the banking system:

"The banking sector was okay because when the banks borrowed foreign currencies, they were always hedged. But it's the customers who borrowed in foreign currencies that did not hedge. So when the baht was devalued, they had to pay more in order to service the debt. And that caused a problem in the corporate sector. And when the corporate sector failed to pay their debt back to the banks, it led back to the problem of nonperforming loans (NPLs) in the banking sector."

The baht devaluation in fact had triple ill effects. It raised corporate distress, led to higher NPLs in financial institutions, and intensified capital outflows as foreign lenders sought repayment. The crisis had turned systemic.

Seeking IMF Assistance

As the crisis mounted, the Chavalit government secretly sought financial assistance from China and Japan. Thanong elaborated on these efforts:

"After the devaluation, we knew that we needed foreign exchange liquidity, especially to deal with lender request to get their money back. They calculated that we needed about USD 12 billion, at the very least, to maintain enough foreign exchange liquidity for the coming years. We then began searching for funding sources. I recommended two directions, in addition to working with the IMF.

One direction was to seek Chinese support. I didn't go there, but the PM sent his team to China to discuss with the Chinese government about financial help. For me, I went to Japan because I had graduated from there. So, I took the liberty of visiting my colleagues and other friends in Japan to seek help. I was received warmly by the then Finance Minister of Japan. He promised to help Thailand, and Vice Minister Sakakibara was instructed to find financial support for Thailand. Sakakibara knew the difficulties of getting Japanese parliament support directly, so he, working in the background with my central bank governor, agreed that we probably had to rely on the IMF, with Japanese support of course."

Despite the stigma of seeking an IMF bailout, the government had no choice but to formally request IMF assistance.

The IMF Program: The Financial Package

It did not take long for an IMF team to arrive in Bangkok to start working on the package. Singh, a member of the team, recalled the hectic pace of the negotiations:

> "We used to work with them (the Thai negotiating team) during the morning, afternoon, and evening. Then, we have to work overnight with our counterparts back in Washington. As the IMF is a very central-ized institution, we had to have all the stuff approved by Washington. We arrived on July 23 or 24, but by August 13, we had the Fund's approval of the program in principle. That was incredible."

The negotiations were stressful for the Thais as well, over issues that would be elaborated on later. Thanong had in various press interviews noted that the IMF negotiations were among the worst moments of his life:

> "So that's why we looked at the IMF, and we started discussions with them after I came back from Japan, and that's how we have been instructed by the IMF, all the programs that we have to go through, with the drafting of the first letter of intent. Certainly it was a very difficult time for me. [laughs] It was a very difficult time."

After the IMF program had been finalized, Japan convened a "Friends of Thailand" conference in Tokyo to announce an assistance package for Thailand. The IMF was committing USD 4 billion to the Stand-By Arrangement, five times the size of Thailand's IMF quota. This, though, was thought to be insufficient. The IMF hence sought, and obtained, supplementary funding as follows: the World Bank and Asian Development Bank (ADB) (USD 2.7 billion); Japan (USD 4.0 billion); Australia, China, Hong Kong, Malaysia, and Singapore (USD 1.0 billion each); and Indonesia and South Korea (USD 500.0 million each). Total funding thus came to about USD 17 billion, of which about 60% were from the regional economies. It was a remarkable show of regional financial support and cooperation.

The IMF program, however, started badly. It was quickly perceived to be underfinanced. The immediate reason was public disclosure of the BOT's forward US dollar commitments. Singh revealed that the IMF was unaware of these commitments when the program was designed:

"When we prepared the program in early August 1997, it was done on the basis of reserves that were not their actual level. Only when the program was announced, with the IMF's endorsement, would Thailand reveal its actual level of reserves. When the numbers came out 3 weeks later, it shocked everybody, including us at the IMF. It made clear that the problem was much deeper. So, it quickly became apparent that what the IMF was putting together to help Thailand would not be enough. It became an underfinanced program."

Confidence in the baht fell as the disclosure revealed that the BOT's usable reserves were much smaller than expected.

The IMF program was, however, underfinanced in a more fundamental way. It underestimated the magnitude of the crisis, the extent of the potential capital outflows, and the intensity of the speculative activity against the currency.

Japanese policy makers were cognizant that the IMF package was inadequate. Kuroda, for instance, observed that even with the additional regional contributions, the final assistance package may fall short:

"The USD 4 billion IMF assistance may be insufficient, so from within the region we mobilized USD 11 billion, but still it was not sufficient. The Thai financial crisis was not contained and spread to other countries, including Indonesia, Korea, and Malaysia. That was so fast and rapid it was more than anticipated."

Kuroda's point was that even though Thailand obtained five times its IMF quota, the quota may have been too low to begin with:

"The second point is as I said, for Thailand, I considered that the IMF quota may be small. In 1995, the IMF provided Mexico with five times of the Mexican quota in financial assistance and it was the largest ever at that time, and so I thought that for Thailand, five times of the quota was equivalent to USD 4 billion. But unlike Mexico, Thailand had a small IMF quota compared with its large economy and the size of financial transactions."

There were consequences of an underfinanced program, as noted by Bandid:

"And then the one thing that I find a little bit disappointing is that the level of financial assistance that they had assembled in the case of

Thailand, which was the first country, was only about USD 17 billion. I think it is very small. The Mexican crisis received USD 50 billion. But now, you know the euro crisis, it is a totally different order of magnitude altogether. But because the market did not see this package to be large enough, it could not maintain the confidence of investors about the new exchange rate system. That's why we had 6 months of very high volatility in the exchange market. You see my point?

So my first remark about the Fund program would be that it didn't account for the perception of markets in the context of, you know, reserves adequacy. Now it's become a standard rule that your announcement of the package should be big enough so that there's no question about the program failing. But this was not the case 20, 25 years ago, with the AFC. That is why it took much longer for the baht to become more stable. But I think that we have learned this lesson if you look at the money they're giving out nowadays. They use, you know, USD 300–400 billion."

The IMF Program: Policies and Structural Reforms

Another controversial issue was the tight monetary and fiscal policies stipulated by the IMF program. Critics saw these policies as the IMF standard "tool kit" that they applied to countries in deficit, nevertheless the Thai situation was different. The negotiations to finalize the first letter of intent, while completed quickly, were hence tense and heated as both sides disputed the degree of austerity that was called for.

The monetary stance called for restricting credit and raising interest rates, which at one point was above 20%. The aim was to deter capital outflows and stabilize the baht. Critics, however, argued that the monetary tightening was contractionary and instead damaged investor confidence, which led to weak baht markets.

Supavud's criticism of the monetary tightening was representative:

"The IMF made a mistake in believing that a high interest rate will keep money in Thailand if the return on the baht is even higher relative to the high interest rate because that kind of interest rate would have caused many companies to default. So, when the interest rates are too high, it actually caused a collapse of the domestic economy."

At that time though, as Singh mentioned, the IMF team saw little leeway to do otherwise.

> "But to be fair, this was the first major crisis since Mexico. Money was leaving the country and it looked odd from an economic point of view to say: 'Money is leaving the country, therefore lower interest rates and expand government spending.' It took a long time for economists to understand the situation. Very few people went out in the open to say: 'Money is leaving, stop the capital from leaving, lower interest rates and raise government spending.' Not many people said that, but now they are."

The IMF's fiscal policy recommendation was even more controversial. It called for a fiscal surplus of 1% of GDP through a value-added tax (VAT) hike and restraints on public spending. The intent was to raise revenues to fund financial sector reform. The issue, however, was that the Thai crisis was not due to fiscal profligacy, as in Latin America. It was basically a balance sheet problem of Thai companies. The fiscal contraction would squeeze the economy and compound these balance sheet difficulties. Indeed, the Thai economy contracted by 10% in 1998, far lower than IMF forecasts.

Bandid saw the IMF-recommended fiscal measures as evidence that the IMF had not yet clued into the essence of the crisis:

> "I think that it was a new thing to them as well. I mean they came in with a mindset like it was similar to Mexico, where there was a question of a fiscal deficit, public indebtedness, and the country cannot pay and needs some foreign currency inflows from the IMF to smooth out the balance of payments in order to pay back the debt."

Continuing, Bandid emphasized that the IMF's insistence on cutting the budget to reduce the current account deficit was misguided:

> "They still focused on cutting the budget. Because they did not realize that once you float the exchange rate, then the mechanics of expenditure switching will take over. And that the new levels of the exchange rate would fix the current account deficit. But they were still focusing on cutting the budget, increasing taxes, you know, to try to reduce spending because they did not understand that the issue was mainly one of liquidity and confidence more than overspending by the government. That is why if you look at the subsequent letters of intent, the fiscal targets were under revision all the time."

Thanong, in recounting the negotiations, hinted at the difficult negotiations his team encountered on the IMF policy prescriptions:

"But the IMF came with very strong austerity measures. That meant we had to balance the budget in a negative growth environment. This was not beneficial at all because Thailand already ran a fairly balanced budget. The Finance Ministry was very frank and realistic on this — we needed the financial package to restructure our economy and it had to come from the government budget. But the IMF didn't allow us to do it, and we had a very heated discussion on this. The IMF team insisted that we accepted it. Otherwise, it would not get approved by the IMF Board of Directors.

Eventually, I only succeeded in negotiating for things that were really important for the poor such as bus fare, train fare, utilities, and facilities that poor districts needed the most. We managed to maintain the prices for these public services."

Like many, Kuroda had similar comments about the inappropriateness of tight fiscal policy:

"As you know, the Thai finance ministry had always emphasized fiscal discipline and even at that time, the Thai fiscal position was not so bad, but the IMF insisted on fiscal austerity for Thailand, like Mexico or Latin American countries. It was unnecessary. So, there was insufficient amount of financial support, not much financial system support or change, and also stringent fiscal policy.

The IMF also pushed for structural reforms, a stance that Neiss explained as follows:

"In the IMF's view, it was also essential that the crisis was taken as an opportunity to implement long overdue structural changes. In particular, bank restructuring, corporate restructuring, and improvements in the operations of public institutions. (The same view was held in the case of Indonesia and Korea.) These are politically difficult measures which, when everything is going well, tend to be postponed. But the pressure during a crisis makes these reforms possible, at least to some extent. I think their implementation has been of lasting benefit to the country."

Critics, however, questioned whether it was appropriate to undertake these reforms during a crisis. In fact, the measures could be disruptive and undermine confidence.

Another controversial issue regarding reforms was the perception among Thai policymakers of pressure to privatize or sell Thai companies at fire-sale prices, as observed by Thanong:

"The other thing that the IMF recommended was for us to privatize the commercial banks and the public enterprises. Among our public enterprises, only one was profitable, so who was going to buy them, especially in a downturn? [laughs]

In the end, we closed down most of the finance and security companies because they were small lenders. We did not close the commercial banks as we looked for joint venture partners for them. But the IMF pressured us to put them on the liquidation market. But a bank is very big and when you have NPLs of about 40% and higher, you really have nothing left. You have to give a lot more incentives to prospective buyers than ever before to buy these banks. That's why we didn't like it. We thought there were better ways to restructure the financial sector. We tried to improve ongoing concerns, buying time for them to clean up their balance sheets. So, it took us quite a long time. I think later the IMF agreed with the governments after me that there were more flexible options."

Nevertheless, reforms were pursued, of which the most important were for the financial sector. Here, the government closed 56 insolvent finance companies and set up two entities, the Financial Sector Restructuring Authority and the Asset Management Corporation, to deal with the impaired assets of these finance companies.

Other important reforms to improve prudential standards and bank supervision were also started. The efforts would take several years to bear fruit, but an important step had been taken. Neiss' "biggest worry was that the banking system reform would not succeed. Fortunately, it was done alright. That was the most important structural reform."

The tight macroeconomic stance, as noted by Supavud, led to a more severe downturn than anticipated by the IMF:

"That's why the GDP collapsed by about 10% in 1998 whereas the initial IMF estimate called for Thailand's economic recovery in 1998. They had to revise their forecast for 1998 economic growth about four or five times, and it ended up being –10%. It was causing companies to become unviable."

To be fair, the IMF ultimately realized its mistakes and would later revise its programs several times to allow for more expansionary fiscal policy.

Thai financial and economic indicators were still dismal several months into the crisis. In January 1998, the baht fell to a record low, the stock market had halved, GDP was expected to fall by 11%, and retrenchments were rife. It was a difficult business environment, as elaborated by Supavud, as he referred to the overall corporate sector and the fortunes of the brokerage firm he was working for:

> "Well, we had to tell the truth that the recession was very, very severe and that what had happened was this. You have a situation where the government made even the best Thai banks and corporates shaky. Suddenly, they became unviable businesses, and they were all in need of massive capital injection. That's why asset prices had to fall, so we have to advise basically that. And personally speaking, even Petra at the time, we didn't survive. Petra was a finance and securities company. What we had to do was to split the finance side from the company, and the finance part had to be managed down and basically closed down.
>
> And by selling the security side to Merrill Lynch, we sold half of ourselves to Merrill Lynch who gave the money to manage down the finance side, and we survived with huge injury and with huge down-sizing. So, my own research section, which had about 50 to 60 people, was cut down to less than 10. It had to be huge downsizing everywhere in the industry."

Policy Leadership

Thai political developments influenced the course of the crisis. The Chavalit government had been lukewarm about its commitment to the IMF program. This made for policy drift and was negative for investor sentiment. A new coalition government, led by Chuan Leekpai, was elected in November 1997. Despite its slim majority, its policies would underpin the recovery.

The key economic appointment was Tarrin Nimmananahaeminda as Finance Minister. The appointment was viewed by Singh as a turning point:

> "Until the government changed, I think it was in early November, the fiscal numbers would not change. As soon as the new government

came in, Tarrin became the Finance Minister. Instantly, numbers and policies were changed and market confidence came back fairly fast. So, what I'm saying is, in both Thailand and Korea, when the political elites accepted the problem, recovery has proven to be quick.

He was trusted by the PM completely. He wanted to keep us, too. In those years, the government was strong and we managed to push some policies to transform the economy. Things then changed politically and it became more difficult for us."

Another critical appointment was M.R. Chatu Mongol Sonakul, who took over as Governor of the BOT in May 1998. It was a difficult time for the institution. Chatu Mongol recalled the high public disaffection with the BOT then and the need to lift the morale of staff:

"At that time the whole thing was bad. Taxis wouldn't take passengers to the central bank. People who wanted to go to the central bank by taxi had to get off some distance and walk to the BOT because the taxi drivers were so mad at the central bank. They wouldn't even carry passengers to the central bank.

All the lights were turned off. And my first 'rescue' was to turn on the lights by the river. Everything was turned off. Life was turned off, as far as I could see. It was bad. Nobody — you know, when an organization dies, everything just stopped. Why turn off the lights by the river? So, I turned it on."

Chatu Mongol also took it upon himself to replace the old monetary policy framework with one based on inflation targeting:

"We began to stabilize the economy. I then decided to implement inflation targeting since the government wasn't functioning. I appointed a committee by myself and put in some private sector people so that they can say what's going on. And one of them actually was an ex-central banker. And he was an engineer as well by training. And he actually became governor later."

A monetary policy framework around inflation targeting would be formalized later. Also, noting that inflation had fallen, Chatu Mongol lowered money market rates to substantially below the 16–17% levels prevailing then. The lower interest rates would be validated by the IMF's fifth letter of intent of December 1998. It allowed for interest rates of 4–6% and a fiscal deficit of 5% of GDP.

Recovery and Reforms

By mid-1999, signs of economic recovery had emerged. Export volumes rose partly because, as Supavud put it, "currency depreciation did its magic" and partly due to strong US and European economic growth. Fiscal stimulus supported demand. The Chuan government's commitment to stay the course boosted market confidence. In June 1999, the government ceased drawing on IMF funding, a year ahead of schedule.

Bandid elaborated on the decision to end the IMF program early:

"I think that the thinking mainly is that we have now regained the confidence of financial markets. And the long-term program is now no longer needed. Because we don't need subsequent inflows of IMF disbursement.

Because the investor money will be returning. And we have been able to maintain sort of a stable exchange rate. But we are committed to continue with the reform program. And so, I think it's a win-win for both. It's a win-win that Thailand was able to recover. And it's a win-win for the IMF that they could now focus their attention onto somewhere else. We also saved on the interest payments."

The aftermath of the crisis was marked by significant reforms in several areas. The BOT consolidated the monetary policy framework centered on inflation targeting. Bandid elaborated on some of the changes introduced:

"We introduced inflation targeting and floating exchange rate regime as our new monetary policy framework. And you know, with the modalities of open communication, the qualities of good monetary policymaking is all there. We put in place this position of spokesperson. And I was the first spokesperson. And we would have regular releases of economics and financial data. Weekly, monthly, and so on, very systematic. And we adopted the IMF scheme of data releases — the Special Data Dissemination Standard (SDDS).

The need for communication came very clearly before the crisis. Because there were so many questions about the data. And all these market analysts were writing about everything, everywhere, you know? So it's good to have a regular communication platform that the market would listen to in addition to the usual Monetary Policy Committee Press Conference."

The banking sector was strengthened. Banks were better capitalized. Banking supervision and prudential standards were raised to conform to international standards. Fiscal policy would be subject to a Fiscal Sustainability Framework that set guidelines on government borrowing.

Corporate governance standards were also upgraded, as Bandid explained:

"Because you know the indebtedness of companies came as a result of failure in corporate governance. Borrowed too much and spent the money unwisely. So as I was saying, there was a huge reform in corporate governance as well, which I became involved in from the very beginning up to 3 years ago."

Conclusion

All in, the reforms reflected a remarkable resilience to make good of a crisis that was unprecedented and severe. As Bandid observed: "It would have been a missed opportunity if the crisis happened, and nothing came of it."

Chapter 4

Indonesia

This chapter draws on the interviews of six persons: Ginandjar Kartasasmita, Joseph Soedradjad Djiwandono, Dennis De Tray, Hubert Neiss, Eisuke Sakakibara, and Jim Walker. During the 1997 Asian financial crisis, Ginandjar was the Minister of State for National Development Planning before becoming Coordinating Minister of the Economy, Finance, and Industry in the latter part of the crisis. Soedradjad was the then Governor of Bank Indonesia. De Tray was the Director and subsequently Country Head of the World Bank's Indonesia Resident Unit, Neiss was the Director of the Asia Pacific Department at the International Monetary Fund, Sakakibara was Japan's Vice Minister of Finance and International Affairs, and Walker was chief economist at the Hong Kong-based Credit Lyonnais Securities (Asia) Ltd during the crisis.

Indonesia, unlike Thailand, had shown no signs of a brewing crisis. However, it would soon be engulfed by an exceptionally virulent crisis, mainly because the financial crisis would trigger a political crisis that would in turn exacerbate financial instability. Hence, the Indonesian narrative is a powerful illustration of how an incipient crisis that seemed containable escalated into one so severe because of the interaction of economic and political forces. Yet, Indonesia overcame the crisis and, in the process, emerged as a well-functioning democracy and emerging market economy.

Pre-Crisis Fundamentals

When the Thai baht was floated on July 2, 1997, Indonesian policymakers were sanguine that they would not be much affected. Joseph Soedradjad Djiwandono summed up the sentiments at the central bank:

"At that time, we were still confident about what we had been doing because we thought we had faced these kinds of things before. In late 1994 during the Mexican peso crisis, or the 'Tequila crisis,' we also felt some effects. Our economy was very open, our capital account was very open, so it was easy for our foreign exchange market to be disrupted by these headwinds. But we were very successful in dealing with them. We had run a managed float, putting the rupiah in a certain band, with an upper and lower limit. Whenever the band was touched, it was usually facing depreciation, not appreciation. We of course intervened, which cost our reserves, but we still were doing okay."

Ginandjar Kartasasmita cited various reasons why the outbreak of the Thai crisis was at first not taken seriously by the business community or policymakers:

"...most of the vital economic figures indicated sound fundamentals in Indonesia. From 1989 to 1996, annual real gross domestic product (GDP) growth averaged 8%, spurred by strong investment behavior. The overall fiscal balance was in surplus after 1992, and public debt fell as a share of GDP as the government used privatization proceeds to repay large amounts of foreign debt. Inflation, which hovered around 10%, was a little higher than those of other East Asian economies, but was still low by developing country standards. Moreover, since the Indonesian economy had been subjected to various crises in the past and had always come out stronger, the general atmosphere was one of confidence in the resilience of the economy."

Not only were its fundamentals sound, Indonesia also had a reputable economic team in charge. Dennis De Tray thought highly of the team's caliber. Headed by Widjojo Nitisatro, one of the most revered Indonesian economists, the "Berkeley Mafia" as it was informally known, was rated by De Tray as

"among the best set of economists I've worked with anywhere in the world during my tenure at the World Bank. They were absolutely spot-on, so it's not that I or the International Monetary Fund (IMF) or anybody else had to tell them what to do. They knew what to do, and they were doing it. Mar'ie Muhammad was the Minister of Finance at the time."

Preemptive Measures

The baht devaluation was followed by selling pressure on the regional currencies, not just the rupiah. Indonesian policy makers reacted promptly to support the currency with a battery of measures considered credible by international media and analysts. First, unlike the Bank of Thailand, Bank Indonesia (BI) widened the intervention margins of the crawling peg regime of the rupiah to allow more scope for the market to determine an acceptable rupiah level.

However, the rupiah was persistently hitting the lower bound, which called for continuous BI intervention to keep the rupiah within the specified band. It was contrary to BI's earlier experiences when the rupiah would move toward the upper bound whenever the band had been shifted. This was an ominous sign, as recalled by Soedradjad:

> "In July 1997, we still thought we were managing things well. We widened the band again as we thought it would give more freedom to the market to determine what kind of exchange rate was acceptable. However, we started to feel that it didn't work like before. I remember during that period, there were a lot of people who said, 'Yeah, you're doing okay.' But that was at the start before things went downhill."

On August 14, 1997, Soedradjad, with the approval of President Suharto, did away with the crawling peg system. BI had sensed that intervention to support the system would be mostly a case of squandering its reserves. BI then floated the currency, as elaborated by Soedradjad:

> "By August 1997, when we knew that band widening didn't really work, meaning that the rupiah kept depreciating, we decided to completely float it. There was debate about this, but I thought it was important to not continue depleting our foreign exchange reserves."

To support the now free-floating rupiah, BI also raised interest rates and tightened liquidity by transferring large amounts of public sector deposits out of commercial banks into state banks. The government next announced in September 1997 the "10 policy" measures to bolster investor confidence. These included the postponement of large infrastructure projects, which in aggregate would cost about USD 13 billion. Ginandjar, who was tasked with selecting the canceled projects, noted the market's response to the cancellation:

> "It was received by the market as a positive sign of the government's determination to prevent further deterioration of the economy, especially as some of the projects were linked to the President's family. The authorities' initial response to the threat of contagion was widely praised for being prompt and decisive."

Still, as Ginandjar observed, the slew of measures thus far implemented did not stem rupiah weakness:

> "These measures failed to restore market confidence in the rupiah. It continued to depreciate; and by early September, the rupiah had moved beyond IDR 3,000 per United States (US) dollar, more than 20% below the average for the first 6 months of the year."

What was undermining the efforts of policy makers was the incessant selling of rupiah for foreign currencies. This was not just by the hedge funds. The more worrying development was Indonesian corporates taking steps to hedge their foreign currency debts.

The Achilles' Heel: Unhedged External Corporate Debt

Indications were that the official statistics understated the foreign currency borrowings of Indonesian corporates. Jim Walker gave a reason why:

> "That was the interesting thing, Indonesia looked perfectly okay on the published numbers. This was largely down to how the reporting of offshore borrowing was handled in Indonesia. It definitely beats me. I didn't see it coming.
>
> A lot of people had concluded that Indonesia looked as if it had perfectly acceptable short-term external borrowing. But what was happening was that it had contracted huge amounts of syndicated loans, mostly from Japanese banks but aided by European and American banks as well, which never really got reported in the official statistics for whatever reason."

De Tray noted that Indonesian companies had been borrowing overseas in large amounts for years:

> "Another thing worth mentioning is that Indonesia's case was not a public debt crisis. It was a private debt crisis. Indonesian firms had borrowed in US dollar for years, with their income streams denominated in rupiah. It was cheaper to have this arrangement and they were arbitraging the cost. But, when the rupiah started to collapse, many companies went bust. Also, the Indonesian court system was not designed to deal with bankruptcies. So, a gridlock emerged in the system, exacerbating the country's decline."

Soedradjad acknowledged that external corporate debt was Indonesia's Achilles' heel as a large portion was unhedged. In addition, he disclosed that BI did not have good data on how much private sector debt was unhedged:

> "To me, Indonesian conglomerates' foreign exposure, loans denominated in dollars, was the core of the problem. For Indonesia, the conglomerates were the ones who were deeply leveraged.
>
> Maybe it's moral hazard. Maybe they trusted the economic management in the beginning too much that they thought that everything was okay. Of course, our interest rate in general was much higher than the interest rate of the developed world, so it was natural that they borrowed abroad. Additionally, our capital account was very free; you can borrow whatever that you liked at that time. For the business groups, it was much easier and cheaper to finance their operations using loans denominated in foreign currencies. That's why they became so leveraged. A lot of these loans were also short-term loans, creating even more pressure on the foreign exchange market when the contagion spread from Thailand.
>
> Actually, when I announced in August 1997 that Indonesia was to free float the rupiah, many business leaders confronted me and asked, 'Mr. Governor, how could you do this? This whole thing is not a good idea'. I immediately asked them, 'You mean you've never really covered your exposure?' I almost fainted when their answer was, 'Of course not.'"

The floating of the rupiah and the raising of interest rates hence led to an unintended consequence: a rush by Indonesian corporates to hedge their foreign currency loans. Instead of stabilizing the currency, these measures contributed to further rupiah weakness. In early October, the rupiah had passed IDR 3,800 to the US dollar, a depreciation of more than 30% since July.

Approaching the IMF

Earlier in September 1997, the government had approached the IMF for a "precautionary" arrangement. This was viewed as a means of getting informal IMF advice on proposed policies without the strict conditionality that comes with a formal arrangement. Soedradjad was a proponent of this approach:

> "I was arguing for an IMF precautionary arrangement. That means the IMF will be approving our condition and almost like a blessing,

which is the thing that we needed at that time. As I said, we needed the support of the international community for our foreign exchange market and the economic management. So, to me, that will be good enough because I understood the conditionality of a stand-by arrangement, and I thought my boss, President Suharto, wouldn't really like all this conditionality. So, I said, let's have that. But then, the dynamics of the decision changed very fast."

Soedradjad's intuition that Suharto would be averse to IMF conditionalities would materialize later in the crisis. In fact, the President's vacillating responses to IMF conditionalities would be a major reason for the crisis turning for the worse.

Nevertheless, in October 1997, growing alarm about the gravity of the situation caused the government to formally request for a regular IMF program. After about 3 weeks of negotiations, a letter of intent (LOI) was signed on October 31. Under the financial assistance package, the IMF and World Bank would provide USD 10 billion and USD 8 billion, respectively. A second line of finance was also made available if needed. Its contributors were Japan and Singapore, USD 5.0 billion each; US, USD 3.0 billion; Brunei, USD 1.2 billion; Australia, Malaysia, China, and Hong Kong, USD 1.0 billion each.

Ginandjar revealed that the IMF negotiations were a closely-guarded secret:

"You may not believe it, but when the Indonesian government negotiated with the IMF, no outside minister was involved. It was almost like a secret. Nobody knew that negotiations were going on. It was Coordinating Minister Saleh Afiff, Finance Minister Mar'ie Muhammad, and BI Governor Soedradjad who negotiated with the IMF, but it was also very clear that Soedradjad — with Ali Wardhana by his side — was supervising their negotiations with the IMF. So the rest of the cabinet, including the Chairman of Bappenas (me), was in the dark. In fact, the entire Indonesian nation was kept in the dark. I was only once asked to sit in on a meeting with an IMF representative at the invitation of Soedradjad. But at that time, we were not given the impression of the gravity of the situation."

Markets greeted the signing of the IMF program with tentative optimism. The rupiah strengthened from around IDR 3,800 to IDR 3,200 against the US dollar. However, the optimism quickly subsided as questions arose as to whether the government would see through the conditions. This was because of the program's wide ambit. It focused not just on the usual macroeconomic adjustments but also on the reform of the banking sector and structural reforms of the economy. Each of these — banking reform, macroeconomic policies, and structural reforms — would be a source of tension and controversy.

Banking Reform

The IMF made banking reform a priority. Soedradjad revealed that the IMF ratified the Agreement only after he and the Minister of Finance signed an undertaking to take action on insolvent banks:

> "Bank closure was part of the so-called 'prior action.' The rationale was that if you are really serious about your plan, then you have to show some commitment. So, prior action from our side meant that we agreed on bank restructuring, which included the closing of insolvent banks. We had to decide, after looking into the balance sheets of 238 banks, in under 2 weeks. Of course, we knew about the health of these banks, but the dynamics were so volatile that the balance sheets would change by the hour. We had to make a final decision on which banks to close, which we did on November 1, 1997."

So, on November 1, the government announced the closure of 16 banks that were facing liquidity problems. Although they were only small banks, the closure led to events that destabilized the banking system and brought the crisis to the man in the street.

Initially, the closure of the insolvent banks was viewed favorably, especially as three of the banks were connected to the President's family. However, the closures soon fanned depositor panic. De Tray blamed the IMF for not being cognizant of the complexity of the banking system in Indonesia:

> "Let me tell you what went wrong. Indonesia had many banks, and many of them were pocket banks serving an individual or a small group of people. They were not well-managed. So, the Indonesians were suspicious of their banking system anyway. Then the IMF comes along and closes something like 20 banks, putting some of them under receivership. This spooked everyone and the people started

withdrawing their cash and putting them in the international banks. This imperiled the local banks, with some of them suffering bank runs. It was a wholly predictable outcome, at least that's what the World Bank thought. Yes, the banking system was weak and needed reforms. Yet, half-measures like those pushed by the IMF only worsened the problem."

However, the manner in which the policy was carried can also be questioned. The President's son was allowed to reopen his bank, though in a different name. In addition, the President reversed the cancellation of some projects connected to his inner circle, a sign that he was intent on protecting their interests. Later, weak banks were kept afloat through a liquidity support scheme. Ginandjar noted that BI had, by the end of January 1998, provided support equivalent to "5% of GDP and 100% of base money." The liquidity expansion led to loss of monetary control and higher inflation. It also fueled capital flight, weakening the rupiah.

Commenting on how events unfolded, Hubert Neiss made the point that politics undermined the bank reform effort:

"I think the underlying cause was the great political uncertainty. Now the first IMF program didn't fare well despite all the right measures and all the right intentions. But from the beginning, for political reasons, the implementation didn't really work well. The first bank closures were mishandled. Some closed banks were reopened by the President and so on. So all the efforts by other countries to help, including joint foreign exchange market intervention by Japan and Singapore to help the rupiah, it didn't help because there was mistrust and uncertainty in the government."

Ginandjar also referred to the mistakes made in implementing the policy:

"I think the closure of the failing banks itself was the right policy. But the way we did it was the problem."

It was a difficult time for BI. In truth, it was figuratively fighting a host of battles with at least one arm tied behind its back as it had to counter policy indecisiveness and inconsistency as well. Soedradjad recalled the hectic period for BI staff during the crisis:

"It was almost like sleeping at the central bank for months. And we even had some new patterns of work. The board meeting at BI, at the time, was once a week. During the crisis, I met with the members of the board, plus the staff, twice a day. There were the morning calls and evening calls, which allowed us to check what has been going around in the markets. That's how we knew the contagion has spread from the foreign exchange market to the banking sector. Worse, the banking shocks then spread to the society, creating lots of political problems such as the May 1998 demonstrations against the government. But the unrest had already started in December 1997."

Macroeconomic Policy

The macroeconomic policies recommended by the IMF were the standard ones it applied to debtor countries. These aimed to reduce aggregate demand through fiscal restraint and stabilize the currency through tighter monetary policy. Like for Thailand, these polices did not address the fundamental issues of corporate debt and volatile capital flows. The tight policies in fact pushed banks and corporates into further difficulties, which in turn led to the rupiah weakening, as commented by Ginandjar:

"On the contrary, the loss of value became more severe than generally anticipated. In retrospect, I would agree with the observation of many writers that both the IMF and the Indonesian government misjudged the depth and nature of the crisis."

Eisuke Sakakibara, who was the Vice Minister at the Japanese Ministry of Finance, was also a critic of the IMF approach:

"Yes, the IMF insisted on tightening fiscal policy and also insisted on closure of some of the bad banks. But again, if you close banks at the time of the crisis, it will generate more debt as the financial crisis is developing. And that is exactly what happened. And tightening the fiscal policy at the time of the crisis is the wrong policy as well. You should use the fiscal fund to solve the problem; rather than tighten, you should loosen the fiscal policy. But I don't know, the IMF has made serious mistakes."

Structural Reforms

The IMF program also called for reforms of the real economy. It was a wide-ranging request, covering the elimination of monopolies to removal of restrictions on imports, as noted by Soedradjad:

> "And the conditionality of the IMF loan to Indonesia, maybe, was the most stringent. I think it became more curious that the IMF supported structural conditionality, which is related to the structure of the economy. It was criticized by many. That is not the expertise and the jurisdiction of IMF, talking about the real sector, restructuring, etc. And we can check in the LOI, the structural conditionality of Indonesia is like a checklist. More than a hundred something items. You have to get rid of the monopoly of clove imports, and a lot of other silly things. I mean, it's true that you should do that, but to put that as a condition for a loan or a liquidity loan, is not really that great."

Sakakibara saw the imposition of structural reforms as an ill-timed attempt to tackle what was termed as "crony capitalism." He was of the view that the US Treasury was prodding the IMF to push for such reforms:

> "I've been very critical of the IMF's handling of the Asian financial crisis (AFC), particularly the Asian department of the IMF that handled the problem. And they tried to sort of take advantage of the crisis to impose some form of propositions on Asian countries, that is, to structurally reform what they, at that time, called the crony capitalism. It was the wrong approach at that time — to try to change the structure of the economy during a crisis is very difficult. And so their trying to change the Asian economies during the crisis was the wrong approach, as adopted by the IMF. Probably, at that time, the US government supported the IMF."

Financial and Political Crisis

Beginning late November 1997, matters would go seriously wrong. Indonesia would be in the grip of a currency, banking, and corporate crisis. To these would be added a political crisis. Contagion from attacks on regional currencies also played a part in clouding market confidence in the rupiah and Indonesian stock market. By December 1997, the rupiah was trading within a range of IDR 5,000–6,000 against the US dollar.

The next critical development was the announcement of the Budget for fiscal year (FY) 1998/99 on January 6, 1998. It was the trigger for a historic plunge in the value of the rupiah. Even Ginandjar, who was involved in preparing the budget, saw the budget as unrealistic:

> "I was involved in the preparation of the budget because the development budget came under my responsibility. My job was to prepare development programs under the designated parameters. But even then I could see that the government budget was so unreasonable. There was no deficit and a 4% growth was projected. Of course, the market did not believe it. As a result, the rupiah took a nosedive."

The market in fact saw the proposed budget as expansionary, contravening the IMF's condition for a budget surplus. It confirmed doubts about President Suharto's commitment to the IMF program. On January 8, 1998 ("Black Thursday"), the rupiah plunged 25% to breach the psychological barrier of IDR 10,000 to the US dollar. This set off fears of hyperinflation, leading to panic buying of groceries and food in Jakarta. There were also riots.

At this point, international leaders began calling President Suharto to urge him to stay the course with the IMF. On January 8, 1998, US President Bill Clinton spoke to him. Other leaders that called included German Chancellor Helmut Kohl and Japanese Prime Minister Ryutaro Hashimoto. Their common message to Suharto was that he could bring the country out of its troubles, but only if he worked with the IMF. Suharto then agreed to do so.

Over the following week, the IMF and Indonesian teams worked on a second LOI. This would come to be known as the "50-point Plan." Apart from the usual macroeconomic targets, the LOI is famously known for its comprehensive list of reforms aimed at removing the concessions enjoyed by the President's family and his inner circle. These included withdrawal of tax privileges for the national (Timor) car project; the elimination of cement, paper, and plywood cartels; the withdrawal of support for the aircraft industry; and other governance and structural reforms. Much criticism has been laid on the IMF for loading the LOI with reform conditionalities, including by Paul Volcker, former Chairman of the US Federal Reserve.

Ginandjar also noted the unusual manner as to how the final contents of the LOI were finalized and what it conveyed about President Suharto's state of mind with regard to his ministers:

"What was extraordinary about the event was that the final content of the LOI was decided not between the Indonesian authorities and the IMF staff, as it normally would be, but directly in a meeting between the President and Stanley Fischer, first Deputy Managing Director of the IMF. Surprisingly, even to his ministers, the President agreed to sign the whole package as presented by the IMF.

Some read this unusual chain of events surrounding the signing of the January 1998 LOI as a signal of the growing distrust of the President toward his economic team at that time. In private discussions I had with the President, he complained not only about their competence but also the sincerity of some of the economic team members."

On January 15, 1998, Suharto signed the second LOI with IMF Managing Director Michel Camdessus as witness. The event was nationally televised. Unfortunately, its enduring image was that of a seemingly imperious arm-crossed Camdessus peering at President Suharto signing off on all the conditions placed on him. As Neiss puts it, it conveyed the impression of an "imperialist" IMF, both in Indonesia and across the region:

"I participated in the signing ceremony, and nothing strange occurred to me then. But when I saw the picture the next day in the Indonesian paper, I realized that this could give the unfortunate impression that the IMF was dominating the policies of Indonesia. And unfortunately, this impression actually prevailed in the public. Certainly the Managing Director did not intend it."

As significantly, the image was also perceived as symbolic of an enfeebled President who had lost control of events. Adding to rumors that he was in poor health, it reinforced the perception that the Suharto era was ending. The possibility of a regime change added a political element to the crisis.

The signing of the second LOI also did not bolster confidence. In fact, the rupiah fell by about 6% the day of the signing and about 5% the next day. There were two reasons for the disappointing reactions. First, it was quickly perceived, as pointed out by Ginandjar, that the program, for all its numerous stipulations to correct distortions in the economy, did not address the underlying causes of the crisis:

"The January IMF program was designed to restore confidence in the government by showing that the government was ready to break with the past. Although it was extensive in outlining structural reform programs with a specific timetable for implementation, it did not include a clear agenda for dealing with bank and corporate debt restructuring, which lay at the core of the crisis. At this point the crisis had clearly become systemic."

Second, markets were skeptical that Suharto would honor his promises contained in the second LOI. These instincts would soon be validated. Ginandjar revealed that from the beginning Suharto saw his concessions to the IMF as a temporary retreat, to be reneged later at an opportune time:

"It became clear that President Suharto had no intention of adhering to the structural conditionality of the January program, even though he had signed it himself. In a closed-door meeting in which I was present, he drew an analogy of his dealings with IMF as a 'guerrilla war.' Guerrilla warfare incorporates retreat and advance as normal tactics. A retreat does not necessarily imply defeat but a temporary way out of a difficult situation. His signing of the LOI and its conditionality was just a tactical retreat for him. He said that the promises could be circumvented later when we were in a stronger position."

In late January 1998, with the rupiah remaining weak, President Suharto's relationship with the IMF soured further. The President then surfaced the idea of a currency board system (CBS) as a means of stabilizing the rupiah. Steve Hanke, an American economist and currency board advocate, was appointed as a consultant. As Ginandjar pointed out, the floating of the CBS idea led to more confusion and to heightened acrimony between President Suharto and the IMF:

"On the other hand, Camdessus publicly declared that if the government adopted the CBS, the IMF would discontinue its program in Indonesia. But the President, desperate to find a quick fix to the exchange rate problem, developed enthusiasm for the CBS. In February, the President publicly introduced the idea. He made it more official in his accountability speech to the Parliament on March 1, 1998. With the CBS concept in mind he spoke about an 'IMF plus' strategy. The ensuing CBS controversy not only added uncertainty to the already confused public, but also served to distract the government from moving ahead with implementing reforms and regaining monetary control."

Soedradjad and his BI colleagues were against the idea, albeit privately. Objective opinion would agree with his arguments why Indonesia was not ready for a CBS:

> "First, we didn't have enough foreign exchange to back it up when I heard that the idea was to peg the rupiah from IDR 10,000 to IDR 5,000 against the US dollar. My God! And then I'm afraid that President Suharto didn't understand well what the currency board means.
>
> The way I understood, the currency board should be like in a plane on autopilot. The minute you believe in the autopilot, you don't intervene. And at that time, I was, again, I didn't dare to say it in public, but I think the propensity to intervene by President Suharto in economic management is too huge.
>
> Then, if I said, 'Okay, go ahead,' my understanding is that the family also has a lot of foreign exchange exposure. They will come to BI saying, 'Hey, I need to buy dollars based on the more favorable rate.' They will want to buy more dollars. How could I say no to him? So, I said, okay, I'm checking. But that's how I felt. That was the real reason I didn't really agree with the currency board."

World leaders pressed on President Suharto to abandon the CBS idea. President Clinton and a host of world leaders urged him to follow the IMF's counsel. Eventually, the CBS idea was quietly dropped but the controversy it had generated weakened Suharto's credibility even more.

Another blow to market confidence was the dismissal of Soedradjad as Governor of BI. He was a highly respected central banker, even more so because of the extremely difficult circumstance that BI had to operate under. Soedradjad recalled how he was, in his words, "fired":

> "I was summoned by President Suharto when he told me that I was discharged. I never really forget the date — it was February 11, 1998. Only the two of us were there. He said, 'It will take a little while for the new government to be set up, and I'll like to replace you with someone else. Thank you for your service of 10 years with me.' I was very well-prepared because I had first wanted to resign in December 1997 when the pressure was so overbearing. Four of my seven managing directors were fired by him, without my prior consultation. Then, he sent in new people whom I don't agree with. I was acting like a real

Javanese when you fight against your boss. You do it very elegantly. You don't try to get mad or whatever. You stay as calm as possible.

I was discharged only about 6 weeks before my term as BI Governor was over. I don't think he has a good reason to remove me, however. Even if you count the liquidity support which I agreed with and a lot of people claimed was bad, it was continued by my successor. That is the way I saw things. He is a clever politician. He didn't say he fired me. I was discharged with honor. But in my interpretation, I was fired."

In March 1998, Suharto was reelected, though not in propitious circumstances. The IMF had withheld the disbursement of the second tranche of the IMF program. Suharto remained defiant, choosing a cabinet that included his daughter and close business associates. Rising unemployment and rising prices of consumer goods sparked riots. There were calls for the President to step down.

The international community made efforts to persuade President Suharto to work with the IMF again. There was concern about the political instability that could occur if Suharto was deposed.

Through the crisis, the IMF had sought advice from Singapore leaders on how it could work better with President Suharto. Neiss recounted a suggestion from Lee Kuan Yew, then Singapore's Senior Minister, that Suharto chair a high-level crisis team so that he could take ownership for its decisions:

"Suharto's mistrust of the technocrats only arose during the crisis. At a meeting of the IMF Managing Director with Lee (where I was also present), this was discussed and the proposal arose that Suharto himself should be the leader of the crisis team of technocrats. Then, whatever was decided would be Suharto's program, his decision.

This proposal was actually implemented. A 'Resilience Council' was established. It included the economic team of technocrats and Prabhakar Narvekar, IMF Deputy Director. Its regular meetings were chaired by Suharto. The idea was, since Suharto was the head of the group, he would see to it that whatever was decided would actually be implemented.

But sad to say, after some time, it became obvious that it didn't work. The measures were just dragged out, changed, or not taken at all. That was not foreseen at the meeting in Singapore, when there were high hopes, that with this council under Suharto's leadership, Indonesia could maneuver itself out of the crisis."

As demonstrations continued to call for his resignation, Suharto agreed to a third LOI with the IMF on April 3, 1998. It did not ease the situation. President Suharto began publicly criticizing the IMF. Then, he raised fuel and electricity prices, one of the conditions of the LOI, probably to foment popular anger against the IMF. Instead, this led to wider student demonstrations demanding Suharto's resignation. There were also riots directed at the ethnic Chinese population. More capital flight ensued, a phenomenon that De Tray observed was a reminder of a past episode:

"The population was also very conscious of what had happened the last time Indonesia had a regime change, when power gravitated from Sukarno to Suharto. Hundreds of thousands of people were killed then, many of whom were ethnic Chinese. When the AFC was combined with a collapsing rupiah, in addition to a possible regime change (which eventually took place), the ethnic Chinese said, 'Not again.' Many of them then moved their wealth to Singapore, wreaking havoc on the financial system. For several months, BI bled foreign exchange, and initially it didn't do anything to try to stop this outflow. By the time people realized how bad things were, the foreign reserves were gone."

Amid growing calls for his resignation, even from his former supporters, Suharto stepped down on May 21, 1998, handing power over to his Vice President Bacharuddin Jusuf Habibie. Few had expected this outcome at the start of the crisis as Suharto had been a decisive leader, as observed by Neiss:

"I remember earlier times, when I was Resident Representative of the IMF in Indonesia in the 1970s. There was the Pertamina crisis then and also a rice crisis later. On these occasions, Suharto was very decisive and effective, trusted his technocrat advisors, and everybody in the government was behind a common action plan. That was all missing during the Asian crisis. So Suharto had changed."

Resolution and Recovery

Habibie inherited a nation in deep crisis. The markets were depressed with the rupiah falling to around IDR 17,000 against the US dollar in June 1998. Domestic banks were weak and the corporate sector was insolvent. The economy had contracted by close to 8% and 17% in the first and second quarters of 1998, respectively. Unemployment and poverty levels had risen.

The new President tackled these challenges decisively and rationally. He committed to work with the IMF. It was a positive turnaround, as Neiss noted:

"Effective policy measures only happened after Suharto had resigned ('stepped down' in his words), and Habibie became President. At my first meeting with him I was very encouraged by his determination to work with the IMF and to implement the program. And this was subsequently done, with the effort of his new team, in particular, the Coordinating Minister Ginandjar."

The Habibie administration embarked on a series of measures to stabilize the financial sector and the economy. Basically, the economic team resumed the recovery program that had been undertaken by the previous government before it was interrupted by the political crisis leading to the change in government.

The team's agenda, as Ginandjar pointed out, consisted of five programs:

"1) restoring macroeconomic stability; 2) restructuring of the banking system; 3) resolution of corporate debt; 4) continuing with structural reform; and 5) stimulating demand and reducing the impact of the crisis on the poor through the social safety net."

Neiss noted the role of the international community in reviving the economy:

"Yes, the turnaround occurred after a new government took over. The political situation became more settled and the IMF program was gradually implemented. In addition, the international community was effective in helping to provide not only more loans through the international institutions, but also loans and grants on a bilateral basis. Some countries also provided technical assistance to Indonesia to advise on financial and other reforms."

When Habibie stepped down as President in late 1999, Indonesia was no longer in crisis mode. The rupiah had stabilized at a level between IDR 6,500 and IDR 7,000 per US dollar, not a small achievement considering that in May 1998, when Habibie's government took charge of the economy, the rupiah was at IDR 17,000 per US dollar.

The more settled rupiah, as Ginandjar noted, reflected fundamental improvements:

> "This principally was the result of market forces, not government intervention in the market for foreign exchange. Sustained commitment to conservative monetary policies and a gradual return of capital from abroad had been attributed to the recovery of the exchange rate."

Politically, President Habibie laid the groundwork for a democratic system, as De Tray noted:

> "Suddenly, with Suharto leaving, Habibie was President. I knew Habibie well. I went to see him shortly after he became President. Even then you could tell he was uncomfortable with being President. But he was the person who launched real democracy in Indonesia, setting up relatively open and fair elections. Indonesia settled into a decent democratic pathway. People began to realize their votes mattered and they had some decent leadership since."

Indonesia had surmounted the trauma of the AFC and had transitioned from an autocratic regime to a democracy while the economy stabilized and gradually recovered from the depths of the financial crisis.

Chapter 5

Korea

This chapter draws on the interviews of eight persons: Chang-yuel Lim, Duck-koo Chung, Yang-ho Byeon, Kyung-wook Hur, Joong-Kyung Choi, Hubert Neiss, Eisuke Sakakibara, and Haruhiko Kuroda. During the 1997 Asian financial crisis, Lim was the Korean Deputy Prime Minister-cum-Minister of Finance and Economy. Chung was the then Vice Minister of Finance and Economy. Byeon was the then Director General of Finance Bureau, Ministry of Finance and Economy. Hur and Choi were both senior officials at the Ministry of Finance and Economy. Neiss was the then Director of the Asia Pacific Department at the International Monetary Fund. Sakakibara was Japan's Vice Minister of Finance and International Affairs. Kuroda was then Director General of the International Bureau at the Japanese Ministry of Finance.

Having just joined the Organization for Economic Co-operation and Development (OECD) in 1996, Korea was expected to sidestep the regional crisis. However, not only did the crisis spread to Korea, but the country nearly went into sovereign default, an event that could have had global financial and security consequences. The default was averted by a concerted international effort. Nevertheless, Korea suffered a deep downturn. As remarkable though was the speed of the country's recovery, reflecting the leadership of a charismatic President who was firmly committed to the International Monetary Fund (IMF) program and determined to push through comprehensive reforms.

The Unexpected Crisis

Prior to the crisis, the Korean economy appeared to be robust, with yearly gross domestic product (GDP) growth of 7–9%, moderate inflation, and balanced budgets in the 3 years before the crisis. In addition, Korea's admission into the OECD in 1996 confirmed its status as an advanced industrial economy.

Hubert Neiss, citing Korea's impressive economic performance over the years, saw the crisis as a "big surprise":

> "Yes, Korea was really a big surprise. Not only to the Korean government and the Koreans, but also to the international community. Korea had been admired as an 'Asian Tiger,' rapidly taking off after the Korean War, expanding industrial development, becoming a member of the OECD, being classified as an industrial country by the World Bank and the IMF — and suddenly we saw the star performer beginning to collapse. Nobody foresaw its suddenness and seriousness."

Kyung-wook Hur expressed the sentiments of his peers by describing the occurrence of the crisis as a "great shock":

> "It was a great shock. All of us were really shocked: we joined the OECD back in 1996, but more than that, I think in 1994 or 1995, the World Bank came up with a report on 'The East Asian Miracle.' We were one of the four tigers mentioned in the report. We also had the Article IV consultation with the IMF back in 1996, and they all said that we had great fundamentals, even though there were some vulnerabilities."

In addition, Hur referred to the burgeoning Korean semiconductor industry as another confidence booster for the country, particularly with Samsung showing signs of becoming a world champion in the field:

> "In addition, there was the 'illusion' arising from semiconductors. Between 1993 and 1995, semiconductors were booming. We also had Samsung, which was turning into a global champion at around that time. In 1995, Korea broke the USD 100 billion export record for the first time."

Vulnerabilities

Korea's sound fundamentals, however, masked vulnerabilities. Reflecting on the situation then, Hur pinpointed three weaknesses that reinforced each other to produce an exceptionally severe crisis:

> "(W)e had a banking problem, an industrial problem, and a void in political leadership. All of these things combined to form the perfect storm. Of course, many of us were complacent too."

Troubled Corporate Sector

The industrial problem was the parlous state of the *chaebols*, the family-owned conglomerates that dominated the Korean economy. From the early 1990s, the *chaebols* had gone on a debt-financed investment binge. Most had set up multiple subsidiaries to venture into sectors deemed prestigious, but which would be marked by excess capacity and thin margins, as observed by Hur:

> "But when we liberalized in the 1990s, the government toned down these industrial policies, believing that the privatized banks will scrutinize the lending better than the government. However, the banks, with no clear majority owners, were lending almost freely to the conglomerates, who were backed up by cross-guarantees. This indirectly caused overlapping, uncoordinated investments from other aspiring conglomerates. For semiconductors, there used to be only Samsung, but with a freer market, firms like LG and Hyundai jumped in. The overlapping investments also occurred in other major industries like automobile, shipping, and petrochemicals."

As concerning as their unprofitable ventures was the level of debt built up by the *chaebols*, "with most of the conglomerates reaching 300% (of debt-to-equity ratios) on the eve of the Asian financial crisis (AFC)," as noted by Hur. In fact, debt-to-equity ratios above 500% were common.

In 1996, *chaebol* difficulties became evident when a drop in international prices of Korea's main exports, which included semiconductors and steel, hit their earnings. Declining revenues, investment losses, and high debt burdens led to a spate of bankruptcies. In early 1997, six of the 30 *chaebols* entered into bankruptcy proceedings. These included the sixth and eighth largest *chaebols*, SsangYong and Kia Motors, respectively.

It was not just overambitious, imprudent management that caused the difficulties of the *chaebols*. Yang-ho Byeon noted that weak banking practices and permissive regulatory oversight also contributed to the problems:

> "I think it was due to the lax corporate management. Korea also faced a crisis as the banking sector, the government, and politicians did not punish the non-competitive companies and just kept them operating until the crisis erupted."

Over-Extended Banking Sector

The troubled *chaebol* sector precipitated a banking crisis. Korean banks had extended long-term won loans to the *chaebols* funded through short-term external borrowing. They were thus exposed to a double maturity and currency mismatch, a situation that left them vulnerable when foreign creditor banks began withdrawing their funds.

Korean banks resorted to borrowing short-term, instead of long-term, funds as the Korean government had chosen to liberalize short-term inflows ahead of long-term inflows, as Haruhiko Kuroda observed:

> "Once a country becomes a member of the OECD, they would be told of the necessity to free up their capital (account). At that time, the Korean government liberalized the holding of short-term funds by banks. Secondly, with that situation as background, as Korean banks started to lend money to Korean companies, American banks provided short-term United States (US) dollar funds for a week or a month. On the other hand, there was long-term lending to the companies."

It was a profitable venture. Banks opened foreign branches to tap onto foreign funds. More dramatic was the proliferation of merchant banks that were allowed to engage in foreign exchange transactions. Thus, within a few years, close to 30 merchant banks, some set up by *chaebols*, had been established. Their sole purpose was intermediating cheaper foreign currency funds into long-term domestic loans. Byeon noted:

> "Korean merchant banks made huge profits by borrowing a lot of foreign funds short term and then giving long-term loans to businesses. Few people anticipated the problem as the merchant banks were making so much money."

The problem did emerge in the form of rising nonperforming loans (NPLs) in the banking sector as more *chaebols* ran into difficulties. Korean banks also faced a growing liquidity crunch as foreign banks became reluctant to roll over their loans. Byeon recalled that the liquidity squeeze was already perceptible in September 1997.

Actually, there were also other warning signs that a crunch was about to break out, Chang-yuel Lim mentioned:

"There had been several warnings about the foreign exchange crisis throughout 1997. In April 1997, Park Young-cheol, the President of the Korea Institute of Finance, wrote in his special report that these practices and situations could lead to a Mexico-style financial crisis. But all of these warnings were ignored by the responsible government officials."

Political Void

The political situation in Korea in 1997 revolved around the presidential election scheduled for December. It was contested by three candidates. This made for a charged political environment as political parties jockeyed for support of their candidates. The result was political gridlock and indecisive responses to deal with the impending crisis.

At a Harvard Kennedy School seminar where he was asked whether a crisis would have occurred if there had been no presidential election, Duck-koo Chung replied:

"Had it not been for the political situation with the upcoming presidential election at that time, the Blue House might not have been malfunctioning. The Blue House's 'malfunctioning' had allowed the handling of very pressing issues to be politicized. I don't think there would have been such a problem without the presidential election. For this reason, good plans and measures such as a payment guarantee for the banks' external debt could not be properly discussed and executed. There was such a plan in September 1997, but it did not go anywhere."

Hur elaborated on how the politics at that time leaned toward populist measures:

"In addition, we were entering a new election year, with the prospect of a new President. However, these structural issues were not properly addressed because of the need to capture votes, populist ones especially. When the companies were facing bankruptcy, politicians would seek protection for them, saying they're national champions, big employment generators, and they don't want to see mass unemployment before the election."

Inception of Crisis

Ineffectual government responses stirred negative market perceptions. The government's decision on October 22, 1997 to bail out near-bankrupt Kia Motors turned out to be significant. Hur recalled:

> "This dealt a big blow to us. It signaled that the Korean government could not rein in companies that were considered too big to fail."

Two days later, Standard & Poor's (S&P) downgraded Korea's sovereign rating, further depressing market confidence. Foreign banks accelerated their withdrawals from Korean banks.

By November 1997, Korea was in crisis mode. Market confidence in won assets had plummeted. Adding to the pessimism were the speculative attacks on currencies elsewhere in the region. Foreign banks refused to roll over their loans to Korean banks. Capital flight by both foreign investors and domestic residents intensified. The Bank of Korea (BOK) intervened in the spot and forward markets to support the won but to little effect. It came under greater pressure. The banking crisis had thus become a currency crisis. Not only that, Korea was also on the verge of default — the BOK was running out of reserves to meet the debt obligations of its banks.

Calling in the IMF

There had been resistance among some Korean officials to seek IMF help. Lim recalled the series of critical meetings he had over 2 days before he could recommend for Korea to seek IMF assistance:

> "I was appointed as Deputy Prime Minister on November 19, had a meeting with Assistant Secretary of the US Treasury Timothy Geithner, prepared a report for the President on November 20, got approval from the President and the agreement from all the presidential candidates on November 21, and made the announcement at the press conference that night. It took me 2 days to do all these things."

An IMF team then arrived in Seoul. Its immediate task was to verify the BOK's reserves holdings. The team, as Neiss recalled, was taken aback by its findings:

> "When we finally had to rush there in a hurry to negotiate a stand-by arrangement, we had to establish the true reserves situation. On

the first evening we arrived, our staff went to the Central Bank and found out that a large part of the foreign exchange shown had been deposited with branches of Korean banks abroad. The branches had to use them, now more frequently, because the roll-overs, which they had relied upon before, had become rarer and rarer.

These reserves were, therefore, not usable for other transactions by the BOK. We could roughly estimate that by the end of the year, usable reserves would be close to zero. This was, of course, a great shock to the mission. I immediately sent a secret report to management to explain the situation.

Since it was impossible to get a quick bridge loan from other central banks (as was the case during an earlier crisis in India), the only alternative to a default was to get timely financial support through a quickly-negotiated agreement with the IMF, to be rushed to the Executive Board for approval, so that the money could be paid out before the BOK ran out of reserves."

Hur explained why the BOK had placed part of its reserves with overseas branches of Korean banks and its consequences:

"Korean policymakers thought we could better mobilize our reserves by lending part of the reserves on a short-term basis, totaling about USD 10 billion at that time, to the Korean banks. The rationale was that the banks could then better utilize these reserves. So, the Korean banks could borrow not only from overseas, but also from the government's reserves, creating a win-win situation. It was a win-win so long as we did not have a reserves problem.

But when the government needed this pool of money and attempted to pull it out from the banks, the latter could not give us the money, at least not immediately. I was really shocked to discover this… So, from that point on, the IMF used the concept of 'useable reserves.'"

Exploring a Second Option and the US' Influence

Lim revealed that, even after the IMF negotiations had started, he had explored a second option of seeking bilateral assistance from Japan:

"Japan's banks held the biggest amount of short-term foreign debt. So, we went to Japan and asked for its cooperation. The situation would have been very different if Japan had put a hold on the collection of the bank loans at that time. I visited Japan around November 28 and 29, during the negotiations with the IMF. With Neiss' agreement, we reported to the President and then went to Japan to discuss with the Minister of Finance of Japan."

The attempt did not succeed. In Lim's view, one reason was the US' insistence that Korea should only work with the IMF:

"I heard that while I was in Japan, the US Secretary of State called our Minister of Foreign Affairs and said, 'The US doesn't want Korea to get support from both sides.' In this regard, we couldn't go forward with getting support from Japan and had no choice but to receive assistance from the IMF."

Lim also disclosed that US officials had wanted to attend the IMF negotiations:

"(T)he US ambassador to Korea came to me and asked if US representatives could attend the negotiations. I rejected, 'No. There has been no case in which a specific country sits down at the negotiating table as part of the IMF negotiation. If this happens, Koreans will blame the US for Korea getting the IMF loans, and the IMF will lose its credibility. There will be a misunderstanding that Washington is using the IMF to put what it wants into the negotiation agenda.'"

Lim succeeded in keeping US officials from attending the negotiations, an achievement he saw as important:

"I still think I made a great decision to reject the US' demand. Had I agreed, we would have lost the credibility of the negotiations with the IMF. Of course, the US had indirect talks, but at least it didn't officially join the IMF negotiation team. If Washington had attended the negotiations, the Korean people would not have trusted the IMF at all."

Nevertheless, as Lim observed wryly, the US exerted its influence on the IMF team behind closed doors:

"The US representatives didn't attend the negotiations. But the US Under Secretary of the Treasury, David Lipton, was upstairs while I was negotiating with the IMF at Hilton Hotel. It seemed that the IMF team went back and forth to get the green light from the US during the talks with Korea."

Korean officials discerned that up to then, US policy on the crisis was shaped by the US Treasury. They found this problematic as its approach was Wall Street–oriented, which favored the opening of markets for US banks and investors. Thus, there were differences of emphasis between them and the IMF, as Chung noted:

"In my opinion, the US Treasury Department and the IMF seemed to have different views on the bailout issue in Korea. While the IMF focused on how to extinguish the fire as firefighters, the US Treasury Department took this opportunity to open up and restructure the Korean market.

When I asked the US Treasury what they wanted, they said that they were not interested in the restructuring issues, but their main focus was market opening and government-owned corporations. So I asked to what extent they wanted to open the market in Korea, and the US Treasury said opening about 50% of the market would be satisfactory."

There were also differences in emphasis between the US Treasury and the US State Department. The latter saw Korea as an important strategic ally, a vital base for US troops in the region. Korean officials consequently went on a campaign to emphasize Korea's strategic role to the US, as Chung revealed:

"So, it seemed that there were two camps even within the White House — the view of the US Treasury Department that the US should take this opportunity to reform Korea, and the view of the State Department which believed that the US could lose Korea strategically, the largest bridgehead against China and Russia.

Since the US Treasury Department's position was stubborn, we had to somehow get the issue to the attention of the White House. Therefore, we mobilized as many people as we could in order to approach the Clinton administration's diplomatic and security officials, including the US Secretary of State Madeleine Albright. Eventually, Secretary Albright persuaded President Bill Clinton to prioritize diplomatic and security considerations."

Chung added that the US approach moved toward the US State Department's views after the election of the new President, Kim Dae-jung, in mid-December 1997:

> "It should be said that the US started to drastically change its view when Kim became President in Korea and President Clinton came to realize that Korea could be in an irreversible predicament. Until then, it appeared that the US Treasury Department led the push for reforms which meant painful torture for us."

Negotiations with the IMF

It had become urgent to finalize the IMF program as Korea was close to a debt default. The urgency called for round-the-clock negotiations conducted in secrecy, Neiss recalled:

> "We had to negotiate day and night during that time. In addition, we had to avoid the journalists, who were constantly around. The Korean delegation had moved into the hotel, where we were staying, and we met in a secret room in the basement (to which we had to move through the kitchen), so no journalist had any idea where we were."

The negotiations were hard on the members of the Korean team. There was, as Joong-Kyung Choi recalled, a sense that they had let the country down:

> "My colleagues and I had a sense that we had sinned. We blamed ourselves that as public servants we had not done our best to prevent a crisis."

Hur admitted to a feeling of resentment, having to seek advice about economic policy from outsiders:

> "When we began to work with the IMF delegation, it was really humiliating. For the bureaucracy, we had pride in managing our economy pretty well for decades and all of a sudden, we were dictated by people who did not necessarily know about the Korean economy as much as we did. So, in every discussion with the IMF, it was very hard, for them and us. We challenged some of their prescriptions as they had a tendency, at the beginning especially, to impose their methods rather

than spending time to listen to our story. Previously, the IMF consultation said that we had a clean bill of health, and now they came out and said that everything was wrong. But later, it got better because we trusted each other more and we began to cooperate more."

Neiss agreed that over time, the two sides were joined by a common purpose to find solutions in the best interests of the country:

"They knew that we both had the same goal: to work in a hurry, to prevent a default of Korea. And cooperation worked very well. In general, during our negotiations, there was a common purpose and a common desire to come to an agreement quickly. Despite the stress and a tense atmosphere, our encounter was friendly and never hostile."

IMF Policies

During the negotiations, the IMF team pressed for tight macroeconomic policies and reforms to address structural weaknesses in the Korean economy. The Korean team challenged the IMF's understanding of the situation, as Hur observed:

"I suspected that the IMF did not have a full picture about how the Korean economy was impacted more by sudden capital outflows rather than structural flaws."

Nevertheless, after intense negotiations, the IMF team essentially pushed through its proposals. First, it called for a fiscal surplus, even though tax revenue was expected to fall because of an economic slowdown. This meant large spending cuts, a policy that Hur said was "dead wrong":

"They wanted us to keep a fiscal surplus, in addition to high interest rates. That's dead wrong. Korea was different from the Latin American cases, where fiscal profligacy was one of the main causes of economic malaise. Our fiscal position was very sound then. It was the wrong prescription from the IMF. After some time, the IMF loosened its stance as it might have realized what we knew all the while."

More controversial was the IMF's insistence on tight monetary policy, in effect raising interest rates to a high enough level to arrest the currency's weakness. Chung noted that despite strong protests, they "had to implement high interest rates of 30% or higher for about 100 days. The government tried hard to solve the problems caused by higher interest rates from the outset in November 1997, but it was not that easy."

Lim admitted that his encounters with then IMF Managing Director Michel Camdessus on the austerity program, especially on interest rates, were the most intense in his experience. The only concession he obtained was that the high interest rate policy would be "temporary":

> "I told him, 'The IMF has a very limited understanding of the prom-issory note system in Korea. Corporate transactions are made using promissory notes as credit. So, if the IMF makes companies insolvent with its high interest rates, the post-dated cheques issued by these companies will cause other businesses to go bankrupt and all sound businesses will collapse. Then this will lead to the insolvency of banks. If this happens, it is only a matter of time before the Korean economy collapses, and people will blame the IMF for destroying the Korean economy.' I kept insisting on this during the negotiations and finally was able to include in the agreement the condition of 'temporary' high interest rates."

The IMF also called for reforms of the banking system, the corporate sector, and other sectors like the labor market. The need for such reforms was accepted by the Koreans although there were differences in emphasis and manner of implementation. In fact, a comprehensive financial sector reform bill would be passed later by the Legislature and the newly-elected President would make it his mission to implement wide-ranging reforms. However, the attempt to implement structural reforms amid contractionary macroeconomic policies worsened the economic downturn.

On the whole, the Korean team resisted the IMF conditionalities, but as Chung pointed out, they had little bargaining power:

> "In this way, after continuous negotiations, the Korean government had no choice but to agree on a few things and reached an agreement with the IMF which became like an occupation force. The Korean government eventually initialed the agreement under pressure from the IMF, but in hindsight, I think that it was wrong."

The IMF also stipulated that the IMF program could only be formalized after all the presidential candidates agreed in writing to its terms. Chung disclosed that while the other two candidates did so, Kim, who would eventually win the elections, agreed only after he was able to send "his own advisors to figure out whether all the numbers and reports were true."

On December 4, 1997, Camdessus and Lim signed a 3-year IMF Stand-By Program. It provided for a financial assistance package of about USD 57 billion — USD 21 billion from the IMF, USD 14 billion from the World Bank and Asian Development Bank (ADB), and a "second line of defense" of USD 22 billion comprising bilateral arrangements with the Group of Seven (G7) governments. Nominally, it was an impressive amount: the total package was equivalent to about 20 times Korea's IMF quota and the IMF portion was the largest it had extended to a single country. But it did not ease the liquidity crunch that the BOK faced.

First, it appeared that the G7 bilateral contingency lines would not be easily activated, Chung commented:

"What Camdessus did most wrong was to seek support from the G7 countries. It seemed that the IMF had never done such a large-scale rescue package before. Since it was difficult for the IMF to get all the necessary funds in a short time, it tried to get support from the G7 countries. But at that time, I argued that the IMF shouldn't include money to be provided only years later in the rescue package. Moreover, it could be more complicated if the parliaments of the G7 countries opposed it."

Second, the IMF's cash disbursements in December 1997 were sufficient only to meet loan withdrawals by foreign creditor banks. As Hur explained,

"At the end of 1997, the IMF came up with the first payment to rescue Korea, but a lot of it went straight back to the foreign lenders."

Foreign creditor banks were increasingly not rolling over their loans to Korean banks, instead demanding repayment of their loans.

Kuroda said the consequent capital outflows exceeded what the IMF had catered for:

"It was a huge IMF loan that was thought to solve the problem but did not work. This was because the short-term loans of banks were not renewed. That was the situation and even though the IMF lent 20 times the quota, the outflows did not stop."

Averting Default

Within a week of the signing of the IMF Agreement, the won resumed its decline. By the second week, the BOK's reserves had reached a perilous level, pushing sovereign default, once an unthinkable scenario, closer to reality.

Two critical developments helped avert a default. First were the actions that President Kim took after he won the elections on December 18, 1997. The day after, he publicly promised that the IMF conditions would be complied with. He then spoke to President Clinton to seek US support. The latter was sympathetic to Kim's request, the outcome of which was stronger US action to aid Korea. Chung saw the good relationship developed with the US president as a significant achievement by President Kim:

> "The biggest contribution President Kim made was to strengthen the relationship with President Clinton. Kim emphasized to Clinton that the Korean government wanted to overcome the crisis with the help of the US, and asked the US to give Korea its support. Additionally, President Kim promised to faithfully carry out reforms for the market economy and democracy in Korea and to act as an evangelist of democracy and market economy in Asia. To be honest, Korea would have been in big trouble without the help of US President Clinton and Secretary Albright."

Second, a Korean default was forestalled because of a coordinated effort, led by the US Federal Reserve, to exert pressure on banks to roll over their loans to Korean banks. Neiss highlighted the role of G7 central banks in convincing the banks under their jurisdiction to do so:

> "But the difficult issue was that the banks should not be forced by the authorities to do that. Instead, they should do it voluntarily. That meant the process had to rely on persuasion by the central banks.
>
> This was accomplished. In this effort, the US government played an important role, and the G7 was very helpful. I think this was a decisive achievement. Of course, it was in everybody's interest, not just Korea's, because a Korean default could have caused a major financial crisis in the region and, maybe, worldwide."

The mission to get a critical mass of banks to agree to a rollover was finally completed, on December 24. The rollover would be extended to end

March 1998. Eisuke Sakakibara vividly remembered that day:

"The agreement was reached on Christmas Eve. I clearly remember that, Christmas Eve of 1997. It was a very memorable occasion, you know, since it was Christmas Eve."

The same day, the IMF, together with the World Bank and the ADB, announced that they would accelerate their disbursements. Lim characterized the events on Christmas Eve as a "Christmas present" for Korea. He remembered the dinner after the press conference:

"Back then, all the staff of the Ministry of Finance and Economy worked very hard in preparing and holding the press conference late at night. When we went to a restaurant to have a very late dinner after that event, other people who were already having a meal at other tables gave us a big hand for our efforts and also paid for our dinner."

Debt Rescheduling

In mid-January 1998, Korea began negotiations with creditor banks to convert their short-term claims into sovereign debt of 1–3 years of maturity. Chung, who led the negotiations, recalled that US support was critical:

"Some people said that the negotiations went well thanks to our negotiation skills. However, the most important factor was rebuilding market confidence and the rapport between President Clinton and President-elect Kim Dae-jung. President Clinton consequently favored the views of the State Department and State Secretary Albright over those of the Treasury Department and Treasury Secretary Robert Rubin.

Furthermore, the Korean negotiators worked very professionally to come up with credible plans for financial restructuring and banking supervision. Many Wall Street professionals noted that they could not imagine how Korea could have fallen into such a serious crisis when we have this group of highly trained and educated government officials. To this day, I am very proud of my colleagues who worked together with me during the crisis in 1998."

Byeon recapped the case the Korean team made to banks at major financial centers. This was that essentially Korea had good fundamentals — it had a solid manufacturing base, healthy fiscal balances to recapitalize corporate balance sheets, and a capacity to absorb foreign funds:

"We went to New York, London, Frankfurt, Hong Kong, Singapore, Paris, and Milan to explain everything and this persuasion worked well. Indeed, creditors and investors were thinking along the same lines."

During the negotiations, the Korean team impressed the bank negotiators with its ability to deliver real-time data on the short-term debt owed by every Korean bank. Chung described how this was done:

"We created a system in which the debt figures of each bank were compiled by the minute. Byeon then sent these data to the global financial community including Wall Street via emails titled 'Email Service from Mr. Byeon' every day. With these efforts, people came to have trust in the numbers (data) that we presented, the accuracy of statistics, and the real-time access to our statistics and data."

The campaign to reschedule the debt was concluded in end-January 1998, in time for the inauguration of the new President.

Economic Hardship

Despite the debt extension, macroeconomic policies remained contractionary till later, as Hur noted:

"However, only after we formally signed the debt rescheduling in March 1998, then only were we allowed to reduce interest rates by the IMF. During those months, many companies went bankrupt. Some of them deserved it, but many of them would have survived if interest rates had been gradually lowered. This would have meant less people getting laid off. But at that time, we were talking to deaf ears."

Korea endured a devastating downturn in 1998. GDP growth declined 6.4% that year. Almost half the *chaebols* went under. In turn, many firms dependent on them for business had to shut down and unemployment rose steeply, Hur recalled:

"When you looked at the stock market, when you looked at the exchange rate, all these numbers were falling rapidly. You could see your private savings disappear overnight, every night. So, this was really painful, plus you lost your job. Our unemployment rate was about 2.5% before the crisis, translating to about 400,000 unemployed people. At the height of the crisis, it was over 1.7 million people — a 400% increase. The conglomerates had also fallen. Out of the top 30, I think 14 were gone."

To this day, the pain from the IMF austerity policies still evoked strong emotions from the interviewees. Thus, Choi noted that "the massive displacement of workers caused by widespread bankruptcy of business firms brought about many cases of broken families. The IMF should apologize to the Korean people officially for its serious mistake."

In the same vein, Chung recalled telling Stanley Fischer, the then IMF First Deputy Managing Director, that the initials IMF among Koreans "were an abbreviation of I aM Fired, not 'International Monetary Fund.' And I heard that even teenagers were praying for the IMF to leave Korea."

Hur, on the other hand, thought it was unfair to blame the IMF for the crisis:

"For the benefit of the IMF, I try to be fair. We called this crisis the 'IMF Crisis' in Korea. This is unfair because the fire was there, and the IMF came to put out the fire. However, we complained when, in the process of putting out the fire, trees and other things were broken. The IMF didn't cause this crisis. It was caused by our own internal problems and by the rapid capital flows."

To their credit, Korean officials set aside their divergent views on the IMF polices and worked as a team, led by the newly-elected President, to resuscitate the country out of the crisis.

Spirited Response Under a New President

Kim Dae-jung's presidency ushered in a period of sweeping reforms that laid the foundations for sustainable recovery. Before Kim assumed office, both the incumbent and incoming presidents put aside their political differences to work together for the good of the country. The joint committee they formed ensured a smooth transition of power. Lim explained:

"Although Kim Young-sam and Kim Dae-jung were long-time political rivals, they worked together very well with cooperative efforts in order to overcome the crisis. I think this should be appreciated in history. Just two days after Kim Dae-jung was elected, he and then-incumbent President Kim Young-sam agreed to form a 12-member Emergency Economic Committee (EEC). The outgoing and incoming administrations specified that they would faithfully implement the agreement with the IMF without any interruptions."

Taking office in early February 1998, President Kim Dae-jung committed his administration to keeping to the tight monetary and fiscal policies as stipulated in a revised letter of intent (LOI) with the IMF. Not only that, he promised wide-ranging structural reforms. He had the reputation of being left-leaning, a critic of past governments, and a reformist, and there were fears that he would upset investors with populist proposals. However, on becoming President, he pushed ideology aside and did what was needed, Chung commented:

"President Kim was liberal, holding left-wing views; but after taking office, he postponed all the things he wanted to execute, such as the introduction of a new welfare system or reform of the labor system. He only focused on overcoming the crisis. Of course, 3 years after, when the crisis was over, he pushed some of his political agenda. I think during the crisis he abandoned all his political philosophies as a liberal politician. Instead he came to accept that crisis resolution had become his historical mission."

To fulfil his promise for fundamental reforms, President Kim had to circumvent two powerful roadblocks, the trade unions and the *chaebols*. Lim explained why he succeeded:

"In fact, President Kim successfully implemented both labor and *chaebol* reforms. The reason why he could push through both reforms was that he had not received any help from *chaebols* in his political career and hence was not indebted to them, and the labor community agreed to 'a grand compromise' since he was the president of their choice. President Kim secured the tripartite agreement among labor, management, and government."

Hur noted that the tripartite agreement was rooted in President Kim's concept of "burden sharing":

"The idea was that the reforms were painful, but we should share the pain. It was a persuasive plan that eventually got the buy-in from all sides."

Lim recalled that the critical moment was when the trade unions "made the tough decision to allow businesses to fire their members" for the sake of corporate survival.

Subsequently, as Hur recalled, Korean officials worked closely with the IMF on implementing structural reforms, especially in the financial and corporate sectors:

"What was interesting as the crisis went on was the feeling that it should not be wasted away. We thought it was an opportunity to push through some structural issues. In private talk, some IMF staff said that they were really surprised that we had not only already identified all the structural issues, but also prepared the solutions. Additionally, they were surprised that these reforms never really got implemented. Therefore, both sides began to see eye to eye"

The banking sector saw several reforms. Hur summarized the thrust of these reform:

"On one hand, we consolidated all the weak banks. On the other, we had much stricter criteria for the surviving ones. The goal was to resume the lending cycle while not draining too much off the public coffers. Otherwise, the economy could not be restored."

Corporate sector reforms centered on dealing with the weaknesses of the *chaebols* that had led to the crisis. The priority was ensuring that the *chaebols* became more transparent, got rid of cross-guarantees, focused on core businesses, and trimmed overlapping investments. The Securities Exchange Act was revised to require large listed companies to appoint independent board members, establish Audit Committees, and have compliance officers.

The scale of reforms was unprecedented. President Kim's success in attaining credible policy and comprehensive reforms made him a special leader, Chung noted:

> "He was an iconic figure in terms of building the credit worthiness and trust in Korea. At that time, President Kim was also revered as a person who completed democracy in Korea, to such an extent that he could be called the Nelson Mandela of Asia."

Recovery

By the end of 1998, signs of recovery had emerged. The won had strengthened from its low of KRW 1,965 to the US dollar on December 24, 1997 to KRW 1,200 at the end of 1998. In 1999, growth rebounded to around 10.9%. Unemployment fell. Korea's V-shaped recovery was the fastest among the crisis-hit economies. The current account had turned into surplus, enabling the country to replenish its reserves. Korea made its last drawing on IMF funds in May 1999 although the IMF program was scheduled to end on December 4, 2000.

A combination of factors accounted for the robust recovery. Korea's export-oriented economy benefited from a favorable external environment, as Hur mentioned:

> "For one, it was not a global financial crisis. Foreign demand was still there and once we began to regain trust by aggressively addressing all these reforms, we could export our way out of troubles."

The tight macroeconomic policies helped turn the current account shortfall into a surplus, observed Byeon:

> "I think one of the reasons why Korea was able to repay IMF bail-out money so quickly was because the Korean government implemented a policy of curbing domestic demand tightly in the early stages. As a result, the current account improved and turned into a surplus."

President Kim's commitment to reform, which led to sweeping structural reforms to tackle the weaknesses that contributed to the crisis, was critical. The reforms bolstered investor confidence and laid the foundations for sustainable growth. Essentially, these reforms paved the way for a more outward-looking and revitalized Korea. Choi saw these changes as critical. His analysis was that Korean macroeconomic policy had failed to recognize that "OECD membership had transformed the Korean economy from a closed economy into a small open economy as it significantly increased cross-border capital mobility. Hence, the Korean government's fixation on attaining per capita income goals led to an overvaluation of the Korean won, balance of payment deficits, and accumulation of short term external debt." As Choi saw it, Korean policymakers should have orientated macroeconomic policy toward external equilibrium as well, instead of focusing almost wholly on internal macroeconomic objectives.

Most importantly, the President's leadership helped galvanize a collective spirit to overcome the crisis. Hur puts that spirit into context:

"The most important factor was the spirit of the people. They bore the burden and persevered with the pain from the adjustment process. The Korean spirit was very moving, and the crisis would not have been surmounted without the people's sacrifice."

That spirit was epitomized by the inspiring gold-collecting campaign, noted Lim:

"Speaking of the public sentiment and role of the Korean people at that time, it is impossible to talk about the crisis without recalling the gold-collecting campaign. This campaign greatly contributed to improving Korea's credibility. Usually, people tend to take care of themselves in a crisis. They will panic and buy gold when faced with a foreign exchange crisis. However, the Korean public even brought their children's gold rings (traditional gifts for babies to celebrate their first birthday in Korea) to donate these as if they were fighting for independence as in the Japanese colonial period. Consequently, Korea gained the trust of the international community that 'Korea will never fail.' Other countries marveled that Koreans were donating their gold for their country in a situation when the country was at risk of going down. It was very meaningful as this showed the unity of the Korean people in a difficult time for the country."

Chapter 6

Malaysia

This chapter draws on interviews with six persons: Lin See-Yan, Andrew Sheng, Ooi Sang Kuang, Nor Shamsiah, Eisuke Sakakibara, and Jim Walker. During the Asian financial crisis, Lin was Chairman of the Pacific Bank Group, after retiring as the Deputy Governor of Bank Negara Malaysia in 1994. Sheng was the then Deputy Chief Executive of the Hong Kong Monetary Authority after a stint at the World Bank as a senior manager of the Financial Sector Development Department. Ooi was the then Head of Regional Research in RHB Securities. He concurrently sat on the boards of several RHB Group companies, one of the largest companies in Malaysia. In 2002, Ooi returned to Bank Negara Malaysia as its Deputy Governor. He is now the Chairman of Singapore-based Oversea-Chinese Banking Corporation Limited. Shamsiah was then in the Banking Regulation Department at Bank Negara Malaysia before serving as its departmental director in the latter periods of the Asian financial crisis. Since July 2018, she has been the Bank Negara Malaysia Governor. Sakakibara was Japan's Vice Minister of Finance and International Affairs while Walker was chief economist at the Hong Kong-based Credit Lyonnais Securities (Asia) Ltd during the crisis.

Malaysia's economic fundamentals going into the Asian financial crisis (AFC) were relatively sound. Still, no different from the other regional economies, it was not spared the speculative attacks on its financial markets. Conventional polices failed to deter the speculators and this eventually led to a deep recession. Malaysia then charted an unorthodox course, eschewing the International Monetary Fund (IMF) and its one-size-fits-all approach. It instead imposed selective exchange controls and pegged the Malaysian ringgit to the United States (US) dollar, measures that were widely criticized then. The measures provided room for policymakers to take expansionary fiscal and monetary policies and the latitude to implement reforms to strengthen the banking and corporate sectors. One year later, Malaysia was on the recovery path.

Pre-Crisis

On the eve of the AFC, the prevailing sentiment on the Malaysian economy and financial system was relatively optimistic. Between 1994 and 1996, annual gross domestic product (GDP) ranged between 9% and 10%, inflation was around 3%, and the fiscal surplus was also as high as 2.7% of GDP. The banking sector was well capitalized and provisioned: its risk-weighted capital ratio was more than 10.0% and nonperforming loans (NPLs) were computed by Bank Negara Malaysia (BNM) to be around 3.6% of total loans outstanding, with loan provisions for the NPLs close to 100.0%.

Significantly, Malaysia had a healthier external debt profile than other crisis-hit economies. External debt was low, amounting to only 43.6% of gross national income (GNI). Another feature that stood out was its low level of external short-term debt. This was due to a longstanding policy to restrict foreign borrowing by the private sector, explained Ooi Sang Kuang:

> "We had a restrictive policy on foreign borrowing by corporates. Unless they had a natural hedge, the central bank would not approve of them doing so. We had, what I would call, some form of control on foreign borrowing. But there was no capital control on foreign companies — they could remit their profits and bring in capital. I think this partially protected Malaysia."

Controls on short-term external borrowing also explained another source of resilience for Malaysia. Its current account deficits were mainly financed by foreign direct investments (FDI) and long-term debt.

Credit Binge and Stock Market Highs

Nevertheless, there were vulnerabilities in the system. Leading up to the AFC, the Malaysian economy had shown signs of overheating fueled by a credit boom, elevated investment spending, and asset price bubbles.

Between 1990 and 1997, lending by Malaysian banks and other financial institutions to the private sector rose sharply from about 70% to 124% of GDP. The credit boom had two perceptible effects. First was the rise in debt-financed private sector investments, especially in property and construction. Coincidentally, public investment spending, marked by mega infrastructure projects, was also high. Thus, investment spending formed a relatively high proportion of GDP then.

Second, the credit boom fueled speculation in real estate and the stock market. Reports suggest that between 1990 and 1996, house prices more than doubled while the stock market rose by more than 140%. Annual credit growth for the purchase of properties and shares exceeded 29% and 30%, respectively, prior to credit ceilings imposed by the central bank in April 1997. Thus, going into the AFC, financial institutions had a big exposure to property and stocks.

A critical feature of the boom in the Malaysian stock market was that it was not just driven by local money. The other propellant was foreign funds, as noted by Andrew Sheng:

"The asset bubble was clearly fueled by incoming (foreign) money."

Ooi also recalled the period of the mid-1990s when he was promoting Association of Southeast Asian Nations (ASEAN) stocks as an asset class to overseas fund managers. Malaysia was a popular investment destination:

"On the Morgan Stanley Capital International (MSCI) index, I remember, the Malaysian stock index in the MSCI Asia ex-Japan had a weight of about 11%–12%. And there was a period later when I was managing funds, many of us were overweighted on Malaysia for as high as 15%. So, funds were flowing in, and I mean basically into those five major ASEAN countries. At that time, Korea was closed; Taiwan Province of China was closed; China, nobody looked at it. So if you invested in an ASEAN fund, you would be overweight on the five ASEAN countries."

Jim Walker elaborated that Malaysia was then considered a top draw for overseas fund managers:

"At that time, Malaysia really was one of the main destinations for portfolio investment in Asia because it was one of the big, liquid markets. People have forgotten this over the last 20 years but on some days, the Malaysian stock market showed higher turnover than Hong Kong. That was purely in Malaysian stocks but listed on two bourses, Singapore and Kuala Lumpur.

As I say, turnover was sometimes higher than in Hong Kong but remember China H-shares didn't exist in those days. So, you know, Malaysia was a real foreign capital attractor. That was the source of most of Malaysia's short-term capital flows."

BNM data show that nonresident holdings in the Kuala Lumpur Stock Exchange averaged about 19% of GDP between 1990 and 1996, among the highest percentages of the regional stock markets. The large proportion of foreign holdings had a sting in the tail for policy makers. The subsequent herd-like exit of these foreign portfolio funds not only affected stock market sentiment but also put tremendous pressure on the ringgit. As Ooi noted, this occurred because the majority of portfolio managers were not long-term investors as professed. They would cut their stocks exposure indiscriminately at short notice:

> "I remember fund managers telling me they were long term investors. They would say they buy good companies and stay with them for years. But actually, many of them are very short term. They look at yearly performance and the moment they suspect something is not right, they will quickly pull out and stocks are so liquid, which is very different from direct real investment. If I build a cement factory, I'm stuck there for good. I cannot pull out. But equity investors can pull out easily."

Preemptive Measures

Alerted to the risks posed by an overheating economy, beginning in 1995, Malaysian policymakers promptly worked for the reduction of the current account deficit and restraint of rapid credit growth. Large public sector projects were put on hold. This led to the current account deficit falling from 9.7% of GDP in 1995 to 4.4% in 1996 and to an overall government budget surplus, averaging 1.3% of GDP from 1995 to 1997.

Nor Shamsiah recalled how BNM tightened monetary policy and credit conditions to moderate the exposure of banks to property and shares:

> "The Statutory Reserve Requirement (SRR) ratio was raised from 8.5% in 1993 to 13.5% in 1996 and this move was complemented by the imposition of limits on banks for loans granted to the broad property sector (not exceeding 20% of their outstanding loans) and the purchase of shares (not more than 15%) effective April 1, 1997. By the end of 1997, the over-exposure of loans to property and shares had moderated, with the outstanding loans for property and shares accounting for 13.1% and 8.9% of total loans, respectively."

However, selling pressure had already hit the stock market by April 1997 and would spill over to the ringgit soon after. Nevertheless, the cooling measures were important buffers that enabled Malaysia to later pursue an autonomous approach in managing the crisis.

Attacks on the Ringgit and Stock Market

BNM attributed the start of the selling pressure on Malaysian financial markets to the repatriation of funds by foreign equity managers in early 1997, when the Thai baht first came under fire. Stocks and the ringgit subsequently declined precipitously. The Kuala Lumpur Composite Index fell by 79.30% from a high of 1,271.57 in February 1997 to a low of 262.70 on September 1, 1998. This was the biggest fall among regional stock markets, attesting to the impact of the sell-off by both resident and foreign equity holders. The ringgit depreciated by about 74% from MYR 2.5235 per US dollar in June 1997 to MYR 4.8800 in January 1998.

Shamsiah attributed the unprecedented plunge in stocks and currency to short-term speculative capital flow and sudden shift in investor sentiment "perceiving the region as a homogenous asset class":

> "I can still remember it distinctly given the severity and speed in which the crisis spread across the region. Also, the AFC was triggered by external factors, mainly due to the short-term speculative capital outflows brought about by herd-like behavior by portfolio investors which subsequently led to a banking system crisis. No doubt there were some vulnerabilities arising from credit expansion and investment activities, which were registering double-digit growth, but in itself, these were insufficient to trigger the crisis."

Sheng concurred:

> "Over in Malaysia, the asset bubble was clearly fueled by incoming money. You see that in the stock exchange. So, are you really surprised that when markets elsewhere tanked, money began to leave Malaysia?"

Ineffectual First Responses

Malaysia's initial policy responses to the crisis mimicked conventional IMF prescriptions. Monetary policy was tightened in an attempt to stabilize the ringgit and reduce credit-driven spending. Fiscal spending was cut to restrain aggregate demand in order to mitigate the current account deficit.

However, these polices failed to stem the turmoil surrounding the ringgit and the stock market. The ringgit and the stock market continued to decline through 1997 with worsening impact on the real economy. The steep depreciation of the ringgit led to higher consumer and producer prices while the negative wealth effects of falling asset prices dampened domestic demand.

Shamsiah recalled the perverse effects of the orthodox approach:

> "The combination of tight monetary policy and fiscal restraint was doing more harm than good to the economy. The measures had instead worsened businesses' cash flows, that were already affected by the ringgit depreciation, decline in stock prices, and weaker external demand. As a result, private sector activity contracted significantly."

Shamsiah also noted how difficulties in the corporate sector spread to the banking sector through rising NPLs and banks consequently cutting back on lending:

> "The effects then spilled over to the banking and corporate sector as deterioration in asset quality led to rising NPLs. This contributed to a vicious cycle in which banks became overly cautious in extending new loans, even to viable businesses in productive sectors, causing banking system loan growth to turn negative from 26.5% at end-1997 to –1.8% at end-1998. This led to a significant halt in economic activity. It became evident that Malaysia was facing a recession for the first time in 13 years when the GDP of the second quarter (Q2) of 1998 was announced in August that year."

Two Different Viewpoints

As the Malaysian economy continued to stutter into the second half of 1998, uncertainty was also generated by the tussle between two groups on how to deal with the crisis, a divergence that had political overtones. One group coalesced around the then Deputy Prime Minister and Finance Minister, Anwar Ibrahim. The other was led by the then Prime Minister Mahathir Mohamad.

The group associated with Anwar, which included the then leadership of BNM, leaned toward orthodox policies espoused by the IMF. In other words, it was "more of the same" approach. Ooi expressed sympathy with the dilemma the central bank's leadership found itself in pursuing a path contrary to the Prime Minister's:

> "We were all brought up in that context. That was the framework of analysis and the IMF had shown us in the past how they got the Latin American countries out of crisis. There were no alternative models, right? The IMF came down hard on the developing countries. They were like demigods and demanded harsh conditionalities."

Mahathir, on the other hand, harbored a repugnance to the IMF approach. He saw first-hand that the austerity policies applied to Thailand and Indonesia had resulted in high job losses and corporate distress. Ooi explained that Mahathir was concerned about the potential for widespread business failures from IMF policies:

> "So, one thing about Mahathir, as a politician he mixed a lot with the businessmen. They basically said that at interest rates of 10–15%, they will all 'die.' And Mahathir being a practical person said, 'If all my corporates die and have to be bailed out or sold to foreigners, my whole economy will collapse. This cannot be right.' So in effect, he said, 'You should lower interest rates. Malaysia should not move toward the IMF way.' So, there was this struggle."

Ooi mentioned another repercussion of IMF policies in Thailand that Mahathir found disturbing. This was the risk that viable Malaysian businesses could be disposed off to foreigners at fire-sale prices, as was happening to Thailand then:

> "IMF policy basically helped to 'plunder' the country in time of crisis because it forced you to do fire sales. Thailand was very, very sore. They have not forgotten it. They had to sell many businesses at fire-sale prices. And the American companies bought them, for a song."

Speculation through Offshore Markets

Mahathir was critical of the orthodox polices pursued for another reason. They ignored the "elephant in the room" that was plaguing Malaysian financial markets: the destabilizing effects of speculation. He had publicly blamed speculators like George Soros for the regional crisis as early as Q3 1997. However, his remarks then were counterproductive. They only provoked the speculators, noted Ooi:

> "Mahathir is a fighter. If you check statements he made before and at the IMF World Bank meeting in Hong Kong, he was basically telling the hedge funds to challenge him. But he did not realize that the hedge funds were able to create chaos and panic, and a run on the domestic currency and on the domestic financial markets and financial institutions.
>
> And I remember, the more statements he made, not only the ringgit dropped but also the other ASEAN currencies. I would say that Malaysia would not have experienced such a big fall in the ringgit and capital outflows if he had kept quiet and re-assured investors. Instead, he went and challenged them."

Despite the criticisms, Mahathir would prove to be fundamentally correct about the large role speculators played in aggravating the crisis in Malaysia. That role was amplified by the presence of active offshore markets in the ringgit and Malaysian stocks, noted Shamsiah:

> "The internationalization of the ringgit and the ability of non-resident investors to short-sell in the equity markets also increased the suscepti-bility of Malaysian financial markets to speculative activities."

Ooi explained how the offshore ringgit market facilitated capital flight from Malaysia and gave hedge funds the means to short the ringgit:

> "What happened is very interesting. The hedge funds, while they were closely watched in Malaysia by BNM, used banks in Singapore to attract Malaysian capital. So the offshore ringgit deposits rates were 20% or higher while the onshore rates were much, much lower. People in Johor Bahru walked across the Causeway to Singapore and deposited ringgit and got 20% or more for 3 months. The better educated Malaysians in Kuala Lumpur and elsewhere also started transferring ringgit down to the banks there. Then of course the banks would lend the ringgit to the hedge funds at a premium. The hedge funds then borrowed and shorted the ringgit. They were prepared to pay these high interest rates because they felt the ringgit could fall even more."

Another source of capital outflow was the offshore stock market operating out of Singapore. Ooi recalled:

"A hedge fund can short Malaysian shares in Singapore. Or, if you are Malaysian and have Malaysian shares, you sell them in Singapore and take out your money. So, there was outflow and an opportunity to short the ringgit."

Ooi also recalled how the hedge funds used every opportunity to short the Malaysian stock market, quoting an example when the Malaysian authorities, with the objective of liberalizing the capital market, allowed stock lending and borrowing in 1996:

"So the hedge funds were very smart. They borrowed the stocks and then shorted them. And, of course, Mahathir was very angry when he was told about it — that the large domestic institutions were lending the stocks just to make money but giving the country more problems."

It was a befuddling situation for Mahathir, who was experienced in politics but not in finance. To his credit, he sought advice from experts on the nuts and bolts of foreign exchange trading and the intricacies of offshore currency markets. He then decided that Malaysia had to do the unorthodox to thwart the speculators.

Turning Point: Selective Exchange Controls

Mahathir's radical policy shift was expressed in two moves. First, he changed the leadership of the central bank, recalled Lin See-Yan:

"You're right on the two camps. The existing camp in BNM was quite orthodox, so Mahathir did not find them very helpful. The problem was not of an orthodox nature, and he wanted somebody who would listen to him to run the central bank. Therefore, rapid changes were made to the management setup. I remember he always asked the new governor: 'Would you implement these policies? If you are not able to, you are not the man for me.'"

Second, on September 1, 1998, the Malaysian government imposed selective exchange controls. The next day it fixed the ringgit exchange rate at MYR 3.80 to the US dollar. It was uncertain times for the central bank, though Shamsiah recalled the policy shift as a turning point:

"For me personally, as much as we hope our policies are well-designed, a change in strategy may at times be warranted to achieve the intended outcome. As a policymaker, we must have the willingness to accept that certain policies might not have worked and could have worsened the situation. For me, this was an important turning point."

Of course, these moves shocked the international financial community. The capital control measures, in particular, were criticized by the majority of Western commentators and media. Rating agencies downgraded Malaysia's credit and sovereign ratings. The stock market plunged on the news.

On the other hand, among others, Eisuke Sakakibara commended Malaysia for adopting a solution that fitted its circumstances:

"We, at the (Japanese) Ministry of Finance, supported Malaysia. We implicitly supported the Malaysian government's decision to close the border and try to avoid the crisis by sticking to its own principles rather than following the IMF instructions. Even at that time I was really very critical of the IMF approach."

Sheng also saw merit in what Malaysia did:

"When Malaysia clamped down on exchange control, the bleeding stopped. There were very different ways of handling the crisis, but at that point of time, the IMF didn't quite understand the situation. It just applied the same old medicine applied to Mexico some years before."

Indeed, the selective exchange control measures focused precisely on crimping the outflow of ringgit from onshore to offshore markets. The measures included the non-internationalization of the ringgit, which meant that offshore ringgit deposits would not be recognized by the central bank; the imposition of a minimum holding period of 1 year on foreign investors' portfolio investment; restrictions on the import and export of ringgit notes by travelers; and the need for residents investing abroad to seek approval from BNM.

The control measures were also nuanced to avoid disrupting trade and direct investments, reiterated Shamsiah:

"They were selective in nature to contain speculative short-term capital flows and were not intended to disrupt flows related to real economic activity such as trade and FDI. There were no controls imposed on current account transactions such as trade in goods and services, repatriation of profits, dividends and interests, and long-term FDI flows."

Lin observed that despite the exchange controls, Malaysia had not turned its back on its tradition of being an open economy:

"Malaysia has always been open, right from the beginning. We were an Article 8 member (of the IMF); never had current account controls at all. We had capital account controls now and then, but never on FDI. We always made sure that whatever we did didn't adversely affect the inflows and outflows of FDI. That's part of the success story of Malaysia. However, short-term capital flows and offshore ringgit were something we could not control. When both swung wildly, the only way left for us was capital controls. We really had no choice."

Lin then noted the efforts of the Malaysian leadership to reassure the investment community that the country still welcomed long-term investors:

"The balance was delicate, I admit. We made it clear that we were targeting short-term capital which we didn't want; FDI was not touched. In fact, Mahathir held a number of high-profile meetings with foreign direct investors who were already here and those thinking of coming to Malaysia. He made it very clear that we will not touch their capital. He also stressed that by stabilizing short-term capital flows, their business will prosper. They were told that they were welcome here despite the capital controls. When the crisis appeared to be over, we took the controls off. We removed it rather quickly, which regained some of our credibility."

Breathing Space to Recover and Reform

The measures announced on September 1–2 marked a turning point in the crisis, noted Shamsiah:

"These exchange control measures provided crucial breathing space for Malaysia to undertake structural reforms to reinforce the economic recovery from the AFC without the undue pressure from volatile short-term capital flows."

A National Economic Action Council (NEAC), established in early 1998, served as the de facto command center of formulating and coordinating a recovery plan for the country. One of its key recommendations was the easing of monetary and fiscal policies.

In fact, the exchange control measures and a pegged currency gave BNM the flexibility to pursue an accommodative monetary policy. It consequently lowered its intervention rate progressively from 11.0% to 5.5% and the statutory reserve requirements for banks from 13.5% to 4.0%. Monetary easing was complemented by expansionary fiscal policy. Shamsiah added the recovery package "was also financed mainly through domestic, non-inflationary sources such as the pension and insurance funds, and the banking system. Furthermore, there was no recourse to deficit financing by BNM."

Equally important were the structural reforms implemented. The priority was, as Shamsiah commented, to "strengthen the financial system, given the critical role of the banking system in supporting the economic recovery."

A major NEAC initiative was the setting up of three agencies to strengthen the balance sheets of banks and corporates. These were Danamodal, to recapitalize banks; Danaharta, to assist banks reduce their NPLs; and the Corporate Debt Restructuring Committee (CDRC), to restructure large corporate loans.

Shamsiah recalled some of the achievements of these agencies. Danamodal injected capital into 10 banking institutions, effectively restoring their capacity to perform the intermediation function of supporting the economic recovery. Danaharta managed to carve out around 70% of total NPLs, bringing down the NPL ratio for the banking system from a peak of 11.4% in August 1998 to below 5.0% by the time the agency was wound up. The CDRC provided a mechanism for both banks and debtors to work out voluntary debt restructuring solutions without resorting to legal proceedings.

It was, as Shamsiah recalled, an intense period for BNM:

"In response to the crisis, it was all hands on deck... the Bank was also in charge of establishing, coordinating, and overseeing (the) three agencies to maintain financial intermediation during the crisis. In particular, I remember the process that led to the establishment of Danaharta, where my team and I received help from the Swedish authorities. To help formulate a holistic strategy to resolve the crisis, for the first time, the Bank conducted macro stress tests to assess and identify risks and vulnerabilities, including potential spillovers, as well as determining system-wide capital and liquidity needs under stress conditions. Last but not least, the Bank also played a key role in the implementation of the exchange control measures."

A feature of the bank recapitalization exercise was that it was largely financed by the banks, as Lin observed:

"Malaysian borrowings were mainly in local currency, and so from that angle, it was easier to handle. So, we set up three agencies, i.e., Danaharta, Danamodal, and the CDRC, to restructure private debts. I think more than 50% of the NPLs of banks were sold to Danaharta, with some equity from the central bank. Similarly with Danamodal, we ensured that the banks were capitalized properly. We didn't want to use government funds, so the banks got together and the Central Bank put in some money. Most of these agencies were led by the Central Bank. The Central Bank wanted the banks, both local and foreign, to participate in this exercise. It took no more than 20% of the capital. The rest of the capital came from the banks."

For Ooi, the three agencies basically helped the banking system recapitalize and the corporate sector restructure their liabilities in an orderly fashion:

"So, instead of fire sales, it was an orderly management of the debt work-out. If all the major companies had collapsed, the banking system would also have gone down. The parties sat down and worked it out — how do we extend short-term debt, how do we share the haircut? I think it was the right thing to do: to resolve the debt crisis in an orderly manner without undermining the banks or the corporates. There were a few things we did that were unconventional. But I think it helped. It helped avoid an economic collapse. And it helped reduce the pain of fire sales."

All in all, Danaharta, Danamodal, and the CDRC worked in tandem to strengthen the balance sheets of banks and corporates. In addition, under them, the cost of bank restructuring was lower than the IMF estimates, noted Shamsiah:

"The cost of restructuring the Malaysian banking sector during the AFC (including the resolution of NPLs by Danaharta and recapitalization of banks by Danamodal) amounted to only about MYR 12.5 billion or 3.0% of GDP, which was far less than the IMF's estimate of 18.0%."

Recovery

The pro-growth policies took effect as early as mid-1999. Subsequently, Malaysia's recovery from the crisis was among the strongest in the region. Its GDP growth rebounded to 6.1% in 1999 from −7.4% in 1998, the pace of the rebound comparable to the speed of decline a year earlier.

The rapid recovery was buttressed by strong external demand. An upswing in the first half of 1999 in the global demand for electronics, a major Malaysian export, was a contributing factor. The pegging of the ringgit at MYR 3.80 to the US Dollar also favored Malaysian exports, noted Walker:

"[G]oing from MYR 2.5 to MYR 3.8, when they really didn't have a dramatic current account problem in the way that Thailand had, left the ringgit in a highly competitive position."

The overall balance of payments also improved as the selective exchange controls were not aimed at trade or long-term investment flows, Shamsiah noted:

"Given that no controls were imposed on current account transactions with non-residents, the current account balance improved significantly. This was evidenced by the shift in the balance of payments position to a surplus of MYR 17.8 billion or USD 4.7 billion, driven by a favorable external trade balance from MYR 58.4 billion in 1998 to MYR 72.3 billion in 1999, and a larger net inflow of long-term capital from MYR 10.6 billion in 1998 to MYR 11.7 billion in 1999."

Walker observed that Malaysia continued to attract long-term investments although equity inflows had not recovered since exchange controls were introduced:

"The closing of the capital account, and the fixing of the exchange rate at MYR 3.8 to a dollar certainly bought Malaysia significant competitiveness. In terms of confidence among foreign investors, direct investors always had a very good experience in Malaysia and I think that continues. But for portfolio investors, that capital control decision was a real shocker. Malaysia has never recovered."

Ooi also found foreign fund managers less interested in Malaysian equities, but also noted that many equity investors are not as long term as they profess to be:

"Interestingly, even 10 years later, up to 2010, when I went overseas to visit fund managers, many of them still had in mind that capital controls were still there. They didn't want to put money in Malaysia. But part of the reason too is that other Asian markets have opened up.

But I have come to the conclusion that while it's useful to have an active equity market, it is a 'good friend' only when you are okay but not when you are seen to have problems. Hence, the equity market can be a source of long-term capital but one should not be too reliant on it."

An encouraging development took place in May 1999, when a team went on a worldwide road show to market a Malaysian government bond issue. The move signaled confidence by policymakers in the durability of the recovery. The roadshow was also viewed as an opportunity to address misperceptions and promote global investors' interest and confidence in Malaysia. The timing of the planned issue turned out to be inauspicious for emerging market debt in general as there were expectations then that US interest rates would rise and fears of a default by Argentina. In the event, the issuance of USD 1 billion of 10-year notes was well-received and oversubscribed more than three times. The engagement with global investors paved the way for another bond issue in 2000 on better financing terms.

In short, Malaysia's unorthodox policy approach during the AFC — which Shamsiah characterized as "to do what needed to be done at the right time, even if it meant doing it alone" — worked.

Chapter 7

Philippines

Four persons were interviewed in the preparation of this chapter: Roberto F. de Ocampo, Amando M. Tetangco, Jr., Diwa C. Guinigundo, and Gil S. Beltran. During the 1997 Asian financial crisis, de Ocampo served as the Secretary of Finance. Tetangco was the then Managing Director of the Bangko Sentral ng Pilipinas, in charge of the Department of Economic Research and the Treasury Department. He served as Bangko Sentral ng Pilipinas Governor from 2005 to 2017. Guinigundo was the then Director of the Department of Economic Research at the Bangko Sentral ng Pilipinas. He was appointed as the Deputy Governor from 2005 until his retirement in 2019. Beltran was then an assistant secretary at the Philippines' Department of Finance and served as Undersecretary from 2005 until he retired in October 2021.

The Philippines was less affected by the Asian financial crisis (AFC) than other regional economies. A seemingly paradoxical reason cited for this, as observed by Roberto F. de Ocampo, was that it was viewed as the "laggard economy of Southeast Asia." However, the economy was also relatively more resilient to the ensuing contagion from the AFC because of reforms and policies pursued earlier. The AFC in turn was the impetus for further reforms to strengthen its economy and financial system when conditions had settled.

Pre-Crisis

The Philippines was more insulated from the AFC than its neighbors partly because, compared to the other regional economies, it had been largely bypassed by investors and international banks up to the start of the 1990s. The country then was still shadowed by the political uncertainties and the debt crisis of the 1980s. As Amando M. Tetangco, Jr. observed, the Philippines consequently was less leveraged as it did not receive as much capital inflows in the pre-crisis period:

> "One of the reasons the Philippines was not that highly leveraged compared to other countries is that we were a 'latecomer' to the Asian

party. For instance, the real estate boom started much earlier and bigger in neighboring countries. In the Philippines, the industry was basically responding to demand for residential and office space until they saw what was happening in the other countries. Then the boom started to catch up here also. As for capital inflows, we were only able to go back to the international capital markets in the early 1990s, after our own debt crisis of the mid-1980s. Portfolio flows started coming in around that time and increased in the mid-1990s. This was, however, cut short by the Mexican tequila (debt) crisis (in 1994). Soon after it started to recover post-tequila crisis, the AFC came knocking."

The lagged inflow of capital was good for the Philippines in two ways. First, asset bubbles there started later and were more restrained than in other regional economies. Second, the Philippines was saved from the massive outflows of capital that would beset the more affected countries. The Philippines was also better protected against the AFC contagion, as Gil S. Beltran commented, due to the comprehensive economic reforms that began in the late 1980s and continued into the 1990s:

"Luckily for us, we implemented economic reforms earlier. We reduced tariffs and removed quotas for two decades in the 1980s and 1990s which made our exports competitive and imports tempered by foreign exchange (FX) movements. Also, we dismantled monopolies and privatized government corporations. In addition, we strengthened our banks with capitalization increases."

Diwa C. Guinigundo noted that the reforms laid in the pre-AFC period were broad, ranging from economic competitiveness to poverty alleviation:

"The period before the crisis was a period of growth and stability. Real gross domestic product (GDP) growth was at positive levels and the external payments position strengthened with a surplus. These demonstrated the positive impact of policy and structural reforms and of progressive governance. Macroeconomic imbalances were greatly reduced while labor, financial, and goods markets' rigidities were also addressed.

At the same time, the Philippines was also beginning to examine issues of poverty and income inequality through agrarian reform, modernization of agriculture, and greater access to education. Under the administration of then President Fidel V. Ramos, the country was undergoing moral recovery from bad governance and from what some economists and sociologists described as 'damaged culture.'"

Just as significantly, the Philippine financial sector was also in relatively better shape going into the crisis. Banks had been conservative in their lending. Tetangco noted that the central bank, Bangko Sentral ng Pilipinas (BSP), had also preemptively tightened prudential standards like limiting loan-to-value (LTV) thresholds for loans to real estate:

> "On the loans side, I think it was a conscious effort on the part of Philippine banks that they remained conservative, which proved very helpful in minimizing the excesses of bad credit leading up to the crisis. There were other measures like the LTV ratio which was adopted shortly before the breakout of the AFC. Some officials in the BSP had heard from foreign sources that a crisis was looming in the region. I guess these sources were keen observers of developments in the Asian region. They looked at the numbers and began to see that something was not moving in the right direction. So the Monetary Board decided to adopt an LTV ratio for bank loans to the property sector before it got too bubbly. Therefore, market intelligence is important in assessing potential sources of financial stress."

In addition, the Philippines had both a rigorous debt monitoring system and a relatively healthier debt profile at the start of the AFC, as pointed out by Tetangco:

> "The BSP had put up an external debt monitoring system as early as, I believe, the 1970s. The system contained information on foreign borrowings of both the public and the private sectors that had to be registered and approved by the central bank for borrowers to be able to buy FX for debt servicing from the banking system. Unregistered foreign obligations could not be serviced using FX coming from the banks.

> Looking at foreign debt metrics, the numbers would show that we were likewise not highly leveraged. The debt equity ratio of Philippine corporates, for instance, was only 1.9% in 1997, the lowest in the Asian region. In terms of total debt to GDP, while the Philippines had a relatively high ratio, most of the debt was owed to multilateral and bilateral agencies.

Private non-guaranteed debt to GDP, prior to the crisis, specifically 1996, was only 6% in the case of the Philippines. Comparable ratios were much higher in the other countries, more than double or triple in some cases. Debt maturity in the Philippines was also tilted toward longer maturities; short-term debt to total debt was only 19%. The ratio of foreign liabilities to reserves of the Philippines was less than 1."

Overall, the country's debt profile mitigated the effects of the AFC on Philippine corporates and banks.

The Contagion

Philippine policymakers were therefore initially largely sanguine that the Thai crisis would not spill over to the Philippines in a big way, as recalled by de Ocampo:

"Our first reaction was, well, big deal. We have just made our economy pretty strong. Our reserves are pretty good. Our exchange rate is fine. It's actually pretty stable and relatively strong, so we are not likely to be affected. Our first inclination was to assure the public and the media that while things are going wrong among the emerging tigers, particularly with Thailand, that's Thailand's problem, not ours. Our main defense was to assure that our domestic economy was fine. Unfortunately, that's not how things turned out, and one after another, this domino effect ensued."

But, as Guinigundo remarked, the contagion from the AFC led to speculative attacks on the peso:

"But despite the fundamental resiliency of the Philippine economy, the country was not spared from heavy speculative attacks due to the contagion. I would say that during this time, market players and specu-lators did not benefit from careful evaluation of country dynamics and fundamentals. There was little discrimination between and among the economies in the region."

Tetangco recalled that the BSP felt the selling pressure on the peso the very day the baht was floated and soon discovered that other regional central banks were also experiencing similar pressures on their currencies. It was the contagion effect at work:

"The Philippines was not spared and the peso suffered speculative attack. It was capital flight that was behind heavy selling of the Philippine peso for the United States (US) dollar. There was continuing downward pressure on the local currency, which we subsequently learned was not confined to the Philippine peso. Because of capital flight, other currencies in the region were also experiencing depreciation pressures. We came to know from our counterparts in other regional central banks that they were being confronted by the same issue. This was the first time that the currencies in the region came under pressure at the same time."

The BSP's first reaction was to intervene in the currency market and to raise interest rates to support the currency. But the intervention did not quell capital outflows. After a few days, as narrated by Tetangco, the BSP decided that intervention would be ineffectual as the problem was negative market sentiment and loss of confidence in Asian markets. Intervention would only deplete much-needed reserves:

"The initial reaction of the BSP at that time was to try and stabilize the exchange rate by intervening in the FX market and raising the policy rate. Such FX intervention was not sustained because we were also conscious about the level of international reserves. At that time, we didn't have a significant level of international reserves.

But it became apparent that continuing to do this would deplete our reserves in a way that would not be helpful. It was, after all, market sentiment and loss of confidence in Asian markets that was exerting downward pressure on the peso. We decided to be more pragmatic, especially given that what was happening was not confined to the Philippines, but was region-wide."

Tetangco added that little time was taken to get the BSP's decision approved:

"It was a collegial monetary board decision because the Bangko Sentral is an independent monetary authority. What the Governor and some of the monetary board members, particularly the Cabinet representative in the Monetary Board, did was to inform the President the day before the announcement of the FX rate system. The President told them, 'If that's what you think is the right thing to do, then go ahead.' So, the decision was adopted. The Cabinet was not involved in that decision."

With its decision on the peso approved, the BSP ceased intervening to support it, allowing it to find its market-driven level. As Tetangco recalled, the impact on the peso was immediate and startling:

"But on the day that the BSP announced the policy to no longer intervene in the FX market and to allow market forces to determine the rate, the peso quickly fell in value against the US dollar. I remember this because we were in the Office of the Governor watching the Reuters screen on the day the policy was announced. On that first day of the new FX policy, the exchange rate went from around PHP 26 to the dollar to about PHP 29 quickly. This was a move never seen before. On that day, the exchange rate closed at PHP 30 to the dollar. It depreciated further thereafter."

Guinigundo added that even the International Monetary Fund (IMF) team assigned to the Philippines was taken aback by the sharp peso depreciation:

"At that time, IMF representatives were actually in the Philippines when the BSP decided to cease FX market intervention. The mission members were astonished at the rapid depreciation of the peso despite their hope and expectation that it would come around and stabilize at about PHP 30 to a dollar. Instead, the peso stabilized at a much lower level. The bloodbath in Asia was unprecedented and reverberated even through the goods market and the real estate industry."

The Crunch

The shift to a more flexible exchange rate did not stop capital flight. In fact, capital outflows quickened, raising the stakes for policymakers. Between July and December 1997, the peso depreciated by about 40%. It was a precipitous fall with implications for inflation and foreign currency borrowers.

Tetangco, in close touch with the trading room of the BSP, sensed the incoming strong orders for US dollars:

"When we adopted a more flexible exchange rate, it was because we didn't want to deplete our reserves defending the currency. The strong demand for US dollars was sustained. It was difficult to ascertain where the demand was coming from, but we knew it was mainly from offshore. Transactions in the local FX market were largely done by Philippine branches of foreign banks and the larger domestic banks, who were supposedly servicing 'client demand.'"

Capital flight, as de Ocampo remarked, was a manifestation of the contagion sweeping the region. It led to currency depreciation and volatility. He remembered the consequent inflationary impact as the Philippines was import-dependent for oil:

"But as the exchange rate deteriorated, everything became much more affected. For example, since we rely a lot on importation of fuel, that particular bill suddenly went overboard. The exchange rate volatility also affected the prices of everything else, causing a big problem. We then experienced our own capital flight. This is the contagion effect. No matter how we tried to convince those that were exiting that they should hang on, they didn't. The sentiment I had at that time was displeasure. Those that had come to Asia in order to benefit just suddenly exited, indiscriminately thinking of Asia as one homogeneous place and just saying 'Asia, we are not sure; Asia, we're getting out of here.'"

Tetangco referred to the intricate balancing act the BSP had to juggle with in the face of persistent capital flight:

"Policymakers had to balance trade-offs in responding to the intense pressure on the peso. Allowing too deep a currency fall would further erode market confidence in the currency. It would also intensify inflation through higher import prices. However, the BSP was concerned about expending its reserves if it intervened too aggressively to support the currency."

With the peso under continuing pressure, policymakers then coupled exchange rate intervention with tighter monetary and fiscal policies to shore up market confidence. As Tetangco remarked, these meant lower economic growth but were necessary to buttress confidence:

"FX intervention was accompanied by a tightening of monetary policy. The BSP interest rate on reverse repos was raised significantly in an attempt to make peso instruments more attractive. Such a policy certainly had important implications on business activity and economic growth, as did contractionary fiscal policy. Increasing local interest rates to attract more funds to the local currency translated to higher cost of funds for businesses, affecting profitability and viability. Trade-offs were important concerns."

Beltran added that when the fiscal policy was tightened, a major concern was the impact on lower income groups. Thus, measures were taken to restrain price increases for essential goods:

"We had also just introduced a new tax regime which allowed us to have the first consecutive years of budget surplus in our history. So, we did have at least a fairly healthy surplus for us to weather the storm. Nevertheless, the general population was affected because once we started moving a large part of our budget to defend the economy, it had serious implications on the social aspects of the budget. Among other things, we had to introduce, not exactly price control, price discipline, so that those that were planning to take advantage of the situation didn't make the situation even more burdensome for the poorer segment of society."

As with other regional economies, the Philippine corporate sector was squeezed on multiple fronts. However, as Tetangco added, it withstood the crisis without major insolvencies as it was relatively less leveraged:

"As you can imagine, the corporate sector was hit from multiple sides: from the currency side, particularly if they had high foreign obligations; on the domestic side, they faced higher costs following the increase in domestic interest rates. They were likewise affected by the decline in demand as economic activity went down. In the case of the Philippines, while an increase in nonperforming loans (NPLs), was seen after about a year after the breakout of the crisis, the NPL ratio didn't really go up that much until about 3 or 4 years later. Hence, there was a gradual build-up in NPLs, which was an indication that Philippine corporates were not as highly leveraged. In hindsight, I think this is one of the factors why the Philippines was moderately affected by the AFC compared to other countries."

In December 1997, the BSP also introduced a currency protection facility for companies. It enabled the BSP to enter into nondeliverable forward contracts with supervised banks, with their FX obligations as underlying transactions. This relieved the pressure on companies to buy foreign currencies in the spot market to cover their future payments.

The Philippines also had an IMF program in place when the crisis started. It was extended during the crisis as a precautionary measure, to enable access to IMF funds if needed. The funding provision was not invoked. As Beltran explained, it was felt that, based on its fundamentals, the country could get by without IMF financing. Policymakers did not want to be subject to conditionalities that called for deeper fiscal spending cuts:

"We did not draw from the precautionary line, although we could have done so. Initially, they were asking us to have a current account surplus, but we had a deficit then. It's a huge task to turn it into a surplus, considering the fact that we have a deficit of 2% of GDP in our consolidated public sector deficit for about 20 or 30 years. We would have to cut social services and employment significantly to turn it to a surplus, and we cannot afford to do so. So, eventually, we did not touch the IMF facility.

Due to these reforms, we did not need to go to the IMF to borrow. However, we maintained and extended the facility with the IMF only as a precautionary measure. We did not actually borrow from the IMF. After our experience and what we saw in our neighboring countries, we thought that it's a good idea to pull our resources together and help each other in future crises."

Resolution

Of the regional economies, the Philippines was among the first to recover. The impact of the tightening policies on the economy was manageable. They did not deepen the slowdown significantly. Thus, economic contraction was considerably less severe, with economic growth in 1998 registering −0.5%.

Tetangco elaborated on the recovery path:

"It didn't take us that long to restore economic growth. By the fourth quarter (Q4) of 1998, we started to post positive growth on an annual basis which continued and gathered pace. We increased government spending as meeting the fiscal targets under the IMF program subsequently bought us spending leeway to support growth.

In fact, since Q4 1998, the Philippine economy has had uninterrupted economic growth up to 2019, just before the coronavirus disease (COVID-19) pandemic. Of course there was some slowdown during the tech bubble in the early 2000s, but the GDP didn't go into negative territory."

Guinigundo remarked that polices turned pro-growth quickly when the crisis was subsiding:

"From an essentially crisis-management mode, monetary policy pivoted to help economic recovery as FX trading stabilized and speculation quelled. With this policy space, the BSP started normalizing its policy rate and liquidity management. Regulatory support was also undertaken to incentivize banks to be more transparent and reduce their lending rates and encourage both corporate and individual borrowings."

Even as the economy recovered, policymakers continued with reforms of the economy and financial sector. Beltran referred to the reforms to make the external sector more competitive:

"We adopted so many reforms. For example, we cut down on the tariff rates from over 100% to 10% over a period of 30 years. We also removed many of the restrictions on the marketing of fuel products and liberalized petroleum pricing. For the peso, we made it more market-oriented. Instead of protecting importers, we were helping the exporters more, so our exports rose significantly, mainly parts of all the electronics products, so suddenly our exports of electronic products became our biggest export item. In the past, we exported mainly agricultural, forest, and mineral products. Later, we became an exporter of manufactured products including electronics. Most of these exports went to China for further processing."

The BSP, as Tetangco pointed out, shifted its monetary policy framework:

"And when inflation started to ease after the crisis, we shifted our monetary policy framework — abandoning the monetary aggregate targeting method and instead adopted the inflation targeting framework to focus on price stability."

Tetangco also outlined how the central bank tightened its supervision framework:

"The AFC revealed weaknesses in banking supervision among Asian jurisdictions, including the Philippines. As a response, like other banking supervisors in the region, we set out to enhance the mandate of banking supervision, generally guided by the Basel Principles of Effective Banking Supervision issued by the Basel Committee. The broad set of strategic reforms were aimed at promoting transparency, systemic stability, institutional safety and soundness, and protection of the public. One of the major initiatives in this area was the adoption of risk-based supervision. Specific measures included increasing bank capitalization, fostering good governance practices, promoting greater disclosure and adoption of international accounting standards, among others."

Beltran referred to a policy to accumulate foreign reserves as a strategic contingency measure:

"Additionally, we started stocking up on reserves as we know that we can only rely on ourselves when a problem strikes. From a buffer of only 2.6 months' worth of imports of goods and services in 1997, it has increased to about 10 months. Furthermore, we opened up FX restrictions so that our investors can invest anywhere in the world. Instead of restricting outward movement of investible funds, we allowed them to invest in other countries. This has borne fruit — there is currently a growing percentage of our FX inflows coming from dividends accrued from those investments made abroad. We're now trying to remove other remaining restrictions to allow for freer movement of FX across borders."

Chapter 8

Hong Kong

This chapter draws on the recollections of three persons: Norman T. L. Chan, Andrew Sheng, and Jim Walker. During the 1997 Asian financial crisis, Chan and Sheng both served as Deputy Chief Executives of the Hong Kong Monetary Authority. Chan was in charge of monetary management, payment and settlement systems, debt market, administration, and finance. He was assigned to orchestrate the unprecedented move by the Hong Kong Monetary Authority to purchase index stocks and futures contracts at the height of the speculative attacks on the Hong Kong markets. Sheng was responsible for reserves management, external affairs, and information technology matters. In late 1998, Sheng was appointed as the Chairman of the Securities and Futures Commission of Hong Kong. Walker was chief economist at the Hong Kong-based Credit Lyonnais Securities (Asia) Ltd during the crisis.

Hong Kong was the quintessential example of how a fundamentally sound economy could have been brought to its knees through speculative attacks on its currency and stock markets. Ironically, it was the sophistication of Hong Kong's financial markets that gave speculators an array of means to attack the system. Through adroit responses, however, policymakers beat the speculators at their own game. Not only that, the operations resulted in a windfall for government coffers and a long-term investment product for Hong Kong residents.

Pre-Crisis

Pre-crisis, Hong Kong's economic fundamentals were robust: steady gross domestic product (GDP) growth, budget surpluses, no sovereign and low corporate external debt, and ample foreign reserves.

Hong Kong's well capitalized banking system was also reassuring, as Norman T. L. Chan recalled:

"When the Asian financial crisis (AFC) first started in Thailand and later spread to Indonesia and Korea, many people in Hong Kong and in the Hong Kong Monetary Authority (HKMA) thought that the crisis hit these countries because of their weak financial systems. We thought that as Hong Kong had a much more mature and robust financial system, the AFC should not affect us that much and, even if it would, Hong Kong would be able to withstand the shockwaves."

Andrew Sheng disclosed that the HKMA had, in addition, girded itself for market dislocations of some sort, following the 1994 Mexican crisis and in anticipation of the handover of Hong Kong to China in July 1997:

"Well, I think the exact timing was unexpected, although we knew that it was going to come. As you know, those of us in Hong Kong monitoring the global financial markets after the Mexican crisis of 1994, knew that it was only a matter of time. That's why Hong Kong was very, very prepared because Hong Kong was prepared for the handover on July 1. We were building up reserves, testing that all the systems, etc. were okay."

Sheng elaborated on the length the HKMA had gone to in stress testing the financial system:

"We monitored all these positions. We stress tested the situation to make sure that the brokers don't fail and the banks won't fail because of liquidity issues. We stress tested every single angle. The payment systems, the banking systems, the stockbroking system, etc. The point was when the stresses came, we were not caught by surprise. We wanted to make sure that the brokers didn't fail and the banks didn't fail because of liquidity issues."

The Speculators' Targets

Although Hong Kong was in a relatively stronger position than its Asian peers prior to the AFC, there were, as Chan pointed out:

"[O]bvious fault lines — a huge property bubble; households that were heavily indebted mainly due to mortgage borrowings; corporates, especially property developers that were over-geared; and prevailing trade deficits running at around 3% of GDP... This indicated a clear overheating of the economy and a loss of competitiveness of the Hong Kong dollar versus the United States (US) dollar."

In addition, there was the Hong Kong's Linked Exchange Rate System (LERS). The LERS was essentially a currency board system (CBS) with the Hong Kong dollar pegged within a narrow band of HKD 7.85–7.75 to the US dollar.

The LERS became an obvious target for currency speculators for two reasons. First, speculators were emboldened to take on another US dollar pegged currency system after their successful attacks on the Thai baht and the Indonesian rupiah. Second, they saw the Hong Kong property bubble and the debt leverage associated with it as weaknesses that could be exploited. Essentially, an attack on the LERS would cause interest rates to rise which, if high enough, would destabilize the property market, cause financial distress for households and property developers, and lead to a sharp economic downturn. Policymakers would then be under pressure to abandon the LERS.

Chan also noted that "the not-too-big and not-too-small size and high liquidity of the Hong Kong dollar markets, coupled with total freedom of movement of funds in and out, made Hong Kong a very attractive target."

The Speculative Attacks

Thus, Hong Kong came to be in the crosshairs of speculators, who trained their sights on the LERS. The first wave of attacks began in August 1997 and lasted for around 2 months, culminating in the week of October 20 with concerted, intense selling of Hong Kong dollars. These attacks triggered the LERS' automatic defense mechanism where essentially the shorting of Hong Kong dollars leads to the monetary base contracting, causing interbank rates to rise and hence raise the cost of shorting the currency. The liquidity squeeze in late October was so intense that on October 23 ("Black Thursday"), overnight rates shot up to nearly 300%. With the costs of shorting so high, the speculators retreated.

Chan recalled that after the speculators withdrew,

> "the overnight Hong Kong Interbank Offer Rate (HIBOR) then fell back to 5–6% a few days later, but one-month HIBOR still stayed above 10%, which was significantly higher than the level before the attack. It was clear that ultra-high Hong Kong dollar interest rates would significantly alter the economics of shorting, but it was also obvious that such high funding costs would do a lot of harm to

the real economy and the financial system if they should last for a prolonged period of time."

There was a period of relative calm in the Hong Kong dollar exchange rate until August 1998. However, the HKMA was becoming increasingly concerned about two disquieting trends in the intervening period, as Chan noted:

"First, the one-month HIBOR, which was the key benchmark for the funding costs of banks for their mortgages and other loans, remained at an elevated level of over 10% in the few months after October 1997. This put enormous pressure on banks to raise their prime rates by several percentage points, which inevitably would deal a further blow to the already collapsing property market (which dropped by almost 50% in 12 months from its peak in 1997). While the banks held back the increase in prime rates, they could not hold for long if HIBORs did not ease back.

Secondly, the stock market was steadily dropping, accompanied by a significant fall in the trading volume, with daily turnover shrinking from an average of HKD 15 billion in 1997 to just HKD 4 billion in July 1998. At the same time, the Hang Seng Index (HSI) futures market saw its total open positions gradually rising from 59,000 contracts at the end of 1997 to 98,000 contracts at the end of July 1998."

The open positions being accumulated were mainly short positions on Hong Kong stocks. It was a puzzling but disconcerting development, as Chan recollected:

"It was not entirely clear to us at that time what was going on, but there was a clear sense of unease with a hunch that a new wave of speculative attacks, likely to be different and on a larger scale than the October 1997 episode, was about to hit Hong Kong."

In August 1998, the attacks resumed, with a twist. It was a double play strategy of shorting both the Hong Kong dollar and stocks. Speculators, learning from their October 1997 experience, had, as Chan elaborated, changed their strategy in two major ways:

"(a) they had built up major short positions in the stock market as well as the HSI futures market, aiming to profit from a sharp fall in both markets when the currency attack began, with the resultant sharp rise in interest rates; and

(b) learning from the inhibitive high cost of shorting back then, they had 'prefunded' themselves with Hong Kong dollars (believed to be to the tune of around HKD 30 billion) by borrowing in the money markets during the 'quiet' months before their attack. So a rise in HIBOR during the attack should do them little harm."

It seemed a "sure-win" proposition for speculators; they would win even if the currency peg held as the consequent high interest rates would cause stocks to fall, and they would win more if the peg broke.

The double play attack revealed a facet of Hong Kong's financial markets that, as Sheng observed, the HKMA had initially overlooked. This was the use of the futures market by the speculators:

"[W]hat we did not see from the HKMA side was the problem with the futures exchange. There was a Hong Kong futures exchange separate from the Hong Kong stock market. And, the futures exchange index became the most liquid index.

The classical problem was that if you don't have a unified view of financial markets, you're going to die. Let me explain. The securities regulation is by the Securities Futures Commission. The Hong Kong stock market is huge, valued at several times of Hong Kong's GDP. There was a separate Hong Kong Futures Exchange. The HKMA is in turn in charge of the Hong Kong dollar and the banking system. But the stock market has massive ups and downs, with a 5% daily fluctuation a normal affair. Fluctuation aside, the bigger issue was whether the market clears."

As Sheng explained, hedge funds had been using the Hong Kong stock futures index as an indirect way of shorting other regional stock markets:

"So, what we didn't understand at that particular point in time was that when the hedge funds were speculating in the rest of Asia, they used the Hong Kong stock futures index as a proxy hedge. This means that if they were to short, let's say the Kuala Lumpur market, the Jakarta market, the Thai market, but these did not have a market to enable them to short the market, the best proxy instrument was the Hong Kong stock futures market.

The result was when the Asian stock markets fell, the Hong Kong stock market took bigger pressure than it would have on its own. You see, that's the true contagion effect, the network effect."

Prepared with their positions, speculators waited for the right time to attack the Hong Kong markets. This came in August 1998 when public sentiment had turned extremely bearish about the currency peg and the stock market. Media reports had been rife of a potential devaluation of the renminbi and the demise of the LERS. Chan observed that speculators themselves were involved in manufacturing these rumors. They stirred pessimism by "collaborating with certain media 'friends' to spread rumors and unwarranted fear in the community."

The double play strategy began in early August. Speculators simultaneously sold short the Hong Kong dollar and Hong Kong stocks. These attacks led to interest rates rising and stocks declining. On August 13, 1998, the stock market fell by 60%. This was what speculators were planning on, as observed by Jim Walker:

"I think the real attack was on the stock market. Fund managers talked a lot about shorting the Hong Kong dollar and that just frightened people into selling the stock market. And that's where they made the real money."

With the Hong Kong dollar and Hong Kong stocks under severe pressure, the risk was a loss of confidence among Hong Kong residents and companies about the LERS and consequent panic outflow of capital. The Hong Kong government had to respond to the speculative attacks decisively.

Bold, Unexpected Response

The next day, the Hong Kong government reacted. It was a bold, unexpected response. The government gave the HKMA the authority to deploy the reserves from the exchange fund to buy the index stocks and futures contracts.

Chan, who was put in charge of the operations, told the story of how it began with his meeting with the chief executives of the three largest brokers in Hong Kong that morning:

"On Friday, August 14, 1998, the CEOs of the three largest stock brokers in Hong Kong were invited to the China Club in Central to attend a breakfast meeting called, at very short notice, by the Financial Services Bureau of the Hong Kong SAR government. When they arrived, they were surprised to see me, and me alone. Hitherto the HKMA had had no dealings with the stock brokers in Hong Kong, as the exchange fund did not make any investments in equities at all. I asked them to finish their coffee and switch off their mobile phones, and then took them to the HKMA office. They were told, in strict confidence, that the government had decided to intervene in the stock and futures markets to counter the double play. They would need to go back to their offices and open stock and futures trading accounts for the HKMA immediately, as we would soon be starting the operation on the very same day. That was the beginning of the stock market operation."

That day, the HSI reversed its declining trend and closed about 8.5% higher. But the battle was not over. The operation would last for 10 trading days, ending on August 28, 1998. Chan gave some details on what he termed the "unprecedented and hazardous endeavor":

"Prior to that, the exchange fund had not directly invested in or held any equities. So we did not even have any stock trading account with anybody anywhere. Besides, the HKMA dealing room was designed to trade only foreign exchange, forwards, interest rates, and bonds. So we did not have the trading facilities for stocks and HSI futures. Obviously the stock market operation was hugely market sensitive and we needed to maintain absolute confidentiality until the launch day. We could only involve very few people within the HKMA who were sworn to secrecy. We set up half a dozen telephone lines with make-shift recording facilities for orders to be made to our stockbrokers. Our mission was clear: to stand in the market and buy and thereby prevent the speculators' manipulative trading strategies from causing excessive falls in the stock and HSI futures markets, which would destabilize our financial system."

Throughout the 10 days, the HKMA and speculators was engaged in a battle of wills, even up to the last day of the operations, August 28. That day was in fact the most stressful, as related by Chan:

"On that single day the selling pressure reached an unprecedented level, with the stock market turnover at a historical high of over HKD 79 billion and with the HKMA almost being the only buyer in town. It was indeed a harrowing day in Hong Kong's financial history."

Still, the HKMA beat down the sellers that day and the HSI closed at 7,830, about 18% above when the operations started, and about double the 4,000 level that the speculators were believed to have been aiming for. Speculator activity then quietened.

During those 10 trading days, the government had mobilized HKD 18 billion or about 18% of the total assets of the exchange fund at that time to buy 33 constituent stocks of the HSI. This amount did not include the money deployed for building long positions in the HSI futures market, all of which were unwound by the end of September 1998.

Even after that, however, the HKMA remained on alert. It was perturbed by the unusually large open positions in the futures market. This suggested that despite their huge losses, the speculators remained a latent threat. External events, however, intervened to reduce their potency. These were Russia's default on its bonds and devaluation of the ruble in 1998 and the collapse of the highly leveraged US hedge fund, Long-Term Capital Management (LTCM). These mishaps forced banks to cut the credit lines that were funding leveraged activities globally. The result was a massive unwinding of the short positions in the Hong Kong and other Asian markets. Hong Kong interest rates then returned to normal levels and the stock market stabilized.

Hong Kong's defeat of the speculators was a crucial victory. That the LERS remained intact was critical. If it had been broken, the loss of public confidence would have led to massive capital outflows with wider destabilizing effects on the economy and the financial system. Apart from financial operations to stave off speculators, the backing that the Hong Kong government received from China was of significant aid in fending off the speculators. This was through the open pledge by the then Chinese Premier, Zhu Rongji, that China stood ready to mobilize its reserves to aid Hong Kong. It was a powerful statement of support.

In 1997, the creation of an agency, the Hong Kong Mortgage Corporation, played a role in alleviating the effects of sharply falling property prices on banks. It helped to relieve banks of their troubled home mortgages and from having to seek liquidity from the HKMA, a reason Sheng gave for no bank failures in Hong Kong then:

> "Can you imagine, at the height of a crisis and in a fully transparent system, the representatives of the troubled bank were seen visiting the central bank? Outside the central bank office, there were all these reporters with their TV cameras showing which banker came in to borrow money. The next thing that's going to happen is a run against that particular bank. When some of the smaller banks were hit during the episode, they just sold the mortgages over the phone to the Mortgage Corporation. The Mortgage Corporation gave them liquidity straight away, so there were no bank failures in Hong Kong."

Challenges Arising from Stock Buying Operation

The stock buying operation proved successful but gave rise to two major challenges for Hong Kong policymakers. First, the unconventional move met with international criticism. Among others, Alan Greenspan, then Chairman of the US Federal Reserve, commented that Hong Kong had abandoned its free market principles in seeking to defend the stock market. Hong Kong officials subsequently went overseas to explain the circumstances and the speculative forces they had to counter. International opinion soon turned positive, especially after the US Fed itself deviated from its nonintervention stance to bail out the LTCM.

In addition, the HKMA's intervention was seen as "out of the box" and its timing excellent as Hong Kong stocks were oversold, as observed by Walker:

> "The stocks were all oversold, and the speculators were over-leveraged. The HKMA dealt them a hammer blow, with great timing, by buying the stock market completely out of the blue. I mean, this was probably one of the most brilliant pieces of policymaking during the course of the Asian crisis.
>
> They just blew the stops away. That cost the speculators an absolute fortune. The HKMA bought the market and continued to buy the market, although they didn't need to buy anywhere near as much as they ended up with, but they weren't to know that in the first instance. That arrested the falling equity prices. And I think it also gave away the reality that there was not much in the way of currency pressure."

The second major challenge was to decide what to do with the shares that the exchange fund had bought. Concerns were expressed that the government had become the largest single shareholder of most of the companies that were constituents of the HSI. On March 16, 1999, the government declared that it would neither nominate Directors to the Boards of these companies nor interfere in their operations unless these materially affected government's interests.

It was, however, recognized that the long-term solution was for the government to divest these shares to the private sector and in a manner that would not disrupt markets. A company, the Exchange Fund Investment Limited (EFIL), was set up to pursue this objective. Subsequently, Chan was tasked with devising a suitable share disposal scheme, the outcome being the creation of an open-ended exchange-traded fund (ETF) called the Tracker Fund of Hong Kong (TraHK). TraHK was listed on the Hong Kong Stock Exchange in November 1999. Later, a Tap facility was introduced to allow more shares to be released based on a market pricing formula.

Chan alluded to the success of the launch of TraHK:

"The initial public offering (IPO), launched in November 1999, was a great success even without the sweetener of an instant discount. We sold TraHK units amounting to HKD 33.3 billion, making it the largest IPO in Asia (ex-Japan) at that time. Thanks to a marketing campaign that highlighted the importance of creating long-term investments for the next generation, more than 184,000 Hong Kong retail investors took part. Those who have held on to their TraHK investments up to today enjoy an annualized rate of return of 7.6%, inclusive of dividends, loyalty bonus units, and unit price rises."

Chan also summed up the monetary consequences of the stock-buying operations after the shares acquired had been released to the market:

"By that stage, the proceeds that the exchange fund received from the TraHK IPO and Tap facility had totaled HKD 140.4 billion (with an additional HKD 24.6 billion received as dividends and other income on the shares). This helped the exchange fund achieve unprece- dented investment returns of HKD 103.8 billion in 1999 and HKD 45.1 billion in 2000. The entire process of stock market operation and subsequent share disposal not only enriched the government's coffers substantially, but also underlined the crucial point that the operation was a right move made at the right time."

Economic Impact

Although the speculative attacks had been rebuffed, they imposed a heavy toll on the economy. As recalled by Chan, Hong Kong went through a severe economic downturn:

> "Hong Kong was very badly hit by the AFC. Despite the success of the market operations by the Hong Kong SAR government, the real economy was severely affected. The property market fell by almost 70% across the board from peak to bottom over a 6.5-year period. The unemployment rate went up to historical high level of almost 9%. Consumer price index (CPI) fell by around 15% over several quarters largely due to sharp shrinkage of domestic demand caused by the bursting of the property bubble and downturn of the economy."

In fact, Hong Kong was among the slowest of the crisis-hit economies to recover. This was mainly because of the Hong Kong dollar's peg to the US dollar. As the regional currencies had fallen sharply against the US dollar during the crisis, the Hong Kong dollar became less competitive. Thus, as Walker remarked, Hong Kong had to regain its trade competitiveness through wage and price deflation, which was slow and painful:

> "Hong Kong was left to deflate its way to competitiveness and that's a much, much more painful, longer-term process. Wages fell. Bonuses disappeared. All other prices fell as well and, effectively, it was an extremely painful, long-lasting price adjustment that eventually brought Hong Kong back into line with the rest of the region. It was only in 2004 that Hong Kong finally recovered. Everybody else in the region had recovered by 1999."

The Hong Kong economy pulled through eventually partly due to the strength of its export markets and the fall in US interest rates, and hence HK interest rates. US interest rates fell dramatically after the bursting of the dot-com bubble in 2000. However, as Chan noted, the inherent strengths of the Hong Kong economy were the fundamental reasons driving its recovery:

> "However, the most important factor for the resilience of Hong Kong was a highly flexible economy, especially its labor and products markets, that could adapt to shocks, whether internally or externally induced, and regain new equilibrium very swiftly through repricing or other appropriate means. Of course, persistent fiscal discipline (similar to Singapore) that had led to considerable fiscal reserves also helped to withstand negative shocks."

Chapter 9

Singapore

Three persons were interviewed in the preparation of this chapter: Teh Kok Peng, Hoe Ee Khor, and Kishore Mahbubani. During the 1997 Asian financial crisis, Teh and Khor were the Deputy Managing Director and the Executive Director, respectively, at the Monetary Authority of Singapore. Mahbubani was the then Permanent Secretary at the Singaporean Ministry of Foreign Affairs.

As a small, open economy and financial center, Singapore inevitably experienced a downturn in a region-wide crisis. However, it did not suffer as much duress as its neighbors because of its strong economic fundamentals. But the Asian financial crisis (AFC) had a longer-term impact that prompted a reorientation of Singapore's long-term economic strategies. The crisis also saw Singapore play a prominent role in giving feedback and advice to the international community, including the International Monetary Fund (IMF), on solutions to the crisis. Singapore also participated in the financial assistance programs for Thailand and Indonesia and, like the other regional economies, actively supported cross-border financial surveillance and capacity building in the post-AFC era.

Dividend of Good Economic Management

Pre-AFC, Singapore had impressive economic fundamentals. The government had no external debt. Singapore had run current account and fiscal surpluses for many years. These translated into the country having ample reserves. The country also had a triple A credit rating.

Singapore business groups were also relatively prudent, with a noticeably lower gearing ratio compared to their counterparts in other AFC economies. In particular, the banking sector was among the best capitalized not only in the region but also globally. The Monetary Authority of Singapore

(MAS) was also reputed for its rigorous prudential standards. Thus, while Singaporean banks invariably had loans exposed to the regional economies, these loans were adequately provided for, as Hoe Ee Khor remarked:

> "So Singapore was not a debtor country. We don't have any external debt. But some of our banks had exposure in the region. Especially Malaysia where some of our banks have big branches, big operations and also in Indonesia. So from that perspective, we have an interest to make sure that our banks were able to manage the losses to their balance sheets. So MAS was very active in that sense, in terms of working with our own banks to make sure that they are doing okay."

A significant policy intervention in May 1996 was the introduction of measures to curb speculation in the property market. These measures included the tightening of credit for local and foreign buyers, a hike in stamp duties, and treating as taxable income gains within 3 years from purchasing properties.

Teh Kok Peng explained why these curbs were implemented and their effectiveness:

> "We didn't anticipate the AFC. But we saw the property prices going up because in this region, there were a lot of capital inflows across Asia, including Singapore. There was a lot of speculation on property.
>
> The way we operate in Singapore, it was all under one roof in a central bank. We were far more prepared to use what we would now call macroprudential measures to put a limit on lending. These actually put a lid on residential property appreciation. I remember there were a lot of complaints at that time, but in retrospect, we did the right thing because otherwise, the prices would have gone up further. The banking system would have been more badly affected when the property prices came down during the crisis."

The measures deflated an incipient property bubble. It was timely. If the speculation in property had continued into the following year when the AFC emerged, banks and investors would have been exposed to more damage on their balance sheets.

Impact of the AFC

The AFC had both an immediate, short-lasting impact on the Singapore economy and a more significant impact on Singapore's long-term economic orientation. The short-term impact was an inevitable by-product of Singapore's economic and financial links across the region, as Khor stated:

> "[W]e were hit because of the spill-over effects. I mean all these countries were major trading partners of Singapore. So when they went down, they pulled us down as well. So that's the impact on us. We also went into a downturn, but that was the short-term impact, which was quite light in a way, because we had a relatively shallow downturn."

The slowdown cut across the economy, from construction to petrochemical to financial services. Tourist arrivals fell sharply because of the downturn in the regional economies, the main source of visitors for Singapore. Policy response to the crisis took the form of supporting households and reducing business costs. Key measures included a 10% corporate tax rebate, wage reduction of 5%–8%, and cuts in a wide range of government rentals, rates, and fees. Individuals and households also received help, ranging from a 5% personal income tax rebate to rebates on governmental service and conservancy charges.

As it turned out, Singapore's gross domestic product (GDP) suffered a 1.5% contraction in 1998. Unemployment rose to 3.2% in 1998. The impact on the economy was not as severe as the other regional economies. This primarily reflected strong economic and financial fundamentals.

Re-Inventing Singapore

The more significant outcome of the AFC on Singapore was that it spurred a revisiting of its economic strategies. The catalyst was the structural effects of the strength of the Singapore dollar relative to the regional currencies. Essentially, MAS had pursued a policy where the Singapore dollar was stable, in that it depreciated much less than the currencies of its regional trading partners against the United States (US) dollar.

Teh offered some insights on the policy:

> "The fact is the downturn was more due to what's happening in the region. So, we had a recession. But at the same time, I think, because

it's external and not internal driven, and in this kind of crisis, you don't want the exchange rate to come down because then there will be a loss of confidence leading to capital outflows, which will worsen internal conditions. Unlike the 1985–1986 recession when speculators attacked the Singapore dollar, I think we kept it quite strong. I mean, we did allow it to go down on a trade-weighted basis somewhat. But we didn't attempt to let the currency depreciate as much as that of our neighbors. But the results were actually, we appreciated quite a bit against the neighboring countries. But clearly, it also came down quite a bit against the US dollar."

Khor further elaborated on the MAS' exchange rate strategy during the AFC and its rationale:

"We widened the band but we didn't want the exchange rate to move too much because we wanted to keep the exchange rate strong. As I said, we are a financial center, and we want to maintain investor confidence in the Singapore dollar, and so there was a cost that we deliberately absorbed in a way, until I think 1999."

A stronger currency vis-à-vis its regional counterparts had a hollowing-out effect on Singapore's labor-intensive industries. This would dampen Singapore's economic growth trajectory. In fact, as pointed out by Khor, up to 2005, Singapore's growth lagged that of several regional economies:

"But the result of that policy was that a lot of our labor-intensive industries moved out of Singapore to Malaysia and other lower-cost locations. So Singapore has hollowed out for a few years, there was very little growth between 1997 to 2003.

A lot of our industries moved offshore. So when you look at the numbers, we were growing at 7–8% a year previously. All of a sudden, our growth collapsed to 3% or 4%. For several years we were not able to revive the growth. So in relative terms, I think the cost was quite high whereas if you look at the other countries like Malaysia, Malaysia actually bounced back very quickly."

The government responded to the structural issues by convening a major economic review in 2001. Chaired by the then Deputy Prime Minister and now Prime Minister Lee Hsien Loong, the review was broad ranging, the assessment being that Singapore needed no less than to reinvent itself to succeed in a post-AFC era, as Khor recalled:

"I think the assessment then was that we needed to reinvent ourselves. The old model was not working anymore, because we had moved to a regime where we needed to move up the value chain if we're going to be competitive. And that's when they decided to allow the casino to come in to develop the hospitality sector and to try to attract a whole new group of manufacturing industries, biomedical, chemical, and the high-end semiconductor industries.

But of course you cannot plan everything in advance, because I still remember when we were doing the review, we were expecting that for the Marina Bay area, the development would take about 10–20 years. But it happened so quickly, within 5–10 years. Most of the area was fully developed by then. So that came as a surprise and that was when I think we opened up the labor market to allow more foreign worker inflow. So if you look at the numbers, between 2005 and 2010, the foreign labor inflows was huge, about 200,000 a year, but that was to support the high growth at that time."

The financial sector was another area that saw transformative changes. In fact, the momentum for reforms here began before the AFC. It was initiated by the then Senior Minister, Lee Kuan Yew, who, through his observations from his wide contacts with financial statesmen and as Board Member of JP Morgan, opined that the Singapore financial sector needed a revamp to be internationally competitive. MAS, under the lead of then Deputy Prime Minister Lee Hsien Loong, took up the quest to remold the financial sector.

As Khor remembered, the reforms started with the move toward a more transparent and accountable regulatory approach. This established the groundwork for encouraging a broader set of financial services:

"Because we wanted to be a financial center. I mean you cannot change the world so we just have to adapt ourselves and make sure that our framework is keeping up with what's happening out there.

And so with the changes that were made, we actually developed more. The financial sector grew very rapidly. We set up the Financial Promotion Department which was responsible for growing or developing the asset management industry, and which is now one of the biggest in the world.

And so those are changes that we made in terms of regulatory framework that helps to make the financial sector more competitive relative to others. Of course there are certain areas like investment banking where we don't have the same advantage that Hong Kong has. But in other areas, we were able to maintain the edge."

Aside from the financial sector reforms, MAS also modernized its monetary policy framework toward an inflation targeting approach. This called for more transparency and accountability and a more rigorous surveillance system to support the policymaking process.

Helping the Neighbors Out

Singaporean policymakers were also actively engaged in watching regional developments with the objective of looking for ways to help its neighbors. As Khor put it, this was of mutual benefit:

"Well, the crisis affected Singapore because we have a strong vested interest in the prosperity of the region. We are a regional financial center, we are a gateway to the region. And we can only do well if the region is doing well, in a way. So when the region is in trouble, it is in our self-enlightened interest to help the region and to try to see how we can do it."

Singapore was valued as a sounding post for regional developments and prospective solutions. Hence, there were active communication lines between Singapore's policy makers and officials from the IMF missions, US Treasury, Japanese Ministry of Finance, and other countries. Khor revealed how his work at MAS took on a new dimension in this period:

"We went from surveillance to surveillance-plus-crisis management. I mean, although Singapore was not hit directly, we had a front row seat, and not just a front row seat, we were actually very actively involved. We were involved in terms of talking to the IMF missions and also the US Treasury officials, who would stop over in Singapore to seek the views of the Senior Minister and the Prime Minister about the situation in the region. We would be supporting the Prime Minister's Office (PMO) in terms of writing briefing notes for them.

So we also engaged, very much engaged, with the IMF because they tended to stop over in Singapore on the way either to Kuala Lumpur or to Jakarta. And we had conversations with them about what's going on and how we see the situation. So in that sense, we were active. I mean, not in terms of making policy but in terms of influencing policymaking."

As Singapore's largest neighbor, Indonesia merited much attention and support. There were close ties between the leaders as well as the importance of the country to the region, as Teh added:

"I would say Lee Kuan Yew was pretty keen to be helpful to President Suharto because he was an old friend. Bilateral relations were very good. Also, because Indonesia is at the center of the Association of Southeast Asian Nations (ASEAN), the fulcrum. If Indonesia goes down for whatever reason, ASEAN would be affected."

IMF officials, including Michel Camdessus, interacted frequently with Singapore's leaders about ways to alleviate the crisis in Indonesia. One solution, alluded to in the earlier chapter on Indonesia, suggested by Lee, was to have President Suharto take charge of decisions. Goh Chok Tong, then Prime Minister, also put in place a scheme to facilitate trade financing for Indonesian banks.

US Treasury officials also visited Singapore to discuss the AFC. Khor noted that they were noticeably more concerned as the crisis developed but were constrained from providing financial assistance because of potential congressional objections:

"However, as I said, the Treasury was very active, especially when it came to Indonesia. They were not as active when the crisis first broke in Thailand, but when the contagion swept through the region they were, I think, really alarmed… So Larry Summers and his staff came by Singapore several times. But their hands were tied because Congress was very opposed to bailing out countries after Mexico."

Singapore also participated in the financial assistance packages for Thailand and Indonesia. Khor recalled that Singapore was ready to help

Thailand from the start:

> "Well Singapore was, as I said, an interested party in the whole thing from the very beginning. I went to Thailand in December 1996 to meet up with the Bank of Thailand (BOT) to understand the problem and we were also working with them in terms of defending the baht. So when the crisis hit, I think we were actually open to helping out.
>
> And so when it turned out that the IMF money was not enough, and the Japanese wanted to mobilize regional support, we were ready to chip in."

When Indonesia came under severe stress, "Singapore was of course very concerned about things getting bad there," said Kishore Mahbubani. He explained:

> "There were financial assistance packages coming out for Indonesia and we said that we would contribute."

Indeed, the financial assistance for Indonesia was larger than that for Thailand, as Khor detailed:

> "And then, when Indonesia came under attack, again we were very interested. But for Indonesia, for some reason the financing from the Fund was more adequate. But they decided to have a second line of defense to strengthen the resources, because Indonesia started off with a much lower level of reserves, and it was very much depleted during the crisis. So they decided to have a second line of defense which would help to strengthen confidence amongst the investors that there was more than just what the IMF was providing. And that second line of defense actually is bigger. And so we chipped in the second line of defense at USD 5 billion. That's a lot of money. But it turned out when Suharto fell, they had to renegotiate the program, and they never drew on the second line of defense."

Singapore actively supported efforts to foster regional financial cooperation. It supported Japan's proposal for an Asian Monetary Fund (AMF), as recalled by Khor:

> "They were willing to put money behind it so they came up with the idea of an AMF, the Asian Monetary Fund. And so when they came by

Singapore to explore whether we would support it, we said we would. Because we were also an interested party, we have a big stake in the region, and we were willing to go along."

Although supporting the concept, Singapore also pointed out where the proposal needed to be firmed up to be accepted as workable, as the feedback from Teh about the first draft indicated:

"It was just a two-pager. It was so sketchy, vague. I mean, what are you going to do? And to build a capability to match that of the IMF takes years, decades. From Asia, how are they going to set up an organization in the midst of the crisis? They're trying to fight the fire, right? How can you build a fire brigade from nothing?"

Japan eventually withdrew the proposal for an AMF due to objections from the US Treasury and the IMF. But Asian policymakers recognized the usefulness of forging more formal arrangements to promote regional financial cooperation. Singapore, like its other regional partners, contributed to the realization of these objectives.

Chapter 10

Japan

This chapter draws on the interviews of four persons: Eisuke Sakakibara, Haruhiko Kuroda, Hiroshi Watanabe, and Jim Walker. During the 1997 Asian financial crisis, Sakakibara was Japan's Vice Minister of Finance and International Affairs. Kuroda was the then Director General of the International Bureau at the Japanese Ministry of Finance, before taking over the position of Vice Minister of Finance and International Affairs from Sakakibara in 1999. Watanabe served as the executive secretary to the then Minister of Finance, Kiichi Miyazawa. Walker was chief economist at the Hong Kong-based Credit Lyonnais Securities (Asia) Ltd during the crisis.

Japan's engagement in the Asian financial crisis (AFC) was multidimensional and consequential. On the one hand, a turnaround in Japanese bank lending contributed to the big swings in capital flows to the region. The bursting of the Japanese asset bubble in 1989–1990 caused Japanese banks to withdraw capital from the region where previously they had been major lenders. On the other hand, when the crisis erupted, Japanese policymakers were very proactive. They organized financial assistance initiatives for the crisis-hit economies and provided leadership to lay the groundwork for regional financial cooperation.

Role of Japanese Banks in the Crisis

Japanese bank lending in the region in the pre-AFC period went through two distinct phases. The first was from the second half of the 1980s to the mid-1990s. Japanese banks were major lenders then, surpassing American and European banks.

Jim Walker recalled the ubiquitous presence of Japanese banks in the region during the period:

"It was the same in Singapore, and in Jakarta, and in Bangkok. Japanese banks were all over the place. Japanese bank names were on every building, it seemed to me. Hardly any of them exist anymore. But you know, banks like the Long-Term Credit Bank of Japan and Industrial Bank of Japan were hugely involved in lending activity. I think it was largely because there wasn't that much lending activity in Japan. And so, essentially, they had contributed to the Asian crisis because they were taking advantage of the high growth in the region."

The surge in Japanese bank lending accounted for a significant proportion of the massive capital inflows into the region then. Hiroshi Watanabe noted some country differentiation in the focus of the Japanese banks. Among the Association of Southeast Asian Nations (ASEAN) countries, Thailand was the most favored:

"At that time, there were still about 20 banks in Japan and around 14 went overseas, and it was a fact that all of them rushed to give out loans. The rate of increase of Japanese bank lending was higher than that of American and European banks, but when the banks withdrew, they did it in one go, and I think that caused distress.

They did not go to Indonesia and Malaysia so much. Malaysia was a mid-sized country. As the country is small, and there was no keen interest in selling and exporting cheap products without much value added, there was not much investment in the country. Of course there was a time when Panasonic production formed 1% of Malaysia's gross domestic product (GDP) and there were investments then, but there wasn't much overlending by Japanese financial institutions that led to dire consequences."

The second phase was from the mid-1990s when Japanese banks reversed their lending stance. They reduced their loan exposures, repatriating significant capital from the region. The reason for this was rising nonperforming loans (NPLs) and weaker balance sheets back home. Domestic banking problems were exemplified by the failure in November 1997 of Sanyo Securities, Hokkaido Takushoku Bank, Yamaichi Securities, and Tokuyo City Bank.

The weakness of Japanese banks was more due to the bursting of the Japanese asset bubble in 1989–1990 than from losses incurred from impaired loans in the AFC, as observed by Watanabe:

> "The proportion of investment into Asian countries is somewhat limited in comparison with total assets of the Japanese banks. I think even though there was some loss in the operation in Thailand and Indonesia, they did not have a big impact on the domestic financial crisis in Japan. In the case of Japan, I think the bursting of the bubble in the asset prices, especially for real estate, was the bigger reason for the Japanese domestic crisis."

However, as Eisuke Sakakibara noted, Korea was a more serious proposition. There, Japanese banks had a much larger exposure. This signified that Japanese banks would be hard hit if their loans to Korean banks went delinquent:

> "The exposure of the Japanese banks, particularly to Korea, was really large, so that as the crisis spread from Thailand, Indonesia, to Korea, we thought that the Japanese banking system or Japanese financial system could be hit quite seriously... Japanese banks were very closely connected with Asian economies, particularly with Korea. So with the start of the Korean crisis, the Japanese financial system was starting to be hit quite seriously."

Aiding Crisis-Struck Countries

Japan took the lead in organizing and extending financial assistance to the crisis countries during the AFC. To be sure, the strong Japanese engagement reflected the fact that Japan's economic health, as Watanabe pointed out, had depended on the rest of Asia doing well:

> "Already in the 1990s the Japanese companies' operations in Asia was growing rapidly, and also the Japanese trade with Asia was nearly half the total trade of Japan. So I think Asia is definitely important to Japanese economic operations. If Asia has some economic difficulties, the negative impact for Japan would be great. So we would like to minimize the negative damage in the region. It was our big concern. This has been the position of Japan for some time."

At the same time, Sakakibara observed that Japanese policymakers also felt a responsibility to provide the leadership to lift the region out of the economic crisis. It was willing to use its financial heft to do so:

> "Some things to reflect on when looking back are that it can't be helped when we were in confrontation with the US on regional problems, and it can't be helped when we were in confrontation with an international organization like the International Monetary Fund (IMF). But that doesn't mean we should just leave things as they were just because we were in confrontation. As a big country, that is a responsibility that we have to bear. We did our best at that time."

Japan was active in assisting crisis countries from the start of the AFC. Sakakibara revealed that "when the crisis erupted, we sent a mission. We sent a mission to Thailand. We found out that the crisis was quite serious." Japan then took the initiative to organize a "Friends of Thailand" group, which supplemented IMF funds with a financial assistance package of about USD 7 billion.

In the case of Indonesia, Japan had a team on the ground. Sakakibara noted:

> "The Indonesian government was quite shaky at that time. That really aggravated the problem. And I remember that David Lipton, Charles Langerin, and myself, US, Germany, and Japan, and other Japanese representatives were together in Indonesia to work on the Indonesian problem jointly. It didn't really work out that well."

Japan also participated in the second line of defense to back IMF financial assistance for Indonesia.

Japanese officials engaged their Malaysian counterparts as the crisis spread to the country. Sakakibara disclosed:

> "[W]e supported Malaysia's decision to impose capital controls. Well, as a matter of fact, we, at the Ministry of Finance, supported Malaysia. And at that time, Malaysian Prime Minister was Mahathir. We also contacted Zeti Akhtar Aziz quite often. She was the Governor of Bank Negara Malaysia. We implicitly supported the Malaysian government's decision to close the border and try to avoid the crisis by sticking to their own principles rather than following the IMF prescriptions. So that you know, even at that time, I was really very critical of the IMF approach. So I was in agreement with Zeti and Prime Minister Mahathir to sort of adopt their own policies rather than following the IMF."

Japan's and the IMF's Approach to the AFC

Japan's approach to the AFC was to supplement the financing available to the crisis countries from the IMF. This is of telling significance as it is indicative of the differences between Japanese policymakers and the IMF about the causes of the AFC and the appropriate measures to tackle the crisis.

Haruhiko Kuroda's view of the causes of the AFC expresses a Japanese Ministry of Finance (JMOF) theme. That is, the AFC did not originate from fiscal or monetary profligacy but from problems caused by adherence to a United States (US) dollar-pegged exchange rate system in a period of massive capital flows:

> "[W]e have seen many currency crises in the last 20-30 years, particularly in Latin America and Africa. But the AFC was a bit different as is often said. It's not caused by overvalued currencies. It's not caused by excessive monetary easing, it's not caused by inflation. It's not caused by sloppy fiscal policy. I mean the economy was growing, fiscal policy was quite disciplined, and monetary policy was not very expansionary. It was the US dollar-pegged system that was the cause of the problem. Very large capital inflows into those economies created some kind of financial bubble."

Watanabe expresses another commonly shared view that the AFC was more a liquidity than a solvency crisis:

> "In the case of the Asian crisis, it was a liquidity crisis. But in the case of Latin America, most of the countries had an insolvency crisis. So in the case of liquidity crisis, if you pump money appropriately, it can stimulate recovery. But if you misunderstand the situation as an insolvency issue, they have to reduce the budget deficit and they have to minimize demand.

> So I think that could be the misunderstanding at that time. Of course in the early 1950s, 1960s in Europe, and also 1970s, 1980s in Latin America, most of the countries had insolvency issues. But in the case of the ending period of the last century, maybe even the first two decades of this century, most of the countries were facing liquidity crisis. So in that case, I think the measures to be taken by the IMF should be quite different. But I think this was not so well understood by the IMF."

Kuroda also pointed out the importance of the contagion effect in the spread of the crisis through the region:

"I think if the Thai currency crisis had not happened, there is a possibility that crises would not have taken place in Malaysia, Indonesia, and Korea. In Indonesia, the current account deficit was only around 3% of GDP and their finances were healthy. In Thailand, the budget deficit was not significant but the similarity was that they were dollar-pegged and there were inflows of capital from overseas, and that was a fact."

In essence, Japanese policymakers were critical of the IMF approach in two respects. First, in pushing for contractionary fiscal and monetary policies, the IMF had adopted a standard template applied to other regions and did not address the proper causes of the crisis. On the contrary, these policies aggravated the liquidity squeeze arising from capital outflows. The second shortcoming of IMF programs, as viewed by JMOF officials, was that they were underfinanced. The Japanese response was evident from the beginning, when the Thai crisis emerged and Japan then organized the "Friends of Thailand" group to supplement IMF funds. Japan also initiated a stand-by credit line for Indonesia.

As Sakakibara recounted, Japan recognized the limitations of providing financing on an ad hoc basis:

"The Ministry of Finance, particularly its international section, initiated the effort to assist the countries... but unfortunately, the assistance we provided did not settle the crisis. And one of the problems for that is, looking back, the IMF assistance was seriously deficient. Rather than solving the problem, they aggravated the situation."

Japan consequently proposed the formation of an Asian Monetary Fund (AMF).

The Asian Monetary Fund

The AMF was conceived to be a regional financial safety net. It would be a backstop facility, funded mainly, but not only, by Asian countries. Japan proposed an AMF during the IMF–World Bank meeting in Hong Kong in September 1997. However, the proposal would be stillborn as it was opposed principally by the IMF and the US.

Kuroda disclosed that the need for such a regional fund had been germinating in JMOF circles even before the AFC:

"And even at that time, Japan was of the view that some kind of regional financial safety net was necessary because as you know, Southeast Asian economies grew very fast and their IMF quotas were lagging behind. So for those countries' economies, we felt that their IMF quotas were small. So even if the IMF could provide some assistance money, or emergency assistance, that would be insufficient. So already before July 1997, I thought some kind of regional financial safety net was necessary. I thought it would be something like an AMF. In that sense, I was not surprised by the July 1997 Thai financial crisis or currency crisis."

The idea of an AMF gained impetus, as Kuroda recounted, from the feedback received from participants at the "Friends of Thailand" meeting:

"The most important element why Japan proposed to establish the AMF during the September 1997 IMF–World Bank meeting in Hong Kong was that, during the Friends of Thailand meeting in August 1997 in Tokyo, already some participants, some Asian participants told me that this kind of ad hoc financial support to crisis-hit economies may not be appropriate. This is because for some countries, such kind of emergency assistance would require not just government decision but also parliamentary decision. It is quite complicated and time-consuming while emergency assistance must be timely. If it is delayed for several months, that would not be good. So a few participants from within the Asian region told me that some sort of standing facility may be necessary."

Sakakibara added that another argument for the AMF was that being regionally-based, it would be more attuned to the needs and circumstances of its Asian member countries as compared to a globally-oriented IMF:

"Well we thought that a global organization like the IMF and the World Bank do not necessarily know the region, particularly the Asian region, that well. So that, rather, like the Asian Development Bank (ADB), we thought that it might be necessary to have an AMF... It was just a financial version of the ADB."

As Kuroda recalled, the proposal was tabled at a meeting in Hong Kong. Invitees to the session were the countries that had provided assistance to Thailand and others who went as observers. The IMF and Group of Seven (G7) participated in the meeting. But the proposal fell through.

Kuroda acknowledged that participants had less than 2 months, between the initial discussions in Thailand and the Hong Kong meeting, to assess the proposal thoroughly. Compared to the ASEAN countries, other participants were not given much opportunity to discuss it beforehand:

> "So we had little time to discuss with other countries. Although with ASEAN countries, we had extensive discussions, because just before the Hong Kong IMF–World Bank meeting, there was the Asia–Europe Meeting (ASEM) in Bangkok, and there, our finance ministers talked with ASEAN ministers, and ASEAN decided that they would support establishing the AMF. So already before the Hong Kong meeting, ASEAN countries agreed, but in that sense, it was only ASEAN. The major possible participants, China and Australia, they took a somewhat neutral position during our meeting in Hong Kong. However, the IMF and US opposed."

IMF and US objections to the AMF were critical. The basic objection they gave was the risk of moral hazard, implying that the AMF could turn into a vehicle for disbursing loans on lax terms, unlike IMF loans that hinged on strict conditionalities. Thus, Watanabe's comment:

> "The IMF and the Treasury of the US were opposed to the establishment of the AMF. The basic reason for their objections was that, if the AMF were established, they thought Japan would give rather easy money to the Asian economies. IMF financing, however, would come with big conditionality for their assistance. But in the case of Asia, they thought Japan would propose a solution to give easy money even though the countries might not be in a good position to recover and restore their economic situation. That was the reason behind the two entities' objections."

There was also an unspoken reason for its rejection by the IMF and US — an AMF would most likely reduce the latter's influence in the region. Sakakibara brought this motive up as he recalled the episode:

> "The major difference was that the US wanted to operate through the

IMF, and by working through the IMF, they thought that they could sort of maintain their strong influence over Asia. But we were very critical of the IMF's handling of the Asian crisis and so we wanted to establish some institution, which was called, at that time, the AMF, which is independent, relatively independent from the IMF. And as you know, the US didn't like it. I still remember the telephone call with Larry Summers. He was very critical of our idea."

As Sakakibara put it, the US objected strenuously and its objections were fatal to the AMF proposal:

"The US was afraid that creation of the AMF would reduce their influence on the Asian region. I clearly remember because, at that time, I contacted Summers quite frequently and he was vehemently opposed to the creation of the AMF. If he agreed, we probably would have been able to establish the institution, but with the strong opposition by the US government, it was impossible."

The fate of the AMF proposal also hinged on the response from China. Here, as Sakakibara noted:

"China abstained, but if it abstained, then the proposal couldn't proceed. China did not oppose nor support it. If China had agreed to it, the AMF would have been set up even with opposition from the US. ASEAN was supportive and we had the agreement from Korea."

Sakakibara ventured that the US may have contacted China about its response to the proposal:

"I don't know whether that's true or not, but you know, I thought at that time, US sort of contacted the Chinese government and conveyed their message that they were against this idea of creating the AMF."

Acknowledging that establishing an AMF would be "very challenging with strong opposition from the US and without participation by China," Sakakibara noted that the proposal was finally dropped.

Japan and the US' Views on the AFC

JMOF and the US Treasury had differences in views not only on the AMF but also on the wider context of the causes of the AFC. These differences molded their policy responses to the crisis. Sakakibara noted that initially the US saw the AFC as fundamentally the fault of weak economic management and poor governance standards in the region:

> "The US thought that Asian economies were very vulnerable and believed this was the cause of the crisis. However, we did not think so. As I mentioned, we thought the worsening of balance of payments and attacks by hedge funds were the causes instead. The crisis occurred because of those two factors. I think the Asian economies were basically sound but the US did not think so. They thought it was crony capitalism and unorthodox capitalism, so that was a significant difference."

In answer to a question as to whether the US position was that the Asian economies were basically "paper tigers," Sakakibara replied that he thought it was probably so and added:

> "The US government did not think that the Asian economies were fundamentally strong. But there wasn't a pinpointing of who and where this view was held."

Consequently, the US approach to the crisis was marked by an emphasis on belt-tightening policies and structural reforms. Sakakibara was critical of the US approach of looking at the crisis as an opportunity to push for reforms:

> "At least at the time of the Asian crisis, you know, tightening fiscal policy was the wrong policy. You should spend during the time of the crisis to try to solve the problem. The problem was that the US government and IMF tried to take advantage of the crisis to impose some orthodoxy on the Asian countries rather than trying to solve the problem.
>
> I don't know why they tried to push some reforms. They thought those were the sort of orthodox policies and they tried to impose those policies on Asia because they thought the Asian policies, the Asian way of doing things, was unorthodox. But it was the unorthodox policies, including Malaysia's capital control, that did work."

To be fair, US engagement in the AFC was more nuanced than outright distancing. It had not participated in the "Friends of Thailand" supplementary loan to avoid Congressional criticisms that had surfaced in the wake of the US loan to Mexico. Sakakibara noted:

"The US participated in solving the Asian crisis. I remember quite clearly that at the time of the Indonesian crisis, I met with an American representative and a German representative and the three of us together, you know, co-operated to try and solve the Indonesian crisis."

The US, however, was more interventionist when it came to Korea. Here, it saw eye-to-eye with Japan on the need to settle the liquidity crisis that Korean banks were facing. The stakes were also higher as more international banks, including US banks, had loans to Korean banks. A Korean default would hit confidence in the international banking system. Sakakibara recalled the coordinated response to the Korean crisis:

"When the crisis spread to Korea, finally, the US government started to agree with us and co-operate with us to solve the crisis. I talked to Robert Rubin and Summers at that time and they agreed to assist Korea through the IMF and the agreement was reached on Christmas Eve. I clearly remember that Christmas Eve of 1997. It was very memorable occasion, you know, since it was Christmas Eve, I clearly remember that."

In recent years, the US view of Japanese efforts to help the regional economies seemed to have become more positive, as observed by Sakakibara:

"Well, at the time of the Asian crisis, there was a very strong opposition from the IMF and the US government. The US government was adamantly opposed to the creation of the regional institutions because they thought their influence in the region would be reduced by the creation of regional institutions. But I think they have learned a lesson and their view has changed somewhat now so that it is quite different from 1997–1998. The ADB and ASEAN+3 Macroeconomic Research Office (AMRO) are the right institutions to solve the regional problems, and the US government now recognizes that."

New Miyazawa Initiative

Despite their unsuccessful AMF proposal, JMOF officials did not give up the idea of setting up a fund to aid the crisis-hit regional economies. Realizing that a multilateral approach was difficult to organize, Japan switched to a bilateral assistance mode using Japanese funds. The result was the New Miyazawa Initiative (NMI), named after Finance Minister Kiichi Miyazawa. He announced the Initiative at the IMF–World Bank Annual Meeting in October 1998.

The NMI consisted of two parts: a USD 15 billion tranche earmarked for long-term assistance mainly for investment and another USD 15 billion for short-term trade financing. Kuroda revealed that Miyazawa personally urged his peers to tap into the funds provided:

> "I still remember when Minister Miyazawa spoke to the ministers of Korea, Thailand, Malaysia, and Indonesia in October 1998, and he made a very interesting political statement. He said, 'Please use the money budgeted for. Because it is of course helpful to your countries to revive your economic growth. That will also help the Japanese economy. So without hesitation, without any guilt, please freely use the USD 30 billion.' It was of course a political statement. No bureaucrat can make such a statement, but Miyazawa made a very impressive statement, without a prepared text."

This time, the IMF strongly supported the idea as it did not encroach into the IMF's domain of emergency financial support. The NMI was aimed instead at supporting economic growth. And the money would be provided by the Japanese government. So, the IMF, World Bank, and ADB also supported the proposal.

Kuroda noted that the first tranche of USD 15 billion dollars was quickly disbursed, particularly to Thailand, Malaysia, Indonesia, and Korea. Projects and programs were quickly identified:

> "I think this helped those economies. They were critical in helping the recovery. However, not all of the other USD 15 billion, earmarked for short-term trade financing, was used. Korea and Malaysia mobilized some of the fund for currency swaps, which later became the prototype for currency swap arrangement under the Chiang Mai Initiative (CMI)."

The Chiang Mai Initiative

By the end of 1998, most Asian economies were recovering from the AFC. Attention then turned to forming a regional self-help mechanism to avert similar crises. This time, it was a collective regional effort, coalescing around the ASEAN+3 group, the outcome being the CMI.

Kuroda shared an anecdote of how the name was chosen:

"I briefed Minister Miyazawa before we went to Chiang Mai in May 2000 for the ASEAN+3 Finance Ministers Meeting about the plan. But I also mentioned that we had not come up with a suitable name for the new regional financial support mechanism. Very interestingly, Minister Miyazawa quickly told me that it must be the Chiang Mai Initiative. Why? Because the meeting would take place in Chiang Mai, in Thailand. He also pointed out that the Thai Finance Minister then was Tarrin whose constituency was in Chiang Mai, so as a politician, Miyazawa immediately told me, 'Oh, it must be the Chiang Mai Initiative because the meeting will take place in Chiang Mai and Chiang Mai is Tarrin's constituency.'"

Chapter 11

China

Two persons were interviewed in the preparation of this chapter: Zhu Guangyao and Wei Benhua. During the 1997 Asian financial crisis, Zhu served first as the Deputy Director General of Department of National Debt and Finance before becoming the Director General of International Department at the Ministry of Finance of China. Zhu was the Vice Finance Minister of China between 2010 and 2018. Wei was the Director General of International Department at People's Bank of China during the crisis and later served as the first Director of the ASEAN+3 Macroeconomic Research Office from May 2011 to May 2012.

While China was relatively insulated from the Asian financial crisis (AFC), its exports to the region slowed sharply during the crisis. China, however, refrained from devaluing the renminbi (RMB), a critical decision that relieved pressure on the regional currencies. The AFC was also the driving force for a breakthrough in a meeting of minds on regional financial cooperation among China, Japan, and Korea.

Relative Insulation from the Turmoil

China was relatively unaffected by the AFC. While its gross domestic product (GDP) decelerated from the previous year, growth was moderate, at 7.8% and 7.6% in 1998 and 1999, respectively. The RMB was also stable. Two main reasons underlie China's relative insulation. First, its capital account was closed. The RMB was thus shielded from speculative attacks. Second, China had low external debt. Its foreign currency exposure was due more to foreign direct investments than loans.

Although the AFC had a fairly modest impact on the economy, it had a powerful influence on Chinese financial policy in several key areas. First, the AFC put China's policymakers on the alert against potential trouble spots in its financial system. The high level of nonperforming loans (NPLs) in the state-owned banks was viewed as one, and Wei Benhua recalled the priority given to resolve the issue:

> "We had to make a strategic decision to get rid of the NPLs state-owned banks. You know the state-owned banks played a crucial role in the national economy. In order to make them better prepared to overcome the crisis, the authorities decided to help them to get rid of those NPLs. Hence, we established financial assets management companies. We established these for each of the four largest banks. Later on, through such a platform, those NPLs could be dealt with in a better way."

Wei noted that except for the Bank of China, the other state-owned banks did not have overseas loans. Nevertheless, it was thought prudent to address the NPL issue as a preemptive measure:

> "However, for a financial institution, you have to be sound, with its own assets, domestically. At that time, except for the Bank of China, the other state-owned banks didn't have much overseas exposure. However, today is a different situation where they are expanding their operations in Asia and in many other parts of the world.
>
> So this is one of the lessons I believe the Chinese authorities put much emphasis on. They knew at that time that they really had to make great efforts to make their financial markets stable and to make their financial institutions capable of overcoming currency volatility. Then after dealing with that, they could come back to deal with the other issues or problems in the economy."

Second, observing the potency of capital flows in destabilizing markets during the AFC, Chinese policymakers saw the need for caution in liberalizing the capital account, as pointed out by Zhu Guangyao:

> "For China itself, the real mission was current account liberalization. We kept pace with this. However, when it came to capital account liberalization, we realized from the AFC that we ought to be more careful, especially when it involved portfolio money."

Third, the AFC spurred Chinese policy to focus on attaining two primary economic targets, or "slogans." These concerned GDP growth and RMB policy, as explained by Zhu:

"Despite the challenges, China had two very important goals in 1998. First, keep economic growth at 8%. Second, to not devalue the yuan. Eventually we realized both goals — output for 1998 grew at 7.8% and the yuan was not devalued. Our policy of keeping the value of the yuan stable helped the region a lot. Yes, Chinese exports decreased because the regional currencies were more competitive, but it boosted overall confidence in the region. This opened up more opportunities for cooperation."

Fourth, as articulated by Zhu, the AFC led to Chinese policymakers concluding that regional cooperation was needed for solutions for the crisis:

"However, the event helped us rethink how to deal with external pressure and to better handle relations among the regional economies. Most importantly, Japan, China, and Korea learned how to better cooperate with each other as well as with the Association of Southeast Asian Nations (ASEAN)."

The following sections will deal with Chinese policy on RMB exchange rate and regional financial cooperation.

Keeping the Renminbi Exchange Rate Constant

One of the pivotal developments in the evolution of the AFC was China's decision to keep the RMB level steady, not to devalue it. Domestic considerations argued for a devaluation as export growth had fallen from around 21.0% in 1997 to 0.5% in 1998. As Zhu mentioned, the pressure to devalue the RMB was high as other regional currencies had fallen sharply:

"In a normal situation, it is normal to devalue your national currency if you want to maintain market share. I remember some world-renowned economists had asked us to devalue it because that was a region-wide trend."

An RMB devaluation, however, would have put untold pressure on already-shaky regional currencies. It could have led to a vicious cycle of currency depreciations throughout the region. As the Hong Kong narrative shows, rumors of a RMB devaluation had triggered pessimism about Hong Kong markets. If the rumor had come to pass, speculators attacking Hong

Kong markets would have had a field day.

In the event, China made the decision to keep the RMB exchange rate stable. It was, as Wei elaborated, a decision that came from the highest political level and one that was explicitly based on consideration for the impact on the region:

> "We needed to maintain a stable exchange rate, because China is the largest developing economy in this region. If we had devalued our exchange rate, then it would have a direct impact on the region. You remember at that time the Prime Minister was Premier Zhu Rongji. He made a solemn promise or announcement to the world that China would not devalue its own currency under any circumstances. Instead, we opted to resolve the difficulties within our economy. We didn't take a beggar-thy-neighbor policy, since under those competitive devaluation policies, the region would indeed be in a disastrous situation. I believe the authority's decision was the right one."

Perhaps, not known to many, as revealed by Zhu Guangyao, Larry Summers, then United States (US) Treasury Secretary, conversed with Premier Zhu when the latter was in Lanzhou, a tourist site, to convey the message that the US was supportive of China's decision to keep the RMB stable:

> "At that time, US Treasury Secretary Summers was supportive of our move to not devalue. He, too, was worried of regional disorder if the yuan was devalued. He conveyed this message to Premier Zhu in Lanzhou when the latter was inspecting the city. I was part of the team that went to Lanzhou. This was also the time when we negotiated with the US on the possibility of us joining the World Trade Organization."

The decision not to devalue the RMB was significant. It lent tremendous support to Hong Kong's battle against the speculators. It also removed an uncertainty hanging over regional currencies. Zhu Guangyao, reflecting on this pivotal decision, also emphasized that it went beyond national considerations:

> "Of course, policymaking is based on national interest. However, there are times when we also have to consider the interests of neighboring countries and the global economy."

The Asian Monetary Fund

As mentioned in other narratives, Japanese authorities floated the idea of the Asian Monetary Fund (AMF) at the time of the International Monetary Fund (IMF)–World Bank Annual Meeting in Hong Kong. But the idea did not materialize. Wei considered that there were two main reasons why it was a nonstarter. First, the proposal did not garner regional consensus and there were objections from the US and IMF as well. Second, Wei also thought that the proposal was too rushed. It didn't give countries enough time to give it proper consideration:

> "At that time already, Asia was a very diversified region with many countries in this region, with very diversified historical and cultural background. For such an important proposal, you need a lot of time to prepare to talk with different countries, different economies, and win their support. I don't think the preparatory process was adequate for Japan at that time. Their proposal was too rushed."

A Breakthrough

Although the AMF proposal failed, the ongoing crisis would catalyze a breakthrough in the level of dialogue among China, Japan, and Korea on financial matters. Zhu recalled the paucity of information sharing between China and Japan up to 1997 due to historical issues. However, the AFC led to him meeting his Japanese and Korean counterparts, Zenbee Mizoguchi, then Director General of Financial Bureau of the Japanese Ministry of Finance, and Yong-duk Kim, then Director General of International Financial Bureau, Korean Ministry of Finance, to consider various forms of cooperation to deal with the regional crisis.

As Zhu recalled, it was after several rounds of contact among the three parties that a trilateral meeting was agreed upon. This all-important first meeting among the three was kept out of public eye. It formed the basis for more substantial meetings:

> "At the margins of international meetings, we began to discuss the possibility of operational action to deal with the financial crisis. Finally, all three sides agreed to have a trilateral meeting in Beijing, but there was to be no public announcement. This first meeting was held in

Diaoyutai Hotel. The only topic discussed was how to deal with the AFC. This type of cooperation was very different from the traditional types.

In the traditional format, we would establish basic cooperation in trade before upgrading it to financial cooperation as the process needs policy support. Unfortunately, trade cooperation at that time was not so active. The onset of the AFC forced us to think outside the box. So, we began by discussing cooperation. I should say that Mizoguchi and Kim both had ambitions to promote more extensive forms of regional cooperation. However, all three countries were mindful of domestic public sentiments. That's why at the start we decided on a private meeting. As the crisis deepened, we, together with the public, realized the urgency of strengthening regional cooperation. We came away from the Beijing meeting that we should have more contact with each other. It is very important as trust is based on communication. Although it was limited in scope, it kick-started more regular and meaningful communication amongst us."

As Zhu elaborated, the trilateral meetings with his Japanese and Korean counterparts culminated in a "ASEAN+3" Finance Ministers' Meeting that endorsed the inception of the Chiang Mai Initiative (CMI):

"I remember that meeting in Chiang Mai, that's a ASEAN+3 Finance Ministers' Meeting. Mizoguchi, Kim, and myself accompanied our Finance Ministers to this meeting. Through the trilateral dialogue, we had reached a basic understanding amongst ourselves and our ASEAN peers to talk about expanding bilateral swap arrangement to a multilateral level.

All the countries had gone through severe hardships during the AFC. Those receiving IMF loans had to observe very strong policy conditionality. We all agreed that it was time to establish a regional mechanism. When the name of this mechanism was mooted, then Chinese Minister of Finance Xiang Huaicheng suggested that we name it after Thai Minister of Finance Tarrin Nimmanahaeminda. However, Tarrin wanted a deeper connection with Thailand. Eventually, during dinner, we all agreed that we should name it after Chiang Mai. That was how the CMI began. To start things off, we began with bilateral swaps amounting to about USD 100 billion that was also 20% de-linked."

Zhu alluded to the importance of trust and use of an unorthodox approach as reasons why the success of the CMI proposal was a surprise:

"Firstly, there is the issue of trust. Unfortunately, at that time, there was still mistrust between some of the countries. Secondly, we approached regional cooperation through an unorthodox way. Instead of the traditional model, where we started from the bottom using trade cooperation, we began by pushing high-level financial cooperation. To reach an agreement, under those constraints, was a surprise to everyone."

ASEAN+3 Macroeconomic Research Office

The ASEAN+3 Macroeconomic Research Office (AMRO) was also a product of the AFC and the resulting push for closer regional collaboration. As the first Director of AMRO, serving between 2011 and 2012, Wei described in anecdotal terms how he envisaged the organization within the regional financial architecture:

"It is very difficult to anticipate a financial crisis. Before a crisis, everything might look good, look peaceful. How to be warned of risks beforehand…

I believe if we had something like AMRO at that time, we could have had better economic intelligence to find out what was going on in the regional economies before the crisis. And we could have had a better chance to identify any significant risks. Really, but that doesn't mean AMRO is smarter, or more clever than the member authorities.

It is like going to the doctor. Sometimes we need a second opinion and it is good for the patient itself. If one goes to another doctor and he gives the same assessment as the first, then it's more convincing. And for the economic issues, today we have AMRO. It serves the same purpose, since one of the major purposes for AMRO is conducting economic surveillance of the economies in this region. I believe it was a necessity for us to have established AMRO."

When asked on the circumstances leading to his appointment, Wei explained that it was a pleasant surprise for him. It was also a good opportunity for him to contribute to nation- and region-building:

"I would say that the person leading AMRO would need some background in dealing with surveillance issues. I believe that I could have been considered since I worked with the IMF on two occasions. First, I served as Alternate Executive Director for 4 years. Then later on, I was Executive Director for another period of more than 4 years, so all together, I had gotten more than 8 years' experience in dealing with surveillance issues. These experiences had allowed me to participate actively during my term at the IMF in discussions and to make suggestions to help member authorities to overcome crises. I believe those experiences, in turn, helped me to come to work in AMRO."

Wei faced two urgent challenges in his leadership role. The first was getting good quality staff members:

"First, since you need to conduct economic surveillance, you do need good qualified staff, a team of economists to do the work. So in order to realize this purpose, we needed to establish rules and regulations about this new institution. Since we started from scratch, really from zero, we had to consider the experiences in the IMF, the Asian Development Bank (ADB), and the Organisation for Economic Co-operation and Development (OECD), and draw on their experiences and adapt them to our situation. Based on the criteria we set then, we went to recruit qualified staff to conduct the work.

Fortunately, we managed to organize ourselves well. So, from the middle of my only one-year term, we already had more than 10 economists to work with. Then, we went to the member economies' capitals to conduct economic surveillance."

The second, and perhaps more critical, challenge involved AMRO establishing a good relationship with the various member authorities. There was a lot of dialogue involved to build trust as well as credibility, and to get them to understand what AMRO was about. The key was to convince the member authorities that AMRO was a partner that had the region's best interest at heart.

When it came to economic surveillance, Wei viewed that AMRO had certain advantages, as compared to the IMF, in its surveillance of the regional economies:

"Of course, the IMF is also conducting such surveillance reports. However, I do believe we have some advantages over the IMF staff, since our staff are mainly from the region, coming from the local authorities such as the ministry of finance, central bank, and other economic institutions. They tend to have a deeper understanding or insight of domestic policies. So when we worked together with member authorities, we were able to discuss the issues in a deeper manner. This enabled us to present, I believe, more informative reports to member authorities. So if we understand their economic issues in a correct manner, then there is trust. I believe that's the most important point, and then based on that trust, we can have closer relations with member authorities."

Chapter 12

International Monetary Fund

Two persons were interviewed in the preparation of this chapter: Hubert Neiss and Anoop Singh. During the 1997 Asian financial crisis, Neiss and Singh were the Director and Deputy Director of the Asia Pacific Department at the International Monetary Fund (IMF), respectively. Both had led missions to the crisis-hit economies and coordinated financial rescue efforts with their East Asian and international counterparts.

The IMF's View of the Asian Financial Crisis

Did the IMF see a regional crisis coming? How did your views about the crisis evolve?

Hubert Neiss:
It came after the first stand-by arrangement (for Thailand) was concluded. The arrangement involved a strong program and major loan from the IMF, supported by pledges of bilateral aid from other countries. So, we expected market turbulence would disappear. But when this did not happen, and indications of contagion appeared, we feared major difficulties for Thailand and the whole region. So, we considered "precautionary stand-by arrangements" with other countries in the area, in particular Indonesia. (These are stand-by arrangements without any disbursement. But disbursement would be triggered if the countries were to run unexpectedly into difficulties.)

Anoop Singh:
In my view, Thailand was not a surprise to us. It was not a surprise to all those people who had lent money to Thailand. From the beginning of 1997, if you looked at Bangkok, many buildings went unoccupied. Some of the financial institutions were also in terrible shape. The surprise was the situation in Indonesia and Korea. It took us a long time to understand that this was a much deeper situation than had been anticipated.

Singh (on the situation in Thailand):

It was a financial crisis, which we were late in recognizing. There was the initial view that this was more a case of excess government spending; it was not. The problem was simply that there wasn't governance from the IMF side or from the Thai side on the supervision of the financial sector. It comes back to what we see even today or what people had feared in China the last 5 years. If you are having debt-financed growth, it's not going to work, at least over the long run. It may work in Japan because Japan is a relatively domestic-driven economy. But, if you're having credit-financed growth as Thailand was having, it's not going to work. When money goes out and you don't have the buffers, it will end badly.

In what way was the Asian financial crisis (AFC) distinct from other financial crises?

Neiss:

The surprise of the outbreak, the difficulties of assessing the seriousness of the situation from the available indicators, the reluctance of the authorities to call for IMF assistance early, the delay in acting decisively on policies, the regional contagion, the international repercussions, and the strong support of the international community. These features distinguish the AFC from the earlier crises in the Philippines and India. But the prolonged denial of governments, that a crisis may be coming, was a common feature.

How would you respond to the criticism that the IMF-stipulated tight monetary and fiscal policies were not appropriate as the regional economies did not have huge fiscal deficits or inflation issues? Comparisons have also been made to the expansionary polices adopted by the United States (US) and the European Union (EU) during the global financial crisis (GFC) and more recently the coronavirus disease (COVID-19) situation.

Neiss:

First, the programs that were negotiated with Asian countries were certainly not flawless (nor were other IMF programs flawless), but by and large, they were appropriate in the situation of a severe balance of payments crisis (more specifically, a capital account crisis) to turn developments around and move countries in the right direction. The subsequent developments in each country bear this out. Also, the programs were not just for "deficit countries," as you mentioned. (This may have wrongly been inferred from the programmed initial fiscal tightening, which was controversial, as I explained earlier.)

Second, the financial resources which were provided to Asian countries were determined by the estimates of financing needs, as well as by the possibilities within the lending constraints of international institutions, and the political constraints to lending by individual governments. I am not aware of any serious complaints that the resources provided were insufficient, or that Asia "was left on its own." On the contrary, there were complaints about too much outside interference.

Whether some bigger effort, however desirable, could have been made, is an open question. But, as I said, under prevailing circumstances, as much was provided as was feasible, and it was enough to stave off the default of the countries and to help them to restore their external viability. So I wouldn't be so negative.

Singh (on the comparison with the US and EU):
You can't compare different economies easily. For the US and the Eurozone, you have a different situation regarding their currencies. Their central banks have the ability to print money, and inflation is not a problem for these countries. The external situation is also not a problem for them, at least in the short run. Lack of growth is the problem.

When inflation goes up again in the EU and the US, the policies will be tightened. They have done this before, and have the experience. But we cannot easily compare the advanced countries with Indonesia, India, and so on. If you're concerned about your debt ratio, it will be worse if you have negative growth than if you have a higher debt ratio because of higher fiscal spending — this is the case in EU and the US. In summary, don't worry about the debt, focus on the short-run situation. That is my, and I may be wrong, understanding.

Singh (on tight monetary policy):
But to be fair, this was the first major crisis since Mexico. Money was leaving the country and it would look odd from an economic point of view to say, money is leaving the country, therefore lower interest rates and expand government spending. It took a long time for economists to understand the

situation. Very few people went out in the open to say: "Money is leaving, stop the capital from leaving, lower interest rates, and raise government spending." Not many people said that, but now they are.

Structural Reforms

Comment on the view that the IMF went beyond its domain in pushing for structural reforms in the crisis-hit economies during the AFC. These proposed reforms, it was argued, were also a source of political distraction.

Neiss:
In the IMF's view, it was also essential that the crisis was taken as an opportunity to implement long overdue structural changes. In particular, bank restructuring, corporate restructuring, and improvements in the operations of public institutions. (The same view was held in the cases of Indonesia and Korea.) These are politically difficult measures which, when everything is going well, tend to be postponed. But the pressure during a crisis makes these reforms possible, at least to some extent. I think their implementation has been of lasting benefit to the country.

Maybe economic policymaking was a bit overburdened by the requirements to implement structural performance criteria. But in essence, the reforms were necessary, because the shortcomings in the economy were contributing to the crisis. And the IMF was of the view that this was an opportunity to tackle these problems in the interests of longer-term sustained growth (as was the case in the other crisis countries). So, there were two sides of the argument.

I would agree that some measures could have been set aside for later. But not essential ones, like making the economy more competitive and making institutions more effective, including making the central bank more independent. These reforms are essential for sound economic development. But I remember the furious debate, and even the IMF (Executive Board) decided later to limit the number of structural performance criteria in programs.

Singh:
The IMF was proven wrong in Indonesia for 3 months or 4 months, in the early phases of engagement. Then, they went to the other extreme, working on structural issues. We went into areas, perhaps not in our domain, but it

was really not that difficult. You know, and Singapore knows, if you have cronies, the markets would want you to open the economy. Without that, money is not going to come in. It is a universal issue.

Importance of Politics

What part did local politics play in shaping the course of the crisis in the different countries?

Singh:
In all three countries (Indonesia, Korea, and Thailand), the government and the central banks refused to recognize that there was a problem. It was just as much a political issue. If you have an IMF program, with a government that does not recognize the problem, that program is not going to succeed.

Things became better when the new government was installed in early November 1997. Chuan Leekpai became the Prime Minister and Tarrin Nimmanahaeminda was his Finance Minister. We had absolutely no difficulty in agreeing on the subsequent reviews with Tarrin. We had long, difficult discussions, but never once was there a time when Tarrin told us, "Please get out. I can't do this." We were always trying to discuss what were the best ways to promote recovery, and so on. It was a joint effort. I was not involved in the IMF team that dealt with Korea. But in Korea, after the President changed, the government changed, it was the same. Things became easier. To some extent, the IMF team sent to Indonesia also experienced a similar situation when President Suharto stepped down. I can firmly say that if there were mistakes made during that time, they were joint mistakes.

I would say recognition of the problem, in addition to political support for dealing with it, which includes dealing with vested interests. Put these two things together, the markets will be convinced. If you have political support and you recognize the problem, markets understand. Until there's recognition of the problem, you're not going to get the market convinced. If you deny the problem and don't reveal the data, no one can solve it.

The Negotiations

Give us a sense of the stress and pressure you, your IMF colleagues, and your counterparts on the other side of table encountered in the negotiations to finalize the IMF Stand-By Arrangements.

Neiss:

The unpredictable and rapidly changing events, as well as the urgency of finding an agreement between the positions of the authorities and of the international community (which had to provide the financing), added to the stress. Some of us (including myself) had to cancel planned vacations.

Things were also difficult, as you said, because of the time difference. So, we had to be on the telephone at night either in Washington with Asia or in Asia with Washington. We had very little time to be with our families, even during Christmas. But I think we never felt we were suffering. We were happy, when progress could be made, and then we felt it was all worth it. Stress and tension in these circumstances were unavoidable, and we did not complain about it.

Both parties knew each other's constraints. The government negotiators were under pressure to achieve a result that was politically acceptable in their countries. And we from the IMF had to achieve a result that would pass the review of senior staff, be acceptable to IMF Management, to the IMF Executive Directors, and ultimately to the IMF member countries — on their instructions, their Executive Directors had to vote yes or no on the program and the funds to be disbursed to the country. These constraints were clear to both sides on the negotiating table. Because of this awareness, we could work well together and without any personal problems. In fact, with some of our counterparts we developed good friendships.

We had a common goal, and we shared this common goal with our counterparts in the respective countries. Whether it was the Indonesian, Korean, or Thai delegation, we developed good personal relationships, and this helped us to get through the tensions more easily.

Singh:

We used to work with them during the morning, afternoon, and evening. Then we have to work overnight with our counterparts back in Washington.

As the IMF is a very centralized institution, we have to have all the stuff approved by Washington. We arrived on July 23 or 24, but by August 13, we had in-principle fund approval of the program. That was incredible.

Changes in the IMF Since the AFC

What adjustments did the IMF make to its operational protocols in the light of its experiences during the AFC?

Singh:
There's been a lot of changes. The Fund has changed hugely, in my view.

Number one, because of the AFC, the IMF created a financial sector assessment program (FSAP), which examines the financial sector of major economies every 1–3 years. Right now, almost all countries have agreed to have it done, although the US hasn't formally agreed to this yet. The net result is that we can look at the financial sector much more carefully.

Number two, our work on Basel III has helped in protecting banks. We have a better idea now on how to get a more structurally robust macro-economic setting.

Number three is transparency. Almost everything the Fund does now is transparent. Only a few countries in the world don't allow the IMF to publish the concluding statement of a normal Article IV consultation, one of them — I hate to say this — is India. China allows you to publish the concluding statement of a team, which sometimes is shorter and more cautious than the staff report. Having said that, we still need regional institutions. We need the Association of Southeast Asian Nations (ASEAN), the ASEAN+3 Macroeconomic Research Office (AMRO), and so on to do a lot more.

Role of the International Community

How would you respond to the perception that the international community, in particular the US, did not do as much to assist the crisis-hit countries during the AFC as it did in other crises, like the Mexican crisis of 1982 and its Tequila crisis of 1994?

Neiss:

I don't think there was a different approach by the international community as a whole, but there was a difference between the US approach to Mexico and to Asia. That difference had political reasons, because when the US government supported Mexico, it ran into difficulties with Congress. Therefore, it was more cautious on Asia. (For instance, the US did not participate in the bilateral package of the Thai program.) Otherwise the US government was supportive on many occasions. (For instance, in the roll-over of the short-term debt of Korean banks, and its approval of the loans by the international Institutions.) The administration (including President Bill Clinton) gave great attention to events during the Asian crisis.

I think that the role (of the international community) during the crisis was positive and very supportive. First, especially in the case of Indonesia, many governments pressed the Indonesian government to persist in implementing measures. Second, the countries, through their Executive Directors, approved large loans by the IMF as well as by the World Bank and by the Asian Development Bank. These disbursements were vital to get through the crisis. Third, governments also provided bilateral loans and technical assistance.

But, of course, I was not the only one "in the frontline." There was intense involvement of IMF staff and management, of IMF Executive Directors, who represented the member governments of the IMF, and also of various government officials of member countries, in particular, Japan, the US, and Germany. Great international attention was given to events in Asia after the outbreak of the crisis.

Lessons for Policymakers

What lessons should policymakers take away from the AFC?

Neiss:

Regarding crisis prevention: maintain a well-supervised banking system and act early on any irregularities; make sure you have always up-to-date statistical information on developments to be able to detect weak points early and act quickly; maintain a flexible exchange rate and keep a sufficient level of reserves to be able to smooth out temporary market fluctuations; if a crisis comes, turn to the international community for assistance as early as possible.

Regarding crisis management: keep policies flexible, be ready to adapt them to events that can move very fast and unpredictably during a crisis; explain the measures and the reasons for them to interest groups in the country and to the broader population to get support for the government's policy (an important lesson that seems to have been forgotten in Europe during the financial crises); take effective measures to support the weakest parts of society to maintain social stability.

There are also lessons for the international community: be aware of the regional and global implications of any country's difficulties and do everything possible, at an early stage, to assist the country in its financing efforts and its policies; regarding the international financial system, try to institute suitable measures to guarantee a "bail-in" of commercial banks; work on further measures to adapt the international financial system, so it can deal flexibly and effectively with any disturbances in the global economy. I hope all these lessons will continue to be taken.

Singh:

I think the independence of central banks, which is a very important shift in the last 20 years, must rank as one of them. An independent central bank provides an important constraint on governments. If you don't have an independent, strong central bank, it is because the government doesn't want to be open.

Personal Memories

Share with us an anecdote about your involvement in the AFC.

Singh:

On a lighter note, I went to Thailand and it was virtually my first trip to the country. We went inside the famous Mandarin Oriental Hotel in Bangkok. I told my secretary that we needed to send an important fax to Washington right now — we were still not into computers that much in those days. It was quite late in the evening and the hotel people told us the business center was closed. So, the next day I called a very nice lady, the assistant manager, who's still there and said, "This is a crisis. We're not staying in your hotel unless we have four things by this evening. We want a huge copy machine outside the secretary's office in three hours. We want a fax machine in three hours. We want your business center open 24 hours and we want free laundry for the entire time. We haven't got time to count, but there should be more. If you don't give us these four, we're moving across the street to another hotel."

It took her half an hour to give us all that we requested. It was a very crazy time then! I was told they still have the fax machine in my name in the Oriental Hotel in the room, which says "Anoop Singh's fax machine, 1997!"

Neiss:

When I had my early morning jogs (in Jakarta), I usually stopped at a market and checked what goods were available, how prices had evolved, and so on. And it became obvious that the situation was steadily deteriorating. Well, the key was rice prices, of course. And they were rising. One reason was that, unfortunately, at that time the rice harvest turned out to be bad, and there was not enough foreign exchange available for quick imports. Also, no spare parts could be imported for the trucks that had been transporting rice to the cities. A bit outside of my assignment, I asked for a meeting with General Wiranto, to suggest that he authorize the use of army trucks for rice transports, and he agreed.

Chapter 13

Policy Insights from
the Asian Financial Crisis

We conclude with quotations from our interviewees on the lessons and policy insights drawn from the Asian financial crisis. These are organized under several broad themes.

Preventing Financial Crises

Norman T. L. Chan

"It is clear that financial crises can take many different forms, but the core feature or cause remains similar: over-exuberance in asset markets, fueled by excessive or unchecked leverage provided by the financial system. So the main lesson that one can learn from the Asian financial crisis (AFC) (or for that matter the global financial crisis (GFC)) is that authorities must make sure that the financial system is adequately regulated so that it will not provide excessive leverage to fund exuberant markets or investments."

Joong-Kyung Choi

"Financial institutions should be watched closely through tightly-designed prudential regulatory framework."

Joseph Soedradjad Djiwandono

"I believe that a crisis always reveals the weakest links of an economy. In their book *This Time is Different*, Kenneth Rogoff and Carmen Reinhart looked into the data of hundreds of years of financial disturbances, and tried to identify one thing which everyone agreed on. They found that a crisis is always led by high leverage, either short term or long term, but in the end, some kind of day of reckoning will take place when the market decides that the leverage has gone overboard."

Lin See-Yan
"Without a strong banking system, no matter how good your economic growth is, you will eventually fail."

Handling Capital Flows

Yang-ho Byeon
"I cannot agree with the view that it was wrong to open the capital market as prescribed by the International Monetary Fund (IMF). It is difficult for a country to attract foreign capital when its capital market is not open. If foreigners invest, they should be able to withdraw their investments later. It will be hard for foreigners to invest when the capital market is not open."

Roberto F. de Ocampo
"[T]here was recognition that it was the speculative capital inflows that could not be totally controlled. They have their pluses and minuses, but the domestic economy and the regional economy must develop mechanisms that can handle such flows. These mechanisms include the development of capital markets, number one. Number two, governance systems within the banking community that would allow for a better and more judicious examination of movements of capital. This was what sparked the Asian Bonds Market Initiative as well as the Chiang Mai Initiative, where currencies of individual countries are allowed to be much more freely exchanged via closer connections among the central banks of the ASEAN+3."

Ooi Sang Kuang
"Taking the perspective of policymakers seeking long-term economic stability and growth, you cannot be over-reliant on equity market inflows and short-term debt as sources of capital inflows. More stable sources are long-term bonds and foreign direct investments. Ultimately, you must rely on domestic savings and have manageable external debt. Your banks must have sound risk management."

Policy Responses in a Financial Crisis

Diwa C. Guinigundo

"Defense of the domestic currency through foreign exchange (FX) intervention producing less than desirable results was another painful lesson during the AFC. The exchange rate is just a market price that reflects the economy's fundamentals. No amount of FX intervention can shore up the exchange value of a domestic currency if it is not supported by market fundamentals. Those who adhered to this strategy found it enormously expensive; and the drawdown of heavy reserves to defend local currencies virtually was not very useful. Supporting this with tight monetary policy was not sustainable over the long run."

Kyung-wook Hur

"Financial markets are driven by sentiments. So the policy measures we take must be credible. Confidence returns when market players realize that our reserves are adequate, that there are swap arrangements in place, and that the government fully backs adjustment measures."

Chang-yuel Lim

"The important thing was to acknowledge the problems of the policy and to promptly take corrective actions. The cause of the crisis was a policy failure and the crisis was resolved by correcting the policy. I think this is a right understanding of that situation. Without that policy change, we would have failed to overcome the crisis."

Nor Shamsiah

"It is critical for policy advice to be tailored according to a country's unique conditions and fundamentals. Back then, the IMF's one-size-fits-all approach was perhaps not the most optimal and involved painful short-term costs and trade-offs to the affected economies. Instead, the prescribed policy responses to Asia should have been tailored to suit each country's economic structure and circumstance to address country specific risks as well as vulnerabilities."

Self-Reliance

Kishore Mahbubani
"You know, until then (the AFC), Asian countries assumed that they just had to listen to Washington D.C., Brussels, London, Paris, Berlin. I think it sort of broke the psychological dependence on the Western capitals, in some ways."

Andrew Sheng
"We have to think strategically for ourselves. We cannot assume that Washington will think for all of us, which we did before. In the AFC, we thought that the US Federal Reserve (Fed) would provide us with dollars. It didn't. Even today, some of us know that, the Fed has not provided swaps for everybody. What does that tell you? That means you have to rely on your own resources. It is not that Asians do not want to be friends with everybody, but if you don't look after your own house, nobody else will. That's reality. So, in my view, we need to take care of our own house. We need to fix the roof. We need to strengthen the foundations, etc. But Asians are true good neighbors, we help each other. That's why we should begin with regional cooperation."

M.R. Chatu Mongol Sonakul
"You better help yourself first, behave properly. Because when you are in trouble, people don't really help you. And if they help you, they will probably expect something in return."

Be Prepared

Gil S. Beltran
"Yes, it's good to have a good fiscal position because that is where you run to when you're in trouble. That's also why in good times you should start building up fiscal reserves."

Haruhiko Kuroda
"So one thing I think we have learned from the AFC is that something unexpected could happen and then regional countries must cooperate

because those kind of things would quickly spread through the region. You cannot make the world economy or world system free of any future crisis or problem. But during the AFC, we learned that we should better cooperate."

Amando M. Tetangco, Jr.
"[A] crisis can happen anytime. So you've got to be vigilant and constantly monitor developments, both local and foreign, to be able to quickly take action in case there are brewing stress points. [T]he best time to prepare for a crisis is in good times."

Wei Benhua
"It is very difficult to anticipate a financial crisis. Before a crisis, everything might look good, look peaceful. This is the lesson we draw from the AFC, from the GFC as well."

Role of Politics

Duck-koo Chung
"From my perspective, the biggest lesson is that politics has a huge impact on international finance. International finance is closely related to other aspects of international politics such as diplomacy and security."

Dennis de Tray
"My bottom line is that what matters is not economics but political economics. You have to take into account the interplay between politics and economics."

Ginandjar Kartasasmita
"The collapse of the Indonesian economy illustrated the need for combining measures of globalization and international integration with a concerted effort to strengthen institutional frameworks, such as an independent and reasonably competent judiciary, strengthened corporate governance and banking sector oversight, as well as a political system open to continuous public scrutiny and not averse to change."

How the AFC Strengthened the Regional Economies

Hoe Ee Khor

"The way [Asian governments] have responded is very admirable because they basically decided that they need to build up the reserves. And they strengthened their fundamentals. They strengthened their regulatory framework and some of them adopted the inflation targeting framework. And then they strengthened the governance system to make sure that the corporates didn't go out and borrow excessively. As a result, almost all the countries in the region now require some kind of prior approval or reporting system. They also rebuilt the fiscal policy space. So they actually strengthened the macroeconomic fundamentals quite significantly after the crisis, and because of that, when the GFC hit, they were better positioned to weather the spill-over effects."

Hubert Neiss

"After the AFC, the [Asian] economies have become stronger and also more efficient and more flexible as a result of the reforms taken during the crisis. That helps in any subsequent crisis. Also, following a lesson learned, the authorities created ample budgetary scope during good times, so that they could afford a major budgetary expansion to support the economy in a crisis, without getting into an unsustainable debt situation."

Bandid Nijathaworn

"But that's why I said that it (the AFC) was a successful crisis. Because it led to changes that were important for longer term sustainability of the region's economy. Had we not experienced the crisis sooner, we could have perhaps experienced a bigger crisis afterwards."

Supavud Saicheua

"I think it had a huge impression on us, people like me who still remember what happened. We are now all very cautious, and as you know, the Thai banks are now very well-capitalized, we're very cautious, and we remain so. The Bank of Thailand is the same. They remain super cautious, maintain a very tight monetary policy, and they're willing to tolerate a strengthening baht."

Teh Kok Peng

"The countries in this part of the world bit the bullet, took the bitter pill. In the sense they showed a social discipline to take the bitter medicine: the savings rate went up, the current account deficits shrank, and the result was to build up a lot of reserves. The consequence was when the GFC hit, the regional economies were ready for it. I mean, clearly there was a hit from the GFC, but there wasn't much of a loss of confidence compared to the AFC. Even now I think our macroeconomics situation, in general, is pretty good."

Jim Walker

"The crisis gave rise to very significant, very positive policy changes. That has contributed to my belief that, at the present time, Asia has never looked better as an investment home. I said that 5 years ago and, even more so now, I would say it again. Partly because of the coronavirus disease (COVID-19) crisis where there's been deft policy management, we did not see mass panic. It's quite astounding to me. Asian governments in particular learned the lessons of the AFC in 1997. Especially places like Indonesia, Thailand, and to a certain extent the Philippines. Fiscal rectitude has been exemplary over the course of the last 25 years."

Hiroshi Watanabe

"I think one of the major consequence of the AFC is that Asian countries have accumulated more foreign reserves. Even after the establishment of the Chiang Mai Initiative, my estimate is that most regional economies have foreign reserves that are more than four or five times larger than in 1997. I think that is a big factor that has strengthened their resilience. The average reserve holdings among Asian countries is more than 6 months or 7 months of imports comfortably above the IMF norm for reserve adequacy. However, too large an accumulation of reserves can also be inefficient use of the country's savings. So I think countries will need to work out a balance."

Regional Financial Cooperation

Thanong Bidaya

"All these initiatives to promote joint cooperation between the Association of Southeast Asian Nations (ASEAN) and the other regional and international players are good. What can be done more is to create some kind of Asian Monetary Fund (AMF). Our region is prosperous enough. There are rich economies like China and Japan and emerging ones like India and ASEAN. We have the potential to create an AMF out of the Chiang Mai Initiative and other monetary agreements. The idea should be studied and put forward so that financial stability can be maintained in this part of the world. We should also be able to adapt based on our own experience. Relying on practices devised by the West might not be appropriate for us. We can even consider more about digital currencies that might work for all of us."

Eisuke Sakakibara

"The other thing is, you know, the need for regional solutions. They (Asian governments) recognize that a regional approach is important. I have previously said that I was very critical of the IMF. Excessive sort of dependence on worldwide institutions like the World Bank and the IMF are not, in some occasions, appropriate. Regional institutions are quite important and the Asian Development Bank (ADB) and the ASEAN+3 Macroeconomic Research Office (AMRO) should operate in case of regional crises."

Anoop Singh

"Now that we have the Regional Comprehensive Economic Partnership (RCEP), which is focused on trade, it is timely that you have something similar to promote financial cooperation. You can do it through AMRO. We need to build up a relationship so that a dialogue can be had with the central banks every few months. The IMF can't get into all that. It's not easy, but you can. I think you should be pressing for it in the next ASEAN+3 Meeting, you should push it forward."

Zhu Guangyao

"Perhaps the pandemic is the new financial crisis. It has hit us not only directly, but also created long-term repercussions that will hold growth back for some time. Loose money is a concern, in the sense that it doesn't solve the problem; it merely postpones the problem. In this regard, I think that regional financial cooperation must be strengthened. There is a need for real policy coordination."

Part III

The Asian Financial Crisis and the Global Financial Crisis

Experiences from the ASEAN+3 Economies

Chapter 14

Thailand
Crisis, Recovery, and Reforms

Chalongphob Sussangkarn

Introduction

Over the past six decades, Thailand's economic development can be roughly divided into four sub-periods (Figure 14.1). The first 25 years, from 1960 to 1985, was a period of basic modernization. Basic infrastructures were built, including transportation and utilities, as well as social infrastructures that provided basic healthcare and education for most of the population. Core economic policy institutions, such as the National Economic and Social Development Board (planning agency) and the Bureau of the Budget, were established. During this period, the Thai economy grew at one of the fastest paces in the world, averaging about 7% per annum.[1]

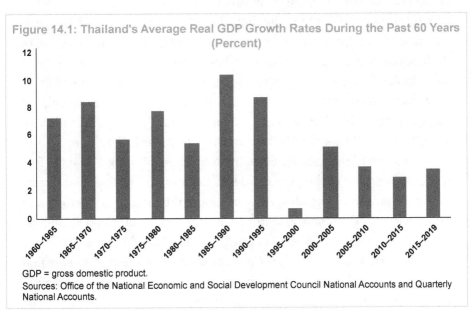

Figure 14.1: Thailand's Average Real GDP Growth Rates During the Past 60 Years (Percent)

GDP = gross domestic product.
Sources: Office of the National Economic and Social Development Council National Accounts and Quarterly National Accounts.

---

[1] Though this was still slower than growth of the Asian newly industrialized economies (NIEs) (South Korea, Taiwan Province of China, Hong Kong, and Singapore).

The next decade, from 1985 to 1995/1996, was a period of accelerated industrialization driven by the realignment of major global currencies resulting from the Plaza Accord in 1985. Huge inflows of foreign direct investment (FDI) came into Thailand. Manufactured export and economic growth accelerated, and confidence boomed. However, the second part of this period also coincided with rapid increases in financial globalization. Huge amounts of short-term funding flowed into Thailand, as well as into other emerging market economies. This was exacerbated by policy mistakes that encouraged more and more short-term foreign borrowing, leading to asset price and real estate bubbles and the increased accumulation of short-term foreign debt that became larger than the total amount of foreign reserves. The burst of the bubble and the futile attempt to defend the value of the baht triggered the Asian financial crisis (AFC) in 1997. Thailand basically ran out of useable foreign reserves and had to enter an International Monetary Fund (IMF) supervised program.

The post-crisis period, from 1997 to about 2005, was a period of gradual clean up and recovery from the crisis. The economic growth engines changed significantly from the pre-crisis period. Exchange rate depreciation made export more competitive, and the ratio of export (goods and services) to gross domestic product (GDP) rose by about 30 percentage points after the crisis. On the other hand, pre-crisis over-investment and the financial difficulties of the business sector led to a collapse in investment. The investment to GDP ratio declined by about 30 percentage points and has remained low up to the present. In contrast, the post-crisis turnaround in the external balance was quite rapid. Foreign reserves increased rapidly, and by the middle of 1999, Thailand did not need further drawings from the IMF rescue package.

Recovery of the broader economy took longer. It took 5 years before real GDP returned to the pre-crisis level. Recovery of the financial sectors took even longer, taking about 8 years before the ratio of nonperforming loans (NPLs) of the financial sector fell below 10%. By 2005, one could say that most of the severe hangovers from the crisis have dissipated.

The period since 2005 to the present is one of the continuing turmoil due to a variety of factors. The global financial crisis (GFC) was obviously very important although luckily Thailand (and most economies in East Asia) avoided major exposures to the sub-prime toxic assets that triggered the crisis. However, the GFC led to severe shortages in United States (US) dollar liquidities, which led to sharp downturns in global trade in 2009, and Thailand was affected along with everyone else. Another factor of particular concern to foreign investors has been the continuing political turmoil. Military coups in 2006 and 2014 and street protests by various groups have lasted for almost a decade and a half now with no clear resolution in sight. Finally, as a country that relies heavily on foreign trade and tourism to drive growth, travel disruptions from measures to control the coronavirus disease (COVID-19) have hit the Thai economy particularly hard. All of the above factors are negative factors affecting the Thai economy. From one of the star performers in ASEAN, Thailand has now become one of the group's worse performers.

This report looks in some detail at developments that led to the AFC as well as crisis resolution measures. The role of the IMF is also examined as controversies and dissatisfaction concerning conditionality of the IMF program were important push factors that led to financial cooperation among ASEAN+3 countries and the setting up of the Chiang Mai Initiative (CMI), its multilateralisation (CMIM), the launch of the ASEAN+3 Macroeconomic Research Office (AMRO), and the transformation of AMRO into an International Organization (IO).[2]

The report also discusses post-AFC challenges, particularly in relation to volatile capital flows, which have created numerous problems for emerging market economies even before the onset of the GFC. The GFC led to US dollar liquidity shortages globally, although direct impact on most countries in East Asia was relatively mild compared to Western countries. However, indirect impact on trade channels was much more widespread, leading to global recession, though relatively short-lived. The GFC demonstrated that US dollar liquidity shortages can occur unexpectedly and regional cooperation initiatives, such as CMIM and AMRO, provide additional surveillance and safety nets that can be very valuable to help countries cope with such episodes.

The Path to Crisis

Part of the reason for the crisis may have come from the very success that Thailand had experienced. Thailand's strong economic performance over

---

[2] See Sussangkarn (2011) for the discussions of East Asia regional financial cooperation.

many decades led to over-confidence. By the early 1990s, Thailand had become an important production center in the region, and exports were booming. To complement its role on the production side, the Thai authorities also wanted to turn Bangkok into a major regional financial center to rival Hong Kong and Singapore. A program of financial liberalization was embarked upon while the risks inherent in this process were not foreseen. The main mistakes were financial liberalization pursued without an adequate supervisory framework over financial institutions and without appropriate monetary and exchange rate policies. These mistakes substantially increased the risks to economic stability, resulting eventually in the 1997 crisis.

Many financial liberalization measures were carried out, and by 1993, most foreign exchange controls on current account and capital account transactions had been lifted. In March 1993, the Bangkok International Banking Facilities (BIBF) was established to serve as a means to develop Bangkok into an international financial center. Tax privileges were given to BIBF transactions to enable it to compete with other financial centers. It was hoped that the BIBF would result in greater in–out financial flows, so that Bangkok could become a financial center providing financing to other regional economies. Instead, most of the flows were out–in, fueling the economic bubble, leading to a rapid increase in short-term foreign debt, which were the key elements that brought about the crisis.

Controls on financial institutions were also reduced. Interest rate ceilings were eliminated by mid-1992 and rules on credit extension became more relaxed. It was hoped that these liberalization measures would lead to greater competition in the domestic financial system and stronger domestic financial institutions and would make Bangkok a leading regional financial center.

However, two key issues were overlooked. First, whether existing financial institutions were ready for a more liberalized system, and second, whether the supervisory system of the authorities was adequate. It turned out that most commercial banks and finance companies in Thailand at that time lacked adequate experience or maturity, and had poor corporate governance. Intra-affiliate lending was prevalent and most of their clients also lacked proper financial discipline and corporate governance. Financial mismanagement and so-called "crony capitalism" were widespread. Worse yet, the central authorities at that time did not have the capacity to effectively supervise financial institutions. Such deficiency led to widespread imprudent lending by financial institutions and contributed to excessive speculative investment, particularly in real estate projects, fueling an asset price bubble.

Another crucial mistake by the authorities was their decision to liberalize capital flows across borders while sticking to a fixed exchange rate system and also trying to pursue an independent monetary policy. Achieving all three, that is, free international capital flows, a fixed exchange rate, and independent monetary policy, is impossible. This is, of course, the classic Mundell's "impossible trinity" (Mundell 1963).

Thailand had successfully used a fixed exchange rate system since the end of the Second World War. This had contributed to economic stability and was an important foundation for economic growth for many decades. However, these successes were mostly in a global environment of modest financial capital flows. The mistake was to stick to this old paradigm in the 1990s when capital flows became very large and very volatile.

Prior to the crisis, the baht was fixed to a basket of currencies with the US dollar having by far the largest weight in the basket resulting in a fairly stable baht/US dollar rate for many years prior to the crisis. However, Thailand also tried to pursue an independent interest rate policy, keeping interest rates high in a futile attempt to deal with the overheating economy. This can be seen from the gap between the Thai overnight inter-bank rate and the US overnight fed fund rate. This gap averaged about 3.97% between January 1989 and June 1997 (the last month before the float of the baht) and sometimes reached up to 10.00% (Figure 14.2). With liberalized capital flow, this inevitably led to huge amount of capital flows into Thailand.

Net capital inflows between 1990 and 1996 averaged 10% of GDP each year, much higher than the average current account deficit of about 7% of GDP for the same period. The large inflows masked the external imbalance problem as it resulted in rapid increases in foreign reserves. At that time, the authorities were viewing the external balance situation with a current account paradigm, basically comparing foreign reserves to months of imports. As reserves were running around 6 or more months of imports in the early to the mid-1990s, this was perceived as a sign of strength. What was not realized at that time was that the increase in reserves came hand in hand with an increase in foreign debt, particularly short-term debt (with maturities of less

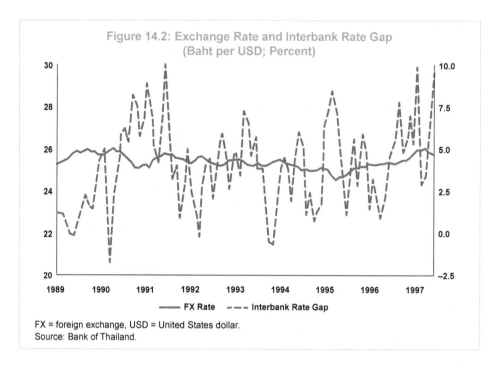

Figure 14.2: Exchange Rate and Interbank Rate Gap
(Baht per USD; Percent)

FX = foreign exchange, USD = United States dollar.
Source: Bank of Thailand.

than one year).[3] As a result, short-term foreign debt increased very rapidly. By 1995, short-term foreign debt was already larger than total official reserves. By the end of 1996, total short-term foreign debt was about USD 47.7 billion compared to total official foreign reserves of about USD 38.7 billion. Even after taking into account the foreign assets of the banking system, the total foreign asset (official and private) was less than the amount of short-term foreign debt of the country. If the short-term foreign debt was not rolled over, there would not be enough foreign assets in the country to service the debt.

The large capital inflows spurred an investment and real estate bubble. Financial institutions were lending excessively and imprudently, leading to rapidly deteriorating asset quality. The central bank made matters worse by trying to shore up ailing financial institutions. The strengthening of the US dollar relative to other major currencies starting in 1995 and China's rapid emergence into the world market also weakened Thailand's competitiveness. In 1996, exports declined by about 1.3% compared to over 20.0% growth in

---

[3] The provisioning requirement for risky assets of the Basel Capital Accord encouraged short-term lending to emerging markets. For lending to financial institutions in developing countries, short-term lending only required 20% provisioning, while long-term lending required 100% provisioning. Because of this, there was a build-in incentive for cross-border bank lending to developing countries to be short term.

both 1994 and 1995. The weak economic fundamentals led to pressures on the baht, and market perception was that the baht needed to be devalued, and speculators attacked the baht in various waves. Aggravating the situation, the Bank of Thailand (BOT) tried to stubbornly defend the value of the baht by forward-selling more and more official foreign reserves. By the end of June 1997, almost all of the country's reserves had been used to defend the value of the baht, and official foreign reserves net of committed forward obligations declined to about USD 2.8 billion. The country basically ran out of foreign reserves to service the foreign currency obligations as there was still about USD 48.5 billion in short-term foreign debt and the current account deficit was about USD 1 billion per month. As a result, the baht had to be floated on July 2, 1997, and Thailand had to seek assistance from the IMF.

Crisis Resolutions and the Role of the IMF[4]

Pre-Crisis Surveillance

The role of the IMF in relation to the Thai crisis was highly controversial.[5] In addition to the harsh conditionality imposed on Thailand (see the next page), many questioned why the IMF did not foresee the crisis and give sufficient warning to the Thai authorities. IMF staff publicly stated that warnings were given about potential problems, particularly the high current account deficits and signs of asset price bubbles, but they could not get serious attention from the Thai authorities.[6] As was earlier indicated, the Thai authorities were viewing the situation from the wrong paradigm. Although current account deficits were high, they saw reserves increasing and took this as a sign of strength. It was necessary to explain clearly the risks arising from rapid inflows of short-term foreign debts and the need to have sufficient reserves to back up these debts. This extends to the double mismatches that arose from foreign borrowing, that is, borrowing short-term to fund long-term projects (particularly in real estate) and borrowing in foreign currency for projects that generated local currency earnings. However, at that time there was less understanding about these problems than in hindsight. In fact, data on short-term debt was not

---

[4] This section draws on Sussangkarn (2002).

[5] This was also the case for South Korea and Indonesia.

[6] See, for example, Fisher (1998).

systematically collected until after the crisis. Possibly the IMF should have explained it better to the authorities, but given the current account paradigm prevalent at the time, this might have been too tall an order.

Conditionality

The IMF package for Thailand was tied to a harsh conditionality. Thailand was required to adopt many policy reforms, such as fiscal and monetary policy tightening as well as structural reforms of the financial and real sectors. These included increased prudential standards, improved governance, foreign access, and privatization. These various measures were meant to restore confidence as well as generate increases in foreign exchange reserves so that the country can meet her foreign currency obligations.

However, the nature of the IMF conditionality that was applied to Thailand (and also to Indonesia and South Korea) was rather controversial and was much debated in the aftermath of the crisis. Critics point to a number of areas, such as[7]:

- the harsh nature of tight fiscal and monetary policies without due regard for social or political consequences;
- unwillingness to allow nonmarket-based interventions such as controls on capital flows;
- imposition of full guarantees for creditors of financial institutions;
- imposition of relatively rapid structural reform measures, such as stringent financial standards and corporate restructuring as well as privatization of state owned enterprises; and
- lack of input from within the region (East Asia), and thus the programs did not take sufficient account of the socio-political realities of the affected countries.

While many of these criticisms are valid up to a point, there is no denying that once a country runs out of foreign reserves, the solution will inevitably involve pain. The critical issue is how to turn around the foreign exchange position so that the country can fully participate in the international

---

[7] For various discussions, see, for example, Sachs (1997), Feldstein (1998), Krugman (1998c), Stiglitz (1998), UNCTAD (1998, Chapter 4), and Stiglitz (2002).

economic and financial system again, and what policies are necessary to do this with as little pain as possible.

The IMF's Recovery Scenarios and Structural Reforms

Some economic contraction appeared inevitable for Thailand as the economy recovered from bank and corporate bankruptcies, and therefore the IMF's policy package should not be criticized for having caused the recession per se. Where one can be more critical of the IMF is that it had a very wrong picture of the recovery process in Thailand from the beginning, and this wrong scenario may have led to a combination of policies that led to more serious economic and social problems than necessary.

Table 14.1 shows some key macroeconomic targets for 1998 from the various Letters of Intent that the Thai government signed with the IMF. In the first Letter of Intent in August 1997, the IMF was still expecting a positive real GDP growth of 3.5%, a current account deficit of USD 5.3 billion, and a capital account surplus of USD 1.8 billion in 1998. These numbers turned out to be the complete opposite to the actual figures for 1998, as shown in the last row of Table 14.1.

Table 14.1: Expected Macroeconomic Targets for 1998 in Various LOIs and Actual Values

Expected 1998 Growth in LOI and Actual	Date	Real GDP Growth (Percent)	Current Account Balance (USD Billion)	Capital Account Balance (USD Billion)	Overall Public Sector Balance (Percent of GDP)
LOI-1	Aug 1997	3.5	−5.3	1.8	1.0
LOI-2	Nov 1997	0.0 to 1.0	−2.5	0.3	1.0
LOI-3	Feb 1998	−3.0 to −3.5	4.4	−12.0 to −14.0	−2.0
LOI-4	May 1998	−4.0 to −4.5	8.5	−14.0 to −16.0	−3.0
LOI-5	Aug 1998	−7.0	11.0 to 12.0	...	−3.0
LOI-6	Dec 1998	−7.0 to −8.0	13.5	...	−5.0
Actual	1998	−10.5	14.3	−9.7	...

... = not available, GDP = gross domestic product, LOI = letter of intent, USD = United States dollar.
Sources: Bank of Thailand and National Economic and Social Development Board.

Making inaccurate forecasts is normal in the economics profession, and at the start of the Thai crisis, just about every institution made wrong forecasts. However, the IMF was supposed to have a better knowledge of the true situation in Thailand than almost everyone else. In particular, it knew about the almost complete depletion in Thailand's net foreign reserves.[8] If one took the targets in the first Letter of Intent at face value, it would appear that the IMF had too much faith in the market confidence in its program. The target current account deficit of USD 5.3 billion meant that it did not expect the severe depreciation of the baht that ensued. Similarly, the target surplus in the capital account meant that it seriously overestimated the rollover of the country's short-term external debt. Both these targets were surprising, since part of the IMF package called for the BOT to begin to reveal key economic information on a regular basis, including data on foreign reserves. Once the market began to figure out that net foreign reserves were almost depleted, the USD 17.2 billion package from the IMF could not generate much confidence, particularly since the amount was to be drawn over a period of 34 months and Thailand still had about USD 35 billion in short-term external debt. The fact that the IMF projected a current account deficit to continue only made the situation worse, since it was hard to imagine how an excess supply of foreign currency could arise. Only when the current account turned into a sizeable surplus would the supply of foreign currencies begin to exceed demand and strengthen the baht.

An internal evaluation report of the IMF program admitted that the IMF badly misjudged the severity of the economic downturn.[9] One reason given was that the IMF did not expect the contagion to spread to other countries. However, the report also made the cryptic statement that the misjudgment may be "perhaps, partly a concern to avoid damaging confidence through gloomy forecasts."[10] This statement was quite disturbing. The IMF had been insisting to countries such as Thailand to be transparent with regard to the release of key information. Yet, if what the statement suggested were true, then it implied that the IMF might have been trying to mislead the market by deliberately distorting the projected economic scenario. Hopefully, the misreading of the scenario stemmed from errors in assumptions and analysis rather than a deliberate distortion.

---

[8] The first Letter of Intent explicitly stated that "as at 19 August 1997, forward obligations over the next 12 months totaled USD 23.4 billion." This compared to gross reserve of about USD 26 billion at the end of July 1997.

[9] Lane et al. (1999), section IX.

[10] Lane et al. (1999), p. 120.

Whatever the reason behind the misjudgment, it had important implications for the structure of the IMF package. If the current account were to
remain in deficit, then how could Thailand turn around her foreign currency
position? Basically, the program had to rely on tight fiscal and monetary
policy to control the current account, the generation of a high rollover
rate of short-term foreign debt, and also the attraction of new medium- to
long-term investment through foreign buyouts of domestic enterprises and
privatization of state enterprises.

The IMF was much criticized for the tight fiscal and monetary policies
(Sachs, 1997). Certainly, if the IMF had used an economic scenario that was
closer to what subsequently happened, it would have made sense to prescribe
a much easier fiscal stance, particularly for social safety net programs. The fact
that it continued to underestimate the severity of the ensuing recession up to
the end of 1998 (Table 14.1) meant that the easing of the fiscal target occurred
fairly slowly. Taken in conjunction with substantial time lags for fiscal targets
to be translated into actual spending due to normal administrative lags, the
cushioning of the social impact was not very effective.[11]

The tight monetary policy was regarded as essential to dampen capital
outflows. By September 1997, short-term interest rates had increased by
about 1,000 basis points from pre-float levels and continued at high levels
until about the third quarter of 1998. Some analysts, such as Krugman
(1998b), saw this as being necessary to try to stem capital outflows at a time
when net foreign reserves had almost been depleted. The tight monetary
policy fitted in with the IMF's strategy of trying to maximize the rollover
of short-term debt, given that it was expecting the current account deficit
to continue. However, the strategy was not particularly effective. Once the
market realized that net foreign reserves had almost been depleted, the baht
depreciated rapidly (Figure 14.3). An increase in interest rates by about
1,000 basis points was hardly a sufficient incentive to continue to keep baht
denominated assets. From the start of the float to January 1998, the US
dollar strengthened against the baht by more than 100%, so baht interest
rates would have had to be extremely high to be effective. With the rapid
depreciation of the baht, domestic borrowers of foreign currencies were
also facing mounting debt in baht terms, so it was logical for lenders to try

---

[11] Though luckily for Thailand, the increases in the baht price of most agricultural commodities in 1998
due to the depreciation of the baht enabled families in the agriculture sector to provide some safety
nets for relatives who had previous worked in the urban areas and were made redundant as a result of
the crisis (Siamwalla and Sopchokchai, 1998).

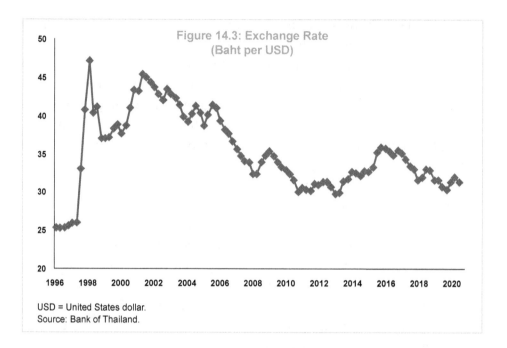

Figure 14.3: Exchange Rate (Baht per USD)

USD = United States dollar.
Source: Bank of Thailand.

to recall their debt as soon as possible in case borrowers became insolvent from the mounting debt. Thus, the tight monetary policy was not very effective in dampening capital outflows, and in fact, the net capital outflow in 1997 was about USD 9 billion compared to a net capital inflow of about USD 19.5 billion in 1996.

Nevertheless, a fairly tight monetary policy seemed to be necessary. This was not so much for providing effective incentives to prevent net capital outflows, but rather to control inflation so that the potential benefits of a weaker baht would not be wiped out through inflation getting out of control.

Another strategy of the IMF package was more problematic. This was the need to generate foreign exchange through medium- to long-term foreign investment in business enterprises and privatization of state enterprises. In late 1997, full foreign ownership of financial institutions was permitted for 10 years, with a grandfather clause protecting the absolute amount of the foreign owner's equity holding. Assets of closed down financial institutions were being auctioned off (to both domestic and foreign buyers). Privatization of state enterprises was also highlighted as a medium-term strategy.[12]

---

[12]This was already stated in the summary of important measures attached to the first Letter of Intent signed by the government (Bank of Thailand 1997).

This strategy came under considerable attack from various social and business groups such as non-governmental organizations (NGOs), labor unions, and some academics. As the baht depreciated and the recession became more severe, critics highlighted this IMF strategy as a "fire-sale" tactic to benefit foreign investors.[13] To push for foreign buyouts at a time when the economy was at its weakest and the baht at its lowest was likely to lead to very low prices for domestic enterprises. Actually, as with the tight fiscal stance at the beginning of the IMF program, if a large recession and a current account surplus had been perceived at the time when the IMF program was drawn up, this strategy should have been downplayed. It made implementation of the adjustment program much more difficult on political–economy grounds. In particular, the program to privatize state enterprises had been ongoing in Thailand well before the crisis. The rationale at that time was much more socially acceptable, that is, to reduce the burden on public expenditures, increase efficiency, and improve services. Once privatization was linked to the IMF program, those with vested interests in opposing privatization were given new potent ammunition to strengthen their arguments.

Financial Sector Restructuring

The financial sector was already weak before the baht's float, with large amounts of credit extended to nonviable projects. Runs on weak financial institutions had started before the baht's float, and 58 finance companies had been suspended by the second half of 1997. The IMF program included many measures to restructure and reform the financial sector. The idea was that a strong and stable financial sector was a prerequisite for recovery. This was a relatively new area for the IMF, and many questions remained about the way the IMF program went about financial sector restructuring and the impact this had on the financial and business sectors. Some have strongly criticized the IMF's financial restructuring measures given its mandate and lack of experience in this area, for example, Feldstein (1998). Some of the key measures included a full guarantee of all depositors and creditors of financial institutions; upgrading prudential regulations on financial institutions, in particular on definitions and classifications of NPLs, provisioning requirements and capital adequacy ratios to reach

---

[13]For some discussion of the issue, see Krugman (1998a).

international standards by the end of the year 2000; bond issuance of more than TBH 1 trillion to help the Financial Institution Development Fund (FIDF); bond issuance of up to THB 300 billion to help the re-capitalization of financial institutions; and the passage of new laws, particularly on bankruptcy procedures and foreclosure, to help encourage debt restructuring.

The full guarantee for depositors and creditors was meant to generate confidence in the financial sector. However, many see the full guarantee for creditors as absolving the foreign creditors of much of the risks that they should be responsible for. As is now clear, the rapid increase in short-term foreign debt since the beginning of the 1990s was one root cause of the crisis in East Asia. Much of these short-term borrowings were used to finance long-term nonviable projects with full approval of the creditors. The huge short-term debt together with foreign exchange mismanagement by the authorities led to the crisis, yet these creditors were protected. This, together with the elements of a fire-sale strategy in the IMF program as already mentioned, led to a broad mistrust of the IMF, with many claiming that the IMF program was more designed for the benefit of foreign investors rather than for Thailand's recovery. The full guarantee for depositors and creditors had also reduced the government's options in dealing with insolvent financial institutions. Closing them down simply shifted the full liability to the government.

The rapid move toward international prudential standards by the end of the year 2000 led to a severe malfunctioning of the financial sector. With the large depreciation of the baht and the ensuing economic recession, the financial and business sectors were moving closer toward insolvency. When the baht was floated, the private sector had about USD 75.6 billion in foreign debts (short and long term). From mid-1997 to January 1998, the baht had weakened from 25.8 baht/US dollar to about 54.1 baht/US dollar. Thus, their debt in baht terms had increased by about THB 2.14 trillion or about 44% of GDP. In this situation, there was little chance for those businesses with large amounts of foreign debt to remain solvent. Non-NPLs in the system were increasing rapidly. Financial institutions were hard-pressed to provide adequate provisioning for NPLs, particularly with the increased prudential standards. Banks and finance companies hardly extended new lending even to credit-worthy companies — afraid that this would lead to new NPLs and hence the need for more provisioning — and tried to keep their assets as liquid as possible. The economy went into a vicious downward spiral, with economic recession leading to more NPLs, leading banks to struggle further with provisioning and capital increases, becoming even more reluctant to lend to the production sector. This in turn led to more liquidity problems for businesses and to more bank loans becoming NPLs.

Recovery from Foreign Reserves Depletion

When Thailand floated the baht and asked for IMF assistance, the country basically ran out of useable foreign reserves. Tackling the problem of almost complete depletion of foreign reserves had to be the main priority of the IMF program. For this purpose, the IMF put together a lending package of USD 17.2 billion for Thailand.[14] The IMF package was meant only as a relatively short-term liquidity support, with repayment for each drawing due in 3 years. Thus, Thailand had to enact a stringent reform package to turn around its foreign reserve position. As discussed earlier, the scenario that the IMF envisaged was very different from actual outcomes. This led to a much harsher reform package than was necessary. In actual fact, due mainly to the baht depreciation and the deep recession in 1998, Thailand recovered relatively quickly from the de facto depletion of foreign reserves.

Data in Table 14.2 show that by the beginning of 1999 the country was well on the way to recovery from foreign exchange depletion. Official foreign

Table 14.2: End Quarter Net Official Foreign Reserves (USD billion)

Year	Quarter	Net Official Reserves
1997	Q1	24.1
	Q2	2.8
	Q3*	1.8
	Q4	1.9
1998	Q1	2.8
	Q2	5.4
	Q3	6.8
	Q4	11.7
1999	Q1	14.1

Q = quarter.
Note: Net reserves are gross reserves net of outstanding forward commitments and borrowing from the IMF package (including drawings from the IMF package contributed from other sources).
*Drawing from the IMF package started in September 1997.
Source: Bank of Thailand.

[14]USD 4 billion of this total amount came from the IMF's own resources, the rest being contributions from countries from the Asia-Pacific region as well as from the World Bank and the Asian Development Bank.

reserves net of forward commitments and net of drawings from the IMF package had increased to about USD 14 billion by the end of March 1999. Including drawing from the IMF package, total net official reserves became larger than short-term debt by the middle of 1999 (Figure 14.4). Given the controversial nature of the IMF program, Thailand decided in September 1999 that no further drawing from the IMF package was needed, so the country exited the IMF program, including all the conditionality attached to it. By that time, Thailand had drawn USD 14.1 billion out of the total package of USD 17.2 billion.

The main reason for the rapid improvement in the country's foreign reserve position was that the current account turned into a substantial surplus starting in the last quarter of 1997 (Table 14.3). This was due to the sharp depreciation of the baht and the recession. Compared to the situation before the baht's float, the turnaround in the current account generated an additional net foreign exchange inflow into the country of about USD 2 billion per month. This helped to offset continued capital outflows due to repayment of outstanding foreign debt. The current account continued to be in substantial surplus for many years until 2005 when oil prices began to increase sharply.

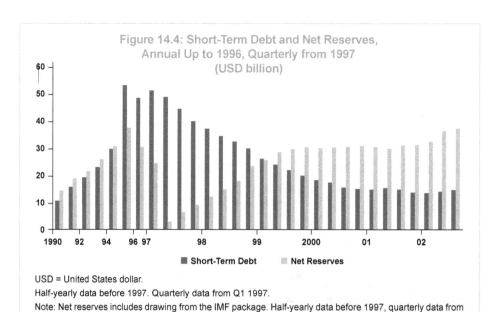

Figure 14.4: Short-Term Debt and Net Reserves, Annual Up to 1996, Quarterly from 1997 (USD billion)

USD = United States dollar.
Half-yearly data before 1997. Quarterly data from Q1 1997.
Note: Net reserves includes drawing from the IMF package. Half-yearly data before 1997, quarterly data from the first quarter of 1997.
Source: Bank of Thailand.

Table 14.3: Real GDP Growth and Current Account

Year	Quarter	Real GDP Growth (%yoy)	Current Account (USD million)
1995	Q1	9.56	−2,356
	Q2	12.33	−3,908
	Q3	9.57	−2,959
	Q4	5.86	−4,011
1996	Q1	4.72	−3,333
	Q2	6.53	−4,802
	Q3	7.83	−3,544
	Q4	4.61	−2,671
1997	Q1	1.00	−2,101
	Q2	−0.58	−3,134
	Q3	−1.61	−746
	Q4	−4.19	2,871
1998	Q1	−7.08	4,210
	Q2	−13.88	2,811
	Q3	−13.92	3,410
	Q4	−7.17	3,860
1999	Q1	−0.21	3,972
	Q2	3.45	2,218
	Q3	8.41	3,026
	Q4	6.42	3,250
2000	Q1	6.49	3,302
	Q2	6.13	1,677
	Q3	2.43	2,165
	Q4	4.05	2,184

GDP = gross domestic product, Q = quarter, USD = United States dollar, yoy = year-over-year.
Sources: Bank of Thailand and Nation Economic and Social Development Board.

The turnaround in the current account and in the country's foreign reserve position was achieved at a very high cost in terms of a severe economic contraction. Real GDP growth started to decline from the second quarter of 1997, and registered a decline of 10.5% in 1998. It could be argued that the economic contraction and attendant social impact could have been less with an alternative recovery package, for example, with less stringent monetary and fiscal targets as had been suggested by Sachs (1997). However, it was very unlikely that the country's rapid recovery of foreign reserves could have been achieved without a certain amount of economic contraction.

The quick exit from the IMF program raised questions about the appropriateness of structural reform measures that were part of the IMF conditionality, such as structural reforms of the financial sector and privatization. These needed time to implement, and given their controversial nature, once Thailand no longer needed additional drawing from the IMF, these reform measures could no longer be enforced.

An important lesson was that, for an export-oriented economy like Thailand, the exchange rate was the critical variable that could bring about quick adjustment to the external balance. So exchange rate flexibility in times of stress is critical.

While Thailand's foreign exchange position turned around relatively quickly, it took much longer to clean up problems in the economy. The depreciation of the baht put a severe strain on much of the financial and production sectors. Those with unhedged foreign debt were driven to bankruptcy. It took 5 years before real GDP returned to the pre-crisis level. If one assumed that without a crisis real GDP would have grown at about 7% per annum, which was the average growth rate for Thailand during 1960–1985 (before the boom period leading to the crisis), then the loss (measured by the difference between the GDP that could have been achieved and actual GDP) in 5 years amounted to about 40% of real GDP.

Restructuring corporate debt was another crucial element for both financial sector reform and economic recovery, because successful debt restructuring helped reduce NPLs of financial institutions and resuscitate economic activities simultaneously. The process was not straight forward,[15] and it took 8 years, until 2005, before the NPL ratio declined to a level below 10% (Figure 14.5).

By 2005, one can say that most of the severe hangovers from the crisis had dissipated. The cleanup cost of the financial system was sizeable. The government had to issue bonds totaling about THB 1.5 trillion to pay for the clean up (about 20% of GDP) and more than THB 740 billion of these bonds are still outstanding.[16] If the interest costs on these bonds are included, then the clean up cost, once completed, could be close to 35%–40% of nominal GDP.

---

[15]See Vichyanond (2002) for discussions of complications involved in debt restructuring.

[16]The Yingluck government transferred all the responsibilities for these bonds (principal and interest) to the BOT in 2012.

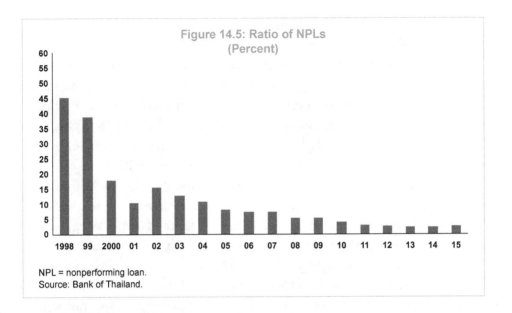

Figure 14.5: Ratio of NPLs (Percent)

NPL = nonperforming loan.
Source: Bank of Thailand.

Lessons and Reforms

While severe economic and social impact resulted from the 1997 crisis, there were also many useful lessons that were not well understood prior to the crisis. This led to reforms and improvements that made the country, and the East Asian region in general, better able to prevent a similar crisis in the future. Experiences during the GFC bore this out. Some main areas of improvements are highlighted as follows.

Risks from Financial Globalization

The most important lesson was probably related to the risks from financial globalization. While financial globalization can bring benefits from access to international financial markets, it can also bring about a lot of volatilities and risks, and needs extremely prudent management. Given Thailand's past development successes based on real sector globalization (through trade and FDI), the country was regarded as an example of the so-called "East Asian Economic Miracle" (World Bank 1993) and was praised internationally as being a model that other countries should emulate. Given these successes, the authorities may have become overconfident and embarked on policies of financial liberalization in the hope of turning Bangkok into a major financial center for the region. Unfortunately, there was insufficient understanding of the implications of financial liberalization, and an incorrect policy regime was pursued and this eventually led to the crisis.

As discussed earlier in this chapter, the authorities were looking at the economy with the wrong paradigm. The external balance situation was viewed with a current account perspective rather than a capital account perspective, and macroeconomic policies did not pay sufficient attention to Mundell's impossible trinity, leading to excessive short-term capital inflows. These large capital inflows fueled the economic bubble in Thailand.

As capital flows increased, foreign reserves also increased as the foreign borrowings were converted into local currency to be invested in the country. The authorities were viewing this as a sign of strength and were looking at the adequacy of foreign reserves in terms of the number of months of imports that they covered (a current account paradigm).

The fact that foreign reserves were also needed to cover foreign debt, particularly short-term debt (a capital account paradigm), was not well understood. This was a painful lesson from the crisis. After the crisis, the country's short-term debt was carefully monitored to make sure that the country would not return to a situation anything like the pre-crisis one. A decade after the crisis, the ratio of foreign reserves to short-term external debt increased substantially to almost five to one at the end of 2008, from much less than one to one just before the crisis.

To avoid a similar crisis, economic management needs to be much more prudent, and appropriate sequencing of policy changes is needed. The authorities need to understand and look out for various risks to the economy. Major policy changes (like financial liberalization prior to the crisis) need to be carefully studied to understand the full implications and risks involved.

Better Data for Risk Assessments and Economic Management

An important lesson from the crisis is the importance of having appropriate and timely data. Prior to the crisis, data essential for risk assessments and economic management were woefully inadequate. GDP data were only available on an annual basis, and with a time lag of a year or so. Regularly available quarterly or monthly data were extremely limited, and critically important data on short-term foreign debt were not collected in any systematic manner.

After the crisis, significant improvements were made. Many monthly and quarterly data series were collected and made publicly available. Vast amounts of monthly official data are now accessible for downloading through the Internet from public agencies, particularly from the BOT. The public availability of these data is very important. It enables nonpublic sector organizations (including businesses, media, and academia) to better track economic developments and make more accurate risk assessments. This has led to a more balanced view compared to a situation where most of the information was only available to the government and public sector organizations.

New Monetary Policy Regime

A clear lesson from the crisis is that under a fixed exchange rate system, politicians find it very difficult to devalue the currency when necessary. Protecting the value of the currency is regarded as an important symbol of national pride. Also, when the currency is under attack by speculators, governments normally regard devaluation as a capitulation to the speculators and will therefore be even more stubborn in defending the value of the currency.

Thailand had to de-peg the currency in July 1997 as net foreign reserves were almost completely depleted. A managed float system was introduced and continued to be used to this day. Under such a system with liberalized capital flows, the role of monetary policy becomes very important in order to underpin a monetary anchor under the managed float system.

The BOT formally introduced an "inflation-targeting" monetary policy framework on May 23, 2000. The framework targeted "core" inflation, which excluded fresh food and energy prices, and the inflation target was set at 0.0%–3.5%. The policy rate is the 1-day bilateral repurchase rate, and the BOT carries out a monetary operation framework in order to steer short-term money market rates in line with the policy interest rate.

The inflation-targeting framework was very new for Thailand, which had been under a fixed exchange rate regime since the end of the Second World War. It was necessary to get the market (as well as policymakers, academics, and the public in general) to understand the system. It was also very important to establish credibility of the system as the BOT had lost most of its credibility as a result of the crisis.

The choice of a broad target range of 0.0%–3.5% was to make sure that it would not be difficult to meet the target over the first few years. During that time, NPLs were still very high, with a lot of excess liquidity in the banking system and production capacity utilization was rather low, so core inflation was low and in fact remained within the target range for almost all of the first decade and a half of the inflation-targeting period except for just a few months. The inflation targets have been fine-tuned a number of times and the current target range set in 2020 is 1%–3% for headline inflation.

The inflation-targeting framework received legal foundation through the revised BOT Act (2008), which provided more operational independence for the BOT and for its Governor. The revised Act tried to provide checks and balances on the appointments of the Governor and outside expert board members. Prior to the revised Act, the Governor could be replaced by the Cabinet for "appropriate reasons." Under the 2008 Act, the Governor can still be removed by the Cabinet but upon the recommendation of the Minister of Finance due to wrongful misconduct or dishonest performance of duties. The Governor can also be removed by the Cabinet upon the recommendation of the Minister or by the proposal of the Minister upon the recommendation of the BOT Board due to gross incompetence in the performance of duties or incapability, provided that an explicit reason shall be specified in the order. So it is much more difficult now to remove the Governor. Operational independence is important for the conduct of monetary policy. There have been episodes of conflicts between the Government and the BOT over the direction of monetary policy leading to the sacking of the Governor.

A noteworthy case related to inflation targeting was when the Thaksin government came into power in early 2001. At that time, the global economic condition was very weak, so Thai exports and economic growth were weak, and inflation was low. However, for whatever reason, the government wanted to see a stronger currency and pressured the BOT to increase the policy rate. After several months of political pressure and the continued refusal by the BOT to increase the policy rate, the Governor was sacked. Under the BOT Act at that time, the sacking of the Governor by the Cabinet could be done for "appropriate reasons." The policy rate was hiked by 100 basis points under a new Governor, but as this was inappropriate for the underlying economic conditions, the policy rate was quickly reversed and lowered to below the level when the sacking of the Governor happened. The political interference in monetary policy created a lot of confusion at the time.

Moreover, it was not clear under Thaksin Shinawatra whether the inflation-targeting framework would remain or the monetary policy framework would move back to something like an exchange-rate-targeting framework. However, the BOT officially stuck to the inflation-targeting framework, and after a while, the market regained confidence in the system and the system has remained in operation to the present.

Even after the revised 2008 Act came into force, there were many episodes of conflicts between the Minister of Finance and the BOT, to the extent of the Minister at the time saying that he would like to sack the Governor several times in public. However, the revised BOT Act gave sufficient protection to the Governor so that he could not be replaced by the government.

Apart from the revised BOT Act, there were other important new financial laws that were passed at about the same time as the BOT Act. These aimed to improve the financial regulatory regimes in line with new financial environments and risks. The main ones were the Financial Institution Business Act (2008), the Deposit Insurance Act (2008), the Credit Information Business Operation Act (2008), and the Securities and Exchange Act (2008).[17]

Development of Long-Term Capital Markets

The crisis also showed the importance of developing a well-functioning long-term capital market as an alternative financing source to bank lending. In particular, if a country has a savings deficit (i.e., a current account deficit), the deficit needs to be funded from foreign borrowings. If these borrowings are mainly from bank lending, then most of them tend to be short term (because of the Basel Capital Accord provisioning requirement) and create risks. Therefore, policies that help build the capacities of domestic companies to raise external long-term capital in place of a reliance on foreign bank lending are crucial to prevent another similar crisis.

Prior to the crisis, the domestic bond markets in Thailand (and most of the emerging market economies in the region) were very thin or almost

---

[17]See Sussangkarn and Vichyanond (2007) for detailed discussions of various financial reforms.

nonexistent. The Thai government ran budget surpluses for 9 consecutive years prior to the crisis, so the supply of government bonds to provide liquidity and benchmarks to the market was not available.

However, the situation is now very different. After the crisis, the government had to issue bonds to finance large cleanup costs and thus was forced to deepen local-currency bond markets. The domestic bond market is now much deeper and more liquid than before. The bond market as a whole has grown from 12% of GDP in 1997 to 91% of GDP as of September 2020. And for the corporate bond market, the outstanding amount has expanded from 3% of GDP in 1997 to 25% of GDP presently. Meanwhile, the stock market capitalization has also grown from 24% of GDP to 86% of GDP during the same period and the reliance on bank lending has declined from 128% of GDP in 1997 to 107% of GDP as of September 2020.

Post-Crisis Changes in Growth Drivers

The crisis of 1997 not only put an end to the hyper-growth era, it led to one of the most abrupt and profound restructurings of the Thai economy. After the baht was floated in 1997, it depreciated rapidly and fell by more than 50% in the first 6 months (Figure 14.3). Firms that relied on foreign borrowing to finance their investments faced huge balance sheet problems. Most of these firms could not service their debt including domestic bank loans, which then became nonperforming. Many corporations ceased to operate and vanished. Many of these corporations used to be among the country's leading firms that drove economic growth.

As a result, aggregate investment fell sharply and the economy contracted by more than 10% in 1998. Even though the foreign reserve position recovered fairly quickly, recovery of the broader real economy took longer; almost 5 years before output recovered to its pre-crisis peak, and 8 years before the NPL ratio declined below 10%. With a slow recovery in the output level, there was excess capacity in the economy and little need for new investment. At the same time, much of the corporate sector was going through debt restructuring and did not have the financial resources for new investment either. Thus, investment declined substantially from the pre-crisis level and contributed little to the post-crisis recovery.

The share of real investment to GDP declined by about half from the pre-crisis level; from about 50% pre-crisis to around 25% on average after the crisis, and has remained so to the present (Figure 14.6). While the pre-crisis ratio was too high, given the speculative bubble at that time, the current ratio is still much lower than what one might expect in a normal situation; for example, the average ratio of real investment to GDP from 1980 to 1990 was about 30%. Also, the average savings rate has been around 30%–35% over the past couple of decades, so an investment to GDP ratio of around 30% can certainly be sustained without any external balance problem.

Apart from investment, another possible source of domestic growth driver is consumption (public and private). In the case of Thailand, Figure 14.7 shows that the ratio of real consumption to GDP does not vary much over time and has ranged around 66%–69%, both before and after the AFC. This suggests that in the case of Thailand, consumption tends to follow overall economic growth rather than lead growth.

While domestic demand had played a relatively minor role in post-crisis growth, it has been the external sector (exports of goods and services) that has provided the growth impetus since the crisis. This is not too surprising. Thailand was an export-led economy prior to the crisis, so that with further

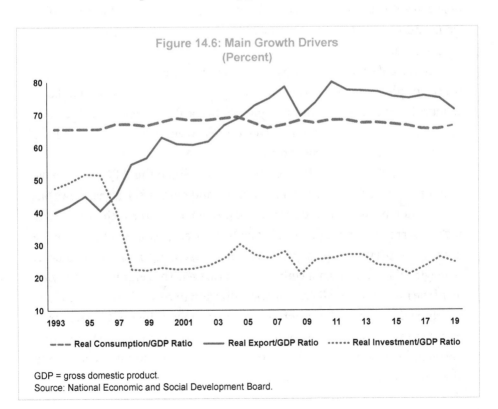

Figure 14.6: Main Growth Drivers
(Percent)

GDP = gross domestic product.
Source: National Economic and Social Development Board.

stimulus coming from the depreciation of the baht, the export sector was able to easily respond and provided the impetus for the growth and recovery of the economy. Given that investment has not yet fully recovered, the export sector has continued to be the main (or only) engine of growth.

With exports as the main growth driver, the share of real export of goods and services (including tourism) to GDP rose from around 40%–45% before the crisis to around 75% at present, an increase of 30–35 percentage points, which is very large. This is in spite of major disruptions to world trade in 2009–2010 during the GFC.

Challenges from Volatile Capital Flows and the GFC

Capital Flows and Capital Controls

Since the AFC, export has become the only effective engine of growth for Thailand. Variables that affect export performance are widely monitored and scrutinized by many groups, including policymakers, business and financial groups, academia, and the media. These variables include the global trade and financial environment as well as factors affecting the country's competitiveness.

A variable that attracts particular attention and has often been the source of policy conflicts is the exchange rate. This is understandable as changes in the exchange rate directly affect the local currency value of exports and imports, and affect the relative competitiveness between competing countries, at least in the short term.

Capital flows also affect exchange rates. Since the AFC, there have been many episodes of large capital inflows and outflows. Large inflows put appreciation pressure on the currency value. For a country such as Thailand, with export as the main driver of growth, political pressures to manage the inflows and prevent large appreciation of the exchange rate can be intense. Managing the inflows is not without cost, however. The central bank's buying up of the inflows normally requires sterilization to control domestic money supply, and given very low interest earnings from holdings of US Treasuries or other advanced economy bonds, the relatively high cost of sterilization normally leads to a loss for the central bank. For many countries, including Thailand, this has fiscal implications.

Inflows can also reverse unexpectedly, such as during the GFC. So making sure that there are enough foreign reserves to back up the inflows and prevent severe exchange rate volatilities is also important. All of these considerations make managing volatile capital flows a particularly delicate exercise.[18]

Thailand suffered from many episodes of capital inflows leading to large currency appreciation and policy conflicts between the central authorities. The most noteworthy case occurred in 2006, leading to the imposition of capital controls on December 18, 2006, and a partial reversal of the controls a day later.

The challenge for exchange rate management was particularly acute in 2006. There were large capital inflows into the country. Although the BOT had been buying foreign currencies to ease the strength of the baht, the currency still strengthened from about 41 baht/US dollar at the end of 2005 to about 37.6 baht/US dollar at the end of the third quarter of 2006. The capital inflow became even more rapid in the last quarter of 2006. Between the beginning of October and the middle of December, the BOT intervened extensively in the foreign exchange market to buy up about USD 800 million per week for 10 consecutive weeks. Yet, the baht strengthened at the most rapid pace ever, reaching about 35.2 baht/US dollar by the middle of December.

Because of the baht appreciation, the authorities were under tremendous political pressures from businesses to intervene more and more. The loss of export competitiveness through currency appreciation from rapid capital inflows was seen to be unrelated to any economic fundamentals, and as export was Thailand's main engine of growth, the loss of this engine would have had wide implications for the economy as a whole.

So on December 18, 2006, Thailand imposed capital controls on capital inflows by copying measures that Chile had used in the early 1990s. Inflows were subject to a 30% unremunerated reserve requirement (so only 70% of the inflows could be invested) and were needed to be kept in the country for at least 1 year, otherwise there would be a fine equal to 10% of the inflow amount. Not surprisingly, the stock market crashed the next day by 15% and the authorities had to reverse the controls on those inflows coming to the stock market.

---

[18]For discussions on maintaining economic stability under volatile capital flows, see Sussangkarn (2017).

In hindsight, it seems that the authorities did not really understand that the requirement to keep the capital inflow in the country for at least 1 year was extremely stringent. This was because very few investors could afford to park their money in one place for that long period without the flexibility to move it if needed. The inflow controls also created distortions and administrative challenges for the authorities, particularly when different inflows were treated differently and there were possibilities of leakages of one type of inflow into another.

One can argue that when a country has to deal with very large capital inflows (or outflows), capital control measures should not be ruled out per se, as they can provide an added valuable instrument for the authorities to maintain the stability of the economy. However, it is very dangerous to simply copy measures that may have worked for some country at some point in the past. The financial system changes so rapidly and financial globalization is now much more extensive than in the early 1990s, so measures that might have worked then may be counter-productive in the present day. If capital controls are to be introduced, then they must be very well designed and the authorities must be very sure of how the market will respond to them. In the Thai case, the capital controls were eventually removed in March 2008 when conditions were more favorable, as the trade balance turned into a deficit following large increases in world oil prices.

Impact of the GFC

It was fortunate that the Thai financial system was not significantly affected by the subprime crisis. NPLs of Thai banks remained low (Figure 14.5). One small bank had to be re-capitalized due to exposures to toxic assets. Most of the other banks avoided significant exposures to these assets. People were certainly going around trying to sell the various collateralized debt obligations (CDOs) to financial institutions. That Thai financial institutions avoided falling prey to these toxic assets must be related to the lessons that were learned from the 1997 crisis.

From the painful experiences of that crisis, the Thai financial sector became much more risk adverse than before. Also being less sophisticated than those in the West, there was not much understanding of what these debt instruments were, and because of the risk aversion, financial institutions generally avoided them.

The stock market was of course affected in line with stock markets around the world. As financial markets in the advanced economies experienced liquidity crunches, there was a massive liquidation of investment assets in the emerging markets and a massive outflow of capital.

Fortunately, having learned from the AFC about the need to have sufficient reserves, Thailand had more than enough foreign reserves to cover capital outflows, and depreciation pressures on the baht could be managed fairly easily.

Even though the financial system managed to avoid the direct impacts of the subprime crisis, Thailand was seriously affected by the crisis indirectly through the trade channel. This became very apparent in the last quarter of 2008. Prior to that, Thai exports were still growing rapidly at more than 20% year on year in dollar value. In the fourth quarter of 2008, export fell 10.4% (year on year) and GDP shrank by 2.0% (Table 14.4).

As an economy highly dependent on export of goods and services, the Thai economy could not avoid the fallout from the decline in world trade, and the declines were certainly steep. Luckily, the decline in world trade only lasted for four quarters, from the fourth quarter (Q4) 2008 to Q3 2009. Once the shortages of US dollar liquidity that led to declines in trade finance were taken care of, global trade bounced back and Thai export resumed growth quite rapidly.

Once world trade recovered in Q4 2009, and when it looked likely that Thailand would get back to a high export growth path, an unexpected shock occurred just to show that nothing was certain. This was the flood in 2011 which was completely unexpected. Again, the impacts did not linger too long, lasting about a year.

Shocks have not gone away and Thailand is in the midst of a couple of shocks that hopefully will not linger too long. One is the street protest by young left-wing leaning groups. This continues the political turmoil that has lasted a decade and a half. The other is the COVID-19 shock, which has hit Thailand's star industry, tourism, extremely hard. Again, depending on how vaccines work out, it is hoped that life can get back to normal soon.

Table 14.4: Export and Real GDP Growth

Year	Quarter	Nominal Export Growth (% yoy)	Real GDP Growth (% yoy)
2006		17.0	5.0
2007		18.2	5.4
2008	Q1	23.7	3.3
	Q2	28.6	3.5
	Q3	26.1	2.2
	Q4	−10.4	−2.0
2009	Q1	−19.6	−4.3
	Q2	−25.6	−3.1
	Q3	−17.0	−0.5
	Q4	12.8	5.1
2010	Q1	30.6	12.2
	Q2	40.6	9.0
	Q3	21.2	5.8
	Q4	19.3	3.4
2011	Q1	25.8	3.3
	Q2	16.9	1.8
	Q3	24.2	2.4
	Q4	−5.7	−4.0
2012	Q1	−1.3	2.9
	Q2	1.5	6.0
	Q3	−3.8	5.0
	Q4	17.4	15.5

GDP = gross domestic product, Q = quarter, yoy = year-over-year.
Sources: Bank of Thailand and the National Economic and Social Development Board.

References

Bank of Thailand. 1997. "IMF's Approval of the Stand-by Arrangement for the Macroeconomic Adjustment Program." Announcement No. 56/1997, Bank of Thailand.

Feldstein, M. 1998. "Refocusing the IMF." *Foreign Affairs* 77 (2): 20–33.

Fisher, S. 1998. "The IMF and the Asian Crisis," Paper presented at the Forum Funds Lecture, UCLA. https://www.imf.org/external/np/speeches/1998/032098.htm (last updated March 27, 2015).

Krugman, P. 1998a. "Fire-sale FDI." Paper presented at the NBER conference on capital flows to emerging markets.

Krugman, P. 1998b. "Will Asia Bounce Back?" Speech for Credit Suisse First Boston, Hong Kong.

Krugman, P. 1998c. "Saving Asia: It's Time to Get Radical," *Fortune*, September 7, 74–80.

Lane, T. et al. 1999. *"IMF-Supported Programs in Indonesia, Korea and Thailand: A Preliminary Assessment."* International Monetary Fund, Washington, DC: International Monetary Fund.

Mundell, R. A. 1963. "Capital Mobility and Stabilization Policy under Fixed and Flexible Exchange Rates." *Canadian Journal of Economics and Political Sciences* 29: 475–485.

Sachs, J. D. 1997. "The Wrong Medicine for Asia," *New York Times*, November 3.

Siamwalla, A. and O. Sopchokchai. 1998. *Responding to the Thai Economic Crisis.* Bangkok: United Nations Development Programme.

Stiglitz, J. 1998. *Must Financial Crises Be This Frequent and This Painful?* Pittsburgh, PA: McKay Lecture.

Stiglitz, J. 2002. *Globalization and its Discontents.* W. W. Norton & Co.

Sussangkarn, C. 2002. "Economic Crisis and Recovery in Thailand: The Role of the IMF." In *Asian Economic Recovery: Policy Options for Growth and Stability*, edited by Tan Kong Yam. The Institute of Policy Studies, Singapore University Press, pp. 204–221.

Sussangkarn, C. 2011. "The Chiang Mai Initiative Multilateralization: Origin, Development and Outlook." *Asian Economic Policy Review* 6 (2): 203–220.

Sussangkarn, C. 2017. "Managing Economic Stability Under Volatile Capital Flows: East Asia Perspectives." *Asian Economic Papers* 16 (1): 174–192.

Sussangkarn, C. and P. Vichyanond. 2007. "10 Years After the Financial Crisis in Thailand: What Has Been Learned or Not Learned?" *Asian Economic Policy Review* 2 (1): 100–118.

UNCTAD. 1998. *Trade and Development Report, 1998* (Chapter 4). New York, NY and Geneva, Switzerland: United Nations Publication.

Vichyanond, P. 2002. *Non-Performing Loans (NPL) and Debt Restructuring in Thailand.* Bangkok: Thailand Development Research Institute.

World Bank. 1993. *The East Asian Miracle: Economic Growth and Public Policy.* New York, NY: Oxford University Press.

Chapter 15

Indonesia
A Tale of Three Crises

Iwan J. Azis

Introduction

Frequent currency crises occurred since the early 1980s, peaking in 1981 with 45 episodes. Sovereign debt crises were also common during that decade, peaking in 1983 with 10 debt crises. The so-called savings and loans crisis in the United States (US) also took place throughout the 1980s into the early 1990s, then the stock market crash (the "Black Monday") erupted in 1987, followed by the 1989 junk bond collapse, which resulted in a significant recession in the US. But a high frequency of financial crises with greater regional and global impact occurred during the decade of 1990s, starting with the European Monetary System (EMS) crisis in Europe where the national central banks could no longer control their domestic (short-term) interest rates, then the 1994 Tequila crisis in Mexico, followed by the 1997-98 Asian financial crisis (AFC).

For Indonesia, the AFC was a major critical event from the economic, political, and social perspectives. As the crisis erupted, the deteriorating economic conditions were exacerbated by the continuing sluggish growth in Japan, the most important trading partner and source of foreign assistance at the time. Instead, the support came from the International Monetary Fund (IMF) with strict conditionalities. The severity of the AFC went beyond trade and financial terms. Declining real wages, massive unemployment, rising poverty, and a sharp decline in the quality of life, not to mention the deterioration in social capital, all contributed to the real hardship of millions of Indonesians who had nothing to do with the creation of vulnerabilities that caused the crisis, let alone the propagation of the crisis.

What and who created the vulnerabilities and how they eventually brought about the crisis are the topics discussed in the next two sections. The bulk of the narratives in the subsequent section is devoted to the chronological events and the unfolding of the crisis, followed by the discussions on the post-AFC development in the section that follows. The latter sets the stage for the subsequent 2008-09 global financial crisis (GFC). After discussing the policies and the effects of the GFC, the role of the ultra-easy money and quantitative easing (QE) policy taken by the advanced economies (AE) as a response to the GFC is highlighted. The repercussion of those unconventional and unprecedented measures on capital flows and global liquidity was significant, and it had played a central role in the ensuing 2013 crisis known as the "taper tantrum" (TT). The unfolding event following the speech by Ben Bernanke, former Chair of the Federal Reserve, about the Federal Reserve's (Fed's) plan to taper its asset purchases rattled the Indonesian financial market. The TT crisis was a vivid reminder of the importance of securing the country's financial stability in a world financial system with free flows of capital, and the analysis shows that an external shock could clearly generate contagion and financial spillovers. The last section compares the scale and nature of the financial spillovers during the three crisis episodes, using the case of the exchange rate and the shock and volatility in the equity market.

Early Liberalization

Early on, Indonesia had an open capital account, aimed primarily at attracting foreign direct investment (FDI) to boost the economy from a sharp downturn in the 1960s. The Investment Law was promulgated in 1967 to attract FDI in mining (mostly in oil) and in selected manufacturing sectors. The government realized that to stimulate the economy, the country needed a strong industrial base supported by some heavy industries, the operations of which required foreign capital and technology. As soon as the establishment of an industrial base began, growth was reversed from negative to positive.

The upward trend continued toward the 1970s and received a further boost in 1974 when the world's oil price quadrupled following the war in the Middle East. The oil crisis (which was an oil boom for Indonesia) boosted government revenues to finance basic infrastructure — hard and soft. Problems emerged during the second half of the 1980s when the price of crude oil fell back to its 1974 level in 1986. This led to a major change in the country's development strategy.

On the financial side, the strategy began in June 1983 with domestic financial liberalization (DFL). The central bank, Bank Indonesia (BI), allowed deposit and lending rates to gradually move freely, and direct credit controls were removed, so were controls on credit allocation and rules for opening new banks. However, the state-owned banks continued to dominate. The move was soon followed by the introduction of new instruments in the money market such as daily auctions through more market-based interest rates and exchange rates, and the installment of relevant institutions for capital market operation. By the mid-1980s, only few selective controls applied to capital inflows, for example, imposing domestic ownership requirements, limiting foreign borrowings, and prohibiting the purchase of equity by foreign investors in the local stock market. But overall, the capital flow regime was fairly liberal during the period.

A major shift also took place in trade policy. After devaluing the currency in 1983 (by 28%) out of the fear of a balance of payment (BOP) crisis, a series of current account and trade liberalization (CTL) measures were taken. The resulting increase of exports, however, was short-lived. As the world oil price plunged from USD 30 to USD 10 per barrel in 1986, the government devalued the currency again, this time by 31%, and took a series of measures to reduce the economy's heavy reliance on the oil sector. The diversification measures were intended to stimulate labor-intensive exports and enhance the role of the private sector.

Realizing the large import content of most industries, firms exporting more than 85% of their products were exempt from import duties and could import inputs free of licensing restrictions. The share of foreign ownership in exporting enterprises was raised to 95%, and permits for FDI operations were extended to 30 years.[1] In addition to lowering import duties and simplifying export-licensing procedures, the government allowed companies established with foreign investments to export products manufactured by other companies and to establish joint-venture companies to export those manufactured products. Many nontariff barriers were replaced by tariffs, which would also gradually be reduced.

Both DFL and CTL entailed the pursuit of coordinated financial and exchange rate policies to provide a stable macroeconomic environment

---

[1] In addition, FDI firms exporting more than 65% of their products were allowed to hire foreign workers/experts.

necessary to sustain growth and to diversify the economy. The exchange rate was allowed to move more flexibly, and the swap premium was shifted to a market-based system with an extended maximum maturity. The encouraging results of the export strategy through greater reliance on market forces and openness to foreign investors raised government confidence to proceed with further liberalization.

A sweeping measure in the financial sector was subsequently taken in October 1988. The policy package, known as PAKTO (or *Paket Oktober*), was intended to improve the functioning and supervision of the banking system and money market, and to allow greater foreign participation through the licensing of new banks and their branches, all of which were meant to create a level playing field for all banks. For state banks, this would pose a challenging task as they could no longer maintain wide margins through thin competition as before.[2] The impact of PAKTO on private banks was significant. The number of bank branches sprouted, forcing them to compete for customers by offering a host of new services. Foreign participation was also encouraged, allowing foreign banks to have rupiah savings schemes, which was previously prohibited, and to participate in other nonbank financial institutions (NBFIs). To diversify the economy, the government required new branch offices of foreign banks to extend at least 50% of their loans to finance nonoil exports. At the same time, FDI companies were allowed to sell their foreign exchange directly to foreign exchange banks without having to sell it to the central bank (BI).

The government also broadened the range of market makers in the capital market and lengthened the maturity of money market instruments. One of such measures was to extend the maximum maturity of money market securities to 6 months. In order to supplement daily auctions, the government introduced weekly auctions of money market instruments, and the NBFIs were authorized to issue rupiah certificates of deposits (CDs). The allowance for foreign banks to receive rupiah savings had a major impact on the country's savings rate as it was accompanied by a drastic reduction in reserve requirements from 15% to 2% on foreign currency deposits and current liabilities (time and saving deposits) of all banks.

---

[2] For example, public enterprises were allowed to hold up to 50% of deposits at nonstate financial institutions.

Although liberalizing trade and liberalizing the financial sector are fundamentally different, the results of both were encouraging. Supported by an improved macroeconomic condition (low inflation and small current account deficits (CADs)), the growth impact was undisputable particularly during the first 2 years after PAKTO. The removal of credit controls resulted in an outpouring of bank lending that led to a surge in consumption and investment, while tariff cuts and reductions in nontariffs barriers helped spur exports (Figure 15.1).

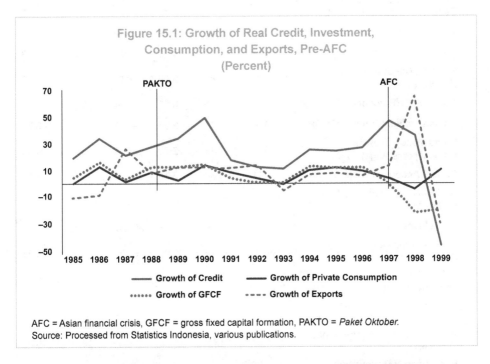

Figure 15.1: Growth of Real Credit, Investment, Consumption, and Exports, Pre-AFC (Percent)

AFC = Asian financial crisis, GFCF = gross fixed capital formation, PAKTO = Paket Oktober.
Source: Processed from Statistics Indonesia, various publications.

However, imports also surged (Table 15.1) as a considerable portion of inputs had to be imported due to the low elasticity of substitution in most exporting sectors. It was during this period that many well-managed and competitive manufacturing firms producing a wide range of labor-intensive goods for world markets flourished. FDI increased, money market improved, and the stock market surged, although with some volatility. Higher growth and investment expanded employment opportunities for a huge number of the labor force, raising real wages and lifting millions of people out of poverty.[3]

---

[3] It should be noted, however, although employment in manufacturing increased, the opposite occurred in the agricultural sector. Combined with a rapid growth of services, the employment ratio of tradable to nontradable sectors declined, while the wage ratio showed the opposite trend (Azis 2006).

Table 15.1: Selected Economic and Social Indicators, 1985–1999

Item	1985	1986	1987	1988	1989	1990
Growth of Real GDP (Percent)	2.50	5.88	4.93	5.78	7.46	7.24
Growth of Real Private Consumption (Percent)	0.00	12.15	1.68	7.74	2.04	13.57
Growth of Credit to Private Sector (Percent)	19.71	33.82	20.96	28.57	34.14	49.08
Growth of Real Government Consumption (Percent)	17.69	−1.10	−12.04	0.75	12.40	8.90
Growth of Real Gross Fixed Capital Formation (Percent)	4.60	16.26	3.37	13.43	13.60	14.82
Growth of Real Exports (Percent)	−10.81	−8.74	25.82	7.78	11.94	12.25
Growth of Real Imports	−5.88	3.72	14.56	4.91	11.24	19.33
Inflation, Consumer Prices (Annual percentage)	4.72	5.82	9.28	8.05	6.42	7.82
Total Deficit (Percent of GDP)	1.28	3.27	0.52	2.34	0.71	−1.25
Primary Deficit (Percent of GDP)	−0.52	0.36	−2.23	−0.79	−2.12	−3.78
Broad Money Growth (Annual percentage)	29.06	19.48	22.79	24.32	38.17	44.56
Current Account/GDP (Percent)	−2.25	−4.89	−2.76	−1.66	−1.17	−2.82
Real Effective Exchange Rate (2015 = 100)	231.90	178.80	130.70	126.00	126.90	123.60
Stock Index	66.53	69.69	82.58	305.12	399.69	417.00
School Enrollment, Primary (Percent net)	97.83	97.22	98.05	97.77	97.88	96.23
School Enrollment, Lower Secondary (SMP) (Percent net)	...	...	...	...	...	...
School Enrollment, Upper Secondary (SMA) (Percent net)	...	...	...	...	...	...
Pupil-Teacher Ratio, Preprimary (Percent)	21.84	21.57	18.56	18.89	19.26	16.84
Prevalence of Underweight (Percent of children under 5)	...	...	35.90	...	31.00	...
Prevalence of Underweight (Percent of adults)	23.10	22.80	22.50	22.20	21.90	21.60
Mortality Rate, Under 5, Female (Per 1,000 live births)	94.70	91.30	87.90	84.50	80.90	77.40
Mortality rate, Infant, Male (Per 1,000 live births)	80.90	78.40	75.80	73.20	70.70	68.00
Life Expectancy at Birth, Total (Years)	60.29	60.70	61.11	61.51	61.92	62.32
Poverty Gap at USD 3.20 a Day (2011 PPP) (Percent)	...	...	47.70	...	...	39.40
Gini Index (World Bank estimate)	...	...	30.60	...	...	31.20

... = not available, GDP = gross domestic product, PPP = purchasing power parity, SMA = *Sekolah Menengah Atas*, SMP = *Sekolah Menengah Pertama*.
Source: Author's compilation from various sources.

1991	1992	1993	1994	1995	1996	1997	1998	1999
6.91	6.50	6.50	7.54	8.22	7.82	4.70	−13.13	0.79
8.14	4.21	−0.84	9.69	11.65	9.18	3.56	−4.54	9.95
17.47	12.20	10.33	24.97	24.21	26.58	46.73	35.99	−46.72
2.47	10.90	0.98	−3.30	4.42	4.21	−5.32	−27.72	16.92
3.83	0.51	−0.05	12.82	11.59	12.27	0.12	−21.96	−20.18
11.01	13.85	−5.99	6.56	7.41	5.82	12.95	65.17	−32.42
10.68	9.04	−6.66	14.77	17.95	3.11	11.41	33.45	−36.03
9.42	7.52	9.67	8.53	9.42	7.97	6.23	58.45	20.48
0.88	1.23	0.52	−1.00	−1.32	−0.76	−0.58	1.38	2.84
−1.34	−1.00	−1.35	−2.60	−2.78	−2.00	−2.30	−2.06	−1.05
17.53	19.62	20.06	20.20	27.52	27.08	25.25	62.76	12.23
−3.65	−2.17	−1.33	−1.58	−3.18	−3.37	−2.27	4.29	4.13
121.10	117.40	121.80	121.10	117.20	126.00	119.50	57.50	84.50
247.00	274.00	588.00	469.00	513.00	637.00	401.00	398.04	676.92
95.32	94.46	93.25	93.79	93.61	92.52	92.46	...	...
...	...	...	50.03	50.96	54.53	57.84	56.96	59.23
...	...	...	33.22	32.60	34.80	36.61	37.23	38.49
17.37	17.28	17.58	16.70	16.96	16.81	17.29	17.74	...
...	29.80	...	...	...	30.30	...	25.80	22.80
21.30	21.00	20.70	20.40	20.00	19.70	19.30	19.00	18.60
73.80	70.30	67.00	63.70	60.70	57.80	55.00	52.40	50.10
65.40	62.80	60.30	57.90	55.50	53.20	51.00	48.90	46.90
62.73	63.13	63.53	63.92	64.29	64.64	64.95	65.24	65.51
...	...	39.20	...	...	32.60	...	44.20	29.80
...	...	32.00	...	...	34.50	...	31.10	31.10

Indeed, an encouraging trend also occurred in the nonmacroeconomic front. Prior to the AFC, Indonesia achieved substantial progress in poverty reduction and improved income distribution and other social conditions especially in health and education (Table 15.1). The combined sustained growth, stable macroeconomic conditions, and improved income inequality led the World Bank to include Indonesia in the list of "Miracle" countries in their well-known publication *The East Asian Miracle: Economic Growth and Public Policy* (World Bank 1993).

To discern the true and precise forces behind this impressive performance, however, is more complex than it seems. Some argued that it was driven by fundamental factors such as the stable macroeconomic environment, the legal framework for competition, and increased investments in people (education and health). These factors, as the argument goes, helped improve the country's productivity and resource allocation. Others, however, associated the performance with the expected dynamic gains of activist government policies through, among others, industrial policies that altered the industrial structure, even at the expense of static allocative efficiency.

While both views carry some elements of credibility, it is a gross exaggeration to claim that Indonesia's achievements were entirely caused by market-based competition and orthodoxy. The government had in fact continued to intervene extensively in both product markets and factor markets. A business network of personal and political favoritism was widespread, and state-owned enterprises continued to hold monopoly power in some sectors. In the financial sector, despite PAKTO, only a few commercial banks continued to control a large share of an oligopolistic market structure, and their shareholders were large industrial groups (conglomerates). Indeed, the structure of banking and nonbanking financial institutions corresponded very closely to the pattern of distribution of economic power.[4] Either in a quasi or direct way, these conglomerates were the largest borrowers. In general, Indonesia's industrial organization structure — marked by a high industrial concentration — shaped the nature of the country's financial structure, not vice versa.

The fact that bank loans constitute almost two-thirds of total corporate finance tells a lot about the nature of Indonesia's corporate finance during

---

[4] There was no anti-monopoly law until after the AFC (Law Number 5/1999 Concerning the Prohibition of Monopolistic Practices and Unfair Business Competition).

the time. Moreover, while the official prudential requirements for domestic banks were basically in line the Basel Committee recommendations, weak enforcement simply added to the problem. Data show that prior to the AFC, 15 out of 240 banks failed to meet the minimum CAR, and 41 did not comply with the legal lending limit.

Equally inaccurate is to assert that the selectivity in industrial policy to promote "winners" by providing incentives across and among sectors (similar to what Japan, Korea, and Singapore did) was behind the success. The government did not really possess the knowledge about what would be the winning sectors, what specific interventions were needed (in addition to the existing ones), let alone how the positive spillover effects of those sectors would compensate for any inefficiencies generated by the interventions.

The country's industrial policies at the time were actually not that different from those adopted in other developing countries: not properly integrated with trade policy, rampant with poor governance, and inefficient competitors continued to be among the most active and effective players to gain the government's special treatments. As discussed in the next section, some of them, especially the big "conglomerates," had actually played an important role in setting the stage for the 1997 crisis. At any rate, evidence that industrial policy had systematically promoted sectors with high productivity was either very weak or nonexistent.

A more accurate assertion would be a mixture of some elements of both. Improvements in macro fundamentals clearly provided the necessary environment to mobilize resources to boost spending for the country's social overhead capital (e.g., health and education), and high concentration of few players controlling corporate empires allowed the economy to grow fairly strongly. These conglomerates often owned a family bank that received state revenues, foreign aid and foreign direct, and portfolio investments, and had a better access to offshore banks and diverse sources of finance such as derivatives. Absent proper regulations, most of these family-run banks allocated a large portion of loans to either single individuals, select groups, or closely related firms of their own. By 1995, it was reported that almost half of all private bank's assets had been in-house lending, consumed by loans to related firms.

It is also important to note that steady growth achievements did not happen smoothly. The process following liberalization exposed some policy trade-offs. To support higher growth of credit, consumption, and investment, which allowed gross domestic product (GDP) growth to hover above 7% per annum, money supply (M2) had to increase. The early 1990s case was a notable example where inflation surged, the real exchange rate (RER) appreciated, and the CAD increased as a result.

When the economy overheated, the authority had to implement a tight monetary policy (TMP). As it turned out, making the policy effective was more difficult than originally thought.

Because of the export-bias trade policy, some sort of trade-off emerged. The early attempt to raise the interest rates failed to sustain inflation reduction, even though active open market operations (OMO) were supported by nonconventional policy (e.g., redeeming central bank promissory notes purchased from state-owned enterprises). The inflation rate jumped to reach close to 10% in 1990 and 1991. A persistent increase in subsidized export credit to support exports was among the reasons behind the failure to lower inflation, and the authority finally decided to eliminate the currency swap mechanism.

In the meantime, a sharp increase in nonbudgetary spending exposed an inconsistency between monetary and fiscal policy. Technocrats in charge of macroeconomic policy tried to resist nonbudgetary spending and succeeded in terminating export credit. The move, however, was not without costs: some important positions in the post-election cabinet were lost. As downward pressures on the exchange rate mounted, the authority widened the band repeatedly, the last one before the AFC occurred in 1996, in which the rupiah was allowed to fluctuate within a 5% range.

But overall credit, consumption, and investment failed to revive GDP growth, forcing the authority to lower the interest rates in 1993. As expected, some macroeconomic indicators began to deteriorate: inflation surged to reach a double-digit figure in the following year before it gradually declined to less than 7% in 1996.

The CAD persistently widened to reach USD 7.6 billion in the same year. Hence, the Indonesian experience with policy trade-off at the time — between controlling inflation and boosting nonoil exports — reflects a typical small open economy case.

Building Up Vulnerability

The mixture of increased reliance on market forces — albeit with interventions — and the dominance of few players in some sectors worked fairly effectively to produce growth. But the system gradually divulged weaknesses that soon became the ingredients of vulnerability.

First of all, pressures to maintain high growth led to explicit and implicit public guarantees to many private projects. In some cases, the projects also received subsidies. Credits were directed to favored firms with little consideration over costs, risks, and externalities. The close links between public and private institutions gave a strong impression that associated projects were somewhat "insured" against adverse shocks. To sustain such a system, capital accumulation continued even when the profitability of new investment projects was low. In an undercapitalized economy with investment opportunities, financing capital accumulation with borrowing was considered an optimal course of action. In the end, the combination of excess investment and increased debt inflows resulted in a wider CAD.

Much of the debt inflows were facilitated by financial intermediation. It was during that period that many Indonesian conglomerates established finance houses, insurance and leasing-factoring subsidiaries, and other forms of securities firms. They managed to arrange large syndicated loans as international banks were more than willing to lend large amounts of funds and paid little attention to sound risk assessment. It was a moral hazard at play, where the key influential factors were the implicit guarantee or potential bail-out (either by the government or by external parties such as the IMF).

As shown in Table 15.2, Indonesia's private external debt increased dramatically and more than tripled during the period of 1990–1997. At the time, falling interest rates in AE (especially Japan) lowered the cost of capital and prompted large inflows into Asian countries including Indonesia. A considerable portion of the flows was in the form of debt, channeled through either the banking sector or the direct transfers to corporate borrowers. Most were short term and used to finance projects with questionable social benefits but were profitable from the private point of view. The largest lenders to Indonesia were Japanese banks, followed by the European and the US banks. For borrowers, the relatively stable exchange rate lowered the risk premium on dollar-denominated debt and eliminated the need to hedge. The intriguing question is, given the risks of such a large increase of short-term debt, why did the authority allow that to happen?

On this issue, some argued that the only information about corporate debt that the authority (in this case BI) had at the time was only the debt made with loan contracts, and the published data on other corporate debt were also incomplete. It was reported that the authority had requested large debtors (mostly conglomerates) to report the details of their external borrowing. Indeed, data on private debt were actually available from as far back as 1970, as shown in the World Bank's debt data. But the accepted concept about the key indicators of vulnerability did not include private debt at that time. It was not about data being unavailable but about misconceiving the risks of crisis.

In the end, the debt figures were released and appeared in the first letter of intent (LOI) between the government and the IMF (discussed in the next section): USD 140 billion, about 60% of GDP, of which USD 33 billion was short term (defined as having less-than 1-year maturity). The estimated private portion of the total debt was roughly USD 80 billion. Based on the yearly data from the World Bank shown in Table 15.2, Indonesia's total external debt for the entire year of 1997 was recorded at USD 136.3 billion, of which the public share of long-term debt was around USD 56 billion, and the private share was USD 44.5 billion. The bulk of the remaining short-term external debt, almost USD 33 billion out of USD 36 billion, was private debt.

Another intriguing question is: Were Indonesia's macroeconomic "fundamentals" strong at that time, and if so, why did the country fall into crisis? Most analysts are of the view that macroeconomic data on Indonesia during the years before the AFC did not show signs of vulnerability. In addition to data on the growth of consumption, investment, and GDP, the traditional measures of macroeconomic "fundamentals" should include the current account, fiscal balance, and inflation; these were considered the "usual suspects." Based on such indicators (Table 15.1), one could not classify Indonesia as fundamentally vulnerable prior to the AFC. Up to 1996, the country's inflation rate was fairly low, consistently at a single-digit level, mainly because of the government's prudent management of the budget. In some years, the fiscal balance was even in surplus. Trade diversification also worked well: exports grew steadily until 1995, before slowing down in 1996. As a result, the CAD was kept low although it slightly increased in 1996 to 4.3%. Reasons behind the export slowdown in 1996 were detected: more than 40% devaluation of Chinese yuan in 1994, stronger US dollar, capital inflows that put upward pressure on exchange rate, and increased competition from other emerging markets (EMs). Also important to note is that the slight widening of CAD occurred because of increased imports, particularly those of the capital and intermediate goods category, reflecting strong investment and import-dependent exports.

Historical experience suggests, however, that to evaluate a country's "fundamentals" one should go beyond simply looking at the "usual suspects." A high economic growth could still weaken the "fundamentals" as the episode of Indonesia's overheating economy during the 1990s have shown. Also, the traditional view that strong economic growth makes the CAD sustainable deserves clarifications.

The question of sustainability should be approached by looking at the intertemporal decisions underlying the CAD. Since the current account balance is equal to the difference between savings and investment, any fall in savings or increase in investment could affect the current account balance. Sustainability is less problematic if external borrowing is used to finance productive capacity that increases exports. On the other hand, if the increased CAD is driven by falling savings, the country's "fundamentals" tend to weaken. A slightly trickier way to look at sustainability associated with the CAD is by linking the deficit with the size of debt and real interest rates. If the debt-to-GDP ratio is high, the gap of the real interest rates and the GDP growth is wide, and the current account surplus that is required to stabilize the debt-to-GDP ratio in the long run would tend to get larger. The difference between the real interest rate and output growth for Indonesia, which was 3.3% before the AFC, is relatively high but not too high by a normal standard.

Another view is that a better and more appropriate approach to evaluate a country's "fundamentals" should include information beyond traditional indicators. One such approach is to focus on selected key variables that reflect a stricter interpretation of "fundamentals": the RER, the strength of the banking system, and the size of foreign reserves. An appreciation of the first, combined with weakness of the second, would quality for weak "'fundamentals."

Figure 15.2 helps put these indicators in perspective. If there was no real appreciation and/or the banking system was not weak, Indonesia's "fundamentals" would be classified as strong. Whether capital outflows have significant negative impact on the economy or not depends on the country's size of foreign reserves. A possible scenario would be having capital outflows but only of limited amount, such that no devaluation expectation or speculative crisis would occur. On the other hand, if Indonesia suffers from an excessive and sustained real exchange rate appreciation and/or having a weak banking system, the country's "fundamentals" would be considered weak. If, however, foreign reserves were ample, the best it could expect was to have a limited amount of capital outflows. Otherwise, a large outflow would occur when the size of foreign reserves is small, in which case a multiple equilibria scenario driven by a circularity mechanism is likely to happen: that is, devaluation depends on capital outflow, but outflow itself depends on the expectation of devaluation. As soon as a self-fulfilling panic took place,

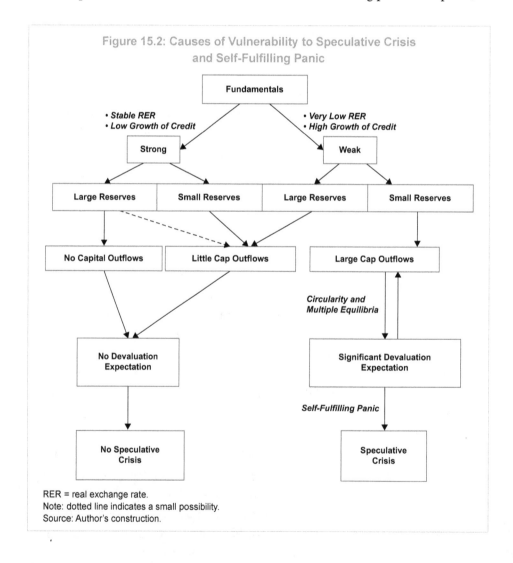

Figure 15.2: Causes of Vulnerability to Speculative Crisis and Self-Fulfilling Panic

RER = real exchange rate.
Note: dotted line indicates a small possibility.
Source: Author's construction.

a speculative crisis would occur. The rationale of the above framework is similar to Sachs, Tornell, and Velasco (1996).

Based on such a framework, Indonesia's annual growth of credits since the early 1990s was roughly 18%, before it accelerated to 26.6% in 1996. No RER appreciation was detected before the AFC.[5] Hence, using a stricter interpretation, one cannot conclude that Indonesia had weak "fundamentals" before the AFC.

What about the size of foreign reserves? This can be evaluated in different ways. In addition to using a traditional measure (the size of reserves converted into the number of months of imports), foreign reserves should also be compared to the domestic currency deposit. Given the quasi-fixed exchange rate system and full convertibility of Indonesia's capital account, a depositor could withdraw rupiah from banks and convert it into dollars at the announced parity (currency substitution). Unless there were sufficient foreign reserves to honor such a demand, a financial system could suffer from illiquidity if it held excessive domestic liabilities. Hence, the ratio of M2 over foreign reserves matters (Azis 2006). Looking at the Indonesian data, the ratio before the onset of the AFC was around 6.3. While it was high compared to those in other Asian crisis countries (except Korea), it was clearly below the ratio in Mexico before the country suffered from the 1994 crisis. Hence, even when considering the possibility of currency substitution, Indonesia's "fundamentals" were not the raison d'être for its vulnerability.

Yet another approach is to consider the size of foreign reserves as a measure of the country's capacity to repay external debt. As discussed earlier, the size of short-term external private debt had increased, mostly incurred by the large corporate sector (conglomerates). Following financial liberalization, the ratio between the short-term external debt and foreign reserves had been persistently higher than unity, implying that the short-term debt was greater than readily available foreign reserves. By 1996, the ratio had reached 166% before peaking at 188% in 1997, which easily put Indonesia into a vulnerable category. Note that the ratio of total private debt-to-foreign reserves in those 2 years reached 189% and 254%, respectively (bottom rows of Table 15.2).

---

[5] Using the consumer price index (CPI), J.P. Morgan found that Indonesia's real effective exchange rate (REER) had depreciated by 5.4% (Azis 2002a). By applying a monetary model and using data on a purchasing power parity (PPP) basis, Chinn (1998) showed that even if the rupiah were overvalued, the size of the overvaluation was smaller than in crisis-free countries. In particular, the overvaluation was less than 5%, way below what happened in the country during the AFC.

Table 15.2: Debt and Foreign Reserves, 1990–1999

Item	1990	1991	1992	1993
External Debt (ED) (USD million)	69,848.51	79,528.20	87,987.35	89,157.13
1. Short Term (ST)	11,135.30	14,314.80	18,057.10	17,987.00
2. Long Term (LT)	58,219.29	65,047.86	69,930.25	71,170.13
3. LT – Public (PB)	47,958.79	51,871.86	53,649.25	57,141.13
4. LT – Private (PR)	10,260.50	13,176.00	16,281.00	14,029.00
5. Others (OTH)	493.91	165.54	0.00	0.00
6. Lending Banks				
a. Japan	15,124.00	16,730.00	16,767.00	16,401.00
b. United States	1,228.00	1,552.00	1,961.00	2,414.00
c. Europe	3,861.00	4,276.00	4,540.00	5,521.00
d. Others	1,955.00	2,172.00	2,594.00	3,349.00
Foreign Reserves (FR) (USD million)	8,656.79	10,357.99	11,482.02	12,474.06
ST/FR	1.29	1.38	1.57	1.44
PR/FR	1.19	1.27	1.42	1.12

USD = United States dollar.
Source: World Bank and author's compilation from various sources.

Then there is a question about measuring the health of the banking system. Although the growth of the bank's credit was relatively low, the allocation of it — by extension also the size of nonperforming loans (NPLs) — matters, so does the bank's capital ratio. Using such measures, data show that Indonesia's banking system was indeed far from healthy. Note, however, that data on NPLs were problematic; the difference between official data and alternate estimates from other institutions was fairly large. For example, according to the official data, the NPLs in 1996 and 1997 were 9.5% and 8.1%, respectively, while according to the IMF and the BIS, they were 12.9% and 14.0%.[6] Meanwhile, data of the bank's capital ratio CAR show that it fell from 11.8% to 9.2% during the same period. In terms of allocation, the proportion of credit going to the property sector increased, reaching between 25% and 30%. Even these statistics did not do justice in describing the overall banking

---

[6] Another problem with NPLs is that poor loan portfolios can be disguised until they are recognized when the crisis arrives. Hence, it does not really measure the health of the banking system at the time the data show.

1994	1995	1996	1997	1998	1999
107,819.78	124,399.50	129,003.51	136,339.70	151,484.84	151,806.50
19,457.00	25,966.30	32,230.44	32,865.00	20,112.70	20,029.08
88,362.78	98,433.20	96,773.07	100,504.37	122,282.15	121,201.17
63,921.83	65,310.01	60,078.73	56,035.60	67,553.85	73,936.30
24,440.95	33,123.19	36,694.34	44,468.77	54,728.30	47,264.87
0.00	0.00	0.00	2,970.34	9,089.99	10,576.25
18,351.00	20,974.00	22,035.00	22,018.00	16,403.00	12,494.00
2,454.00	2,778.00	5,279.00	4,893.00	3,537.00	3,454.00
6,201.00	8,841.00	13,106.00	13,003.00	10,586.00	9,280.00
5,059.00	7,721.00	10,296.00	12,509.00	11,164.00	13,459.00
13,321.14	14,907.56	19,396.15	17,486.80	23,605.84	27,345.10
1.46	1.74	1.66	1.88	0.85	0.73
1.83	2.22	1.89	2.54	2.32	1.73

system as it overlooked the quality and enforcement of bank regulation. As argued earlier, most conglomerates set up their own banks to finance their excessive spending and accumulate the external debt. Financing own affiliated companies was a common practice at the time, especially among big companies belonging to the same people or group who also own the banks. The fact that it was allowed to occur suggests that the country had a questionable regulatory and supervisory framework, making the banking system and corporate governance weak.

In sum, Indonesia's vulnerability prior to the AFC was associated with increased private external debt as a result of poor governance (implicit guarantees, which downplayed the price signals) and a weak banking system following DFL and CTL (intermediating funds with lax regulation), both of which were enabled by the external conditions at the time (low interest rates abroad). All these occurred in an environment where Asia was generally seen as a region with stellar records, as elucidated in the "East Asian Miracle," hence Indonesia continued to be a favorite destination to invest.

Chronicle of Events: Contagion and Unfolding the AFC

Some analysts argue that reversed expectations of market players over future investment profitability played a key role in triggering the AFC (Corden 1999; Krugman 1999; McKibbin and Stoeckel 1999; Woo, Sachs, and Schwab 2000). While that may be true, the question remains: what caused the changes in expectations? For Indonesia, the contagion from Thailand that began in July 1997 is often quoted as the trigger. The floating of the Thai baht on July 2 (first time in 14 years) intensified the pressure on the rupiah. How big was the scale of the spillover?

By applying the variance decomposition based on vector autoregression (VAR) for the period of July 1997–June 1998, and focusing on the shock volatility (Azis et al. 2013; Azis, Virananda, and Estiko 2021), Table 15.3 displays the results that can help answer the question. Looking at Thailand as the transmitter (the column) and other countries as receivers (the row), the effect of exchange rate spillover from the baht on the Indonesian rupiah did not actually occur directly but indirectly through the baht's effect on the Singapore dollar and the Philippines peso. As shown in Table 15.3, the percentage shares of forecast error variance of the spillover from the Thai baht to those two currencies were 0.140% and 0.070%, and the percentage shares of the spillover effects of the two on the rupiah were 0.080% and 0.040%, respectively, higher than the direct spillover from the Thai baht on the rupiah (0.016%).

Table 15.3: FX Spillover Index, July 1997–June 1998

Item	FX_JP	FX_CN	FX_IN	FX_KR	FX_ID	FX_TH	FX_MY	FX_PH	FX_SG
FX_JP	0.8492	0.0041	0.0126	0.0201	0.0335	0.0002	0.0712	0.0001	0.0089
FX_CN	0.0137	0.8969	0.0245	0.0306	0.0007	0.0276	0.0019	0.0003	0.0038
FX_IN	0.0035	0.0109	0.7431	0.1096	0.0491	0.0008	0.0560	0.0012	0.0258
FX_KR	0.0220	0.0717	0.0422	0.7924	0.0134	0.0068	0.0112	0.0122	0.0282
FX_ID	0.0711	0.0024	0.0268	0.1459	0.6294	0.0016	0.0034	0.0403	0.0791
FX_TH	0.0430	0.0079	0.0060	0.1926	0.0409	0.6696	0.0072	0.0172	0.0157
FX_MY	0.0559	0.0006	0.0285	0.1256	0.2418	0.1200	0.4054	0.0208	0.0014
FX_PH	0.0892	0.0062	0.0503	0.1819	0.1160	0.0718	0.0610	0.3933	0.0303
FX_SG	0.1820	0.0129	0.0002	0.0672	0.1030	0.1375	0.1656	0.0211	0.3105

FX = exchange rate, CN = China, ID = Indonesia, IN = India, JP = Japan, KR = Korea, MY = Malaysia, PH = the Philippines, SG = Singapore, TH = Thailand.
Note: Each cell denotes the percentage share of forecast error variance from spillover.
Source: Author's calculations.

The spillover effect, however, went beyond the exchange rate. To evaluate the effects on variables such as GDP growth rate and the inflation rate, the impulse response function (IRF) was calculated by using the Cholesky decomposition in the following order: exchange rate → GDP growth → inflation rate. To the extent a contagion process always occurred during a crisis, it is also of interest to compare the spillovers among Asian countries under different crisis episodes.[7] Using the period that covers the AFC (1991–2000), one covering the GFC (2001–2010), and 2011–2020 to cover the TT and the ongoing coronavirus disease (COVID-19) crisis, the scale of macro spillover during the period covering the AFC appears to be quite considerable. The scale is bigger than during the GFC and is, for now, only slightly smaller than the spillover during the period covering the TT and the ongoing COVID-19 crisis (Figure 15.3).[8] Hence, while the Thai baht devaluation in early July indeed sparked a contagion in Indonesia, albeit indirectly, the spillover effect went beyond just the exchange rate to include other macroeconomic variables, the detailed events of which are described in Figure 15.3.

Fearful that the currency would continue to lose value against the US dollar, many Indonesian companies with external debt began to sell the local currency in increasing quantities. In response, the monetary authority took a standard tightening policy, that is, raising the interest (*Sertifikat Bank Indonesia* (SBI)) rates from 6% to 15% for a 6-day period, and from 7% to 10% for a period of more than a week, intervening in the foreign exchange market (with some USD 500 million sold), and widening the exchange rate band (to 12%). In addition, BI also froze commercial papers (*Surat Berharga Pasar Uang* (SBPU)) and called on domestic banks to support the rupiah. Ironically, more intervention caused more intensified speculative attacks. As the repeated attempts to defend the rupiah failed, and as foreign reserves continued to deplete, on August 14, the government finally gave in and let the rupiah float.

[7] The Spillover Index is calculated from the variance decomposition based on VAR estimation of quarterly data of inflation, GDP growth, and foreign exchange (USD:IDR). The variance decomposition allows us to split the forecast error variances of each variable into parts attributable to the various system shocks (i.e., fraction of error variance x_1 that is contributed from x_1, x_2, and so on). The i,j-th value within the spillover matrix is then constructed from the error variance of the 10-period-ahead returns. The Spillover Index is subsequently calculated by dividing the off-diagonal sum with the total sum of this matrix. The off-diagonal column sums denote the contribution *to* others and the off-diagonal row sums denote the contribution *from* others. Given the directional spillover from the columns and rows, the net spillover for a given variable can be calculated as the difference between its contribution *to* others and its contribution *from* others.

[8] Due to differences in the nature and the coverage of each crisis episode, however, the US was included in the calculation as another potential transmitter of spillovers. Note also that two crisis episodes were covered in the 2011–2020 period; the 2013 "TT" and COVID-19.

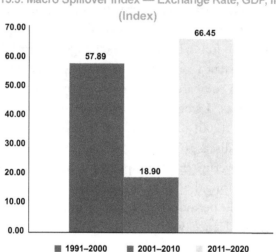

Figure 15.3: Macro Spillover Index — Exchange Rate, GDP, Inflation (Index)

GDP = gross domestic product.

Notes: The index indicates the extent to which the variance or fluctuation of each variable is caused by the spillover of volatility in the other variables. Hence, an index of 57.89 during 1991–2000 means that 57.89% of the exchange rate variance is due to the spillovers from gross domestic product and inflation volatility, not from the exchange rate volatility itself.

Source: Author's calculations.

The praise from IMF strengthened BI confidence that it was doing the right thing, despite the fact that it actually made things worse as the rupiah depreciated further and interest-sensitive businesses started to feel the pinch of higher rates.[9] Alas, with confidence, BI raised the interest rates again, from 10.5% to 20% for 1 week, and from 22% to 30% for 2 weeks. It also restricted the forward selling transactions of foreign currency from local banks to foreigners by putting a cap at USD 5 million per customer and per position per bank (swap transactions for foreign trade and investment were exempted). The rupiah, however, continued to slide.[10]

---

[9] In the IMF News Brief No. 97/18, August 14, 1997, Stanley Fischer, the IMF's acting Managing Director, remarked, "The management of the IMF welcomes the timely decisions of the Indonesian authorities. The floating of the rupiah, in combination with Indonesia's strong fundamentals, supported by prudent fiscal and monetary policies, will allow its economy to continue its impressive economic performance of the last several years."

[10] At that point, some people began to question the conventional wisdom of an open economy often cited in macroeconomic textbooks that raising interest rates would reduce, if not reverse, capital outflows and thence strengthen the country's currency. Argued by Kindleberger (1996), this conventional wisdom holds only during normal times, and the relationship is actually reversed during a financial panic. A similar argument was made by Sachs (1999). Referring to the AFC episode, Furman and Stiglitz (1998) found that in 13 crisis episodes in 9 emerging markets, the temporarily high interest rates were associated with exchange rate depreciation, not appreciation. Gould and Kamin (1999) showed that the exchange rates in the region were not affected by changes in the interest rate but were influenced by credit spreads and stock prices.

Facing a severe liquidity problem, many state-owned companies withdrew IDR 12 trillion deposits from BI, almost half of their total deposits. To alleviate the liquidity crunch, BI began to lower the SBI rate from 39% to 27% for 1 month, and from 28% to 25% for 3 months (a rollback of monetary tightening).

But few banks were actually lending, because market confidence had already been shattered. Even with ministers' repeated announcements that the government would postpone several infrastructure projects to restore confidence, market reacted skeptically, and speculative attacks continued. This led President Suharto to announce on September 22 that some 81 infrastructure projects worth more than USD 17 billion would be postponed as part of a reform package. That did not stop the rupiah from sliding.

Apparently the market was more concerned with something else. In several interviews, many brokers clearly expressed their concern toward the mounting short-term external debt. They believed that the amount was much larger than reported. Indeed, the power of information (or lack thereof) was on full display. As the BI Governor conceded, he simply had no idea about it, and there was nothing the government could do to make the debt disappear; investors rushed for the exits, and Indonesia saw its first defaults. While market intervention continued, the authority also tried to attract foreign currencies from exporters to boost foreign reserves by introducing swap facilities awarding exporters and forward buying facilities for imports if the imported goods were used to produce export products. But the repeated failure to restore confidence made the government no longer able to stomach the market reaction. On October 8, the government officially asked the IMF for assistance. Indonesia was entering the new saga.

After a technical mission was sent to Jakarta, Michel Camdessus (the then IMF Managing Director) continued to declare that Indonesia's fundamentals were sound, despite the rupiah's new low of IDR 3,845 against the dollar (a more than 30% depreciation). As many had predicted, the government and the IMF had to go through difficult negotiations on the conditions for aid. In late October, Japan and Singapore pledged USD 5 billion each, and Malaysia and Australia USD 1 billion each, probably in the hope that President Suharto would declare that he needed only expertise and not money from the IMF (Vatikiotis 1997). But by the end of the month, a LOI had been submitted along with a Memorandum on Economic and Financial Policies (MEFP), which contained conditionalities as prerequisites for receiving IMF financial support. By that time, the cumulative depreciation of the rupiah since the crisis began in July had already exceeded 30%, and the stock market had fallen by 35%, both indicating the largest declines in the region.

In addition to a standard macroeconomic policy of tightening, the LOI essentially comprised of two components: dealing with the financial sector (insolvent banks and bank supervision) and dealing with the real sector of the economy (overcoming structural rigidities, including governance issues). On the policy of tightening, it appears that the experience of handling the Latin American crisis just 3 years before the AFC had convinced the IMF that a traditional policy mix of monetary tightening and fiscal restraints was appropriate for Indonesia and other crisis countries in Asia.[11] On removing structural rigidities, the experience with policy reform in Eastern Europe and the former Soviet Union (to shift from a socialist to a market economy) during the 1990s could have inspired the IMF to do the same with Indonesia.

One of the sticking points in the negotiation was about the IMF's demand to close insolvent banks. While the proposal made sense, the counterarguments pointed to the risk of bank run due to the fact that at the time, Indonesia did not have a formal deposit insurance scheme in place. After long and difficult negotiations, on November 5, the authorities agreed to enter into a 3-year Stand-By Arrangement with the IMF for USD 10 billion, which was augmented by USD 1.4 billion in July 1998. In addition, multilateral institutions pledged USD 8 billion and bilateral donors USD 18 billion as the second line of defense."[12] The government finally agreed to close 16 banks as demanded by the IMF.

What was feared about bank runs quickly came into reality: bank closures prompted a panic. Savings of thousands of people had to be frozen, and it cost 6,000 bank employees their livelihoods. In a matter of days, panic shifted to the government. While originally it was announced that no guarantee would be given to deposits, the government changed its position

---

[11]Nobel laureate James Tobin believed that the IMF's Asian packages were based on its experiences with Mexico in 1994 (Tobin and Ranis 1998).

[12]The total dollar amount of the rescue package was unclear. The popularly known amount was USD 43 billion, consisting of SDR 7.3 billion for a 3-year stand-by loan from the IMF (through an emergency procedure) which amounted to USD 18 billion when combined with support from the World Bank and the Asian Development Bank (ADB), Indonesia's own reserves for BOP support amounting to USD 5 billion, and the remaining amount from bilateral supporters in a second line of defense, which in the end was never been used.

by guaranteeing deposits up to IDR 20 million per depositor account at 16 closed banks. However, a panic bank run deepened. As the public realized that larger deposits would not be guaranteed, a rush of withdrawals from many banks occurred. Even at the country's largest private institution, Bank Central Asia, account holders pulled out and headed for the safety of state banks. Prompted by such development and the fear of possible systemic impact of it, in January 1998, the government changed its position again by declaring that it would provide a blanket coverage of all deposits in all domestic banks (a so-called blanket guarantee). Ironically, on the same day of the announcement the government also declared that some 15 infrastructure projects that were originally postponed would now be given the go-ahead.

Entering 1998, the deteriorating market began to hit many firms and companies. According to one estimate, three out of four companies were deemed unhealthy. The crisis also spilled over across countries and assets (regional prices of commodities fell). As depicted in Figure 15.4A and 15.4B, the accelerated drop in investment began during the first quarter of the year and the largest fall occurred in the third quarter. In the last quarter, the fall continued, and the decline of GDP was made more severe by the steepest drop in consumption (the largest GDP component). As a result, for the entire year, the overall GDP fell by more than 13%, largest among the Asian crisis countries.

Poverty increased dramatically as indicated by a jump in the poverty gap. By sector, the utilities sector of electricity, gas, and water supply was the only one that avoided a negative growth for the year.

The three sectors suffering from the largest fall were trade-hotel-restaurant, construction, and manufacturing. In all three, the fall occurred persistently in every quarter of the year. Notable in Figure 15.4B is the growth pattern of the agricultural sector. In the second and fourth quarters, the sector managed to register an increase despite the severe prolonged effect of the El Niño drought in that year.[13] Part of the reason was most of the adverse impacts of the crisis hit the main island of Jawa, not the agriculture-dominated non-Jawa region where the majority of plantations were located.

---

[13] Together with the economic crisis, the El Niño phenomenon contributed to the deterioration of food supply situation and a major forest fire. The World Bank estimated that up to 50 million Indonesians faced problems in maintaining an acceptable caloric intake, while the haze layer caused by the forest fire expanded over an area of more than 3,000,000 km² (1,200,000 sq mi), covering large parts of Sumatra and Kalimantan, and reached Malaysia, Singapore, Brunei, Thailand, and the Philippines, as well as Sri Lanka. The cause of the fire, however, was not only caused by El Niño but also man-made sources.

Together with some mining products, plantation and other agricultural exports enjoyed greater competitiveness due to the weakening rupiah. This partly explains why income inequality slightly improved as indicated by a fall of the Gini index from 34.5 in 1996 to 31.1 in 1998.

As shown in Figure 15.4A, in every quarter during 1998, exports were the only component experiencing a positive growth. On the other hand, the fall of investment led to a sharp drop in imports during the fourth quarter. As a result, for the first time in more than a decade, the current account balance turned positive (surplus), which lasted for more-than a decade before returning to deficit in 2012.

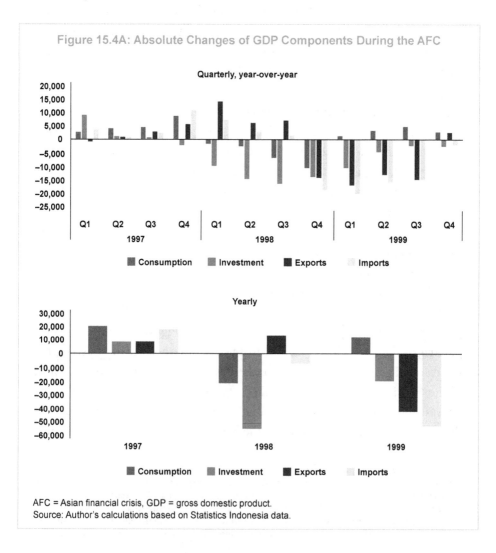

Figure 15.4A: Absolute Changes of GDP Components During the AFC

AFC = Asian financial crisis, GDP = gross domestic product.
Source: Author's calculations based on Statistics Indonesia data.

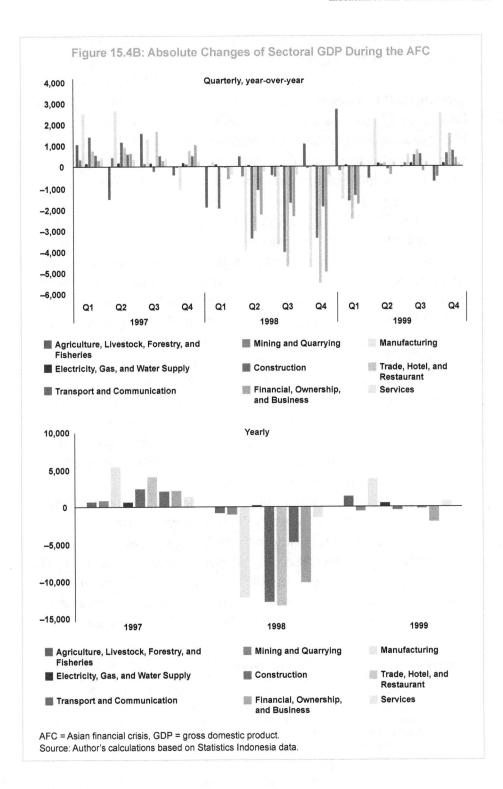

Figure 15.4B: Absolute Changes of Sectoral GDP During the AFC

AFC = Asian financial crisis, GDP = gross domestic product.
Source: Author's calculations based on Statistics Indonesia data.

Over a 5-day period, the rupiah plunged to IDR 10,000 to the dollar, down more than 70% since the crisis began in July 1997. This prompted a talk among market players that Indonesia might declare a debt moratorium. The effects of the IMF program on the socio-economic and political environment began to bite. In particular, the IMF austerity program heightened the likelihood of social unrest prior to the March presidential poll. It caused panic buying of food as people feared that prices would spiral. The perception was strong that the Indonesian government was not tough enough to negotiate with the IMF over the demanded austerity program.

In the midst of widespread doubt that the government would implement the agreed IMF program, a glimmer of hope appeared when it was reported that US President Bill Clinton called the Asian leaders, and President Suharto later pledged his commitment to implement the economic reforms. But the hope was short-lived, as Stanley Fischer arrived in Jakarta on January 11 with additional reform measures. Among others, the new proposal called for significant new structural reforms, including lifting subsidies for energy, dismantling domestic trade restrictions in several industries, establishing greater independence for BI, reducing selected foreign investment barriers, and ending support for Indonesia's national automobile program and national aircraft program. Most of these proposed reforms had very little to do with recovering the tattered economy, especially those areas that were outside IMF expertise and mandate. If anything, they created confusion and consequently worsened the already gloomy public mood.[14]

Pressures for Indonesia to quickly implement the reform intensified, including from US Defense Secretary William Cohen, and Deputy Treasury Secretary Lawrence Summers, who met with Suharto. The whole saga culminated on January 14, when Michel Camdessus met with Suharto. The event was later captured in a photo laden with heavy symbolism of Western "imperialism" in which Indonesia surrendered to the IMF's austerity measures.[15] Most analysts viewed that the photo heightened — or even triggered — the

---

[14] The extent of this proposed reform was characterized by the World Bank's James Wolfensohn as broad-based. A Fund staffer confessed that the structural reforms did not address the real problems: banking system weaknesses and the corporate debt burden (Blustein 2001 reviewed in Azis 2002b).

[15] In the photo, Camdessus, with his arms crossed, peered over the shoulder of a visibly cowed Suharto. He said of the meeting that "the immediate priority of my visit is to arrest and turn around the tremendous loss of confidence, and stabilize the market through monetary discipline and a dramatic acceleration of long overdue structural reforms."

reason for the anti-IMF stigma, especially in Asia, that has lasted until today.

The market, however, was not amused. The Jakarta stock exchange slumped and the rupiah slid further to IDR 8,650 to the US dollar. The main reason it failed to impress was because it did not address the key issue, which was Indonesia's USD 133 billion debt, especially the private short-term share of it. Since USD 9.6 billion of such debt would mature in 2 months' time, the amount of rupiah needed to change into dollars to pay the principal, not including interest payment, increased significantly because the debt was made when the rupiah was still IDR 2,400 per US dollar. This raised the possibility of debt moratorium or mass bankruptcies. Some analysts estimated that 228 companies faced problems servicing debt, and out of them only 22 did not have liabilities exceeding assets.

As Suharto announced that he would run for a seventh 5-year term in office, and rumors spread that Minister Habibie would be his vice president, the rupiah tumbled to a record low of IDR 11,800 to the dollar. Even with the renewed government commitment to implement the new IMF package, no signs indicated that such a package would alleviate market confidence since the resolution of the private debt was nowhere mentioned. The only news that the market received was that the government would soon announce guidelines to resolve liquidity and solvency problems in the private banking sector. The combination of the above events brought the rupiah to another record low of IDR 17,000 to the US dollar, dragging down other Asian currencies as well.

The effect of the worsening financial condition on the real sector soon became deeper. Because the country's exports were highly import-dependent, many exporters were unable to conduct their business as foreign lenders ceased accepting letters of credit (LC) from Indonesian banks. Upon the initiative of then Singapore Prime Minister Goh Chok Tong, a multilateral committee of eight countries was established to guarantee LCs issued by Indonesian banks.

A meeting between Indonesian officials led by Radius Prawiro (Suharto's debt adviser) with representatives from 20 big banks took place on January 27 in Singapore.

Indonesia announced a temporary freeze on debt servicing until a new framework was worked out between lenders and Indonesian borrowers, and the government would guarantee the security of both depositors and creditors. Borrowers would be able to roll debt forward and postpone payments. This was a significant move as it was the first time the key issue contributing to the deepening of the crisis was finally addressed. But there was another significant announcement made: the government committed to allow more foreign ownership in Indonesian banks. Not long after that, the government declared that it would establish the Indonesian Banking Restructuring Agency (IBRA), which would be responsible for restructuring banks unable to restore themselves before bringing (selling) them back in the market (to the private sector). Intended to avoid massive bank liquidation, the practical meaning and implications of the two announcements were soon proven by the evidence: many banks in Indonesia would be owned, either majority or partly, by foreigners.[16]

It was also announced that the International Finance Corporation (IFC) and other banks would provide USD 42 billion in credit for 42 domestic companies, and the government would set up a bankruptcy law. A series of banking rules and regulations followed, for example, higher minimum paid up capital for banks (to enhance bank's capital structure to anticipate mergers) and 12% capital adequacy ratio (CAR), both of which had to be met in 1 to 3 years. The market reacted positively. The rupiah strengthened by 28% to reach IDR 7,450 to the US dollar.

The growing rumors that the country might adopt the currency board system (CBS) created mix reactions: positive because it was seen as a possibility that the rupiah would stabilize but also negative because to ensure every unit of local currency issued backed by the equivalent in foreign reserves — which was the premise of CBS — would require a huge amount of foreign reserves which BI did not have. There was a risk that the government would not be able to keep the rupiah at the rate they wanted. Also, to prevent outflows under the CBS, the interbank rates would have to go up to a very high level and that would exacerbate the already serious NPL problem in many banks.

When the ruling Golkar party named Research and Technology Minister, Habibie, as vice presidential candidate, the stock market fell. As the CBS rumors got stronger, the IMF sent a strong signal that it disagreed with the idea and threatened to pull the plug on its rescue effort. Disagreement was also expressed by Lawrence Summers, Robert Rubin, and Federal Reserve Chairman Alan Greenspan (the last two made their remarks during their

---

[16]Some 54 banks (39 private, 4 state-owned, and 11 provincial-run) were placed under IBRA, and more followed before some of them were merged.

testimony to the Congress). Acting defiantly, the government announced that it would quickly establish a currency board. Even when President Clinton phoned Suharto urging him not to establish the CBS, Suharto's position was to drop the plan only if the US and other developed countries helped and came up with an alternative that would work. A similar response was delivered to the IMF.

On February 17, a new Governor of BI, Syahril Sabirin, was appointed. Following the commitment of Japan, the US, and Australia to grant export credits (in addition, Japan also pledged new loans totaling USD 2.36 billion), on February 21, the government suspended its plan to implement the CBS. It also guaranteed a payout on all legal deposits in the 16 liquidated banks (a major change from the previously announced coverage which was only up to IDR 20 million in each account). The government also requested the G-7 nations to help. A few days later, another meeting took place between the representatives of foreign bankers and Indonesian corporate borrowers, from which both sides expressed optimism about resolving the USD 73 billion private borrowing. On debt data, efforts would be made to compile a complete inventory of Indonesia's debt data.

While financial and economic uncertainty lingered, social unrest erupted in various places throughout the country, driven mostly by soaring prices of basic commodities and deeper economic hardship. Demonstrators burned cars, shops (especially those owned by ethnic Chinese), and attacked churches. Although official data showed that the year-to-year inflation reached slightly above 30%, the actual prices in many places had actually increased much higher. Interestingly, in his speech to the People's Consultative Assembly (MPR) on March 2, President Suharto raised again the possibility of using the CBS in combination with the IMF reform; he called it the "IMF-Plus."[17] The rupiah fell again to IDR 10,000 per US dollar as uncertainty grew about whether the IMF would go on with the second USD 3 billion assistance. In the meantime, riots and demonstrations continued to erupt almost everywhere, including in university campuses where students began to demand for political reform.[18] As socio-economic

---

[17] Once again, Washington tried to persuade Suharto to abandon the CBS idea by sending Walter Mondale as an envoy to Indonesia. About the meeting, Mondale later said, "I was able to make our case. But what their decision will be I do not know."

[18] Frustrated, Suharto was quoted as saying that the IMF's economic reform was not in agreement with the constitution because it supported a "liberal" economic system that was in contrast with the constitution-mandated "family-oriented" system.

conditions worsened, the IMF began to show its flexibility and promised to pay more attention to the humanitarian aspects of the crisis. This was apparent during the discussions about the scheduled release of another installment of its loan.

At the end, however, the IMF suspended the USD 3 billion disbursement because of its disappointment with the pace of reform. This time, however, Indonesia's response was stronger than ever: the country was ready to suffer the consequences of the IMF pull out rather than accede to the IMF's economic-liberalization agenda! The newly appointed Cabinet, including Habibie as the Vice President, was seen as another signal of Indonesia's disappointment with the IMF program and pressure. Fearing region-wide consequences, former Japanese Prime Minister Ryutaro Hashimoto and former senior financial ministry official Eisuke Sakakibara visited Jakarta to persuade President Suharto to stand by his agreements with the IMF. By this time, the second USD 3 billion installment had not been decided yet. One of the sticking points was the IMF 's insistence not to relax the limits of fiscal expenditures that included an increase of subsidy for food and medicine.

By mid-March, former Coordinating Minister for Economy, Finance, and Industry Ginandjar Kartasasmita tried to convince the IMF team that the CBS would not be implemented due to the country's limited foreign reserves. At the same time, the IMF conceded that it would have to relax certain fiscal and other requirements in light of Indonesia's social needs. The country's deteriorating socio-economic conditions must have been behind the IMF's change of stand. The IMF finally agreed that the government could maintain state subsidies for nine essential food categories and basic medicines. At the same time, the World Bank pledged to coordinate humanitarian relief to supply imports of food and other essentials worth USD 1.5 billion.

As the second USD 3.0 billion tranche was finally agreed upon, including USD 2.5 billion from the World Bank and the Asian Development Bank, Indonesia seemed to be back to the orthodox IMF policy. BI's subsequent decision to raise interest rate (again) was quickly praised by the IMF. As to the issue of external private debt, the then new minister for state-owned enterprises, Tanri Abeng, announced that the government would make it compulsory for corporations to report their debts and would not conduct any bailout or take any credit risk.

Post-AFC

As the economy slowly recovered, there remained much unfinished work, one of which was to complete the design and execute the plan of bank recapitalization based on the CAR (after existing shareholder equity has been written down commensurately with adequate provisioning for NPL and other assets). According to the plan, the government's contribution to the recapitalization program — up to 80% — would be in the form of long-term bonds including both market-linked and indexed bonds. There were three types of bonds: floating rate bonds up to IDR 95 trillion (using 3-month SBI rate for 3–10 years), fixed rate bonds up to IDR 9 trillion (12% for 5 years and 14% for 10 years), and index-linked bonds amounting to IDR 54 trillion (3% above inflation for 20 years). The first group of eligible banks was recapitalized to at least 4% CAR. Confusion abound about when those bonds could be sold in the market. Decades after the AFC, few large banks, especially the state-owned ones, continue to hold some of these bonds. Indeed, this is one of the problems from the AFC that continues to burden the government coffers even until today.

There was a serious governance issue arising from the whole restructuring policy as it failed to transform the institutional structure of the corporate economy. Even with the 1998 bankruptcy law, the 1999 anti-monopoly and law, and the rule that the NPL should be transferred before banks and corporates were restructured, the protracted negotiations over the restructuring allowed the heavily indebted conglomerates and family firms to move capital out, contributing to capital outflows. After refusing to meet payments, they reassembled and raised loans abroad. At the same time, the government had to decide how to dispose of the non-performing assets but also wanted to avoid insolvency of the fear of workers bearing the brunt of liquidation. All these problems resulted in a business environment where the high-leverage conglomerates continued to be dominant and have monopolistic market power with high asset concentration. On the other hand, many smaller and weaker firms had either collapsed or faced insurmountable difficulties to get credit. The subsequent 2003 law on corporate restructuring did not change the setting as it primarily dealt only with the state-owned enterprises.

On debt management, a Debt Management Office (DMO) was established within the Ministry of Finance in July 2006. It was tasked to manage the central government debt to ensure the achievement of fiscal sustainability. But it was the private external debt that caused great concern due to its role in the AFC. On this front, improvements had been made with the introduction of the External Debt Information System (EDIS) in 2002 and the initiative to publish monthly indicators.[19] Yet, the breakdown of debt components remains sketchy (e.g., distinguishing between scheduled and actual debt service, estimating the accumulation/reduction of private sector payments arrears, and estimating rescheduling and debt reductions from external creditors). More importantly, given the continuing dominance and influence of large businesses cited above, which typically have numerous subsidiaries and complex financial transactions, the accuracy of information is subject to question.

On the macroeconomic front, even with the low base level due to the crisis, the GDP growth rate in the early years of post-AFC never reached the pre-AFC level, far lower than the needed rate to absorb the growing labor force (Azis 2008). Figure 15.5 shows that until the onset of the GFC, Indonesia's GDP growth in PPP terms lagged behind that of other Asian-crisis countries.

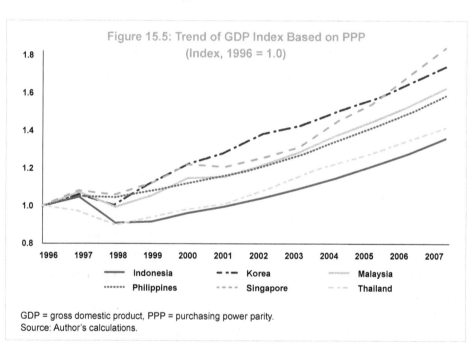

Figure 15.5: Trend of GDP Index Based on PPP
(Index, 1996 = 1.0)

GDP = gross domestic product, PPP = purchasing power parity.
Source: Author's calculations.

---

[19] Through Bank Indonesia Regulation No. 14/21/PBI/2012 (later replaced by Bank Indonesia Regulation No. 21/2/PBI/2019), any banks, NBFIs, and nonfinancial institution companies conducting activities in foreign exchange activities are required to deliver complete, accurate, and timely reports, information, and data on such activities to BI. Also, through BI Regulation No. 1/4/PBI/1999, Article 10, paragraph 1, BI has the right to request information and data object from the respondent through a survey. The final data on external debt are then compiled in accordance with the guidelines published by the IMF.

By components, the accelerated growth since early 2000s occurred only in exports due to the favorable commodity prices and weak rupiah (Table 15.4). If we compare the periods of 2002–2004 and 2004–2006, government consumption had increased, but the surge was not for countercyclical purposes, but rather for the 2004 tsunami disaster-related spending, financing of the newly implemented decentralization policy, and debt payment. On the other hand, the growth of investment and private consumption (largest component of GDP) tumbled due to the restrictive macroeconomic policy, a disconnect between monetary policy and real sector, and the lure of higher returns from investing in financial assets, each of which is discussed in Table 15.4.

A tight fiscal policy was evident since 2001. An expanded aggregate demand through fiscal policy was virtually nonexistent as the deficit never exceeded 2% of GDP despite the 3% limit stipulated in the State Finance Law and Government Regulation 23/2003. On the monetary side, following Act 23/1999 concerning the central bank (BI)'s legal independence, a single objective of price stability, and the prohibition for BI to extend credit to the government and the private sector (Alamsyah et al. 2001), the policy leaned toward tightness. Although Act 23 also mentioned inflation targeting (IT), the implementation of the policy did not occur until 2005. Insofar accountability, transparency, and managing expectation are key for an independent central bank, the authority felt that a number of necessary steps had to be taken to improve the BI communication policy first before implementing the IT. Indeed, the country's transparency of monetary policy had improved over time, and the gap between market expectations and the actual policy had narrowed down, making the monetary policy more predictable.[20]

On the exchange rate, although the floating system had formally replaced the crawling peg regime, attempts to defy "the impossible trinity" dictum continued; when signs of weakening rupiah emerged, the authority did not refrain from intervening the market. A case in point was in December 2001, when BI raised the policy rate (SBI rate) to over 17% despite no serious sign of inflation.[21] At the time, the pressure on the rupiah to depreciate escalated

---

[20] Despite these improvements, the BI's press releases on the monetary policy still contained long sentences and complex wording structures. More importantly, monetary policy surprises had a significant impact only on the short-term money market rates, not on the bonds market and the exchange rates, which indicates that the country's yield curve remained incomplete (Ahokpossi et al. 2020).

[21] The inflation began to rise only when the government removed the domestic fuel subsidy in October 2005 that caused a 120% jump in the domestic fuel price.

Table 15.4: Selected Macroeconomic Indicators, 2002–2017

	2002	2003	2004	2005	2006	2007	2008
Real GDP (Percentage change)	4.50	4.80	5.00	5.70	5.50	6.30	6.10
Domestic Demand (Percentage change)	2.40	6.00	5.40	5.30	3.30	4.10	7.60
Of Which:							
Private Consumption (Percentage change)	3.80	3.90	5.00	4.00	3.20	5.00	5.30
Gross Fixed Investment (Percentage change)	4.70	0.60	14.70	10.80	2.90	9.40	11.90
Net Exports (Percentage change)	0.80	1.80	−2.10	1.10	1.40	0.60	0.70
Consumer Prices (12-month average)	11.80	6.80	6.10	10.50	13.10	6.20	9.80
Central Government Balance (Percentage of GDP)	−1.60	−2.00	−1.40	−0.30	−1.00	−1.20	−0.10
Primary Balance (Percentage of GDP)	3.40	1.60	1.30	2.10	1.40	0.80	1.70
Base Money (12-month percentage change end period)	8.30	19.80	20.40	21.90	22.20	26.50	−2.90
Private Sector Credit (12-month percentage change end period)	25.10	22.10	30.40	19.70	14.40	27.50	30.50
Current Account (Percentage of GDP)	0.40	3.40	0.60	0.10	2.70	2.40	0.00
Rupiah/USD	9,314.00	8,575.00	8,933.00	9,705.00	9,165.00	9,141.00	9,439.00

GDP = gross domestic product, USD = United States dollar.
Source: Author's compilation from various sources.

because of the rising demand of imported oil by the state oil company Pertamina, which led to a surge in dollar requirements. The trauma of currency depreciation, weak balance sheet of banks and firms, and large size of external debt had made the authority edgy. Evidence also showed that the crawling peg rate headed toward a soft US dollar peg, casting doubt about the official claims that the rupiah was managed under a floating regime. Obviously, such a system required a substantial size of international reserves. As countries having big reserves often did better to withstand the contagion during a crisis, reserves accumulation became the preferred policy.

Despite the SBI rate increase, however, the lending rates did not change much and credit and investment continued growing until the early 2002. Since then, an anomaly occurred: the interest rates fell (causing the gap between

2009	2010	2011	2012	2013	2014	2015	2016	2017
4.50	6.20	6.50	6.30	5.60	5.00	4.90	5.00	5.10
5.30	5.40	6.10	7.90	4.70	5.00	4.20	4.60	5.00
4.90	4.70	4.70	5.30	5.50	5.30	4.80	5.00	5.00
3.30	8.50	8.80	9.70	5.00	4.40	5.00	4.50	6.20
1.20	0.90	1.50	−1.40	0.60	−0.20	1.00	0.10	0.30
4.80	5.10	5.40	4.00	6.40	6.40	6.40	3.50	3.80
−1.60	−0.60	−1.10	−1.90	−2.20	−2.10	−2.60	−2.50	−2.50
0.10	0.80	0.10	−0.60	−1.00	−0.90	−1.20	−1.00	−0.90
17.20	28.90	18.30	14.90	16.70	11.60	3.00	4.60	9.70
7.20	19.60	25.40	22.30	20.00	11.80	10.30	7.70	8.70
2.00	0.70	0.20	−2.80	−3.20	−3.10	−2.00	−1.80	−1.60
10,354.00	9,086.00	8,774.00	9,375.00	10,414.00	11,862.00	13,391.00	13,306.00	13,383.00

the lending rates and the SBI rate to widen) while the growth of credit and investment fluctuated and fell (Figure 15.6). The real investment recovered only briefly in the third quarter of 2004 before it fell again for the next three quarters.

That episode of disconnect between interest rates and investment provides an important lesson, that is, due to high agency costs, macroeconomic shocks tend to curtail the ability of banks to supply loans even years after the crisis is over. High leverage and weak balance sheet of firms and banks, asset prices that have not fully recovered, and the disappearance of large borrowers have all raised the agency costs imposed by the asymmetric information between borrowers and lenders. Combined with the bank's large holding of recap bonds and SBI, this significantly reduced the effectiveness of monetary policy (Azis 2008). The lure of returns on financial assets also diverted liquidity away from real investment. Based on the flow of fund data, Figure 15.7 shows that among business and household sectors, the share of financial investment (as opposed to real investment) in total investment has increased dramatically since the AFC.

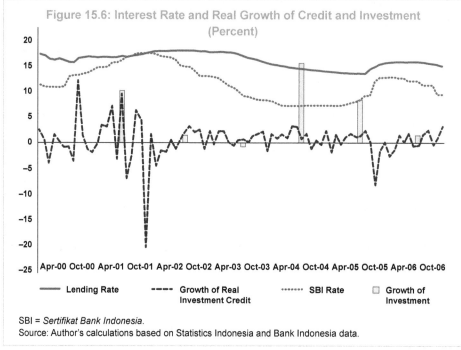

Figure 15.6: Interest Rate and Real Growth of Credit and Investment (Percent)

SBI = *Sertifikat Bank Indonesia*.
Source: Author's calculations based on Statistics Indonesia and Bank Indonesia data.

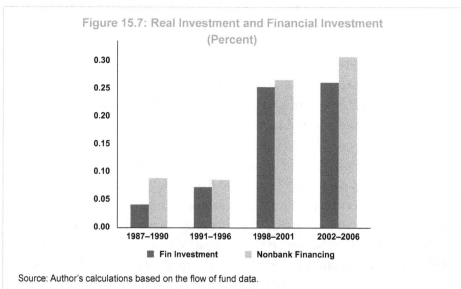

Figure 15.7: Real Investment and Financial Investment (Percent)

Source: Author's calculations based on the flow of fund data.

There was a major and dramatic policy change that altered the country's institutional arrangement after the AFC. Given the highly centralized system in the past, many had expected that a shift toward a decentralized system in Indonesia would have to be made. To minimize the risks of a sudden change, however, such a shift would need to be gradual. But to the dismay of many observers, the new government under Habibie made a drastic decision to flip the system upside down immediately. Through Law No. 22/1999 and Law No. 25/1999, the central government quickly devolved some of its major functions and a large share of national revenues to subnational governments. On the political front, local leaders would be elected directly (no longer appointed by the central government), where the local elections would be done in stages, starting in few districts and municipalities before reaching a full swing in all regions in 2005. No doubt, the change was dramatic. Some international organizations and observers coined it a "big bang" decentralization.

Interestingly, such a drastic decision was not driven by pressures from governors, regents, mayors, and local elites; rather it was motivated by the ambition of President Habibie's supporters to win voters by making his administration appear reformist. While in a large and diverse country like Indonesia there are clearly potential governance benefits from decentralizing, the resulting welfare performance has not been encouraging. Most of the elected leaders were unable to play a robust role in promoting local development and improving the general welfare of their constituents. "Local capture" and money politics were widespread, the number of conflicts increased, and the progress in improving the various aspects of the human development index (HDI) and economic growth in many regions had been dismal (Azis and Pratama 2020). Poor preparation, low quality of human capital, a lack of transparency and accountability, and higher dependency of some districts on intergovernmental grants also led to a growing number of corruption cases.[22]

Overall, the post-AFC period saw some changes in policies and institutional arrangements, but many also remained unchanged. The macroeconomic environment was relatively fine, with 6% average growth during the last 2 years before the GFC. The inflation rate continued to decline, although

---

[22] Some outside observers argued that Indonesia's decentralization was successful based on their conclusion on the fact that the early prediction of a collapse in local service functions did not materialize. They undermine the spread of weakening institutions that have undercut the effectiveness of many economic policies since then.

it temporarily spiked in 2005 (17.1%) due to a drastic cut in domestic fuel subsidy. The latter did not only cause domestic fuel prices to surge, but also interrupted the upward trend of economic growth (which fell from 5.7% in 2005 to 5.5% in 2006). The current account was persistently in surplus due to favorable commodity prices, and the fiscal deficit was kept below 2% of GDP along with the persistent surplus in the primary balance. More importantly, especially from the perspective of the AFC experience, the external debt was under control. Having the reserve accumulation be the preferred policy, the ratio of short-term external debt to foreign reserves was on a declining trend, with the exception in 2005 when the ratio spike to 97%. By the time the GFC was about to happen, the ratio was down to 63%.

From GFC to Taper Tantrum

With the above post-AFC backdrop, Indonesia was in a better initial position to confront the shock during the GFC. The overall impact of the shock was mild, although the effect in the financial sector was quite significant. During July 2007–December 2008, the interest rate spread rose significantly, where the J.P. Morgan Emerging Markets Bond Spread jumped from 168 basis points to more than 920 basis points, recorded as the largest in emerging Asia. Other financial indicators also showed the extent of the impact: the stock market was down by 50.0%, bank CAR fell from 21.6% in January to 16.8% in November 2008, and the bank's return on assets (ROA) dropped from 3.2% to 2.6% during the same period. As the scandal of Bank Century emerged, confidence fell.[23] The interbank transactions dropped by almost 60%, causing the deposit rate to spike, and the growth of credit declined from above 30% to only 10%.

---

[23] The scandal involving Indonesia's 13th largest bank, Bank Century, was the poster child of the impact of the GFC on the banking sector. When the bank reported a negative CAR one month after the Lehman collapse, at first the government seized and placed the bank under the care of Indonesia's deposit insurance company (Federal Deposit Insurance Corporation (FDIC) equivalent). As foreign investment started to pull out, and terrified of a repeat of the AFC, the government decided to bail out the bank. But the bailout quickly turned rotten as one of the bank's cofounders was found guilty of issuing fake LC, and the bailout cost (IDR 6.76 trillion or USD 737 million) turned out to be almost 10 times more than the original estimates. A subsequent parliament vote on whether the bailout was warranted resulted in a resounding vote of no confidence, implying that the decision created some political costs. Perhaps because of that unpleasant experience, when another bank (Bank IFI) failed to increase its capital following the GFC, BI decided to close it down.

Although the overall banking system has been resilient, with less than 4% NPL, 77% loan-to-deposit ratio, and 17% CAR, the highly segmented banking system left the smaller banks to remain vulnerable to liquidity risk due to their narrow funding options and difficulties to get market access during distress. It was at that point that the Indonesia Deposit Insurance Corporation (IDIC) raised the maximum amount of deposit insured to IDR 2 billion per depositor per bank.

Although the impact of the GFC on the financial sector was greater than the impact through the trade channel (explained in the following paragraph), there was no panic in Indonesia's financial market and no widespread insolvencies. The growth of the economy remained positive, only slowing from 6.3% in 2007 to 6.1% and 4.5% in 2008 and 2009, respectively (Table 15.4). The positive growth was supported primarily by a steady growth of private consumption. The latter received a boost in the first quarter from the election-related spending and lower taxes as part of the government's fiscal stimulus. Despite the loosening of monetary policy (the interest rate was reduced from 9.5% to 6.5%) and a sharp increase in private credit, the growth of investment dropped rather sharply. But the country's capacity to withstand the external shock from the GFC was enhanced by the fact that the share of exports in GDP was less than 30% during 2008–2009, far lower than in most countries throughout Emerging Asia (EA). The share fell further since then to reach below 20%, until now.

Insofar the GFC hit industrial countries whom EMs relied on for their exports, the contagion through trade channel had significantly affected the export-oriented countries in EA but not Indonesia. In fact, Indonesia's nonoil exports increased due to the more open trade policy, greater flexibility of the exchange rate, greater global supply chain networks, and, most importantly, a strong economic recovery in China that led to increased demand for Indonesian products. At any rate, these factors and the dependence on domestic consumption had helped Indonesia withstand the effect of the GFC.

With moderate fiscal stimulus, loose monetary policy, and increased flexibility of the exchange rate combined with judicious use of reserves, the economy should have been reverting back to its medium growth path. Under normal circumstances, that should have also boosted the country's financial stability. Yet, the circumstances were far from normal. Although economic growth was relatively stable, averaging around 6%, the financial risk structure had changed as the global liquidity surged following the ultra-easy money policy adopted by the AE.

It all began with the aggressive move by the US Federal Reserve to push down the already low interest rates to 0.25% following the Lehman collapse in the fall of 2008. A similar move was made by the Eurozone by lowering the rates to 1%. Realizing the scale of the crisis and the risk of entering a depression, the Fed kept those low rates for several years, while in the Eurozone the rate was further lowered to 0.25% in 2013 and 0.15% in 2014. To deal with the financial institutions' deteriorating balance sheets caused by the subprime crisis, in November 2008 the Fed implemented a quantitative easing-1 (QE-1) policy, in which it would purchase the long-term Treasury securities, agency securities, and mortgage-backed securities (MBS). QE-1 was subsequently proceeded by QE-2 that lasted from June 2009 until March 2010, followed by a reinvestment program in August 2010.[24]

The market response to the low interest rates and the QE policy was expected: a massive amount of capital left AE to EM including EA and Indonesia. Unlike the case before the GFC, where most inflows to EM were intermediated through banks, this time the flows were predominantly entering through the capital market including the local currency bond market. The consequence of surging inflows was a large expansion of liquidity and a lower cost of borrowing which, in turn, spurred credit creation and economic growth. The growth of private credit surged from a single-digit rate to 20.0% and 25.4% in 2010 and 2011, respectively, and the growth of investment jumped from 3.3% in 2009 to 8.5% and 8.8% during the same period. As a result, GDP growth increased from 4.6% to 6.2% and 6.5% in 2010 and 2011 respectively (Table 15.4). At the same time, the pressure on the exchange rates to appreciate also increased: the rupiah strengthened by 14.5% in 2010, and it further strengthened by 3.6% in 2011. The surge of net foreign assets (NFA) almost doubled the growth of base money, causing the inflation rate to jump.

But the implied risks went beyond the standard macroeconomic hazards of an overheating economy. With plenty of liquidity and low costs of borrowing, the overall risks to financial stability increased. The flow of funds data showed that banks, nonfinancial companies, and households shifted their preference toward financial and risky investments. The low cost

---

[24]Since any increase in the Fed's balance sheet through asset purchases would ultimately be removed when the purchased assets mature, the reinvestment policy will act to keep the QE policy from undoing itself naturally.

of borrowing also led the government to accelerate the issuance of sovereign bonds and to undertake "maturity adjustment." While all were enjoying the "party" of ample liquidity, however, the risks of the winding down of AE's easy money policy did not seem to be in the radar screen.

Such risks turned into a crisis during the summer of 2013 when the former Fed Chair, Ben Bernanke, announced the Fed's intention to reduce its asset purchases. As soon as the news was out, the capital market was rattled and the exchange rate tumbled. The stock market became volatile as capital outflows surged. The shock, known as taper tantrum (TT), was felt particularly hard in the local currency bond market because the market was shallow and the foreign ownership was around 40%. Any amounts of outflows could easily rattle the market. The resulting slower growth of GDP persisted until several years later. Indeed, while the impact of the TT on the financial market was relatively brief, if we compare with the period before TT, during TT the Indonesian economy was marked by slower average economic growth (5.0% versus 6.0%) and lower credit growth (9.6% versus 18.6%). Moreover, the surplus in current account and primary balance was turned into a deficit since 2013.

In retrospect, comparing the three crisis episodes, the effect of the shocks on economic growth was most severe during the AFC and least severe during the TT (Figures 15.8A and 15.8B). So was the effect on the overall macroeconomic indicators such as the exchange rate (Figures 15.9A and 15.9B) and the inflation rate (Figures 15.10A and 15.10B). Much of the contagion effects had been transmitted through the financial channel than the trade channel. Consequently, as the financial market post-AFC grew bigger, the effects of the shocks in the financial market became more apparent.

Interestingly, the resulting spillovers on the exchange rate during the GFC were different from those during the TT in that in the latter, the size and the volatility exceeded those during the GFC (Figure 15.11A). The shock and the volatility in the rupiah during the TT also affected the currencies in other Asian countries. Similarly, the received shock and volatility in Indonesia's equity market during the TT generated spillovers to other countries' equity market. In terms of the shock magnitude, during the TT the transmitted spillover from Indonesia was greater than what the country received, but during the GFC the opposite was the case. In terms of volatility, in both the GFC and the TT the transmitted volatility was greater than the received one.

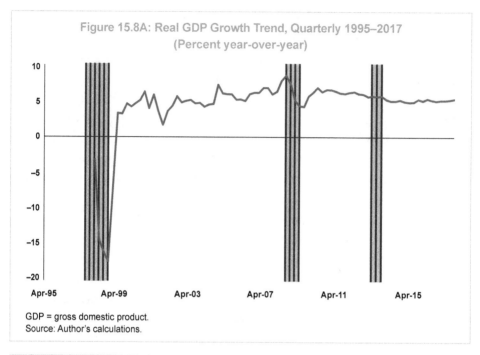

Figure 15.8A: Real GDP Growth Trend, Quarterly 1995–2017 (Percent year-over-year)

GDP = gross domestic product.
Source: Author's calculations.

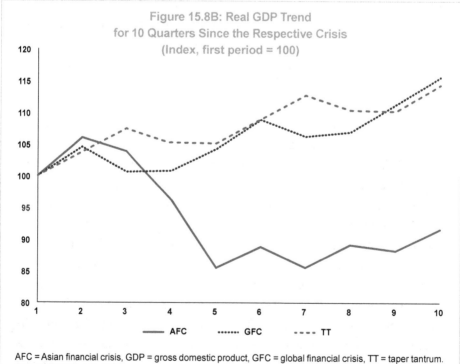

Figure 15.8B: Real GDP Trend for 10 Quarters Since the Respective Crisis (Index, first period = 100)

AFC = Asian financial crisis, GDP = gross domestic product, GFC = global financial crisis, TT = taper tantrum.
Source: Author's calculations.

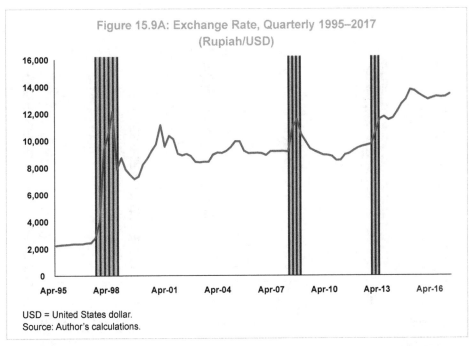

Figure 15.9A: Exchange Rate, Quarterly 1995–2017 (Rupiah/USD)

USD = United States dollar.
Source: Author's calculations.

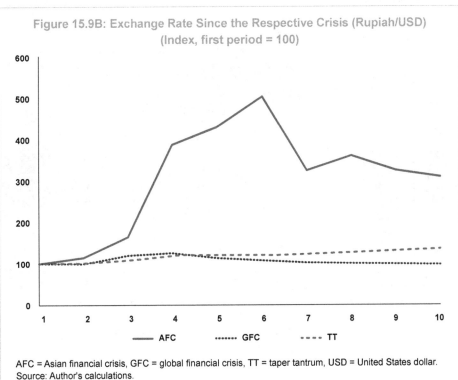

Figure 15.9B: Exchange Rate Since the Respective Crisis (Rupiah/USD) (Index, first period = 100)

AFC = Asian financial crisis, GFC = global financial crisis, TT = taper tantrum, USD = United States dollar.
Source: Author's calculations.

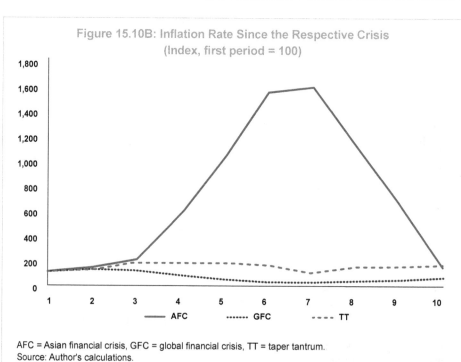

Figure 15.10A: Inflation Rate, Quarterly 1995–2017
(Percent year-over-year)

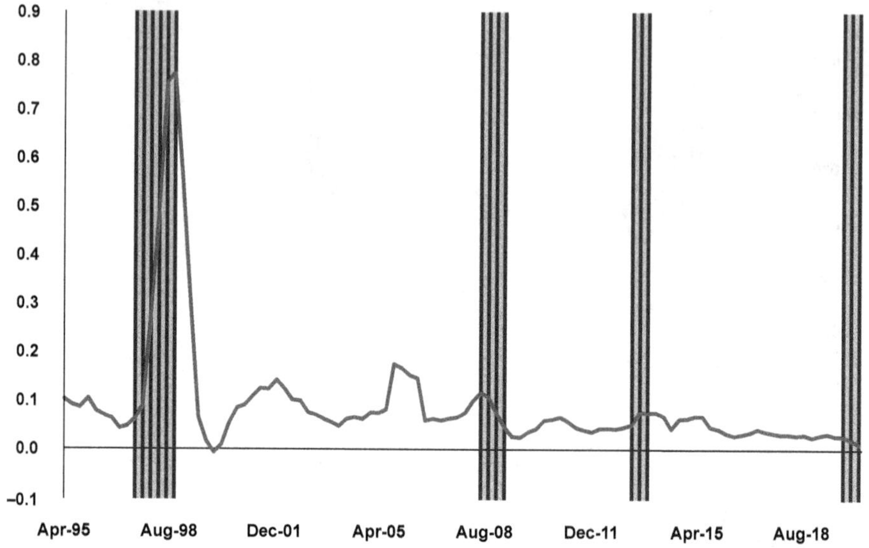

Source: Author's calculations.

Figure 15.10B: Inflation Rate Since the Respective Crisis
(Index, first period = 100)

AFC = Asian financial crisis, GFC = global financial crisis, TT = taper tantrum.
Source: Author's calculations.

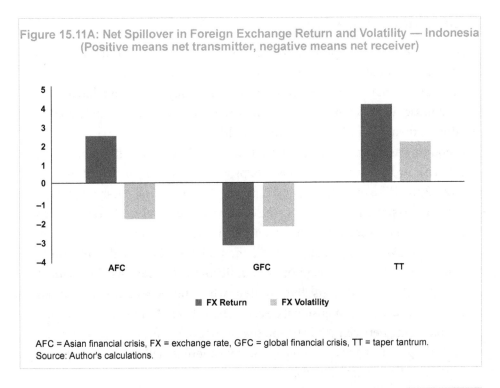

Figure 15.11A: Net Spillover in Foreign Exchange Return and Volatility — Indonesia (Positive means net transmitter, negative means net receiver)

AFC = Asian financial crisis, FX = exchange rate, GFC = global financial crisis, TT = taper tantrum.
Source: Author's calculations.

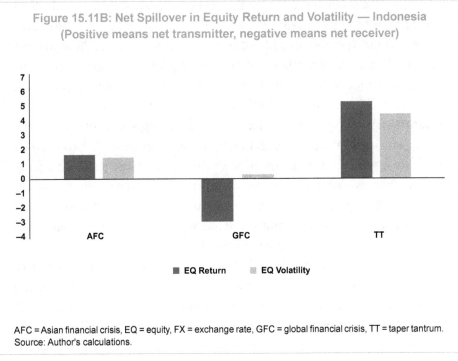

Figure 15.11B: Net Spillover in Equity Return and Volatility — Indonesia (Positive means net transmitter, negative means net receiver)

AFC = Asian financial crisis, EQ = equity, FX = exchange rate, GFC = global financial crisis, TT = taper tantrum.
Source: Author's calculations.

Concluding Remarks

Before summer 1997, praises toward Asian economies including Indonesia appeared in many articles, books, and reports, including those published by international financial institutions (IFIs). Policymakers overlooked the weaknesses in the country's economic and governance affairs, and failed to address them. So did the IFIs. They could not correctly predict where the economy was heading, let alone how it could fall into a crisis. It was only after the crisis broke out that they began to propagate a sharply different analysis (Azis 2018). The previously praised policies and performances were swiftly turned into something featuring the country's structural weaknesses, based upon which a sweeping institutional reform was demanded as a condition to receive IMF financial support. As the policy packages failed to restore confidence, the overall economic conditions worsened. As the ensuing socio-political conditions deteriorated, what started as a financial crisis turned into a multi-dimensional disaster. Aside from the misguided policies, the bickering between the IMF and the Indonesian officials over what to do in dealing with the precipitous fall of the economy had contributed to the depth and length of the crisis.

After the shock receded, and the economy gradually recovered, albeit slower than in other Asian crisis countries, the government made some changes in macroeconomic and institutional policies. Some of those changes produced better results; others did not. The improvements in the economic front placed Indonesia in a better position to deal with the subsequent shocks during the GFC and the TT, but the persistent weaknesses that plagued the institutional setting, and had clearly played an important role during the AFC, remained intact. The effect of, and the response to, the AFC failed to make a significant improvement in the country's governance affairs. Big companies with high leverage continued to dominate, and rampant money politics and the practice of "capture" during local elections post-decentralization posed a serious obstacle for improving the constituents' welfare in many regions throughout the country.

To the extent the nature and intensity of the shocks during the three crisis episodes were not the same, the policy response was also different. The misguided policy during the AFC brought about the most significant impact on the country's economy and socio-political conditions. The policy direction was toward monetary and fiscal tightening, combined with structural changes unrelated to the crisis. The effect of the GFC shock was milder because of the better initial macroeconomic conditions before the crisis, as well as the boost from greater demand from other Asian countries, particularly China. As a result, the general direction of the policy was the opposite toward loosening monetary and fiscal policy while maintaining the exchange rate flexibility and securing financial stability. The overall impact of the TT shock was also generally mild. But due to the nature of the shock, the country's financial sector felt a more significant jolt than during the GFC, and the significant spillovers received were also transmitted to other countries. Accordingly, the policy direction was toward monetary tightening, keeping the fiscal balance in check, and minimizing the exchange fluctuations through encouraging the use of hedging, among others.

An important lesson from the three crises was that monitoring standard indicators ("measured risks") may not be sufficient. "Hidden risks" emerge and are exposed in a crisis. Another lesson, a country's domestic financial safety net could be far from sufficient to deal with the contagion and spillovers from external shocks. As shown in this chapter, financial spillovers, including the indirect ones, were large and significant during a crisis. It is in this respect a regional financing arrangement can and should play a complementary role in securing financial stability in the individual countries throughout the region. An effective regional cooperation is one that plays an assisting role in overcoming its members' challenges during a crisis.

References

Ahokpossi, Calixte, A. Isnawangsih, M. S. Naoaj, and T. Yan. 2020. "The Impact of Monetary Policy Communication in an Emerging Economy: The Case of Indonesia." IMF Working Paper 20/109, June

Alamsyah, H, C. Joseph, J. Agung, and D. Zulverdy, D. 2001 "Towards Implementation of Inflation Targeting in Indonesia." *Bulletin of Indonesian Economic Studies* 37 (3): 309-324.

Azis, I. J. 2002a. "What Would Have Happened in Indonesia if Different Economic Policies had been Implemented When the Crisis Started?" *The Asian Economic Papers*, MIT Press.

Azis, I. J. December 2002b. "Review: The Chastening: Inside the Crisis that Rocked the Global Financial System and Humbled the IMF." *Journal of Economic Literature* 60.

Azis, I. J. 2006. "Indonesia's External Liberalization: Policy Dynamics and Socio-Economic Impact." In *External Liberalization in Asia, Post-Socialist Europe, and Brazil*, edited by Lance Taylor, Oxford University Press.

Azis, I. J. 2008. "Indonesia's Slow Recovery after Meltdown." *Asian Economic Papers* 6 (3), MIT Press.

Azis, I. J. 2018. "Coping with the Dangerous Component of Capital Flows and Asia's Ineffective Cooperation." In *Critical Junctures in Mobile Capital*, edited by J. F. Pixley and H. Flam. Cambridge University Press.

Azis, I. J., and Alvin Pratama. May 2020. "Polarization and Local Conflicts in Post Decentralization Indonesia." In *Peace Economics, Peace Science and Public Policy*. Vol. 26. De Gruyter.

Azis, I. J., I. G. S. Virananda, and F. I. Estiko. 2021. "Financial Spillover in Emerging Asia: A Tale of Three Crises." *Asian Economic Papers*, MIT Press.

Azis, I. J., S. Mitra, and A. Baluga. 2013. "Global Shock and Regional Spillovers." In *Peace Economics, Peace Science and Public Policy*, edited by De Gruyter, Vol. 19, 183-211.

Blustein, P. 2001. *The Chastening: Inside the Crisis that Rocked the Global Financial System and Humbled the IMF*, Public Affairs, New York.

Chinn, M. D. 1998. "Before the Fall: Were East Asian Currencies Overvalued?" NBER Working Paper No. W6491, April.

Corden, M. 1999. "*The Asian Crisis: Is There a Way Out?*" Singapore: Institute of Southeast Asia.

Diebold, F. X, and K. Yilmaz. 2009. "Measuring Financial Asset Return and Volatility Spillovers, with Application to Global Equity Markets." *The Economic Journal* 119 (534): 158-171.

Furman, J. and J. Stiglitz. 1998. "Economic Crises: Evidence and Insights from East Asia." *Brookings Papers on Economic Activity* 2: 1–114.

Gould, D. M and S. B. Kamin. 1999. "The Impact of Monetary Policy on Exchange Rates during Financial Crisis." 1999 Pacific Basin Conference, San Francisco, September.

Kindleberger, C. P. 1996. *Manias, Panics, and Crashes: A History of Financial Crises*. New York: John Wiley & Sons.

Krugman, P. 1999. "*Analytical Afterthoughts on the Asian Crisis.*" mimeo, MIT. http://web.mit.edu/krugman/www/MINICRIS.htm.

McKibbin, W. and A. Stoeckel. 1999. "East Asia's Response to the Crisis: A Quantitative Analysis." Paper presented at the ASEM Regional Economist's Workshop, 15–17 September, Denpasar, Indonesia.

Sachs, J. D. 1999. "Creditor Panics: Causes and Remedies." *Cato Journal* 18 (3): 337-390.

Sachs, J. D., A. Tornell, and A. Velasco. 1996. "Financial Crises in Emerging Markets: The Lessons From 1995." *Brookings Papers on Economic Activity* 1.

Tobin, J. and G. Ranis. 1998. "The IMF's Misplaced Priorities: Flawed Funds." *The New Republic.* http://www.geocities.ws/mugajava.geo/edisi04/tobin01.htm.

Vatikiotis, M. 1997. "Pacific Divide." *Far Eastern Economic Review*, November 6.

Woo, W. T., J. D. Sachs, and K. Schwab, eds. (2000). *The Asian Financial Crisis: Lessons for a Resilient Asia.* Cambridge: MIT Press.

Chapter 16

Malaysia
Managing Global Financial Vulnerabilities and Regional Financial Cooperation

Sukudhew Singh

Introduction

The Asian financial crisis (AFC) was a watershed moment for regional economies and how they thought about regional financial cooperation. The previously strong performing economies had not anticipated the dire consequences of financial globalization in terms of creating vulnerabilities that ultimately undermined the entire economy. However, a decade later, they saw developed countries go through a similar experience as excessive financial activity, with the risks poorly understood by market participants as well as regulators, created a financial crisis that undermined economic growth for many years. The lessons of both crises for regional policymakers were that a healthy financial system is critical to a well-functioning economy and that financial excesses need to be preemptively managed to avoid disastrous outcomes. In the context of financial globalization, regional financial cooperation became necessary not only for consultation but also for policy cooperation, for having an international voice, and to create common defensive mechanisms against the vagaries of globalized finance.

The Malaysian Economy and Financial System at the Onset of the AFC

In the 10 years prior to the AFC, that is, 1988–1997, the real gross domestic product (GDP) of Malaysia had grown at an average annual rate of 9.3% with rapid growth in the manufacturing (13.9%), construction (12.9%), and services (10.8%) sectors. Aside from global developments like the Plaza Accord, the reforms undertaken to drive industrialization, liberalize foreign direct investment (FDI), and promote exports were key factors that came

287

together during the decade to pull in significant FDI flows and shift the economy structurally away from agriculture and mining into manufacturing and services. Consequently, the share of manufacturing in GDP increased from 19.8% in 1987 to 29.9% in 1997, and the share of the services sector grew from 45.3% to 51.8% during the same period.

Given the rapid pace of economic growth, strong demand conditions, high capacity utilization, and low unemployment, the economy did experience inflationary pressures. However, a combination of macro-economic and demand management policies was successful in preventing inflation from escalating. Although inflation was above the 4% level in 1991–1992, the average for the decade was 3.4%. More problematic was the increase in asset price inflation, which, aside from being fueled by a rapid growth in bank credit, was also supported by strong portfolio investment inflows.

The strong demand pressures also leaked out into the external sector with the current account of the balance of payments posting a deficit for almost the entire decade. Between 1990 and 1995, public investment grew by 14.9% annually, while private investment grew by 17.4% per annum. Even though gross national savings averaged around 35% of gross national product (GNP), the high rate of investment led to a negative savings–investment gap that was reflected in the current account deficit. Portfolio investment flows were a source of vulnerability, and policymakers in Malaysia were challenged in dealing with the size and volatility of these flows. Portfolio flows were attracted to Malaysia by its strong economic growth, interest rate differentials, the steady rise in the stock market, and the upward trend of the ringgit exchange rate. The net inflow of these funds during 1992–1993 was MYR 26 billion. To moderate the resulting pressure on the exchange rate, Bank Negara Malaysia (BNM), the central bank, intervened in foreign exchange markets. However, trying to sterilize the liquidity arising from these operations proved to be challenging. BNM lacked sufficient instruments and there was also a significant fiscal cost due to the higher domestic interest rates. Despite the statutory reserve requirement (SRR) ratio for banking institutions being raised progressively from 3.5% in January 1989 to 13.5% in June 1996, liquidity accumulated in the banking system. This provided fuel for the high credit growth. BNM faced a policy dilemma: it needed to maintain high interest rates to dampen rising inflationary pressures and mitigate asset price bubbles, but the high interest rates also contributed to attracting substantial amounts of short-term portfolio funds.

In early 1994, BNM introduced a series of exchange control measures to manage the short-term capital inflows. These measures were helpful in driving out most of the short-term funds. Unfortunately, when the Central Bank relaxed the measures in the later part of 1994, it led to a resurgence of inflows and the re-emergence of the imbalances the Central Bank was trying to manage. As a result, at the dawn of the AFC, despite the series of subsequent fiscal and macro-prudential measures, the imbalances persisted and proved to be a source of vulnerability for the financial system and the Malaysian economy.

In summary, before the currency crisis washed onto its shores, most of Malaysia's economic and financial fundamentals were sound:

- Real GDP had grown by 8% in the first half of 1997.
- External debt stood at 43.2% of GNP at the end of 1996.
- Inflation was on a moderating trend and stood at 2.1% in July 1997.
- The government had 5 years of fiscal surpluses.
- The average risk-weighted capital ratio of the banking system was at 12% in June 1997.
- Net nonperforming loans (NPLs) of the banking system were at 2.2% of total loans with 100% provisioning.
- Due to stringent foreign borrowing regulations, most corporates and banks did not have unhedged foreign currency borrowings.

However, there were also several structural imbalances, which, while being addressed, were a point of vulnerability when the crisis hit:

- Large capital inflows as a result of capital account liberalization.
- The current account deficit was 10% of GNP in 1995, which had declined to 5% in 1996 due to policy measures.
- Growing signs of asset price inflation with sharp increases in equity and property prices.
- The banking system experienced high credit growth.

Economic and Financial Impact of the AFC

Following the sharp decline in the exchange rate of the Thai baht starting in May 1997, other regional currencies faced sustained selling pressure from foreign investors and currency speculators, who did not care to distinguish between the varying macroeconomic and financial conditions among regional economies.

The ringgit also came under sustained selling pressure, which was particularly intense in May 1997 and July 1997. Intervention to support the ringgit during these episodes caused overnight interest rates to spike to 18.75% and 40.00%, respectively. By the end of August 1997, the ringgit had depreciated by 40.00% against the United States (US) dollar compared to its level in June 1997. The stock market was even more adversely affected with the Kuala Lumpur Stock Exchange Composite Index (KLSE CI) declining by 79.3% from 1,272 at the end of February 1997 to 263 on September 1, 1998.

In early 1997, as the crisis unfolded, policymakers in Malaysia adopted several standard prescription policies in the hope of reducing vulnerabilities, gaining investor confidence, and minimizing the risk of contagion. These included measures to decrease the current account deficit in the balance of payments, tighter fiscal and monetary policies, as well as tighter prudential standards for the recognition of, and provisioning for, NPLs by banking institutions. The Malaysian economy continued its momentum and grew by 7.8% in 1997. However, sustained instability in the external and financial sectors began to take its toll on the economy in 1998. The combination of a weakening exchange rate and the sharp sell-down in the capital market not only had a negative wealth effect but also adversely affected confidence among businesses, investors, and consumers. In addition, the policy measures the authorities adopted also played a dampening role. By the middle of the year, the economy was in a recession. Real GDP fell by 7.5% in 1998, the first negative growth since 1985. At the same time, the depreciation of the exchange rate caused the inflation rate to increase, peaking at 6.2% in June 1998.

The financial sector also proved to be not invulnerable in the face of the significant external shock. Once the economy started to feel the negative effect of the external volatility, it set a cycle of vulnerabilities between the economy and the financial system, which led to a deterioration in both.

Given the sharp contraction in the economy, the volatility in the financial markets, the large depreciation of the exchange rate, and the strong pre-crisis growth in bank credit to the asset markets, it was not surprising that there was a deterioration in bank assets. Asset quality deteriorated as corporates experienced a contraction of their cash flows due to the economic downturn, and the sharp fall in the stock market reduced the value of shares pledged as collateral for loans. Despite the Central Bank's injections of liquidity, lending rates increased sharply and this also contributed to the rise in NPLs. By June 1998, the net NPL ratio of the banking system had increased to 8.9%, compared to 4.7% at the end of 1997 (BNM Annual Report 1998). A significant portion of these NPLs came from loans extended to the construction sector, real estate, and for purchases of shares. The increase in NPLs eroded the capital base of banking institutions. The situation was exacerbated by a flight in deposits from the smaller financial institutions, although this was successfully managed with policy measures involving liquidity support and the provision of a blanket guarantee of deposits.

The banking sector experienced a pre-tax loss of MYR 2.3 billion in 1998, and the net NPL/total loans ratio increased to 9% by the end of 1998. Total Tier-1 capital fell by MYR 4.3 billion, although the core capital ratio remained healthy at 8.7% compared to the BIS prescribed minimum of 4% (BNM 2008, p. 586). Behind these average numbers, several banking institutions did face problems and had to be rescued by the Central Bank and the institutions set up specifically to recapitalize and rehabilitate banks. The deterioration in asset quality led to banking institutions pulling back on lending to conserve capital, and it would have led to a credit crunch if not for the preemptive action of the Central Bank.

As has already been mentioned, the stock market experienced a sharp contraction, which was greatly exacerbated by the outflow of portfolio funds. The KLSE CI dropped to 202.70 on September 1, 1998, its lowest level in 11 years. However, after the imposition of exchange controls and reforms in the market, sentiments improved and by October 19, 1999, the KLSE CI had bounced back by 181.1% to 738.28 points (BNM 1999, p. 299).

Activity in the bond market also moderated sharply with net funds raised dropping from MYR 33.5 billion in 1997 to MYR 17.8 billion in 1998. Private debt securities (PDS) issued by corporates that now had difficulty in servicing their debt were downgraded by rating agencies. Domestic yields increased sharply with the Petronas 2006 bond's benchmark yield spread over the equivalent US Treasury bond rising sharply from 66 basis points in May 1997 to over 1,000 points in September 1998 (BNM 1999, p. 328).

By the middle of 1998, it was becoming increasingly obvious that the conventional measures adopted by the authorities had not been successful in reducing the volatility in the external sector and the ringgit continued to be under speculative pressure. Without addressing volatility in the external sector, it was difficult for policymakers to undertake necessary measures to rehabilitate the financial system and economy. A change in policy strategy was needed.

Policy Response to the Crisis

One of the core challenges faced by countries affected by a crisis is formulating a coordinated policy response. This requires a centralization of information flows and appropriate expertise, decision-making, and communications. In January 1998, the National Economic Action Council (NEAC) was set up to holistically formulate a policy response to the crisis and put the Malaysian economy back on the path of growth. In July 1998, the NEAC announced a comprehensive National Economic Recovery Plan to expedite economic recovery.

The Plan had six policy priorities. In the short term, the priority was given to stabilizing the ringgit, restoring market confidence, and maintaining financial stability. Over the longer term, the plan focused on promoting structural reforms to strengthen economic fundamentals, revitalizing key sectors of the economy, and persevering with socioeconomic priorities.

Given the nature of the crisis, BNM took a leading role in dealing with the crisis. There were several parts to its strategy:

(1) Restore stability in the external sector

In 1998, the Malaysian economy had entered a recession. Yet, the Central Bank was constrained in its ability to reduce interest rates due to concerns about exacerbating resident and nonresident capital outflows and adding to ringgit exchange rate instability. It became clear to policymakers in Malaysia that without addressing the root causes of the instability in the external sector, they would be constrained in their ability to address issues in the financial system and the economy. As a result, several measures were undertaken:

- August 4, 1998: Limit of USD 2 million on nontrade-related swap transactions.

- September 1, 1998: Selective exchange controls on short-term capital flows, including:

  * noninternationalization of the ringgit;

  * requirement for foreign portfolio funds invested in Malaysia to remain in Malaysia for 1 year;

  * elimination of offshore ringgit trading through disallowing:

    ◆ the transfer of funds between external accounts, that is, ringgit accounts held by nonresidents in banks in Malaysia, to stop the lending and borrowing of ringgit for currency trading and speculation;

    ◆ the net settlement of currency trades through the external accounts; and

    ◆ the offshore trading of Malaysian equities with the subsequent closing of the over-the-counter (OTC) offshore market in Malaysian equities in Singapore, which was known as the Central Limit Order Book (CLOB).

- September 2, 1998: The exchange rate of the ringgit against the US dollar was pegged at 3.80.

- July 1999: Demonetization of the MYR 500 and MYR 1,000 currency notes to prevent large sums of ringgit being easily taken offshore.

To guard against the possible development of a black market for the US dollar, the Central Bank ensured that there was an ample supply of the US currency to meet demand.

The selective exchange controls were not intended to hamper the movement of funds related to real investment, trade, and normal economic activity. For instance, the flow of FDI and the repatriation of interest, profits, and dividends continued to be guaranteed. The changes were directed at containing speculation on the ringgit and minimizing the impact of short-term capital flows on the domestic economy.

In fact, with the restoration of stability, in February 1999, less than a year after they were imposed, BNM started loosening the exchange control measures by converting the 1-year holding period for nonresident portfolio funds into a graduated levy based on the length of time the funds have been in Malaysia. Later, in September, even this was removed. Why did Malaysia not resort to the International Monetary Fund (IMF) assistance? For one thing, its foreign exchange reserves were still at healthy levels and it had low external indebtedness. Furthermore, in IMF consultations, it became clear to Malaysian policymakers that the proposed restrictive policies recommended by the IMF would further undermine the economy that was already in recession but would not address the speculative pressures on the ringgit.

Some observers said that Malaysia essentially imposed exchange controls after most of the portfolio funds had already left. This was certainly not how it looked to Malaysian policymakers when the controls were imposed given the continued volatility in the ringgit exchange rate, signs of continued speculation against the currency in the offshore markets, and the selling down of Malaysian equities. The restoration of stability in the external sector was a necessary preamble to measures to support the economy and financial system and toward ensuring the success of these measures.

(2) Ease fiscal and monetary policies to support the economy

Prior to the AFC, the Malaysian government had maintained fiscal surpluses for 5 successive years. Given the initial focus of policy was not on supporting growth but rather on addressing vulnerabilities — containing inflation, high credit growth, the current account deficit, and the volatility in the financial markets — Malaysia adopted a largely standard IMF policy prescription for crisis countries. This entailed higher interest rates and a reduction in government expenditure. The government cut its operating expenditures and deferred several infrastructure projects.

By early 1998, as signs of a sharp contraction in the economy became evident, the government reversed course and undertook additional fiscal spending, going against the IMF advice. The fiscal stimulus resulted in the development expenditure ceiling of the Seventh Malaysia Plan being increased from MYR 22 billion to MYR 184.5 billion during the mid-term review of the plan (BNM 1999, p. 46). The expansionary fiscal policy created a fiscal deficit of 1.8% of GDP in 1998 and 3.2% in 1999. These deficits were largely financed from domestic sources, with some additional funds coming from external borrowings.

Similarly, monetary policy adopted a more expansionary stance. BNM eased liquidity conditions by reducing the SRR of the banking institutions from 13.5% at the beginning of the year to 8.0% by July 1. Although the Central Bank's 3-month intervention rate (policy rate) was lowered from 11.0% to 9.5% in August 1998, interest rates remained high relative to what would have been optimal for the weak state of the economy. Concerns about exacerbating volatility in the external sector prevented the Central Bank from undertaking a more aggressive easing of monetary policy.

All that changed after the imposition of exchange controls. BNM undertook a series of interest rate reductions and continued to do so into 1999. By August 1999, the intervention rate had fallen to 5.5% and as a result, the average base lending rate (BLR) of commercial banks was almost halved to 6.8%, compared to August 1998. The combined impact of the stimulative macroeconomic policies helped support domestic demand. With stability in the external sector, exporters were able to take advantage of steady external demand. Consequently, in 1999 the economy bounced back strongly from the recession in 1998.

(3) Prevent the banking system from choking on its loan problems and undermining the economy

To deal with the bad loans problem in the banking system, BNM set up three institutions to address the problem in a holistic manner:

- **Pengurusan Danaharta Nasional (Danaharta)**: An asset management company set up in June 1998. At the completion of its acquisitions of problematic assets in March 2000, Danaharta was managing MYR 47 billion in NPLs, equivalent to about 44% of the total NPLs of the banking system.

- **Danamodal Nasional (Danamodal)**: Set up in August 1998 to recapitalize banking institutions. By the end of 2000, it had injected MYR 7.1 billion into 10 financial institutions.

- **Corporate Debt Restructuring Committee (CDRC)**: Also set up in August 1998 to facilitate the restructuring of large corporate loans. By the end of 2000, it had resolved 42 cases involving debts of MYR 27 billion in total.

These three agencies, which were overseen by a steering committee chaired by the Governor of BNM, were effective in realizing their ultimate objective of ensuring that the banking system continued to perform its financial intermediation role without disruption.

(4) Consolidation of the banking system

It was apparent during the crisis that many financial institutions were too small financially to compete and had low resilience to shocks. However, left to their own devices, there was very little enthusiasm among the financial institutions to increase their financial strength through consolidation or by increasing their capital. Therefore, in 1999, BNM provided the push toward consolidation by increasing the capital requirements from MYR 20 million to MYR 2 billion. The measure had its intended outcome, resulting in 10 core banking groups making up the Malaysian banking system.

Key Policy Initiatives Post-Crisis

Once stability was restored in the external sector with a stable exchange rate, things started turning around for the Malaysian economy and financial system. With financial intermediation sustained due to measures undertaken by BNM and supported by expansionary monetary and fiscal policies, business and investor confidence returned. Sustained growth in most of Malaysia's major export market economies allowed the economy to experience an export-led growth. The economy grew by 6.1% in 1999 and 8.9% in 2000. The multinational companies that were prominent in the manufacturing sector, and dominant in the electronics sector, were less affected by both the crisis and capital controls (which specifically excluded all trade and business-related flows). An upturn in the global electronics cycle also helped. Therefore, the surge in FDI into Malaysia prior to the crisis and the significant consequent presence of multinational corporations in Malaysia's manufacturing sector appear to have been instrumental both to mitigating the impact of the crisis on the economy and its quick recovery from the crisis.

With the restoration of stability in the domestic financial system and the resumption of economic growth, the urgency of undertaking substantial economic reforms seemed to have largely dissipated. The sense of urgency, however, did not dissipate for the financial sector, as the Central Bank wanted to ensure that the likelihood of an event like the AFC would be minimized and should it again occur, the financial system would be robust enough to weather it. That transformation started first within the Central Bank itself.

Transformation and Cultural Change in the Central Bank

After having dealt with the AFC, and while it was building the resilience of the financial system, BNM was very aware that it needed to build its own resilience and capabilities given the highly uncertain globalized environment where events like the AFC could happen unexpectedly. Accordingly, BNM started thinking about its future role and functions and tried to determine the forces of change affecting not just central banking but also the economy and financial system.

In 2000, the management set up a taskforce to look into the role and functions of BNM over the next decade. After extensive consultations with other central banks, and intensive internal research and discussions, the outcome was a plan for the transformation of the Central Bank that was not dissimilar from its master plans for the transformation of the financial system.

Over the next 10 years, the Bank achieved greater clarity and focus on its core functions. It became a more performance-based organization by assessing its own performance, and that of its people, based on outcomes achieved. It enhanced both its managerial and policy governance and adopted greater public transparency and accountability. It also looked into modernizing its legislation, resulting in the new Central Bank of Malaysia Act 2009.

New Interest Rate Framework

As the Central Bank looked at unpegging the exchange rate, it took the opportunity to also look at what would be the optimal monetary policy framework for Malaysia in a period where the exchange rate would be more flexible. The outcome was a new interest rate framework that was announced on April 23, 2004. The new framework adopted the overnight policy rate (OPR) as the indicator of the Central Bank's monetary policy stance, with the Central Bank undertaking monetary operations to bring the overnight interbank rate into alignment with the OPR. A corridor of ±25 basis points around the OPR and the availability of standing facilities helped to minimize the deviations of the overnight money market rates from the OPR. This helped to improve the transmission of changes in the policy rate to other market rates. Any changes in the OPR would be announced by a monetary policy statement following a meeting of the Bank's Monetary

Policy Committee. Under the new interest rate framework, interest rates in the banking system were liberalized and individual banking institutions could determine their own BLRs.

Removal of the Ringgit Peg

By the time the Central Bank freed the exchange rate from its peg in 2005, the framework for flexible domestic financial prices was already in place to complement greater flexibility in the exchange rate. On the peg itself, soon after the immediacy of the crisis had waned, work started within the Central Bank on not just the conditions and timing of the removal of the peg but also on what the new exchange rate regime should be. Numerous policy papers were produced to update the Bank's leadership on the prevailing and anticipated conditions and developments, and their implications for the peg. It became increasingly clear that despite the proliferation of exchange rate indices, administratively determining the fundamentally appropriate value for the ringgit exchange rate would be difficult. The thinking started to shift toward a more autonomous exchange rate regime. At the same time, it was equally clear that Malaysia would continue to be a trade-dependent economy. Given the then recent experience with currency volatility due to speculative short-term capital flows, the exchange rate was too important to be left entirely to markets. Therefore, consensus developed around a managed float of the ringgit.

The timing came down to looking for an opportunity to cleanly exit the peg with the least amount of economic and financial disruption. Apart from generally stable economic and financial conditions, one consideration that loomed large was any change to China's yuan/US dollar peg. A change to China's exchange rate regime would have potentially adverse implications for the ringgit peg. Recognizing this, work began within the Central Bank to prepare for the transition, right down to preparation of the press release announcing removal of the peg. As a result of this preparation, in just over an hour after China announced the change to its peg on July 21, 2005, Malaysia was able to announce removal of its own peg.

Once the unpegging was announced, the immediate critical question was how to manage the transition. There were those in the Central Bank who argued that the markets were expecting a 2% appreciation of the ringgit and that unless actual outcome met this expectation, there would be instability in the exchange rate. Others argued that giving markets what they expected could lead to self-fulfilling beliefs among market participants, which could be difficult to manage. Therefore, the Central Bank should resist large movements in the exchange rate immediately after the removal of the peg. Fortunately, the latter group won the day, the Central Bank intervened to maintain ringgit stability, and the transition from the peg turned out to be uneventful. Consequently, over time, the Central Bank was able to allow the exchange rate to move more fully in response to changes in fundamental conditions.

Transforming the Financial System

The genesis of many of the major financial reforms that took place after the AFC lay in the Central Bank's Financial Sector Master Plan (FSMP) and the Securities Commission's Capital Market Master Plan (CMMP). These plans laid out a decade-long vision of the evolution of the financial system. The FSMP envisaged a diversified, well-regulated, and resilient financial system operating in a competitive environment to meet the diverse financing needs of the Malaysian economy.

It is important to note that the underlying assumption in the FSMP was that the Malaysian economy and the financial system would, over the next decade, become more integrated regionally and internationally. Therefore, the challenge was to prepare the Malaysian financial system for the anticipated more competitive environment. The plan was implemented in three stages:

- Phase 1: Building the capacity of domestic banking institutions.
- Phase 2: Increasing competition among domestic banking institutions.
- Phase 3: Increasing integration with international financial markets and allowing in new foreign players.

Figure 16.1 shows that there were significant achievements in transforming the financial system in the years from the AFC to just before the global financial crisis (GFC) in 2008. It is worth pointing out that many of these reforms were intended to benefit consumers of financial services. The left-hand side of Figure 16.1 identifies some of these key achievements in terms of increasing access to financing, providing consumers with information they need to make wise financial decisions, and setting up institutions for the protection of consumers of financial services.

Turning to the financial markets, some of the key developments are again summarized in the bottom right-hand side of Figure 16.1. The most

Figure 16.1: Key Developments in the Malaysian Financial System Post-AFC Until 2007

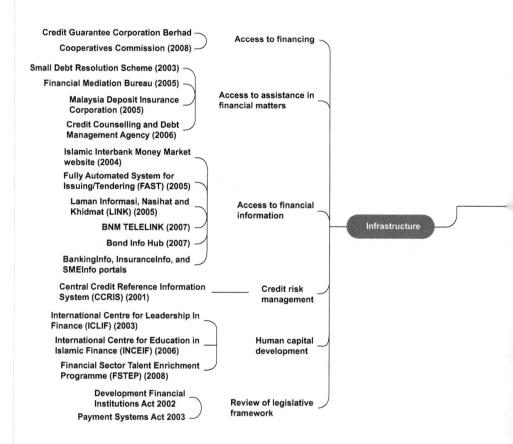

AFC = Asian financial crisis, DFI = development finance institutions, GDP = gross domestic product.
Source: Bank Negara Malaysia (BNM) Financial Stability and Payment Systems Report, 2007, p. 78.

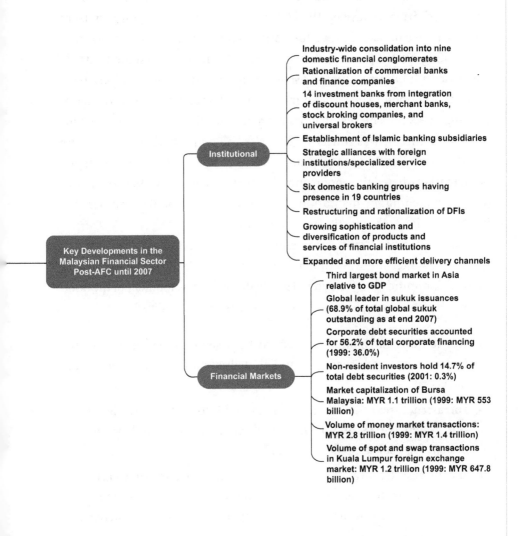

important of these was the development of the domestic bond market. In the aftermath of the AFC, the Central Bank and other agencies undertook several significant measures to support the development and growth of the local currency (LCY) bond market, including putting in a comprehensive legal and regulatory framework. There were several motivations behind the authorities' drive to develop the LCY bond market. Arising directly from the experience of the AFC was the desire to diversify credit risk away from the banking system, particularly for projects that had long gestation periods and posed a funding mismatch risk for banks. For funding these long-term projects, the bond market was a more efficient and lower-cost provider of funding. Also, for a market that has been historically dominated by government securities, it was timely to diversify the bond market toward more private sector bonds. From the perspective of investors, a well-developed bond market offered the opportunity for portfolio diversification and better liability matching for institutions like insurance companies and pension funds, as well as other institutional investors.

The Securities Commission and BNM undertook numerous reforms in the years after the AFC to make this goal a reality. The National Bond Market Committee was formed in 1999 to drive the development of the bond market. The following were some of the key transformations:

- **Regulations and standards**: Such as the issuance of guidelines for the issuance of various securities and guidelines on regulated short selling of securities.

- **Infrastructure**: Establishment of the bond information and dissemination system (BIDS) and the introduction of web-based fully automated system for issuing/tendering (FAST).

- **Incentives**: Removal of withholding tax on interest income earned by nonresidents, tax incentives to encourage issuance of Islamic papers, and measures to ensure that the principal dealers played an active role in the market.

- **Increasing market participants**: Universal brokers were allowed into the OTC market, multilateral institutions were allowed to issue ringgit-denominated bonds, and principal dealers were introduced to spur market activity.

The Central Bank played a particularly active role, even coming up with a mechanism to unlock the securities held by large institutional investors, so that they can then be made available for trading in the market.

Figure 16.2 summarizes the key structural transformation achieved by the FSMP.

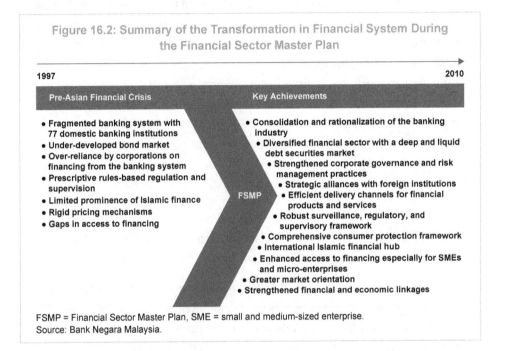

Figure 16.2: Summary of the Transformation in Financial System During the Financial Sector Master Plan

1997   2010

Pre-Asian Financial Crisis   Key Achievements

- Fragmented banking system with 77 domestic banking institutions
- Under-developed bond market
- Over-reliance by corporations on financing from the banking system
- Prescriptive rules-based regulation and supervision
- Limited prominence of Islamic finance
- Rigid pricing mechanisms
- Gaps in access to financing

FSMP

- Consolidation and rationalization of the banking industry
- Diversified financial sector with a deep and liquid debt securities market
- Strengthened corporate governance and risk management practices
- Strategic alliances with foreign institutions
- Efficient delivery channels for financial products and services
- Robust surveillance, regulatory, and supervisory framework
- Comprehensive consumer protection framework
- International Islamic financial hub
- Enhanced access to financing especially for SMEs and micro-enterprises
- Greater market orientation
- Strengthened financial and economic linkages

FSMP = Financial Sector Master Plan, SME = small and medium-sized enterprise.
Source: Bank Negara Malaysia.

Malaysia also participated in efforts to develop regional bond markets through the two Asian Bond Funds (ABFs) that were issued under the auspices of the Executives' Meeting of East Asia-Pacific Central Banks (EMEAP), a grouping of 11 regional central banks. While ABF1 was primarily intended to diversify a small portion of central bank reserves back into the region in US dollar, ABF2 was intended to offer investors a new asset class in the form of a basket of regional-currency bonds.

All these efforts had the desired outcome of deepening financial markets. By 2007, as a percentage of GDP, the Malaysian bond market was the largest in the Association of Southeast Asian Nations (ASEAN) and the third largest in Asia. As an international Islamic financial hub, 69% of total global sukuk (Islamic bonds) issuances were done in Malaysia. The share of financing through issuance of private LCY debt securities (PDS) more than doubled from 5% of total financing in 1997 to 12% in 2007. Commensurately, the share of bank loans in overall financing declined from 43% to 35%. As a result of incentives and measures undertaken by BNM and the government to promote the development of the Islamic financial industry, the share of Islamic finance also increased rapidly.

The structural changes in the financial system transformed the structure of financing for the economy in several ways. As the bond market developed, companies started relying on it more to finance their longer-term financing needs. At the same time, the banks shifted their focus from financing large companies toward providing more financing to small and medium-sized enterprises (SMEs) and households. The share of household loans in total banking loans increased from 33% in 1997 to 56% in 2007. The share of financing provided by nonbank institutions, that is, the development finance institutions (DFIs), insurance companies, and housing credit institutions, also increased.

The GFC and Significant Developments in the Malaysian Economy and Financial System

When the speculative housing bubble in the US first started to deflate in 2007, the Malaysian economy was largely unaffected. Real GDP grew by 6.3%, with private consumption and private investment growing by 10.8% and 9.8%, respectively. Rising global prices for primary and food commodities increased the current account surplus and strong FDI, and portfolio investment inflows led to the buildup of BNM's foreign exchange reserves.

Inflation was on a downward trend at 2%. This good performance continued into the first half of 2008 but the impact of the financial crisis was fully felt in the second half of 2008 and into the first half of 2009. The deterioration in the global economic and financial conditions spilled over into the domestic economy. Commodity and oil prices fell sharply. There was also an outflow of portfolio funds and foreign exchange reserves fell. Growth of private investment moderated sharply to just 1.5% in 2009 and both exports and industrial production also fell significantly. The economy grew by 4.6% in 2008 but contracted by 1.7% in 2009.

There was a strong macroeconomic response from the Malaysian authorities to support domestic demand. The Central Bank reduced its OPR by 150 basis points to 2% and cut the SRR by 3 percentage points between

November 2008 and March 2009. This was accompanied by a strong fiscal stimulus with the budget deficit increasing to 7% of GDP in 2009. The financial markets were affected by contagion from the crisis, primarily through the outflow of portfolio funds, which pulled down the stock market. However, both the extent of the portfolio outflows and the downturn in the stock market were of a smaller magnitude compared to the AFC. Given the reforms that had been undertaken in the financial sector and the fact that Malaysian financial institutions also did not have exposure to sub-prime collateral debt obligations, the financial sector continued its intermediation function. In 2008, net financing to the private sector through bank loans and the private PDS market grew by 12.7%.

Things started to improve in the second half of 2009 as policies under-taken by the governments in advanced and emerging economies provided crucial support to the global economy. In the region, most notably, the strong fiscal and monetary response by the Chinese government spilled over to many of its trading partners, including those in the region. The Malaysian economy rebounded, growing by 4.5% in the fourth quarter of 2009 and by 7.2% in 2010. With economic growth having resumed, and even though inflation was just 1.7%, BNM started normalizing its policy rate by increasing it in three steps to 2.75%, deeming it unhealthy for the economy and financial system to have too low interest rates for too long.

Transformation of the Financial Sector After the GFC

The reforms of the financial sector that BNM and the Securities Commission had undertaken continued, and in 2011, both regulators launched new 10-year plans to build on the achievements of their previous 10-year master plans. Although maintaining the focus on building a robust financial system, the GFC did have an impact on how BNM saw the role of the financial system. Unlike the 2001 master plan, which talked of the financial system as the "driver of growth," meaning that growth of the financial system was a key contributor to GDP, the new Blueprint saw the financial system as being a facilitator or catalyst of growth. There was a recognition that unconstrained growth of the financial system that was not linked to the economy was not healthy. The Blueprint gave greater focus to the financial system being balanced, inclusive, and sustainable. There was also increased attention to developing talent for the financial industry, particularly for Islamic finance.

Another key development was the coming into force of the new Central Bank of Malaysia Act 2009 (CBA) on November 25, 2009. The new legislation provided BNM with the powers and autonomy to effectively pursue its mandates of monetary and financial stability. It clarified the Central Bank's role in nine key areas, which included, aside from monetary and financial stability, responsibility for oversight over the payment system and promoting a sound, progressive, and inclusive financial system.

One of the key outcomes of the Act was the creation of a new governance framework for the Central Bank's key policy responsibilities (Figure 16.3). This governance framework made it very clear who was accountable for

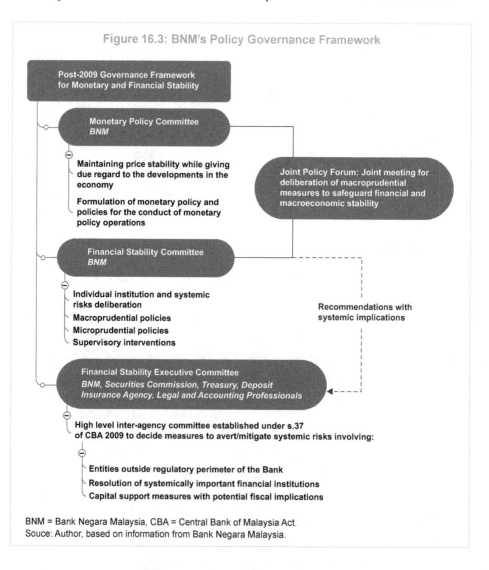

Figure 16.3: BNM's Policy Governance Framework

BNM = Bank Negara Malaysia, CBA = Central Bank of Malaysia Act.
Souce: Author, based on information from Bank Negara Malaysia.

which area of policy. The Financial Stability Executive Committee proved to be very helpful when the problem areas transcended the regulatory purview of BNM. It ensured that all key stakeholders were represented at the table when decisions on systemic issues were made.

In carrying out its financial stability mandate, an area of priority for the Central Bank was ensuring that key parts of the financial system had appropriate laws to govern the business as well as to provide the regulatory powers needed by BNM. Older laws that lagged behind the developments in the financial system were updated by new laws. Figure 16.4 provides an overview of the key legislations that were enacted post-AFC as well as their

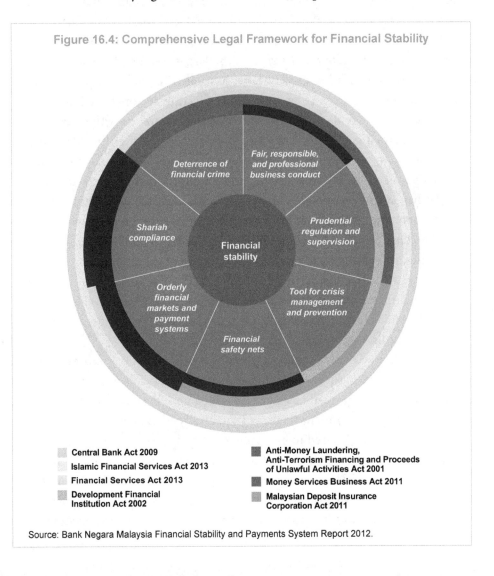

Figure 16.4: Comprehensive Legal Framework for Financial Stability

Central Bank Act 2009
Islamic Financial Services Act 2013
Financial Services Act 2013
Development Financial Institution Act 2002

Anti-Money Laundering, Anti-Terrorism Financing and Proceeds of Unlawful Activities Act 2001
Money Services Business Act 2011
Malaysian Deposit Insurance Corporation Act 2011

Source: Bank Negara Malaysia Financial Stability and Payments System Report 2012.

role in the comprehensive legal framework for financial stability. The most notable and wide-ranging of these legislations were the Financial Services Act 2013 and the Islamic Financial Services Act 2013.

Transformations in the Malaysian Economy

Given the two decades that have passed since the AFC, it is possible to reflect on some of the structural changes that have occurred in the economy over this period.

Figure 16.5 compares the structure of the Malaysian economy in 2017 to just before the AFC in 1996. The most important change has been the increased role of the services sector and the reduced role of manufacturing. Within the services sector, while the wholesale and retail trade and the finance and real estate sectors remain the largest sectors, the share of the former has grown while that of the latter has fallen. The shares of government services and the transport and telecommunication sectors have increased. The decline in manufacturing is reflected in the slower growth of exports. While Malaysia has diversified its export destinations after the AFC, with the regional economies and China playing a bigger role compared to the developed economies, it has also lost some manufacturing activity to China and other ASEAN economies. There has been a move to higher value-added manufacturing, which may have slowed but not stopped the contraction in the contribution of the manufacturing sector to GDP. Therefore, the increased role of the services sector is reflective of the greater dependence on domestic demand in driving economic activity. This may in part explain the structural shift to a lower level of economic growth after the AFC (Figure 16.6). Cumulative average annual growth that was 8.39% in the decade before the AFC declined to 4.58% in the years after the AFC.

Another structural change after the AFC has been in government finances. Figure 16.6 shows that compared to the 5 years of fiscal surplus before the AFC, the government has had a sustained period of fiscal deficits since 1998. Clearly, government finances structurally weakened after the AFC. This has so far not proved to be a vulnerability due to the largely domestic financing of these deficits, aided by the development of capital markets and the presence of large institutional players, both domestic and foreign. However, the increase in government debt and the associated servicing costs will have implications for future government spending and the economy.

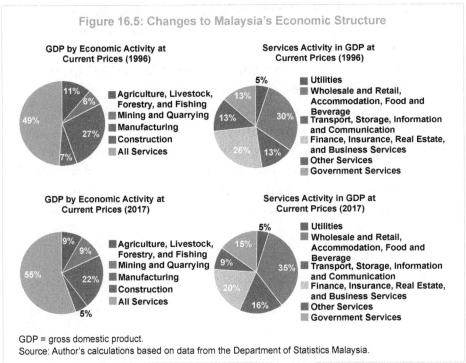

Figure 16.5: Changes to Malaysia's Economic Structure

GDP by Economic Activity at
Current Prices (1996)

- Agriculture, Livestock, Forestry, and Fishing
- Mining and Quarrying
- Manufacturing
- Construction
- All Services

Services Activity in GDP at
Current Prices (1996)

- Utilities
- Wholesale and Retail, Accommodation, Food and Beverage
- Transport, Storage, Information and Communication
- Finance, Insurance, Real Estate, and Business Services
- Other Services
- Government Services

GDP by Economic Activity at
Current Prices (2017)

- Agriculture, Livestock, Forestry, and Fishing
- Mining and Quarrying
- Manufacturing
- Construction
- All Services

Services Activity in GDP at
Current Prices (2017)

- Utilities
- Wholesale and Retail, Accommodation, Food and Beverage
- Transport, Storage, Information and Communication
- Finance, Insurance, Real Estate, and Business Services
- Other Services
- Government Services

GDP = gross domestic product.
Source: Author's calculations based on data from the Department of Statistics Malaysia.

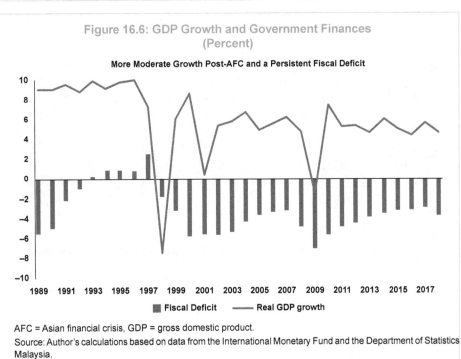

Figure 16.6: GDP Growth and Government Finances
(Percent)

More Moderate Growth Post-AFC and a Persistent Fiscal Deficit

Fiscal Deficit —— Real GDP growth

AFC = Asian financial crisis, GDP = gross domestic product.
Source: Author's calculations based on data from the International Monetary Fund and the Department of Statistics Malaysia.

The other significant structural change in the period after the AFC has been in the balance of payments. The most notable thing in Figure 16.7 is the persistent current account surplus since 1998. This surplus has been on an increasing trend from 2003 and peaked in 2008. After the GFC, the current account surplus has been generally on a shrinking trend.

Figure 16.7 also shows the exchange rate of the ringgit against the US dollar. It is obvious that once the ringgit was unpegged in 2005, it started appreciating on the back of the growing current account surplus. For the period after 2008, the moderating current account surplus is also reflected in the weaker ringgit. Could the ringgit have strengthened more than it did? It could have had it not been for the outflows on the financial accounts.

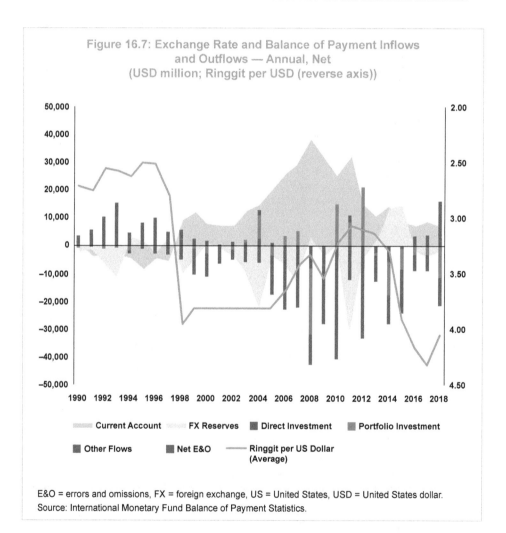

Figure 16.7: Exchange Rate and Balance of Payment Inflows and Outflows — Annual, Net
(USD million; Ringgit per USD (reverse axis))

E&O = errors and omissions, FX = foreign exchange, US = United States, USD = United States dollar.
Source: International Monetary Fund Balance of Payment Statistics.

Most notably, the "other flows" were significantly negative for most of the period since 2005. Some of these flows may reflect the foreign exchange operations of the banking institutions as a result of financial liberalization, which allowed more of the foreign exchange inflows to stay in the banking system — effectively a decentralization of reserves. It could also reflect the transactions of Malaysian banks with their subsidiaries outside of Malaysia, in line with the growing presence of Malaysian financial institutions in other regional countries. Along the same line, net FDI has also been negative for most of the period since 2005, having turned positive only in 2016. Aside from possibly weaker inflows of FDI, this again reflects the growing direct investments abroad by Malaysian corporates looking at expanding their operations beyond the Malaysian borders.

Therefore, the value of the ringgit largely reflected the interplay of inflows and outflows on the balance of payments. During times when the current account surplus was growing, the ringgit strengthened but to a lesser extent due to significant offsetting outflows on the financial accounts. Correspondingly, the ringgit continued to appreciate in 2010–2011 despite a falling current account surplus because of additional impetus from large portfolio inflows. In 2014–2015, large financial outflows overwhelmed the current account surplus and the Central Bank had to intervene using its reserves to prevent a sharp depreciation of the ringgit. Overall, the fundamental support for the ringgit exchange rate since the AFC has come from the current account surplus.

Lessons for Policymakers from Malaysia's Crises Experiences

The Malaysian experience in managing the AFC provides an important counternarrative to the standard understanding of how to deal with a currency crisis. Clearly, the selective use of capital controls can be effective if applied appropriately. It should be noted though that to maintain the exchange controls[1] and a fixed exchange rate like Malaysia did, a country must not have significant external vulnerabilities. In Malaysia's case, its foreign exchange reserves were still healthy and the level of external indebtedness was relatively low. After the crisis, the current account also turned positive,

---

[1] Malaysia has referred to its capital flow restrictions as "exchange controls" rather than capital controls due to their selective nature and the fact that residents were also affected by these measures.

which was helpful. Without these fundamentals, the path Malaysia chose would not have been feasible.

When using exchange control measures, there is always the risk that these measures will be maintained too long. But as the Malaysian experience in the early 1990s showed, there is also the risk of prematurely removing the controls. If the conditions that are attracting the strong inflows, or creating the outflows, have not normalized, it is likely that once the controls were removed, the flows would resume. In terms of the pace of removal of these controls, a gradual and phased approach is more cautionary and preferred.

Once a country decides to impose these controls, it must make good use of the policy space provided to ensure that the financial system and the economy are on more solid footing for when those controls are eased or removed. Without such urgency, weaknesses in the financial system and economy will become vulnerabilities when the controls are removed. If the controls are maintained for extended periods, the incentives to evade them will increase over time, especially if the domestic fundamentals like inflation and currency value are not managed well.

In a crisis like the AFC, policymakers need to worry not only about what nonresident investors would do but also what their own residents would do. When the exchange rate depreciates like it did during the AFC, residents can be expected to take funds out of the domestic currency and even try to place those funds abroad. This would put additional pressure on the exchange rate and foreign exchange reserves.

During the AFC, with financial institutions in Singapore offering high interest rates on ringgit deposits, some Malaysians were even willing to carry currency notes across the Causeway. Hence, the necessity of making the exchange controls also applicable to residents and the demonetization of large denomination currency notes.

In designing exchange control measures, policymakers must balance between what is needed to restore stability, and at the same time avoid damaging the economy. To avoid hurting the economy, the measures must allow normal flows related to trade and investment activity to continue unhampered. This was the case with the Malaysian controls. It does open a potential loophole but that can be managed through having the necessary administrative measures in place.

In small open economies like Malaysia, financial integration has increased external influence on domestic financial conditions. Large capital flows pose a dilemma for central banks in these economies because of their impact on the exchange rate, domestic asset prices, and incentives to borrow from abroad.

Does having larger financial systems help? It does, to the extent that they are able to effectively intermediate capital inflows and outflows, with the presence of large domestic institutional players supporting stability of domestic financial markets.

However, deeper financial systems can also be a double-edged sword — increased availability of financial instruments and higher liquidity could attract increased capital inflows. The large presence of nonresidents in domestic financial markets can be a vulnerability, as Malaysia found out during the AFC. Central banks in small open economies with large financial systems need to hold more foreign exchange reserves as a buffer against potentially higher volatility in their exchange rates.

Floating exchange rates are optimal for most Emerging Market Economies (EMEs) but cannot guarantee full monetary policy autonomy. In normal times, a combination of a floating exchange rate, foreign exchange market intervention, and liquidity sterilization provides some degree of policy independence. However, since the AFC, there have been few, if any, "normal times." Prolonged exchange rate misalignment can turn the exchange rate from being a shock absorber into a shock propagator. Floating exchange rates guarantee monetary policy autonomy only if there is a high tolerance to significant exchange rate volatility and misalignment.

Even developed economies have shown that they have limited tolerance, especially for exchange rate appreciation. Such tolerance also depends on economic structure — it is higher for commodity exporters than for exporters of manufactured goods (or being part of global value chains). Malaysia exports commodities, but it is a bigger exporter of manufactures, and therefore can be expected to have limited tolerance to significant and sustained volatility in its exchange rate.

Building a strong and resilient financial system pays off in supporting growth when extreme negative developments like the AFC and the GFC happen. During the AFC, some fundamental weaknesses of the Malaysian financial system, such as its fragmented nature and the concentration of lending in some sectors, undermined its ability to support the economy during the crisis. However, the reforms, especially the creation of larger and better capitalized banking groups through consolidation and better risk-based regulation, ensured that economic activity was well-supported during the GFC and the subsequent debt crisis in the developed world starting in 2007.

There are a couple of areas that Malaysia probably did not do so well post-AFC. One was in terms of fiscal management. Compared to the 5 years of fiscal surpluses before the AFC, once the budget went into a deficit in 1998, it has remained in a deficit over the more than 20 years since. Even during years when economic fundamentals were relatively favorable (good economic growth, high commodity prices, and high oil prices), there was a large budget deficit. Therefore, fiscal management deteriorated after the AFC.

Another area that represented a missed opportunity was using the crisis to make the economy more efficient and competitive. Although there was a significant restructuring and transformation of the financial system, the same cannot be said for the rest of the economy. Despite some privatization, today, there is the continued large presence of monopolies, government-linked companies, and middlemen in the economy.

While the IMF approach of the fire sale of public assets is questionable, Malaysia could have benefited from a crisis-induced structural transformation of the economy that has otherwise proved difficult due to resistance from powerful vested interest groups. That failure has since manifested itself in lost productivity, a less competitive business environment, and the waste of public funds for rescuing government-linked businesses that have no business being in business.

Regional Financial Cooperation in the Aftermath of the AFC

During the AFC, Malaysia contributed USD 1 billion in foreign exchange funding to both Thailand and Indonesia. Thailand drew down the loan in full, whereas Indonesia did not. This loan was on top of the funds that the IMF was providing. Other regional countries also extended bilateral loans to the crisis-affected countries. Given the difficulties countries faced in getting the support they needed during the crisis, there was support for Japan's proposal for an Asian Monetary Fund that would be able to step in when the need arose. However, the Fund idea never got off the ground due to opposition from the US and a failure to gain support from China.

Nevertheless, there are other areas where regional cooperation has had better success after the AFC.

Increased Dialogue on Financial Cooperation

In the immediate aftermath of the AFC, there was increased urgency among regional policymakers for dialogue with their regional peers. This can be traced to several factors related to the experience of the AFC:

- It increased the sense of interdependence. A crisis that affected one regional economy quickly spread to other regional economies. Regional policymakers could no longer ignore what was happening across the border. This gave rise to the idea of peer surveillance.

- It created a sense of shared destiny and an understanding that global factors affected them similarly and that the consequences were also shared. For example, following the speculation on the Thai baht, the selling pressure spread to the Philippines peso, the Indonesian rupiah, the Malaysian ringgit, the Singapore dollar, the Korean won, the Hong Kong dollar, and the Taiwan dollar. Similarly, the contagion in the regional financial markets was also widespread.

- Countries like Malaysia, which was battling global consensus due to its unconventional choice of policies to deal with the crisis, found that having the support of other regional countries made for a stronger voice internationally.

- In responding to the crisis, there was a lot of sharing of information on policy issues, including on reform of the banking sector, avoiding currency instability, and managing short-term capital flows.

- The shock of the "East Asian Miracle" being ended by the crisis led to regional policymakers coming together to look for answers as to what had gone wrong and coming to an understanding of what domestic and global financial conditions had played a role.[2]

There were several regional forums that became key to facilitating these discussions among regional policymakers. These included the ASEAN

---

[2] The same thing happened among Western policymakers shocked at the devastation caused by the 2008 financial crisis in the developed world.

Finance Ministers' Meeting (AFMM), the Manila Framework, and the Asia-Pacific Economic Cooperation (APEC). Among regional central banks, the key ones were the ASEAN Central Bank Forum (ACBF), EMEAP, and South East Asian Central Banks (SEACEN). Some of the issues that received attention at these forums included:

- appropriate exchange rate regimes;
- sequencing of capital account liberalization;
- restructuring the financial and corporate sectors;
- importance of peer surveillance for crisis prevention;
- reform of the international financial architecture;
- conduct of monetary policy in an environment of large and volatile capital flows; and
- the role of temporary capital controls.

An example of where these discussions resulted in the ASEAN+3 countries adopting a common stand on an issue was after the 18th ASEAN+3 Finance Ministers and Central Bank Governors' meeting in Baku, Azerbaijan on May 3, 2015. The joint statement after the meeting recognized the role of capital flow management measures as part of the policy toolkit: "…while dealing with macroeconomic and financial stability risks arising from large and volatile capital flows, the necessary macroeconomic policy adjustments could be supported by macro-prudential measures and capital flow management measures, where appropriate."

Transformation of the SEACEN as a Regional Central Banking Forum

The SEACEN Research and Training Centre, which started in 1966 as a forum among a few regional central banks, has grown to become a key part of the regional central banking community. It provides a forum for regional policymakers to discuss issues affecting the regional central banks. It also provides training and research.

At the time of the AFC, SEACEN had 10 regional central banks as members. After the AFC, the number of member central banks increased to 19. SEACEN now includes the People's Bank of China, the Hong Kong Monetary Authority, the Reserve Bank of India, and the Bank of Korea.

In recognition of its growing importance to the regional central banking community, a revamp of SEACEN was undertaken in 2013–2014. This was to ensure that it had the internal expertise, governance, and organizational structure to meet the higher expectations of its members in the post-GFC world. Over the years, through its many activities, SEACEN has also been instrumental in building relationships among regional central bankers at all levels.

Regional Currency Cooperation

In the immediate aftermath of the AFC, there was great interest among regional policymakers to find ways to collaborate to avoid the volatility of their currencies that tends to disrupt trade and investment activity. Given that the Euro was launched on January 1, 1999, there was interest to determine if a similar option was feasible for ASEAN. The ASEAN central banks were tasked to investigate its feasibility. A taskforce was set up to carefully study the issue. In fact, over a period of 9 years (2001–2009), three different taskforces[3] were set up in sequence to study the issue of currency cooperation[4]:

2001–2003: Taskforce on ASEAN Single Currency

2004–2006: ACBF Exchange Rate Mechanism Taskforce

2009–2010: ASEAN Taskforce on the Use of Regional Currencies for Trade Settlement

The study produced by the Taskforce on ASEAN Single Currency was comprehensive in its assessment of the current state of ASEAN economic and financial integration as well as the preconditions for a successful regional currency. The essential finding was that the current state of ASEAN economies, including the level of economic and financial integration, would make it difficult to sustain a common currency.

The report of the Taskforce contained recommendations on the progressive stages of integration that ASEAN economies would need to

---

[3] The author of the current paper chaired these three taskforces with membership coming from ASEAN central banks.

[4] Since all three of the reports were classified as confidential by the ASEAN central bank governors, it is not possible to go into the details beyond describing the key outcomes and providing a logical sequence to the thinking of ASEAN policymakers as they explored currency cooperation through sequentially setting up the three taskforces.

undergo. Important to the process was building trust and deep political commitment to integration and policy coordination. A path to this could be through more immediate cooperation in areas such as resource pooling and peer surveillance. Given the finding that ASEAN was not yet ready for a common currency, in June 2003, ASEAN central bank governors gave a new mandate to the Taskforce to look at possible currency arrangements that could further facilitate and promote intra-regional trade and deepen regional economic integration. The Taskforce examined various exchange rate arrangements, including by clustering the ASEAN economies. However, in every case, the heterogeneity of the economies and their trade patterns made it difficult to recommend a particular arrangement.

The Taskforce noted that compared to exchange rate stability, far greater progress could be made in increasing regional trade and investment by addressing key impediments such as tariff and nontariff barriers and differences in standards and regulations across countries. Nevertheless, the Taskforce did not discount the possibility of currency cooperation, noting however, that it would only be beneficial after greater economic and financial integration among the ASEAN economies had been achieved. The report was accepted and endorsed by ASEAN central bank governors in March 2006.

The ASEAN Taskforce on the Use of Regional Currencies for Trade Settlement presented its report to ASEAN central bank governors in April 2010, identifying three possible mechanisms for the greater use of regional currencies in trade among ASEAN countries and the pre-requisites for operationalizing them. The Taskforce emphasized that the success of any of these mechanisms will depend on private sector acceptance. In the current author's view, the findings of the Taskforce reinforced the realization among many ASEAN central banks that it would be onerous to put such a mechanism in place and may not be justified by the economic gains. To the author's knowledge, there was no further follow-up at the regional level on this issue. By that time, focus had shifted to integrating banking systems and payment systems as offering bigger payoffs in facilitating trade and investment among regional economies.

ASEAN Banking Integration Framework

A key initiative under the Financial Sector Blueprint was to increase regional and international financial integration with the ultimate objective of supporting trade and investment between Malaysia and partner economies. In 2016, the Bank entered bilateral arrangements with Otoritas Jasa Keuangan (OJK — Indonesia's banking regulator), the Bangko Sentral ng Pilipinas (BSP), and the Bank of Thailand (BOT) under the ASEAN Banking Integration Framework (ABIF). These agreements created an opportunity for Malaysian banks to become Qualified ASEAN Banks (QABs) in these three countries, and conversely, suitably qualified banks from these countries can apply to operate in Malaysia as QABs. So far, the arrangement with OJK has resulted in two Malaysian banks becoming the first QABs in the region.

Supervisory Cooperation

As Malaysian financial institutions have set up operations in other jurisdictions to take advantage of business opportunities, it has become necessary for BNM to strengthen cooperative arrangements with other central banks and supervisory authorities to ensure the sound operations of these cross-border financial groups and to mitigate cross-border transmission of risks. As a result, over the years, BNM has both hosted supervisory college meetings for Malaysian banks that are operating in other regional countries and has itself participated in supervisory college meetings related to foreign financial institutions that are operating in Malaysia.

Local Currency Settlement Framework

In March 2016, BNM established a Ringgit-Baht Local Currency Settlement Framework (LCSF) with the BOT. This was followed by a Ringgit-Rupiah LCSF with Bank Indonesia (BI) in December 2017. As of 2019, BNM was still engaged in discussions to have a similar arrangement with the BSP.

Under these arrangements, businesses and investors in the signing countries can use LCYs for settlement of trade and investment, thereby bypassing the use of major currencies. It is up to the private sector to decide whether using LCYs makes economic sense in terms of reducing transaction costs and foreign exchange risks.

Swap Arrangements

Malaysia has undertaken several bilateral currency swap arrangements with regional countries. Most of the swaps are with the +3 economies of China, Japan, and Korea as shown in Figure 16.8. First, there are the long-standing swap arrangements under the Chiang Mai Initiative (CMI). However, Malaysia has also negotiated additional swap arrangements with these countries. Malaysia was among the first countries to sign a renminbi swap with China. The swap arrangements with China and Korea have been renewed several times. The first one with Japan was signed in 2020. The 2019 swap arrangement with BI was therefore unique, in the sense that it was the first between Malaysia and another ASEAN country.

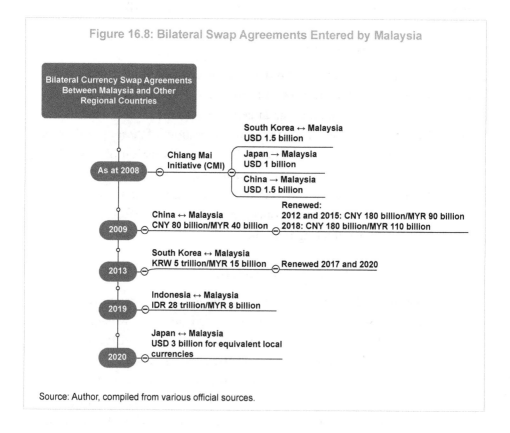

Figure 16.8: Bilateral Swap Agreements Entered by Malaysia

Source: Author, compiled from various official sources.

Conclusion

Given the small size of the domestic economy in Malaysia, regional and global economic and financial integration is a necessity for the continued growth of the economy. However, such integration is not without its risks as experienced during the AFC and GFC. In this respect, the post-AFC experience has shown clear benefits of regional economies coming together to cooperate and mitigate those risks.

Following the GFC, as noted in BNM's Financial Sector Blueprint, there was a recognition within the Central Bank that the emerging market economies, particularly those in Asia, would be key drivers of global growth. Within ASEAN, it envisioned greater economic integration and, along with that, greater financial integration. The regional financial system will have a critical role in ensuring that regional and global savings in the region are channeled into productive uses across the region. Given that the ASEAN economies are still a long way from realizing the full potential of economic and financial integration, the recent Regional Comprehensive Economic Partnership (RCEP) free trade agreement could provide the needed impetus for that integration. A higher level of financial integration would require greater cooperation among the regional central banks and financial regulatory authorities to not only jointly chart the path of the cross-border financial system but also to ensure that such a system is well regulated and does not pose risks of cross-border financial contagion.

References

Bank Negara Malaysia. 2000. *Financial Sector Masterplan 2001–2010*. Kuala Lumpur.

Bank Negara Malaysia. 2008. *Bank Negara Malaysia: Bulwark of the Nation: 1959–2017*. Kuala Lumpur.

Bank Negara Malaysia. 2010. *Financial Sector Blueprint 2011–2020*. Kuala Lumpur.

Bank Negara Malaysia. 1991–2019. *Annual Report*. Kuala Lumpur.

Bank Negara Malaysia. 2006–2019. *Financial Stability and Payments System Report*. Kuala Lumpur.

Hassan, Ali Abul. 1998. "The Way Forward." Governor of BNM's speech at the National Congress on Economic Recovery, Kuala Lumpur.

National Economic Action Council. 1998. *National Economic Recovery Plan: Agenda for Action*. Kuala Lumpur: Economic Planning Unit, Prime Minister's Department.

Securities Commission. 2000. *Capital Market Masterplan*. Kuala Lumpur.

Securities Commission. 2010. *Capital Market Masterplan 2*. Kuala Lumpur.

Securities Commission. 2007–2019. *Annual Report*. Kuala Lumpur.

Chapter 17

Korea
Tiding Over the Asian and Global Financial Crises

Joon-Ho Hahm and Hyeon-Wook Kim

Introduction

Korea is praised as an Asian miracle country that was unexpectedly sacrificed in the tsunami of the Asian financial crisis (AFC). While the 1997 Korean crisis was triggered by foreign creditors' run on Korean banks' short-term debts, it would not have been propagated into a full-blown crisis without the structural vulnerabilities already latent in the pre-crisis Korean economy.

Korea became a "poster child" for the International Monetary Fund (IMF) thanks to its remarkable economic recovery after the AFC. However, reconstruction of the damaged bank and corporate balance sheets did not guarantee the full transition of its outmoded financial system into an efficient and robust one. Notwithstanding the reform efforts to ensure macroeconomic flexibility and financial stability, new risks and vulnerabilities were growing in Korea's post-AFC economic environment. Indeed, with its fairly open and globally integrated financial system, Korea was severely hit again by the global financial crisis (GFC) in 2008. The trauma from the AFC unsettled financial market sentiment and an economic contraction followed. However, the Korean economy rebounded successfully with unusual resilience immediately after the sharp contraction in the final quarter of 2008. Korea was one of the few among peer countries that successfully kept its 2009 growth rate from falling into negative range.

As such, the propagation and economic consequences of the two major crises were quite contrasting in Korea. While the shockwave in the GFC was much larger and stronger than the regional shockwave emanated from Thailand in the AFC, Korea was more deeply hurt and suffered an extreme contraction in the AFC. In this vein, the aim of the present study is to identify the differences and draw lessons by investigating the nature of shocks, pre-crisis structural vulnerabilities, and the main factors behind

323

the heterogeneous and contrasting post-crisis dynamics. We also critically assess the transition of the Korean financial system by looking at the shift in fund flows over the AFC and the GFC.

Among many lessons that can be drawn from the Korean experience, we emphasize the following: First, financial deregulation and liberalization without strong market discipline may lead to significant misallocations of credit and structural vulnerabilities. This is even more so when the legacy of government guarantee and "too-big-to-fail" moral hazard distort the market incentives as witnessed in the pre-AFC financial markets in Korea. Second, albeit the drastic post-crisis restructuring of the banking and corporate sector along with institutional reforms of the supervisory and governance systems, a lack of macroprudential capacity to oversee and monitor systemic risk potential can lead to structural vulnerabilities. Indeed, new risks were emerging from the exposure to overly procyclical capital flows, herd behaviors of banks, and concentration of risks at the onset of the GFC. Third, although it cannot be a perfect barrier, the balance sheet soundness of banks and corporate sectors plays a critical role in blocking the spread of an external shock. Swift and flexible macroeconomic policy responses along with securing a credible foreign currency liquidity line also contribute much to the resilience and rapid recovery in open emerging economies.

The Causes and Propagation of the AFC

The Nature of the Crisis in 1997

The sudden reversal of capital flows in the last quarter of 1997 triggered a full-fledged currency and banking crisis in Korea. The unexpected nature of the crisis raised many questions as to its true nature and causes: Was it caused by the panic-driven shift to a bad equilibrium? Or was it caused by weak fundamentals of the Korean economy?

According to the bad equilibrium view, a crisis may materialize as a consequence of self-fulfilling shifts in expectations when multiple equilibria exist (Cole and Kehoe 1996; Obstfeld 1996; Sachs, Tornell, and Velasco 1996). Radelet et al. (1998), for instance, analyzed the Asian crises with this framework and suggested intrinsic instability in international financial markets as a source of panic. Indeed, in the absence of domestic runs, foreign creditors ran to Korean banks and merchant banking corporations forcing them to reduce their short-term external debts by more than 40% over the last 2 months of 1997.

The weak fundamentals view, on the other hand, blames deteriorations of economic fundamentals as a main culprit of the financial crisis. Corsetti, Pesenti, and Roubini (1999), for instance, emphasized the terms of trade shock, lending booms, and the maturity and currency mismatches of the financial and corporate sectors as main factors behind the deteriorating fundamentals in Korea before the AFC. They argued that the weak fundamentals could fully explain the crisis.

In hindsight, it would be fair to say that the Korean crisis shared both features emphasized by these two views. Without its weak fundamentals, the scar of the bad equilibrium should not have been so deep and should not have lasted long. Likewise, weak fundamentals alone cannot explain the sudden and rapid collapse of the entire financial system, let alone the dramatic recovery after the crisis.

Alternatively, there exists a view that emphasizes both weak fundamentals and the possibility of a nonlinear disruption that can be propelled by the vicious cycle of market failures. Mishkin (1996) defines a financial crisis "to be a nonlinear disruption to financial markets in which the asymmetric information problems of adverse selection and moral hazard become much worse, so that financial markets are no longer able to efficiently channel funds to those who have the most productive investment opportunities." According to this view, in emerging open economies a financial crisis typically develops along two paths — either through the mismanaged financial liberalization and globalization, or through fiscal deficits and government debt.

Applying the asymmetric information view, Hahm and Mishkin (2000) analyzed the propagation of the AFC in Korea and argued that the first path explains the Korean crisis particularly well. Although macroeconomic performance appeared fine and the government was maintaining strong fiscal discipline, uncertainty was rising amid deteriorating corporate and bank balance sheet fundamentals at the onset of the AFC. Credit market disruptions in the midst of a series of major corporate defaults had already occurred since early 1997. Foreign creditors suspecting the debt service capacity of Korean banks began running on them. The nonlinear financial market disruptions culminated in November and December 1997, when interest rates soared to an unprecedented level, and stock markets plunged while credit flows to the corporate sector ceased abruptly. The sharp depreciation of the Korean won further worsened the asymmetric information problems on account of the high dependency of Korean banks and the corporate sector on foreign currency debts. The collapse of credit intermediation and economic activities was propagated into a full-fledged financial crisis.

Structural Vulnerabilities and Policy Factors Before the AFC

Discussions above lead us to ask the question: What were the structural vulnerabilities latent in the Korean economy at the onset of the AFC? In this section, following Hahm and Mishkin (2000), we use the balance sheet approach to describe those structural vulnerabilities and underlying policy factors leading to them.

External Balance Sheet: Short-Term External Debt and Maturity Mismatch

Despite the apparently robust macroeconomic performance evidenced by stable gross domestic product (GDP) growth and inflation, Korea was vulnerable to external shocks due to growing weaknesses in its external balance sheet. As Figure 17.1 shows, its gross external debts began swelling significantly after 1994 along with the government policy of comprehensive capital account liberalization. Its external debt-to-GDP ratio reached a level close to 30% in 1997. Widening current account deficits driven by strong corporate investment since 1994 and the terms of trade shocks in 1996 and 1997 also caused the expansion of external debts. Although the level of external debts itself was probably not in an unsustainable level as argued by Radelet et al. (1998), the structure of external debts was quite vulnerable. The persistently high short-term debt ratio harboring over 45% signaled a serious refinancing risk and foreign currency liquidity problems. The external vulnerability was also revealed by the sharply rising ratio of short-term external debt to foreign reserves that reached 286% in 1997.

An important factor that brought about external vulnerabilities was the poorly sequenced and asymmetric deregulation of the capital account in the 1990s. While the government comprehensively liberalized overseas borrowing by financial firms, overseas borrowing by nonfinancial firms, long-term borrowing in particular, was tightly controlled. This asymmetric deregulation was partly based upon the concern that large business groups' discretionary access to low-cost overseas financing may accelerate the concentration of economic power (Choi 2002). External borrowing through financial firms was also preferred as the government wanted to maintain its

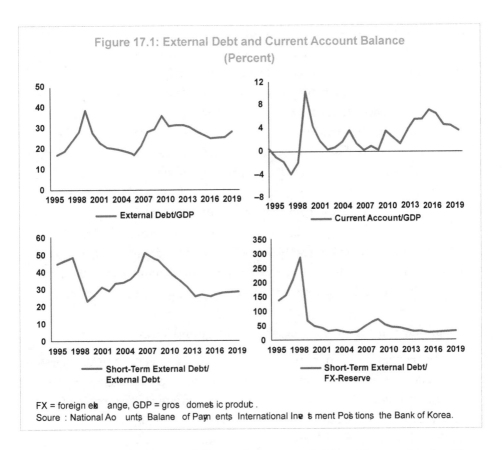

Figure 17.1: External Debt and Current Account Balance
(Percent)

FX = foreign e**x**   ange, GDP = gros   domes ic produ**c**t .
Soure : National Ao   unts Balan**c**e of Pa**y**n ents International In**v** s ment Po**s** tions the Bank of Korea.

control over volatile capital flows. Consequently, the risk associated with external funding was concentrated in the financial sector.

Furthermore, in an attempt to manage capital flows, explicit ceilings on financial firms' long-term borrowing were maintained while short-term borrowing was liberalized. The deregulation of corporate trade credits and aggressive short-term borrowing by less regulated nonbank financial institutions (NBFIs) gave an impetus to the rapid accumulation of short-term debts, which exposed the Korean economy to foreign currency liquidity risk.

Due to the regulation limiting Korean banks' net open currency positions, most of the currency mismatch risks were transferred to the corporate sector in the form of foreign currency loans. However, the maturity mismatch risks across foreign currency assets and liabilities remained serious in the banking sector. Banks often extended long-term foreign currency loans to the corporate sector with funds raised from short-term external debts. To make things worse, the foreign currency liquidity regulations imposed on commercial banks requiring the ratio of short-term foreign currency assets to short-term foreign currency liabilities above 70% were not applied to merchant banking corporations. Thus, they aggressively invested in foreign long-term high-yield assets such as emerging market debts by funding from short-term debts.

Another key propagating channel of the external debt crisis was the sharp increase in offshore borrowings of Korean banks via overseas branches. When foreign creditors rushed to collect the loans of overseas bank branches, the Bank of Korea offered emergency liquidity support, significantly diluting the usable amount of official foreign reserves. While the official foreign reserves fell to USD 24.4 billion as of November 30, 1997, the actual amount of usable reserves after subtracting the central bank's deposits at the overseas branches of Korean banks was only USD 7.3 billion. Uncertainty and rumors regarding the actual size of overseas branch borrowing and usable amount of official foreign reserves became a devastating factor triggering the foreign creditors' run.

Corporate Balance Sheet: Excessive Leverage and Terms of Trade Shock

Another factor leading to the pre-AFC structural vulnerability was the investment boom in 1994–1996 and rapidly rising corporate leverage to finance the boom. Figure 17.2 shows the private corporate investment-to-GDP ratio and the private corporate credit-to-GDP ratio. Corporate credit was measured as the sum of loans, corporate bonds, and commercial papers of private nonfinancial firms. As can be seen, the rapid accumulation of corporate debts was closely related to the 1994–1996 investment boom driven by overly optimistic capital expenditures of Korean large business groups *(chaebols)*, which accelerated corporate leverage in the years leading to the AFC. During the 1990–1995 period, the debt-to-equity ratio of all listed firms was already high at around 300%. It further rose to 384% in 1997 due to declining profits amid rising debt at the onset of the AFC.

The top 30 *chaebols'* average debt-to-equity ratio was even higher at a level around 400%, which signaled a serious risk latent in the corporate balance sheet. *Chaebols* pursued a size growth by aggressively raising debts via cross-guarantees among subsidiary firms and investing in a few similar industries such as semiconductors, petrochemicals, steels, and automobiles.

The overly optimistic investment of *chaebols* and the subsequent negative terms of trade shocks in 1996 and 1997 caused serious damage to corporate balance sheets. As Hahm and Mishkin (2000) argued, the

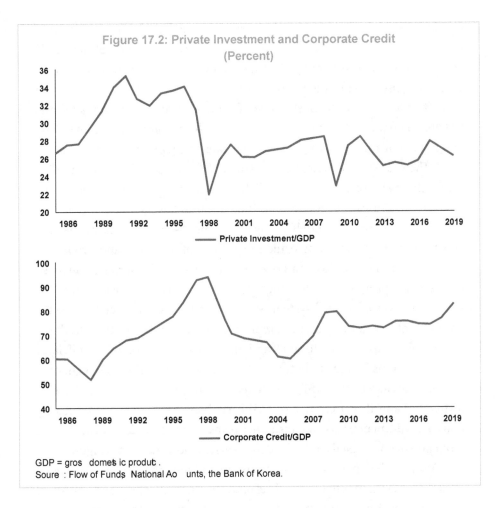

Figure 17.2: Private Investment and Corporate Credit (Percent)

GDP = gross domestic product.
Source: Flow of Funds National Accounts, the Bank of Korea.

incremental capital output ratio, which is a measure of aggregate investment efficiency, was deteriorating since 1992, and overall corporate profitability was also declining.

Along with the business cycle downturn, major terms of trade shocks hit the Korean economy in 1996 and 1997. During the 2 years, the prices of major Korean export products such as semiconductor chips, steel, and chemical products plummeted approximately 30%. This severe terms of trade shock caused irreparable harm to the profitability of Korean *chaebols*, which was already deteriorating. The return on equity of all listed firms fell from 8.7% in 1995 to 2.7% in 1996 and then to −2.9% in 1997.

Major corporate bankruptcies began materializing from early 1997. Starting from the 14th largest *chaebol* Hanbo in January, five other large *chaebols* went bankrupt in 1997, foretelling the end of the "too-big-to-fail" regime for *chaebols*. The corporate default rate soared nearly 50% in 1997 compared to the last year, indicating the degree of worsening corporate viability at the onset of the crisis.

Then what were the deep-rooted factors leading to the aggressive and unfettered financing behavior of Korean *chaebols*? According to Hahm (2003), two notable features characterized corporate financing patterns before the AFC. The first was the increasing share of NBFI-related corporate funding (both lending and direct financing via NBFIs) and the second was shortening maturity structure of corporate debts (both local and overseas). These features were in fact outcomes of the changing government–business risk partnership and asymmetric financial deregulation policies of the 1980s and 1990s.

In the 1980s, the Korean government introduced a series of financial liberalization programs in the recognition of the problems associated with the state control over financial system. While privatizing commercial banks, the government did not let go of the reins over bank credits and tried to divert credit flows from *chaebols* to small and medium-sized firms. As a result, large business groups increasingly turned to financing via NBFIs. Deregulation of entry barriers to the NBFI sector resulted in the expansion of *chaebols*' ownership and direct control of NBFIs such as merchant banks, security houses, investment trusts, and insurance firms. By the early 1990s, the share of NBFI borrowing in total corporate debts reached more than 50% (Figure 17.6).

With capital market deregulations, direct financing also emerged as an attractive financing scheme for *chaebols*. Commercial papers and corporate bonds became important alternatives to bank credits, and the share of direct financing in corporate external funding rose significantly. In particular, the surge in commercial paper issuance in 1995 and 1996 signaled substantial shortening of corporate debt maturity at the onset of the crisis (Figure 17.6). Important NBFIs in this context were merchant banking corporations as they were principal underwriters in commercial paper issuing markets.

The changing corporate financing patterns implied that *chaebols* gradually became independent in their major investment decisions from the screening of outside financiers. This shift was, however, signaling serious moral hazard risks as the legacy of "too-big-to-fail" policy for *chaebols* still existed in the financial markets. As Hahm and Lim (2006) stated, "This explosive combination of 'de-control without de-protection' had serious implications for the financial system."

Bank Balance Sheet: Latent Bad Loans and Overestimated Capital Adequacy

As reflected in the rising corporate credit-to-GDP ratio at the onset of the crisis, financial institutions kept supplying credit despite deteriorating corporate profitability. In an environment of weak credit culture and lax supervision, persistently high credit growth and accumulation of bad loans led to the deterioration of financial sector balance sheets. Although all the banks were satisfying the regulatory capital ratio until 1996, the bank loan classification criteria and loss provisioning requirements were quite lenient in the pre-crisis period, implying that bank capital adequacy was overestimated.

For instance, bank lending to the firms whose interest coverage ratio was less than one was increasing fast at the onset of the crisis. This false credit due to rollovers of the loans of ailing firms was not appropriately reflected in the official bank balance sheets. Hahm and Mishkin (2000) showed that once the latent bad loans were appropriately recognized, the bank capital ratio would decline below the 4% minimum requirement from 1995. Subsequently, the capital ratio declined more dramatically to 3.5% in 1996 and 2.3% in 1997. Clearly, bank balance sheets were deteriorating substantially at the onset of the AFC. Along with lenient financial supervision, inefficient corporate exit mechanisms led to the delayed resolution of ailing firms.

There were two other sources of vulnerabilities in the financial sector balance sheet. First, the banking sector with its large external debts became increasingly exposed to the risk of local currency depreciation. Although currency mismatches were tightly regulated for banks as described previously, they were hardly safe from the depreciation of the Korean won since borrowing corporate firms left most of their foreign currency-denominated bank loans unhedged. The depreciation of the won and immediate deterioration of corporate balance sheets in turn led to the rise in credit risks of assets held by financial institutions.

Another source of financial vulnerability was the growing share of NBFIs in financial intermediation as mentioned previously. Relative to commercial banks, NBFIs' balance sheets were much more vulnerable as they were subject to less-stringent regulation and supervision. As many authors (Cho 1999; Choi 2002; Lee et al. 2002) pointed out, deregulation policies were unbalanced between commercial banks and NBFIs, and the asymmetric nature of financial liberalization policies fed into the emergence of NBFIs. The regulatory authority applied much less-stringent standards to NBFIs in their business and risk management. As a result, NBFIs were able to offer more attractive yields on their products such as commercial papers, which shifted financial savings from banks to loosely supervised NBFIs. Consequently, the rising volume of NBFI intermediated credits came with magnified risks for the entire financial system.

In sum, credit flows failed to reflect the true risk-return tradeoff given the "too-big-to-fail" hypothesis based on the implicit government guarantee extended to *chaebols*. The *chaebols*, in turn, exploited NBFI financing to undertake their large-scale investment projects. There were no effective disciplining forces to control misallocation of funds — neither banks, nor supervisors, not to mention financial markets. Globalization accentuated this process. Most foreign banks made loans to Korean banks without proper screening in turn, expecting implicit government bailout. The asymmetric nature of the financial liberalization policies in combination with the legacy of government guarantee of banks and large business conglomerates contributed to the buildup of vulnerabilities at the onset of the AFC.

The Post-AFC Reform and Financial System Transition

During the interim period between the AFC and the GFC, remarkable progress was made to reform Korea's outmoded financial system. The government's financial restructuring program that mobilized massive public funds resulted in rapid consolidation and conglomeration of the financial system. It also contributed to a marked improvement in the capital adequacy and profitability of banks and NBFIs. Drastically open capital markets also grew rapidly both in size and deepness. In particular, the bankruptcy and restructuring of ailing *chaebols* served as a clear signal for the market that the traditional paradigm based on the implicit government guarantee would no longer persist.

IMF Austerity Program and Macroeconomic Adjustments

As the Korean government requested emergency financial assistance from the IMF in November 1997, most of the initial policy responses were led by the IMF programs. The most imminent policy goal of the IMF program was to resolve foreign currency liquidity problems (Fischer 1998). Priority in macroeconomic policies was also given to stabilizing the balance of payments by tightening aggregate expenditures.

On the monetary front, the Bank of Korea raised the inter-bank overnight call rate from 13% to 30%. While contributing to the stabilization of financial market sentiment, the high interest rate policy began exerting serious negative consequences on the highly leveraged corporate sector. The IMF also maintained a stance of contractionary fiscal policy to reduce current account deficits and secure fiscal resources for financial restructuring. Along with macroeconomic tightening, the IMF introduced measures to fully liberalize capital accounts including short-term money markets.

The drastic IMF austerity program was controversial and criticized by many experts and scholars both in Korea and abroad. The criticisms were made largely on the ground that Korea's external debt crisis was a liquidity problem rather than an insolvency problem. Thus, simply applying the old conventional austerity program employed in Latin America would not be appropriate. Another criticism was that the IMF was going beyond the lender of last resort role by demanding structural reforms that would intrude political processes (Feldstein 1998; Radelet at al. 1998). Furman and Stiglitz (1998) argued that the high interest rate policy was not appropriate and could even have destabilizing effects by lowering corporate net worth and local currency values. Cho (2010) also argued that while the high interest rate policy was unavoidable to cope with the shortage in foreign currency, the tight fiscal policy was not desirable given that a short-term fiscal expansion to stabilize the sharp contraction in aggregate demand would not have intensified the foreign currency liquidity crisis given the fiscal soundness of Korea.

In hindsight, it was the success of the external debt rescheduling policy that provided a critical momentum in breaking the watershed to mitigate the liquidity crisis. The Korean government and the IMF pursued external debt rescheduling to convert short-term debts of Korean banks into medium- to long-term debts. On the eve of Christmas in December 1997, 13 advanced countries agreed to provide an USD 8 billion secondary liquidity fund and persuade major creditor banks of respective countries to reschedule short-term debts of Korean banks. The negotiation was successfully completed in New York in January 1998. 134 creditor banks in 32 countries finally agreed to convert 96% of short-term bank debts (USD 21.8 billion) into 1-year (17%), 2-year (45%), and 3-year (38%) maturity debts guaranteed by the Korean government.

The successful debt rescheduling became a watershed allowing the government to use more flexible macroeconomic policies focusing on domestic economic conditions. The IMF and the government began to ease the fiscal stance from February 1998. The monetary stance was also eased subsequently. As Figure 17.3 shows, the overnight call rate was lowered to

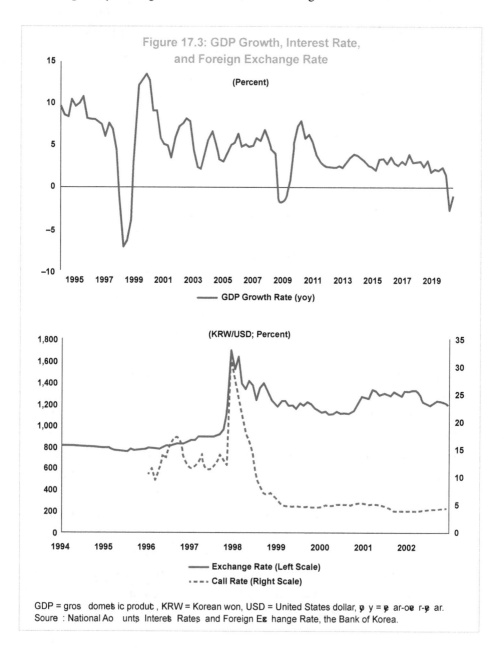

Figure 17.3: GDP Growth, Interest Rate, and Foreign Exchange Rate

GDP = gros domes ic produc , KRW = Korean won, USD = United States dollar, ｙ ｙ = ｙ ar-oｅ r-ｙ ar.
Soure : National Ao unts Interes Rates and Foreign Eꭗ hange Rate, the Bank of Korea.

20% in May and 15% in July 1998. Along with the adjustment in macroeconomic policies, economic activity and GDP growth began recovering fast.

Bank Recapitalization and Financial Consolidation

Along with the IMF austerity program, the government conducted drastic structural reforms with the goal of reconstructing a more robust and balanced financial system. Korea's post-AFC restructuring policy was characterized as follows:

- First, the government mobilized a massive amount of public funds and intervened aggressively for swift identification and closure of insolvent financial institutions.

- Second, priority was given to commercial banks in cleaning up bad loans and recapitalizing while owners were held accountable for the restructuring of NBFIs.

- Third, corporate restructuring was pursued indirectly via the recapitalized banks.

- Fourth, unlike countries where financial consolidation naturally took place in the market as a way of reaping economies of scale and scope, bank consolidations in Korea responded to government impetus. The government pursued bank consolidation and conglomeration in the process of recapitalization by exercising supervisory measures such as merger and acquisition (M&A) and purchase and assumption (P&A) orders.

- Finally, comprehensive governance and capital market reform measures were introduced to foster a more balanced financial system between its traditional bank-based system and the arm's length market-based system.

During the restructuring period of 1998–2006, a total of KRW 168.3 trillion (USD 133 billion) of public funds, approximately 30% of Korea's GDP in 2000, was spent on financial restructuring.[1] The two main agencies for government-led restructuring were the Korea Asset Management Corporation (KAMCO) and the Korea Deposit Insurance Corporation (KDIC). Out of the total amount of fiscal support, KRW 82 trillion was used for the recapitalization of banks in the process of the government-directed

---

[1] As of March 2021, KRW 117.3 trillion or 69.5% of public funds has been recovered.

M&As and P&As, KRW 56 trillion for the purchase of nonperforming loans (NPLs) and other assets, and KRW 30.3 trillion for the deposit repayments for closed institutions.

The number of financial firms declined by 37.5% from 2,103 in 1997 to 1,315 by the end of 2006, and a total of 899 insolvent financial institutions were closed or merged in the restructuring process.

As Figure 17.4 shows, as an outcome of drastic restructuring, both the profitability and the capital soundness of commercial banks improved remarkably. Considering that the asset classification standard was significantly upgraded during the restructuring period, rapid reduction in the NPL ratios indicated that a massive amount of NPLs was resolved in the aftermath of the AFC. It is also noteworthy that, despite losses from massive sell-offs of NPLs, the Bank for International Settlements (BIS) capital ratio of commercial banks increased remarkably alongside recoveries in profitability.

One outcome of the drastic consolidation process was higher market concentrations in the commercial banking and insurance industries. The Herfindahl–Hirschman Index (HHI) in the commercial banking industry rose from 707 in 1996 to 1,454 in 2006, transforming the industry from a "competitive" to a "moderately concentrated" industry. The market

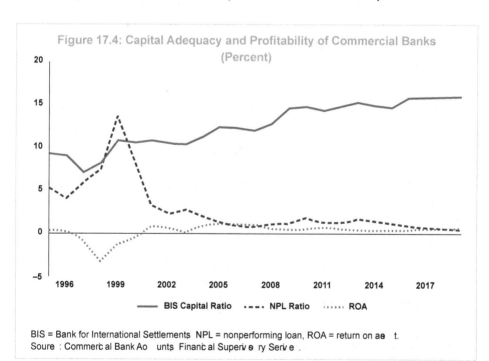

Figure 17.4: Capital Adequacy and Profitability of Commercial Banks (Percent)

BIS = Bank for International Settlements, NPL = nonperforming loan, ROA = return on ae t.
Soure : Commerc al Bank Ao   unts Financ al Superv s ry Serv e .

concentration in the insurance industry, which was already high in 1997, increased further as smaller-sized companies were restructured.

Corporate Restructuring and Reforms in Governance and Exit Systems

Thanks to drastic restructuring policies following the crisis, much was achieved in restoring the soundness of corporate balance sheets as well. In February 1998, the government and large business conglomerates agreed to the corporate restructuring guideline to strengthen transparency and accountability of major shareholders and management. It also aimed at reducing financial leverage and eliminating cross debt guarantees among the subsidiaries of *chaebols*. Following the government's strong policy initiatives, *chaebols* also made voluntary efforts including asset revaluation, debt reduction, and restructuring in investment and employment. Consequently, overall leverage of Korean companies declined substantially. As Figure 17.5 shows, the average debt–equity ratio of corporate firms listed in the stock market declined from nearly 400% in 1997 to 107% in 2007, and the average interest coverage ratio improved from barely 130% in 1997 to 435% in 2007, indicating that the overall credit risk of corporate firms has dramatically fallen compared to the level at the onset of the AFC.

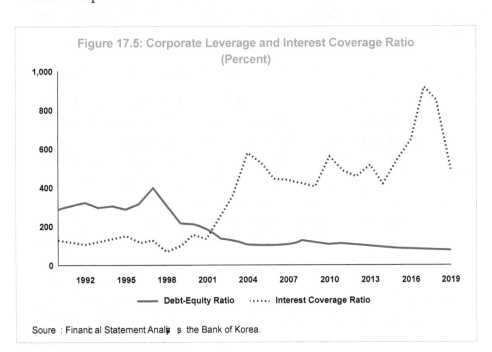

Figure 17.5: Corporate Leverage and Interest Coverage Ratio (Percent)

Soure : Financial Statement Analysis the Bank of Korea.

With the recognition that the exit of insolvent firms was critical to a reduction in vulnerabilities, institutional arrangements to facilitate corporate exits and reorganizations were also streamlined. Hostile and foreign takeovers were allowed and the bankruptcy code was revised to introduce an "economic test" in determining a firm's viability for reorganization, and the out-of-court workout procedure was introduced. The number of corporate reorganizations, compositions, and bankruptcies increased substantially, and M&As including numerous cross-border cases also increased subsequently. In particular, Daewoo Group, the second largest *chaebol* at that time, was finally allowed to go bankrupt and put into the workout program in August 1999, which signaled credible exit threats even for largest *chaebols*.

The progress in corporate restructuring was accompanied by improved governance and ownership structures of large business conglomerates. Shareholders' rights were reinforced and the appointment of outside directors was required to improve the overseeing role of the board of directors. The reform measures put considerable pressure for *chaebols* to improve their mode of governance along with maintaining the soundness of their balance sheets. For instance, Choi et al. (2007) found that the effects of outside directors on firm performance after the reform were strongly positive, while the effects of indigenous institutions such as *chaebol* or family control became much weaker.

Reforms in Financial Supervision and Deposit Insurance Systems

The government also pursed various reform measures to overhaul the outmoded financial regulatory infrastructure. In order to establish a consolidated financial supervisory authority, existing supervisory bodies were merged into a newly established Financial Supervisory Board (FSB) in January 1999, which was superintended by the Financial Supervisory Commission (FSC). The consolidation of supervisory functions under a single agency was a step forward to reflect the reality that the previous segmentation within the financial industries had become increasingly blurred in light of financial innovations and deregulation.

Along with the institutional reform, contents and standards of prudential regulations were significantly upgraded. Prompt corrective action schemes were established for commercial banking and merchant banking industries in April 1998, which were subsequently extended to other NBFIs. Asset classification standards were also upgraded to include forward-looking criteria, according to which the future debt service capacity of debtors must be assessed regardless of current repayment status.

In order to strengthen the transparency of information in the financial market, the accounting and disclosure standards were strengthened to conform to globally best-practiced standards.

A closely related measure with the supervisory reform was the over-hauling of the deposit insurance system. After integrating sector-specific deposit insurance schemes into the KDIC in 1998, the KDIC was given a bigger role as a financial safety net provider. The KDIC, with its expanded resolution capacity, played a critical role in mobilizing public funds by issuing KDIC bonds and recapitalizing ailing financial institutions. The KDIC also began scaling down the protection of deposits from the temporary full blanket system introduced with the outbreak of the AFC. The improvement was a desirable step to mitigate moral hazard problems and strengthen depositors' oversight over the financial institutions.

Policy Lessons and Shifts in Flow of Funds After the AFC

In hindsight, the IMF programs were beneficial in the sense that it accelerated long-delayed structural reforms of the Korean economy. In particular, the reconstruction of financial and corporate balance sheets played a pivotal role in mitigating the impact of the GFC as we discuss in the following section. However, the programs were also experimental at least in the following two respects.

First, the austerity program ignored the potential vicious cycle that could arise from the high interest rate policy through financial accelerator mechanisms. It is now widely recognized that shocks to asset prices and interest rates could generate amplified aggregate impacts in the real economy due to financial frictions. For instance, Gertler, Gilchrist, and Natalucci (2007) showed that the combination of high interest rate policy to defend exchange rate and financial accelerator mechanism could well explain the severity of economic distress that Korea experienced during the AFC. While Korea allowed its exchange rate to float, the drastic propagation of shocks through credit channels could have been mitigated if the central bank had maintained its accommodative monetary policy from the start.

Second, the program was also based on the naïve assumption that immediate and complete opening and liberalization of financial markets would make the economy more efficient and robust. However, the recent findings indicate that it is hard to find robust support for large quantifiable benefits of global financial integration while it apparently raises financial instability risks in open emerging economies (Rey 2015). While Korea upgraded its supervisory standards after the AFC, a lack of macroprudential capacity to oversee and monitor risks associated with capital flows and cross-border financial spillovers exposed the economy again to external shocks at the onset of the GFC.

Irrespective of the potential flaws and side effects, the IMF program turned out to be most successful in Korea among the AFC-affected countries. Both external and internal factors contributed to this outperformance. First, thanks to Korea's strong manufacturing production capacity and substantial depreciation of the Korean won, Korea was able to record a large current account surplus immediately after the crisis, which was instrumental in restoring external credibility. For instance, Korea's current account surplus-to-GDP ratio surged from −1.9% in 1997 to 10.4% in 1998 and 4.4% in 1999.

Second, even before the AFC, consensus was emerging among policymakers and stakeholders on the urgency of structural reforms. The government was conscious that the economy could not sustain growth over the long term without serious restructuring. The pre-crisis debates and the policy capability within the government certainly provided the driving force to implement drastic reform measures mitigating resistance from various interest groups. As a case in point, at the onset of the AFC, a comprehensive financial reform package was prepared by the Presidential Commission for Financial Reform. Subsequently, with the outbreak of the AFC, this package was fully endorsed by the IMF, and the 13 financial reform bills were passed at the National Assembly as a conditionality of the IMF program.

Indeed, the extensive financial and corporate restructuring along with various reform measures introduced after the AFC brought about structural shifts in the pattern of corporate financing and bank asset structures.[2]

The first notable change in the corporate financing pattern after the AFC is the significant increase in reliance on direct financing. The first panel in Figure 17.6 shows the share of direct financing in total corporate external financing (in terms of stock measures). Due to statistical changes in various

---

[2] This section extends Hahm (2008) to recent periods and characterizes the shifting patterns in fund flows.

versions of the system of national accounts (SNAs), the trend for the entire period cannot be tracked. However, the share of direct financing seems to have structurally increased, converging to a level around 50% since 2010. Along with the rapid expansion of capital markets, large companies have become much more dependent upon direct financing.[3]

The second notable change in the corporate financing pattern is the improvement in the maturity structure in direct financing as shown in the second panel of Figure 17.6. As discussed previously, the share of short-term financing increased to an unusually high level before the AFC. The subsequent fall, first triggered by the paralysis of the commercial paper market, continued as firms became more dependent on corporate bonds and stocks. This trend of an improved maturity structure in direct financing also reflected the change in risk attitudes of corporate firms as they recognized the risks of high leverage centered on short-term debts.

Also as an outcome of the government's bank-centered restructuring policy, the commercial banking industry reclaimed its share in financial intermediation. As discussed previously, the sharply rising share of NBFIs before the AFC reflected asymmetric deregulations favorable to NBFIs and *chaebols'* dominance in the NBFI industry. As market participants began to recognize inherent risks of NBFI products amid massive failures of insolvent NBFIs, the share of NBFIs fell substantially in the post-AFC period as shown in the third panel in Figure 17.6. Depositors' increased awareness of risks helped commercial banks to regain their market share, especially as they substantially improved capital soundness with the help of the recapitalization program.

The AFC also brought about a set of noticeable changes in the balance sheets of commercial banks. In particular, as shown in Figure 17.7, household loans expanded substantially after the crisis and gained a greater share relative to corporate loans from 2002. This structural shift reflected both large corporate firms' increased access to direct financing and banks' change in risk attitude toward more diversified household loans. This trend continued until the occurrence of the GFC, resulting in the rapid accumulation of household

---

[3] The share of direct financing fluctuated substantially immediately after the AFC. In 1997, the commercial paper market was paralyzed with the bankruptcies of merchant banking corporations, which caused severe credit and liquidity crunches for ailing *chaebols*. As corporate debtors refinanced their commercial papers by issuing corporate bonds and stocks, the share of direct financing increased temporarily in 1998 and 1999. The ratio fell sharply again in 2000 in the aftermath of the bankruptcy of Daewoo Group. The share of direct financing increased substantially before the GFC but plunged once again with the outbreak of the crisis in 2008. The share recovered its pre-crisis level soon after and has been subsequently stabilized at the 50% level.

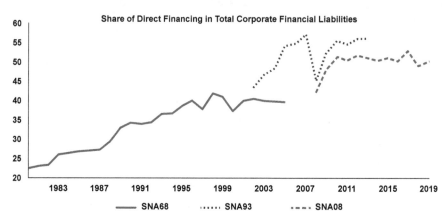

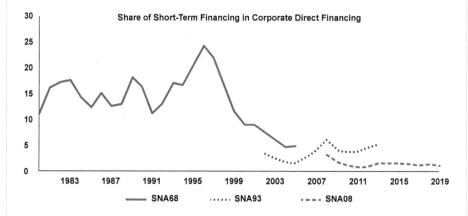

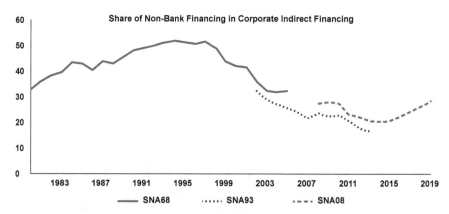

AFC = Asian financial crisis, SNA = system of national accounts.
Soure : Flow of Funds the Bank of Korea.

debts. With the strengthening of prudential regulations on housing-related loans such as the loan-to-value (LTV) and debt service-to-income (DTI) ratios, the share of household loans has been stabilized subsequently at around 50%.

As for corporate loans, the share of SME loans substantially increased after the AFC. As the lower panel in Figure 17.7 shows, the temporary fall in the share of SME loans during the AFC soon recovered, and the share further increased to almost 90% before the GFC. While improved risk management capacity and risk-based pricing helped banks extend SME lending, the

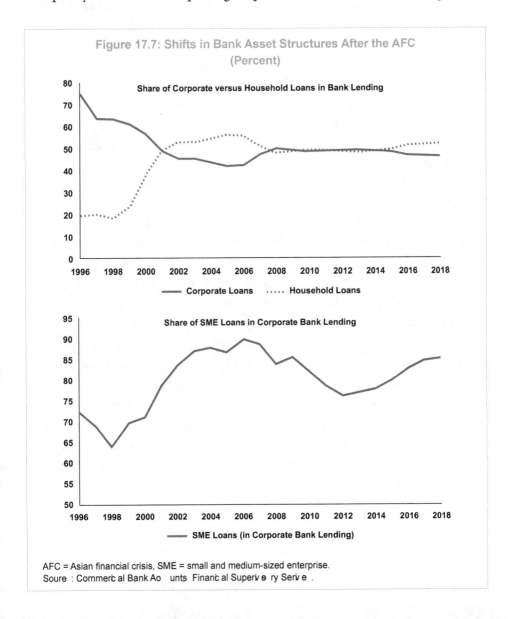

Figure 17.7: Shifts in Bank Asset Structures After the AFC
(Percent)

AFC = Asian financial crisis, SME = small and medium-sized enterprise.
Soure : Commerc al Bank Ao unts Financ al Superv e ry Serv e .

dominance of SME loans in bank lending also partially reflected decreasing loan demand from large good credit firms as they became more dependent on direct sources of funding.

The GFC and Vulnerabilities of the Korean Economy

Korea is a small open economy and as such, it provides greater flexibility to the economy by having the rest of the world as its overall markets, but at the same time, such openness makes the Korean economy more susceptible to adverse external environment. Even after the AFC, when the flexible exchange rate scheme was implemented to ensure macroeconomic flexibility and various restructuring efforts had been made in all sectors of the economy to enhance its soundness and stability, the economy could not be free from the constant flow of external shocks such as business cycles of surrounding economies, global commodity prices, and turmoil in international financial markets.

Indeed, Korea was very badly hit again by the GFC. In the fourth quarter of 2008, exports collapsed, stock prices plunged, and even the trauma from the 1997 crisis resurged. Sentiments in the Korean foreign exchange (FX) market were driven to the extreme. *The Economist* (2009) ranked Korea fourth on its list of emerging market economies which were most likely to turn out as the hopeless victims of the GFC, as recalled by Cho (2012). However, the Korean economy began to rebound immediately, attaining about 8% growth in a year from the second quarter of 2009 to the first quarter of 2010. Indeed, Korea successfully overcame the 2008 crisis, which was especially contrasting to the 1997 crisis when Korea suffered severe and lasting pain.

Then, what are the major factors that made the Korean economy vulnerable to global economic turbulence and enabled its rapid and successful recovery possible? By examining Korea's adjustment to the GFC, this section seeks some clues to how Korea mitigated the impact of external shocks brought about by the GFC.

Crisis Spreading Channels

In the literatures on the economic crisis, economies can be infected via two different channels of contagion: the international trade channel and the international financial market channel. Considering Korea's export-oriented economic structure and open financial markets, both channels played consequential roles in transmitting turbulences of the GFC to the Korean economy.

International Trade Channel

Until the third quarter of 2008, Korea's export had maintained a steady pace of expansion, while the growth of domestic demand had slowed down due to the rapid oil price hike. In fact, Korea's exports in the third quarter of 2008 increased by 27% year-on-year. However, the global market panic in September 2008 changed the whole environment. With high external dependencies, it came as no surprise that the Korean economy was severely hit by the GFC. While most advanced countries experienced a massive asset price plunge and negative growth rates, the Korean economy witnessed a serious contraction in its export demands. The year-over-year growth rate of exports plunged from 27.6% in September to 7.8% (−0.8%, month-to-month) in October and further to −19.5% (−22.3%, month-to-month) in November. This drastic collapse in Korea's exports raised concerns about its capability to obtain foreign currencies, serving as the main basis for the excessively pessimistic outlook and exacerbating investor sentiments in Korea's FX market.

International Financial Market Channel

International financial markets also underwent a terrible shock as panicked financial institutions were desperate to secure United States (US) dollar liquidity by any means possible, which caused rapid capital outflows from emerging markets. As one of the small open economies, Korea was dragged into drifts of the GFC and witnessed rapid and massive capital outflows. According to Kim and Lee (2011) and Cho (2012), the net capital outflow from Korea in October 2008, just one month, was about USD 25 billion, which was far more than the USD 6.4 billion in December 1997, the worst month for the Korean economy during the AFC.

The rapid and massive capital outflows caused concerns about the foreign currency liquidity situations in Korea and strong depreciation pressures on the value of the Korean won against hard currencies. Consequently, the exchange rate of Korean won against US dollar rose by more than 30%, and official foreign reserves plunged by 20% during the period from September to December 2008.

Although the rapid capital outflows in the aftermath of the GFC were accompanied by the contraction of economic activities signaling a possible economic crisis in Korea, the rapid outflows could not be fully explained by domestic macroeconomic factors alone. In retrospect, there existed financial market conditions at home and abroad before the GFC that led to the rapid rise in short-term external debts, which eventually ended up causing extensive capital outflows with the outbreak of the GFC. The integration into the global financial markets not only heightened the volatility of capital flows but also exposed the Korean economy to more serious spillover effects from overseas.

Vulnerabilities in the Foreign Exchange Market at the Onset of the GFC

Prior to the GFC, Korea did not need external borrowing as its current account position comfortably remained in surplus, and the government and the central bank believed that the official foreign reserves that was more than USD 240 billion was sufficient to protect its economy from external turbulence.

However, the impact of the crisis was more severe than expected, accompanying the abrupt and massive capital outflows. Such large-scale capital outflows may have seemed inevitable as these were mainly caused by the severe credit crunch in advanced countries during the GFC. Moreover, Korea suffered a stigma effect from the 1997 crisis, which may have worsened negative views of foreign investors. Nevertheless, there are more issues that need to be analyzed to understand why the Korean economy was hit by the GFC more severely than many other countries.

As reported by Shin and Shin (2011), contrary to the common perception that massive capital outflows mainly resulted from foreign investors' withdrawal of their investments from the Korean stock market, it was Korean banks that played a crucial role in increasing the foreign currency liquidity strain during the GFC. In the fourth quarter of 2008, capital outflows from the Korean banking sector were USD 50.4 billion. This was bigger than the decrease in official foreign reserves from USD 239.7 billion at the end of the third quarter to USD 201.2 billion at the end of 2008. The Korean stock market, in fact, experienced net capital inflows during the same period. In this regard, more important to analyze are the causes and structures of capital inflows into the Korean banking sector during the mid-2000s. These made the abrupt and massive capital outflows possible during the GFC.

Rapid Rise in Short-Term External Debt in the Banking Sector

With the outbreak of the GFC, the most critical concern issued by commentators and investors was that Korea was highly likely to default on external debt due to the foreign currency liquidity problem of its banking sector. As Figure 17.8 shows, from the mid-2000s, Korean banks rapidly increased external debt so that the total external debt recorded USD 366 billion at the end of the second quarter in 2008, increased from USD 160 billion at the end of 2005. The total external debt-to-GDP ratio increased from 17% in 2005 to 30% in 2008 and 36% in 2009, before decreasing steadily from 2010 onward. The external debt-to-GDP ratio was as high as the one during the AFC when the ratio rose to 39% in 1998.

The maturity structure of Korea's external debt was more problematic. For example, short-term external debt recorded USD 187.8 billion at the end of the third quarter of 2008, increased from USD 65.1 billion at the end of 2005. This resulted in the short-term debt ratio being 52% of the total external debt, amounting to 78% of official foreign reserves.

Foreign investors also observed that the rapidly increased external debts were mostly from short-term borrowing by banks, as shown in Figure 17.9. They viewed the Korean economy as vulnerable to the global credit crunch. As Lee and Song (2012) described, for example, *Financial Times* (2009) reported that although Korea had the world's sixth largest official foreign reserves, the economy had one of the thinnest external debt coverage ratios among emerging market economies in September 2008 due to the massive amount of short-term external debt (Figure 17.10).

Among the elements contributing to the rapid expansion of Korean banks' external debts during the 2006–2008 period, an indirect but more fundamental one was the exuberant global liquidity and low interest rate environment supported by expansionary monetary policies in advanced economies, which provided procyclical capital flows to emerging market economies.[4] In addition, under the low interest rate environment in the

---

[4] For instance, using Korean banks' liability data, Hahm et al. (2013) showed that the noncore bank liabilities such as external debts were not only highly procyclical but were also affected by the US interest rate. This implies that the pre-crisis expansion of global liquidity provided an impetus for the excessive increase in external debts of Korean banks.

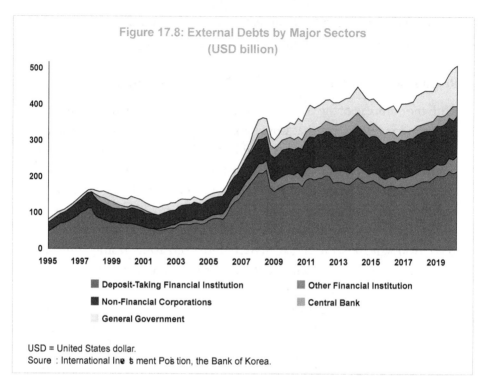

Figure 17.8: External Debts by Major Sectors
(USD billion)

■ Deposit-Taking Financial Institution   ■ Other Financial Institution
■ Non-Financial Corporations   ■ Central Bank
  General Government

USD = United States dollar.
Soure : International Ine s ment Pos tion, the Bank of Korea.

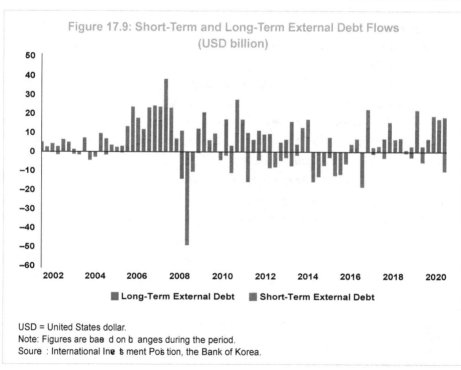

Figure 17.9: Short-Term and Long-Term External Debt Flows
(USD billion)

■ Long-Term External Debt   ■ Short-Term External Debt

USD = United States dollar.
Note: Figures are bae d on b anges during the period.
Soure : International Ine s ment Pos tion, the Bank of Korea.

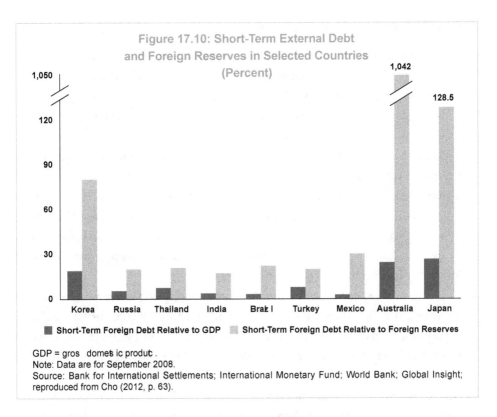

Figure 17.10: Short-Term External Debt and Foreign Reserves in Selected Countries (Percent)

GDP = gros domeš ic produt .
Note: Data are for September 2008.
Source: Bank for International Settlements; International Monetary Fund; World Bank; Global Insight; reproduced from Cho (2012, p. 63).

mid-2000s, global banks in advanced countries also tried to expand their businesses in emerging market countries including Korea to find more profitable business opportunities. As Table 17.1 shows, according to the BIS database, the average annual growth rate of global banks' lending to Korea was 25% during 2000–2007, which was much higher than that of their total lending, implying that there had been excessive bank capital inflows to Korea.

Table 17.1: Global Banks' Overseas Lending, Annual Average Growth Rate (Percent)

	1984–1989	1990–1997	1998	2000–2007	2008	2009–2010
Total	10.7	10.1	−4.1	17.5	−11.9	2.1
Developed Countries	17.7	11.2	11.2	18.0	−12.9	0.0
Developing Countries	5.4	10.0	−2.5	18.9	−6.1	9.5
Offshore Regions	19.5	10.9	−10.6	15.0	−12.9	8.2
Korea	1.4	16.2	−18.2	24.7	−21.9	11.6

Soure s Cons lidated foreign b aims of Bank for International Settlements reporting banš on indiv dual o untries by nationality of reporting banš Bank for International Settlements reprodue d from Lee and Hong (2011).

Surge in Demands for FX Risk Hedging

Among other elements that motivated Korean banks to pile up external debt from mid-2000s, one of the most frequently pointed out was the rapid expansion of demand for FX forward contracts in Korea. If an exporting company is reluctant to be exposed to exchange rate risk, it can open an FX forward contract of selling US dollars (export proceeds) for Korean won with a Korean bank. This means that the bank is now exposed to exchange rate risk in the future. If the bank wants to hedge the risk in its forward position, it must make an arrangement to sell US dollars it expects to receive in the future, and one way to do so, which many Korean banks adopted then, is to borrow in US dollars today and make repayment by using the dollars to be delivered by the exporting company in the future. These transactions inevitably increased external debt of banks.[5]

The most spearheaded Korean companies that massively increased FX forward contracts were shipbuilders who observed their order books expanding following the upturn of the global demand cycle for ships. As Korean shipbuilders had the largest global market share, the sizes of their shipbuilding contracts were substantial. Their production cycles were long enough to expose Korean shipbuilders to large exchange rate risks, and thus they needed to hedge them through the FX forward contracts.[6] Along with Korean shipbuilding companies, domestic asset management companies (AMCs) also massively increased FX forward contracts from 2006. Foreign securities investment of Korean investors rose from USD 1.5 billion in 2005 to USD 13 billion in 2006, and further to USD 27 billion in 2007 following the policy that encouraged overseas investment announced in January 2007. Korean AMCs increased FX forward contracts for a large part of these investments and contributed to the rapid expansion of Korean banks' external debts. In this sense, currency risks of exporting firms and AMCs were converted into foreign currency liquidity risks of banks.

---

[5] Because importers found it relatively easy to pass through the fluctuations in the exchange rate into changes in import prices, the hedging ratio for import transactions was relatively low compared with that for export transactions. While FX forwards sold by exporters rose to 32.3% of exports in 2007 from 24.7% in 2005, FX forwards bought by importers declined from 16.5% of imports to 15.4% during the same period. The expectation of a weaker US dollar, to be mentioned in the following section, contributed to the low hedging ratio for Korean importers.

[6] According to the Bank of Korea (2010), the shipbuilding orders received by Korean companies rose to USD 62 billion (by 97%) in 2006 and to USD 98 billion (by 58%) in 2007. At the same time, the total amount of forward contracts by shipbuilding companies rose to USD 35 billion in 2006 and USD 53 billion in 2007.

Moreover, expectations of the Korean won's appreciation also led the shipbuilders and AMCs to rapidly expand their hedging demand, building up a massive amount of external debts in the banking system. The gradual but solid appreciation of the Korean won against the US dollar from 2003 prompted anticipations on further appreciation of the Korean won accompanied by an almost threefold increase of foreign reserves. Such expectations were further built up in the FX market due to the increased FX forward sold by Korean exporters and AMCs.

Table 17.2 shows the net purchase of FX forward positions by domestic banks along with their external borrowings before the GFC. It can be observed that most of the external borrowings of the Korean banks were financed by short-term external debts. The FX forward contract-related short-term external debts were considered as safe at that time because they could be repaid with US dollar payments delivered by shipbuilding companies and AMCs at the date of maturity.

Massive Capital Inflows Through Foreign Bank Branches

To hedge the large exchange rate risk due to the rapid increase in FX forward sold by shipbuilders and AMCs, Korean banks attempted to square their positions by either borrowing foreign currency funds directly in the international financial markets, typically done by foreign bank branches (FBBs), or taking short positions by entering FX swap contracts, typically done by domestic banks. FBBs in Korea were functioning as intermediaries

Table 17.2: FX Forward Positions and External Borrowing of Korean Banks (USD 100 million)

	2002	2003	2004	2005	2006	2007	2008
Net Purchase of FX Forward Positions	7.2	7.2	529.1	481.7	810.1	1291.8	740.5
Bank External Borrowing	70.8	48.1	9.2	41.9	450.0	391.9	−203.2
Change in Short-Term Debt	79.4	26.2	36.8	68.3	448.2	378.9	−210.1

FX = foreign ex ange, USD = United States dollar.
Sources: the Bank of Korea; reproduced from Cho and Hahm (2016, p. 173).

of foreign currency funding for domestic banks. However, the FBBs were criticized for amplifying foreign currency liquidity risks as they were loosely regulated and monitored in comparison to domestic banks. In fact, it was believed that FBBs could easily raise foreign currency funds because they had access to ample FX liquidity through their respective headquarters, and it was assumed that foreign currency liquidity risks of FBBs must be monitored and controlled also by their headquarters. Therefore, the financial supervisory authorities in Korea did not pay much attention to the potential foreign currency liquidity risk of FBBs.

In addition, none of the foreign currency liquidity-related regulations that applied to domestic banks were applied to FBBs, and only the combined positions of FX spot and FX futures were regulated by the financial supervisory authority. FBBs in Korea thus could relatively freely expand the supply of foreign currency funds in the form of FX swaps and obtain risk-free profits from the foreign currency-related derivative trading.

The FBBs also borrowed foreign currency funds in the short term as interest rates and the perceived liquidity risk were low given that those funds were usually interoffice loans from their respective headquarters. In this regard, it can be said that the asymmetric FX market regulation

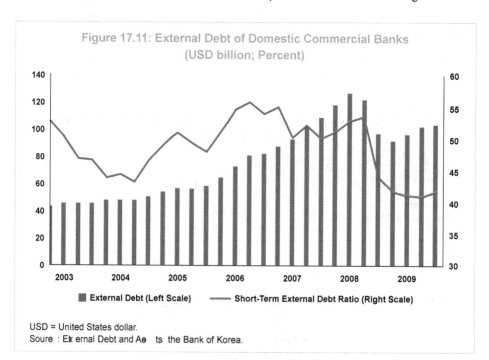

Figure 17.11: External Debt of Domestic Commercial Banks (USD billion; Percent)

■ External Debt (Left Scale)　——— Short-Term External Debt Ratio (Right Scale)

USD = United States dollar.
Soure : Ek ernal Debt and Ae ts the Bank of Korea.

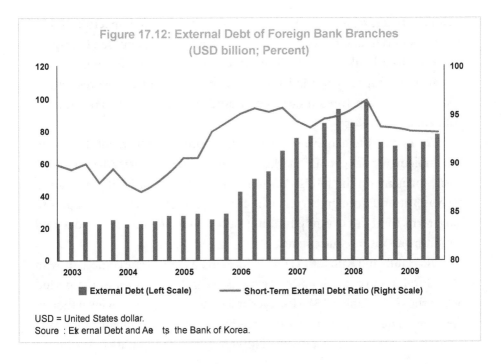

Figure 17.12: External Debt of Foreign Bank Branches (USD billion; Percent)

USD = United States dollar.
Soure : Ek ernal Debt and Ae ts the Bank of Korea.

between domestic banks and FBBs contributed to the rapid increase in short-term external debts and led to large maturity mismatches in foreign currency-denominated assets and liabilities of the Korean banking sector.

Another problem of the rapid expansion in FX swap transaction was that they increased the interconnectedness among financial institutions and markets at the onset of the 2008 crisis. As domestic banks needed more Korean won funds to finance FX swap transactions, the expansion in FX swaps led to the increase in noncore liabilities of domestic banks such as certificates of deposits (CDs) and bank debentures. These Korean won funds raised by domestic banks through noncore liabilities were swapped with the FBBs' foreign currency-denominated funds, and the FBBs in turn invested these Korean won funds in domestic financial markets. Consequently, it can be said that the supply of foreign currency fund by the FBBs through the FX derivatives significantly raised vulnerability of the overall Korean banking sector to the shocks from the international financial market.

Behind the Scenes: Lack of Considerations on Macro-Prudence

As in other emerging market economies, commercial banks are major players in the financial markets in Korea. Considering such a bank-oriented financial structure, it is not difficult to imagine that small uncertainties or problems in refinancing foreign currency liabilities of banks led the whole economy to a banking crisis. Therefore, enhancing the FX-related risk management capacity of the banking sector and securing the regulatory system to restrain foreign currency liquidity risks are crucial tasks for policymakers in Korea.

As an effort to achieve such aims, the Korean government developed and implemented a set of FX market regulations in the aftermath of the 1997 crisis, focusing on the foreign currency liquidity risk of individual banks, such as 3-month foreign currency liquidity ratio requirement, medium- to long-term foreign currency funding ratio requirements, and 7-day and 1-month gap ratio requirements.

As Hahm and Kim (2011) reported, Korean banks were complying with these foreign currency liquidity regulations and guidelines in the period before the GFC (Table 17.3). However, it deserves attention that even though there was general compliance with banking regulations, Korean banks were distressed because they ran short of foreign currency liquidity in the fourth quarter of 2008.

Table 17.3: Foreign Currency Liquidity Indicators Before the GFC

	2007	2008	2009[5]	Supervisory Guidance
3-Month Foreign Currency Liquidity Ratio[1]	102.7	98.9	106.0	≥ 85.0
Medium- to Long-Term Foreign Currency Funding Ratio[2]	125.1	105.6	110.6	≥ 80.0
7-Day Gap Ratio[3]	3.7	3.3	2.0	≥ 0.0
1-Month Gap Ratio[4]	2.9	0.4	2.5	≥ −10.0

GFC = global financial crisis.
Notes
[1] Foreign currency assets less than 3 months due divided by foreign currency liabilities less than 3 months due.
[2] Foreign currency funding longer than 1 year divided by foreign currency loans with maturity longer than 1 year.
[3] Foreign currency assets less than 7 days due minus foreign currency liabilities less than 7 days due, divided by total foreign currency assets
[4] Foreign currency assets less than 1 month due minus foreign currency liability less than 1 month due, divided by total foreign currency assets
[5] March 2009.
Sources: the Bank of Korea; reproduced from Hahm and Kim (2011, p. 289).

Overall, the massive increase in short-term external debts of Korean banks would have been a less acute problem if it had been matched by a similar increase in external assets. In fact, foreign currency assets and liabilities were almost balanced for the economy as a whole. However, mismatches in foreign currency balance sheets of individual sectors were expanding considerably, especially in the banking sector. The relatively large official foreign reserves accumulated by the central bank and thus improved aggregate level FX soundness indicators masked the foreign currency liquidity risk concentrated in the banking sector (Figure 17.13).

In this sense, regulatory measures implemented after the AFC were mainly microprudential policy tools focusing on the soundness of individual banks' FX balance sheets. These microprudential measures focusing on the solvency of the individual banks proved not to be sufficient to deal with financial risks enlarged by the factors like herd behavior of banks and procyclicality of capital flows. After the GFC, financial supervisory authorities in Korea were asked to devise macroprudential measures to limit foreign currency liquidity risk exposures of banks and make banks install adequate internal systems to monitor and control currency and maturity mismatches.

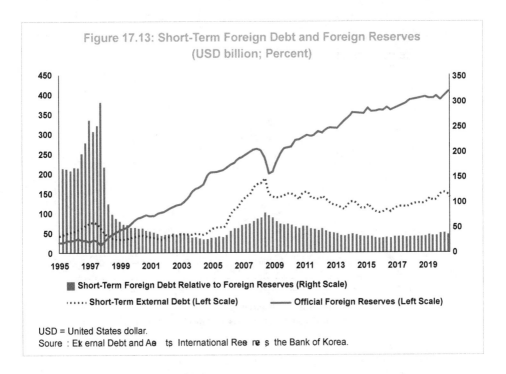

Figure 17.13: Short-Term Foreign Debt and Foreign Reserves
(USD billion; Percent)

Short-Term Foreign Debt Relative to Foreign Reserves (Right Scale)

Short-Term External Debt (Left Scale)   Official Foreign Reserves (Left Scale)

USD = United States dollar.
Source : External Debt and Assets International Reserves the Bank of Korea.

The Macroeconomic Impacts of the GFC

Comparisons of Macroeconomic Impacts of Crises

When it came to the Korean economy, while the 1997 crisis was mainly driven by the asset side problems that amplified credit risks of banks as well as the double mismatch problems in the FX liabilities of banks and corporates, the 2008 crisis was mainly triggered by the liability-side problems and liquidity risks reflected in the FX funding structures of banks. Therefore, different from the recovery from the 1997 crisis that required an enormous amount of time and financial resources to address latent bad loans and rebuild damaged capital adequacy, recovery from the 2008 crisis was achieved at a faster pace, supported by liquidity provisions from the central bank and the government.

In addition, Korea's credit market was largely immune to the GFC. Shocks to the FX market did not develop into a full-fledged financial market crisis. As Figure 17.14 shows, while bank loans continued to expand, no apparent rises were witnessed in either the ratio of NPLs or the ratio of dishonored promissory notes. No banks were bailed out by the government, and no indications of bank-runs were recognized. Therefore, for the Korean economy, the 2008 crisis was far from a credit crisis or banking crisis, and this was the most essential difference from the 1997 crisis.

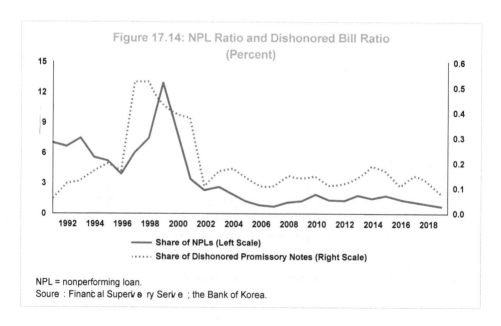

Figure 17.14: NPL Ratio and Dishonored Bill Ratio (Percent)

——— Share of NPLs (Left Scale)

⋯⋯⋯ Share of Dishonored Promissory Notes (Right Scale)

NPL = nonperforming loan.
Soure : Financ al Superv e ry Serv e ; the Bank of Korea.

Along with the recovery of neighboring emerging market economies such as China from January 2009, Korea's exports also started to rebound at a relatively faster pace. Although the recovery process of the Korean economy was not the best among countries, excluding advanced countries, the stability of the Korean economy, such as growth rates and inflation rates, could be second to none in the world.

While recovery was possible based on the stabilization of global financial markets and the recovery of global trade, the structural reforms and restructuring, which had been carried out steadily in Korea since the AFC, gave the economy a buffer and enhanced capacity to respond to the crisis and avoid a prolonged recession. In addition, comprehensive and timely implementation of expansionary macroeconomic policies of the central bank and the government contributed to making the recovery faster than expected (Kim 2012).

Factors of Shock Mitigation During the GFC

Various factors worked in mitigating the negative consequences of the GFC in Korea. A set of factors contributed to preserving the domestic banking sector, and others made the recovery of exports relatively faster. As Cho (2012) argued, these factors can be broadly classified into two categories: pre-crisis fundamentals and post-crisis macroeconomic policy reactions. The pre-crisis fundamentals include improved financial soundness of the corporate sector and banking sectors, large official foreign reserves, and modest rise in housing prices, while the post-crisis policy reactions include monetary and fiscal policies that were carried out on time and effectively stabilized the economy.

Progress in Economic Restructuring Since the AFC

According to Hahm and Kim (2011), Cho (2012), and others, the progress in economic restructuring achieved since the 1997 crisis was the key factor that saved the Korean economy from the GFC. Such achievements in economic restructuring include enhancement in financial soundness of corporates and banks, for instance.

The financial soundness of the corporate sector was essential in mitigating the negative impact of the GFC on the economy. Since the 1997 crisis, Korean companies had executed serious financial restructuring, including asset revaluation and debt repayment under the government's restructuring program, and significantly improved their financial soundness as shown earlier in Figures 17.5 and 17.6. This achievement greatly supported the Korean corporate sector to withstand the financial constraints and demand contraction posed by the GFC.

Banks also secured stronger buffers to cushion shocks in 2008 than in 1997. With significantly enhanced capital adequacy and profitability as shown in Figure 17.4, the banking sector was able to avoid a critical situation. Hahm and Kim (2011) reported that Korea belonged to a group of countries with a banking sector showing the lowest NPL ratio in 2008 and no significant rise in the ratio in 2009. Considering that the GFC was triggered by the housing market adjustment and rapid deleveraging of household loans in advanced countries, Korea's relatively stable housing market largely contributed to the soundness of the banking sector.

All in all, the improved financial soundness of banking and corporate sectors played crucial roles in protecting Korea's foreign currency crisis from spreading into a banking crisis. This also helped in sustaining domestic demand during the GFC, despite tremendous shocks flooding into Korea through trade and foreign currency liquidity channels.

Flexible and Timely Macroeconomic Policy Responses

Flexible and timely macroeconomic policy responses also contributed to effectively mitigating the negative impact of the GFC. In particular, the expansionary stance taken by fiscal and monetary authorities during the 2008 crisis was quite in contrast to the contractionary policies during the 1997 crisis.

Monetary Policy

Among the numbers of policy responses during the 2008 crisis, monetary policy was the most contrasting to the one during the 1997 crisis. While the central bank's short-term interest rate was increased from around 12% to almost 30% in 1997, the policy rate was lowered from 5.25% to 2.00% at the onset of the GFC. There is no suspicion that the expansionary monetary policy in the GFC was essential in protecting the Korean economy from the external turbulence, whereas the monetary tightening aggravated the AFC.

The expansionary monetary policy helped to alleviate fears of a credit crunch, but abundant liquidities also lowered domestic interest rates and thus weighed depreciation pressure on the Korean won. Therefore, it could be said that the critical difference in the monetary policy environment was the overall foreign currency liquidity situation reflected in the foreign reserves when the crisis was triggered. Given the imminent depletion of official foreign reserves, the contractionary monetary policy in December 1997 may have been inevitable. However, the Korean economy had space to manage on this front in 2008.

In fact, the Korean government's stance to the FX market was the most important factor that led to different foreign reserve situations. During the 1997 crisis, the government believed that it could, and should, control the FX market and maneuvered a gradual depreciation before the IMF conditionality was imposed. This stance only created speculations in FX market and precipitated foreign reserve depletion. During the 2008 crisis, in contrast, the government allowed the exchange rate to move freely to buffer against external shock.[7] This eventually secured monetary policy flexibility as well as the automatic adjustment role of the exchange rate.

Fiscal Policy

The Korean government's stances of fiscal policy were not as contrasting as those of monetary policy across the AFC and the GFC. During both crises, expansionary fiscal policies were adopted and the budget deficits, about 3% of GDP, were also similar. However, the procedures to these similar consequences were different.

During the AFC, the IMF recommended that the Korean government preserve a budget balance when fiscal stimulus was most desired. The expansionary fiscal stance and a budget deficit were allowed in February 1998 after the recession was taken hold and deepened.

In 2008, in contrast, the government announced its expansionary fiscal stance as soon as the GFC broke out and executed the fiscal stimulus. A supplementary budget of KRW 10 trillion, about 1% of GDP, was raised and carried out in November 2008, and an additional supplementary budget of KRW 28.4 trillion, about 2.8% of GDP, was arranged in March 2009. Considering time lags in implementation, the early implementation of fiscal expenditure must have contributed to stabilizing the economy in 2009.

Numerous efforts of the government also contributed to alleviating the disruptions in the financial market during the GFC. The government

---

[7] According to Kim (2012), even before the GFC, the Korean government limited its intervention in the FX market by allowing the exchange rates to be determined by supply and demand conditions in the market.

announced that it would provide provisional guarantees in rolling over the short-term external debts of domestic banks until the end of June 2009 (later extended to December 2009). Although no banks were hinged on government funds, this policy helped attenuate anxieties of international investors. Also, a fund of KRW 10 trillion was raised for Korean bond market stabilization, from which only KRW 5 trillion was utilized before the dissolution. In addition, the government strengthened capital bases of public credit guarantee agencies and even attempted to persuade Korean banks to roll over their loans to SMEs.

Expansion of Foreign Reserves and a Swap Arrangement with the Federal Reserve Board

The enlarged official foreign reserves contributed to reducing the negative effects of a sudden stop in capital flows to Korea. And the mode of deploying foreign reserves was also advanced. As mentioned earlier, unlike in 1997, the government did not deplete foreign reserves by targeting a certain level for the exchange rate. Rather than fighting against the market, the government focused its efforts on supporting Korean banks by providing foreign currency liquidity. Therefore, it was not a surprise to observe that the decrease of official foreign reserves by about USD 40 billion during the period from September to December 2008 was almost the same as the decrease of Korean banks' short-term external debt. In addition, the Korean government and the Bank of Korea secured more foreign currency liquidity through currency swaps with the US and other countries. What made the biggest contribution to the stabilization of the FX market was the announcement that the Bank of Korea had signed a currency swap contract with the Federal Reserve Board amounting to USD 30 billion on October 29, 2008 at the height of the GFC.[8] The Bank of Korea also worked out to extend the currency swap arrangement with the Bank of Japan on December 12, from USD 3 billion

---

[8] Considering that Korea accumulated official foreign reserves of over USD 250 billion before the GFC, it was difficult to examine how meaningful the currency swap of USD 30 billion was. In fact, the stabilizing effect of the currency swap contract of USD 30 billion did not persist long. Only after the Federal Reserve Board (FRB) announced that it would extend the currency swap agreement with the Bank of Korea in February and June 2009, foreign investors' confidence in the Korean banking sector strengthened, and the FX market stability could be secured. Nevertheless, considering that global financial institutions were desperate to secure US dollar liquidity by any means possible at the onset of the GFC and most of Korean banks' external debts were denominated in the US dollar, it would be appropriate to argue that the currency swap contract with the FRB contributed to stabilizing panicked financial institutions.

to USD 20 billion, and announced a currency swap contract to be signed with the People's Bank of China.[9]

Macroprudential Measures Adopted After the GFC

Our discussions so far illustrate that the magnitude of external shocks is not the sole or most significant factor in identifying economic consequences of a crisis. The two different crisis experiences of the Korean economy — the 1997 crisis when the overall economy confronted the crisis prompted by a comparatively modest external shock (AFC) and the 2008 crisis when economic resilience was undeterred by the tremendous external shock (GFC) — demonstrate a key lesson that sound economic fundamentals are essential for stability in an open economy and, therefore, should not be undermined. Contrary to many advanced countries, the fact that Korea did not suffer severe deleveraging or an asset price meltdown during the GFC was definitely an important factor that allowed the Korean economy to rebound early.

Based on earlier discussions in this study, we can also draw policy implications as follows: First, maintaining sound balance sheets of individual financial institutions is a prerequisite to secure financial and economic stability. Second, financial soundness of individual financial institutions alone does not guarantee stability of the whole financial system and macroeconomic soundness, and therefore, there should be systemic risk management. Third, as an open economy, it is necessary to develop a macroprudential regulatory framework to address systemic risk potential and procyclicality that result from the fluctuations in global financial cycles and international capital flows.

Macroprudential Policy Measures

Strengthening FX Liquidity Regulations

As we discussed previously, although individual banks satisfied required soundness in their FX balance sheets, the government should have noticed

---

[9] Again, it is not clear how effective the currency swap arrangements with the Bank of Japan and the People's Bank of China were. However, the Korean government diagnosed that it was urgent to recover the confidence of panicked foreign investors to stop rapid capital outflows and sought the currency swap arrangements with large economies rather than the IMF rescue program or the Chiang Mai Initiative (CMI) support.

the system-wide vulnerability resulting from the rapid accumulation of short-term external debt in the Korean banking sector during the period leading to the GFC. Hence, in the aftermath of the crisis, one of the greatest challenges for the government was to manage excessive growth of foreign currency-denominated assets and liabilities in the banking sector and to devise policy measures to counter the problem in an effective manner. To respond to these challenges, the Korean government introduced an enhanced policy framework which included tightening of foreign currency liquidity regulations and implementation of macroprudential policy measures on FX transactions.

In 2010, the regulation and supervision over the FX-related soundness of individual banks were greatly strengthened. The government set an explicit upper limit on the FX derivative positions of banks, strengthened regulations on foreign currency-denominated loans, and implemented prudential regulations to enhance the FX-related risk management capacity of individual financial institutions.[10]

Ceilings on FX Forward Positions and Macroprudential Levy

The episode at the onset of the GFC also reminded Korean financial supervisory authorities of the necessity to introduce a set of macroprudential regulations such as ceilings on FX derivative positions and a macroprudential levy on noncore foreign currency-denominated liabilities.[11]

In June 2010, the Korean government announced that new macroprudential regulations would be introduced to moderate the excessive volatility and procyclicality of capital flows as well as to reduce short-term external debts of the banking sector. These new regulations included the maximum

---

[10]Regarding the FX liquidity ratio regulations, differentiated liquidity weights were newly designed for respective foreign currency-denominated assets. The minimum required level of medium- to long-term foreign currency funding ratio was raised from 80% to 90% and subsequently to 100%. Other measures were also intended to constrain the expansion of short-term external debt of banks by requiring banks to obtain more equity capital. In addition, new standards were imposed to discourage excessive FX-derivative transactions of commercial banks through a ceiling of 125% of actual hedging demands of corporates in January 2010, which was lowered to 100% in August 2010. The government also implemented a minimum requirement for holdings of safe foreign currency-denominated assets effective from July 2010, which must be more than 2% of the total amount of foreign currency-denominated assets or maximum possible capital outflows within 2 months.

[11]In addition, prudential measures were needed to mitigate the procyclical bank leverage financed by wholesale funding. For instance, Hahm, Shin, and Shin (2013) found that the noncore liability ratio has significant predictive power for subsequent currency and credit crises based on a panel probit study of emerging and developing economies.

ceilings on FX forward positions effective from October 2010. The ceilings on the FX forward positions were set at 50% of equity capital for domestic banks and 250% for FBBs in October 2010, which were lowered to 40% and 200%, respectively, in July 2011.

Furthermore, in December 2010, the Korean government announced that it would introduce a macroprudential levy on the foreign currency-denominated liabilities of domestic banks and the FBBs, along with the reinstatement of taxation on domestic bond investments by foreign investors in January 2011. The macroprudential levy was to curb procyclical wholesale foreign currency funding of domestic banks and the FBBs and to improve the maturity structure of external debts of the Korean banking industry. After the legislation process of the National Assembly of Korea, the macroprudential levy became effective from August 2011.[12]

Assessments of Macroprudential Policy Measures

There had been some important cyclical and structural changes in the Korean banking sector since the GFC, which led to a significant reduction in vulnerabilities such as foreign currency liquidity mismatches and their linkage to FX market volatility. For instance, Korean shipbuilders' demand for medium- to long-term FX hedging decreased due to a steep decline in ship orders. The decline helped to lessen foreign currency liquidity mismatches of the FBBs. Along with this, it is noteworthy that macroprudential measures implemented after the GFC have also contributed to the decline in the vulnerability.

As shown in Figures 17.11 and 17.12, since the implementation of strengthened supervisory and macroprudential measures, short-term external debts of domestic banks and the FBBs have declined substantially. Along with the decrease in short-term external debt ratios, domestic banks' foreign currency liquidity position has also improved. Overall, the introduction of ceilings on FX derivative transactions and FX forward positions could be assessed to have notable success in restraining Korean banks' practice of hedging US dollar forward positions by holding Korean won carry trade positions, funded with short-term US dollar borrowings. As the funds supplied by the

---

[12]The rate for the macroprudential levy was determined as 20 basis points for short-term foreign currency-denominated liabilities of maturity up to 1 year, and the rate could go down to 5 basis points for long-term foreign currency-denominated liabilities of maturity exceeding 5 years.

FBBs through FX swap contracts and derivative transactions had previously increased the vulnerability of domestic banks and volatility of the Korean FX market, the macroprudential measures were evaluated as effective.

In addition, since the implementation of strengthened policy measures including the macroprudential levy, the debt structure of the Korean banking sector has improved substantially. For instance, Hahm and Cho (2014) conducted a counter-factual vector autoregression (VAR) analysis and found that the macroprudential levy implemented in Korea after the GFC has indeed contributed to the significant decline in noncore funding of domestic banks.

Concluding Remarks

For the Korean economy, the impacts of the AFC and the GFC looked alike on the surface in that sudden and excessive capital outflows triggered serious foreign currency liquidity problems that were propagated into the simultaneous collapse of financial asset values and real economic activities. However, the problems inherent in the financial system at the onset of each crisis were different in nature, so that the magnitude and duration of the domestic economic hardship also differed a great deal across the two crises.

The 1997 crisis in Korea was fraught not only with double mismatch problems in the FX liabilities of banks and corporate firms but also with asset side problems in the balance sheet of financial institutions, and thus could be characterized as a credit crisis as well as an external debt crisis. In contrast, the 2008 crisis in Korea was driven by liability problems such as noncore, wholesale FX funding of banks, and thus could be characterized as mainly a foreign currency liquidity crisis. Consequently, recovery from the AFC took considerable time and required enormous public resources to address latent bad loan problems and reconstruct damaged balance sheets of banks and corporate firms. On the other hand, recovery from the GFC occurred at a faster pace, with the help of foreign currency liquidity provision from the central bank, supported by the bilateral currency swap arrangement with the US Federal Reserve.

Furthermore, while the 1997 crisis was a crisis rooted in both the microprudential problems of individual financial institutions and the macroprudential problems worsened by the exchange rate risk, the 2008 crisis mainly reflected the macroprudential systemic problems. This implies that, despite the post-AFC restructuring effort greatly enhancing the soundness of individual financial institutions, policy responses were focused on the microeconomic problems so that there remained system-wide problems. These include exposure to procyclical capital flows and excessive dependence on short-term external financing accelerated by the herd behavior of financial institutions, which were witnessed at the onset of the GFC.

Discussions in this study suggest that Korea's experience over the AFC and the GFC yields a set of valuable policy lessons for open emerging economies. First, financial deregulation and liberalization without proper establishment of strong market discipline can lead to significant misallocations of credit and structural vulnerabilities. This is even more so when the legacy of government guarantee and "too-big-to-fail" moral hazard distort the incentives of market participants as witnessed in the pre-AFC financial markets in Korea.

Second, albeit the drastic restructuring of the banking and corporate sector along with institutional reforms of the supervisory and governance systems, the lack of macroprudential capacity to oversee and monitor systemic risk potential can lead to structural vulnerabilities such as exposures to overly procyclical capital flows, herd behavior of banks, and concentration of risks. The Korean experience provides a case in point showing that liquidity risk management at individual banks tends to ignore shifts in aggregate liquidity situations resulting from system-wide shocks and their endogenous interaction with asset prices such as exchange rates. During the GFC, FX swap transactions became a main transmission channel of global liquidity shocks in Korea, through which domestic banks were put under excessive pressure to meet foreign currency needs for additional margin requirements and unwinding derivative positions caused by the sharp depreciation of the Korean won. The off-balance sheet channels of interconnectedness among financial institutions and financial markets, and potential propagation mechanism of foreign currency liquidity shocks should have been identified and closely monitored.

The Korean experience strongly suggests that a macroprudential approach is necessary and instrumental in safeguarding the financial system in open emerging economies. Indeed, the post-GFC policy measures introduced in Korea, such as a macroprudential levy, have been effective in mitigating the procyclical noncore wholesale funding of domestic banks.

However, macroprudential regulations would not be a panacea in coping with rapid and large capital inflows. These may also exert efficiency costs for the economy. The optimal macroprudential framework must focus also on consolidating the institutional capacity, along with reducing the risk of overkill and closing loopholes.

Third, although it cannot be a perfect barrier, the balance sheet soundness of banks and corporate sectors and the swift and flexible macroeconomic policy responses must be the first line of defense. In the GFC episode, along with securing foreign currency liquidity line, the significantly improved capital adequacy of Korean banks and NBFIs acted as an effective shock absorber in preventing external shocks from propagating into a full-fledged financial crisis.

Finally, in designing a policy framework to safeguard the financial system, as policy changes in one country could have significant spillover effects on other countries through trade and financial channels, a certain degree of global cooperation may be required. In this globally integrated economic environment, for each country's government to design and implement effective domestic policies, an accurate understanding of global economic conditions such as spillovers from global financial cycles is of remarkable importance. In that regard, the sharing of timely information about macroeconomic and financial market conditions and policy stances among countries should be especially instrumental in pursuing international cooperation for financial stability.

References

Bank of Korea. 2010. "The Effect of FX Risk Hedge of Shipbuilders on Foreign Exchange Market in Korea." *Monthly Economic Bulletin.*

Cho, Dongchul. 2010. "Overcoming the 1997–1998 Crisis: Macroeconomic Policy Adjustments," Korea Knowledge Sharing Program Report, Ministry of Strategy and Finance and Korea Development Institute.

Cho, Dongchul. 2012. "Responses of the Korean Economy to the Global Crisis: Another Currency Crisis?" In Chapter 3, *Global Crisis: Impacts, Transmission and Recovery,* edited by Obstfeld, Cho, and Mason. Northampton: Edward Elgar Publishing Ltd.

Cho, Sungbin, and Joon-ho Hahm. 2016. "Foreign Currency Liquidity Risk and Prudential Regulation of Banks." In Chapter 8, *Macroprudential Regulation of*

International Finance: Managing Capital Flows and Exchange Rates, edited by Dongsoo Kang and Andrew Mason. Northampton: Edward Elgar Publishing Ltd.

Cho, Yoon-Je. 1999. "An Analysis on the Financial Liberalization Policies in the 90s and the Financial Crisis in Korea." *Journal of Korean Economy Studies* 2: 61–86.

Choi, Doo-Yull. 2002. *Asymmetric Regulations on Corporate Financing and the Currency Crisis*, Korea Economic Research Institute.

Choi, Jongmoo Jay, Sae Woon Park, and Sean Sehyun Yoo. 2007. "The Value of Outside Directors: Evidence from Corporate Governance Reform in Korea." *Journal of Financial and Quantitative Analysis* 42 (4): 941–962.

Cole, Harold, and Timothy Kehoe. 1996. "A Self-Fulfilling Model of Mexico's 1994–1995 Debt Crisis." *Journal of International Economics* 41: 309–330.

Corsetti, Giancarlo, Paolo Pesenti, and Nouriel Roubini. 1999. "What Caused the Asian Currency and Financial Crisis?" *Japan and the World Economy* 11: 305–373.

Economist. 2009. "Domino Theory: Where Could Emerging Market Contagion Spread Next?" *Economics Focus in The Economist*.

Feldstein, Martin. 1998. "Refocusing the IMF." *Foreign Affairs* 77 (2).

Financial Times. 2009. "Korea's Debt." *The Financial Times*.

Fischer, Stanley. 1998. *The Asian Crisis: A View from the IMF*. Washington: IMF. www.imf.org/en/News/Articles/2015/09/28/04/53/sp012298

Furman, Jason, and Joseph E. Stiglitz. 1998. "Economic Crises: Evidence and Insights from East Asia." *Brookings Papers on Economic Activity* 1–114.

Gertler, Mark, Simon Gilchrist, and Fabio M. Natalucci. 2007. "External Constraint on Monetary Policy and the Financial Accelerator." *Journal of Money, Credit and Banking* 39 (2–3): 295–330.

Hahm, Joon-Ho. 2003. "The Government, Chaebol and Financial Institutions in Pre-Crisis Korea." In Chapter 3, *Economic Crisis and Corporate Restructuring in Korea*, edited by Stephan Haggard, Wonhyuk Lim, and Euysung Kim. Cambridge: Cambridge University Press.

Hahm, Joon-Ho. 2008. "Ten Years after the Crisis: Financial System Transition in Korea." In *Ten Years after the Korean Crisis*, edited by M. D. Y. IMF and KIEP, pp. 65–99.

Hahm, Joon-Ho, and Sungbin Cho. 2014. "Foreign Currency Noncore Bank Liabilities and Macroprudential Levy in Korea." *Emerging Markets Finance and Trade* 50 (6): 5–18.

Hahm, Joon-Ho, and Hyeon-Wook Kim. 2011. "Soundness of Financial Institutions and Impact of External Shock." In Chapter 7, *Korea's Capacity to Cope with Crises in a Globalized Environment*, edited by Dongchul Cho and Hyeon-Wook Kim. Seoul, Korea: Korea Development Institute.

Hahm, Joon-Ho, and Wonhyuk Lim. 2006. "Turning a Crisis into an Opportunity: The Political Economy of Korea's Financial Sector Reform," In *From Crisis to Opportunity: Financial Globalization and East Asian Capitalism*, edited by Jongryn Mo and Daniel Okimoto. Shorenstein APARC distributed by Brookings Institution Press.

Hahm, Joon-Ho, and Frederic S. Mishkin. 2000. "The Korean Financial Crisis: An Asymmetric Information Perspective." *Emerging Markets Review* 1: 21–52.

Hahm, Joon-Ho, Hyun Song Shin, and Kwanho Shin. 2013. "Noncore Bank Liabilities and Financial Vulnerability." *Journal of Money, Credit and Banking* 45 (S1): 3–36.

Kim, Hyeon-Wook. 2012. "Macroeconomic Policies of Korea to Cope with the Crisis." In Chapter 9, *Global Crisis: Impacts, Transmission and Recovery*, edited by Maurice Obstfeld, Dongchul Cho, and Andrew Mason. Northampton: Edward Elgar Publishing Ltd.

Kim, Hyeon-Wook, and Jae-Joon Lee. 2011. "Korea's Monetary Policy to Cope with Global Financial Crisis." In Chapter 8, *Korea's Capacity to Cope with Crises in a Globalized Environment*, edited by Dongchul Cho and Hyeon-Wook Kim. Research Monograph, No. 2011–03. Seoul, Korea: Korea Development Institute.

Lee, Chung H., Keun Lee, and Kangkook Lee. 2002. "Chaebol, Financial Liberalization and Economic Crisis: Transformation of Quasi-Internal Organization in Korea." *Asian Economic Journal* 16 (1): 17–35.

Lee, Hangyong, and Ki Seok Hong. 2011. "External Shocks Spreading through Financial Markets." In Chapter 3, *Korea's Capacity to Cope with Crises in a Globalized Environment*, edited by Dongchul Cho and Hyeon-Wook Kim. Research Monograph, No. 2011–03. Seoul, Korea: Korea Development Institute.

Lee, Hangyong, and Min-Kyu Song. 2012. "How did Korean Financial Markets get Infected by the Global Financial Crisis?" In Chapter 5, *Global Crisis: Impacts, Transmission and Recovery*, edited by Maurice Obstfeld, Dongchul Cho, and Andrew Mason. Edward Elgar Publishing Ltd.

Mishkin, Frederic S. 1996. "Understanding Financial Crises: A Developing Country Perspective." NBER Working Paper 5600.

Obstfeld, Maurice. 1996. "Models of Currency Crises with Self-Fulfilling Features." *European Economic Review* 40 (3–5): 1037–1047.

Obstfeld, Maurice, Jay C. Shambaugh, and Alan M. Taylor. 2009. "Financial Instability, Reserves, and Central Bank Swap Lines in the Panic of 2008." *American Economic Review* 99 (2): 480–486.

Radelet, Steven, Jeffrey Sachs, Richard Cooper, and Barry Bosworth. 1998. "The East Asian Financial Crisis: Diagnosis, Remedies, Prospects." *Brookings Papers on Economic Activity* 1998: 1–90.

Rey, Helene. 2015. "Dilemma not Trilemma: The Global Financial Cycle and Monetary Policy Independence." NBER Working Paper 21162.

Sachs, Jeffrey, Aaron Tornell, and Andes Velasco. 1996. "The Mexican Peso Crisis: Sudden Death or Death Foretold?" *Journal of International Economics* 41: 265–283.

Shin, Hyun Song, and Kwanho Shin. 2011. *Procyclicality and Monetary Aggregates*. NBER Discussion Paper No. 16836. Cambridge: National Bureau of Economic Research.

Chapter 18

Philippines
Rising Above the Challenges
During the Asian and Global Financial Crises

Wilhelmina C. Mañalac

Introduction

This chapter on the Philippines seeks to explore the causes and consequences of both the Asian financial crisis (AFC) and the global financial crisis (GFC), including the policy responses implemented by the government to mitigate their impact on the Philippine economy.

The AFC in 1997 was characterized by extremely turbulent economic developments that transpired in much of East and Southeast Asia, leaving a profound impact on the economic, social, and political arena of affected countries. Economic activity contracted in the region and resulted, among others, in firm closures and increased unemployment that led to social consequences including a rise in poverty incidence.

This chapter seeks to find out the reasons why, as history would relate, the Philippines performed better than the rest of the region during the AFC. In particular, the Philippine debt crisis that transpired more than a decade prior to the AFC will be considered to provide some ground on the greater resiliency exhibited by the country during the course of the AFC relative to its regional peers. In addition, policy responses to the crisis will be discussed, which assisted the Philippine government to rise above the challenges posed by the AFC.

In 2007, after a span of 10 years from the onset of the AFC, the GFC took place that led to a period of extreme stress in the global financial markets and banking systems. While the GFC emanated from the advanced economies, the crisis spread into a global economic shock, resulting in declines in gross domestic product (GDP) worldwide, plummeting of international trade, soaring of unemployment, and rise in poverty levels. Similar to its performance during the AFC, the Philippines was largely spared from the worst effects of this crisis.

The narrative on the Philippines' development during the GFC will cover a statistical recount of the capital flow trends in the country, the impact on the economy, as well as the policies and actions implemented in response to the crisis to explain the relative flexibility and resilience of the Philippine economy.

Finally, efforts to align policies regionally and internationally guide the Philippines' active participation in the regional financial cooperation that was established largely due to the occurrence of the various crises.

The Philippine Economy: Pre-AFC, 1983–1996

Documenting the Philippines' economic performance and its various challenges and responses in the years prior to 1997 is important in explaining how the country surmounted the adverse impact of the AFC.

Trends in Various Economic Indicators

Over more than two decades prior to the AFC, the Philippines tracked a difficult path toward sustainable growth. There were numerous internal and external challenges, some of which were not within the government's direct control. These played a significant role in the country's economic performance, which largely followed boom and bust cycles. While these developments uncovered weaknesses in the economy, the same events highlighted the country's capacity to adjust in the face of adversities.

During this period, economic growth largely depended on the government's expanded public development investment program, majority of which relied on external financing. As a result of readily available foreign funding and aid flows particularly after the proclamation of martial law, the Philippines was able to generate a domestic annual growth of 6.1% from 1973 to 1979. However, when the external environment turned to worse after the second oil price shock in 1980, the country's economic situation deteriorated sharply. The accumulation of foreign debt, which commenced in the 1970s under the Marcos administration (1965–1986) and continued in the early 1980s, led to the Philippine debt crisis in 1983.

With the Philippines' growth lagging way behind its neighbors and confidence in the Marcos administration waning considerably, which was made worse by the assassination of Benigno Aquino in 1983, the peso depreciated sharply by 30.1% in 1983 and a further 50.3% in 1984. Given the state of disarray, no one wanted to lend to the Philippines.

Consequently, while the growth of its neighbors came to be known as the "Asian miracle," the Philippines earned the label, "the sick man of Asia." Such a title prevented Philippine companies from borrowing foreign currency as early and as easily as other countries.

The Debt Crisis of 1983–1985

A chronic balance-of-trade deficit which traced its roots to the oil price crunches of 1974 and 1979, the continued increase in short-term debt particularly by the public sector, and political instability led the government to declare a 90-day moratorium on its principal repayments on debts owed to foreign banks and other financial institutions starting on October 17, 1983. This move prepared the way for rescheduling certain foreign obligations of the country. Succeeding years were marked by government efforts to reduce the country's foreign debt with the use of various debt reduction schemes that included debt for nature, debt-equity swaps, and debt buybacks, among others.

The country likewise participated in the Brady Initiative where countries with sound adjustment programs were given access to debt and debt-service reduction facilities supported by international financial institutions and official creditors. The process generally made use of a market-based, negotiated "menu" of options that enabled debtor countries to take advantage of secondary market discounts. Under the Initiative, international commercial banks were given greater incentive to make voluntary reductions in the outstanding debts of heavily indebted developing countries and to grant them fresh money (Frenkel 1989).

Reeling from the debt crisis, the country's real growth rate decelerated to 1.9% in 1983 from 3.7% in 1982 (Figure 18.1). Real growth turned negative in 1984 and 1985 when the full impact of the crisis took its toll.

The negative growth trend was largely a result of restrictive monetary policy and contractionary fiscal policy, imposition of higher reserve requirements, reduced credit availability from the Central Bank (CB), restraint in government investment expenditure, as well as new tax measures adopted during the period. Meanwhile, the decline in real economic growth was

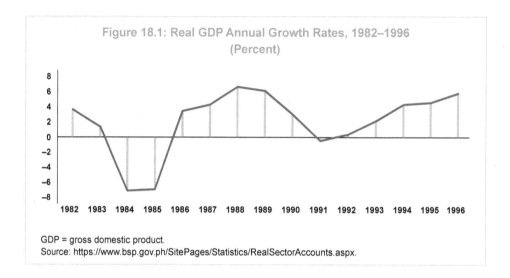

Figure 18.1: Real GDP Annual Growth Rates, 1982–1996 (Percent)

GDP = gross domestic product.
Source: https://www.bsp.gov.ph/SitePages/Statistics/RealSectorAccounts.aspx.

accompanied by high inflation rates of 49.8% and 22.5% in 1984 and 1985, respectively (Figure 18.2) and a general rise in average domestic bank lending rates. The significantly high inflation rate in 1984 reflected spillover effects of the substantial depreciation in the exchange rate in 1983 of 30.1%, which persisted through 1984 (50.3%), raising fuel prices, power rates, transportation fares, and wages.

The imbalance in the country's external sector resulted in a significantly large current account (CA) deficit in 1983 (Table 18.1). This deficit was reduced in the following year because of emergency temporary measures. In particular, the merchandise trade account improved due to better export performance and reduction in imports because of an import prioritization

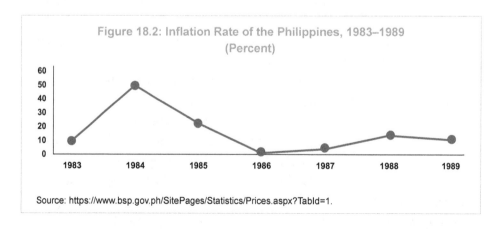

Figure 18.2: Inflation Rate of the Philippines, 1983–1989 (Percent)

Source: https://www.bsp.gov.ph/SitePages/Statistics/Prices.aspx?TabId=1.

Table 18.1: BOP, 1982–1985
(USD million)

Item	1982	1983	1984	1985
I. Current Transactions				
A. Merchandise Trade	−2646	−2482	−679	−482
Exports	5021	5005	5391	4629
Imports	7667	7487	6070	5111
B. Services	−1040	−740	−823	26
C. Transfers	486	472	386	379
Current Account, Net	−3200	−2750	−1116	−77
II. Nonmonetary Capital, Net	1302	499	1205	1685
III. Others	277	183	169	693
IV. Overall BOP Position	−1621	−2068	258	2301

BOP = balance of payments, USD = United States dollar.
Note: Based on the Fourth Edition of the Balance of Payments Manual.
Sources: For 1985: Bangko Sentral ng Pilipinas, Balance of Payment, BOP Old Concept, Main Table Historical EXCEL, https://www.bsp.gov.ph/SitePages/Statistics/External.aspx?TabId=1; for 1984: Central Bank of the Philippines (CBP) Thirty-Seventh Annual Report, 1985 page 6; for 1983: CBP Annual Report 1984, page 7; for 1982: CBP Annual Report 1983, page 9.

scheme employed by the authorities. There was a further narrowing of the CA deficit in 1985 due to improvements in the services account that accompanied a continued decline in the trade gap.

The economic recovery program in 1985 called for the adoption of a cautious monetary policy aimed at balancing the apparently conflicting objectives of lowering inflation rates and restoring economic activity. In addition, to further the adjustment in the external account, a foreign exchange (FX) policy that eased FX restrictions and allowed the floating of the exchange rate was put in place. To complement these policies, the monetary authorities undertook measures to restructure external debt and access a moderate amount of new financing. Finally, to make sure that financial stability was achieved and economic efficiency was promoted, fundamental changes were introduced in credit policy and banking supervision. The authorities' efforts to bring about economic recovery were supported by the International Monetary Fund (IMF) Stand-By Program approved in December 1984 amounting to SDR 615 million.

The New Government: 1986–1989

In 1986, the government of Ferdinand Marcos was replaced. President Corazon Aquino's democratic and open political regime (1986–1992) as well as outward-looking and market-oriented reforms brought in new investor and international confidence. While the Aquino government was not without setbacks, its shift in policy direction was the basis for comprehensive reforms implemented in the following decade.

Economic turnaround was apparent in the beginning of the third quarter of 1986. It became more pronounced in the fourth quarter as a result of stable domestic prices, interest rates, and the exchange rates (BSP 1986). This provided a stable environment for investment and growth.

Real GDP grew by an average of 5.2% during the four-year period 1986–1989, a reversal of the preceding 2 years' negative growth. Growth was mainly attributed to capital formation combined with strong export performance. The latter mitigated the effect of import expansion that accompanied a growing economy. Inflation was drastically reduced to 1.1% in 1986 from 22.5% in 1985 and averaged 7.4% from 1986 to 1989 (Figure 18.2).

In the same period, the balance of payments (BOP) yielded surpluses owing to marked improvement in the capital and financial account arising from an expansion in earnings from the net investments account.

As a consequence, gross international reserves (GIR) reached a comfortable level of USD 2.4 billion at the end of 1989, equivalent to 1.9 months' worth of imports of goods and services. This helped sustain stability of the peso–dollar exchange rate, which stood at PHP 21.74/USD at the end of 1989 from PHP 20.38/USD at the end of 1986 (Figure 18.3).

The Philippine Economy in the 1990s

After growth bounced back in 1986–1989, recovery faltered in 1990–1991 owing to a string of natural disasters, three external shocks, and renewed political instability (Rodlauer 2000). The setback was made worse by policy slippages, for example, a sharp widening of the fiscal deficit, expansionary monetary policy, and average currency appreciation of 12.4% for the 2-year period, leading to a sharp increase in the CA deficit, which totaled USD 3.4 billion; a jump in inflation to a 2-year average of 16.5%; and a reversal in the BOP to a deficit in 1990. Structural constraints such as the country's high dependence on imports and an underdeveloped capital market were also

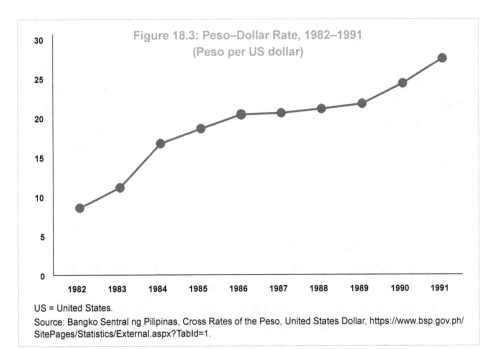

Figure 18.3: Peso–Dollar Rate, 1982–1991
(Peso per US dollar)

US = United States.
Source: Bangko Sentral ng Pilipinas, Cross Rates of the Peso, United States Dollar, https://www.bsp.gov.ph/SitePages/Statistics/External.aspx?TabId=1.

factors that led the country to return to a "boom-and-bust" cycle.

In 1991, the effects of the Gulf War in January, the eruption of Mount Pinatubo in June, and other adverse developments bore heavily on the economy as real GDP for the first three quarters of the year dropped by 1% relative to the previous year's level. Toward the end of the year, the economy gradually recovered and recorded positive developments particularly on the external front.

In the same year, the BOP yielded a surplus of USD 2.1 billion, a marked turnaround from the USD 93 million deficit registered in 1990. This was made possible by the narrowing of the merchandise trade gap, improvement in the services account because of the notable increase in workers' remittances, and the positive developments in all items of the capital account. These items consisted of medium- and long-term loans, foreign investments due to significant gains in nonresidents' reinvested earnings as well as debt conversions and portfolio investments (PIs), and short-term capital inflows. In particular, exports positively responded to government incentives while imports contracted, reflecting the slowdown in domestic economic activity and imposition of the import levy during the year.

As of 1991, GIR registered a record high of USD 4.5 billion, sufficient to finance 3.3 months' worth of imports of goods and services (Figure 18.4). As part of efforts to reduce the debt burden and arrive at a comprehensive resolution of the country's debt problem, the authorities reached an agreement with the IMF on a new 18-month Stand-By Arrangement amounting to SDR 334.2 million to support the country's economic stabilization program. With the approval of the IMF loan, the Philippine Assistance Program (PAP) session was successfully completed and resulted in some USD 3.3 billion in pledges by donor countries in the form of financial assistance. The PAP was initiated by the United States (US) and evolved into a multilateral pool of assistance facilities to be contributed by the US and its security partners, especially Japan (Magallona 1989).

In addition, the country's obligations with the Paris Club amounting to some USD 1.5 billion were successfully rescheduled in June 1991, contingent on the extension of the IMF program until 1992. In the same month, extension of the USD 3 billion trade facility, which ensured continuous access to credits necessary to facilitate trade transactions, was positively endorsed by the country's foreign creditor banks. Finally, in August of 1991, the country reached an agreement with the country's Bank Advisory Committee, composed of the 12 foreign private banks with the biggest loan exposure to the Philippines, on a comprehensive commercial bank financing package,

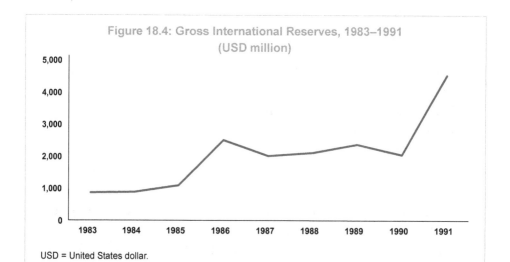

Figure 18.4: Gross International Reserves, 1983–1991 (USD million)

USD = United States dollar.
Source: Bangko Sentral ng Pilipinas, International Reserves of the BSP, Historical EXCEL, https://www.bsp.gov.ph/SitePages/Statistics/External.aspx?TabId=1.

which involved debt and debt service reduction as well as the inflow of new money (BSP 1991).

Period of Relative Growth and Stability: 1992–1996

From 1992 until the onset of the AFC in 1997, the Philippines enjoyed positive growth rates, that is, until the full effect of the AFC set in, rendering a negative growth of 0.5% in 1998. For the 5-year period, real GDP growth recorded an average of 3.5%.

It is noteworthy that in 1996, growth accelerated to about 6% and the external position significantly strengthened to a BOP surplus of USD 4.1 billion, brought about by strong export growth and continued increase in GIR.

The positive economic indicators recorded during the period resulted from the various economic and structural reforms put in place by the successor governments after the dictatorship, which made the economy more liberalized, market-based, and competitive, in contrast to the totalitarian and bureaucrat capitalist government of the Marcos regime.

Policy Measures During the Period Leading to the AFC

The new government led by President Fidel Ramos (1992–1998) embraced a comprehensive reform strategy to further open up the economy, reduce macroeconomic imbalances, and address other structural rigidities (Rodlauer 2000). This program, supported since 1994 by an Extended Fund Facility (EFF) from the IMF amounting to SDR 791.2 million, enabled significant reduction in the fiscal deficit particularly in 1992 (Annex 1), acceleration in privatization, the liberalization of a number of important sectors, and the restructuring of the CB provided for under a new law that included, among others, a clearer specification of its mandate of price stability and its recapitalization.

In general, the period was characterized as one with substantially reduced government economic intervention, reestablished competitive markets, renewed emphasis on rural development and on equitable allocation of benefits resulting from sustained recovery, and the creation of a more competitive and outward-looking economy through trade and FX liberalization as well as flexible exchange rate policies.

Monetary Policy

During the period preceding the AFC, monetary and fiscal policy instruments were flexibly adopted. To stimulate investment and productive activities, the thrust toward market orientation, deregulation, and privatization was pursued more resolutely in monetary policy.

More specifically, interest rate ceilings were eliminated to encourage competition and efficiency in bank intermediation. Measures were adopted to reform the rediscounting window and utilize this instrument for liquidity control rather than for credit allocation. In terms of open market operations, there was a gradual phase out of CB bills, which until then were the main instruments of open market operations, and the revival of the auction method for Treasury Bills.

Another notable reform enacted during the period was the restructuring of the Central Bank of the Philippines (CBP) in 1993 into the Bangko Sentral ng Pilipinas (BSP), under which the BSP was granted full policy instrument independence as well as increased fiscal and administrative autonomy from other sectors of the government. This law prohibited the BSP from engaging in the quasi-fiscal activities that it performed consistent with the policies of the National Government (NG) at that time, which had led to the technical insolvency of the old CB. These activities included FX forward cover contracts and swaps entered into by the CBP with certain banks and government-owned and -controlled corporations, the CBP's assumption of the FX liabilities of some of these corporations and private sector companies during the Philippine FX crisis in the 1980s, development banking and financing by the CBP, and the CBP's conduct of open market operations and incurrence of high interest expenses on its domestic securities issued in connection with such operations (Tetangco 2003). In addition, pursuant to the New Central Bank Act, the BSP was no longer permitted to engage in development banking or financing. The formulation and implementation of the country's monetary policies rested with the Monetary Board (MB), the members of which would not be affected by changes in government. Two government representatives, including the BSP Governor and a cabinet member appointed by the president, and five full-time members from the private sector comprised the members of the MB in the BSP. This compared with the MB in the CBP, whose members had consisted of four government representatives plus three part-time members from the private sector (Malacañang 1972).

Fiscal Policy

In 1986, the Tax Reform Program (TRP) was adopted to "simplify the tax system" and make it more equitable (Bureau of Internal Revenue (BIR) website). The TRP aimed to strengthen the elasticity of the tax structure through higher tax exemptions for low-income earners, simplify the tax structure, increase taxes on nonessential items, abolish export taxes except on logs, and remove tax and duty exemptions and grant tax amnesty in the second half of 1986 (BSP 1986).

Under the TRP, a major reform was the introduction of the value-added tax (VAT), then set at 10%. The 1986 TRP led to reduced fiscal imbalances and higher tax effort in the succeeding years. In particular, the NG cash operations reversed from a deficit of PHP 21.9 billion or 1.3% of GDP in 1993 to a surplus of PHP 16.3 billion (0.9% of GDP) in 1994 and remained in surplus until 1997 (Annex 1).

The Government's policy to sell sequestered assets of President Marcos and his so-called cronies increased the share of nontax revenues to about PHP 20 billion. Another important reform was the 1991 Local Government Code, which led to fiscal decentralization that increased the taxing and spending powers of local governments, increasing local government resources.

External Sector Policy

In the external sector, a flexible exchange rate system continued to be adopted. Likewise, a series of FX liberalization measures was implemented to promote exports, mobilize FX resources, particularly remittances of Overseas Filipino (OF) Workers. Among others, the monetary authorities issued a circular that allowed FX receipts, acquisitions, or earnings, including those of commodity and service exporters, to be deposited into foreign currency accounts in the Philippines or abroad. This was a complete reversal of the prior requirement for commodity and service exporters to surrender their earnings to the banking system. Likewise, measures were put in place to encourage foreign investments including streamlining of procedural requirements.

Import liberalization or the gradual lifting of quantitative restrictions for a more tariff-based protection system to maximize efficiency of domestic industries and enhance competitiveness was likewise introduced. Reforms that lowered tariffs on major commodities were also continued (BSP Circular No. 1993).

Financial Sector Reforms

Further strengthening of the financial system came in the form of privatization of government-owned and -controlled banks, rehabilitation of rural banks and liberalization of rules on opening branches by banks and establishment of new banks, and increase in the required capitalization of expanded commercial banks.

External Debt Management

A positive outcome of the debt crisis was the refinement of external debt statistics, which prior to the crisis lacked detailed information on private sector debt particularly banks. Further refinements in subsequent years have provided authorities with sufficient information to implement the necessary policies that would make the external debt environment manageable and sustainable, ensuring that the crisis would not be encountered again.

In general, external debt policy remained supportive of the goal to restore the viability of the country's external payments position. Efforts were geared toward raising the required FX resources crucial to sustaining economic recovery and obtaining payments relief on debts already outstanding.

Structural Reforms

Proclamation No. 50 dated December 8, 1986 formalized the Philippine Privatization Program, crafted for speedy disposition and privatization of certain government corporations and assets. The process resulted in the sale of corporations such as Philippine Airlines, Philippine National Bank, and Union Bank of the Philippines. The proceeds from asset sales financed the government's Comprehensive Agrarian Reform Program.

The Foreign Investments Act of 1991 (Republic Act (R.A.) No. 7042) was signed into law by President Aquino on June 13, 1991. It sought to liberalize the foreign investment climate in the country while maintaining specific safeguards provided for in the Constitution and other laws. It simplified investment rules by (1) opening all investment areas and activities to 100% foreign equity participation, except for those sectors/activities specified in a negative list; and (2) further streamlining registration procedures.

R.A. No. 7925, otherwise known as the "Public Telecommunications Policy Act of 1995," was enacted to promote and govern the development of the Philippines' telecommunications industry as well as to provide basic policies for the delivery of efficient public telecommunications service.

R.A. No. 8479, entitled "Downstream Oil Industry Deregulation Act of 1998," was approved on February 10, 1998. In deregulating the oil industry, the Philippine government effectively reduced control on oil-related pricing activity and trade restrictions. In the initial phase, oil importation was liberalized and the automatic pricing mechanism was implemented. In the full deregulation phase, controls on oil price setting were similarly lifted, the FX cover was removed, and the Oil Price Stabilization Fund (OPSF) was abolished. The OPSF was a budgetary allocation maintained by the NG to automatically absorb any price change incurred by oil companies in importing crude oil, which was not reflected in the selling price. Deregulating the oil industry stabilized and provided reasonable prices, encouraged competition and investments, and removed cross product subsidies (Caparas 2000).

These reforms since the late 1980s, which intensified in the 1990s, have borne and continue to bear fruit with the help of skillful crisis management.

The Philippine Economy During the AFC: 1997–1998

Start of the Crisis

Contagion

The devaluation of the Thai baht sparked contagion in the region because of the loss of confidence in Asian economies. This resulted in capital flight with heavy selling pressures affecting local currencies. Moreover, levels of international reserves declined as regional CBs acted to ensure that the economy could supply needed FX.

The peso–dollar exchange rate was allowed to depreciate by 11.5% 9 days after Thai authorities' action on their currency in July 1997. This occurred even as the monetary authorities attempted to defend the rate in the first few days after the devaluation of the baht. With the significant depreciation of the peso, the monetary authorities tolerated a wider band for the trading of the local currency and allowed the market to fully operate in determining the value of the peso to the dollar. Likewise, it was made known that the CB would not intervene except to moderate excessive fluctuations of the rate, a major reason being to preserve the country's international reserves (Holley 1997).

Increase in Domestic Interest Rates

In stabilizing the FX market amid a highly speculative environment, Philippine authorities implemented measures to influence local interest rates to move upward, attracting more funds to the local currency. Moreover, higher interest rates translated to higher cost of funds for borrowers, including businesses, that affected their profitability and viability. As a result of the peso depreciation and higher interest rates, the debt burden of borrowings denominated in foreign currencies considerably increased and further aggravated the financial crisis for banks and firms.

Accumulation of FX Liabilities

In the run up to the crisis, investors from developed countries sought higher rates of return on their funds, particularly from economies experiencing the Asian economic miracle. They thus shifted massive amounts of capital into the Asian region. Cheap short-term foreign currency funds led to acceleration of foreign borrowings that mostly went to nonprofitable plant investments and speculative activities in real estate and the stock market.

In the case of the Philippines, its external debt escalated from USD 28.5 billion in 1990 to USD 46.3 billion at the end of 1998, or by 62.6% (Figure 18.5). Short-term debt rose by 87.2% vis-à-vis the level at the start of the decade, while medium- and long-term debt was higher by 59.5%. Private

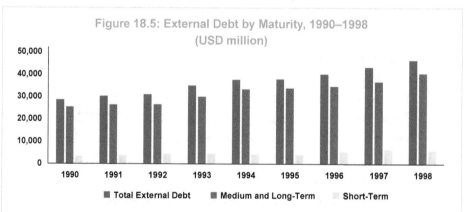

Figure 18.5: External Debt by Maturity, 1990–1998 (USD million)

USD = United States dollar.

Source: Bangko Sentral ng Pilipinas, External Debt: External Debt (by Type of Borrower, Creditor & Country Profile), Historical EXCEL, https://www.bsp.gov.ph/SitePages/Statistics/External.aspx?TabId=1.

sector debt also expanded by more than three times the level at USD 16.2 billion in 1998 compared to only USD 5 billion in 1990. It is to be noted, however, that while short-term borrowings increased significantly, its share to total debt averaged only 12.6% from 1990 to 1998.

When the crisis set in, borrowers of short-term loans faced a more difficult time in repaying their debt as a result of the depreciation in the exchange rate. In addition, the same borrowers who could have availed of hedging instruments to protect against currency risk faced higher costs due to the lack of a well-developed forward market. The rush to cover foreign currency liabilities when the exchange rate started to depreciate aggravated the fall in the currencies, creating a vicious cycle in the economy.

Other weaknesses included an underdeveloped capital market that contributed to vulnerability of the country's financial market as short-term investments were primarily the type of instruments available to investors. This was particularly true for the private corporate bond market, which remained small and narrow.

Growth and the Fiscal, External, and Financial Sectors During the AFC

The Philippines managed to grow by an average of 2.3% during 1997–1998 or the AFC. Growth was recorded at a respectable rate of 5.2% in 1997 but succumbed to the effects of the crisis in the following year as growth turned negative but by a slight 0.5% vis-à-vis more severe declines recorded in the growth of other countries in the Association of Southeast Asian Nations (ASEAN). Growth was weighed down by a severe drought that reduced agricultural output by 7% in 1998. Industry also declined (by 2.7%), while services managed to remain buoyant (growing by 2.9%). On the demand side, growth was supported largely by household consumption expenditure, which rose by 5.3% and a decline in imports by 13.2% due to a sluggish economy. Gross domestic capital formation, however, fell sharply by 14.8%, and unemployment rose to 10.3%. Reflecting the impact of a drought which resulted in higher food prices, inflation reached 9.4% in 1998.

The NG's fiscal position was in surplus from 1994 to 1997. Recorded at PHP 1.6 billion or 0.1% of GDP, the surplus in 1997 was, however, lower than the previous year's surplus of PHP 6.3 billion (0.3% of GDP). The impact of the crisis caused a turnaround in the fiscal position during the following year when it recorded a deficit of PHP 50 billion, or 1.7% of GDP (Figure 18.6).

In the external sector, merchandise exports showed strong growth at 16.9%, while imports declined by 18.8% in 1998. The external sector showed improvement in its CA position, which recorded a significant turnaround to a surplus of 2.3% of gross national product (GNP), and in its overall BOP position, as a result of its improved trade position and net foreign investments. The accumulated stock of GIR initially declined to USD 8.8 billion in 1997 as a result of government actions prior to the depreciation in July of that year. However, as the economy gained ground, GIR increased to USD 10.8 billion by the end of 1998 or 3.1 months of imports of goods and services (Figure 18.7).

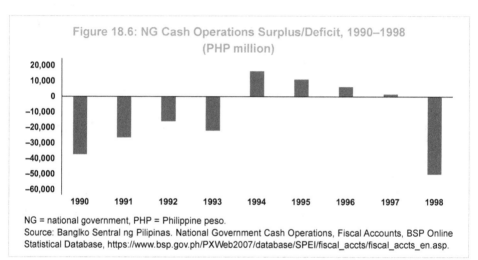

Figure 18.6: NG Cash Operations Surplus/Deficit, 1990–1998 (PHP million)

NG = national government, PHP = Philippine peso.
Source: Banglko Sentral ng Pilipinas. National Government Cash Operations, Fiscal Accounts, BSP Online Statistical Database, https://www.bsp.gov.ph/PXWeb2007/database/SPEI/fiscal_accts/fiscal_accts_en.asp.

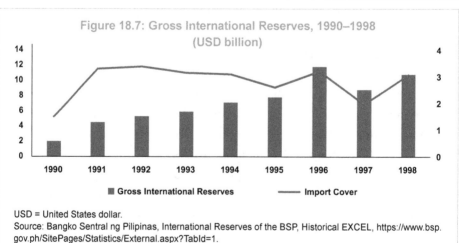

Figure 18.7: Gross International Reserves, 1990–1998 (USD billion)

■ Gross International Reserves   —— Import Cover

USD = United States dollar.
Source: Bangko Sentral ng Pilipinas, International Reserves of the BSP, Historical EXCEL, https://www.bsp.gov.ph/SitePages/Statistics/External.aspx?TabId=1.

The country's external debt profile continued to improve steadily. As of the end of 1998, total external debt was estimated at USD 46.3 billion. The external debt service burden was reduced to just 11.7% of exports of goods and services from 27.2% in 1990. In addition, the level of short-term external debt was kept moderate at 12.6% of total FX liabilities (Figure 18.8). It is to be noted that short-term external debt as a ratio of gross international reserves sharply fell from 152.7% in 1990 to 54% in 1998 as short-term debt declined while the country beefed up its FX reserves, ensuring the availability of foreign currency to pay for short-term liabilities should any FX crisis occur.

Meanwhile, the financial system remained strong, expanding its resources and operating network. While the ratio of nonperforming loans (NPLs) to total loans rose to 10.4% in 1998 from 2.8% in 1996 (Annex 2), banks were able to build loan-loss provisions to 4% of total loans and improved their capital adequacy ratio to 17.7%. The latter was well above the statutory requirement of 10% and the international standard of 8%, reflecting the positive benefits of measures implemented as a result of the external debt crisis in the mid-1980s. These earlier reforms included increased minimum

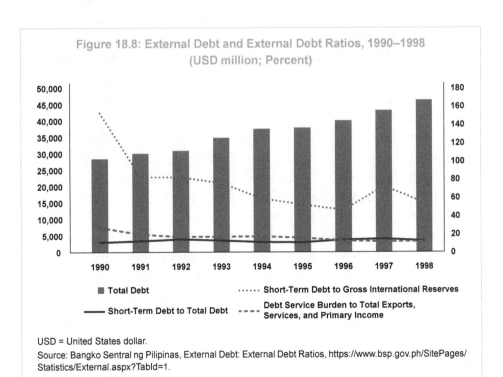

Figure 18.8: External Debt and External Debt Ratios, 1990–1998
(USD million; Percent)

USD = United States dollar.
Source: Bangko Sentral ng Pilipinas, External Debt: External Debt Ratios, https://www.bsp.gov.ph/SitePages/Statistics/External.aspx?TabId=1.

capitalization requirements, liberalization of bank branching, and the entry and operation of foreign banks, which resulted in enhanced competition from both local and foreign players, reduction in reserve requirements, and tightening of bank supervision.

The Philippines' Policy Response to the Crisis

The authorities aimed to stabilize the situation through contractionary monetary policy in the form of increased borrowing rates and liquidity reserve requirements. Monetary policy during this period would "lean against" pressures in the FX market by raising interest rates without attempting aggressively to resist market forces (Rodlauer 2000). The BSP adopted a policy that allowed market forces to determine the exchange rate and for the BSP to intervene in the FX market only to stabilize the rate in any direction. That is, no large-scale intervention would be undertaken to defend any particular level of the exchange rate.

Thus, on July 11, 1997, the BSP reaffirmed its market-oriented exchange rate policy by allowing the rate to move within a wider range. The measure was adopted to remove speculation against the peso, eventually leading to a gradual reduction in the interest rates as financial markets stabilized.

After the sharp depreciation of the peso that followed the decision to allow it to be traded within a wider range, foremost among the BSP's concerns was the restoration of order and stability in the FX market. Several measures were pursued to cool down speculative activities and reduce undue pressure on the peso while adding FX liquidity into the market.

On December 22, 1997, the BSP introduced the currency risk protection program (CRPP). The CRPP was a nondeliverable forward contract between the BSP and commercial banks with FX obligations of bank clients as the underlying transaction.[1] The facility was aimed at relieving some of the pressure on the spot market created by market players wanting to frontload their future foreign currency requirements and by borrowers wanting to cover foreign currency obligations that were not yet due (Tuaño-Amador 2009).

As the exchange rate stabilized, the policy stance shifted gradually toward supporting recovery through a gradual reduction in liquidity reserves to influence the downward direction of interest rates. Moreover, to further

---

[1] The coverage of the CRPP was subsequently expanded to provide a hedging mechanism for a broader group of users including oil importers.

influence the reduction in interest rates, banks were mandated to publish their cost of funds for more transparency. Stiffer penalties were imposed on banks violating the overbought/oversold FX positions. Likewise, sanctions were introduced on violations of regulations on loans obtained by directors, officers, stockholders, and related interests as these would be considered self-dealing or insider transactions. A mechanism to report and address abuses of irresponsible banks was established by the BSP and the Bankers Association of the Philippines. Components of intermediation costs were lowered and rediscounting privileges provided by the BSP were linked to the banks' performance in lowering their lending rates.

The tight fiscal policies during the early part of the crisis were gradually relaxed by revising the previous target of a fiscal surplus of 1% of GNP to an eventual deficit target of 3% of GNP. Efforts were made to improve tax administration.

In addition, the Ramos administration focused on strengthening the banking sector. Furthermore, decisive action was taken to contain the crisis and restore confidence. In particular, additional prudential measures were put in place to further improve bank asset quality, reduce concentrated lending, achieve better loan loss provisioning, better define the responsibilities of bank directors, and align prudential rules with international standards. This included passage by the BSP of regulations that tightened criteria for determining past-due loans. Moreover, a general loan-loss provision over and above the provision for probable losses linked to individually identified uncollectible accounts was required, and a policy intended to enhance banks' ability to absorb losses in case of default was adopted.

Because of policies requiring 100% cover on foreign currency deposit liabilities of banks — which accounted for the bulk of bank foreign liabilities — and mandating that 30% of this be kept in liquid form, banks managed their FX exposure on the liability side fairly well.

To prevent banks from overexposure to the real estate sector, the BSP directed commercial banks to grant loans for real estate, valued at not more than 60% of the appraised value of the real estate property used as collateral for the loan, compared to 70% prior to the crisis, exclusive of individual loans not exceeding PHP 3.5 million. Furthermore, the BSP imposed a regulatory limit on banks' loans to the real estate sector to not more than 20% of a bank's total loan portfolio, exclusive of loans to finance the acquisition or improvement of residential units amounting to not more than PHP 3.5 million.

However, the aggregate real estate loans, inclusive of those loans for residential units amounting to not more than PHP 3.5 million, should not exceed 30% of the banks' total loan portfolio. Exempted from the ceilings were housing loans extended or guaranteed under the government's National Shelter Program, as these were considered nonrisk assets.

The BSP also issued guidelines governing responsibilities and duties of the board of directors of banks to improve bank management. Meanwhile, a proposed bill to amend the 52-year old General Banking Act (GBA) to make it adhere to internationally-accepted standards with respect to risk-based capital requirements and ensure sound banking practices was submitted by the BSP to Congress for deliberation. The General Banking Law of 2000, otherwise known as the GBA, was subsequently signed into law on May 23, 2000. The Law provided the BSP with greater flexibility in supervising the banking industry, improve business practices, and upgrade the country's banking laws to meet global standards, as well as opened the banking sector to more foreign investment.

The country likewise availed of a USD 1 billion Stand-By Arrangement from the IMF approved in March 1998 to help cement implementation of reforms. The objective of the program was primarily to address the dual goals of managing the current crisis while creating the conditions for sustained growth over the medium term. The authorities' intention was to treat the arrangement as precautionary, with drawings to be executed only if necessary.

The Philippines' Resiliency During the Crisis

External Debt

Mijares (1999) cited the following comparative statistics, which explain the Philippines' economic and financial resiliency during the AFC:

- Although the ratio of its total external debt to GDP was high, much of this was in the form of government debt to multilateral aid agencies. In terms of private nonguaranteed debt to GDP, as of the end of 1996, it was only about 6%, compared this to about 20% for Thailand, 16% for Indonesia, and 13% for Malaysia. Furthermore, the proportion of short-term debt to total debt was also low. At the end of 1996, it was about 19% while that for South Korea was 48%, Thailand was 41%, Malaysia was 28%, and Indonesia was 25%.

- The currencies were vulnerable as the ratio of short-term foreign liabilities to FX reserves increased. By mid-1997, South Korea's short-term borrowings amounted to about 2.1 times its reserves; Indonesia about 1.8 times, Thailand about 1.5 times, the Philippines about 0.9 times, and Malaysia about 0.6 times.

- In terms of foreign currency deposit liabilities in the Philippines' commercial banking system, more than 86% were owed to residents (depositors), and only less than 14% to nonresidents, as of the end of 1996, and many of these residents were exporters. Thus, the Philippines' deposit system was less subject to capital flight compared to Thailand. By borrower, the largest share of Foreign Currency Deposit Unit (FCDU) loans was availed of by exporters. As of September 1996, 60% of FCDU loans were drawn by exporters, who were adequately hedged against export earnings.

Financial Sector Reforms

As a result of prudential regulations adopted by the BSP earlier, banks' exposure to the real estate sector in the Philippines was lower at 15% of total assets in 1997, compared to other countries such as Malaysia and Thailand, both at 30%–40%. Additionally, collateral valuation in the Philippines was more conservative at 70%–80%[2] of market value, compared to 80%–100% for the others (Mijares 1999). Philippine property developers utilized other forms of financing and were not reliant only on bank financing compared to their counterparts in ASEAN. In particular, Filipino developers would prominently finance their projects by preselling. It was not, and still is not, uncommon for buyers to be offered condominium units for sale before developers have even broken ground, or very early in construction, years before the building would be ready for occupancy. Being more risk-averse than their other Asian counterparts, property developers in the Philippines were thus better assured that they would not end up with largely unsold and unoccupied buildings once these were completed (Habito 2017). Thus, these developers were not as highly leveraged compared to their Asian neighbors.

The reasons why the Philippines exhibited resiliency during the AFC are summed up as follows (Mijares 1999): (1) The Philippines had a stronger

---

[2] This was later brought down to 60%.

financial system; thus, credit available was not reduced to the extent of its neighbors; (2) the Philippines had much fewer short-term foreign currency borrowings. Moreover, half of the foreign currency liabilities of the private sector was to residents, and most of the foreign currency deposit loans were availed of by exporters, who were naturally hedged; (3) compared to its peers, most of the loans in Philippine banks were directed to more productive sectors of the economy such as manufacturing. Loans to the real estate sector were relatively smaller, and the growth in real estate investment was basically due to real demand; and (4) the Philippines had a large overseas workforce remitting foreign currency that more than covered present interest payments on public debt.

The Philippine Economy After the Storm: 1999–2006

Instead of throwing the Philippine economy off course, the difficult conditions it encountered prior to the AFC enabled authorities to recognize systemic frailties and adopt appropriate corrective measures. Apart from addressing existing problems, authorities employed necessary actions in a timely manner based on macroeconomic warning signals. They strategically implemented monetary, fiscal, and FX policies, which served to check potential sources of instabilities in the economy. While the Philippines was not able to escape the full impact of the AFC, the 1997 crisis became an opportunity not only for employing effective "crisis management" but also for further strengthening the economy, ensuring that its growth prospects could be sustained for the long haul.

As financial markets stabilized, the year 1999 saw encouraging signs that most Asian economies affected by the financial crisis have swung back to growth. The Philippine economy displayed good macroeconomic performance in 1999, a turnaround from the economic slowdown that followed the 1997 crisis. The recovery of the Philippine economy was also partly aided by external developments, as demand for Philippine exports continued to be strong.

From 1999 to 2006, real economic growth averaged 4.6%. In most years, the recovery was led by a rebound of agriculture and the sustained growth of the service sector. The industry sector likewise showed a strong expansion, driven by the growth performance of the manufacturing sector.

On the demand side, growth was driven by consumption expenditures and exports (Table 18.2). Based on the Philippine Labor Force Survey in 1998, the unemployment rate, which was estimated at 10.3%, declined to 8% in 2006 due to job creation fueled by improved economic performance.

Inflation generally stayed within a single-digit territory, averaging 5% for the 8-year period, driven largely by favorable weather conditions, which supported the recovery of agriculture.

In 2006, the cash operations of the NG posted a PHP 64.8 billion deficit (1% of GDP), which showed a decline of almost half, compared to the deficit of PHP 146.8 billion, or 2.6% of GDP, recorded in the previous year. This arose as the Government continued to increase expenditures to pump-prime the economy, even as revenues likewise grew by 20%.

Price stability paved the way for lower interest rates. Given prevailing favorable macroeconomic conditions, monetary authorities adopted measures to further reduce banks' intermediation costs and induce a decline in interest rates. These measures included reduction in banks' reserve requirements on deposit and deposit substitute liabilities and in the BSP's policy rates, that is, BSP borrowing and lending rates under the reverse repurchase and repurchase facilities, respectively. In 2002, the BSP shifted to

Table 18.2: GDP by Expenditure at Constant 2018 Prices, Annual Percentage Change, 1999–2006

	Item	1999	2000	2001	2002	2003	2004	2005	2006	Ave.
I.	Household Final Consumption Expenditure	4.0	5.2	3.9	5.1	5.4	5.9	4.4	4.2	4.8
II.	Government Final Consumption Expenditure	−3.6	−1.0	−1.3	−3.7	4.2	2.1	3.0	12.2	1.5
III.	Gross Capital Formation	−13.1	1.1	20.5	6.7	−0.4	6.1	−4.3	−10.3	0.8
IV.	Exports of Goods and Services	10.2	13.7	−2.2	4.8	9.2	6.5	12.5	10.1	8.1
V.	Less: Imports of Goods and Services	1.7	11.8	8.6	7.1	5.3	3.3	3.9	0.4	5.3
VI.	Statistical Discrepancy	...	...	...	...	...	...	...	...	...
	GDP	3.3	4.4	3.0	3.7	5.1	6.6	4.9	5.3	4.5

... = not available, GDP = gross domestic product.

Source: Bangko Sentral ng Pilipinas, Gross National Income by Expenditure Shares (at Constant Prices), Historical EXCEL, https://www.bsp.gov.ph/SitePages/Statistics/RealSectorAccounts.aspx.

inflation targeting to place more emphasis on price stability and less weight on intermediary monetary targets.

As a result of continuing reforms in the banking system and the generally strong macroeconomic fundamentals, the financial system displayed increasing resiliency and strength. While the ratio of NPL to total loans of universal and commercial banks continued to peak in 2001 at 17.4% due to the lingering effects of the regional crisis, the banking system remained stable and poised to support sustained economic growth. The NPL ratio declined until it settled at 5.7% in 2006. Asset quality improved as shown by the sustained decline in commercial banks' NPL ratio due to the implementation of the Special Purpose Vehicle law.

The BSP remained unwavering in its efforts to further strengthen the banking system. It undertook necessary reforms to enhance its ability to intermediate funds and manage risks as well as make it a more efficient channel of monetary policy. The banking system's total resources continued to rise on the back of a growing deposit base and higher capitalization.

In the same period, the country's external transactions generally recorded surpluses, resulting from the improved CA position, which turned positive in 2003, and the net inflow in the capital and financial account. The former was driven mainly by sustained growth in export earnings while the latter was due to higher net inflows of direct investments (DIs) and PIs. Improvements in the external sector allowed the BSP to build GIR to record levels of USD 23 billion or 5.1 months import cover and short-term external debt cover of three times the amount of short-term debt as of the end of 2006. These factors resulted in the exchange rate remaining generally stable.

FX liabilities of the country continued to be manageable, with outstanding liabilities at the end of the period recorded at USD 61.4 billion equivalent to 48.1% of GDP. The liabilities were largely medium term in nature (87.8%) and with 34% of total owed to official creditors, whose loans carried more favorable terms.

One important milestone was BSP's prepayment in full of its outstanding obligations to the IMF at the end of 2006 amounting to USD 219.9 million under its post-program monitoring, 4 months ahead of schedule. This allowed the BSP to exit early from its Post-Program Monitoring Arrangement with the Fund. The prepayment likewise marked the end of the country's borrower status with the Fund, after nearly four and a half decades.

The event likewise conveyed a strong signal to the international community that implementation of macroeconomic and structural reforms have firmly taken root to lessen dependence on IMF resources. The country's prepayment in full of its outstanding obligations to the IMF further provided signals to the international community that the Philippines was serious in the implementation of reforms that would ensure sustainable growth.

The country's sustained positive growth after the AFC is testament of the effects of policies adopted as early as the 1980s despite numerous internal and external challenges that beset the country from 1999 to 2006, including renewed uptick in oil prices, hostilities in the southern part of the Philippines, and questions on public governance.

Given structural reforms and numerous policies in place, the Philippine economy similarly proved resilient during the GFC. It continued to exhibit relatively strong macroeconomic fundamentals amid the negative impact brought about by the volatility of capital flows. It may be noted, however, that in spite of the many reforms instituted by government in response to the various challenges it faced at different points in time, the authorities have not exhausted the list of other policy changes that it still has to adopt. Many other reforms stand to be implemented including: strengthening public financial management, increasing tax revenues, enhancing competitiveness through stronger regulatory capacity, reducing the cost of doing business, addressing infrastructure and service delivery bottlenecks, and improving workers' skills, thus making them more employable (World Bank 2012).

Capital Flows Pre-GFC: 2005–2006[3]

Net direct investments (DIs) and net PIs recorded inflows of USD 869.9 million and USD 1.3 billion in 2005 and USD 1.6 billion and USD 3 billion in 2006, respectively. As a result of significant inflows, authorities encouraged both the private and public sectors to prepay their outstanding external debts to counteract the effects of capital inflows on the economy, particularly on the exchange rate. At the same time, local banks extended a significant amount of loans to nonresidents. Consequently, the other investment account

---

[3] For consistency of BOP data, only these 2 years were covered as the BOP statistics based on Balance of Payments Manual Sixth Edition (BPM6) date back to only 2005.

that included loan availment and repayment showed significant outflows. Recording net outflows of USD 4 billion and USD 6.2 billion in 2005 and 2006, respectively, these negated the net inflows from DIs and PIs. The 2-year period prior to the GFC thus ended up registering total net outflows in the total financial account of USD 1.8 billion in 2005 and USD 1.7 billion in 2006 (Figure 18.9; Annex 3).

The significant net outflows in the other investment account during the 2-year period resulted largely from (1) loans extended by local banks to nonresidents; (2) currency and deposit placements abroad by banks and other private entities; and (3) loan repayments by private corporations and the NG.

On DIs, nonresidents' investments in Philippine equities and debt instruments, or foreign direct investments (FDIs), amounted to USD 1.7 billion in 2005, while Philippine residents' outward DIs abroad registered USD 794.1 million. The increase in inward FDI compared to the previous year reflected positive sentiment generated by various reforms, particularly the sin tax and the reformed VAT[4] in the fiscal sector.

For the following year 2006, the country's strong economic fundamentals translated into a significant rise in inward FDIs into the country, which

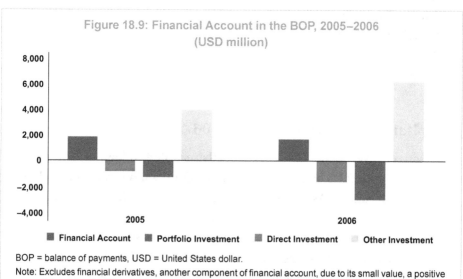

Figure 18.9: Financial Account in the BOP, 2005–2006 (USD million)

BOP = balance of payments, USD = United States dollar.
Note: Excludes financial derivatives, another component of financial account, due to its small value, a positive amount denotes net outflows while a negative amount denotes net inflows.
Source: Bangko Sentral ng Pilipinas, Balance of Payments BPM6 Format, New Concept, Main Table, Historical EXCEL, https://www.bsp.gov.ph/SitePages/Statistics/External.aspx?TabId=1.

---

[4] This refers to the law increasing the VAT coverage to include oil, power, and transportation.

rose significantly to USD 2.7 billion or by about 62.7%. These inflows were channeled mainly to manufacturing, services, real estate, financial intermediation, mining, and construction industries. The major investors during the review period were those from the US, Japan, the Netherlands, the United Kingdom, Switzerland, and Germany.[5] Resident investments abroad rose by a smaller percentage of 34.5%, or from USD 794.1 million to USD 1.1 billion. A pronounced acceleration in inward FPIs was also observed, where nonresident inflows increased by 21.6% (USD 3.6 billion) in 2006 from USD 2.9 billion in 2005.

Into the GFC: 2007–2008

Net capital inflows arising from nonresidents' inward DIs to the country continued to increase in 2007, recording an unparalleled amount of USD 2.9 billion for the decade. This peak was attributed to significant net equity capital placements and reinvested earnings. In particular, gross equity capital placements expanded by 24.9% to USD 2.2 billion during the year. These were channeled largely into manufacturing, services, construction, mining, real estate, financial intermediation, and agricultural industries. The bulk of these inflows came from Japan and the US.[6]

The rise in residents' investments in equity and fund shares following the acquisition of shares of a foreign power company,[7] as well as in debt instruments amounting to USD 5.4 billion, more than offset nonresident investments, thereby resulting in net outflows for DIs.

Meanwhile, even as inward FPIs declined in 2007 by 52% vis-à-vis 2006 due to increased investor risk aversion, PIs still posted net inflows of USD 1.6 billion. Factors that contributed to this included continued placements by nonresidents in equity securities of private corporations and lower outward FPI flows by residents.

In addition, since the other investment account reversed to a net inflow, the financial account posted a net inflow of USD 169.9 million in 2007, an improvement from a net outflow of USD 1.7 billion in 2006. Contributory factors included (1) disbursements of program loans to the NG from official

[5] BSP 2006, https://www.bsp.gov.ph/Media_And_Research/Annual%20Report/annrep2006.pdf, page 34.

[6] BSP 2007, https://www.bsp.gov.ph/Media_And_Research/Annual%20Report/annrep2007.pdf, page 34.

[7] BSP 2007, https://www.bsp.gov.ph/Media_And_Research/Annual%20Report/annrep2007.pdf, page 34.

creditors (i.e., USD 250 million Development Policy Loan from the World Bank, USD 250 million Development Policy Support Loan from the Asian Development Bank (ADB), and USD 295 million Power Sector Development Loan from the Japan Bank for International Cooperation; (2) loan availment by corporations (USD 5.3 billion), and (3) lower residents' lending (USD 1.1 billion). These inflows were partly offset by loan repayments by the NG (USD 1.2 billion) and private corporations (USD 2.5 billion).

In 2005–2007, significant capital inflows exerted upward pressure on the peso–dollar exchange rate as well as the expansion in domestic liquidity. Averaging PHP 55.09/USD in 2005, the peso appreciated against the US dollar by 16.2% to PHP 46.15/USD in 2007. In addition, inflows from OF remittances contributed to currency appreciation.

In the wake of the GFC, the financial account in 2008 reversed to a net outflow of USD 1.4 billion, weighed down by investors' sentiment, which remained cautious particularly in the last quarter of the year. Except for other investments, components of the financial account recorded net outflows, including FDIs and FPIs. Both DIs and PIs posted net outflows of USD 630 million and USD 1.6 billion, respectively. The deterioration in the DI account emanated from residents' DIs abroad, which exceeded DIs by nonresidents in domestic enterprises. The PI account turned around to a net outflow vis-à-vis the previous year's position mainly as a result of the NG's and local banks' net redemption/repayment of debt securities issued to nonresidents as well as the net withdrawal by nonresidents of their equity securities holdings in banks and private companies. Notwithstanding net outflows recorded in the financial account, the exchange rate continued to appreciate by 3.6% as the overall BOP position remained in surplus, albeit by only USD 88.7 million as a result of the CA surplus.

After the GFC: Capital Flow Movements

Periods of Capital Inflows — 2009–2012

Emerging markets in Asia, the Philippines included, experienced substantial capital inflows. The financial account registered net inflows of USD 895.9 million in 2009 to USD 11.5 billion in 2010, after which the amount of net inflows was reduced to an average of USD 6 billion for the 2 following years.

The surge in capital inflows resulted mainly from the effect of the highly accommodative monetary policy adopted in advanced economies in the form of significant interest rate cuts, as well as quantitative easing, to prop up their economies. These actions gave rise to large interest rate differentials between these economies and those of emerging markets, resulting in capital inflows to the latter as investors pursued higher rates of return. In addition, the US subprime crisis prompted institutional investors to purchase financial assets including bonds and equities from emerging markets as these were deemed more attractive.

Other factors that contributed to substantial capital inflows were the country's strong macroeconomic fundamentals, upgrades on credit ratings received by the Philippines, and expected continued growth prospects of the country. Moreover, the efficient handling of the crisis through monetary and fiscal measures provided greater investor confidence.

Buoyed by the strong inflows of FX from OF workers' remittances, business process outsourcing revenues, and tourist receipts and net capital inflows, the exchange rate mainly recorded appreciations for the period, from an average of PHP 47.64/USD in 2009 to an average of PHP 42.23/USD in 2012.

Facing Capital Outflows — 2013–2016

The trend in capital flows for the next 4 years was largely influenced by several factors, including (a) moderation in the growth momentum of emerging market economies, particularly China, notwithstanding the growth recovery in some advanced economies; (b) divergence in monetary policy in developed economies as a consequence of the different levels and speed of recovery in their economies; and (c) the drastic fall in international prices of oil, which raised concerns on risks of deflation in the midst of an already sluggish external demand conditions (BSP Annual Reports 2013–2016).

These external headwinds resulted in bouts of volatility in capital flows, the exchange rate, and the stock market, all of which presented serious challenges. These events did not take place only in the Philippines as there were similar occurrences in the rest of the emerging markets in Asia. From 2013 to 2016, the net financial account registered outflows, reversing inflows recorded during previous years.

For this 4-year period, DIs continued to post net inflows due largely to nonresidents' investments in the country, except for 2014, when nonresidents' inward FDI was surpassed by residents' outward FDI. This came as a result of the taper tantrum toward the end of 2013. Meanwhile, with the exception of 2013, FPIs registered net outflows due to the net redemption by the NG of its debt securities and withdrawal by nonresidents of their investments in debt securities and other equities, compounded by residents' acquisition of financial assets abroad.

These actions were largely influenced by the tapering off of the US Federal Reserve's (US Fed) bond purchases under its quantitative easing program. While the US Fed communicated its plans to normalize monetary policy in response to signs that the US economy was strengthening, there were uncertainties as to the magnitude and timing of the return to normalcy. The increased risk aversion resulted in bouts of volatility due to portfolio rebalancing and search for higher returns. Moreover, the combined effect of a stronger US dollar and the uptick in interest rates provided impetus for investors to shift their funds back to the US markets and withdraw from emerging markets, including the Philippines.

The peso–dollar rate depreciated by an average of 3% during this period as a result of recorded capital outflows.

Return to Capital Inflows — 2017–2019

The 3-year period 2017–2019 saw a reversal of capital outflows from 2013 to 2016 as shown in the net financial account. This occurred despite the unwinding of accommodative policies of advanced economies, which caused volatility in capital flows in emerging markets, including the Philippines, as investors expected interest rates abroad to increase.

In 2017, capital flows to the Philippines, as recorded in the total financial account, reversed to a net inflow of USD 2.8 billion from a net outflow of USD 175 million in the previous year. This was mainly a result of the substantial inflows of DIs resulting from the country's strong macroeconomic fundamentals and prospects for positive growth.

The reversal in flows came mainly from the marked improvement in net inflows of FDIs, which soared to USD 7 billion in 2017, arising from the annual growth of 23.9% in inward FDI or a record high of USD 10.3 billion. More particularly, investments in net equity and investment fund shares and debt instruments expanded by 29% and 20.5%, respectively. Gross placements of about USD 3.7 billion originated largely from the Netherlands, Singapore, the US, Japan, and Hong Kong. These were channeled mainly to gas, steam, and air-conditioning supply; manufacturing; real estate; construction; and wholesale and retail trade activities.[8]

The improvements in DIs more than offset net outflows in both the portfolio and other investment accounts. As for the former, residents increased placements in equities and investment fund shares issued by nonresidents and local corporates recorded lower amounts of prepayment/repayment of long-term debt securities held by nonresidents.

The total financial account again recorded net inflows in 2018, arising from the reversal of the other investment account to net inflows from net outflows in 2017, resulting from higher loan availment by residents from foreign creditors. In addition, portfolio investments recorded lower net outflows as nonresidents increased their placements in debt securities issued by local banks. These improvements more than offset the lower net inflows of DIs.

Net inflows in the total financial account continued to be recorded in 2019 as all the components recorded net inflows except the other investment accounts. The amount of USD 7.3 billion, however, was lower than the net inflows in 2018 of USD 9.3 billion.

A contributory factor to the net inflows witnessed during the year was the continuing amendments in the FX regulatory framework, which further liberalized rules on inward and outward investments by a broadening of their coverage, among others. As of 2019, there were a total of 11 waves of FX reforms to ensure that regulations remained responsive to the needs of a dynamic and expanding economy. A timeline of capital flows is shown in Figure 18.10.

Policy Responses to Capital Flows

FX Reforms

Given the surge in capital inflows, the BSP implemented measures to reduce the supply of FX and simultaneously increase its demand through a series of FX reforms. These reforms were instituted notwithstanding uncertainties brought about by the GFC.

---

[8] BSP 2017, https://www.bsp.gov.ph/Media_And_Research/Annual%20Report/annrep2017.pdf, page 29.

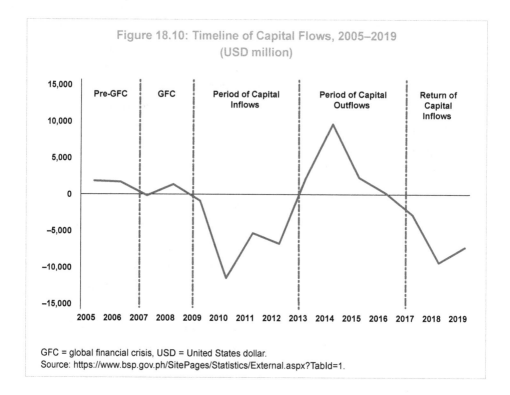

Figure 18.10: Timeline of Capital Flows, 2005–2019
(USD million)

GFC = global financial crisis, USD = United States dollar.
Source: https://www.bsp.gov.ph/SitePages/Statistics/External.aspx?TabId=1.

In the initial period preceding the GFC, the BSP adopted policies to create a regulatory environment more responsive to the needs of an expanding and more dynamic economy increasingly integrated with global markets (ASEAN Working Committee on Capital Account Liberalization (WC-CAL) 2019).

More specifically, the changes introduced were intended to (a) further diversify PIs; (b) provide banks with greater flexibility to manage their FX exposure; and (c) facilitate nontrade CA transactions and outward investments of Philippine residents. Among measures to increase FX demand was prepayment of foreign borrowings. In particular, the BSP fast-tracked payment of some of its outstanding foreign obligations. At the same time, the BSP likewise encouraged the NG and the private sector to take advantage of their strong external liquidity position to prepay their foreign debts (WC-CAL 2019).

Following these amendments to the FX regulatory regime, the BSP continued to review, liberalize, and rationalize the FX regulatory framework, ensuring that the regulations remained in pace with domestic and global developments while taking international standards and best practices into consideration. FX reforms included measures designed to (a) encourage outflows to temper upward pressures on the peso and allow freer and more efficient capital flows in the long term; (b) facilitate access to banking system resources for funding of legitimate transactions; (c) expand available financing options; and (d) offer greater opportunities for portfolio diversification. Mindful of the disadvantages that can accompany liberalization, the BSP ensured that prudential regulations and supervision (monitoring/ reporting/registration) remained in place. Continuing to implement such processes would allow monetary authorities to capture data required for policy review, formulation, statistics, and detection of any imminent crisis brewing in the horizon (WC-CAL 2019).

From 2013, further liberalization measures were introduced by the BSP to (a) facilitate the use of banking system resources to fund legitimate FX transactions, both trade and nontrade, and improve data capture; (b) provide residents in the Philippines greater flexibility to manage FX cash flows as well as to transact in FX; (c) allow the use of FX to fund resident-to-resident transactions that used to be strictly regulated; and (d) make it easier to avail of FX loans to fund projects and activities intended to support economic growth.

Reserve Accumulation

The BSP, having been tasked to manage the country's GIR, allowed the latter to rise to comfortable levels as a first line of defense in instances where extreme stress is observed in the FX market.

Monetary Policy

During the GFC, the BSP implemented a series of policy rate cuts starting in December 2008, totaling 200 basis points (bp), which brought down the overnight borrowing or reverse repurchase rate to 4% and the overnight lending or repurchase rate to 6% in July 2009. The downward movement in interest rates became possible with the easing of price pressures as a result of subdued demand. The rate reductions were aimed at stimulating economic growth and/or dampening the slowdown in economic activity by bringing down the cost of borrowing, thus reducing the financial burden of firms and households. Reduced policy rates also helped mitigate the negative feedback loop between weakening economic conditions and a more cautious financial sector (Guinigundo 2011). The action also paved the way for consumer confidence to improve.

Liquidity measures were fine-tuned by expanding access to its Special Deposit Account (SDA)[9] to trust entities of financial institutions under the BSP's supervision. Funds deposited with these entities were siphoned off once placed with the BSP's SDA. Because SDAs offered relatively higher rates, the amounts of deposits to this account grew rapidly. Consequently, nonresidents' placements were prohibited from being deposited in the SDA.

The Credit Surety Fund Program (CSFP) was also launched in the second half of 2008 to ensure that small businesses had access to financing. The CSFP is a credit enhancement scheme that allows micro, small, and medium enterprises that are members of cooperatives to borrow from banks even without traditional collateral. Loans granted by banks under the program are eligible for rediscounting with the BSP (Guinigundo 2011). Dollar liquidity measures were also introduced to infuse dollars into the domestic financial system to assist banks with dollar liquidity needs. Increased dollar liquidity likewise made it easier for domestic firms to manage their FX risks. These measures included among others (a) making available the BSP's US dollar repo facility (Guinigundo 2011); (b) promoting the use of banks' hedging facilities and increasing the budget for the exporters' dollar and yen redis-counting facility; and (c) allowing the use of foreign-denominated sovereign debt securities as collateral for loans.

The reduction in interest rates and the provision of liquidity were viewed as confidence-building moves — evidence that the BSP was fully committed to ensuring that there was sufficient money supply to boost the economy's growth. These also signaled the BSP's intent to maintain low interest rates to cut borrowing costs of firms and households and therefore support investment and consumption growth.

---

[9] The SDA was a monetary policy instrument implemented by the BSP for the purpose of managing excess domestic liquidity in the financial system and not intended for investment activities funded from nonresident sources. In 2006, the SDA, which so far had been used by monetary authorities as an important instrument to regulate the level of liquidity in the system, was replaced by the term deposit facility when the Interest Rate Corridor (IRC) was adopted. An IRC is a system for guiding short-term market interest rates toward the CB target/policy rate. It consists of a rate at which the CB lends to banks (typically an overnight lending rate) and a rate at which it takes deposits from them (deposit rate) (Revised Framework for Monetary Operations Under the BSP IRC System).

Macroeconomic Policies

Philippine authorities developed the Economic Resiliency Plan (ERP) in February 2009 as a response to the GFC. Amounting to PHP 330 billion (USD 6.9 billion[10] or 4.1% of GDP), the fiscal package was geared to stimulate activities to spur economic growth, through a mix of government spending, tax cuts, and public–private partnership projects. The ERP led the government to postpone its medium-term balanced budget goal to 2011 (Doraisami 2011). More specifically, the Plan included: (a) a PHP 150 billion budget allocation to fund government employment, rehabilitation of public buildings, social services, infrastructure and development, and various forms of agriculture support; (b) a PHP 100 billion infrastructure fund to be pooled from government corporations, financial institutions, and the private sector; (c) PHP 40 billion in the form of corporate and individual tax cuts (including doing away with the withholding taxes and actual taxes of minimum wage earners); (d) PHP 30 billion temporary additional benefits from social security institutions; and (e) PHP 250 million reintegration and livelihood assistance program for displaced OF workers (Lim 2010). The plan centered on the importance of infrastructure as a means of generating jobs. The ERP was implemented by the Department of Finance and the National Economic and Development Authority.

Exchange Rate Flexibility

The BSP maintained a market-determined exchange rate and allowed FX flexibility while guarding against speculative flows that would contribute to volatilities and undermine the inflation target (WC-CAL 2019). The local currency's competitiveness was monitored through the use of real effective exchange rates vis-à-vis the country's trading partners and competitor countries.

Recognizing the pitfalls of a fixed exchange rate system as experienced in the years prior to the AFC, the implementation of a market-determined exchange rate was also found to be consistent with the country's thrust toward FX liberalization and the independent monetary policy as contained in the New Central Bank Act.

---

[10]Using the average exchange rate of PHP 47.58/USD in February 2009.

Macroprudential Management

Several tools were employed to ensure that banks do not engage in transactions that could lead to credit booms or banks incurring excessive leverage. These included (a) limits to banks' exposure to real estate loans and stress test limit for real estate exposures; (b) provisions for loan losses; (c) requirements on banks' capital adequacy; (d) rules on derivatives activities, where among others, thresholds for banks of nondeliverable forward transactions at 20% and 100% of unimpaired capital for domestic banks and foreign bank branches, respectively, were set; (e) establishment of a framework to deal with domestic systemically important banks; (f) generation of Residential Real Estate Price Index; and (g) adoption of Basel III requirements.

The BSP likewise issued new guidelines on banks' internal capital adequacy assessment process and its supervisory review process. It also made use of tools to aid macroprudential risk assessments, such as: (i) the Financial Stability Report to enhance the public's understanding of financial stability risks and vulnerabilities; (ii) macro-stress tests to assess vulnerability of banks to shocks; and (iii) Senior Bank Loan Officers' Survey, which monitors changes in overall credit standards of banks (WC-CAL 2019).

Capital Market Deepening

The BSP supported initiatives related to the development of the domestic and regional bond markets, particularly the introduction of a broader range of financial products to further encourage market activity and advance improvements in market depth, breadth, and liquidity.

Regulatory Forbearance

To ensure that confidence in the banking system remained, guidelines were formulated to allow financial institutions to reclassify financial assets from categories measured at fair value to those measured at amortized cost. This measure eased pressure on financial institutions' balance sheets. The maximum deposit insurance coverage was also increased from PHP 250,000 to PHP 500,000.

Communication and Cooperation

To ensure a coordinated domestic response to the GFC, the BSP consulted with partners such as banks in the implementation of measures adopted to mitigate the effects of the crisis. The BSP strengthened participation in discussions with regional peers to share information, consider emerging developments, and pooling of resources, if warranted, including FX reserves. Clear communication with the market provided important information that the BSP was adhering to its mandates, ensuring sufficient liquidity to fund growth in a manner consistent with price stability.

Economic and Financial Literacy Program

The Economic and Financial Literacy Program (EFLP), launched in 2010, is one of the BSP's key programs to support its financial inclusion policy agenda. This is in line with the BSP's drive to promote greater awareness and understanding of essential economic and financial issues that will help the Filipino public acquire the knowledge and develop the skills to make well-informed economic and financial decisions and choices.

The program is composed of learning sessions aimed at different audiences. Modules involve the two major categories of economic information and financial education. The first includes programs that aim to promote awareness and appreciation of basic economic concepts, issues, and concerns, with particular emphasis on the BSP's roles and responsibilities and how these affect the lives of Filipinos. The second category involves programs that aim to educate the public on personal financial management (i.e., budgeting, saving, and investing), as well as on consumer protection (i.e., rights and responsibilities of financial consumers, safeguarding against unsafe banking practices, frauds, and scams).

For instance, the program has helped increase the awareness among OF households of the importance of saving part of the remittances they receive. From as low as 10.7% in the first quarter of 2007, the savings rate increased to 31.4% during the fourth quarter of 2019. The BSP collaborates with the Department of Education to include financial literacy lessons in the school curriculum and embed financial literacy sessions in the regular training programs for teachers and nonteaching personnel.

The Philippines: Participation in Regional Cooperation

The Philippines' involvement in regional cooperation has been influenced largely by developments in global and regional monetary and financial conditions. In many instances, the occurrence of a crisis served as a major push for the establishment of various cooperation efforts.

The AFC underscored the widespread effect and virulent nature of a contagion. The region witnessed how FX volatility and financial market instability in one country could be easily transmitted to the rest of the region as a result of linkages in trade and financial markets that subsequently gave rise to declines in output, corporate distress, and financial system failures. Since the negative impact was geographically concentrated, the establishment of a regional grouping that could offer financial support was considered appropriate. Moreover, regional cooperation was seen to reduce dependence on international financial institutions such as the IMF, with which some countries in the region had controversial dealings with at the time of the AFC. Such regional cooperation was likewise viewed as a better option to IMF borrowings as conditionalities imposed were seen to be more tailored to the circumstances existing in the region.

Immediately after the AFC, a proposal for regional response was made by Japan to create an Asian Monetary Fund. The proposal was for an institution to be formed to work toward setting up a regional network funded by Asian countries to overcome current and future economic crises (Narine 2001).

This was later rejected and subsequently replaced by another possible framework for regional cooperation — the Manila Framework Group or MFG. The MFG was established in 1997 to promote financial stability in Asia and dialogue with the West (Reuters 2004). The Group was formed by the East Asian countries, the United States, Canada, Australia, and New Zealand. The MFG was later disbanded in December 2004 when members agreed that its objectives could be achieved in similar existing groups.

Participation in these two fora took place at the same time that the Philippines was already a member of, and was participating in, international financial institutions such as the IMF and the World Bank, which the country joined in 1945. The Philippines is likewise the host country of the ADB established in 1966, starting with membership of 31 countries, growing to encompass 68 members as of 2020.

As the landscape of the global economy drastically changed from the time of the CBP to the present-day BSP, so has the latter's participation in various fora and regional mechanisms. Alongside regional economies building up reserves as a first line of defense against external fluctuations, stand-by regional agreements and pooling facilities were established, aimed at reducing the pressure of accumulating reserves at the national level as safeguards to volatilities in the external environment. Such arrangements were seen as regional financing facilities that would be able to deliver timely and adequate support in time of extreme need.

After the AFC, the Chiang Mai Initiative (CMI) was the first regional currency swap arrangement launched by the ASEAN+3 countries in May 2000 to address the short-term liquidity difficulties in the region and to supplement the existing international financial arrangements (BSP 2019). It is composed of (a) the ASEAN Swap Arrangement (ASA)[11] among ASEAN countries; and (b) a network of bilateral swap arrangements (BSAs) among the ASEAN+3 countries. Under the CMI, the total amount of the ASA was raised to USD 1 billion in November 2000 from USD 100 million in 1977. In 2002–2004, the BSP acted as the Agent Bank for the ASA[12] and thus coordinated its renewal in 2004. The financing arrangement was further expanded to USD 2 billion in May 2005. Meanwhile, the BSA is a facility in the form of swaps of US dollars with the domestic currencies of the ASEAN+3 member countries. Repurchase agreements were meant to provide liquidity support through the sale and buyback of US treasury notes or bills, with a remaining life of no more than 5 years, and government securities of the counterparty country. The swap arrangement is meant to supplement existing international financial facilities, including those provided by the IMF and ASA. By October 2003, 13 BSAs had been successfully concluded with a combined total size of roughly USD 35 billion (Sussangkarn 2010). As of September 22, 2020, BSAs amounted to USD 325.4 billion.

---

[11] The ASA is a reciprocal currency or swap arrangement which allows member CBs to swap their local currencies with major international currencies for a period of up to 6 months and for an amount up to twice their committed amounts under the facility. The duration, coverage, and amount of the ASA have expanded significantly since the agreement was signed. The effectivity, which was originally intended to be for 1 year, has been extended to 2 years and remains in effect to date, providing a USD 2 billion short-term liquidity support for ASEAN's 10-member nations.

[12] In order to coordinate the implementation of the ASA, an Agent Bank is appointed on a rotation basis based on alphabetical order for a term of 2 years and is tasked specifically to inform and consult with the rest of the members on the assessment and processing of a member's swap request as expeditiously as possible.

In May 2006, the ASEAN+3 member countries agreed to initiate discussions on how to evolve the CMI into a more effective mechanism or a more advanced version of the CMI. A year hence, the members agreed "on the principle of converting the bilateral schemes of the CMI into a multilateralized self-managed reserves pooling scheme governed by a single contractual agreement, or the Chiang Mai Initiative Multilateralisation (CMIM)" (Sussangkarn 2010).

The rationale for multilateralizing the CMI is to (a) increase the certainty of funding; (b) enlarge the amount of funds available; (c) send a strong signal of regional cooperation and policy coordination; (d) simplify the activation mechanism through operation of a central coordinating body and an automatic triggering mechanism with adequate safeguards and surveillance arrangements; (e) play a complementary role vis-à-vis international financial institutions in providing liquidity support to crisis economies and conduct surveillance; and (f) facilitate the evolution of CMI into higher forms of regional monetary and financial cooperation (BSP 2019). In these endeavors, the BSP actively co-chaired, with the Bank of Korea, the working group on the self-managed reserve pooling arrangement that considered options on the size of the CMI, deliberated on how to determine individual country contributions, and looked into the sourcing of additional resources.

Following active deliberations on the issue, the CMI became the CMIM in 2009 with the signing of the Articles of Agreement on December 28, 2009, which came into effect on March 24, 2010. The CMIM parties agreed on an initial size of USD 120 billion, which was later doubled to USD 240 billion during the 15th ASEAN+3 Finance Ministers' and CB Governors' Meeting held in Manila on May 3, 2012. During this same event, CMIM features were enhanced involving introduction of a crisis prevention facility; and increase in the IMF De-Linked Portion (IDLP) from 20% to 30%. Thus, the CMIM currently has the option to tap two financing facilities: (1) for crisis prevention or the CMIM Precautionary Line; and (2) for crisis resolution or the CMIM Stability Facility.

Following this milestone agreement, continuing consultations have been held by ASEAN+3 members to further enhance the CMIM framework. The Philippines has been vigorously involved in all these dialogues, particularly on the further increase of the IDLP, specifically from 30% to 40%. This increase in the IDLP has been agreed to by the ASEAN+3 members in 2020, and this will come into force in 2021 after signing has been completed by all members.

The Philippines also participates in the ASEAN Surveillance Process under the ASEAN Finance Ministers' Process, and the Economic Review and Policy Dialogue Process under the ASEAN+3 Finance Ministers' Process, which are policy dialogue-based and peer review structured forms of surveillance.

Also noteworthy is the country's participation in the ASEAN+3 Macroeconomic Research Office (AMRO), which is an evolving regional surveillance mechanism of the CMIM. Lastly, the BSP participates in selected policy exchange and information sharing activities under key CB regional forums such as the Executives' Meeting of East Asia Pacific (EMEAP) CBs and the Bank for International Settlements (BIS) (BSP 2019). Needless to say, the BSP regularly participates in the ASEAN CB Forum.

To strengthen policy dialogue with peers in the ASEAN region and enhance surveillance, the Philippines keenly participated in discussions that gave rise to the document "The Declaration of ASEAN Concord II" in 2003 in Bali, Indonesia, which aimed to build a regional community based on three pillars composed of politics, the economy, and the sociocultural field. The Philippines, as one of the original founders of the ASEAN, was greatly involved in the adoption of the ASEAN Economic Community (AEC) Blueprint 2008–2015, which set the guidelines and strategic plan of action to achieve regional economic integration. Subsequently in November 2015, the ASEAN member states adopted the AEC Blueprint 2025, succeeding the Blueprint 2015, laying the groundwork for further cementing the results achieved in the earlier blueprint and ensuring that the strategic objectives laid down for the next decade would be achieved.

On the basis of the Blueprint, which included ensuring the freer flow of capital, the ASEAN Finance Ministers' Meeting in 2003 endorsed the creation of the WC-CAL. As part of its roadmap for monetary and financial integration of ASEAN, WC-CAL was aimed at removing and relaxing restrictions in the CA, FDIs, FPIs, and other capital flows. The end goal of WC-CAL in the AEC Blueprint 2025 is to achieve substantial liberalization in the capital accounts of ASEAN member states and to strengthen policy dialogue and information exchange mechanisms.

The BSP chaired as well as co-chaired the WC-CAL with the Bank of Thailand (BOT) and the State Bank of Vietnam from 2011 until 2019. Over the period, the Committee continued discussions on the CAL Framework, which provided guidance on the individual liberalization processes, including drafting of the CAL Heatmap spearheaded by the BSP. The CAL Heatmap is a tool to assess the level of openness of the capital account regime in ASEAN and to monitor the CAL process. The Heatmap also serves as a tool to identify gaps between the demand for and supply of capacity-building measures. Likewise, under the BSP's chairmanship, a policy dialogue on capital flows and safeguard mechanism for CAL was established to discuss current trends in capital flows and capital flow management measures.

In addition to economic integration under ASEAN and ASEAN+3, the Philippines remains actively involved in other regional arrangements that involve surveillance of regional and individual economies as well as the provision of intellectual support. One of these arrangements is the Monetary and Financial Stability Committee (MFSC) under the EMEAP, composed of EMEAP Deputies, established in 2007. The MFSC is tasked to assist EMEAP Governors in promoting monetary and financial stability in the region by highlighting issues, identifying areas of vulnerabilities, and recommending broad policy options in the areas of regional macro-monitoring, risk management, crisis management, and crisis resolution (BSP 2019).

Under the BSP's chairmanship in the MFSC, a Data Template of Weekly Financial Market Developments in EMEAP economies was initiated in August 2009. This template was to track quick-moving financial indicators to pinpoint possible risks to regional stability, including exchange rates, stock market indices, credit default swap spreads, emerging market bond indices, interest rates, and computations of the carry-to-risk ratio for individual EMEAP economies. Over time, several changes have been made in the report to make it more meaningful and efficient.

The BSP co-chaired, with Bank Negara Malaysia (BNM), the Task Force on Milestones Toward ASEAN Monetary and Financial Integration under the ASEAN CB Forum in 2009. During its co-chairmanship, the BSP steered the conduct of a study that provided a thorough and critical assessment of the current state of financial services liberalization, capital market development, and CAL in the ASEAN member countries. Completion of the study took 2 years and it was finally endorsed by the ASEAN CB Governors in April 2011.

Results of the study showed that ASEAN member countries started from different initial conditions and required different necessary preconditions to achieve specific milestones toward achieving financial integration. As a result, the ASEAN Financial Integration Framework was crafted, where each member country defined its own milestones and timelines to achieve a semi-integrated financial market by 2020 based on their initial conditions and at their own pace.

The BSP also co-chaired the Working Committee on ASEAN Banking Integration Framework (WC-ABIF) with the State Bank of Vietnam for 2016–2018. During its co-chairmanship, the WC-ABIF deliberated on possible bilateral arrangements to ease entry of Qualified ASEAN Banks (QABs) in addition to implementing other concessions on banking consistent with the ABIF Guidelines.

The BSP and BNM signed a Heads of Agreement (HOA) on March 14, 2016, covering guidelines on entry of QABs between the Philippines and Malaysia. The HOA allowed up to three QABs from each jurisdiction to operate in the other country. In 2017, the BSP signed the ABIF accord with BNM, BOT, and Indonesia Financial Services Authority (OJK). In particular, the Declaration of Conclusion of Negotiations on the entry of QABs between the two countries was signed by both the BSP and BNM. Letters of Intent between the BSP and the BOT and between the BSP and OJK were signed, expressing intent to begin bilateral negotiations between the two countries. This is expected to provide more access to financial services and products for Filipinos, create jobs in the financial services sector, and expand market opportunities for Philippine banks across the region (BSP 2019).

To assist the individual ASEAN member states in their journey toward achieving semi-financial integration in 2020, and cognizant of the flexibility each member is given in achieving this target based on their initial conditions, the ASEAN Senior Level Committee on Financial Integration was established in April 2011. This high-level committee composed of ASEAN CB Deputies and Officials aimed to ensure that the needed capacity and institution-building essential to achieve timelines set by each member would be available to assist members in achieving their goals. The BSP co-chaired this Committee with BNM in the first 2 years of its existence, after which co-chairmanship has been rotated among the rest of the ASEAN members.

Conclusion

The external debt crisis which the Philippines faced in the early 1980s brought to fore the weaknesses and vulnerabilities of the economy. However, the same challenges underscored the capability of the country to rise above the challenges and adopt appropriate corrective measures.

The courses of action that the authorities took focused on crisis management and resolution. These policies, among others, involved maintaining a flexible exchange rate, adopting prudential measures toward achieving a healthy financial system, strengthening the fiscal sector, ensuring a sustainable external debt situation, and providing a responsive FX regulatory environment, which helped shape the performance of the Philippines during the AFC and the GFC. In particular, the Philippine economy was able to exhibit greater resiliency vis-à-vis its peers arising from the lessons it drew from the earlier crisis and the consequent responses it generated.

The successive economic growth for 21 years commencing in 1999 is a testament of the fruits borne by the numerous reforms undertaken by the government in response to the weaknesses and problems observed in the economy.

While advances have been made on many fronts, Philippine authorities realize that more work needs to be done. A long list of essential reforms continues to face the Philippines, among which are the need to build sufficient infrastructure and reduce poverty levels and income inequality.

The authorities are fully committed to implement the necessary reforms to ensure that the country is able to transcend the emerging challenges it may face in the future, including continued active participation in regional and international financial initiatives.

References

Akyüz, Y. 2000. "Causes and Sources of the Asian Financial Crisis." UNCTAD, Geneva, paper presented at the Host Country Event: Symposium on Economic and Financial Recovery in Asia UNCTAD X, Bangkok.

Association of Southeast Asian Nations Working Committee on Capital Account Liberalization. 2019. "Capital Account Safeguard Measures in the ASEAN Context."

Bangko Sentral ng Pilipinas (BSP). 1986. Annual Report.

Bangko Sentral ng Pilipinas. 1991. Annual Report.

Bangko Sentral ng Pilipinas. 1993. Circular No. 1389.

Bangko Sentral ng Pilipinas. 2013. Annual Report.

Bangko Sentral ng Pilipinas. 2014. Annual Report.

Bangko Sentral ng Pilipinas. 2015. Annual Report.

Bangko Sentral ng Pilipinas. 2016. Annual Report.

Bangko Sentral ng Pilipinas. 2019. Annual Report.

Bangko Sentral ng Pilipinas. 2019. *The Story of Philippine Central Banking: Stability and Strength at Seventy.*

Bergsten, C. F. 1998. "Reviving the 'Asian Monetary Fund'." *Policy Brief, Peterson Institute for International Economics* 98–98.

Bureau of Internal Revenue. Website, Transparency, BIR History, Aquino Administration.

Caparas, Ma. Teresa D. 2000. Oil Price Deregulation, Philippine Institute for Development Studies, Economic Issue of the Day, No. 2.

Clarete, Ramon, L., Emmanuel F. Esguerra, and Hal Hill. 2018. *The Philippine Economy, No Longer the East Asian Exception?* Singapore: ISEAS — Yusof Ishak Institute.

Corsetti, Giancarlo, Paolo Presenti, and Nouriel Roubini. 1999. "What Caused the Asian Currency and Financial Crisis?" *Japan and the World Economy* 11.

Doraisami, Anita. 2011. *The Global Financial Crisis: Countercyclical Fiscal Policy Issues and Challenges in Malaysia, Indonesia, the Philippines, and Singapore.* ADB Institute Working Paper No. 288.

Espinosa, Ray C. 1993. "The Further Liberalization of FX Control Regulations in the Philippines." *The International Lawyer* 27 (3): 771–774.

Frenkel, Michael. 1989. *The International Debt Problem: An Analysis of the Brady Plan.* ECONSTOR.

Guinigundo, Diwa C. 2011. *The Impact of the Global Financial Crisis on the Philippine Financial System — An Assessment.* BIS Papers No. 54.

Habito, Cielito F. 2017. "Recalling the Asian Financial Crisis." *Philippine Daily Inquirer.*

Holley, David. 1997. "Philippine Peso Succumbs to Weight of Thai Devaluation." *Los Angeles Times.*

Kawai, M. 2015. *From the Chiang Mai Initiative to An Asian Monetary Fund.* ADB Institute.

Lim, Joseph Anthony. 2010. *The Impact of the Global Financial and Economic Turmoil on the Philippines: National Responses and Recommendations to Address the Crisis.* TWN Global Economy Series 23.

Magallona, Merlin M. 1989. *U.S. Marshall Plan for the Philippines: U.S. Military Bases and Foreign Monopoly Capital.* Quezon City: New Horizons Research and Publications.

Malacañang, 1972. Presidential Decree No. 1972.

Mijares, Roy. 1999. "Philippine Resiliency to the Asian Financial Crises." Sakura Institute of Research, Inc.

Narine, Shaun. 2001. "ASEAN and the Idea of an "Asian Monetary Fund: Institutional Uncertainty in the Asia Pacific." *Non-Traditional Security Issues in Southeast Asia* 227–254.

Noland, Marcus. 2000. "The Philippines in the Asian Financial Crisis: How the Sick Man Avoided Pneumonia." *Asian Survey* 40 (3).

Ofreneó, Rene E. 1984. "The Philippines: Debt Crisis and the Politics of Succession." *Philippine Sociological Review* 32 (1/4): 7–17.

Reuters. 2004. "Manila Framework Group Ends."

Rodlauer, Markus. 2000. *Philippines: Toward Sustainable and Rapid Growth.* IMF Occasional Paper 187.

Sussangkarn, Chalongphob. 2010. *The Chiang Mai Initiative Multilateralization: Origin, Development and Outlook.* ADB Institute Working Paper Series.

Tetangco, Amando M. Jr. 2003. *The Tax Exempt Status of the Central Bank in the Philippines.* BIS Paper No. 20.

Tetangco, Amando M. Jr. 2005. *The Composition and Management of Capital Flows in the Philippines.* BIS Paper No. 23.

Tuaño-Amador, Ma. Cyd 2009. Asian Financial Crisis of 1997–1998 and the Philippine Economy: Causes, Consequences and Challenges, Central Banking in Challenging Times: The Philippine Experience (The Macroeconomic Perspective by Governor Amando M. Tetangco, Jr.).

World Bank. 2012. "Philippines: Reforms Urgently Needed to Achieve Higher Growth to Improve Lives of More Poor Filipinos — World Bank." *Press Release,* March 2012.

Yap, Josef T., Celia M. Reyes, and Janet S. Cuenca. 2009. *Impact of the Global Financial and Economic Crisis on the Philippines.* Discussion Paper Series No. 2009–30. Philippine Institute for Development Studies.

Note: A complete set of annexes can be found at https://www.worldscientific.com/worldscibooks/10.1142/12753#t=suppl

Annex 1. National Government Cash Operations
(PHP million, unless otherwise specified)

Item	1990	1991	1992	1993	1994	1995	1996	1997	1998	1999
A Revenues	180,902	220,787	242,714	260,405	336,160	361,220	410,449	471,843	462,515	478,502
(Percent year-over-year)	19	22	10	7	29	8	14	15	-2	4
A.1 Tax Revenues	151,700	182,275	208,705	230,170	271,305	310,517	367,894	412,165	416,585	431,686
Tax Effort (Percent of GDP) [1, a]	13	13	14	14	15	15	15	15	14	13
A2 Non-Tax Revenues[2]	29,202	38,512	34,009	30,235	64,855	50,703	42,555	59,678	45,930	46,816
B Expenditures	218,096	247,136	258,680	282,296	319,874	350,146	404,193	470,279	512,496	590,160
(Percent year-over-year)	27	13	5	9	13	10	15	16	9	15
B.1 Current Operating Expenditure	191,322	212,533	219,505	234,563	277,275	289,053	353,062	419,401	467,920	524,240
B.2 Interest Payments	71,114	74,922	79,571	76,491	79,123	72,658	76,522	77,971	99,792	106,290
B.2.1 Domestic	53,323	56,347	63,113	56,183	59,806	51,376	59,002	58,350	73,525	74,980
B.2.2 Foreign	17,791	18,575	16,458	20,308	19,317	21,282	17,520	19,621	26,267	31,310
B.3 Net Lending and Equity	2,768	5,964	-6,949	9,902	8,993	8,420	3,176	2,960	1,098	4,725
C Surplus/ Deficit (-)	-37,194	-26,349	-15,966	-21,891	16,286	11,074	6,256	1,564	-49,981	-111,658
(Percent of GDP)[a]	-3	-2	-1	-1	1	1	0	0	-2	-3
D Financing[3]	19,270	41,248	152,638	-15,656	-21,939	10,969	43,319	-27,113	88,896	181,698
D.1 Net Domestic Borrowings	15,144	34,368	138,248	-28,566	-10,361	24,315	49,324	-20,295	76,550	98,898
D.1.1 Gross Domestic Borrowings	30,096	64,722	148,146	-16,992	4,620	58,653	62,584	-2,430	105,311	160,450
D.1.2 Amortizations	14,952	30,354	9,898	11,574	14,981	34,338	13,260	17,865	28,761	61,552

2000	2001	2002	2003	2004	2005	2006	2007	2008	2009	2010
514,762	567,481	578,406	639,737	706,718	816,159	979,638	1,136,560	1,202,905	1,123,211	1,207,926
8	10	2	11	11	16	20	16	6	-7	8
460,034	493,608	507,637	550,468	604,964	705,615	859,857	932,937	1,049,189	981,631	1,093,643
13	13	12	12	12	12	14	14	14	12	12
54,728	73,873	70,769	89,269	101,754	110,544	119,781	203,623	153,716	141,580	114,283
648,974	714,504	789,147	839,605	893,775	962,937	1,044,429	1,149,001	1,271,022	1,421,743	1,522,384
10	10	10	6	7	8	9	10	11	12	7
585,396	652,642	...	...	...	...	...	...	...	...	...
140,894	174,834	185,861	226,408	260,901	299,807	310,108	267,800	272,218	278,866	294,244
93,575	112,592	119,985	147,565	169,997	190,352	197,263	157,220	170,474	164,703	175,673
47,319	62,242	65,876	78,843	90,904	109,455	112,845	110,580	101,744	114,163	118,571
3,170	4,428	4,112	8,243	5,720	1,897	3,692	13,479	16,084	6,423	11,407
-134,212	-147,023	-210,741	-199,868	-187,057	-146,778	-64,791	-12,441	-68,117	-298,532	-314,458
-4	-4	-5	-4	-4	-3	-1	-0	-1	-4	-4
203,815	175,235	264,158	286,823	442,046	471,737	325,500	292,793	417,671	473,045	621,388
119,459	152,320	155,045	142,961	360,879	379,072	204,746	236,631	426,873	320,568	488,340
164,888	206,358	235,989	290,283	383,780	396,819	370,306	326,963	429,261	458,473	661,757
45,429	54,038	80,944	147,322	22,901	17,747	165,560	90,332	2,388	137,905	173,417

continued on next page

Annex 1: *continued*

	1990	1991	1992	1993	1994	1995	1996	1997	1998	1999
D.2 Net External Borrowings	4,126	6,880	14,390	12,910	-11,578	-13,346	-6,005	-6,818	12,346	82,800
D.2.1 Gross External Borrowings	24,406	23,086	34,143	38,223	12,285	16,833	21,955	22,995	48,302	120,354
D.2.2 Amortizations	20,280	16,206	19,753	25,313	23,863	30,179	27,960	29,813	35,956	37,554
E Change in Cash: Deposit/ Withdrawal (-)	-13,065	18,142	90,659	-24,240	-39,772	-17,232	30,676	-32,564	-17,089	38,984
(Percent of GNI)[a]	-3	-2	-1	-1	1	1	0	0	-2	-3

GDP = gross domestic product, GNI = gross national income, NG = National Government, PHP = Philippine peso.
Notes: GDP-related ratios are computed based on the revised National Account series (2000 = 100).
[1] Revised series to compute tax effort as percent of GDP (instead of GNI in the old series); to be consistent with international practice adopted by the Department of Finance (DOF).
[2] Including grants.
[3] Starting 2004, data are based on the revised financing, which are sourced from the National Government Cash Operations of the Bureau of the Treasury (BTr) to conform with the Government Finance Statistics Manual (GFSM) 2014 concept where reporting of debt amortization reflects the actual principal repayments to creditor including those serviced by the Bond Sinking Fund (BSF), while financing includes gross proceeds of liability management transactions such as bond exchange.
[4] Refer to accounts not included in the NG budget, e.g., sale, purchase or redemption of government securities, but included in the cash operations report to show the complete relationship in the movements of the cash accounts.
[a] Latest comparative GDP/GNI ratios refer to the January-September data.
Source: Bureau of the Treasury.

Annex 2. Nonperforming Loans and Loan-Loss Provisions of Universal and Commercial Banks; End of Period
(PHP billion, unless otherwise specified)

Year	TLP	NPL	LLP	LLP to NPL	NPL to TLP
1996	1,221.76	34.21	15.15	44.29%	2.80%
1997	1,573.14	73.60	34.78	47.25%	4.68%
1998	1,542.49	160.00	61.33	38.33%	10.37%
1999	1,582.89	195.39	91.04	46.59%	12.34%
2000	1,628.21	245.81	107.21	43.61%	15.10%
2001	1,625.05	281.91	127.41	45.20%	17.35%
2002	1,639.38	245.10	125.46	51.19%	14.95%
2003	1,747.15	245.51	130.01	52.96%	14.05%
2004	1,784.24	227.03	137.12	60.40%	12.72%
2005	1,872.74	153.68	119.08	77.49%	8.21%
2006	2,073.35	117.41	97.03	82.64%	5.66%
2007	2,194.78	97.63	91.12	93.33%	4.45%

NPL = nonperforming loans, LLP = loan loss provision, PHP = Philippine peso, TLP = total loan profile.
Source: Bangko Sentral ng Pilipinas.

2000	2001	2002	2003	2004	2005	2006	2007	2008	2009	2010
84,356	22,915	109,113	143,862	81,167	92,665	120,754	56,162	-9,202	152,477	133,048
125,876	68,482	200,267	240,122	199,533	218,317	284,081	118,414	71,311	251,366	357,410
41,520	45,567	91,154	96,260	118,366	125,652	163,327	62,252	80,513	98,889	224,362
3,810	-22,229	-1,706	25,767	-19,412	22,329	6,063	106,951	47,477	-66,027	37,166
-3	-3	-4	-4	-3	-2	-1	-0	-1	-3	-3

	TLP	NPL	LLP	LLP to NPL	NPL to TLP
2008	2,502.33	88.19	88.20	100.01%	3.52%
2009	2,724.87	80.91	90.90	112.34%	2.97%
2010	2,801.71	80.22	95.04	118.48%	2.86%
2011	3,221.78	71.94	90.90	126.36%	2.23%
2012	3,650.76	100.61	128.46	127.68%	2.76%
2013	4,256.96	90.51	130.44	144.12%	2.13%
2014	5,117.88	93.06	132.54	142.43%	1.82%
2015	5,719.67	91.60	129.22	141.07%	1.60%
2016	6,706.31	93.80	135.70	144.67%	1.40%
2017	7,867.08	97.53	145.84	149.53%	1.24%
2018	9,017.78	113.52	148.34	130.67%	1.26%
2019	9,953.96	156.53	170.52	108.94%	1.57%

Annex 3. Balance of Payments for Periods ———
(USD million, unless otherwise specified)

Item	2005	2006	2007	2008	2009	2010	2011
A Current Account	1990.39	6962.85	8071.94	144.02	8448.16	7179.16	5642.72
(Percent of GNI)	1.68	4.99	4.74	0.07	4.29	3.09	2.17
Percent of GDP	1.85	5.45	5.17	0.07	4.79	3.44	2.40
Exports	50329.66	61356.68	68329.36	70774.65	66602.74	79211.37	83835.87
Imports	48339.27	54393.82	60257.42	70630.63	58154.57	72032.21	78193.14
A.1 Goods, Services, and Primary Income	-9644.00	-6280.76	-6373.73	-15575.06	-8121.54	-10416.65	-12924.29
Exports	38513.78	47874.59	53696.68	54738.07	49631.85	61241.49	64791.64
Imports	48157.78	54155.35	60070.41	70313.14	57753.40	71658.15	77715.94
A.1.1 Goods and Services	-9998.07	-6982.40	-8008.13	-16675.07	-8962.22	-11094.11	-13866.04
(Percent of GNI)	-8.47	-5.00	-4.71	-8.42	-4.56	-4.78	-5.34
(Percent of GDP)	-9.30	-5.46	-5.13	-9.21	-5.08	-5.32	-5.92
Exports	33772.64	41798.66	46304.28	47733.53	43226.99	54553.95	57154.67
Imports	43770.72	48781.07	54312.42	64408.61	52189.21	65648.06	71020.72
A.1.1.1. Goods	-12145.63	-11459.15	-13966.18	-18645.61	-13860.14	-16859.20	-20428.03
(Percent of GNI)	-10.30	-8.22	-8.21	-9.41	-7.05	-7.27	-7.87
(Percent of GDP)	-11.30	-8.97	-8.95	-10.30	-7.86	-8.09	-8.72
Credit: Exports	25161.77	30734.44	32802.57	34678.75	29142.86	36771.71	38276.47
Debit: Imports	37307.40	42193.60	46768.75	53324.36	43003.01	53630.91	58704.50
A.1.1.2 Services	2147.55	4476.75	5958.04	1970.53	4897.92	5765.08	6561.98
Credit: Exports	8610.87	11064.22	13501.71	13054.78	14084.13	17782.24	18878.20
Debit: Imports	6463.32	6587.47	7543.66	11084.25	9186.20	12017.15	12316.21
A.1.2 Primary Income	354.07	701.63	1634.40	1100.01	840.67	677.46	941.75
Credit: Receipts	4741.13	6075.92	7392.39	7004.53	6404.85	6687.54	7636.97
Debit: Payments	4387.05	5374.28	5757.99	5904.52	5564.18	6010.08	6695.22
A.2 Secondary Income	11634.39	13243.62	14445.67	15719.08	16569.71	17595.81	18567.02
Credit: Receipts	11815.88	13482.09	14632.68	16036.57	16970.88	17969.87	19044.22
Debit: Payments	181.48	238.47	187.00	317.48	401.17	374.06	477.19
Capital Account	79.27	103.10	36.44	110.06	89.88	88.49	159.88
Credit: Receipts	81.27	127.10	81.44	127.06	97.88	98.49	188.88
Debit: Payments	2.00	24.00	45.00	...	8.00	10.00	29.00
Financial Account	1833.50	1683.71	-169.93	1369.76	-895.86	-11490.77	-5318.58
Net Acquisition of Financial Assets	6383.13	5414.66	8559.77	-4598.30	2620.64	945.39	593.09

2012	2013	2014	2015	2016	2017	2018	2019
6949.48	11383.50	10755.93	7265.67	-1198.87	-2142.96	-8877.04	-3386.25
2.38	3.58	3.24	2.12	-0.33	-0.58	-2.31	-0.81
2.65	4.00	3.61	2.37	-0.37	-0.65	-2.55	-0.89
95137.43	97885.58	107546.49	105850.71	108905.17	124126.44	129979.73	136361.51
88187.95	86502.07	96790.56	98585.03	110104.04	126269.41	138856.78	139747.77
-12550.18	-9689.88	-12026.48	-15997.42	-25926.41	-28295.47	-35695.44	-31096.03
75080.46	76205.84	84100.75	81764.74	83494.02	97229.28	102372.99	107864.94
87630.64	85895.73	96127.23	97762.16	109420.44	125524.75	138068.43	138960.98
-12747.42	-10647.20	-12753.92	-17854.38	-28505.66	-31521.65	-39364.38	-36423.25
-4.38	-3.35	-3.84	-5.22	-8.05	-8.64	-10.25	-8.79
-4.86	-3.75	-4.28	-5.82	-8.94	-9.59	-11.34	-9.66
66823.49	67847.55	75321.79	72262.15	73938.02	86645.90	90373.83	94505.05
79570.91	78494.76	88075.72	90116.53	102443.69	118167.56	129738.21	130928.31
-18926.07	-17661.97	-17330.40	-23309.22	-35548.81	-40214.78	-50972.49	-49313.23
-6.50	-5.56	-5.22	-6.82	-10.04	-11.02	-13.28	-11.90
-7.22	-6.22	-5.82	-7.60	-11.15	-12.24	-14.69	-13.08
46384.28	44512.40	49823.70	43197.10	42734.42	51814.26	51976.74	53475.24
65310.36	62174.37	67154.11	66506.32	78283.23	92029.05	102949.24	102788.47
6178.65	7014.77	4576.48	5454.83	7043.14	8693.13	11608.11	12889.97
20439.20	23335.15	25498.09	29065.04	31203.60	34831.64	38397.08	41029.80
14260.54	16320.38	20921.61	23610.21	24160.46	26138.51	26788.96	28139.83
197.23	957.31	727.44	1856.96	2579.25	3226.17	3668.93	5327.21
8256.97	8358.28	8778.96	9502.59	9555.99	10583.37	11999.16	13359.88
8059.73	7400.96	8051.51	7645.62	6976.74	7357.19	8330.22	8032.66
19499.66	21073.39	22782.41	23263.09	24727.54	26152.50	26818.39	27709.78
20056.96	21679.74	23445.74	24085.96	25411.14	26897.16	27606.74	28496.57
557.30	606.34	663.33	822.86	683.60	744.65	788.34	786.78
94.81	133.79	107.88	84.27	62.08	69.24	64.86	84.90
110.81	151.37	120.54	99.45	76.83	102.82	102.77	104.56
16.00	17.57	12.66	15.17	14.74	33.58	37.91	19.65
-6748.01	2230.22	9631.16	2300.54	175.00	-2798.48	-9332.47	-7260.28
3845.76	6336.63	15004.24	6138.57	5658.39	6716.54	7522.33	9279.96

continued on next page

Annex 3: *continued*

Item	2005	2006	2007	2008	2009	2010	2011
Net Incurrence of Liabilities	4549.62	3730.95	8729.71	-5968.07	3516.50	12436.16	5911.68
C.1 Direct Investment	-869.88	-1639.10	2453.94	630.00	-167.49	1641.77	342.49
Net Acquisition of Financial Assets	794.11	1068.31	5372.66	1970.03	1897.12	2712.16	2349.64
Net Incurrence of Liabilities	1664.00	2707.41	2918.72	1340.02	2064.62	1070.38	2007.15
C.2 Portfolio Investment	-1297.81	-3019.13	-1575.41	1587.16	-2054.05	-4890.30	-3663.23
Net Acquisition of Financial Assets	1643.80	559.23	141.14	-1604.87	234.16	1468.22	-563.15
Net Incurrence of Liabilities	2941.62	3578.36	1716.55	-3192.03	2288.22	6358.52	3100.08
C.3 Financial Derivatives	43.00	138.00	288.00	113.74	-30.15	193.63	-1004.67
Net Acquisition of Financial Assets	-98.00	-159.00	-170.00	-539.83	-400.87	-427.77	-1541.70
Net Incurrence of Liabilities	-141.00	-297.00	-458.00	-653.58	-370.71	-621.40	-537.02
C.4 Other Investment	3958.20	6203.95	-1336.46	-961.15	1355.84	-8435.87	-993.15
Net Acquisition of Financial Assets	4043.20	3946.12	3215.96	-4423.63	890.22	-2807.22	348.31
Net Incurrence of Liabilities	85.00	-2257.82	4552.43	-3462.47	-465.61	5628.65	1341.46
Net Unclassified Items	2173.83	-1613.25	277.23	1204.34	-3013.33	-3515.42	278.80
Overall BOP Position	2410.00	3769.00	8555.56	88.66	6420.57	15243.00	11400.00
(Percent of GNI)	2.04	2.70	5.03	0.04	3.26	6.57	4.39
(Percent of GDP)	2.24	2.95	5.48	0.04	3.64	7.31	4.86
Debit: Change in Reserve Assets	1621.00	2934.00	8548.75	1596.40	4910.09	15242.00	11399.00
Credit: Change in Reserve Liabilities	-789.00	-835.00	-6.81	1507.73	-1510.48	-1.00	-1.00
Memo Items:							
F Change in Net Foreign Assets (NFA) of Deposit-Taking Corporations, Except the Central Bank	3387.99	4101.61	441.18	-958.26	3714.38	-5362.88	-5675.93
F.1 Change in Commercial Banks' (KBs) NFA	3313.04	4335.33	310.80	-1100.90	3774.4338	-5306.90	-5696.98
F.2 Change in Thrift Banks' (TBs) NFA	28.23	91.24	93.37	-261.18	-76.48	-22.17	7.00

2012	2013	2014	2015	2016	2017	2018	2019
10593.78	4106.40	5373.07	3838.03	5483.39	9515.03	16854.81	16540.24
957.80	-90.42	1014.34	-99.65	-5882.81	-6951.71	-5832.90	-4376.10
4173.22	3646.94	6753.92	5539.50	2396.73	3304.73	4115.69	3309.22
3215.41	3737.37	5739.57	5639.15	8279.54	10256.44	9948.59	7685.33
-3205.03	-1001.14	2708.28	5470.92	1480.20	2454.35	1447.84	-3486.01
964.04	-637.77	2704.86	3342.71	1216.39	1658.01	4740.19	3979.49
4169.07	363.37	-3.41	-2128.20	-263.81	-796.34	3292.35	7465.50
-13.67	-87.96	3.98	5.61	-32.19	-50.66	-53.41	-172.89
-277.18	-312.42	-292.88	-530.92	-700.78	-503.47	-679.19	-873.75
-263.50	-224.45	-296.87	-536.53	-668.59	-452.80	-625.78	-700.85
-4487.12	3409.76	5904.54	-3076.33	4609.80	1749.53	-4894.00	774.73
-1014.31	3639.88	5838.34	-2212.72	2746.06	2257.27	-654.36	2864.99
3472.80	230.12	-66.19	863.61	-1863.74	507.74	4239.64	2090.25
-4556.31	-4202.15	-4090.64	-2432.92	273.88	-1587.61	-2826.08	3884.39
9236.00	5084.92	-2857.99	2616.48	-1037.90	-862.84	-2305.79	7843.33
3.17	1.60	-0.86	0.76	-0.29	-0.23	-0.60	1.89
3.52	1.79	-0.96	0.85	-0.32	-0.26	-0.66	2.08
9235.00	5085.00	-2857.99	2616.47	-1037.59	-861.81	-2305.13	7842.74
-1.00	0.07	-0.00	-0.00	0.30	1.02	0.65	-0.58
-3670.89	2039.94	5997.82	-1064.77	1381.22	432.65	-476.13	1588.86
-3833.29	2185.68	6069.20	-1164.56	1421.01	399.98	-462.69	1620.50
72.72	-66.98	-75.31	168.18	-166.08	58.22	-25.50	27.47

continued on next page

Annex 3: *continued*

Item	2005	2006	2007	2008	2009	2010	2011
F.3 Change in Offshore Banking Units' (OBUs) NFA	46.71	-324.96	37.00	403.83	16.43	-33.79	14.04
G Personal Remittances	13094.80	14988.30	15852.63	18063.64	19077.71	20562.88	21922.20
G. 1 Of which: OF Cash Remittances Channeled Through the Banking System	10689.00	12761.30	14449.92	16426.85	17348.05	18762.98	20116.99

Details may not add up to total due to rounding.

... = not available, BOP = balance of payments, GDP = gross domestic product, GNI = gross national income, OF = overseas Filipino, USD = United States dollar.

Technical Notes:

[1] Balance of payments statistics from 2005 onwards are based on the International Monetary Fund's Balance of Payments and International Investment Position Manual, 6th Edition.
[2] Financial account, including reserve assets, is calculated as the sum of net acquisitions of financial assets less net incurrence of liabilities.
[3] Balances in the current and capital accounts are derived by deducting debit entries from credit entries.
[4] Balances in the financial account are derived by deducting net incurrence of liabilities from net acquisition of financial assets.

2012	2013	2014	2015	2016	2017	2018	2019
89.68	-78.75	3.93	-68.39	126.29	-25.55	12.05	-59.12
23352.20	25368.84	27272.71	28308.48	29706.00	31288.36	32213.46	33467.24
21391.33	22984.03	24628.05	25606.83	26899.84	28059.78	28943.11	2483.61

[5] Negative values of net acquisition of financial assets indicate withdrawal/disposal of financial assets; negative values of net incurrence of liabilities indicate repayment of liabilities.

[6] Overall BOP position is calculated as the change in the country's net international reserves (NIR), less non-economic transactions (revaluation and gold monetization/demonetization). Alternatively, it can be derived by adding the current and capital account balances less financial account plus net unclassified items.

[7] Net unclassified items is an offsetting account to the overstatement or understatement in either receipts or payments of the recorded BOP components vis-à-vis the overall BOP position.

[8] Data on deposit-taking corporations, except the central bank, consist of transactions of commercial and thrift banks and offshore banking units (OBUs).

Source: Bangko Sentral ng Pilipinas.

Chapter 19

Hong Kong:
Weathering the AFC and the GFC
Facing a Storm, Building Credibility, and Staying Resilient

Hans Genberg[1]

Introduction and Summary

This chapter is about the experiences of Hong Kong during the financial crises in Asia in 1997–1998 and in the United States (US)/Europe in 2008–2009. In both cases, global trade declined sharply, which impacted all economies that were highly dependent on exports revenues for economic growth and prosperity, Hong Kong being no exception.

Each crisis started first and foremost with a disruption in financial markets that reverberated throughout the global financial system and affected economies that were closely integrated with that system. Hong Kong is a prime example given its large financial sector and complete openness to international capital flows. Yet, as the chapter seeks to show and explain, Hong Kong was much more affected by the Asian financial crisis (AFC) than the great (global) financial crisis (GFC).[2]

In the lead-up to the AFC, the Hong Kong economy could be seen as sharing some of the vulnerabilities characterizing the economies in the region that were severely scarred by the crisis. The economy appeared to be overheating as indicated by an investment boom, high inflation, a trade balance deficit, and sharp appreciations of asset prices, principally of residential property and equities, all of which were accompanied by rapidly increasing bank lending to the private sector.

---

[1] Comments on earlier drafts from Lillian Cheung, John Greenwood, Dong He, Cho-Hoi Hui, as well as members of the Steering Committee are gratefully acknowledged.

[2] Throughout the chapter, the GFC is referred to as the great financial crisis (to preserve the acronym) rather than the more common global financial crisis. The reason is that while the AFC started and was mostly the result of financial disruptions in Asian economies, the origin of the GFC was primarily in the US and Europe. Their effects were transmitted to Asia through their effects on trade in goods and dislocations in the global US dollar funding market.

The economy also operated with a fixed exchange rate that, in the case of Thailand for example, turned out to be the proximate trigger of the crisis in the region. In the eyes of financial market participants, an economy with a fixed exchange rate was seen as a candidate for a currency crisis.

But the similarities were more apparent than real. The next section of the chapter argues that the reason why Hong Kong ended up having to face a severe exchange rate crisis was not due to inherent vulnerabilities but rather due to contagious speculative attacks on the Hong Kong dollar (HKD).

The section also describes how the Hong Kong authorities reacted in very unorthodox ways to preserve the fixed exchange rate system by intervening directly in spot and forward markets for both foreign exchange and equities on the Hong Kong Stock Exchange. These actions drew sharp criticism at the time from commentators who felt that the authorities had done damage to the market-friendly reputation of Hong Kong. But in the end, the fixed exchange rate system prevailed against speculation on its demise.

The episode did, however, reveal certain shortcomings in the institutional and operational framework of the system. With the peak of the crisis behind them, the authorities set out to enact reforms with the objective to render it more robust. The description of the measures and their effects on the operations of concludes that rendering the system more rules-based made it stronger and more credible in the eyes of financial markets.

The chapter next turns to the GFC. For Hong Kong and indeed much of Asia, the origins of the macroeconomic effects during this crisis were principally violent contraction in international trade. The principal financial aspects of the crisis were, at least initially, confined to the US and Europe. When they did propagate to the rest of the world, the system the authorities in Hong Kong had reformed after the AFC turned out to be resilient, validating the importance of rules-based institutional design.

The chapter concludes with some general lessons from the experience of Hong Kong during the two crises.

Hong Kong During the AFC: An Innocent Bystander?

Hong Kong experienced a sharp economic contraction during the AFC. Following a speculative attack on the HKD in October 1997, residential property prices fell sharply and equity prices declined precipitously, leading to loss of wealth, declining consumption and investment, an outright contraction in gross domestic product (GDP) in 1998, and protracted high unemployment and consumer price index (CPI) price deflation.

Were these developments the inescapable consequences of vulnerabilities built up in the years before the crisis, or did they result from contagion from the crises in other countries?

This is the question this section tries to answer while giving an overview of the economic and financial developments in the years before, during, and immediately after the crisis.

Macroeconomic Developments

Macroeconomic developments in Hong Kong during the periods before, during, and immediately after the AFC can be described in terms of four phases (Table 19.1, more detailed data in Appendix 19.1): the early part of the 1990s characterized by steady growth and no particular signs of trouble ahead, a transition period from 1994 to 1997 with slowing economic growth and a deteriorating external balance and rising asset prices, the crisis year in 1998, and the subsequent recovery.

During the first 3 years of the decade, Hong Kong experienced steady economic growth at close to 6% on average, fueled by strong export performance. The external balance, measured in Table 19.1 by net exports of goods and services, posted a surplus of close to 4% of GDP. The unemployment rate was low at less than 2% on average during these years.

The nominal interest rate at the 3-month horizon declined during the period from slightly over 8.0% to slightly below 3.5%, following the similar decline in the 3-month US dollar London Interbank Offered Rate (LIBOR) as dictated by the Linked Exchange Rate System (LERS).[3]

The only cloud on the horizon was the relatively high rate of inflation, which, at close to 10% on average, implied an appreciating real exchange rate and negative real interest rates.

During the transition phase from 1994 to 1997, economic growth continued at a respectable rate of close to 5% per year. Contrary to the previous period where growth had been underpinned by export growth, the 1994–1997 period was one in which export growth had declined. Instead, the

---

[3] The LERS is described in the next section.

principal sources of growth were domestic final consumption expenditures and gross fixed capital investment. Both of these were accommodated by a sizable increase in bank credit.[4]

As growth in consumption and investment expenditures increased, while total output growth remained at previous levels, the result was an increase in domestic absorption relative to income, and therefore, by definition, a deterioration in net exports. The increase in domestic spending relative to income was accompanied by a further real appreciation of the HKD.

Table 19.1: Macroeconomic Indicators at the Time of the AFC

Item	1991–1993	1994–1997	1998	1999
GDP (% yoy growth)	5.8	4.7	−5.3	3.0
Exports of Goods and Services (% yoy growth)	16.9	8.3	−4.3	3.7
Net Exports, Goods and Services (% of GDP)	3.7	−3.8	−1.0	6.9
Imports of Goods and Services (% yoy growth)	17.0	9.4	−6.3	−0.2
Final Consumption Expenditures (Ratio to GDP, %)	66.0	60.0	70.0	70.0
Gross Capital Formation (Ratio to GDP, %)	27.0	33.0	29.0	25.0
Banking Institutions, Claims on Private Sector (Ratio to GDP, %)	134.0	155.0	167.0	153.0
CPI Inflation (% yoy)	9.9	7.5	2.9	−4.0
Unemployment (%)	1.9	2.5	4.4	6.2

AFC = Asian financial crisis, CPI = consumer price index, GDP = gross domestic product, yoy = year-over-year.
Source: International Monetary Fund, International Financial Statistics.

The third phase in this macroeconomic overview featured the sharp decline in economic growth in 1998 as export growth turned negative during the acute face of the AFC. The negative economic growth was accompanied by an equally sharp increase in unemployment as well as a decrease in inflation from over 7% pre-crisis to just under 3% in 1998.

---

[4] Gerlach and Peng (2003) study the causal relationship between bank lending and housing prices in Hong Kong during the period between 1984 and 2001 and argue that the causality runs primarily from housing price movements to bank lending growth.

Economic growth returned in 1999, but it would take until mid-2000 before the pre-crisis level of real GDP was reached.[5] Notwithstanding the resumption of growth, economic slack remained as shown by the increasing rate of unemployment and declining inflation into negative territory. Export growth resumed but imports were stagnant in part as a consequence of declining investment spending that returned to pre-crisis levels as a percent of GDP.

Does the macroeconomic narrative of the lead-up to the crisis provide answers to why the HKD was eventually drawn into the AFC? There are indeed some similarities in the experiences of the economies most affected by the crisis. The slowdown in economic growth on the back of declining export performance; rapid increases in domestic demand, especially investment expenditures accompanied by rapid growth in bank credit; real currency appreciation; and a deteriorating net export position feature prominently in all cases. In combination with fixed or heavily managed nominal exchange rates, these conditions have similarities with the so-called first-generation models of speculative attacks on a fixed exchange rate (Krugman 1979).[6]

Notwithstanding these similarities, it is unlikely that the macroeconomic developments in Hong Kong by themselves would have led to the kinds of pressures on the currency that would materialize in 1998. Part of the reason is that the imbalances in Hong Kong were not as large as in other economies. But the more important reason, in the view of this author, is that the managed exchange rate regime in Hong Kong was based on a much more robust institutional structure than those in other affected economies.

To explain why requires an explanation of the Hong Kong LERS.

Exchange Rate, Interest Rate, and Asset Price Developments
The Linked Exchange Rate System

Since 1983, Hong Kong's monetary regime has been defined by the LERS. This is a currency board arrangement whereby both the level and the change

---

[5] Compared to what it would have been based on the pre-crisis trend growth, the actual level of real GDP has never caught up. According to Cerra and Saxena (2008), this permanent loss of output following a financial crisis is a general phenomenon observed in a variety of contexts. See also Cerra et al. (2020).

[6] While Krugman's formal model emphasized persistent government budget deficits as the principal source of external payment deficits, loss of international reserves, and the eventual currency crisis, excess private sector demand fueled by bank credit could have similar consequences for external payments and pressures on the currency.

in the HKD Monetary Base are backed by official international reserves.[7] This feature makes the LERS more robust in the face of possible speculation against the system. The monetary base is defined as the sum of bank notes issued by note-issuing commercial banks, notes and coins issued by the Hong Kong government, the aggregate value of the clearing accounts held by commercial banks with the Hong Kong Monetary Authority (HKMA), and Exchange Fund Bills and Notes which are HKD fixed income securities issued by the HKMA.

As note-issuing commercial banks can issue notes by purchasing certificates of indebtedness from the HKMA at the rate of 7.8 HKD/USD, this rate is intended to serve as the anchor of the system. Together with the absence of restriction on international capital movements, the exchange rate anchor implies that interest rates in Hong Kong will follow the corresponding US dollar interest rates closely as long as the system is viewed as credible. The credibility of the currency board system is a result of the full backing of the monetary base by international reserves. Larger-scale sales, by the private sector, of HKDs against the US dollar in anticipation of a depreciation of the HKD would not cause a depletion of official international reserves as it could in a typical fixed exchange rate regime, where the stock of international reserves only covers a fraction of the monetary base that could be converted to foreign exchange. In situations where there was a sale of HKD for US dollar, the monetary base would automatically contract, leading to a tightening of monetary conditions in Hong Kong, raising domestic interest rates. In normal times (i.e., times when the 7.8 parity would be considered credible), the increase in local interest rates would attract capital inflows, replenishing official international reserves.

(Relative) Calm Before the Storm: The Linked Exchange Rate System in the Pre-AFC Period

As noted, full international capital mobility combined with a fixed HKD/USD exchange rate should lead to a convergence of HKD interest rates with corresponding USD rates, provided the fixed exchange rate is credible. Data for the interest rate differentials in Figure 19.1 show that this was indeed the normal state of affairs during the pre-AFC period under review. The

---

[7] For a history of the system, see, for example, HKMA (2005) and Greenwood (2008).

3-month interest differential exceeded 200 basis points only twice during the first 7 years of the 1990s: first, in May–June 1991 in connection with the closure of the Hong Kong branch of the Bank of Credit and Commerce International (BCCI), and second, in January 1995 following the devaluation of the Mexican peso in December the year before. In each case, the significant interest rate spread was largely eliminated within a month. During the period, the exchange rate was also stable — trading within a narrow band of 7.72–7.76 from 1992 onwards.

If the exchange rate movements and interest rate differentials did not foreshadow any troubles, the same cannot be said for other asset prices. Residential and equity prices experienced substantial fluctuations related to the evolution of real interest rates and capital inflows. Between 1991 and mid-1994, residential property prices more than doubled, implying an annual growth rate of close to 30%, before falling by a cumulative 13% in the following year and a half (Figure 19.2A). This evolution mirrors that of real HKD interest rates described in the previous section.

Residential property prices began rising again in 1996 and accelerated into the first half of 1997 supported by ample bank finance, capital inflows, and a general optimism about economic growth in Hong Kong following the handover of the colony to China on July 1, 1997.

The evolution of the Hang Seng equity price index shown in Figure 19.2B mirrors closely that of property prices. Together, these asset price movements illustrate the general proposition that international financial conditions are transmitted forcefully to economies that are highly integrated into the international financial system. This would be demonstrated even more strongly as the financial crisis took hold in Thailand and other regional economies in 1997 and 1998.

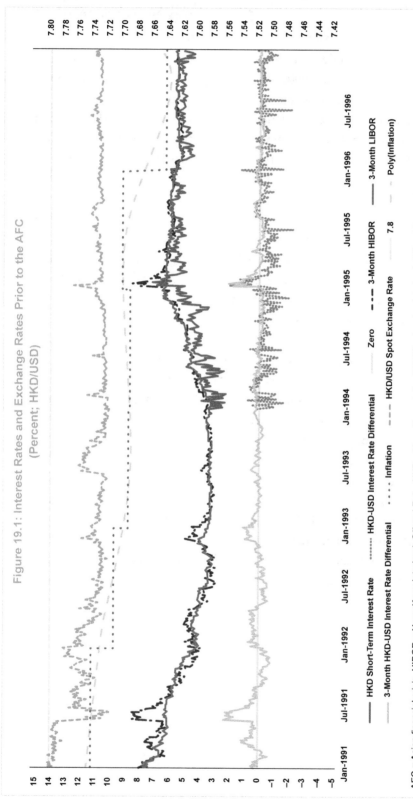

Figure 19.1: Interest Rates and Exchange Rates Prior to the AFC
(Percent; HKD/USD)

AFC = Asian financial crisis, HIBOR = Hong Kong Interbank Offered Rate, HKD = Hong Kong dollar, LIBOR = London Interbank Offered Rate, USD = United States dollar.

Notes: Interest rates, the interest rate differential, and inflation are measured on the left axis, and the exchange rate is measured on the right axis. Poly(inflation) represents a fourth-order polynomial fitted line through the inflation data.

Source: Author's calculations based on data from the Hong Kong Monetary Authority website, CEIC, and Bloomberg.

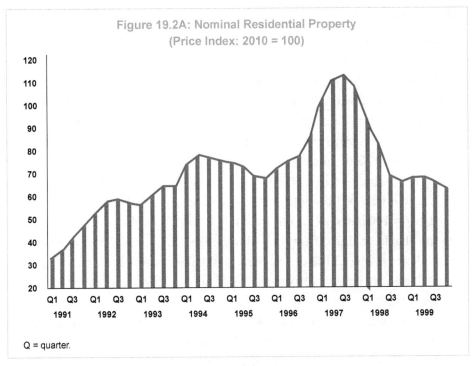

Figure 19.2A: Nominal Residential Property
(Price Index: 2010 = 100)

Q = quarter.

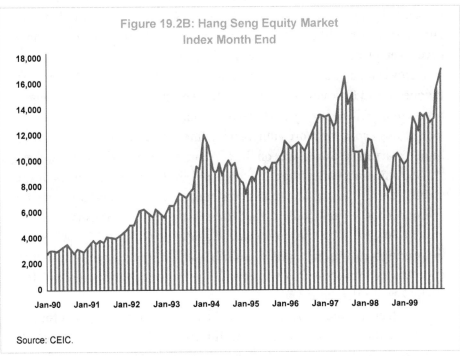

Figure 19.2B: Hang Seng Equity Market
Index Month End

Source: CEIC.

Facing the Storm

Massive speculation against the Thai baht took place on May 13–14, 1997. This was preceded by deteriorating economic growth, increasing difficulty of Thai companies to honor their debt obligations, and, as a direct consequence, increasingly precarious balance sheet positions of Thai financial institutions. The fixed exchange rate of the baht was finally abandoned on July 2, a date that has become synonymous with the onset of the AFC.

In Hong Kong, meanwhile, there were few outward signs of trouble: the HKD exchange rate was stable, and, more importantly, the interest rate differential vis-à-vis US dollar rates was inconsequential, generally staying well below 100 basis points until late July, 3 full weeks after the devaluation of the Thai baht. The differential, which, to recall, is an indicator of market confidence in the LERS, did not reach 200 basis points until mid-August but fell back to the 100–150 range throughout September and early October (Figure 19.3).

In the author's view, this lack of pressure on the HKD constitutes the argument that developments internal to the Hong Kong economy would not alone have triggered a speculative attack on the LERS. True, the sharp increases in domestic asset prices (Figure 19.2A and 19.2B) did appear unsustainable, but like in 1994, price corrections in these markets could have taken place without endangering the LERS.

However, as the financial crisis spread to Malaysia, the Philippines, Indonesia, and Korea in July and August, the macroeconomic consequences began to be felt in the form of declining export demand, rendering the Hong Kong economy more vulnerable to interest rate increases that would be necessary in case pressures on the currency were to manifest themselves.

Speculators understood the logic and underlying mechanics of the spread of the financial and macroeconomic stress throughout the region and, indeed, the world, and further stress in the foreign exchange markets ensued. For the HKD, the stress came to a head on October 23, 1997, when the overnight interest rate spiked upwards to about 300% as banks scrambled to obtain HKD to cover short positions. The Hang Seng Index immediately fell by 29% on the same day.

Reflecting uncertainties about the longer-term prospects for the currency, the 3-month Hong Kong Interbank Offered Rate (HIBOR) increased from 6% in the first half of the year to the 8%–12% range during

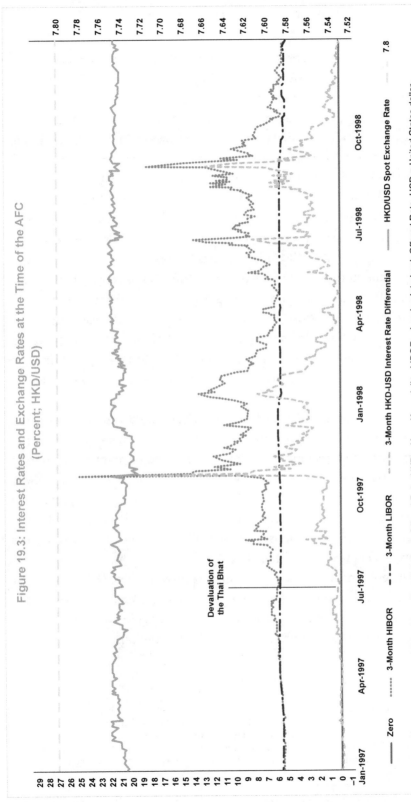

Figure 19.3: Interest Rates and Exchange Rates at the Time of the AFC
(Percent; HKD/USD)

AFC = Asian financial crisis, HIBOR = Hong Kong Interbank Offered Rate, HKD = Hong Kong dollar, LIBOR = London Interbank Offered Rate, USD = United States dollar.
Notes: Interest rates and the interest rate differential are measured on the left axis, and the exchange rate is measured on the right axis.
Source: Author's calculations based on data from the Hong Kong Monetary Authority website, CEIC, and Bloomberg.

the remainder of 1997 and first 2 months of 1998. As actual and expected inflation had declined by this time, the implied real interest rates increased sharply, causing considerable harm to the economy. Residential housing prices fell by close to 40% from the third quarter of 1997 to the third quarter of 1998, foreshadowing a decline in consumption and investment spending with a knock-on effect on employment and overall economic growth.

After a 2-month lull in the spring of 1998, speculation against the HKD picked up in June, leading the 3-month HIBOR-LIBOR spread to widen again. Further damage to the economy bolstered beliefs in some quarters that the pain would be too great for the Hong Kong government to tolerate and that the LERS might have to be abandoned. Thus, a financial strategy took hold whereby speculators would simultaneously take short positions both in HKDs and in Hong Kong equities. Speculators would stand to gain on the short position in HKDs if the LERS was abandoned and the currency was left to depreciate. On the other hand, they would gain on their short equity position if the authorities were to defend the exchange rate by raising interest rates further, thereby leading to a decline in equity prices.

To the authorities, this "double-play," as it became called, was considered an attack on the very foundation of Hong Kong's monetary and financial system. Authorities responded by carrying out a "double counter play" during a 10-day period starting in late August.[8] This was executed by the HKMA by intervening in both the spot and futures market for equities, preventing further declines in share prices while simultaneously making sure that the automatic adjustment process built into LERS continued to function so as to prevent a depreciation of the HKD.

The government ended up owning approximately HKD 120 billion worth of shares in various companies at the end of August. Subsequently, the government started selling those shares by launching the Tracker Fund of Hong Kong, making a profit of about HKD 30 billion.

---

[8] Later Joseph Yam, the Chief Executive of the HKMA at the time, would write that the intervention was executed to deter "currency manipulation by those who have built up large short positions in the Hang Seng Index futures.... . There is no doubt that there has been manipulation in our currency to engineer extreme conditions in the interbank market and high interest rates in order that profits could be made in the large short positions that have been built up in stock index futures" (as quoted in Greenwood 2008, p. 279).

The end result of the actions of the HKMA was a retreat of the speculators and an end to the speculative attacks on the HKD. By year-end, the interest differential with the US had been essentially eliminated. The massive interventions in the equity and foreign exchange market had "saved Hong Kong."[9]

Assessment: "An Innocent Bystander"?

It is time to return to the question posed at the beginning of this section, namely whether the economic and financial developments in Hong Kong during the AFC were the inescapable consequences of vulnerabilities built-up in the years before the crisis, or whether they were the results from contagion of the crises in other countries?

The tentative answer this author reaches is that absent a region-wide financial crisis, the build-up of imbalances in Hong Kong during the first part of the 1990s was not of a scale and nature to lead to a full-blown currency crisis. It is true that bank credit and asset price developments seemed to be based on excessively optimistic scenarios, but the speed and extent of the reversals would almost certainly have been smaller in the absence of speculative contagion from the crises that enveloped neighboring economies.

The LERS would also not likely have come under the kind of severe strains as it did solely on the basis of imbalances in the Hong Kong economy. This assessment is based in part on the timing of the first signs of pressures on the system. These materialized well over 2 months after the devaluation of the Thai baht in the beginning of July 1997, an event that was followed in short order by similar pressures in Indonesia, Malaysia, and the Philippines.

But saying that the pressure on the LERS was principally due to contagion from crises elsewhere does not mean that this system could not be changed to become more resilient. It could and it did, as will be discussed in the next section.

---

[9] *Intervention to Save Hong Kong: The Authorities' Counter-Speculation in Financial Markets* is the title of a book published in 2003, which presents a detailed account of the events that led up to this unprecedented intervention and of the exact mechanics of the HKMA's actions. It also contains detailed analysis of the effects of the intervention on the behavior of asset prices, and an overall assessment in terms of its impact on speculators, its profitability, and its influence on the reputation of Hong Kong as a financial center. See Goodhart and Dai (2003).

Building Credibility of the LERS

Reforming the System

The performance of the LERS during the AFC led to reforms that began as early as in the fall of 1998. The reforms culminated in 2005 with a consequential modification of the system.

A number of features of the system came under scrutiny. One of these was the behavior of overnight interest rates in the interbank market. When the HKD came under selling pressure, liquidity would tighten in the interbank market. Because the total supply of liquidity in the market was relatively inelastic, interest rates would increase sharply, as for example in the October 1997 episode discussed in the previous section. With the objective of dampening interest rate volatility, a discount window mechanism was, therefore, included as one of a set of reforms to the LERS introduced in September 1998. The reforms also contained measures that made it possible for banks to borrow from the HKMA against collateral and to manage their liquidity needs more flexibly, thereby introducing a shock absorber mechanism in the relationship between domestic interest rates and capital flows.[10] The reforms effectively introduced some rules-based elements into the system's adjustment mechanism, which until then had been subject to a certain degree of discretion by the HKMA.[11]

Another significant aspect of the 1998 reforms was the exchange rate mechanism itself. Recall that the anchor of the system was the fixed exchange rate between the certificates of indebtedness against which note-issuing banks could issue HKD notes. The fixed exchange rate of 7.8 HKD/USD had been in effect since the inception of the LERS, but as can be seen in Figures 19.1 and 19.3, the market rate had been on the strong side of this conversion rate for almost the whole of the period before and during the crisis.

According to Greenwood, a close observer of monetary affairs in Hong Kong for more than four decades, "[i]f the authorities had been entirely confident about the robustness of the system, they could have allowed the exchange rate to trade much closer to the official conversion rate, and even fall below it, but between 1990 and 1998 this was not permitted to occur.... This was the canary in the coalmine that told the market that there was an

---

[10]HKMA (1998).

[11]Latter (2007) and Greenwood (2008).

inherent vulnerability in the system. The maintenance of the market rate at this elevated level seemed to indicate that the authorities needed a protective buffer between the market rate and the official rate — just in case something serious happened, which it inevitably did."[12]

The reforms introduced in 1998 also contained an element that addressed this issue. It introduced a firm weak-side commitment (convertibility undertaking, CU) to prevent the exchange rate from depreciating beyond 7.75 HKD/USD, a rate that would be moved by small daily amounts starting in April 1999 until it reached 7.8 in August 2000 (Figure 19.4). This was another measure that removed a discretionary element from the system. More was to come in response to currency developments during the first part of the 2000s.

As illustrated in Figure 19.4, after the introduction of the weak-side CU, the spot exchange rate in the market followed that rate closely, and the HIBOR-LIBOR differential was inconsequential until the autumn of 2003 and again in late 2004 and early 2005. At that time, as a consequence of expectations in the market that the Chinese yuan would appreciate and the possibility that an appreciation of the HKD would follow, a forward premium on the HKD materialized and HKD interest rates fell below corresponding US dollar rates.[13] Absent a firm commitment by the HKMA to intervene to stabilize the currency, the HKD appreciated sharply in late 2003. The strength of the HKD resumed in late 2004. At that time, the appreciation did not reach beyond the rate 7.75 HKD/USD, however. This was perhaps in anticipation of the introduction (in May the following year) of a commitment to prevent the HKD from appreciating beyond that rate.

The last major reform of the LERS was thus introduced on May 18, 2005 when a symmetric convertibility zone (a target zone in the jargon of the academic literature) was introduced with 7.80 as the midpoint, and 7.75 and 7.85 as the edges. The HKMA undertook to keep the market exchange rate within these limits of the target zone with unlimited interventions if necessary but allowed for the possibility of intra-zone interventions.

The move to an almost completely rules-based exchange rate system was thus competed.

The next section discusses whether this achieved the objective of building credibility.

---

[12]Greenwood (2008), pp. 273–274.
[13]HKMA (2013).

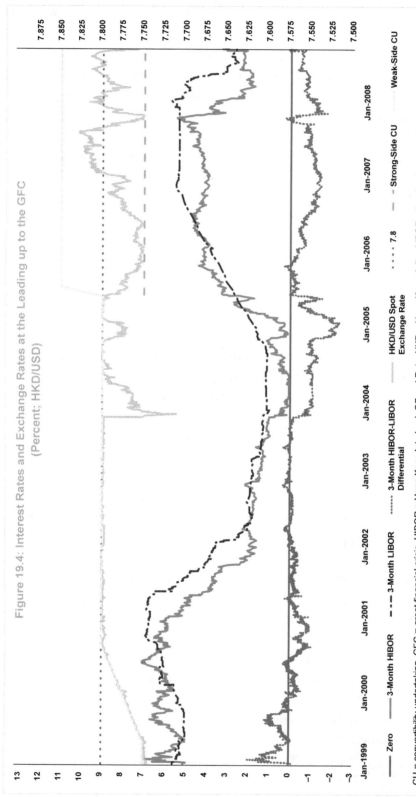

Figure 19.4: Interest Rates and Exchange Rates at the Leading up to the GFC
(Percent; HKD/USD)

CU = convertibility undertaking, GFC = great financial crisis, HIBOR = Hong Kong Interbank Offered Rate, HKD = Hong Kong dollar, LIBOR = London Interbank Offered Rate, USD = United States dollar.
Notes: Interest rates and the interest rate differential are measured on the left axis, and the exchange rate is measured on the right axis.
Source: Author's calculations based on data from the Hong Kong Monetary Authority website, CEIC, and Bloomberg.

Did the Reforms Have the Intended Effects?

Did the reforms increase the credibility of the exchange rate system? In the absence of a counterfactual, this question is difficult to answer conclusively.

Superficially, it might be argued that the absence of a serious speculative attack on the LERS since the introduction of the reforms is an indication of its robustness. This ignores, however, the possibility that lack of speculative attacks could be the consequence of a benign external environment. What about the fact that the exchange rate did not seem to converge to the mid-point of the target zone after its introduction, but rather fluctuated significantly within the band, and even approached the strong side on several occasions? Does that not constitute evidence against the idea that the system has become more credible? Based on academic modeling of the exchange rate target zone system, this interpretation is incorrect. Such models suggest, on the contrary, that in a target zone system, the exchange rate will spend most of the time close to the boundaries of the zone.

What is needed to answer the question in the title of this section, therefore, is to base an assessment on information about market expectations related to the performance of the system. This is what was attempted in the study by Genberg and Hui (2011), using information imbedded in spot, futures, and derivative instruments related to the exchange rate and to HKD and US dollar interest rates. The authors set out to answer four questions: (i) Did forward-looking market expectations of exchange rate movements become more centered around the weak-side CU during the 1996–2005 period?[14] (ii) Did forward-looking market expectations of exchange rate movements become bounded by the edges of the target zone after they were introduced in 2005? (iii) Did interest rate volatility decrease after the September 1998 measures that, inter alia, increased the elasticity of supply in the interbank credit market? (iv) What was the nature of the relationship between the volatility of interest rates and the volatility of the exchange rate after the introduction of a more rule-based system?

To answer the first two questions, Genberg and Hui utilized information imbedded in currency options contracts to estimate (i) the implied probability distribution of market expectations of the future HKD/USD exchange rate and (ii) the maximum appreciation/depreciation of a currency

---

[14] Note that this is different from asking whether the actual spot rate itself moved more in step with the weak-side CU, which is obviously the case by inspection of Figure 19.4.

expected in the financial market based upon a first-passage-time approach.[15] By carrying out the estimation for time periods before and after reforms of the LERS were introduced, the general conclusion the authors reached was affirmative to both questions.[16]

To answer the third and fourth questions about interest rate and exchange rate volatility, the authors estimated univariate and bivariate Exponential GARCH (EGARCH) models for the HKD/USD interest rate differential or the change in the HKD/USD exchange rate. The estimation results showed that interest rate volatility did indeed decrease after September 1998, suggesting that the improved liquidity provision measures had their intended effects. As to the fourth question, there was no indication that more confidence in the stability of the exchange rate regime came at the expense of increased volatility of interest rates. This is contrary to what is sometimes asserted as a drawback of a fixed exchange rate system.

All in all, the empirical evidence presented in Genberg and Hui (2011) led the authors to the conclusion that the "credibility of the LERS as revealed by asset prices seems to have increased over time" (p. 186). The next section will show that the increased credibility served Hong Kong well during the GFC of 2008–2009.

Resilience During the GFC

For the Hong Kong economy, the period of the GFC was much less turbulent than that of the AFC. Not only was the macroeconomic impact less severe, but the impact on the exchange rate and other assets was, with some exceptions, more muted. There are several possible reasons for this. First, the GFC was a financial crisis principally in the US and Europe. For Hong Kong as well as Asia more generally, the crisis was mostly due to a massive decline in global trade leading to a precipitous decline in demand for exports from the region with knock-on effect on the overall macroeconomy and financial markets. While it is true that the decline in exports was in part due to the reverberations of the crisis on the trade credit market, the effects on

---

[15]On the first-time-passage approach, see Hui and Lo (2009).

[16]When the seven technical measures were introduced on September 14, 1998, exchange rate expectations became more centered on the CU, and when the three refinements (including the target zone for the exchange rate) were introduced on May 19, 2005, most of the probability distribution of the expected exchange rate was confined within the target zone. Furthermore, the maximum and minimum expected changes of the HKD were well within the target zone after it was introduced.

the banking systems in Asia were generally less consequential. Second, for Hong Kong, the reforms of the exchange rate system had rendered it more robust and credible, and therefore more resilient to shocks as argued in the previous section. Third, since the GFC was not primarily a financial shock in Asia,[17] the contagion that spread the AFC throughout the region did not take place during the GFC.

Economic Developments During the GFC

The GFC was transmitted to the Hong Kong economy principally through the reduction in international trade, and hence, Hong Kong's exports. From a pre-crisis steady growth rate of over 10% per annum, exports shrank at an average annual rate of close to 3% during 2008 and 2009, a sharper decline than during the AFC (Table 19.2). As a result, GDP growth decreased from slightly over 7% pre-crisis to just below zero during the two principal crisis years.

Table 19.2: Macroeconomic Indicators at the Time of the GFC

Item	2004–2007	2008–2009	2010–2012
GDP (% yoy growth)	7.40	−0.17	4.43
Exports of Goods and Services (% yoy growth)	11.65	−2.88	8.52
Net Exports, Goods and Services (% of GDP)	8.88	8.32	4.62
Imports of Goods and Services (% yoy growth)	10.69	−2.32	9.43
Final Consumption Expenditures (Ratio to GDP, %)	68.00	68.00	70.00
Gross Capital Formation (Ratio to GDP, %)	23.00	22.00	23.00
Banking Institutions, Claims on Private Sector (Ratio to GDP, %)	140.00	148.00	195.00
CPI Inflation (% yoy)	1.15	1.45	4.67
Unemployment (%)	5.38	4.32	3.73

CPI = consumer price index, GDP = gross domestic product, GFC = great financial crisis, yoy = year-over-year.
Source: International Monetary Fund, International Financial Statistics.

---

[17]Based on an analysis of deviations from covered interest parity, Hui et al. (2011) concluded that "... funding liquidity risk was lower in... Hong Kong, Japan, and Singapore [than] in the US, [reflecting] that these markets became alternative dollar funding sources as borrowing in the European economies became more difficult."

While there had been a bank-financed investment boom in Hong Kong before the AFC, leading to a turn-around in net exports from a surplus to a deficit, this was not the case in the GFC period. As a result, net exports stayed positive throughout. The evolution of residential property prices and equity price was similar to what transpired during the AFC (Figure 19.5A and 19.5B).

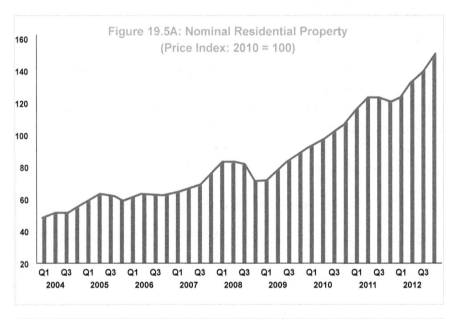

Figure 19.5A: Nominal Residential Property (Price Index: 2010 = 100)

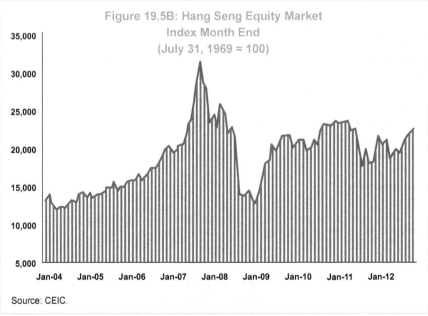

Figure 19.5B: Hang Seng Equity Market Index Month End (July 31, 1969 = 100)

Source: CEIC.

Both dropped as the GFC progressed, residential prices by less than during the AFC but equity prices more. Both recovered as the macroeconomic effects of the GFC faded, and as it became clear that the financial market consequences were contained.

The economy rebounded rapidly starting in 2010 supported by rapid expansion of bank lending.

Exchange Rate and Interest Rate Developments[18]

US dollar interest rates went through a roller coaster ride prior to and during the GFC. The Federal Funds target rate of the Federal Reserve increased in 17 rapid steps from 1.00% in early 2004 to 5.25% in July 2005, before starting an even sharper decline from September 2007 to reach 0.25% by end 2008. As expected given the currency board arrangement, Hong Kong interest rates closely followed the same path. (See Figure 19.6, which shows 1-month HIBOR (green) and US dollar LIBOR (blue) rates.) Reflecting the credibility of the LERS, the interest rate differential was mostly consistent with expectations that the exchange rate would be bounded by the target zone band.

Figure 19.6 also shows that the exchange rate never breached the target zone bands. Most of the time it stayed on the strong side of the band, reflecting the emerging status of the HKD as a safe haven currency (HKMA 2013). On numerous occurrences, the automatic adjustment mechanism of the LERS would be triggered as heavy capital inflows pushed the exchange rate to the 7.75 strong side intervention point. While the size of the required interventions was, on occasion, very large, there was never any serious risk that the target zone band would be broken. The reformed LERS proved resilient during the GFC.

Resilience in Spite of Volatile Real Estate Prices: The Role of Macroprudential Policies

Real estate prices in Hong Kong have historically been very volatile, subject, as we have seen, to wide fluctuations associated with large inflows and outflows of capital and growth of bank credit. These fluctuations are, by

[18]Based on the theoretical exchange rate target zone model developed in Lo et al. (2015), HKMA (2018) provides a comprehensive description of the operation of the LERS after the introduction of the symmetric convertibility zone in 2005. The article concludes that the operation of the LERS is consistent with "... recently developed target zone model, which can adequately describe the exchange rate dynamics and its associated interest rate differential in a credible target zone. ... Overall, our findings suggest that making the policy environment less discretionary does have benefits in terms of increased credibility and hence greater robustness" (HKMA 2018, pp. 9–10).

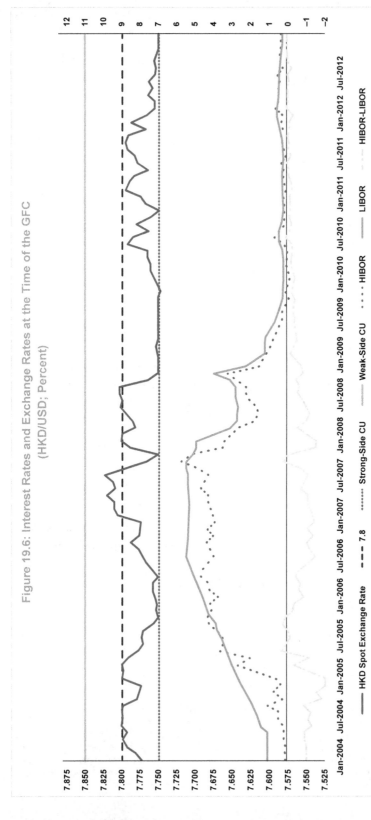

Figure 19.6: Interest Rates and Exchange Rates at the Time of the GFC
(HKD/USD; Percent)

CU = convertibility undertaking, GFC = great financial crisis, HIBOR = Hong Kong Interbank Offered Rate, HKD = Hong Kong dollar, LIBOR = London Interbank Offered Rate, USD = United States dollar.
Note: Interest rates are measured on the left axis, and the exchange rate is measured on the right axis.
Source: Author's calculations with Hong Kong Monetary Authority and Federal Reserve Bank of St. Louis data.

an order of magnitude, larger in Hong Kong than in other economies for which we have data.

As an illustration, Figure 19.7 depicts a measure of the swings in residential real estate prices for economies for which the Bank for International Settlements (BIS) publishes monthly date going back to 1993 (1994 for Israel and 1995 for the United Kingdom). Whereas the deviations from trend lie mostly within a ± 5% band for seven of the economies in the sample, those for Hong Kong are much wider.

The frequency of significant price declines is also much higher in Hong Kong. The number of months in the sample for which the year-over-year decline is larger than 10% is 56 for Hong Kong, whereas it is just 13 for Japan, the economy with the second largest number of such declines.

As commercial banks provide the bulk of finance for the purchase of real estate, they are vulnerable to potential increases in nonperforming mortgage loans when real estate prices fall precipitously. In view of the volatility of residential real estate prices in Hong Kong, it is therefore instructive to identify the reason why its banking sector has been as resilient as it has.

While there is no single reason for the resiliency, the use of macro-prudential policies in Hong Kong is without doubt an important one. It has been well documented that the implementation of such policies took place earlier in Asia than in other parts of the world (Zhang and Zoli 2014), in part as a result of lessons learned from the AFC.

Recognizing the importance of mortgage lending for the Hong Kong banking sector and the risks associated with volatile prices of real estate, the Hong Kong authorities had already introduced loan-to-value (LTV) regulations in the early 1990s. Originally, the maximum LTV was set at 90%, but soon a more stringent maximum 70% level was adopted as industry standard at the urging of the Hong Kong government. Since the AFC and later the GFC, changes in LTV standards and differentiating them according to the type and value of the underlying property have been actively used by the Hong Kong authorities.[19]

Empirical studies at the HKMA on the effects of the LTV policies on mortgage loan delinquencies at Hong Kong banks have confirmed the beneficial effects of these policies on the resiliency of the banking system to property price shocks. Interestingly, the studies also suggest that the LTV

---

[19]See He (2014) for a chronology of the changes and for an analysis of their effects. See also Hui (2013).

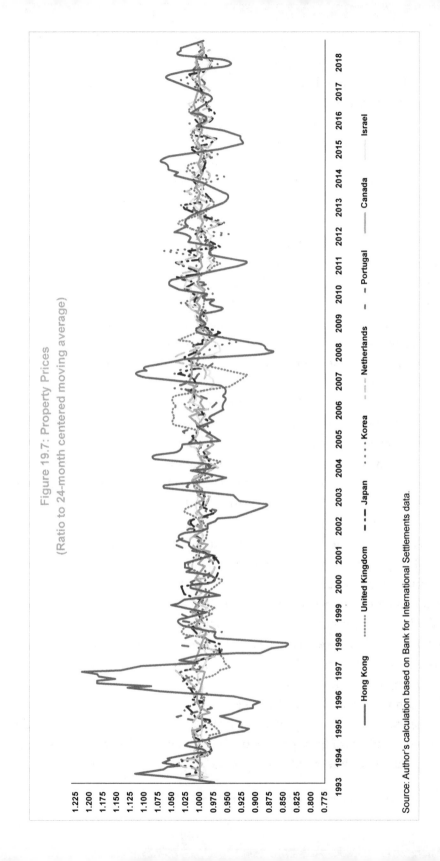

Figure 19.7: Property Prices
(Ratio to 24-month centered moving average)

Hong Kong   United Kingdom   Japan   Korea   Netherlands   Portugal   Canada   Israel

Source: Author's calculation based on Bank for International Settlements data.

policies have not had a material impact on price developments themselves, implying that the beneficial effects on financial stability have come through reducing borrowers' leverage.[20]

Lessons

As much as exchange rate pressures during the AFC were traumatic, those that materialized during the GFC seemed more like a nonevent by comparison. This paper has argued that the fundamental reason for this difference was contagion from the regional turmoil and not unsustainable domestic economic conditions leading up to the earlier crisis. Even though there were signs of overheating in the economy during the years before the AFC, the imbalances could have been unwound in an orderly fashion in the absence of the regional turmoil.[21]

The crisis spread to Hong Kong because its LERS was conflated with the heavily managed exchange rate policies pursued in the economies most strongly affected by the crisis, and by a contagious process the HKD came under speculative attack.[22]

The first lesson from this experience is that contagion should be assumed to be a regular feature in financial markets, and it can happen even if fundamentals of the economy are sound.[23]

Why then was the LERS more resilient during the GFC? The argument in this paper is that the experiences during the AFC led Hong Kong authorities to introduce changes in the operations of the LERS to make it less discretionary and more predictable. The changes effectively removed ambiguities that led speculators to test the resolve of Hong Kong authorities during the AFC, with the result that they saw no reason to doubt the currency peg during the GFC.

The second lesson, therefore, is that resilience of a policy regime does not only mean strong economic fundamentals. These must be accompanied

---

[20]See He (2014), HKMA (2017), and references therein.

[21]This assessment is based on the strong fiscal position of the Hong Kong government, the ample foreign exchange reserves held by the Exchange Fund, and the notorious flexibility of prices and wages in the territory.

[22]That the epicenter of the AFC was in Southeast Asia was likely also a contributing factor.

[23]This points to the importance of international cooperation in the exchange of information and analysis about emerging threats to financial stability and about policies that are being considered by individual countries and in international regulatory agencies to counter such threats. Such cooperation is pursued in numerous regional and international fora in which Hong Kong authorities are active participants. Appendix 2 provides a brief summary.

by transparent and credible policy rules. In the case of Hong Kong, that meant making the operations of the LERS less discretionary and more predictable. More generally, however, policy regimes must have clearly stated objectives and be designed so that the operation of the regime is transparent and consistent with the stated objectives. In the case of Central Banks, this is true whether the regime is about targeting inflation, designing macroprudential policies, introducing capital flow management policies, or intervening in the foreign exchange market.

Finally, in spite of a high concentration of mortgage loans on the balance sheets of Hong Kong banks and notoriously volatile property prices, the Hong Kong banking system turned out to be resilient during both the AFC and the GFC. One reason can be traced to the early implementation of macroprudential policies in the form of LTV restrictions. These reduced the leverage of borrowers and thereby reduced the frequency of nonperforming loans. This points to a third lesson from Hong Kong's experience during the two crisis periods and their aftermath: the importance of preemptively introducing safeguards in the financial system will dampen the impact of shocks that are transmitted to the economy through the global financial system.

References

Cerra, Valerie, Antonio Fatás, and Sweta Saxena. 2020. "Hysteresis and Business Cycles." IMF Working Paper No. 20/73.

Cerra, Valerie, and Sweta Chaman Saxena. 2008. "Growth Dynamics: The Myth of Economic Recovery." *American Economic Review* 98 (1): 439–457.

Genberg, Hans, and Cho-Hoi Hui. 2011. "The Credibility of Hong Kong's Link from the Perspective of Modern Financial Theory." *Journal of Money Credit and Banking* 43: 185–206.

Gerlach, Stefan, and Wensheng Peng. 2003. "Bank Lending and Property Prices in Hong Kong." HKIMR Working Paper No. 12/2003.

Goodhart, Charles, and Lu Dai. 2003. *Intervention to Save Hong Kong — The Authorities' Counter-Speculation in Financial Markets*. Oxford: Oxford University Press.

Greenwood, John. 2008. *Hong Kong's Link to the US Dollar: Origins and Evolution*. Hong Kong University Press.

He, Dong. 2014. "The Effects of Macroprudential Policies on Housing Market Risks: Evidence from Hong Kong." In *Macroprudential Policies: Implementation and Interaction, Financial Stability Review*. Banque de France, pp. 105–119.

Hong Kong Monetary Authority, 2008 Annual Report.

Hong Kong Monetary Authority. 2005. *HKMA Monetary Brief No. 1*, Second Edition, November.

Hong Kong Monetary Authority. 2008. "Strengthening of Currency Board Arrangements in Hong Kong." *Press Release*, September 5.

Hong Kong Monetary Authority. 2013. "Monetary Operations under the Currency Board System: The Experience of Hong Kong." In *Bank for International Settlements, Market Volatility and Foreign Exchange Intervention in EMEs: What Has changed?* BIS Papers No 73.

Hong Kong Monetary Authority. 2017. "Hong Kong's Property Market and Macroprudential Measures". In *Macroprudential Frameworks, Implementation and Relationship with Other Policies*. BIS Papers No. 94, pp. 141–152.

Hong Kong Monetary Authority. 2018. "Linked Exchange Rate System Operations — Mechanisms and Theory." *HKMA Quarterly Bulletin* 97.

Hui, Cho-Hoi. 2013. "Macroprudential policies and their effectiveness: Hong Kong SAR." In *Macroprudential Frameworks in Asia*, edited by Rodolfo Maino and Steven A. Barnett. Washington: International Monetary Fund.

Hui, Cho-Hoi, and Chi-Fai Lo. 2009. "A Note on Estimating Realignment Probabilities — A First-Passage-Time Approach." *Journal of International Money and Finance* 28 (5): 804–812.

Hui, Cho-Hoi, Hans Genberg, and Tsz-Kin Chung. 2011. "Funding Liquidity Risk and the Deviation from Interest-Rate Parity during the Financial Crisis of 2007–2009." *International Journal of Finance and Economics* 16: 307–23.

Krugman, Paul. 1979. "A Model of Balance-of-Payments Crises." *Journal of Money, Credit and Banking* 11 (3): 311–325.

Krugman, Paul. 1991. "Target Zones and Exchange Rate Dynamics." *Quarterly Journal of Economics* 106: 669–682.

Latter, Tony. 2007. "Rules Versus Discretion in Managing the Hong Kong Dollar, 1983–2006." HKIMR Working Paper No. 2/2007, January.

Lo, Chi-Fai, Cho-Hoi Hui, Tom Fong, and S. W. Chu. 2015. "A Quasi-bounded Target Zone Model — Theory and Application to Hong Kong Dollar." *International Review of Economics and Finance* 37: 1–17.

Zhang, Longmei, and Edda Zoli. 2014. "Leaning Against the Wind: Macroprudential Policy in Asia." IMF Working Paper, WP/14/22.

Appendix 1

Table A1: Key Indicators for Hong Kong, 1991–2000

Indicator	1991	1992	1993	1994	1995	1996	1997	1998	1999	2000
GDP Growth (% yoy)	5.1	6.3	6.1	5.4	3.9	4.5	5.0	-5.3	3.0	10.4
Exports of Goods and Services (% yoy)	17.3	19.8	13.5	10.4	12.0	4.8	6.1	-4.3	3.7	17.1
Net Exports, Goods and Services (Percent of GDP)	3.9	2.9	4.0	-1.7	-4.8	-2.7	-5.9	-0.9	6.9	7.2
Imports of Good and Services (% yoy)	19.4	19.4	12.0	13.5	12.7	4.4	6.9	-6.3	-0.2	16.7
Final Consumption Expenditures (Ratio to GDP, %)	66	67	66	67	70	70	69	70	70	68
Gross Capital Formation (Ratio to GDP, %)	27	28	27	31	34	32	34	29	25	28
Banking Institutions, Claims to Private Sector (Ratio to GDP, %)	137	130	135	144	149	157	169	167	153	150
CPI Inflation (yoy)	11.2	9.7	8.8	8.7	9.1	6.3	5.8	2.9	-4.0	-3.7
Unemployment (%)	1.7	1.9	1.9	1.9	3.0	2.8	2.2	4.3	6.2	5.1

CPI = consumer price index, GDP = gross domestic product, yoy = year-over-year.
Source: Author's calculations based on International Monetary Fund, International Financial Statistics.

Table A2: Key Indicators for Hong Kong, 2005–2012

Indicator	2005	2006	2007	2008	2009	2010	2011	2012
GDP Growth (% yoy)	7.4	7.0	6.5	2.1	-2.5	6.8	4.8	1.7
Exports of Goods and Services (% yoy)	12.2	10.2	8.2	3.5	-9.3	17.6	4.8	3.2
Net Exports, Goods and Services (Percent of GDP)	10.0	10.7	9.4	9.8	6.8	6.2	4.7	2.9
Imports of Good and Services (% yoy)	9.3	9.9	9.1	3.3	-7.9	18.4	5.7	4.3
Final Consumption Expenditures (Ratio to GDP, %)	68	66	67	67	69	69	70	72
Gross Capital Formation (Ratio to GDP, %)	23	23	22	22	22	22	23	24
Banking Institutions, Claims to Private Sector (Ratio to GDP, %)	143	137	137	140	155	186	202	199
CPI Inflation (yoy)	0.8	2.0	2.0	4.3	0.6	2.3	5.3	4.1
Unemployment (%)	5.7	4.8	4.1	3.4	5.2	4.4	3.4	3.3

CPI = consumer price index, GDP = gross domestic product, yoy = year-over-year.
Source: Author's calculations based on International Monetary Fund, International Financial Statistics.

Appendix 2

Hong Kong in Regional and Global Financial Fora

The HKMA actively participates as a full member of a number of regional and international initiatives and institutions focused on cross-border financial cooperation. Examples of regional fora are ASEAN+3 Macroeconomic Research Office (AMRO), Asia-Pacific Economic Cooperation (APEC), the Chiang Mai Initiative Multilateralisation, and Executives' Meeting of East Asia-Pacific Central Banks (EMEAP).

Global fora in which the HKMA represents Hong Kong authorities include the BIS in Basel and the various BIS-hosted institutions such as the Basel Committee on Banking Supervision and the Financial Stability Board.

The Hong Kong authorities also participated in the activities of the IMF as part of the Chinese delegation.

In international standard setting institutions, Hong Kong is represented by the HKMA in the Basel-based Committee on Payments and Market Infrastructure (CPMI), the Islamic Finance Services Board (IFSB), and the Securities Exchange Commission in the International Organization of Securities Commissions (IOSCO).

Finally, the HKMA is active in capacity building institutions for central banks and financial regulators through the South East Asian Central Banks (SEACEN) Centre in Kuala Lumpur and the Financial Stability Institute in Basel.

Chapter 20

Singapore
Braving the Asian Financial Crisis, Emerging Stronger

Lam San Ling[12]

Preamble

One lesson from the Asian financial crisis (AFC) of 1997, and the global financial crisis (GFC) a decade later, is that one does not, and cannot, predict the timing of a financial crisis with any level of useful accuracy. Did the two crises take central bankers and financial regulators by surprise? Not really. The warning signs were there. The Thai baht had been under pressure as early as mid-1996. Current account deficits and rising external debt in the region were indications that hitherto stable exchange rates would be increasingly vulnerable to volatile capital flows. Likewise, the GFC came on the heels of the United States (US) subprime mortgage crisis in 2007; Lehman Brothers was not the first entity to succumb. Yet, few economists, let alone financial regulators, predicted the currency and economic turmoil that shook the region after mid-1997. Right up to July, and even a few months into the crisis, many hoped for — or at least could not preclude — a more orderly re-alignment of exchange rates (and exchange-rate regimes) and a less disruptive resolution of the macroeconomic imbalances that were by then apparent. It was much easier to explain and rationalize, *with the benefit of hindsight,* the economic and financial conditions that laid the foundation for a crisis and the chain of events that eventually precipitated the AFC. This

[1] The views and commentary expressed in this paper belong solely to the author and do not reflect the positions of ASEAN+3 Macroeconomic Research Office or the Monetary Authority of Singapore (MAS). The author is grateful to members of the AMRO History Project Steering Committee for substantive and editorial comments. Any and all remaining errors belong to the author.

[2] The author was an economist in MAS' Economics Department (heading its external economies division) when Thailand devalued the baht on July 2, 1997, and a securities regulator (heading MAS' capital markets intermediaries supervision) when Lehman Brothers filed for bankruptcy on September 15, 2008. The author would like to record her thanks to individuals who shaped her experience during the AFC: Dr. Teh Kok Peng and Mr. Tharman Shanmugaratnam, Deputy Managing Director and Head of Economics Department, respectively, when the author joined MAS; and Freddie Orchard and Dr. Hoe Ee Khor, who led the department in the years leading up to the AFC.

acknowledgement of the limitations of economic forecasting is not intended to cast doubt on the importance of regular surveillance and assessments of countries and markets, the need to develop leading indicators of crises, or the relevance of the economics profession. Far from it, financial crises are painful and should be averted as far as possible. However, since crises are difficult or impossible to predict, efforts at crisis prevention must go-hand-in-hand with crisis mitigation and safety nets, a dose of humility, and a willingness to learn and not make the same mistakes. Countries in the region — their central banks and policymakers — took to heart lessons from the Asian crisis. These lessons shaped their development and regulatory philosophies, and would stand them in good stead through subsequent global shocks.

This chapter is organized as follows. "The East Asian Miracle" describes, from Singapore's vantage point, the region in the half dozen years before the crisis. "The East Asian Mirage?" chronicles the abrupt shift in narrative that was bewildering at the time and yet inevitable in hindsight. "Riding Out the Storm" recounts Singapore's experience in navigating the financial and economic contagion as crisis gripped the region. "Strengthening the Financial Sector" focuses on Singapore's financial and regulatory journey as it transitioned through the crisis to build a stronger and more vibrant financial center. "AFC Aftermath and Legacy" reflects on how the crisis has shaped Asia's approach to globalization and regionalization. "Lessons From the GFC" concludes with an update on Asia and Singapore in the post-GFC policy landscape.

The East Asian Miracle

Asia in the 1990s — and Singapore in particular — was a unique place to be in. Singapore, according to the International Monetary Fund (IMF) in 1991, was one of "seven rapidly growing economies."[3] The World Bank in 1993 published the *East Asian Miracle: Economic Growth and Public Policy*, a research on the relationship between government, the private sector, and the market in "eight high-performing Asian economies."[4] In the May 1997

---

[3] International Monetary Fund (1991). The seven rapidly growing economies in developing Asia were Indonesia, Malaysia, Thailand, and the four newly industrializing economies (Hong Kong, Korea, Singapore, and Taiwan Province of China).

[4] World Bank (1993). The eight high-performing Asian economies (HPAEs) refer to Japan, the four Asian tigers (Hong Kong, Korea, Singapore, and Taiwan Province of China) and the newly industrializing economies or NIEs (Indonesia, Malaysia, and Thailand).

World Economic Outlook, the IMF moved Hong Kong, Korea, Singapore, and Taiwan Province of China to the new "advanced economies" group.[5] It was a period of economic optimism in Asia.

The Singapore economy was expanding at high single-digit rates comparable to growth in the rest of the Association of Southeast Asian Nations (ASEAN) region.[6] While its ASEAN neighbors had current account deficits, Singapore enjoyed current account surpluses (since the mid-1980s) and had little or no net external debt. This was not deemed unusual, given their different stages of development. In the two decades after independence, Singapore also ran sizable current account deficits close to 10% of gross domestic product (GDP), reflecting higher domestic investment needs than could be financed by national savings alone. Singapore in the 1990s was an archetypal open economy, with exports and imports several times its GDP. Singapore had no exchange controls, although it continued to maintain a policy of noninternationalization of the Singapore dollar (SGD).[7]

Within East Asia, the strong belief in globalization was mingled with a sense of pride in the recognition from the global community that countries in the region had "arrived," so to speak, and were role models for the rest of the developing world. Their achievement was proof that an outward-looking trade policy had advantages over protectionism. The East Asian Miracle economies had achieved current account convertibility by the mid-1990s, and many were heading to open capital accounts if they had not done so earlier. With China's acceptance of the IMF's Article VIII obligations in late 1996, nearly 70% of developing country trade in 1997 was carried out under current account convertibility, compared to 30% in 1985.[8] By mid-1997, the IMF was in the process of garnering broader support for an amendment to the Articles of Agreement that would promote the liberalization of capital flows.

If there was a wrinkle in the international endorsement of the development model in East Asia, it would be that of the role of government.

---

[5] IMF (1997a). The IMF relabeled the previous "industrial countries" to "advanced economies" in recognition of the declining share of employment in manufacturing.

[6] Singapore's growth rate in the 3 years before the AFC (1994–1996) averaged 8.8% per annum (p.a.), compared to the 8%–9% p.a. in Indonesia, Malaysia, and Thailand.

[7] Singapore had removed all exchange controls by 1978. The SGD noninternationalization policy, related to the extension of SGD credit to nonresidents for activities outside Singapore, was not a restriction on the capital account; residents and nonresidents were free to remit funds into and out of Singapore.

[8] IMF (1997a).

The World Bank acknowledged in its 1993 publication that "activist public policies" were an element in some of the success stories in East Asia, especially Japan, Korea, Singapore, and Taiwan Province of China. This raised complex and potentially controversial questions concerning the relationship between government, the private sector, and the market. The World Bank was cautiously neutral, if slightly disapproving, on the role of government in promoting selected industries, citing the lack of convincing evidence that industrial policy would accelerate growth. However, the nature of public policy in East Asia was often to improve the functioning of markets, to favor export promotion over import substitution, and to be steadfastly open to foreign direct investment and technology. In other words, there was no contradiction between government intervention and free markets if public policy was nudging economies toward embracing globalization.

Looking back now, Asia had an overly narrow, perhaps naïve, view of what globalization entailed. An outward-looking development strategy was often synonymous with lower tariffs and few or no nontariff barriers, and pro-export policies. The "global" in globalization would thus focus on the *advanced* economies that provided the markets for exports and the capital and technology to drive export industries. Other developing economies, including those in the immediate region, mattered less, except as competitors. This view, that *regional* developments were much less relevant compared to what was happening in major economies, would be proven horrendously wrong before the decade was over.

Before the AFC, the risks of contagion, especially through financial markets, were not well understood. The word "contagion" was not widely associated with anything other than communicable diseases; financial interconnectedness across jurisdictions was a little-known subject then. It was also generally assumed that there would be symmetry in the upside (gains) and downside (risks) of globalization; for example, greater openness would be associated with incrementally higher growth and slightly higher inflation due to economic overheating. Few economists fully grasped the risks of *financial* globalization, let alone the potentially devastating consequences of tail risk events. Why would they? Economists in central banks were trained in micro- and macroeconomics, international trade, and development economics, and were a vocation apart from their finance-trained regulatory colleagues who resided in separate departments, or even separate institutions.

Policymakers in Asia were schooled in the advantages of free cross-border flows and market-friendly policies for trade, investment, and growth. They only learned the hard way that sudden surges and reversals in capital inflows could lead to financial chaos in recipient countries and unprecedented economic hardship. It would take another 10 years, and a GFC, for the rest of the world to learn similar lessons.

In the years leading up to the AFC, the Monetary Authority of Singapore (MAS) was paying close attention to the economic and financial developments in the region — not that it would be able to influence developments, but simply because the external outlook, both global and regional, had a huge impact on the Singapore economy. China was gaining economic strength and influence, and the ASEAN countries were booming.

The East Asian Mirage? The Narrative Changes

The fall of the baht, when it happened, was not a surprise — it was a matter of "when" rather than "if." Devaluations in emerging economies were not uncommon, and the baht was last devalued in 1984 to relatively little fanfare. What shocked many, on July 2, 1997, and in the following 6 months, was the financial and economic havoc it wreaked in Thailand, and the speed and magnitude of the contagion to turn the devaluation of a single currency into a full-blown regional financial crisis.

More than 20 years later, with hindsight and the wisdom gained from the GFC, it is not difficult to rationalize the AFC. We now know more about financial globalization, herd behavior, systemic risks, and black swan events. However, Asia in the 1990s was focused on maximizing the growth dividends from open markets and international trade, and there was no playbook on what to do when capital flows took on a life of their own.

The swiftness with which financial markets and world opinion turned against the East Asian story in 1997 was both devastating and sobering. Reflecting on the crisis, then-Senior Minister in Singapore, Mr. Lee Kuan Yew, would ask in his memoirs, "Was the Asian miracle in fact a mirage?"[9] As events unfolded, there would be a subtle but distinct change in the

---

[9] Lee Kuan Yew (2000). Mr. Lee also shared in his memoirs that at Thailand's request in March 1997, MAS intervened in the foreign exchange markets (with funds provided by Thailand) to support the baht. This worked for a while, but the baht came under attack again in May 1997.

narratives surrounding familiar macroeconomic fundamentals, including the exchange rates, private investments, and current account deficits. For example:

- *Stable exchange rates*, in the East Asian success stories, were evidence of good macroeconomic management and sound policies.[10] However, after the baht fell, the exchange rate regimes in crisis-hit economies were roundly criticized: the *stability* that was previously conducive to international trade and foreign investment became a vulnerability when its *inflexibility* triggered speculative attacks and massive capital outflows.

- *Private investments* were a good thing, according to the old narrative,[11] especially when the alternative was heavy reliance on state-owned enterprises or state-directed spending on pet projects. In the revised narrative, the private sectors in crisis-hit economies turned out to be greedy and imprudent in their borrowing and investment decisions, and corrupt governments were blamed for their lax oversight.

- *Current account deficits* were natural, especially in developing economies where foreign capital inflows were needed to supplement domestic savings to finance growth-inducing investments. (This was, after all, the case for Singapore up to the mid-1980s.) Unfortunately, current account deficits and foreign currency debt in Asia alarmed investors and contributed to the collapse in market confidence — and with good reason, since capital inflows and easy credit found their way to domestic real estate projects and other less-than-productive investments.

The above shifts in narratives pre- and post-AFC would put into context the blind spots in macroeconomic analysis at the time, and why central bankers and economists were caught off guard. In particular, it is accepted today that the exchange-rate regimes in Indonesia, Malaysia, and Thailand (described as fixed or relatively fixed; formally or informally pegged to the US dollar) contributed to the AFC. Why was this not obvious in the years before the

---

[10]For example, World Bank (1993) cited "the remarkable stability of real exchange rates since 1970 in Korea, Malaysia, and Thailand" and their "pragmatic macroeconomic management" in the chapter on macroeconomic stability and export growth.

[11]For example, the World Bank (1993) attributed higher economic growth in the HPAEs partly to its high rates of investment, particularly private investments, compared to other developing countries.

crisis? How did central bank officials in Asia rationalize their exchange rate policies back in the early 1990s? The following statements from a central bank seminar in 1992 provide a snapshot[12]:

> IMF: *"Whereas most [Southeast Asian] economies were pegged to a single currency in the mid-1970s, by the mid-1980s, all had adopted more flexible arrangements."*

> Indonesia: *"Since the 1986 devaluation, the government has provided more room for gradual exchange rate adjustment to reflect the development in the market."*

> Malaysia: *"The floating exchange rate regime for Malaysia did give greater flexibility in monetary management and made domestic stabilization policies more effective."*

> Thailand: *"From Thailand's experience over the past twenty years, it may be concluded that fixed exchange rates have not been sustained without a number of problems... The subsequent shifts towards more flexible exchange rate regimes have not only helped alleviate these problems but also allowed more timely and appropriate monetary adjustments."*

Significantly, the Bank of Thailand participants had added:

> *"An important precondition to [an even more flexible regime] is perhaps that the appropriate hedging instruments should first, if not simultaneously, be made available at market prices before such a system can be developed further."*

Central bank officials clearly understood the merits of market-driven exchange rates. Perhaps some countries did not go far enough, over the following years, to move in that direction. Alternatively, in the absence of adequate market hedging tools, central banks had taken it upon themselves to mitigate exchange risks by keeping the rates stable for the benefit of trade and investments. It could also be argued that had the baht, rupiah, and ringgit been allowed to float, they might not have moved in the "right" direction to avert a crisis.

Up till late in 1996, market sentiments and the policy debate were centered on whether governments might have kept exchange rates artificially

---

[12]See South East Asian Central Banks Research and Training Centre (SEACEN) (1992).

low to gain export competitiveness, rather than whether currencies in the region were overvalued.[13] East Asia was enjoying robust private capital inflows, including into their emerging bond markets.[14] Reserves accumulation was strong (current account deficits notwithstanding) and the decision confronting central bankers was how much, if at all, to allow exchange rates to appreciate in response to short-term flows. Academics and policymakers did not anticipate just how swift the reversal in flows would be, less than a year later.

While economists were analyzing and pondering current account balances and other slow-moving macroeconomic fundamentals, a group of currency traders were focusing on short-term (and volatile) capital flows and the valuation of the exchange rates. One of them was George Soros, reputedly the man who "broke the Bank of England" by shorting the British pound in 1992. By his own account, he turned his attention to Asia and started selling the baht short in January 1997.[15]

The abrupt change in narrative, from *miracle economies* to *emerging economies with vulnerable currencies*, triggered and propelled the AFC. However, while speculators and currency traders were among the first to act on the revised narrative, empirical studies since then have found no support for the hypothesis that Soros or hedge fund managers as a group were responsible for the crisis by uniformly taking positions on and profiting from the collapse of the currencies in the summer and fall of 1997.[16] Indeed, Soros' Quantum Fund reportedly lost money or did not profit from his rupiah and ringgit trades, and was unsuccessful in Hong Kong. Other currency traders, international investors, and market analysts took a second, and third, look at the economic and financial data in Southeast Asia, and started questioning the sustainability of capital flows and exchange rate in these economies.

---

[13]See, for example, Hicklin et al. (1997) and Montiel (1997). At the conference organized by the IMF and Bank Indonesia on "Macroeconomic issues facing ASEAN countries" in Jakarta on November 7–8, 1996, Peter Montiel addressed the question whether the stability in the real effective exchange rate (REER) in five ASEAN countries despite capital inflows *reflected active management of the nominal exchange rate in pursuit of a competitiveness objective* (emphasis added), or if it was an equilibrium phenomenon; the author saw no evidence of misalignment in the REER. One central bank participant (from Malaysia) highlighted the dilemma facing policymakers whether to allow the exchange rate to adjust partly or fully to short-term flows.

[14]See, for example, Dalla and Khatkhate (1996).

[15]Hargreaves (2016). Soros was the most prominent but not the only speculator to hold positions against the baht.

[16]See, for example, Brown et al. (1998).

Amid the currency turmoil, two economies steadfastly stuck to their exchange rate regimes. Singapore had adopted an exchange rate-based monetary policy since 1981, managing the SGD against a trade-weighted basket of currencies with price stability as the overriding objective. Hong Kong adopted the currency board system, linking the Hong Kong dollar to the US dollar in October 1983 to provide a firm monetary anchor and reduce foreign exchange risk.[17] Both Singapore and Hong Kong pulled through the crisis with the exchange rate regimes intact, and their currencies relatively unscathed — though not without a show of resolve by their respective governments.

Riding Out the Storm

As an open economy with extensive trade and financial linkages with the region, Singapore was not spared the fallout from the crisis. The stock market plunged 50%, while the SGD weakened 16.5% against the US dollar in the course of 1997.[18] However, the eventual adverse impact of the crisis on Singapore would be more economic than financial.

Favorable macroeconomic fundamentals shielded Singapore from the worst of the currency turmoil that engulfed the region in the months following the baht devaluation. Perhaps luck and timing played a part. Current account deficits earlier in Singapore's development were financed by longer-term foreign direct investment rather than short-term capital flows. Singapore in the years preceding the AFC was running current account and fiscal surpluses,[19] had low inflation and no public external debt, and possessed significant foreign exchange reserves.

Thailand's experience showed that reserves alone were no defense against determined capital outflows, speculative or otherwise. While hedge fund activities exposed the vulnerability of the Thai currency, it was the general market selloffs of emerging market currencies by investment funds and corporates that spread the financial contagion to Malaysia, Korea,

---

[17] The Hong Kong dollar was floated in November 1974 after being briefly pegged to the US dollar in July 1972 following the dismantling of the sterling area.

[18] The SGD fell to SGD 1.68 against the US dollar from SGD 1.40 earlier in 1997, and further to SGD 1.81 during the height of the crisis in January 1998.

[19] Over the period 1994–1996, current account and fiscal surpluses in Singapore averaged 16.0% of GDP and 6.5% of GDP, respectively.

and Indonesia. What these economies had in common — current account deficits and a rapid build-up of external debt — made them indistinguishable to nervous investors. Never mind that right up to the crisis, these countries had healthy savings rates and manageable inflation, and the governments were not running large fiscal deficits.

Thailand turned to the IMF in August 1997, agreeing to financial sector restructuring and monetary and fiscal tightening to narrow the savings-investment gap and restore market confidence. The economic and financial crisis was expected to be over quickly. The IMF-led financial package for Thailand received financial support from most countries in the region — including those that subsequently grappled with the fallout from the contagion.[20] While no stand-by credit facility could match the volume of private flows, it was thought that Thailand's adoption of the managed float, and commitments given under the IMF program, would restore confidence and stem further panicked capital outflows.

The IMF program for Thailand would be the first of several in connection with the AFC. Indonesia signed agreements in October 1997 and in January 1998. Korea accepted a program in December 1997. The IMF programs emphasized macroeconomic discipline and structural reforms, and reaffirmed (or accelerated) the countries' export-oriented development strategy and capital account liberalization. Singapore extended a USD 1 billion bilateral swap line to Thailand as part of the IMF package and pledged USD 5 billion to the package for Indonesia.

In January 1998, at the height of the crisis, then-Senior Minister Lee Kuan Yew was invited to speak in Bangkok, Thailand, on his views and outlook for the region.[21] Mr. Lee Kuan Yew was characteristically blunt in his assessment of why the crisis spread as quickly as it did. "The computer and information technology had speeded up the globalization of financial markets and allowed capital to move swiftly from one center to another for higher returns," he said. "Once [international investors] lost confidence in Thailand, they sold out their assets in all ASEAN countries, which are classified together as 'emerging markets.'" Indeed, Mr. Lee was describing the

---

[20] Pledges were received from Japan, China, Australia, Hong Kong, Malaysia, Singapore, Indonesia, and Korea, as well as from the World Bank and the Asian Development Bank.

[21] Lee Kuan Yew (1998). Mr. Lee was accompanied on the trip by a delegation that included his then-personal private secretary, Mr. Heng Swee Keat, and this author.

herding behavior of portfolio managers, who often disregarded economic fundamentals once markets have been spooked.[22]

Singapore During the Crisis

Singapore took a pragmatic and hard-nosed approach throughout the crisis as the financial turbulence played out. Singapore was also an emerging market in the eyes of the financial community. The authorities acted quickly to reassure markets and investors. Amid heightened volatility in foreign exchange markets, MAS allowed the SGD to fluctuate within a wider band. The SGD weakened against the US dollar, but the exchange rate on a trade-weighted basis appreciated slightly between the middle and the end of 1997. Interest rates in Singapore rose sharply in reaction to the regional contagion, hitting a peak in the early part of 1998 but trended downward as international financial markets stabilized.[23]

Hong Kong had much less wiggle room with the Hong Kong dollar peg than Singapore did with the trade-weighted managed float. In August 1998, the Hong Kong authorities called the hedge funds' bluff in a way Singapore did not have to. Their decision to support the stock and futures markets, in response to what they saw as market manipulation with little regard to Hong Kong's economic fundamentals,[24] might today be deemed acceptable unconventional monetary policy, but at the time drew criticisms for its departure from free market philosophy. The move paid off. The Hong Kong dollar peg held, and the shares acquired in the intervention were subsequently liquidated.

MAS' longstanding policy of not encouraging the internationalization of the SGD likely helped to avert similar attacks on the SGD — by making it harder for would-be speculators to short the SGD. Mr. Lee Hsien Loong,

---

[22] A key reason is the fact that most fund managers are evaluated based on "relative performance," that is, they are less likely to be penalized for an unprofitable investment decision if other fund managers make the same mistake. Harmes (2001) studied the short-term and herd behavior of institutional investors during the 1992 European Exchange-Rate Mechanism (ERM) crisis, the 1994 Mexico crisis, and the 1997 AFC.

[23] The 3-month interbank rate reached 9% at the end of January 1998 but had moderated to 5% by March. The rate climbed to more than 6.00% in May when rioting broke out in Indonesia, before trending down to 1.72% by the end of 1998.

[24] The speculators had engaged in "double play" whereby they shorted stocks and Hang Seng Index futures and, at the same time, short-sold Hong Kong dollar to push up interest rates, with a view to creating panic in the market such that they could make huge profits either from their short positions in stock/index futures or the Hong Kong dollar in the event the peg broke.

then-Singapore Deputy Prime Minister and MAS Chairman, explained in 2001, "We could not afford to assume that speculation in international markets was invariably self-stabilising."[25] Singapore was not unfamiliar with currency speculators. More than a decade earlier, in September 1985, during Singapore's first recession since independence, MAS dealt decisively with foreign banks who had bet on a devaluation of the SGD to boost export competitiveness.[26]

To shore up confidence in the financial system, MAS dialed up disclosure and transparency requirements in the banking sector. From 1998, banks were instructed to disclose information on their reserves (including previously "hidden" reserves[27]), the market value of their investments, and their provisions for regional loans. This was to enable investors to judge for themselves the value of the banks' assets. Since the local banks had large capital buffers and were fully provisioned should loans turn bad, the enhanced disclosure standards and increased transparency provided the assurance to markets that the Singapore banking system was sound.[28]

Singapore averted what might have been a more serious crash in the property market by pricking the property bubble in 1996, a year before the AFC. Like other countries in the region, Singapore had experienced a real estate boom in the early-1990s. Property prices soared by an average 30% per annum over 1993–1995 and was becoming dangerously overheated by the early 1996. The authorities introduced property cooling measures in May 1996 to curb excessive bank credit and discourage speculation in the property market. They included housing loan-to-value (LTV) limits (capped at 80%) for lending by financial institutions, and a new seller's stamp duty (SSD) tiered at 1%–3% on residential properties sold within 3 years of purchase. The government also tightened the rules for public housing (including on financing and the resale levy) to curb demand.

---

[25] Lee Hsien Loong (2001).

[26] In the September 1985 episode, MAS engineered an appreciation of the Singapore dollar and forced speculators to pay punitive rates in the interbank markets to make good their short sales.

[27] MAS-convened Committee on Banking Disclosure (1998). Singapore banks had built up undisclosed or hidden reserves by recording investments at cost or written-down values, and taking realized profits to "other liabilities" or "assets" instead of to the profit and loss account.

[28] At the end of 1997, the aggregate loan exposure of the local banking groups to Malaysia, Indonesia, Thailand, Korea, and the Philippines accounted for 16% of their total assets. The banks had capital ratios above the mandated 12% and were fully provisioned for the classified loans, which represented 2.3% of their global assets.

Singapore's property cooling measures in 1996 would today be called *macroprudential policy*, defined by the IMF as the use of primarily prudential tools to limit systemic risk. The property price inflation in Singapore moderated to 5% in 1996. Perhaps Singapore was ahead of the curve. Had similar measures been implemented in other parts of the region, they might have prevented excessive credit and over-investment in property projects and altered the course of the AFC. Property prices in Singapore fell 12% in 1997 while GDP growth registered a still-robust 8% during the year.

Singapore investors were hit by an unexpected shock in 1998 even as the country weathered the financial storm and navigated the property cycle. Malaysia, like others in the region, was the target of currency and stock market sell-off after the baht devaluation. Unlike Thailand, Korea, and Indonesia, Malaysia eschewed an IMF program to chart its own path out of the crisis — by pegging the ringgit to the US dollar in September 1998 and imposing capital controls, a move that was heavily criticized by the international community at the time, including the IMF. In the context of the trilemma of international finance, Malaysia made a policy decision during the AFC to restrict cross-border flows in favor of monetary policy autonomy (allowing domestic interest rates to come down) and control over the exchange rate. However, Malaysia's closure of the offshore market in ringgit and ringgit assets brought the trading of Malaysian shares in Singapore to a sudden halt. The suspension of accounts on the Central Limit Order Book (CLOB)[29] would affect more than 170,000 investors in Singapore with positions on CLOB, valued then at an estimated USD 4.5 billion. The matter was resolved bilaterally over the next 2 years as Malaysia gradually relaxed its capital control measures.[30]

Singapore slid into a recession in the second half of 1998. The impact of the crisis was wide-ranging. Singapore had strong regional links, and the economic collapse in neighboring countries translated into declines in trade, bank lending, and other financial services. The crisis took a toll on the stock market and the property market. Domestic demand contracted

---

[29] CLOB was an over-the-counter market established by the Stock Exchange of Singapore (SES) on January 2, 1990, following the split between the Kuala Lumpur Stock Exchange (KLSE) and the SES, to facilitate continued investments by Singapore investors into Malaysian shares.

[30] An agreement was reached between the two countries in the early 2000 for a staggered release of CLOB securities into individual investors' securities accounts (DPM Lee Hsien Loong's reply on CLOB to the Committee of Supply, March 8, 2000).

as private investment activities fell, unemployment rose, and household incomes and wealth took a hit. Economic growth for the year registered a small negative (Table 20.1).

Table 20.1: Singapore, 1996–2000

Macroeconomic Variable	1996	1997	1998	1999	2000
GDP Growth (Percent)	7.8	8.3	−1.4	7.2	10.0
Inflation (Percent)	1.4	2.0	−0.3	0.0	1.3
Current Account (Percent of GDP)	15.0	15.5	22.2	17.4	11.6

GDP = gross domestic product.
Source: IMF (2006), *World Economic Outlook* database, September.

Singapore relaxed the property cooling measures in 1998 and implemented a host of measures to provide relief to businesses and households. MAS maintained the 80% LTV limit on residential property loans from financial institutions, but the government suspended the seller SSD, relaxed some rules on the sale of public housing, and deferred land sales to arrest property price declines. To reduce business costs, the government offered corporate and property tax rebates, and implemented a 10% cut in employers' contribution to the mandatory Central Provident Fund (CPF) for employees. Households were granted rebates on personal income tax and on other government fees.

Singapore and other countries in the region staged a convincing recovery in 1999 after a deep but relatively short-lived contraction in 1998. The Singapore economy expanded by 7% in 1999. After the AFC, Singapore would enter a new phase of financial sector reform and development.

Strengthening the Financial Sector

The AFC put the spotlight on capital account liberalization and the risks posed by short-term (and footloose) cross-border flows. Strong macroeconomic fundamentals were absolutely essential, but open economies would also need to ensure that their financial systems (and banks, in particular) were adequately regulated and supervised and sufficiently sound to withstand shocks from financial globalization.

The IMF had remained a staunch proponent of open capital accounts as the AFC unfolded. It was initially thought that the regional currency turmoil following the baht devaluation would blow over quickly. Then-IMF First Deputy Managing Director Stanley Fischer, in a September 1997 speech in Hong Kong, made the case for amending the IMF Articles of Agreement to promote capital account liberalization, the benefits of which, he argued, would outweigh the risks.[31] This proposal was quietly dropped as the crisis progressed.

The narrative, and key factors blamed for the crisis, turned from macroeconomic fundamentals and the exchange rate policy to weaknesses in the financial sector. In its interim assessment of the crisis in December 1997, the IMF pointed to inadequacies in the regulation and supervision of financial institutions, and the mispricing and mismanagement of risks by lenders.[32] Imprudent bank lending, with little regard for currency risks and maturity mismatches, led to low-quality and excessive investments, and eventual reckoning in the face of adverse external developments. In Thailand, Indonesia, and Korea, the magnitude of the problem in the financial sector was not realized until it was too late, due to lack of transparency, or simply lack of data. The IMF credited stronger financial sectors in Singapore and Hong Kong for the respective economies' relative success in containing the contagion.

Singapore: Safeguarding the Financial Sector During the AFC

Singapore had an open capital account very early in its economic and financial journey, having removed exchange controls by 1978. Singapore had little choice. As a young nation with no natural resources, Singapore made a policy decision to embrace globalization and leverage on foreign direct investment to create industry and employment for its people. Mindful that it could be vulnerable to the risk of large and volatile cross-border flows and exchange rate movements that might be out of sync with economic fundamentals, Singapore put in place two important safeguards.

---

[31] Fischer (1997).

[32] IMF (1997b).

First, Singapore adopted a policy of noninternationalization of the SGD since the early 1980s.[33] This referred to MAS' policy of not encouraging the development of an offshore SGD market and the use of SGD outside Singapore for activities unrelated to its real economy, including speculation against the currency. For example, as part of the policy, banks were required to consult the central bank before extending credit facilities exceeding SGD 5 million to nonresidents for use outside Singapore. The policy was aimed at ensuring that the growth of the SGD market would be commensurate with the development of the economy, and not compromise MAS' management of the trade-weighted SGD exchange rate.

Looking back, the SGD noninternationalization policy could be deemed a form of macroprudential policy. It served the country well in the early phase of its financial development by deterring short-term capital flows that could be disruptive to domestic economic and financial activities — as was indeed the case for some countries during the AFC. In later years, as the SGD gained strength and market confidence was preserved on the basis of sound macroeconomic fundamentals and a credible exchange rate policy, MAS would re-assess the SGD noninternationalization policy.

Second, Singapore maintained strong supervisory oversight over domestic financial institutions. MAS was a strict gatekeeper, granting licenses in the early years of its financial development to only large (well-capitalized) and reputable institutions, and supplementing this with regular examination and monitoring of their lending and investment practices.[34] MAS' high regulatory standards, its reputation for surprise inspections, and its officers' close scrutiny of banks' books, while dreaded by banks in normal times, provided a much-welcomed level of assurance to markets during the crisis. Singapore's financial sector emerged from the AFC battle-scarred but resilient, poised for a new chapter of growth.

Singapore: Promoting Financial Sector Competitiveness Post-AFC

The period of the AFC coincided in Singapore with a fundamental review of its financial sector policies. Singapore established the Financial Sector Review Group (FSRG) in August 1997, and MAS worked with industry

---

[33]Ong (2003); IMF (2017a).

[34]MAS credited Mr. Koh Beng Seng, its chief financial regulator through the 1980s and 1990s, for steering the financial sector through many crises, including the AFC, before he left the organization in February 1998.

players and experts to re-assess its policies toward regulating and developing the financial sector to keep up with the rapid changes in the global financial landscape. Mr. Lee Hsien Loong became the Chairman of MAS in January 1998, when Asia was still reeling from the regional crisis.

MAS pressed ahead with financial sector liberalization in 1998, in spite of or because of the AFC, cognizant of the urgency to enhance Singapore's competitiveness as a financial center while maintaining high regulatory and supervisory standards. MAS reiterated Singapore's commitment to building a strong and competitive banking industry, promoting its asset management industry, and broadening and deepening the capital markets.[35] Many of the proposals MAS adopted following the review would reaffirm and update the policies that saw Singapore through the crisis — retaining key elements while allowing for more innovation and growth.

MAS reviewed the policy of noninternationalization of the SGD, progressively relaxing restrictions from August 1998. The basic thrust of not encouraging speculation against the SGD remained, but the policy was liberalized to facilitate development of capital market activities, including SGD equity listings and bond issues, and transactions in SGD interest rate derivatives. Banks were allowed to make SGD loans to nonresidents for investment in Singapore, thereby broadening the investor base for SGD assets. MAS renamed the policy in 2004 to reflect the revised and more targeted objective of only restricting SGD lending to nonresident financial institutions *for the purpose of speculating in the SGD.* [36]

MAS shifted the focus of its supervision from a system based on prescriptive regulation to one that was risk-based. MAS would move away from extensive regulation of all aspects of individual institutions' business activities to an emphasis on the adequacy of their internal controls and risk management, and the standard of disclosure and corporate governance. The capital market and asset management industries were expanding, and a risk-based approach would allow MAS to adapt supervision to a more

---

[35] *MAS Annual Report 1998/99*, Chairman's statement.

[36] The MAS Notice on the "Non-internationalisation policy of the Singapore dollar" was renamed "Notice on lending of SGD to non-resident financial institutions." Two key requirements remained: first, financial institutions may not extend credit facilities exceeding SGD 5 million to nonresident financial entities where they have reason to believe that the proceeds may be used for speculation against the SGD; and second, nonresident financial entities must convert SGD proceeds from loans (exceeding SGD 5 million), equity listing, and bond issuances to foreign currency before using these funds outside Singapore.

diverse financial sector with banks and nonbank financial institutions of varying sizes, business models, and target clientele.

MAS also announced that it would provide greater transparency and accountability into its monetary policy framework by issuing a monetary policy statement and a macroeconomic policy review report twice a year. The first monetary policy statement was issued in February 2001, and the inaugural Macroeconomic Review published in January 2002, to provide greater clarity to the markets on MAS' monetary policy stance and the basis for its decision.

Equally important, MAS enhanced its internal capacity to deal with the new economic and financial landscape. MAS made key organizational changes in 1998 to synergize and strengthen coordination between its central banking and supervisory functions. MAS was a central bank and an integrated financial regulator, one of very few in the world but had not fully harnessed the advantages of this arrangement. Mr. Tharman Shanmugaratnam, former Singapore Deputy Prime Minister and current MAS Chairman, described MAS departments in the 1990s as distinct "silos" that were individually well-run but had minimal interaction with each other and were protective of their turf.[37] To MAS' credit, the departments and senior management in MAS charged *respectively* with monetary policy and financial supervision did an admirable job during the AFC.[38] However, they could be even more effective *working together*, and the financial sector review was an impetus for MAS to function more effectively as a central bank-cum-financial regulator to anticipate the challenges ahead.

As part of the restructuring exercise in MAS, regular meetings were instituted where senior management from different functions would exchange information and debate policy issues, that is, for monetary policy to talk to supervision, and vice versa. This practice, so ingrained in MAS today, was a game changer then. Departments retained primary responsibility for their mandates but could tap on a broader spectrum of expertise and views before finalizing policy decisions. Officers across disciplines and functions

---

[37]MAS (2011). Mr. Tharman himself spent many years in MAS' economics department and was MAS' Deputy Managing Director for financial supervision, and subsequently MAS Managing Director, before he joined politics in 2001.

[38]Internal communication and policy coordination likely took place through more informal channels. For example, Dr. Teh Kok Peng shared that the need for property cooling measures in 1996 was discussed by MAS senior management in both economic policy and banking supervision.

consulted each other or worked on projects together, and staff mobility within MAS became the norm.[39]

Economists and regulators in MAS would discover they had much to learn (and unlearn) from each other. For example, economists tended to view capital flows and exchange rates through a *macroeconomic* lens, focusing on measurable variables in their analysis and modeling; institutions (often complex and evolving) and individuals (not always rational) were a lot harder to capture in equations. The AFC was a lesson that bank runs (which regulators were more alert to) could happen to countries and not just institutions. At the same time, financial supervisors began to appreciate that the tools of economic analysis could help them anticipate and stress-test how economic and financial shocks, and regulatory policy, might affect market outcomes. The *macroprudential* perspective of the financial sector and the behavioral economics of herd instincts were examples of what the two disciplines (economics and financial supervision) combined could contribute to understanding financial crises.

AFC: Aftermath and Legacy

Asian economies paid a heavy price for the AFC. Commenting on the crisis in 2000, Mr. Lee Hsien Loong said, "The punishment meted out by the markets was out of proportion to the crime. The damage was not just the 9% shrinkage in the GDP of the crisis countries, but the social dislocation and political turbulence that followed."[40]

The AFC was largely over by 1999. Yet, it left a deep scar in Asia that went beyond that associated with an economic and financial shock, and the subsequent recovery.

First, Asian countries emerged from the AFC more vigilant and more mindful of financial shocks. The crisis was a cautionary tale about the risks of globalization, especially financial openness and unfettered capital flows. However, Asia had come too far to turn its back on globalization. For Asia, it was a case of once bitten, get the repellent (or antidote) ready. Post-AFC,

---

[39]This author left the economics department in July 1998 for the human resources department (to work on training and career development initiatives for MAS officers) and subsequently spent 10 years in securities regulation.

[40]Lee Hsien Loong (2000).

Asian countries were more cautious and more determined to avert the fury of financial markets by committing to macroeconomic prudence and financial resilience.

For example, in the decades after the crisis, Asian economies strived to run current account surpluses, even at the expense of lower domestic investment, persistent infrastructure gaps, and lower growth.[41] Asian central banks re-assessed the adequacy of their reserves, once measured by months of imports, and concluded that more is necessary to cushion the economy against large gross capital outflows. Events such as the "taper tantrum" of 2013 (when the US Treasury bond yields surged following indications that the Fed would taper its quantitative easing), while thankfully short-lived, continued to reaffirm the Asian countries' resolve for self-insurance through reserves accumulation.

Second, Asia woke up to the fact that the region, and *regionalization*, was a vital and unavoidable component of globalization. Asian countries might have thought they were individual success stories (of outward-oriented growth strategy) that happened to be in the same vicinity, but in a crisis, they were "emerging Asia" to speculators and asset managers.[42] Whether by geographical proximity, cultural affinity, or economic similarity, the collective *Asia* would matter more to Asian countries than the sum of its individual GDPs and markets.

After the crisis, the region has become more integrated and more interconnected than ever — in trade and investments, and in their financial markets.[43] What was a regional liability during the AFC has since evolved into an advantage, with the rise of Asia as the world's production hub (*Factory Asia*) and as the fastest growing market for goods and services (*Shopper Asia*).[44] Governments in Asia have come to recognize this dual aspect of regional integration. If ASEAN was born in the post-independence years to promote political and economic cooperation, then the ASEAN+3

---

[41] AMRO (2019). Chapter 2, "Building Capacity and Connectivity for the New Economy," discusses the legacy of the AFC on public and private investments in Asia.

[42] Singapore today is still classified as "emerging market economies" in Bank for International Settlements (BIS) annual reports, as are Hong Kong, Korea, and Taiwan Province of China. Singapore and Hong Kong are included in MSCI's developed markets Pacific index.

[43] See, for example, Rana (2006) on regionalism in East Asia in the years after the AFC. For more recent discussion on economic and financial integration in Asia, see Asian Development Bank (2021).

[44] AMRO (2020). Chapter 2, "ASEAN+3 in the Global Value Networks," discusses *Factory Asia, Shopper Asia* as the new growth paradigm.

Macroeconomic Research Office (AMRO) (headquartered in Singapore) is the equivalent for economic and financial cooperation of the ASEAN+3 countries in the post-crisis era.[45]

Third, Asia was forced to reassess the accountability of and relationship between central banking and financial supervision. The Asian crisis posed many difficult questions. Were central bankers overly complacent? Were bank regulators sleeping on the job? Why were both parties blindsided? True, economists could point to lax financial oversight and prudential rules (not under their purview) for compounding the problems of macroeconomic imbalances and tipping the countries into a full-blown crisis. Equally true, supervisors would be rightly aggrieved that they were not alerted to the dire consequences of exchange rate mismanagement and external imbalances (which they were not responsible for) on the banking system before it was too late.

For central banks and regulatory authorities in Asia, the AFC underscored how important it was for them to communicate regularly, identify risks early, and work together to preempt and resolve crises. Central bankers and regulators could be individually competent, and yet operate sub-optimally by working separately. In Singapore, MAS strengthened its internal communication and policy coordination in tandem with efforts to diversify and deepen its financial sector. Asian central banks and financial regulators would revisit the issue of the appropriate institutional and governance structure to deal with financial crises after the GFC.

Could the AFC have been avoided? Perhaps not. The IMF conceded in its interim assessment in December 1997 that "neither economic forecasts nor the pricing of assets in financial markets foretold the depth and breadth of the economic and financial difficulties" and that "it may well be that such developments are inherently nonforecastable." Both the AFC and the GFC have been deemed Black Swan events — alongside the dot-com crash (in 2000), 9/11 attacks (2001), and Brexit (2016). Black swans are the "unknown unknowns" — events that are difficult if not impossible to predict but have far-reaching consequences.[46] Arguably, many of these events, including the

---

[45] ASEAN was formed in 1967 by Indonesia, Malaysia, the Philippines, and Thailand to promote political and economic cooperation and regional stability. Other countries joined later. AMRO was established in April 2011 and became an international organization in February 2016.

[46] The term black swan was coined by Nassim Nicholas Taleb, a former Wall Street trader, in his 2001 book, *Fooled by Randomness*, and elaborated on in his 2007 book, *The Black Swan*.

AFC, could be explained with the benefit of hindsight. More recently, the term "pink flamingos" has been attached to "known knowns," or predictable events that are brightly lit but remain studiously ignored by policymakers due to group cognitive biases.[47] It mattered little whether the AFC or the GFC were black swans, or pink flamingos, or both. Perhaps, more than 20 years after the AFC, governments and central bankers in Asia could take comfort from the fact that the GFC similarly took policymakers in the US and Europe by surprise, even though the warning signs were also there.

Lessons From the GFC

The AFC has been credited for why Asian economies fared much better when another financial crisis, this time of global proportions, struck a decade later. Countries in Asia knew better than most that international capital flows could magnify the risks from existing distortions in domestic financial and asset markets. While Asia was not immune to the GFC, it averted the catastrophic financial instability and economic contractions that characterized the AFC. Asian economies had stronger macroeconomic fundamentals at the start of the GFC and more policy space during the crisis for an accommodative monetary and fiscal stance.[48] Financial systems in Asia were more resilient, as banks were stronger and better supervised, and the capital markets more developed.

However, the GFC shed further light on financial stability risks that were not previously well understood or researched — or thought to be relevant only to emerging economies. The policy and academic discourse since the GFC have sharpened the world's understanding of the risks of financial innovation, globalization, and systemic risks, and focused effort on tools to deal with financial crises. International organizations, national authorities, and academia have joined in contributing to the empirical work and policy discussion on trade (real) globalization vs financial globalization, how they interact, and how their risks intertwine.[49]

---

[47]The term pink flamingo was coined by Frank Hoffman, a US defense expert, when writing in 2015 about US military strategy and predictable situations that a senior leader or group or leaders may wish to avoid or be in denial about.

[48]See, for example, Rhee and Posen (2013).

[49]BIS (2017b). Chapter IV, "Understanding globalisation," discusses the trends, risks, and other implications of international trade and finance.

The rest of this section discusses the policy landscape on financial stability after the GFC, highlighting key elements relevant to the AFC, and Singapore's response.

The institutional framework to address financial crises has improved after the GFC as international organizations and national authorities adopted financial stability as an explicit mandate. The Financial Stability Board (FSB)[50] was established in April 2009 to promote international financial stability; it monitors and makes recommendations about the global financial system. The IMF's mandate was updated in 2012 to include all macroeconomic and financial sector issues that bear on global stability.

In Singapore, MAS formalized financial stability as an explicit mandate in the MAS Act in 2013.[51] MAS put in place governance arrangements to monitor and mitigate systemic risks, including a Board-level Chairman's Meeting that makes major policy decisions on financial stability, a management-level Financial Stability Committee that supports the Chairman's Meeting, and a macroprudential surveillance department that works closely with monetary policy and supervisory departments. Elsewhere in Asia, the relevant authorities also reviewed and made changes to the legal and institutional arrangements for financial stability, taking into account coordination with the monetary policy mandate and financial supervisory function where they reside in more than one entity.[52]

A key element of the global response to the GFC was to develop policies to address the "too-big-to-fail" problem posed by large institutions. Asia found out the hard way, during the AFC, that bank failures and bank closures could trigger a wider financial and economic crisis. The GFC post-mortem gave rise to the identification of systemically important financial institutions, defined as institutions whose disorderly failure, because of their

---

[50] The FSB monitors and makes recommendations about the global financial system, and was successor to the Financial Stability Forum (FSF) founded in 1999. The FSB was formed to place the FSF on stronger institutional ground with an expanded membership. FSB members in Asia include China, India, Hong Kong, Japan, Korea, and Singapore (FSB website: www.fsb.org).

[51] MAS Act section 4(b) was amended in April 2013 to reflect "to foster a sound and reputable financial centre and to promote financial stability" as one of four principal objects of the Authority. [Amendment as underlined.] The other principal objects are: 4(a) to maintain price stability conducive to sustainable growth of the economy; 4(c) to ensure prudent and effective management of the official foreign reserves of Singapore; and 4(d) to grow Singapore as an internationally competitive financial center.

[52] BIS (2017a). The compilation of case studies on the financial stability and macroprudential framework in different jurisdictions include contributions from China, Hong Kong, Indonesia, Korea, Malaysia, the Philippines, Singapore, and Thailand.

size, complexity, and systemic interconnectedness, would cause significant disruption to the wider financial system and economic activity. The FSB, in consultation with the Basel Committee on Banking Supervision (BCBS), published its first list of 29 global systemically important banks (G-SIBs) in November 2011,[53] and has updated this list on an annual basis. Notably, the number of Chinese banks on the G-SIBs list has increased from just one in 2011 to four since 2015. The FSB and BCBS continue to make recommendations to national authorities on policy measures (including capital requirements, supervisory intensity, and resolution planning) to address the systemic and moral hazard risks associated with GSIBs.

To complement the G-SIB framework, the BCBS sets out principles for countries to tailor a framework to identify and address the risks posed by domestic systemically important banks (D-SIBs) to the local financial system and the local economy.[54] In 2015, MAS published the framework identifying and supervising D-SIBs in Singapore, as well as the list of these banks.

In 2010, the IMF made it mandatory for members with systemically important financial sectors to undergo assessments under the financial sector assessment program (FSAP) every 5 years.[55] Members would be assessed on the resilience of their (banking and non-banking) financial sectors, the quality of the regulatory and supervisory framework, and the capacity to manage financial crises. The number of jurisdictions with systemically important financial sectors was increased to 29 (from 25) in 2013, after a review of the methodology to place greater emphasis on interconnectedness. Singapore completed its most recent FSAP assessment in 2019. Other jurisdictions in Asia, including those hardest hit during the AFC, have also undergone FSAP assessments.

The GFC drew attention to financial stability risks posed by nonbank financial intermediaries (previously "shadow banks"). In the years preceding the crisis, the assets and activities associated with nonbank financial intermediation grew rapidly, especially in the US and Europe.[56] Systemic risks could arise directly from these entities, as well as from their

---

[53] FSB (2011).

[54] BCBS (2012).

[55] IMF (2010).

[56] FSB (2012). By the FSB's estimate, the size of the global shadow banking system rose from USD 26 trillion in 2002 to USD 62 trillion in 2007. A search for yield and stricter regulation of banks were some of the reasons cited for the increase.

interconnectedness with banks. Following the global crisis, the FSB took on the task of monitoring the global trends and risks in nonbank financial intermediation, and making recommendations for its oversight and regulation. Singapore has participated in the FSB annual survey on nonbank financial intermediation since 2012. The result of a parallel survey focusing on nonbank financial intermediation activities in Asia was published in 2014.[57]

There were calls after the AFC for Asian countries to develop their capital markets in order to provide another source of funding (as an alternative to bank loans) for businesses and to improve the efficiency and allocation of savings. The GFC was a reminder that nonbanks themselves, and credit intermediation through nonbanks, could be a source of financial stability risk. The development of capital markets and nonbank entities in the financial ecosystem (alongside banks) must therefore go hand-in-hand with adequate monitoring, surveillance, and supervision.

The world, including Asia, has benefited post-GFC from a robust review and development of policy tools to address financial stability risks. Macroprudential policy includes old measures that have been retooled and enhanced, as well as more recent regulatory initiatives to contain systemic risks globally. The BCBS developed Basel III requirements for banks to strengthen regulation, supervision, and risk management within the banking industry.[58] The countercyclical capital buffer (CCyB), introduced in 2011 to address procyclicality and interconnectedness in the banking systems, would be the first macroprudential policy that entails multilateral cross-border reciprocity. MAS included the CCyB in its macroprudential policy toolkit from 2016.

In Singapore, the property market has been identified to be of systemic importance to the financial sector and domestic economy. Following the GFC, Singapore saw a 60% run-up in property prices from the second quarter (Q2) of 2009 to Q3 2013. MAS introduced new restrictions on debt-to-income (DTI) ratios, caps on loan tenures, and new calibrations to

---

[57]FSB Regional Consultative Group for Asia (2014). A total of 15 jurisdictions in Asia (including Singapore) participated in the survey.

[58]BCBS (2010).

the existing loan-to-valuation (LTV) ratios.[59] The government announced property supply measures through government land sales and fiscal (tax) measures on property purchases. The latter includes a new additional buyer's stamp duty (ABSD) on property purchases based on the number of properties an individual owns and his/her citizenship. Likewise, in other jurisdictions in Asia, macroprudential measures focused on the property sector have also featured prominently, with the most popular being LTV and DTI caps.[60]

In 2012, the IMF proposed an institutional view on the liberalization and management of capital flows following calls to review its approach and advice on capital flows.[61] The main points captured in the IMF document would, in hindsight, neatly sum up Asia's experience during the AFC: capital flows have substantial benefits for countries, capital flows carry risks, and capital flow liberalization is generally more beneficial and less risky if countries have reached certain levels of financial and institutional development.

With this institutional view, the IMF would take a more nuanced approach toward the use of capital flow management measures (CFMs) during financial crises. The IMF conceded that "in *certain circumstances* (emphasis added), introducing CFMs can be useful for supporting macroeconomic adjustments and safeguarding financial system stability." However, CFMs should be *temporary*, and not a substitute for sound macroeconomic policies. The IMF has also provided guidance on the relationship between CFMs and macroprudential measures (including situations when they overlap), and how countries may exit from one or both policies.

Concluding Remarks

The GFC and the global policy discussions post-GFC on systemic and contagion risks have much to offer Asian countries — in providing an analytical framework to understand the AFC, as well as in averting and mitigating future financial crises. However, the resilience and determination of countries in the region in the face of adversity are uniquely Asian.

A common element of the AFC and GFC is that they took the countries, and the governments, by surprise. If there is one key difference between

---

[59] An inter-agency task force comprising MAS, the Ministry of Finance, and the Ministry of National Development would discuss and coordinate the appropriate policy response for the property sector. For a list of macroprudential policies in Singapore since 1996, see https://www.mas.gov.sg/publications/macroprudential-policies-in-singapore.

[60] BIS (2017a).

[61] IMF (2012).

the two crises, it would be how their aftermath has shaped countries' views toward globalization. Post-AFC, Asian countries stayed firmly on the path of globalization, pursuing an outward-oriented growth path while re-engaging the confidence of international markets. Singapore was not alone within Asia in liberalizing and allowing the financial sector to take off further. In contrast, the decade following the GFC has coincided with an increase in trade tensions and protectionist pressure as the world came to terms with the gains, risks, and distributional implications of globalization.

The COVID-19 pandemic is a rude reminder, to Asia and the world, of yet another element to global interconnectivity, besides trade and financial globalization. Asian countries have demonstrated time and again that they have a steep learning curve and are able and willing to do what is necessary to pull through a crisis. Asia will emerge, again, stronger and wiser in the post-pandemic new normal. In this, perhaps Asia has something to offer the world.

References

ASEAN +3 Macroeconomic Research Office. 2019. *ASEAN+3 Regional Economic Outlook 2019.*

ASEAN +3 Macroeconomic Research Office. 2020. *ASEAN+3 Regional Economic Outlook 2020.*

Asian Development Bank. February 2021. *Asian Economic Integration Report 2021: Managing Digital Platforms Work for Asia and the Pacific.*

Basel Committee on Banking Supervision. December 2010. *Basel III: A Global Regulatory Framework for More Resilient Banks and Banking Systems.*

Basel Committee on Banking Supervision. October 2012. *A Framework for Dealing with Domestic Systemically Important Banks.*

Bank for International Settlements. December 2017a. "Macroprudential Frameworks, Implementation and Relationship with Other Policies." BIS papers no. 94. https://www.bis.org/publ/bppdf/bispap94.htm.

Bank for International Settlements. June 25, 2017b. *87th Annual Report.*

Brown, Stephen J., William N. Goetzmann, and James Park. 1998. "Hedge Funds and the Asian Currency Crisis of 1997." NBER working paper no. 6427.

Dalla, Ismail, and Deena Khatkhate. 1996. "The Emerging East Asian Bond Market." *Finance and Development* 11–13. https://www.imf.org/external/pubs/ft/fandd/1996/03/pdf/dalla.pdf.

Financial Stability Board. 2010. "Reducing the Moral Hazard Posed by Systemically Important Financial Institutions." October 20.

Financial Stability Board. 2011. "Policy Measures to Address Systemically Important Financial Institutions." November 4.

Financial Stability Board. 2012. "Global Shadow Banking Monitoring Report 2012." November 18.

Financial Stability Board Regional Consultative Group for Asia. 2014. "Report on Shadow Banking in Asia." August 22.

Fischer, Stanley. September 19, 1997. "Capital Account Liberalization and the Role of the IMF." A Speech at the Seminar "Asia and the IMF," Hong Kong. https://www.imf.org/en/News/Articles/2015/09/28/04/53/sp091997

Hargreaves, Rupert. 2016. "Here's How George Soros Broke the Bank of Thailand." *Business Insider,* September 7.

Harmes, Adam. 2001. "Institutional Investors and Polanyi's Double Movement: A Model of Contemporary Currency Crises." *Review of International Political Economy* 8: 3.

Hicklin, John, David Robinson, and Anoop Singh, editors. 1997. *Macroeconomic Issues Facing ASEAN Countries.* International Monetary Fund. https://www.elibrary.imf.org/view/books/071/04390-9781557756374-en/04390-9781557756374-en-book.xml

International Monetary Fund. October 1991. *World Economic Outlook.*

International Monetary Fund. May 1997a. *World Economic Outlook.*

International Monetary Fund. December 1997b. *World Economic Outlook.*

International Monetary Fund. June 2000a. "Recovery from the Asian Crisis and the Role of the IMF." https://www.imf.org/external/np/exr/ib/2000/062300.htm

International Monetary Fund. October 2000b. *World Economic Outlook.*

International Monetary Fund. September 2006. *World Economic Outlook Database.*

International Monetary Fund. August 27, 2010. "Integrating Stability Assessments under the Financial Sector Assessment Program into Article IV Surveillance." https://www.imf.org/external/np/pp/eng/2010/082710.pdf

International Monetary Fund. November 14, 2012. *The Liberalization and Management of Capital Flows: An Institutional View.*

International Monetary Fund. June 27, 2017a. *Singapore: Selected Issues.*

International Monetary Fund. September 2017b. *Increasing Resilience to Large and Volatile Capital Flows: The Role of Macroprudential Policies.* https://www.imf.org/en/Publications/Policy-Papers/Issues/2017/07/05/pp060217-increasing-resilience-to-large-and-volatile-capital-flows

International Monetary Fund Article IV Consultation with Singapore Public Information Notices (PINs). 1998–2002.

Lee, Hsien Loong. 2000. "Post Crisis Asia — The Way Forward." William Taylor Memorial Lecture in Basel, Switzerland.

Lee, Hsien Loong. 2001. "Credibility, Confidence, Dynamism: MAS in the New Economic and Financial Landscape." Keynote Address at MAS 30th Anniversary Conference.

Lee, Kuan Yew. 1998. "How and When will East Asia Recover?" Speech by Senior Minister Mr Lee Kuan Yew at the Thai National Defence College.

Lee, Kuan Yew. October 3, 2000. *From Third World to First: The Singapore Story: 1965–2000*.

Monetary Authority of Singapore. "Annual Reports, Speeches, Policy Papers, Replies to Questions from Parliament, Committee of Supply." www.mas.gov.sg

Monetary Authority of Singapore. 2011. *Sustaining Stability Serving Singapore: MAS 1971–2011*. 40th Anniversary Publication. Singapore: Straits Times Press.

Monetary Authority of Singapore Committee on Banking Disclosure. 1998. "Report on Banking Disclosure." May.

Montiel, Peter. 1997. "Exchange Rate Policies and Macroeconomic Management in ASEAN Countries." In *Macroeconomic Issues Facing ASEAN Countries*, edited by John Hicklin, David Robinson, and Anoop Singh. International Monetary Fund.

Ong, Chong Tee. 2003. "Singapore's Policy of Non-Internationalisation of the Singapore Dollar and the Asian Dollar Market." *China's Capital Account Liberalization: International Perspectives* 15: 93–98. https://www.bis.org/publ/bppdf/bispap15l.pdf

Park, Donghyun, Arief Ramayandi, and Kwanho Shin. 2013. "Why did Asian Countries Fare Better During the Global Financial Crisis than During the Asian Financial Crisis." In *Responding to Financial Crisis: Lessons from Asia Then, the United States and Europe Now*, edited by Changyong Rhee and Adam S. Posen. Washington: Peterson Institute for International Economics.

Rana, Pradumna B. July 2006. "Economic Integration in East Asia: Trends, Prospects, and a Possible Roadmap." ADB Working Paper Series on Regional Economic Integration no. 2.

Rhee, Changyong, and Adam S. Posen, editors. October 2013. *Responding to Financial Crisis: Lessons from Asia Then, the United States and Europe Now*. Washington: Peterson Institute for International Economics.

South East Asian Central Banks Centre. January 17–19, 1992. "Recent Issues in Exchange Rate Policies in SEACEN Countries." Report on the SEACEN-IMF Seminar, Kuala Lumpur.

World Bank. 1993. *The East Asian Miracle: Economic Growth and Public Policy*.

Chapter 21

ASEAN's Newer Members in Two Crises
Impact, Response, and Lessons

Jayant Menon[1]

Introduction

Apart from the coronavirus disease (COVID-19) pandemic that hit in 2020 and is currently ongoing, the Association of Southeast Asian Nations (ASEAN) region has been through two major crises in the last quarter century that have had major economic and financial effects: the 1997–1998 Asian financial crisis (AFC) and the 2008–2009 global financial crisis (GFC).

The AFC is often identified with the ASEAN region, although its effects extended beyond it. The impact of the AFC varied across ASEAN, with the newer members less affected than the original ones. This chapter focuses on the experience of these five newer members — Brunei Darussalam, Cambodia, Lao People's Democratic Republic (PDR), Myanmar, and Vietnam, or BCLMV — with the AFC and the GFC. The literature has largely ignored the experience of these newer members, with respect to both the AFC and the GFC, and this chapter aims to fill this gap.

BCLMV are a diverse grouping but are discussed together because of one important commonality: they represent the ASEAN member countries that were indirectly as well as the least affected by the AFC.[2] This is also true of the GFC, but the indirect channel of transmission of this crisis applies to all ASEAN members. BCLMV could be thought of as crisis-affected rather than crisis-hit countries because they suffered less and only from contagion that swept through the region and beyond.

---

[1] I am particularly grateful to Diwa C. Guinigundo and Masahiro Kawai for extensive written comments. I also received very useful comments and suggestions from Hoe Ee Khor and Thiam Hee Ng. Anna Cassandra Melendez provided excellent research assistance. Any remaining errors are my own.

[2] Even among the original members of ASEAN, there are significant differences in impact from the AFC. For instance, the Philippines and Singapore were less affected than Thailand, Indonesia, or Malaysia.

For the first time, a systematic analysis of the experience of the newer members of ASEAN relating to the AFC and the GFC focusing on impact, policy response, and lessons is here provided. Their participation in regional financial cooperation initiatives in helping prevent or mitigate the impact of future crises and how these need to be enhanced to better serve BCLMV are also considered.

The remainder of the chapter has five sections. It begins with an overview of BCLMV economies and the two crises to lay the groundwork for the ensuing analysis is provided. The impact of the AFC on each of the five countries and how they responded while drawing out similarities and differences are then examined. The section following that looks at the same but in relation to the GFC. Lessons from the crises and the resulting regional financial cooperation initiatives and ways in which they can be enhanced to better serve BCLMV are then analyzed. The final section concludes.

The AFC, GFC, and BCLMV: An Overview

A good way to introduce BCLMV is to start with ASEAN and their points of entry into it. ASEAN was established in 1967 after the signing of the Bangkok Declaration by the five original members, namely Indonesia, Malaysia, Philippines, Singapore, and Thailand. Although these five countries are referred to as the founding fathers, ASEAN was always open to expanding its membership and finally did so in 1984 with the accession of Brunei. More than a decade passed before ASEAN expanded further, and this occurred when Vietnam joined in 1995. Although the AFC is deemed to have started on July 2, 1997, the turmoil did not affect the accession of Lao PDR and Myanmar later that month. Cambodia was supposed to also join at this time, but an internal political rift delayed their accession by almost 2 years, and they were finally accepted on April 30, 1999. The original membership had doubled to 10 with the accession of these five countries over a 15-year period.[3]

The AFC began as a currency crisis in Thailand on July 2, 1997, when the Thai baht came under severe selling pressure and the Bank of Thailand was forced to abandon the peg to a basket of currencies dominated by the

---

[3] ASEAN's membership could extend further if it accepts Timor Leste's application to become its 11th member.

United States (US) dollar, leading to a massive, immediate depreciation. It set off a series of currency devaluations and massive flights of capital, initially affecting Malaysia, Indonesia, Singapore, the Philippines, and Korea.[4] It later spread to Hong Kong, Chinese mainland, and even Russia and Brazil. Many other countries in the region and beyond were affected, although ASEAN continues to be identified as the focal point of the crisis until today.

Unlike most economic and financial crises emanating in developing countries,[5] the GFC of 2008–2009 started in the US and affected the world economy. Excessive risk-taking behavior combined with the bursting of the US housing bubble caused values of securities tied to US real estate to fall sharply, damaging financial institutions globally. It initially led to the bankruptcy of Lehman Brothers on September 15, 2008, and an international banking crisis ensued. It produced the Great Recession, the worst economic downturn since the Great Depression. The worst impact was felt in the US and other developed countries such as members of the European Union (EU), although the developing countries were not spared. Although all ASEAN countries were only indirectly affected this time, the impact was felt in varying degrees among members.

As noted earlier, BCLMV are a diverse group. The theoretical grouping includes one high-income country (Brunei) and four transitional economies, of which one has joined the high human development index (HDI) group (Vietnam)[6] and the remaining three are still classified as less developed countries (LDCs) (Cambodia, Lao PDR, and Myanmar). CLMV are still largely agrarian economies despite structural transformations that have resulted in the share of agriculture and related industries in gross domestic product (GDP) consistently declining over the years (Table 21.1). Even in 2018, the rural sector continued to employ more than half of the labor force in Lao PDR and Myanmar, and a third in Cambodia and Vietnam.

---

[4] In the first 6 months of the crisis, the value of the Indonesian rupiah was down by 80%, the Thai baht by more than 50%, the Korean won by nearly 50%, and the Malaysian ringgit by 45%. Collectively, the economies most affected saw a drop in capital inflows of more than USD 100 billion in the first year of the crisis.

[5] See, for instance, Edwards (2007) and Bird and Mosley (2004).

[6] The HDI ranks economies based on a weighted average measuring life expectancy, education, per capita income, gender gap, and poverty. Vietnam passed the threshold of 0.7 in 2019 to join the high HDI group.

Table 21.1: Sector Share of GDP and Employment, Selected Years

Country	Sector	% of GDP					% of Employment				
		1995	2000	2005	2010	2018	1995	2000	2005	2010	2018
Brunei	Agriculture, hunting, forestry, fishing	1.1	1.0	0.9	0.7	1.0	1.6	1.2	0.9	0.7	1.4
	Industry	53.4	64.5	72.0	67.4	62.2	23.9	21.7	20.6	19.3	16.0
	Services	45.5	34.5	27.1	31.9	36.7	74.5	77.1	78.5	80.0	82.7
Cambodia	Agriculture, hunting, forestry, fishing	51.4	37.8	32.4	36.0	23.5	79.0	73.5	62.0	57.3	33.7
	Industry	12.9	23.0	26.4	23.3	34.4	6.1	8.5	13.2	16.0	28.3
	Services	35.7	39.1	41.2	40.7	42.1	14.9	18.0	24.8	26.7	38.1
Lao PDR	Agriculture, hunting, forestry, fishing	42.8	33.6	29.1	23.6	17.7	85.4	81.6	77.3	71.5	63.2
	Industry	15.7	24.1	26.2	30.9	35.5	3.5	4.5	6.0	8.3	11.6
	Services	41.5	42.2	44.7	45.5	46.8	11.1	13.8	16.7	20.2	25.1
Myanmar	Agriculture, hunting, forestry, fishing	60.0	57.2	46.7	36.9	26.3	66.6	61.5	57.1	53.5	49.7
	Industry	9.9	9.7	17.5	26.5	34.7	10.5	13.2	16.3	17.7	16.0
	Services	30.1	33.1	35.8	36.7	39.0	22.8	25.4	26.6	28.8	34.3
Vietnam	Agriculture, hunting, forestry, fishing	24.5	22.5	19.3	21.0	16.2	67.1	65.3	54.8	48.7	38.6
	Industry	26.1	34.0	38.1	36.7	38.1	11.8	12.4	18.8	21.7	26.8
	Services	49.4	43.5	42.6	42.2	45.7	21.1	22.3	26.4	29.6	34.6

GDP = gross domestic product, Lao PDR = Lao People's Democratic Republic.
Source: United Nations Conference on Trade and Development (UNCTAD) Statistics database, data downloaded November 27, 2020.

The structural transformation in CLMV has been driven by economic and financial reforms that have supported growth through increases in trade (Figure 21.1) and foreign direct investment (FDI) (Figures 21.2A and 21.2B). This has resulted in remarkable achievements in the social sphere, especially in terms of poverty reduction (Table 21.2). While poverty headcount ratios (either USD 1.90 per day or national poverty line estimates) were above 50% in the early 1990s in CLMV, they have fallen sharply to below 20% by 2018. Financial systems had also been very weak prior to the AFC but matured in the decade leading up to the GFC and have continued deepening since (Table 21.3).

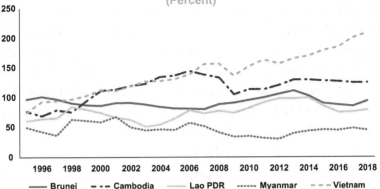

Figure 21.1: Share of Total Trade in Goods and Services (X + M) in GDP (Percent)

250
200
150
100
50
0
1996 1998 2000 2002 2004 2006 2008 2010 2012 2014 2016 2018
Brunei
Cambodia
Lao PDR
Myanmar
Vietnam

GDP = gross domestic product, Lao PDR = Lao People's Democratic Republic.
Source: United Nations Conference on Trade and Development (UNCTAD) Statistics database, data downloaded November 27, 2020.

Figure 21.2A: FDI Flows as a Percentage of GDP, 1995–1999 (Percent)

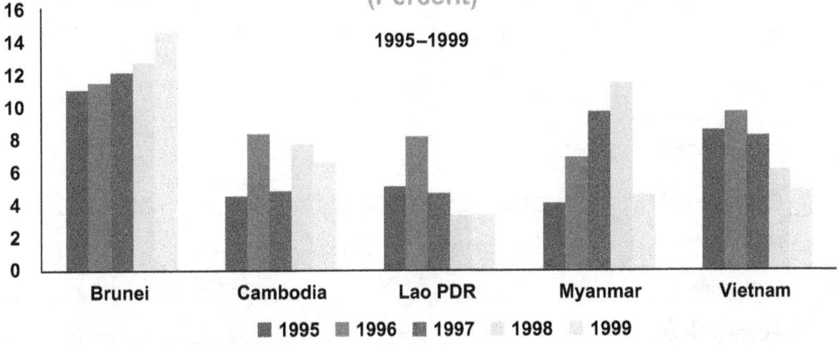

1995–1999
16
14
12
10
8
6
4
2
0
Brunei
Cambodia
Lao PDR
Myanmar
Vietnam
1995
1996
1997
1998
1999

FDI = foreign direct investment, GDP = gross domestic product, Lao PDR = Lao People's Democratic Republic.
Source: United Nations Conference on Trade and Development (UNCTAD) Statistics database, data downloaded November 27, 2020.

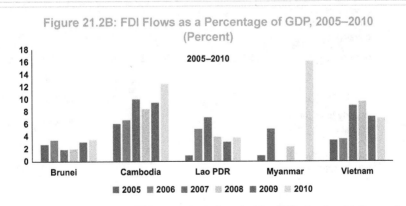

Figure 21.2B: FDI Flows as a Percentage of GDP, 2005–2010 (Percent)

2005–2010
18
16
14
12
10
8
6
4
2
0
Brunei
Cambodia
Lao PDR
Myanmar
Vietnam
2005
2006
2007
2008
2009
2010

FDI = foreign direct investment, GDP = gross domestic product, Lao PDR = Lao People's Democratic Republic.
Source: United Nations Conference on Trade and Development (UNCTAD) Statistics database, data downloaded November 27, 2020.

One of the consequences of a weak financial system is dollarization or the multiple currency phenomenon, whereby the US dollar and/or the currency of other countries serve the function of money in the domestic economy. Dollarization or the multiple currency phenomenon was present in varying degrees in CLMV during the AFC and GFC, although more pernicious during the former. Cambodia is highly dollarized, and both the US dollar and Thai baht serve as money in Lao PDR (see Menon 2008a,

Table 21.2: Human Development Indicators, Selected Years

Country	Indicator	1990s				2000s
		1992	1995	1997	1998	2002
Brunei	GDP per capita	72,704.700	72,446.400	69,940.900	67,984.200	70,770.600
	HDI	0.777	0.790	0.794	0.794	0.807
Cambodia	GDP per capita	...	1,182.400	1,228.300	1,252.3 00	1,642.600
	HDI	0.377	0.391	0.401	0.406	0.457
	Poverty headcount ratio at national poverty lines	...	...	...	...	...
Lao PDR	GDP per capita	2,046.700	2,330.200	2,555.300	2,608.000	3,106.000
	HDI	0.415	0.432	0.453	0.460	0.486
	Gini index	34.300	...	34.900	...	32.600
	Poverty headcount ratio at $1.90 a day	...	...	50.400	...	31.800
Myanmar	GDP per capita	658.100	774.700	849.500	887.800	1,336.200
	HDI	0.363	0.380	0.392	0.396	0.432
	Poverty headcount ratio at national poverty lines	...	...	...	...	...
Vietnam	GDP per capita	1,847.600	2,252.600	2,587.100	2,701.800	3,269.900
	HDI	0.504	0.537	0.547	0.567	0.602
	Gini index	35.700	...	...	35.400	37.000
	Poverty headcount ratio at $1.90 a day	51.900	...	...	34.400	37.100
	Poverty headcount ratio at national	...	...	...	...	...

continued on next page

... = not available, GDP = gross domestic product, HDI = Human Development Index, Lao PDR = Lao People's Democratic Republic.

2008b). Vietnam and Myanmar had lower degrees of dollarization but had highly managed exchange rates. Brunei has a Currency Board Arrangement whereby its currency is pegged to the Singapore dollar through a Currency Interchangeability Arrangement. These differences in monetary and exchange rate and control arrangements affected the ability of BCLMV to respond to crises through the conduct of monetary stabilization policies.

Table 21.2: *continued*

			2000s				
2003	2004	2005	2006	2007	2008	2009	2010
71,483.600	70,616.800	69,787.400	71,843.300	71,052.100	68,855.600	66,850.400	67,751.300
0.813	0.818	0.822	0.825	0.825	0.825	0.827	0.827
1,752.000	1,902.100	2,120.600	2,313.300	2,511.900	2,640.600	2,603.600	2,716.700
0.470	0.482	0.494	0.506	0.520	0.525	0.528	0.539
50.200	...	...	45.000	...	34.000	23.900	22.100
3,245.200	3,399.300	3,584.300	3,830.400	4,052.800	4,296.500	4,542.200	4,850.200
0.494	0.503	0.512	0.514	0.527	0.535	0.545	0.552
...	...	...	...	35.400	...	...	...
...	...	...	...	25.500	...	...	...
1,507.100	1,696.900	1,912.000	2,146.600	2,388.400	2,617.100	2,874.800	3,129.900
0.442	0.452	0.461	0.471	0.482	0.493	0.504	0.515
...	...	48.200	...	...	...	...	42.200
3,462.900	3,689.700	3,931.800	4,167.100	4,422.300	4,628.000	4,830.300	5,089.400
0.611	0.620	0.624	0.632	0.640	0.647	0.659	0.661
...	36.800	...	35.800	...	35.600	...	39.300
...	25.800	...	18.800	...	14.100	...	4.000
...	...	...	...	...	...	...	20.700

Notes: GDP per capita and purchasing power parity (PPP) are at constant 2017 international dollar. Gini index data are based on World Bank estimates. Poverty headcount ratio is estimated at USD 1.90 a day (2011 PPP).

Sources: World Development Indicators, data downloaded November 27, 2020; United Nations Development Programme Human Development Index, data downloaded January 11, 2021.

Table 21.3: Financial Depth Indicators, Selected Years

Country	Indicator	1995	1999	2000	2005	2007	2010
Brunei	Central bank assets to GDP (%)	...	1.1	0.8	0.0	0.0	0.0
	Deposit money bank assets to deposit money bank assets and central bank assets (%)	...	98.1	98.2	100.0	100.0	100.0
	Deposit money banks' assets to GDP (%)	...	54.2	43.1	36.5	33.5	38.5
	Domestic credit to private sector (% of GDP)	...	60.2	50.3	40.3	37.5	36.9
	Liquid liabilities to GDP (%)	...	69.4	64.8	53.4	43.2	60.6
	Private credit by deposit money banks and other financial institutions to GDP (%)	...	54.2	43.1	35.8	32.5	37.0
	Private credit by deposit money banks to GDP (%)	...	54.2	43.1	35.8	32.3	36.8
Cambodia	Central bank assets to GDP (%)	2.5	2.1	2.0	1.1	0.9	0.6
	Deposit money bank assets to deposit money bank assets and central bank assets (%)	55.3	71.5	75.1	88.3	94.2	97.7
	Deposit money banks' assets to GDP (%)	3.2	5.4	5.9	8.6	14.0	25.0
	Domestic credit to private sector (% of GDP)	3.5	5.7	6.3	9.0	18.2	27.6
	Liquid liabilities to GDP (%)	6.4	10.0	11.6	18.1	25.6	38.0
	Private credit by deposit money banks and other financial institutions to GDP (%)	3.1	5.3	5.9	8.2	13.9	25.0
	Private credit by deposit money banks to GDP (%)	3.1	5.3	5.9	8.2	13.9	25.0
Lao PDR	Central bank assets to GDP (%)	0.8	4.8	4.4	2.4	2.1	6.1
	Deposit money bank assets to deposit money bank assets and central bank assets (%)	87.3	66.0	65.7	77.3	77.7	75.7
	Deposit money banks' assets to GDP (%)	5.4	9.3	8.5	8.2	7.4	19.1
	Domestic credit to private sector (% of GDP)	9.1	8.4	8.9	7.4	6.5	20.9
	Liquid liabilities to GDP (%)	6.7	14.0	13.7	16.7	18.5	29.8
	Private credit by deposit money banks and other financial institutions to GDP (%)	3.9	7.0	6.5	5.5	5.1	17.0
	Private credit by deposit money banks to GDP (%)	3.9	7.0	6.5	5.5	5.1	17.0

continued on next page

Table 21.3: *continued*

Country	Indicator	1995	1999	2000	2005	2007	2010
Myanmar	Central bank assets to GDP (%)	22.3	12.1	13.2	13.3	11.9	13.8
	Deposit money bank assets to deposit money bank assets and central bank assets (%)	26.6	41.5	41.1	24.4	21.9	40.3
	Deposit money banks' assets to GDP (%)	8.1	8.6	9.2	4.3	3.3	9.3
	Domestic credit to private sector (% of GDP)	7.6	8.1	9.5	4.7	3.4	4.8
	Liquid liabilities to GDP (%)	27.1	19.7	23.2	16.4	14.6	20.1
	Private credit by deposit money banks and other financial institutions to GDP (%)	6.3	6.6	7.1	3.5	2.8	3.9
	Private credit by deposit money banks to GDP (%)	6.3	6.6	7.1	3.5	2.8	3.9
Vietnam	Central bank assets to GDP (%)	2.1	3.0	2.6	2.1	1.4	3.7
	Deposit money bank assets to deposit money bank assets and central bank assets (%)	90.6	89.5	92.5	96.6	98.2	96.7
	Deposit money banks' assets to GDP (%)	19.9	25.5	32.0	59.9	77.4	108.3
	Domestic credit to private sector (% of GDP)	18.5	28.2	35.3	60.5	85.6	114.7
	Liquid liabilities to GDP (%)	19.1	30.1	38.7	63.0	83.0	101.1
	Private credit by deposit money banks and other financial institutions to GDP (%)	18.1	24.0	30.3	53.6	69.7	100.0
	Private credit by deposit money banks to GDP (%)	18.1	24.0	30.3	53.6	69.7	100.0

... = not available, GDP = gross domestic product, Lao PDR = Lao People's Democratic Republic.
Source: Global Financial Development database, data downloaded November 27, 2020.

The Asian Financial Crisis

BCLMV Regional Overview

When the AFC hit in 1997, the financial systems of BCLMV were fairly underdeveloped and not well linked to global financial markets (Table 21.3). Therefore, there were limited channels through which the worst effects of the regional crisis could be transmitted domestically. The so-called double mismatch problem, involving long-term borrowings in foreign currency being financed by short-term domestic currency loans, did not exist in these countries due to nascent domestic financial systems. BCLMV also did not experience the rapid and disruptive flight of volatile, short-term capital that crippled other Asian countries because the amount of portfolio capital in these countries was nonexistent or small, since they did not have stock or debt securities markets at the time (ADB 2010; Jeasakul et al. 2014; Okonjo-Iweala et al. 1999).

On the positive side, the large rural sectors that characterized the developing nature of CLMV served as a cushion against the worst effects of the AFC. Although the share of the agricultural sector in GDP in CLMV continues to decline, it was still quite high when the AFC hit, ranging between 40% and 60% in CLM and 25% in Vietnam (Table 21.1). The share of the labor force employed in agriculture was much higher than its share in GDP, signifying its even greater importance. Agriculture employed about 80% of the labor force in Cambodia and Lao PDR, and more than 60% in Myanmar and Vietnam, just before the AFC hit. A large agricultural sector provides a buffer during external crises because demand for output is generally inelastic and a significant share of demand is domestic.

However, the crisis hit at a time when CLMV were slowly becoming linked to the region through trade (Figure 21.1) and FDI (Figure 21.2A). This growth in trade and FDI helped fuel years of sustained development in CLMV. However, growing interconnectedness also made them increasingly reliant on economic growth and stability elsewhere in the region and, therefore, more vulnerable to external shocks. The AFC also hit CLMV while these countries were in the process of undertaking market-oriented reforms. With many reforms unfinished or delayed, CLMV came into the crisis with weak macroeconomic fundamentals and long-standing structural vulnerabilities (Okonjo-Iweala et al. 1999).

The temptation to retreat behind borders and raise tariff and nontariff barriers (NTBs) to protect domestic output and employment is heightened during times of economic crisis. Some of the Mekong countries succumbed to this temptation by raising temporary tariffs and other NTBs, although there was no major shift in the overall thrust of their policies to continue liberalizing and reforming their economies. Most of the protection measures were removed soon after the effects of the AFC had dissipated.

The borders of the countries in the Mekong region are porous, with large numbers of workers crossing them regularly, sometimes on a daily basis. Pre-AFC, there was a significant number of people from CLMV working in crisis-hit countries, especially Thailand. The economic downturn in these countries affected migrant workers more than domestic workers. The contractual arrangements applying to legal migrant workers made them easier to retrench. Policy changes in response to rising unemployment in Thailand and other crisis-hit countries resulted in a reduction in the number of legal migrant workers they were willing to accept during the crisis.

A significant proportion of workers from Cambodia, Lao PDR, and Myanmar are believed to be working in Thailand illegally. The crisis resulted in an intensification of efforts to crackdown on illegal migrant workers. For instance, Thailand announced in February 1998 that it would repatriate 300,000 illegal workers from Myanmar and Cambodia over a 6-month period.[7] Other ASEAN countries such as Malaysia and Singapore also tightened restrictions on legal migration or intensified efforts to curtail illegal migrant workers. Both legal and illegal migrant workers were forced to return home to local conditions that were worse than when they left. This resulted in the replacement of a valuable flow of remittances with an increase in the pool of the locally unemployed. The reported fall in remittances may also be underestimated to the extent that illegal or unrecorded migrant workers were forced to return home.

In the case of CLMV, the impact on their real economies was aggravated by a weakened capacity to implement a countercyclical macroeconomic policy. At least some of the tools of macroeconomic stabilization were either blunt or unavailable in these countries. Varying degrees of dollarization and the multiple currency phenomenon in Cambodia and Lao PDR, in particular, but also Myanmar and Vietnam, and the Currency Board Arrangement in Brunei complicated the conduct of monetary policy.

The monetary and exchange rate conditions in these countries made it difficult for their real exchange rates to adjust quickly or adequately to exogenous shocks and, therefore, to work as stabilizers in moving their

---

[7] Reported in "Repatriation of Burmese workers blasted," *Bangkok Post*, February 16, 1998, page 1.

respective economies back toward pre-shock conditions. That is, in these economies, nominal exchange rate changes could not play much of a role in delivering the required real exchange rate adjustments, and the burden of adjustment fell on factor prices instead (Menon 2012).

For instance, the real exchange rate depreciation required to correct growing current account deficits had to involve changes to factor prices, especially wages, and this was often slow, if not difficult to implement. Even in Brunei, the currency peg to the Singapore dollar limited discretionary adjustments to the nominal exchange rate, although the depreciation of the Singapore dollar during the AFC flowed through domestically, and indirectly assisted in the adjustment.

Limited fiscal headroom due to difficulties in collecting taxes constrained the ability of fiscal policy to play a significant role in limiting the growth slowdown. On top of this, mistakes were also made where inappropriate policy responses were pursued, sometimes aggravating the situation and adding to economic and social costs.

BCLMV Country Experiences

Brunei

Brunei entered the AFC in a somewhat good position, with the economy growing by around 3% (Figure 21.3A) on the back of strong construction and services, benign inflation, and a healthy current account surplus. Although the AFC affected the economy in 1998, oil and gas export revenues and an increase in net foreign assets largely insulated the economy, with the Brunei Investment Agency providing a buffer that cushioned the immediate impact of the shock. Brunei had a relatively liberal trade policy regime following its membership of the General Agreement on Tariffs and Trade (GATT) in 1993. This, combined with the currency peg to the Singapore dollar, helped provide stability.

Nonetheless, the AFC led to a further decline in economic activity, particularly in construction, with Brunei being the only country among the BCLMV to suffer a recession. Although the government had initially planned to reduce public expenditures before the crisis hit, authorities decided to forgo this in favor of increased spending to help fuel the sluggish economy (IMF 1999a).

Cambodia

Between 1990 and 1996, Cambodia's economy was growing at an average of 5.4% a year (Figure 21.3A), supported by strong growth in trade and investment.

The AFC led to slower economic growth, a depreciation in the riel, and an increase in inflation. However, severity of the crisis' effect was relatively muted compared to other countries. This was due to several factors. First,

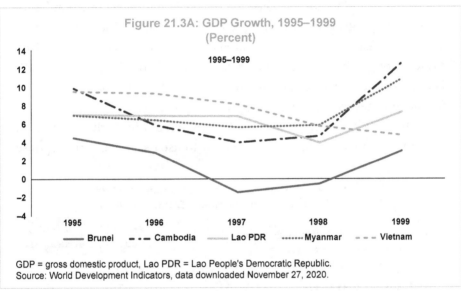

Figure 21.3A: GDP Growth, 1995–1999 (Percent)

GDP = gross domestic product, Lao PDR = Lao People's Democratic Republic.
Source: World Development Indicators, data downloaded November 27, 2020.

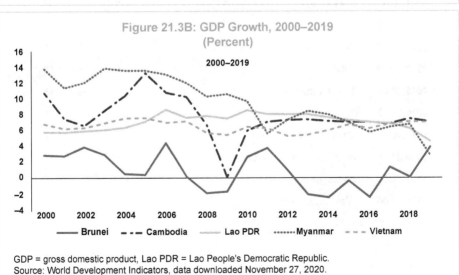

Figure 21.3B: GDP Growth, 2000–2019 (Percent)

GDP = gross domestic product, Lao PDR = Lao People's Democratic Republic.
Source: World Development Indicators, data downloaded November 27, 2020.

Cambodia's exports were not significantly affected by the crisis (Figure 21.1). Cambodia's main exports were garments, and these were mainly exported outside the region to markets in the EU and the US. With tariff-free access under the Generalized System of Preferences (GSP), these exports were relatively unaffected and remained buoyant despite the AFC. The booming garments sector allowed Cambodia to increase its reserves to 2.5 months of imports in the midst of the crisis (Okonjo-Iweala et al. 1999).

On the import side, there was concern that the sharp depreciation of the Thai baht in particular had left domestic producers of a number of import-competing goods with a significant competitive disadvantage. In an attempt to offset this, tariffs were raised on 12 products that were perceived to face strong import competition from Thailand in particular (Table 21.4). For two of these products, tariffs were increased from 15% to 35%, while for the rest they were more doubled from 7% to 15%.[8]

The AFC, however, revealed certain vulnerabilities in the Cambodian economy, particularly its limited capacity to use fiscal policy in response

Table 21.4: Cambodian Import-Competing Products that Underwent Tariff Increases During the AFC

Code No.	Product Description	Pre-AFC Rate (%)	Post-AFC Rate (%)
1902.30.10	Noodles (packet)	7	15
2501.00.91	Cooking salt	15	35
2523.00.00	Cement	7	15
3917.00.00	Pipes	7	15
3923.00.00	Tubes	7	15
4011.20.00	Tires for trucks or buses	7	15
4011.50.00	Tires for bicycles	7	15
4013.10.00	Cooling or heating coils (vehicles)	15	35
4013.20.00	Cooling or heating coils (bicycles)	7	15
6904.00.00	Bricks (clay)	7	15
6905.00.00	Tiles (clay)	7	15

AFC = Asian financial crisis.
Source: Ministry of Economy and Finance, Royal Government of Cambodia.

---

[8] Since Cambodia did not join the World Trade Organization (WTO) until 2004, the raising of tariffs in this manner did not incur any legal repercussions.

to external shocks. Because the economy is highly dollarized, limiting the use of monetary policy, the government had to rely on fiscal policy to maintain macroeconomic stability. At the time, Cambodia's fiscal position was constrained by weak revenue collection, overspending on the military budget, and a lack of foreign budgetary support, matters made worse by domestic political uncertainty. Faced with these challenges, the government had no choice but to cut spending in order to achieve fiscal balance. This led to a reduction in spending on civilian operations (including health and education) and maintenance outlays (IMF 1999b).

Cambodia also went through a period of political turmoil that coincided with the onset of the AFC. The fighting between troops loyal to joint Prime Ministers Hun Sen and Norodom Ranaridh, which eventually led to the collapse of the coalition government, started on July 5, 1997, only 3 days after the baht collapsed and signaled the start of the AFC. A long period of uncertainty ensued, lasting more than a year, before a new government was formed in November 1998. It was only at this point that public confidence started to slowly return. Economic activity, particularly in tourism and retail trade, took a bit longer and started to pick up only in late 1998 (IMF 1999b). The overlap or coincidence of an independent political crisis and a financial crisis in the neighborhood made it difficult to disentangle or isolate their respective effects on the economy.

Lao PDR

Lao PDR enjoyed a period of fast growth and low inflation from the late 1980s up until 1997, the result of several market-oriented economic reforms encompassing taxation, trade and investment liberalization, and privatization of state enterprises. In 1997, however, reform efforts started to stall and the government began loosening monetary and fiscal policies. This set the stage for a deterioration in macroeconomic conditions that was made worse by the impact of the AFC (IMF 1999c, 1999d). In this sense, the AFC did not cause but accelerated an ongoing trend of economic instability.

Prior to the AFC, the Lao PDR economy was growing at an average rate of 6.4% a year between 1990 and 1996 (Figure 21.3A). This growth slowed to 5.5% in 1997 and 1998, marking the sharpest decline in growth among the newer member countries of ASEAN. Although garments exports helped shore up manufacturing — garments manufacturing actually grew in 1998 with the reinstatement of the EU's GSP — construction declined significantly as investments projects stalled (IMF 1999d). The AFC's impact on the Thai economy delayed investments in hydropower in Lao PDR, leading to a decline in FDI inflows. The AFC led to a decline in FDI from USD 104 million in 1997 to roughly USD 60 million a year in 1998 and 1999 (IMF 1999c).

The Lao PDR government introduced a number of policies relating to the monetary conditions in the country in 1997, although not all were in response to the AFC. In June 1997, just before the onset of the AFC, the Bank of Lao PDR moved to enforce the decree that stipulated that only the local currency, kip, could be used as a medium of exchange in domestic transactions.[9] Although increased policing of the use of the kip increased its use in domestic transactions, it did not stop the use of baht or US dollars. The enforcement measures were designed to curb the depreciation of the kip due to black market speculation, but instead of stemming its depreciation, it accelerated it. Indeed, the kip was perhaps the only currency to have fallen in value against the baht during a time when the baht was depreciating against almost every other currency during the early phase of the AFC (Figure 21.4).

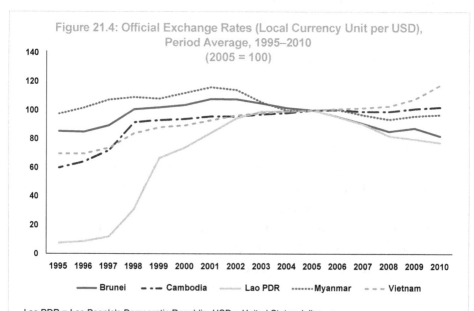

Figure 21.4: Official Exchange Rates (Local Currency Unit per USD), Period Average, 1995–2010 (2005 = 100)

Brunei · · Cambodia — Lao PDR ····· Myanmar · · · Vietnam

Lao PDR = Lao People's Democratic Republic, USD = United States dollar.
Source: Author's calculations using data from the World Development Indicators, data downloaded November 27, 2020.

---

[9] This move was essentially an enforcement measure, as Decree No. 53, dated September 7, 1990, and has always made it illegal to employ foreign currencies in domestic transactions.

The lack of monetary instruments in the form of kip-denominated interest-bearing assets prevents the Bank of Lao PDR from effectively conducting open market operations to control the money supply. Therefore, the government had to employ other tools to try and implement its monetary policy. To offset the anticipated growth slowdown emanating from the AFC, the government tried to pursue an expansionary monetary policy by abandoning bank credit ceilings, a policy that was sustained through to 1998. This led to a rapid growth in broad money and an expansion in credit to both the private and public sectors (IMF 1999d).

Meanwhile, weak fiscal management and the failure to follow through on key revenue reforms led to large public deficits in 1997 and 1998. The government sought to plug this deficit through substantial central bank financing. However, with the economy highly dollarized, under-monetized, and largely dependent on Thailand, this fiscal expansion led to triple-digit inflation and further depreciation in the kip (IMF 1999c, 1999d). Consumer price inflation reached 90% in 1998 and peaked at almost 130% in 1999 (Figure 21.5).

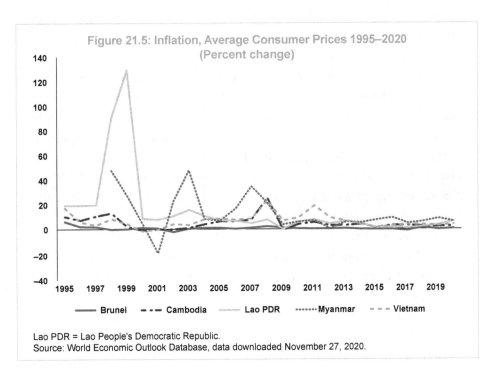

Figure 21.5: Inflation, Average Consumer Prices 1995–2020 (Percent change)

Lao PDR = Lao People's Democratic Republic.
Source: World Economic Outlook Database, data downloaded November 27, 2020.

From the late 1998 to early 1999, the government tried to tighten monetary and fiscal policies in an attempt to stabilize the macroeconomy, but these efforts were difficult to implement and not sustained. Instead, foreign exchange and price pressures were largely addressed through administrative measures, which were ultimately also ineffective. By the third quarter of 1999, renewed efforts at tightening started to finally bear fruit, halting a further depreciation in the currency and easing inflation somewhat (IMF 1999c, 1999d).

Myanmar

Myanmar enjoyed solid economic growth in the years prior to the AFC, although this performance paled in comparison to Cambodia, Lao PDR, and Vietnam (Figure 21.3A).

While CLV were already several years into implementing market-oriented reforms, Myanmar remained a closed and highly controlled economy; many barriers to trade, investment, and currency exchange remained in place. Myanmar's macroeconomic fundamentals were also less sound compared to its neighbors. Net international foreign exchange reserves were low, leading to frequent shortages, and more than a third of international debt was in arrears (IMF 1999e).

Despite starting from a somewhat weaker macroeconomic position, Myanmar appeared to have weathered the AFC better than most other countries. The relatively free market exchange rate depreciated rapidly against the dollar after the Thai baht was floated (Figure 21.4), triggering a rise in inflation (Figure 21.5). By the last quarter of 1998, however, the exchange rate started to strengthen, and inflation began to ease (IMF 1999e). Nongas exports remained buoyant despite the crisis, helping to offset the loss of expected revenues from gas exports due to lower energy demand from Thailand. Although new FDI commitments fell to zero in 1998/1999, FDI inflows from previous commitments held up (Figure 21.2A). Worker's remittances from abroad also continued, as did tourism receipts despite a slow down in the growth of tourism arrivals (Figure 21.6).

Myanmar was able to avoid the worst effects of the AFC mainly due to its continued insularity. For instance, exports were less than 15% as a share of GDP in 1995 and remains low until today (18% in 2018). On top of this, Myanmar employed additional protectionist measures to insulate itself further, such as tightening import controls and revoking foreign exchange licenses of private banks to reduce the demand for foreign exchange (IMF 1999e). While this inward-looking approach prevented Myanmar from participating more fully in the social and economic progress that CLV enjoyed both before and after the AFC, it did significantly limit negative contagion from the AFC permeating its economy.

Vietnam

Vietnam's trade and investment linkages within the region were the strongest among BCLMV. The AFC therefore led to a sharp fall in economic activity, with real GDP growth declining from almost 10% between 1995 and 1996 to 7% between 1997 and 1998 (Figure 21.3A).

As with other countries, however, this drop in economic activity was not purely a result of the AFC. Vietnam was already at a disadvantaged position when the AFC hit, and as such suffered the greatest damage among the newer member countries of ASEAN. FDI was a major driver of Vietnam's growth leading up to the crisis, but these inflows were largely channeled to the nontradeable sector and inefficient import-substituting industries. In addition, most FDI projects had to be done through joint projects with state-owned enterprises (SOEs). The inability of these industries to absorb the large inflow of FDI was already leading to excess capacity when the AFC hit. When the sudden drop in FDI in 1997 revealed major weaknesses in these industries (Figure 21.2A), the government responded by further increasing protection through the use of quotas and licensing. The government also continued to support SOEs through the provision of bank credit (IMF 1999f, 2000), ultimately leading to a build-up of inflationary pressures (Figure 21.5).

The slowdown in growth, expansion in credit, and worsening financial position of SOEs placed added pressure on the banking system that was already grappling with a weak capital base, low profitability, and mounting nonperforming loans (NPLs) (IMF 1999f).

Although the economy began showing signs of recovery by mid-1999, this was largely driven by strong exports and increases in rice production. FDI, domestic demand, and imports remained sluggish, however. Both monetary and fiscal policies were relaxed in 1999 to help spur recovery. Reforms covering trade, private investment, foreign exchange, banking, and SOEs also picked up momentum in order to support recovery.

The Global Financial Crisis

BCLMV Regional Overview

The transition toward a more market-based economy in CLMV gathered pace during the decade between the AFC and the GFC. Trade and investment liberalization were aggressively pursued as part of commitments to the ASEAN Free Trade Area (AFTA), as were other reforms in the real and financial sectors, producing high rates of economic growth (Figure 21.2B). CLMV grew by more than 7.0% on average between 2000 and 2007, while ASEAN as a whole grew at about 5.5%. Brunei was the worst performing economy in ASEAN, however, managing only 2.2% during this period. By the time the GFC erupted in 2008, BCLMV had become more deeply connected with global markets as well. Because of this, and as small, open economies, they were quite susceptible to the vagaries of the GFC, and more so than when the AFC hit (ADB 2010). Brunei fell into a recession, Cambodia's growth fell to zero, and growth in Vietnam and Myanmar slowed significantly.

Trade was the main transmission channel, with exports contracting as demand in advanced economies receded (Figure 21.1). The crisis also dampened tourism and reduced remittances, although remittances remained buoyant and made up for the contraction in exports in some countries. The financial shocks were transmitted through greater volatility in the capital and foreign exchange markets; a contraction in credit, investment, and official aid; and a sharp fall in asset values. Nonetheless, the monetary and financial systems of BCLMV remained largely stable and resilient (ADB 2010; Parulian 2009). Exposure to toxic subprime assets was limited for Asia as a whole. The ADB (2010) estimated that the region's direct exposure to these assets was a mere 0.09%. Deleveraging and capital outflows had a bigger impact on the economies, but these outflows eventually recovered as advanced economies cut interest rates and the US pursued aggressive monetary easing (ADB 2009).

Although the GFC inflicted damage on BCLMV economies, the effects were somewhat milder and recovery was faster for most countries when

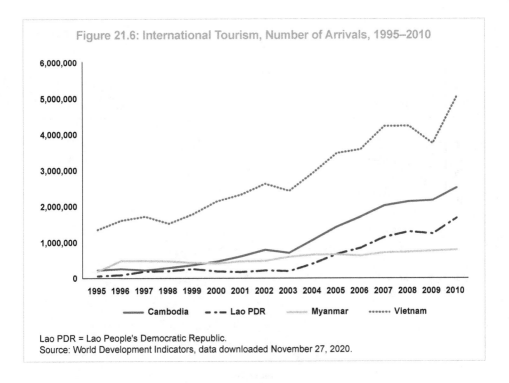

Figure 21.6: International Tourism, Number of Arrivals, 1995–2010

Lao PDR = Lao People's Democratic Republic.
Source: World Development Indicators, data downloaded November 27, 2020.

compared to the AFC. This was mainly because the starting conditions in these countries were better this time around. Across BCLMV, domestic fundamentals were stronger and prudent economic management in the years leading up to the GFC helped mitigate the effects of the crisis. Current account positions in CLV were generally stronger leading up to the GFC (Figure 21.7B) compared to the AFC (Figure 21.7A). Less intervention to support domestic currency values in foreign exchange markets also resulted in greater accumulation of foreign exchange reserves. With the exception of Vietnam, credit expansion was moderate and inflation was benign. Fiscal conditions were also good, with countries enjoying modest deficits and debt burdens leading up to the GFC (Jeasakul et al. 2014; Park et al. 2013). For these reasons, BCLMV had more space and better macroeconomic conditions and instruments to implement countercyclical monetary and fiscal policies to mitigate the impact of the GFC compared to the AFC.

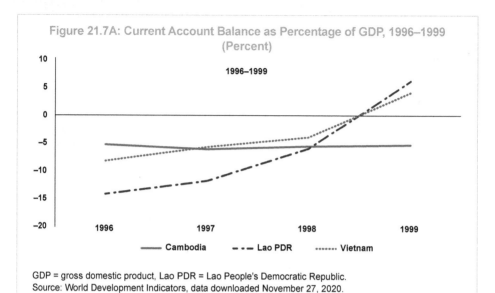

Figure 21.7A: Current Account Balance as Percentage of GDP, 1996–1999 (Percent)

GDP = gross domestic product, Lao PDR = Lao People's Democratic Republic.
Source: World Development Indicators, data downloaded November 27, 2020.

Figure 21.7B: Current Account Balance as Percentage of GDP, 2005–2010 (Percent)

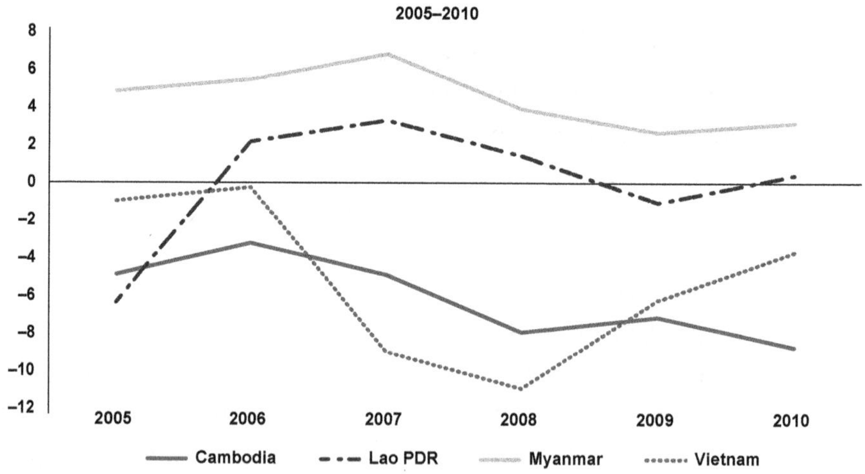

GDP = gross domestic product, Lao PDR = Lao People's Democratic Republic.
Source: World Development Indicators, data downloaded November 27, 2020.

BCLMV Country Experiences

Brunei

As with the AFC, Brunei was the only country among the newer members of ASEAN to have suffered a recession as a result of the GFC. Although growth had started to slow prior to the onset of the GFC, it turned negative and averaged −1.9% in 2008 and 2009 (Figure 21.3B). This was mainly driven by weaker energy demand from traditional markets and maintenance-related stoppages led to a fall in the production of oil and gas and liquified natural gas output. The fall in energy prices resulted in a significant deterioration in Brunei's terms of trade (Figure 21.8). Weaker trade, tourism, and manufacturing slowed growth in the nonenergy sector as well. Lower economic activity also dulled demand for imports.

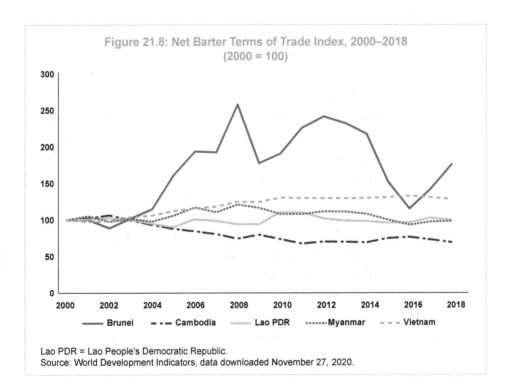

Figure 21.8: Net Barter Terms of Trade Index, 2000–2018
(2000 = 100)

Lao PDR = Lao People's Democratic Republic.
Source: World Development Indicators, data downloaded November 27, 2020.

Large structural liquidity, adequate capital, and limited exposure to toxic assets kept the financial sector stable, while the continuation of price controls and the decline in global commodities prices helped temper inflation. The market value of assets managed by the Brunei Investment Agency was affected by the GFC but eventually rebounded. The peg to the Singapore dollar and the Currency Interchangeability Arrangement continued to keep the currency stable (IMF 2010a).

The government responded to the GFC by reducing the corporate income tax and increasing the implementation capacity and speed of development projects. Financial regulators also worked with banks to develop a financial sector emergency plan and introduce a blanket deposit guarantee along with other countries in the region (IMF 2010a).

Cambodia

Prior to the GFC, Cambodia was experiencing a decade of high growth, with real GDP growing by an average of 9.6% between 2000 and 2007 (Figure 21.3B). Cambodia's growth fell to 6.4% in 2008 and then collapsed to almost zero in 2009 as demand for exports slowed in the US as well as the EU. These were the traditional markets for its exports of garments, textiles, and footwear, which together accounted for most of its exports. Of all the newer members of ASEAN, Cambodia was the country with strongest trade ties with the US, with about half of its exports destined there just prior to the GFC. The US and the EU accounted for about two-thirds of its exports at the time, consisting mostly of garments traded under GSP privileges. This geographical distribution of trade played out as a major negative factor during the GFC as the US and the EU were the worst hit countries. FDI inflows also contracted (Figure 21.2B), as did tourism receipts, *albeit* to a lesser extent (Figure 21.6).

The government sought to cushion the GFC's impact by raising minimum wages and accelerating development spending, causing an increase in the overall fiscal deficit. These were mainly financed through concessional loans and grants, although domestic financing also increased and reached almost 2% of GDP. In addition, the National Bank of Cambodia (NBC) eased reserve requirements from 16% to 12% and introduced an overdraft facility. However, as with the AFC, the government's response was hampered by the limited fiscal revenue base and the high degree of dollarization (IMF 2010b).

Cambodia's economy began bouncing back by 2010. By the end of 2010, exports and FDI inflows had increased by about 20.0% and 50.0%, respectively (Figure 21.2B), while tourist arrivals and tourism receipts rose by about 16.0% and 14.5%, respectively (Figure 21.6). GDP growth bounced back to 6% in 2010, and then 7.1% in 2011, which was about the average growth rate for the remainder of the ensuing decade.

Lao PDR

Like Cambodia, the GFC affected Lao PDR's exports, FDI inflows, and tourism arrivals and receipts. However, Lao PDR managed to weather the GFC relatively well. Although its growth slowed down in 2008, this growth was still one of the highest in Southeast Asia during the GFC (Figure 21.3B). This was mainly due to ongoing projects in the mining and hydropower sectors and accommodative monetary and fiscal policies, which helped boost construction activity and stimulated domestic demand and imports (ADB 2011). Mining and hydropower projects have long gestation periods and are less likely to be greatly affected by a temporary event such as the GFC. Furthermore, both the price and sales of the output of hydropower projects were pre-determined by long-term, binding power purchase agreements (mostly with Thailand) and, therefore, were relatively immune from the impact of the GFC. These special features of the Lao economy created a buffer that insulated it from some of the effects of the GFC.

Accommodative policies put pressure on both the balance of payments and the fiscal deficit, but macroeconomic fundamentals remained largely sound (Figure 21.7B). Lao PDR also did a better job of containing inflation during the GFC compared to the AFC (Figure 21.5).

By 2010, growth returned to pre-crisis levels, led by strong growth in industry at 16%. Tourism rebounded increasing by about 25%, allowing the hotel and restaurant industry to grow by 6% (Figure 21.6). Services as a whole grew by 5% (ADB 2011).

Myanmar

The GFC's impact on Myanmar was mainly transmitted through the economic slowdowns in neighboring countries with which it had some trade and investment linkages. This, together with the collapse in commodity prices (Figure 21.8) and the impact of Cyclone Nargis, led to a reduction in

GDP growth to its lowest level since the AFC in 2008 (Figure 21.3B). The slowdown in Thailand led to a decline in natural gas production and exports, while private consumption was hit due to lower remittances from workers in Thailand, Malaysia, and Singapore. By 2009, growth had recovered on the back of improved performance in the agriculture, mining, manufacturing, and transport and communications subsectors. Demand for exports rose as recovery took hold in Myanmar's neighbors. The government managed to contain inflation by financing part of its fiscal deficit through Treasury bond issues instead of fully relying on money creation (ADB 2010, 2011).

Vietnam

Conditions in Vietnam in the run-up to the GFC were somewhat similar to conditions prior to the AFC. After years of impressive growth fueled by massive FDI inflows, the Vietnamese economy was showing signs of overheating in 2007 (Menon 2009). Aggregate demand pressures, coupled with rising commodity prices, caused inflation to rise to double digits (Figure 21.5). Both the fiscal and current account deficits were on the rise as well (Figure 21.7B). Early in 2008, the State Bank of Vietnam (SBV) began taking steps to stabilize the economy, and the economy entered a contractionary phase in the first half of 2008 (Hung and An 2011; IMF 2008).

The onset of the GFC weakened exports, FDI, remittances, and domestic demand. The trade to GDP ratio was the highest among BCLMV but fell from 157% in 2008 to 136% in 2009 (Figure 21.1). This sharp drop was due to the fact that its main export markets were badly hit by the GFC, namely the US, the EU, and Japan. Imports of intermediate goods also fell sharply, reflecting Vietnam's growing importance in global supply chains.

Growing risk aversion led to massive portfolio investment outflows, and the Vietnam stock index fell about two-thirds in 2008, accompanied by further depreciation in the dong (IMF 2008). The GFC also exposed vulnerabilities in the banking system, which had high loan-to-deposit ratios (Table 21.3) and which relied considerably on short-term interbank funding.

To mitigate the impact of the GFC, accommodative fiscal and monetary policies were pursued. An economic stimulus plan was launched, with a wide range of incentives aimed at supporting exporters (Hung and An 2011). The SBV lowered policy rates and reduced reserve requirements. The SBV also devalued the dong and widened the dong-US dollar trading band to relieve currency pressures.

Exports began rebounding in 2009, driven by textiles, footwear, and electronics and computers. FDI, remittances, and tourism receipts also began to recover (Figures 21.2B and 21.6). The SBV started withdrawing monetary stimulus beginning late 2009, and most fiscal stimulus measures expired by late 2009 (ADB 2011).

Lessons for Policy and Regional Financial Cooperation

Lessons for Policy

Overall, it appears that the AFC had a slightly greater impact on BCLMV than the GFC. This is also related to the fact that the effects were slightly longer lived, or the recovery not as rapid, with the AFC compared to the GFC. But there are several qualifications that need to be made.

First, there were differences in the effects of each crisis across the countries in the group. For instance, Cambodia was clearly more severely affected by the GFC than the AFC, even though the AFC coincided with an independently occurring political crisis at home. On the other hand, Lao PDR appears more severely affected by the AFC as its macroeconomic problems had started before the AFC. While the AFC clearly accelerated and compounded these problems, not all the observed effects can be attributed to the AFC alone. It is also difficult to accurately attribute effects to the AFC or GFC in the other countries as well, since they were all only indirectly affected by both crises. With these caveats in mind, however, there are still some lessons that can be drawn from the experience from these crises.

Despite the impact of the GFC being more pronounced due to greater integration both regionally and globally, this should not be a basis to slow or fear the reforms that supported such integration. There are a number of reasons for this. To begin with, the remarkable achievements in improving economic and social conditions, especially for the poor, were not seriously affected by the GFC. This was largely because these countries were better equipped to deal with the GFC as a result of the very same reforms that increased their exposure to the contagion. The reforms had produced more robust economic and financial systems with more effective macroeconomic policy instruments. The GFC did not last as long as the AFC because it was not misdiagnosed, and so appropriate remedial measures were applied and were done so aggressively in the US and Europe (Grenville 2013). This limited the long-term consequences, or economic scarring, from the crisis.

If the BCLMV had been better prepared to deal with a crisis when the GFC hit, why was the recovery from the GFC only marginally faster than that from the AFC? The fact that recovery speeds were not very different had more to do with the nature of the two crises than preparedness or ability to deal with them. Unlike the GFC, which resulted in a global recession, the growth slowdowns associated with the AFC were mostly regional, confined mainly to Southeast and East Asia. Therefore, crisis-hit countries were able to export their way out of recession, aided by buoyant global demand and highly competitive exchange rates as a result of massive currency depreciations. Just as the negative contagion slowed down growth in BCLMV, so did positive contagion when the rapid recovery set in among their neighbors. BCLMV were able to ride the so-called V-shaped recovery taking place all around them, and quickly regained the growth momentum which they had before the AFC hit. Neither the original members of ASEAN nor the newer ones could export their way out of the GFC because it was a global slowdown that affected most of their export markets.

In both cases, however, the fact that BCLMV, like the original ASEAN members, resisted the temptation to turn inward or raise significant protective barriers created conditions to support recovery. Had these countries succumbed to the protection temptation, then both the speed and the nature of the recovery may have been very different and this could have resulted in long-term consequences that may have delayed their transition toward market-based economies.

Lessons for Regional Financial Cooperation

The AFC prompted the region's policymakers to realize the importance of economic and financial cooperation, given the region's deepening economic interdependence. Following the crisis, ASEAN and the "Plus Three" countries — China, Korea, and Japan — embarked on various initiatives to manage such interdependence and achieve stable economic growth.

In the monetary and financial area, three key initiatives were undertaken by the finance ministers of ASEAN+3 to promote regional financial cooperation:

- Introduction of a regional economic review and policy dialogue process (ASEAN+3 ERPD);

- Establishment of a regional reserve pooling arrangement (Chiang Mai Initiative, CMI); and

- Development of local-currency bond markets (Asian Bond Markets Initiative, ABMI).

All three are interrelated, and serve, in varying degrees, to prevent the recurrence of financial crises. The ASEAN+3 ERPD and the CMI were both launched by the ASEAN+3 Finance Ministers in May 2000. More than the ABMI, the CMI and the ERPD were created to prevent the recurrence of regional financial crises and to contain such crises effectively, if and when they occur.

The ERPD is designed to assist in the prevention of financial crises through the early detection of irregularities and vulnerabilities and the swift implementation of remedial policy actions. The mechanism is intended to facilitate information sharing, exchanges of views, and collaboration on financial, monetary, and fiscal issues of common interest.[10] Although the ERPD is only one of several surveillance mechanisms created in the wake of the AFC, it soon became the core mechanism for regional economic surveillance, due to its linkage to the CMI (Kawai and Houser 2008). The ERPD has worked relatively well but could be improved to better serve its members, especially the newer members.

CLMV are arguably more susceptible to domestic or external shocks as they continue their transition to becoming more mature market economies, with the side note that Brunei is often subject to terms of trade shocks given its heavy reliance on oil exports. For the ERPD to be more effective, its formal processes must move away from the current focus on information exchange to include stronger peer review and due diligence functions. Peer review will allow member countries to identify domestic policies that can impinge on regional economic stability, as well as enable them to persuade poorly

---

[10]The ERPD process encompasses the following five aspects: (i) assessing global, regional, and national economic conditions; (ii) monitoring regional capital flows and currency markets; (iii) analyzing macroeconomic and financial risks; (iv) strengthening banking and financial system conditions; and (v) providing an Asian voice in the reform of the international financial system.

performing countries to take corrective policy measures. ASEAN+3 can use peer review not only to conduct country-by-country examinations but also to assess cross-country thematic issues or broader issues of regional cooperation.

How has this played out in practice? The ERPD has to move away from what critics have referred to as a "beauty contest," where discussions are highly guarded and tend to highlight positive developments while ignoring or even suppressing vulnerabilities or other negative aspects. It is only when there is sufficient trust among members that the peer review process is able to mature into an open and frank discussion of risks and vulnerabilities so that the ERPD can be of maximum value to BCLMV and other members.

Disenchantment with the International Monetary Fund (IMF) programs in crisis-hit countries following the AFC was a key driver in developing the CMI to provide an alternative in the form of a regional financial safety net. The CMI's first major test came in September 2008 when the GFC struck. Members of the CMI that required liquidity support did not turn to it but instead rushed to secure bilateral swaps with, or financial support from, the US, China, Japan, Australia, regional development banks, and other multilaterals. The regional financial safety net appeared to have failed its members.

This brought about various changes, including: (i) multilateralization of the CMI to become the Chiang Mai Initiative Multilateralisation (CMIM) in 2009, with the many swap lines now governed by a single agreement; (ii) a doubling of its size to USD 240 billion, and an increase in the so-called non-linked share, or the share available without an IMF program to 30%; and (iii) the setting up of an independent surveillance unit, the ASEAN+3 Macroeconomic Research Office (AMRO), in 2011. Several other developments took place over the years, increasing its size further and strengthening AMRO and its surveillance role, but will these be enough to ensure that the CMIM will be called upon when the next crisis strikes? This is a key question and is particularly relevant to BCLMV, whose abilities to access alternative sources of liquidity during an emergency are more limited than other members of ASEAN+3.

Furthermore, as noted earlier, the susceptibility of these transition economies to domestic or external shocks is high. They also do not have the kind of foreign exchange reserves compared to original ASEAN members to serve as a first line of defense in the event of a liquidity crisis. Even if they could, this high-cost mercantilist route of self-insurance through excessive holdings of foreign exchange reserves would be particularly burdensome for these transitional economies.

Despite impressive enhancements to the CMIM over the years, concerns over its operability remain. Unfortunately, the CMIM still appears unusable, either as a co-financing facility in tandem with the IMF or as a stand-alone alternative. There are a number of reasons for this (Takagi 2009), but the main one seems to be the fact that it is constituted as a reserve-pooling arrangement — there is no fund but a series of promises. This is not a problem per se but becomes so when there are no rapid response procedures to handle a fast-developing financial emergency (Menon and Hill 2014).

Therefore, the newer members of ASEAN may need to follow the lead of the original members and pursue bilateral swap arrangements in order to guard against future financial crises, assuming that they can. In fact, bilateral swap arrangements have arguably become the main instrument in Asia's financial safety net. If and until the CMIM becomes operable, there appears to be no other option if these countries want an alternative to the global lender of last resort — the IMF.

The ABMI has mainly served the original members of ASEAN, with little direct impact so far on BCLMV. Although this may be mostly a reflection of the early stage of development and lack of depth of local financial markets in these countries, it does pose a challenge that the ABMI should try and address, if it is to be useful to *all* of its members. There is an obvious causality dilemma here, which was only recognized after the GFC, when the Credit Guarantee Investment Facility (CGIF) was created as part of the ABMI.

The CGIF was established in 2010 to provide guarantees on local currency denominated bonds issued by corporations that may not otherwise have been able to do so. These guarantees are designed to help corporations with no or low credit rating to issue local currency bonds with longer maturities (Azis 2012). The CGIF, unlike other initiatives of the ABMI,[11] has been more successful in reaching some of the newer members of ASEAN and in helping corporations in those countries raise local currency financing at home or in the region.

---

[11] Launched at around the same time as the CGIF was the Asian Bond Market Forum (ABMF). The ABMF was set up as a common platform to foster standardization of market practices and harmonization of regulations relating to cross-border financial transactions in the region. Although the central banks and securities and exchange commissions of BCLMV are involved in the ABMF, the core activities have focused on the original ASEAN members.

Vietnam has been the main beneficiary, and so has Cambodia and Lao PDR. This includes guarantees covering 100% of local currency bond issuances for nine unrated Vietnamese firms and two unrated Cambodian firms. The CGIF also guaranteed a bond issuance in the Singapore market for a Lao PDR-based company, Kolao Holdings.[12] It has been able to do this because it is designed to provide credit enhancement to allow the region's less established issuers to issue local currency bonds and the more established ones to issue across national borders and penetrate new markets by overcoming the sovereign credit ceiling. Currently, however, the majority of guarantees are provided to relatively highly rated firms in the original member countries of ASEAN and recently even one to a Japanese firm issuing a yen-denominated bond in the Japanese market.[13] If the CGIF is to realize its main objectives, then the focus of its guarantee operations will need to shift from the more highly rated firms in the more developed member countries of ASEAN+3 to the lower rated ones in the less developed member countries.[14]

As noted earlier, although the double mismatch problem did not exist in BCLMV when the AFC hit, the CGIF can reduce the risk of it happening in the future, as their financial markets develop and corporate financing needs at home increase. In this respect, the newer members may enjoy a latecomer advantage, by not only learning from the mistakes of the past but also benefiting from measures like the CGIF that were created because of the problems that led to the AFC. The size of the operations of the CGIF remains small, however, an increase over time, which includes a shift toward unrated firms in BCLMV, is required. This needs to be done carefully, however, without compromising its risk profile while providing firms in the LDCs in ASEAN, where the domestic banking systems remain underdeveloped, with possibly the only opportunity to raise local currency financing.

---

[12]For the full portfolio of bond issuances guaranteed (either fully or partially) by the CGIF, see the following section on their website: GUARANTEE PORTFOLIO TABLE (cgif-abmi.org).

[13]On December 24, 2020, CGIF guaranteed 15.4 billion yen-denominated 9-year fixed-rate senior unsecured bond issued by GLP Pte. Ltd. in the Tokyo Pro-Bond market. Details are provided in the following press release: cgif-guarantees-first-jpy-bond.pdf (adb.org)

[14]There are a number of interrelated challenges to be overcome that will take time. Market infrastructure that supports corporate bond market development, including credible local rating agencies, secondary markets, and settlement systems, needs to be strengthened. Also, more issuance of public-sector bonds would be needed to forge stable yield curves and encourage more trading in the secondary market. Without the development of a deep public sector bond market, developing a corporate bond market remains difficult.

Conclusion

When the AFC hit on July 2, 1997, only Brunei and Vietnam were members of ASEAN. Although Lao PDR and Myanmar joined within weeks, and Cambodia a couple of years later, the process of integrating with the region was in its infancy and served to shield the newer members from the worst effects of the economic crisis. Insularity can serve as a buffer during periods of crisis. The lower the share of foreign demand as a source of growth, the lower is the domestic impact from a regional or global slowdown.

The financial systems of these countries were also at an early stage of development and were not yet closely linked across borders or to global financial markets. The lack of such financial links limited the transmission of the contagion emanating from the region and into their domestic economies. BCLMV were in no way immune, however. Although trade and FDI did not contract as much as in the original ASEAN member countries, it was sufficient to reduce growth in all of the newer members in 1998, exposing and magnifying existing vulnerabilities in their macroeconomies and nascent financial sectors.

One such vulnerability was the limited capacity of these countries to implement counter-cyclical stabilization policies using conventional instruments of macroeconomic policy. The monetary situation in CLMV was characterized by varying degrees of dollarization and the multiple currency phenomenon, compromising the ability of their monetary authorities to implement a discretionary monetary policy. In these countries, limited fiscal headroom as a result of weak tax collection capacity prevented fiscal policy from playing a bigger role in boosting growth during the slowdown. This was in sharp contrast to the original ASEAN members that entered the AFC with fiscal surpluses. Therefore, the same factors that limited greater contagion of the crisis also played a role in limiting the capacity of national authorities in addressing the negative consequences that affected their respective domestic economies. Nevertheless, the muted impact from the contagion suggests that overall, the newer members of ASEAN got through the AFC with much less economic scarring than the original members.

When the GFC erupted about a decade later, the financial systems in BCLMV had developed to become more deeply integrated with global markets, *albeit* from a low base. Trade and FDI had also grown sharply over the decade as a result of a wide-ranging program of economic and financial reforms. These outcomes led to greater overall integration with the region and beyond. With this greater interdependence came higher risk of contagion, which played out during the GFC. Except for Lao PDR, which kept growing because of FDI pre-commitments in large mining and hydropower projects, growth slowed significantly in Vietnam and Myanmar, fell to zero in Cambodia, and turned negative in Brunei.

Unlike with the AFC, these countries were better prepared to respond to the effects of the GFC, however. This was a result of the maturing of their economic systems, and improvements in the instruments of macroeconomic policy to address the contagion. Both fiscal and monetary policy were able to play a more effective role in mitigating the impact of the GFC, which also assisted with speeding up their recovery.

The AFC highlighted the need to increase economic and financial cooperation in the context of deepening economic interdependence to address common economic and financial shocks. It gave birth to the ASEAN+3 institution and process, and various initiatives designed to prevent or mitigate the impact of future crises. A process of peer review for early detection of emerging vulnerabilities (ERPD), a program to accelerate the growth of local currency financing instruments (ABMI), and a regional financial safety net to provide emergency liquidity assistance (CMIM) were created.

However, all three have had limited value to BCLMV before, during, and after the GFC. Critics lament the peer review process turning into a beauty contest, the regional financial safety net remaining inoperable, and local currency bond market development not reaching BCLMV in any significant way. If trust among the ASEAN+3 countries could increase to allow a more open and frank discussion of domestic and regional risks in the peer review process, this would be particularly beneficial to BCLMV. Not only are BCLMV more likely to be vulnerable to internal and external instability, their capacity to identify and respond to them remains lower than other members. BCLMV would also benefit more than others if the CMIM could be made operable since the alternative sources of liquidity finance available to them are quite limited. Unlike the other members, the foreign exchange reserves of CLMV are insufficient to provide a strong first line of defense. Furthermore, bilateral swap arrangements, which have grown to become the main instrument in the defense armor of other members, are practically nonexistent in CLMV.

The failure of the ABMI to make greater inroads may be due to the early stage of development and lack of depth of local financial markets in BCLMV. There is an obvious causality dilemma with this argument, however, which was finally recognized after the GFC when the CGIF was created as part of the ABMI. The CGIF is the only facility that has been used effectively by some of the newer member countries. It has been able to do this because it recognizes that the underdeveloped banking and financial sectors and the inability to issue local currency bonds are problems that are inter-related. By providing guarantees on local currency denominated bonds issued by corporations that may not otherwise have been able to do so, it attempts to directly address the duality of the problem that pervades BCLMV. There is still room to increase the share of guarantee operations covering unrated issuers in the BCLMV as majority of guarantees continue to cover firms in original member countries with relatively good credit rating.

If the volume of guarantees to unrated firms in the newer ASEAN members can be increased without compromising the risk profile of the facility, then potential exists to make a significant impact on both financial market development and local currency financing in BCLMV. This would complement direct efforts to hasten the development of domestic banking and financial systems, especially in the BCLM. It is only through identifying and addressing market failures such as these that the vulnerabilities that contributed to these crises can be avoided, or the contagion from them effectively mitigated, when the next financial crisis occurs.

References

Asian Development Bank 2009. *The Global Economic Crisis: Challenges for Developing Asia and ADB's Response*. Manila: Asian Development Bank.

Asian Development Bank. 2010. *Asian Development Outlook 2010*. Manila: Asian Development Bank.

Azis, Iwan J. 2012. "Asian Regional Financial Safety Nets? Don't Hold Your Breath." *Public Policy Review, Policy Research Institute, Ministry of Finance Japan* 8 (3): 321–340.

Bird, G., and P. Mosley. 2004. "The role of the IMF in developing countries." In *The IMF and its Critics: Reform of Global Financial Architecture*, edited by David Vines and Christopher L. Gilbert. Cambridge: Cambridge University Press, pp. 288–315.

Edwards, Sebastian. 2007. "Crises and Growth: A Latin American Perspective." NBER Working Paper No. 13019, National Bureau of Economic Research, Cambridge, MA.

Grenville, Stephen. 2013. *Asian Crisis and GFC Compared: All the Wrong Lessons.* The Interpreter, Sydney: Lowy Institute.

Hung, Nguyen Manh, and Pham Sy An. May 2011. "Impacts of the Global Economic Crisis on Foreign Trade in Lower-income Economies in the Greater Mekong Sub-region and Policy Responses: the Case of Vietnam and its Implications for Lao PDR and Cambodia." Asia-Pacific Research and Training Network on Trade Working Paper Series, No. 102.

International Monetary Fund. 1999a. *Brunei Darussalam Recent Economic Developments, 1997–1998.* Washington: IMF.

International Monetary Fund. April 6, 1999b. *Public Information Notice: IMF Concludes Article IV Consultation with Cambodia.* Public Information Notice No. 99/30, IMF, Washington, DC.

International Monetary Fund. December 2, 1999c. "Public Information Notice: IMF Concludes Article IV Consultation with Lao P.D.R." 99/109, IMF, Washington, DC.

International Monetary Fund. 1999d. *Lao PDR Recent Economic Developments.* Washington: IMF.

International Monetary Fund. 1999e. *Myanmar Recent Economic Developments.* Washington: IMF.

International Monetary Fund. 1999f. *Vietnam: Selected Issues.* Washington: IMF.

International Monetary Fund. August 4, 2000. "Public Information Notice: IMF Concludes Article IV Consultation with Vietnam." NO. 00/55, IMF, Washington, DC.

International Monetary Fund. March 17, 2008. "Public Information Notice: IMF Executive Board Concludes 2008 Article IV Consultation with Vietnam." Public Information Notice (PIN) No. 09/36, IMF, Washington, DC.

International Monetary Fund. June 3, 2010a. "Public Information Notice: IMF Executive Board Concludes 2010Article IV Consultation with Brunei Darussalam." No. 10/71, IMF, Washington, DC.

International Monetary Fund. December 14, 2010b. "IMF Executive Board Concludes 2010 Article IV Consultation with Cambodia." Public Information Notice (PIN) No. 10/158, IMF, Washington, DC.

International Monetary Fund. September 8, 2010c. "Public Information Notice: IMF Executive Board Concludes 2010 Article IV Consultation with Vietnam." Public Information Notice (PIN) No. 10/127, IMF, Washington, DC.

International Monetary Fund. January 31, 2011. "Public Information Notice: IMF Executive Board Concludes 2010 Article IV Consultation with the Lao People's Democratic Republic." Public Information Notice (PIN) No. 11/12, IMF, Washington, DC.

Jeasakul, Phakawa, Cheng Hoon Lim, and Erik Lundback. 2014. "Why Was Asia Resilient? Lessons from the Past and for the Future." IMF Working Paper WP/14/38, IMF, Washington, DC.

Kawai, M., and C. Houser. 2008. "Evolving ASEAN+3 ERPD: Towards Peer Reviews or Due Diligence?" In *Shaping Policy Reform and Peer Review in Southeast Asia. Integrating Economies Amid Diversity*. Paris: Organization for Economic Co-operation and Development.

Menon, Jayant. 2008a. "Cambodia's Persistent Dollarization: Causes and Policy Options." *ASEAN Economic Bulletin* 25 (2): 228–237.

Menon, Jayant. 2008b. "Dealing with Dollarization: What Options for the Transitional Economies of Southeast Asia?" *Journal of the Asia-Pacific Economy* 13 (2): 131–146.

Menon, Jayant. 2009. "Managing Success in Vietnam: Macroeconomic Consequences of Large Capital Inflows with Limited Instruments." *ASEAN Economic Bulletin* 26 (1): 77–95.

Menon, Jayant, and Hal Hill. 2014. "Does East Asia Have a Working Financial Safety Net?" *Asian Economic Journal* 28 (1): 1–17.

Okonjo-Iweala, Ngozi, Victoria Kwakwa, Andrea Beckwith, and Zafar Ahmed. 1999. "Impact of Asia's Financial Crisis on Cambodia and the Lao PDR." *Finance & Development* 36 (3).

Park, Donghyun, Arief Ramayandi, and Kwanho Shin. 2013. "Why Did Asian Countries Fare Better during the Global Financial Crisis than during the Asian Financial Crisis?" In *Responding to Financial Crisis: Lessons from Asia Then, the United States and Europe Now*, edited by Changyong Rhee and Adam S. Posen. Washington: Asian Development Bank and Peterson Institute for International Economics.

Parulian, F. July 2009. "Global Financial Crisis and Policy Responses in Southeast Asia: Towards Prudent Macroeconomic Policies." ERIA Policy Brief, No. 2009–04. Economic Research Institute for ASEAN and East Asia, Jakarta.

Takagi, Shinji. 2009. "The Global Financial Crisis and Macroeconomic Policy Issues in Asia." ADB Institute Research Policy Brief 32, ADBI, Tokyo.

Chapter 22

China
Weathering the Financial Crisis — Policy Response and Role in Regional Financial Cooperation

Haihong Gao

Introduction

The Asian financial crisis (AFC) in 1997–1998 came at the time when China was in an early phase of economic reform and opening-up, which began in 1978. Compared with other crisis-hit economies in Asia, China experienced relatively mild shocks thanks to strict capital control and limited external exposure. However, China shared the same domestic financial weaknesses the other countries faced before and during the crisis. Therefore, the AFC was a wake-up call for China to draw lessons from other countries, particularly in the areas of conditions for capital account liberalization and soundness of the domestic financial system.

The global financial crisis (GFC) originated from the United States (US) subprime markets in 2007. It soon turned into a global crisis through various channels of a highly integrated financial system and economic linkages. The Chinese economy was severely affected mainly through channels of trade and investment. In response to the crisis, the government launched a massive fiscal stimulus package to boost the economy. The authorities also accelerated its economic opening-up, with the ambition to maintain domestic growth as well as integrate the Chinese economy with the rest of the world. However, the subsequent unsustainability of the growth model forced authorities to rebalance the economy and increase its tolerance to a slower growth widely accepted as an economic "new normal." In the meantime, renminbi internationalization became a policy objective alongside accelerated currency convertibility and domestic financial reform.

China's participation in Asian financial cooperation was inspired by the regional consensus on managing contagion effects through a regional financing arrangement (RFA) as a supplement to existing international financial institutions like the International Monetary Fund (IMF) (Gao 2004). Political factors that could slow the pace of cooperation in Asia were a consideration, especially China–Japan rivalry (Grimes 2014). And the sluggish establishment of a regional trade bloc was also regarded as a barrier for financial cooperation.

However, policymakers in the region decided to move ahead. The first attempt was an Asian Monetary Fund (AMF) proposed by Japan in 1997 without any success. In May 2000, the finance ministers of Association of Southeast Asian Nations (ASEAN) countries, China, Japan, and Korea (ASEAN+3) established the Chiang Mai Initiative (CMI). The CMI evolved and transformed into the Chiang Mai Initiative Multilateralisation (CMIM), a disciplined framework with a common decision-making process.

The establishment of the ASEAN+3 Macroeconomic Research Office (AMRO) with an integrated surveillance approach enhanced regional financial cooperation to an institutional level. From the Chinese perspective, the country's increasing economic integration in Asia raised a fundamental need and has become important motivation to be actively engaged with the regional approach to providing public goods in the region.

China's regional engagement is concurrent with its role in the global sphere. China has actively utilized global multilateral platforms to join collective actions through international cooperation. In particular, the Group of Twenty (G20) took the lead in response to the GFC. Since the first summit in 2008, G20 leaders have repeatedly expressed their commitment to reform international financial institutions, mitigate financial risks, and secure global financial stability. In September 2013, the G20 Leaders' Declaration in St Petersburg reiterated the importance of RFAs in the Global Financial Safety Net (GFSN).

Meanwhile, the IMF as the center of the GFSN has reformed itself in many aspects since the crisis. It has adjusted its credit lines to be more flexible and adaptable for crisis support. It doubled its quota resource and adjusted its quota allocation in matching the changing economic shares of its members in the world.

For China, the outbreak of the crisis reflected pitfalls of existing international financial institutions. The mismatch between economic weights and rule-making powers actually sowed the seed of fragility of the international financial system. Such reflection has shaped China's positive attitude toward multilateral approaches to voice reform in international financial institutions. It has also motivated China to establish new multilateral financial institutions as supplements to existing ones.

This chapter is organized as follows: the first section discusses policies China adopted before and during the AFC. The content focuses on the restrictions of capital account transactions, the rigidity of exchange rate policy, as well as key lessons China learned from the AFC. The second section examines the Chinese policy response to the GFC and the economic consequences that resulted from massive fiscal stimulus and credit expansion. This section also investigates how China managed capital flows and adjusted exchange rate flexibility to achieve a soft landing. The third section describes China's economic linkages in the region. It provides discussions about possible regional currency cooperation as well as the evolving role of the renminbi in the region. This section also illustrates China's role in regional financial cooperation with emphasis on the process of CMI-CMIM, development of regional policy dialogue and institutional cooperation, and efforts at building a regional financial safety net. The final section concludes the chapter.

Policy Adoption and Reflection on the AFC

The Chinese economy demonstrated resilience during the AFC in 1997–1998. Gross domestic product (GDP) growth rate dropped to 7.8% and 7.7% in 1998 and 1999, respectively, from the previous average of 10.2% over the years of 1978–1997. It soon picked up in 2000 and was back to 10% in 2003.

The limited impact of the AFC on China was mainly due to China's strict capital control before and during the crisis. The renminbi's dollar peg combined with capital control played a role in isolating China from external shock. The quick rebound after the crisis was driven by enthusiasm generated by China's entry into the World Trade Organization (WTO) in 2001. The economy also showed signs of internal and external imbalances due to an export-driven economic strategy and lack of exchange rate flexibility. Although China's economy and the financial system were less affected by the crisis than those of the crisis-hit countries, the AFC taught China lessons in dealing with financial crisis.

Capital Control and Favorable External Position

In December 1996, China accepted IMF's Article VIII and lifted foreign exchange restrictions on current account transactions. A year earlier, China decided to merge its dual foreign exchange markets that had existed for a long time. However, China was very cautious in relaxing foreign exchange restrictions in capital account transactions. China also adopted a general principle of "crossing the river by feeling the stones" and delivered simple guidelines without a timetable on currency convertibility under capital account transactions.

Such cautious financial opening resulted in two features of China's external financial position. First, China's external position is relatively strong. In 1997, China's debt–service ratio and foreign debt-to-trade ratio were at 7.3% and 63.2%, far below the critical levels of 20.0% and 100.0%, respectively. The external debt structure was also relatively healthy — the ratios of short-term foreign debt to total foreign debt were below 23% during 1989–1997 except for 41% in 1985. The ratios of short-term debt to foreign exchange reserves were below one in the same period (Figure 22.1). Such foreign debt structure was formed due to the state's unified external debt plan and a strict registration system.

Second, China has a foreign direct investment (FDI)-dominated capital flow. In the 1990s, China began relaxing controls over inward flows of FDI and allowed nonresidents to invest in China under Sino-foreign joint-venture laws and other relevant regulations upon approval of the Ministry of Commerce of China. This legal framework, combined with many policy-related incentives for inward direct investment, together with China's low-cost skilled labor and relative good infrastructure, played important roles in attracting FDI inflows. Encouraged by the government's favorable policies, FDI inflows were in excess of any other forms of cross-border investments dominating China's cross-border capital movements for decades (Figure 22.2).

China's securities market was completely closed until 1991 when the Shanghai Stock Exchange (SHSE) and Shenzhen Stock Exchange (SZSE) began to offer B-shares, providing foreign investors a legal channel to invest in China's equity markets. In 2002, China introduced the Qualified Foreign Institutional Investors (QFII) program, allowing nonresident institutions to invest in China's capital market. In 2007, China introduced the Qualified Domestic Institutional Investors (QDII) program, allowing domestic institutional investors to invest in overseas markets. Meanwhile, China kept its fixed income securities market closed for nonresidents. Such capital flow regulations protected China from being severely affected by external shocks. Subsequently, the rapid growth of FDI inflows became the most prominent factor in helping China integrate with global and regional markets.

Figure 22.1: China's Foreign Debt Outstanding and Short-Term Debt Ratio to Foreign Exchange Reserves,1989–1998 (USD billion; Ratio)

USD = United States dollar.
Source: State Administration of Foreign Exchange.Second.

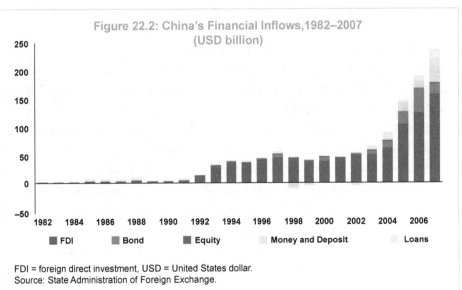

Figure 22.2: China's Financial Inflows,1982–2007 (USD billion)

FDI = foreign direct investment, USD = United States dollar.
Source: State Administration of Foreign Exchange.

Renminbi's Dollar Peg as a Nominal Anchor

China's foreign exchange system was partially liberalized by the time China accepted IMF's Article VIII. On January 4, 1994, China ended its dual currency system (official and unofficial markets), and adopted a single and managed floating exchange rate regime by one-shot devaluation of over 30% (Figure 22.3). The unified foreign exchange market was located in Shanghai, a single exchange rate partially determined by market forces.

The controls on the capital account during this time effectively supported the Chinese authorities' ability to hold on to the pegged exchange rate of the renminbi, based on a series of regulations on selling and purchasing foreign exchange. For instance, foreign exchange demand and supply were subject to strict restrictions of foreign exchange submission. In 1997, the authorities relaxed the mandatory requirement for selling and purchasing foreign exchange incomes for domestic enterprises. However, a strict cap for those who were qualified to retain foreign exchange incomes, such as a certain level of trade volume and capital base, was set. As a result, very few enterprises were qualified to retain their foreign exchange incomes. The stability of the currency's exchange rate also relied on the central bank's intervention. The People's Bank of China (PBC) authorized the State Administration of Foreign Exchange (SAFE) to set and adjust the band based on the daily fluctuation of renminbi exchange rates.

The absence of capital account convertibility limited the instant mobility of capital across borders. Speculators, both foreigners and Chinese, could not short sell currency even if they believed it to be overvalued (Gao 2000). Thus, although Asian currencies experienced sharp devaluations at the time of the AFC, the renminbi was an exception and maintained its pegged rate to the United States (US) dollar.

As the AFC loomed in the region in 1997, Hong Kong's currency board system began facing speculative attacks. The Hong Kong Monetary Authority had to strongly intervene in the foreign exchange market to stabilize the Hong Kong (HK) dollar against the US dollar. But due to the nature of the linked exchange rate system, intervention was accompanied by the high interest rates. In October 1997, the overnight repo rate was once hiked by 300 basis points, which was beyond the theoretical rationales and that neither covered interest parity nor uncovered parity could explain (Yu 1999).

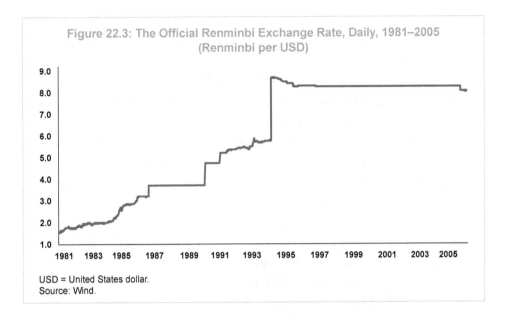

Figure 22.3: The Official Renminbi Exchange Rate, Daily, 1981–2005 (Renminbi per USD)

USD = United States dollar.
Source: Wind.

In March 1998, Premier Zhu Rongji announced at his first press conference that under certain circumstances, if the Hong Kong government asked for help, the central government would sustain Hong Kong's prosperity and stability at any costs, as well as support its linked exchange rate system. On June 26, 1998, in the meeting with the then US Secretary of the Treasury Robert Rubin, Premier Zhu Rongji expressed, "Even though renminbi devaluation could bring China huge benefits, we stay away from it as one who harms the others is doomed to harm oneself" (Zhu 2011).

The central government's commitment to maintain the renminbi peg and secure stability of the Hong Kong financial system played a crucial role in preventing the linked exchange rate system from collapsing. More broadly, the dollar peg of the renminbi was regarded as a stabilizing factor during the AFC, and such a decision helped other economies rebuild confidence against the pressure of further devaluations.

However, China soon realized that the dollar peg came with a price of persistent undervaluation resulting in a distortion of resource allocation. It is true that the renminbi's undervaluation matched the nation's export-oriented growth strategy during the 1990s and the early 2000s, together with a combination of factors, including an increase in production capacity, a lack of effective domestic demand, and the transfer of global manufacturing activity to China due to the availability of low-cost labor. Such an export-oriented strategy became a driving force behind China's double-digit growth rates during the time.

China's entrance into the WTO in 2001 was also a catalyst for the economy to enjoy the benefits of further reform and opening-up. This is because China's entrance into the WTO was built on a series of reform commitments made by the Chinese government. For instance, China promised to reduce tariff rates and eliminate nontariff barriers, permit foreign companies to participate in restricted industries, open China's insurance market, allow foreign banks to access the renminbi business, and so on.

As rapid growth continued to ride on the allocation of resources toward manufacturing and external sectors, China began to experience twin surpluses — surpluses on the current account and the capital and financial account, with massive accumulation of foreign exchange reserves. Running twin surpluses persistently reflected the failure of utilizing domestic savings for domestic investment (Yu 2008).

Lessons China Learned from the AFC

The AFC is regarded as a typical capital account crisis, featuring massive capital outflow, bank and corporate bankruptcies, sharp currency value adjustments, and subsequent policy responses, including abandoning fixed exchange rates and implementing temporary capital controls, as was observed in Malaysia. In most cases, the crisis happened when capital account controls were dismissed without soundness of preconditions. Among many, the following lessons are especially worth noting and have played an important role for China's policy adjustment in the aftermath of the crisis.

First, a fixed exchange rate regime should be replaced by a floating rate system before implementing full convertibility. Experiences in developing countries show that a rigid exchange rate regime should be allowed an orderly shift to regimes with greater exchange rate flexibility before capital account openness, although the actual methods could be different from country to country (Eichengreen and Masson 1998; Eichengreen and Mussa 1998). Before the crisis, most Asian developing countries pegged their currencies to the US dollar, which was a key factor for their record of strong growth. But the lack of exchange rate flexibility also helped to build up problems leading to the financial crisis which began in July 1997 (Gao 2000).

For instance, the Thai government found difficulties in coping with the impossible trinity of macroeconomic policies — choosing high interest rate as a tool contain domestic economic and asset market boom while fixing the exchange rate in the case of less restricted capital inflows. In fact, before the crisis, the real effective exchange rate already appreciated against its competitor currencies, making Thai exports less competitive. For fear of intense speculative pressure and losing domestic confidence, which would have resulted in a huge run on the baht, the Thai government decided to protect the exchange rate system for as long as possible. According to the Bank of Thailand (BOT), such a policy decision was premised on the rationale that a devaluation of the baht would have done more harm than good (BOT 1998). The basic rationale for this decision was that it could buy more time to tackle the fundamental problems in the economy and the financial sector without having to face a currency crisis at the same time. However, the fundamental problems had worsened, the currency crisis inevitably came, and the fixed exchange rate system had to be abandoned (Gao 2000).

Second, implicit guarantees and the resulting moral hazard are key weaknesses in a financial system. The guarantees existed in various areas. For instance, the pegged exchange rate regime provided an implicit guarantee of currency value for banks that faced double mismatches in currency and duration. In Thailand, the exchange risk premium remained low while investors kept up their confidence. However, this guarantee evaporated when large capital outflows occurred. The implicit government guarantee for financial institutions also generated oligopolistic profit reflected in large spreads between deposit and lending rates (Jonson et al. 1997).

Third, vulnerability that accumulated in the bank-dominated financial sector should be addressed before full convertibility. Before the AFC, most developing Asian economies adopted similar domestic financial systems. In 1996, the ratio of domestic credit to GDP was at 157% in Thailand; Korea's ratio was at 134%. Additionally, in Thailand's case, most bank lending was to priority sectors: large manufacturing sectors and export industries (BOT 1998). The collateral-based lending by banks and large relending to the real estate sector by corporations made excessive lending very vulnerable to asset price deflation. Such vulnerability was enlarged by increased foreign capital inflows. Generally, the lack of competition in bank-dominated financial systems would likely result in nonperforming loans (Hu 1998). And nonperforming loans in the banking system became a source for systematic risk, which would lead to a currency crisis in an open environment for capital flows (Wu 1998).

China's financial system suffered from the same weaknesses as most Asian economies before the crisis. In particular, the majority of banks loans, mainly provided by state-owned banks, flowed to the state-owned enterprises (SOEs) that accounted a large share of the economy. The problem of corporate government in the SOEs, such as blurry distinction between managers and supervisors, lack of incentives for entrepreneurs' spirit, and distortions of resources allocation, caused severe profit losses for years. Therefore, the overleveraged SOEs became a major component in accumulating banks' nonperforming loans. At the end of 1997, nonperforming loans accounted for 35% of total outstanding loans of China's financial institutions. This figure was much higher than the pre-AFC levels in the banking systems of Thailand, Korea, and Indonesia. However, poor bank health in China did not lead to a banking crisis or a credit crunch because of public confidence that the state would guarantee individual deposits in the banks (Gao 2000). The outbreak of the AFC sent an alarm for Chinese authorities to separate bad loans from the balance sheet of banks. From 1998–2001, up to CNY 1,400 billion worth of nonperforming loans of four major state-owned banks were separated and passed on to four financial asset management corporations (Ye 2003).

Response to the GFC and Economic Consequences

Although the direct impact of the GFC on China's financial system was limited, the indirect impact on real sectors was immense. In response to the crisis, China adopted a fiscal stimulus policy to boost domestic investment and released a comprehensive reform and open-up agenda. The PBC also started to promote renminbi internationalization in line with the Chinese call for international monetary system reform in the aftermath of the GFC. However, the policy response resulted in subsequent overleverage, financial vulnerabilities, and economic imbalances, requiring further economic adjustments afterward.

Policy Response

China's financial exposure to troubled subprime mortgage-backed securities during the GFC was limited due to three factors. First, there were relatively strict restrictions on cross-border portfolio investment abroad under the capital account. By that time, China had already partially opened its domestic stock and equity markets to foreign institutional investors under the theme of QFII. The resident holdings of foreign assets were mainly attributed to Chinese government entities. The exposure of Chinese private investment to subprime mortgage-related products was relatively small. The share of foreign exchange reserves accounted for 66.5% of China's total foreign asset holdings by the end of 2008. China's holdings of US securities totaling USD 1,205 billion made China the second largest foreign holder after Japan (Morrison 2009). Out of the total holdings, 97.5% was in long-term securities, including agency securities, treasury securities, equities, and corporate securities. Only 2.5% was in short-term debt. While the direct impact of the subprime mortgage crisis was limited, the indirect impacts through trade and investment loomed in the onset of the crisis.

Due to China's export-oriented strategy, China's growth was heavily dependent on export and FDI inflows. China's export as a share of GDP was only 5% in 1978 when China began its reform and opening-up. The share increased thereafter, reaching 21% in 2000, 35% in 2006, and 31% in 2008. Thus, the outbreak of the GFC posed an external demand shock to China. Exports began shrinking in July 2008 until July 2009 (Figure 22.4).

On the other hand, China's actual use of FDI inflows was only USD 40.7 billion by the end of 2000. The number reached USD 92.4 billion in 2008, an increase by 126.9% cumulatively. However, due to the crisis, the actual use of FDI inflows dropped from the peak in January 2008, along with a deep contraction by 32.67% from December 2008 to January 2009. As a result of such a contraction, the GDP growth rate declined concussively from the second quarter of 2008. The GDP growth rate dropped from 10.9% in the second quarter to 9.5% in the third quarter of 2008. The downward trend continued until the third quarter of 2009 when the impact of the stimulus policy to support investment set in.

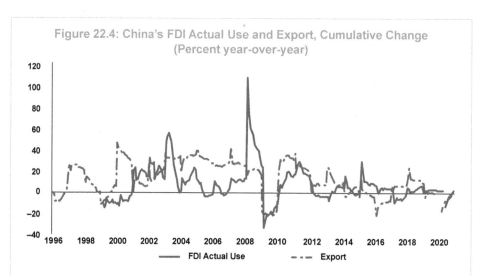

Figure 22.4: China's FDI Actual Use and Export, Cumulative Change (Percent year-over-year)

FDI = foreign direct investment.
Source: Wind.

Stimulus Package

China launched a massive fiscal stimulus package to boost its economy in November, 2008. The National Development and Reform Commission (NDRC), the nation's top economic planning agency, made a statement that the government planned to deliver CNY 4 trillion (USD 586 billion). The NDRC noted that the stimulus plan was to be spent over the following 2 years. The plan was prioritized over projects improving people's livelihood, including those in rural areas, housing projects for low-income earners in urban areas, and social undertakings (Xinhua News Agency 2008).

On November 27, 2008, the NDRC announced the details of the stimulus package (China Daily 2008). The package mainly targeted domestic hard infrastructure such as housing projects, infrastructure in rural areas, highways, railroads, and the power grid. It also included medical care and education, ecological and environmental projects, research and development, and innovation projects. The stimulus plan was based on the NDRC's estimation that China's total domestic investment was expected to reach CNY 16 trillion in 2008 and CNY 18 trillion in 2009, compared with CNY 13 trillion in 2007. The CNY 4 trillion stimulus package was just part of the investment China needed to drive its economy.

The stimulus package was also aided by credit expansion during the time. The PBC set up a higher lending target together with cuts of reserve rate requirements (RRRs) for financial institutions. The PBC lowered RRRs twice by cutting the rates from 17.5% to 13.5% for small- and medium-size financial institutions from September to December 2008. The RRRs for large size financial institutions were also reduced from 17.0% to 15.5% during the time. The money supply M2 to GDP ratio jumped from 18.8% in January to 20.5% in February, 2009. The average monthly M2-to-GDP ratio grew to 26.5% in 2009.

The stimulus policies successfully prevented the Chinese economy from experiencing a deep contraction in the wake of the GFC. However, it sowed seeds of the problems, including overcapacity and overleverage in the economy.

The package was heavily investment-dominated, reflecting that China followed its investment-driven growth model. Fixed capital formation picked up quickly, which contributed to 94.9% in GDP growth in the third quarter of 2009. The rapid increase in investment was mainly achieved by local infrastructure projects, which accounted for 70% of the package. With the incentive to boost the local economy as well to earn credits for performance evaluated by the central government, local government officials created a funding mechanism using land as collateral for obtaining bank loans to finance the projects. The widespread use of such a mechanism resulted in a surge in local government financing vehicles (LGFVs), a local government-owned entity. It also generated crowding-out effects by mobilizing resources for SOEs that were much less productive than private firms (Huang et al. 2017).

Renminbi Internationalization

The outbreak of the GFC reflected deficiency of the existing international monetary system. As part of the effort to reform the international monetary system, the Chinese central bank governor Zhou Xiaochuan proposed a super-sovereign reserve currency (Zhou 2009). He criticized the fundamental flaws of a single currency dominating system — one of the major sources of global imbalance and financial instability that caused the GFC and suggested delinking global financial stability from one country's balance of payment. It was regarded as a theoretical thought to design an ideal system where the Triffin dilemma, an inherent conflict in a national currency also serving as an international currency, would no longer be present. Zhou's proposal also reflected that China had emerged as the major growth engine of the world economy. China had an increasing share in the global trading system and was frustrated with its potential capital loss of massive foreign exchange reserves (Gao and Yu 2002). In fact, in the late 2008 when the economy was in sharp downturn, the Chinese government faced domestic pressure to utilize foreign exchange reserves in profitable ways rather than recycle domestic savings into dollar assets that are subject to volatility of dollar exchange rate. Therefore, renminbi internationalization is regarded as an attempt for a diversified reserve currency system (Gao 2018). The motivations also lay in the desire of the PBC to achieve its own objective without waiting for outsiders' consent (Yu 2014).

Academic studies provided rationales for this line of thought from both theoretical perspectives and historic experiences. For instance, there is rich literature discussing the conditions for currency internationalization and the effects of a dominant currency (Eichengreen 2011; Frankel 1999). The experiences of the Japanese yen internationalization also presented lessons for the Chinese currency (Kawai and Takagi 2011; Takagi 2012).

On the policy front, renminbi internationalization was initially an ad hoc process because the Chinese government wanted to examine the benefits and costs of implementation (Gao 2018). A remarkable policy move was the launch of Administrative Rules on Pilot Program of Renminbi Settlement of Cross-Border Trade Transactions in July 2009, which allowed renminbi to be used in cross-border trade settlement. In January 2011, China launched the Provisional Rules for the Pilot Program of RMB Settlement for Overseas Direct Investment, allowing Chinese banks and enterprises to use the renminbi in overseas direct investments. In February 2004, the central government permitted banks in Hong Kong to provide renminbi services, which was an initial push for Hong Kong to promote offshore renminbi businesses. In 2007, renminbi-denominated offshore bonds, dim sum bonds, were issued in Hong Kong. The renminbi offshore market was also extended to London, Singapore, and other financial markets. A major step took place when the IMF decided to add the renminbi to the special drawing rights (SDR) basket in November 2015. The new basket, made in October 2016, consisted of five currencies: the US dollar, euro, yuan, yen, and pound sterling.

After years of effort, the renminbi now functions as international store of value, medium of exchange, and unit of account. However, compared with other matured international currencies, the renminbi's position in international use is still very limited. Nevertheless, renminbi internationalization has been meaningful because such an objective could only be achieved through China's continuous efforts at liberalizing its financial system and pursuing domestic reforms (Gao 2018). Moreover, the currency's regional use is in line with the advent of policies to promote the use of local currencies in the region (Sussangkarn et al. 2019).

The Grand Reform Agenda

In November 2013, the Third Plenary Session of the Eighteenth Central Committee of the Communist Party announced a comprehensive reform agenda. The key objective of this agenda was to establish a modern market system based on market rules through two major approaches: marketization and liberalization. The agenda covered six reform areas: economic and financial, social, political, cultural, ecological, and national security.

One of its key messages was to reduce reform government intervention in the economy. It also changed the officials' performance evaluation system from one based on GDP growth to an index including resource consumption, overcapacity, and incremental local government debt levels. Such a change reflects the fact that China realized the fallout of stimulus policies post-GFC and has faced challenges of reforming an unsustainable growth driven by local government investment. It also touched upon other challenges such as promoting the key role of the market in factor resource allocation, which required a systematic deviation from the central planning system.

The most distinct element of the agenda is ownership reform. This includes the set-up of state-owned asset management companies, an increase in the share of state capital gains transferred to the social security fund, the conversion of nonpublic-owned enterprises to SOEs, and participation in state investment projects. The SOEs played a significant role in China's economic structure. It has been one of the toughest areas in the agenda because it required reforms across deep waters, including the clarification of the relationships between state and nonstate sectors, and the extent to which the government could play a role in the system to achieve efficient resource allocation and minimum distortions.

In the area of financial sector reform, the agenda included some ambitious reforms, such as setting up privately funded small- and medium-sized banks, promoting a registration-based stock issuance system away from the approval-based one, liberalizing the interest rate, improving market-oriented exchange rate formation, and speeding up renminbi capital account convertibility. In the area of investment and rule of laws, the agenda promised to explore national treatments, adopt a "negative list," improve protection of property rights, and liberalize investment access by setting up unrestricted free trade zones. These measures have partially materialized in subsequent years due to the continuous efforts of decision-making bodies as well as domestic and international market participants.

This grand reform agenda set the tone for China's reforms and opening-up in the following years with significant impact on the Chinese economy and society. It shows that China continues to follow the path of gradual approaches, with more ambitions in the areas that require core reforms.

Economic Rebalancing

The rebalancing efforts were policy adjustments to address the repercussions of post-GFC stimulus actions. The consensus at that time was that the old economic growth model, which was export- and investment-driven and state-owned sector-dominated and was characterized by factor resources misallocation, was not sustainable. For instance, China adopted an export-oriented economic strategy beginning in the 1980s, following East Asia's successful growth models. China's export-oriented strategy was supported by a set of policies, such as tax rebates to provide incentives for Chinese exporters and the pegged exchange rate regime that was subject to the nation's trade policy. The existence of a savings gap and changes of economic cycles were also the factors behind China's current account surplus in the pre-GFC period (Yu 2015). As China's economic growth continued to rely on the external sector, the resultant current account surplus and accumulation of foreign exchange reserves became a source of the country's external imbalance before the GFC.

To rebalance the economy, China launched a number of measures to cut overcapacity, conduct credit deleveraging, and improve the social security system. The decline of China's current account surplus in the post-GFC period was one of the outcomes of economic rebalancing. The factors behind the decline of current account surplus also included the rise of wages and wealth resulting from the past high growth rates, real appreciation of the currency, and the decrease of domestic savings rates beginning in 2009.

Starting from the first quarter of 2011, domestic consumption surpassed capital formation and became the major driver of GDP growth. As this trend continued, the economy moved away from the old growth model (Figure 22.5). The household sector became the major driving force due to social and economic policies that reduced depressive factors for consumption. For instance, China improved social welfare coverage. Thus, savings rates reached a high level. Subsequently, the national savings rates declined from 2010, while household consumption increased relative to disposable income. A shift to a consumption-driven economy implies that China would become a major destination of the world's exports and shift its trade balance from a surplus to a deficit in the future.

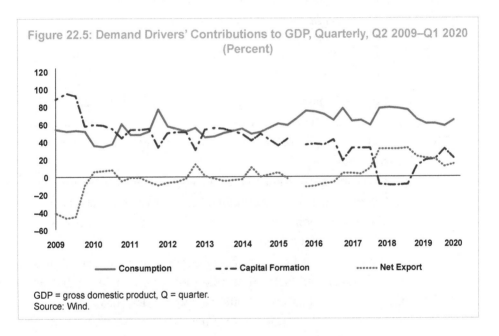

Figure 22.5: Demand Drivers' Contributions to GDP, Quarterly, Q2 2009–Q1 2020 (Percent)

Consumption   Capital Formation   Net Export

GDP = gross domestic product, Q = quarter.
Source: Wind.

On the supply side, the service sector has been steadily surpassing the industrial sector in value-add since 2014 (Figure 22.6). The service sector is comprised of a wide range of activities. One of the activities is related to new services, such as e-commerce and technology services and information and transportation services, indicating an Internet-led new economy. China has actually taken advantage of new technology to upgrade its services. In this area, there is less government intervention, limited regulation, and a high degree of competition. More importantly, the expansion of service

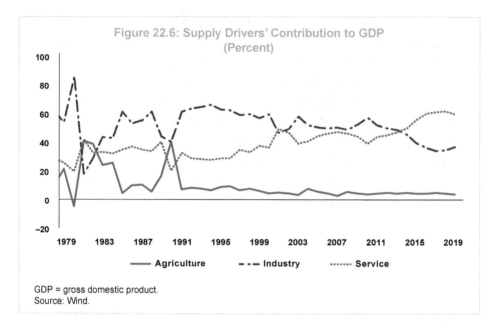

Figure 22.6: Supply Drivers' Contribution to GDP (Percent)

GDP = gross domestic product.
Source: Wind.

activities has created massive novel job opportunities in the economy. However, there are many service activities which are regarded to be attached to lower productivity, implying lower total factor productivity (TFP) in the years to come.

As a part of economic rebalancing, China had to deal with the problem of domestic debt and financial vulnerability. China's over-reliance on fixed investments has been responsible for the accumulation of overcapacity in sectors where output declined faster than the inputs.

Debt accumulation has been a global phenomenon. However, China's debt to GDP has increased faster than many other countries, aided by CNY 4 trillion fiscal stimulation in 2008. Corporate debt has dominated due to an investment-driven model, rapid urbanization, and dominance of SOEs. Roughly half of corporate debts were absorbed by nonprofitable sectors, which were subject to overcapacities (AMRO 2018a).

Concerns about debt default and financial instability have led to a nationwide effort to deleverage the economy starting in 2017 through 2019. The countermeasures include stabilization of the credit-to-GDP growth ratio, cutting overcapacity in the areas of high energy costs, deleveraging local government debt by means of debt-to-bonds swaps, and the promotion of mixed ownerships. Such efforts have resulted in a decline in corporate debt below the peak of 166.4% to GDP in 2016. By the end of 2019, it had come down to 151.3%. However, household debt-to-GDP ratio has increased rapidly, from 44.4% of GDP in 2016 to 55.8% in 2019.

While the banking system was still subject to tight regulation, banks and nonbank financial institutions were given incentives to provide financing to meet the rising need for loans. Shadow banking has developed rapidly, motived by the underling force of regulatory arbitrage to circumvent banks' credit control and the lack of interest rate flexibility. The incentive for regulation arbitrage occurs when banks and nonbank financial institutions want to expand balance sheets without breaking regulatory boundary. Loans were arranged off the balance sheet with much higher returns for investors. For instance, the size of wealth management products (WMPs) increased from 0 to CNY 28.38 trillion in January 2017, which accounted for 28.2% of Chinese total social financing.

Shadow banking had various forms, such as asset management products, entrusted loans, trust loans, banker's acceptances, peer-to-peer (P2P) lending, and leasing. According to the Financial Stability Board (FSB) shadow banking tracker, the size of Chinese shadow banking reached USD 7 trillion in 2016. By the end of 2017, the size of nonbank financial intermediations increased to USD 8.2 trillion (FSB 2018, 2019). The sharp increase in Chinese shadow banking has become a source of financial instability due to the complexity of the definition, changing patterns, high credit risks associated with off-balance sheets, and leveraged and mismatched nature. In particular, the various structured products have been linked to corporate debt that is intertwined with the overcapacity problem (AMRO 2018b).

Facing the increasing challenges to financial stability, China stepped up to improve financial regulatory policies. During the presidency of the G20 summit in 2016, China requested the IMF, FSB, and Bank for International Settlements (BIS) to carry out a comprehensive study on essential aspects and good practices of national macroprudential policies. As a result, these institutions issued the "Elements of Effective Macroprudential Policies: Lessons from International Experience", which provided a guideline covering definitions and objectives, institutional arrangements, operational tools and models, and so on for countries to improve their macroprudential policy frameworks (PBC 2017).

Following the guideline, China strengthened monitoring and assessment of systematic risks and improved macroprudential policy tools. From 2017, the regulators decided to include the off-balance sheet WMPs in the definition of broad credit in the macroprudential assessment (MPA) to mitigate potential systemic risk (PBC 2017). The aim of the MPA is to help prevent financial risks and enhance the soundness of the banking system. In August 2018, the PBC upgraded the MPA by publishing the "Guidelines on Regulating Wealth Management Businesses of Financial Institutions." The updated MPA system exhibited promising improvement of previous quantity-based macroprudential measures (Zheng 2018).

In 2017, China reshuffled its financial regulatory frameworks and established the Financial Stability and Development Committee (FSDC). The FSDC was affiliated to the State Council to enhance the effectiveness of the financial supervisory system. By merging the China Banking Regulatory Commission (CBRC) and the China Insurance Regulatory Commission (CIRC), the new framework aims to close regulatory loopholes, approve important financial reform plans, and coordinate financial regulations and issues concerning monetary policy to serve the real economy as well as safeguard financial stability (PBC 2018).

Managing Capital Flows and Exchange Rate Flexibility

After the GFC, China seized opportunities to promote financial opening and pursue flexibility of the exchange rate regime. In doing so, it had to face a trade-off between financial stability and increasing volatility of cross-border capital flows.

Capital Account Openness

One major breakthrough was establishment of the Shanghai Free Trade Zone (SFTZ) in September 2013. This was the first time China relaxed foreign exchange controls in an onshore free economic zone. The financial institutions and nonfinancial companies registered in SFTZ were granted the rights to open a free trade (FT) account. They enjoyed renminbi transactions services under macroprudential management. The SFTZ is an experimental case for renminbi convertibility and financial liberalization. It hopes to effectively prevent risks from spilling over to areas outside SFTZ and to replicate the partial success of macroprudential measures on capital flows and currency transactions nationwide.

In January 2016, the experiment of SFTZ was extended to Guangdong, Tianjin, and Fujian, allowing 27 financial institutions and all companies registered in the zones to enjoy free renminbi transactions. In May 2016, the PBC rolled out macroprudential management nationwide (PBC 2016).

In the meantime, China continued to open up its interbank market, equity market, and bond issuance by allowing more entities to participate in transactions and by lowering market barriers for the QFII and the QDII. In 2014, China took the first step to unify capital markets through the Shanghai–Hong Kong Connect. In 2015, the interbank market was opened to all foreign central banks, international financial institutions, and sovereign wealth funds with no quota required. In 2016, China further relaxed restrictions of the interbank market to medium- and long-term investments. The openness of equity and bond markets was further broadened through the Shenzhen–Hong Kong Connect and Mainland–HK bond connect. In January 2017, "The Notice of Macroprudential Regulation on the Full Coverage of Cross-border Financing" was published. The new framework covered more financial activities and aimed to facilitate cross-border financing and lower the external financial costs of domestic institutions (PBC 2018).

Starting from April 2018, the US–China tension extended from trade, currency, and technology to financial areas. Against such a worsening environment, China continued to follow its own timetable of financial opening-up. China eventually decided to allow foreign ownership to enter the Chinese financial market a year earlier. The quota requirements were largely lifted for QFII and QDII. China also opened its credit rating market to foreign agencies and allowed American Express to enter the domestic card payment business.

In 2019, the domestic A-share and bond indexes were added to the Morgan Stanley Capital International (MSCI). The Chinese government bonds and policy bank securities were also included in Bloomberg Barclays Global Aggregate Index. Such steps were expected to help the development of a deep and liquid domestic capital market.

Changing Patterns of Capital Flows

It is noticeable that China's financial account structure has a large share of an official asset — almost half of its reserves are invested in low interest rate assets. For instance, the PBC was the biggest foreign holder with USD 1.12 trillion, which accounts for 28% of foreign official holdings of US Treasury marketable and nonmarketable bills, bonds, and notes at the end of 2018. Such an investment pattern fits the basic rules that China has set to manage its foreign exchange reserves for precautionary purposes as the first priority.

Considering both its assets and liabilities, China suffered negative net revenues in its national wealth for a decade: the revenue of its overseas investment was less than the revenue that foreign investors earned in China. For instance, according to Wind statistics, at the end of 2018, the rate of return on liabilities was 5.39% while that on assets was 2.97%, making a net figure at −2.42%. Such phenomena partially supported the argument that China suffered from capital losses, a reason for boosting renminbi internationalization as China wanted to manage its assets in a safe way and to get out of a dollar trap.

China's net capital flows have been correlated with policy steps of opening since 2008. China experienced net capital inflows for a long time due to favorable conditions. However, the net inflows registered a large negative figure in 2012 when China began accelerating capital account convertibility. The situation worsened in 2015 due to a combination of currency depreciation, a weaker growth prospect, stock market turbulence, domestic anti-corruption moves, and the expectation of a Fed rate hike. Starting from 2016, China decided to tighten bureaucratic scrutiny over cross-border capital flows, such as increasing filing requirements for individual foreign exchanges, requirements for additional documentation for foreign companies profit remittance, and requirements for banks in Shanghai to balance renminbi outflows with its inflows. The measures effectively prevented persistent outflows. Non-reserve financial net inflows emerged once again in 2018 from the lowest level (large net outflows) in 2015. Outflows declined due to a number of factors, whilst inflows increased as well (SAFE 2019).

However, effectiveness of capital flow management has been debated. The evidence of loopholes was often judged by "error and omission." The size of error and omission was large during the time that net inflow was smaller or even negative, such as in 2015 and 2016 (Figure 22.7). Another indicator is reflected in the item "other." In times of capital outflows, the net outflow of "others" was often large. Interestingly, this was probably related to capital controls in place, and domestic investors were more sensitive and wanted to move money out of the country.

There were three ways to do so: (1) residents would increase overseas money and deposit holding through activities of Chinese business, (2) banks would increase loans to their subsidiaries overseas, and (3) trade credit would increase due to trade activities. The gross flows also reflected the change in capital account openness. As the IMF warned, the further opening of the capital account would likely create substantially larger two-way gross flows (IMF 2019).

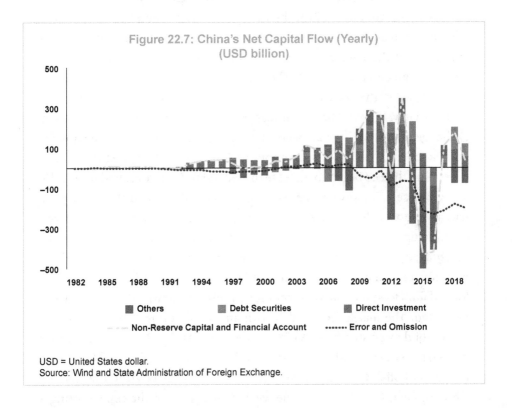

Figure 22.7: China's Net Capital Flow (Yearly) (USD billion)

USD = United States dollar.
Source: Wind and State Administration of Foreign Exchange.

Toward Exchange Rate Flexibility

The renminbi's dollar peg ended in July 2005 when the PBC adopted a managed regime with reference to a currency basket, although the US dollar weight still dominated the basket. The PBC also set the middle price that was based on the previous day's closing market rate and included a market-oriented factor in the exchange rate policy.

From 2008 to 2012, the central bank virtually rolled back to a dollar peg because of fear of instability caused by external shocks and contraction of economic growth. From 2012 to 2014, the central bank widened trading bands several times in order to allow the exchange rate to fluctuate by market forces. Arbitrage activities increased because of the introduction of the renminbi spot exchange rate in the offshore market in Hong Kong in June 2011.

In August 2015, the PBC decided to make a bold move by not intervening in the middle price of the currency. The famous "8/11" exchange rate reform allowed the renminbi to move freely without the central bank's intervention.

Starting from mid-2015, the IMF started the process of SDR review. Whether to include the renminbi in the basket was one of their major considerations. But there were two preconditions: China's trade share should be large enough and the renminbi should be freely usable. A flexible exchange rate was part of the deal, although the requirement was implicit.[1] From this point of view, the PBC had solid reasons to let the exchange rate float, and exchange rate flexibility had been a policy objective for the central bank for quite a long time. However, a proper action was implemented at a wrong time, since the Fed began to increase the federal funds rate around mid-2015. The Chinese economy showed signs of slowing down and the stock price had started to collapse. It was also the time when the capital account was opening up at a fast pace. A flexible exchange rate was supposed to act as a buffer against external shocks and at the same time allow freer capital flows with less capital controls — a desirable policy combination that the PBC longed for. However, market reaction was contrary to what the central bank predicted. The market responded with an overshooting depreciation. The renminbi depreciated by 4.7% in one day (August 11, 2015). Such a move created larger depreciation expectations. The offshore nondeliverable forward (NDF) and offshore Chinese yuan (CNH) rates diverted from the onshore Chinese yuan (CNY) rate on the weaker side most of the time, putting a strong depreciation pressure on CNY (Figure 22.8).

In order to tame expectations, the central bank adopted the traditional measure to inject foreign exchange reserves and at the same time tighten bureaucratic scrutiny over cross-border capital flows. The central bank also

---

[1] In its "Review of the Method of the Valuation of the SDR — Initial Consideration" (August 3, 2015), the IMF pointed out, for SDR valuation purposes, "a market-based 'representative' RMB in terms of the U.S. dollar would be needed to value the RMB against the SDR. The representative rate is currently the onshore fixing rate, i.e., central parity rate, announced daily by the CFETS at 9:15 a.m. However, this rate is not based on actual market trades, and can deviate by up to 2% from the onshore market exchange rate. In the event of SDR inclusion, the Fund, in consultation with the Chinese authorities, would need to identify a market-based exchange rate that could be used as a representative rate for the RMB" (pp. 31–32).

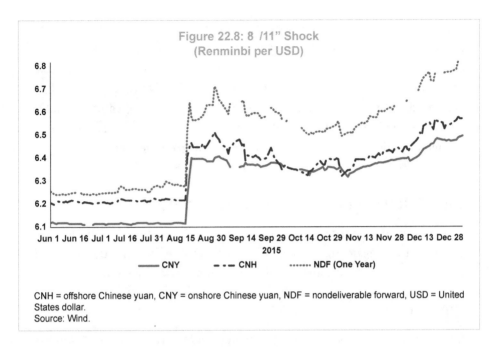

Figure 22.8: 8 /11" Shock
(Renminbi per USD)

CNH = offshore Chinese yuan, CNY = onshore Chinese yuan, NDF = nondeliverable forward, USD = United States dollar.
Source: Wind.

changed the exchange rate formula by introducing a weighted currencies basket — the China Foreign Exchange Trade System (CFETS) index beginning in December 2015 and adding a countercyclical factor in the formula in June 2017.

The CFETS has been designed to be a weighted basket comprising China's major trade partners' currencies. Initially, the CFETS included 13 currencies. Starting from 2017, the basket expanded to include 24 currencies that represented most of China's trading partners. However, inclusion of a countercyclical factor received criticisms because this factor lacked transparency.

Like many other central banks, the PBC constantly faces tradeoffs between stability and flexibility. The original form of impossible trinity put forward by Mundell and Fleming in the 1960s was translated into a policy trilemma by Obstfeld (2005). Theoretically, the relation between the stability of exchange rate, monetary policy autonomy, and free capital flows has been a never-ending debate. For Chinese policymakers, a middle solution was always practically possible. Yi and Tang (2001) searched for possible middle solutions to the triangle problem and indicated that the development of derivatives markets for hedging activities played an important role: the more sophisticated the market was, the more likely the triangle held.

Interestingly, Sun and Li (2017) used a scalene triangle model to argue that capital flows played a bigger role compared with the autonomy of monetary policy and the fixed exchange rates. If free capital flow is chosen, the monetary authority could only achieve a relatively stable exchange rates and a relatively independent monetary policy. Nevertheless, exchange rate flexibility has been China's long-term objective. However, such an objective is also subject to middle solutions considering the pace of capital account liberalization as well as the extent to which the PBC keeps the autonomy of monetary policy — a key lesson China learned from the AFC.

China's Role in Regional Financial Cooperation

China's growing engagement in Asia is rooted in its deep economic integration. Such engagement is part of the collective efforts to build regional financial safety nets to safeguard financial stability in the region.

China's Regional Economic Linkage

Over time, China has emerged as a major trade partner in the region. Its financial links in Asia changed, alongside its continuous financial opening-up as well as the regional effort to develop the local currency financial market. Asia has become China's largest partner in trade, FDI, equity, and bond flows (Figure 22.9). For instance, China's trade with the rest of Asia accounted for 46.5% of China's total trade. China's actual amount of FDI inflows from the Asian region accounted for 77.4%. China's equity and bond inflows from the rest of Asia accounted for 44.4% and 31.1%, respectively (ADB 2020).

In terms of the balance of payments, China had relatively balanced trade with ASEAN before 2011, partly because of their complementarity on value-added chains. In fact, the largest components of both China's exports to and imports from ASEAN reflected close intra-industry linkages between the two partners. However, the balance was tilted to faster growth in China's exports than imports after 2012, reflecting the changing pattern mainly due to the rise of labor costs in China (AMRO 2018a).

The growing cross-border network of production has been part of the formation of global value chains (GVCs) in Asia where China's trade with ASEAN countries has been dominated by intermediate goods. This reflects the fact that China has become a manufacturing hub in the regional supply chain (Figure 22.10). Specifically, China has been in a position to import intermediate goods from other economies and export final goods to the

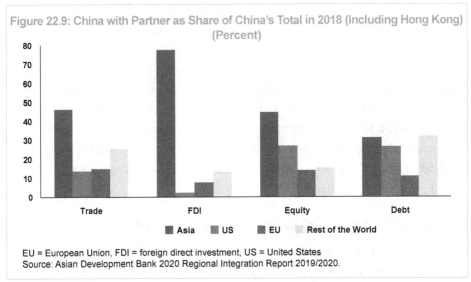

Figure 22.9: China with Partner as Share of China's Total in 2018 (Including Hong Kong) (Percent)

EU = European Union, FDI = foreign direct investment, US = United States
Source: Asian Development Bank 2020 Regional Integration Report 2019/2020.

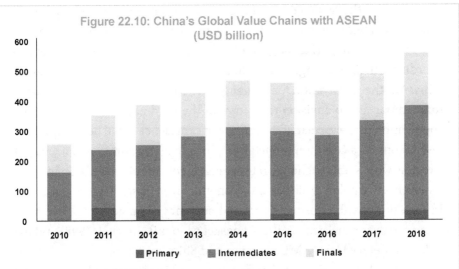

Figure 22.10: China's Global Value Chains with ASEAN (USD billion)

ASEAN = Association of Southeast Asian Nations, USD = United States dollar.
Note: Trade includes import and export; intermediates include semi-final goods and partials; finals include capital and consumption goods.
Source: United Nations Comtrade Database; Qin and Zhao (2020).

US, as suggested by the backward linkages of China and the US. In terms of forward linkages, China's exports to the US are either final goods or intermediate goods that are used by the US for further production. Some of the intermediate goods exported by the US may go back as final goods to the US (ADB 2020).

However, the rise of nationalism and trade tensions between the US and China has created uncertainties and posed negative shocks for China and most other ASEAN+3 economies. One factor that contributed to this is the fact that the US trade deficit with China could be the sum of intermediate goods exported to China from other Asian economies for China's final export to the US (AMRO 2018a). In addition, amid the reduction of global trade, the outbreak of the pandemic also showed the vulnerability of the highly centralized global production network. In particular, the global supply chain began shifting away from China, which brought challenges for both China and economies in Asia.

Regional Currency and the Role of the Renminbi

The possibility of a higher level of monetary cooperation has been discussed among economists in the aftermath of the AFC. Such an attempt has been motivated by the fact that emerging economies in Asia began showing a similar exchange rate framework — a currency basket arrangement after the crisis (Kawai 2005). This has potentially brought up the need for them to coordinate their exchange rate policies so as to avoid competitive devaluations. Another motivation for exchange rate cooperation is that it appeared to be important to envision the future of the roadmap for Asian financial cooperation. In particular, if the European experience could be of any guide, discussions on a common monetary regime, that is, a common objective of a region-wide stable exchange rate arrangement, should have been in place for an effective policy dialogue and economic surveillance (Gao 2004, 2005). In fact, the possible forms of regional currency arrangements have been proposed over time, such as the G3 basket proposal (Ito et al. 1998) and the Asian Monetary Unit (AMU) (Ogawa and Shimizu 2005).

Particularly, China's exchange rate policy has begun to have regional effects. The spillover can be mirrored by exchange rate co-movements — a factor that provides explanation for synchronized shocks across countries. Gao and Li (2020) find correlated movements between the renminbi and other Asian currencies based on China's GVC linkages in Asia. Some other works in the literatures also document the influence of the renminbi from the perspective of regional currency use. Park (2010) emphasized the renminbi denomination of financial assets and suggested a regional approach for renminbi internationalization. Gao and Yu (2012) documented the regional use of renminbi as a result of increasing cross-border trade as well as emerging desires for local currency swaps and local currency bond issuance supported by central banks and finance ministries in Asia. Fratzscher and Mehl (2011) proposed a China "dominance hypothesis" and investigated whether a tripolar international monetary system with the US dollar, euro, and renminbi had already existed. Kawai and Pontines (2014) found that, although renminbi gained some weight in East Asian economies, the US dollar continued to be the dominant anchor currency in the region. McCauley and Shu (2016) assessed the influence of renminbi movements on Asian and non-Asian currencies by taking trade links and business cycle alignments into consideration and suggested that a northeast Asian renminbi zone had been formed since 2017.

On the policy front, Chinese authorities prioritize the renminbi strategy in cross-border trade transactions with neighboring countries. In addition, Chinese loans alongside infrastructure projects under the Belt and Road Initiative (BRI) are stimulators for the use of the renminbi regionally.

Particularly, the renminbi payment system has developed into the Cross-Border Interbank System (CIPS) launched in October 2015. This system is based on real-time settlement to support renminbi payment businesses such as remittance, trade, investment, and financing. The operation of CIPS remains limited in terms of scope of participants and areas. However, as a major setup of financial infrastructure, it facilitates renminbi transactions in an efficient manner. As of the end of 2019, CIPS covered all 10 ASEAN countries and included 71 financial institutions from ASEAN countries as participants.

The renminbi settlement in China's goods trade with ASEAN countries also increased in the past decade. For instance, in 2011, the renminbi settlement in trade with ASEAN was less than CNY 200 billion; the number reached CNY 1,200 billion in 2015, the peak during the period. It declined in the following years but picked up in 2018 and remained in an upward trend, amounting to CNY 620.5 billion in 2019. Compared with trade settlement, the renminbi's use under financial transactions with ASEAN countries is still limited. In 2018, the PBC and the Ministry of Finance released new rules to standardize Panda bonds issuance. ASEAN grasped this opportunity to increase Panda bonds issuances. By the end of 2019, the issuances had covered governments, nonfinancial enterprises, and financial institutions and amounted CNY 8.5 billion, of which CNY 5 billion was issued in 2019 alone (Financial Society of Guang Xi 2020).

Regional Financial Safety Net and China's Participation

The GFSN is a loose network of various sources of financial support aimed to secure global financial stability through a multilayered set of instruments and institutions (Gallagher et al. 2020). Normally, a nation's foreign exchange reserve is regarded as the single most important first line of defense against a crisis. The central banks' bilateral swap lines are the second defense line. They are especially crucial for countries having insufficient foreign reserves. The US dollar is the prominent liquidity source and the Federal Reserve is in the position to perform the lender of last resort function. The regional financing arrangements (RFAs) serve as a third layer and is a core instrument for a group of countries in a region. Notably, the CMIM, European Stability Mechanism (ESM), Latin American Reserve Fund (FLAR), and the Arab Monetary Fund (AMF) are the RFAs that perform similar functions. The IMF with its universal funding source and wider risk sharing is the most important financial safeguard for a broad membership.

China and CMI–CMIM

In the early phase of the CMI, China contributed by signing bilateral swap arrangements (BSAs) with member countries. By the end of July 2007, China signed six BSAs with Japan, Korea, Thailand, Malaysia, the Philippines, and Indonesia, totaling USD 23.5 billion (Table 22.1). At this stage, most contracts were denominated in the US dollar. The local currencies, including the renminbi, were used in few contracts, such as the ones between China and Japan, Korea, and the Philippines.

Table 22.1: BSAs Between China and Other ASEAN+3 Countries as of July 2007

Swaps	Direction	Currency	Amount (USD billion)	Duration
China–Thailand	One-way	USD/Baht	2.0	Concluded: December 6, 2001; Expired: December 5, 2004
China–Japan	Two-way	Renminbi/Yen Yen/Renminbi	6.0	Concluded: March 28, 2002
China–Korea	Two-way	Renminbi/Won Won/Renminbi	8.0	Concluded: June 24, 2002
China–Malaysia	One-way	USD/Ringgit	1.5	Concluded: October 9, 2002
China–Philippines	One-way	Renminbi/Peso	2.0	Concluded: August 29, 2003; Amended: April 30, 2007
China–Indonesia	One-way	USD/Rupiah	4.0	Concluded: December 30, 2003; Amended: October 17, 2006

ASEAN = Association of Southeast Asian Nations, BSA = bilateral swap arrangement, USD = United States dollar.
Source: Bank of Japan, https://www.boj.or.jp/en/announcements/release_2007/data/un0707a.pdf.

In the later phase of ASEAN+3 cooperation, particularly in response to the GFC, the member countries accelerated the pace of updating RFAs. In February 2009, the finance ministers of ASEAN+3 issued the joint statement "Action Plan to Restore Economic and Financial Stability of the Asian Region." In May of the same year, China, Japan, and Korea agreed on their contributions to a common regional reserve pooling. China (including Hong Kong Monetary Authority (HKMA)) and Japan provided USD 38.4 billion each. Korea promised USD 19.2 billion. ASEAN countries' contributions ranged from 0.03% to 3.98% of the total. This joint action helped stabilize the financial market as well as laid out the foundations for the further enhancement of ASEAN+3 cooperation.

The establishment of the CMIM agreement was a milestone for the Asian RFA. CMIM came into effect on March 24, 2010. In 2014, the size of CMIM expanded from USD 120 billion to USD 240 billion. China (including HKMA) and Japan committed USD 76.8 billion each, together with Korea's contribution of USD 28.4 billion and ASEAN countries' total USD 48 billion. The IMF delinked portion of CMIM also increased to 30%.

CMIM's role in the regional financial safety net was further improved when AMRO came into operation in 2011. Since its establishment, AMRO has strengthened its capacity as a regional economic surveillance body and eventually transformed itself into an international organization in 2016. Being a core institution for CMIM, AMRO holds a special position in the regional financial safety net as well as maintains consistency and collaboration with the IMF and other RFAs (Cheng et al. 2018; Henning 2019).

In June 2020, the member countries amended the CMIM Agreement and the Operational Guidelines, thereby increasing flexibility of the financing period of the IMF-linked portion of CMIM. This introduced an overarching legal base for conditionality and for addressing legal issues. Such moves paved the way for CMIM to become a reliable self-help mechanism for ASEAN+3 and an important component of the GFSN (AMRO 2020). Although CMIM has never been activated, the ASEAN+3 countries have more choices of protection if they are in need of support.

China in the Regional Policy Dialogue and Institutional Cooperation

The rationale for strengthening policy dialogue and economic surveillance in Asia has been discussed among scholars and policymakers (Ito 2002; Kuroda and Kawai 2002). It has been commonly recognized that financial instability cannot be contained within national borders. A region-wide early warning system could facilitate the examination of financial vulnerabilities. The regional policy dialogue could help ensure effective implementation of collective policy targets. Moreover, economic surveillance could be a warranty for creditworthiness of borrowers, and regular surveillance would enable quick disbursements in times of crises (Wang and Woo 2003). However, the constraints were also recognized, such as how to coordinate the regional surveillance with existing global multilateral mechanisms like the IMF (Gao 2005).

China has been very supportive of and involved in multiple policy dialogue and economic surveillance mechanisms, ranging from regional to transregional processes, such as the Asia-Pacific Economic Cooperation (APEC); Asia–Europe Meeting (ASEM); Executives' Meeting of East Asia-Pacific Central Banks (EMEAP); South East Asia, New Zealand, Australia Initiative (SEANZA); and ASEAN+3.

Spillovers of China's economic and financial shocks to the region have become significantly important. At the same time, China also exposes itself to potential spillback effects generated in the region. The presence of such mutual spillover effects is an important reason for China's active participation in regional and transregional forums. Another reason for China's engagement lies in rising desire to be heard by the international and regional community and, if conditions are mature, to share more responsibility as a stakeholder in institutional settings. The post-GFC efforts in reforming the existing global financial governance also matched with China's interest.

One contribution that China made was to initiate a new regional financial institution — the Asian Infrastructure Investment Bank (AIIB).[2] In January 2016, the AIIB began to operate. According to its Articles of Agreement, the AIIB is designed to promote public and private investment, in particular for infrastructure and other productive sectors in Asia for development. The AIIB has also injected new ideas in governance by introducing nonresident Board of Directors. Based on the institutional framework and the purpose it serves, the AIIB is expected to be a new standard multilateral development bank (MDB). However, in the early phase of its establishment, the AIIB faced backlash and skepticism. The concerns were mainly centered on China's motivations, its relationship with the existing MDBs, and the issues related to its transparency, standards, and governance (Hong 2015; Weiss 2017). After four years' of operation, skepticism faded away. Its membership expanded to 103 approved members worldwide, although some major economies including the US and Japan have not participated.

PBC's Renminbi Swap Lines

One of the major responses to post-GFC challenges was to set up a network of bilateral swap lines with other central banks. The first bilateral swap was signed between the PBC and the Bank of Korea (BOK) in December 2008, when Korean banks experienced liquidity shortage in the fall of that year. The total amount of the swap was CNY 180 billion or KRW 38 trillion. The PBC's swap line, together with the swap lines the BOK signed with Federal Reserve and with Bank of Japan, helped strengthen Korea's defense against global illiquidity (Kim 2009).

In the following years since 2008, the PBC has signed more bilateral swaps with central banks worldwide. The time length of the PBC's swaps is

2 Another effort that China made was the establishment of New Development Bank (NDB) with Russia, Brazil, India, and South Africa. The NDB was operational in February 2016, with the initial subscribed capital of USD 50 billion shared equally among founding members. The Contingent Reserve Arrangement (CRA) with the initial committed USD 100 billion under the NDB was set to provide liquidity and precautionary instruments for the member countries under short-term balance of payments pressures.

normally 3–5 years. But the swaps can be extended by mutual consent after expiration. By the end of January 2021, the PBC had signed bilateral swaps with 39 central banks with a total amount of CNY 3,838.7 billion (including the extended and enlarged ones), among which eight contracts were signed with the central banks of ASEAN+3 members (Table 22.2).

The motivations behind PBC's established network of swap lines are twofold. One is that the GFC was a wake-up call for the region's central banks to act using local currencies in supporting financial institutions and trade flows. The PBC's participation was part of such efforts (Jin 2012). Like many other central banks' swap lines, the renminbi-denominated bilateral swap lines aim to provide liquidity support for partners in need.[3] The difference is that the role of the renminbi is more symbolic than its actual use due to limited convertibility of the renminbi. This is also because when countries have liquidity problems in the balance of payment, they are often in short of the US dollar. This is probably the reason why renminbi swaps are rarely activated. However, the PBC's swap lines help build confidence by sending a positive signal to the market on the availability of adequate liquidity in times of liquidity crisis. The PBC's swap lines have an additional purpose — to boost renminbi use in bilateral trade and investment by way of cooperation between the PBC and other monetary authorities (Gao 2018). One example was presented in the renminbi swap line signed between the PBC and Turkey's central bank in 2019. During the coronavirus disease (COVID-19) crisis, Turkey's central bank allowed its firms to settle their payment of Chinese imports using renminbi under the currency swap agreement. This is the first time that Turkey used the funding facility for renminbi under the swap line amid increasing global financial uncertainties and liquidity pressure of the US dollar (Global Times 2020).

---

3 In an interview, a PBC senior official explained the background of the PBC–BOK currency swap: "The PBC–BOK currency swap agreement is a remarkable step forward taken by emerging market economies in handling the financial crisis. The arrangement is, on the one hand, beneficial to boosting market confidence in China and Korea, as the move demonstrates both parties' willingness to further cooperation, and on the other hand, conducive to financial stability and economic development in the region as well as the financial stability in the world" (http://www.pbc.gov.cn/en/3688110/3688172/404 8341/3715012/index.html).

Table 22.2: PBC Swap Lines with Central Banks of ASEAN+3

Partner/Country or Region	Siぇ (Including Renewal) (CNY billion)	Date
Korea	360	Dec 8
HKMA	400	Jan 9
Malaysia	180	Feb 9
Indonesia	100	Mar 9
Singapore	300	Jul 10
Thailand	70	Dec 11
Japan	200	Oct 18
Macao	30	Dec 19

ASEAN = Association of Southeast Asian Nations, CNY = Chinese yuan, HKMA = Hong Kong Monetary Authority, PBC = People's Bank of China.
Source: People's Bank of China's various announcements at http://www.pbc.gov.cn and authors' calculation.

China and the Asian Regional Financial Market

After the AFC, China and many other Asian countries realized the importance of developing regional financial markets. It was widely noticed that the AFC indicated fragility of the financial system in Asian countries: the overdependence on bank-intermediated financing and huge foreign currency-denominated short-term financing. Developing regional bond markets would minimize the problems of double mismatches of both maturity and currency. It could help Asia with recycling the accumulated foreign exchange reserves in the region as most of the reserves were first invested in the developed markets and later recycled back to the region in the form of cross-border bank loans, debt and equity securities, and foreign direct investments. Furthermore, the development of regional bond markets could create a regional fundamental need for local currencies and correspondingly reduce overdependency on the US dollar.

The Asian Bond Fund (ABF) implemented in July 2003 was the first effort to foster a regional bond market. It was a transitional stage as no local currency bonds were involved and there was a lack of a secondary market. In June 2005, EMEAP launched the second stage of ABF (ABF2), with the amount of seed money up to USD 2 billion. Moreover, while the bonds issued by sovereign and quasi-sovereign issuers under the ABF1 were denominated only in the US dollar, the ABF2 allowed local currencies to denominate bond issuances in eight markets including China, Hong Kong, Indonesia, Korea, Malaysia,

Philippines, Singapore, and Thailand. The renminbi was correspondingly used in the China Fund issuance. Other major actions included the establishment of the Credit Guarantee and Investment Facility (CGIF) as a trust fund of the Asian Development Bank (ADB) with an initial capital of USD 700 million.

Given the limited size and immaturity of the Chinese domestic bond market in the time around the GFC, China realized that to promote involvement in regional bond market development, the mainland should take full advantage of the well-developed market in Hong Kong (Gao 2004). The issuance of government bonds denominated in renminbi in Hong Kong in 2007 was seen as the first step in promoting the renminbi's involvement in the bond market outside Chinese mainland. China also realized that an active attitude toward regional cooperation in the area of financial market could be a catalyst for the development of a domestic financial market. The two processes can interact with each other. In the years after the GFC, China's financial market developed rapidly, boosted by both financial opening-up policies and the market appetite for returns generated from China's growth. With more foreign participation, especially in the government bond market where the foreign investment ratio exceeded 9%, China's bond market became the second largest in the world. With the ambition of renminbi internationalization and the need for risk diversification in investment, development of the renminbi bond market constitutes a part of the regional efforts towards the development of the Asian local currency bond market.

Conclusion

Over time, China's evolving external financial policy has been following concurrent approaches: regional and global. China's initial "mute" response to Japan's proposal of an AMF reflected China's worry about possible minimization of the role of the IMF in the region (Bowies and MacLean 2017). However, China's attitude toward a regional approach is very positive. China realizes that regional financial stability is a public good that requires regional cooperation. China also learned from the AFC that its exchange rate policy could have a regional spillover effect — the Chinese nondevaluation of the renminbi during the crisis actually played a role in avoiding competitive depreciation in the region. Furthermore, the rationale for China to be engaged in regional cooperation is rooted in Chinese economic integration with the region. Thanks to China's fast growth and continuous economic and financial opening-up, China has become a major trade partner and the hub of GVCs in Asia. The Chinese currency also has regional influence aided by financial integration and favorable policies.

China's contribution to the establishment of regional financial safety nets is part of the collective contribution of ASEAN countries together with Japan and Korea. In the meantime, China joined global efforts to revive the economy and secure financial stability through various institutional setups and multilateral platforms, including the G20, IMF, World Bank, and other international financial institutions. China has also initiated new institutions such as the AIIB and the New Development Bank. China's increasing economic and financial integration with the world has helped the country learn to adopt international standards, rules of games, and best practices, and to realize the importance of a position of bargaining.

However, the rise of nationalism and trade tensions among the major economies threatens the global trading system and multilateral-based financial cooperation. The outbreak of the COVID-19 crisis has further injected uncertainties about policy reactions and economic consequences. Perhaps the most pressing downside effect of the pandemic for China is the pressure of economic decoupling and interruption of globalization. Domestically, China also faces the challenges of making a transition to a technology and innovation-driven economy and coping with an aging population (AMRO 2020). In response to the new challenges, China set out an ambitious economic strategy and focused on a "dual circulation" plan that allows China to maintain integration with the rest of the world while strengthening domestic demand. The spillover effect of such a strategy is too soon to predict. But China's commitment to openness will continue to be a major driver for the country's regional economic and financial engagement. For instance, the reconfiguration of GVCs would bring a certain degree of shocks for China. But it would also bring about an upgrading of China's position in the global supply chains. The positive outcome would also be accompanied with policies that are more transparent and less discriminatory, and would foster a better environment by improving the rule of law and legal system. Another example of a possible outcome is that a domestically demand-driven economy can make the Chinese market a major consumer in years to come, which would have multiple implications for economic relations in Asia.

References

Asian Development Bank. 2020. *Regional Integration Report 2019/2020*. Manila: Asian Development Bank.

ASEAN+3 Finance Ministers and Central Bank Governors. September, 2020. "Joint Statement of the 23rd ASEAN+3 Finance Ministers and Central Bank Governors Meeting." https://www.amro-asia.org/joint-statement-of-the-23rd-asean3-finance-ministers-and-central-bank-governors-meeting-september-18-2020-virtual/.

ASEAN+3 Macroeconomic Research Office. 2018a. *ASEAN+3 Regional Economic Outlook 2018*. Singapore: ASEAN+3 Macroeconomic Research Office.

ASEAN+3 Macroeconomic Research Office. March, 2018b. *AMRO Annual Consultation Report China — 2017*. Singapore: ASEAN+3 Macroeconomic Research Office.

ASEAN+3 Macroeconomic Research Office. March, 2020. *AMRO Annual Consultation Report China — 2019*. Singapore: ASEAN+3 Macroeconomic Research Office.

Bank of Thailand. April–June, 1998. "Bank of Thailand Economic Focus." 2 (2).

Bowies, Paul and Brian K. MacLean. 2017. "China and Asian Financial Cooperation." http://web.isanet.org/Web/Conferences/HKU2017-s/Archive/89f87f58-6374-4886-a029-9c6051197468.pdf.

BRICS. July 15, 2014. *Treaty for the Establishment of a BRICS Contingent Reserve Arrangement*. Fortaleza, Brazil. http://www.brics.utoronto.ca/docs/140715-treaty.html.

Cheng, Gong, Dominika Miernik, Yisr Barnieh, Beomhee Han, Ika Mustika Sari, Faith Qiying Pang, Tigran Kostanyan, Alexander Efimov, Marie Houdart, Alexandra de Carvalho, Carlos Giraldo, and Viviana Monroy. October 10, 2018. IMF-RFA Collaboration: Motives, State of Play, and Way Forward: A Joint RFA Staff Proposal.

China Daily. November 27, 2008. "NDRC Reveals Details of Stimulus Package." http://www.chinadaily.com.cn/business/2008-11/27/content_7246758.htm.

China Daily. January 16, 2014. http://www.china.org.cn/chinese/2014-01/16/content_31213800.htm.

Eichengreen, Barry. 2011. *Exorbitant Privilege: The Rise and Fall of the Dollar and the Future of the International Monetary System*. Oxford University Press.

Eichengreen, Barry and Michael Mussa. 1998. Capital Account Liberalization — Theoretical and Practical Aspects, *IMF Occasional Paper No. 172*.

Eichengreen, Barry and Paul Masson. 1998. Exit Strategies: Policy Options for Countries Seeking Greater Exchange Rate Flexibility. *IMF Occasional Paper No. 168*.

Financial Society of Guang Xi. August, 2020. *2020 Report on Use of RMB in ASEAN Countries*. China Finance Publishing.

Financial Stability Board. 2018; 2019. *Global Monitoring Report on Non-Bank Financial Intermediation*. Basel: Financial Stability Board.

Frankel, Jeffrey A. 1999. "No Single Currency Regime is Right for All Countries or at All Times." *NBER Working Paper Series* 7338.

Fratzscher, Marcel and Arnaud Mehl. 2011. China's Dominance Hypothesis and the Emergence of a Tri-Polar Global Currency System. *Economic Journal* 124.

Gallagher, Kevin P., Gao Haihong, William N. Kring, José Antonio Ocampo, and Ulrich Volz. November, 2020. "Safety First: Expanding the Global Financial Safety Net in Response to COVID-19." *Global Policy*. https://doi.org/10.1111/1758-5899.12871.

Gao, Haihong. 2000. "Liberalising China's Capital Account: Lessons Drawn from Thailand's Experience." *Institute of Southeast Asian Studies Working Paper. Visiting Researchers Series No. 60.*

Gao, Haihong. May-June, 2004. Toward a Financial Architecture in East Asia. *China & World Economy* 12 (3).

Gao, Haihong. July-August, 2005. "A Roadmap for Policy Dialogue and Economic Surveillance in East Asia." *China & World Economy* 13 (4).

Gao, Haihong. 2018. "RMB Internationalization." In *The New Palgrave Dictionary of Economics*, edited by Steven N. Durlauf and Lawrence E. Blume. Palgrave Macmillan.

Gao, Haihong and Yingting Li. 2020. "The Renminbi as a Trading Currency: Evidence from Selected Countries Participating in the Belt and Road Initiative." *China & World Economy* 2 (5): 45-63.

Gao, Haihong and Yongding Yu. January, 2012. "The RMB Internationalisation." In *Currency Internationalisation: Lessons from the Global Financial Crisis and Prospects for the Future in Asia and the Pacific.* BIS Papers No 61.

Global Times. 2020. https://www.globaltimes.cn/content/1192282.shtml.

Grimes, William W. 2014. "The Rise of Financial Cooperation in Asia." In *The Oxford Handbook of the International Relations of Asia*, edited by Saadia Pekkanen, John Ravenhill, and Rosemary Foot.

Henning, C. Randall. 2019. "Regional Financial Arrangements and the International Monetary Fund: Sustaining Coherence in Global Financial Governance." *CIGI Special Report.*

Hong, Yelin. 2015. "The AIIB is Seen Very Differently in the US, Europe and China." https://thediplomat.com/2015/03/chinas-controversial-asian-infrastructure-invest-ment-bank/

Huang, Yi, Marco Pagano, and Ugo Panizza. June 28, 2017. "The Dark Side of the Chinese Fiscal Stimulus: Evidence from Local Government Debt." http://voxchina.org/show-3-17.html.

Hu, Fred. 1998. The Problems of Banks and the Crisis of Asian Financial Crisis. Working Paper No. 199806 (April). National Center for Economic Research at Tsinghua University. Beijing.

International Monetary Fund. January 26, 2010. *Global Financial Stability Report GFSR Market Update: Financial System Stabilized, But Exit, Reform, and Fiscal Challenges Lie Ahead.* Washington, DC: International Monetary Fund.

International Monetary Fund. 2019. External Sector Report.

Ito, Takatoshi. 2002. "Regional Surveillance Mechanisms in East Asia." http://www.mof.go.jp/jouhou/kokkin/tyousa/tyou041f.pdf.

Ito, Takatoshi, Eiji Ogawa, and Yuri Nagataki Sasaki. 1998. "How Did the Dollar Peg Fail in Asia." *Journal of the Japanese and International Economies* 12: 256-304.

Jin, Zhongxia. 2012. "The Use of RMB in International Transactions: Background, Development and Prospect." https://china.ucsd.edu/_files/renminbi/pdf-rmb-report.pdf.

Johnson, R. Botry, Salim M. Darbar, and Claudia Echeverria. November, 1997. "Sequencing Capital Account Liberalization: Lessons from the Experiences in Chile, Indonesia, Korea and Thailand." *IMF Working Paper, No.157.*

Kawai, Masahiro. 2005. "Regional Economic Integration and Cooperation in East Asia." In *Policy Coherence towards East Asia: Development Challenges for OECD Countries,* edited by Kiichiro Fukasaku, Masahiro Kawai, Michael G. Plummer and Alexsandra Trzeciak-Duval. Paris: Development Centre, Organisation for Economic Cooperation and Development, 2005, pp. 289–345.

Kawai, Masahiro and Shinji Takagi. January 10–11, 2011. "The RMB as a Key International Currency? Lessons from the Japanese Experience." Notes prepared for the Asia-Europe Economic Forum. Paris.

Kawai, Masahiro and Victor Pontines. February, 2014. "The Renminbi and Exchange Rate Regimes in East Asia." In *Renminbi Internationalization: Achievements, Prospects, and Challenges,* edited by Barry Eichengreen and Masahiro Kawai. Washington, D.C.: Brookings Institution Press, pp. 159–204. https://www.adb.org/sites/default/files/publication/159835/adbi-renminbi-internationalization-achievements-prospects-challenges.pdf.

Kim, Kyungsoo. 2009. "Global Financial Crisis and the Korean Economy. Conference Volume: Asia Economic Policy Conference on Asia and the Global Financial Crisis (October 19–20)." The Federal Reserve Bank of San Francisco, Santa Barbara, California. https://www.frbsf.org/economic-research/files/Panel_Kim.pdf.

Kuroda, Haruhiko and Masahiro Kawai. 2002. "Strengthening Regional Financial Cooperation in East Asia." *Pacific Economic Papers* No.332 (October): 1–35. Asia Pacific School of Economics and Government, Australian National University. http://apseg.anu.edu.au/pdf/pep/pep-332.pdf.

McCauley, Robert N., and Chang Shu. 2016. Dollars and Renminbi Flowed Out of China. *BIS Quarterly Review* (March): 26–27.

Morrison, Wayne M. 2009. "China and the Global Financial Crisis: Implications for the United States." *Congress Research Service 7-5700*, June 3. www.crs.gov. RS22984.

Obstfeld, Maurice. 2015. "Trilemma and Tradeoffs: Living with Financial Globalization." *BIS Working Papers No 480.*

Ogawa, Eiji and Junko Shimizu. 2005. "AMU Deviation Indicator for Coordinated Exchange Rate Policies in East Asia." *RIETI Discussion Paper, No. 05-E-017.*

Park, Yung Chul. 2010. RMB Internationalization and its Implications for Financial and Monetary Cooperation in East Asia. *China & World Economy* 18 (2): 1–21.

People's Bank of China. 2016. "People's Bank of China Announced to Implement Macro Prudential Management of Cross Border Financing Nationwide." http://www.pbc.gov.cn/goutongjiaoliu/113456/113469/3055696/index.html.

People's Bank of China. 2017. China Financial Stability Report 2017.

People's Bank of China. 2018. China Financial Stability Report 2018.

Qin, Wang and Zhao Xuefei. 2020. "On the China-ASEAN Free Trade Area and Joint Construction of the 'Belt and Road'." *Journal of Xiamen University. No. 5 2020. General Serial No. 261*, 99–106.

State Administration of Foreign Exchange. 2019. *China Balance of Payment Report –2019*. Shanghai: State Administration of Foreign Exchange.

Sun, Guofeng and Zhewen Li. 2017. "Monetary Policy, Exchange Rate and Capital Flow — From 'Equilateral Triangle' to 'Scalene Triangle'." *PBC Working Paper Series. No. 2017/3.*

Sussangkarn, Chalongphob, Junko Shimizu, Lu Feng, Soyung Kim, Beomhee Han, Jae Yong Lee, Jinho Chol, and Hongbo Wang. 2019. "Local Currency Contribution to the CMIM." *AMRO Research Collaboration Program PCP/19-01.*

Takagi, Shiji. 2012. Internationalizing the Yen, 1984-2003: Unfinished Agenda or Mission Impossible? *BIS Paper No. 61*, 75–92.

Wang, Yunjong and Wing Thye Woo. 2003. "Moving Forward on the Establishment of an Effective Surveillance System and an Improved Financial Architecture for East Asia." *Korea Institute for International Economic Policy (KIEP) Discussion Paper 03-05.*

Weiss, Martin A. 2017. "Asian Infrastructure Investment Bank." *Congressional Research Service*, February 2.

Wu, Xiaoling. 1998. "The Influences of Banks' Non-Performing Loans on the Financial System — Lessons from Southeast Asian Financial Crisis." *Working*

Paper No. 199811 (October). National Center for Economic Research at Tsinghua University. Beijing.

Xinhua News Agency. December 10, 2008. "NDRC to Explain Economic Stimulus Measures." http://www.china.org.cn/government/central_government/2008-12/10/content_16924441.htm.

Ye, Yanfei. 2003. *The Way of Dealing with Non-Performing Loans and Its Effects on Macro-statistics in China. May. National Accounts Department.* Beijing: National Bureau of Statistics. https://www.imf.org/external/np/sta/npl/eng/2003/051603a.pdf.

Yi, Gang and Tang, Xuan. 2001. A Theory of Exchange Rate Regime "Conner Solution Hypothesis." *Journal of Financial Research* 8, 5–14.

Yu, Yongidng. 1999. "Another Fight between the Hong Kong Monetary Authority and International Speculators." *Journal of World Economy and Politics. No. 10*, 18–21.

Yu, Yongding. 2008. "Managing Capital Flows: The Case of the People's Republic of China." ADB Institute Discussion Paper No. 96.

Yu, Yongding. 2014. "Why and How Renminbi Internationalization was Brought into Policy Agenda." *ADBI Working Paper 461.*

Yu, Yongding. 2015. Understanding China's External Imbalances. *China Economic Journal* 8 (1): 40–45.

Zheng, Liansheng. March, 2018. "The Macro Prudential Assessment Framework of China: Background, Evaluation and Current and Future Policy." *CIGI Papers No. 164.*

Zhou, Xiaochuan. 2009. "Reform the International Monetary System." *BIS Review 41.*

Zhu, Rongji. 2011. *Zhu Rongji Jianghua Shilu* Vol. 3. People's Publishing House, p. 61.

Chapter 23

Japan
Managing Crises, Reforming Financial Markets, and Promoting Regional Cooperation

Masahiro Kawai and Shinji Takagi[1]

Introduction

This chapter reviews Japan's international economy of the 1990s through the late 2010s, beginning with the period leading to the Asian financial crisis (AFC) and ending with the period of so-called Abenomics that followed the global financial crisis (GFC). The period was a challenging one for Japan, during which it experienced major domestic, regional, and global crises and suffered prolonged economic stagnation. The chapter discusses overarching macroeconomic developments, structural changes in the Japanese economy, and major policy measures taken by the government and the central bank to navigate this period. It also examines Japan's financial cooperation initiatives in supporting Asia's crisis-affected countries and helping to build a regional financial architecture. The role of Japan in addressing the AFC and the GFC and in promoting Association of Southeast Asian Nations (ASEAN)+3 financial cooperation receives a particular focus.

The chapter asks critical questions related to Japan for the period extending from the dawn of the AFC to the aftermath of the GFC. Why did Japan experience a systemic banking crisis during 1997–1998 almost simultaneously with the AFC? Was there any causal relationship between the two crises? Did reversals of Japanese capital outflows trigger the crisis in Thailand and aggravate crisis situations in Asia's four crisis-hit countries, namely Indonesia, Korea, Malaysia, and Thailand? Even though Japan was not

---

[1] This chapter is written for a joint project on regional financial cooperation, hosted by the ASEAN+3 Macroeconomic Research Office (AMRO) and the Asian Development Bank (ADB). The authors are grateful to Mr. Diwa C. Guinigundo, Mr. Haruhiko Kuroda, and other seminar participants for their constructive comments. The views expressed here are the authors' own and do not represent those of AMRO, ADB, or any other institution they may have been affiliated with in the past.

exposed to toxic assets (such as mortgage-backed securities and collateralized debt obligations), why was Japan affected by the GFC much more severely than the United States (US), where the crisis had originated, and other advanced economies? Did substantial monetary easing under Abenomics have negative beggar-thy-neighbor effects on neighboring economies in Asia by creating yen depreciation? During the AFC and in its aftermath, what prompted Japan to assume leadership in supporting crisis-affected countries and in launching and strengthening ASEAN+3 regional financial cooperation?

The chapter proceeds as follows. It first presents a brief overview of Japan's macroeconomic developments as the background against which subsequent discussion will proceed. It then explains factors behind its own banking crisis during 1997–1998 just as the AFC was occurring almost simultaneously, and discusses the relationship between the two crises and the possible impact of Japanese capital outflow reversals on the four crisis-hit countries. The chapter then moves on to examine the state of the Japanese economy and finance in the period before and after the GFC. It next reviews a series of measures the Japanese government adopted to remove the remaining vestiges of restrictions on international financial transactions, further open the Japanese financial market, and promote yen internationalization through what is known as the financial "Big Bang." The penultimate section highlights Japan's international and regional cooperation initiatives during the entire period, including its support for Asia's AFC- and GFC-affected countries as well as its contributions to the design of a regional financial architecture. The final section concludes the chapter.

Macroeconomic and Exchange Rate Developments

Bursting of the Asset Price Bubble

Japan's "bubble economy" of the 1980s burst during the period of 1990–1991. From 1990 to 2019, its annual real gross domestic product (GDP) growth barely averaged 1.1% (Figure 23.1), compared to more than 4.0% during the 1980s, largely reflecting a decline in the capital stock and total factor productivity growth. Real GDP growth appeared to pick up in 1996 only to fall back. In 1998, severe recession set in, with negative growth in 1998 and 1999. Although the Japanese economy experienced the longest expansion in the post–World War II era from February 2002 to February 2008, the recovery was fragile with annual economic growth less than 2%, except in 2004. Then, the GFC tested Japan severely as exports collapsed in the last quarter of 2008, causing real GDP to contract by 1.2% and 5.7% in 2008 and 2009, respectively. The pickup of 4.1% in 2010 was a modest, partial reversal of this sharp contraction. The prolonged stagnation was compounded by sustained deflationary pressure (Figure 23.2). From 1990 to 2019, annual consumer price index (CPI) inflation averaged about 0.5%, and average annual producer price index (PPI) inflation was slightly negative at –0.03%. The level of PPI in 2019 was some 3% lower than the level in 1990, and real GDP stood only 24% higher.

In response to the bursting of the asset price bubble, Japanese authorities eased fiscal and monetary policies. First, the general government budget balance swung sharply from a surplus of 1.7% of GDP in 1991 to a deficit of 10.1% in 1998 (Figure 23.3). The fiscal balance remained in substantial deficit afterwards, averaging 6.0% of GDP, until it worsened in 2009 to a deficit of 10.1% of GDP. This caused the stock of gross public debt to rise steadily during this period from 63% in 1990 to 235% of GDP in 2019. Second, the Bank of Japan (BOJ) cut the discount rate in several steps from 6.0% in June 1991 to 0.5% in September 1995. With no additional room left to maneuver, in February 1999, the BOJ reduced the overnight call rate to virtually zero which, following the full deregulation of interest rates in 1994, had replaced the discount rate as the main policy rate (Figure 23.2).[2]

As the stance of macroeconomic policies continued to be accommodative in the form of deficit spending and conventional monetary easing, any remaining policy space began to evaporate. This meant an increasing reliance on "unconventional" monetary policy as the principal instrument of countercyclical policy. From March 2001 to March 2006, the BOJ, going beyond the zero interest rate policy (ZIRP) that had been re-introduced in February 2001, adopted what became known as quantitative easing (QE) monetary policy. This decision was made against the backdrop of falling stock prices, collapsing exports and industrial production, and a prospect of large losses by major Japanese banks. QE consisted of three pillars: (i) supplying ample liquidity by using current account balances (commercial bank deposits held at the BOJ) as the main operating target, (ii) publicly

---

[2] The BOJ terminated the de facto zero interest rate policy in August 2000.

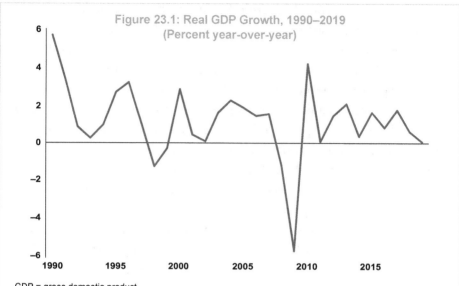

GDP = gross domestic product.
Source: Authors' compilation using data from Cabinet Office, available at www.esri.cao.go.jp/jp/sna/menu.html.

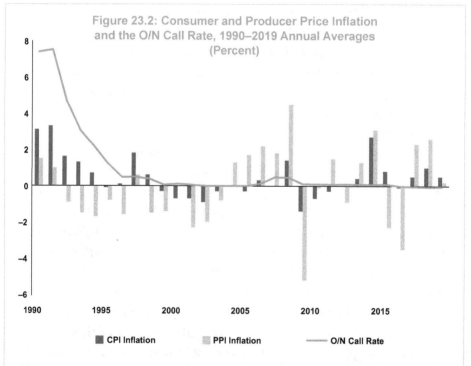

CPI = consumer price index, O/N = overnight, PPI = producer price index.
Sources: Authors' compilation using data from Bank of Japan, available at https://www.boj.or.jp/en/statistics/index.htm; Statistics Bureau, Ministry of Internal Affairs and Communications, available at https://www.stat.go.jp/data/cpi/index.html.

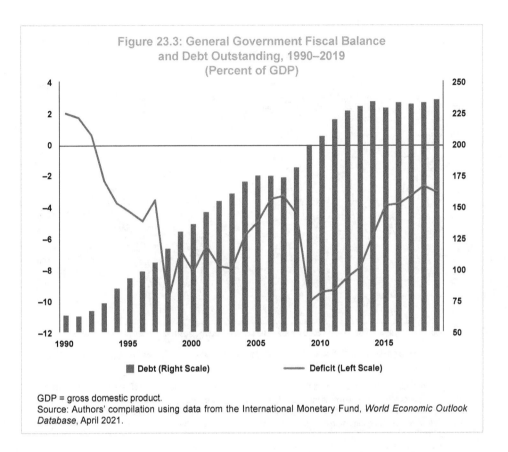

Figure 23.3: General Government Fiscal Balance
and Debt Outstanding, 1990–2019
(Percent of GDP)

Debt (Right Scale)   Deficit (Left Scale)

GDP = gross domestic product.
Source: Authors' compilation using data from the International Monetary Fund, *World Economic Outlook Database*, April 2021.

committing to maintaining ample liquidity until core CPI inflation became zero or higher on a sustained basis, and (iii) increasing purchases of Japanese government bonds (JGBs) to inject liquidity. With the recovery of economic growth in the mid-2000s, the BOJ raised the overnight call rate in August 2006, but the economy was severely affected by the GFC of 2008 and saw another round of monetary easing, as further discussed below.

Cycles of Yen Appreciation and Depreciation

Japan faced several phases of prolonged currency appreciation and depreciation (Figure 23.4). The first of these episodes occurred from mid-1990 to mid-1995, when the yen, on a real effective basis (with the base year 2000 set at 100), appreciated from around 130 in mid-1990 to 85, the most appreciated level since the early 1980s.[3] This was followed by a reversal,

---

[3] The yen–US dollar nominal exchange rate reached JPY 79.75 on April 19, 1995, the then most appreciated level in the post–World War II period.

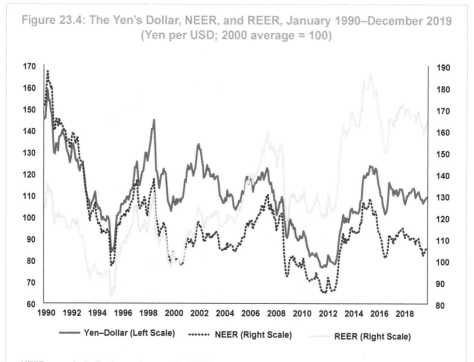

Figure 23.4: The Yen's Dollar, NEER, and REER, January 1990–December 2019 (Yen per USD; 2000 average = 100)

NEER = nominal effective exchange rate, REER = real effective exchange rate, USD = United States dollar.
Note: The yen–dollar exchange rate is the monthly average of daily exchange rates observed in the Tokyo market at 17:00 each day. An increase in value for any of the three measures is defined as a depreciation of the yen.
Source: Authors' compilation using data from the Bank of Japan, available at www.boj.or.jp/statistics/category/market.htm/.

when the yen depreciated on a sustained basis until it approached 130 in the summer of 1998.[4] The depreciation initially started as authorities attempted to counter the appreciation pressure on the yen and continued after the AFC as economic growth decelerated. From late 1997 to mid-1998, the Ministry of Finance (J-MOF) heavily intervened to stem further excessive yen depreciation.

The next cycle began when the yen's real effective exchange rate appreciated toward a level of 100 from the fall of 1999 through much of 2000, even as economic growth remained weak. Then the yen depreciated again from around 100 at the end of 2000 to around 120 during 2002–2005 when nascent economic recovery was underway. This was the backdrop against which QE was adopted, along with the "great intervention" of 2003–2004

---

[4] The yen–dollar exchange rate reached JPY 147.64 on August 11, 1998.

whose cumulative amount reached 7% of Japan's annual GDP and exceeded the corresponding period's external current account surplus. The great intervention in particular, and the intervention of the 2001–2004 period more generally, took place when the monetary base was expanding under QE.[5] It therefore effectively amounted to unsterilized intervention. From 2005 to 2007, the yen depreciated substantially in real effective terms, reaching close to 160 in mid-2007, in part driven by active yen carry trade in which private investors borrowed in yen at low or zero interest rates to invest the proceeds in high-yielding assets in foreign markets (Kawai and Takagi 2009).

The final cycle was observed as the GFC caused the yen's real effective exchange rate to sharply appreciate from around 150 in 2008 to 120 in 2009 and to remain at an appreciated level until 2012. The sharpest appreciation of this episode took place after a devastating magnitude 9.0 earthquake damaged the northeast coast of Honshu (Japan's main island) in March 2011. The material damage from the earthquake — and the successive waves of tsunami it triggered — was believed to be so large as to create investor expectations that Japanese insurance and nonfinancial firms would need to repatriate a substantial amount of capital from abroad. As the yen strengthened, retail investors with positions in foreign currencies faced margin calls, forcing them to close positions by abruptly purchasing yen, thereby exacerbating yen strength.[6] When a new government under Shinzo Abe, who promised to resort to expansionary macroeconomic policies once elected, was expected to be in place, the yen's real effective exchange rate sharply depreciated from around 123 in mid-2012 to 135 in late 2012 and then to 160 in the spring of 2013. Not only did the expectation prove correct, but the BOJ also adopted a new and enhanced round of monetary easing (known as quantitative and qualitative easing monetary policy) in April 2013, which further supported the yen's additional depreciation. In mid-2015, the yen's real effective exchange rate exceeded 180, its most depreciated level in the preceding 35 years, and remained in the range of 160–170 in the next 4 years.

---

[5] From 2001 to 2004, the increase in commercial banks' balance of current accounts of over JPY 44 trillion (about USD 374 billion, converted at the average 2001–2004 exchange rate reported by the BOJ) almost exactly corresponded to the cumulative sale of JPY 42 trillion (about USD 357 billion) in the foreign exchange market.

[6] The yen–dollar exchange rate temporarily reached the then post–World War II high of JPY 76.25 in New York trading on March 17, 2011. The next day, the J-MOF intervened in the market to sell nearly JPY 7 trillion or about USD 86 billion of yen (Takagi 2015) and intervention continued until November of the same year.

The Japanese Banking Crisis and the AFC: Background and Aftermath

From 1997 to 1999, Japan almost simultaneously experienced two crises, namely the AFC (which particularly hit Indonesia, Korea, Malaysia, and Thailand) and a domestic banking crisis. It is not possible to establish exactly how the two crises were connected. The authors' view is that, given the relatively rapid recovery of AFC-hit economies and their relatively small share in Japan's stock of external portfolio assets and bank loans, the AFC was not a predominant cause of Japan's banking crisis. For example, the share of these countries in the stock of foreign portfolio investment (FPI) assets at the end of 1998 (the earliest year for which such stock data are available) was 0.9%, and the share in the stock of total external bank loans at the end of 1996 was 5.0%.[7] The banking crisis was largely Japan's own making.

Japan's Systemic Banking Crisis

The Japanese banking crisis was a result of one of the classic real estate-led boom and bust cycles, accompanied by a stock market boom and bust. Figure 23.5 shows that stock prices peaked in December 1989, while urban land prices, nationwide average, peaked almost 2 years later in September 1991. Stock and land prices had risen by almost 130% and 60% from their respective levels in March 1986. Over the subsequent 20 years, however, stock prices moved on a downward trend toward the pre-1985 level, and land prices lost all of their gains between 1980 and 1991 and continued to decline into the 2010s.

The asset price bubble was driven largely by a steady acceleration of bank loan growth during most of the 1980s. But once asset prices collapsed, in 1991, loan growth began to slump, and growth slid steadily to around zero where it stabilized from 1994 to 1998. Between 1998 and 2005, bank loans fell sharply against the backdrop of a systemic banking crisis, the AFC, the

---

[7] However, Japanese banks' exposures to Thailand and Korea were not insignificant. Japan quickly supported IMF assistance for Thailand in the summer of 1997, as later discussed in this chapter. Japan also responded to Korean banking problems positively as a further worsening of Korea's financial crisis could have had significantly adverse impact on Japanese banks and thus Japan's banking crisis. Japan participated in the Christmas Eve 1997 agreement between Group of Seven (G7) creditor banks and the Korean government that the former would roll over their short-term credits to Korean banks for one month. Subsequently, in January 1998, the Korean government agreed to guarantee Korean banks' short-term debt maturing during 1998, while international banks from seven countries, with that guarantee, agreed to transform the maturity of their short-term loans into one, two, or three years. These agreements had a stabilizing impact on Korea's financial markets.

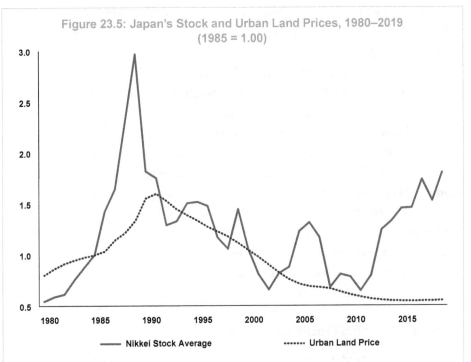

Figure 23.5: Japan's Stock and Urban Land Prices, 1980–2019
(1985 = 1.00)

—— Nikkei Stock Average   ••••••• Urban Land Price

Note: Urban land price is a nationwide average for all purposes (commercial, residential, and industrial).
Source: Authors' compilation using data from Bank of Japan, Economic and Financial Data; Japan Real Estate
Institute, Urban Land Price Index, and Wooden House Market Value Index, various issues.

2000 dot-com bubble burst in the US, and authorities' aggressive policies to
write off nonperforming loans (NPLs) and to recapitalize banks. The fall in
bank loans was a reflection of substantial deleveraging by the nonfinancial
corporate sector. Surprisingly, bank lending continued to contract even after
economic growth resumed in 2003, but finally made a modest recovery in
2006, only to be reversed by the Lehman shock in 2008.

Japan's post-bubble economy had several unique features (Kawai and
Morgan 2013). First, nominal GDP did not increase at all. Although it rose
modestly throughout most of the 1990s and peaked in 1997, it declined
thereafter. Nominal GDP in 2007 was below the 1997 peak before being
further reduced by the GFC. Even so, real GDP steadily rose, given a falling
GDP deflator. Second, the prolonged deflation of goods and services prices
set in (Figure 23.2). Third, private capital investment slowed down sharply,
especially when adjusted for capital depreciation. Thus, the growth of capital
stock slowed down considerably. Fourth, nominal interest rates declined to

extremely low levels (essentially zero for those on short-term instruments, Figure 23.2). Finally, government debt rose to an alarming level (Figure 23.3) as a result of persistently large deficit spending to support aggregate demand and expanding social expenditure related to its rapidly aging population.

Several factors contributed to the Japanese banking crisis: (i) overextension of bank loans in risky investment under the general environment of inadequate supervision and regulation over banks during the bubble period, which later became nonperforming; (ii) severe negative impact of the bursting of the bubble and the prolonged pace of deleveraging, leading to persistent asset price deflation and causing real estate-related bank loans to become nonperforming; (iii) delayed and inadequate monetary policy responses following the bursting of the bubble, failing to prevent price deflation and yen appreciation;[8] (iv) economic slowdown in the 1990s; and (v) a delay in policy action, in the form of regulatory forbearance and "zombie" financing, to decisively contain the banking sector problem.[9]

Japanese Capital Outflows to Crisis-Hit Countries

The AFC occurred in 1997 when Thailand and other countries experienced a sudden reversal of the large capital inflows they had received in previous years. An important question therefore is what role, if any, Japan may have played in the buildup of crisis vulnerabilities and in the triggering of the crisis. To be sure, Japan was a large capital exporter both to the world and to the region. Although it is not possible to identify exactly how much of Japan's global capital outflows were recycled into and out of the AFC-hit countries (e.g., through Hong Kong, Singapore, London, or New York), data suggest that Japanese resident investors largely played a stabilizing role in the AFC-hit countries, except perhaps in Korea.

Two policy actions taken by Japanese authorities may have contributed to the surge in capital outflows from Japan to the world in 1995 and 1996.

---

[8] It was only in March 1995 that the BOJ cut the overnight call rate below 2%.

[9] Kawai (2005) provides several reasons for the delay in decisive policy action in Japan: the initial approach, which was based on the expectation that a resumption of economic growth would restore the financial health of banks and their clients; Keynesian fiscal policy, which supported minimum aggregate demand and helped insolvent corporations ("zombie" firms) survive; and absence of domestic pressure (due to high savings, low inflation, relatively low unemployment, and political and social stability) and external constraints (due to large foreign exchange reserves, a large net external asset position, no prospect for capital flight, and little risk of balance of payments difficulty or currency crisis), which otherwise would have prompted the government to accelerate the resolution of banking sector problems.

Japan had earlier experienced a sustained, sharp real effective appreciation of the yen from 130 in 1990 to 85 in 1995, even as the country was trapped in recession. As a result, authorities attempted to stem the tide of yen appreciation from April 1993 through 1995 by selling yen in the market, including in coordination with other G7 authorities. This was coupled with a further easing of monetary policy and a package of foreign investment promotion measures for Japanese institutional investors, such as: (i) relaxation of rules governing both foreign currency- and yen-denominated external lending by insurance companies, (ii) elimination of restrictions on the repatriation of nonresident euroyen bonds, (iii) revision of the valuation method for foreign bonds held by institutional investors, and (iv) promotion of purchases of foreign bonds by banks by relaxing foreign exchange position controls.

Figure 23.6 depicts Japan's capital outflows to the four AFC-hit countries and Asia during the period 1995–2001 based on its balance of payment (BOP) data (see Box 23.1 for a detailed explanation of the figure). First, a good portion of Japanese investment in Asia was foreign direct investment (FDI), which during 1995–1996 constituted as much as 44% of all Japanese investment in Indonesia, 55% in Malaysia, and 26% in Thailand.[10] FDI was the most stable part of Japanese investment. Second, the withdrawal of FPI by Japanese investors during 1997 was small, amounting to a mere JPY 14.0 billion (USD 0.1 billion), JPY 115.0 billion (USD 0.9 billion), JPY 28.0 billion (USD 0.2 billion), and JPY 42.0 billion (USD 0.3 billion) from Indonesia, Korea, Malaysia, and Thailand, respectively. Third, Japanese financial firms, including banks and institutional investors, maintained their exposure to Indonesia and Thailand throughout 1997, though not to Korea or Malaysia. Indeed, they reduced exposure to the latter two countries in 1997 and 1998 by as much as JPY 290.0 billion (about USD 2.4 billion) and JPY 117.0 billion (about USD 0.9 billion), respectively, in the case of Korea, though the reversal was much more limited for Malaysia. Japanese financial firms began to retreat from global foreign lending only in 1998 as the domestic banking crisis unfolded. Their global external lending in 1997 was larger than the amount during 1995–1996, at JPY 19.7 trillion (about USD 162.6 billion), but precipitously fell to a mere JPY 1.0 trillion (about USD 7.6 billion) in 1998 and turned negative in 1999, amounting to a withdrawal of as much as JPY 30.6 trillion (USD 269.0 billion).

---

[10]The share of FDI in Korea was rather small at 10%, given the country's restrictive investment regime.

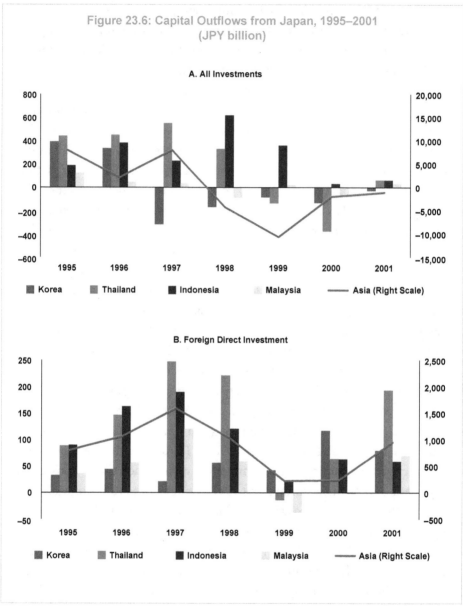

Figure 23.6: Capital Outflows from Japan, 1995–2001
(JPY billion)

A. All Investments

B. Foreign Direct Investment

continued on next page

Figure 23.6: *continued*

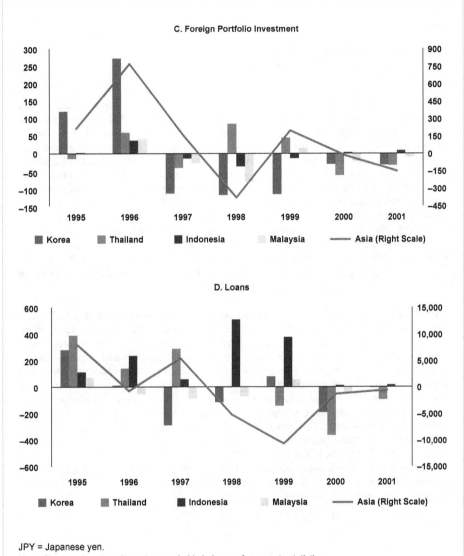

JPY = Japanese yen.

Note: Changes in external assets recorded in balance of payments statistics.

Source: Authors' compilation using data from the Japanese Ministry of Finance, available at www.mof.go.jp/pri/publication/zaikin_geppo/hyou08.htm.

Box 23.1:

Japanese Capital Outflows Before and During the AFC

Japan was a large capital exporter during 1995 and 1996, acquiring external assets globally amounting to JPY 19.9 and JPY 14.6 trillion (or USD 212.0 and USD 134.0 billion, converted at the respective annual average exchange rates), respectively. Of this total (JPY 34.5 trillion or USD 346.0 billion), FDI assets were JPY 4.7 trillion (USD 42.0 billion), FPI assets were JPY 20.5 trillion (USD 200.0 billion), and bank loans were JPY 16.5 trillion (USD 175.0 billion). Even though the amounts directly invested in Asia, including the four AFC-hit countries, during 1995–1996 were modest (JPY 10.1 trillion or USD 104.4 billion for Asia as a whole, JPY 571.0 billion or USD 5.5 billion in Indonesia, JPY 726.0 billion or USD 7.2 billion in Korea, JPY 167.0 billion or USD 1.7 billion in Malaysia, and JPY 887.0 billion or USD 8.7 billion in Thailand, see Figure 23.6), they were sizable in relation to the amounts of International Monetary Fund (IMF) financing requested by Indonesia, Korea, and Thailand, which were USD 11.2 billion, USD 21.0 billion, and USD 4.0 billion, respectively. In addition, part of Japanese capital outflows to the rest of the world were likely intermediated through global financial centers and directed to the crisis-hit countries, although it is not possible to obtain such data.

Among the AFC-hit countries, patterns of change in Japanese capital outflows in 1997–1998 differed from country to country. In the case of Korea, there was a clear capital outflow reversal during 1997–1998, amounting to a total of –JPY 489.0 billion (–USD 3.9 billion). Reversals of loan and FPI outflows to Korea more than offset the FDI outflows to Korea. Japanese banks were part of the mass exodus of short-term credits provided to Korean banks even as they expanded their global exposure in 1997. Malaysia likewise saw a similar pattern to Korea, although the severity of the capital outflow reversal was much more limited as Japanese outflows to the country remained positive in 1997 and saw only a modest reversal in 1998 (amounting to –JPY 91.0 billion or –USD 0.7 billion) driven largely by a withdrawal of FPI. In contrast, overall capital outflows to Thailand declined only marginally from 1995–1996 to 1997–1998 (maintaining a total outflow of JPY 878 billion or USD 7 billion), and turned negative only in 1999 when economic recovery was already underway. More interestingly, Japanese capital outflows to Indonesia rose from 1995–1996 to 1997–1998 (amounting to a total of JPY 848.0 billion or USD 6.6 billion) and remained positive afterwards.

Some have argued that Japanese banks played a role in triggering and aggravating the crisis in the AFC-hit countries by extending excessive loans in the pre-crisis period and withdrawing them quickly at the first sign of trouble. Unfortunately, no BOP data are available on loan outflows by banks. However, the Bank for International Settlements (BIS) provides locational banking statistics (LBS) and consolidated banking statistics (CBS), which can be used to identify changes in cross-border claims on the four AFC-hit countries by residence and nationality, extended by Japanese, US and

European, and other banks (Table 23.1).[11] One can clearly observe, in either set of statistics, a pre-crisis build-up followed by a post-crisis unwinding of all cross-border bank claims for each AFC-hit country. Such a pattern

Table 23.1: Changes in Cross-Border Bank Claims on Residents of the Four AFC-Hit Countries and Major Creditors' Shares

Country	Locational Banking Statistics				Consolidated Banking Statistics			
	All	Japan	United States and Europe	Other	All	Japan	United States and Europe	Other
	(USD billion)	(%)	(%)	(%)	(USD billion)	(%)	(%)	(%)
Korea								
Q4 1993→Q2 1997	72.9	18.7	44.4	36.9	62.6	18.7	34.5	46.8
Q2 1997→Q4 1998	−44.4	10.6	48.2	41.4	−38.5	16.9	32.7	50.1
Thailand								
Q4 1993→Q4 1996	44.8	42.2	9.9	47.8	40.4	53.0	22.0	25.0
Q4 1996→Q4 1998	−47.4	31.0	7.8	61.2	−23.0	65.7	28.3	6.5
Indonesia								
Q4 1993→Q4 1997	27.3	2.6	31.5	65.9	29.4	19.0	30.3	50.7
Q4 1997→Q4 1998	−11.9	1.7	28.6	69.7	−14.3	39.2	20.3	39.9
Malaysia								
Q4 1993→Q2 1997	16.9	18.3	13.6	66.9	15.8	33.5	27.8	38.0
Q2 1997→Q4 1998	−9.3	29.0	14.0	55.9	−8.3	47.0	28.9	24.1

AFC = Asian financial crisis, Q = quarter, USD = United States dollar.

Note: Changes in cross-border bank claims are calculated using data from the Bank for International Settlements' locational banking statistics and consolidated banking statistics. For each Asian Financial Crisis-hit country, the entire period (the fourth quarter (Q4) of 1993 to Q4 1998) is divided into two sub-periods, that is, the period until all cross-border claims reached a peak and the period after the peak. A negative figure means a decline in the stock of cross-border bank claims.

Source: Compiled by authors from the Bank for International Settlements, *Locational Banking Statistics* and *Consolidated Banking Statistics*.
http://stats.bis.org:8089/statx/srs/table/A6.2?c=ID&p=&f=csv
http://stats.bis.org:8089/statx/srs/table/B4?c=ID&p=&f=csv

---

[11] The LBS provides information on banks' balance sheets and the geographical distribution of their counterparties and captures the outstanding financial assets and liabilities of internationally active banks located in reporting countries against counterparties residing in more than 200 countries, in a way consistent with BOP and international investment position data. The CBS captures the worldwide consolidated positions of internationally active banking groups headquartered in reporting countries in a way consistent with the consolidation approach taken by banking supervisors. Both are reported to the BIS at a country level.

of build-up and withdrawal is most visible in numerical terms in the case of Korea and Thailand, followed by Indonesia and Malaysia. Although not shown in the table, both LBS and CBS data reveal that internationally active banks did not withdraw a significant amount of cross-border claims from Thailand between the fourth quarter (Q4) of 1996 (a peak quarter) and Q2 1997, suggesting that the baht crisis of July 1997 was not triggered by the behavior of international banks, including Japanese banks.

Even though the LBS data are compiled in a way consistent with BOP and international investment position statistics, they give information somewhat different from Japanese BOP data on loan outflows. The discrepancy is particularly large in the case of Japanese bank claims on Thailand in 1997 and 1998. The table shows that during 1997–1998 Japanese banks reduced cross-border claims on Thailand by USD 14.7 (= 47.4 × 0.31) billion, suggesting a large capital outflow reversal, whereas the BOP-based loan data presented in Figure 23.6D, including those made by banks, institutional investors, and other financial firms, actually recorded an outflow of USD 2.4 billion. If both sets of data (Japanese BOP and BIS-LBS data) are accepted as accurate, it follows that non-bank loan outflows from Japan to Thailand more than offset the withdrawal of Japanese bank loans from Thailand during 1997–1998.

Further, there is also a discrepancy between the LBS and CBS data, particularly for Japanese banks. The contribution made by Japanese banks to the pre-crisis build-up and the post-crisis withdrawal of cross-border bank loans is larger in the CBS than in LBS data. The discrepancy between the two is most notable in the case of Thailand and Indonesia, where Japanese banks globally contributed more than 50% and close to 20% in the case of the build-up, and more than 65% and close to 40% in the case of the unwinding of cross-border bank loans, respectively. This suggests that, more than their parent banks in Japan, Japanese bank branches and subsidiaries abroad, such as those based in Singapore, Hong Kong, and other global financial centers, played a greater role in the build-up and withdrawal of cross-border bank loans in Thailand and Indonesia. BOP data do not adequately capture banks' lending behavior outside the country's jurisdiction. This is not unique to Japanese banks. The same can be said about the behavior of globally active non-Japanese banks, including those from Europe and the US, before, during, and after the crisis.

In sum, the BOP data show that overall capital outflows from Japan to the AFC-hit countries remained positive in 1997 (with the exception of those to Korea) and in 1998 (except Korea and Malaysia), suggesting that Japanese resident investors, for the most part, played a stabilizing role at least for Indonesia and Thailand. On the other hand, the BIS data on international bank loans suggest the possibility that Japanese banks located abroad withdrew their loans even from Thailand and Indonesia. To make a solid assessment of the role played by Japanese non-resident investors, full information about their behavior, including the extent to which they mobilized Japanese domestic savings, would be needed. In the case of Korea, Japanese banks agreed on rollovers and maturity extension of short-term external debt of Korean banks in late 1997 and early 1998 and thereby contributed to the stabilization of the country's financial markets. In the case of Malaysia, the Japanese government provided financial support to the country under the New Miyazawa Initiative (NMI), to be discussed below, and partially mitigated the potentially negative impact of capital outflow reversals.

Banking Sector Restructuring and the Yen

The yen's depreciation, which had begun in 1995, accelerated during the middle of the AFC and continued through 1998. The depreciation occurred against the backdrop of a fragile banking sector in systemic crisis, caused by prolonged economic stagnation and rising NPLs. With slow growth, deflation, and a collapse of asset prices, especially in the real estate market, the value of NPLs held by banks had declined sharply, putting a large number of banks in difficulty (Hoshi 2001). The problem was likely compounded by the AFC, which caused international investors, rightly or wrongly, to reassess the health of the Japanese banking sector exposed to the region. As foreign investors began to pull out of the Japanese equity market, especially out of financial sector stocks, the Nikkei stock average fell precipitously, for example, from more than JPY 20,000 in June to less than JPY 16,500 in October 1997.

This was a bleak moment for the Japanese economy. Real GDP would fall by 2% in 1998, and negative growth would continue for another year. It was under these circumstances that, in November 1997, three major financial firms — Sanyo Securities, Hokkaido Takushoku Bank, and Yamaichi Securities — failed, bringing down the stock prices of other major financial firms. At the end of the month, the so-called Japan premium, a premium that Japanese banks faced in raising funds in the international wholesale market, reached 1%, virtually squeezing them out of the market (Sakakibara 2000). On the other hand, the yen funding costs for foreign financial institutions edged closer to zero (and reached below zero occasionally). This started the process of foreign financial institutions borrowing yen in the domestic market and investing the proceeds abroad in what became known as the global carry trade, placing further downward pressure on the yen exchange rate.

In February 1998, the Japanese Diet passed a set of laws to address the banking crisis, including an appropriation of JPY 13.0 trillion (about USD 103.3 billion) for the resolution of failed banks. The euphoria turned to disappointment when the injection of public money in March 1998, at a mere JPY 1.8 trillion (about USD 14.0 billion), was perceived to be miniscule compared to the total magnitude of the NPLs in the banking sector (Sakakibara 2000). The yen–dollar exchange rate, which stood at JPY 126 in mid-February, reached JPY 135 in early April. The J-MOF intervened sporadically in the foreign exchange market to stem excessive yen depreciation, even as the Japanese government announced a JPY 16.0 trillion (about USD 121.4 billion) economic stimulus package. The largest single-day yen purchase intervention so far, amounting to JPY 2.62 trillion (about USD 19.90 billion), took place in April 1998.[12] The impact of intervention, if any, was short-lived. In June 1998, the banking crisis flared up again as the difficulties of the Long-Term Credit Bank of Japan (LTCB) was reported in the press (LTCB and the Nippon Credit Bank were eventually nationalized toward the end of the year) and the Japan premium rose sharply.

As the yen reached a new low of JPY 146 per US dollar, Japan secured the commitment of the US Treasury for coordinated intervention in exchange for Japan's pledge to implement further fiscal stimulus measures and a decisive plan to deal with the banking crisis, which took place in June 1998 (Sakakibara 2000).[13] Downward pressure on the yen finally began to subside as Western financial institutions, distressed by the Russian default, evidently started to reverse the yen carry trade (Sakakibara 2000). The yen began to stabilize at a more appreciated level amid news of positive developments

---

[12] Even larger single-day interventions were observed following the Great East Japan Earthquake, namely in August (JPY 4.51 trillion or about USD 58.50 billion) and October (JPY 8.07 trillion or about USD 105.20 billion) in 2011.

[13] Despite these efforts, the yen–dollar exchange rate drifted downward again, recording the post-bubble peak of JPY 147.64 on August 11, 1998.

in the banking sector. In October 1998, the Diet passed legislation to allow JPY 60 trillion (about USD 495 billion) of public money to be injected into troubled banks to augment their capital. The newly created Financial Reconstruction Commission and the Financial Supervisory Agency injected about JPY 7.5 trillion (about USD 62.0 billion) of public funds into 15 large banks in March 1999 before recapitalizing five regional banks with about JPY 290.0 billion (about USD 2.5 billion).[14]

The 1997–1998 banking crisis prompted the government to take a more aggressive policy to tackle the banking sector problem. Authorities focused on banking sector stabilization and restructuring through closure or temporary nationalization of non-viable banks, recapitalization of weak but viable banks, tighter loan classification and loan loss provisioning, acceleration of NPL disposal, and corporate debt and operational restructuring. As a result, by 2003, banks' capital had been strengthened, profitability stopped declining, and the Japanese banking system restored a sense of stability and health, setting the stage for sustained economic recovery. Bank safety nets were fully in place, and credit allocation was made more rational.

Thus, it was 2003 when the stability and functioning of the financial system began to improve. The economy returned to a full-fledged recovery path supported by export-led growth due to global expansion. During the bank and corporate restructuring process, Japanese banks incurred cumulative losses of some JPY 96.0 trillion (about USD 817.0 billion, converted at the 1998–2000 average exchange rate), roughly 20% of Japan's GDP, and the government spent JPY 47.1 trillion (about USD 401.0 billion), of which JPY 25.1 trillion (or 53% of total) was recovered. Judging from the size of fiscal outlays required to resolve the crisis, the cost of addressing the Japanese banking crisis of 1997 was larger than the crisis cost experienced by the US in 2007–2011 but considerably smaller than those experienced by Indonesia, Korea, Malaysia, and Thailand during the AFC or by Greece and Ireland from 2008 to 2012 (Laeven and Valencia 2018).[15]

---

[14]The yen–dollar exchange rate appreciated from JPY 135 at the beginning of October to JPY 114 in mid-month, an appreciation of some 15% in just over 2 weeks (Takagi 2015).

[15]Laeven and Valencia (2018), based on a standard metric of fiscal spending, placed Japan's outlays at 8.6% of GDP, compared to 56.8% in Indonesia, 43.8% in Thailand, 31.2% in Korea, and 16.4% in Malaysia (while comparable figures outside Asia were 37.6% in Ireland, 28.7% in Greece, and 4.5% in the US).

The GFC: Background and Aftermath

Structural Change and Greater Openness of the Japanese Economy

Against the background of sustained yen weakness from around 2001, three important structural changes took place in Japan's external sector. First, not only did the GDP share of exports increase, from around 10% in the early 1990s to over 17% in the second half of the 2000s, but Japan's overall trade openness (the value of exports and imports divided by GDP) also rose from less than 20% to 35% during the same period (Table 23.2). Partly corresponding to the greater openness of the Japanese economy was a declining share of the nontradable goods sector. During the "lost decade" of the 1990s, the share of the nontradable goods sector expanded in a way consistent with a real exchange rate level that was more appreciated than the historical average. As the yen's real effective exchange rate returned to a level more consistent with the long-run average, the share of nontradable

Table 23.2: Japan's Changing External Sector, 1990–2019
(Percent of GDP; Percent share of Asia in total)

Components of the External Sector	1990	1995	2000	2005	2010	2015	2019
Percent of GDP							
Exports	10.4	8.8	10.5	13.8	14.9	17.4	17.4
Imports	9.2	7.6	9.1	12.4	13.6	18.0	17.7
Exports Plus Imports	19.5	16.4	19.6	26.2	28.5	35.4	35.1
FDI Assets Abroad	6.2	5.8	6.0	8.7	13.6	28.2	36.5
FPI Assets Abroad	17.2	16.5	28.0	46.9	53.3	76.5	88.4
Bank Assets Abroad	29.1	24	25.7	39.1	45.7	71.0	76.3
Percent Share of Asia							
Exports	31.1	43.5	41.2	48.4	56.3	53.4	53.8
Imports	28.8	36.9	41.9	44.6	44.8	49.4	48.0
FDI Assets Abroad	n.a.	30.6[1]	17.7	22.7	25.6	28.5	27.8
FPI Assets Abroad	n.a.	n.a.	2.0	1.6	2.7	3.5	3.4
Bank Assets Abroad	3.6	5.7	3.4	2.3	3.5	5.3	5.4

FDI = foreign direct investment, FPI = foreign portfolio investment, GDP = gross domestic product, n.a. = not available.
Note:
[1] For 1996.
Sources: Authors' compilation using data from Japanese Ministry of Finance, Bank of Japan and Cabinet Office. www.mof.go.jp/pri/publication/zaikin_geppo/hyou08.htm; https://www.boj.or.jp/statistics/bis/ibs/index.html/; www.esri.cao.go.jp/jp/sna/menu.html.

goods in Japanese output began to decline from a peak achieved in 2002 (Kawai and Takagi 2011).[16]

Second, Japan's trade integration with other Asian economies deepened as China overtook the US in 2007 as the nation's largest trading partner. Asia's share in Japan's total exports rose by 20 percentage points from the early 1990s to the late 2000s, far surpassing the shares of North America and Europe. This was achieved as part of a larger trend of regional economic integration through the development of supply chains with other Asian economies, where the share of intraregional trade rose from 30% to more than 50% of total trade over three decades. Closely related to supply chain-driven intraregional trade was a rise in intraregional FDI. Japan's direct investment in plants and equipment in other Asian economies created production networks and value chains in industries such as electronics, automobiles, and other machinery products that cut across national borders — a flipside of the growing intraregional trade. As the center of these expanding production networks, over 90% of Japan's exports consisted of highly income elastic products, including industrial supplies, parts and components, and capital goods, not to mention consumer durables.

Third, as part of these developments, the composition of Japan's external current account surplus changed against net exports in favor of net income (Figure 23.7).[17] While the value of both exports and imports expanded substantially, the country's chronic surplus in its trade balance saw a sharp decline after 2007. In the immediate aftermath of the GFC, from the third quarter of 2008 to the first quarter of 2009, Japan even recorded a deficit in its trade balance for the first time in nearly 20 years; this was followed by annual trade balance deficits during 2011–2013. In contrast, the surplus on net income from abroad rose steadily from JPY 3.3 trillion (or USD 23.0 billion) in 1990 to a pre-GFC peak of JPY 15.1 trillion (or USD 128.0 billion)

---

[16] Kawai and Takagi (2011) define the nontradable goods sector to include construction, electricity, gas, water, wholesale and retail trade, banking and insurance, real estate, transportation, telecommunication, and services.

[17] Even though Japan's external current account remained in surplus throughout, the sources of the surplus changed from the savings-investment (S-I) perspective. In the mid-1980s the surplus was largely attributable to high net savings of the household sector and an improved S-I balance in the public sector. In the 1990s the corporate sector improved its S-I balance significantly by raising savings and reducing investment, while the public sector S-I balance deteriorated quickly. In the 2000s, a widening of the current account surplus reflected a massive improvement in the corporate sector S-I balance, which more than offset the deterioration in the household and public sector balances. See Kawai and Takagi (2015).

Figure 23.7: Components of the Current Account Balance, 1990–2019
(Percent of GDP)

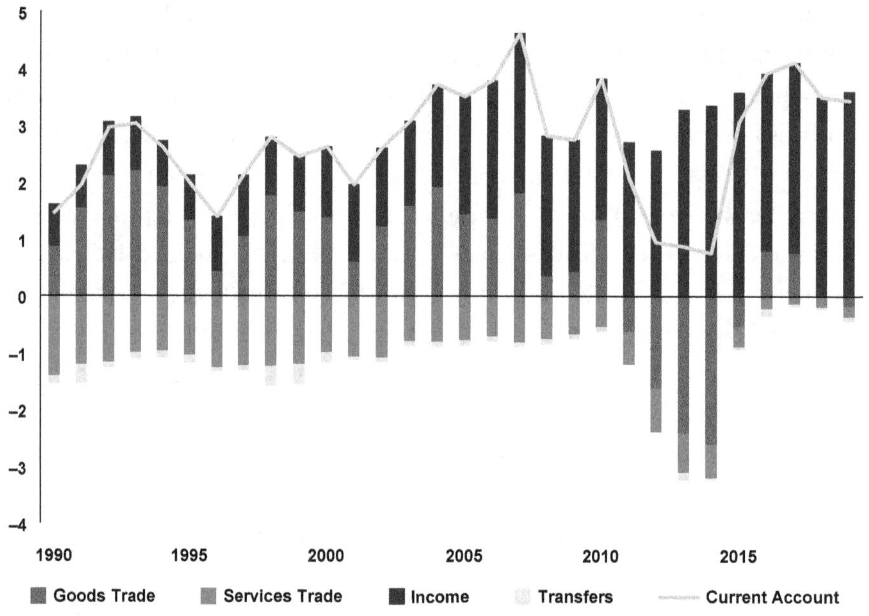

GDP = gross domestic product.

Source: Authors' compilation using current account data from Japanese Ministry of Finance, available at https:// www.mof.go.jp/policy/international_policy/reference/balance_of_payments/bpnet.htm; national income data from Cabinet Office, available at: www.esri.cao.go.jp/jp/sna/menu.html.

in 2007. In 2011, when the nation-wide shutdown of nuclear power plants necessitated significant imports of mineral fuels,[18] the income surplus of JPY 13.5 trillion (or USD 169.0 billion) more than offset the trade balance deficit for goods and services of JPY 3.1 trillion (or USD 39.0 billion), with similar patterns repeating during 2012–2015 and again in 2019.

Higher costs of production in Japan, exacerbated by a higher value of the yen beginning in the late 1980s, encouraged Japanese manufacturing firms to shift their production activities abroad. The ratio of overseas to total output produced and sold by all Japanese manufacturing firms rose steadily

---

[18]The Great East Japan Earthquake on March 11, 2011 was followed by a devastating tsunami that disabled the backup electricity-generating systems at the Fukushima Daiichi Nuclear Power Plant, resulting in the second most serious nuclear accident in world history after the Chernobyl power plant explosion in Ukraine, the former Soviet Union, in 1986. Following the nuclear plant failure, the Japanese government shut down virtually all nuclear power plants throughout the country.

from 3% in 1985 to 18% in 2011 (the rise was from 8% to 32% when only those operating abroad are considered). Likewise, the ratio of overseas to total equipment investment made by all Japanese manufacturing firms rose from 5% in 1986 to 22% in 2011 (Kawai and Takagi 2015). Japanese firms increasingly exported parts and components to their production sites and subsidiaries in the rest of Asia while importing finished products or exporting them from Asian factories to third markets in North America and Europe. The compositional changes in the external current account reflected these developments.

Severe Impact of the GFC on the Japanese Economy

These structural changes explain why Japan was hit so hard by the GFC in late 2008 despite the fact that its financial system was relatively free of toxic assets such as mortgage-backed securities and collateralized debt obligations.[19] Industrial production contracted sharply in the fourth quarter of 2008 and the first and second quarters of 2009 by 15.0%, 34.0%, and 27.6% (year-over-year), respectively. Although the fall in output was attributable to a confluence of factors — including stock price declines that eroded the capital base of commercial banks as well as the lagged impact of a sharp rise in oil and other commodity prices in the summer of 2008 — the primary cause was the negative effect of economic contraction in the US and Europe on world trade. In this environment, Japan was particularly vulnerable because output had become much more responsive to demand shocks coming from abroad (Kawai and Takagi 2011). Japan's exports to the US and European markets were adversely affected, both directly and indirectly. Given Japan's strong trade links to other Asian economies, the collapse of these economies' exports to North America and Europe had a ripple effect on Japan's exports to this region, a large portion of which consisted of industrial supplies, parts and components, and capital goods.

In fact, Japan was the only major advanced economy that experienced negative economic growth for the year 2008. Although most advanced economies experienced recession in 2009, Japan's economic contraction (of 5.4%) surpassed the contractions experienced by the US, the Euro Area,

---

[19]Credit-related write-downs in the banking sector for 2007–2010 were estimated by the IMF to be a mere USD 149 billion for Japan, compared to USD 2,712 billion for the US and USD 1,193 billion for Europe (France, Germany, Italy, the Netherlands, Spain, Switzerland, and the United Kingdom), as quoted in Kawai and Takagi (2011).

and the United Kingdom, where the financial crisis for the most part had originated. Japan recovered part of the output loss in 2010 by growing by 4.2% but experienced negative growth again in 2011 due to the earthquake-related triple disasters. In contrast, most of the major Asian economies fared much better, notably with China, India, and Indonesia maintaining positive growth in 2009. Although Singapore and Taiwan Province of China were deeply affected, they recovered rather quickly, as did Korea.

Even so, the yen appreciated sharply in both nominal and real terms during this period, in part reflecting the perception that the yen was a safe haven currency (Botman et al. 2013), combined with the unwinding of the global yen carry trade as American and European investors repatriated their investments from Asia and other emerging regions (Iwata 2010; Kawai and Takagi 2011). Authorities, refraining in principle from intervening in the foreign exchange market, instead eased fiscal and monetary policies, initially in coordination with the other Group of Twenty (G20) countries. Although the public debt-to-GDP ratio was already high (at about 175.0%), the government expanded fiscal policy substantially, with the deficit widening from 3.2% of GDP in 2007 to 4.5% in 2008 and further to 9.0%–10.0% during 2009–2011. The stimulus measures included cash payments, public works, subsidies for energy-efficient purchases, a higher gift tax exemption to support spending, and vocational training.

Initially, in September 2008, the BOJ expanded the range of eligible JGBs for repo operations and reduced the minimum fee for the Security Lending Facility from 1.0% to 0.5%. In late October, 3 weeks after coordinated interest rate cuts by European and US monetary authorities went into effect, the BOJ cut the call rate by 20 basis points to 0.3% and the discount rate (now renamed the basic loan rate under the complementary lending facility) by 25 basis points to 0.5%. Because the BOJ had not participated in the earlier coordinated interest rate cuts, the yen–dollar exchange rate appreciated sharply from about JPY 100 to about JPY 90 toward the end of October. The call rate and the basic loan rate were further cut to 0.1% and 0.3% in December, respectively, again following similar actions by the other advanced economy central banks.

Additional easing measures ensued. In early December, the BOJ raised its monthly purchases of JGBs from JPY 1.2 trillion (about USD 13.0 billion) to JPY 1.4 trillion (about USD 15.0 billion) and introduced a time-bound measure to provide unlimited liquidity to financial institutions against relaxed collateral requirements. In January 2009, the BOJ began outright purchases of commercial paper (CP) and asset-backed CP up to JPY 3 trillion (about USD 33 billion) and, in February, reinstated the program of purchasing stocks held by financial institutions (through April 2010) and started outright purchases of corporate bonds up to JPY 1 trillion (about USD 11 billion). In March, the BOJ further raised monthly purchases of JGBs to JPY 1.8 trillion (about USD 18.0 billion). Similar actions to introduce additional mechanisms of liquidity provision were announced in 2009 and 2010, including the April 2010 announcement to provide lending at the policy interest rate to financial institutions to encourage them to extend loans in support of "growth" industries.

Seeing the decelerating pace of recovery, in October 2010, the BOJ adopted a "comprehensive monetary easing policy." This consisted of three pillars: (i) a reduction in the overnight call rate from 0.1% to the 0.0%–0.1% range, (ii) maintenance of ZIRP until CPI inflation was judged to remain at about 1% (year-over-year) over the medium term, and (iii) establishment of a JPY 5 trillion (about USD 61 billion) fund on the BOJ balance sheet to purchase assets, including CP, corporate bonds, exchange-traded funds (ETFs), and real estate investment trusts (J-REITs), and an increase in the balance of fixed-rate funds-supplying operations to JPY 30 trillion (about USD 367 billion).

Abenomics and its Impact

In early 2013, after two decades of economic stagnation, then Prime Minister Shinzo Abe unveiled a comprehensive economic policy package to sustainably revive the Japanese economy. This program became known as Abenomics, which had three "policy arrows" targeted at aggressive monetary policy, flexible fiscal policy, and growth strategy including structural reforms. The idea was to tackle the fundamental structural problems of the Japanese economy while creating a supportive macroeconomic environment. Aggressive monetary policy was led by the BOJ, which adopted what it called quantitative and qualitative easing (QQE) monetary policy to achieve a 2% inflation target. Flexible fiscal policy meant a policy of supporting aggregate demand through temporary fiscal stimulus, which together with supporting anti-deflationary monetary policy would provide a breathing space to implement structural reforms. Structural reforms in major economic sectors were intended to enhance productivity and potential GDP growth through measures such as investment in science and technology, research and development (R&D), and human capital; deregulation in labor markets and the health, energy, and agricultural sectors; industrial revitalization and strategic market creation; and the promotion of international trade and investment.

The BOJ had long adopted QE monetary policy at the zero lower bound, but this policy was largely ineffective in combating persistent deflation.[20] The BOJ's New Monetary Policy Framework, announced by Governor Haruhiko Kuroda in April 2013, was intended to make the QE policy more effective and achieve the 2% inflation target, which had been adopted since January 2013, in 2 years. To achieve this, the BOJ started with (i) doubling the monetary base in 2 years at an annual pace of about JPY 60–70 trillion (about USD 614–716 billion), (ii) increasing JGB purchases at an annual pace of about JPY 50 trillion (about USD 512 billion) for all maturities, and (iii) doubling purchases of ETF and J-REIT (though from a small base). The new framework was called QQE, because it was intended not only to increase the monetary base through asset purchases but also to change the asset composition of the BOJ's balance sheet and to affect asset prices.

The new monetary policy framework initially worked well in pushing up stock prices, creating yen depreciation, ending deflation, stimulating nominal GDP growth, and improving labor market conditions. In the event, inflation was prevented from reaching the 2% target by various external shocks (e.g., the taper tantrum of mid-2013, declines in international petroleum prices, the China shock of 2015–2016, the pro-Brexit outcome in the United Kingdom national referendum in 2016, the US–China trade war of 2018–2019) as well as by a hike in the consumption tax rate in April 2014. In response, the BOJ eased monetary policy further in several steps through speeding up the annual pace of monetary base expansion in October 2014, applying a negative interest rate of –0.1% to a portion of commercial banks' current account balances held at the BOJ (called the policy rate balances) in February 2016, and introducing yield curve control by way of maintaining the negative interest rate of –0.1% on the policy rate balances and setting 10-year JGB yields at around 0.0%.

---

[20]The BOJ made the following series of monetary policy decisions over time: adoption of de facto ZIRP in February 1999, termination of ZIRP in August 2000, reintroduction of de facto ZIRP in February 2001, introduction of QE policy in March 2001, termination of QE in March 2006, termination of ZIRP in July 2006, re-introduction of de facto ZIRP in December 2008, re-adoption of QE in October 2010, and introduction of QQE in April 2013.

Abenomics, particularly its monetary policy component, delivered favorable economic outcomes, despite the fact that the target inflation rate of 2% was never achieved. Compared with the pre-Abenomics period of 1990–2012, the Abenomics period of 2013–2019 saw higher CPI and PPI inflation (0.8% and 0.5%, compared with 0.4% and –0.2%, respectively), higher asset price increases (14.1% for the Nikkei stock average and –0.4% for urban land prices, compared with –3.0% and –3.6%), a more depreciated real effective exchange rate (166 compared with 119, with the average for the base year 2000 set at 100), and higher nominal GDP growth (1.6% compared with 0.8%). Real GDP growth was similar at 1.0% compared with 1.1%. Even when the negative economic growth years of 1998–1999 and 2008–2009 are excluded from the pre-Abenomics period, the results remain essentially the same except that real GDP growth becomes somewhat higher in the pre-Abenomics period. Abenomics supported the second longest uninterrupted economic expansion in post–World War II Japan from December 2012 to October 2018.

When the BOJ pursued QQE, some policymakers in emerging Asia expressed concern that such a policy, by depreciating the yen, might have a negative spillover on their economies. The BOJ on its part claimed that QQE focused on the domestic objective of achieving the target inflation rate of 2% and was not designed to stimulate economic growth at the expense of neighboring economies. Nonetheless, the resulting yen depreciation was an important channel for ending deflation, supporting growth, and providing an environment for domestic economic recovery.

McKinnon and Liu (2013) provided econometric evidence showing that Japan's economic growth had positive impact on growth in many Asian economies, while yen depreciation had negative impact on their growth. This finding is consistent with what standard macroeconomics would predict. The BOJ's aggressive monetary easing, including QQE, negative interest rate policy, and yield curve control, resulted in yen depreciation, which may have possibly exerted a negative influence (beggar-thy-neighbor effect) on other Asian economies. At the same time, it also supported Japan's economic growth, which likely had a positive influence (locomotive effect). On balance, the net impact of the BOJ's monetary easing was ambiguous, although Japan's fiscal stimulus, by supporting Japan's economic growth, likely had an expansionary impact on other Asian economies (Kawai 2016). Indeed, Japan's sustained economic expansion for 6 years from the end of

2012 to 2018 likely contributed positively to economic growth in Japan's neighboring economies. Thus, the regional impact of Abenomics may well have been positive overall, and Japan was more a locomotive than a beggar to its neighbors.

Further Financial Market Opening and Yen Internationalization

Japanese authorities took a series of measures to revamp the country's regime for international financial transactions under the rubric of yen internationalization and, from 2003, promoting Tokyo as an international financial center (Takagi 2015). Yen internationalization was a policy adopted in the mid-1980s initially under pressure from the US to open Japan's domestic capital markets. It soon took on a life of its own, and the Japanese government pursued the policy to promote greater use of the yen in international transactions throughout the rest of the 1980s. This policy continued from 1990 to 2003.

The Financial "Big Bang"

The promotion of the yen as an international currency and Tokyo as an international financial center presupposes, in a world of competing international currencies and financial centers, the presence of a highly open capital account and a well-developed domestic financial system that offers a variety of instruments. The efforts therefore took on the character of domestic financial reforms as the capital account only had residual controls to begin with (Table 23.3).

Table 23.3: Selected Measures to Internationalie the Yen and Japanese Capital Markets, 1990–2003

Time of Action	Measures Taken
July 1990	Resident corporations and individuals authorized to hold foreign currency bank deposits abroad for portfolio investment up to equivalent of JPY 30 million without obtaining approval
July 1993	Eligibility criteria for nonresident Euroyen bonds abolished
January 1994	Minimum repatriation period for sovereign Euroyen bonds abolished
	Eligibility criteria relaxed for resident foreign bonds and samurai bonds
March 1994	Freely allowable limit for foreign currency deposits abroad by residents increased to JPY 100 million

continued on next page

Table 23.3: *continued*

Time of Action	Measures Taken
July 1994	Eligibility criteria relaxed for yen-denominated foreign bonds
April 1995	Procedures for approval and notification made flexible for nonresident Euroyen bonds
	Procedures for approval and notification made flexible for nonresident domestic bonds
August 1995	Minimum repatriation period abolished for nonresident Euroyen bonds
January 1996	Eligibility criteria for resident Euroyen bonds abolished
	Eligibility criteria abolished for nonresident domestic bonds
April 1996	Minimum repatriation period for resident Euroyen bonds shortened from 90 to 40 days
	Issuing rules for Euroyen commercial paper (CP) abolished (virtual elimination of all restrictions on bringing proceeds back into domestic market)
	Freely allowable limit for foreign currency deposits abroad by residents increased to JPY 200 million
April 1998	Minimum repatriation period for resident Euroyen bonds abolished
March 1999	Securities transactions tax abolished
April 1999	Public auction of financing bills (FBs) introduced
	Withholding tax abolished for certain types of FBs and Treasury bills (TBs)
September 1999	Income tax exempted for nonresidents on interest on certain Japanese government bonds (JGBs)
October 1999	Commissions fully deregulated in equity market
February 2000	Five-year interest-bearing JGBs introduced
January 2001	Real-time gross settlement (RTGS) introduced to current accounts at Bank of Japan and settlement of JGBs
April 2001	Repo transactions based on repurchase and resale agreements introduced
May 2001	Delivery versus payment (DVP) settlement introduced to listed stocks in Tokyo and Osaka
June 2001	DVP settlement system for CP established (with system coming into operation in March 2003)
January 2003	Requirement of concurrent domestic exchange listing abolished for samurai bonds
	Nonresidents allowed to participate in private placement market for samurai bonds restricted to qualified institutional investors
	Book entry system for settlement in securities introduced
	STRIPS government bonds introduced
July 2003	Securities and insurance companies allowed to participate in offshore market

JPY = Japanese yen, STRIPS = separate trading of registered interest and principal securities.
Source: Adapted from Takagi (2015), Tables 5.5, 5.6, 5.8, 5.9, which are based on information obtained from the Japanese Ministry of Finance.

These efforts were punctuated by a major reform of Japan's foreign exchange regime in 1998. The tremendous transformation of the global financial landscape had made the 1980 Foreign Exchange and Foreign Trade Control Law, which had liberalized all external financial transactions in principle, increasingly obsolete. Even though Japan had achieved a substantial opening of its capital account by the mid-1980s, as a result of efforts made by the Japan–US "Yen–Dollar Committee," domestic financial firms remained segmented by type of transaction. External transactions were in principle free but remained subject to the requirement that they be conducted through authorized foreign exchange banks. Some new financial products, such as interest rate swaps between residents and nonresidents, were subject to control. In the meantime, heavily regulated financial firms had lost incentives to innovate and become increasingly inefficient, and the hollowing-out of financial services followed (Toya 2006). There was increasing awareness that the country was being left out of rapid changes taking place in the rest of the advanced economy world (Sakakibara 2000).

It was with this sense of urgency that the Japanese government unveiled in November 1996 a sweeping reform of Japan's financial system. This reform would be carried out over a 3-year period, starting in April 1998, and cover the banking, securities, and insurance industries, as well as foreign exchange and accounting standards. Called the financial "Big Bang," a term borrowed from the deregulation of London's financial markets in the 1980s, the plan sought to make Japan's financial markets and institutions market-based ("free"), transparent and rules-based ("fair"), and consistent with internationally accepted legal, accounting, and supervisory standards ("global") (Dekle 1998). This would be brought about by removing regulatory barriers separating the activities of various types of financial firms as well as restrictions on the menu of products and services they could offer.

The Big Bang had two phases. The first phase commenced with complete deregulation of foreign exchange transactions in April 1998, while the bulk of other reforms took effect in December 1998, including comprehensive revision of the securities, banking, and insurance laws. The Diet passed the new Foreign Exchange Law in May 1997 (to take effect in April 1998), shifting the legal basis of oversight from prior approval or application to ex-post reporting requirements, if any. Prior approval or notification requirements were in principle abolished; instead, ex-post facto reporting requirements were prescribed for transactions exceeding a stipulated amount for statistical purposes. The systems of authorized foreign exchange banks and designated securities companies were abolished. As a result, nonfinancial institutions, such as multinational corporations and large trading companies, were allowed to deal directly in foreign exchange transactions without intermediation by authorized foreign exchange banks, and the monopoly of banks in foreign exchange businesses was terminated.

Progress of Yen Internationalization

Following the revision of the Foreign Exchange and Foreign Trade Control Law in 1980 and financial market opening, Japan started the market-driven process of yen internationalization. Initially, Japanese authorities were not keen on actively promoting yen internationalization because of fear that higher demand for yen assets might cause the yen to appreciate and that control over monetary policy might be lost. In the 1990s, however, authorities took a more active approach to promoting yen internationalization and achieved certain concrete results. Figure 23.8A indicates a steady increase in the use of yen for import invoicing or settlement in the 1980s and 1990s (the share of yen rose from less than 3% in 1980 to 25% in the early 2000s), although the share of yen on the export side did not rise significantly once it reached the level of the early 1980s (the share remained remarkably stable between 35% and 40%). Figure 23.8B shows that the share of yen in the global foreign exchange market turnover reached 14% in 1989 but has since declined as a trend. The share in global foreign exchange reserves achieved 8.5% in the early 1990s but declined steadily toward 3% in the late 2000s (though it has been edging up to 6% in more recent years). The share of yen denomination in global cross-border bank liabilities exceeded 14% from the late 1980s to mid-1990s, and the share in global international debt issues reached close to about 13% in the mid-1990s.

Thus, while the financial "Big Bang" did produce much concrete results, and despite the authorities' efforts, the initial promising gains in the role of the yen as an international currency or the status of Tokyo as a global financial center in the early to mid-1990s could not be sustained. What became clear in the process is that government policy could only set the necessary conditions for the market's choice of the yen or Tokyo, but the choice would ultimately depend on a variety of factors, including corporate

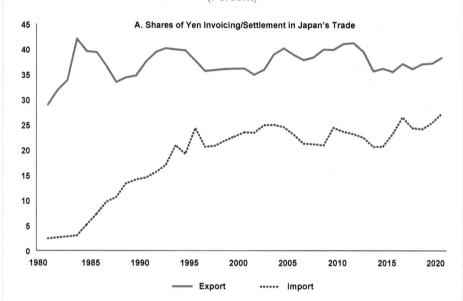

Figure 23.8: Yen Internationalization Indicators, 1980–2020
(Percent)

A. Shares of Yen Invoicing/Settlement in Japan's Trade

—— Export   •••••• Import

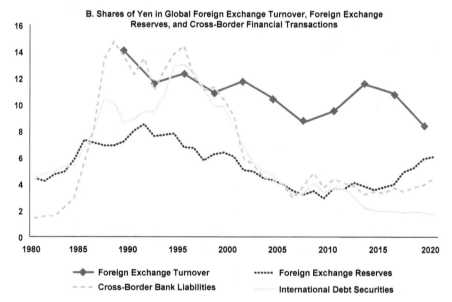

B. Shares of Yen in Global Foreign Exchange Turnover, Foreign Exchange
Reserves, and Cross-Border Financial Transactions

—◆— Foreign Exchange Turnover   •••••• Foreign Exchange Reserves
– – – Cross-Border Bank Liabilities   —— International Debt Securities

Note: Data for export invoicing for 1999 and those for import invoicing for 1981, 1982, 1984, and 1999 are
created through interpolation due to lack of original data for these years. Data for foreign exchange turnover
are available only once every three years from 1989 and these observations are connected through lines.
Data for cross-border bank liabilities and international debt securities are those denominated in yen as shares
in their respective global totals.

Sources: A: Authors' compilation using data from Japanese Ministry of Finance and Ministry of Economy, Trade
and Industry. B: Authors' compilation using data from Bank for International Settlements, *Triennial Central Bank
Survey: Foreign Exchange Turnover*, *Locational Banking Statistics* (LBS_D_PUB) and *Debt Securities Statistics*
(DEBT_SEC2); International Monetary Fund, *Annual Report* (various issues) and *Currency Composition of
Official Foreign Exchange Reserves (COFFER)*.

pricing behavior (including within supply chains),[21] network externalities, regulatory frameworks, tax systems, and even language and culture.

Several reasons can be given for the limited progress of yen internationalization (Eichengreen and Kawai 2015). First, Japan achieved its economic growth in the postwar period as a US dollar zone country, and did not fully grow out of the dollar orientation for a long time. Second, Japan's neighboring countries in Asia were also US dollar zone countries, with the preference to use the US dollar for international transactions including trade with Japan. Third, large Japanese trading companies and multinational corporations have developed the internal capacity to manage currency risks and thus had little need to invoice their trade and investment in yen. Fourth, the stagnation of the Japanese economy after the bursting of the asset price bubble in the early 1990s reduced growth in per capita income, its share in global trade, and the presence of Japanese banks abroad, thereby limiting the overall use of the yen (Ito and Kawai 2016).

It is not warranted, however, to conclude that Japan's currency and capital market internationalization efforts failed. These efforts freed up the Japanese economy from regulatory barriers inhibiting free movement of capital, leading to an accelerated financial integration of Japan with the rest of the world. External assets and liabilities expanded phenomenally, reaching JPY 1,824.0 trillion (USD 16.7 trillion or 326% of GDP) in 2019 (Figure 23.9). The net international investment position (IIP) also rose steadily and reached a peak of JPY 357.0 trillion (USD 3.3 trillion or 64% of GDP) in 2019 (the peak as a percent of GDP, at 68%, was reached in 2014). An increasing participation of foreign investors in the domestic capital market was observed as a trend, and, except for a brief setback around the time of the GFC, the stock of FPI liabilities increased rapidly. Starting from a small base of JPY 63.0 trillion (about USD 614.0 billion or 12% of GDP) in 1995, it reached a pre-GFC peak of JPY 221.0 trillion (about USD 2.0 trillion or 41% of GDP) in 2007 and then JPY 396.0 trillion (about USD 3.6 trillion or 71% of GDP) in 2019. Because of slow growth, the stock of FDI liabilities,

---

[21] Ito et al. (2013), based on a 2009 survey of more than 200 Japanese exporting firms, report that yen invoicing was more prevalent when trade relationships were arm's length, whereas US dollar or trade partner currency invoicing tended to become more common in intra-firm trade. Moreover, the authors find that yen invoicing was less prevalent for larger firms, indicating that they engaged more in intra-firm transactions and chose not to impose foreign exchange risk on their subsidiaries. These large players have the internal capacity to manage currency risks and thus can easily handle the US dollar and other major currencies for international transactions.

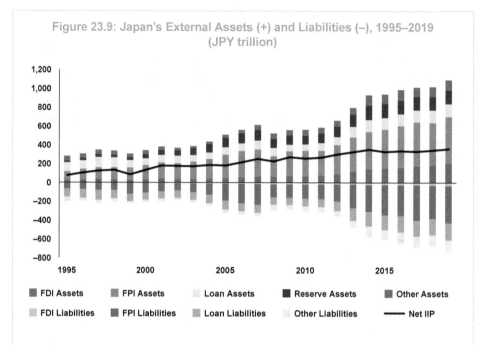

Figure 23.9: Japan's External Assets (+) and Liabilities (–), 1995–2019 (JPY trillion)

FDI = foreign direct investment, FPI = foreign portfolio investment, IIP = international investment position, JPY = Japanese yen.

Sources: Authors' compilation using data from Bank of Japan, available at www.stat-search.boj.or.jp/ssi/cgi-bin/famecgi2?cgi=$nme_a000&lstSelection=BP01; Japanese Ministry of Finance, available at www.mof.go.jp/pri/publication/zaikin_geppo/hyou08.htm.

at JPY 34 trillion (about USD 315 billion or 6% of GDP) in 2019, remained small for the size of the Japanese economy, suggesting that attracting foreign businesses to Japan continues to be a challenge.

The Japanese government has recently adopted an initiative to promote Japan as an international financial center by making Japan an attractive place for foreign professionals, corporates, and funds.[22] The idea is to improve the business and living climate for foreign businesses and professionals by removing taxation and regulatory barriers, enhancing the attractiveness of financial and capital markets, and carrying out corporate governance

---

[22] The government's new economic measures announced in December 2020 included an initiative called "Realization of Japan as a Global Financial Center." The Japanese Financial Services Agency (JFSA) has been engaged in a reform of the Japanese financial and capital markets so as to make them more attractive to foreign financial businesses, particularly asset management companies, and high-skill professionals. See https://www.fsa.go.jp/en/financialcenter/excerpt_fpj.pdf; and https://www.fsa.go.jp/financialcenter/summary.pdf.

reform.[23] This initiative is complemented by local government efforts, as exemplified by the Tokyo Metropolitan Government's "Global Financial City: Tokyo" Vision (November 2017; revised draft July 2021) to transform Tokyo into the world's leading financial city.[24] This local initiative purports to attract mostly Asian financial firms and professionals skilled in finance by providing them with tax and other incentives. It is yet to be seen how successful these initiatives turn out to be, but no country, without making perennial efforts to improve the business environment, can expect to maintain even the status quo, much less to raise its global financial center status.

Japan's International and Regional Cooperation

Japan's Support for ASEAN+3 Economies Hit by the AFC and GFC

Support for the AFC-Hit Countries

Japan actively supported not only Thailand, Indonesia, and Korea within the framework of IMF adjustment programs but also Malaysia, a country that did not seek IMF assistance. Notably, in August 1997, soon after the financial crisis erupted in Thailand, the Japanese government hosted a meeting of the "Friends of Thailand" to reach an agreement on a much-needed IMF financial support package for the country. Under the leadership of Japan, which provided USD 4.0 billion from its own resources, a total of USD 10.5 billion in bilateral support was agreed to by the Friends of Thailand to supplement USD 4.0 billion in IMF financing (Table 23.4).[25] Likewise for Indonesia, Japan offered USD 5.0 billion in a total bilateral support of USD 16.2 billion which

---

[23]The proposed tax measures are designed to make corporate, inheritance, and income taxes more favorable for asset management companies, heirs of foreign residents, and fund managers, respectively. The proposed regulatory policy changes include the provision of one-stop and all-in-English regulatory services and the simplification of market entry procedures for foreign asset managers. The Corporate Governance Code is also revised to encourage companies to improve the quality and quantity of independent directors and to ensure diversity through the promotion of women, foreign nationals, and mid-career hires, and to promote timely and appropriate corporate disclosure. In addition, residence status requirements are relaxed, and company setup and livelihood support is provided, including greater sharing of information in English.

[24]See https://www.seisakukikaku.metro.tokyo.lg.jp/en/pgs/gfct/vision/kousou-kaitei.index.html for the revised draft of the vision which is intended for public communication and comments. The revised vision focuses on promoting green finance and environmental, social, and governance (ESG) investment, the digitalization of finance through fintech, and asset management businesses.

[25]The "Friends of Thailand" were nine economies that extended financial assistance to Thailand in 1997 and included Japan (USD 4.0 billion), Australia, China, Hong Kong, Malaysia, Singapore (USD 1.0 billion each), Brunei, Indonesia, and Korea (USD 0.5 billion each).

was agreed to by six Asian economies, the US, and Australia as a second line of defense to supplement IMF financing.[26] For Korea, Japan made USD 10.0 billion available for a total bilateral assistance of USD 23.2 billion agreed by 13 advanced creditor countries, again to support IMF financing.[27] All in all, Japan provided USD 19 billion for the three countries under IMF programs, accounting for nearly 40% of total bilateral assistance. Outside the framework of IMF programs, Japan provided Malaysia with USD 2.5 billion in short-term financing and additional medium- and long-term financing under the NMI.

Table 23.4: Financial Assistance Packages under the IMF Programs in Mexico and East Asia
(USD billion; Percent of GDP of the year in parenthesis)

Country	Multilateral			Bilateral					Total
	IMF	WB	IDB/ADB	Bi-Total	Japan	China	Korea	ASEAN	
Mexico	17.8	2.0	1.0	30.0	0	0	0	0	50.8
(Feb 1, 1995)	(6%)								(14%)
Thailand	4.0	1.5	1.2	10.5	4.0	1.0	0.5	3.0	17.2
(Aug 20, 1997)	(3%)								(12%)
Indonesia	11.2	5.5	4.5	16.2	5.0	n.a.	0	7.2	42.3[1]
(Nov 5, 1997)	(5%)								(18%)
Korea	21.0	10.0	4.0	23.2	10.0	0	0	0	58.2
(Dec 4, 1997)	(5%)								(13%)

ADB = Asian Development Bank, ASEAN = Association of Southeast Asian Nations, GDP = gross domestic product, IDB = Inter-American Development Bank, IMF = International Monetary Fund, n.a. = not available, USD = United States dollar, WB = World Bank.

Note:

[1] Total for Indonesia includes contribution by the Indonesian government (USD 5 billion).

Sources: Authors' compilation and estimates obtained from World Bank, *Global Development Finance*, 1999, pp. 91–93; International Monetary Fund, *Press Release* No. 95/10, February 1, 1995.

In addition to financing, Japan intervened in Singapore's foreign exchange market in November 1997 to support the Indonesian rupiah by selling US dollars. This action was timed to coincide with the approval of the adjustment

---

[26]The following economies participated in bilateral support for Indonesia: Japan, Singapore (USD 5.0 billion each), the US (USD 3.0 billion), Brunei (USD 1.2 billion), Australia, Malaysia (USD 1.0 billion each), China, and Hong Kong (amounts of contribution not disclosed).

[27]The 13 advanced countries that supported Korea bilaterally were Japan (USD 10.00 billion), the US (USD 5.00 billion), France, Germany, Italy, the United Kingdom (a total of USD 5.00 billion), Belgium, the Netherlands, Sweden and Switzerland (a total of USD 1.25 billion), Australia (USD 1.00 billion), Canada (USD 1.00 billion), and New Zealand (USD 0.10 billion).

program by the IMF Executive Board in order to boost confidence in the rupiah. The data released by the J-MOF show that the intervention lasted for 5 days and amounted to the equivalent of JPY 69.3 billion (or USD 553.0 million). Despite the intervention, however, the rupiah continued to depreciate under the weight of capital flight as the closure of 16 banks as a prior action for Board approval failed to calm investor anxiety. In early 1998, the Japanese government, through the Export-Import Bank of Japan, provided assistance to Indonesia in securing trade credits for its viable firms so that international trade could remain uninterrupted.

Even though the December 1997 financing package for Korea (a total of USD 58.2 billion) was seemingly large, market confidence toward Korea did not improve and even deteriorated because the amount immediately available to the authorities was too small to meet Korean banks' short-term obligations. A major breakthrough was made on the eve of Christmas in 1997, when the authorities of the 13 advanced countries participating in the supplementary support, including the US and Japan, decided to persuade creditor banks in their own countries to extend the maturities of existing short-term claims on Korean banks. Toward the end of December, Japanese banks, which had the largest exposure to Korea, and other major creditor banks agreed to a temporary extension (or rollover) for debt maturing at the end of 1997 until mid-January or end-March 1998. In mid-January, they completed a plan to roll over short-term loans to Korean banks through end-March. Finally in end-January, a total of 134 creditor banks in 32 countries agreed to convert most of short-term bank debts, falling due in 1998, into longer maturity debts guaranteed by the Korean government. The Japanese creditor banks, which attached value to preserving traditional business relationships with Korean banks, strongly supported the extension of debt maturity. The rollovers and debt maturity extension restored confidence and stability to Korean financial markets.

In October 1998, Japan launched the NMI by pledging USD 30 billion to support the ongoing crisis resolution and economic recovery in the crisis-affected Asian countries. Half of the pledged amount was dedicated to short-term financing needs for economic restructuring and reform, while the rest was earmarked for medium- and long-term reforms. Long-term support was extended to assist crisis-affected countries in restructuring corporate debt, reforming financial sectors, strengthening social safety nets, generating employment, and easing the credit crunch. As part of the NMI,

Japan also established a USD 3 billion facility with the ADB to support all crisis-affected countries by raising funds from international financial markets through guarantees, interest subsidies, and other measures. The facility was designed to serve the "Asian Growth and Recovery Initiative" announced jointly by Japan and the US at the Asia-Pacific Economic Cooperation (APEC) Economic Leaders Meeting in November 1998.

Japanese financial support to crisis-affected Asian countries continued under the NMI. In December 1998, at the ASEAN+3 Summit, Japan announced a Special Yen Loan Facility for the total amount of up to JPY 600 billion (USD 5 billion) over 3 years, with an interest rate of 1% and a 40-year repayment period, in order to support growth through infrastructure development, employment promotion, and economic structural reforms. In June and August 1999, the J-MOF committed to providing up to USD 5.0 billion in contingency liquidity support to the Bank of Korea (BOK) and up to USD 2.5 billion to Bank Negara Malaysia (BNM), through bilateral swap arrangements (BSAs) involving US dollars and local currencies. This commitment to Korea later became part of a BSA between Japan and Korea under the Chiang Mai Initiative (CMI). The short-term financial support provided to Korea and Malaysia under the NMI served as a basis for enhanced bilateral currency swap arrangements under the CMI.

All in all, focusing on the immediate crisis period (through the end of 1998), Japan pledged approximately USD 44 billion in financial assistance for the AFC-hit Asian countries. The assistance took the form of bilateral cooperation in the context of IMF-led assistance packages (USD 19 billion), support for private investment, facilitation of trade financing, and support for the socially vulnerable, economic structural reforms, and human resource development. Japan's commitment to provide substantial financial resources, particularly under the NMI, undoubtedly helped stabilize regional markets and economies, thereby facilitating the recovery process.

Support for the GFC-Affected Countries

The collapse of Lehman Brothers in September 2008 affected Korea's financial market hard as foreign investors began to withdraw funds from the country and both domestic currency and foreign exchange liquidity tightened for Korean banks with large wholesale financing requirements. The BOK, which had lost foreign exchange reserves since March 2008, continued to see a decline in reserves. The spread of credit default swap reached a peak of 700 basis points in late October 2008. The won depreciated sharply from a strong KRW 907 per US dollar in October 2007 to KRW 1,483 in November 2008. Korea faced a mini currency crisis.

Unwilling to go to the IMF or CMI (which had a tight link to an IMF program), Korean authorities entered into a USD 30 billion bilateral currency swap arrangement with the US Federal Reserve in October 2008. At the same time, in December 2008, the BOK secured a CNY 180 billion/KRW 38 trillion swap arrangement with the People's Bank of China (PBC) outside the CMI while raising the existing limit of the currency swap arrangement in place with the BOJ from the USD 3 billion equivalent to the USD 20 billion equivalent.[28] The BOK's swap arrangements with the US Federal Reserve, the PBC, and the BOJ had an immediate, stabilizing impact on the market. In 2009, a depreciated won promoted export recovery and reserve accumulation before gradually restoring its value.

Indonesia, on the other hand, did not face financial turmoil or (mini) currency crisis as severe as Korea's, but it too sought a similar bilateral currency swap arrangement with the US Federal Reserve as it faced a sharply depreciating currency. In the event, it was not accorded the same consideration from US authorities, creating room for Japan to step in. In 2009, in order to assist Indonesia overcome difficulty in mobilizing fiscal resources, Japan helped arrange a "stand-by loan facility" ("deferred drawdown options") of USD 5.5 billion by providing USD 1.0 billion from its own resources.[29] The facility, which gave the Indonesian government potential access to financial resources for budgetary support, was in the event not utilized, but it nevertheless provided the Indonesian authorities with a sense of security.

Another measure instituted by the Japanese government for neighboring Asian economies in the aftermath of the GFC was a mechanism established at the Japan Bank for International Cooperation (JBIC) to issue samurai bonds up to JPY 500 billion (about USD 5 billion). Called the "Market Access Support Facility," JBIC used the mechanism to fully guarantee the principals

---

[28]The existing bilateral won–yen currency swap between the BOK and the BOJ was designed for a non-crisis situation.

[29]The remaining balance was provided by the World Bank (USD 2.0 billion), the ADB (USD 1.5 billion), and Australia (USD 1.0 billion).

and partially guarantee the interest payments of Asian sovereign bonds.[30] A maximum of USD 1.5 billion equivalent in yen was committed to Indonesia, allowing the country to issue samurai bonds up to JPY 35 billion (USD 350 million),[31] giving Indonesia an additional mechanism of raising funds at a time of market turbulence.

Japan as an Active Promoter of ASEAN+3 Financial Cooperation

Proposal for an Asian Monetary Fund and the Launch of the CMI

In September 1997, following the successful meeting of the "Friends of Thailand," Japan proposed to establish an Asian Monetary Fund (AMF) designed to supplement IMF resources for crisis prevention, response, and resolution. The aim of the proposed AMF was to pool foreign exchange reserves held by East Asian authorities both to deter currency speculation and, once a crisis had occurred, to contain the crisis and contagion. It was said at the time that the proposed fund would mobilize as much as USD 100 billion.

In the event, the US and the IMF expressed strong opposition to the proposal on the grounds of moral hazard and duplication. They argued, in particular, that an East Asian country troubled by a currency crisis would bypass the tough but necessary conditionality of IMF-supported programs and prefer to receive easy money from the proposed AMF. They also reasoned that an AMF would be redundant in a world where the IMF already exists to play a critical role as an effective global crisis manager. Even though the idea received support from Korea and ASEAN countries, without clear support from China, Japan under these circumstances had little choice but to withdraw the AMF proposal.[32]

---

[30] See https://www.jbic.go.jp/en/information/news/news-2009/0503-2023.html.

[31] In the event that Indonesia was not able to issue bonds, it was agreed that JBIC would participate in a joint lending arrangement (stand-by loan facility) for Indonesia organized by the World Bank and ADB. As things turned out, Indonesia did issue samurai bonds and, thus, did not draw down the facility as stated in the main text.

[32] China did not express a clear view over Japan's proposal. That is, it neither supported nor rejected the idea of an AMF itself. Eisuke Sakakibara, then vice minister of finance for international affairs, stated to one of the authors that if China had supported the proposal, the J-MOF would have gone all the way to creating an AMF despite US and IMF opposition. He also acknowledged that the lines of communication between the finance ministries of Japan and China had not been well established at that time and that the lack of intensive information exchange had prevented China's clear support for the Japanese proposal from being obtained. Taking this as an important lesson, the lines of communication between the two ministries, and those among wider ASEAN+3 authorities, have since deepened considerably.

Instead, in May 2000, the finance ministers of ASEAN+3 countries who met in Chiang Mai agreed to introduce a network of bilateral currency swap arrangements (to be known as the CMI) and an economic review and policy dialogue (ERPD) process as the region's liquidity support and economic surveillance mechanisms, respectively. Initially consisting of an enlarged ASEAN Swap Arrangement (ASA) and a network of BSAs between any of select ASEAN member states and a plus-three country,[33] the CMI evolved in institutional maturity over time. For instance, China, Japan, and Korea concluded BSAs among themselves and with core ASEAN countries. In April 2009, a total of USD 90 billion was made available under CMI BSAs. Japan was again the largest contributor, with its total BSAs amounting to USD 44 billion or nearly 50% of the total (Table 23.5). An important feature of the CMI was that, beyond a certain percentage of the BSA limit (initially set equal to 10%),[34] a member requesting short-term liquidity support is required to seek concurrent IMF support.

Recent years have seen important enhancements to the CMI and the surveillance arrangement. Most importantly, the CMI, as a network of bilateral swaps, was multilateralized as the Chiang Mai Initiative Multilateralisation (CMIM) in March 2010, with a total size of USD 120 billion (with the IMF-delinked portion remaining at 20%). This meant that a set of bilateral arrangements was consolidated into a single multilateral agreement, with a streamlined decision-making process, agreed contributions, and associated voting rights. The CMIM essentially became a US dollar liquidity support arrangement.[35] On the surveillance side, a regional surveillance unit, the ASEAN+3 Macroeconomic Research Office (AMRO),

---

[33] The ASA, established in August 1977 as a multilateral swap arrangement by the central banks of the original five ASEAN countries, with a total facility of USD 100 million, was augmented to a total of USD 200 million in 1978. Under the CMI, ASA membership was expanded to include all ASEAN members, and its facility was further augmented to USD 1 billion. It was agreed in April 2005 to further augment ASA to USD 2 billion. In June and August 1999, under the NMI, the J-MOF committed to providing up to USD 5.0 billion in contingency liquidity support to the BOK and up to USD 2.5 billion to BNM through swap transactions between US dollars and local currencies. The NMI commitment to Korea later became part of the CMI BSA between Japan and Korea, while the NMI commitment to Malaysia did not become a CMI BSA between Japan and Malaysia, as noted in the text.

[34] This IMF-delinked portion was raised to 20% in May 2005, to 30% in May 2012, and further to 40% in May 2021.

[35] At this time, the CMIM was made to include all ASEAN+3 members plus Hong Kong (the CMI BSAs had not previously included Brunei, Cambodia, Lao People's Democratic Republic, Myanmar, Vietnam, or Hong Kong). In May 2012, further modifications were introduced, including a doubling of the total lending limit to USD 240 billion, an increase in the IMF-delinked portion from 20% to 30%, and the introduction of a crisis prevention facility called the CMIM-Precautionary Line.

was established as a limited company in 2011 and was transformed into an international organization in 2016. AMRO is tasked to conduct country and regional surveillance by issuing regular reports and to support ERPD processes and CMIM decision-making.

Table 23.5: BSAs under the CMI, April 2009
(USD billion or its equivalent)[1]

From: To:	China	Japan	Korea	Indonesia	Malaysia	Philippines	Singapore	Thailand	Total
China	...	3.0[2]	4.0[2]	4.0	1.5	2.0[2]		2.0	16.5
Japan	3.0[2]	...	13.0[3,4]	12.0	1.0[4]	6.0	3.0	6.0	44.0
Korea	4.0[2]	8.0[3]	...	2.0	1.5	2.0		1.0	18.5
Indonesia			2.0	...					2.0
Malaysia			1.5		...				1.5
Philippines		0.5	2.0			...			2.5
Singapore		1.0					...		1.0
Thailand		3.0	1.0					...	4.0
Total	7.0	15.5	23.5	18.0	4.0	10.0	3.0	9.0	90.0

BSA = bilateral swap arrangement, CMI = Chiang Mai Initiative, USD = United States dollar.
Notes:
[1] The table does not include the Association of Southeast Asian Nations Swap Arrangement (ASA), which totaled USD 2 billion.
[2] The agreements were in local currencies, and the amounts in the table are expressed in United States (US) dollar equivalents.
[3] Japan–Korea bilateral swap arrangement (BSA) includes both US dollar swaps (USD 10 billion from Japan to Korea and USD 5 billion from Korea to Japan) and local currency swaps (USD 3 billion equivalent each from Japan to Korea and vice versa). The yen–won BSA was raised from USD 3 billion to USD 20 billion equivalent in December 2008 until end-April 2009 and was later extended to end-October 2009, which is not included in the table.
[4] There were also USD 5.0 billion and USD 2.5 billion commitments made by Japan to Korea and Malaysia (made in June and August 18, 1999) under the New Miyazawa Initiative (NMI), which are not included in the table.
Source: Authors' compilation using information obtained from Japanese Ministry of Finance, available at http://www.mof.go.jp/english/.

Japan's Bilateral Currency Cooperation with ASEAN+3 Economies

More recently, Japan has been strengthening bilateral currency cooperation with several ASEAN+3 countries to complement the CMIM and to promote further yen internationalization. These efforts include the renewal or introduction of BSAs with regional central banks and the inclusion of the yen as a swap currency, and the development of markets in which the yen could be exchanged directly for other regional currencies.

As to the renewed or additional currency swaps, the J-MOF and the BOJ contracted such agreements with at least six countries, excluding India, in the region (Table 23.6). For example, the J-MOF renewed BSAs with the Bangko Sentral ng Pilipinas (BSP, October 2017), the Bank of Thailand (BOT, July 2018), Bank Indonesia (BI, October 2018), and the Monetary Authority of Singapore (MAS, May 2021) by adding the yen as an available swap currency, and with the BNM (September 2020) for a US dollar–local currency swap. The BOJ also concluded a BSA with the PBC (October 2018), extended a BSA with the MAS (November 2019), and signed an agreement with the BOT (March 2020), all of which involve yen–local currency swaps.

Table 23.6: Japan's Bilateral Currency Swap Arrangements (as of May 2021)

Country	Contracting Agencies	Currency Used (Amount of Swap Commitment)
Philippines	J-MOF and BSP (Oct 2017)	Japan→Philippines, USD or JPY versus PHP (USD 12 billion equivalent); Philippines→Japan, USD versus JPY (USD 0.5 billion)
Thailand	J-MOF and BOT (Jul 2018)	Japan→Thailand, USD or JPY versus THB (USD 3 billion equivalent) Thailand→Japan, USD versus JPY (USD 3 billion)
Indonesia	J-MOF and BI (Oct 2018)	Japan→Indonesia, USD or JPY versus IDR (USD 22.76 billion equivalent)
India	J-MOF and RBI (Feb 2019)	Japan→India, USD versus INR (USD 75 billion) India→Japan, USD versus JPY (USD 75 billion)
Malaysia	J-MOF and BNM (Sep 2020)	Japan→Malaysia, USD versus MYR (USD 3 billion) Malaysia→Japan, USD versus JPY (USD 3 billion)
Singapore	J-MOF and MAS (May 2021)	Japan→Singapore, USD or JPY versus SGD (USD 3 billion equivalent) Singapore→Japan, USD versus JPY (USD 1 billion)
China	BOJ and PBC (Oct 2018)	Japan↔China, JPY versus CNY (JPY 3.4 trillion, CNY 200 billion)
Singapore	BOJ and MAS (Nov 2019)	Japan↔Singapore, JPY versus SGD (JPY 1.1 trillion, SGD 15 billion)
Thailand	BOJ and BOT (Mar 2020)	Japan↔Thailand, JPY versus THB (JPY 0.8 trillion, THB 240 billion)

BI = Bank Indonesia, BNM = Bank Negara Malaysia, BOJ = Bank of Japan, BOK = Bank of Korea, BOT = Bank of Thailand, BSP = Bangko Sentral ng Pilipinas, CNY = Chinese yuan, IDR = Indonesian rupiah, INR = Indian rupee, J-MOF = Japanese Ministry of Finance, JPY = Japanese yen, MAS = Monetary Authority of Singapore, MYR = Malaysian ringgit, PBC = People's Bank of China, PHP = Philippine peso, RBI = Reserve Bank of India, THB = Thai baht, USD = United States dollar.

Note: The BSA between the J-MOF and the MAS complements the Chiang Mai Initiative Multilateralisation (CMIM) and requires an IMF program if more than 40% of the commitment is to be withdrawn.

Source: Authors' compilation using information released by the Japanese Ministry of Finance, https://www.mof.go.jp/english/international_policy/financial_cooperation_in_asia/bsa/index.htm; the Bank of Japan, https://www.boj.or.jp/en/intl_finance/cooperate/index.htm/.

As to direct trading of yen for regional currencies, the J-MOF in June 2017 announced a comprehensive plan to develop a scheme to further promote yen internationalization. As a start, it signed a memorandum of cooperation with the BOT to promote the use of local currencies in March 2018. In May 2019, it signed a letter of intent with the BSP on the establishment of a yen–peso direct trading framework. This was followed in August 2020 by a joint announcement with BI for the establishment of a framework for cooperation to promote the use of yen and rupiah for the settlement of bilateral trade and FDI.[36] The significance of this joint statement should not be underestimated. It not only stated that "(t)he framework includes, among others, promotion of the direct quotation between the Indonesian Rupiah and the Japanese Yen as well as the relaxation of relevant rules and regulations to enhance the usage of local currencies" but also appointed several banks in each country to conduct cross-currency transactions between the yen and the rupiah. Also significantly, Japan's cooperative efforts with Thailand, the Philippines, and Indonesia effectively helped to expand the ASEAN-led Local Currency Settlement Framework (LCSF) to the wider ASEAN+3 region.[37] The expectation was to reduce foreign exchange risk associated with trade and investment and the costs of foreign exchange transactions and also to contribute to further ASEAN+3 financial integration.

Conclusion

This chapter has reviewed Japan's international economy of the 1990s through the late 2010s, beginning with the period leading to the AFC and ending with the aftermath of the GFC through Abenomics. The Japanese economy suffered from the negative consequences of the bursting of a domestic asset price bubble in the early 1990s and encountered a systemic banking crisis during 1997–1998, the timing of which coincided with the AFC. Faced

---

[36]https://www.mof.go.jp/english/international_policy/financial_cooperation_in_asia/bilateral_financial_cooperation/index.htm.

[37]The LCSF, initially developed by Malaysia and Thailand, later joined by Indonesia and more recently by the Philippines, promotes the use of local currencies for bilateral transactions. It involves a set of bilateral agreements among central banks to use their own currencies for cross-border settlements of mutual trade and FDI through commercial banks designated as appointed cross-currency dealers (ACCDs) tasked to exchange one currency for another and to quote exchange rates. Banks assigned as ACCDs can also provide several foreign currency services for their domestic clients, such as loans and deposit taking in the partner currency as well as currency hedging to help manage exchange risks involving the two currencies.

with an exploding banking crisis, Japanese authorities began to address banking sector problems in earnest, which, coupled with a favorable global environment, helped the economy recover in the early 2000s and achieve sustained growth until it was affected in 2008 by the GFC. In fact, the GFC affected Japan more severely than did the 1997–1998 banking crisis cum the AFC, and its economic contraction during the GFC was deeper than those experienced by the US, European, and other Asian economies. This reflected Japan's increasing export dependence since the early 2000s, especially through the East Asian supply chain countries to which it predominantly supplied intermediate and capital goods.

Japan's prolonged economic stagnation was in part due to policymakers' inaction and indecisiveness in the immediate aftermath of the collapse of the bubble in the early 1990s and their initial reluctance to pursue and maintain aggressive monetary easing in subsequent years. The lack of domestic and external pressure (e.g., from high unemployment, capital flight, or currency crisis risk) was not helpful in this respect as it created a sense of complacency on the part of Japanese authorities. Despite the mounting domestic difficulties, however, Japan remained committed to international and regional financial cooperation. The chapter has highlighted the leadership roles Japan played to support crisis-affected countries, including the successful organization of a "Friends of Thailand" meeting to assist Thailand, the ill-fated proposal to create an AMF, and the further support of AFC-hit countries through the NMI. Measures taken at the time of the GFC included, among others, the provision of a bilateral currency swap to Korea's central bank and the arrangement of a stand-by loan facility to Indonesia.

Aggressive monetary easing and other policies to correct a strong yen led to a massive outflow of capital from Japan during 1995–1996, thereby potentially contributing to the buildup of crisis vulnerability in AFC-hit countries. Japan was not alone in this regard as international investors from Europe, the US, and other financial centers also channeled capital to these countries during the pre-crisis period. Yet there is no evidence to show that Japanese investors triggered the crisis by creating a large capital flow reversal in the first half of 1997. Also, Japanese resident investors kept their capital in the AFC-hit countries perhaps except Korea during 1997–1998 based on Japan's BOP data. On the other hand, the BIS data suggest the possibility that Japanese bank branches and subsidiaries abroad, such as those in Singapore, Hong Kong, and other international financial centers, may have withdrawn their international loans even from Thailand and Indonesia once the crisis erupted. Without full information available, however, it is difficult to comprehensively assess the role played by non-resident, Japan-affiliated investors abroad.

The monetary policy component of Abenomics, that is, the economic policies of former Prime Minister Shinzo Abe introduced in early 2013, may have had a negative spillover on Asia's neighboring economies through yen depreciation, but the net effect was ambiguous, given the positive spillover effect working through Japanese economic recovery. When the positive effect of simultaneous fiscal stimulus, which likely supported Japan's economic expansion for 6 years, is taken into account, the total regional effect of Abenomics may well have been positive overall.

Since the eruption of the AFC, Japan has been an active promoter of regional financial cooperation. The country notably assumed a leadership role in initiating the ASEAN+3 process, launching the CMI and ERPD, and establishing AMRO, among other things. An important motivation for Japan's regional cooperation efforts is the recognition of Asia as a key production base and as an expanding consumer market for Japanese multinational corporations, and the awareness that financial stability in the region is therefore vital to the Japanese economy.

References

Botman, Dennis P. J., Irineu de Carvalho Filho, and W. Raphael Lam. 2013. "The Curious Case of the Yen as a Safe Haven Currency: A Forensic Analysis." IMF Working Paper 13/228. International Monetary Fund, Washington, D.C.

Dekle, Robert. 1998. "The Japanese 'Big Bang' Financial Reforms and Market Implications." *Journal of Asian Economics* 9: 237–249.

Eichengreen, Barry, and Masahiro Kawai, eds. 2015. *Renminbi Internationalization: Achievements, Prospects, and Challenges.* Washington, D.C.: Brookings Institution Press.

Hoshi, Takeo. 2001. "What Happened to Japanese Banks?" *Bank of Japan Monetary and Economic Studies* 19: 1–29.

Ito, Hiro, and Masahiro Kawai. 2016. "Trade Invoicing in Major Currencies in the 1970s–1990s: Lessons for Renminbi Internationalization." *Journal of the Japanese and International Economies* 42: 123–145.

Ito, Takatoshi, Satoshi Koibuchi, Kiyotaka Sato, and Junko Shimizu. 2013. "Choice of Invoicing Currency: New Evidence from a Questionnaire Survey of Japanese Export Firms." Discussion Paper No. 13-E-034. Research Institute of Economy, Trade and Industry, Tokyo.

Iwata, Kazumasa. 2010. *Defure tono Tatakai [Fight against Deflation]*, Tokyo: Nihon Keizai Shimbun Shuppansha.

Kawai, Masahiro. 2005. "Reform of the Japanese Banking System." *International Economics and Economic Policy* 2: 307–335.

Kawai, Masahiro. 2016. "International Spillovers of Monetary Policy: The US Federal Reserve's QE and the Bank of Japan's QQE." In *Managing Complexity: Economic Policy Cooperation after the Crisis*, edited by Tamim Bayoumi, Stephen Pickford, and Paola Subacchi. Washington, D.C.: Brookings Institution Press, pp. 139–176.

Kawai, Masahiro, and Peter Morgan. 2013. "Banking Crises and 'Japanization.'" In *Responding to Financial Crisis: Lessons from Asia Then, the United States and Europe Now*, edited by Changyong Rhee and Adam S. Posen. Washington, D.C.: Peterson Institute for International Economics, pp. 11–55. https://www.adb.org/sites/default/files/publication/31146/responding-financial-crisis.pdf.

Kawai, Masahiro, and Shinji Takagi. 2009. "Kawase Rēto to Kokusai Shūshi: Puraza Gōi kara Heisei Fukyō no Makuro Keizai. [Exchange Rate and Balance of Payments: Macroeconomics from the Plaza Agreement to Heisei Stagnation]." In *Kokusai Kankyō no Henka to Nihon Keizai [Changes in the International Environment and the Japanese Economy]*, edited by Motoshige Ito. Tokyo: Keio University Press, pp. 235–275.

Kawai, Masahiro, and Shinji Takagi. 2011. "Why Was Japan Hit So Hard by the Global Financial Crisis?" In *The Impact of the Economic Crisis on East Asia: Policy Responses from Four Economies*, edited by Daigee Shaw and Bih Jane Liu. Cheltenham and Northampton: Edward Elgar, pp. 131–148.

Kawai, Masahiro, and Shinji Takagi. 2015. "Japan's Current Account Rebalancing." In *Transpacific Rebalancing: Implications for Trade and Economic Growth*, edited by Barry P. Bosworth and Masahiro Kawai. Washington, D.C.: Brookings Institution Press, pp. 119–147.

Laeven, Luc, and Fabian Valencia. 2018. "Systemic Banking Crises Revisited." IMF Working Paper 18/206 (September). International Monetary Fund, Washington, D.C.

McKinnon, Ronald, and Zhao Liu. 2013. "Modern Currency Wars: The United States versus Japan." ADBI Working Paper No. 437 (October). Asian Development Bank Institute, Tokyo.

Sakakibara, Eisuke. 2000. *Nihon to Sekai ga Furueta Hi [The Day When Japan and the World Were Shaken]*. Tokyo: Chūo Kōron Shinsha.

Takagi, Shinji. 2015. *Conquering the Fear of Freedom: Japanese Exchange Rate Policy since 1945*. Oxford: Oxford University Press.

Toya, Tetsuro. 2006. *The Political Economy of the Japanese Financial Big Bang: Institutional Change in Finance and Public Policymaking*. Oxford: Oxford University Press.

Part IV

Assessments of the Crises, and the Development of Regional Financial Cooperation in Asia

Chapter 24

International Capital Flows in ASEAN+3

Soyoung Kim and Hyungji Kim

Introduction

Management of volatile international capital flows is of great concern for the Association of Southeast Asian Nations (ASEAN)+3 economies. Some underwent capital account liberalization prior to the Asian financial crisis (AFC), and relatively high (about 10%) net capital inflows were observed before then. During the AFC in the late 1990s, capital flows were reversed, leading to boom–bust cycles and severe crisis in some ASEAN+3 economies.[1]

After the AFC, another wave of huge capital inflows was observed, partly related to the low United States (US) interest rate policy to overcome its recession in the early 2000s. Later, another episode of capital flow reversals was observed during the global financial crisis (GFC) in the late 2000s.

After the GFC, increased liquidity flowed into the ASEAN+3 economies again, propelled by unprecedented expansionary monetary policy in advanced economies. A few economies experienced some financial market volatility and instability during the 2010s.

More recently, because of the coronavirus disease (COVID-19) pandemic, most economies are facing huge volatility in capital flows and financial instability. As all economies around the world take strong expansionary policies to bounce back from the global pandemic, some economies are likely experiencing huge capital inflows. Then, those economies may experience another episode of capital flow reversals as advanced economies take contractionary positions to return to the normal.

Against this backdrop, this chapter reviews the trends and movements of international capital flows and the economic performance of the ASEAN+3 economies from the 1990s. Focus is on the developments around two most

---

[1] See Kim and Kim (2013) and Kim et al. (2013). Details of boom-bust cycle are discussed in later sections.

important episodes: the AFC and GFC. Based on the reviews, some policy implications are drawn, especially in preparing for upcoming challenges on volatile international capital flows in the post-COVID-19 era.

The chapter is organized as follows. At the start of this chapter, the trends and movements of international capital flows and related policies of the ASEAN+3 economies are documented. Capital account liberalization and capital flow management policies and trends of capital flows to and from the ASEAN+3 before, during, and after the crises are discussed. The trends and properties of various components of capital flows, such as portfolio investment, direct investment, and other investments, and intra-regional versus inter-regional capital flows are also studied.

In the next part of this chapter, the economic performance of the ASEAN+3 economies around the AFC and GFC is documented. The evolution of key macroeconomic variables such as real gross domestic product (GDP), real investment, real consumption, current account, and nominal and real exchange rates to infer the performance of the ASEAN+3 economies during the AFC and GFC is discussed. By reviewing the trends of various key macroeconomic variables, the experience with the typical boom–bust cycles generated by reversals in capital flows is examined. The evolution of policy variables such as short-term interest rate, real government spending, and foreign exchange reserves to infer the policy responses during the AFC and GFC is likewise documented.

In addition to documentation of the performance of the ASEAN+3 economies in the previous part of this chapter, the effects of shocks to capital flows on the ASEAN+3 economies are analyzed by employing structural panel vector autoregression (VAR) models. First, the empirical model is explained in detail. Following that, the empirical results are reported. Substantial parts of the empirical findings of this chapter are based on Kim and Kim (2021). Finally, a summary of findings and policy implications are discussed.

Throughout this chapter, the AFC and GFC are compared. Questions on which crisis affected the ASEAN+3 economies more severely, whether the policy responses were different during the AFC and GFC, in which crisis reversals in capital flow reversals were more severe, which shocks to capital flows or reversals in capital flows affected economies more severely are tackled. In addition, economies that experienced severe currency crisis during the AFC are compared with others to draw some implications on the relation between economic performance and volatile capital flows.

Trends of International Capital Flows and Related Policies in ASEAN+3 Economies

Trends of International Capital Flows

Trends in international capital flows for the ASEAN+3 economies are here examined, with particular focus on changes in international capital flows around the AFC and GFC.

Figure 24.1 shows the average ratio of capital inflows to the trend GDP for the ASEAN+3 economies. Capital inflows are divided against the trend GDP for normalization. Trend GDP (instead of actual GDP) is used as actual GDP is volatile and often falls sharply during a financial crisis. This is done also to show the movements of capital inflows clearly. To construct the trend GDP, Hodrick–Prescott (HP) filter is applied with $\lambda = 100$. The ratio for each economy is calculated and then a simple average[2] for the ASEAN+3 economies is taken. The red line shows the total average for 14 economies (Korea, Japan, China, Hong Kong, Singapore, Malaysia, Indonesia, the Philippines, Thailand, Vietnam, Cambodia, Lao People's Democratic Republic (PDR), Brunei, and Myanmar). In addition, the average for economies that experienced huge depreciation during the AFC ("AFC economies") is represented by the green line. Six economies (Korea, Malaysia, Indonesia, the Philippines, Thailand, and Lao PDR) experienced severe currency crisis (more than 50% depreciation of their currency against the US dollar) during the AFC.[3] The black line shows the average for six other ASEAN+3 economies — Myanmar, Vietnam, Japan, China, Brunei, and Cambodia — excluding Hong Kong and Singapore ("non-AFC economies"). Table 24.1 summarizes the ASEAN+3 economy classification used in this chapter. The size and the volatility of capital inflows (as a ratio to trend GDP) in Hong Kong and Singapore are far larger than those of other ASEAN+3 economies, and the direct comparison with these economies may not be justifiable. Thus, Hong Kong and Singapore are excluded from the non-AFC economies but are included in the average of the ASEAN+3 economies. The capital flows (as a ratio to trend GDP) for Hong Kong and Singapore are provided in Appendix A.

---

[2] A simple average is calculated instead of a weighted average despite a risk of overestimating the weight of small countries. As the size of China's economy is too large compared to other ASEAN+3 economies, a weighted average has the potential to over-represent China's economic indicators as the average of ASEAN+3.

[3] We calculated the depreciation rate from the period before the AFC to the maximum exchange rate during the AFC by using monthly data. The same group of economies is selected when we use the end of period annual data and calculate the deprecation rate from 1996 to 1997.

Table 24.1: Classification of ASEAN+3 Economies

Group	Economies	Notes
AFC	Korea, Malaysia, Indonesia, Philippines, Thailand, Lao PDR	Economies that experienced more than 50% depreciation of their currency against the US dollar during the AFC
Non-AFC	Myanmar, Vietnam, Japan, China, Brunei, Cambodia	ASEAN+3 economies not belonging to the AFC, except for Hong Kong and Singapore
ASEAN+3	AFC + Non-AFC + Singapore, Hong Kong	Includes Hong Kong and Singapore

AFC = Asian financial crisis, ASEAN = Association of Southeast Asian Nations, Lao PDR = Lao People's Democratic Republic, US = United States.

Figure 24.1 reports capital inflows during the period 1990–2018. The average for the AFC economies (green line) shows a clear reversal in capital inflows, but the patterns are slightly different. The increases in the ratio of capital inflows to trend GDP are found up to 1996 when the ratio reaches over 10%. However, it dropped to approximately 2% in 1997 and approximately −2% in 1998. The ratios are still close to 0% in 1999 and 2000.

The average of capital inflows for the non-AFC economies (black dotted line) declines during the AFC. However, the size of declines in capital inflows is far larger in the AFC economies than in the non-AFC economies, which suggests that the AFC economies experienced more severe reversals in capital inflows than the non-AFC economies. In addition, capital inflows did not recover, staying at around 0%, even in 1999 and 2000 in the AFC economies, while capital inflows fully recovered in 2000 in the non-AFC economies.

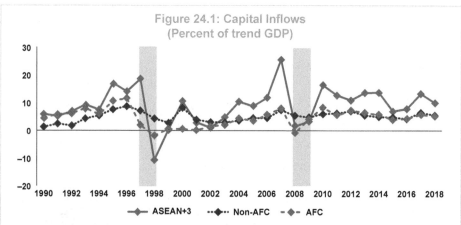

Figure 24.1: Capital Inflows
(Percent of trend GDP)

AFC = Asian financial crisis, ASEAN = Association of Southeast Asian Nations, GDP = gross domestic product, GFC = global financial crisis.
Note: The shaded areas correspond to the AFC and the GFC periods.
Source: International Monetary Fund Financial Statistics, World Bank.

The average for the ASEAN+3 (red line) shows a similar reversal in capital inflows during the AFC. The capital inflows in 1997 amount to approximately 20% of the trend GDP but drop sharply to under −10% of the trend GDP. It recovers to approximately 0% in 1999 and approximately 10% in 2000. However, note that this pattern is due to inclusion of Hong Kong and Singapore, which can be inferred from the gap among the average of the ASEAN+3, AFC, and non-AFC countries.

For the period 2001–2018, capital inflows increased over time and peaked in 2007 but dropped sharply in 2008. Capital inflows recovered in 2010. A huge reversal in capital inflows is observed during the GFC, but the size of the reversal is slightly smaller than during the AFC. Also for the AFC economies, the drop in capital inflows is smaller and less persistent during the GFC than during the AFC. This may suggest that the AFC economies suffered less from the reversal in capital flows during the GFC than during the AFC. For the non-AFC economies, capital inflows declined slightly during the GFC.

However, Hong Kong and Singapore experienced dramatic drops in capital inflows during the GFC (and AFC). This can be inferred from the fact that the average for the ASEAN+3 economies, which includes Hong Kong and Singapore, shows a far larger drop in capital inflows during the GFC than the AFC and non-AFC economies, which do not.

Figure 24.2 shows the averages of the ratio of capital outflows to the trend GDP for the period 1990–2018. For the AFC and non-AFC economies, capital outflows increased in the early 1990s and significant changes were

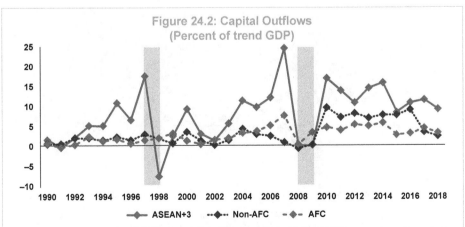

Figure 24.2: Capital Outflows
(Percent of trend GDP)

AFC = Asian financial crisis, ASEAN = Association of Southeast Asian Nations, GDP = gross domestic product, GFC = global financial crisis.
Note: The shaded areas correspond to the AFC and the GFC periods.
Source: International Monetary Fund Financial Statistics, World Bank.

not found during the AFC, but a significant reversal of capital outflows was found for the ASEAN+3 economies, mostly for Hong Kong and Singapore.

For the period 2001–2018, capital outflows of the AFC and non-AFC economies increased in the early 2000s but dropped in 2008 and 2009. This pattern is quite different from that found around the AFC period. A larger reversal is found in the AFC economies than in the non-AFC economies. This suggests that the AFC economies (and the non-AFC economies to some extent) sold foreign assets to mitigate effects of the reversal in capital inflows during the GFC, which was not observed during the AFC.

Figure 24.3 shows the averages of the ratio of net capital flows (capital inflows minus capital outflows) to trend GDP for the period 1990–2018. During the 1990s, net capital flow movements net out capital inflows and outflows, as a decline in capital inflows, was financed by a decline in capital outflows during the AFC. In all economies, net capital inflows decreased during the AFC. During the AFC, net capital flows were over 10% in 1996 but were approximately –4% in 1998.

These were still negative in 1999 and 2000. A larger reversal is found in the AFC economies than in the non-AFC economies. The level of reversal is smaller in the ASEAN+3 economies than the AFC economies, which suggests that a sharp decline in capital inflows in Hong Kong and Singapore is much offset by a decline in capital outflows.

During the GFC, a small decline in net capital flows (1%–2%) was found for the AFC economies in 2008 and recovery in 2009, which contrasts

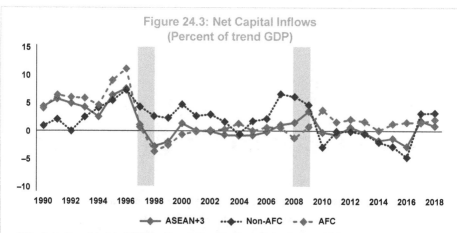

Figure 24.3: Net Capital Inflows
(Percent of trend GDP)

AFC = Asian financial crisis, ASEAN = Association of Southeast Asian Nations, GDP = gross domestic product, GFC = global financial crisis.
Note: The shaded areas correspond to the AFC and the GFC periods.
Source: International Monetary Fund Financial Statistics, World Bank.

to the huge reversal in 1997. However, the capital flow reversal was more serious in the non-AFC economies during the GFC than during the AFC. In the mid-2000s, net capital flows increased and reached approximately 7% in 2007. These declined in 2008 and 2009, further declined in 2010 to approximately −3%, and showed negative numbers until 2016. Interestingly, this reversal is mostly due to the surge in capital outflows after the GFC, which is different from the reversal during the AFC, which is mostly due to a decline in capital inflow during the AFC.

To summarize, capital inflows were reversed dramatically during the AFC and GFC, more in the AFC economies than in the non-AFC economies. Capital outflows were also reversed substantially in most cases to mitigate the size of net capital flow reversals. However, in the AFC economies during the AFC, capital inflows were reversed but capital outflows were not, and thus net capital flows were reversed dramatically. In the non-AFC economies, capital outflows surged after the GFC, which led to huge net capital flow reversals after the GFC.

Trends of Capital Flows Components

Figure 24.4 (1) reports the components of capital inflows for the ASEAN+3 economies for the period 1990–2018. Capital inflows are categorized as direct investment, portfolio investment, financial derivatives, and other investments. Direct investment, portfolio investment, and financial derivatives are further divided into equity and debt instruments/securities. Capital inflows through debt instruments of other investments accounted for the largest parts of capital inflows in the 1990s before the AFC. In 1997 and 1998, capital inflows in debt instruments of other investments show huge negative numbers, which means that foreigners pulled out huge money invested in debts instruments of other investments.

Capital inflows in debt instruments of other investments were the main component of capital inflows reversed during the AFC. Debt instruments of other investments include bank loans. In fact, the reversals of capital inflows in bank loans during the AFC were the main reason that some economies experienced severe financial crisis together with the currency crisis. Huge negative flows in financial derivatives during the AFC can be gleaned from the graph.

For the period 2001–2018, capital inflows in equities of direct investment were stable for all years. Capital inflows in debt instruments of other investments were positive before the GFC but were reversed to negative numbers in 2008 and 2009 during the AFC.

Capital inflows in portfolio investment in the form of debt securities and equity were positive before the GFC but were reversed to negative in 2008. In addition, the size of the negative flows in portfolio investment was even larger than that of negative flows in debt instruments of other investments. This suggests that the main component of capital inflows reversals during the GFC was capital inflows in portfolio investment, instead of capital inflows in debt instruments of other investments which was the main component of capital inflows reversals during the AFC.

Figure 24.4 (2) reports components of capital inflows for the AFC economies for the period 1990–2018. During the 1990s, patterns of capital inflows for the AFC economies were similar to those for ASEAN+3 economies. First of all, the role of capital inflows in debt instruments of other investments during the AFC is clear. They were the major components of capital inflows that reversed during the AFC. Second, capital inflows in direct investment were quite stable. Note that though capital inflows in debt instruments of direct investment were slightly negative in 1998 and 1999, capital inflows in equities of direct investment were positive and large even during the AFC.

For the period 2001–2018, capital inflows in equities of direct investment were the most stable flows, which is also similar to those for ASEAN+3 economies. Capital inflows of portfolio investment, both equities and debt securities, were mostly positive before the GFC, but capital inflows in equities of portfolio investment were negative in 2007 and 2008. The main component of reversals in capital inflows is capital inflows in equities of portfolio investment. Capital inflows in debt instruments of other investments were positive before the GFC, and negative in 2008, but the size of reversals in capital inflows in equities of portfolio investment was far larger than that of debt instrument of other investments.

Figure 24.4 (3) reports the components of capital inflows for the non-AFC economies for the period 1990–2018. For the 1990s, the patterns for the non-AFC economies are somewhat different from the AFC economies. This is partly because the data were not available for the period before the AFC in some of the non-AFC economies. Capital inflows in debt instruments of other investments were negative in 1992, 1993, and 1999. Capital inflows in financial derivatives were also negative from 1996 to 2000.

For the period 2001–2018, capital inflows of equities of direct investment were the most stable flow. Capital inflows in portfolio investment, both equities and debt securities, were positive for the periods before the

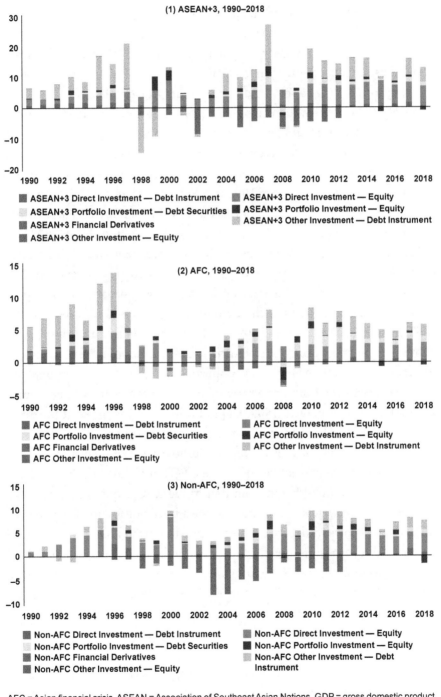

Figure 24.4: Components of Capital Inflows
(Percent of trend GDP)

(1) ASEAN+3, 1990–2018

- ASEAN+3 Direct Investment — Debt Instrument
- ASEAN+3 Direct Investment — Equity
- ASEAN+3 Portfolio Investment — Debt Securities
- ASEAN+3 Portfolio Investment — Equity
- ASEAN+3 Financial Derivatives
- ASEAN+3 Other Investment — Debt Instrument
- ASEAN+3 Other Investment — Equity

(2) AFC, 1990–2018

- AFC Direct Investment — Debt Instrument
- AFC Direct Investment — Equity
- AFC Portfolio Investment — Debt Securities
- AFC Portfolio Investment — Equity
- AFC Financial Derivatives
- AFC Other Investment — Debt Instrument
- AFC Other Investment — Equity

(3) Non-AFC, 1990–2018

- Non-AFC Direct Investment — Debt Instrument
- Non-AFC Direct Investment — Equity
- Non-AFC Portfolio Investment — Debt Securities
- Non-AFC Portfolio Investment — Equity
- Non-AFC Financial Derivatives
- Non-AFC Other Investment — Debt Instrument
- Non-AFC Other Investment — Equity

AFC = Asian financial crisis, ASEAN = Association of Southeast Asian Nations, GDP = gross domestic product.
Source: International Monetary Fund Statistics, World Bank.

GFC, but capital inflows in equities of portfolio investment were negative in 2007 and 2008. Capital inflows in debt instruments of other investments were reversed in 2008, but the size of reversals in capital inflows in equities of portfolio investment was larger than the size of reversals in capital inflows of debt instruments of other investments.

Figure 24.5 (1) reports the components in capital outflows for the ASEAN+3 economies for the period 1990–2018. In the 1990s, capital outflows of debt instruments of other investments grew until 1997 but reversed in 1998 and 1999. Capital outflows in direct investment and both types of portfolios increased in the 1990s. Capital outflows in financial derivatives were negative from 1996 to 2000.

For the period 2001–2018, capital outflows in debt instruments of other investments were positive before the GFC but turned negative in 2008 and 2009. Capital outflows in equities of direct investment and both types of portfolio were positive and relatively stable. They were positive even in 2008 and 2009. Capital outflows in financial derivatives were negative in every year.

Figure 24.5 (2) reports the components of capital outflows for the AFC economies for the period 1990–2018. In the 1990s, capital outflows in debt instruments of portfolio investment and equities of direct investment increased and accounted for a high proportion of capital outflows throughout the 1990s, with only little reversals in capital outflows in debt securities of portfolio investment in 1997. Capital outflows in equities of portfolio investment were relatively small throughout the period.

For the period 2001–2018, capital outflows of debt securities of portfolio investment were positive before the GFC but turned negative in 2009. This pattern is quite different from that of the AFC economies during the AFC, in which reversals in capital outflows were not found. The reversals in capital outflows in debt securities of portfolio investment likely helped finance the reversals in capital inflows during the GFC. Reversals in capital outflows in equities of portfolio investment were found in 2008 but the size of reversals was relatively small. Capital outflows in debt instruments of direct investment were positive in most periods and were small but still positive even in 2008. Capital outflows in equities of direct investment were stable and positive in this period.

Figure 24.5 (3) reports components of capital outflows for the non-AFC economies for the period 1990–2018. Capital outflows in debt instruments of other investments were the main component of capital outflows before the

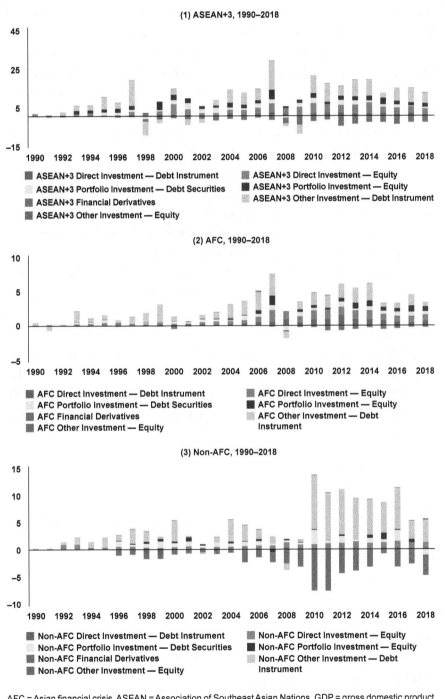

Figure 24.5: Components of Capital Outflows
(Percent of trend GDP)

(1) ASEAN+3, 1990–2018

- ■ ASEAN+3 Direct Investment — Debt Instrument
- ■ ASEAN+3 Portfolio Investment — Debt Securities
- ■ ASEAN+3 Financial Derivatives
- ■ ASEAN+3 Other Investment — Equity
- ■ ASEAN+3 Direct Investment — Equity
- ■ ASEAN+3 Portfolio Investment — Equity
- ■ ASEAN+3 Other Investment — Debt Instrument

(2) AFC, 1990–2018

- ■ AFC Direct Investment — Debt Instrument
- ■ AFC Portfolio Investment — Debt Securities
- ■ AFC Financial Derivatives
- ■ AFC Other Investment — Equity
- ■ AFC Direct Investment — Equity
- ■ AFC Portfolio Investment — Equity
- ■ AFC Other Investment — Debt Instrument

(3) Non-AFC, 1990–2018

- ■ Non-AFC Direct Investment — Debt Instrument
- ■ Non-AFC Portfolio Investment — Debt Securities
- ■ Non-AFC Financial Derivatives
- ■ Non-AFC Other Investment — Equity
- ■ Non-AFC Direct Investment — Equity
- ■ Non-AFC Portfolio Investment — Equity
- ■ Non-AFC Other Investment — Debt Instrument

AFC = Asian financial crisis, ASEAN = Association of Southeast Asian Nations, GDP = gross domestic product.
Source: International Monetary Fund Statistics, World Bank.

AFC like the AFC economies. However, huge reversals in capital outflows of debt instruments of other investments were found in 1998 and 1999, different from the situation in the AFC economies. The reversals in capital outflows of debt instruments of other investments were likely used to counter the reversals in capital inflows in debt instruments of other investments. This likely mitigated the effects of reversals in capital inflows of debt instruments of other investments in the non-AFC economies. Capital outflows of the two types of portfolio investments and capital outflows of equities of direct investment increased over time in the 1990s without any reversals.

For the period 2001–2018, capital outflows of debt instruments of other investments were positive before the GFC but turned negative in 2008 and 2009. The reversals in capital outflows in debt instrument of other investments likely helped finance reversals in capital inflows during the GFC. Capital outflows in equities of direct investment and the two types of portfolio investment were stable and positive in this period. After the GFC, the non-AFC economies had huge capital outflows in debt instrument of other investments, which led to net capital flow reversals.

Figure 24.6 reports the ratio of intra-regional portfolio investment assets to total portfolio assets for the ASEAN+3 economies. The ratio of portfolio assets invested in the ASEAN+3 economy to total portfolio assets is calculated for each ASEAN+3 economies and then the simple average number is calculated. The ratio was approximately 19.8% in 2001,

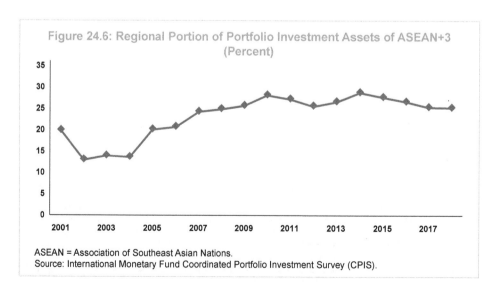

Figure 24.6: Regional Portion of Portfolio Investment Assets of ASEAN+3 (Percent)

ASEAN = Association of Southeast Asian Nations.
Source: International Monetary Fund Coordinated Portfolio Investment Survey (CPIS).

decreased to 12.1% in 2002, but it increased over time. It reached a peak
of 28.7%, then began to decrease slightly, but it was still 25.2% in 2018. In
general, the ratio increased over time. Although it is not clear, considering
that total portfolio investment capital flows tend to increase over time, it's
very likely that portfolio investment capital flows within ASEAN+3 will
also increase over time. In addition, it's likely that the regional portion of
portfolio investment flows of ASEAN+3 increases over time. Various regional
efforts on regional financial cooperation, such as the Chiang Mai Initiative
Multilateralisation (CMIM) and Asian Bond Market Initiative, promote
financial integration within ASEAN+3.

To summarize, the main components of reversals in capital inflows were
debt instruments of other investments during the AFC but debt securities of
portfolio investment during the GFC. During the AFC, reversals of capital
inflows in debt instruments of other investments were financed by reversals
of capital outflows in debt instruments of other investments in the non-AFC
economies but not in the AFC economies. During the GFC, reversals of
capital inflows in debt securities of portfolio investments were financed by
capital inflows in debt securities of portfolio investment and debt instruments
of other investments in the AFC, but mostly by debt instruments of other
investments in the non-AFC economies. After the GFC, the non-AFC economies had capital outflows mostly in debt instrument of other investments,
but the AFC economies had capital outflows in more diverse components.

Trends of Policies on International Capital Flows

In this section, overviews on the evolution of policies on international
capital flows in the ASEAN+3 economies are provided. For this purpose,
the Chinn-Ito index is used. The Chinn-Ito index shows the degree of
capital account openness, which is mostly the consequence of capital flow
liberalization/management/controls policies. Among various measures of
capital account liberalization/controls, the Chinn-Ito index is available for a
relatively long period. From this, the evolution of policies on capital account
openness from periods far before the AFC to the present can be inferred. In
addition, the index is constructed for each economy with the same standard
to easily compare the degree of capital account openness across different
economies. The value of the index lies between 0 and 1. A higher number
represents a higher degree of capital account openness.

Figure 24.7 shows the simple average values of the index for the ASEAN+3, AFC, and non-AFC economies. Capital account openness is higher in the AFC economies than the non-AFC economies. This capital account liberalization trend of the AFC economies seems to have resulted in the trend of sharp increases in capital flows during the mid-1990s. This eventually reversed and made economies suffer from boom–bust cycles during the AFC. A tightening of capital account openness was found in 1996–1998 but it was probably too late to mitigate the devastating effects of capital inflows reversals at that time.

For the period 2001–2018, the simple average for the whole ASEAN+3 shows that the degree of capital account openness again increased over time up to 2008, and then tightened in 2009. Again, these liberalization trends before the GFC could have contributed to an increase in capital flows in the 2000s, which was again reversed during the GFC.

Interestingly, the degree of capital account openness increased more in the non-AFC economies than the AFC economies. In addition, a tightening was clearly shown after the GFC in the AFC economies but not in the non-AFC economies. The AFC economies were more likely to be cautious in further capital account liberalization as they had already experienced a severe currency crisis. Thus, the size of increase in capital flows and reversals in the 2000s were smaller and less persistent in the AFC economies than those in the non-AFC economies.

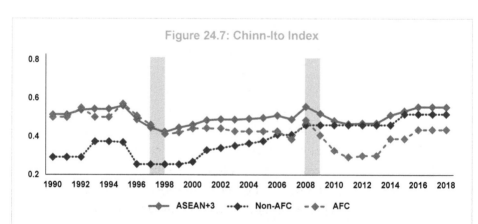

Figure 24.7: Chinn-Ito Index

AFC = Asian financial crisis, ASEAN = Association of Southeast Asian Nations, GFC = global financial crisis.
Notes: The index is normalized to range between zero and one. The shaded areas correspond to the AFC and GFC periods.
Source: Chinn and Ito (2006).

Macroeconomic Outcomes and Policy Responses During the AFC and GFC

Boom–Bust Cycles

In this section, macroeconomic consequences of the AFC and GFC for the ASEAN+3 economies are documented. The time series plots of key macroeconomic variables are examined to infer how these two crises with huge reversals in capital flows affected the ASEAN+3 economies.

While macroeconomic outcomes of the ASEAN+3 economies are investigated, whether some economies experienced boom–bust cycles with reversals in capital flows is of particular interest. Some past studies (e.g., Kim and Kim 2013, Kim et al. 2004, Kim and Yang 2011) documented that capital account liberalization and following surges and reversals in capital flows led to boom–bust cycles in some Asian economies during these crises. Capital account liberalization or loosening of capital flow management policies led to an initial surge in capital inflows. As capital flowed into the economy, domestic credit expanded, which in turn led to consumption and investment booms and surges in asset prices. However, the process was reversed over time. Capital inflows appreciated nominal and real exchange rates, which worsened the current account. This led foreign investors to have a negative view on the economy and withdraw their capital investment. Therefore, capital inflows declined and eventually negative net capital inflows were observed. This reversed the boom stage and initiated the bust stage. As capital flowed out of the economy, there were credit crunches and asset markets crashes, and consumption, investment, and output fell dramatically. Thus, some economies experienced a more severe economic crisis compared to others.

In this chapter, macropolicy responses during the AFC and GFC are examined with attention given to policy variables such as government spending, the short-term interest rate, and foreign exchange reserves. From these, fiscal, monetary, and foreign exchange policy responses are inferred.

To identify the changes of the ASEAN+3 economies brought about by the AFC, differences in macroeconomic outcomes and policy responses of the ASEAN+3 economies for the AFC and GFC are discussed. Macroeconomic outcomes and policy responses of the AFC and non-AFC economies are also compared.

Effects on Macroeconomic Variables

Figures 24.8–24.10 show the simple averages of real GDP, real consumption, and real investment growth rates for the ASEAN+3, AFC, and non-AFC economies for the period 1990 to 2018. During the 1990s, the growth rate of these variables in the ASEAN+3 economies dropped sharply in 1998. Real GDP growth rate was approximately 0%, real consumption growth rate was approximately 3%, and real investment growth rate reached –17% in 1998. The drop in these variables in 1998 was more severe in the AFC economies than in the non-AFC economies. The growth rates of real GDP, real consumption, and real investment of the AFC economies in 1998 were –3%, –6%, and –27%, respectively. In the non-AFC economies, the growth rate also declined in 1997 and 1998, but the decline was moderate. The fall

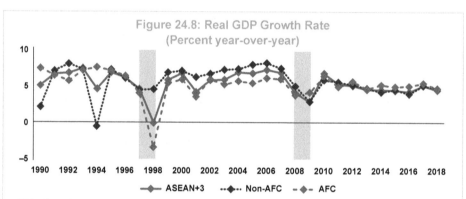

Figure 24.8: Real GDP Growth Rate (Percent year-over-year)

AFC = Asian financial crisis, ASEAN = Association of Southeast Asian Nations, GDP = gross domestic product, GFC = global financial crisis.
Note: The shaded areas correspond to the AFC and GFC periods.
Source: Census and Economic Information Center (CEIC) database, Asian Development Bank database, Central Banks, Asia Regional Integration Center.

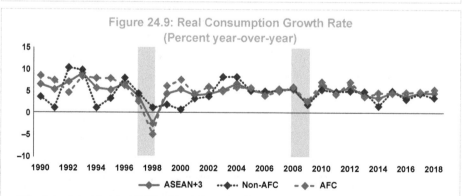

Figure 24.9: Real Consumption Growth Rate (Percent year-over-year)

AFC = Asian financial crisis, ASEAN = Association of Southeast Asian Nations, GFC = global financial crisis.
Note: The shaded areas correspond to the AFC and GFC periods.
Source: Census and Economic Information Center (CEIC) database, Asian Development Bank database, Central Banks, Asia Regional Integration Center.

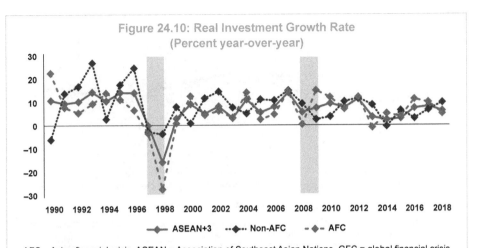

Figure 24.10: Real Investment Growth Rate
(Percent year-over-year)

ASEAN+3 ·····Non-AFC ··◆·· AFC

AFC = Asian financial crisis, ASEAN = Association of Southeast Asian Nations, GFC = global financial crisis.
Note: The shaded areas correspond to the AFC and GFC periods.
Source: Census and Economic Information Center (CEIC) database, Asian Development Bank database,
Central Banks, Asia Regional Integration Center.

in consumption growth rate is lower than that of GDP growth rate due to consumption smoothing behaviors, whereas the fall in investment growth rate is higher than that of GDP growth rate.

For the period 2001–2018, real GDP, real consumption, and real investment growth rates dropped during the GFC, but the size of the drops in those variables was smaller during the GFC than during the AFC. Real GDP growth rate dropped from approximately 7% in 2007 to approximately 4% in 2008 and 3% in 2009 for the ASEAN+3 economies. Also interestingly, the drops in these variables are smaller in the AFC economies than in the non-AFC economies. In the AFC economies, real GDP growth rate was approximately 6.0% in 2007, dropped to approximately 4.0% in 2008, and slightly increased to 4.5% in 2009. In the non-AFC economies, the real GDP growth rate was approximately 7.0% in 2007, dropped to approximately 5.0% in 2008, and further dropped to approximately 2.5% in 2009.

Figures 24.11 and 24.12 report the level of real exchange rate (period average) and the ratio of current account to the trend GDP around the AFC.[4] The real exchange rate of each country in 2018 is normalized to 100, and then the average is reported. During the AFC, the real exchange rate depreciated sharply in 1997 and 1998 and current account improved and turned into approximately 4% surplus in 1999.

---

[4] Real exchange rate of each country is calculated by using the nominal exchange rate against the US dollar and consumer price indexes of each country and the US.

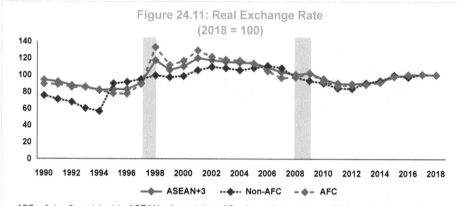

Figure 24.11: Real Exchange Rate
(2018 = 100)

AFC = Asian financial crisis, ASEAN = Association of Southeast Asian Nations, GFC = global financial crisis.
Note: The shaded areas correspond to the AFC and GFC periods.
Source: Bank for International Settlements Statistics warehouse.

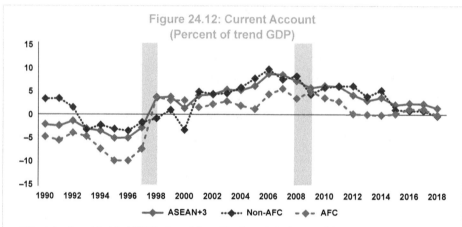

Figure 24.12: Current Account
(Percent of trend GDP)

AFC = Asian financial crisis, ASEAN = Association of Southeast Asian Nations, GDP = gross domestic product,
GFC = global financial crisis.
Note: The shaded areas correspond to the AFC and GFC periods.
Source: International Monetary Fund Financial Statistics, World Bank.

This is a typical pattern found in the usual boom–bust cycles discussed previously. These patterns are appear to be more pronounced in the AFC economies than in the non-AFC economies. The real exchange rate of the AFC economies depreciated by 100% from 1997 to 1999 after showing appreciation during the early 1990s. The turnaround of the current account is also quite dramatic in the AFC economies. The current account worsened until 1996, recording −10% deficits in 1995 and 1996, and then improved in 1997 and 1998, recording 5% surplus in 1998.

For the period 2001–2018, the real exchange rate appreciated before the GFC but only a little reversal was found during the GFC. In addition, a worsening current account was not found before the GFC and the current account recorded a surplus before the GFC. These patterns are different from the patterns found during the AFC. This result suggests that boom–bust cycles with capital flow reversal may not be the main mechanism through which the ASEAN+3 economies suffered.

Figure 24.13 reports the level of nominal exchange rate against the US dollar (period average). The nominal exchange rate of each country in 2018 is normalized to 100, and the average is reported. During the AFC, a sharp depreciation of the exchange rate was found. The depreciation is stronger in the AFC economies, which is not surprising since the AFC economies are defined as those that experienced a huge depreciation during the AFC. On the other hand, during the GFC, only a slight depreciation was found in the ASEAN+3 and AFC economies and no depreciation was found in the non-AFC economies.

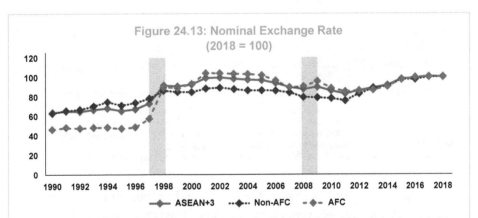

Figure 24.13: Nominal Exchange Rate
(2018 = 100)

AFC = Asian financial crisis, ASEAN = Association of Southeast Asian Nations, GFC = global financial crisis.
Note: The shaded areas correspond to the AFC and GFC periods.
Source: Bank for International Settlements Statistics warehouse.

Effects on Policy Variables

Figure 24.14 shows the growth rate of foreign exchange reserves. Before the AFC, the growth rates of foreign exchange reserves were positive in most cases, which suggests that these economies accumulated foreign exchange reserves over time. However, the growth rate of foreign exchange reserves turned negative, reaching approximately −25% in 1997 for the AFC economies, which means that the level of foreign exchange reserves declined sharply in 1997 in the AFC economies. This suggests that the AFC economies tried to defend the exchange rate depreciation by selling foreign exchange reserves during the AFC.

During the GFC, the growth rate of foreign exchange reserves fell in 2008, although it was still positive on average. Some economies experienced a negative growth rate of foreign exchange reserves, which implies that they tried to defend exchange rate depreciation by selling foreign exchange reserves in the GFC. Interestingly, the growth rate of foreign exchange reserves was negative in 2013 and close to zero in 2014, 2015, and 2016. This may suggest that some countries tried to defend against depreciation pressure, likely generated by the US monetary policy normalization process.

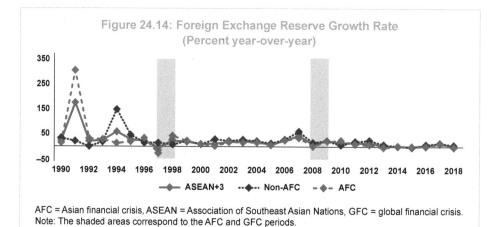

Figure 24.14: Foreign Exchange Reserve Growth Rate (Percent year-over-year)

AFC = Asian financial crisis, ASEAN = Association of Southeast Asian Nations, GFC = global financial crisis.
Note: The shaded areas correspond to the AFC and GFC periods.
Source: International Monetary Fund, Asian Development Bank database, Asian Regional Integration Center.

Figures 24.15 and 24.16 show the call rate and real government consumption growth rate, respectively, for the period of 1990–2018. During the AFC, the interest rate increased sharply in 1998, especially in the AFC economies. In the AFC economies, the call rate reached to approximately 25% in 1998, increasing from 10%–15% before the AFC. Real government spending also fell sharply in 1998, especially in the AFC economies, reaching −4% in 1998. Monetary and fiscal tightening were mostly due to the International Monetary Fund's (IMF) demands on the AFC economies, but with stringent and debatable policy suggestions, the AFC economies suffered from crisis more severely.

During the GFC, the government spending growth rate increased sharply and the interest rate tended to decline. Such a tendency is very clear for the AFC economies. The AFC economies increased the growth rate of real government spending from under 10% before the GFC to over 20% in 2009.

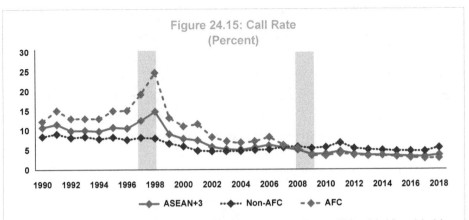

Figure 24.15: Call Rate
(Percent)

AFC = Asian financial crisis, ASEAN = Association of Southeast Asian Nations, GFC = global financial crisis.
Note: The shaded areas correspond to the AFC and GFC periods.
Source: International Financial Statistics.

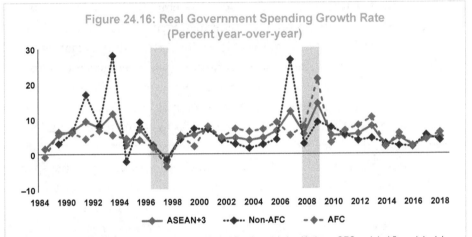

Figure 24.16: Real Government Spending Growth Rate
(Percent year-over-year)

AFC = Asian financial crisis, ASEAN = Association of Southeast Asian Nations, GFC = global financial crisis.
Note: The shaded areas correspond to the AFC and GFC periods.
Source: Census and Economic Information Center (CEIC) database, Asian Development Bank database,
Central Banks, Asia Regional Integration Center.

The AFC economies also increased the interest rate from over 7% before the GFC to approximately 3% in 2009. It seems that the AFC economies learned from the AFC experience with the controversial policy suggestions of IMF, and these monetary and fiscal expansions helped the recovery of the AFC economies from the GFC.

To summarize, the movements of key macrovariables around the AFC, especially in the AFC economies, are consistent with the boom–bust cycle following capital flow reversals. The capital account tended to be liberalized, capital inflow surged, real exchange rate appreciated, and the current account worsened, and then capital inflows were reversed, foreign exchange reserve fell, GDP growth rate dropped dramatically, real exchange rate depreciated, and the current account improved. During the AFC, monetary and fiscal policy tightened, which contributed to the fall in GDP growth rate. However, during the GFC, these patterns are not clearly found, which may suggest that different mechanisms resulted in the fall in GDP growth rate during the GFC.

Empirical Model

Baseline Empirical Model

In order to analyze the effect of shocks to capital flow in the ASEAN+3 economies, structural panel VAR models are employed. Structural panel VAR models have been useful in considering dynamic interactions among variables, identifying shocks to variables of interests, and investigating the effects of the identified shocks while controlling for heterogeneities across countries. In this section, interactions between capital flows and various macroeconomic variables are studied to identify the shocks to capital flows and to investigate the effects of the shocks to capital flows on various macroeconomic variables.

Annual data of 14 ASEAN+3 economies are used and the time span of the data series is relatively short. To increase the degree of freedom in our estimations, the panel structure is exploited by introducing a panel structure in VAR models. Some heterogeneities are assumed among the 14 economies by modeling the individual fixed effect in the panel VAR models. See Appendix B for details on the estimation of panel VAR model.

In the baseline model, three variables, current account as a ratio to the trend GDP (CUR), net capital outflows as a ratio to the trend GDP (CAP), and X, where X is a macroeconomic variable of interests, are included. CAP are included to infer the effect of shocks to capital flow which is the main objective of this chapter. Note that net capital outflows (capital outflows minus capital inflows) are included to show the effects of the unexpected increase in net capital outflows during the AFC and GFC instead of net capital inflows (capital inflows minus capital outflows). CUR is included to control for the capital flow movements that are driven by current account imbalances. Note that current account imbalances are naturally financed by corresponding changes in capital flows. Thus, autonomous capital flows that do not directly correspond to current account movements can be identified in the model. X is included to infer the effects of shocks to net capital outflows on a macroeconomic variable X, which is the main objective of this exercise.

For identification, a recursive structure on contemporaneous structural parameters is assumed, as suggested by Sims (1980). In particular, Cholesky factorization with the order {CUR, CAP, X} is adopted, in which the contemporaneously exogenous ones are ordered first.

The reasons behind the ordering {CUR, CAP, X} are as follows. First, CUR is assumed contemporaneously exogenous to CAP and X, which helps to identify more exogenous components of CAP movements by excluding endogenous movements of CAP caused by CUR movements. Current account imbalances are automatically financed by capital flow movements, and we would like to exclude such endogenous movements of CAP. Second, CAP is assumed contemporaneously exogenous to X to infer the effects of shocks to CAP on X, including the contemporaneous effects of shocks to CAP on X within a year.

These identifying assumptions are similar to those of Kim et al. (2004) who investigated the effects of shocks to capital flows on various macroeconomic variables in Korea. Some alternative identifying assumptions are experimented with, but the main results are not much different qualitatively. Some results are reported in the later part of this chapter.

For X, various macroeconomic variables are considered. In the representative models, real gross domestic product (RGDP) (in the log-differenced form) is used since RGDP is the variable that can show the overall aggregate macroeconomic activities of each economy. In addition to RGDP, the following variables are considered one by one. To discuss general business cycle effects, (i) consumption in real term (in the log-differenced form) and (ii) investment in real terms (in the log-differenced form), in addition to RGDP, are considered.

To compare with the predictions of the boom–bust cycle theory, (iii) the real exchange rate (in the log-differenced form) is considered. To provide discussion in relation to the currency crisis, (iv) the nominal exchange rate (in the log-differenced form) is considered. To infer policy responses to shocks to capital flows, (v) real government consumption (in the log-differenced form), (vi) call rate, and (vii) foreign exchange reserves (in the log-differenced form) are taken into account.

Extended Empirical Models

An extended model that includes capital inflows as a ratio to the trend GDP (CAPI) and capital outflows as a ratio to the trend GDP (CAPO) separately is also analyzed. The effects of capital inflows and those of capital outflows can be different. Here, more focus is on the effects of capital inflows. Capital inflows driven by foreign investors' behaviors are regarded as the main cause of the AFC and crisis led by capital flow reversals. Capital outflows are also included in the model because the effects of capital inflows on the economy also depend on how capital outflows respond to shocks to capital inflows, as mentioned in the beginning of this chapter.

The extended model includes CUR, CAPI, CAPO, and RGDP.[5] Note that the negative sign of capital inflows (as a ratio to the trend GDP) and the negative sign of capital outflows (as a ratio to the trend GDP) are used to be consistent with the baseline model in which net capital outflows are included in the model. By taking the negative sign of capital inflows, the effects of shocks to capital flows on the economy are likely to have a similar sign to that found in the baseline model with net capital outflows. That is, the study shows the effects of decline in capital inflows on the economy during the AFC and GFC. In addition, the negative sign is also added to capital outflows so the correlation between CAPI and CAPO is unaffected.

For identifying assumptions, Cholesky factorization with the order {CUR, CAPI, CAPO, RGDP} is adopted to the structural panel VAR model. The reasons behind the ordering among CUR, CAP (CAPI and CAPO), and RGDP are the same as in the baseline model. Then, CAPI is assumed to be contemporaneously exogenous to CAPO for the following reason. The main focus is on the consequences of shocks to capital inflows, including its effects on capital outflows, and that CAPI is driven by foreign investors' behavior, so CAPI is likely to affect CAPO, not the other way around, especially in the crisis episode.

---

[5] Due to the results of unit root tests, RGDP is used as log-differenced while CAP, CAPI, CAPO, and CUR as levels. See Appendix C for the details on the results of unit root tests.

Furthermore, an extended model that includes each component of capital inflows is considered. The model is similar to the previous four variable models with both capital inflows and capital outflows. In this model, CAPI is replaced with each component of capital inflows (i.e., {CUR, CAPI by component, CAPO, RGDP}). The following four components of CAPI are considered: direct investment, equities of portfolio investment, debt securities of portfolio investment, and other investments. Both equities and debt instruments of direct investment have stable flows. Debt instruments of other investments take up the most part of other investments but equity instruments of other investments take up only a small part of other investments. Thus, there is no need to separate these investments into further details. On the other hand, portfolio investments are of two types, equities and debt securities, because these two types of flows often show different trends and magnitude, and these types of flows increase fast over time and have become very important in recent years.

Sample Periods

The model covers the sample period 1990–2018. The sample of the 1980s was excluded as data were not available for some economies and some economies allowed very limited capital flow movements during the 1980s. Two sub-periods, the period from 1990 to 2004 and the period from 2001 to 2018, are also considered. The period 1990 to 2004 pays close attention to the 7 years before and after the AFC. The period 2001–2018 set with emphasis on the 7 years preceding the GFC to the latest period available.[6] Two lags are included in each model. Appendix D reports the data sources and details.

Empirical Results

Baseline Model with Real GDP

Figure 24.17 (1) reports impulse responses of each variable to shocks to net capital outflows (as a ratio to trend GDP) with 90% probability bands for the

---

[6] We also experiment with the period 2001–2015 in which we consider 7 years before and after the GFC. The results are similar to those for the period 2001–2018, but huge probability bands are found more frequently for the period 2001–2015 than for the period 2001–2018.

full sample period for the ASEAN+3 economies. For differenced variables, the cumulative impulse responses are reported to show the impulse responses of the variable levels. For example, the accumulated impulse responses of differenced (log of) real GDP are reported to show the impulse responses of (log of) real GDP.

For easy comparison of the effects in various cases, impact effect of shocks to net capital outflows on net capital flows is normalized to 1% (of trend GDP). In response to shocks to net capital outflows, net capital outflows increased by 1% but decreased back to the initial level over time, and in about 6 years, net capital flows approached the level close to the initial level. This suggests that the shocks to net capital outflows are temporary in nature. In response to such net capital outflows shocks, real GDP decreased on impact and further declined in the next year. The decline of real GDP in the second year was statistically significant at 5%. The size of the decline in net capital outflows was approximately 0.1% in the second year.

Figures 24.17 (2) and (3) report impulse responses to shocks to net capital outflows with 90% probability bands for the full sample period for the AFC and non-AFC economies, respectively. The effect of shocks to net capital outflows on real GDP was far larger in the AFC economies than in the non-AFC economies. In the AFC economies, real GDP declined by 0.2 % on impact and further declined in the next year by approximately 0.53% and then slowly increases back over time. Even 6 years after the shocks, real GDP declined by 0.4%. The decline is statistically significant at 5% up to 5 years after the shock. In fact, the size of the decline in real GDP is huge, considering that the impact effect on net capital outflows was 1% (of trend GDP). In addition, given that net capital outflow responses were significant only for the first 3 years, the effect on real GDP was quite persistent since the decline in real GDP was statistically significant up to 6 years after the shocks. On the other hand, the effect of shocks to net capital outflows on real GDP was not statistically significant in any horizon in the non-AFC economies.

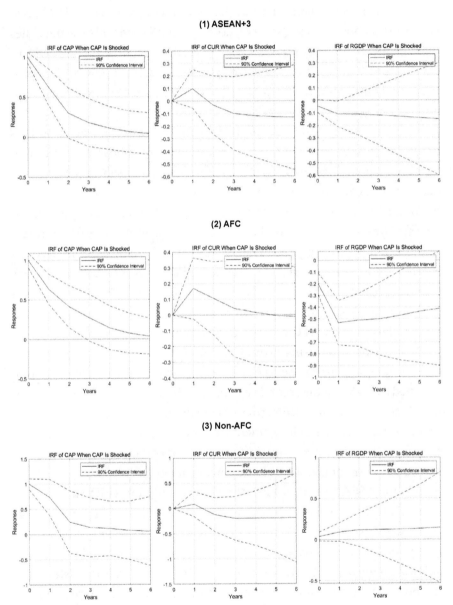

Figure 24.17: Impulse Responses Functions to Shocks to Net Capital Outflows: Baseline Model

(1) ASEAN+3

(2) AFC

(3) Non-AFC

AFC = Asian financial crisis, ASEAN = Association of Southeast Asian Nations, CAP = net capital outflows as a ratio to the trend gross domestic product, CUR = current account as a ratio to the trend gross domestic product, IRF = impulse responses functions, RGDP = real gross domestic product.
Source: International Monetary Fund Financial Statistics, World Bank, Census and Economic Information Center (CEIC) database.

Baseline Model with Other Macroeconomic Variables

The effects of shocks to net capital outflows on various key macroeconomic variables such as real consumption (RCON), real investment (RINV), real government consumption (RGOV), nominal (NEX) and real exchange rates (REX), and the interest rate (CALL) are further examined. Figures 24.18 (1), (2), and (3) show the impulse responses of each variable to shocks to net capital outflows with 90% probability bands in the ASEAN+3, AFC, and non-AFC economies, respectively.

Real consumption and real investment declined significantly. This suggests that shocks to net capital outflows generated business cycles that changed various components of real GDP. In response to shocks to net capital outflows, real consumption declined by 0.1% on impact and further declined by 0.2% in the next period. The decline in real consumption was significant for the first 3 years. In response to shocks to net capital outflows, real investment responded more strongly than real consumption. Real investment declined by 0.4% on impact, and further declined by 0.7% in the next period. The decline in real investment was also significant for the first 3 years. The effects of shocks to net capital outflows on real consumption and real investment were far larger in the AFC economies than the non-AFC economies.

This is not surprising given that the AFC economies experienced a serious recession during the AFC. In the AFC economies, real consumption declined by 0.25% in the second year and real investment declined by 1.60% in the second year. The declines in real consumption were significant for the first 2 years, and those in investment were significant for the first 3 years. In the non-AFC economies, impulse responses of real consumption and real investment were not statistically significant at any horizon.

In the ASEAN+3 economies, the real exchange rate (REX) depreciated significantly in response to shocks to net capital outflows. The real exchange rate depreciated by 0.55% on impact and further depreciated by 1.05% in the next period. The real exchange rate depreciation was statistically significant at 5% at all horizons. The real exchange rate depreciation is consistent with the boom–bust cycle story, together with current account improvement.[7] When capital flows into a country, real exchange rate appreciates and the

---

[7] In Figure 24.17, we can see that the current account tends to improve. In the baseline model, the current account is assumed to be contemporaneously exogenous to net capital outflows, and the effects on current account tend to be weak. But when the net capital outflow is assumed to be contemporaneously exogenous to current account, the increase in current account is significant.

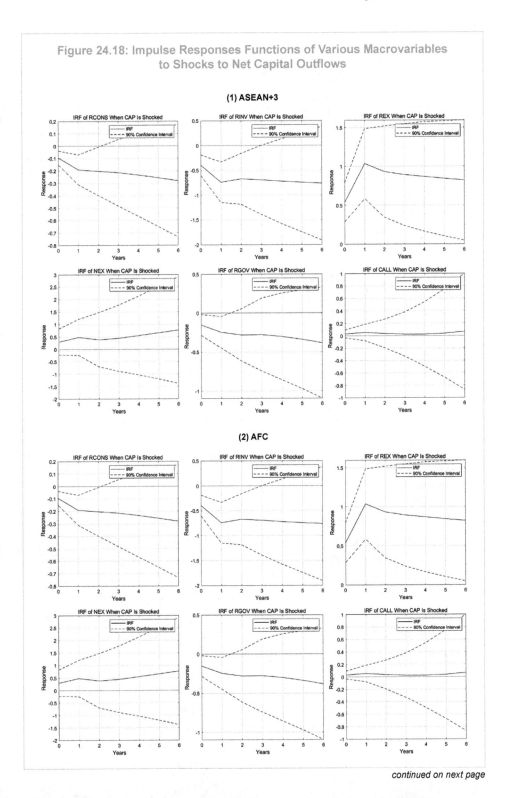

Figure 24.18: Impulse Responses Functions of Various Macrovariables to Shocks to Net Capital Outflows

continued on next page

Figure 24.18: *continued*

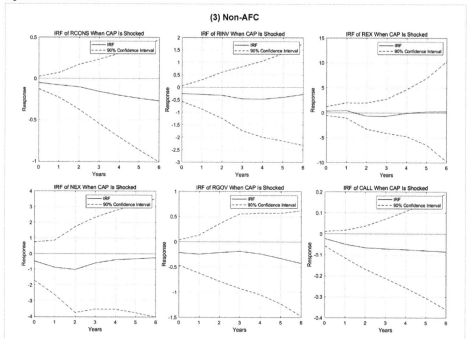

AFC = Asian financial crisis, ASEAN = Association of Southeast Asian Nations, CALL = call rate, CAP = net capital outflows as a ratio to the trend gross domestic product, IRF = impulse responses functions, NEX = nominal exchange rate, RCONS = real consumption, REX = real exchange rate, RGDP = real gross domestic product, RGOV = real government consumption, RINV = real investment.
Source: International Monetary Fund Financial Statistics, World Bank, Census and Economic Information Center (CEIC) database.

current account worsens, but when capital flows reverse, real exchange rate depreciates and current account improves.

In the AFC economies, the nominal exchange rate (NEX) depreciated sharply in response to shocks to net capital outflows. On impact, the exchange rate depreciated by 1.1 %, and further depreciated by 2.4% the next year. The exchange rate depreciation is statistically significant at 5% up to 6 years after the shock. In the ASEAN+3 economies, in response to the shocks to net capital outflows, the nominal exchange rate depreciated but the depreciation is not statistically significant at any horizon. For the non-AFC economies, the impulse responses of nominal exchange rate were not statistically significant at any horizon.

In the ASEAN+3 economies, real government spending (RGOV) fell significantly for the first 2 years in response to shocks to net capital outflows. The magnitude of the decrease was 0.2%–0.4%, which is substantial. This suggests that fiscal policy was not counter-cyclical in response to shocks to net capital outflows. Instead, in response to shocks to net capital outflows, contractionary fiscal policy was taken, which likely generated further negative effects on the economy. The decrease in real government spending was larger in the AFC economies than the non-AFC economies. In addition, the decrease in real government spending was significant in the AFC economies but not in the non-AFC economies.

The call rate (CALL) increased in response to shocks to net capital outflows in the AFC economies. The increase in call rate was statistically significant at 5% for the first 2 years after the shock. This suggests that monetary policy did not pursue output stabilization in response to shocks to net capital flows. Instead of monetary expansion, the monetary authorities of the AFC economies took monetary contractions in response to shocks to net capital outflows that led to a decline in output. In the non-AFC and ASEAN+3 economies, the interest rate responses were not statistically significant at any horizon.

Sub-Period Estimations

The effects of shocks to net capital outflows for two sub-periods, the period around the AFC (1990–2004) and the period around the GFC (2001–2018), are investigated.

Figure 24.19 reports the impulse responses with 90% probability bands for the ASEAN+3, AFC, and non-AFC economies. The shocks to net capital outflows had significant negative effects on real GDP in the period 1990–2004 for the ASEAN+3 and AFC economies. The effect on real GDP for the AFC economies was particularly strong. In response to shocks to net capital outflows, real GDP declined by 0.25% on impact, and further declined by 0.70% in the next year. The decline in real GDP was statistically significant at 5% for the first 4 years after the shocks. However, the shocks to net capital outflows had statistically insignificant effect on real GDP in other periods and groups. These results may suggest that the boom–bust cycles generated from volatile capital flows occurred mostly for the AFC economies during the period around the AFC.[8]

---

[8] Alternative identifying assumptions are experimented with by first considering the model in which CAP is contemporaneously exogenous to all other variables. Second, the model in which all other variables are contemporaneously exogenous to CAP is examined. The results are qualitatively similar. However, under the former identifying assumptions, the effects of net capital outflows shocks on real GDP tend to be more significant and larger than those in the baseline model due to the specification that identified CAP shocks are conditioned on no other shocks. Under the latter identifying assumptions, the effects of net capital outflows shocks on real GDP tend to be less significant and smaller than those in the baseline model due to the specification that identified CAP shocks are conditioned on more shocks. At any rate, it is clear that shocks to net capital flows have statistically significant negative effects in the ASEAN+3 economies, especially in the AFC economies. The results are available upon request.

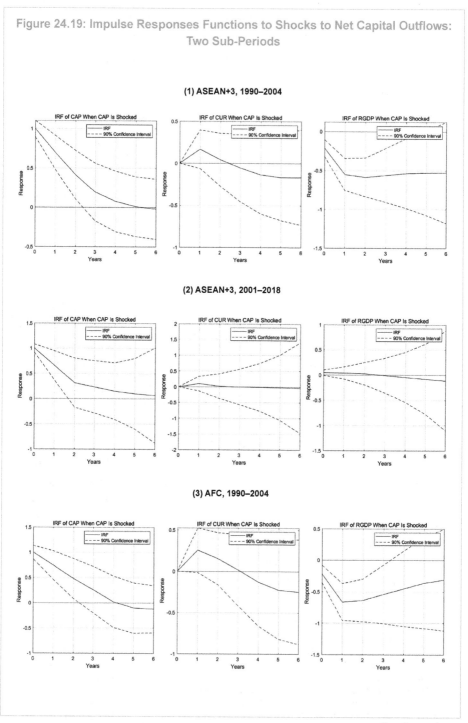

Figure 24.19: Impulse Responses Functions to Shocks to Net Capital Outflows: Two Sub-Periods

continued on next page

Figure 24.19: *continued*

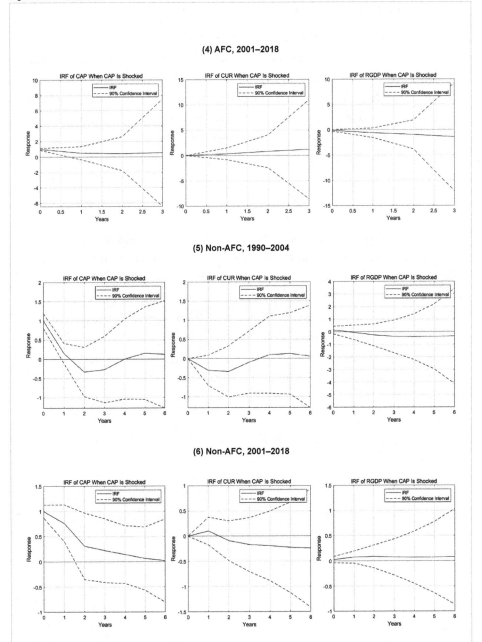

AFC = Asian financial crisis, ASEAN = Association of Southeast Asian Nations, CAP = net capital outflows as a ratio to the trend gross domestic product, CUR = current account as a ratio to the trend gross domestic product, IRF = impulse responses functions, RGDP = real gross domestic product.

Source: International Monetary Fund Financial Statistics, World Bank, Census and Economic Information Center (CEIC) database.

Effects of Capital Inflows

The effects of (negative) shocks to capital inflows in the four-variable model are here investigated. Figure 24.20 reports the impulse responses of each variable to negative shocks to capital inflows with 90% probability bands for the ASEAN+3 economies. In the full sample period and two sub-sample periods, negative shocks to capital inflows had significant effects on real GDP on impact. However, the size of the effects was relatively small. The decline of real GDP on impact was less than 0.05% in the full sample period and two sub-sample periods. In addition, the effects on real GDP were not statistically significant after the first year. The relative weak and less persistent effect of shocks to capital inflows seems to be related to the responses of capital outflows. In response to negative shocks to capital inflows, capital inflows declined but capital outflows also declined. In addition, the size of the decline in capital inflows and capital outflows was similar. Both capital inflows and outflows declined by approximately 1%. Furthermore, the shape of dynamic responses of capital inflows was almost similar to those of capital outflows. If the effects of capital outflows were the opposite to those of capital inflows, capital inflows that led to a similar magnitude of capital outflows likely had relatively small effects on the economy.

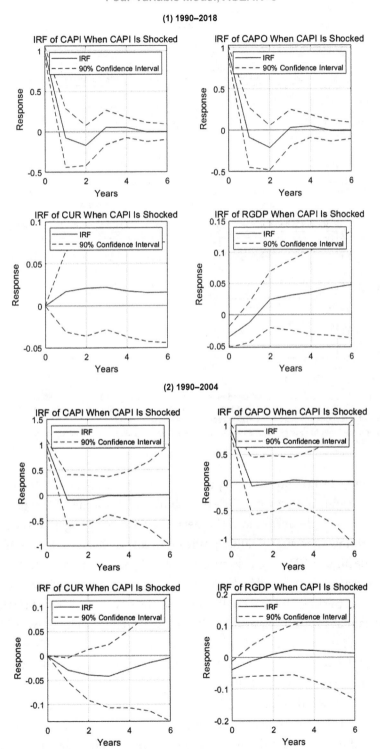

Figure 24.20: Impulse Responses Functions to Negative Shocks to Capital Inflows: Four-Variable Model, ASEAN+3

(1) 1990–2018

(2) 1990–2004

continued on next page

Figure 24.20: *continued*

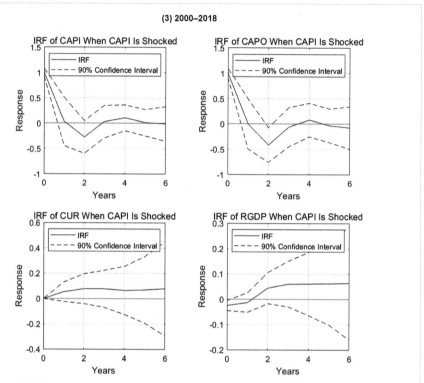

CAPI = capital inflows as a ratio to the trend gross domestic product, CAPO = capital outflows as a ratio to the trend gross domestic product, CUR = current account as a ratio to the trend gross domestic product, IRF = impulse responses functions, RGDP = real gross domestic product.
Source: International Monetary Fund Financial Statistics, World Bank, Census and Economic Information Center (CEIC) database.

Figure 24.21 reports the impulse responses of each variable to negative shocks to capital inflows with 90% probability bands for the AFC economies. In the full sample period and the period 1990–2004, negative shocks to capital inflows had statistically significant negative effects on real GDP. The size of decline in GDP was also substantial and persistent. In the full sample period, real GDP declined by 0.2% on impact, and further declined by 0.4% in the next period. The real GDP decline in the first 2 years was statistically significant at 5%. In the period 1990–2004, real GDP declined by 0.2% on impact and further declined by 0.5% in the next year. The real GDP decline in the first 3 years was statistically significant at 5% significance level.

Interestingly, in the full sample period and the period 1990–2004, capital outflows also declined in response to negative shocks to capital inflows, but the size of decline in capital outflows was far smaller than for capital inflows. In the full sample period, capital outflows declined only by

Figure 24.21: Impulse Responses Functions to Negative Shocks to Capital Inflows: Four-Variable Model, AFC

(1) 1990–2018

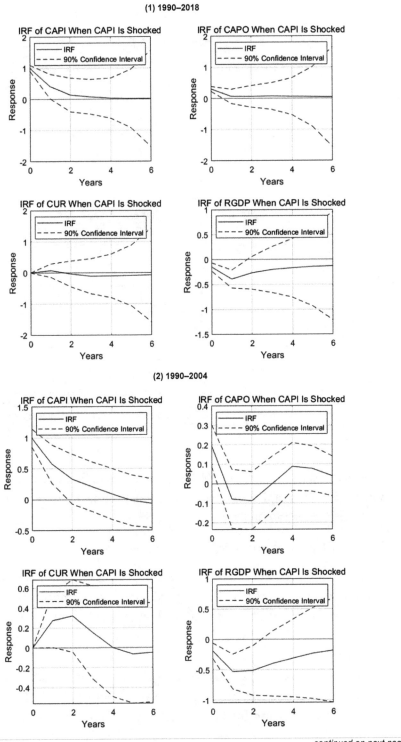

continued on next page

Figure 24.21: *continued*

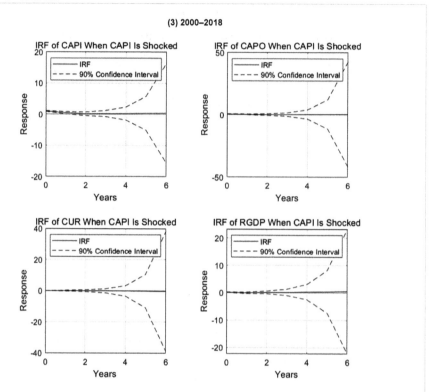

AFC = Asian financial crisis, CAPI = capital inflows as a ratio to the trend gross domestic product, CAPO = capital outflows as a ratio to the trend gross domestic product, CUR = current account as a ratio to the trend gross domestic product, IRF = impulse responses functions, RGDP = real gross domestic product. Source: International Monetary Fund Financial Statistics, World Bank, Census and Economic Information Center (CEIC) database.

0.3% and in the period 1990–2004, capital outflows declined only by 0.2%. A huge decline in capital inflows with a small decline in capital outflows led to a large decline in real GDP.

Effects of Components of Capital Inflows

The effects of (negative) shocks to each component of capital inflows in the four-variable model are here investigated. Figure 24.22 reports the impulse responses of each variable to negative shocks to each component of capital inflows with 90% probability bands for the ASEAN+3 economies for the full sample period.

Negative shocks to capital inflows in direct investment had a significant negative effect on real GDP for the ASEAN+3 economies. Real GDP declined by 0.2% on impact and further declined by 0.4% in the next period. The declines in real GDP were significant for the first 2 years. However, this does not necessarily imply that capital inflows in direct investment played an important role in the AFC or GFC because capital inflows in direct investment were relatively stable even during the AFC and GFC.

Negative shocks to equities of capital inflows in portfolio investment had significant negative effects on real GDP. Real GDP fell by 0.20% on impact and further decreased by 0.25% in the next period. The declines of real GDP in the first 2 years were statistically significant. Negative shocks to capital inflows in other investments also had a statistically significant negative effect on real GDP, but only impact effect was significant and the size of the effect was relatively small since the decline in real GDP is only by 0.03% on impact. Negative shocks to capital inflows in debt securities of portfolio investment

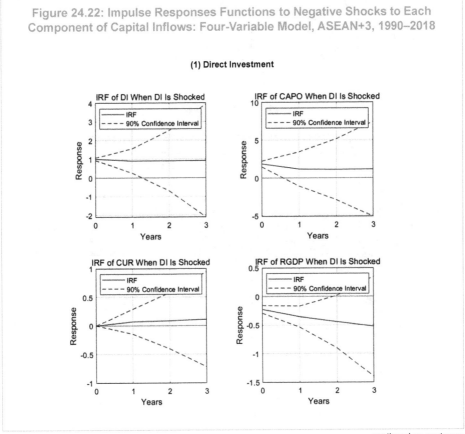

Figure 24.22: Impulse Responses Functions to Negative Shocks to Each Component of Capital Inflows: Four-Variable Model, ASEAN+3, 1990–2018

(1) Direct Investment

continued on next page

Figure 24.22: *continued*

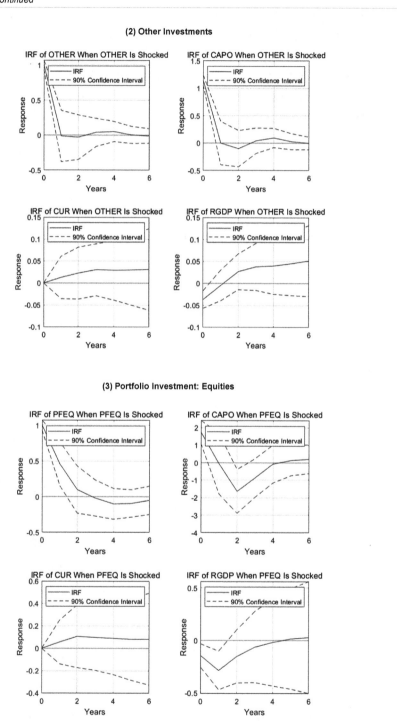

continued on next page

Figure 24.22: *continued*

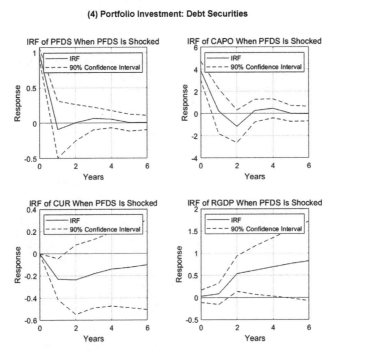

(4) Portfolio Investment: Debt Securities

CAPO = capital outflows as a ratio to the trend gross domestic product, CUR = current account as a ratio to the trend gross domestic product, DI = capital inflows in direct investment as a ratio to the trend gross domestic product, IRF = impulse responses functions, OTHER = capital inflows in other investments as a ratio to the trend gross domestic product, RGDP = real gross domestic product, PFDS = capital inflows in debt securities of portfolio investment as a ratio to the trend gross domestic product, PFEQ = capital inflows in equities of portfolio investment as a ratio to the trend gross domestic product.
Source: International Monetary Fund Financial Statistics, World Bank, Census and Economic Information Center (CEIC) database.

did not really decrease real GDP. Thus, only negative shocks to equities of capital inflows in portfolio investment help to explain the AFC experience.

Figure 24.23 reports the impulse responses of each variable to negative shocks to each component of capital inflows with 90% probability bands for the AFC economies for the period 1990–2004. The results are somewhat different from those for the full sample period. Negative shocks to capital inflows in other investments had a statistically significant negative effect on real GDP as expected, but other shocks did not, which is puzzling. This suggests that reversals in capital inflows in other investments were the main drivers that led the AFC economies to the boom–bust cycles during the AFC. Shocks to capital inflows in other investments indeed had a substantial effect on real GDP. Real GDP declined by 0.25% on impact and further declined to 0.60% in the next year. The declines in real GDP in the first 3 years were

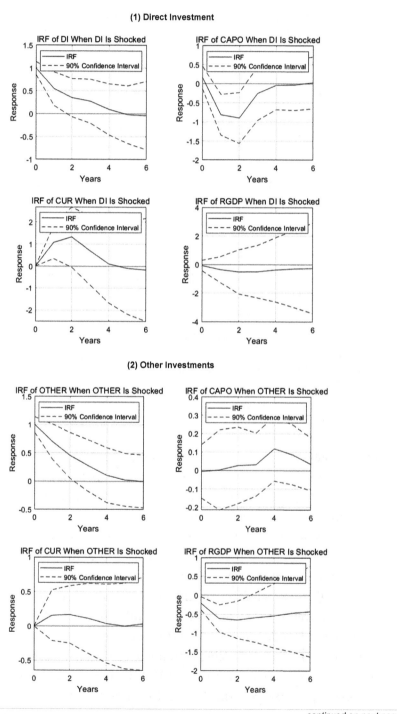

Figure 24.23: Impulse Responses Functions to Negative Shocks to Each Component of Capital Inflows: Four-Variable Model, AFC, 1990–2004

(1) Direct Investment

(2) Other Investments

continued on next page

Figure 24.23: *continued*

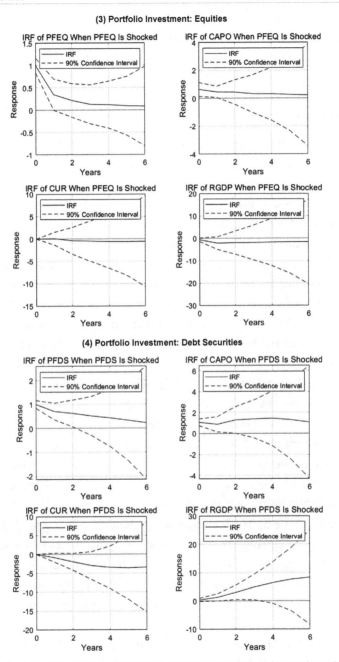

(3) Portfolio Investment: Equities

(4) Portfolio Investment: Debt Securities

AFC = Asian financial crisis, CAPO = capital outflows as a ratio to the trend gross domestic product, CUR = current account as a ratio to the trend gross domestic product, DI = capital inflows in direct investment as a ratio to the trend gross domestic product, IRF = impulse responses functions, OTHER = capital inflows in other investments as a ratio to the trend gross domestic product, RGDP = real gross domestic product, PFDS = capital inflows in debt securities of portfolio investment as a ratio to the trend gross domestic product, PFEQ = capital inflows in equities of portfolio investment as a ratio to the trend gross domestic product.

Source: International Monetary Fund Financial Statistics, World Bank, Census and Economic Information Center (CEIC) database.

statistically significant at 5%. It is also interesting that capital outflows did not respond much to negative shocks to capital inflows in other investments, but capital outflows strongly responded to other shocks.[9]

Conclusion

The trend of capital flows and the performance of the ASEAN+3 economies are documented in this chapter. The effects of shocks to capital flows on the ASEAN+3 economies are investigated by paying close attention to the AFC and GFC. The main results and messages are summarized as follows.

The ASEAN+3 economies suffered from severe economic recession during the AFC and GFC. The economic performance in the ASEAN+3 economies was worse during the AFC than in the GFC. In particular, the AFC economies experienced devastating economic downturns during the AFC.

Capital inflows were reversed dramatically during the AFC and GFC, more in the AFC economies than in the non-AFC economies. Capital outflows were also reversed substantially in most cases, except for the AFC economies during the AFC. Net capital inflows (inflows minus outflows) were reversed dramatically during the AFC (more in the AFC economies than in the non-AFC economies) but not in the GFC.

These results suggest that the capital flow reversal was a very important source of economic downturns during the AFC, especially in the AFC economies. However, the capital flow reversal was not the main source of recession during the GFC, although volatile capital flows still contributed to financial instability during the GFC.

The formal empirical analysis using panel VAR models also supports the conclusion. During the AFC, shocks to capital flows had a substantial effect on key macrovariables on the AFC economies, but not much during the GFC. During the GFC, the decline in the US economy could have affected the ASEAN+3 economies through various channels such as trade and other finance channels.

During the AFC, the AFC economies experienced the typical boom-bust cycle with capital flow reversals. As capital flowed into the economy,

---

[9] When we analyze the effects of shocks to each component of net capital flows, some results are similar but others are different. In the full sample period of the ASEAN+3 economies, only shocks to other investments have a significant effect. In the AFC period of the AFC countries, only shocks to portfolio investments have a significant effect.

domestic credit expanded, which in turn led to consumption and investment booms and surges in asset prices. However, capital inflows caused the appreciation of nominal and real exchange rates, which worsened the current account. Then, foreign investors pulled out their investments, which resulted in negative net capital inflows, credit crunches, and asset markets crashes, and consumption, investment, and output fell dramatically.

The devastating effects of capital flow reversals during the AFC for the AFC economies seem to result from various sources. The AFC economies liberalized capital accounts without enough preparation against volatile international capital flows. Huge reversals in capital inflows in bank loans led to huge instabilities in their financial systems and caused a financial crisis. A relative shortage of foreign exchange reserves may also have contributed to the crisis. A relative shortage of foreign assets and restrictions on capital outflows made it difficult for these economies to utilize foreign assets to counter the effects of reversals in capital inflows. Monetary and fiscal contractions during the AFC, forced by the IMF, make the situation worse.

After the AFC, all the ASEAN+3 economies, especially the AFC economies, paid more attention to capital flows managements. Capital account restrictions were tightened and some measures, which are today called macroprudential policies, were introduced in some cases. Foreign exchange reserves were piled up, and more financial assets were obtained and used in the case of capital outflows. Capital inflows in bank loans were better managed, and more advanced and stable financial systems were developed. It is likely that these economies were less affected by volatile capital flows during the GFC because of these reforms.

In upcoming years, most economies are likely to experience capital flow reversals. Huge expansionary policies from advanced countries during the pandemic and subsequent tapering would result in another episode of capital flow reversals in the ASEAN+3 economies. The GFC experience does not necessarily guarantee that the ASEAN+3 economies will be safe from volatile capital flows in the future. The international financial market environment and the composition of capital flows are changing rapidly. Capital inflows in portfolio investment have been ever increasing. Empirical results suggest that negative shocks in capital inflows in equities of portfolio capital flows can have significant economic effects. As capital inflows in portfolio investment increase, the reversal in portfolio capital inflows can have huge adverse effects. The ASEAN+3 economies also need to pay more attention to capital flows generated by nonbank financial institutions, which are increasing over time but are difficult to regulate and monitor. Capital inflows through offshore debt issuance is also another example of capital inflows that are difficult to monitor (Kim and Shin 2021). The ASEAN+3 economies need to closely monitor changes in international financial market conditions and new channels of capital flows to avoid the adverse effects of volatile capital flows in upcoming years.

Appendix A. Capital Flows for Hong Kong and Singapore

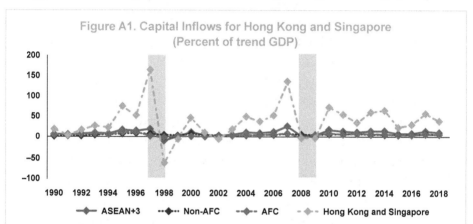

Figure A1. Capital Inflows for Hong Kong and Singapore (Percent of trend GDP)

AFC = Asian financial crisis, ASEAN = Association of Southeast Asian Nations, GDP = gross domestic product, GFC = global financial crisis.
Note: The shaded areas corresponded to the AFC and GFC periods.
Source: International Monetary Fund statistics, World Bank.

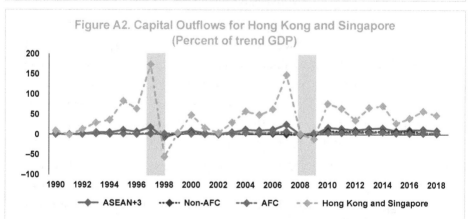

Figure A2. Capital Outflows for Hong Kong and Singapore (Percent of trend GDP)

AFC = Asian financial crisis, ASEAN = Association of Southeast Asian Nations, GDP = gross domestic product, GFC = global financial crisis.
Note: The shaded areas corresponded to the AFC and GFC periods.
Source: International Monetary Fund statistics, World Bank.

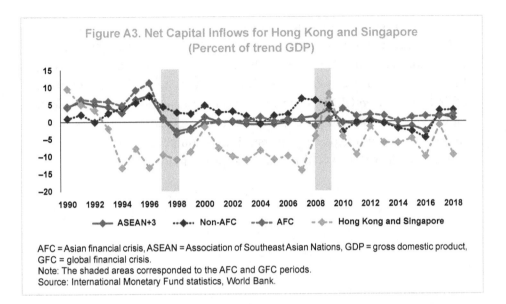

Figure A3. Net Capital Inflows for Hong Kong and Singapore
(Percent of trend GDP)

AFC = Asian financial crisis, ASEAN = Association of Southeast Asian Nations, GDP = gross domestic product,
GFC = global financial crisis.
Note: The shaded areas corresponded to the AFC and GFC periods.
Source: International Monetary Fund statistics, World Bank.

Appendix B. Structural Panel Vector Auto-Regression Models

To estimate the reduced form panel VAR models, the procedure suggested by
Abrigo and Love (2016) is applied. In particular, k-variate homogeneous panel
VAR of lag order p with country-specific fixed effects is estimated as follows:

$$Y_{it} = Y_{it-1}A_1 + Y_{it-2}A_2 + \cdots Y_{it-p}A_p + u_i + e_{it}$$
$$\text{for } i \in \{1,2,\ldots,N\}, t \in \{1,2,\ldots,T_i\}$$

where Y_{it} is a k-dimensional vector of dependent variables of country i at time
t, u_i is a k-dimensional vector of country-specific fixed effects for country
i, and e_{it} is a k-dimensional idiosyncratic error of country i at time t. Note
that $A_1,\ldots,A_p$ are $k \times k$ coefficient matrices to be estimated, and the sample
years, represented by T_i, can be different across economies.

There are two key assumptions under these panel VAR settings. First,
systematic cross-sectional heterogeneity is modelled as u_i, which represents
country-specific fixed effects. These coefficients differ across economies
($i \in \{1,2,\ldots,N\}$), but not for time unit ($t \in \{1,2,\ldots,T_i\}$). Second, the innovations $\{e_{it}\}$ have the following stochastic properties: $E(e_{it}) = 0$, $E(e_{it}'e_{it}) = \Sigma$
and $E(e_{it}'e_{is}) = 0$ for $t > s$ all i. These assumptions imply that the errors are
not serially correlated, especially with its past realizations. That is, weak
exogeneity is assumed.

How the country-specific fixed effects u_i are addressed in panel VAR is as follows. As the country-specific heterogeneity u_i may have some correlations with the innovations e_{it}, u_i in the model should be removed by using the stochastic characteristics of e_{it} described previously. The assumption of first-differenced (FD) transformation can be a solution to this problem. However, as Abrigo and Love (2016) discuss, there can be data loss. Thus, the panel VAR model is transformed into a compact form (i.e., forward orthogonal deviation (FOD) transformation) as follows.

$$Y_{it}^* = \widetilde{Y_{it}^*} A + e_{it}^*$$
$$Y_{it}^* = [y_{it}^{1*} \ y_{it}^{2*} \cdots y_{it}^{k*}]$$
$$\widetilde{Y_{it}^*} = [Y_{it}^* \ Y_{it-1}^* \cdots Y_{it-p}^*]$$
$$e_{it}^* = [e_{it}^{1*} \ e_{it}^{2*} \cdots e_{it}^{k*}]$$
$$A' = [A_1' \ A_2' \cdots A_p']$$

where y_{it}^j, is the jth dependent variable of vector Y_{it}, $y_{it}^{j*} \equiv (y_{it}^j - \overline{y_{it}^{j*}})\sqrt{T_{it}/(T_{it}+1)}$ for all t, i, and j, T_{it} is the number of future observation for panel i from time t, and $\overline{y_{it}^{j*}}$ is the mean of all future observation for panel i from time t.

Next, generalized method of moments (GMM) is used to estimate the panel VAR model. In particular, the GMM estimator is given by

$$A = \left(\widetilde{Y^*}' \ Z \widehat{W} Z' \widetilde{Y^*} \right)^{-1} (\widetilde{Y^*}' \ Z \widehat{W} Z' Y^*)$$

where $Z, N \times L$ (where $L \geq kp$) matrix of instruments, and $\widehat{W}$, an $L \times L$ weighting matrix, which is assumed to be nonsingular, symmetric, and positive semidefinite. The instrument matrix Z is specified as follows. It is known that under the assumption that $E(Z'e) = 0$ and $\mathrm{rank}[E(\widetilde{Y_{it}^*}'Z)] = kp$, the GMM estimator is consistent (Hansen 1982). Thus the first p lags (the lag order of VAR model) of dependent variables are specified as instrument variables, which satisfy the above conditions by the assumptions of e_{it}. For the weight matrix $\widehat{W}$, two step GMM estimation is used.

Appendix C. Unit Root Test and Results

As Blundell and Bond (1998) pointed out, the GMM estimator may suffer from the weak instruments problem when the dependent variables in VAR is a near unit root process. Therefore, the presence of a unit root must be tested in each dependent (or endogenous) variable in the panel VAR models before implementing GMM estimation.

Among a variety of unit root tests, the Im-Pesaran-Shin (IPS) (2003) test seems to be suitable for our analysis. The IPS test allows each panel to have its own ρ_i for $i \in \{1,2,\ldots,N\}$ and eases the assumption of a common ρ, which is a major limitation of the Levin–Lin–Chu (LLC) test and Harris–Tzavalis (HT) test. In addition, the IPS test does not require strongly balanced data, which is the case for our panel data samples. The null hypothesis is that all panels have a unit root.

The IPS test is implemented for various key macro variables of the 14 ASEAN+3 economies during the whole sample period (1990–2018). The list of macro variables are: the log of real GDP (RGDP), the percentage ratio of net capital outflow to trend GDP (CAP), the (negative of the) percentage ratio of capital inflow to trend GDP (CAPI), the (negative of the) percentage ratio of capital outflow to trend GDP (CAPO), and the percentage ratio of current account to the trend GDP (CUR).

The p-values of the IPS test of each variable are as follows: 0.9754 for RGDP (with Z-t-tilde-bar = 1.9665), 0.0000 for CAP (with Z-t-tilde-bar = −4.4770), 0.0000 for CAPI (with Z-t-tilde-bar = −6.1514), 0.0000 for CAPO (with Z-t-tilde-bar = −6.8844), and 0.0067 for CUR (with Z-t-tilde-bar = −2.4705). Therefore, the null hypothesis of the unit root can be rejected at a 95% significance level for CAP, CAPI, CAPO, and CUR. Meanwhile, RGDP is first-differenced and tested again: The p-value of IPS test for first-differenced RGDP is 0.0000 (with Z-t-tilde-bar = −8.1905), which rejects the null hypothesis at a 95% significance level.

Therefore, in subsequent analysis, RGDP is used as first differenced whereas CAP, CAPI, CAPO, and CUR are used as levels. The pvar package in STATA developed by Abrigo and Love (2016) is used to estimate the panel VAR model.

Appendix D. Data and Sources

Variable Name	Source	Notes
Trend GDP	World Bank	Uses an HP (Hodrick–Prescott) filter to nominal GDP (current USD) with λ = 100
Capital Inflows/ Outflows/Net Inflows	IMF Financial Statistics: Balance of Payments	Sums each components of financial account (excludes reserves and related items) in terms of asset (outflows) and liabilities (inflows)
Components of Capital Inflows/Outflows	IMF Financial Statistics: Balance of Payments	
Regional Portion of Portfolio Investment Assets of the ASEAN+3	IMF Coordinated Portfolio Investment Survey (CPIS)	Total Portfolio Investment by Economy of Nonresident Issuer, End-of-Period
Chinn-Ito Index	Chinn and Ito (2006)	The index is normalized between 0 and 1.
Real GDP Growth Rate		
Real Consumption Growth Rate	CEIC database, ADB database, Central banks, Asia Regional Integration Center	
Real Investment Growth Rate		
Real Government Spending Growth Rate		
Current Account	IMF Financial Statistics: Balance of Payments	Excludes reserves and related items
Real Exchange Rate	BIS Statistics warehouse	
Nominal Exchange Rate		
Foreign Exchange Reserve Growth Rate	IMF, ADB database, Asia Regional Integration Center	Excludes gold
Call Rate	International Financial Statistics (IFS)	Uses money market rate for call rates except for Myanmar, China, Lao PDR, Vietnam, Brunei, and Cambodia where the data are not available. For these economies, policy rate data are used instead.

ADB = Asian Development Bank, ASEAN = Association of Southeast Asian Nations, BIS = Bank for International Settlements, CEIC = Census and Economic Information Center, GDP = gross domestic product, IMF = International Monetary Fund, Lao PDR = Lao People's Democratic Republic.

References

Abrigo, M. R., and I. Love. 2016. "Estimation of Panel Vector Autoregression in Stata." *The Stata Journal* 16 (3): 778–804.

Blundell, Richard, and Stephen Bond. 1998. "Initial Conditions and Moments Restrictions in Dynamic Panel Data Models." *Journal of Econometrics* 87 (1), 115–143.

Chinn, Menzie D., and Hiro Ito. 2006. "What Matters for Financial Development? Capital Controls, Institutions, and Interactions." *Journal of Development Economics* 81 (1): 163–192.

Hansen, Lars Peter. 1982. "Large Sample Properties of Generalized Method of Moments Estimators." *Econometrica* 50 (4): 1029–1054.

Harris, Richard D. F., and Elias Tzavalis. 1999. "Inference for Unit Roots in Dynamic Panels Where the Time Dimension is Fixed." *Journal of Econometrics* 91 (2): 201–226.

Im, Kyung So, M. Hasem Pesaran, and Yongcheol Shin. 2003. "Testing for Unit Roots in Heterogeneous Panels." *Journal of Econometrics* 115 (1): 53–74.

Kim, Hyungji, and Soyoung Kim. 2021. "International Capital Flows Shocks and Economic Crisis in East Asian Countries." Working Paper, Seoul National University.

Kim, Soyoung, and Sunghyun H. Kim. 2013. "International Capital Flows, Boom-Bust Cycles, and Business Cycle Synchronization in the Asia Pacific Region." *Contemporary Economic Policy* 31 (1): 191–211.

Kim, Soyoung, Sunghyun H. Kim, and Yunjong Wang. 2004. "Macroeconomic Effects of Capital Account Liberalization: The Case of Korea." *Review of Development Economics* 8 (4): 634–639.

Kim, Soyoung, and Hyun Song Shin. 2021. "Offshore EME Bond Issuance and the Transmission Channels of Global Liquidity." *Journal of International Money and Finance* 112: 102336.

Kim, Soyoung, and Doo Yong Yang. 2011. "The Impact of Capital Inflows on Emerging Asian Economies: Is Too Much Money Chasing Too Little Good?" *Open Economies Review* 22 (2): 293–315.

Levin, Andrew, Chien-Fu Lin, and Chia-Shang James Chu. 2002. "Unit Root Tests in Panel Data: Asymptotic and Finite-Sample Properties." *Journal of Econometrics* 108 (1): 1–24.

Sims, Christopher. 1980. "Macroeconomics and Reality." *Econometrica* 48 (1): 1–48.

Chapter 25

IMF Surveillance and Crisis Lending in Emerging Asia
A Crucible that Inspired an Intellectual Revolution, 1995–2010

Shinji Takagi[1]

Introduction

This chapter revisits, with hindsight of more than 20 years, the role played by the International Monetary Fund (IMF) in Thailand, Indonesia, and Korea during the Asian financial crisis (AFC) of 1997–1998. The crisis, and the IMF's role in it, had a profound impact on the subsequent debate on the nature of economic crises and the design of an international financial architecture to prevent, manage, and resolve them. The crisis was notable in several respects. First, it occurred in the world's then most dynamic region, and above all among "Asian miracle" economies whose annual growth had averaged more than 8% during the preceding years (Figure 25.1). Second, contrary to early expectations that, with IMF intervention, these economies would recover quickly after a small deceleration in growth, they all experienced a sharp fall in output (and none ever recovered to the growth rate of the pre-crisis years). Third, granted that governments are primarily responsible for preventing a crisis in their own countries, the IMF, with vast resources devoted to global economic analysis and monitoring, failed to foresee the magnitude of the impending crisis and the virulence with which it spread from one country to another. The IMF's reputation was badly damaged within Asia and across the world.

The crisis erupted as a precipitous fall in their currencies when the countries, experiencing a sudden loss of investor confidence, saw a sharp reversal

[1] This chapter was prepared for a joint research project on regional financial cooperation, hosted by the ASEAN+3 Macroeconomic Research Office (AMRO) and the Asian Development Bank (ADB), in commemoration of the 22nd anniversary of ASEAN+3 financial cooperation. The views expressed herein are the author's own and do not represent those of AMRO, ADB, or any other institution with which he may have been affiliated in the past. The author thanks Masahiro Kawai and Diwa C. Guinigundo for useful comments on an earlier draft.

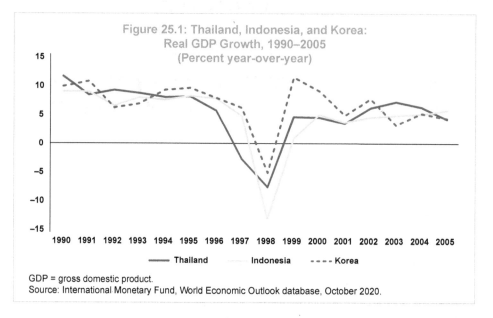

Figure 25.1: Thailand, Indonesia, and Korea:
Real GDP Growth, 1990–2005
(Percent year-over-year)

GDP = gross domestic product.
Source: International Monetary Fund, World Economic Outlook database, October 2020.

of the brisk capital inflows they had previously received. The currency depreciation, coupled with monetary tightening to stabilize the exchange rate, placed a serious strain on their banks and corporations heavily exposed to foreign currency borrowing, a flipside of the large capital inflows of the preceding years, in the process bringing to the surface the fragilities of their economic systems that had been hidden behind the facade of rapid growth, including in the financial sector, corporate governance, and government regulations. They successively approached the IMF for financial assistance. Thailand and Korea did so in July and November, respectively, when their foreign exchange reserves were nearly depleted and their currencies had already depreciated. Indonesia's request for IMF assistance was preemptive. Coming before the eruption of a full-blown crisis, its intention was to use IMF assistance to solidify its initial policy response, which included monetary tightening and a floating of its currency. From August 1997 through the end of 2003, the IMF provided these countries with financial assistance totaling SDR 28 billion (Table 25.1).[2]

---

[2] The chapter does not address the Philippines, which also received financial assistance from the IMF during the AFC. The case of the Philippines was quite different from the other three cases. The country was already in a financing arrangement with the IMF when it was hit by contagion from Thailand. The extended arrangement under the Extended Fund Facility, approved in June 1994, expired at the end of March 1998, and was succeeded by a stand-by arrangement (SBA) in April. The country's situation was such that the SBA was initially treated as precautionary (that is, the Philippine authorities had no intention to draw from the facility). See Manalac (2021).

Table 25.1: Thailand, Indonesia, and Korea: IMF Program Lending, 1997–2003

Program Details	Thailand, 1997–2000	Indonesia, 1997–2003			Korea, 1997–2000
Type of Arrangement	34-month SBA	3-year SBA	26-month EFF	35-month EFF (ext. to 45-month)	3-year SBA
Date of Approval	Aug 20, 1997	Nov 5, 1997	Aug 25, 1998	Feb 4, 2000	Dec 4, 1997
Date of Expiration	Jun 19, 2000 (completed)	Aug 25, 1998 (replaced)	Feb 4, 2000 (replaced)	Dec 31, 2003 (completed)	Dec 3, 2000 (completed)
Amount Approved	SDR 2.9 billion	SDR 7.3 billion	SDR 4.7 billion (aug. to SDR 5.4 billion)	SDR 3.6 billion	SDR 15.5 billion[1]
Amount Drawn (Percent)	SDR 2.5 billion (86%)	SDR 3.7 billion	SDR 3.8 billion	SDR 3.6 billion	SDR 14.4 billion (93%)
		SDR 11.1 billion (100%)[2]			
Year of Full Repayment	2003	2006			2001

EFF = extended fund facility, IMF = International Monetary Fund, SBA = stand-by arrangement, SDR = special drawing rights.
Notes:
[1] Of this amount, SDR 9.95 billion was provided under the supplemental reserve facility (SRF), which carries a higher charge with a shorter maturity.
[2] The total amount drawn is less than the gross amount approved because the first two arrangements had undrawn balances when replaced.
Source: Various International Monetary Fund documents (available at www.imf.org).

The IMF's crisis lending is usually offered within the context of an agreed economic adjustment program supported by a stand-by arrangement (SBA), the Fund's "workhorse" crisis lending vehicle.[3] IMF financing is therefore conditional. A country requesting IMF financial assistance must formulate a package of economic policy measures, which in the IMF's judgment is sufficient to ensure the "revolving" nature of IMF resources. In the case of Indonesia, once the immediate, acute phase of crisis management subsided, the focus of IMF conditionality unambiguously shifted to medium- and longer-term structural issues. This explains why the Fund's involvement in Indonesia, lasting 6 years, was more prolonged than the other cases. The SBA was canceled in 1998 and replaced by an extended arrangement under the Extended Fund Facility (EFF), the IMF's longer-term lending facility with more favorable repayment terms. This was replaced again when a democratically elected Parliament was installed following a political transition.[4]

[3] http://www.imf.org/external/np/exr/facts/sba.htm.
[4] Given the topic of this chapter, we are mainly interested in the 1997 SBA. The structural component of the IMF's 6-year engagement in Indonesia did not materially change over time.

A controversial aspect of the IMF's engagement in Asia was its initial failure to contain the free fall of the currencies (Figure 25.2). Despite the expectations that the Fund, with its massive firepower, would stem the tide of capital flight and calm the market, they continued to fall even after the countries received their first disbursements. The fall was particularly pronounced for the Indonesian rupiah, which depreciated from IDR 3,600 per United States (US) dollar before the IMF agreement in November 1997 to IDR 10,375 in January 1998 and, in the midst of a political crisis, to IDR 14,900 in June 1998. Then, in 1998, all three countries under the tutelage of IMF programs suffered a sharp contraction in output, with GDP falling by 8% for Thailand, 13% for Indonesia, and 5% for Korea in 1998. These outcomes, coupled with the IMF's policy prescription of macroeconomic austerity and extensive structural conditionality perceived overly intrusive to national sovereignty, created a considerable backlash against the IMF in Asia. The stigma of going to the IMF prompted countries across the region to accumulate foreign exchange reserves in the years following the AFC to preempt any future need for IMF assistance.

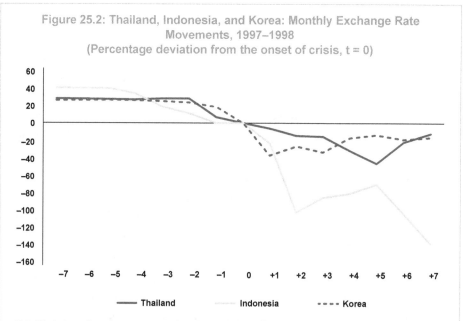

Figure 25.2: Thailand, Indonesia, and Korea: Monthly Exchange Rate Movements, 1997–1998
(Percentage deviation from the onset of crisis, t = 0)

Note: End-of-month exchange rates against the United States dollar expressed as a percentage deviation from the onset of crisis (*t* = 0 defined as July 1997 for Thailand and November 1997 for Indonesia and Korea).
Source: Author's calculation based on International Monetary Fund, *International Financial Statistics*, monthly issues.

For good or ill, the AFC was a watershed event in the history of international monetary cooperation. Volumes have been written on questions such as why IMF surveillance failed to sound alarm bells with sufficient clarity ahead of time, why initial IMF intervention failed to stabilize the situation, and whether the IMF's overall approach to crisis management was appropriate. The crisis led to profound changes in the way we think about economic crises and to numerous policy and institutional adjustments and adaptations over the subsequent decades within the IMF. With the passage of more than 20 years, any adversarial sentiment against the IMF is no longer intense, allowing us to revisit the IMF's controversial role in a more nuanced way, from the perspective of what has since transpired in our intellectual thinking and institutional innovations. A caricature of the IMF as an institution clueless about building vulnerabilities, and uncreative in applying a cookie-cutter approach of austerity to managing a new type of crisis rooted in the capital account, is unhelpful.

This chapter takes the view that the AFC represented a new type of crisis which, unlike the old type, was driven by capital (as opposed to trade) flows. In such a crisis, market expectations matter a great deal, and crisis resolution requires restoring investor confidence. To be sure, the AFC was not the first of its kind. Three years prior, Mexico had experienced a crisis which Michel Camdessus, the IMF's former Managing Director, famously called "the first financial crisis of the twenty-first century."[5] And even earlier in 1992 and 1993, the currencies participating in the exchange rate mechanism of the European Monetary System (EMS) had been attacked by speculative capital flows. Untested by the Mexican crisis (where the United States immediately provided USD 20 billion from its Exchange Stabilization Fund to calm the market) or the EMS crises (where the countries involved could borrow internationally in their own currencies), the effectiveness of the IMF's conventional crisis management tool was tested for the first time in Asia against this new type of crisis.

The AFC did not prove to be the last of this kind. It was soon followed by similar crises in Russia, Brazil, Turkey, and Argentina, among other places, before the whole world was engulfed in 2008 by a crisis that originated from the financial markets of the largest advanced economies. The soul searching prompted by the AFC has indeed been an ongoing process. We begin our

---

[5] As quoted in Fischer (2001)'s Robbins Lectures at the London School of Economics.

review with the IMF's pre-crisis surveillance informed by the aftermath of the Mexican crisis in 1985 and take it through the aftermath of the global financial crisis (GFC) in about 2010, covering the major policy and institutional changes of the post-AFC period while also reflecting on more recent developments where relevant.

IMF Pre-Crisis Surveillance, 1995–1997

Policy Developments

Surveillance is an activity of the IMF to "oversee the international monetary system" and to "monitor the economic and financial policies" of member countries through analysis, dialogue, and communication.[6] The IMF conducts its surveillance through two principal vehicles: (i) multilateral surveillance of global developments mainly through its periodic flagship publications and (ii) bilateral surveillance mainly through Article IV consultations held in principle annually with all member countries individually. Multilateral and bilateral surveillances are expected to be integrated as the global economy consists of individual parts and it is the interlinkages between them that have an important bearing on the whole. Surveillance's effectiveness is determined by the accuracy of analysis as well as the extent to which member countries incorporate the advice into actual policymaking for their own good and the good of the international community. Governments are typically subject to competing voices. IMF surveillance, as one of many such voices, generally does not have a lot of influence on policy outcomes in member countries except when access to IMF resources is at stake.

The prevailing sentiment about IMF surveillance in the immediate aftermath of the Mexican crisis focused on the need to strengthen the analysis of financial conditions. This is well illustrated by what is stated in the communiqué issued by the heads of government or state of the Group of Seven (G7) advanced industrial countries in June 1995 at Halifax, Nova Scotia. The G7 summit, noting how the Mexican crisis had "sharpened our understanding" of the "risks inherent in the growth of private capital flows [and] the increased integration of domestic capital markets," called upon

---

[6] https://www.imf.org/en/About/Factsheets/IMF-Surveillance.

the IMF to develop "an improved early warning system, so that we can act more quickly to prevent or handle financial shocks," through "improved and effective surveillance of national economic policies and financial market developments, and fuller disclosure of this information to market participants." The communiqué observed that this could best be achieved by establishing "benchmarks for the timely publication of key economic and financial data."

The Special Data Dissemination Standard (SDDS), launched in June 1996, was a response to this call. The SDDS is meant to serve as a standard of data disclosure which countries seeking access to international capital markets are expected to follow. Though subscription to the SDDS is voluntary, once subscripted, adherence to the prescribed standards of data quality, coverage, periodicity, timeliness, and public accessibility becomes mandatory. The idea is twofold: (i) if bad information is routinely released to the public, there will not be a surprise that triggers a panic and (ii) public dissemination of data will discipline national governments to pursue prudent policies. This data disclosure initiative, however, came too late to matter for Asia. While all three crisis countries subscribed to the SDDS during the course of 1996, they did not meet the SDDS benchmarks before the eruption of crisis in 1997.[7] At a minimum, had Thailand and Korea been compliant with the SDDS in 1997, IMF intervention, if any, might have taken place well before their official reserves were nearly depleted.[8]

The 1995 G7 communiqué highlighted the surveillance of "financial market developments." A report on the background to the Mexican crisis commissioned in early 1995 attributed part of the IMF's failure to detect the emerging crisis to the IMF's near exclusive focus on macroeconomic developments and its insufficient appreciation of financial market developments.[9] Following the IMF Executive Board's 1995 Biennial Surveillance

---

[7] They met the benchmarks during the course of program engagement: 1999 for Korea and 2000 for Indonesia and Thailand.

[8] The true picture of their foreign exchange reserve positions was not transparent because both Thailand and Korea had been making off balance-sheet transactions in foreign exchange through the forward market (in Thailand) or by advancing foreign exchange to commercial banks experiencing a loss of market access (in Korea). The market would have caught these transactions earlier if the countries had been SDDS-compliant.

[9] The findings of the internal report, prepared by Alan Whittome, are summarized in the IMF's 1995 Annual Report (IMF 1995).

Review (BSR) and the Interim Committee's April 1995 meeting,[10] the IMF took measures, among other things, to "give more attention to members' financial policies and the soundness of their financial sectors" (IMF 1995). Two years later, the Board, in the context of the 1997 BSR, called for increased attention to financial and banking system issues. This led to the issuance of a staff operational guidance note in July 1997, which stipulated that staff reports for Article IV consultations "should include assessments of financial market developments and prospects as well as of problems and policy issues in the banking and financial sector" (IMF 1997). These initiatives, of course, came too late for Asia's crisis countries.

Surveillance of Thailand, Indonesia, and Korea

The immediate pre-crisis years in the three crisis countries were characterized by large current account deficits even while their fiscal policy remained in small surplus (Figure 25.3). The large current account deficits were a counterpart of large net private capital inflows, which had roughly commenced in 1988 for Thailand, 1990 for Indonesia, and 1990–1991 for Korea. The magnitude of capital inflows experienced by Thailand was particularly massive, amounting cumulatively to an estimated 51.5% of average annual GDP from 1988 to 1995. Though considerably smaller, the capital inflows experienced by Indonesia and Korea were also significant at around 10% of GDP cumulatively over the same period (Takagi and Esaka 2001).

The countries experienced a surge in capital inflows in an environment where they progressively removed impediments to cross-border financial transactions while fostering the development and liberalization of their domestic financial markets (Azis 2021; Hahm and Kim 2021; IEO 2005; Sussangkarn 2021; Takagi 2004). Thailand had already attained a relatively open capital account by the late 1980s with respect to inflows. From then on, especially in the early 1990s, it actively took measures to promote capital inflows through the creation of special mutual funds, an amendment of the Investment Promotion Act, various tax incentives, and the 1993 establishment of a Bangkok International Banking Facility in an attempt to make Bangkok a major regional financial center rivaling Hong Kong and Singapore. Indonesia, having removed most controls on capital outflows

---

[10]The Interim Committee was transformed into the International Monetary and Financial Committee in 1999.

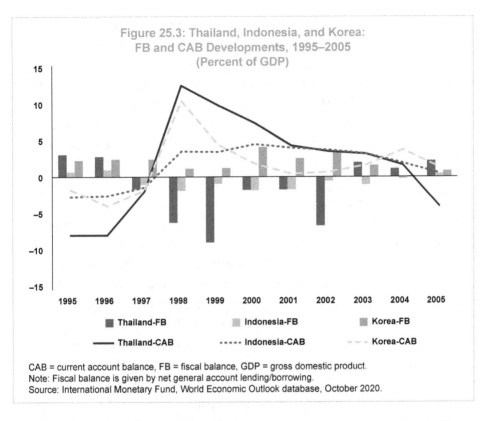

Figure 25.3: Thailand, Indonesia, and Korea:
FB and CAB Developments, 1995–2005
(Percent of GDP)

CAB = current account balance, FB = fiscal balance, GDP = gross domestic product.
Note: Fiscal balance is given by net general account lending/borrowing.
Source: International Monetary Fund, World Economic Outlook database, October 2020.

by the late 1980s, liberalized inflows related to foreign direct investment from the late 1980s. Korea took a gradualist approach to capital account liberalization in the context of its 1996 accession to the Organization for Economic Co-operation and Development (OECD), beginning with capital outflows, followed by foreign investment in the domestic stock market and short-term trade-related borrowing.[11]

This was a period during which the IMF sought to amend its Articles of Agreement in order to give itself an additional mandate to promote the liberalization of capital flows and jurisdiction over restrictions in the capital account. Clear support emerged in the context of the Madrid Declaration of the Interim Committee in 1994, and the issue assumed a priority in the IMF's work program from 1996. With the backing of the vast majority of industrial countries, the Interim Committee's support for the amendment reached its height in September 1997, following the onset of the AFC, at its

---

[11] At the time of the 1997 crisis, Korea retained a number of reservations to the OECD Code of Liberalization of Capital Movements, particularly regarding the liberalization of long-term capital inflows.

annual meeting in Hong Kong when it issued a communiqué instructing the Executive Board to prepare and submit a draft amendment. Had there not been a crisis in Asia at the time, capital account liberalization would have likely become an obligation of IMF membership, with any capital controls subject to IMF oversight and approval. With the severity of the AFC, the risks of capital account liberalization began to weigh on the minds of policymakers who had previously given disproportionate weight to its benefits (IEO 2005).

This is not to suggest that the IMF, through its surveillance, pressured individual countries to pursue capital account liberalization against their better judgements. The IMF Independent Evaluation Office (IEO) report in 2005 concluded, based on a sample of some 27 countries for 1990–2002, that there was no evidence of IMF staff pressuring national authorities to remove impediments to capital flows before the AFC; on the contrary, they often alerted the authorities to the risks of premature liberalization when proper institutions were not in place. The point is that the authorities in Thailand, Indonesia, and Korea liberalized their capital account to pursue their own national objectives in a manner suitable to their individual circumstances (Azis 2021; Hahm and Kim 2021; Sussangkarn 2021). At the same time, there was clearly a global rhetoric extolling the virtues of an open capital account throughout the pre-crisis period of the 1990s. The possibility cannot be ruled out that this intellectual climate limited the menu of available policy options for the crisis countries in 1997 when they faced a free fall of their currencies.

Stanley Fischer, writing in mid-1998 as the IMF's first Deputy Managing Director, stated that the IMF "had warned Thailand of potential problems, but the government took no action," and that it had also warned the governments of the prospective crisis countries "about financial sector weaknesses" (Fischer 1998b). There is little doubt that the IMF was aware of the potential risks of large net capital inflows as reflected in a large current account deficit. By the early 1990s, there was large academic literature on what came to be known as the "capital inflow problem." Famously in 1991, Chile introduced a celebrated unremunerated reserve requirement to stem the tide of short-term inflows, which was followed by Colombia in 1993. The causes of such inflows and what to do with them were being hotly and widely debated in the early 1990s (Isard 1995; Calvo et al. 1996). It is hardly surprising that the IMF too noticed the implications of large net capital inflows on their sustainability and their potentially adverse impact on the quality of bank loans, especially in the real estate sector.

A more relevant question for us to ask is whether IMF surveillance provided added value beyond the platitude of unsustainable capital inflows overheating the economy and adversely affecting the balance sheets of banks. The types of problems that became critical as the crisis unfolded — the maturity composition of foreign debt, balance sheet exposure to foreign currency borrowing, weak enforcement of financial regulations, central bank foreign exchange on-lending to private banks, central bank forward sales of dollars, and the like (Azis 2021; Hahm and Kim 2021) — could have only been quantified with better access to what was then proprietary information. This is not to belittle the IMF. It was aware, at least confidentially, of banking sector issues,[12] weak corporate governance, Indonesia's pervasive corruption and cronyism, and Korea's heavily leveraged conglomerates (*chaebol*) that dominated the economy. Whatever the understanding of these weaknesses and vulnerabilities may have been, IMF surveillance clearly underestimated their adverse impact on investor confidence.

The IMF's headline messages remained cautiously optimistic about the economies' macroeconomic performance. At a meeting of the Indonesia Consultative Group in Tokyo in July 1997, the IMF representative, while recognizing the "need to guard against changes in market sentiment, weaknesses in the banking system, relatively high external debt and increased financial market turbulence in the region," stated that "financial market confidence in Indonesia [remained] strong." Likewise, the Article IV Mission that visited Seoul in October 1997 concluded that Korea would avoid being seriously affected by the crisis then spreading through Southeast Asia, provided that the authorities moved promptly to address the problems in the financial sector and demonstrated a firm commitment to reform.[13] To

---

[12] Drawing on earlier technical assistance work, the background paper for the 1997 Article IV consultation correctly observed that the main problems of the Indonesian banking sector were reflected in a high share of nonperforming loans, incomplete compliance with prudential requirements by some banks, concentrated bank ownership and connected lending, continued operation of problem banks, and large exposure of banks to property loans.

[13] This Mission included a financial sector expert who examined the vulnerabilities in the financial sector to a degree that was unusual at that time. The staff report was prepared by the Mission but never presented to the Executive Board as it was overtaken by events. The Mission's confidential assessment communicated to the headquarters that Korea was "relatively well equipped" to handle further external pressures was clearly informed by its lack of access to data on the official reserve position. At this time, "usable" reserves (reserves net of advances to commercial banks) were being rapidly depleted. See IEO (2003).

rectify the lack of full access to data, surveillance could have explored more proactively what was happening on the ground by utilizing what little was publicly available by way of market indicators,[14] or by engaging with market participants and other experts outside the official sector.[15] This was not done.

IMF Adjustment Programs, 1997–2000

The Nature of the IMF Crisis Programs

IMF crisis management programs seek to strike a balance between financing and adjustment. A total bailout would mean that a country experiencing a large net outflow of capital has no need to make macroeconomic adjustment as the capital outflow is fully financed by official inflows. There would be no need for current account adjustment or exchange rate depreciation, and any adverse impact on the real economy would be mitigated. This, however, is not the benchmark of success for an IMF adjustment program. If there was a fundamental macroeconomic imbalance to begin with, some correction of that imbalance must take place. Except in the case of a pure liquidity crisis, zero adjustment is not the objective of a crisis management program. Ex-post macroeconomic adjustment reflects both the *outcome* and the *policy design* of IMF intervention. The objective of crisis intervention is to facilitate a smoother adjustment of the underlying imbalances by providing official financing.

Take the example of a large fiscal balance (FB). Any fiscal adjustment (through a combination of an expenditure cut and a tax hike) would necessarily exert a contractionary impact on output. Thus, a fall in GDP cannot be equated with a failure of the IMF program. A more sensible assessment of the contribution of the IMF program would be possible if the counterfactual were known, namely, how much the output would have fallen in the absence of the IMF intervention. Even then, there is no way of determining whether the IMF program should have let the output fall more or less. Likewise, some

---

[14]Such publicly available market indicators included the yield spread of state-guaranteed obligations denominated in dollars over US treasuries and the expected won depreciation implied by prices in the offshore nondeliverable forward market (IEO 2003).

[15]In Korea, with international banks increasingly concerned, Korean banks started experiencing difficulty rolling over their short-term loans from early 1997.

downward adjustment of the nominal exchange rate would be necessary if the real exchange rate was substantially overvalued to begin with. But too rapid a depreciation of the nominal exchange rate could exert a severe contractionary impact on real output if the country's external liabilities were denominated in foreign currencies. A case can be made that a free, uncontrolled fall in output or the exchange rate is a failure of IMF intervention, but how much fall in either should be tolerated would be a judgment call.

Qualitatively, all three countries shared a remarkably similar adjustment program, consisting of (i) "exceptional" IMF financing,[16] supplemented by additional official financing; (ii) initially tight monetary and fiscal policies, eased over time; (iii) financial sector restructuring, arguably the most prominent element of IMF engagement; and (iv) other structural reforms of various intensity. Given the logic presented above, the magnitude of required fiscal adjustment is not independent of the size of financing, which in turn depends on the size of the capital flow reversal that is expected to take place over the course of the program. Because investor confidence is critical in determining the size of the capital flow reversal, ultimately not all financing may be used if the programmed path to adjustment is credible enough to convince foreign investors to stay put in the country. There are several moving parts to a program, and they are mutually dependent and cannot be assessed in isolation.

Financial Support

Mitigating the full brunt of a capital account crisis (caused by a sharp reversal of cross-border capital flows) requires some official international financial support. Loss of investor confidence means that the country under crisis can no longer access international capital markets. If capital were allowed to flow out of the crisis economy freely, the requirement of external adjustment would cause a sharp contraction of output in order to compress imports and thereby generate a narrowing of the current account deficit. The IMF's crisis lending plays a critical role in this effort to limit the outflows and provide room for a smoother adjustment of output and external adjustment. Yet, IMF financial support cannot be without bounds. It is only meant to be catalytic. With a credible adjustment program, it attempts to convince foreign investors

---

[16]In IMF parlance, exceptional financing generally means financing in excess of 100% of the quota in a year or 300% of the quota cumulatively. Exceptional finance policy was only formalized in the early 2000s.

to stay put in the country, if not to bring in additional flows. Without a credible program, no amount of IMF financing would be sufficient.

The IMF provided "exceptional" financing to Thailand, Indonesia, and Korea during the AFC while catalyzing additional official financing, including from the World Bank, the ADB, and some bilateral sources (Table 25.2).[17] Financing was highly front-loaded for an IMF facility. In Thailand, for example, 72% of the amount actually drawn (or 62% of the amount approved) was disbursed during the calendar year 1997 even though the program started in August (Figure 25.4). What made these large front-loaded disbursements possible was the Emergency Financing Mechanism (EFM), an innovation developed in response to the G7's 1995 Halifax summit, which enabled not only an expedited approval of IMF lending by the Executive Board (within days, not customary weeks, of the submission of a proposed program)[18] but also a larger than normal access and a more front-loaded disbursement.

Korea's financing package appears disproportionately large in relation to quota, but this is deceptive. The quota was unreasonably small relative to the size of the economy because it had not kept up fast enough with Korea's rapid rise from a low-income to a high-income country. In order to access much larger IMF resources, it availed itself of another innovation under

Table 25.2: Thailand, Indonesia, and Korea: IMF and Other Official Financing, 1997 (USD billion, unless otherwise noted)

	IMF Financing	In Percent of:[1]				Total, Including Other Official (in Percent of GDP)
		IMF Quota	GDP	Imports	Current Account Deficit	
Thailand	4	505	2.2	6.3	27.2	17.2 (9.5)
Indonesia	10	490	4.5	22.6	130.5	28.0 (12.6)[2]
Korea	21	1,939	4.0	14.5	90.5	35.0 (6.7)[3]

GDP = gross domestic product, IMF = International Monetary Fund, USD = United States dollar.
Notes:
[1] GDP, imports, and current account balance are for 1997.
[2] Excluding USD 17 billion designated as the "second line of defense" and USD 5 billion drawn from its own foreign exchange reserves.
[3] Excluding USD 20 billion designated as the "second line of defense."
Source: Author's estimates based on the International Monetary Fund's initial program documents.

---

[17]Unless noted otherwise, IMF "program documents" in this and other tables refer to the relevant letters of intent, press releases and, where available, staff reports that are published following the Executive Board's approval of IMF-supported programs.

[18]Korea's program, when it was submitted to the Board, was not fully specified. A full program was developed only in January 1998.

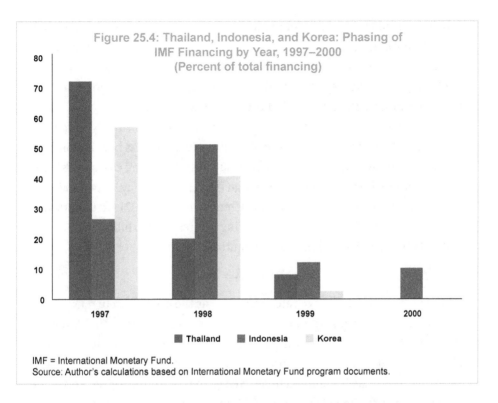

Figure 25.4: Thailand, Indonesia, and Korea: Phasing of IMF Financing by Year, 1997–2000 (Percent of total financing)

IMF = International Monetary Fund.
Source: Author's calculations based on International Monetary Fund program documents.

consideration at the time the program was approved on December 4. The Supplemental Reserve Facility (SRF), approved on December 17, allowed Korea to receive immediate large-scale financing on near market terms with a shorter repayment period without regard to quota, based solely on the IMF's judgment of its needs and ability to repay. Relative to other metrics (such as GDP and imports), the scale of financing provided to Korea was smaller than Indonesia, though larger than Thailand. Despite these innovations, however, IMF and other official financing proved insufficient in all three cases, given the parameters of the programs (see the following subsection).

Macroeconomic Assumptions and Conditionality

Monetary and fiscal policies were both programmed to be tight initially. Tight monetary policy was the choice of the authorities in all three counties. The countries approached the IMF after having raised interest rates when faced with depreciation pressure on their currencies. All three programs kept the tight monetary stance and called for a further hike in interest rates in an attempt to halt the downward spiral of currency depreciation, a decision soon criticized by several prominent economist as misguided (Furman and Stiglitz 1998). In Indonesia, however, the central bank, faced with a systemic banking crisis from late November, began to provide liquidity support to banks experiencing deposit withdrawals, undermining the tight stance of monetary policy, and a free fall of the rupiah continued.

The debate on high interest rate policy remains and is likely to remain unsettled. The interest rate defense of a falling currency has been a standard practice in many contexts and has been successful in some cases. In Korea, there is some evidence to suggest that high interest rate policy helped stabilize the exchange rate (Cho and West 2000; Chung and Kim 2002). To understand the issues involved, think of the following interest rate arbitrage condition across two countries with no capital controls:

$$s_t = s^e_{t+1} - r_t + rp_t \qquad (1)$$

where s is the spot exchange rate (expressed as the domestic currency price of foreign currency), s^e the expected future exchange rate, r the domestic interest rate (plus 1), and rp the risk premium on the domestic currency, all expressed in natural logarithms; t and $t + 1$ are time subscripts; and the foreign interest rate is assumed to be fixed (hence, with appropriate normalization, its natural logarithm is zero). Equation (1) is an open interest rate parity condition adjusted for a risk premium.

Equation (1) shows that, in order for the spot exchange rate to remain stable, capital flight (indicated by a rise in rp_t) requires an offsetting rise in the domestic interest rate, given the expected future spot rate. If the expected future spot rate increases too, the domestic interest rate must be raised that much higher. But these relationships assume that the risk premium (which may be thought of as a propensity to take capital out of the country) is independent of the level of the domestic interest rate, that is, $(\partial rp/\partial r) = 0$. If the risk premium is endogenous to the domestic interest rate, a high interest rate policy could (e.g., by further damaging the banking sector or reducing aggregate demand) instead precipitate additional capital flight and additional depreciation. The success or failure of an interest rate defense likely depends on a complex set of these and other factors.[19]

---

[19] Gregori (2009) modeled the problem as a war of attrition between speculators and monetary authorities, highlighting the roles played by the level of the interest rate, the associated private costs to both parties, and the rate of expected depreciation by the speculators when the defense fails.

Another controversial aspect of macroeconomic conditionality was its fiscal component. Furman and Stiglitz (1998) and Ito (2007), among others, have argued that a tight fiscal policy as initially programmed (in the sense of programming a small surplus) was unwarranted not only in view of a prospective deceleration of growth, which did in fact materialize, but also given the fact that FBs were initially in surplus and that fiscal prodigality was not a cause of the crisis. A policy that proves to be an error ex-post may not be an error ex-ante. To call initially tight fiscal policy an error is unhelpful without providing an explanation of why such a policy was advocated in the first place.

To understand the rationale for initially tight fiscal policy in the IMF's adjustment programs in Asia, think of the following accounting identity:

$$CAB = (SP - IP) + (T - G) \tag{2}$$

where CAB is the current account balance (that is, net exports plus net foreign income from abroad), SP private national saving, IP private investment, T tax revenue, and G government expenditure. Equation (2) states the CAB must be equal to the sum of net private saving and the FB. The evolution and resolution of a capital account crisis involves a rise in CAB as a counterpart of a fall in net capital inflows, in an environment where exports cannot expand quickly to offset the capital outflows. This means either a smaller current account deficit or a reversal of the capital account balance from deficit to surplus (i.e., $\Delta CAB > 0$). The IMF explained that a small fiscal surplus ($T-G > 0$) was needed to ease the burden of external adjustment on the private sector. What proved to be an error is not tight fiscal policy per se, but rather the highly benign underlying assumptions about capital flow reversals and real economic growth (Table 25.3).

The IMF's most egregious misjudgment was to grossly underestimate the capital flow reversals during the course of the crisis (Table 25.3, upper panel). For example, they projected the CABs to remain in moderate deficit in 1998, that is, a modest adjustment (in percentage points of GDP) of 2.9 for Thailand, 2.2 for Indonesia, and 1.8 for Korea from 1997 to 1998. In reality, the adjustment (in actual realized values) amounted to more than 14, about 5, and more than 12, respectively, with all countries experiencing a swing from deficit to surplus (Figure 25.2). Three factors were responsible for this misjudgment. First, they did not fully understand the nature of a capital account crisis as a massive reversal of capital flows. Second, they overestimated the expansionary effect of currency depreciation on exports (Boorman et al. 2000). Third, they

Table 25.3: Thailand, Indonesia, and Korea: Macroeconomic Assumptions Under IMF Programs, 1997[1]

Country	Preceding Year, Actual	Program Year, Projected or Programed	Following Year, Programed
Current Account Balances (USD billion; Percent of GDP in parenthesis)			
Thailand	−14.7 (−7.9)	−9.0 (−5.0)	−5.3 (−3.0)
Indonesia	−7.7 (−4.9)	−5.8 (−2.7)	−4.9 (−2.2)
Korea	−23.7 (−4.9)	−13.8 (−3.1)	−2.3 (−0.6)
Real GDP Growth (Percent year-over-year, per annum)			
Thailand	6.4	2.5	3.5
Indonesia	8.1	5.0	3.0
Korea	7.1	6.0	2.5
Fiscal Balances (Percent of GDP)			
Thailand	2.2	1.0	1.0
Indonesia	1.2	1.0	1.0
Korea	0.3	0.8	0.2

GDP = gross domestic product, IMF = International Monetary Fund, USD = United States dollar.
Note:
[1] Calendar or fiscal year, as indicated in the program documents.
Source: International Monetary Fund program documents.

overestimated the positive confidence ("catalytic") effect of IMF financing on foreign investors, who in this case clearly saw that either the IMF programs were deficient or that the size of financing was inadequate. Understandably, they felt justified in taking the money out to protect themselves.

The optimistic growth projection was a natural consequence of this underestimation of the capital flow reversals (Table 25.3, middle panel). The IMF projected the annual rate of real GDP growth in 1998 to be 2.5% for Thailand, 5.0% for Indonesia, and 6.0% for Korea, while the realized growth turned out to be −7.6, −13.1, and −5.1%, respectively (Figure 25.1). In the absence of a quick export expansion, a CAB improvement can only be generated by a fall in imports, which requires a fall in domestic demand. Moreover, the IMF staff underestimated the negative balance sheet effect of currency depreciation, given the history of significant unhedged foreign currency borrowing.[20]

---

[20]The negative wealth effect of exchange rate devaluation when there is net external debt in foreign currencies was first recognized over half a century ago by Diaz-Alejandro (1963). Among development economists, the possible contractionary impact of currency depreciation was a well-known empirical regularity even at the time of the AFC (Edwards 1989).

As a result, all three programs provided for a small fiscal surplus for 1998 (Table 25.3, bottom panel). Yet, as the extent of the external adjustment and output contraction became evident, the programmed fiscal adjustments were substantially eased during the course of the program (Figure 25.5 for

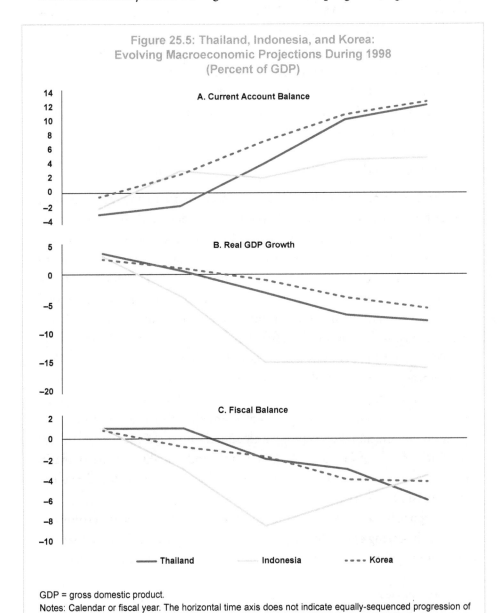

Figure 25.5: Thailand, Indonesia, and Korea:
Evolving Macroeconomic Projections During 1998
(Percent of GDP)

A. Current Account Balance

B. Real GDP Growth

C. Fiscal Balance

——— Thailand   Indonesia   - - - - Korea

GDP = gross domestic product.
Notes: Calendar or fiscal year. The horizontal time axis does not indicate equally-sequenced progression of time; depending on the country, projections were adjusted at various times throughout 1998; the final value is a provisional actual given some months after the end of 1998.
Source: Author's estimates based on International Monetary Fund program documents.

1998 only). Looking only at the calendar or fiscal year 1998, the first full year of the program, the growth projection for Thailand was progressively lowered from +3.5% to −10.4%, while the programmed fiscal surplus of 1.0% of GDP was allowed to move to a deficit of 3.3%. For Korea, the adjustment was from a surplus of 0.8% of GDP to a deficit of 5.0%. The trajectory was somewhat different for Indonesia. Even though the FB was allowed to move from a surplus of 1.0% of GDP to a deficit of 8.5%, the government could not fully utilize the fiscal space created. At the end of the program, the deficit was only 3.6%. In all three countries, fiscal policy was quickly and substantially eased so that initially tight fiscal policy could not have been a major cause of the contraction of output experienced.[21]

Structural Conditionality

All three programs included financial sector restructuring and extensive structural reforms in other areas to improve efficiency and competitiveness. In the AFC countries, weaknesses in the financial sector were widely viewed as central to the crises, and tackling these was thought crucial not only to resolve the damage done by the crisis but also to regain investor confidence and support sustained economic recovery. Thailand had already suspended 16 unviable finance companies in June and an additional 42 companies in early August before they concluded the program with the IMF, Indonesia closed 16 unviable banks as a prior condition for the approval of the IMF program at the beginning of November, and Korea suspended nine insolvent merchant banks the day before the IMF program was approved. Rightly, financial sector restructuring was a major focus of the programs, but structural conditionality went beyond addressing the critical problems of the financial sector (Table 25.4). Structural conditionality was particularly extensive for Indonesia, where a number of measures were included relating to cronyism and corruption.

Arguably, some of these measures were useful to crisis resolution, such as the easing of restrictions on foreign equity participation in financial institutions, a measure included in all programs. Others did not seem as

---

[21]It is interesting to note in this context that a similar pattern of economic growth was observed in Malaysia, an Asian crisis country that did not seek IMF assistance. Malaysia's real GDP fell by 7.5% in 1998 while there was a fiscal deficit amounting to 1.8% of GDP. This suggests that a contraction in economic activity is inherent to an exceptionally large capital flow reversal irrespective of the stance of fiscal policy. See Singh (2021).

Table 25.4: Thailand, Indonesia, and Korea: The Scope of Structural Conditionality, 1997–2000

Country	Structural Reform Measures
Thailand	• Financial sector restructuring (including easing of restrictions on foreign equity participation in troubled financial institutions) • Corporate restructuring (including the privatization of state-owned enterprises and greater private sector participation in transportation, power, and other key sectors) • Civil service reform • Data disclosure, including Bank of Thailand balance sheets and the adoption of SDDS
Indonesia	• Financial sector restructuring (including closure of 16 banks, with partial deposit guarantee, as prior action; intensified supervision of remaining weak but viable banks; strengthening, including privatization, of state and regional development banks; improved prudential standards; and capital market development) • Fiscal structural reforms, including tax administration • Governance (including greater transparency and more competitive bidding for public sector procurement and contracting, bankruptcy and judicial reforms for commercial disputes) • Trade and investment liberalization • Domestic deregulation and privatization (including phasing out of agricultural and domestic marketing monopolies)
Korea	• Financial sector restructuring (including central bank independence, consolidated financial supervision, improved corporate accounting standards, closure or recapitalization of troubled financial institutions) • Trade and capital account liberalization • Corporate governance and corporate restructuring (including *chaebol* reforms) • Labor market reform

SDDS = Special Data Dissemination Standard.
Source: International Monetary Fund program documents.

relevant, such as the termination of the so-called import diversification program in Korea.[22] The structural component assumed greater centrality as the immediate crisis management ended but the programs themselves continued for some time. Thailand and Korea implemented these reforms successfully, but implementation in Indonesia faced political resistance from vested interests and capacity constraints. To be sure, many of these measures were structural benchmarks (SBs) untied to the disbursement of funds. The number of structural performance criteria (SPCs), the observance of which

---

[22] The term was a euphemism for the effective ban on imports of finished products from Japan. The work this author directed at the IMF Independent Evaluation Office found no evidence that the Japanese government had played a role in the inclusion of this measure (IEO 2003).

was required for disbursement, was relatively small at each review. Even so, the distinction between the two was immaterial for the majority of foreign investors who, given the opaqueness of IMF loan documents, saw both of them as indistinguishable parts of the IMF package.

Two opposing views have been expressed on structural conditionality in the AFC programs. One view holds that some of the structural reform measures were unrelated to the immediate problem of crisis resolution and distracted attention from the core macroeconomic and financial issues, and these were felt to be an encroachment into domestic decision-making, creating an unnecessary opposition, and may also have damaged investor confidence by signaling to the markets that the situation was worse than they had feared (Feldstein 1998; Radelet and Sachs 1998). The other view argues that restoring investor confidence requires the demonstration of a will to tackle the structural causes of crisis vulnerabilities in the economy (Goldstein 2002; Summers 1999). The issue will never be fully resolved, although the balance of opinion has shifted to the former view during the course of a post-AFC policy debate within the IMF (see the following section for a discussion).

At the time of the crisis, the latter view held sway within the IMF. The Managing Director, speaking in February 1998, stated that "the centerpiece of each program [in Asia was] not a set of austerity measures to restore macroeconomic balance, but a set of forceful, far-reaching structural reforms to strengthen financial systems, increase transparency, open markets, and, in so doing, restore market confidence," adding that "these reforms will require a vast change in domestic business practices, corporate culture, and government behavior, which will take time" (Camdessus 1998). Just a few weeks later, the First Deputy Managing Director echoed the same voice by stating that "because [these] problems … lie at the heart of the economic crisis in each country," "it would not serve any lasting purpose for the IMF to lend to these countries unless these problems were addressed." Remarkably, likely referring to Indonesia, he explained the program's failure to bring stability as caused by the market's skepticism that "reform efforts are … incomplete or half-hearted" (Fischer 1998a).[23]

---

[23]Such sentiment was reflected in Indonesia's letter of intent dated January 15, 1998 (when it was evident to everyone that the initial macroeconomic program had hopelessly gone off-track), calling for "bolder, and faster, reform" and stating the government's decision to "accelerate" planned measures and supplement them with "additional actions."

Capital Controls and Private Sector Involvement

In retrospect, use of capital controls was the elephant in the room that nobody either saw or wanted to see. As noted, this was a period in which the international community, led by the majority of industrial countries, was about to agree to amending the IMF Articles of Agreement, giving the Fund a mandate to promote capital account liberalization. In an environment like this, the authorities of the crisis countries, not to mention the IMF staff, could not possibly have proposed capital controls as an instrument to deal with a falling currency, especially when they involved unilateral administrative restrictions.[24] With capital controls, which would separate domestic from foreign markets, an arbitrage condition of the type given by Equation (1) would not have to hold, cutting off the negative feedback loop from a high interest rate to the banking and corporate sectors. With a stoppage of capital outflows, moreover, there would not be an output contraction working through a fall in aggregate demand and import compression. Neither would there be a need for exceptionally large official financing. A sudden imposition of capital controls, of course, would create a myriad of legal issues, but the cost of legal work would be a small fraction of the amount that needs to be provided in the absence of capital controls. Yet, the intellectual climate was such that, when Malaysia introduced a 12-month holding period restriction for the repatriation of the proceeds from the sale of Malaysian securities in September 1998, the international community reacted negatively by downgrading the country's credit rating and removing it from major investment indices (Kawai and Takagi 2004; Singh 2021).

In Korea, however, when the initial attempt to calm the market had failed, an idea soon emerged to roll over foreign banks' outstanding short-term credits to Korean banks. Around Christmas time 1997, American, European, and Japanese banks agreed to roll over short-term credits to Korean banks at current levels, with the central banks and the IMF monitoring the enforcement of the agreements. And, in January 1998, these banks agreed to convert virtually all short-term credits into medium-term bonds guaranteed by the Korean government (Hahm and Kim 2021). The Korean crisis was virtually over when the rollover agreements were reached with major banks. The agreements were voluntary, but they effectively worked as

---

[24]From May 1997 to January 1998, Thai authorities curtailed banking system sources of baht credit to be used by foreign speculators in the swap market (Kawai and Takagi 2004).

a capital control to halt capital flight. This type of capital control has assumed a more respectful name of private sector involvement (PSI), which does not carry the stigma associated with heavy-handed administrative controls. In Thailand as well, there was an understanding that foreign banks would maintain their exposure during the crisis, but the commitments did not seem to amount to much.

Post-Crisis Reforms and Innovations, 1998–2010

Surveillance Reforms

Attempts to strengthen IMF surveillance, in light of its failure to anticipate the AFC, began in early 1998. In April, and then in October, the Interim Committee called upon the Fund to intensify its surveillance of financial sector issues, including policy interdependence and risks of contagion, and to widen its scope to cover the regulation and supervision of the financial sector. In June, the IMF released for the use of its staff a "Guidance Note for the Monitoring of Financial Systems under Article IV Surveillance," stressing the need to identify "conditions and developments in the banking and the financial system and markets that may impinge upon macroeconomic conditions and policies" and "macroeconomic conditions and developments that may have detrimental effects on the financial system" (IMF 1998). In 1999, the IMF, jointly with the World Bank, launched the Financial Sector Assessment Program (FSAP) as an initiative to identify financial system vulnerabilities (IMF and World Bank 2000).[25]

Strengthening the coverage of financial sector issues in surveillance became a recurring call. The 2004 BSR, for example, observed that the IMF was not adequately integrating financial sector analysis into bilateral surveillance. In response, in 2005, the IMF issued a revised surveillance guidance note, in which the scope and modalities for covering financial sector issues in bilateral surveillance were clarified. The guidance note, for instance, stated that the "range of issues" to be covered included "financial sector issues" and "financial sector developments and policies," focusing on "assessing financial sector conditions, linkages with macroeconomic developments and prospects, and measures to address weaknesses" (IMF 2005b).

---

[25]It was initially launched on a 1-year pilot basis. The pilot included 12 countries: Cameroon, Canada, Colombia, El Salvador, Estonia, Hungary, India, Iran, Ireland, Kazakhstan, Lebanon, and South Africa.

In 2006, the Managing Director proposed that "the coverage of financial sector issues in Article IVs ... be elevated to a higher level" to "give financial issues coverage that is at least on par with, say, the traditional fiscal policy analysis" (IMF 2006). In 2007, an interdepartmental taskforce, based on a stocktaking of the existing state of financial surveillance, proposed a broad organizing framework for integrating finance into Article IV surveillance, highlighting, inter alia, the need to address: (i) the channels of interaction between the macro-economy, financial markets, and financial sector; (ii) the role of the financial sector in initiating, amplifying, or muting disturbances to the economy; (iii) the diagnostic information from financial markets and the financial sector about the risks of financial crises; and (iv) the role of the financial sector in facilitating or retarding growth (IMF 2007).

The GFC of 2008 provided an occasion for serious reflection and soul searching on the part of the IMF. It was apparent that, despite the years of efforts to strengthen surveillance, the IMF had insufficiently appreciated the severity of the vulnerabilities in the financial systems of major countries and their interconnectedness. To remedy the identified weaknesses, the IMF developed new analytical tools to assess macro-financial risks (Takagi 2018). To strengthen the surveillance of all countries with systemic financial systems, the FSAP, for which participation had been voluntary, was reformed in two stages. First, in 2009, the administration of the FSAP was made more flexible, with a clearer delineation of responsibilities between the IMF and the World Bank, allowing the Fund to conduct financial stability modules separately from financial development modules by the Bank. Second, in 2010, the Executive Board made financial stability assessments under the FSAP a "regular and mandatory part of the Fund's surveillance for members with systemically important financial sectors" (IMF 2010).[26]

A New Access Policy

The early 2000s was a benign period for emerging market economies when, recovering from the capital outflows they had experienced from the late 1990s, they received a plentiful of international capital inflows. The IMF provided no crisis lending. This changed with the Lehman shock of

---

[26]Initially, a total of 25 jurisdictions were identified as having systemically important financial sectors, based on a methodology that combines the size and interconnectedness of each country's financial sector, covering nearly 90% of the global financial system and 80% of global economic activity. In 2013, the number of countries with systemic financial sectors was increased to 29.

September 2008. Over the period 2008–2010, nearly 30 countries, including some small industrial ones, sought financial assistance from the Fund. The size of financing the IMF provided to these countries, especially those receiving assistance during the last months of 2008, was large when headline numbers are considered. The size of financing under the first four European programs (Ukraine, Hungary, Iceland, and Latvia) was three to five times larger in relation to GDP than the size of financing under the AFC programs (Takagi 2016). The first 14 programs were all exceptional access cases, even after the access limits were doubled in March 2009.[27]

Headline numbers, in relation to GDP, quota, or the size of an expected capital flow reversal, can be a misleading benchmark of comparison. For example, the larger access of the early GFC programs may be reflective of a higher openness of these countries, their greater interconnectedness (and hence the risk of contagion), the less favorable external economic environment (when practically the whole world economy was contracting), their larger initial imbalances (and therefore greater required adjustment), and the like, compared to the AFC countries. The difference, in and of itself, says little about the lesson the IMF may have learned from the AFC. To account for the difference properly, the headline numbers must ideally be adjusted for influences other than the program's identity as an AFC or a GFC program.

To estimate such a difference, De Resende and Takagi (2018) regressed IMF financing (as a percent of GDP) over the CAB, real GDP growth, a change in international reserves, the balance of external debt, the FB, and a dummy variable for post-GFC programs. Depending on whether current or 1 year lagged values are used, they found that, based on annual data containing 159 observations for 1997–2013, the size of financing after September 2008 was larger by 1.1–1.2 percentage points of GDP when all arrangements are considered (Table 25.5). The difference was 3.3–3.6 percentage points for SBAs alone. Although IMF financing is necessarily catalytic and cannot be without bounds, this is an indication that the IMF had learned from the AFC that inadequate upfront financing could fail to restore investor confidence and arrest capital outflows.

---

[27]Normal lending limits (100% of quota annually and 300% of quota cumulatively) were doubled in March 2009.

Table 25.5: The Size of IMF Financing, Pre-GFC versus Post-GFC Programs (Percentage points of GDP, unless otherwise specified)

Coefficient/Summary Statistic	All IMF Programs		Stand-By Arrangements Only	
	Current Values	Lagged Values	Current Values	Lagged Values
Post-2008 Programs (Probability)	1.141 (0.007)	1.180 (0.003)	3.274 (0.003)	3.608 (0.000)
NOB	159	159	48	52
R-Squared	0.354	0.331	0.359	0.505

GDP = gross domestic product, GFC = global financial crisis, IMF = International Monetary Fund, NOB = number of observations.
Notes: Ordinary least square (OLS) estimates, for the period 1997–2013, of the coefficient for the dummy variable for post-September 2008 programs obtained by regressing the size of International Monetary Fund financing (as a percent of GDP) on the dummy, current account balance (as a percent of GDP), real GDP growth, percentage change in reserves (as a percent of GDP), external debt (as a percent of GDP), and fiscal balance (as a percent of GDP), based on White heteroskedasticity-consistent standard errors and covariances. Two sets of results are reported, one with current values for the independent variables (other than the dummy) and the other with 1-year lagged values.
Sources: De Resende and Takagi (2018), Table 1.

Realistic Macroeconomic Assumptions and Conditionality

During the GFC, the IMF correctly forecast negative growth for the countries experiencing capital outflows, indicating that it understood the nature of a capital account crisis as one in which the attendant CAB improvement necessitates an import compression and a contraction of aggregate demand (Takagi et al. 2014). Even so, the GFC programs on average still overpredicted growth by 1.4% (3.3% for the first eight programs) for the subsequent year. Affecting a multitude of countries simultaneously, the contractionary impact of the crisis was unprecedented. As it took the IMF (and much of the world) time to fully grasp the magnitude of the impact, early optimism is understandable. This may explain why later programs did not display the same growth optimism of the early programs, at least to the same extent. The IMF likewise forecast a large improvement in the CAB, though these forecasts too turned out to be optimistic on average by 5.6 percentage points of GDP for the second year of the program.

The larger financing, coupled with a negative economic growth forecast, explains why the GFC programs provided for substantial fiscal deficits (Table 25.6). This too reflects a lesson from the AFC, where it had initially called for a small fiscal surplus. Unlike the AFC countries, most GFC countries had a (sometimes large) fiscal deficit to begin with. The loss of investor confidence was not unrelated to their perceived fiscal fragilities.

Thus, fiscal conditionality attempted to manage the tradeoff between supporting the economy during a downturn and achieving medium-term fiscal sustainability; it was calibrated to country-specific circumstances.[28] The logic was to tighten fiscal policy moderately but to accommodate a sizeable deficit and to target a gradual deficit reduction over the course of the program. The uncertain costs of bank restructuring were excluded from fiscal conditionality (whereas in the AFC programs additional tightening was programmed precisely to contain such costs), allowing the countries to increase fiscal spending flexibly without violating the terms of conditionality.

Allowance for sizable deficits was based on realism, not on the disregarding of the need for fiscal adjustment in countries with underlying fiscal fragility. The programs for 25 countries on average called for an initial fiscal tightening of 1% of GDP from the first to the second year of the program, and 1.8% of GDP from the second to the third (see Table 25.6). Roaf (2012) notes that as the immediate impact of the GFC dissipated, fiscal policy became less accommodative of adverse shocks, and that the post-GFC programs were tighter than past crisis cases in cyclically adjusted terms. The magnitude of the initial fiscal imbalances meant that the outcome was a generally tighter stance of fiscal policy throughout the subsequent period. Truman (2013), based on a smaller set of countries, argues that compared to the AFC programs, fiscal conditionality was tighter ex-post for post-GFC programs.

Table 25.6: Programmed/Projected versus Actual Fiscal Balances in Post-AFC Programs, from *t* (Program Year) to *t* + 3 (Percent of GDP, simple averages)

Fiscal Balance	*t* = Program Year	*t* + 1	*t* + 2	*t* + 3
Programmed/Projected	−5.3	−4.3	−2.5	−2.0
Actual	−5.5	−4.1	−3.3	−3.5

GDP = gross domestic product.
Note: Based on 25 crisis programs during the global financial crisis.
Sources: De Resende and Takagi (2018), Table 6.

---

[28]For example, the program did not allow the deficits to continue in Ukraine. The special case of Latvia should be noted. Latvia had a national goal of joining the euro area by 2012, which required both meeting the Maastricht criteria and maintaining the peg to the euro. Under the IMF program, a fiscal adjustment equivalent to 7% of GDP was carried out for the 2009 budget (compared with the original budget).

A New Approach to Structural Conditionality

The pros and cons of structural conditionality were hotly debated in the aftermath of the AFC. Crisis has often been used as a convenient opportunity for politically difficult reforms. In Indonesia, where the scope of structural reform was extensive, much of the inputs came from a team of senior Indonesian economic officials who saw a need for reform but had faced formidable political resistance. In Korea, too, there was a group of reform-minded officials who had already produced a home-grown program for financial sector restructuring. The IMF's structural conditionality thus became a contest between vested interests and domestic reformers supported by the international community. Indonesia's fragile political system could not quite handle the tension, and a downfall of the incumbent president was the outcome. Irrespective of their intrinsic merits, one can legitimately ask if the programmed reforms in these countries, especially Indonesia, went too far.

The idea that emerged out of this debate was the concept of national ownership, which the IMF (2001) defined as a "willing assumption of responsibility for an agreed program of policies" by responsible officials in a borrowing country. To demand a policy measure to which a government (and the society it represents) cannot fully commit itself, no matter how desirable it may be to the national economy, would increase the chance of program failure and might end up undermining investor confidence. This is a lesson of the AFC. The IMF proposed to streamline conditionality as a way to strengthen the national ownership of IMF programs as an essential element of successful intervention. The policy may or may not be homegrown. It can be a product of negotiation but must be owned by the authorities.

The streamlining initiative began in earnest with the interim guidance note of September 2000, which called for focusing structural measures on the IMF's areas of competence on the basis of "macro-relevance." In 2002, the new guidance note changed the basis from "macro-relevance" to "macro-criticality," noting that only conditions that are of "critical importance for achieving the macroeconomic goals of the program" should be included in a program. Further, the note highlighted the "principle of parsimony," which requires "program-related conditions" to be "limited to the minimum necessary to achieve the goals of the Fund-supported program or to monitor its implementation" (IMF 2002). The IMF's internal review of conditionality, comparing structural conditionality in IMF programs between 1995–1997 and 2001–2003, noted that major shifts had occurred in the direction of "greater focus on criticality" (IMF 2005a).

During the middle of the GFC, in March 2009, the IMF Executive Board adopted a decision to terminate SPCs in all IMF financing arrangements. Following this decision, some existing SPCs in ongoing programs were converted to SBs. The decision was more symbolic than substantive, however, because there is an alternative way to make disbursements conditional on the progress of structural reforms by converting SBs into binding prior actions (PAs) at succeeding reviews. In the event, the post-GFC programs were lighter on structural conditionality than the AFC programs, based on a sum of SPCs, SBs, and PAs as a measure of intensity, though the number of structural conditions tended to increase as the immediate impact of the crisis dissipated (Takagi et al. 2014). The average number rose from 5.2 per year for programs approved in 2008 to 8.5 per year for those approved in 2010 (the corresponding number was 15.3 per year for the AFC programs approved in 1997).

Use of Exchange and Capital Controls

The IMF took a highly accommodative attitude toward the use of capital controls in some GFC programs. Part of this was the fuller recognition of the nature of a capital account crisis as a reversal of capital flows. In the absence of capital controls, a crisis-driven rise in the risk premium could make it all but impossible to use a reasonable set of macroeconomic policy measures to contain a free fall of the domestic currency (see Equation (1)), which would in turn adversely affect the balance sheets of banks and corporations exposed to foreign currency debt. In the aftermath of the AFC, the IMF devoted considerable resources to developing a tool (the "balance sheet approach") to analyze the implications of currency and maturity mismatches in the balance sheets of various sectors in an economy. The balance sheet approach may well be the single most important analytical development within the IMF that came out of the AFC (Allen et al. 2002; Rosenberg et al. 2005). With this understanding, stemming a sharp currency depreciation subsequently began to receive priority in IMF crisis programs, including through temporary use of capital and even exchange controls if necessary.

In 2008, Iceland and Ukraine were allowed to retain the restrictions they had introduced prior to approaching the IMF on capital outflows and payments for some current transactions; Latvia also retained the exchange control related to the frozen bank deposits. Exchange restrictions related to current transactions (except those approved under the transitional arrangements of Article XIV) are in violation of Article VIII of the IMF Articles of Agreement, and are normally not permitted in IMF programs as "measures destructive of national or international prosperity" (IMF 2002). Yet, they were permitted in these cases on the condition that they would be removed as soon as practical. Although capital controls do not violate the IMF Articles as long as they do not restrict payments for current transactions, the IMF had generally taken a position unfavorable to any administrative measure that interfered with the free movement of capital. The intellectual opposition to the use of capital controls, characteristic of the earlier decades, had dissipated by this time.[29]

Also, as a voluntary form of capital control, PSI was attempted from the outset. This limited the magnitude of capital outflows and helped arrest the extent of exchange rate depreciation, hence the adverse impact on bank and corporate balance sheets. In Korea, PSI was tried and proved critical to stabilizing the foreign exchange market, but only after IMF financing had proved inadequate. With this experience, PSI of one type or another became a standard feature of IMF programs to deal with a capital account crisis, starting with the Brazilian crisis in 1999. During the GFC, Hungary, Latvia, and Ukraine, where foreign-owned banks constituted a significant share of the banking sector, sought a commitment from the parent banks to maintain their exposure to their local subsidiaries.[30] A successful PSI requires transparency, on the part of the government and the IMF, with respect to the content of the adjustment measures. It has since become a standard practice for senior government and IMF officials to go on "roadshows" to major financial centers to convince foreign investors of the credibility and viability of the program as worthy of their support.

Following the GFC, in December 2012, the IMF clarified its position on the use of capital controls by issuing an "Institutional View" on the

---

[29]In 1998, at the height of the AFC, many observers believed that the IMF was hostile to the introduction of a capital outflow control by Malaysia (IEO 2005).

[30]This was formalized in 2009 as the Vienna Initiative, which would cover all of Emerging Europe (Aslund 2010; Berglof 2012; de Haas et al. 2012). In Hungary, foreign banks injected capital into their Hungarian subsidiaries in the range of EUR 2–EUR 3 billion and many times more in the form of loans, which exceeded the combined amount of IMF–EU tranches utilized. See http://hvg.hu/gazdasag/20130225_Simor_Az_orszag_erdeke_volt_az_adatok_ata.

liberalization and management of capital flows. The Institutional View, which is primarily concerned with capital controls — called capital flow management measures (CFMs) — to manage surges in inflows, endorses "a temporary role for the introduction of CFMs on outflows" when a country is "in crisis situation, or when a crisis may be imminent." It states that CFMs "in response to disruptive flows" must be both "comprehensive" and "temporary," and must be introduced as "part of a broader policy package that also includes macroeconomic, financial sector, and structural adjustment to address the fundamental causes of the crisis," adding that they are meant to "provide breathing space" (IMF 2012). The benefits of such a prescriptive approach to the use of capital controls can be debated, but capital controls, if introduced within the framework of an IMF program, would carry greater respectability and may militate against damaging investor confidence.

More Effective Cooperation

During the GFC, the IMF collaborated with other multilateral institutions and bilateral donors in at least 17 programs supported by SBAs. The program for Hungary represented the first case of IMF–European Union (EU) collaboration, which set a precedent for future requests for financial support by EU members.[31] Likewise, the program for Latvia was part of a coordinated international effort, in which the European Commission actively participated, along with representatives from the European Central Bank (ECB), the World Bank, and Nordic countries. The EU's financial support was not confined to EU members — it was part of six financing packages, while the World Bank participated in 15 packages. The IMF has had a long history of co-financing, but the innovation of GFC programs was the participation of official partners from the program design stage. During the AFC, the programs were negotiated almost exclusively by the IMF staff and the authorities of the countries concerned, with limited direct participation by other stakeholders, and the IMF did not share certain information on confidentiality grounds.

The IMF staff enumerated these additional sources of financing in a transparent way. When the amount was less than certain (Angola and

---

[31] The onset of crises in the euro area from 2010 saw an intensification of the IMF's collaborative efforts with European institutions in an informal arrangement that came to be known as the "troika," consisting of the IMF, the European Commission, and the ECB (IEO 2016; Kincaid 2017).

Mongolia), they clearly stated that the amount needed to be reassessed at a subsequent review. The documents further stated that several stakeholders, such as the EU, the ECB, the World Bank, and Nordic countries, had participated in the preparation of the programs, giving credibility to the amount to be provided by these entities. The program documents clearly stated the amount of financing needs and how the gap was to be filled. The transparent manner in which the IMF collaborated with official donors contributed to the effectiveness of SBA-supported programs in building investor confidence (Takagi et al. 2014; Takagi 2016). During the AFC, in contrast, foreign investors questioned the credibility of the total official financing provided under the IMF programs, given the lack of transparency about the backing of the numbers and the ambiguity with which conditions for access to financing were specified.[32]

Formalizing the Modality of Cooperation with RFAs

The IMF's engagement with the euro area during the crises in Greece, Ireland, and Portugal from 2010 became the background against which the Fund's modality of cooperation with regional financing arrangements (RFAs) saw greater formalization on the basis of the "Principles for Cooperation between the IMF and RFAs," as endorsed by the Group of Twenty (G20) finance ministers and central bank governors in October 2011.[33] The G20 principles were intended to provide high-level guidance for IMF–RFA collaboration, in light of not only a recent proliferation of RFAs[34] but also the involvement of European institutions in IMF lending operations in the euro area, where

---

[32] In Thailand, total official financing of USD 17.2 billion was less than half the amount of short-term external liabilities (USD 38 billion at the end of May 1997). In Indonesia and Korea, though the World Bank and the ADB agreed to provide financing, the amount included the funds that had already been committed before the crisis; bilateral financing (USD 17 billion for Indonesia and USD 20 billion for Korea) was designated as the second line of defense, and was to be activated only when financing from all other sources proved insufficient, but the conditions for activation were not specified, causing the market participants to question not only their availability but also the credibility of the official financial packages. See IEO (2003).

[33] These consist of six nonbinding principles, among which are found: (1) need to respect the roles, independence, and decision-making processes of each institution; (2) need to include open sharing of information and to benefit from the comparative advantages or relative expertise of each institution; (3) need to be consistent in lending conditions in order to prevent arbitrage and facility shopping while maintaining flexibility; and (4) need to respect the preferred-creditor status of the IMF.

[34] There exist seven RFAs: Arab Monetary Fund (established in 1976); BRICS Contingent Reserve Arrangement (2014); CMIM (2000, 2010); Eurasian Fund for Stabilization and Development (2009); EU Balance of Payments Facility (2002); European Stability Mechanism (2012); and Latin American Reserve Fund (1978). See IMF (2017a, 2017b).

the opaque nature of the collaboration raised the issue of legitimacy and accountability (IEO 2016; Kincaid 2017).

Despite an urging by the International Monetary and Financial Committee to do so in April 2011, and the preparation of a staff paper raising the topic for discussion in May 2013 (IMF 2013), the IMF Executive Board did not develop a formal modality of engagement with RFAs as it saw the extent and form of such cooperation as "the most difficult question to answer" (as quoted in Kincaid 2017). Much of the difficulty came from the overlapping mandates of the IMF and RFAs as crisis manager, which presented the possibility that their judgments and approaches could differ, a situation that would not generally arise in the case of collaboration between the IMF and development banks where the division of labor was more clearly understood.[35] In a common currency area, moreover, there was an additional complication that the member countries might be subject to union-wide policy rules (such as the Stability and Growth Pact, and the associated Excessive Deficit Procedure, in the euro area).

Concrete steps have been taken to make IMF–RFA collaboration operational. In 2016, the IMF was invited to participate in a test run with the Chiang Mai Initiative Multilateralisation (CMIM), where a borrower is required to conclude an adjustment program with the IMF when the borrowing exceeds 30% of the maximum drawable amount;[36] the test run revealed the challenges posed by the CMIM's shorter repayment periods and program length (IMF 2017a). In July 2017, the Executive Board formally discussed a set of staff papers, which noted, among other things, the importance of having a single program framework including aligning the qualification standards for lending instruments and the need for mutual respect of institutional independence and capacity (IMF 2017a, 2017b). The Board endorsed the proposed principles "as an important first step" and encouraged continued dialogue with RFAs and joint test-runs to gain further experience and to identify emerging issues (IMF 2017c).

These were followed, in October 2017, by the signing of a formal memorandum of understanding with AMRO and the European Stability Mechanism. The understanding between the IMF and AMRO included

---

[35] Typically, the IMF takes the lead in designing a macro framework while the development bank assumes primary responsibility for designing structural reforms.

[36] In September 2020, the IMF de-linked portion was raised to 40%.

the agreement to "enhance cooperation to promote the common goal of regional and global financial stability" through "advancing cooperation and leveraging of each other's expertise" (IMF 2017d). The cooperation is said to involve exchanging views related to macroeconomic surveillance, providing training and staff exchange opportunities, and joint research projects. Fully aligning the competing mandates and approaches of different institutions remains a difficult task. Only time can tell how these and further efforts will enhance the efficacy of the global financial safety net, of which the IMF is increasingly becoming only a part.

Conclusion

This chapter has revisited, with a hindsight of more than 20 years, the IMF's controversial role in Thailand, Indonesia, and Korea during the AFC of 1997–1998. The experience gained from its less-than-impeccable intervention inspired a large number of policy and institutional innovations over the subsequent decades within the IMF. The chapter, after reviewing the IMF's pre-crisis surveillance and crisis programs in the three crisis countries, has traced these developments through the aftermath of the GFC. A comparative review of programs during the GFC has identified what the IMF had learned from the Asian experience to improve the effectiveness of crisis management programs. With the lessons learned, the IMF's surveillance became increasingly focused on financial sector issues. Its crisis programs became more realistic about macroeconomic assumptions and conditionality, informed by a better understanding of the nature of economic crisis driven by a capital flow reversal. Structural conditionality became more streamlined and focused on the IMF's core areas of competence. The IMF became more transparent in its engagement with official partners and private investors. It became more accommodative of the use of capital controls to stem capital outflows. By its very nature, a new crisis will inevitably happen from causes not sufficiently understood or anticipated. Attempts to improve surveillance and to strengthen crisis management capacity must be an ongoing process.

References

Allen, Mark, Christoph Rosenberg, Christian Keller, Brad Setser, and Nouriel Roubini. 2002, "A Balance Sheet Approach to Financial Crises," Working Paper 02/210, International Monetary Fund.

Aslund, Anders. 2010. *The Last Shall Be the First: The East European Financial Crisis.* Washington: Peterson Institute for International Economics.

Azis, Iwan J. 2022. "Indonesia: A Tale of Three Crises." In *Trauma to Triumph — Rising from the Ashes of the Asian Financial Crisis,* edited by Hoe Ee Khor, Diwa C. Guinigundo, and Mashiro Kawai. Singapore: World Scientific, 237–285. See Chapter 15 of this volume.

Berglof, Erik. 2012. "Filling the Gaps: The Vienna Initiative and the Role of International Financial Institutions in Crisis Management and Resolution." In *The Global Macro Economy and Finance,* edited by F. Allen, M. Aoki, J. Fitoussi, N. Kiyotaki, R. Gordon, and J. E. Stiglitz. New York: Palgrave Macmillan, 211–223.

Boorman, Jack, Timothy Lane, Marianne Schulze-Ghattas, Ales Bulir, Atish R. Ghosh, Javier Hamann, Alex Moumouras, and Steven Phillips. 2000. "Managing Financial Crises: The Experience in East Asia." *Carnegie-Rochester Conference Series on Public Policy* 53: 1–67.

Calvo, Guillermo A., Leonard Leiderman, and Carman M. Reinhart. 1996. "Inflows of Capital to Developing Countries in the 1990s." *Journal of Economic Perspectives* 10: 123–139.

Camdessus, Michel. 1998. "The IMF and Its Programs in Asia." Speech given at the Council on Foreign Relations, New York, February 6.

Cho, Dongchul, and Kenneth D. West. 2000. "The Effect of Monetary Policy in Exchange Rate Stabilization in Postcrisis Korea." In *Korean Crisis: Before and After,* edited by I. Shin. Seoul: Korea Development Institute.

Chung, Chae-Shick, and Se-Jik Kim. 2002. "New Evidence on High Interest Rate Policy During the Korean Crisis." In *Korean Crisis and Recovery,* edited by D. T. Coe and S. J. Kim. Washington and Seoul: International Monetary Fund and Korea Institute for International Economic Policy.

de Haas, Ralph, Yevgeniya Korniyenko, Elena Loukoianova, and Alexander Pivovarsky. 2012. "Foreign Banks and Vienna Initiative: Turning Sinners into Saints?" Working Paper 12/117, International Monetary Fund.

De Resende, Carlos, and Shinji Takagi. 2018. "Assessing the Effectiveness of IMF Programs Following the Global Financial Crisis: How Did It Change Since the Asian Crisis?" Working Paper No. 838, Asian Development Bank Institute.

Diaz-Alejandro, Carlos F. 1963. "A Note on the Impact of Devaluation and the Redistributive Effect." *Journal of Political Economy* 71: 577–580.

Edwards, Sebastian. 1989. *Real Exchange Rates, Devaluation, and Adjustment: Exchange Rate Policy in Developing Countries*. Cambridge, MA and London: MIT Press.

Feldstein, Martin. 1998. "Refocusing the IMF." *Foreign Affairs* 77: 20–33.

Fischer, Stanley. 1998a. "The IMF and the Asian Crisis." Speech presented in Los Angeles, March 20.

Fischer, Stanley. 1998b. "The Asian Crisis and the Changing Role of the IMF." *Finance and Development*. 35: 2–5.

Fischer, Stanley. 2001. "International Financial System: Crises and Reform." The Robbins Lectures, London School of Economics, October.

Furman, Jason, and Joseph Stiglitz. 1998. "Economic Crises: Evidence and Insights from East Asia." *Brookings Paper on Economic Activity* 2: 1–135.

Goldstein, Morris. 2002. "IMF Structural Programs." In *Economic and Financial Crises in Emerging Market Economies*, edited by M. Feldstein. Chicago: University of Chicago Press, 363–458.

Gregori, Tullio. 2009. "Currency Crisis Duration and Interest Defense." *International Journal of Finance and Economics* 14, 256–267.

Hahm, Joon-Ho, and Hyeon-Wook Kim. 2022. "Korea: Tiding Over the Asian and Global Financial Crisis." In *Trauma to Triumph — Rising from the Ashes of the Asian Financial Crisis*, edited by Hoe Ee Khor, Diwa C. Guinigundo, and Mashiro Kawai. Singapore: World Scientific, 323–369. See Chapter 17 of this volume.

Independent Evaluation Office. 2003. "The IMF and Recent Capital Account Crises: Indonesia, Korea, Brazil." Evaluation Report, International Monetary Fund.

Independent Evaluation Office. 2005. "The IMF's Approach to Capital Account Liberalization." Evaluation Report, International Monetary Fund.

Independent Evaluation Office. 2016. "The IMF and the Crises in Greece, Ireland, and Portugal." International Monetary Fund.

International Monetary Fund. 1995. "Annual Report of the Executive Board for the Financial Year Ended April 30, 1995."

International Monetary Fund. 1997. "Staff Operational Guidance Note Following the 1997 Biennial Surveillance Review."

International Monetary Fund. 1998. "Guidance Note for the Monitoring of Financial Systems Under Article IV Surveillance."

International Monetary Fund. 2001. "Strengthening Country Ownership of Fund-Supported Programs."

International Monetary Fund. 2002. "Guidelines on Conditionality."

International Monetary Fund. 2005a. "Review of the 2002 Conditionality Guidelines."

International Monetary Fund. 2005b. "Surveillance Guidance Note."

International Monetary Fund. 2006. "The Managing Director's Report on Implementing the Fund's Medium-Term Strategy."

International Monetary Fund. 2007. "Report of the Taskforce on Integrating Finance and Financial Sector Analysis into Article IV Surveillance."

International Monetary Fund. 2010. "IMF Expanding Surveillance to Require Mandatory Financial Stability Assessments of Countries with Systemically Important Financial Sectors," Press Release No. 10/357.

International Monetary Fund. 2012. "The Liberalization and Management of Capital Flows: An Institutional View."

International Monetary Fund. 2013. "Stocktaking the Fund's Engagement with Regional Financing Arrangements."

International Monetary Fund. 2017a. "Collaboration Between Regional Financing Arrangements and the IMF."

International Monetary Fund. 2017b. "Collaboration Between Regional Financing Arrangements and the IMF — Background Paper."

International Monetary Fund. 2017c. "The Chairman's Summing Up: Collaboration Between Regional Financing Arrangements and the IMF." Executive Board Meeting 17/68, July 26.

International Monetary Fund. 2017d. "The International Monetary Fund (IMF) and the ASEAN+3 Macroeconomic Research Office (AMRO) Agree to Enhance Cooperation," Press Release No. 17/395.

International Monetary Fund and World Bank. 2000. "Financial Sector Assessment Program (FSAP) — A Review: Lessons from the Pilot and Issues Going Forward."

Isard, Peter. 1995. *Exchange Rate Economics.* Cambridge: Cambridge University Press.

Ito, Takatoshi. 2007. "Asian Currency Crisis and the International Monetary Fund, 10 Years Later: Overview." *Asian Economic Policy Review* 2: 16–49.

Kawai, Masahiro, and Shinji Takagi. 2004. "Rethinking Capital Controls: The Malaysian Experience." In *East Asia's Monetary Future: Integration in the Global Economy,* edited by S. Chirathivat, E. Claassen and J. Schroeder. Cheltenham and Northampton: Edward Elgar, 182–214.

Kincaid, G. Russell. 2017. "The IMF's Role in the Euro Area's Crisis: What Are the Lessons from the IMF's Participation in the Troika?" In *Background Papers for the IMF and the Crises in Greece, Ireland, and Portugal,* edited by M. J. Schwartz and S. Takagi. Washington: International Monetary Fund, 137–207.

Mañalac, Wilhelmina C. 2022. "Philippines: Rising Above the Challenges During the Asian and Global Financial Crises." In *Trauma to Triumph — Rising from the Ashes of the Asian Financial Crisis,* edited by Hoe Ee Khor, Diwa C. Guinigundo, and Mashiro Kawai. Singapore: World Scientific, 371–427. See Chapter 18 of this volume.

Radelet, Stephen, and Jeffrey D. Sachs. 1998. "The East Asian Financial Crisis: Diagnosis, Remedies, Prospects." *Brookings Papers on Economic Activity* 1: 1–90.

Roaf, James. 2012. "Crisis Programs Review." Presentation to the IMF Executive Board, July.

Rosenberg, Christoph B., Ioannis Halikias, Brett E. House, Christian Keller, Jens Nystedt, Alexander Pitt, and Brad Setser. 2005. "Debt-Related Vulnerabilities and Financial Crises." Occasional Paper No. 240, International Monetary Fund.

Singh, Sukudhew. 2022. "Malaysia: Managing Global Financial Vulnerabilities and Regional Financial Cooperation." In *Trauma to Triumph — Rising from the Ashes of the Asian Financial Crisis,* edited by Hoe Ee Khor, Diwa C. Guinigundo, and Mashiro Kawai. Singapore: World Scientific, 287–322. See Chapter 16 of this volume.

Summers, Larry H. 1999. "Reflections on Managing Global Integration." *Journal of Economic Perspectives* 13: 3–18.

Sussangkarn, Chalongphob. 2022. "Thailand: Crisis, Recovery, and Reforms." In *Trauma to Triumph — Rising from the Ashes of the Asian Financial Crisis,* edited by Hoe Ee Khor, Diwa C. Guinigundo, and Mashiro Kawai. Singapore: World Scientific, 205–235. See Chapter 14 of this volume.

Takagi, Shinji. 2004. "Capital Account Liberalization: Lessons from Two Giants and Four Tigers." In *Financial Interdependence and Exchange Rate Regimes in East Asia,* edited by M. Kawai. Tokyo: Policy Research Institute, Japanese Ministry of Finance, 103–129.

Takagi, Shinji. 2016. "Applying the Lessons of Asia: The IMF's Crisis Management Strategy Following the Global Financial Crisis." *International Economic Journal* 30: 409–428.

Takagi, Shinji. 2018. "IMF Bilateral Financial Surveillance." Background Paper 18-02/01, Independent Evaluation Office, International Monetary Fund.

Takagi, Shinji, and Taro Esaka. 2001. "Sterilization and the Capital Inflow Problem in East Asia, 1987–97." In *Regional and Global Capital Flows: Macroeconomic Causes and Consequences,* edited by T. Ito and A. O. Krueger. Chicago and London: University of Chicago Press, 197–226.

Takagi, Shinji, Carlos De Resende, Jerome Prieur, Franz Loyola, and Tam Nguyen. 2014. "A Review of Crisis Management Programs Supported by IMF Stand-By Arrangements, 2008–11." Background Paper 14/12, Independent Evaluation Office, International Monetary Fund.

Truman, Edwin M. 2013. "Evolution of the Asian and European Financial Crises: Role of the International Monetary Fund." In *Responding to Financial Crisis: Lessons from Asia Then, the United States and Europe Now*, edited by C. Rhee and A. S. Rosen. Manila and Washington: Asian Development Bank and Peterson Institute for International Economics, 179–212.

Chapter 26

The CMI and CMIM

Beomhee Han

Background

During the 1997 Asian financial crisis (AFC), the five crisis-hit economies — Indonesia, Korea, Malaysia, the Philippines, and Thailand — experienced a combined loss of around 30% of gross domestic product (GDP).[1] Many were of the view that the AFC was not a traditional current account crisis such as those earlier seen in Latin America. Rather, it was viewed as a capital account crisis driven by investor panic and an erratic shift in market expectation that portrayed a negative aspect of financial globalization, compounded by underlying weak macroeconomic fundamentals in the crisis-hit economies.[2] The crisis that began in Thailand in early 1997 quickly spread to neighboring countries by way of contagion. The interconnectedness in trade and finance in the region brought on a regional economic downturn as a whole.

Following these turbulent events, Thailand went to the International Monetary Fund (IMF) for a bailout in July 1997. There was widespread dissatisfaction with the IMF bailout programs in the region. The IMF, assuming the role of global crisis manager, could not provide swift and large-scale liquidity support to prevent and resolve the crisis in Asia. The lending conditions contained a comprehensive structural reform agenda, including not only the measures to address underlying weakness in financial systems but also corporate restructuring and governance reform, disclosure and accounting standards, trade and capital account liberalization, competition policy, privatization, labor reform, and so on. They were believed by many to be inadequate, too stringent, and without regard for the specific circumstances of each country.[3]

---

[1] Asian Development Bank (1998).

[2] Kuroda and Kawai (2002).

[3] Feldstein (1998), Sussangkarn (2010), Park (2008). Indeed, there was a counterargument that the program focusing on structural issues was immediately required to strengthen market confidence (IMF 2000).

Given that the AFC was largely a capital account crisis, excessively high interest rates and deflationary measures imposed by the IMF led to a sharp downturn in economic activities.

The scope and timing of IMF policy conditionality were based on a standard set of "structural performance criteria" in keeping with the Washington Consensus, which was seen as "intrusive in national affairs" and damaged the national ownership of the IMF program.[4] In fact, even if structural reforms were relevant, it was considered not necessarily ideal to implement them in a time of crisis. This led to "IMF stigma," which has prevented several of the region's governments from going into an IMF program for fear of being discredited by their own national constituents (political stigma) or financial markets (financial market stigma).[5] Indeed, Dominique Strauss-Kahn, former Managing Director of the IMF, acknowledged in 2010 that it had "made some mistakes" in handling the AFC.[6]

Regional policymakers agreed that an effective regional framework could have averted the crisis or could have, at the very least, brought it under control sooner and more effectively. The use of a regional framework would have also replaced or supplemented the IMF's role. An alternative arrangement would have taken into account country-specific factors. Prior to the AFC, the level of regional financial cooperation did not correspond to increasing economic interdependence in the region through trade, investment, and finance. The AFC provided a strong incentive for Association of Southeast Asian Nations (ASEAN)+3 members to accelerate the development of their own crisis management framework, which gave birth to the Chiang Mai Initiative (CMI) and CMI Multilateralisation (CMIM).

In this chapter, we first look at the initial ideas for a regional mechanism, and focus on how regional and global policymakers tried to bridge the gaps in understanding the expected role of any liquidity mechanism. Second, we outline the progress of the CMI, which was put forward as a regional solution in the form of a liquidity backstop. The next section describes the background to the CMIM and outlines its main features. Finally, we touch upon the issue of institutional lightness in the CMIM and suggest a few issues to be considered in enhancing the role of the CMIM as a regional liquidity mechanism.

---

[4] Goldstein (2003).

[5] ECB (2018).

[6] Address by Dominique Strauss-Kahn, Managing Director of the IMF at the Asia 21 Conference, Daejeon, Korea, July 12, 2010 (https://www.imf.org/en/News/Articles/2015/09/28/04/53/sp071210).

Developing Regional Initiatives During the AFC

Following the AFC, East Asian countries started to seek a regional mechanism that would provide sufficient and timely liquidity support, and extend adequate lending conditions. This quest is traced back to the second line of defense for Thailand during the AFC, discussions of an Asian Monetary Fund (AMF), the Manila Framework Group (MFG), and the New Miyazawa Initiative. All these efforts consolidated to become part of the ASEAN+3 financial cooperation framework within which the CMI and CMIM were established.

The Second Line of Defense in the Bailout Package for Thailand: Prototype of Bilateral Financing

Before the collapse of the Thai baht in July 1997, Thailand came under a series of increasingly serious speculative attacks and markets lost confidence in the economy. By the end of June 1997, more than 90% of its foreign reserves had been used in trying to shore up the baht's value. Thailand was eventually forced to switch to a flexible exchange rate system on July 2, 1997, and the Thai baht was immediately devalued by 20%.[7] The Thai government was unable to manage the crisis on its own. Therefore, it sought external assistance from the IMF.

However, the IMF alone was unable to provide sufficient funds in a timely manner to arrest Thailand's crisis.[8] The IMF and interested parties drew out a rescue package for Thailand at their meeting on August 11, 1997 in Tokyo, Japan. More than 60% of the package came from bilateral arrangements with East Asian economies and Australia, and this was termed as a "second line of defense." This was an arrangement made on an ad hoc basis.[9]

---

[7] The value of the baht declined persistently from then that to reach a low of THB 48.8 per United States dollar in December that same year, its lowest value since Thailand started keeping record in 1969.

[8] The IMF's lending capacity hinges on its member countries' quota subscriptions, and bilateral borrowings and increasing funding sources is always challenging because of political economy. Thus, in most cases, the IMF's role includes catalyzing additional support from the international community — including the private sector and other international financial institutions, including the World Bank, conditional to an IMF-supported program for policy adjustment for the borrowing country.

[9] Brunei, China, Hong Kong, Indonesia, Japan, Korea, Malaysia, and Australia participated in the rescue package, totaling USD 17.2 billion. The United States participated in the meeting but did not contribute any funds for the "second line of defense." The "second lines of defense" for Korea and Indonesia were not disbursed.

Table 26.1: Quota, Access Limit and Surcharge in IMF Lending in 1997 (USD billion)

Country	IMF Quota 1997	SBA Access Limit	Approved Amount	Total	IMF Surcharge
Korea	SDR 799.6 million (USD 1.0 billion)	1.0 (annual) 3.2 (cumulative)	21.1[1] (19 times of quota)	58.4	
Thailand	SDR 573.9 million (USD 780.0 million)	0.7 (annual) 2.3 (cumulative)	4.0 (5 times of quota)	17.2	SRF[1]'s surcharge 300–500 bps
Indonesia	SDR 1.5 billion (USD 2.0 billion)	2.0 (annual) 6.2 (cumulative)	10.1[2] (5 times of quota)	36.1	

bps = basis points, IMF = International Monetary Fund, SBA = Stand-By Arrangement, SDR = special drawing rights, USD = United States dollar.

Notes:

[1] Until 2009, IMF SBA's annual access limit was capped at 100% of quota, and cumulative at 300% of quota. On December 3, 1997, Korea requested a three-year SBA from the IMF in an amount of SDR 15.5 billion under exceptional access policy, which was later institutionalized into the supplemental reserve facility (SRF) under discussion in the Manila Framework Group.

[2] This was augmented by about USD 5 billion under the Extended Fund Facility in February 2000.

Source: Author's calculations for IMF quota, SDR rates, SBA access limit, and SRF's surcharges based on IMF data in the website (https://www.imf.org/).

Table 26.2: Public Financial Assistance During the AFC[1]

		Thailand (Aug 1997)		Indonesia (Nov 1997)		Korea (Dec 1997)	
		(USD billion)	(Percent)	(USD billion)	(Percent)	(USD billion)	(Percent)
First line of defense	Sum	6.7	39.0	18.1	50.1	35.3	60.4
	IMF	4.0	23.3	10.1[2]	28.0	21.1	36.1
	World Bank	1.5	8.7	4.5	12.5	10.1	17.3
	ADB	1.2	7.0	3.5	9.7	4.1	7.0
Second line of defense	Sum	10.5	61.0	18.0	49.9	23.1	39.6
	Japan	4.0	23.3	5.0	13.9	10.0	17.1
	US	...	...	3.0	8.3	5.0	8.6
	Singapore	1.0	5.8	5.0	13.9	...	...
	Others	5.5[3]	31.9	5.0	13.9	8.1	13.9
	Total	17.2	100	36.1	100	58.4	100

... = not available, ADB = Asian Development Bank, AFC = Asian financial crisis, IMF = International Monetary Fund, US = United States, USD = United States dollar.

Notes:

[1] The sizes of the financial packages vary, subject to calculation and timing of agreements and sources. Table 26.2 shows the amounts in the original package, which differed from actual disbursements.

[2] On November 5, 1997, Indonesian authorities entered into a three-year stand-by arrangement with the IMF for USD 10 billion. This amount was augmented by about USD 1.4 billion in July 1998. In February 2000, a new three year extended arrangement for about USD 5 billion with the IMF was approved.

[3] USD 5.5 billion: Australia 1, Brunei 0.5, China 1, Hong Kong 1, Indonesia 0.5, Korea 0.5, and Malaysia 1.

Source: ADB (2017), IMF (2000).

Notably, a group of countries in East Asia, including Australia, joined, but the United States (US) did not participate in the bilateral financing for Thailand's rescue package. This was in contrast with the 1995 Mexican peso crisis, when it provided large bridge loans.[10] Bilateral financing, to supplement the IMF lending, was also applied to the rescue package for Indonesia and Korea in 1997 and later by the CMI in 2000. In short, the second line of defense demonstrated the IMF's lending limitation at the time, and the need for an additional liquidity mechanism at the regional level that could also supplement the IMF.

The Proposal for an AMF — An Exclusive Regional Fund

The idea for an AMF had existed long before the AFC. The idea for creating an IMF equivalent in Asia can be traced to the time when the Asian Development Bank (ADB) was established in 1966. However, the role of a regional monetary fund could not be clearly envisioned in the 1960s in Asia, given the stage of regional economic development. This idea was shelved for a long time. In September 1995, Bernie Fraser, former Governor of the Reserve Bank of Australia, proposed an Asian version of the Bank for International Settlements to members of the Executives' Meeting of East Asia-Pacific Central Banks (EMEAP).[11] The "Fraser Proposal" was about establishing a regional liquidity mechanism equipped with surveillance capabilities.[12] This proposal did not prosper, owing to insufficient support because emerging Asian economies had little experience in receiving conditional loans from the IMF until 1995. The Fraser Proposal actually portended what would happen in 1997.

Subsequently, Japan's Ministry of Finance developed an idea for an Asian version of the IMF and this idea gained momentum during the AFC. The US' initial passive stance[13] was considered to be a green light for an AMF. Japan

---

[10] Since securing funds for the Mexican peso bailout had involved a tough political battle in the US, another substantial commitment to bailing out an economy — in which the US clearly had a lesser stake — would have been hard to win Congressional approval (Altbach 1997).

[11] The EMEAP, established in 1991, comprises the central banks and monetary authorities of China, Hong Kong, Indonesia, Japan, Korea, Malaysia, the Philippines, Singapore, Thailand, New Zealand, and Australia. It is a forum to foster mutual relationships and information sharing on economic and financial issues among regional central banks without the involvement of finance ministries.

[12] Seen as of November 5, 2020, at https://www.rba.gov.au/speeches/1995/sp-gov-250995.html.

[13] "Japan's Vice Minister for International Finance at the time was Eisuke Sakakibara, whose personal view was that Japan should pursue a greater leadership role in Asia, independent of the US. The United States refrained from contributing to the bilateral aid effort for Thailand, lending support to Sakakibara's personal preference to set up a regional institution absent the United States." (Amyx 2002).

put forward the AMF proposal at the meeting held in Tokyo on August 11, 1997, at which the rescue package for Thailand was agreed upon. The AMF plan comprised the following components[14]:

(i) The IMF surveillance mechanism will be supplemented by local surveillance by the AMF in the region;

(ii) In accordance with the IMF economic adjustment program, participants of the AMF will be engaged in financial support of troubled countries in the region; and

(iii) A permanent secretariat.

The AMF proposal intended to set up a regional backstop starting at USD 100 billion, almost equivalent to the sum of all rescue packages during the AFC (Table 26.2). This would be achieved by pooling East Asian countries' foreign exchange reserves in a fund to deter currency speculation and to mobilize resources during crises. This was a logical solution to address the IMF's lending problems, such as resource adequacy and timely activation. An ad hoc arrangement of bilateral financing, such as the one for Thailand, would take time to coordinate.

In mid-September 1997, prospective members of the AMF included Australia, China, Hong Kong, Indonesia, Japan, Korea, Malaysia, the Philippines, Singapore, and Thailand. The US was excluded because it had chosen not to contribute to the second line of defense for Thailand.[15] While Japan, Korea, and most ASEAN countries supported the proposal at the formal preparation meeting,[16] China[17] and Australia maintained a neutral position, making general comments without indicating support or opposition.

The US[18] and the IMF were against the proposal, citing a moral hazard problem and the redundancy of the proposed AMF's role vis-à-vis the

---

[14]Hamada (1999).

[15]Amyx (2002).

[16]It was convened between 10 prospective members and the United States, and the IMF as the observer on the occasion of the IMF–World Bank annual meetings in Hong Kong from September 20–25, 1997.

[17]Agence France-Press, "China Cautious on Proposed Asian Monetary Fund," November 18, 1997, quote from a government official: "The parties concerned have yet to conduct studies on this issue." Another view was that China was concerned about the role played by Japan in the region which could sidestep China's position. As China was seeking a membership of the World Trade Organization (WTO), they did not want to go against the US stance (See note 15).

[18]It is reported that after obtaining the unofficial AMF outline paper, the US intended to participate in forming an "Asia Pacific Cooperative Framework" for crisis resolution by sending out a letter signed by then Treasury Secretary Robert Rubin and Federal Reserve Chairman Alan Greenspan to all Asia-Pacific Economic Cooperation finance ministers.

IMF.[19] They, as well as many European countries, suspected an AMF would attach softer conditionality to crisis financing. In their view, it would simply promote moral hazards, provide "easy money," and divide creditors. Then US Treasury Secretary Lawrence Summers and Under Secretary Timothy Geithner argued that overlapping mandates would, in turn, undermine the IMF's central role in the global financial system, in the process framing the discussion as an AMF versus IMF tussle.

This dissenting argument was partly overblown. An AMF would not trespass on the IMF's key function since it would be "in accordance with the IMF economic adjustment program." It was also premature to discuss the moral hazard issue in the heat of the crisis, which could be resolved by formulating a framework in which an AMF would complement the IMF. Regional arrangements in Latin America[20] and Arab[21] states had already co-existed alongside the IMF since the late 1970s. Nonetheless, the detailed criteria an AMF would apply when making a decision for financing and policy adjustments were still unknown.

Part of the reason for the AMF proposal not being accepted was that it came at the wrong time, with insufficient lead time for background work and preparation.[22] The IMF was already arranging and implementing the rescue package for Thailand when this proposal was announced. As a result, there was insufficient time for informal discussions and lobbying of key stakeholders.[23]

Meanwhile, some people held the view that the unspoken motivation for the objection to an AMF was that the US and the IMF were deeply concerned about their possibly diminished roles in Asia following its creation.[24] In fact, the US did not oppose the creation of an AMF itself, but challenged the idea of an AMF without US membership. The US did not favor a framework

---

[19] It is reported that Stanley Fischer, the First Deputy Managing Director of the IMF, said the proposed AMF could undermine the authority and effectiveness of the IMF itself (See note 15).

[20] The Latin American Reserve Fund was first established in 1978, comprising Bolivia, Colombia, Costa Rica, Ecuador, Paraguay, Peru, Uruguay, and Venezuela to provide balance of payments support, grant loans, or guarantee loans from third parties.

[21] The Arab Monetary Fund was founded by Arab states in 1976 in context of the 1970s' oil price boom. It was initially established to provide low-interest loans to less prosperous Arab countries experiencing balance of payments problems.

[22] Sussangkarn (2010).

[23] Mr Eisuke Sakakibara recalled in an interview that "in retrospect, Japan lacked contacts with top Beijing officials. We asked their counterparts in Hong Kong to connect us with them so that we could explain our intention but it did not work." (June 22, 2017, Nikkei Asian Review).

[24] See note 15.

that sought an East Asian model of economic and financial management on the ground that it might go against the then existing global framework, particularly from a financial liberalization agenda standpoint.[25]

The rise and fall of the AMF proposal made it clear that a regional arrangement could be successfully launched with more solid and unified support of members under collaborative capabilities. Nevertheless, the AMF proposal had set the approach for expanding a regional self-help mechanism, which was elaborated on further in the MFG and then the New Miyazawa Initiative, which eventually led to the CMI's creation.

Manila Framework Group — A More Inclusive Framework

Once the AMF proposal failed to take flight owing to the US' opposition, the US had to reinforce its engagement with East Asia to maintain its status and regional clout. The US proposed an alternative arrangement called the MFG. The MFG was established in Manila, the Philippines, on November 25, 1997, at a meeting convened immediately after the Asia-Pacific Economic Cooperation (APEC) Leaders' Meetings. It was a forum for deputies from finance ministries and central banks of 14 APEC economies, comprising the contributors to the Indonesian rescue package. It therefore included the US and Canada, which was the APEC Chair at that time.[26] The meeting also included international financial institutions (IFIs) such as the IMF, World Bank, ADB, and the Bank for International Settlements.

The MFG did not suggest creating a regional pool of funds under a permanent secretariat. Instead, it sought a mechanism for regional surveillance to complement the IMF's global surveillance.[27] Since the IMF played the role of a loose secretariat for surveillance purposes, its surveillance and crisis financing practices were to be followed. Regional participants, meanwhile, felt they were regularly scrutinized by the IMF and the US [28]

As the AFC eased and then passed and economic recovery and structural adjustment progressed, members' interest in the MFG waned. In 2000, the group stopped releasing a joint statement at the conclusion of

---

[25]Bergsten (1998). He was a close aide to the Clinton Administration and Head of the Institute for International Economics (IIE) in Washington. Lee (2006).

[26]The participants to the MFG were Australia, Canada, New Zealand, the US, Brunei, China, Hong Kong, Indonesia, Japan, Korea, Malaysia, the Philippines, Singapore, and Thailand (14 economies).

[27]Official summary of the discussion at the inaugural meeting in Manila, November 1997. (https://www.mof. go.jp/english/international_policy/financial_cooperation_in_asia/manila_framework/if000a.htm)

[28]Wang and Woo (2004).

its semi-annual meetings. At its final meeting in November 2004, members decided to discontinue the MFG after noting that its objective was largely achieved. At around that time, crisis-hit economies under IMF bailout packages emerged successfully out of the crisis and from relevant IMF programs.

New Miyazawa Initiative and Changed Circumstances

In 1998, global policymakers also noticed the financial crisis had extended beyond East Asia to Russia and Brazil. The US had to shift its focus to international financial stability, which assumed greater priority than concerns relating to the Washington Consensus. In October 1998, financial authorities from the Group of Seven (G7) countries held the first meeting of the Financial Stability Forum.[29] The authorities clearly recognized the need to make the international financial system less vulnerable by strengthening regulatory and supervisory measures for highly leveraged hedge funds, offshore markets, and short-term capital flows.

Under the changed circumstances, Japan reaffirmed its active position and decided to provide further support to crisis-hit economies.[30] On October 3, 1998, it announced the New Miyazawa Initiative at the meeting of finance ministers and central bank governors attended by Indonesia, Malaysia, the Philippines, Korea, and Thailand. This initiative included a financial support package totaling USD 30 billion, named after Japan's then Finance Minister Kiichi Miyazawa. By mid-1998, US officials had also begun to better appreciate Japan's efforts in stabilizing East Asia.[31] This was illustrated by the US–Japan joint announcement to establish the Asian Growth and Recovery Initiative in collaboration with the World Bank and ADB in November 1998.[32]

By the end of 1998, most affected countries had emerged out of a severe crisis situation. However, there was still a paucity of funds, because of which

---

[29] The Financial Stability Forum (FSF) under G7 was first convened in April 1999 in Washington, D.C., consisting of major financial authorities. After the GFC, the Financial Stability Board (FSB) was established in April 2009 under the Group of Twenty (G20), as the successor to the FSF with an expanded membership and broadened mandate. Since then, the FSB has assumed a key role in promoting the reform of international financial regulation and supervision.

[30] Katada (2001).

[31] Kikuchi (2002). The announcement sought to quickly restore economic growth by restructuring regional corporations and banks, and mobilizing private sector funding. This effort also resulted in the establishment of the Asian Currency Crisis Support Facility, which was housed within the ADB and was funded by Japan, drawing funds from the New Miyazawa Initiative.

[32] "Asian Growth and Recovery Initiative," accessed on December 27, 2020, https://japan.kantei.go.jp/e1e055.html.

Table 26.3: Path Toward the CMI

Date	Main Developments
Jul 1997	• Thailand devalued the baht and requested assistance from the IMF. • Malaysia intervened to defend the ringgit. • The Philippine peso was floated.
Aug 1997	• Thailand agreed to the IMF program with tough economic measures, including a second line of defense (without the United States). • Indonesia's rupiah plunged. • Japan proposed an "Asian Monetary Fund (AMF)."
Sep 1997	• A formal preparatory meeting for AMF was convened, but did not reach consensus.
Oct 1997	• Indonesia asked the IMF for emergency liquidity support. • Korean's won began to weaken.
Nov 1997	• Manila Framework Group was established (discontinued from 2004). • IMF approved a rescue package for Indonesia, including a second line of defense (including the United States). • Korea requested IMF aid.
Dec 1997	• IMF approved a bailout package for Korea, including a second line of defense (including the United States), the largest in history. • First ASEAN+3 Summit was held in Malaysia.
Oct 1998	• Japan announced the New Miyazawa Initiative.
May 1999	• First ASEAN+3 Finance Ministers' Meeting (AFMM+3) was held, aiming to create a regional emergency financing facility.
Nov 1999	• Third ASEAN+3 Summit formally initiated the ASEAN+3 financial cooperation, seeking to enhance self-help mechanism in East Asia.
May 2000	• ASEAN+3 finance ministers launched the CMI.

ASEAN = Association of Southeast Asian Nations, CMI = Chiang Mai Initiative, IMF = International Monetary Fund.

they were unable to forge ahead with economic development initiatives or tide over prevailing economic woes. Half the funds under the New Miyazawa Initiative were made available for medium- to long-term financial assistance for capital investment needs. The other half was set aside to provide short-term financial support, if required, when countries were in the process of implementing economic reform.[33] In particular, this took the form of bilateral currency swap arrangements — the Japan–Korea swap for USD 5.0 billion and Japan–Malaysia swap for USD 2.5 billion.

---

[33] Along with the New Miyazawa Initiative, Japan provided USD 3 billion for the establishment of the Currency Crisis Support Facility at the ADB for guarantees and interest subsidies. Additionally, in December 1998, Japan announced a Special Yen Loan Facility, totalling approximately USD 5 billion, as assistance for economic structural reform. "Official Development Assistance (ODA)," Ministry of Foreign Affairs, Japan, https://www.mofa.go.jp/policy/oda/summary/1999/ov2_2_01.html#chart_19.

This currency swap represented a shift from simply providing liquidity assistance during a crisis on an ad hoc basis to establishing a permanent swap network for future crises. While this was not a separate fund like the AMF proposal, the Miyazawa swap network was another step toward a permanent regional financing arrangement (RFA) — a key component of the CMI.[34] The requirements for receiving funds from the New Miyazawa Initiative were simply commitments to economic reform, taking into account the situation in each country. This was in contrast to the intrusive, meticulous conditionality of IMF programs.

Path Toward the CMI

Various ideas and regional initiatives were seen from the time the AFC broke out in 1997 until the CMI emerged in 2000. Some were successful while others were not. For instance, bilateral financing came to the fore in a more structured way. It offered a practical means of emergency financing that supplemented IMF lending. However, the idea of a separate Asian fund failed. To meet large-scale emergency financing needs, bilateral financing was provided on an ad hoc basis as a second line of defense. Such financing was used for Thailand in August 1997 and employed again by the Manila Framework for a cooperative financing arrangement that would supplement IMF resources. This was transformed into two pre-arranged currency swap lines under the New Miyazawa Initiative. The next step was the expansion of these initiatives with more regional partners under the CMI, which was launched since May 2000.

Regional and global policymakers began to share a common understanding of the causes of the AFC and how it should have been addressed.[35] Global policymakers gradually embraced the concerns of East Asia that rapid and upsized liquidity support was essential to fend off capital account crises since the IMF could not manage these on its own. There was a strong need for reform in international financial regulation and supervision given the scale of the crisis, which also engulfed Russia and Brazil. At the global level, reforms for crisis prevention, response, and resolution were proposed and

---

[34]The currency swaps under the New Miyazawa Initiative were the predecessor of CMI, a network of bilateral swaps. In countries that already had IMF programs in place, the Miyazawa swap lines complemented IMF lending. They were extended to Malaysia, Vietnam, and Myanmar, where IMF programs were not in place. Malaysia, having rejected IMF support and imposed capital controls in September 1998, welcomed the swap lines as they could be disbursed quickly without any linkages to IMF conditionality. In Malaysia's case, the initiative actually substituted IMF lending, rather than supplement it.

[35]Grimes (2009).

put in place. They focused on managing the forces of financial globalization, particularly in a world of rapid short-term capital flows. The IMF had consistently increased its lending capacity through quota reforms and borrowing schemes, although it was yet to reach an optimal level.[36] At the same time, there was growing awareness in East Asia that large-scale liquidity support on a short-term basis alone would be insufficient to avert a crisis and that, to a certain extent, policy adjustments, such as financial sector reforms, though painful, are necessary to address domestic weaknesses.

CMI Under the ASEAN+3 Process

ASEAN+3 Financial Cooperation Process

A regional concept based on East Asia was originally put forward by Malaysia's then Prime Minister Mahathir Mohamad. This was around the same time the APEC was established in 1989. The East Asian Economic Caucus (EAEC) was meant to comprise East Asian countries — ASEAN countries, China, Japan, and Korea — but was not realized in the early 1990s. It was reported that the US and Australia quickly opposed the EAEC because they were excluded from the new grouping.[37] On the occasion of the APEC Osaka meeting in 1995, the Thai government hosted an informal meeting among ASEAN+3 leaders, a similar grouping to the EAEC, in preparation for the prospective Asia–Europe Meeting (ASEM), whose first summit was held in Bangkok in March 1996. In March 1996, heads of ASEAN+3 met on the occasion of ASEM Summit, now regarded as the start of ASEAN+3 regional cooperation. They decided to meet again at the ASEAN Summit in December 1997. This was the first time that only East Asian leaders — that is, leaders from the ASEAN+3 — had gathered in one place.

It was in the backdrop of the AFC that the first ASEAN+3[38] summit was held in Malaysia in December 1997. The countries discussed regional financial cooperation, but there was no significant outcome. Since the AMF proposal was unsuccessful in September 1997 and the MFG became the main

---

[36]The IMF introduced a standing borrowing arrangement with official lenders called the New Arrangements to Borrow, effective November 1998, and the General Arrangements to Borrow.

[37]Terada (2003), Yoshida (2004).

[38]Nine ASEAN member countries plus China, Japan, and Korea. Cambodia joined ASEAN only on April 30, 1999.

forum for crisis management, there was no further initiative taken during that first summit. Momentum in favor of an RFA gathered again at the second ASEAN+3 summit held in Hanoi, Vietnam in December 1998. In the context of changed circumstances in the US and global concerns around financial stability, the importance of the New Miyazawa Initiative was reaffirmed at this meeting. The idea of a separate regional fund was re-bundled into a form of pre-arranged swap lines while reflecting the MFG process. China proposed that deputies from ASEAN+3 finance ministries and central banks meet on a regular basis to explore possibilities for regional financial cooperation.[39]

Subsequently, the first ASEAN+3 Finance Deputies' Meeting (AFDM+3) was held in March 1999. This meeting led to the first ASEAN+3 Finance Ministers Meeting (AFMM+3) held immediately on the occasion of the ADB annual meeting in Manila, the Philippines in May 1999. It set three core goals: strengthening regional bond markets, promoting monetary policy cooperation, and creating an emergency financing facility. CMI emerged from these goals. At the third ASEAN+3 Summit held in November 1999 in Manila, ASEAN+3 leaders formally initiated the ASEAN+3 financial cooperation process. The leaders sought to enhance self-help and support mechanisms in East Asia through the ASEAN+3 Framework in the areas of monetary and financial cooperation.

The CMI

In May 2000, the ASEAN+3 finance ministers launched the CMI, which defined the scope of financial cooperation within ASEAN+3. The CMI was a solution proposed to meet the need for large and timely financing, if required, to address short-term liquidity difficulties in the region and supplement existing international facilities (such as IMF lending), comprising two components: (i) expanding and enhancing the ASEAN Swap Arrangement (ASA) and (ii) establishing a network of bilateral swap arrangements (BSAs).[40]

This initiative was cautiously welcomed by the US and the IMF.[41] Randall Henning, a professor of international economic relations at the American University in the US, documented that the US Department of

[39] Henning (2002).

[40] The Joint Ministerial Statement of the ASEAN+3 Finance Ministers Meeting, May 6, 2000, Chiang Mai, Thailand.

[41] See note 1; "U.S., IMF Cautiously Welcome Asia Currency Swap Plan," Dow Jones International News, May 8, 2000.

Treasury, which chiefly blocked the AMF proposal, remained aloof and cautious about the CMI in early 2000. Then Assistant Secretary for international affairs, Edwin M. Truman, who represented the US at the ADB annual meeting in May 2000, said the CMI as a regional initiative would be "perfectly appropriate." He said "the devil is in the details" and "if they are supportive of prompt financing and economic adjustments, then I think they are to be commended." An IMF representative welcomed the CMI as well, noting it was intended to work with the IMF.[42]

Expanded ASA

The ASA dates back to 1977 when it was established by the five original ASEAN members (Indonesia, Malaysia, the Philippines, Singapore, and Thailand), serving as a symbol of ASEAN solidarity. The ASA is a reciprocal currency swap arrangement to "provide short-term foreign exchange liquidity support for member countries that experience balance of payment difficulties." This is accomplished by exchanging local currency with US dollars, similar to the CMI. At the initial stage, each member was equally committed to contributing USD 20 million toward a total amount of USD 100 million in 1977. The contribution amount was increased to USD 40 million per country in 1978, taking the total to USD 200 million.

Table 26.4: ASEAN Members' Contribution to the ASA Since 2005

Participating Members	Commitment Amount (USD million)	Proportion of Total Commitment (Percent)
Indonesia, Malaysia, the Philippines, Singapore, Thailand, Brunei	300	15.0
Vietnam	120	6.0
Myanmar	40	2.0
Cambodia	30	1.5
Lao PDR	10	0.5
Total	2000	100.0

ASA = ASEAN Swap Arrangement, ASEAN = Association of Southeast Asian Nations, Lao PDR = Lao People's Democratic Republic, USD = United States dollar.
Source: Association of Southeast Asian Nations Documents Series 2005, found at www.asean.org.

During the AFC, the ASA — of USD 200 million — was too small to address financing needs. This amount increased to USD 1.0 billion in November 2000 and to USD 2.0 billion in May 2005 but was still far smaller

---

[42]See note 39.

than the size of Thailand's rescue package (USD 17.2 billion). These concerns led ASEAN economies to turn to an expanded regional financial cooperation under the CMI with the so-called "Plus Three Countries," comprising China, Japan, and Korea.

Network of BSAs Under the CMI

The finance ministers of the ASEAN+3 launched a regional network of BSAs, which formed the core of the CMI, in Chiang Mai, Thailand in May 2000. The BSA network was taken as a "functional equivalent" of the original AMF idea in terms of providing large-scale financing in a timely manner.[43] The modality of bilateral financing by swaps was an extended form of the New Miyazawa Initiative. The CMI affirmed the central role of the IMF in crisis management following the MFG discussion, which was reflected in BSA objectives and the existence of the IMF-linked portion. IMF centrality implicitly indicated the IMF would take the lead and decide on the macroeconomic framework and policies. Regional and bilateral donors, meanwhile, would contribute to the scheme.

CMI BSA Objectives and Participants

The objective of CMI BSAs was twofold. The swap arrangement would (i) provide "short-term liquidity support" as a self-help mechanism in the form of swaps to a member in need of balance of payments or short-term liquidity support[44] and/or (ii) supplement existing international facilities such as those provided by the IMF and the ASA.

The first objective assumed the occurrence of a liquidity crisis — one that was mainly brought about by contagion risks and was less connected with macroeconomic mismanagement. As foreign capital would be rapidly exiting the country, it would need a quick short-term liquidity injection. Theoretically, this "innocent bystander" would, therefore, not need rigorous policy adjustments and conditionality. Meanwhile, the assumption for the second objective was that something could go wrong with macroeconomic policy. In such an event, BSA donors would rely on an IMF-supported

---

[43] Krauss and Pempel (2000).

[44] ASEAN countries strongly argued that providing "short-term liquidity support" should be included in the CMI's objectives during the discussion after May 2000, in addition to the objective of "supplementing the IMF."

program to adjust the recipient's policy in a more desirable way. The objectives of CMI were later relayed without change to the CMIM created in 2010 onward.

The BSA participants were the five original members of ASEAN — Indonesia, Malaysia, the Philippines, Singapore, and Thailand — and China, Japan, and Korea. The five newer members of ASEAN — Brunei, Cambodia, Lao People's Democratic Republic (Lao PDR), Myanmar, and Vietnam — did not participate in the CMI on the ground that the possibility of so-called "capital account crises" was low for them. This was because these economies were still not deeply integrated with global markets, and so there were less pull factors for short-term capital flows in the early 2000s. Thus, concessional lending by other IFIs was more appropriate for most of them at the time.[45]

Financing Design and Size

Contracting parties to the BSAs enjoyed flexibility in designing each individual swap according to specific needs. Unlike ordinary BSAs among central banks, ASEAN+3 had developed rules and procedures to govern BSAs for a collective influence from the start. These included conditions for BSA activations, linkages to the IMF program, and maturity and interest rates. These were gradually modified and finalized at the meeting in Hyderabad, India in 2006.[46] This half-baked collective nature was later addressed by consolidating BSAs into a single agreement, the CMIM, in 2010.

Most CMI participants opted for a BSA (currency swap) between the US dollar and their local currencies, or between local currencies,[47] governed bilaterally by swap donors and recipients.

The total size of BSAs stood at USD 36.5 billion in May 2004 and increased to USD 84 billion by the end of 2007. This amount was over twice

---

[45] All those nonparticipants to CMI BSAs have participated in the CMIM since 2010.

[46] The Joint Ministerial Statement of the 9th ASEAN+3 Finance Ministers' Meeting, held on May 4, 2006 in Hyderabad, India.

[47] Available types of financing arrangement included a repurchase agreement of US Treasury securities and repurchase agreement of sovereign securities denominated in local currency. Under repos, one party sells eligible securities for cash to a counterparty with the understanding that the securities will be repurchased in future. Since the transaction is a security-for-cash deal, it takes the nature of a loan with the security providing the collateral. Similar to the BSA, the repos were to be concluded by two parties as a bilateral arrangement. However, unlike currency swap for US dollars, it is unknown how many repos were arranged and what terms and conditions were under the CMI. The CMI participants focused their discussion on BSAs to provide US dollar liquidity support.

Table 26.5: Network of BSAs Under the CMI as of November 2007 (USD billion)

Donor \ Recipient	China	Japan	Korea	Indonesia	Malaysia	Philippines	Thailand	Singapore	Committed Amount
China		RMB/JPY (3.0)	RMB/KRW (4.0)	4.0/IDR	1.5/MYR	RMB/PHP (2.0)	2.0/THB	...	16.5
Japan	JPY/RMB (3.0)		10.0/KRW; JPY/KRW (3.0)	6.0/IDR	1.0/MYR	6.0/PHP	6.0/THB	3.0/SGD	38.0
Korea	KRW/RMB (4.0)	5.0/JPY; KRW/JPY (3.0)		2.0/IDR	1.5/MYR	2.0/PHP	1.0/THB	...	18.5
Indonesia	...	...	2.0/KRW						2.0
Malaysia	...	...	1.5/KRW	...					1.5
Philippines	...	0.5/JPY	2.0/KRW	...	...				2.5
Thailand	...	3.0/JPY	1.0/KRW	–	–	–			4.0
Singapore	...	1.0/JPY	...	...		...	...		1.0
Receivable Amount	7.0	15.5	23.5	12.0	4.0	10.0	9.0	3.0	84.0
IMF SBA 1997[1]	4.6	11.2	1.1	2.1	1.1	0.9	0.8	0.5	22.2
IMF SBA 2009[2]	12.1	19.9	4.4	2.2	2.2	1.3	1.6	1.3	45.0

BSA = bilateral swap arrangement, CMI = Chiang Mai Initiative, IDR = Indonesian rupiah, IMF = International Monetary Fund, JPY = Japanese yen, KRW = Korean won, MYR = Malaysian ringgit, PHP = Philippine peso, RMB = renminbi, SBA = Stand-By Arrangement, SGD = Singapore dollar, THB = Thai baht, USD = United States dollar.

Notes:

[1] SDR = USD 1.357710 as of December 1, 1997 IMF Stand-By Arrangement, annual access limit: 100 of quota.

[2] SDR = USD 1.49192 as of January 30, 2009 IMF Stand-By Arrangement, annual access limit: 100 of quota, after quota reform in 2008.

Sources: Reports from ASEAN+3 Financial Cooperation Meetings.

what the IMF disbursed during the AFC and comparable to the proposed size of an AMF. In this network of swaps, the countries in crisis could borrow (purchase) pre-determined amounts of their counterparts' US dollar reserves for 90 days. This was renewable seven times for up to two years with government guarantees. These maturity and renewable times were adopted by the original CMIM in 2010 without change.

The initial drawdown and the first renewal after 90 days of maturity were set at 150 basis points (bps) over the London Interbank Offered Rate (LIBOR). Subsequently, a time-based rate was charged at additional renewals, specifically 50 bps for two renewals, capped at 300 bps. The swaps were not cheap, compared to ASA (LIBOR+25 bps). But it was accepted as reasonable at that time because it was meant to be a type of countercyclical financing. The applied charges from the IMF started from around 8.82% from the first tranche of the IMF loans during the AFC.[48] These rates were applied to the original CMIM in 2010.

Timely Activation and Collective Nature

At the initial stage, activating the BSAs was entrusted to purely bilateral action. This gave rise to concerns over procedural delays in activation. Moreover, there was no guarantee that BSAs would be activated simultaneously by all donors as any providing country would be able to turn down the swap request or demand different terms and conditions. In response, the ASEAN+3 adopted a coordination mechanism in 2006, under which two coordinating countries would be appointed — one each from each of ASEAN and the Plus Three members on a rotation basis — and be in charge of administration and coordination.[49] A collective decision-making mechanism was also introduced in 2006. If consensus was not reached in two weeks, the next step was to make a decision by weighted voting rights within four weeks, allocated on a pro rata basis for swap providers. But it was not legally enforceable so that each party to BSAs could move ahead to lend, back out, or not lend, irrespective of the outcome of the collective decision-making process.

---

[48] Borrowing cost is calculated from IMF policy as of 1997, comprising 5.32% of basic rate (SDR interest rate 1997 4.32% + 1.00%), 3.00% of surcharge, and 0.50% of service charge. The IMF traditional surcharge policy was to encourage early repayment once borrowers regain access to private capital markets and to mitigate the risks to the IMF financing resources, associated with policy adjustment programs.

[49] The role of two coordinating countries was equivalent to the agent bank in the ASA.

ASEAN+3 introduced an opt-out clause while adopting the above-mentioned collective decision-making procedure. A member could choose to either provide a partial contribution or opt out due to exceptional financial circumstances, such as difficulties in maintaining balance of payments or insufficient safeguard measures. If so, the shortfall would be met by the remaining donors, subject to their maximum committed amount. These activation procedures have been generally reflected in the CMIM since 2010.

IMF Linkage and Surveillance

The CMI introduced an IMF linkage as a condition for full access to individual bilateral swaps. This might seem at odds with the stigma associated with borrowing from the IMF. However, one of the two CMI objectives was to supplement IMF lending.[50] Second, there was growing understanding that the IMF had evolved ever since the AFC — enhancing financial market surveillance, adjusting quotas, and starting to review conditionality policy and lending facilities to reduce the stigma effect. Third, it was more realistic for potential swap donors to rely on the IMF's conditionality to address potential concerns over moral hazard and to ensure repayment capacity in terms of their domestic accountability to taxpayers in each country. Indeed, a regional surveillance process, called the Economic Review and Policy Dialogue (ERPD), was launched in May 2000. However, this was rather a forum for information sharing and peer pressure and not mature enough to conduct due diligence for recommending policies and monitoring the correction process. Lastly, the value of local currencies, swapped for US dollar liquidity support as quasi-collateral, was low, particularly because they would depreciate in crisis time and some local currencies were partly nonconvertible.

That said, CMI participants were faced with a contentious issue — the degree of linkage with the IMF. Potential donors insisted that swap arrangements be closely linked to IMF programs, while ASEAN countries preferred either weak linkages or none at all.[51] In April 2001, they agreed

---

[50]Unlike the AMF proposal, then IMF Managing Director Horst Köhler, at his opening remarks at the Japan National Press Club in Tokyo, Japan in January 2001, openly supported the CMI on the condition that it remained complementary to the IMF's financial assistance that would help undertake adjustment efforts (accessed on January 30, 2021, https://www.imf.org/en/News/Articles/2015/09/28/04/53/sp011201).

[51]Back in 1997, Malaysia chose to avoid an IMF program in the aftermath of the crisis and was therefore not happy with the IMF being introduced for the CMI.

the swap requesting party could immediately obtain short-term liquidity support for the first 10% of each BSA.[52] The so-called IMF de-linked portion was increased to 20% in May 2005.[53] This increase came together with the enhanced regional surveillance framework. The ERPD, the regional surveillance framework, was formally integrated into the CMI in anticipation of being utilized for actual operation of the CMI in 2005. This indicated that ASEAN+3 could go further to intensify the CMI's role in its sole operation by enhancing the CMI's surveillance function. The CMI created the institutional basis for regional financial cooperation on a solid basis, which could be further developed by its own efforts.[54]

Conditions for Lending

Following the IMF linkage, swap donors would assess the economic and financial situation of a recipient and judge whether there was a reasonable prospect that an IMF program be established in the very near future, or if there would be no need for one. If the source of the liquidity problem was deeply associated with structural issues that would justify policy adjustments, swap donors could borrow credibility from the IMF. For judgment on the IMF de-linked portion, a surveillance process kicked in following the integration of the ERPD into the CMI process in 2005. A swap recipient was required to have "undertaken the implementation of sound economic measures to counter unusual downward pressure on foreign reserves" and "hold and maintain access to private market financing."

Assessment and the Path Toward the CMIM

Establishing the CMI by bilateral swaps was less burdensome than creating a monetary fund under a treaty. Participating central banks did not need

---

[52] It was reported that at the first discussion, China insisted the CMI be 100% linked to IMF programs without the IMF de-linked portion. ASEAN countries preferred no linkage to the IMF. Malaysia was particularly upset by the introduction of the IMF linkage at this stage since it did not go for an IMF program during the Asian crisis. Under pressure from then Malaysian Prime Minister Mahathir Mohamad and other prospective borrowers, it was agreed that participants could borrow 10% of funds from CMI BSAs without an IMF program for up to six months (Bergsten and Park 2002).

[53] It was reported that ASEAN countries, including Thailand and Malaysia, wanted the IMF de-linked portion to be increased to 50%.

[54] Nemoto Yoichi, the former ASEAN+3 Macroeconomic Research Office Director during 2012–2016, argued that "the pursuit of economic surveillance and policy dialogue might lead the ASEAN+3 authorities to construct tailored conditionality distinct from what the IMF critics called one-size-fits-all conditionality" (2003).

legislative ratification to establish swaps with each other. It was inexpensive to maintain swaps because central banks keep reserves on hand, without transferring a portion of reserves. There were many precedents for swaps — for example, the ASA — which made them less problematic to potential objectors inside or outside the region. The US alone has entered into over 115 swaps between the creation of the Exchange Stabilization Fund in 1934 and 1995.[55] The CMI was an outcome of a process of trial and error and that might have brought about a degree of imperfection. No CMI swap was ever activated. CMI participants lacked confidence in it and continued to stockpile foreign exchange reserves to self-insure themselves.

There were a few reasons for this. First, the CMI lacked financing certainty as it was only a stand-by, unfunded arrangement. Each swap donor had full discretion over whether or not to release liquidity. Second, each swap was just a bilateral contract between two authorities. To mobilize funds during crises, a swap requesting party had to be involved in time-consuming negotiations with multiple counterparties. A coordination process and collective decision-making was adopted in 2006. However, as these were not legally mandated to be reflected in individual swap arrangements, it was not sufficient to ensure timely liquidity support in crisis time. The need for a rule-based activation process was even more pertinent when there were multiple requests for funding as the crisis could be contagious. Third, an IMF program was required to be in place to access the full swap quota in the CMI BSAs; the issue of IMF stigma made members reluctant to go into CMI BSAs linked to an IMF-supported program.

The CMIM

Over the past decade, the CMIM, which provides insurance against financial shocks and contagion effects and supplies rapid and large-scale emergency financing in case of crises, has been a key component of the ASEAN+3 finance process. The CMIM is an incremental advancement on the pre-existing network of bilateral swaps of the CMI but not a full-fledged monetary fund, as the term "multilateralisation" in its name denotes.

---

[55]See note 39.

Changed Circumstances in 2005

ASEAN+3 members first announced the CMIM process in May 2005 while confirming to increase the IMF de-linked portion of BSAs from 10% to 20%. This was a regional collective voice that requested the IMF to undertake more reforms, particularly in terms of its governance structure for relatively fair representation of the AEAN+3 economies.[56]

"We called for an urgent review of the quota of the Asian countries in the IMF to properly reflect the current realities and their relative positions in the world economy. This would strengthen the mutual understanding between Asia and the IFIs."[57] (Joint Ministerial Statement of the AFMM+3, 2005, Istanbul, Turkey)

It is true that representation is not just about voting power, but it is also related to the persuasiveness of arguments.[58] Despite it, formal voting procedures have had a key influence over decision-making in the IMF because power relationships are determined by relative voting strength. The intent for the CMIM process itself might have fueled some skeptics' concerns in the IMF. However, those concerns were alleviated by the fact that the CMIM process would be incremental, the CMIM would keep the IMF linkage, and the IMF regularly participates in the biannual ASEAN+3 deputies' meetings, which would continue.[59] Back then, Indonesia, Thailand, and Korea had just emerged out of IMF programs, harboring IMF stigma. These countries, along with other neighbors, fully supported the CMIM process. By 2005, though, China had become one of the world's largest foreign exchange reserve holders and an increasingly key player in the ASEAN+3 region, which incentivized it to invest more in regional cooperation to help avert a regional crisis.

---

[56] Decisions in the IMF are taken either as consensus or with special voting majorities (usually 85%). Back in 2005, while the US and Europe as a bloc possessed a veto over decisions requiring 85% majority, the ASEAN+3 region did not have such a veto with 13% of the total voting powers. Since the 14th quota review took effective on January 26, 2016, the share of ASEAN+3 voting powers in the IMF has reached 18.15% and thus the ASEAN+3 economies have acquired veto power collectively.

[57] Japan's Finance Minister, Mr. Sadakazu Tanigaki, already requested for fairer representation of East Asian countries in the IMF quota at the 11th meeting of the International Monetary and Financial Committee (IMFC) held on April 16, 2005. This statement was conveyed to the Joint Ministerial Statement of the AFMM+3 in 2005 (https://warp.ndl.go.jp/info:ndljp/pid/11194366/www.mof.go.jp/english/international_policy/imf/imfc/20050416st.htm).

[58] Fischer (2001).

[59] Ciorciari (2011).

Lessons from the GFC

The global financial crisis (GFC) reminded the ASEAN+3 economies of contagion risk problems. It also highlighted that even countries with strong economic fundamentals could face short-term liquidity pressures stemming from unanticipated events outside of their control. Domestic policy options were largely insufficient and inefficient in the face of massive volatility of capital flows and an additional buffer for liquidity supply was needed.[60]

But the CMI was not tapped. Experts noted there were inherent weaknesses in the CMI's institutional setting.[61] Besides, the total size of BSAs reached only USD 84 billion at the end of 2007. While the sum would have been sufficient to cover the IMF's financing portion in tackling the AFC, it would have been insufficient in addressing the impacts of the GFC. This raised concerns over the CMI in preventing a speculative attack and calming market nervousness. Then Thai Finance Minister Chalongphob Sussangkarn described the CMI as "more symbolic than truly effective."[62] It was the USD 30 billion bilateral currency swap arrangement with the US Federal Reserve in October 2008 that had an immediate, stabilizing effect on the financial markets in Korea.[63] Singapore also established a swap line of USD 30 billion with the US Federal Reserve to relieve pressures in global funding markets in October 2008.[64]

A More Effective Regional Liquidity Mechanism

When the CMI was launched in 2000, ASEAN+3 members recognized that a network of CMI bilateral swaps was a very loose form of crisis financing.

---

[60] In 2008, Korea was in a better position to weather financial distress as compared to the position before the AFC, supported by ample foreign reserves, improved policy frameworks, and limited exposure to "toxic assets" such as mortgage-backed securities originating in advanced economies. However, given its trade and financial integration with the rest of the world, market confidence in Korea deteriorated severely, investors began to repatriate funds from Korea in a "flight to quality" as global deleveraging intensified, and global economic growth slowed. By November 2008, the Bank of Korea had lost large amounts of reserves, the Korean won had depreciated rapidly, and the stock market had collapsed.

[61] Kawai (2015).

[62] Sussangkarn (2010).

[63] Korea also entered into bilateral swaps with the Bank of Japan and the People's Bank of China in December 2008. In 2009, the low won helped export recovery and reserve accumulation and the Korean won began to restore its value gradually in 2009 (see note 61).

[64] However, Indonesia failed to get a similar swap from the US and turned to bilateral swaps with China and Japan. The experience of Indonesia made it clear that the Fed swap would not be always available, particularly to developing economies (Sussangkarn and Chalongphob 2011).

In response, individual BSAs of the CMI were consolidated into a single arrangement by multilateralisation in 2010. Since then, members have been collectively committed to providing emergency financing and its certainty has improved. Second, a weighted voting system and a coordination process have been institutionalized for efficient activation. Third, the initial CMIM's size was set at USD 120 billion in 2010, which was increased to USD 240 billion in 2014. ASEAN+3 has continuously increased the IMF de-linked portion from the initial 20% to 30% of each member's swap quota in 2014 and to 40% in March 2021.

Through the CMIM process, ASEAN+3 members created an institutional basis for regional cooperation in a more concrete way, which can be further developed by its own efforts. In particular, the CMIM has brought about a permanent regional institution for regional surveillance in support of its operation, called the ASEAN+3 Macroeconomic Research Office (AMRO). Since 2011, AMRO has complemented the CMIM by conducting economic surveillance of member economies and the region as a whole, and supports the CMIM's operation.

There was still no central secretariat for the CMIM process. The ASEAN+3 authorities instead launched the CMIM Taskforce (TF) in November 2006 to function as the focal point of discussion in hammering out details. The "ASEAN Way" of seeking consensus was preferred at each stage of the discussion, which, though sluggish, has helped secure general agreement among members. A strong commitment to "consensus" helped avoid leaving small members stranded and added to their collective influence. The multilateralisation process continued for five years starting from 2005. The original CMIM Agreement came into force on March 24, 2010.[65] (See Annex: Progress on the CMIM and Further Developments.)

Main Features of the CMIM as a Regional Liquidity Mechanism

Participants and Modest Objectives

The CMIM has inherited two objectives of the CMI without change: (i) address short-term liquidity difficulties in the region as a regional self-help mechanism and (ii) supplement existing international financial

---

[65]The original CMIM Agreement became effective after 90 days from the date on which CMIM parties of all Plus Three countries and five or more ASEAN countries completed signing.

arrangements.[66] The first is to maintain regional autonomy so that the CMIM, in its sole operation, is able to promptly decide whether immediate action is needed. ASEAN+3 has, thus, gradually increased the IMF de-linked portion to 40% of each member's swap quota while enhancing regional surveillance functions. Following the second objective, the CMIM has made it abundantly clear that it is not an alternative to the IMF but is instead supplementing IMF lending, being a part of the global financial safety net (GFSN) that places the IMF at its center. Technically, the function of a self-help mechanism — which may suggest some form of competition with the IMF — is limited to the size of the IMF de-linked portion.

Unlike the CMI, the CMIM includes all ASEAN+3 financial authorities, particularly the five newer members: Brunei, Cambodia, Lao PDR, Myanmar, and Vietnam.[67] Hong Kong also joined the CMIM, only at the deputy level, not at the ministerial level.

Financial Arrangement — Lightness in the Form of Multilateralisation

The top priority in the CMIM process was to enhance the certainty of financing in times of crisis. It created a single contractual arrangement under which ASEAN+3 agreed to certain collective principles and procedures. To determine how the members would mobilize and disburse funds, three options were suggested in 2006: (i) earmarking akin to the ASA, (ii) self-managed reserve pooling arrangement (SRPA) modeled after the European Monetary Cooperation Fund (EMCF),[68] and (iii) centrally managed reserve pooling with upfront funding. At the first round of discussions in early 2007, the second option was adopted, which would form a virtual fund as an accounting arrangement, with a separate legal entity under a uniform agreement. Each monetary authority would transfer the legal title of ownership of a certain amount of its reserve assets to a virtual fund. In return, each central bank would obtain a claim on the fund while retaining full powers in managing pooled reserves.

---

[66] The Joint Ministerial Statement of the 10th ASEAN+3 Finance Ministers' Meeting May 5, 2007 in Kyoto, Japan.

[67] Chabchitrchaidol, Nakagawa, and Nemoto (2018).

[68] Established in 1973, one of the EMCF's functions was to provide short-term financing between central banks, leading to a concerted policy on reserves. The Fund was dissolved on January 1, 1994 when its roles were taken over by the European Monetary Institute, while the Bank for International Settlements continued to operate as an agent for a transitional period until May 15, 1995.

The SRPA model could offer greater financing certainty than earmarking could. Some members' concerns about the depletion of reserves and the differing priorities of reserve investments were allayed because the pledged amount would continue to count as part of each authority's reserves. In 2009, however, the SRPA model was dropped[69] mainly because some jurisdictions did not allow central banks to transfer legal ownership of the reserve assets to a nondomestic entity without an international legal personality or to exchange promissory notes with each other. They also recognized that setting up an SRPA would take up a great deal of time and slow down the CMIM process in the context of the GFC. Instead, it was agreed that the monetary authorities would issue to and exchange commitment letters with each other. The CMIM is now a relatively decentralized financing arrangement, as a stand-by and unfunded liquidity arrangement, similar to earmarking.

Legal Modality

Three options were considered for a legal modality, in line with the options for financial arrangement: (i) memorandum of understanding (MOU), (ii) contractual agreement, and (iii) treaty. Amid the GFC, members did not consider it realistic to establish an international organization either for financing arrangements or for economic surveillance. The second model — a private contractual agreement — was adopted for the CMIM, to which the contracting parties would be participating central banks and finance ministries.[70] Under this model, members' commitment was legally binding through the jurisdiction of English law, but it did not require an additional ratification process by "sovereign states" as is required by a treaty. The CMIM Agreement, however, does not have the legal status of a law in each member country's domestic jurisdiction, unlike a treaty. At the same time, it was perceived to be accompanied with a lesser degree of commitment than would be the case with a treaty.[71]

---

[69]During the final round of discussion, the term SRPA was deleted from the draft CMIM Agreement in 2009.

[70]AFMM+3, Kyoto, May 2007.

[71]Separately, in relation to the CMIM's available size, whether to allow the CMIM to borrow was discussed. This issue was related to the issue of forms of financing arrangements and legal modality. The CMIM would be able to borrow from markets only when it would become an independent legal personality.

Financing Design: Total Size, Shares, and Voting Power

A bigger-sized crisis financing facility is desirable to cope with simultaneous requests for funds, but it needs to be balanced with members' capacity to contribute. In 2008, the planned CMIM's total size was set at USD 80 billion. Following the GFC, it was increased to USD 120 billion in February 2009.[72] This amount further increased to USD 240 billion in 2014.

In terms of the contribution ratio of individual members, three options were proposed in 2007: (i) IMF quota formula, (ii) United Nations contribution formula, and (iii) tiered contributions. By any means, China and Japan would account for more than four-fifths of the contribution in terms of their economic size, substantial holdings of reserves, or openness in trade and finance. China and Japan agreed to go "underweighted" relative to their economic size. Thus, a tiered contribution model was adopted in 2008. Members noted that other arrangements such as the ASA, the EMCF, and the Latin American Reserve Fund (FLAR) had also adopted a tiered contribution structure.

In this model, members are first categorized into groups based on the sizes of their economies and their capacity to pay. Thereafter, a factor of fair representation was also considered. As such, contribution shares of the ASEAN and Plus Three countries were firstly set at a 20:80 ratio[73] and then individual members' shares were determined in each tiered group. This made it possible to allow for meaningful shares for smaller economies, achieving a degree of equity between members and helping avoid one single leadership. As a consequence, the original five ASEAN members had an equal share of 3.793% each. This was in line with a guiding principle of consensus on the "ASEAN Way" that member states should be equal in decision-making, rather than relying on a notion of "hegemonic stability."[74]

Both China and Japan sought to be the largest contributor to the CMIM and to have corresponding influence and standing.[75] To resolve the deadlock, the Plus Three countries reached an agreement on their shares through

---

[72] Joint Media Statement, Phuket, Thailand, February 2009, "Action Plan to Restore Economic and Financial Stability of the Asian Region" (https://www.amro-asia.org/joint-media-statement-action-plan-to-restore-economic-and-financial-stability-of-the-asian-region/).

[73] AFMM+3 Joint Ministerial Statement, Madrid, Spain, May 2008.

[74] Ciorciari (2011) (see note 59).

[75] Kuroda and Kawai (2002); Grimes (2011).

negotiations. Japan would provide 32% of the funds and be the largest single contributor. China was allowed to bring Hong Kong into the arrangement as a separate member, and together they would contribute 32%. With Hong Kong as part of its team, China became one of the two "co-equal largest contributors." [76] Korea, meanwhile, would contribute 16% of the funds.

Voting power was also a contentious issue. There was a need to alleviate ASEAN's concerns around dominance by the Plus Three members in the Executive Level Decision Making Body's (ELDMB's) day-to-day decision-making, including the approval of swap requests. Voting power was based on the sum of "basic votes," equally distributed, and the "votes based on contribution." As a result, ASEAN countries were able to have more voting power (28.41% in total) than their financial contribution (20%), whereas the Plus Three's voting power (71.59% in total) was smaller than its financial contribution (total of 80%). Given the majority two-thirds voting system in the ELDMB, no single member has been given a veto. This has enabled individual ASEAN governments to raise their voice as a unified group in negotiations and to avoid leaving individual members stranded in negotiations.

Borrowing Quota — Demand Side

Regarding the maximum amount (swap quota) that members could borrow, two options were discussed: (i) one single multiple of commitment for all members and (ii) tiered multiples according to the size of commitment. The second option was chosen in 2009 as it met the different financing needs of members — a higher multiple was assigned to members with smaller contributions.

Collective Decision-Making and Activation Procedures

A two-tier decision-making structure was introduced in 2007 with separate responsibilities among representatives from finance ministries and central banks. Fundamental issues, including total size, contribution, borrowing multiples, membership and terms of lending, and the like, are to be determined by "consensus" approval by finance ministers and central bank governors.[77] One

---

[76]Ciorciari (2011).

[77]In May 2011, ASEAN+3 finance ministers agreed to invite central bank governors to ASEAN+3 meetings from 2012. Following this, the amended CMIM Agreement to include central bank governors in the Ministerial Level Decision Making Body (MLDMB) became effective in July 2014.

Table 26.6: Financial Contribution
(After the First Amendment of 2014)

ASEAN+3 Members	Financial Contribution (USD billion)	Financial Contribution (Percent)	Purchasing Multiple	Maximum Arrangement Amount (USD billion)	Basic Votes (No. of votes)	Votes Based on Contribution (No. of votes)	Total Voting Power (No. of votes)	Total Voting Power (Percent)
China	China (excluding Hong Kong)* 68.400	32.000 { 28.500	0.5	34.20	3.20	68.400	71.600	25.430
	HK 8.400	3.500	2.5	6.30	0.00	8.400	8.400	2.980
Japan	76.800	32.000	0.5	38.40	3.20	76.800	80.000	28.410
Korea	38.400	16.000	1.0	38.40	3.20	38.400	41.600	14.770
Plus 3	192.000	80.000		117.30	9.60	192.000	201.600	71.590
Indonesia	9.104	3.793	2.5	22.76	3.20	9.104	12.304	4.369
Thailand	9.104	3.793	2.5	22.76	3.20	9.104	12.304	4.369
Malaysia	9.104	3.793	2.5	22.76	3.20	9.104	12.304	4.369
Singapore	9.104	3.793	2.5	22.76	3.20	9.104	12.304	4.369
Philippines	9.104	3.793	2.5	22.76	3.20	9.104	12.304	4.369
Vietnam	2.000	0.833	5.0	10.00	3.20	2.000	5.200	1.847
Cambodia	0.240	0.100	5.0	1.20	3.20	0.240	3.440	1.222
Myanmar	0.120	0.050	5.0	0.60	3.20	0.120	3.320	1.179
Brunei	0.060	0.025	5.0	0.30	3.20	0.060	3.260	1.158
Lao PDR	0.060	0.025	5.0	0.30	3.20	0.060	3.260	1.158
ASEAN	48.000	20.000		126.20	32.00	48.000	80.000	28.410
Total	240.000	100.000		243.50	41.60	240.000	281.600	100.000

ASEAN = Association of Southeast Asian Nations, Lao PDR = Lao People's Democratic Republic, USD = United States dollar.
*Hong Kong's purchasing is limited to the IMF de-linked portion because it is not a member of the IMF.
Source: Author's calculations based on Joint Statements of the ASEAN+3 Finance Ministers' Meeting in Tashkent, Uzbekistan in May 2010, and Manila, the Philippines in May 2012.

level below them is an ELDMB in charge of day-to-day decisions, comprising the deputy-level representatives. The ELDMB decision includes the activation of the CMIM swap, which needs a two-thirds majority of effective votes.

The CMIM does not have a formal secretariat in charge of all aspects of activation. Instead, two coordinating countries are appointed each year to oversee the decision-making process. The difference in coordination is assisted by AMRO's technical secretariat support, if requested, and the process becomes legally enforceable, unlike in the CMI's case. In exchange for adopting legally binding collective decision-making, the CMIM also allows each party to opt out from contributing to a swap request. However, it must be approved in advance by the ELDMB's voting. In exceptional cases such as an extraordinary event or in the event of force majeure and domestic legal limitations, however, opting out is still possible without obtaining the ELDMB's approval.[78] If one or more participants opt out and the swap is still approved, others must make up the difference, provided this additional burden does not exceed their contribution limits. The CMIM inherited activation procedures set by the CMI BSAs in 2006, but it has consolidated them. Still, it remains relatively decentralized and "institutionally light" compared to peer RFAs.

Financing Terms, Interest Rates, and Maturity

The CMIM has followed most financial terms for CMI BSAs. A CMIM party that intends to request for drawing has to meet a set of conditions precedent — substantive and procedural — before the vote to approve a swap request. These include the completion of a review of the economic and financial situation of the swap recipient and no events of default. After the disbursement of funds, the recipient is obliged to comply with a set of covenants. For example, each CMIM party needs to submit periodic surveillance reports, with AMRO's support, and to participate in the regional surveillance process, that is, the ERPD, convened bi-annually.[79] In determining financing conditions, the term "conditionality" was avoided in the original CMIM in 2010. Even if it was economically justified and had "buy-in" from a borrower, it was thought that it could result in associations being drawn with the IMF stigma.

---

[78] From Annex 1 of the Joint Ministerial Statement of the 13th ASEAN+3 Finance Ministers' Meeting in Tashkent, Uzbekistan on May 2, 2010.

[79] Joint Statement of the 13th ASEAN+3 Finance Ministers' Meeting on May 2, 2010, Tashkent, Uzbekistan.

The CMIM bears above-market interest rates resulting from its nature of countercyclical liquidity support in times of crises. Interest rates of CMIM funds equal to 1.5% plus the LIBOR, increasing by 0.5% each 180 days to a maximum of LIBOR + 3.0%.[80] Under the original CMIM in 2010, drawings under the IMF-linked portion had a maturity of 90 days, renewable up to seven times so that the maximum supporting period was just two years. The IMF de-linked portion had the same maturity but was renewable up to three times so that the maximum supporting period was only one year.

IMF Linkage — IMF De-Linked Portion

The CMIM took over the IMF linkage as well from the CMI. In late 2007–2008, the ASEAN+3 authorities had another chance to determine the extent of IMF linkage for multilateralisation. Three options were on the table: (i) initial drawdown of up to 20% of borrowing quota without IMF programs, (ii) pre-approved initial drawdown of up to 50% without IMF programs, and (iii) completely de-linked from IMF programs. The first option was agreed upon in which a swap recipient would be able to draw down only 20% of each member's swap quota without IMF linkage.[81] The second and third options were available upon pre-qualification assessments, but at that time, the prospect for having a robust surveillance function for pre-qualification was not clear.[82]

Dissenting views to the first option were that (i) the initial tranche of funds — 20% of each borrowing quota — might be smaller than needed, (ii) if linked to an IMF program, it would take a longer time before disbursement from the second tranche, and (iii) the linkage would limit the autonomy of the region as well. On the other hand, there were concerns that RFAs, including the CMIM, would hand out easy money and undermine economic discipline and reform.

This is the issue of moral hazard — specifically "'facility shopping" or "conditionality shopping," which could discourage borrowers' anti-crisis actions, lower the efficiency of using creditors' resources, and dampen repayment capacity. A solution was that the CMIM, following the CMI, would outsource the negotiation of conditionality unless such a function

---

[80] Hill and Menon (2012).

[81] Joint Media Statement, Phuket, Thailand, February 2009.

[82] The gradual increase of the delinked portion to 30% in 2014 and 40% in 2020 has been achieved by enhancing the regional surveillance function of AMRO and conditionality framework.

was well developed within the CMIM itself.[83] The original CMIM explicitly stipulated it would establish an independent regional surveillance unit. It noted that the CMIM's role, as a regional self-help mechanism, was further intensified by enhancing the economic surveillance function. It was hinted that the de-linked portion could increase to above 20% when a surveillance and monitoring mechanism would become better. This materialized with the creation of AMRO in 2011, a surveillance arm of CMIM, and the IMF de-linked portion was gradually increased.

Most other RFAs also require IMF involvement in their lending operations either explicitly or implicitly.[84] The CMIM may operate by itself to the extent of the IMF de-linked portion without an IMF-supported program. The difference from other RFAs lies in that to access beyond the IMF de-linked portion, the CMIM requires an IMF-supported program to be in place as one of the legal conditions.

Three Amendments to the CMIM (2012–2021)

Through the GFC, ASEAN+3 has continually sought to address the remaining gaps of the original CMIM's limited function as a crisis lender.[85] In May 2012, ASEAN+3 countries unanimously agreed to amend the original CMIM Agreement, which became effective in July 2014 after members signed the amended CMIM Agreement.

The second amendment in 2015–2020 focused on adjusting CMIM's financing terms in line with the IMF facilities and addressing remaining legal ambiguities. For instance, a confidentiality clause was clarified to allow CMIM-related information to be used for media coverage to help bolster market confidence when the CMIM is activated. In 2021, a much-awaited increase of the IMF de-linked portion from 30% to 40% became effective, together with the adoption of the CMIM conditionality framework. CMIM members also decided to use the members' local currencies for CMIM crisis financing, in addition to the US dollar.

---

[83] Eichengreen (2010). The IMF linkage is called a "nesting strategy" — nesting CMIM in the international financial system with the IMF at the center. This enabled shifting tough choices to the IMF, while reducing the risk that imposing conditionality would lead to political objections. See Grimes (2011).

[84] A member of the BRICS Contingent Reserve Arrangement (CRA) can request more than 30% of its maximum access only if a corresponding IMF program is in operation. The US Treasury portion of North America Framework Agreement (NAFA) requires an IMF letter expressing confidence in the economic policies of the borrower before activating the swap line.

[85] ADBI (2010).

Financing Design: Doubling the Size and Use of Local Currency

Some members' swap quotas under the USD 120 billion of the CMIM size were modest, compared to the USD 157 billion package for Greece or the USD 121 billion package for Ireland during the GFC. The 2014 amendment doubled the size of the CMIM to USD 240 billion, while leaving contribution shares, purchasing multiples, and voting powers unchanged.

Another breakthrough in 2021 was the members' decision to allow the use of local currencies, in addition to the US dollar, for CMIM crisis financing. This provides more funding options for members and lowers their burden to draw from their international reserves. The decision was made in the context of the growing demand for local currency usage in regional cross-border transactions, several mutual agreements on initiatives relating to promotion of local currency usage, and a greater role for local currencies as reserve currency.[86]

New CMIM Facility for Crisis Prevention

The ASEAN+3 introduced a crisis prevention facility called the CMIM Precautionary Line (CMIM-PL).[87] When a request for a CMIM-PL is approved, swap lines will be established between a recipient and donors. The recipient may make a drawing of US dollars from the swap lines upon prior notice without another ELDMB's approval.

In financial crises, as much as in illness, an ounce of prevention is worth a pound of cure. The CMIM-PL was introduced on the understanding that the qualifying member, in the face of potential liquidity pressure, would have implemented sound macroeconomic policies and would regain economic soundness, although it may still display moderate vulnerabilities. Thus, more emphasis was placed on ex-ante conditionality — modeled after the IMF precautionary facilities. This would enable the CMIM members to act pre-emptively in order to mitigate contagion and to minimize the costs of crises.[88]

The ERPD Matrix framework was endorsed in 2019. This framework is used for ex-ante qualification criteria upon any member's request for access to the CMIM-PL. AMRO contributed to developing qualification criteria

---

[86] Sussangkarn, Shimizu, and Kim (2019).

[87] The ASEAN+3 Informal Seminar for the Deputies on "A Possible Crisis Prevention Function for CMIM," July 22, 2011 in Tokyo, Japan; CMIM TF on September 14, 2011 in Bali.

[88] The ASEAN+3 Informal Seminar for the Deputies on "A Possible Crisis Prevention Function for CMIM," July 22, 2011 in Tokyo, Japan; CMIM TF on September 14, 2011, in Bali, Indonesia.

following explicit instructions from the ASEAN+3 authorities.[89] The process ensures that a CMIM member does not build up unsustainable imbalances during peace time. The adoption of the ERPD matrix framework indicates that the CMIM, particularly in its sole operation, will determine whether a requesting party has taken sound economic measures on its own for CMIM-PL.

Table 26.7: CMIM Arrangements

CMIM-SF	CMIM-PL
• Currency swap for actual short-term liquidity and/or BOP difficulties	• Swap lines for potential short-term liquidity and/or BOP difficulties
• May attach ex-post conditionality	• Ex-ante qualification based on five areas and may attach ex-post conditionality
• For full swap quota, the ILP and financing terms must be consistent with the IMF	
• For the IDLP, there must be no prospect of IMF-supported programs being introduced, possibly evidenced by the assessment that a borrower has implemented "sound economic policies."	

BOP = balance of payments, CMIM = Chiang Mai Initiative Multilateralisation, CMIM-PL = CMIM Precautionary Line, CMIM-SF = CMIM Stability Facility, IDLP = International Monetary Fund de-linked portion, IMF = International Monetary Fund. Source: Author's summary based on Joint Statements of ASEAN+3 Finance Ministers and Central Bank Governors' Meetings.

Financing Terms: Extending Maturity

The maturity period of 90 days, adopted from the time of the CMI BSAs, was a radical expression that the CMIM would also address "urgent short-term liquidity difficulties" on the assumption that a swap requesting party would be a "pure innocent bystander." But the GFC showed that such a case is not entirely realistic because, as always, "innocence" is difficult to determine in a real situation. The 2014 amendment allowed the maturity to be extended from 90 days to 360 days for the IMF-linked portion, renewable twice. The supporting period for the IMF de-linked portion was increased from 90 to 180 days, renewable up to three times.

Coordination with the IMF-Supported Programs

While the IMF-linked portion of the CMIM was intended to co-finance with the IMF since its creation in 2010, the operational specifics had remained unclear. A series of financing terms and conditions of the CMIM have been upgraded to enable it to fully match relevant IMF-supported programs. For

---

[89] See note 67.

instance, the supporting period is flexibly adjusted by allowing multiple renewals as needed, and disbursement dates can be switched to secure consistency with the IMF-supported program (Table 26.8).

Table 26.8: Maturity and Duration of CMIM Arrangements

Item	IMF-Linked Portion (ILP) (Up to 100%)	IMF De-Linked Portion (IDLP) (Up to 40%)
Maturity of Each Drawing Under CMIM-SF[1]/CMIM-PL[2]	360 days (For SF only, renewable multiple times following the matching IMF-supported program after 2020)	180 days (For SF only, renewable three times, up to 2 years)
Swap Lines Under CMIM-PL[2]	180 days *ILP: renewable multiple times following the matching IMF-supported program after 2020; IDLP: renewable up to three times, up to 2 years	

CMIM = Chiang Mai Initiative Multilateralisation, CMIM-PL = Chiang Mai Initiative Multilateralisation Precautionary Line, CMIM-SF = Chiang Mai Initiative Multilateralisation Stability Facility, IMF = International Monetary Fund.
[1] CMIM-SF (Stability Facility) means a crisis resolution facility in response to actual crises.
[2] CMIM-PL (Precautionary Line) means a crisis prevention facility in response to potential crises.

From 2016 to 2018, the CMIM and IMF conducted joint test runs (Box 26.1) to work out a cooperation mechanism in terms of burden sharing, financing conditions, and information sharing.[90] A set of CMIM operational guidelines was adopted for the information sharing process with the IMF, tuned to a coordination mechanism, in December 2018. This mechanism enables both sides to have a shared view of the policy adjustment path, financing needs, and the associating conditionality for the IMF-linked portion. The guidelines were prepared, referring to the 2011 Group of Twenty (G20) principles for cooperation between the IMF and RFAs, and the IMF policy on the exchange of documents between the IMF and RFAs.

Increasing the IMF De-Linked Portion and CMIM Conditionality

The IMF de-linked portion was increased from the original 20% in 2010 to 30%, effective from July 2014, and to 40% in 2021. Members' growing faith in AMRO's surveillance and analytical capacity has supported the decision, which makes the CMIM more readily available as a self-help mechanism. The 40%

[90]Since 2013, the CMIM members have been conducting test runs annually. This is a simulation exercise of the activation of CMIM facilities based on a mock scenario. The test run has contributed to familiarizing members with CMIM activation procedures and identifying gaps in the operational readiness of the CMIM.

increase came together with the adoption of the CMIM conditionality. After the CMIM was created in 2010, there was uncertainty around whether CMIM liquidity support would be provided with any conditionality, particularly in its sole operation without an IMF linkage. The amendment in 2014 formally introduced a legal basis for CMIM-PL to attach conditionality. This legal basis expanded into the CMIM crisis resolution facility, called the CMIM-SF, in 2019. Following this, ASEAN+3 members viewed that adoption of the CMIM conditionality framework would be one of core prerequisites for further increasing the IMF de-linked portion.[91] Under this framework, AMRO will support the ELDMB to ascertain whether the potential borrower is broadly illiquid but solvent and to determine what policy adjustments are required.

There was an argument that neighbors in an RFA would likely not choose to impose painful conditions on one another.[92] While this remains

---

Box 26.1:

Lessons from the CMIM–IMF Joint Test Runs

Under the CMIM, tapping more than a certain percent of the full swap quota (40% as of 2021) by any member (called the "IMF-linked portion") is allowed only if an IMF-supported program is in place or is expected to be put in place in the very near future. For this IMF-linked portion, the CMIM needs to be "consistent" with the relevant IMF-supported program, mainly in its financing terms and program design. However, both sides had been silent on how to coordinate and bring consistency until 2016. The three joint test runs in 2016–2018 highlighted the issues that had to be addressed to ensure consistency and smooth operations. The test runs were based on a hypothetical setting in which a member experienced a shock that was large enough to require co-financing and needed both financing and policy adjustments.

1. Consistency in financing terms

The test runs revealed that a few specific CMIM financing terms were not compatible with those of IMF lending. While the maturity of IMF lending can be extended flexibly, the CMIM supporting period was fixed at three years. The CMIM had no basis for phased drawings in tranches. Following the IMF's lending policy, the CMIM was required to provide "financing assurance" that CMIM be provided throughout the entire period of the IMF-supported program while accepting the "preferred creditor status" of the IMF in repayment.

2. Collaboration process and information sharing

Following the joint test run, CMIM members adopted a scheme of early information sharing in 2018. This enabled both institutions to come to a shared view of the policy adjustment path, financing needs, and the associated conditionality and program reviews. The IMF also endorsed a policy of "Exchange of Documents Between the Fund and Regional Financing Arrangements" in December 2017.

continued on next page

---

[91] The IMF approach to conditionality evolved since a review in 2009. This change might have laid a foundation for ASEAN+3 members to adopt a CMIM conditionality framework, finalized in 2020.

[92] See note 83.

Box 26.1: *continued*

3. Conditionality framework for the IMF-linked portion
The CMIM and the IMF applied the lead agency model during the joint test runs, which was proposed by the IMF in 2017 ("Collaboration between Regional Financing Arrangements and the IMF"). In this model, the IMF took the lead in preparing a macroeconomic framework and core policies and associated conditionality, while the CMIM focused on aspects within its areas of comparative advantage. Based on this experience, the CMIM, with the IMF's support, developed a framework for program design and conditionality setting for the IMF-linked portion in 2020. This framework placed utmost emphasis on ensuring full accountability in the CMIM's decision-making body. The IMF indicated that the lead agency model could evolve to become a "coherent program design model" as applied during its co-financing with the European Union authorities, provided CMIM/AMRO gain experience in program design and implementation.

to be seen in actual crisis situations, the CMIM has gradually taken steps to address such concerns.[93] At the same time, a technical guidance for program design and conditionality setting for the IMF-linked portion was separately adopted in August 2020 following lessons learned from CMIM-IMF's joint test runs during 2016–2018 (Box 26.1).

Future Developments of the CMIM

In the past decade, the ASEAN+3 authorities have improved the CMIM's effectiveness in keeping with its two objectives: (i) a regional self-help mechanism and (ii) to supplement IMF lending. Both objectives have been achieved simultaneously, and not exclusively or at the expense of the other. The first has been achieved by multilateralisation itself, evolving from a network of BSAs, and increasing the IMF de-linked portion, underpinned by AMRO's surveillance, and the conditionality framework. An assessment tool for ex-ante qualification for the CMIM-PL is already in place, called the ERPD matrix framework. Local currencies can be used for CMIM crisis financing, the detailed procedures for which are partly completed as of late 2021. In keeping with the second objective, an IMF linkage has been maintained. The CMIM held joint test runs with the IMF, bringing about an information-sharing mechanism and the CMIM conditionality framework for the IMF-linked portion.

Evolving Circumstances and the Case for the CMIM

The ASEAN+3 region weathered the GFC better than other regions, backed by ample reserves and policy tools for relatively robust macroeconomic

---

[93] As evidenced in the case of the Greek experience with the troika, European neighbors did implement strong loan conditionality in accordance with the European Stability Mechanism treaty.

fundamentals. The ASEAN+3 policymakers have broadly implemented sound monetary policies, fiscal policies, and flexible exchange rates to manage capital flows since the AFC and GFC. Following the GFC, capital flow management measures and macroprudential measures have been widely adopted in East Asia. Such policy tools are important for crisis prevention. Separately, the ASEAN+3 economies have also accumulated large foreign reserves as self-insurance for possible financial crises.[94] Reserves remain the single most important form of financial insurance for most regional economies and help reduce the probability of a full-blown liquidity crisis.

Additionally, the number of BSAs among central banks outside the CMIM has proliferated since the GFC. Today, the total value of BSAs involving ASEAN+3 economies is around USD 373 billion, larger than the CMIM (based on AMRO staff calculations as of October 2021).

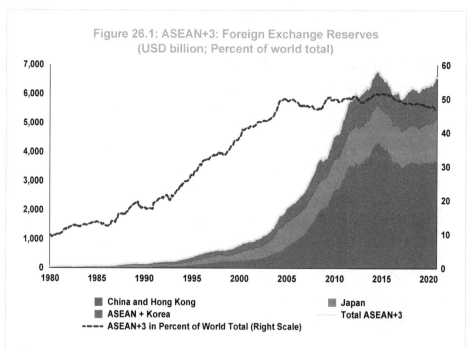

Figure 26.1: ASEAN+3: Foreign Exchange Reserves (USD billion; Percent of world total)

ASEAN = Association of Southeast Asian Nations.
Note: Data as of September 2020.
Source: International Monetary Fund via Haver Analytics; ASEAN+3 Macroeconomic Research Office staff calculations.

---

[94] A paper by Aizenman and Lee (2007) compares the importance of precautionary and mercantilist motives in the hoarding of international reserves by developing countries. Overall, empirical results support precautionary motives; in particular, a more liberal capital account regime results in increased international reserves.

The IMF will continue to be at the apex of the GFSN, playing a central role in emergency financing and policy coordination at the global level. The size of funds available for ASEAN+3 members, in the IMF stand-by arrangement under the normal access limit, has grown especially since the 14th IMF quota reform, effective from January 2016.[95]

Table 26.9: Financing Size : CMIM versus IMF Loan (USD billion)

ASEAN+3 Economies	IMF 1997 SBA 300%[1]	IMF 2010 SBA 300%[2]	IMF GFC SBA 600%[2]	CMIM 2010 MAA	IMF 2020 SBA[3]435%	IMF 2020 PLL[3]500%	CMIM 2020 MAA
China	13.79	36.21	72.42	17.10	187.21	215.19	34.20
Hong Kong	...	...	...	3.15	...	...	6.30
Japan	33.57	59.58	119.17	19.20	189.29	217.57	38.40
Korea	3.26	13.10	26.20	19.20	52.71	60.59	38.40
Indonesia	6.10	6.70	13.41	11.38	28.55	32.81	22.76
Thailand	2.34	4.84	9.68	11.38	19.73	22.67	22.76
Malaysia	3.39	6.65	13.31	11.38	22.32	25.65	22.76
Singapore	1.46	3.86	7.72	11.38	23.90	27.47	22.76
Philippines	2.58	3.94	7.88	11.38	12.55	14.42	22.76
Vietnam	0.98	1.47	2.95	5.00	7.08	8.14	10.00
Cambodia	0.26	0.39	0.78	0.60	1.07	1.24	1.20
Myanmar	0.75	1.16	2.31	0.30	3.17	3.65	0.60
Brunei	0.61	0.96	1.93	0.15	1.85	2.13	0.30
Lao PDR	0.16	0.24	0.47	0.15	0.65	0.75	0.30
Total	69.25	139.11	278.23	121.75	550.09	632.28	243.50
Total (excl. China and Japan)	21.89	43.32	86.64	82.30	173.58	199.52	164.60

... = not available, ASEAN = Association of Southeast Asian Nations, CMIM = Chiang Mai Initiative Multilateralisation, GFC = global financial crisis, IMF = International Monetary Fund, Lao PDR = Lao People's Democratic Republic, MAA = maximum arrangement amount of CMIM swap quota, SBA = Stand-By Arrangement.
Notes:
[1] SDR = USD 1.357710 as of December 1, 1997.
[2] SDR = USD 1.49192 as of January 30, 2009.
[3] SDR = USD 1.41187 as of September 22, 2020.
Source: Author's calculations.

---

[95]On February 7, 2020, the Board of Governors of the IMF adopted a resolution concluding the 15th General Review of Quotas with no increase in IMF quotas. Instead of a quota increase, they decided to double the New Arrangements to Borrow, considering a further temporary round of bilateral borrowing beyond 2020 to maintain the Fund's lending capacity of about USD 1 trillion.

To get around the perceived stigma associated with IMF lending, the IMF's lending toolkits have also been reformed to provide precautionary lending, such as through the Flexible Credit Line (FCL) and Precautionary Credit Line (PCL).[96] In April 2020, the IMF introduced a new precautionary arrangement, called the Short-Term Liquidity Line (SLL), to fill a gap in the toolkits for short-term, moderate, and repeated potential capital flow volatility. With global uncertainty high and protracted, the SLS is designed as a swap-like liquidity facility for members with very strong policies and fundamentals to manage temporary liquidity shocks by providing assurances of quick liquidity provision and a signal of strength to markets. While the CMIM has become a more robust regional liquidity mechanism, other layers of the GFSN have been also strengthened.

As a regional mechanism for collective insurance, the fact that the CMIM has not been tapped does not necessarily mean it has become less important. In the face of possible crises, the value of the CMIM stems largely from its unique status as a regional self-help mechanism, supplementing the IMF. It serves as a regional financial stabilizer with ample resources, in addition to other financing resources. The CMIM is more cost-effective than individual self-insurance.[97] Regional ownership helps avoid the potential stigma associated with IMF borrowing. The CMIM, backed by AMRO's surveillance function, is expected to quickly address the regional spread of crises. The value of the CMIM as a regional financial safety net is confirmed along the following four lines of consideration.

First, traditional policy tools cannot fully substitute the liquidity backstop as it usually takes a relatively longer time to have an impact. It has been difficult to correct global economic imbalances through global policy coordination, partly due to political economy constraints. There is a limit in using capital flow management measures as well. The CFMs should be temporary and transparent, take spillover effects into consideration, and be

---

[96] Since the late 1990s, the IMF has considered facilities to help members with strong policies deal with financial market volatility. The first such facility was the Contingent Credit Line, established in 1999 after the AFC. The Short-Term Liquidity Facility was subsequently established during the GFC, and quickly replaced by the FCL and the PCL. The PCL was further replaced by the Precautionary Liquidity Line (PLL) in 2014.

[97] The costs can be divided into servicing cost, which is the difference between the return on reserves and the borrowing cost of the sovereign; the social opportunity cost of public capital, which is the difference between the yield on reserves and the social return on capital and a currency valuation risk. This is since reserves expose a central bank to capital losses should the domestic currency strengthen (Bank of England 2016).

reviewed regularly.[98] The effectiveness of macroprudential measures decreases over time due to market expectations.

Second, self-insurance remains the single most important form of financial insurance. However, holding excessive foreign reserves is less efficient, and entails potential systemic costs. In an actual crisis, self-insurance funds may not be fully tapped because a certain maximum level of reserves of a country would be often interpreted by the markets as the minimum level that the country needs to hold.[99]

Third, the BSAs in the region are distributed very unevenly. Most BSAs are either between the Plus 3 and ASEAN-5 countries, or between the ASEAN-5 countries themselves. A few smaller economies (Brunei, Cambodia, Myanmar, and Vietnam) are left outside of the BSA network. More fundamentally, simpler in format by nature, BSAs are less reliable for countercyclical liquidity support than the CMIM or IMF as they are more likely bound by domestic policy considerations.[100]

And finally, in addition to the stigma problem, the IMF has limitations in addressing any global crisis alone as the lender of last resort. This may be partly due to the overall size of the IMF's lending capacity, and ultimately because the IMF is not a global central bank that issues a global currency. Rather, it is an intermediary of global liquidity, mainly the US dollar as the key currency.

Table 26.10: Four Layers of the Global Financial Safety Net

FX Reserves for Self-Insurance	BSAs	RFA (CMIM)	IMF
Remains the single most important form of a safety net	Relatively quick to avail of, effective during the GFC	Designed for quick disbursements	Global insurance by a centralized party
An expensive safety net; hard to assess the adequacy of reserves	Subject to counterpart's domestic mandate (not for fiscal financing) due to credit risk borne by swap provider	Local knowledge by regional surveillance Limited to short-term liquidity problems in its sole operation	May take more time to negotiate ex-post lending conditions Negative signaling effects or stigma associated with use of IMF resources

BSA = bilateral swap agreement, CMIM = Chiang Mai Initiative Multilateralisation, FX = foreign exchange, GFC = global financial crisis, IMF = International Monetary Fund, RFA = regional financing arrangement.

---

[98] "G20 Coherent Conclusions for the Management of Capital Flows Drawing on Country Experiences" and "The Liberalization and Management of Capital Flows: An Institutional View," November 14, 2012.

[99] Eichengreen and Woods (2016).

[100] IMF (2016).

The CMIM has been steadily reviewed and strengthened, but there remains room for further development in its financing arrangement and activation procedures.

Financing Design — Financial Arrangement

The CMIM has brought about a degree of centralization by streamlining swap activation procedures in the CMI BSAs, adding an element of financing certainty.[101] At least, the likelihood that an individual member would choose not to release funds at a time of crisis is significantly reduced, compared to the CMI. This is because all members are formally committed to providing emergency financing. A weighted voting system in the ELDMB and AMRO's surveillance is in a way a departure from the ASEAN way of consensus.

At the same time, certain limitations are also observed. The CMIM is not a virtual fund as an accounting arrangement, nor a real fund with upfront contribution. Rather, it comprises a number of formal commitments held together by the execution of the CMIM Agreement and a commitment letter. It is not a legal entity, which enables it to be fully insulated from members' domestic foreign exchange policy. This is in contrast to peer RFAs such as the Arab Monetary Fund, European Stability Mechanism (ESM), and Latin American Reserve Fund (FLAR), which have been established with paid-in capital under a treaty and with the legal status of international organizations. The concern is that the CMIM's swap structure, still involving multiple transactions among members at the time of activation, is likely to generate a degree of uncertainty in crisis financing.

It has always been said that "the best time to repair the roof is when the sun is shining." The ASEAN+3 authorities are recommended to revisit the original option for a financial modality for the CMIM — the SRPA model for more financing certainty. A prerequisite for this is to transform the CMIM Agreement into a type of treaty which will grant a legal entity to the CMIM. This may enable CMIM financing to be insulated to some extent from member authorities' domestic policy and thus increase financing certainty. In the long run, when political commitments are certified, it would be worth discussing the possibility of introducing a real fund with subscribed paid-in capital equipped with legal personality on a pilot basis.

---

[101]Henning (2011).

Total Size and Swap Quota

An increase in the CMIM's size to USD 240 billion was a huge step up from the the CMI and also from the initial CMIM in 2010, and it is the second largest RFA globally today. In 2012, the members decided to double the size without having to wait for the full staffing and capability enhancement by AMRO. This was because they fully realized the importance of having a large and substantial facility. However, on a mid- to long-term basis, the CMIM size may be revisited if such a necessity arises, considering risk factors and collaboration with BSAs and the IMF.

An alternative is that the CMIM allows each member's swap quota to be flexibly adjusted under a new ceiling, in particular for small economies, while maintaining the current total size and "tiered contribution" system. In exchange, robust measures could be employed to safeguard the resources contributed. The current system of the fixed swap quota seems to be based on the assumption that all members could request for assistance simultaneously, but this appears to be a very conservative view.

At the same time, the ASEAN+3 member economies may consider adopting a collaboration framework between the CMIM and BSAs, given the large number and amount of BSAs in the region, which amounts to about USD 373 billion as of late 2021. They had already agreed to maintain and enhance BSAs, if each party would consider BSAs necessary during the CMI multilateralisation process till 2010.

Objectives and Lending Facilities

There is room for CMIM facilities to be further diversified to respond to the changing nature of crises and to meet various demands of countries at different stages of economic development. The CMIM mandate, in its sole operation, has been limited to address short-term liquidity problems. It has two facilities whose financing terms are prescribed at the agreement level: CMIM-SF for crisis resolution and CMIM-PL for crisis prevention, whose supporting period is 180 days, renewable up to three times.

Recognizing the relatively narrow scope of the CMIM facilities set by the existing mandate, the ASEAN+3 authorities are recommended to explore the possibility of introducing new instruments to help members better deal with macro-critical structural issues. A new financing instrument, free of any limits arising from the use of members' foreign reserves, may provide a

Box 26.2:

CMIM Mandate

The CMIM mandate is narrower than those of the IMF and other RFAs. While the IMF exercises wide discretion in determining whether there is a balance of payments need or not, which triggers IMF lending to a member country in trouble, another mandate is to provide concessional lending to low-income countries to reduce poverty and promote economic growth. Other RFAs' objectives are diverse, including economic development and regional integration, together with correcting balance of payments problems. By contrast, the CMIM focuses only on addressing urgent short-term liquidity and/or balance of payment difficulties in the region and to supplement IMF lending. Following multiple objectives, it was easier for the IMF and other RFAs to take diverse and proactive steps, including providing fiscal support, to address the impacts of the COVID-19 pandemic in 2020. The difference in objectives may partly explain why the CMIM has not been activated in response to the pandemic since 2020.

Regional Financing Arrangements' Mandate and Responses to the Pandemic

Institutions	Objectives	Responses to the COVID-19 Pandemic in 2020
European Stability Mechanism (ESM) 2010	Mobilize funding and provide stability support to members that are either experiencing or are threatened by severe financing problems in order to safeguard the financial stability of the euro area	[Pandemic Crisis Support] Support domestic financing of direct and indirect healthcare services, cure and prevention related due to the pandemic
Latin American Reserve Fund (FLAR) 1978	Correct disequilibria in balance of payments/improve investment conditions of foreign exchange reserves/policy coordination	Help member countries overcome balance of payments difficulties arising from the pandemic
Eurasian Fund for Stabilization and Development (EFSD) 2009	Help member states overcome the negative impact of global financial and economic crises/ensure members' long-term economic stability, and promote regional economic integration	Support the governments' measures to counter the impacts of of the pandemic
Arab Monetary Fund 1976	Short- and medium-term credit to overcome members' balance of payments problems/exchange rate stability/regional economic integration/regional financial markets development/regional monetary cooperation/payment system to promote intra-regional trade	Support governments in their response to the pandemic

Sources: Websites of each institution (ESM: https://www.esm.europa.eu/; FLAR: https://flar.com; EFSD: https://efsd.eabr.org; Arab Monetary Fund: https://www.amf.org.ae/en).

longer supporting period than that of the current CMIM. Since such a new financing instrument is likely to stand outside the existing CMIM mandate, attempts to introduce it would need to secure critical mass of political commitments of ASEAN+3 members.

IMF Linkage and Cooperation with the IMF

Since the ASEAN+3's request for IMF quota reform in 2005, which came with the announcement of the CMIM project, the IMF has continuously reformed its governance structure, although modestly. It gave larger shares to China, Korea, Mexico, and Turkey in 2010, which were much underrepresented relative to the size of their economies. The IMF also gave more voting shares to "underrepresented" countries, including many in Asia. Meanwhile, the CMIM and IMF have developed an early information-sharing process and a conditionality framework for co-financing. This will determine how the CMIM and IMF will work together in providing co-financing and designing a program, and monitoring conditionality.

One practical question left to address with respect to the adopted cooperation framework is how the CMIM and IMF will resolve differences if both have divergent views on surveillance, program, and conditionality. Given their overlapping mandates, such as economic surveillance in particular, it is challenging to have some division of labor in which the two institutions would defer to one another in their respective areas of comparative advantage. Currently, both sides have agreed to apply the lead agency model. Here, the IMF takes the lead in program design and the CMIM/AMRO complements it to the degree that consistency is ensured, similar to that of the IMF–World Bank co-financing model. The lead agency model can be transitioned to a more advanced form — a coherent program design model — once CMIM/AMRO gains sufficient experiences in program design and implementation.[102] In this upgraded model, both sides may adopt certain guiding principles, rather than formulate rigid rules, that allow for a coherent program design. Meanwhile, the guiding principles must respect one another's independence and different lending practices to resolve differences, if any, as practiced by EU–IMF co-financing.

---

[102]IMF (2017).

There is an alternative view that challenges the notion that the fragmented GFSN layers should be stitched together, particularly RFAs and the IMF.[103] In this view, the GFC in 2007–2008 induced inconsistent and ad hoc discontinuities in global financial governance and the incoherence can be productive rather than debilitating. A more complex and multipolar form of global financial governance may expand possibilities for policy and institutional experimentation, policy space for economic development, financial stability and resilience, and financial inclusion, according to this view.

Integration of CMIM and AMRO

Under the current CMIM, if there is a request for CMIM liquidity support, AMRO, as its surveillance unit, is not only tasked to analyze the economic and financial situation of a swap recipient and provide its recommendation to the CMIM decision-making body but also to provide technical support for CMIM implementation. Concerns have been raised that the CMIM lacks a permanent secretariat in charge of all aspects of CMIM activation and rotating two coordinating countries would be less efficient in handling a contingency situation or retaining institutional memory. To stabilize the coordination function for CMIM activation and to fully utilize AMRO's organizational capacity, a new governance structure under which AMRO takes on a broader role in support of CMIM or serves as a CMIM secretariat could be considered. If the CMIM is transformed into a legal entity based on a treaty in the long run, AMRO can be integrated as a part of the newly created entity.

More Collaboration with Regional Initiatives

A number of regional initiatives have emerged, along with the CMIM. Apart from the CMIM and AMRO, ADB serves as a secretariat for the ASEAN+3 Asian Bond Markets Initiative (ABMI); the Credit Guarantee and Investment Facility (CGIF) was established to provide credit guarantees for local currency denominated bonds issued by investment grade companies in ASEAN+3 countries; the Asian Bond Fund (ABF) is operating under the auspices of the Executives' Meeting of East Asia and Pacific Central Banks (EMEAP); and the Asia Region Funds Passport (ARFP) in APEC has been established to support the development of an Asia region funds management industry through improved market access and regulatory harmonization

---

[103]Grable (2018).

since 2013. As such, there are various ongoing initiatives and endeavors in East Asia and the Pacific. Closer cooperation with them may further enhance the effectiveness of each initiative's implementation and create synergy.

Conclusion

RFAs have been actively operating in recent decades, particularly after the AFC and GFC. Among them are the CMIM and its surveillance arm, AMRO, which provide a financial safety net for the ASEAN+3 region.

Even though the IMF-supported programs during the AFC were a "blessing in disguise"[104] to some countries, in hindsight, many of the ASEAN+3 members became disenchanted with the IMF.[105] The IMF, many in East Asia believed at that time, did not represent their interest in a proper way, partly due to underrepresentation in its voting structure. Second, irrespective of its necessity and adequacy, the regional economies have harbored bitter memories of IMF-supported programs during the AFC, called the IMF stigma, which had a cookie-cutter approach without regard to region-specific considerations. Lastly, the most immediate issue was that the IMF did not have enough resources to rescue countries during the AFC. These considerations propelled the ASEAN+3 policymakers to establish their own regional liquidity arrangement, called the CMI, set up as a web of BSAs between member authorities in 2000.

The CMI was multilateralized into the CMIM in 2010. The CMI was only stand-by and unfunded, lacking in financing certainty and faced with procedural issues. Access to the CMI was also discouraged by the low level of the IMF de-linked portion. Not surprisingly, the CMI was never tapped during the GFC. Learning from those lessons, individual BSAs of the CMI were consolidated into a single arrangement in 2010. Since then, in accordance with the two CMIM mandates, the ASEAN+3 members have continued to enhance the CMIM — particularly by doubling the CMIM size to USD 240 billion from USD 120 billion, and increasing the IMF de-linked portion to 40%, broadly in line with the progress made in terms of economic surveillance and the adoption of the CMIM conditionality framework, and allowing the use of local currencies for CMIM liquidity support, together with USD. They also addressed the GFSN agenda by adopting a set of

---

[104]"The Wall Street Journal (1998).

[105]Suk and Paradise (2020).

collaboration mechanisms with the IMF. In doing so, members sought to maintain a good balance between the concern over moral hazard and the need for a strong regional self-help mechanism.

Despite these achievements, there are remaining challenges, and room for further enhancement of the CMIM. First, the financing modality of the CMIM is still in a lighter form. As it is not an independent real fund, nor a legal entity, there is room for further enhancement in terms of financing arrangement and legal structure.

Second, given the increasing magnitude of capital flows in the region, discussions on accessibility may be important, and in the mid to long term, the size of the CMIM may be revisited. For this, it would be worth considering to introduce flexible multiples of swap quota for small economies and adopting a collaborative mechanism with BSAs in the region.

Lastly, the CMIM and the IMF may revisit the modality of collaboration on a long-term basis. Besides, it is recommended for AMRO to take on a broader role in support of CMIM and be positioned to serve as the CMIM secretariat. Closer cooperation with other regional initiatives may further enhance the effectiveness of each initiative's implementation by creating synergy.

There is no substitute for a strong financial safety net to help avert financial stress arising from large and volatile capital flows. As global financial networks have become more complex and integrated, cross-border capital flows have increased substantially, relative to world GDP. Given growing interconnectedness in trade and financial activity across economies, sudden stops and reversals of capital flows are real risks, and with contagion effects. It is no surprise, therefore, that global policymakers have focused on creating a stronger GFSN. This will also help reduce a reserve accumulation spree and lower sovereign risk premia, which in turn will help reallocate capital to where it might be most productive. Therefore, the goal to have a stronger liquidity support mechanism in the region is not only desirable, but it is also urgent. It is imperative therefore for the ASEAN+3 members to advance the CMIM further, to make it a more active, more centralized, and more collaborative liquidity mechanism.

Annex: Progress on the CMIM and Further Developments

The first AFMM+3 was held on the occasion of the ADB annual meeting in May 1999 on an annual basis. This meeting process has been expanded to

Date	Main Developments of the CMIM
May 2005	• ASEAN+3 members embarked on a CMIM process
May 2007	• Agreement on a form of financial arrangement and legal modality • Reiterated commitment to maintain the two core objectives of the CMI
May 2008	• Agreement on the proportion of contribution coming from ASEAN countries and the Plus Three countries to be 20:80
May 2009	• Agreement on all the main components of the CMIM, with its total size set at USD 120 billion, and its implementation • Agreement to establish an independent surveillance unit
March 2010	• On December 24, 2009, six ASEAN countries, the Plus Three countries (China, Japan, Korea) and Hong Kong signed the original CMIM Agreement, which entered into force on March 24, 2010
May 2010	• Agreed to establish AMRO as a company, the surveillance unit of CMIM
May 2011	• Endorsed the Operational Guidelines for CMIM (OG)
May 2012	• Participation of central bank governors in the ASEAN+3 process • Agreement to strengthen the CMIM through doubling the total size to USD 240 billion, increasing the IDLP to 30%, and introducing a crisis prevention facility (CMIM-PL (first amendment))
May 2013	• Finalization of the first amendment of the CMIM Agreement, and agreement to transform AMRO to an international organization • The first CMIM test run was conducted in 2013
May 2014	• The first amendment of CMIM entered into force on July 17, 2014 • Completion of the revised Operational Guidelines • Endorsed the Guidelines for the further cooperation with the IMF
May 2015	• Developed the ERPD Matrix — ex ante qualification criteria for CMIM-PL • Continued the test run, OG revision, and CMIM peace-time preparation
May 2016	• Established AMRO as an international organization on February 9, 2016 • Studied how CMIM can be better integrated into global financial safety net • A joint test run with the IMF kick-started (2016–2018) • Discussed the increase of the IDLP
May 2017	• Clarified the activation process of IDLP • Endorsed the plan on the first periodic review of the CMIM Agreement
May 2018	• Agreed on the main contents of the first CMIM periodic review, enhancing consistency with the IMF-supported program and creating an explicit legal basis for CMIM conditionality
May 2019	• Adopted the Guiding Principles of the CMIM conditionality framework • Adopted the ERPD Matrix Scorecard as a qualification reference • Adopted an information sharing mechanism with the IMF • Acknowledged the progress of review of the future direction of the CMIM • Endorsed the General Guidance on local currency contribution to the CMIM
May 2020	• The amended CMIM Agreement entered into force on June 23, 2020 • Completed the CMIM Conditionality Framework (Technical Guidance for IDLP and ILP) • Conducted test runs for funds transfer (2019–2020)
May 2021	• The amended CMIM Agreement entered into force on March 31, 2021, including (i) increased IDLP from 30% to 40 % and (ii) institutionalized local currency contributions for the CMIM crisis financing • Discussed a new CMIM reference interest rate to replace LIBOR and reviewed the interest margin, preparing the OG for the use of local currency for CMIM • Discuss how to further develop the CMIM in the future

AMRO = ASEAN+3 Macroeconomic Research Office, ASEAN = Association of Southeast Asian Nations, CMI = Chiang Mai Initiative, CMIM = Chiang Mai Initiative Multilateralisation, CMIM-PL = Chiang Mai Initiative Multilateralisation Precautionary Line, ERPD = Economic Review and Policy Dialogue, IDLP = International Monetary Fund de-linked portion, ILP = International Monetary Fund linked portion, IMF = International Monetary Fund, LIBOR = London Interbank Offered Rate.
Source: Joint Statement of ASEAN+3 Finance Ministers (and Central Bank Governors) Meetings, various years.

the ASEAN+3 Finance Ministers and Central Bank Governors (AFMGM+3) since 2012, acting as the governing forum for all CMIM developments.

References

Asian Development Bank. 1998. "The Financial Crisis in Asia." *Asian Development Outlook*: 19–37.

Asian Development Bank. 2010. "Policy Recommendations to Secure Balance and Sustainable Growth in Asia."

Altbach, Eric. December 19, 1997. "The Asian Monetary Fund Proposal: A Case Study of Japanese Regional Leadership." *JEI Report* 47.

Aizenman, Joshua, and Jaewoo Lee. 2007. "International Reserves: Precautionary Versus Mercantilist Views, Theory and Evidence." *Open Economies Review*.

Amyx, Jennifer. 2002. "Moving beyond bilateralism? Japan and the Asian Monetary Fund." *Pacific Economic Papers*, no. 331. Australian National University.

Bank of England. 2016. "Stitching Together the Global Financial Safety Net." Financial Stability Paper No. 36.

Bergsten, Fred. 1998. "Reviving the Asian Monetary Fund." *International Economy,* November–December.

Bergsten, Fred and Yung Chul Park. 2002. *Toward Creating a Regional Monetary Arrangement.* ADBI, pp. 31–33.

Chabchitrchaidol, Akkharaphol, Satoshi Nakagawa, and Yoichi Nemoto. 2018. "Quest for Financial Stability in East Asia: Establishment of an Independent Surveillance Unit 'AMRO' and Its Future Challenges."

Ciorciari, John D. 2011. *Chiang Mai Initiative Multilateralization: International Politics and Institution–Building in Asia.* University of Michigan.

European Central Bank. 2018, "Stigma? What Stigma? A Contribution to the Debate on Financial Market Effects of IMF Lending." Working Paper Series No. 2198.

Eichengreen, Barry 2010. *The International Financial Architecture and the Role of Regional Funds.* Berkeley: University of California.

Eichengreen, Barry, and Ngaire Woods. 2016. "The IMF's Unmet Challenges." *Journal of Economic Perspectives* 30 (1): 29–52.

Feldstein, Martin. March/April 1998. "Refocusing the IMF." *Foreign Affairs* 77 (2).

Goldstein, Morris. 2003. "IMF Structural Programs", Ed. *Economic and Financial Crises in Emerging Market Economies.* University of Chicago Press.

Grable, Ilene. 2018. *When Things Don't Fall Apart: Global Financial Governance and Developmental Finance in an Age of Productive Incoherence*. The MIT Press.

Grimes, William W. 2009. "Lending Into Crises, The Chiang Mai Initiative." In *Currency and Contest in East Asia*. Cornell University Press.

Grimes, William W. 2011. "The Asian Monetary Fund Reborn?: Implications of Chiang Mai Initiative Multilateralization." *Asia Policy*, no. 11..

Hamada, Koichi. 1999. "From the AMF to the Miyazawa Initiative: Observations on Japan's Currency Diplomacy." *The Journal of East Asian Affairs* 13 (1).

Hill, Hal, and Jayant Menon. 2012. *Financial Safety Nets in Asia*. Australian National University.

Henning, C. Randall. 2002. "East Asian Financial Cooperation," Peterson Institute Press: Policy Analyses in International Economics, Peterson Institute for International Economics, number pa68, July.

Henning, C. Randall. 2011. "Coordinating Regional and Multilateral Financial Institutions." Working Paper WP 11-9, Peterson Institute for International Economics, Washington, D.C., March.

International Monetary Fund. 2000. "Managing Financial Crises: The Experience in East Asia."

International Monetary Fund. 2010. "Address by Dominique Strauss-Kahn." Managing Director of the IMF at the Asia 21 Conference, Daejeon, Korea, July 12.

International Monetary Fund. 2016. "Adequacy of the Global Financial Safety Net."

International Monetary Fund. 2017. "Collaboration between Regional Financing Arrangements and the IMF."

Katada, Saori N. 2001. *Banking on Stability: Japan and the Cross-Pacific Dynamics of International Financial Crisis Management*. The University of Michigan Press.

Kawai, Masahiro. 2015. "From the Chiang Mai Initiative to an Asian Monetary Fund." ADBI Working Paper Series, No. 527.

Kikuchi, Tsutomu. 2002. "East Asian Regionalism: A Look at the ASEAN Plus Three's Framework." *Japan Review of International Affairs* 16 (1).

Krauss, Ellis S., and T. J. Pempel. 2000. *Beyond Bilateralism: U.S.-Japan Relations in the New Asia-Pacific*. Stanford University Press Education.

Kuroda, Haruhiko, and Masahiro Kawai. 2002. "Strengthening Regional Financial Cooperation in East Asia." Pacific Economic Papers, No. 332 (October).

Lee, Young Wook. 2006. "Japan and the Asian Monetary Fund: An Identity-Intention Approach." *International Studies Quarterly* 50.

McKinsey Global Institute. 2017. "The New Dynamics of Financial Globalization."

Nemoto, Yoichi. 2003. *An Unexpected Outcome of the Asian Financial Crisis.* Princeton Institute for International and Regional Studies.

Park, Yung Chul, and Charles Wyplosz. 2008. "Monetary Financial Integration in East Asia: The Relevance of European Experience." *European Economy Economic Papers* 329.

Suk, Hyun, and James F. Paradise. 2020. "Toward an Asian Monetary Fund: Ideas for Transition." *Asian Economics Papers* 19 (2).

Sussangkarn, Chalongphob. 2010. *The Chiang Mai Initiative Mulilateralization: Origin, Development and Outlook.* ADBI.

Sussangkarn, Chalongphob. 2011. *Institution Building for Macroeconomic and Financial Cooperation in East Asia.* Thailand Development Research Institute.

Sussangkarn, Chalongphob, Junko Shimizu, Lu Feng, Soyoung Kim, Beomhee Han, Jae Young Lee, Jinho Choi, and Hongbo Wang. 2019/ AMRO Research Collaboration Program RCP/19-01, "Local Currency Contribution to the Chiang Mai Initiative Multilateralisation." https://www.amro-asia.org/local-currency-contribution-to-the-chiang-mai-initiative-multilateralisation.

Terada, Takashi. March 2003. "Constructing an 'East Asian' Concept and Growing Regional Identity: From EAEC to ASEAN+3." *The Pacific Review.*

Wang, Yunjong and Wing Thye Woo. 2004. "A Timely Information Exchange Mechanism, an Effective Surveillance System, and an Improved Financial Architecture for East Asia." In *Monetary and Financial Integration in East Asia: The Way Ahead.* Vol. 2. Houndmills and New York: Palgrave MacMillan, 426-458.

Yoshida, Tadahiro. March 2004. *East Asian Regionalism and Japan.* APEC Study Center–Institute of Deveoloping Economies, JETRO.

Chapter 27

Institutionalizing ASEAN+3 Regional Financial Cooperation and the Birth of AMRO

Yoichi Nemoto[1] and Faith Pang Qiying[2]

Introduction — Laying the Groundwork (1997–2006)

Within the Association of Southeast Asian Nations (ASEAN)+3 region, the Asian financial crisis (AFC) in 1997–1998 was a watershed moment. Besides highlighting the danger sudden changes in the direction of cross-border private capital flows and foreign exchange rates play in causing foreign currency liquidity and financial crises, the AFC also prompted regional monetary and financial authorities to consolidate the respective economic policy and financial supervisory framework(s) in their own jurisdiction(s). It also led to the genesis of the ASEAN+3 financial cooperation process.

In December 1998, ASEAN+3 Leaders met in Hanoi and agreed that their Finance Deputies and Deputy Central Bank Governors should meet to discuss financial and macroeconomic matters of concern to the region. The first meetings of the ASEAN+3 Finance and Central Bank Deputies and the ASEAN+3 Finance Ministers took place in March 1999 in Hanoi and May 1999 in Manila.[3] In November 1999, the ASEAN+3 financial

[1] Nemoto acknowledges the Japan Society for the Promotion of Science (JSPS) Kakenhi Grant Number 19K01621 for the support for his study of regional financing arrangements.

[2] The authors are previous and current staff of AMRO, respectively. However, the views expressed here are solely those of the authors in their private capacity and do not in any way represent the official views of AMRO nor the ASEAN+3 authorities. The information contained in this chapter is based on public knowledge, publicly available information, the authors' personal observations, or the knowledge the authors had already possessed before working for AMRO. No confidential information they received during their tenure at AMRO is disclosed in this paper. The information provided by AMRO (IO) is explicitly mentioned.

[3] The Deputies' meeting exchanged views on ways to monitor short-term capital flows and the international financial architecture. For details, see the Joint Statement of the first ASEAN+3 Deputy Finance Ministers and Deputy Central Bank Governors' Meeting, March 18, 1999, Hanoi, Vietnam (https://www.amro-asia.org/the-joint-statement-of-the-1st-asean3-finance-ministers-and-deputy-central-bank-governors-meeting-march-18-1999-afdcm-3-ha-noi-vietnam/). The Finance Ministers did not make a public statement in 1999.

cooperation process was institutionalized following the affirmation of the importance of regular engagements to increase opportunities for cooperation and collaboration, with the aim of promoting peace, stability, and prosperity in the region. Leaders agreed to strengthen policy dialogue, coordination, and collaboration on financial, monetary, and fiscal issues of common interest, reform the international financial architecture, and enhance self-help.[4]

The regional financial cooperation process advanced after the Leaders' announcement. At the ASEAN+3 Finance Ministers' Meeting (AFMM+3) in Chiang Mai in May 2000, the Finance Ministers agreed to establish a regional financing arrangement to supplement existing international facilities to strengthen the region's self-help and support mechanisms.[5] This was the birth of the Chiang Mai Initiative (CMI).[6]

In May 2002, the modality of the ASEAN+3 financial cooperation process was strengthened when the Finance Ministers announced at their meeting in Shanghai that their Finance and Central Bank Deputies would meet informally to discuss economic and policy issues under the framework of the Economic Review and Policy Dialogue (ERPD).[7] The establishment of a regular surveillance policy dialogue and the regional self-help mechanism thus took root within 4 years of the Leaders' announcement in 1999. This is an achievement in itself, considering the deliberate nature of decision-making among state actors in the international arena.

Under this framework of regional financial cooperation, the CMI and EPRD progressed steadily.[8] At the behest of the Finance Ministers, the

---

[4] For details, see the Joint Statement on East Asia Cooperation, November 28, 1999, Manila, Philippines (https://www.amro-asia.org/the-joint-statement-on-east-asia-cooperation-november-28-1999-manila-philippines/).

[5] The AFMM+3 has been convened annually since 1999 mostly at the sidelines of the Asian Development Bank's (ADB) Annual Meetings. In 2012, the AFMM+3 was renamed as the ASEAN+3 Finance Ministers' and Central Bank Governors' Meeting (AFMGM+3) to reflect the expanded participation of Central Bank Governors in the process. The Deputy-level and working-level meetings have always involved both monetary and financial authorities.

[6] The CMI consisted of (a) an expanded ASEAN swap arrangement and (b) a network of bilateral swap agreement (BSA) facilities among ASEAN countries, China, Japan, and Korea. For an early assessment of the CMI establishment, see Henning (2002) and Nemoto (2003).

[7] For details, see the Joint Statement of the fifth AFMM+3, May 10, 2002, Shanghai, China (https://www.amro-asia.org/the-joint-state).

[8] See Grimes (2009) for the development of the CMI network and regional surveillance in the 2000s.

ASEAN+3 Research Group (RG)[9] embarked on two studies aimed at strengthening financial resilience in the region. The first explored ways to enhance the effectiveness of the CMI in the medium term, with multilateralization of the CMI as a key recommendation.[10] The second study proposed institutional designs for surveillance and policy dialogue for future consideration. In the second study, five key recommendations were made: (1) link the regional surveillance process to CMI, (2) invite Central Bank Governors to the AFMM+3, (3) *create an independent secretariat as centralized surveillance institution*,[11] (4) take gradual steps toward establishing reserve pooling (or ear-marking), and (5) adopt regional contingent credit lines.[12] The RG's third recommendation is regarded as one of the earliest ideas of an independent surveillance institution for the ASEAN+3 region. These reports were submitted to the ASEAN+3 Finance Deputies in April 2005.

In May 2005, the Finance Ministers announced four key actions to deepen and expand regional financial cooperation, in line with the RG's recommendations. One of these recommendations was to integrate and enhance ASEAN+3 economic surveillance into the CMI framework to enable early detection of irregularities and swift remedial policy actions, *with a view to developing effective regional surveillance capabilities to complement the work of other international financial institutions (IFIs)*.[13]

This 2005 Finance Ministers' statement can be regarded as recognition at the highest level of the need to create an independent surveillance office

---

[9] The ASEAN+3 RG was launched at the AFMM+3 in August 2003, with the aim of identifying and exploring subjects for possible regional financial cooperation from the medium- to long-term points of views by mobilizing knowledge and expertise of private researchers and research institutions. The RG was terminated in November 2014, following ASEAN+3 members' conclusion that the RG had successfully accomplished its goal of rooting research culture into the ASEAN+3 finance process. The ASEAN+3 process may have been deprived of academic and innovative inputs by this termination.

[10] For details, see Exploring Ways to Enhance the Functions of the Chiang Mai Initiative in the medium-term summary report (https://asean.org/wp-content/uploads/2012/10/17889.pdf).

[11] The italics are the authors' own emphasis.

[12] This study was initiated in 2004. For details, see the Economic Surveillance and Policy Dialogue in East Asia summary report (https://asean.org/wp-content/uploads/2012/10/17902.pdf).

[13] The italics are the authors' own emphasis. The other actions announced by the Finance Ministers are to (1) clearly define the swap activation process and to adopt a collective decision-making mechanism of the current BSA network as a first step of multilateralization so that the relevant BSAs would be activated collectively and promptly in case of emergency, (2) significantly increase the size of swaps, and (3) raise the swap amount that can be drawn without a linkage to an International Monetary Fund program from 10% to 20%. For an interpretation of the ASEAN+3 financial authorities' intention behind this Joint Statement, see Kenen and Meade (2008), pp. 153–156.

in East Asia.[14]

Opportunity In Crisis (2007–2009)

In less than a decade, the ASEAN+3 finance process evolved from an ad hoc response to the AFC to an institutionalized regional forum, working to implement key initiatives to transform the international financial architecture.

In 2007, progress on the CMI front advanced. In May 2007 in Kyoto, the ASEAN+3 Finance Ministers announced that the total size of the CMI increased to USD 80 billion. They also agreed in principle that a self-managed reserve pooling arrangement governed by a single contractual agreement would be an appropriate form of multilateralization and tasked their Deputies to forge ahead with its implementation.[15]

As the ASEAN+3 Deputies conducted in-depth studies and discussed the key elements to multilateralize the CMI, the spectre of another financial crisis was looming ahead. In the midst of this uncertainty, the ASEAN+3 Finance Ministers gathered in Madrid in May 2008 and reiterated their commitment to accelerate the work to reach consensus on the Chiang Mai Initiative Multilateralisation (CMIM) elements.[16] They also agreed to strengthen the ERPD by increasing the frequency of dialogues and developing a standardized format for the provision of necessary information and data to contribute to smooth and efficient decision-making for the CMIM.[17]

The outbreak of the global financial crisis (GFC) in September 2008 reminded ASEAN+3 financial authorities of the threat posed by sudden changes in the direction of cross-border private capital flows, especially in

---

[14]Discussions on the multilateralization of the CMI — that is the CMI Multilateralisation (CMIM) — commenced in 2005, following the Finance Ministers' instructions to their Deputies to study various possible routes toward this. Discussions continued from 2006, as Deputies were charged with establishing a new task force to further study various possible multilateralization options, as well as to enhance regional surveillance capacities. For details, see the Joint Statement of the 9th AFMM+3, May 4, 2006, Hyderabad, India (https://www.amro-asia.org/the-joint-statement-of-the-9th-asean3-finance-ministers-meeting-may-4-2006-hyderabad-india/).

[15]For details, see the Joint Statement of the 10th AFMM+3, May 5, 2007, Kyoto, Japan (https://www.amro-asia.org/the-joint-statement-of-the-10th-asean3-finance-ministers-meeting-may-5-2007-kyoto-japan/).

[16]These elements include the concrete conditions eligible for borrowing, and contents of covenants specified in borrowing agreements.

[17]For details, see the Joint Statement of the 11th AFMM+3, May 4, 2008, Madrid, Spain (https://www.amro-asia.org/the-joint-statement-of-the-11th-asean3-finance-ministers-meeting-may-4-2008-madrid-spain/).

view of the interdependent nature of cross-border financial transactions. During the GFC, neither the CMI nor International Monetary Fund (IMF) facilities were activated. On one hand, this was a positive sign that the region had taken the lessons of the AFC to heart and had adopted prudent financial and monetary policies in the intervening years that enabled them to build strong and sound macroeconomic and financial fundamentals. On the other hand, it suggested two lessons. First, neither the CMI nor IMF facilities were particularly attractive to ASEAN+3 authorities who turned to ad hoc financial arrangements — that is, dollar liquidity swap lines — with the United States (US) Federal Reserve instead. Under these dollar liquidity swap lines, the US Federal Reserve could unconditionally provide liquidity, unlike the CMI and IMF facilities, which set certain conditions for drawing.[18] Second, the authorities must have noticed that they needed an objective third-party assessment of economic and financial developments by an independent surveillance unit located in the region.[19]

As the GFC intensified, there was recognition on the part of ASEAN+3 authorities that it was imperative to strengthen the region's financial safety net and to enhance the region's economic surveillance capabilities. At a special ad hoc meeting in February 2009 in Phuket, ASEAN+3 Finance Ministers emphasized the importance of operationalizing the CMIM and agreed to (1) increase the size of the CMIM from USD 80 billion to USD 120 billion, (2) *strengthen the regional surveillance mechanism into a robust and credible system that will facilitate the prompt activation of the CMIM through the establishment of an independent regional surveillance unit*,[20] and (3) increase the IMF delinked portion above the current limit of 20% once the surveillance unit is fully effective.[21]

With this announcement, the link between objective, independent

---

[18]See Ito (2017), Chabchitrchaidol et al. (2018), and McDowell (2019) for bilateral swaps after the GFC. The dollar liquidity swap lines were regarded as temporary and offered only to Korea, Singapore, Brazil, and Mexico, while different swap lines were offered to the central banks of Canada, Europe, Japan, Australia, and New Zealand. In March 2020, the Federal Reserve offered the swap lines to the same emerging economies as in 2008 (Korea, Singapore, Brazil, and Mexico). For more details, see the Federal Reserve's press releases in October 2008 (https://www.federalreserve.gov/newsevents/pressreleases/monetary20081029b.htm) and March 2020 (https://www.federalreserve.gov/newsevents/pressreleases/monetary20200319b.htm).

[19]See Kawai (2009) for the reasons the ASEAN+3's ERPD process did not work during the GFC.

[20]The italics are the authors' own emphasis.

[21]For details, see the Joint Media Statement, Action Plan to Restore Economic and Financial Stability of the Asian Region, February 2, 2009, Phuket, Thailand (https://www.amro-asia.org/joint-media-statement-action-plan-to-restore-economic-and-financial-stability-of-the-asian-region/).

surveillance and the provision of financial support under the CMIM became by far more explicit to external parties. It set the wheels in motion for the establishment of an ASEAN+3 regional surveillance unit as financial authorities sought to strengthen the region's buffers against increasing global uncertainty.

Taking The First Steps (2009–2010)

The notion of establishing an independent regional surveillance unit was not new.[22] The GFC merely served as a catalyst for its prompt implementation as the idea was first seeded in 2005, together with the CMIM in the RG report as well as the Finance Ministers' statement, as indicated in the section earlier.

Following the February 2009 announcement, progress in the establishment of this surveillance unit accelerated. In May 2009, ASEAN+3 Finance Ministers reiterated their commitment to establish an independent regional surveillance unit as soon as possible to monitor and analyze regional economies and support CMIM decision-making.[23] A year later, there were two major milestones. First, the CMIM Agreement took effect as of March 24, 2010. Second, the ASEAN+3 Macroeconomic Research Office (AMRO), the region's independent surveillance unit, would be located in Singapore to monitor and analyze regional economies for the early detection of risks, swift implementation of remedial actions, and effective decision-making of the CMIM. AMRO was expected to commence operations in early 2011.[24]

It is important to consider the external environment during this time. When the announcement of the establishment of a regional surveillance unit was made, the global economy was reeling from a banking crisis and credit crunch that prompted government bailouts of banks in the US and Europe. Borrowing costs were rising and financing was drying up. In Europe, as the situation deteriorated, the European Financial Stability Facility (EFSF) was

---

[22] See Katada and Nemoto, "Finance and Japan" in *The Oxford Handbook of Japanese Politics* for the 1998 report by the Asian Financial and Capital Markets Subcommittee at the Japan Ministry of Finance (JMOF).

[23] For details, see the Joint Statement of the 12th AFMM+3, May 3, 2009, Bali, Indonesia (https://www.amro-asia.org/the-joint-statement-of-the-12th-asean3-finance-ministers-meeting-may-3-2009-bali-indonesia/).

[24] For details, see the Joint Statement of the 13th AFMM+3, May 2, 2010, Tashkent, Uzbekistan (https://www.amro-asia.org/the-joint-statement-of-the-13th-asean3-finance-ministers-meeting-may-2-2010-tashkent-uzbekistan/).

established in response to the sovereign debt crisis in June 2010 to provide temporary assistance to struggling Eurozone countries.[25] At the same time, the global sentiment toward the role of regional financing arrangements as part of the global financial safety net was changing. While the IMF had opposed the establishment of a strong regional initiative in 1997, the Eurozone crisis seemed to have led to the recognition that regional surveillance and combined firepower could contribute toward global economic stability. In October 2010, the International Monetary and Financial Committee (IMFC) called on the IMF to cooperate with regional financing arrangements,[26] signalling the acceptance of regional financing arrangements as an integral part of the global financial safety net.[27] Meanwhile, the IMF's 14th General Review of Quotas was kept on hold despite its completion in December 2010 due to delays in US Congress approval (the conditions for implementing this quota increase were finally met in January 2016).

Against this backdrop of uncertainty and shifting winds, the general sentiment was that a robust regional crisis prevention and crisis resolution mechanism needed to be in place before a crisis strikes, and that the time was ripe to do so. It also underscored the need to strengthen surveillance and monitoring to identify risks and vulnerabilities early. These considerations could have contributed toward the swift decision-making among the authorities, especially considering the consensus model of decision-making prevalent in the region.[28]

---

[25] The European Stability Mechanism (ESM), established in October 2012, is the successor to the EFSF. EFSF is a company incorporated in Luxembourg under Luxembourgish law on June 7, 2010 (see https://www.esm.europa.eu/sites/default/files/2016_02_01_efsf_faq_archived.pdf) while ESM is an international organization established by the treaty (see https://www.esm.europa.eu/about-us/history). See Henning (2017) on the development of the EFSF and ESM, and their relationship with the IMF. Legal resemblances between EFSF/ESM and AMRO (public company limited by guarantee, company for non-profit activities)/AMRO (international organization) turned out to be a useful reference for AMRO and ASEAN+3 authorities during their transformation.

[26] For details, see the press release of the IMFC Communiqué from October 2010 (https://www.imf.org/en/News/Articles/2015/09/14/01/49/pr10379).

[27] The momentum for this initiative would continue and in October 2011, the G20 issued the G20 Principles for Cooperation between the IMF and Regional Financing Arrangements (http://www.g20.utoronto.ca/2011/2011-finance-principles-111015-en.pdf). See IMF (2013) and IMF (2016) for the IMF's stocktaking of regional financing arrangements (and bilateral swaps).

[28] Grimes and Kring (2020) place the CMIM and AMRO as a departure from an "Asian way" of decision making.

Building the Foundations (2011)

Fourteen months after ASEAN+3 Finance Ministers announced the creation of the region's independent surveillance unit, AMRO was established in Singapore in April 2011. AMRO's purposes were to (1) monitor and analyze ASEAN+3 regional economies, (2) contribute to the early detection of risks, (3) provide policy recommendations for remedial actions, and (4) support the effective decision-making of the CMIM.

AMRO started out as a public company limited by guarantee (CLG, company for non-profit activities),[29] hereafter referred to as AMRO (CLG), and was governed under Singapore's laws. Mr Wei Benhua, the former Deputy Administrator of the State Administration of Foreign Exchange (SAFE) of the People's Republic of China, was appointed as AMRO's first Director. When Mr Wei arrived in Singapore, he had only two colleagues[30] to assist with setting up the office's operations. While Singapore's financial and monetary authorities, in their capacity as the host country, offered advice and assistance with respect to navigating Singapore's laws and business practices, the lean AMRO team had to draft and secure the budget, open bank accounts, complete AMRO's registration under the Singapore Companies Act, recruit staff, propose AMRO's logo for members' approval, set up AMRO's website, convene the AMRO Advisory Panel (AP) meetings,[31] as well as procure equipment for the office. They were backed by strong support from its member authorities.

In August 2011, after AMRO's fiscal year (FY) 2011 budget was approved by ASEAN+3 authorities, AMRO received the first transfer

---

[29] According to Singapore law, AMRO was classified as a public company limited by guarantee (CLG) because it was formed for the purpose of carrying out non-profit activities. We use CLG, company for non-profit activities, in this chapter because "public" and/or "private" may also refer to the form of shareholding in certain other legal contexts.

[30] Counselor Dr Yoichi Nemoto, from the Japan Ministry of Finance, and Mr Satoshi Nakagawa, Asian Development Bank Consultant, joined Mr Wei in Singapore to help with establishing the AMRO office. The ASEAN+3 authorities had requested for Dr Nemoto to join Mr Wei from the onset to help with setting up the office and its surveillance activities to ensure consistency throughout his term, which was scheduled to commence after a one-year period.

[31] The first AMRO AP meeting was held in August 2011, one month before the first economist's arrival. AMRO's AP comprise of six members (three from ASEAN member states and one each from China, Korea, and Japan) who are distinguished and respected economists. According to the AMRO (IO) Agreement, the AP members are appointed by AMRO's Executive Committee for a term of two years, with the mandate of providing timely strategic, technical, and professional input to AMRO's macroeconomic assessments and recommendations to AMRO's Director. The list of AMRO's current AP members can be found at https://www.amro-asia.org/about-amro/who-we-are/advisory-panel/.

of funds to support its manpower operations. One month later, the first recruited economist arrived in Singapore to start work. In September 2011, AMRO also received the first transfer of its office-related funds from Singapore authorities.[32] A significant portion of the office-related funds was allocated to information and database resources, which could have been a response to the data and statistical reporting problem that contributed to the European sovereign debt crisis. In October 2011, AMRO welcomed five more surveillance staff to its office and conducted its first consultation visit to Vietnam.

Despite the delays in the budget process,[33] AMRO participated in the ASEAN+3 Finance and Central Bank Deputies' Meeting (AFCDM+3) in Sendai in December 2011. At the meeting, AMRO presented on the regional economic outlook and submitted country surveillance reports for each of its 14 member economies for the Deputies' deliberation at the ERPD session (see the later section on the progress in AMRO's surveillance capabilities).

Taking Flight (2011–2012)

AMRO's establishment as a public CLG should have enabled it to commence operations swiftly. Being subject to the laws of Singapore, however, led to two major constraints in building AMRO's surveillance capacity — (1) human resources and (2) information and data access. As a CLG,

---

[32] AMRO is funded annually by its member authorities. Its budget comprises the manpower-related budget (funded by ASEAN+3 member authorities) and the office-related budget (funded by the host authorities — the Monetary Authority of Singapore and Singapore Ministry of Finance).

[33] The initial design of the budget process was far from ideal and resulted in a delay in AMRO's start-up by almost half a year. Neither ASEAN+3 authorities nor the host country provided AMRO with liquidity after its establishment in April 2011.

The 2011 budget process was as follows: (1) AMRO submitted its requests for both manpower and office-related budgets to ASEAN+3 authorities, (2) ASEAN+3 authorities would then examine and approve both budgets, and (3) ASEAN+3 authorities then proceeded with their internal budget processes before transferring money to AMRO's accounts. This meant that AMRO had to start its operations and establish its office (including during the process of preparation of budget requests and participation in the meetings organized by ASEAN+3 authorities) without any cash during this period.

This delay in AMRO's start-up, together with the restrictive publication policy (until 2017; see the later section), may have led to pessimistic observations vis-à-vis AMRO's future by outsiders (Eichengreen (2012); at the same time, Eichengreen and Woods (2016) recognized AMRO's steady progress and development after one of the authors visited AMRO's office in 2015).

Nonetheless, this delay may have ultimately helped to promote AMRO's transformation into an IO from a CLG because some authorities seemed to (mistakenly) attribute the delay to the fact that AMRO had yet to obtain IO status, rather than to the far from ideal design of the budget process.

AMRO was constrained by Singapore's immigration policy, which saw a tightening in the number of foreign workers within the country during that period. Second, the fact that AMRO (CLG) was governed by Singapore's laws was potentially sensitive, as there could be reluctance among other ASEAN+3 member authorities to share their confidential information or policy plans, which is crucial for AMRO to carry out its purpose and functions. Finally, AMRO (CLG) and its staff were subject to Singapore's laws, such as freedom of speech.

AMRO's CLG status was regarded as temporary and its transformation into an international organization (IO) was the next task.[34] As early as May 2011, ASEAN+3 Finance Ministers instructed their Deputies "to launch a study to strengthen the legal status of AMRO to constitute an international organisation with an international legal personality."[35]

IOs are generally constituted or created by way of an international agreement. Although IOs are not sovereign states and do not enjoy sovereign immunity, it has become practice to confer certain privileges and immunities (P&Is) to IOs for them to carry out their functions fully and independently. This generally includes immunity from legal processes in respect of acts performed in its official capacity, inviolability of its premises and official archives, and exemption from certain taxes and duties. Since these P&Is will be granted not only by the host country but also by other members, it would be ideal for this international agreement to be formulated by all involved parties.

ASEAN+3 member authorities recognized that transforming AMRO into an IO would raise AMRO's profile internationally and would allow it to contribute effectively to the global community. This would help AMRO gain credibility and establish networks with peer institutions, thereby facilitating effective exchange of knowledge, information, and best practices.

After the ASEAN+3 Finance Ministers' and Central Bank Governors' Meeting (AFMGM+3) in Manila in May 2012, preparations to draft an

---

[34]There seemed to be a variety of views regarding the timing of "the next." Some members wanted to transform AMRO (CLG) into IO as soon as possible while others viewed it to be a long-term agenda, similar to the transformation of the ASEAN Secretariat. The ASEAN Secretariat was first housed at the Department of Foreign Affairs of Indonesia in Jakarta in 1976 and the current ASEAN Secretariat at 70A Jalan Sisingamangaraja, Jakarta, was established and officiated in 1981.The ASEAN Charter (treaty) entered into force in 2008. See ASEAN's website at http://asean.org/asean/asean-secretariat/.

[35]For details, see the Joint Statement of the 14th AFMM+3, May 4, 2011, Hanoi, Vietnam (https://www.amro-asia.org/the-joint-statement-of-the-14th-asean3-finance-ministers-meeting-may-4-2011-ha-noi-viet-nam/).

international treaty to transform AMRO from a CLG to an IO began in earnest. At this meeting, Finance Ministers and Central Bank Governors called to accelerate the preparation work to institutionalize AMRO as an IO and urged AMRO and Singapore (as host country) to work together on the first draft of the treaty.[36] With regard to legal modality vis-à-vis the institutionalization of AMRO as an IO, they agreed to establish a treaty agreed upon by member governments and endorsed by their Parliaments to grant AMRO international legal personality via a legally binding instrument (see Table 27.2 on comparisons of international institutions affiliated with the regional financing arrangements).

Metamorphosis (2012–2013)

Treaty Drafting

Although the treaty drafting process was co-led by AMRO and Singapore authorities, it required consensus among all 14 member authorities before it could be finalized (by the Ministers' signing of the treaty). ASEAN+3 working-level officials held several intensive discussions between May 2012 and May 2013 to reach consensus on the "Agreement Establishing ASEAN+3 Macroeconomic Research Office" (hereafter referred to as the "AMRO Agreement").[37]

Since AMRO (CLG) already started its operations under its Articles of Agreement (AoA), ASEAN+3 members agreed that it would be prudent and expedient to retain the key policy decisions made at the point of AMRO (CLG)'s establishment. At the same time, a clause allowing AMRO (IO) to

---

[36] ASEAN+3 Finance Ministers and Governors "instructed the Deputies to accelerate the preparation to institutionalize AMRO as an international organization. In this regard, [they] endorsed the Deputies' decisions to urge AMRO to prepare a work plan, including a concrete timeline, and Singapore to work with AMRO to come up with the first draft of the treaty. [They] also affirmed the importance of concluding the Host Country Memorandum of Understanding (MOU) between AMRO and Singapore to clearly define the responsibility of the Host Country." For details, see the Joint Statement of the 15th AFMGM+3, May 3, 2012, Manila, the Philippines (https://www.amro-asia.org/the-joint-statement-of-the-15th-asean3-finance-ministers-meeting-may-3-2012-manila-philippines/).

[37] At the 16th AFMGM+3 in Delhi, India, May 3, 2013, it was announced that Finance Ministers and Central Bank Governors had reached consensus on the draft of the AMRO Agreement and will proceed with the necessary domestic processes as early as possible for its prompt signature and entry into force. This would enable AMRO to conduct objective surveillance as a credible, independent international organization, contributing further to the regional financial stability along with the strengthened CMIM. See the Joint Statement of the meeting for details (https://www.amro-asia.org/the-joint-statement-of-the-16th-asean3-finance-ministers-and-central-bank-governors-meeting-may-3-2013-delhi-india/).

carry out the necessary activities to fulfil its functions without amending the treaty would be included.[38] In this regard, it was agreed that the AMRO Agreement would adopt a "two-tier approach" — that is, fundamental issues would be defined in the treaty, while other details would be prescribed in the secondary rules to allow members to flexibly decide and amend nonfundamental rules as AMRO (IO) evolves in the future. As a result, the text of the AMRO (IO) Agreement was reduced to a third, compared with that of the AoA of AMRO (CLG).[39]

This was a practical decision because the AMRO (IO) Agreement would be signed by the governments of member authorities, rather than just the financial and monetary authorities to grant AMRO (IO) full legal personality under international law, as well as full legal capacity. AMRO (IO) would be allowed to enter into contracts, acquire and dispose of immovable and movable property, and institute legal proceedings.[40] However, this also meant that should amendments be made to the treaty, members would have to undergo a lengthy and administratively burdensome process. They would need to go through their domestic processes to obtain the instrument of full powers to sign the amendment. Even after signing the amendment, the instruments of ratification, acceptance, or approval was needed for the amendments to be effective. Having non-fundamental details in a second-tier, that is, the Secondary Rules of the AMRO Agreement, would accommodate AMRO's future growth and development in a more flexible manner.

ASEAN+3 members also agreed to grant P&Is to AMRO (IO) to enable it to carry out its work objectively in the territories of all its members. Under the AMRO Agreement, AMRO (IO) was provided immunity from legal process; its property and assets were immune from search, requisition, confiscation, expropriation, and seizure; its archives and documents were inviolable; and its official communications were protected from censorship. In addition, AMRO (IO)'s staff were granted functional immunity to protect them in the course of their work.

---

[38] For example, Article 3(d) of the AMRO Agreement states that one of AMRO's functions is "to conduct such other activities necessary for achieving the purpose of AMRO as may be determined by the Executive Committee."

[39] The information in this paragraph was provided by AMRO (IO) for this chapter.

[40] This is enshrined in Article 17, Legal Status of AMRO in the AMRO Agreement (see https://amro-asia. org/wp-content/uploads/2016/09/amro-agreement.pdf).

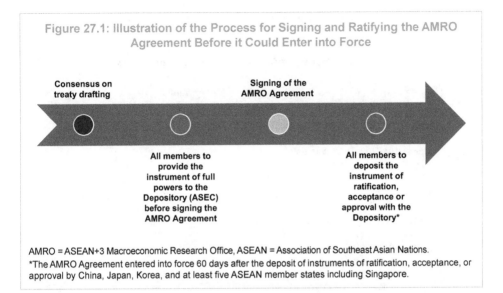

Figure 27.1: Illustration of the Process for Signing and Ratifying the AMRO Agreement Before it Could Enter into Force

Consensus on treaty drafting

Signing of the AMRO Agreement

All members to provide the instrument of full powers to the Depository (ASEC) before signing the AMRO Agreement

All members to deposit the instrument of ratification, acceptance or approval with the Depository*

AMRO = ASEAN+3 Macroeconomic Research Office, ASEAN = Association of Southeast Asian Nations.
*The AMRO Agreement entered into force 60 days after the deposit of instruments of ratification, acceptance, or approval by China, Japan, Korea, and at least five ASEAN member states including Singapore.

The AMRO Agreement also obliges member authorities to cooperate with AMRO (IO) to ensure that it would be able to fulfil its purposes and functions. Article 4 of the AMRO Agreement mandates that each member "shall cooperate with AMRO in good faith" and "provide AMRO with relevant information and assistance as may reasonably be required for its surveillance and other activities."[41] By including this Article, AMRO's members were not only signaling their trust in this newly established institution but also demonstrating their commitment to develop AMRO (IO) into an independent, credible, professional, and effective regional organization.

Since AMRO (CLG and IO) is headquartered in Singapore, AMRO (CLG) and Singapore authorities agreed on the text of Headquarters Agreement (HQA) for AMRO (IO) in May 2013. The HQA seeks to ensure the smooth headquarters operations of AMRO in Singapore and commits both parties to work together to this end. The HQA would be executed and

---

[41] Article 4 (Cooperation of Members) states, "(1) Each member shall provide AMRO with relevant information and assistance as may reasonably be required for its surveillance and other activities provided for under Article 3 to the extent permissible under its applicable laws and regulations. Members shall be under no obligation to provide information in such detail that the affairs of individuals or corporations are disclosed. (2) Each member shall cooperate with AMRO in good faith in AMRO's surveillance and other activities provided for under Article 3." (https://amro-asia.org/wp-content/uploads/2016/09/amro-agreement.pdf).

enter into effect concurrent with the AMRO Agreement.[42]

Table 27.1: Process of AMRO's Transformation to an IO

Year	Month	Key Milestones
2009	Feb	AFMM+3 decided to establish an independent regional surveillance unit.
2011	Apr	AMRO (CLG) was established.
	May	AMRO (CLG) started operation.
2012	May	AFMGM+3 instructed to accelerate the preparation to institutionalize AMRO as an IO.
	Sep	Working-level discussion started on drafting a treaty.
2013	May	AFMGM+3 agreed to transform AMRO to an IO.
	Nov	Consensus was reached on the AMRO Agreement draft.
2014	Oct	The AMRO Agreement was signed by ASEAN+3 member authorities. ASEAN+3 authorities started their domestic processes to ratify the AMRO Agreement.
2016	Feb	AMRO (IO) was established.

AFMGM+3 = ASEAN+3 Finance Ministers' and Central Bank Governors' Meeting, AFMM+3 = ASEAN+3 Finance Ministers' Meeting, AMRO = ASEAN+3 Macroeconomic Research Office, ASEAN = Association of Southeast Asian Nations, CLG = company limited by guarantee, IO = international organization.
Source: Based on Chabchitrchaidol et al. (2018) and Joint Statements of AFMM+3 and AFMGM+3.

Treaty Signing, Ratification and Entry into Force (2013–2016)

Subsequent to the May 2013 announcement, the text of the AMRO Agreement was finalized in November 2013, following minor adjustments at the technical working level. The next step was for members to obtain the instrument of full powers to the delegated signing authority.

---

[42] See the Joint Statement of the 16th AFMGM+3. Legally speaking, AMRO (CLG) was not protected by the HQA between 2011 and 2013. In the end, this helped to rationalize the IO conversion process because AMRO (CLG) and Singapore authorities could discuss the text for the Host Country MOU for AMRO (CLG), the HQA for AMRO (IO), and the treaty concurrently. In the Joint Statement of the 15th AFMGM+3 on May 3, 2012, Ministers and Governors "affirmed the importance of concluding the Host Country Memorandum of Understanding (MOU) between AMRO and Singapore to clearly define the responsibility of the Host Country" and also "welcomed Singapore's commitment to provide the necessary host country support which AMRO deems critical to pursue its mission as an independent surveillance unit, for example to provide budget and liquidity support, protect the member countries' data and information, and facilitate employment pass process" (for details, see https://www.amro-asia.org/the-joint-statement-of-the-15th-asean3-finance-ministers-meeting-may-3-2012-manila-philippines/). The Host Country MOU was concluded in May 2013 and provided AMRO (CLG) with legal protection until its reconstitution as an IO (see the Joint Statement of the 16th AFMGM+3, May 3, 2013 for details: https://www.amro-asia.org/the-joint-statement-of-the-16th-asean3-finance-ministers-and-central-bank-governors-meeting-may-3-2013-delhi-india/).

After all 14 members completed their domestic processes to obtain the instrument of full powers,[43] the signing of the treaty to transform AMRO into an IO was successfully convened on October 10, 2014, in Washington, D.C., at the sidelines of the IMF/World Bank (WB) annual meetings. The next step was for members to enter into their respective domestic processes to ratify this treaty.

The AMRO Agreement came into effect on February 9, 2016, following the ratification by the minimum requisite number of members required for entry into force as per Article 26 of the AMRO Agreement.[44] Dr Yoichi Nemoto, then Director of AMRO (CLG), assumed the position as Director of AMRO (IO). The opening ceremony for AMRO took place on February 19, 2016 in Singapore to commemorate this milestone event.[45] ASEAN+3 Finance and Central Bank Deputies, members of the diplomatic corps, and representatives from other IOs,[46] financial institutions, and institutions of higher learning attended the ceremony. Singapore's then Minister for Finance, Mr Heng Swee Keat, delivered the welcome remarks at the event.[47]

Table 27.2 compares institutions affiliated with regional financing arrangements that were established after the GFC.[48] Despite their diverse backgrounds (due to various reasons), it is safe to conclude that AMRO (IO) has acquired the commensurate legal foundation (indicated by its establishment by international agreement), governance (as indicated by the clearly pre-determination of supermajority rule), and transparency (as

---

[43] It is reported that it took 10 months from the technical level's consensus on the text of the Agreement to its signing due to a situation whereby one member required its Minister to obtain approval from the Parliament to sign for finalization (not approval of the treaty), as the lower house was dissolved for a certain period.

[44] Article 26 of the AMRO Agreement states, "This Agreement shall enter into force on the sixtieth (60th) day following the deposit of instruments of ratification, acceptance or approval by the People's Republic of China, Japan, the Republic of Korea, and at least five ASEAN Member States including the Republic of Singapore."

[45] See AMRO's website for more details on the opening ceremony (https://www.amro-asia.org/amros-opening-ceremony/).

[46] The European Stability Mechanism (ESM), IMF, Asian Development Bank (ADB), Asian Development Bank Institute (ADBI), Economic Research Institute for ASEAN and East Asia (ERIA), and Credit Guarantee and Investment Facility (CGIF) sent representatives to attend the opening ceremony.

[47] Mr Heng's speech can be found on AMRO's website (https://www.amro-asia.org/welcome-remarks-by-his-excellency-heng-swee-keat-minister-for-finance-for-singapore-at-amros-opening-ceremony/).

[48] Grabel (2017) compares characteristics of the regional financing arrangements. Kring and Grimes (2019) compare the Latin America Reserve Fund (FLAR) and CMIM/AMRO in terms of members, scope, centralization, control, and flexibility and examine their impact on the global liquidity regime.

Table 27.2: Institutions for RFAs Established After the GFC

International Organizations/ Institution	Year of Establishment	Region	Legal Bases	Whether Arrangements and Institutions are Described by the Single Legal Source	Governance Decision-Making	Economic Research Report Publication
European Financial Stability Facility (EFSF) (Company set up under Luxembourg law)	2010	Euro members (19 countries)	Contract ("Framework Agreement")	Same	Special majority	No
European Stability Mechanism (ESM) (Public international organization)	2012	Euro members (19 countries)	International Treaty	Same	Special majority	Yes
ASEAN+3 Macroeconomic Research Office (AMRO) (Company established under Singapore law (2011–2016), public international organization (2016))	2011	ASEAN, China, Japan, and Korea	Contract ("Articles of Agreement") (2011–2016) International Treaty (2016)	Separate	Consensus (special majority in case consensus is not reached)	Limited (2011–2017) Yes (2017–)
Eurasian Fund for Stabilization and Development (EFSD) (Not a legal entity, Eurasian Development Bank manages resources)	2009 (name changed in 2015)	Former CIS countries (6 countries)	International Treaty	No provisions for institutions (financial arrangements only)	Special majority	Yes (they appear on both EFSD's and the Eurasian Development Bank's homepage)
(Cf.) Latin America Reserve Fund (FLAR) (Public international organization)	1978 (name changed in 1991)	8 countries in Central and South America	International Treaty	Same	Special majority (one country, one vote)	Yes
(Cf.) Arab Monetary Fund (AMF) (Public international organization)	1976	22 countries in MENA region	International Treaty	Same	Special majority	Yes
(Cf.) BRICS Contingent Reserve Arrangement (CRA) (Not a legal entity)	2014	Brazil, Russia, India, China, and South Africa	International Treaty	No provisions for institutions (financial arrangements only)	Consensus and special majority (depending on items)	No
(Cf.) International Monetary Fund (IMF) (Public international organization)	1946	All regions	International Treaty	Same	Majority and special majority (depending on items)	Yes

ASEAN = Association of Southeast Asian Nations, CIS = Commonwealth of Independent States, GFC = global financial crisis, MENA = Middle East and North Africa, RFA = regional financing arrangement.
Source: Based on Grabel (2017), Kring et al. (2019), Tominaga (2020), and the organizations' homepages.

indicated by the publication of its economic reports).[49, 50]

Table 27.3 compares the process to establish the IMF, Asian Development Bank (ADB), and AMRO. While the duration between the start of discussion and operationalization in the case of the IMF and ADB are 4 years and 3 years, respectively, the duration between the ASEAN+3 Finance Ministers' decision (February 2009) and establishment of the company (April 2011) was 2 years, and it took almost 5 more years to complete the transformation to an IO. Chabchitrchaidol et al. (2018) suggest the reason why AMRO was initially founded as a company in Singapore, rather than an IO, is because the Finance Ministers might have anticipated that setting up an IO would require a long preparation period. They argue that "AMRO was desired to start operations promptly in light of the underlying economic and financial condition surrounding the region (after the GFC). "

Table 27.3: Establishment of the IMF, ADB, and AMRO: A Comparison

	IMF	ADB		AMRO
Start of Discussion	Mar 1943	Dec 1963	**Establishment as Company**	Apr 2011
Signing of Treaty	Jul 1944	Dec 1965	**Start of Discussion on Transition to IO**	May 2012
Establishment	Dec 1945	Aug 1966	**Signing of Treaty**	Oct 2014
Operationalia tion	Mar 1947	Dec 1966	**Transition to IO**	Feb 2016

ADB = Asian Development Bank, AMRO = ASEAN+3 Macroeconomic Research Office, IMF = International Monetary Fund, IO = international organization.
Source: Chabchitrchaidol et al. (2018) based upon International Monetary Fund (1996), McCawley (2017), Watanabe (1973), Joint Statements of ASEAN+3 Finance Ministers' Meeting, and ASEAN+3 Finance Ministers' and Central Bank Governors' Meeting.

---

[49] The appointment of the Directors of AMRO (IO), Dr Chang Junhong (2016–2019) and Mr Toshinori Doi (2019), are "guided by the principles of meritocracy, transparency and openness." This is enshrined in Article 11(2) of the AMRO Agreement.

[50] One notable difference is the fact that an institution and a financial arrangement are prescribed separately (see the discussion in the "Looking Forward" section).

IO versus CLG (Company for Non-Profit Activities) (2016–2020)

With AMRO's transition to an IO in February 2016, the formation of its legal framework was firmly grounded. The AMRO Agreement enshrines AMRO's rights and functions, and is succinctly captured in Article 5(c), which states that "AMRO, independently and without undue influence of any member, shall prepare such reports as it deems desirable in carrying out its purpose and functions, and communicate its views informally and confidentially to any member on any matters arising under this Agreement that may affect such member." It reaffirms AMRO's role in supporting the CMIM, as articulated in Article 3(c), which states that AMRO shall "support members in the implementation of the regional financing arrangement."[51] It also guarantees the autonomy of AMRO's personnel, stating that the "Director and the staff shall, in the discharge of their functions, owe their duty entirely to AMRO and to no other authority. Members shall respect the international character of this duty and shall refrain from all attempts to influence any of the staff in the discharge of these functions."[52]

Since its transformation to an IO, AMRO's operations have changed significantly, reflecting the Articles above and its international legal status. This section will examine the key changes.

Enhanced Transparency and Accountability

AMRO's status as an IO engendered greater openness in its operations. In their paper "Institutionalizing Financial Cooperation in East Asia: AMRO and the Future of the Chiang Mai Initiative Multilateralisation," Grimes and Kring (2020) point out that AMRO, as an IO, is transparent in what it does and this has established AMRO as an authoritative and professional organization among its member authorities and peers.

Since 2017, AMRO (IO) started to publish some key indicators of its activities, such as expenditures and human resource capacity in its corporate annual report.[53] This document details the organization's key developments

---

[51] See the AMRO Agreement for details. Kawai (2015) expects impartial surveillance by an objective, independent, international organization.

[52] See Article 11(5) of the AMRO Agreement.

[53] AMRO's corporate annual reports are available on its website (https://www.amro-asia.org/publications/corporate-documents/amro-annual-report/).

and achievements. In the same year, AMRO started to publish its annual consultation reports on its member economies as well as its flagship ASEAN+3 Regional Economic Outlook (AREO).[54]

This is a conscious decision on AMRO's part as it seeks to promote transparency and accountability in its activities and documents, strengthen its effectiveness by providing stakeholders and the public with access to AMRO's functions and relevant activities, support the quality of surveillance by subjecting AMRO to external review, and raise AMRO's public profile and visibility through various channels. It was also acknowledged that for AMRO to be recognized as a peer of other IFIs, it was crucial to ensure that its publication policy was on par with theirs. In the years since AMRO (IO) set its publication policy in 2017, it has expanded the categories of publications in its website to include analytical notes, working papers, blogs, and speeches.

Publication Policy

One of the policy issues raised following AMRO's establishment as an IO was its publication policy. ASEAN+3 members put in place a highly restrictive publication policy for AMRO (CLG) when they designed its governance structure. This is attributed to three factors. First, there was a need for an objective third-party view of the region's economic and financial development (as described in the Opportunity in Crisis section), even as the external environment was clouded with uncertainty. ASEAN+3 members wanted to keep the reports and discussions frank and expedient, but confidential to enable open and candid exchange of views. Second, member authorities wanted to avoid unnecessary market speculation that the publication of its reports could bring. Third, it was possible that member authorities did not want to undergo the process of reviewing and editing AMRO (CLG)'s surveillance reports to prepare it for publication, as it was doing with the other IFIs.

As a result, AMRO (CLG) was required to obtain explicit approval from all member authorities to publish any external publications.[55] Thus, AMRO only managed to publish two reports during its first 5 years of

---

[54] AMRO's AREO reports are available on its website (https://www.amro-asia.org/publications/asean3-regional-economic-outlook/).

[55] This makes this chapter challenging, especially for the AMRO (CLG) period as it is based upon publicly available information (see footnote 2).

operations.[56] AMRO (CLG) and its member authorities recognized that the publication policy of AMRO (CLG) was greatly restrictive and inadequate to accommodate the ambitions for AMRO (IO). Accordingly, they stipulated that "AMRO shall publish such reports as it deems desirable for carrying out its purpose and functions in accordance with subparagraph (2)(f) of Article 8" for AMRO (IO).[57]

Thus, AMRO's Executive Committee agreed to revise AMRO's publication policy to strike a balance between boosting AMRO's visibility while ensuring confidentiality of information per the AMRO Agreement. The revised publication policy of AMRO (IO) came into effect in January 2017.[58] The impact of the change in policy was clear. AMRO (IO) published 58 reports in the first three and a half years its operations, a stark contrast to its CLG years. See Table 27.4

Table 27.4: Number of Economic Reports Published by AMRO (CLG) (2011–2016) and AMRO (IO) (2016–2019) (as of December 31, 2019)[59]

Category of Reports	2011	2012	2013	2014	2015	2016 (Company)	2016 (IO)[1]	2017	2018	2019
Regional	0	0	0	0	0	0	0	1	9[2]	6
Country	0	0	0	0	0	0	0	8	11	13
Research	0	0	0	0	1[1]	1	0	2	6	2
Total	0	0	0	0	1	1	0	11	26	21

AMRO = ASEAN+3 Macroeconomic Research Office, CLG = company limited by guarantee, IO = international organization.

Note:

[1] ASEAN+3 Macroeconomic Research Office (AMRO) (IO)'s publication policy was being discussed during this period, and only came into effect in January 2017. This explains the lack of publications during this time. Authors moved the publication year of a report titled "Understanding Banking Supervisory Priorities and Capacities in ASEAN+3 Economies" from 2016 to 2015. The report was uploaded on AMRO's homepage in 2016 although the report was completed and made public in 2015 (as indicated on the cover page of the report).

[2] This includes monthly regional outlook updates.

Source: Based on information provided by AMRO. The shaded areas indicate AMRO during the stage when it was a company (CLG).

---

[56] Technically speaking, 2011–2016 (5 years) is the period between the establishment of AMRO (CLG) and the establishment of AMRO (IO). After 2016, AMRO (CLG) and AMRO (IO) coexisted for about 4 years until AMRO (CLG) was formally dissolved on December 24, 2019.

[57] Subparagraph (2)(f) of Article 8 states, "The Executive Committee shall maintain strategic oversight of and set policy directions for AMRO and, in particular: set the publication policy of AMRO." See the AMRO Agreement for more details.

[58] Although AMRO's Executive Committee described the process as a "revision" because AMRO (IO) followed AMRO (CLG)'s publication policy until January 2017, the process could have been referred to as "creation," in light of the substantial changes to AMRO's publication policy.

[59] The information of this table was provided by AMRO (IO) for this chapter.

for the number of economic reports published annually during AMRO's time as a company (CLG, 2011–2016), and the early years of its reconstitution as an IO (2016–2019).[60] This is a new and significant development, considering that the gaps in the publication of reports in previous years had been viewed as a hindrance in tracking, even in an informal way, the sophistication or accuracy of AMRO's surveillance efforts over time.[61]

Credibility and Legitimacy for Partnerships, Outreach, and Communications

AMRO's formal establishment as an IO via a treaty with full legal personality and legal capacity for carrying out its purpose and functions also provides it with legitimacy as a regional actor and reflects its member authorities' commitment and support. This is significant because it confers AMRO with a greater sense of respectability in its interactions with peer IOs, the media, academia, global and regional fora, and financial institutions as it seeks to build capacity, gain credibility, and enhance capabilities.

As AMRO expands its engagement with these groups, it is able to assert its voice on a larger stage and this reinforces AMRO's reputation as a trusted advisor to ASEAN+3 member authorities. For instance, AMRO has been invited to participate in several high-level fora since being reconstituted as an IO to disseminate its views on the regional economy and the global financial safety net.[62] These include the Asia-Europe Meeting (ASEM) Finance Ministers' Meeting, the Asian Infrastructure Investment Bank (AIIB) Annual Meetings, Group of Twenty International Financial Architecture Working Group (G20 IFA WG) Meetings, ADB Annual Meetings, IMF/WB Annual Meetings,[63] and the United Nations Economic and Social Commission for Asia and the Pacific (UNESCAP) meetings.

With the ability to enter into contracts, AMRO as an IO has been able to institutionalize several key partnerships as well. AMRO has entered into

---

[60] These numbers are based on AMRO's homepage as of December 2020 (https://amro-asia.org/publications/).

[61] See Grimes and Kring (2020). The consultation reports of all member economies have become accessible from the AMRO homepage (as of December 2020).

[62] The AMRO (CLG) Director has been invited to ASEAN Finance Ministers' Meetings since April 2013.

[63] AMRO has participated in the IMF/WB meetings as an observer since 2013. During AMRO's early years as a CLG, AMRO and IMF gradually established informal channels of communication at the ground level. These informal channels of communication include AMRO staff visiting IMF's representative offices during their trips to member economies, and the IMF mission team stopping by AMRO's office before or after their Article IV missions. The first meeting between the heads of AMRO and IMF took place in July 2012, when AMRO Director and IMF Managing Director met, 1 year after the start of AMRO (CLG).

Memoranda of Understanding (MoUs) with the ADB, ESM, FLAR, IMF, and the Trilateral Cooperation Secretariat (TCS)[64] and cultivated win–win relations to ensure mutually beneficial outcomes through joint activities (e.g. joint seminars, joint research), information sharing and exchange on surveillance, crisis management support and other pertinent thematic issues, and corporate enhancement in the form of staff exchange, secondments, and exchange of best practices.

As AMRO (IO)'s visibility and profile increased, it began to attract attention from mainstream media outlets. The greater autonomy conferred to AMRO meant that it was able to accept requests for interviews while practicing the necessary discretion to safeguard confidential information. AMRO has featured in several interviews with high-profile media outlets, including Reuters, CNA, Chosun Biz, and ABS-CBN.[65] This has further helped assert AMRO as an authoritative voice in the region and bolster its reputation as the premier surveillance unit for ASEAN+3.

This three-prong approach of leveraging on its IO status to enhance its partnerships, communications, and outreach has entrenched AMRO's position as an independent, credible, and professional regional organization, acting as a trusted policy advisor to its member authorities. As AMRO has gained a wider audience and has built a deeper understanding and support for its role and operations, it has been able to compete with peer IOs and attract talent from the region, especially since it is no longer bound by Singapore's immigration laws. This ability to pick the crème-de-la-crème of talent bodes well for AMRO's future development.

Table 27.6 compares the key functions of AMRO (CLG) and AMRO (IO). Some functions are enabled by parliamentary approval and others are enabled by specific provisions in the AMRO Agreement.

---

[64] See AMRO's website for more details on partnership engagements (https://www.amro-asia.org/about-amro/what-we-do/#partnerships).

[65] For details on AMRO's interviews, see its website (https://www.amro-asia.org/news-events/interviews/).

Table 27.5: AMRO's Partnerships — MOU Signed by AMRO (IO)[66]

MOU	Areas of Cooperation	Modality of Cooperation	Remarks
AMRO-ADB MOU (May 3, 2017)	Surveillance and research, capacity building	Information sharing and consultation, joint activities, staff exchange	MOU was renewed on January 1, 2021
AMRO-IMF MOU (October 10, 2017)	Surveillance, capacity building, regional and global financial safety nets	Information sharing and exchange of views, training and staff exchange, joint activities	MOU was renewed on October 11, 2020
AMRO-ESM MOU (October 11, 2017)	Dialogues between RFAs and between RFAs and the IMF, research, capacity building	Joint activities, technical cooperation, information sharing, staff exchange	MOU was renewed on October 11, 2021
AMRO-FLAR MOU (October 5, 2018)	Dialogues between RFAs and between RFAs and the IMF, research, capacity building	Joint activities, technical cooperation, information sharing, staff exchange	
AMRO-Trilateral Cooperation Secretariat (April 17, 2019)	Regional economic and financial affairs, capacity building	Research, joint activities, information sharing and consultation	

ADB = Asian Development Bank, AMRO = ASEAN+3 Macroeconomic Research Office, ESM = European Stability Mechanism, FLAR = Latin American Reserve Fund, IMF = International Monetary Fund, IO = international organization, MOU = memorandum of understanding, RFA = regional financing arrangement.
Source: ASEAN+3 Macroeconomic Research Office's partnership page (https://www.amro-asia.org/about-amro/what-we-do/#partnerships) and authors' own information.

Table 27.6: Comparison of AMRO (CLG) and AMRO (IO) on Key Functions

Key Functions	AMRO (CLG)	AMRO (IO)	Remarks
Protection from member authorities' interference (e.g., staff's arrest, document confiscation)	n.a. (No legal protection)[1]	Explicit protection by AMRO Agreement (legally protected)	Enabled by parliamentary ratification
Member authorities' obligation to submit to AMRO the same information to the IMF	Based on private agreement among central banks (articles of agreement)	Based on international treaty ratified by Parliament	

continued on next page

---

[66]The information of this table was provided by AMRO (IO) for this chapter.

Table 27.6: *continued*

Key Functions	AMRO (Company)	AMRO (IO)	Remarks
Information exchange and various cooperation with other international organizations (e.g., IMF)	n.a.	Allowed to establish cooperative relations as AMRO	
CMIM secretariat function	n.a.[2]	Explicit provision in AMRO Agreement	Enabled by provisions in AMRO Agreement
Support to other ASEAN+3 activities	n.a.	Explicit provision in AMRO Agreement	
External publication including economic reports	Strict condition. practically difficult for timely publication	Allowed to publish as per pre-set publication policy	

AMRO = ASEAN+3 Macroeconomic Research Office, ASEAN = Association of Southeast Asian Nations, CLG = company limited by guarantee, CMIM = Chiang Mai Initiative Multilateralisation, IMF = International Monetary Fund, IO = international organization, n.a. = not available.

Note:

[1] A memorandum of understanding (MOU) was signed between AMRO (CLG) and Singapore in May 2013.

[2] With the explicit instruction by ASEAN+3 authorities, AMRO (CLG) prepared a set of indicators to assess ASEAN+3 members' qualification for the CMIM's crisis prevention facility (called the Economic Review and Policy Dialogue (ERPD) Matrix).

Source: Chabchitrchaidol et al. (2018) based on the AMRO Agreement.

As The Number of Economists Exceeds the Number of Member Economies...[67]

Until its transformation into an IO in 2016, the priority of AMRO's (CLG) surveillance work was mainly given to support regional surveillance discussions at the ERPD session — a peer review surveillance session among the Deputies at the AFCDM+3. As described in an earlier section, an AMRO surveillance team made its first annual consultation visit to one of its member economies, Vietnam, in October 2011 and AMRO began to submit a regional surveillance report titled "ASEAN+3 Regional Economic Monitoring (AREM) Report" and 14 individual country reports for the member economies to the AFCDM+3 meetings biannually, only with six surveillance staff in total (two senior economists and four economists) in December 2011. AMRO's (CLG) human resources were preoccupied with conducting annual visits to 14 member economies and producing quarterly surveillance reports on the region and individual economies.

With the transition to an IO in February 2016, AMRO was better positioned to further enhance its surveillance capacity. Key enabling factors are as follows:

---

[67] The information in this paragraph was provided by AMRO (IO) for this chapter.

First, AMRO's top management structure evolved from a single directorship to a senior management system, consisting of a Director, Deputy Director 1 (Administration), Deputy Director 2 (CMIM, Strategy and Coordination), and Chief Economist (Surveillance). Second, AMRO's surveillance capacity was significantly strengthened in both staffing and organizational structure. The number of surveillance staff increased from 6 in December 2011 to 23 by December 2016, and then further expanded to 41 (including 9 secondees) in August 2020. In the second half of 2016, AMRO also bolstered its regional and sectoral surveillance capacity by establishing dedicated teams for these functions (e.g., financial surveillance, regional surveillance, and fiscal affairs). Third, AMRO has been able to publish its surveillance reports under the new publication policy since 2017 as described in the previous section.

With greater resources at its disposal, AMRO was also able to strengthen its support toward enhancing the CMIM, in particular, the work on the ERPD Matrix. After agreeing to introduce the CMIM Precautionary Line (CMIM-PL) in 2012, ASEAN+3 Deputies explicitly tasked AMRO (CLG) to develop this Matrix, consisting of economic indicators of all ASEAN+3 economies to facilitate assessment of members' qualification for the CMIM-PL.[68] Subsequently, this work by AMRO (CLG) was transferred to AMRO (IO) and has since become one of AMRO's (IO) core tasks, with AMRO working closely with member authorities to refine the assessment framework.

As mentioned earlier, the ERPD Matrix was first introduced as a quantitative "scorecard" on financial stability to be applied in determining access to the CMIM-PL. It has since been enhanced and expanded to include both quantitative and qualitative analyses and currently consists of three components. First, a purely quantitative "scoring" of a suite of macro-financial indicators, representing pre-defined macroeconomic and financial soundness criteria for members, relative to designated peer economies. Second, analyses from AMRO's regular bilateral surveillance of member economies and third, qualitative assessments of member economies' data

---

[68] For details, see the Joint Statement of the 16th AFMGM+3. In 2012, ASEAN+3 authorities needed to explicitly task AMRO (CLG) to develop this ERPD Matrix. The AoA of AMRO (CLG) defined AMRO's (CLG) functions within a narrow scope and the work on the ERPD Matrix fell outside of it. On the other hand, the Agreement establishing AMRO (IO) prescribes that one of its functions is "to support members in the implementation of the regional financing arrangement" (see Article 3(c) of the AMRO Agreement). In the context of AMRO and the ASEAN+3 region, the regional financing arrangements refer to the CMIM. See also Table 27.6 on the previous page for a comparison of the key functions of AMRO (CLG) and AMRO (IO).

adequacy and quality of financial supervision.[69]

In 2018, the EPRD Matrix framework was integrated into AMRO's surveillance work.[70] The convergence of the ERPD Matrix with AMRO's regular surveillance of member economies provides the basis for more in-depth analysis to assess qualification to the CMIM-PL.[71] AMRO continued to support members with respect to CMIM activation and in 2019, the ASEAN+3 Finance Ministers and Central Bank Governors announced that they had adopted the ERPD Matrix Scorecard as a qualification reference for the CMIM-PL, which was made possible because of AMRO's efforts.[72]

AMRO's progress in enhancing its surveillance capacity has therefore enabled it to serve as a trusted advisor to members, especially in ensuring the operational readiness of CMIM activation. In 2020, ASEAN+3 Finance Ministers and Central Bank Governors shared that a policy and review function would be introduced within AMRO to strengthen the governance of its surveillance process and reinforce support for CMIM programs.[73] Following the global outbreak of the coronavirus disease (COVID-19) pandemic, AMRO has provided timely analyses on the impact of the pandemic to its member authorities. These surveillance products have also been made available on AMRO's homepage as part of its efforts to establish itself as a trusted policy advisor for within the region.[74] This demonstrates the value and importance ASEAN+3 members place in AMRO's contributions.

---

[69]Li Lian Ong and Laura Grace Gabriella, AMRO Working Paper: The ERPD Matrix "Scorecard": Quantifying the Macro-Financial Performance of ASEAN+3 Economies (https://www.amro-asia.org/wp-content/uploads/2020/04/AMRO-Working-Paper-20-01_ERPD-Matrix-Scorecard_Ong-Gabriella_final.pdf).

[70]See Joint Statement of the 21st AFMGM+3, May 4, 2018, Manila, Philippines (https://www.amro-asia.org/the-joint-statement-of-the-21th-asean3-finance-ministers-and-central-bank-governors-meeting-may-4-2018-manila-philippines/).

[71]See Ong and Gabriella (2020) for more details on the ERPD Matrix framework, in particular the framework and methodology for the Scorecard component.

[72] See Joint Statement of the 22nd AFMGM+3, May 2, 2019, Nadi, Fiji (https://www.amro-asia.org/joint-statement-of-the-22nd-asean3-finance-ministers-and-central-bank-governors-meeting/).

[73]See 23rd AFMGM+3 Joint Statement, September 18, 2020, virtual (https://www.amro-asia.org/joint-statement-of-the-23rd-asean3-finance-ministers-and-central-bank-governors-meeting-september-18-2020-virtual/).

[74]AMRO refocused its efforts to better support members by providing information on the latest developments on the COVID-19 pandemic, informing national authorities on the impact of the COVID-19 pandemic on their economic activities and financial stability, deepening its analytical capabilities by stocktaking pandemic policies undertaken by ASEAN+3 member authorities and developing surveillance tools, as well as enhanced monitoring on vulnerable countries in the region. A wide array of new surveillance products that addressed the impact of the pandemic were also introduced and a microsite that collates these products was established on its homepage at https://www.amro-asia.org/covid-19-in-focus/.

Looking Forward

The past decade has been a whirlwind of activity for AMRO. Despite its achievements, there is scope for AMRO to enhance its effectiveness and support to members in the long run. This section will examine some of them.

AMRO's core mission is to contribute to the macroeconomic and financial stability of the region through conducting macroeconomic surveillance and supporting the implementation of the regional financing arrangement. To do so, AMRO must continue to accumulate expertise and knowledge on crises, program design, and policy advice. In detecting risks and vulnerabilities, AMRO's advantage lies in its close relations with member authorities, which has fostered close and regular dialogues among them. At the same time, it is imperative that AMRO remains objective in its assessments and continues to provide candid and frank views to member authorities.

Given the importance of accurate reporting of data and statistics for effective surveillance, AMRO has scaled up its technical assistance (TA) program in recent years. AMRO's TA program seeks to create a platform to strengthen members' macroeconomic surveillance capacities and facilitate knowledge sharing among members and other IOs through the programs. The heterogeneous nature of AMRO's member economies means that some members may require more assistance in this regard. The need to enhance the coverage, frequency, and quality of data and statistics will continue to be a long-term agenda for AMRO.

Finally, there is a need for ASEAN+3 members to consider the future direction of AMRO with respect to its role in supporting the CMIM. As mentioned, the vision of creating an independent secretariat as a centralized surveillance institution linked to the CMIM, with reserve pooling and regional contingent credit lines, was mooted in the early years of the ASEAN+3 financial process (i.e., in the 2004–2005 recommendations of the ASEAN+3 RG). To date, AMRO and the CMIM exist as separate entities — inexorably linked together yet unable to unify as one. The CMIM is a quasi-public contract among central banks while AMRO's treaty was approved by the respective Parliaments of its member authorities.[75] Should ASEAN+3 desire a smoother activation process for AMRO and the CMIM, it

---

[75]Article 3(c) of the AMRO (IO) Agreement stipulates that one of AMRO's functions is "to support members in implementation of the regional financing arrangement."

is worthwhile to consider legally upgrading the CMIM and to pool together a portion of the CMIM's total size to ensure the swift disbursement of funds.

If there is one key lesson to take away from the AFC, GFC, and the Eurozone crisis, it is that we must make hay while the sun shines. The ASEAN+3 region has shown remarkable resilience in the years following the AFC and has competently navigated the uncertainty and challenges in the global economy since. It has built a strong foundation and sound macroeconomic fundamentals and strengthened the various layers of the regional financial safety net to create strong self-help buffers. Perhaps it is timely to consider further enhancing and integrating its regional facilities so that AMRO/CMIM can take its place as a credible regional monetary fund that complements the global financial safety net. The COVID-19 pandemic is expected to accelerate these discussions and efforts to strengthen the CMIM as its members recognize the importance of ensuring its relevance in the face of the fast-changing global environment. It is noted that rule-based multilateral systems are more difficult to maintain, but they are more resilient against various shocks even in critical periods.[76]

References

ASEAN+3 Macroeconomic Research Office. "Agreement Establishing ASEAN+3 Macroeconomic Research Office (AMRO)." https://amro-asia.org/wp-content/uploads/2016/09/amro-agreement.pdf.

ASEAN+3 Macroeconomic Research Office. "ASEAN+3 Joint Statements." https://www.amro-asia.org/news-events/asean3-documents/asean3-joint-statements/.

ASEAN+3 Research Group. 2004–2005a. "Economic Surveillance and Policy Dialogue in East Asia." https://asean.org/wp-content/uploads/2012/10/17902.pdf.

ASEAN+3 Research Group. 2004–2005b. "Exploring Ways to Enhance the Functions of the Chiang Mai Initiative in the Medium Term." https://asean.org/wp-content/uploads/2012/10/17889.pdf.

Board of Governors of the Federal Reserve System. 2008. "Federal Reserve, Banco Central do Brasil, Banco de Mexico, Bank of Korea, and Monetary Authority of Singapore Announce the Establishment of Temporary Reciprocal Currency Arrangements." https://www.federalreserve.gov/newsevents/pressreleases/monetary20081029b.htm.

---

[76]See Nemoto (2015). Grabel (2019) is of the view that emergent coherence is (on balance) productive with respect to development and stability, rather than debilitating.

Board of Governors of the Federal Reserve System. 2020. "Federal Reserve Announces the Establishment of Temporary U.S. Dollar Liquidity Arrangements with other Central Banks." https://www.federalreserve.gov/newsevents/pressreleases/monetary20200319b.htm.

Chabchitrchaidol, A., S. Nakagawa, and Y. Nemoto. 2018. "Quest for Financial Stability in East Asia: Establishment of an Independent Surveillance Unit 'AMRO' and Its Future Challenges." *Financial Review* 133: 170–201.

Eichengreen, B. 2012. "Regional Financial Arrangements and the International Monetary Fund." ADBI Working Paper, no. 394.

Eichengreen, B., and N. Woods. 2016. "The IMF's Unmet Challenges." *Journal of Economic Perspectives* 30 (1): 29–52.

European Financial Stability Facility . "European Financial Stability Facility FAQs." https://www.esm.europa.eu/sites/default/files/2016_02_01_efsf_faq_archived.pdf.

European Stability Mechanism. "History." https://www.esm.europa.eu/about-us/history.

Grabel, I. 2017. *When Things Don't Fall Apart: Global Financial Governance and Development Finance in an Age of Productive Incoherence.* Boston, MA: The MIT Press.

Grabel, I. 2019. "Continuity, Discontinuity, and Incoherence in the Bretton Woods Order: A Hirschmanian Reading." *Development and Change, Special Issue on "Beyond Bretton Woods: Complementarity and Competition in the International Economic Order"* 50 (1): 46–57.

Grimes, W. W. 2009. *Currency and Contest in East Asia: The Great Power Politics of Financial Regionalism.* Ithaca, NY: Cornell University Press.

Grimes, W. W., and Kring, W. N. 2020. "Institutionalising Financial Cooperation in East Asia: AMRO and the Future of the Chiang Mai Initiative Multilateralization." *Global Governance* 26: 428–448. https://www.bu.edu/pardeeschool/files/2020/09/Grimes-Kring_proof-final9.2020.pdf.

Group of Twenty Information Centre. 2011. "G20 Principles for Cooperation between the IMF and Regional Financing Arrangements." http://www.g20.utoronto.ca/2011/2011-finance-principles-111015-en.pdf.

Henning, C. R. 2002. *East Asian Financial Cooperation.* Peter Institute Press: Policy Analyses in International Economics, Peterson Institute for International Economics, number pa68, July.

Henning, C. R. 2017. *Tangled Governance: International Regime Complexity, the Troika, and the Euro Crisis.* New York, NY: Oxford University Press.

International Monetary Fund. 1996. *The International Monetary Fund 1945–1965: Twenty Years of International Monetary Cooperation Volume I: Chronicle.* International Monetary Fund.

International Monetary Fund. 2010. "Press Release: Communique of the Twenty-Second Meeting of the International Monetary and Financial Committee of the Board of Governors of the International Monetary Fund." https://www.imf.org/en/News/Articles/2015/09/14/01/49/pr10379.

International Monetary Fund. 2013. "Stocktaking the Fund's Engagement with Regional Financing Arrangements." https://www.imf.org/external/np/pp/eng/2013/041113b.pdf.

International Monetary Fund. 2016. "Adequacy of the Global Financial Safety Net." http://www.imf.org/~/media/Files/News/Seminars/adequacy-of-the-global-financial-safety-net.ashx?la=en.

Ito, T. 2017. "A new financial order in Asia: Will a RMB bloc emerge?" *Journal of International Money and Finance* 74: 232–257.

Katada, S., and Yoichi N. 2021. "Finance and Japan," in *The Oxford Handbook of Japanese Politics*, edited by Robert J. Pekkanen and Saadia Pekkanen. Oxford: Oxford University Press.

Kawai, M. 2009. "Reform of the International Financial Architecture: An Asian Perspective." ADBI Working Paper, no. 167.

Kawai, M. 2015. "From the Chiang Mai Initiative to an Asian Monetary Fund." ADBI Working Paper, no.527.

Kenen, P. B., and E. E. Meade. 2008. *Regional Monetary Integration*. Cambridge University Press.

Kring, W. N., and W. W. Grimes. 2019. "Leaving the Nest: The Rise of Regional Financial Arrangements and the Future of Global Governance." *Development and Change* 50 (1): 72–95.

McCawley, P. 2017. *Banking on the Future of Asia and the Pacific: 50 Years of the Asian Development Bank*. Asian Development Bank.

McDowell, D. 2019. "The (Ineffective) Financial Statecraft of China's Bilateral Swap Agreements." *Development and Change* 50 (1): 122–143.

Nemoto, Y. 2003. "An Unexpected Outcome of the Asian Financial Crisis." Princeton Institutes for International and Regional Studies, Program on U.S.-Japan Relations, Monograph Series, Number 7, Princeton University.

Nemoto, Y. 2015. "The International Monetary System and the Role and Challenges of Regional Financial Safety Nets in Asia." The Next 70 Years, Reinventing Bretton Woods Committee, Bretton Woods.

Ong, L. L., and L. G. Gabriella. 2020. "The ERPD Matrix "Scorecard": Quantifying the Macro-Financial Performance of the ASEAN+3 Economies." AMRO Working Paper. https://www.amro-asia.org/wp-content/uploads/2020/04/AMRO-Working-Paper-20-01_ERPD-Matrix-Scorecard_Ong-Gabriella_final.pdf.

Tominaga, T. (2020), "ASEAN+3 Macroeconomic Research Office and Future of Regional Financial Cooperation", *Finance* 657, 51–55 (in Japanese). https://www.mof.go.jp/public_relations/finance/202008/202008k.pdf.

Watanabe , T. 1973. *Diary of the ADB President*. Nihon Keizai Shimbun (in Japanese).

Chapter 28

EMEAP and the Financial Crises

Diwa C. Guinigundo

"Never let a good crisis go to waste"
— Winston Churchill

Introduction

Literature on political science and international relations has often linked economic crises with the development of regional cooperation mechanisms. For instance, the punctuated equilibrium theory states that the evolution of institutions, which are relatively slow and stable, is punctuated or accelerated by short bursts of revolutionary processes. Such a view has underscored the role crises can play in catalyzing institutional change (Emmers & Ravenhill, 2011).

According to Henning (2011), crises can potentially provide the perfect conditions that trigger a shift to a new and durable equilibrium, which in turn can lead to the creation of new regional institutions and arrangements. First, crises give rise to demands for state actions that are satisfied more effectively when coordinated regionally. Second, these events create new information about preferences and behaviors of regional partners. Third, tail events can affect countries within a region similarly, which creates a common interest to devise some common response. Fourth, crises can stimulate communication, discourse, and negotiation among policymakers within a region. Lastly, they can also lead to ideational convergence that facilitates the creation of regional institutions.

The Asian financial crisis (AFC) in 1998 and the global financial crisis (GFC) in 2008 are perfect examples of a crisis that led to the enhancement of regional cooperation in the Asian region. Although the two crises elicited varied and arguably divergent responses, both have generally reinforced regional cooperation among Asian economies.

In the run-up to the AFC, Asian countries shared common vulnerabilities that made the region susceptible to systemic risks and contagion. Rapid domestic credit growth and inadequate supervisory oversight in individual economies resulted in a build-up of financial leverage, as reflected in mounting current account deficits and piling up of external debt. Such overreliance on foreign borrowing, often at short maturities, exposed corporations and banks in the region to foreign exchange and funding risks (Carson and Clark 2013). When speculative attacks led to a sharp depreciation of Asian currencies, firms saw sharp increases in the local currency (LCY) value of their external debts, leading many into distress and even insolvency.

These shared vulnerabilities, which were exposed during the AFC, also revealed underlying weaknesses within the region's economic and financial cooperation mechanisms. While scholarly opinion remains divided in attributing the cause of the crisis between external and internal factors, the AFC was generally viewed as a crisis internal to the region, and the problems encountered during this period could have been better addressed by regional policies (Emmers and Ravenhill 2011). For instance, most Asian economies shared a common vulnerability of overreliance on foreign or external sources of funding, which for many policymakers in the region largely contributed to the escalation of AFC into a full-blown regional crisis. Such recognition of these common problems quickly led to calls for greater regional focus of monetary and economic policies (Angrick and Nakabayashi 2017). In fact, one of the popular mantras that emerged at the onset of the AFC has been the need for regional solutions to regional problems (Lin and Rajan 2010). Moreover, the crisis also highlighted the undersupply of public good services such as adequate mechanisms for preventing and managing financial crises, as well as guaranteeing macroeconomic and financial stability on a regional scale (Ocampo 2006).

Meanwhile, the GFC is an event considered as external to the region and its impact is viewed to be less severe than that of the AFC. The external nature of the GFC conditioned a response for Asian countries that was focused on a broader global effort to prevent a global financial meltdown. This is not to say, however, that economies in the region were not affected by the GFC and its aftermath. Confronted with the effective zero lower bound, the United States Federal Reserve (US Fed) resorted to massive asset purchases or quantitative easing (QE) to provide the much-needed monetary stimulus for the US economy. This led to excess global liquidity and an ultra low interest rate environment, which in turn stimulated large and volatile capital flows in emerging market economies (EMEs) in Asia. For instance,

Fernandez (2015) found empirical evidence that the US Fed's QE, via the interest rate channel, had significant and persistent effects on total gross portfolio inflows in the Philippines. For all of these reasons, the crisis also triggered regional institutions, including the EMEAP, to enhance monetary and economic cooperation at the regional level in the form of strengthening regional safety nets and further enhancing Asian financial stability.

Consequently, all of these prompted the impetus for a stronger regional identity and cooperation, which in turn led to the enhancement of regional cooperation mechanisms that were focused on regional financial forums such as the Executives Meeting of Asia-Pacific (EMEAP) Central Banks.

EMEAP and its Evolution

EMEAP is a cooperative organization of central banks and monetary authorities in the Asia-Pacific region comprising the following 11 members: (1) Reserve Bank of Australia (RBA), (2) People's Bank of China (PBOC), (3) Hong Kong Monetary Authority (HKMA), (4) Bank Indonesia (BI), (5) Bank of Japan (BOJ), (6) Bank of Korea (BOK), (7) Bank Negara Malaysia (BNM), (8) Reserve Bank of New Zealand (RBZ), (9) Bangko Sentral ng Pilipinas (BSP), (10) Monetary Authority of Singapore (MAS), and (11) Bank of Thailand (BOT).

The organization's primary objective is to strengthen cooperation among its members. In particular, the organization aims to enhance regional surveillance, exchanges of information and views, and promotion of financial market development. Since its official establishment in 1991, its structure and activities have significantly evolved in response to the demands of the region's changing economic and financial environment.

Unlike other regional financial organizations, EMEAP started on an informal basis. Initially, it was created as a platform for information consultations and exchanges among central bank executives on issues relating to economic and financial developments in the region. In October 1990, the BOJ initiated the idea of establishing a regional central bank forum and consulted various Asian central banks through various visits by BOJ officials. According to Hamanaka (2011), this initiative suggested that the BOJ already realized the importance of East Asian regionalism even before the establishment of the East Asia Economic Caucus (EAEC) was proposed in December 1990.

In February 1991, the BOJ hosted the first central bank forum in the East Asia and Pacific region in Tokyo, Japan. Half-yearly meetings were conducted thereafter with the goal of nurturing relationships among regional central banks and exchange economic and financial information, including results of macroeconomic surveillance. Likewise, the BOJ's feedback on Bank for International Settlements (BIS) and Basel matters were also an important agenda in these meetings. Thus, this forum became a platform for other participating economies to have access to international policy agenda during the time.

Another important feature of the forum was its membership, which was purely composed of countries from the East Asia and Pacific region. In this sense, the forum was perceived by some observers as the first successful regional forum in the region (Hamanaka 2011).

In 1995, then Governor of the RBA, Bernie Fraser, spurred EMEAP's development by proposing to upgrade financial cooperation in the region that followed a BIS model. This meant an institution with its own capital and balance sheet. While this suggestion did not materialize, this led to the strengthening of the structure of EMEAP with its formal institutionalization in the following year with the launching of the annual governors' meeting. EMEAP's activities are centered on these annual meetings, along with the deputies' meetings and various working groups. Unlike other regional institutions, EMEAP has no permanent secretariat and secretariat functions are shared by member central banks.

Establishment

In July 1996, the first EMEAP Governors' Meeting was held in Tokyo, Japan. The agenda of the meeting was to review economic and financial developments in the region and to discuss means to enhance cooperation to strengthen financial stability and foster market developments. The involvement of the governors was crucial to the forum's recognition as an organization. During the first meeting, the governors found the event very useful and agreed to hold the governor's meeting annually, as well as gradually increase the activities conducted by the group. The central bank governors also decided to establish two working groups (Financial Market Development and Central Banking Operations) and one study group (Banking Supervision) to conduct studies on the primary functions of central banks.

The structure of these working groups is similar to the structure of the working groups in the BIS. The three groups' functions and objectives are detailed as follows (EMEAP 1996):

1. **Working Group on Financial Market Development:** This group studies the development of financial markets (i.e., bond, money, foreign exchange) to promote their further development. The EMEAP governors recognized the need for a healthy and efficient financial infrastructure. In particular, robust payment and bond clearing and settlement systems are crucial to intermediate savings effectively and mobilize capital within and outside the region.

2. **Working Group on Central Banking Operations:** This group focuses on facilitating exchange of information and technical expertise on market innovation and interdependence. Likewise, the group looks at how these developments affect the delivery of central banking services.

3. **Study Group on Banking Supervision:** This group conducts research on banking supervision issues that are of interest to member central banks. It aims to enhance knowledge and capacity on technical banking supervision issues in the region through the sharing of information, techniques, and experience.

Over the years, EMEAP has continually undergone enhancements to better serve its objective of promoting cooperation in the region.

EMEAP and the AFC

In the aftermath of the AFC, the EMEAP governors affirmed the importance of EMEAP activities in promoting information exchange and developing mutual trust among the economies in the region during the Third Governors' Meeting held on July 14, 1998. Given its membership consisting of central banks, EMEAP had the comparative advantage of enhancing policy analysis and providing advice on operational and institutional issues for crisis-affected member countries (EMEAP 1998).

During this meeting, the governors endorsed their deputies' proposals to re-organize its existing working groups into the following:

1. First, the Working Group on Financial Market (WGFM) Development was restructured as the Working Group on Payments and Settlements (WGPS) in order to focus primarily on payment system issues.

2. Second, the Working Group on Central Banking Operations was replaced by the new WGFM. This group was expected to focus on conducting comparative studies of central bank services amid increasing market innovation and independence, as well as financial market developments, which was previously covered by the WGFM Development.

3. Third, the Study Group on Banking Supervision was given a more permanent status and was renamed the Working Group on Banking Supervision (WGBS). This change reaffirmed the fact that the AFC underscored the importance of improving the conduct of banking supervision in the region.

The establishment of an EMEAP website was also endorsed during this meeting. This facilitated the creation of a virtual secretariat for EMEAP, through which members could exchange information among each other. Likewise, the BOJ suggested a new facility for yen liquidity, wherein the BOJ would purchase Japanese government bonds and bills from the region's central banks and monetary authorities at their request either outright or under repurchase agreements. This facility was expected to enhance the use of the yen in the region and promote regional financial stability. In 2001, an additional working group was established to study information technology (IT)-related developments and their potential applications in central banking.

During the period 2003–2005, EMEAP also paved the way for the establishment of the Asian Bond Fund (ABF), in line with its vision of enhancing LCY bond market development in the region. The ABF was composed of two bond-type funds, invested jointly by members as a way of fostering regional bond markets and diversifying members' official reserve portfolio. The ABF offered EMEAP member central banks an opportunity to invest in diversified regional investment products for their reserves management.

The ABF's first stage (called ABF1) was established and launched in July 2003 (EMEAP 2003). It had an initial size of USD 1 billion and its investments were limited to US dollar-denominated bonds issued by EMEAP member governments and governmental institutions. However, Japan, Australia, and New Zealand were excluded since these markets were already developed. ABF1 was managed by the BIS on behalf of EMEAP central banks and an oversight committee was formed within EMEAP to monitor the fund's performance.

The establishment of ABF1 was an important step toward greater regional cooperation. It was a stepping stone to the establishment of the ABF's second stage (called ABF2). The initial structure of ABF2 was announced on April 15, 2004, and was launched in December 2004 (EMEAP 2004). ABF2 had two components, namely: (1) a Pan Asia Bond Index Fund (PAIF) and (2) eight single-market funds. The PAIF was a single bond fund to be invested in sovereign and quasi-sovereign LCY-denominated bonds issued in the eight emerging EMEAP markets (China, Hong Kong, Indonesia, Korea, Malaysia, Philippines, Singapore, and Thailand). Meanwhile, each of the eight single-market funds was to be invested in sovereign and quasi-sovereign LCY-denominated bonds issued in the concerned EMEAP market (EMEAP 2005). ABF2 was to be managed by private sector fund managers with the BIS as the administrator and initially started as a USD 2 billion bond-type fund financed by foreign exchange reserves of member central banks.

EMEAP and the GFC

In the run-up toward the GFC in 2007, EMEAP established the Monetary and Financial Stability Committee (MFSC) composed of EMEAP deputies. The MFSC aimed to assist the EMEAP governors in promoting monetary and financial stability in the region by highlighting issues, identifying areas of vulnerabilities, and recommending broad policy options in the areas of regional macromonitoring, risk management, crisis management, and crisis resolution.

The GFC in 2008 underscored the importance of stepping up regional cooperation and surveillance efforts to jointly monitor the developments of the GFC and assess its impact on regional economies and its implications for EMEAP central banks (EMEAP 2008). Consequently, the MFSC reaffirmed its commitment to maintaining monetary and financial stability in the region and enhancing its surveillance framework.

In August 2009, EMEAP started a data template of weekly financial market developments in the EMEAP economies under the BSP chairmanship in the MFSC, which tracked quickly moving financial indicators to pinpoint possible risks to regional stability. The data template was provided to the EMEAP deputies through electronic mail, summarizing the previous week's developments. The indicators tracked on a weekly basis included exchange rates, stock market indices, credit default swap (CDS) spreads, emerging market bond indices, interest rates, and computations of the carry-to-risk ratio for individual EMEAP economies. Over time, the EMEAP report was revised to better serve the information needs of the deputies and revisions included a crisis reference period as benchmark, a narrative highlighting crucial developments during the period, and a change in the submission period from a weekly to monthly and then to a quarterly basis to minimize possible duplication with other monitoring reports of EMEAP member economies.

In 2011, EMEAP also conducted an informal meeting of governors and heads of supervision. This was in response to the realization during the GFC that monetary and financial stability objectives could have potential tradeoffs. For instance, macroprudential policies to safeguard financial stability likely had significant impact on inflation, potentially creating significant challenges for policymakers during episodes where low inflation coincides with buoyant credit growth. Hence, in this informal meeting, heads of supervision, in jurisdictions where such a mandate was not under the central bank, were invited to take on a more idiosyncratic approach and foster better policy coordination.

Present-Day EMEAP

At present, EMEAP is a multi-tiered forum without a dedicated secretariat. A proposal to establish a formal secretariat was once again made. However, the governors decided to sustain the informality of EMEAP meetings and this was affirmed during the 12th EMEAP Governor's Meeting held in September 2007 in Cebu, Philippines. In the conduct of the periodic meetings of the governors, deputy governors, and various working groups, the host member country would be expected to continue handling the secretariat functions. The governors decided that this arrangement remained efficient and effective. EMEAP is currently conducting the following activities:

1. **EMEAP Governors' Meetings**: Annual meetings wherein most recent economic and financial developments and issues relevant to the region's economies are discussed. The meetings also act as the highest decision-making of policies relating to EMEAP activities.

2. **EMEAP Deputies' Meetings**: Bi-annual meetings closely monitor EMEAP activities and provide guidance to its various working groups. This is EMEAP's core forum.

3. **EMEAP Monetary and Financial Stability Committee**: Established in 2007 to enhance macromonitoring and crisis management mechanisms in the region. The committee produces the Macromonitoring Report, which provides information on recent macrofinancial developments in member countries. The committee meets twice a year and is subsumed and held back-to-back with the Deputies' Meeting. In these meetings, the committee discusses policy implications at the regional and national level, macroeconomic forecasts, and outlook for member economies, among others.

4. **EMEAP's Working Groups**: These groups were established to address specific concerns relating to key central bank functions.

   a. **Working Group on Financial Markets**: This working group is mainly responsible for implementing the ABF, which has contributed to the deepening of financial and capital markets in the region. With the closure of the ABF initiative, the working group is actively pursuing research on financial market developments such as the report on EMEAP money markets survey and EMEAP Repo Market State of Play Report.

   b. **Working Group on Banking Supervision**: This working group's studies on supervisory issues are of interest to central banks and share members' experiences in the implementation of new regulatory frameworks, in particular Basel III. The working group also conducts surveys on EMEAP members. Over the years, the governments of some EMEAP member countries have moved to separate banking supervision functions from the central bank and placed them with a specialist supervisory agency. In this connection, although the working group is still mainly comprised of central banks, representatives from the supervisory agencies of some countries have also been invited to the working group.

   c. **Working Group on Payments and Market Infrastructures (WPMI)**: This working group was evolved from the WGPS. It oversees developments in domestic and cross-border payment and settlement systems as well as domestic business continuity/crisis management arrangements. It is responsible for compiling the EMEAP Red Book a comprehensive survey of member countries' payment and settlement systems. In addition, the working group now provides opportunities for member central banks to communicate regional perspectives and cooperate with other multilateral institutions and international forums on matters related to payments and market infrastructures.

    d. The IT Directors' Meeting (ITDM): This meeting was established in 2001 to study IT-related matters and their application to member central banks. This includes topics such as data and statistics management and cybersecurity, among others.

EMEAP continues to review its direction and activities to ensure that the group fosters greater regional cooperation. Such a review included the recent decision made during the 23rd EMEAP Governors' Meeting in August 2018 in Manila to minimize reporting on recent economic and financial developments and instead focus more on strategic issues to ensure continued relevance of EMEAP to its constituency central banks and the region in general.

EMEAP's Contribution

Following Ocampo (2006), the organization's contribution in regional cooperation can be mainly classified in two groups, namely: (1) development financing, such as initiatives to enhance regional bond markets through the ABF and (2) strengthening crisis management regimes, which include policy dialogues and macroeconomic surveillance, among others.

Capital Market Development and the ABF

The AFC underscored the importance of having well-developed bond markets in the region. According to policymakers, the presence of deep and liquid capital markets in the region could have mitigated the drying of dollar liquidity during the crisis and cushioned its negative impact on the regional economy (Shirakawa 2012).

    Prior to the crisis, Asian countries exhibited a variety of interconnected financial activities. First, many of them relied heavily on external sources of borrowing. Although not necessarily bad, local banks heavily borrowed from foreign financial institutions, often in the form of short-term foreign currency borrowings with maturities of a year or less. According to Borst (2017), between 1993 and 1996, 87% of the deficits of Association of Southeast Asian Nations (Indonesia, Malaysia, the Philippines, and Thailand) (ASEAN-4) and Korea were financed by short-term foreign borrowings. With the over-reliance on short-term external borrowing, countries in the region faced both currency and maturity mismatches referred to as the "double mismatch" problem. Thus, when Asian currencies significantly depreciated during the crisis, the burden of foreign currency debt was shouldered by debtors while creditors refused to roll over short-term loans, which were mostly tapped to fund long-term projects. These contributed to the severity of the financial crisis.

Second, the region also heavily relied on banks and less on capital markets because domestic capital markets in the region were small, illiquid, and underdeveloped. This led to a problem referred to as the missing "spare tire." In the 1990s, firms in the region faced constraints in accessing funding and were mostly limited to equity issuance and bank borrowing for their financing. Thus, when the region experienced large capital outflows and bank credit crunch, the lack of access to alternative sources of funding seriously impaired firms' production and investment activities. Lastly, during the height of the crisis, the large capital outflows suffered by domestic markets dried up dollar liquidity. Tight dollar liquidity fueled more serious investor panic, which in turn caused further capital outflows and speculative attacks on Asian currencies. All of these factors caused currencies, asset prices, and economic activity in the region to plunge precipitously more than what was warranted by prevailing economic fundamentals.

To help address these issues, Asian policymakers placed the development of bond markets at the forefront of national and regional policy agenda. These included measures to help develop a more robust and efficient market infrastructure at the national and regional levels such as the creation of standardized debt instruments, the establishment of rating agencies, the improvement of foreign exchange transactions and settlements, the creation of credit guarantee mechanisms, the provision of technical assistance, and the role of multilateral development banks, foreign government agencies, and Asian multinational corporations in issuing bonds in local markets and local currencies (Eichengreen 2004). These would in turn lessen member economies' reliance on external sources of funding and provide insurance from currency and maturity mismatches, as well as provide members with more options with respect to crisis response mechanisms by ensuring access to sufficient liquidity, especially during periods of speculative attacks (Sivalingam and Ismail 2016).

EMEAP, therefore, decided to establish the ABF, a fund comprising portions of foreign exchange reserves held by its member central banks. The fund's objective was to broaden investor participation through: (1) identifying and removing impediments to cross-border capital flows and (2) harmonizing regulations, withholding tax provisions, accounting practices, rating conventions, and clearing settlement systems (BIS 2011). According to Eichengreen (2004), these initiatives addressed key issues involving liquidity, efficiency, and growth prospects that made it difficult for small countries to develop deep and liquid bond markets. EMEAP member countries could not address these issues individually given their small size and limited liquidity. Hence, the consolidation of EMEAP member markets was considered appropriate in overcoming the size and liquidity challenges.

The ABF's initial objective was to provide an innovative, low-cost, and efficient product in the form of passively managed index bond funds so as to broaden investor participation, identify impediments to bond market development in the EMEAP economies, and act as a catalyst for regulatory reforms and improvements to market infrastructure (BIS 2011). According to EMEAP itself, the ABF promoted financial market deepening in several ways (EMEAP 2005). First, it promoted new products. The PAIF and the eight single-market funds represented a new asset class in Asia. For instance, the PAIF was a convenient and cost-effective investment fund for investors who wanted to have a well-diversified exposure in EMEAP bond markets. Second, ABF2 has improved market infrastructure through the establishment of transparent, replicable, and credible benchmarks such as the iBoxx ABF indices.

The region has seen several advancements since the launch of the ABF initiative. They include (1) accelerated tax reforms to exempt nonresident investors from withholding tax, (2) enhancement of the regulatory framework for exchange-traded funds, (3) liberalization of foreign exchange administration rules, (4) improvements in regional market infrastructure, and (5) the adoption of documentation in line with international best practices (Kuroda 2017). A case study by Sivalingam and Ismail (2016) found that the ABF could not only facilitate the development of Asian bond markets in order to keep Asian international reserves in Asia but could also potentially provide the much-needed liquidity in the event of another speculative attack on their currencies.[1] Despite the limited size of the ABF funds, the idea was to draw the interest of both regional and extra-regional investors in the EMEAP capital markets and, from there, grow in size. Development of Asian bond markets was also expected to help diversify Asian financial systems away from a bank-based system, which had exposed these countries to currency and maturity mismatches during the AFC triggered by sudden reversals of portfolio flows and high bank leverage.

A BIS Report (2011) assessing the effectiveness of ABF2 was prepared at the request of the then Assistant Governor of the BOJ and Chair of the EMEAP WGFM. The report indicated that the ABF2 had served as a catalyst for bond market development in the region. The size of LCY bond markets has grown significantly in the eight ABF2 economies since its inception from USD 2.1 trillion in 2005 to USD 16.0 trillion in 2019 (Figure 28.1). Of course, other factors could also be at play.

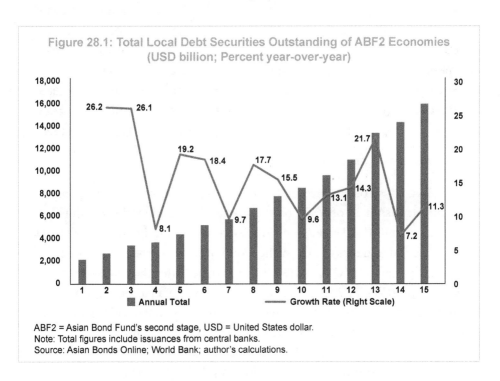

Figure 28.1: Total Local Debt Securities Outstanding of ABF2 Economies
(USD billion; Percent year-over-year)

ABF2 = Asian Bond Fund's second stage, USD = United States dollar.
Note: Total figures include issuances from central banks.
Source: Asian Bonds Online; World Bank; author's calculations.

---

[1] Nonetheless, there remains the issue whether the size of ABF amounting to a total of USD 2 billion can sufficiently counter tail events similar to the AFC.

In terms of the type of issuance, both government and corporate bond issuances have significantly increased in the ABF2 economies. However, government bonds continued to dominate the total issuances, comprising around 61% of total issuances as of the end of 2019 (Table 28.1). This suggests that while ABF2 sparked the development of government bond markets, corporate bond market development has lagged behind in the region (Amstad et al. 2016). Nonetheless, since the establishment of ABF2 in 2005, the growth rate of the total volume of local debt securities outstanding for participating member countries has consistently remained positive.

Table 28.1: Amounts of LCY Debt Securities Outstanding (USD billion)

Economy	2005			2019		
	Corp.	Gov.	Total	Corp.	Gov.	Total
China	49.6	878.4	928.0	4,337.0	7,753.1	12,090.0
Hong Kong	69.2	16.3	85.6	139.1	151.7	290.8
Indonesia	5.9	48.3	54.2	32.1	206.7	238.8
Korea	360.8	392.9	753.7	1259.4	823.6	2083.0
Malaysia	45.6	61.3	107.0	174.1	189.0	363.1
Philippines	1.0	41.1	42.1	29.7	101.5	131.2
Singapore	36.2	46.9	83.1	127.3	212.3	339.6
Thailand	14.1	64.9	79.0	127.4	318.2	445.6
Total	582.4	1,550.2	2,132.6	6,226.2	9,755.9	15,982.1

Corp. = corporate, gov. = government plus central banks, LCY = local currency, USD = United States dollar.
Source: Asian Bonds Online.

An analysis of variance (ANOVA) is employed to determine the impact of the establishment of ABF2 on the size of LCY bond markets in the eight participating EMEAP economies. This exercise tests for the equality of means of LCY bond issuances in the eight economies before the establishment of ABF2 (first quarter (Q1) of 1999–Q4 2003) and after the establishment of ABF2 (Q1 2004–Q4 2020). The ANOVA is implemented on: (1) total LCY bond issuances, (2) total LCY government bond issuances, and (3) total LCY corporate bond issuances for each country. Data are expressed as ratio of gross domestic product (GDP) to control for GDP growth.

Table 28.2 summarizes the ANOVA results. The results suggest that the creation of the ABF2 helped the LCY bond markets grow at a substantial pace and size relative to pre-ABF. Total bond issuances grew significantly for the majority of the eight countries over the period in review.[2] In particular, Korea, China, Thailand, and Singapore recorded the largest increase in total bond issuances after the establishment of the ABF2. The same trend can be observed for LCY government and corporate bonds as issuances significantly grew in most of the eight countries.

Table 28.2. Analysis of Variance on EMEAP Member Economies

Economy	Government Bonds		Corporate Bonds		Total	
	Pre-ABF	14.8967	Pre-ABF	0.2811	Pre-ABF	15.1778
China	Post-ABF	35.3507	Post-ABF	15.0076	Post-ABF	50.3584
	Difference	20.454***	Difference	14.7265***	Difference	35.1806***
	Pre-ABF	0.0000	Pre-ABF	26.2668	Pre-ABF	26.2667
Hong Kong	Post-ABF	2.1997	Post-ABF	34.4229	Post-ABF	36.6226
	Difference	2.1997***	Difference	8.1561***	Difference	10.3559***
	Pre-ABF	8.8931	Pre-ABF	21.7736	Pre-ABF	30.7043
Korea	Post-ABF	31.5675	Post-ABF	56.9563	Post-ABF	88.5238
	Difference	22.6744***	Difference	35.1827***	Difference	57.8195***
	Pre-ABF	20.2743	Pre-ABF	1.5843	Pre-ABF	21.8586
Indonesia	Post-ABF	16.7111	Post-ABF	2.1708	Post-ABF	18.8818
	Difference	−3.5632*	Difference	0.5865*	Difference	−2.9768
	Pre-ABF	40.4075	Pre-ABF	36.7900	Pre-ABF	77.1975
Malaysia	Post-ABF	46.2763	Post-ABF	40.0916	Post-ABF	86.3679
	Difference	5.8688*	Difference	3.3016	Difference	9.1704
	Pre-ABF	32.0975	Pre-ABF	0.1600	Pre-ABF	32.2575
Philippines	Post-ABF	30.7363	Post-ABF	4.3457	Post-ABF	35.0821
	Difference	−1.3612	Difference	4.1857***	Difference	2.7946*
	Pre-ABF	27.1914	Pre-ABF	21.9486	Pre-ABF	49.1400
Singapore	Post-ABF	33.5978	Post-ABF	30.1920	Post-ABF	63.7898
	Difference	6.4064**	Difference	8.2434***	Difference	14.6498***
	Pre-ABF	23.9762	Pre-ABF	4.6900	Pre-ABF	28.6662
Thailand	Post-ABF	30.3176	Post-ABF	14.5591	Post-ABF	44.8768
	Difference	6.3414***	Difference	9.8691***	Difference	16.2106***

*, **, and *** indicate significance at a 90%, 95%, and 99% confidence bound, respectively.

Notes: All figures are measured in billions of United States dollars. Data used for the analysis of variance (ANOVA) were obtained from Asian Bonds Online. All calculations were done by the author. The time span used would be the first quarter (Q1) of 1998 until Q4 2020. Adjustments to the time span were made for countries that lacked data pre-2000 (i.e., Indonesia, Malaysia, and the Philippines). Central bank issuances were excluded in the ANOVA to solely focus on the analysis on government and corporate issuances.

Source: Author's estimations.

---

[2] Meanwhile, results for Indonesia (negative growth) and Malaysia are not significant. The insignificant results could be explained by the lack of a longer series for both countries prior to ABF2.

The results suggest that the ABF has generally contributed to the growth of the region's capital markets. Despite the GFC in 2008, the growth of the region's bond markets was not hampered. In fact, the size of the overall bond markets grew steadily after the GFC. This is not to say that the ABF initiative was the singular driver of the region's capital market growth. The member countries must have also realized the importance of further developing and deepening their domestic capital markets to enhance their capacity to manage future financial market shocks. Yet, in this regard, the EMEAP initiatives to make member countries' respective tax regimes more conducive to capital market development must have also helped. Post-ABF developments including appropriate regulatory changes, liberalization of foreign exchange regulations, and strengthening of regional market infrastructures also contributed to the overall efforts to cultivate greater interest in the region's capital markets.

Macrofinancial Surveillance and Policy Dialogue

The AFC and to some extent the GFC provided policymakers in the region with valuable lessons about the nature of crisis and crisis management. These events highlighted the vulnerability of small open economies to capital inflow surges and reversals. They also showed how investor sentiment can quickly shift and how interconnectedness can easily propagate shocks to other neighboring jurisdictions. In response, Asian countries have made collaborative efforts for resolving and preventing occurrence of future crises. Cooperation in this area has focused on two pillars, namely establishing a regional financial arrangement and strengthening a monitoring and surveillance framework.

The need for a mechanism for regional surveillance was first raised during a meeting of the so-called Manila Framework held on November 18–19, 1997. During this time, it was agreed that an Asian Surveillance Framework that complemented the general framework of the International Monetary Fund (IMF) with the assistance of the Asian Development Bank (ADB) should be established (Manupipatpong 2002). This led to the creation of the Asian Surveillance Process within the Manila Framework, which was operationalized in March 1999.

Following the AFC, policymakers realized that effective surveillance could help reduce the probability of a crisis and enhance crisis management response policy. Regular surveillance would help formulate and mobilize timely and appropriate crisis response. For instance, international institutions would be more willing to lend resources to member countries if they had enough knowledge of the true conditions of their economies.

Since the AFC, a number of surveillance framework have emerged in the region. A report by the Association of Southeast Asian Nations (ASEAN) Secretariat (2005) characterized surveillance frameworks in the region into three levels, namely: (1) information sharing, (2) peer review and peer pressure, and (3) conditions for contingent credit line wherein surveillance has a strong element of due diligence.

Information sharing is the weakest form of policy dialogue. It involves specific information exchange with regard to attitudes and views on economic performance and policymaking. It is nonetheless the first step for deeper policy dialogue. Peer review and peer pressure can be described as the systematic examination and assessment of the performance of member countries with the ultimate goal of helping member countries improve their policymaking, adopt best practices, and comply with established standards and principles (OECD 2008). Meanwhile, conditions for contingent credit line would represent the highest form of surveillance. They involve due diligence and specific enforcement mechanisms. An example of this is the IMF's Contingent Credit Line.

EMEAP has made significant progress in building a system for economic and financial surveillance in the region. In the previous section, it was indicated that in April 2007, EMEAP's MFSC, composed of deputy governor-level staff of member central banks, was launched. This committee now handles regional monetary and financial monitoring, and also pursues activities promoting risk and crisis management and resolution.

In May 2007, the MFSC decided to launch a regional monetary and financial monitoring system. The committee was to discuss recent economic and financial developments based on its Macromonitoring Report containing macroeconomic and financial information provided by member countries. The committee had been meeting twice a year, back-to-back with the Deputies' Meetings.

In November 2007, its members agreed to build a regional crisis management and resolution network (Jung 2009). This network was to be composed of a high-level team and a technical level crisis management team (TLCMT). The role of high-level team was to advise members on policy alternatives in dealing with crises and also provide them with a point of contact with the international financial institutions (IFIs). The role of TLCMT was to support the high-level team through data collection and execution of business continuity plans (BCPs) in times of crisis.

According to some observers, the EMEAP surveillance process has its strengths. Hamanaka (2011) claimed that EMEAP was among the institutions that had a pure regional perspective as it was able to keep the US outside of its membership. The value of having a purely regional surveillance is that member countries tend to be more frank and open to each other as they tend to focus on issues of common interest. This has contributed to more knowledge sharing among member central banks.

Moreover, unlike other Asian regional groupings, EMEAP has a unique membership composition that shares a strong sense of central bank community. Central banks have specific expertise in monetary, financial, and exchange rate policy management and in delivering high-level surveillance. Its membership also includes advanced economies such as Japan and Korea in Asia as well as Australia and New Zealand in the Pacific, a membership structure that enables other members to gain insights from those with more developed and mature financial markets.

Indeed, EMEAP has contributed significantly in improving policy dialogue and cooperation through its surveillance framework. EMEAP surveillance, through its periodic meetings and working groups, has become an important platform for enhancing information sharing, peer review, and peer pressure in the region.

Effective Representation in International Policymaking Bodies

The establishment of EMEAP has also provided the region with greater representation and bargaining position in international forums. The EMEAP central banks have also launched joint efforts to ensure that their views are duly considered in policymaking at the global level.

In 1996, the WGBS was duly recognized by BIS as one of its regional supervisory groups (Hamanaka 2011). This gave EMEAP members leverage in terms of shaping the outcome of international best practices in banking supervision that would be beneficial for the region. For instance, in 2001, the working group was able to effectively communicate their comments on the draft of the New Basel Accord and successfully raised the concern among

Asian countries that some aspects of the new accord were unfavorable to Asian commercial banks. The WGBS submitted a consultative paper that outlined issues and concerns by EMEAP economies on some specific aspects of the new accord, particularly on Pillar 1. These issues covered the following topics, among others (EMEAP WGBS 2001):

- *On implementation.* The complexity of the New Accord will have significant resource implications for supervisors in the EMEAP region. Thus, the WGBS suggested that the BIS develop a centralized "model" of guidelines and legislation on matters relating to amending bank legislation, developing relevant supervisory policies, and devising new bank returns.

- *On proposed risk assessment.* The proposed internal ratings approach (IRB) could subject capital adequacy ratios to greater economic fluctuations which, in turn, could potentially be subject to misinterpretations.

- *On credit risk mitigation.* Proposed use of real estate collateral for credit mitigation can potentially be less effective compared to applying appropriate haircuts.

Moreover, EMEAP also extends its efforts to represent the region to central bank groupings outside the region. EMEAP has periodic joint meetings with its counterparts in Europe, enabling EMEAP members to communicate their views on major factors that may impact the Asia and the Pacific regions. Given global interconnectedness, these activities help promote policy coordination, especially when there is a major threat to the global financial system.

Market Awareness

Greater representation in international fora has also led to more awareness of EMEAP markets. For instance, the WGPMI compiled the EMEAP Red Book, which covered the payment systems of EMEAP members, which was not covered by the BIS Red Book. The EMEAP Red Book is an accomplishment of collective study over the past years by the EMEAP WGPMI and promotes further understanding of payments and settlement systems as well as market infrastructure in the EMEAP region.

The WGFM also regularly publishes reports on EMEAP money markets. This report aims to record the state of play in the money markets, together with policy initiatives taken by EMEAP central banks. While acknowledging that money markets have evolved in a manner unique to each jurisdiction, this report provides a reference to assist with further development of money markets in the region. At the same time, the report provides information on the latest developments in the EMEAP members' respective financial markets.

Capacity Building

EMEAP has contributed to the capacity building of its members. All of its working groups conduct their respective regular studies on various topics that relate to central bank policies and operations. The research findings can help improve members' respective operations and improve policy collaboration. In addition, in their periodic meetings at various levels, relevant resource persons are invited to speak on the latest issues on global and regional economies, financial technology, digital currencies, and other related topics.

Having members from advanced economies such as Japan also benefits other EMEAP members in terms of spillover of technical knowledge. For instance, the BOJ regularly hosts three workshops and seminars annually with a view to furthering technical assistance and cooperation among the member central banks in the Asia and the Pacific regions. These learning events covered topics on central banking and capital market, economic statistics and its analysis, and various issues related to central banking operations.

Member central banks also conduct short-term research and training sessions on various central banking operations. EMEAP central banks also dispatch their staff and subject matter experts to workshops and seminars held at various central banks within and outside the region.

Challenges and Future Directions

Notwithstanding EMEAP's significant contributions, there is scope to further advance the cause of regional cooperation in the areas of: (1) bond market development and (2) a regional scheme for macroprudential policies.

In the area of bond market development, more work remains in developing corporate bonds. EMEAP can work on fostering corporate bond markets with initiatives such as expanding the range of credit quality and developing infrastructure bonds in order to deepen the primary market. Meanwhile, liquidity in the secondary market can be enhanced by developing regional mechanisms to increase post-trade transparency and developing hedging markets (Amstad et al. 2016).

In addition, EMEAP has the potential to develop a regional scheme for macroprudential policies of its members. It provides a platform for regular communication among the governors and deputy governors of the region. Frequent meetings and exchanges of information and collaboration could foster greater macroprudential policy coordination, which is often required in a timely manner.

According to Chutikhamoltham (2017), EMEAP's scope of work overlaps with those of ASEAN+3 Macroeconomic Research Office (AMRO) and South East Asian Central Banks (SEACEN). For instance, EMEAP's working groups conduct studies that are similar to those of the two organizations, particularly on the payments and settlements systems and banking supervision. The macroeconomic surveillance it conducts also appears to overlap with AMRO. While the overlap of functions could hardly be avoided, it is suggested that EMEAP could improve its collaboration with other organizations or focus on an agenda that is distinct from the other two.

While there could be unavoidable overlaps, observers argue that compared to AMRO and SEACEN, the scope of surveillance conducted by EMEAP differs in terms of coverage. Hence, there could be scope to strengthen communication between AMRO and EMEAP to enhance early warning systems in the region and improve crisis management response. EMEAP benefits from its unique membership that includes more developed economies like Australia, Japan, Korea, and New Zealand, which, in turn, gives the group a unique perspective. Moreover, EMEAP working groups have more sustained research initiatives compared to one-off training programs offered by other regional institutions. These initiatives conducted by working groups tend to be a series of activities that are often long term in nature.

There is also the impression that public information about EMEAP's work is rather limited. Its website contains limited information on its recent publications and initiatives. Observers suggest that EMEAP can benefit from greater transparency in its current programs and initiatives. Toward this end, EMEAP has taken significant measures to improve its transparency. These include the regular publication of press releases for its various meetings such as the Governors Meeting and Deputies Meeting, as well as regular publication of the working groups' research studies in the EMEAP website.

Conclusion: Not Letting Crises Go To Waste

Since its inception, EMEAP has significantly contributed to fostering economic and financial cooperation in the region. Its efforts and initiatives have contributed to the deepening of regional bond markets, enhancing regional macrofinancial surveillance, and increasing information sharing and capacity-building activities in the region.

Indeed, EMEAP has taken advantage of the lessons learned from both the AFC and the GFC to put forward reforms that have contributed to greater cooperation among its member central banks. It can be said that the institution resonated with Winston Churchill by not letting a single crisis go to waste.

References

Amstad, M., S. Kong, F. Packer, and E. Remolona. 2016. "A Spare Tire for Capital Markets: Fostering Corporate Bond Markets in Asia." BIS Paper No. 85.

Angrick, S., and S. Nakabayashi. 2017. "20 Years After the Asian Financial Crisis, How has Financial Cooperation Evolved?" Diplomat, June 3. https://thediplomat.com/2017/06/20-years-after-the-asian-financial-crisis-how-has-financial-cooperation-evolved/.

Association of Southeast Asian Nations Secretariat. 2005. "Economic Surveillance and Policy Dialogue in East Asia." March.

Bank for International Settlement. 2011. "Local Currency Bond Markets and the Asian Bond Fund 2 Initiative." BIS Report prepared for the Chair of the EMEAP Working Group on Financial Markets, July 14.

Borst, N. 2017. "Capital Flows, Bond Markets, and Financial Stability in Asia." Asia Focus, Federal Reserve Bank of San Francisco, November.

Carson, M., and J. Clark. 2013. "Asian Financial Crisis." Federal Reserve Bank History, November. https://www.federalreservehistory.org/essays/asian-financial-crisis

Chutikamoltham, S. 2017 "Effectiveness of Regional Mechanisms for Multilateral and Regional Governance." ADBI Working Paper Series No. 719.

Eichengreen, B. 2004. "The Development of Asian Bond Markets." BIS Paper No. 30.

Emmers, R., and J. Ravenhill. 2011. "The Asian and Global Financial Crisis: Consequences for East Asian Regionalism." Contemporary Politics 17 (2): 133–149.

Executives Meeting of Asia-Pacific Central Banks. 1996. "Press Release — First Governors' Meeting on 19 July 1996, Tokyo, Japan." http://www.emeap.org/index.php/press-releases/.

Executives Meeting of Asia-Pacific Central Banks. 1998. Press Release — Third EMEAP Governors' Meeting on 14 July 1998, Tokyo Japan. http://www.emeap.org/wp-content/uploads/2015/04/14jul98.pdf.

Executives Meeting of Asia-Pacific Central Banks. 2003. "Press Release — EMEAP Central Banks to Launch Asian Bond Fund," June 2. http://www.emeap.org/wp-content/uploads/2015/04/02june03.pdf.

Executives Meeting of Asia-Pacific Central Banks. 2004. "Press Release — EMEAP Central Banks Announce the Initial Structure of Asian Bond Fund 2," April 15. https://www.emeap.org/wp-content/uploads/2015/04/15apr04.pdf.

Executives Meeting of Asia-Pacific Central Banks. 2005. "Press Release — Asian Bond Fund 2 has moved into Implementation Phase," May 12. http://www.emeap.org/wp-content/uploads/2015/04/12may05.pdf.

Executives Meeting of Asia-Pacific Central Banks. 2008. "Statement of the MFSC," October 30. http://www.emeap.org/wp-content/uploads/2015/04/EMEAPJointStatement2008-10-30.pdf.

Executives' Meeting of East Asia-Pacific Central Banks Working Group on Banking Supervision. 2001. "Comments on the Second Consultative Package of the New Basel Accord by EMEAP Working Group on Banking Supervision." Comments sent to the Secretary General, Banking Committee on Banking Supervision, Bank for International Settlements dated 28 May 2001.

Fernandez, J. R. A. 2015. "US Quantitative Easing and Philippine Capital Inflows: The Role of US Long-Term Interest Rates." BS Review-2015. Bangko Sentral ng Pilipinas.

Hamanaka, S. 2011. "Asian Financial Cooperation in the 1990: The Politics of Membership." *Journal of East Asian Studies* 11 (1): 75–103.

Henning, C. 2011. "Economic Crisis and Institutions for Regional Cooperation." ADB Working Paper Series on Regional Economic Integration No. 81.

Jung, J. 2009. "Regional Financial Cooperation in Asia: Challenges and Path to Development." BIS Papers No. 42.

Kuroda, H. 2017. "Asian Financial Markets — 20 Years since the Asian Financial Crisis, and Prospects for the Next 20 Years." Keynote Speech at the 2017 Annual General Meeting of Asia Securities Forum, Tokyo, Japan.

Lin, C., and R. Rajan. 1999. "Regional Responses to the Southeast Asian Financial Crisis: A Case of Self-Help or No Help?" *Australian Journal of International Affairs* 53 (3): 261–281. DOI:10.1080/00049919993854.

Manupipatpong, W. 2002. "The ASEAN Surveillance Process and the East Asian Monetary Fund." *ASEAN Economic Bulletin*, 19 (1): 111–122. Rethinking the Asian Development the East Asian Development Model.

Ocampo, J. A. 2006. "Regional Financial Cooperation: Experience and Challenges." In Chapter 1, *Regional Financial Cooperation. United Nations Commission for Latin America and Caribbean*. Washington: Brookings Institution Press.

Organisation for Economic Co-operation and Development. 2008. *Shaping Policy Reform and Peer Review in Southeast Asia: Integrating Economies amid Diversity*. Paris: OECD Publishing. https://doi.org/10.1787/9789264039445-en.

Shirakawa, M. 2012. Welcome Remarks delivered during the Joint Bank of Japan-Bank for International Settlements High Level Seminar on "The Development of Regional Capital Markets."

Sivalingam, G., and I. Ismail. 2006. "The Asian Bond Fund: A Case Study of Successful Economic and Financial Cooperation in Asia." *Investment Management and Financial Innovations* 3.

Chapter 29

Asian Bond Markets Initiative

Satoru Yamadera

Introduction

The Asian Bond Markets Initiative (ABMI) is a notable example of regional cooperation by the Association of Southeast Asian Nations (ASEAN) plus China, Japan, and Korea — collectively known as ASEAN+3. The 1997–1998 Asian financial crisis (AFC) revealed that, in addition to the importance of sound economic management, a well-functioning domestic bond market is indispensable to prevent major financial risks.

The ASEAN+3 finance ministers launched ABMI at the ASEAN+3 Deputies Meeting in Chiang Mai, Thailand, in December 2002 to mitigate the risks. Regional cooperation under ASEAN+3 had two goals: one goal was to prevent a contagion of financial market failure in the short run. The other was to facilitate a more stable financial environment in the long run. The Chiang Mai Initiative Multilateralisation mainly addressed the former, while ABMI addressed the latter.

ABMI can be seen as a journey to respond to the original sin hypothesis by Eichengreen and Hausmann (1999). They claimed there might be an incompleteness in international financial markets "in which the domestic currency cannot be used to borrow abroad or to borrow long term, even domestically." But they also suggested another solution "to build deep and liquid domestic markets in long-term domestic-currency-denominated securities," which ASEAN+3 began to pursue, although it appeared as a difficult journey.

This chapter explains ABMI and its achievements as well as remaining challenges. As a part of regional cooperation to support the local currency (LCY) bond market development, the Executives' Meeting of East Asia-Pacific Central Banks (EMEAP) also established the Asian Bond Fund (ABF). ABF supported LCY bond market development by playing a catalytic role to create a real demand. It paved a way to bring foreign funds to domestic LCY bond markets. The contribution of ABF to develop LCY bond markets is explained further in Chapter 28.

This chapter explains the background of the ABMI and how the AFC created momentum for regional cooperation. Then, the chapter explains the original sin hypothesis and the need for various reforms. It also explains the role of regional cooperation to support the development of LCY bond markets. Subsequently, it provides the history of ABMI; the initial phase of ABMI; the progress of ABMI after 2008; and achievements of ABMI. The chapter concludes with remaining challenges.

The AFC as an Impetus to Regional Cooperation

In the early 1990s, massive short-term private capital from developed markets flew into emerging Asia, driven by optimism on strong macroeconomic fundamentals, interest rate differentials, and a belief that quasi-fixed exchange rate regimes would be sustained. The capital inflows led to the increase of short-term external debt (Figure 29.1). Moreover, indiscreet liberalization of domestic financial markets and capital accounts exacerbated problems associated with capital inflows. The huge capital inflows created excessive credit expansion and risk-taking by financial institutions and led to inefficient investments in real estate and corporate activities (Yoshitomi and Shirai 2001).

But once the sustainability of the quasi-fixed exchange rate regime and optimism on the economic fundamentals were questioned, capital flows were

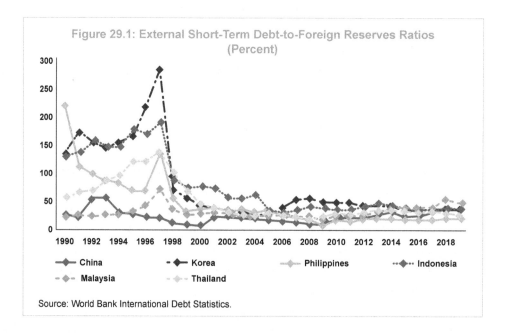

Figure 29.1: External Short-Term Debt-to-Foreign Reserves Ratios (Percent)

Source: World Bank International Debt Statistics.

suddenly reversed. The transformation of short-term liabilities into long-term credits is one of the functions of the banking system, but the banking systems in these economies could not cope with such sudden reversal of capital flows because these liabilities were denominated in foreign currencies. They faced a sudden sharp decline in exchange rates, which drained foreign reserves, worsening market confidence. Thus, these economies fell into vicious cycles of financial crises.

In sum, "currency and maturity mismatches related to external borrowing and inefficient investment it financed were among the root causes of the crisis" (ADB 2020a). Of course, the double mismatch alone should not be seen as the only cause of the crisis. With weak fundamentals, the double mismatch exacerbated the situation and trapped the economies in the crisis.

Policymakers in ASEAN+3 recognized that changes from short-term to long-term finance and from foreign currency to LCY finance were necessary. In other words, LCY bond markets were needed to be developed in the region to avoid the recurrence of the crisis.

Original Sin Hypothesis and Need for Various Reforms

The development of well-functioning LCY bond markets was imperative to replace foreign currency-denominated bank loans. LCY bond markets could minimize the currency and maturity mismatches that had made the region vulnerable to the sudden reversal of capital flows. However, this was not an easy task. The original sin hypothesis by Eichengreen and Hausmann (1999) claimed that there might be an incompleteness in international financial markets "in which the domestic currency cannot be used to borrow abroad or to borrow long term, even domestically. In the presence of this incompleteness, financial fragility is unavoidable because all domestic investments will have either a currency mismatch (projects that generate pesos will be financed with dollars) or a maturity mismatch (long-term projects will be financed with short-term loans)" (Eichengreen and Hausmann 1999).

They claimed that the way out from the original sin was to dollarize the economy or build "deep and liquid domestic markets in long-term domestic-currency-denominated securities" like Australia. But to do so, countries needed to adopt "securities-market regulations that discourage insider trading, market cornering, and market manipulation in order to make participation attractive to investors." They also noted "the need of reforming monetary and fiscal institutions in ways that enhance the independence, transparency, and credibility of the policy-making authorities, and acquiring a track record of following sound and stable policies," which seemed very difficult, if not impossible.

Role of Regional Cooperation to Support the Development of LCY Bond Markets

Developing an LCY bond market is basically a national agenda. But regional cooperation can help alleviate development challenges by dealing with the problems collectively. As the original sin hypothesis claims, the development of LCY bond markets is not an easy task. But regional arrangements can support and often complement the efforts of individual countries.

For instance, highlighting LCY bond market developments under ABMI has resulted in greater support from various stakeholders and established better coordination not only among the ASEAN+3 member economies but also within each individual jurisdiction. In addition, regional arrangements can reinforce commitments of the governments involved, which also increased commitments by market participants. In other words, regional cooperation and regional arrangements can reduce the uncertainty associated with the development of the markets. Furthermore, joint efforts and collective action under regional arrangements can attract more attention and increase recognition of the efforts to develop the markets. These supports and commitments would not have been possible by a single action of a solo emerging market.

Initial Phase of the ABMI (2002–2007)

During the initial phase of the ABMI, ASEAN+3 policymakers focused on establishing a common understanding of building blocks needed to develop a market, such as basic market infrastructures and regulations for LCY bond markets. Six voluntary working groups (WGs) were established to examine necessary elements for bond market development: WG1 for new securitized debt instruments chaired by Thailand, WG2 for regional credit guarantee and investment mechanism chaired by Korea and China, WG3 for foreign exchange transaction and settlement issues chaired by Malaysia, WG4 for issuance of bonds denominated in LCYs by multilateral development banks and foreign government agencies chaired by China, WG5 for rating systems and dissemination of information chaired by Singapore and Japan, and WG6 for technical assistance coordination chaired by Malaysia, Indonesia, and the

Philippines. In 2004, the ABMI Focal Group was established to coordinate the activities of the six WGs. In May 2005, these WGs were reorganized into four WGs because WG5 ceased to exist as its objective was achieved, and WG6 was moved under the ABMI Focal Group.

In determining policies and activities to promote the development of the region's bond markets, ASEAN+3 policymakers met regularly and conducted policy dialogues and discussions. They also held seminars and conferences to solicit views from academics, think tanks, and market participants. Once policymakers reached a consensus on policies to support under ABMI over the medium term, a road map outlining necessary policy actions was prepared for members to implement over a 3-year period. Though ASEAN+3 officials did not specify numerical targets for the member economies, the economies were encouraged to implement the recommended policy measures. To ensure relevance and effectiveness, the policymakers undertook a periodic review of the progress made under the road map.

Progress of the ABMI After 2008

In 2008, the four WGs were rearranged into four new task forces focusing on four key areas: (i) promoting the issuance of LCY-denominated bonds (supply side), (ii) facilitating the demand for LCY-denominated bonds (demand side), (iii) improving the regulatory framework, and (iv) improving related infrastructure for bond markets (Figure 29.2).

In 2008–2009, the ASEAN+3 economies faced another crisis, that is, the global financial crisis (GFC). Thanks to the efforts made by the ASEAN+3 member economies, the region showed relative resilience against the crisis and registered a strong and quick recovery. At this point, the region could support their respective economies by public expenditure which was financed by LCY government bond issuances. Corporate bond issuance also expanded as a spare tire to ensure multiple channels of financial intermediation since the banking sector was more severely impacted by the GFC (Figure 29.3).

After the GFC, the importance of LCY bond market development was clearly recognized as a global policy agenda. The Group of Twenty (G20) highlighted that LCY bond markets could play an important role in diversifying financial intermediary channels and mitigating the impact of a financial crisis on the real economy. To increase the benefit of globalization while preventing and managing risks that could undermine financial stability and

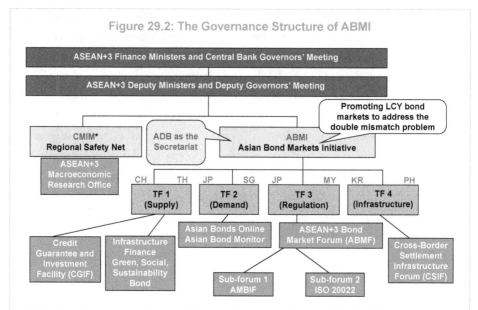

Figure 29.2: The Governance Structure of ABMI

ABMI = Asian Bond Markets Initiative, ADB = Asian Development Bank, AMBIF = ASEAN+3 Multi-Currency Bond Issuance Framework, ASEAN = Association of Southeast Asian Nations, CH = China, CMIM = Chiang Mai Initiative Multilateralisation, JP = Japan, KR = Korea, LCY = local currency, MY = Malaysia, PH = the Philippines, SG = Singapore, TF = task force, TH = Thailand.
Source: Asian Development Bank.

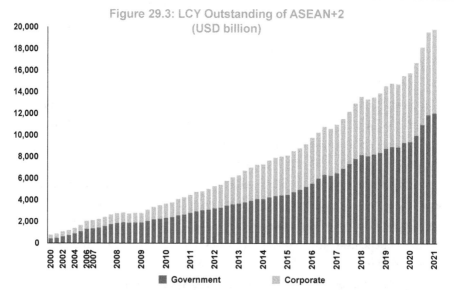

Figure 29.3: LCY Outstanding of ASEAN+2 (USD billion)

ASEAN = Association of Southeast Asian Nations, LCY = local currency, USD = United States dollar.
Note: Based on the end of period for the annual data from 2000 to 2006 and the quarterly data from the first quarter of 2007 to the first quarter of 2021; ASEAN+2 includes the ASEAN countries, China, and Korea.
Source: AsianBondsOnline.

sustainable growth at the national and global levels, at the Cannes Summit in 2011, the G20 leaders launched an initiative to prepare an action plan for the development of LCY bond markets (International Monetary Fund and World Bank 2020).

After 2008, policies supported under ABMI shifted toward more technical discussions to create more tangible outputs. Various initiatives were undertaken by the four task forces. Particularly, attention was given to the development of corporate bond markets because too much dependence on the banking system showed vulnerability. Corporate bonds can supplement and substitute for bank loans, thus creating another financial intermediary channel. The corporate bond market can also support financial stability when the banking system is malfunctioning. The following sections explain the initiatives and activities under each task force in detail. (Summary of each task force is shown in Table 29.1.)

Table 29.1: ABMI Task Forces

Task Force	Co-Chairs	Mandate	Activities
Task Force 1	China, Thailand	Promoting the issuance of local currency (LCY) bonds	Establishment of Credit Guarantee and Investment Facility to facilitate LCY corporate bond issuance. Promotion of sustainable bonds to help recycle funds within the region.
Task Force 2	Japan, Singapore	Facilitating demand for LCY bonds	Information dissemination through AsianBondsOnline as the regional market information hub. Market research on Asian markets. Organizing bond conferences.
Task Force 3	Japan, Malaysia	Improving the regulatory framework	Organizing ASEAN+3 Bond Market Forum. Promotion of the ASEAN+3 Multicurrency Bond Issuance Framework. Promotion of international standards.
Task Force 4	Korea, Philippines	Improving related infrastructure for the bond market	Organizing Cross-Border Settlement Infrastructure Forum to discuss establishment of the regional settlement intermediary. Asia Prime Collateral Forum to study the possible use of regional government bonds as collateral for cross-border transactions.

ABMI = Asian Bond Markets Initiative, ASEAN = Association of Southeast Asian Nations.
Source: Asian Development Bank.

Task Force 1: Promoting the Issuance of LCY Bonds

Task Force 1 focuses on promoting the issuance of LCY bonds, co-chaired by China and Thailand. LCY bonds were considered useful to finance infrastructure investment. To maintain their growth momentum, eradicate poverty, and respond to climate change, ASEAN countries needed to fill the infrastructure investment gap, which was estimated at USD 102 billion per year (ADB 2017a). Due to limited public finance resources, more than half of the investment gap would have to be financed by private investments. However, the ability of domestic financial institutions in the region to supply needed infrastructure finance was still restricted by their limited risk-taking capacity. Thus, LCY bonds could fill the gap. To help promote the issuance of LCY bonds, the Credit Guarantee and Investment Facility (CGIF) was established in November 2010 as a trust fund of the Asian Development Bank (ADB) to provide credit enhancement. CGIF was designed to provide guarantees to LCY corporate bonds issued by companies in ASEAN+3 member economies. It aimed to help these companies secure long-term LCY financing to reduce their dependency on short-term foreign currency borrowing and address currency and maturity mismatches by recycling savings within the ASEAN+3 region more efficiently.

Credit Guarantee and Investment Facility

The CGIF was established by ASEAN+3 and ADB in November 2010 as a trust fund of ADB. CGIF enjoys ADB's privileges and immunities as an international organization, but its operation is independent from ADB. CGIF's Meeting of Contributors is the highest decision-making body, and CGIF's own Board of Directors as well as its management team and staff are separated from that of ADB.

Credit rating agencies recognize CGIF as an entity independent from ADB. CGIF is currently rated AA by Standard and Poor's in the global rating scales and AAA by domestic rating agencies in ASEAN economies in their national rating scales. LCY corporate bonds guaranteed by CGIF can enjoy the high credit standing of CGIF as a guarantor, enabling them to access investors who might otherwise find it difficult to invest in the bonds.

When CGIF started its guarantee operations, its initial guarantee capacity was limited to USD 700 million, given the USD 700 million in capital provided by its contributors (shareholders) without any leverage.

This resulted in the ability to support only a very small number of bond issuers despite its ambitious mandate. As the guarantee capacity limitation constrained CGIF's business development, its contributors decided in November 2013 to increase CGIF's guarantee capacity to USD 1.75 billion by increasing the leverage ratio from 1:1 to 2.5:1. However, this increase was also found to be insufficient; thus, CGIF contributors agreed in December 2017 to increase CGIF's guarantee capacity to USD 3.0 billion by increasing its capital to USD 1.2 billion. This capital increase implementation is underway, with plans for completion by 2023 (ADB 2019a).

CGIF guarantees have achieved notable developmental impacts on LCY corporate bond markets across ASEAN, which can be categorized as follows:

- **Supporting first-time issuers in tapping the domestic bond market:** Many creditworthy companies in ASEAN still find it difficult to tap their domestic bond markets because institutional bond investors in these markets tend to have conservative investment policies with high thresholds for rating requirements or are reluctant to invest in companies or businesses that they are not familiar with. CGIF guarantees have helped ASEAN companies overcome these barriers and tap on their domestic bond markets for the first time.

- **Enabling access to long-term funds:** CGIF guarantees have helped ASEAN companies raise long-term funds to match their investment needs when such long-term funds are otherwise not easily available in the market.

- **Broadening the investor base:** For prospective bond issuers in ASEAN's LCY corporate bond markets, the universe of potential bond investors is still limited because domestic institutional bond investors require high credit ratings, and foreign investors are constrained by their country risk exposure policies.

- **Supporting cross-border transactions:** Despite the progress of economic integration in the ASEAN+3 region and the expansion of ASEAN+3 companies into neighboring economies, cross-border bond issuances by ASEAN+3 companies are still very rare. Cross-border LCY bond issuances in other ASEAN markets are particularly useful when the depth of the domestic bond market is insufficient to meet the company's funding needs or there are very limited funding options in the domestic market. To encourage intraregional bond issuance, the CGIF promotes the ASEAN+3 Multi-Currency Bond Issuance Framework (AMBIF) to promote standardized issuance procedures by utilizing a common document for submission (for further details, please refer to the paragraphs below on the AMBIF). They also help the local operations of ASEAN+3 companies to raise bonds in matching currencies in the economy they have invested in.

- **Introduction of new debt instruments**: In ASEAN's LCY bond markets, the available types of debt instruments are still limited. Due to legal uncertainty and unfamiliarity, structured debt instruments like project bonds and securitization cannot be created easily despite their importance as vital funding tools to meet critical investment needs in the region. CGIF has been actively promoting the introduction of these new types of debt instruments in the ASEAN's LCY bond markets by supporting credit risk reduction and collaboration with ADB to build necessary institutional arrangements. Pilot cases for green and social bonds will be created through collaboration with other activities under ABMI.

By the end of 2020, CGIF is expected to guarantee more than 40 bonds and support more than 30 corporate bond issuers from Cambodia, Hong Kong, Indonesia, Japan, Korea, Lao People's Democratic Republic (PDR), China, Malaysia, Myanmar, the Philippines, Singapore, Thailand, and Vietnam.

Support for the Development of Thematic Bond Markets

Another important initiative Task Force 1 is currently highlighting is the development of thematic bond markets. Many ASEAN+3 member economies are vulnerable to climate risk. The region has suffered from big earthquakes, volcano eruptions, large typhoons, and health threats from pollution. According to the Global Climate Risk Index 2020, Japan and the Philippines are the two most affected countries in 2018 (Eckstein et al. 2020). For the period 1999–2018, Myanmar, the Philippines, Vietnam, and Thailand were included in the top 10 of the most affected countries as indicated by the annual Climate Risk Index average scores. Therefore, the region needs to consider a new approach to mobilize intermediate funds to create more environmentally friendly finance.

In addition, social bonds are receiving more attention because the ASEAN+3 member economies need to consider other important social values aligned with the Sustainable Development Goals adopted by the United Nations. Examples are gender, healthcare, and education for their development.

The outbreak of the novel coronavirus disease (COVID-19) clearly increased awareness of social bonds. To combat COVID-19 and recover from it, while the governments are facing the accumulation of public debt, raising money from private investors to address social needs is critically important. As a reaction to COVID-19, social bond issuance has increased globally. Social bonds need to bring the power of private capital to urgently needed healthcare services, better sanitation, and recovery of small and medium-sized enterprises (SMEs). Though it is still at the early stage of development, social bonds are expected to grow in ASEAN+3.

Task Force 2: Facilitating Demand for LCY Bonds

Task Force 2 focuses on facilitating the demand for LCY bonds, co-chaired by Japan and Singapore. To disseminate information and outputs produced under ABMI and to promote investment in LCY bonds, the AsianBondsOnline (ABO) website (https://asianbondsonline.adb.org/) was launched in 2004. The ABO disseminates data and various information on ASEAN+3 bond markets. Meanwhile, the Asian Bond Markets Summit was organized in 2005 and has been held annually since then to discuss market developments and challenges.

AsianBondsOnline

ABO is a web portal functioning as a one-stop clearinghouse of information on the government and corporate bond markets in ASEAN+3. It was created in 2004 and is managed by ADB as the ABMI Secretariat. The goal is to provide relevant information to various stakeholders and users to better guide their decision-making processes as well as to enhance awareness of ASEAN+3's bond markets. It presents both regional and market-specific information and data in a structured format, giving market participants and potential investors a clear and up-to-date perspective of the ASEAN+3 markets. Government and private sector initiatives to enhance market depth and liquidity are also detailed.

The technical assistance supporting ABO aims to support bond market development in ASEAN+3 markets by (i) providing information on the region's bond markets in the ABO portal, (ii) creating knowledge products such as Asia Bond Monitor (ABM), and (iii) engaging in capacity building activities in less financially developed economies (ADB 2017c). The website is targeted at institutional and individual investors, sovereign and corporate issuers, financial intermediaries, credit rating agencies, market regulators, policymakers, multilateral institutions, academic researchers, and journalists, both in local markets and outside the region. ABO is widely recognized by its many stakeholders as a key source of information for ASEAN+3 LCY bond markets (ADB 2019b).

Task Force 3: Improving the Regulatory Framework

Task Force 3 focuses on improving the regulatory framework, co-chaired by Japan and Malaysia. To facilitate market integration, ASEAN+3 policymakers looked to the experience of the European Union (EU) in harmonizing and coordinating the diverse interests of member economies and financial institutions. Based on the experiences of the EU, the policymakers established a Group of Experts on Cross-Border Bond Transactions and Settlement Issues in 2008 to provide advice to governments to foster regional bond market development and integration. Based on the Group of Experts' recommendations, the policymakers established the ASEAN+3 Bond Market Forum (ABMF) in 2010 as a common platform to foster standardization of market practices and harmonization of regulations relating to cross-border bond transactions in the region (ADB 2019a).

ASEAN+3 Bond Market Forum

The ABMF was established in May 2010 as the only regional platform at which actions and recommendations are reported to the ASEAN+3 policymakers. It functions to integrate the ASEAN+3 markets through standardization and harmonization of regulations and market practices as well as market infrastructures relating to cross-border bond transactions. ABMF consists of two forums: Sub-Forum 1 (SF1) and Sub-Forum 2 (SF2). SF1 focuses on regulatory issues related to bond issuance while SF2 focuses on technical issues related to standardization and market infrastructures for payments and settlements.

Normally ABMF meetings are held three times a year, bringing together more than 100 experts from the ministries of finance, central banks, securities market regulators, central securities depositories (CSDs), securities exchanges and market operators, financial market associations, as well as major financial institutions and information technology (IT) vendors in the region. The forum is open to experts who are interested in bond market developments and regional financial cooperation.

Since its establishment, ABMF has produced various outputs and created impacts. In 2012, ABMF released the *ASEAN+3 Bond Market Guide*, the first officially recognized publication of bond market regulations and settlement procedures in the ASEAN+3 member economies (ADB 2012). The market guide helped narrow information gaps and increase market transparency, which was often regarded as the biggest barrier to market entry. In 2013, ABMF published the SF1 Phase 2 Report, Proposal on ASEAN+3 Multi-Currency Bond Issuance Framework (ADB 2013a), in which an AMBIF was proposed as a regionally standardized bond issuance framework. And the SF2 Phase 2 Report, ASEAN+3 Information on Transaction Flows and Settlement Infrastructures, was published to deepen our understanding of the market infrastructures in the region with the aim to increase interoperability among them (ADB 2013b). Through these publications, ABMF gradually created a common understanding of what needs to be standardized and harmonized to integrate the markets. In 2015, ABMF released two Phase 3 reports, Implementation of the AMBIF: ABMF SF1 Phase 3 Report (ADB 2015a) and Harmonization and Standardization of Bond Market Infrastructures in ASEAN+3: ABMF SF2 Phase 3 Report (ADB 2015b). Based on the SF1 Phase 3 report, the Single Submission Form (SSF) was proposed as a common bond issuance document to be utilized where AMBIF is recognized. The SF2 Phase 3 report identified and recommended key financial technical standards such as ISO 20022 for linking and integrating market infrastructures to facilitate cross-border financial transactions.

Thanks to the efforts of the ABMF members, the ASEAN Economic Community Blueprint 2025 adopted by the ASEAN Leaders stated that:

"Payment and Settlement Systems will be further enhanced in several areas such as promoting standardisation and developing settlement infrastructure for cross-border trade, remittance, retail payment systems and capital markets. This will provide an enabling environment to promote regional linkages and payment systems that are safe, efficient and competitive. This will also require a certain level of harmonisation of standards and market practices based on international best practices (such as ISO 20022) to foster stability and efficiency within as well as outside the region."

ASEAN+3 Multi-Currency Bond Issuance Framework

The AMBIF aims to promote cross-border bond issuance and investment. Local markets are different because each jurisdiction may have a different regulatory framework, different currency, and different language. Thus, to make a cross-border transaction, investors and issuers need to understand the differences.

In reality, this is not easy. However, by focusing on similarities among the different markets, a common market may be created even in different jurisdictions without harmonization of regulations and currencies.

Based on such an understanding, ABMF agreed to focus on the development of professional bond market segments for corporate bonds. By focusing on professional investors, regulations can be lighter. For example, the regulators can assume that professional investors understand international accounting rules and the differences between these and local rules. Professional investors have a deeper knowledge of finance and understand the risks associated with various financial products and bonds. Professional investors can negotiate with an issuer and receive appropriate information for investment. Professional investors have greater capacity than retail investors to follow changes in market circumstances and take measures to hedge.

By creating a professional investor market segment, ASEAN+3 member economies can standardize and harmonize their individual markets for greater efficiency. Since definitions, regulations, and investor protections for professional investors are relatively similar across jurisdictions, the establishment of such markets would lead to further bond market integration across ASEAN+3. By creating a professional investors-only bond market, the level of investor protection can be reduced so that professional investors and issuers can enjoy easier and timelier issuances. In addition, regulators can assume that professional investors understand English as well as a common language of finance; thus, disclosure in English is acceptable in a professional investors-only market. Through this, AMBIF promotes the establishment of professional investors-only bond market in each ASEAN+3 market.

Consequently, the application of the AMBIF concept led to the acceptance of a standardized document for submission, the SSF, as a common language for finance and information disclosure based on international financial reporting standards. This should make the assessment of issuers and individual issues much easier. Of course, issuance procedures for bonds offered to professional investors are different from market to market, but the procedures are clearly documented in the AMBIF Implementation Guidelines for participating markets, which explain these procedures step-by-step. The guidelines increase transparency in the regulatory process and address the problem of information asymmetry that often prevents investors from coming to an emerging market.

From an investor perspective, AMBIF is expected to increase investment opportunities. Unlike publicly offered bonds, underwriters can solicit professional investors and create various instruments across a number of tenors in response to investor demand. From an issuer's perspective, the cost associated with producing issuance documentation and disclosure information is lower than the cost of a public offering, which would require additional information for the purpose of investor protection. In addition, the time to market can be much shorter, which enables timely issuance. From a regulator's perspective, the governance of the market can be delegated to a self-regulatory organization, which makes the market more responsive to changes and increases the effectiveness of market governance. Defined and standardized documentation, as well as more standardized market practices, will amplify the potential benefits of AMBIF. In particular, issuers who already produce an SSF in their home market can issue a bond to professional investors in other AMBIF markets more easily. This cannot happen without AMBIF.

Since its establishment in 2015, AMBIF has been recognized in seven markets, namely Cambodia, Hong Kong, Japan, Malaysia, the Philippines, Singapore, and Thailand. To expand AMBIF in the rest of the ASEAN+3 markets, ADB provides technical support to establish a necessary regulatory framework, starting from the establishment of professional investors concept, then appropriate regulatory exemption for professionals, including the acceptance of English and the SFF. To expand the recognition of AMBIF, the CGIF promotes AMBIF in its guarantee operations. The bonds issued under AMBIF are listed on the ABO website.

Task Force 4: Improving Related Infrastructure for the Bond Market

Task Force 4 focuses on improving related infrastructure for the bond market, co-chaired by Korea and the Philippines. ABMI has conducted several studies on establishing a regional settlement intermediary (RSI). The development of efficient and sound market infrastructure for regional securities settlement is regarded as one of the key components of ABMI. The Group of Experts on Cross-Border Bond Transactions and Settlement Issues published a report in April 2010 that analyzed possible RSI models from the viewpoint of legal and business feasibility (ADB 2010). The report published identified potential market impediments as well as cross-border transaction costs and provided models for RSIs to be considered in the future. After the publication of the report, a series of reassessments were made, and the establishment of a Cross-Border Settlement Infrastructure Forum (CSIF) was endorsed at the ASEAN+3 Finance Ministers' and Central Governors' Meeting in Delhi in May 2013. The CSIF aims to discuss the improvement of cross-border bond and cash settlement infrastructure in the region, including the possibility of establishing an RSI.

Cross-Border Settlement Infrastructure Forum

The CSIF consists of the central banks and national CSDs of ASEAN+3 member economies, with market regulators and officials from the region's ministries of finance joining as observers.

The CSIF aims to: (i) enhance the dialogue among policymakers and operators of bond and cash settlement infrastructure in the region, (ii) assess existing settlement infrastructure and identify comprehensive issues and requirements to facilitate cross-border bond and cash settlement infrastructure in the region, (iii) develop common basic principles for cross-border bond and cash settlement infrastructure with medium- and long-term perspectives, and (iv) discuss prospective models, an overall roadmap, and an implementation plan for the establishment of cross-border bond and cash settlement infrastructure in the region.

Since its inception, the CSIF has submitted the following reports to ABMI TF4: (i) Basic Principles on Establishing a Regional Settlement Intermediary and Next Steps Forward in May 2014, (ii) Progress Report on Establishing a Regional Settlement Intermediary and Next Steps: Implementing Central Securities Depository (CSD)–Real-Time Gross Settlement (RTGS) Linkages in ASEAN+3 in May 2015, (iii) Common Understanding on Cross-Border Business Continuity Planning and Cybersecurity in May 2018, (iv) Common Understanding on International Standards and Gateways for Central Securities Depository and Real-Time Gross Settlement Linkages in May 2019, and (v) Next Step for ASEAN+3

Central Securities Depository and Real-Time Gross Settlement Linkages in July 2020. Along with the discussions, the CSIF has been stepwisely establishing a common understanding on how CSD–RTGS linkages can be built in ASEAN+3.

Thanks to the efforts of CSIF members, ASEAN+3 member economies are now ready to implement the international standard. CSD and RTGS system operators in the region are supporting their participants' migration to ISO 20022. The related discussions focus more on how to maximize the expandability of data exchanges under ISO 20022.

As a pilot case of CSD–RTGS linkage, the Bank of Japan and the Hong Kong Monetary Authority (HKMA) announced the first cross-border cross-currency delivery versus payment (DvP) link on April 1, 2021. The link helps eliminate settlement risk by ensuring simultaneous delivery of Hong Kong dollars (HKD) and the Japanese government bonds, which was not possible because cross-border transactions are normally executed through a chain of command of correspondent banking networks. More importantly, the link will facilitate banks in conducting a cross-currency repurchase (repo) transaction to obtain HKD funds immediately with a repo using Japanese government bonds as collateral. The linkage will not only reduce cross-border settlement risks and costs but also provide a funding tool that can reduce a buildup of financial stress, as banks can swiftly mobilize foreign currency liquidity in exchange for their LCY bond holdings.

Further, amid the current regulatory trend of collateralization in cross-border transactions, the CSIF has discussed freeing up the region's domestic collateral pools for use in cross-border transactions. As economic and financial linkages within ASEAN+3 are increasing, collateral demands for cross-border transactions and the need for LCY liquidity will increase. Therefore, CSIF members have studied and discussed the possibility of using collateral in one economy to obtain liquidity in another, which is referred to as cross-border collateral.

As the next step, the CSIF will need to consider the implications of recent advancements in financial technology. Distributed ledger technology and blockchain will soon be employed as part of payment and settlement infrastructure in the region. For example, the National Bank of Cambodia officially introduced a blockchain-based payment infrastructure called Bakong in 2020. The Bank of Thailand launched the world's first block-chain-based platform for government savings bonds in 2020. Given these rapid developments, the CSIF will take stock of the varied experiences of the ASEAN+3 member economies (ADB 2020b).

Asian Prime Collateral Forum

Task Force 4 also launched the Asian Prime Collateral Forum in 2017 to study the possible use of regional government bonds as collateral for cross-border transactions. As financial markets in the region are integrating, it is necessary to discuss LCY-to-LCY liquidity management to facilitate more cross-border transactions and improve the region's safety net.

Technical Assistance Coordination Team

Since 2003, under the Japan–ASEAN Financial Technical Assistance Fund, the ASEAN Secretariat has been providing technical assistance to some ASEAN member states. The Technical Assistance Coordinating Team (TACT), consisting of the ASEAN member states, decides necessary capacity building for selected member countries to strengthen market foundations and address constraints to bond market development. For example, TACT, together with ADB, supported the creation of the corporate bond market in Cambodia in 2018 and revisions of the Securities Law in Vietnam in 2019. ADB and TACT shared the experiences of other ASEAN markets and provided technical assistance in customized approaches to help develop these markets.

As explained, the structure of the four task forces, namely supply, demand, regulations, and infrastructures, plus capacity building under TACT, encompasses all the necessary ingredients for LCY bond market development. But to strengthen the functionality of the markets and deepen market integration in the region, all four aspects have to be tackled simultaneously. For example, to develop a green bond market, it is necessary to find not only an issuer, that is, supply, but also an investor, that is, demand. To promote green bond issuance, it must have an appropriate framework of how to recognize a green bond, that is, regulations. In addition, a proper marketplace for disclosure and trade, that is, infrastructure, is necessary. In this regard, it is worth noting the function of the Secretariat of ABMI, which connects all activities, mobilizes necessary resources, and produces tangible outputs, with a strong backup by the ASEAN+3 member states under the TF framework. To deepen and integrate the markets, organic interactions of all task force activities are indispensable.

Achievements and Assessment of the ABMI to Date

Since the establishment of ABMI, the five original members of ASEAN, namely Indonesia, Malaysia, the Philippines, Singapore, and Thailand, plus China, Korea, and Vietnam (ASEAN+2), have achieved remarkable progress in developing their respective domestic bond markets. The total size of these LCY bond markets climbed to USD 18.7 trillion at the end of September 2020 (ADB 2020c). The total size is comparable to the United States (US) Treasury bonds and euro-denominated bonds issued by the residents of the Euro Area (Figure 29.4).

Among this grouping, Indonesia and Thailand have made concerted efforts to develop their markets, including the establishment of strong public debt management capacities. Korea and Malaysia have developed bond markets that are well balanced between the government and corporate segments, with significant depth in both. China's LCY bond market has become one of the largest in the world and still has room to grow. Thanks to these efforts, it is notable that the size of LCY bond markets of some of these economies as a ratio of gross domestic product (GDP) has exceeded those

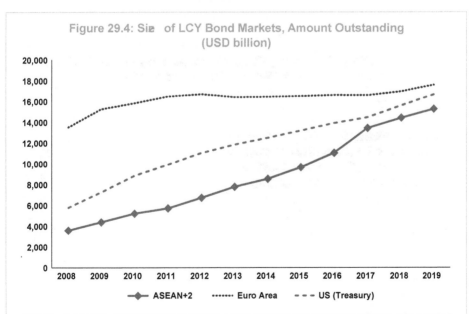

Figure 29.4: Size of LCY Bond Markets, Amount Outstanding (USD billion)

ASEAN = Association of Southeast Asian Nations, LCY = local currency, US = United States, USD = United States dollar.
Sources: AsianBondsOnline, CEIC, European Central Bank, International Monetary Fund, and Securities Industry and Financial Markets Association.

of some European countries. In terms of market development relative to the economic size, these ASEAN+3 markets can be considered as comparable to developed markets (Figure 29.5). As a testament of significant development of Asian bond markets, the inclusion of Malaysian and Chinese government bonds in world government bond indexes can also be noted.

Between 2003 and 2008, capital inflows from developed economies into emerging Asia increased again, given the region's strong growth prospects. These flows ended abruptly with the onset of the GFC. Economic growth in emerging East Asia dropped sharply due to a collapse in external demand.

However, thanks to timely policy stimulus measures, the ASEAN+3 member economies weathered the crisis and experienced a V-shaped recovery from the sharp downturn of late 2008 and early 2009. China implemented a sizable fiscal stimulus package, and the ASEAN member economies introduced a variety of fiscal measures to stimulate their economies in 2009. Fiscal stimuli created budgetary deficits across the region, but most of them were financed domestically. Thanks to the prudent budget management following the 1997–1998 AFC and concerted efforts toward

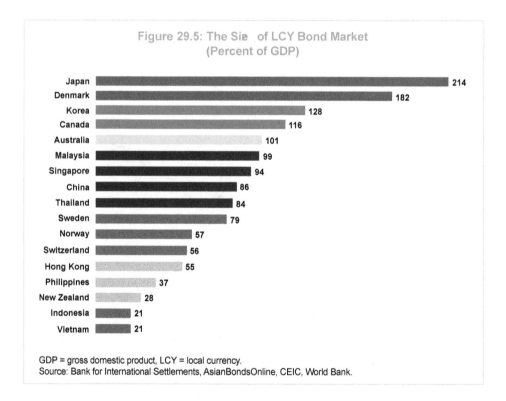

Figure 29.5: The Size of LCY Bond Market
(Percent of GDP)

Country	Percent of GDP
Japan	214
Denmark	182
Korea	128
Canada	116
Australia	101
Malaysia	99
Singapore	94
China	86
Thailand	84
Sweden	79
Norway	57
Switzerland	56
Hong Kong	55
Philippines	37
New Zealand	28
Indonesia	21
Vietnam	21

GDP = gross domestic product, LCY = local currency.
Source: Bank for International Settlements, AsianBondsOnline, CEIC, World Bank.

the development of LCY bond markets, they could finance fiscal expansion without causing much stress (Figure 29.6).

Since the 1997–1998 AFC, the ASEAN+3 member economies have made significant efforts to improve the resilience and soundness of the region's financial system. Having said that, the GFC inevitably affected the banking sector in the region, with credit growth ultimately contracting. However, unlike the 1997–1998 AFC, corporate bond markets could supplement financial intermediation, thus supporting a V-shaped recovery in the region.

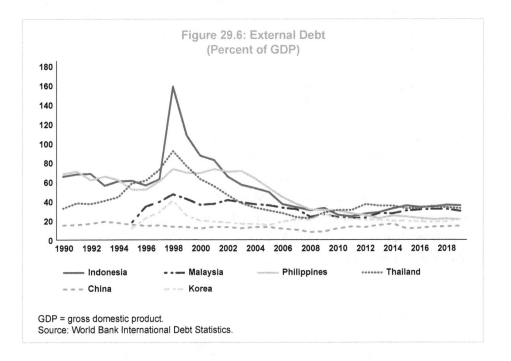

Figure 29.6: External Debt (Percent of GDP)

GDP = gross domestic product.
Source: World Bank International Debt Statistics.

ABMI has supported not only the growth of market size but also the functions of LCY bond markets. Yield curves have become more reliable and bond maturities have been gradually lengthened in most economies (Figure 29.7). In addition, there is now a wider range of benchmark issues, which has also allowed the creation of benchmark indexes across many regional markets.

There is a wider range of bonds issued in the region, including inflation-linked bonds, green bonds, asset-backed securities, and sukuk (Islamic bonds).

Liquidity has also markedly improved. Based on the ABO annual bond market liquidity survey, the bid-ask spread for on-the-run government

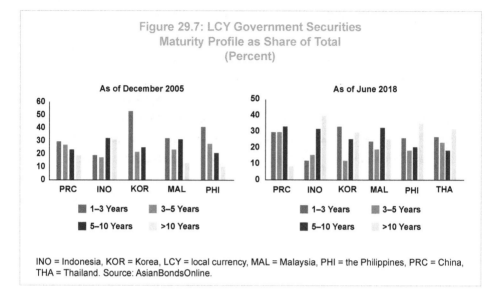

Figure 29.7: LCY Government Securities Maturity Profile as Share of Total (Percent)

INO = Indonesia, KOR = Korea, LCY = local currency, MAL = Malaysia, PHI = the Philippines, PRC = China, THA = Thailand. Source: AsianBondsOnline.

bonds narrowed considerably in most economies in ASEAN+3 between 2000 and 2019. The spread dropped from 15.0 basis points to 1.1 basis points in China, from 15.2 basis points to 2.1 basis points in Indonesia, from 4.9 basis points to 2.7 basis points in Malaysia, from 47.5 basis points to 2.8 basis points in the Philippines, from 7.3 basis points in 2004 to 2.7 basis points in Thailand, and from 75 basis points in 2008 to 5.5 basis points in Vietnam (Figure 29.8).

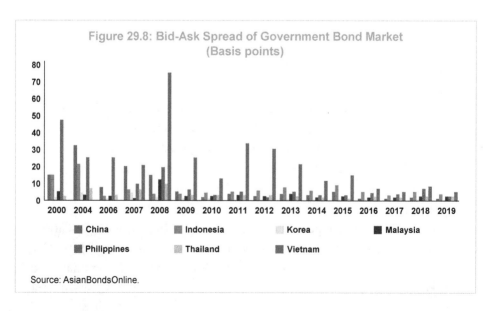

Figure 29.8: Bid-Ask Spread of Government Bond Market (Basis points)

Source: AsianBondsOnline.

The original sin hypothesis predicted that "the domestic currency cannot be used to borrow abroad or to borrow long term, even domestically;" thus, financial fragility would remain because the double mismatch would continue. However, most of the ASEAN+3 governments no longer need to rely on foreign currency finance. They can finance by themselves with their local currencies. The share of foreign currency government bond against the LCY government bond outstanding declined continuously (Figure 29.9).

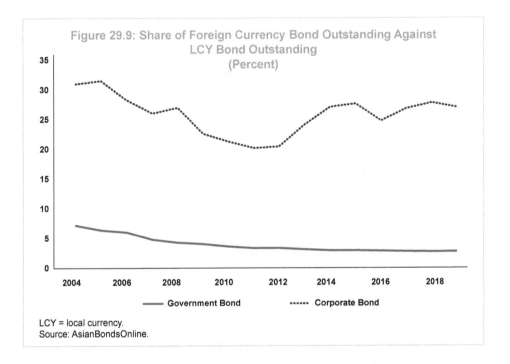

Figure 29.9: Share of Foreign Currency Bond Outstanding Against LCY Bond Outstanding (Percent)

LCY = local currency.
Source: AsianBondsOnline.

The foreign currency corporate bond outstanding has increased in recent years, but this should be seen as a result of increasing international activities by the Chinese companies, not due to the constraint of fund availability (Figure 29.10).

Finally, thanks to the efforts toward various financial reforms and improvements in economic fundamentals, the region could attract foreign capital into domestic markets (Figure 29.11). The expansion of LCY bond markets shows that the ASEAN+3 member economies have made a great deal of progress in mitigating the original sin.

Figure 29.10: Foreign Currency Corporate and Outstanding (USD billion)

USD = United States dollar.
Source: AsianBondsOnline.

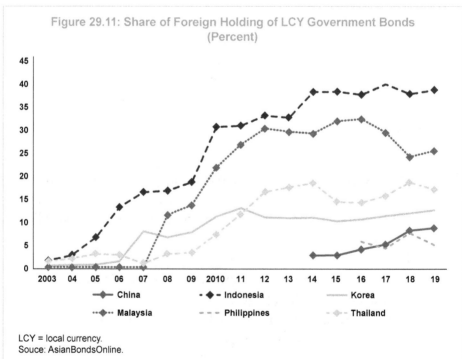

Figure 29.11: Share of Foreign Holding of LCY Government Bonds (Percent)

LCY = local currency.
Souce: AsianBondsOnline.

Remaining Challenges

As shown, ABMI has made great progress. However, there are still remaining challenges. In 2019, ASEAN+3 ABMI Medium-Term Road Map, 2019–2022 was adopted. While the road map acknowledged the progress of LCY bond market development, it also indicated the remaining challenges to be tackled as follows:

a. **Different levels of bond market development within the ASEAN+3 region:** LCY bond market development across ASEAN+3 has not been even. Brunei, Cambodia, Lao PDR, and Myanmar have only recently begun meeting the challenges of starting a bond market. Some of the other economies need to develop corporate bond markets further to support their infrastructure investment. The rest of the economies need to improve the functionality of the markets and liquidity by linking market infrastructures and facilitating more cross-border funding and investments.

Having said that, ABMI is gradually bringing forth fruit. For example, ABMF supported the creation of the LCY bond market in Cambodia in 2018, starting from a corporate bond market. Normally, it is recommended to develop an LCY bond market from government bonds. But a thorough analysis of the financial regulations by ABMF provided an opportunity to create the market even before creating the government bond market. The approach to developing a bond market from scratch requires a deep analysis of the financial sector and close communication with the authorities because the prescription and policy advice for the market development must be tailor-made. Also, close coordination among regulators such as the central bank as a banking regulator, securities market regulator, insurance regulator, and ministry of finance is indispensable because impediments often fall under jurisdictions of different authorities. In addition, thanks to a collaboration with CGIF, further corporate bond issues were realized under the AMBIF in Cambodia. It is expected Cambodia will take steps toward government bond issuance soon to develop the market further.

Similarly, ABMI supported other markets under the effective collaboration of ADB and TACT to narrow the development gap among the markets. Research under ABMI, particularly the bond market guides by theABMF, provide the basis of communication and establish a common understanding of what is missing and what needs to be developed.

b. **Large infrastructure investment gap:** According to ADB's estimate, ASEAN requires USD 3.1 trillion or USD 210 billion annually from 2016 to 2030 for climate change-adjusted infrastructure investment. And the estimated financing gap is USD 102 billion per year, which needs to be filled by the active participation of the private sector (ADB 2017a).

Moreover, COVID-19 has made a significant impact on the region's economy. Relative to a pre-COVID-19 baseline, ADB estimated a loss of 8.6% to 12.7% of ASEAN GDP in 2020 and a loss of 6.1% to 11.0% in 2021. These are equivalent to USD 253 billion to USD 374 billion and USD 178 billion to USD 322 billion, respectively (ADB 2020d). The recovery from COVID-19 will require faster infrastructure building to help the vulnerable. In addition to the immediate support to healthcare, it is necessary to improve social infrastructures, including sanitation, water supply, and hospitals. Also, improved logistics to support the region's value chain with more advanced information technologies is also necessary to build back better.

However, the ability of domestic financial institutions in the region to supply needed infrastructure finance is still restricted due to their limited risk-taking capacity. To enhance the risk-taking capacity of the private sector, a more innovative approach may be necessary.

For example, more active involvement of CGIF in project finance from the start of a project, that is, at the greenfield stage, may be considered. The most common use of project bonds is to refinance when construction is completed or the original syndicated bank loan matures, that is, at the brownfield stage, because cash flows are more predictable (ADB 2015c). CGIF's earlier involvement would reduce risks at the greenfield, hence bankable projects may increase. But it would require expansion of its guarantee not only to bonds but also to bank loans because it is not easy to find bond investors who invest in greenfield projects. In addition, CGIF would require enhancing risk analysis and risk-taking capacity as well as further collaboration with more experienced private sector experts. To invigorate infrastructure finance, GCIF may consider participating in a project at a much early stage. A project faces various risks such as construction and completion risk, operating risks, demand risk, political and regulatory risk, and environmental risk.

It may not be possible to cover all risks involved, but a risk related to a country risk may be considered if CGIF can leverage its position under the ASEAN+3's regional cooperation mechanism.

c. **Need for sustainable finance:** Many ASEAN+3 member economies are vulnerable to climate risk. ASEAN+3's coastal populations are facing more risks to increasingly frequent and more powerful typhoons. Hence, recovery strategies from COVID-19 must build back better, not build back to the previous one. The region needs to consider a new approach to mobilize and intermediate funds to create a more environmentally friendly, socially impactful, natural disaster-resilient, and sustainable economy. It requires building new institutional arrangements, guidelines, market practices, as well as awareness and a good understanding of market participants. It is expected to create pilot issues of thematic bonds to develop the markets in the region under ABMI.

d. **Low degrees of intraregional portfolio investment:** ASEAN+3 needs to utilize the region's vast savings to expand business opportunities and growth of the region. However, intraregional portfolio investment remains relatively low compared to the intraregional trade, which is comparable to that of the European Union (Figure 29.12).

To support the recycling of vast savings within the region to lead infrastructure finance, measures to remove a number of impediments to attract foreign investors, particularly foreign exchange risk mitigation measures, must be considered. This said, the efforts require thorough investigation because the elimination of such causes would often conflict with other policy objectives.

For example, restrictions on inbound and outbound capital flows may be due to consideration for exchange rate stability. In the region, there is no strict capital control, but there are cumbersome reporting procedures and prior registration requirements that would discourage smooth capital flows. The so-called real demand principle, that is to substantiate underlying transactions of foreign exchange transactions, would reduce speculative transactions, but it also inhibits over-hedging or under-hedging because foreign exchange transactions must meet the value of underlying transactions. As a result, it would reduce market liquidity, particularly when a market is under stress. As a small open economy, it is justifiable to watch the market closely and keep safeguard measures against volatile market movements. But more importantly,

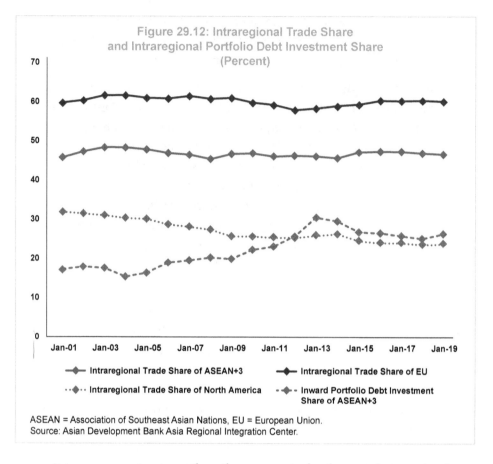

Figure 29.12: Intraregional Trade Share
and Intraregional Portfolio Debt Investment Share
(Percent)

ASEAN = Association of Southeast Asian Nations, EU = European Union.
Source: Asian Development Bank Asia Regional Integration Center.

it is necessary to strengthen the economic fundamentals to make the economy resilient against a speculative attack. In addition, the search for a market monitoring tool that is less damaging to market efficiency needs to be considered, along with technological advancement.

Also, the lack of and too expensive hedging tool is often pointed out as an impediment for cross-border transactions. This is a difficult problem because the root cause is not stemming from the foreign exchange market but due to the inefficiency and inactiveness of the short-term money market as well as the secondary bond market. To construct a foreign exchange (FX) swap and cross-currency basis swap, the market must have an efficient yield curve from the short-end based on active market transactions, which enables the modeling of the term structure. But invigorating the market would require the accumulation of financial assets and trading experiences and more diversified market participants. This would require structural changes in the regulatory framework, trading practices, market participants, market platform, and economic fundamentals, which cannot be solved overnight.

In addition, there may be a home country bias, a tendency of investors to favor companies from their own country over those from other countries due to familiarity and information asymmetry, as well as inertia in market practices to favor precedents. Besides, the inability of long-term investors to invest in projects in neighboring markets may be due to regulations related to insurance and pensions, such as rating requirements for investable assets. AMBIF is expected to reduce the asymmetry and the market inertia by creating common regional practices as well as a common understanding of how to and where to invest regionally.

e. **Heavy reliance on US dollar for intraregional transactions**: To facilitate further intraregional transactions, appropriate LCY-to-LCY transaction facilities need to be considered. The expansion of the LCY bond market may alleviate some foreign exchange risks but not all. Foreign exchange risk can be transferred to foreign investors, but it would still create market volatility in the domestic financial market. Contrary to trade integration within the region, most intraregional financial transactions are still denominated in US dollar (Figure 29.13).

Previously, goods produced in Asia were consumed mostly in the US and Europe. In such a case, it was justifiable to transact and settle in US dollar or euro. However, Asia is now becoming the largest destination for final goods produced by Asia. ASEAN is becoming a large consumer market, and China has become the largest trade partner for all other ASEAN+3 member economies. In such cases, transaction and settlement for intraregional transactions by US dollar may become a source of potential risk.

To mitigate the risk, ASEAN+3 may consider LCY-to-LCY settlement. However, this is not easy because liquidity in LCY-to-LCY transactions is much less compared with LCY-to-USD transactions. Like the barter trade system, it is not easy to match LCY sell and LCY buy. Therefore, it is worth considering cross-border collateral more actively to access LCY liquidity without exchanging to US dollar. For example, by pledging Japanese government bonds to Thai banks, Japanese

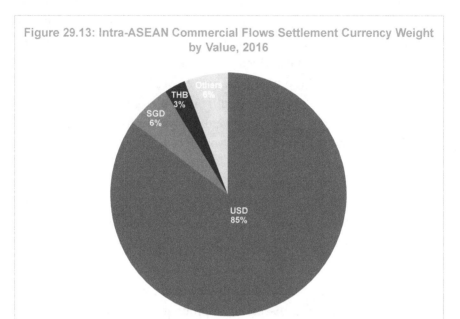

Figure 29.13: Intra-ASEAN Commercial Flows Settlement Currency Weight by Value, 2016

ASEAN = Association of Southeast Asian Nations, SGD = Singapore dollar, THB = Thai baht, USD = United States dollar.
Source: SWIFT (2016). Achieving Financial Integration in the ASEAN Region. SWIFT discussion paper.

banks may receive Thai baht liquidity from Thai banks. Contrary to a cash transaction through foreign exchange, which normally takes two days because of the involvement of US dollar transactions, liquidity provision via cross-border collateral can be made on the same day because ASEAN+3 member economies are in almost the same time zone. Currently, the use of cross-border collateral arrangements by the central banks in ASEAN+3 is limited to an emergency. Thus, more routinely operationalized cross-border collateral arrangements such as the correspondent central banking model established by the European Central Bank may be considered. To this end, the CSIF will conduct a study on central bank collateral eligibility.

Conclusion

The development of a bond market is not easy and requires enormous efforts. All relevant parties must understand what they need to do and work closely together. In addition, they must establish a consensus on how to develop the market. Commitments from the securities market regulator alone cannot create a successful market. It must be built together with other public authorities and the central bank, as well as all market participants and financial institutions.

Based on the experiences of ABMI, there is no one-size-fits-all approach to the development of an LCY bond market. Given different levels of market development and financial circumstances, as well as different legal and regulatory environments, it is not practical to apply the same prescriptions to all. Therefore, careful diagnostics, analysis, and strategies are necessary for each country before applying policy measures. The key challenges and areas of focus for each ASEAN+3 markets further develop LCY bond markets, which are summarized in Table 29.2.

Table 29.2: Key Characteristics, Challenges, and Area of Focus for LCY Bond Market Development

Economy	Strength	Weakness	Challenges and Area of Focus
Brunei	Accumulated domestic wealth	The limited size of the economy	Increase in LCY transactions Creation of CSD to safekeep LCY assets
Cambodia	The openness of the economy	Heavy dollarization	Issuance of government bonds Creation of a custodian Development of long-term investors such as insurance and pension funds
China	Large economic and market size and growth	Segregation of onshore and offshore renminbi markets	Building a benchmark interest rate Promotion of intraregional transactions Acceptability of English
Hong Kong	Well-established international financial market	No significant weakness	Further connection to Chinese mainland through the Bond Connect
Indonesia	High demand for credit	Low credit creation relative to its economic size	Further development of the professional investors-only market Derivative market development for hedging Acceptability of English
Japan	Large and liquid government bond market	Small corporate bond market relative to its economic size Lack of credit demand	Promotion of professional bond market Promotion of new technology

continued on next page

Table 29.2: *continued*

Economy	Strength	Weakness	Challenges and Area of Focus
Korea	The well-developed corporate bond market	Relatively low participation of foreign issuers in the market compared to the high participation of Korean issuers outside of Korea	Promotion of intraregional transactions Promotion of new technology
Lao PDR	Potential to become a regional corridor	A very early stage of market development Shortage of capacity	Improvements in regulatory frameworks, institutional arrangements, and market infrastructures Developing long-term investors such as insurance and pension funds Development of professional investor concept
Malaysia	The well-developed corporate bond market	A "real demand principle" — the foreign exchange transaction must be linked to a qualifying underlying asset or transaction	Promotion of intraregional transactions Promotion of new technology
Myanmar	High demand for credit	A very early stage of market development Shortage of capacity	Improvements in regulatory frameworks, institutional arrangements, and market infrastructures. Developing long-term investors such as insurance and pension funds Development of professional investor concept
Philippines	High demand for credit	Low credit creation relative to its economic size	Diversification of investor base including promotion of corporate bond investments by institutional investors Derivative market development for hedging
Singapore	Well-established international financial market	No significant weakness	Promotion of new technologies
Thailand	The well-developed corporate bond market Mekong Subregional bond issuance	Restriction on cash holding by nonresidents	Derivative market development Promotion of new technology
Vietnam	High demand for credit	Limited diversification of investors	Further development of the professional investors-only market Diversification of investor base, including the development of institutional investors Derivative market development for hedging

CSD = central securities depository, Lao PDR = Lao People's Democratic Republic, LCY = local currency.
Source: Partially extracted from the ASEAN+3 Bond Market Guides by the author.

ABMI has demonstrated the role of regional cooperation, which can address the problem of coordination failure and lack of knowledge and experience. Furthermore, it can push member countries toward achievements through peer pressure. Shared knowledge and experiences can support the identification of problems and provide appropriate policy advice.

To overcome the remaining challenges of ABMI and deepen regional market integration, the scope of the regional initiative needs to be expanded. As discussed, necessary policy measures are not limited to the bond markets. To create more useable and cheaper hedging tools to mitigate FX risk, it is necessary to create a more active interbank market, short-term money market, interest rate swap market, as well as a liquid bond market. To create more LCY-to-LCY transactions, it is necessary to expand access to LCY liquidity; thus, cross-border collateral needs to be considered by utilizing the increasing amount of high quality liquid assets, thanks to the development of LCY government bond markets in the region. Moreover, to facilitate cross-border movement of capital flows, it is necessary to strengthen market confidence and reduce frictions due to various restrictions. Therefore, the ASEAN+3 economies must continue their efforts to improve financial market structure and economic fundamentals. ABMI should consider a more holistic approach. Along with the market development of ASEAN+3, including the rapid advancement of financial technology, ABMI will need to evolve and lead a regional discussion to ensure the region's financial development and stability in the long run.

References

ASEAN+3. 2003. *ASEAN+3 Chairman's Press Release on the Asian Bond Markets Initiative.*

ASEAN+3. 2004. The Joint Ministerial Statement of the ASEAN+3 Finance Ministers Meeting, May 15, Jeju, Korea.

Asian Development Bank. 2005. *Technical Assistance Report Harmonization of Bond Standards in ASEAN+3.* Manila.

Asian Development Bank. 2010. *Asian Bond Markets Initiative Group of Experts (GoE) Report for Task Force 4.* Manila.

Asian Development Bank. 2012. *ASEAN+3 Bond Market Guide.* Manila.

Asian Development Bank. 2013a. *Proposal on ASEAN+3 Multi-Currency Bond Issuance Framework*. Manila.

Asian Development Bank. 2013b. *ASEAN+3: Information on Transaction Flows and Settlement Infrastructures*. Manila.

Asian Development Bank. 2015a. *Implementation of the ASEAN+3 Multi-Currency Bond Issuance Framework: ASEAN+3 Bond Market Forum Sub-Forum 1 Phase 3 Report*. Manila.

Asian Development Bank. 2015b. *Harmonization and Standardization of Bond Market Infrastructures in ASEAN+3: ASEAN+3 Bond Market Forum Sub-Forum 2 Phase 3 Report*. Manila.

Asian Development Bank. 2015c. *Local Currency Bonds and Infrastructure Finance in ASEAN+3*. Manila.

Asian Development Bank. 2017a. *Meeting Asia's Infrastructure Needs*. Manila.

Asian Development Bank. 2017b. *The Asian Bond Markets Initiative: Policy Maker Achievements and Challenges*. Manila.

Asian Development Bank. 2017c. "Supporting the Development of Asian Bond Markets through AsianBondsOnline." Technical Assistance Report. Manila.

Asian Development Bank. 2017d. *Box 4.1: Asia's Cross-Border Collateral Agreements. Asian Economic Integration Report 2017*. Manila.

Asian Development Bank. 2019a. *Good Practices for Developing a Local Currency Bond Market: Lessons from the ASEAN+3 Asian Bond Markets Initiative*. Manila.

Asian Development Bank. 2019b. *Box A2.1. AsianBondsOnline. Good Practices for Developing a Local Currency Bond Market: Lessons from the ASEAN+3 Asian Bond Markets Initiative*. Manila.

Asian Development Bank. 2020a. *Asia's Journey to Prosperity: Policy, Market, and Technology Over 50 Years*. Manila.

Asian Development Bank. 2020b. *Next Step for ASEAN+3 Central Securities Depository and Real-Time Gross Settlement Linkages: A Progress Report of the Cross-Border Settlement Infrastructure Forum*. Manila.

Asian Development Bank. 2020c. *Asia Bond Monitor November 2020*. Manila.

Asian Development Bank. 2020d. "The Impact of COVID-19 on Developing Asia: The Pandemic Extends into 2021." ADB Brief No. 159. Manila.

Association of Southeast Asian Nations. 2015. *ASEAN Economic Community Blueprint 2025*. Jakarta.

Credit Guarantee and Investment Facility. http://www.cgif-abmi.org/#about-usEckstein, D., V. Künzel, L. Schäfer, and M. Winges. 2020. *Global Climate Risk Index 2020*. Germanwatch.

Eichengreen, B., and R. Hausmann. 1999. "Exchange Rates and Financial Fragility." Proceedings, Economic Policy Symposium, Jackson Hole. Federal Reserve Bank of Kansas City, 329–368.

International Monetary Fund and Work Bank. 2020. *Staff Note for the G20 International Financial Architecture Working Group.* Washington.

Yoshitomi, M., and S. Shirai. 2001. *Technical Background Paper for Policy Recommendations for Preventing Another Capital Account Crisis.* Tokyo: Asian Development Bank Institute.

Part V

Conclusion and Challenges Ahead

Chapter 30

ASEAN+3 Regional Financial Cooperation in Retrospect

Hoe Ee Khor, Diwa C. Guinigundo, Masahiro Kawai, and Jinho Choi

Introduction

The Asian financial crisis (AFC) has had a profound impact on both the foundation and the path of regional economic growth and integration. This crisis has taught us important lessons that have influenced the perspectives of public policy on crisis management in the past 20 plus years. In particular, the AFC revealed the dramatic changes that had taken place in global financial markets since the breakdown of the Bretton Woods system in 1971 and the need for countries to strengthen their macroeconomic fundamentals, reform their financial systems, and build up foreign reserves as buffers against capital flow volatility shocks. It also highlighted the imperative for stronger regional financial cooperation in crisis management. While Japan's early proposal in 1997 to create an Asian Monetary Fund (AMF) was not broadly accepted by the international financial circle, the idea was revived in 2000 with the establishment of the Chiang Mai Initiative (CMI) under the Association of Southeast Asian Nations (ASEAN)+3 Finance Process. It was further strengthened by the CMI's subsequent expansion to the Chiang Mai Initiative Multilateralisation (CMIM) Agreement in 2010. To support the Agreement, the ASEAN+3 Macroeconomic Research Office (AMRO) was created in 2011 as an independent macroeconomic surveillance body.

The importance of "holding hands" among regional peers to prevent and resolve financial crises cannot be overemphasized. Based on the experience of the past two decades, ASEAN+3 should continue to enhance the effectiveness of the regional financial safety net to better meet the needs of the members. In related literature, Ocampo (2006) provides a comprehensive summary of key arguments in support of regional financial cooperation. He argues that more active regional financial arrangements can strengthen the international financial architecture, which would in turn benefit regional economies in several aspects. First, fortifying regional defenses against financial crises explicitly internalizes the effects of domestic macro-financial policies on regional partners. Strong regional defenses also secure regional reserve funds and swap arrangements as a second or third line of defense against crises, which would serve as "regional public goods" (Mistry 1999). Second, regional financial cooperation develops the financial infrastructure to support domestic financial development and expands regional capital markets (Sakakibara 2003). Third, a regional financial arrangement benefits small- and medium-sized economies by providing a broader menu of alternative funding sources for crisis management, enhancing their bargaining power against "global public goods" (Griffith-Jones et al. 1999; Ocampo 2002).

In this context, it is necessary to take stock of how the ASEAN+3 region's financial cooperation has developed. Assessing how regional cooperation has benefited from establishing a regional safety net with a complementary economic surveillance body will help guide us in addressing the remaining agenda of regional financial cooperation and charting appropriate courses of action for the future. This chapter, therefore, concludes this volume with reflections on what has been achieved thus far, and what gaps and challenges remain ahead. This chapter aims to catalyze discussions in order to help further advance regional financial cooperation.

The outline is as follows: the next section describes the key achievements of ASEAN+3 during the post-AFC period, focusing on increased resilience of the region's macro-financial foundations and the launch of regional financial cooperation. The subsequent section discusses the challenges ahead, particularly those revealed by the coronavirus disease (COVID-19) pandemic crisis. The last section concludes the chapter.

Reflection on Key Achievements of ASEAN+3 After the AFC

Handling Economic Challenges

The AFC was a critical milestone for Asian economies. It provided many valuable lessons to policymakers and shaped their thinking on how to prevent and combat financial crises, not only in the region but also in other emerging market economies.

One key lesson is that policymakers should pay more attention to the dynamics of cross-border capital flows and developments in global financial markets. Most issues preceding the AFC were related to excessive government spending, which had led to high inflation and large fiscal and current account deficits. During the AFC, serious problems were caused by excessive borrowing in foreign currency by the banking and corporate sectors, followed by a sudden halt, massive capital flow reversals, a collapse in asset prices, and unexpected contagion spreading across the region. Starting with Thailand, the crisis spread quickly throughout the region. Financial markets suddenly became a source of major risk and volatile capital flows a main cause.

Another lesson is that the exchange rate should be more flexible and supported by ample reserves and policy buffers. During the AFC, regional exchange rates were pegged too tightly against the United States (US) dollar, which led to a huge loss of foreign exchange reserves when central banks attempted to defend their currencies against speculative attacks and/or large capital outflows.

Enhanced Macro-Financial Policy Framework

In the aftermath of the AFC, regional policymakers overhauled their policy frameworks and institutions to strengthen financial systems and macroeconomic fundamentals while improving flexibility in their policy mixes to deal with external shocks. Among these changes were more disciplined monetary policy frameworks coupled with more flexible exchange rate regimes, fiscal consolidation to rebuild policy space, a strengthening of the financial regulatory framework, and better prudential oversight to deal with emerging financial stability risks (AMRO 2017a).

First, regional policymakers became more skillful at managing the trilemma of exchange rate stability, independent monetary policy, and capital mobility. Indonesia, Malaysia, the Philippines, and Thailand moved from tightly pegged exchange rate regimes to more flexible arrangements, albeit at different paces. This allowed them to gain greater monetary policy autonomy in the context of more open capital accounts. Thailand, Korea, Indonesia, and the Philippines also adopted inflation targeting frameworks to handle the new dynamics of inflation and enhance the credibility of monetary policy and central banks.

Second, the crisis-hit economies — Indonesia, Korea, Malaysia, and Thailand — also implemented fiscal reforms to strengthen their fiscal positions. Indonesia, Malaysia, and Thailand, as well as the less-affected Philippines, set ceilings on fiscal deficits and/or debt-to-gross domestic product (GDP) ratios. Some countries also broadened and diversified their tax bases, especially those highly dependent on oil and gas revenue. These measures anchored fiscal policies and stabilized debt-to-GDP ratios at lower and more sustainable levels.

Third, regional policymakers strengthened their financial systems' resilience to shocks through a series of regulatory reforms in the financial and corporate sectors. Following the AFC, the crisis-hit economies implemented financial and corporate restructuring, adopted new laws to strengthen corporate governance and improve corporate bankruptcy procedures (Table 30.1), and carried out institutional reforms to improve risk management capabilities. Meanwhile, many countries strengthened their supervisory and regulatory powers by creating financial supervisory agencies, and also established deposit insurance schemes. These policy efforts to reform the financial system, combined with fiscal consolidation efforts, led to stronger balance sheets in both the public and private sectors, which provided countries with firmer foundations to weather the 2008–2009 global financial crisis (GFC).

Table 30.1: Institutional Frameworks for Bank and Corporate Restructuring After the AFC

Country	Major Support Institution	Agency for Bank Recapitalization	Asset Management Company	Agency for Voluntary Corporate Restructuring
Indonesia	Indonesian Bank Restructuring Agency (IBRA)	Direct from Bank Indonesia (BI) or via IBRA	IBRA	Jakarta Initiative Task Force (JITF)
Malaysia	Bank Negara Malaysia (BNM)	Danamodal	Danaharta	Corporate Debt Restructuring Committee (CDRC)
Thailand	Bank of Thailand (BOT)	Financial Restructuring Advisory Committee (funded by FIDF)	FRA to take assets of closed finance companies; unsold assets moved to AMC and good assets to RAB. TAMC for commercial banks	Corporate Debt Restructuring Advisory Committee (CDRAC)
Korea	Financial Supervisory Service (FSS)	Korea Deposit Insurance Corporation (KDIC)	Korea Asset Management Corporation (KAMCO)	Corporate Restructuring Coordination Committee (CRCC)

AFC = Asian financial crisis, AMC = Asset Management Corporation, FIDF = Financial Institutions Development Fund, FRA = Financial Sector Restructuring Authority, RAB = Radanasin Bank, TAMC = Thai Asset Management Corporation.
Source: Kawai (2000).

Fourth, ASEAN+3 economies were most active in adopting macro-prudential measures to manage financial stability risks. After the GFC, the ASEAN+3 region saw sustained capital inflows amid ample global liquidity triggered by unconventional monetary policies in advanced economies. Massive and sustained capital inflows could yield benefits such as low-cost financing, but they also generate financial vulnerabilities in recipient economies and increase the risk of sudden stops and capital flow reversals. In particular, the "taper tantrum" episode that started in May 2013 high-lighted the risk that emerging economies with large current account and fiscal deficits and high inflation were highly vulnerable to sudden shifts in market sentiments. This was observed in the capital outflows and currency depreciation in the so-called "fragile five" — Brazil, India, Indonesia, South Africa, and Turkey. To manage financial stability risks from sustained capital inflows, ASEAN+3 economies deployed capital flow management measures (CFMs) to discourage short-term inflows and macroprudential policy measures (MPMs), such as loan-to-value ratios, debt servicing ratios, reserve requirement ratio, and minimum liquidity buffers, to avoid a credit boom or asset price bubble while engaging judiciously in foreign exchange interventions to counter excessive market volatility. The ever-increasing interlinkages in the global financial market, the large and volatile capital flows caused partially by easy monetary policies of the US Federal Reserve and other major central banks, and the small sizes of their financial markets provided a strong rationale for ASEAN+3 economies to use CFMs and MPMs while intervening judiciously in the foreign exchange market to defend themselves from massive external shocks and maintain financial stability.

Solid Economic Recovery and Deep Deleveraging with Stronger External Buffers

Continuing and often painful policy reforms by the affected economies after the AFC and the GFC have enabled them to strengthen macroeconomic fundamentals, improve the governance and regulatory frameworks, and rebuild policy buffers. During the first 10 years after the AFC, exports led the recovery in crisis-hit economies, mainly driven by strong global demand and boosted by a deepening of regional value chains, aided by China's World Trade Organization accession in 2001. The move toward more flexible exchange rate regimes enhanced external resilience and competitiveness. The GFC led to a collapse in external demand in the US and Europe and a rebalancing of growth toward domestic demand. ASEAN+3 economies became more integrated with each other due to the rapid growth of the middle class in the region, especially in China and ASEAN countries, and the deepening of regional supply chains through intra-regional trade and investment.

It is noteworthy that crisis-hit economies successfully recovered from the devastation of the AFC, as evidenced in key macroeconomic and financial indicators. These economies regained growth momentum, reaching their pre-AFC output levels within 5 years or so. On the financial front, ASEAN+3 economies restored financial health through a deep deleveraging process after the AFC. As a result of aggressive financial and corporate sector restructuring, banking sector health was restored. Reflecting the effects of exchange rate devaluation and bank recapitalization, public sector debt rose sharply in the crisis-affected countries but gradually stabilized after the AFC, falling to below 60% of GDP in subsequent years.

Associated with the rapid credit expansion in the pre-AFC period was an equally rapid rise in domestic investment. The AFC led to a massive reduction in investment in all crisis-hit economies, mainly due to the protracted rebuilding of damaged corporate balance sheets, as well as disruptions in domestic and external sources of financing. This downward adjustment in investment was in turn reflected in a sharp improvement of the current account balance in the region. Indeed, the ASEAN+3 region's external position strengthened with a significant build-up in foreign exchange reserves, mainly attributable to solid current account surpluses in the post-AFC period and large capital inflows, the latter following the adoption of unconventional monetary policy in the US and other advanced economies in response to the GFC.

The ASEAN+3 region's foreign exchange reserves increased 10-fold from USD 625.5 billion in 1997 to USD 6.8 trillion in 2020, accounting for 47% of the world's total foreign exchange reserves. China and Japan were key contributors to the region's stronger external buffers. ASEAN and Korea also saw a significant expansion in their combined foreign exchange reserves from a total of USD 168.5 billion in 1997 to USD 1.5 trillion in 2020. According to the International Monetary Fund's (IMF) reserve adequacy metric, the ASEAN+3 region has maintained moderate to ample foreign exchange reserves which serve as a first line of defense against external shocks.

Launch of Regional Financial Cooperation

The AFC, by bringing the region together to support crisis-hit economies and engage in policy dialogues, has encouraged the development and institutionalization of ASEAN+3 regional financial cooperation over the past two decades. Stronger regionalism around the world in the 1990s, as witnessed in stronger trade and economic integration through the North American Free Trade Agreement in 1994 and the launch of the European Economic and Monetary Union in 1999, has also encouraged Asian countries to engage in more active discussions of regional financial cooperation (Jung 2008). Yet another reason for closer regional financial cooperation is that, despite having built up external buffers with enhanced policy frameworks since the AFC, the ASEAN+3 region witnessed the disruptive destabilization of financial markets when global market conditions deteriorated sharply as seen during the GFC and the taper tantrum episode.

Against this backdrop, ASEAN+3 countries have made significant progress in deepening regional financial cooperation, especially in three key areas: (i) financial safety net, (ii) economic and financial surveillance, and (iii) financial market development (Kawai and Morgan 2014; Morgan 2018).

Strengthening the Region's Financial Safety Net

Ever since the AFC, ASEAN+3 economies have long desired to establish their own liquidity support mechanism to supplement existing international facilities, aiming at self-help crisis prevention and resolution in the region. Unfortunately, Japan's proposal for creating an AMF during the AFC failed to take off, mainly owing to opposition from the US and the IMF. Nevertheless, such early efforts to establish a regional financial safety net, which led to the establishment of the Manila Framework Group and the New Miyazawa Initiative, eventually contributed to the launch of the CMI at the ASEAN+3 Finance Ministers' Meeting in May 2000. The CMI is aimed to: (i) expand and enhance the ASEAN Swap Agreement (ASA) and (ii) establish a regional network of bilateral swap arrangements (BSAs).

In May 2007, ASEAN+3 members agreed on a form of financial arrangement and legal modality for consolidating individual CMI BSAs into one single multilateralized arrangement, namely the CMIM. The first version of the CMIM, effective March 2010, was equipped with only a crisis resolution facility, called the CMIM Stability Facility (CMIM-SF), with a total size of

USD 120 billion. The CMIM-SF is accessible only when a member economy is hit by a temporary balance of payments problem. In 2014, ASEAN+3 finance and central bank authorities introduced a crisis prevention facility, called the CMIM Precautionary Line (CMIM-PL), under which short-term liquidity could be provided on a precautionary basis to a member economy in anticipation of a potential liquidity shock. After three amendments in 2014, 2020, and 2021, the CMIM has been strengthened in a significant way. First, the total size of the CMIM Agreement has increased to USD 240 billion since 2014. Second, the IMF de-linked portion, i.e., the amount of the allocation that can be drawn down without an IMF program, has been raised to 40% from March 31, 2021. The twin liquidity facilities of the CMIM-SF and the CMIM-PL equipped the ASEAN+3 region with both a crisis resolution and a crisis prevention tool. With the IMF de-linked portion increasing from the initial 10% (under the CMI) to 40%, CMIM has been strengthened as a self-help mechanism to help meet members' urgent financing needs, with lesser reliance on an IMF program.

Upgrading Economic and Financial Surveillance

Several regional forums and organizations have been established over the years for the purpose of information exchange, economic monitoring, research and training, and policy dialogue to develop expertise and build capacity for better policymaking. Many ASEAN+3 members have been engaged in multiple regional cooperation forums and organizations, including ASEAN's and ASEAN+3's finance and central banks forums, the Executives' Meeting of East Asia-Pacific Central Banks (EMEAP), and the South East Asian Central Banks Research and Training Center (SEACEN), as shown in Figure 30.1. Among the various forums with overlapping memberships, the ASEAN and ASEAN+3 finance processes and EMEAP have been the main ones for regional financial cooperation in East Asia.

In May 2000, ASEAN+3 finance ministers established the Economic Review and Policy Dialogue (ERPD) process to discuss macroeconomic and financial issues in East Asia. From 2012 onward, the central bank governors of ASEAN+3 members joined this forum. On a separate track, ASEAN and ASEAN+3 finance and central bank deputies have been meeting twice a year. The policy dialogue and surveillance process among ASEAN+3 members were in transition from the "information sharing" stage to the "peer review and peer pressure" stage. The "due diligence" process has yet to start in a serious

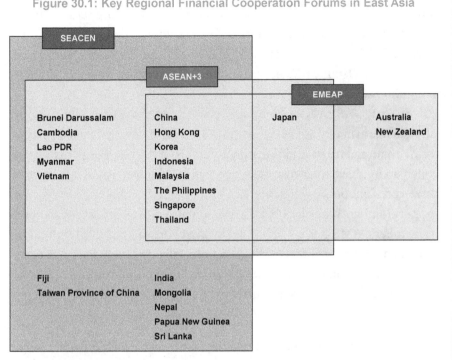

Figure 30.1: Key Regional Financial Cooperation Forums in East Asia

ASEAN = Association of Southeast Asian Nations, EMEAP = Executives' Meeting of East Asia-Pacific Central Banks, Lao PDR = Lao People's Democratic Republic, SEACEN = South East Asian Central Banks Research and Training Center.
Note: For SEACEN and EMEAP, the members are only central banks whereas for ASEAN and ASEAN+3, those comprise both central banks and ministries of finance.
Source: Authors.

manner (Kawai and Houser 2008).

Another key forum is EMEAP, a cooperative group of central banks and monetary authorities in the Asia-Pacific region, comprising Australia, China, Hong Kong, Indonesia, Japan, Korea, Malaysia, New Zealand, the Philippines, Singapore, and Thailand. Since its establishment in 1991, EMEAP is perceived as the first successful regional forum in the region (Hamanaka 2011). In the aftermath of the AFC, EMEAP governors affirmed the importance of its activities in promoting information sharing on economic and financial issues and developing mutual trust among regional central banks (EMEAP 1998). According to Ocampo (2006), the key contributions of EMEAP to regional cooperation can be grouped into two areas, namely: (i) development financing to enhance regional bond markets through the Asian Bond Funds (ABF) Initiative and (ii) strengthening macroeconomic management through policy dialogues and macroeconomic surveillance. Up to now, EMEAP has continued to pursue its goal of building greater regional cooperation under the modality of a multitiered, informal forum without a dedicated secretariat. Current EMEAP activities are undertaken at three levels: the Governors' Meetings, the Deputies' Meetings, and the Monetary and Financial Stability Committee and Working Groups.

In 2011, ASEAN+3 members established AMRO as the regional surveillance arm of the CMIM. AMRO is a legal entity established through an international treaty and is distinguished from the other regional forums which do not have their own full-time staff and budget. AMRO focuses on three core functions, which are to conduct macroeconomic surveillance, support implementation of the CMIM, and provide technical assistance to its members. AMRO was established in Singapore in April 2011, initially as a company limited by guarantee. It was officially designated as an international organization (IO) in February 2016. Since becoming an IO, AMRO has expanded and developed further in terms of organizational structure and capacity:

- First, AMRO's top management structure has evolved from a single director to a four-member senior management team. Since May 2016, AMRO's senior management has comprised Director, Deputy Director 1 (administration), Deputy Director 2 (CMIM, strategy and coordination), and Chief Economist (surveillance).

- Second, AMRO has significantly strengthened its surveillance capacity by revamping its overall surveillance framework and developing analytical toolkits (see Box 30.1 on "AMRO's Key Achievements toward a More Systemic Surveillance Framework"). It has also ramped up staff resources to accommodate members' growing needs. The number of surveillance staff has significantly increased from 6 in December 2011 to 43, including 10 secondees, in June 2021. In 2016, AMRO bolstered its regional surveillance capacity by establishing a dedicated team for this function.

- Third, AMRO started publishing its surveillance reports under a new publication policy in 2017. AMRO launched the ASEAN+3 Regional Economic Outlook (AREO) in May 2017 as its annual flagship report, covering both regional economic outlook and thematic issues. Since then, the number of AMRO surveillance reports published has increased rapidly. In 2019, for the first time in AMRO's history, annual consultation reports were published on all member economies, and since then, most of the reports have been made available on the AMRO website. Besides the annual consultation reports, AMRO has also published more analytical notes, blogs, and research papers to provide timely analyses on topical economic issues and developments.

- Fourth, AMRO has stepped up efforts to strengthen international cooperation with the Asian Development Bank (ADB), the IMF, and Regional Financing Arrangements (RFAs) (AMRO 2017b, c, d; IMF 2017). AMRO has enhanced collaboration with the IMF through staff exchange programs, participation in the Article IV mission,[1] joint test runs, and exchange of views on policy issues affecting members and the region. AMRO has also actively engaged with other RFAs under various platforms such as annual High-Level Dialogues since 2016 and Research Seminars since 2017, and has conducted collaborative research projects.[2] Furthermore, AMRO has continued to raise its profile in regional policy dialogue by presenting its assessment of the regional outlook at the ASEAN+3 Finance Ministers' and Central Bank Governors' Meeting and by providing policy notes for the ASEAN+3 Leaders' Summit and other regional forums.

In terms of institutional arrangements, AMRO has been uniquely endowed with a formal mandate to perform regional surveillance. This is key to mobilizing full support and cooperation of ASEAN+3 members. According to Choi et al. (2020), most RFAs have no formal surveillance mandate, except for AMRO and the European Commission (EC).[3] Most RFAs conduct on-site surveillance on an informal ad-hoc basis in normal times, while AMRO has established regular surveillance cycles and procedures, which is essential in guiding surveillance during a crisis. ASEAN+3 economies have made rapid progress in regional integration in terms of trade, direct investment, and capital flows, increasing the need to support the macroeconomic and

---

[1] Since 2013, AMRO has deployed an economist to participate in parts of the IMF's Japan mission. The arrangement expanded into a cross-participation format in 2019 when the IMF also started sending an economist to join parts of AMRO's annual consultation visit to Japan. Several ASEAN+3 members have agreed to support AMRO's participation in IMF missions scheduled in 2021.

[2] These include, among others, Cheng et al. (2018), Giraldo and Contreras (2020), and Choi et al. (2020).

[3] The EC has a legal mandate for economic surveillance operating in the context in the European Semester. In contrast, the European Stability Mechanism (ESM) does not have a surveillance function but has monitoring tasks for program countries.

financial stability of individual economy for the common interest of all members. This, in turn, implies the need to boost AMRO's capacity to detect adverse spillovers in a timely manner.

While related literature on the effectiveness of AMRO remains scarce, the view of Grimes and Kring (2020) is worth noting. They stated that AMRO's latest development in its surveillance and program design capabilities disproved skeptical views made at the time of AMRO's establishment. Positive assessments have been given to: (i) the quality of selected published country reports, showing a level of professional competence and objective

---

Box 30.1:

AMRO's Key Achievements Toward a More Systemic Surveillance Framework

1. Revamping Country Surveillance Cycles

In September 2016, under the guidance of a new senior management, AMRO recalibrated its country surveillance cycle to synchronize the reporting cycles for all 14 economies with their respective annual consultation visits. Until that time, all country reports had been prepared twice a year to support ERPD sessions conducted at the ASEAN+3 Finance and Central Bank Deputies Meetings (AFCDM), usually held in April and December, with no close links to the annual consultation visits. The new reporting cycle allowed 14 individual country reports to be submitted to all member authorities once a year for review, around two months after each consultation visit (similar to the IMF Article IV Report).

2. Adopting a Systemic Surveillance Framework

In 2017, AMRO formally launched its first surveillance framework by adopting the Guidance Note for AMRO Country Surveillance Consultation. The Guidance Note provided formal guidance to AMRO staff on how to conduct annual consultations of member economies, with a focus on the macroeconomic and financial stability of member economies. It also stipulated detailed processes, timelines, guidelines, and formal requirements for country surveillance while advising AMRO staff to enhance engagement and communication with various stakeholders to achieve AMRO's vision of being a trusted advisor. AMRO also strengthened its internal policy review practices and further streamlined processes around the annual consultations visits to member economies. In March 2021, the Guidance Note was revised to reflect AMRO's experiences and lessons of the past four years, incorporating feedback from members on the effectiveness and relevance of the surveillance work, and also to include a new assessment framework called the ERPD Matrix framework.

3. Developing a Suite of Analytical Toolkits

AMRO's surveillance capacity has been strengthened greatly, as shown in its enhanced forward-looking analysis and policy recommendations, the growing number of publications, and active participation in policy dialogue and international conferences. AMRO improved its surveillance capacity through the development of analytical frameworks, such as the Global/Country Risk Map, the ERPD Matrix framework, debt sustainability analysis, trade spillover analysis using global vector autoregressive models, the financial stress index approach, business and credit cycle characterization, and the policy space assessment framework.

economic analysis; (ii) management's efforts to seek objective analysis through internal reviews while mitigating home country bias and clientelism; (iii) closer cooperation with other international financial institutions; and (iv) enhanced transparency in publishing surveillance reports and cooperating with external parties. The authors concluded that given a lack of actual experience in managing a regional currency crisis, it might be too early to judge AMRO's capability as a crisis manager.

Financial Market Development

The AFC exposed the structural vulnerabilities of some ASEAN+3 economies arising from their high dependence on foreign short-term debt particularly in the form of bank loans, as well as "double mismatches" in maturity and currency, due in part to underdeveloped financial markets in the region. This led to the recognition of the need for policymakers and market participants to develop regional local currency bond markets as an alternative source of financing for the corporate and public sectors. Key progress made in this area includes the Asian Bond Markets Initiative (ABMI) and the ABF initiative.

In August 2003, ASEAN+3 finance ministers agreed to launch the ABMI to mitigate double mismatches and help to channel the region's large savings into financing its own investment needs. Over the past two decades, ASEAN+3 members have developed both primary and secondary local currency bond markets. Three key achievements made under the ABMI were the launch of the AsianBondsOnline website in 2004, the formation of the Credit Guarantee and Investment Facility (CGIF) in May 2010 as a trust fund of the ADB, and the establishment of the ASEAN+3 Bond Market Forum (ABMF) in 2010. The first two components of the ABMI have aimed at facilitating both the supply of and demand for local currency bonds through information dissemination and enhancing credit, respectively. The third component, i.e., the ABMF, was intended to provide a common platform to foster standardization of market practices and harmonization of regulations relating to cross-border bond transactions in the region, and produce stock-taking reports on regional bond markets.

Another achievement in strengthening the demand side of local currency bond markets was the creation of the ABF under the initiative of EMEAP. In 2003, ABF-1 was created with a USD 1 billion bond fund that invested in sovereign and quasi-sovereign US dollar bonds issued by eight of the EMEAP members. Further progress was made under ABF-2, created in 2004 with a fund size of USD 2 billion. The second fund invested in sovereign and quasi-sovereign local currency bonds issued by the same eight members.

These policy initiatives have been relatively successful, as the size of local currency bond markets has significantly expanded with varying maturities, diversifying issuer and investor bases, and deeper market liquidity. That said, Kawai (2019) pointed out that smaller ASEAN economies — such as Brunei, Cambodia, Lao People's Democratic Republic (Lao PDR), and Myanmar — still face the basic challenge of creating well-functioning local currency government bond markets. For other ASEAN+3 economies, deepening local currency corporate bond markets remains a priority, while regional integration of markets is also being pursued.

Remaining Challenges and the Future of Regional Financial Cooperation

Navigating the COVID-19 Pandemic

When the COVID-19 pandemic hit, ASEAN+3 economies had the advantage of increased resilience of financial systems, significant policy cushions, and foreign exchange reserves, benefiting from financial sector reforms and solid policymaking over many years. Prudent macroeconomic policy management, sound banking and corporate sectors, and strengthened regulatory, institutional, and governance frameworks since the AFC have created sufficient policy space for regional authorities to support their respective economies (AMRO 2021). Many of the region's banking systems had built up robust capital and liquidity buffers — the result of lessons learned from both the AFC and GFC — putting them in a strong position to absorb the impact to their loan books and volatility in funding markets.

The moderate to ample policy space enabled ASEAN+3 economies to swiftly respond to the COVID-19 pandemic with substantial economic stimulus packages. On the fiscal front, governments rolled out relief measures for households, including cash transfers, debt relief, and tax deferrals. To support the corporate sector, job retention programs, the provision of low-cost loans, and moratoria on debt repayments were implemented. Central banks eased monetary policies and recalibrated macroprudential policies to absorb adverse shocks to financial and credit markets and support economic activities. Financial regulators afforded banks forbearance to temporarily ease pressure on their balance sheets exerted by rising credit risks.

Post-Pandemic Policy Challenges

As the COVID-19 pandemic is still spreading, ASEAN+3 policymakers are continuing to provide urgent, multi-faceted support such as protecting people's lives through containment policies and mass vaccination programs and supporting the economy through targeted policy mixes. However, once the pandemic is well contained and economic activity resumes, policymakers should shift their attention toward: (i) formulating an exit strategy to support the economic recovery, (ii) addressing high public and private debt accumulated during the COVID-19 pandemic, and (iii) rebuilding a more resilient economy through structural reforms.

- *Formulating an exit strategy*: The question as to when and how to exit smoothly from stimulus policies without triggering a cliff effect is a challenging one. It requires policymakers to follow some broad guiding principles. Safeguarding public health remains the top priority amid the risk of another COVID-19 outbreak. Although the rapid development of efficacious vaccines is encouraging, many economies will likely remain highly susceptible to waves of infections — requiring renewed containment measures — until the bulk of the population has been vaccinated and herd immunity is achieved. However, extensive and indefinite policy stimuli to support economic recovery is not sustainable, given the narrowing policy space and rising debt burden. The dilemma for policymakers is that any premature withdrawal of existing stimulus measures could undermine the nascent economic recovery.

- *Managing sovereign debt and financial risks*: The long-term impact of prolonged economic stimulus policies on indebtedness, financial stability, and macroeconomic management will likely be significant. As economies emerge from the current crisis, both public and private debts are expected to increase significantly. The financial system will also likely become more fragile owing to loan losses and the impaired balance sheets of lenders. Once regulatory forbearance and moratoria on debt servicing are lifted, a spike in bad loans from corporate bankruptcies may put significant strain on the banking systems. In addition, a prolonged period of accommodative monetary policy may also lead to rising financial imbalances.

Macroeconomic management would be very challenging, especially if inflationary pressures were to emerge against the backdrop of highly indebted public and private sectors and a weakened financial system.

- *Rebuilding a more resilient economy*: Rebuilding the post-pandemic economy should take account of structural issues. These are structural reforms and investment in the necessary hard and soft infrastructures to facilitate the transition to the new digital economy (AMRO 2020a). Unviable businesses should be phased out, and workers need to be reskilled and encouraged to migrate from sunset industries to emerging sectors. During this period, social safety nets should be strengthened to support the transition. The COVID-19 pandemic demonstrates the importance of resilient economic systems, the achievement of which should be one of the ultimate goals of structural reforms in a post-pandemic world. AMRO (2021) highlights that a more resilient post-pandemic economy can be achieved by four key strategies: (i) reconfiguring global value chains (GVCs), (ii) harnessing adaptive technology, (iii) strengthening healthcare and social protection, and (iv) rebuilding policy space. In particular, the COVID-19 pandemic forces a shift from physical to contactless interactions, made possible by digital technology. Governments could facilitate continuing transition by providing appropriate incentives and the requisite infrastructure. The pandemic also underscores the importance of developing strong healthcare capacities and enhancing social security systems to preserve lives and livelihoods.

Enhancing the CMIM/AMRO as a Regional Liquidity Mechanism

The effectiveness of the CMIM facility needs to be further enhanced with greater flexibility to better accommodate members' diverse needs. Since its creation in 2010, the CMIM's liquidity support facility has never been used by ASEAN+3 members even in the midst of the 2013 taper tantrum, and not even during this COVID-19 pandemic. There are divergent views on the reasons for the nonutilization of the facility. The nonutilization is mainly attributable to stronger external buffers and improved CFM in the region. Kawai and Morgan (2014) pointed out two problems with the CMIM's financing design: the link to IMF conditionality, given that the "IMF stigma" still remains, and the cumbersome and untested process for drawing funds. In contrast,

Henning (2020) noted that the usage of CMIM facilities should not be judged as the most significant measure of effectiveness. This is because precautionary arrangements are most effective if they sustain market confidence. Therefore, it can be argued that they never have to be drawn — if the CMIM and the surveillance process that underpin the CMIM are truly effective.[4]

With only 10 years since its establishment, AMRO has proven its ability to function as an autonomous and effective regional surveillance organization, as acknowledged by the Joint Statement of ASEAN+3 Finance Ministers' and Central Bank Governors' Meeting in May 2021.[5] In line with the phases of organizational development set out in Kawai (2015), over the past decade, AMRO has moved beyond simple "information sharing" to a more demanding "peer review and peer pressure" stage. That said, AMRO should further step up its institutional capacity to achieve greater rigor in conducting "due diligence" to facilitate the operational readiness of the CMIM. Against this backdrop, the following subsections discuss remaining challenges for the CMIM and AMRO to tackle so as to fulfill their mandates.

Expanding the CMIM's Toolbox with Greater Flexibility

The CMIM is designed to focus solely on addressing balance of payments and/or short-term liquidity difficulties that are temporary and attributable to factors exogenous to the member's policy management. Thus, its toolbox is narrowly limited, compared with the IMF and other RFAs. The CMIM may have some scope to expand the scope and range of its financing facilities for crisis prevention and resolution in tandem with the different financing needs of ASEAN+3 members (Cheng et al. 2020). Table 30.2 indicates that even with crisis resolution tools, some RFAs have loan programs to address long-run structural reforms and sector-specific issues, and give assistance to low-income countries. Many RFAs have additional tools such as investment loan grants, sovereign securities purchases and grants customized for each region and members' needs. In this context, the CMIM's facilities for managing a

---

[4] Henning (2020) claims that the CMIM serves as a focal point around which ASEAN+3 policymakers confer and develop common strategies for crisis prevention and response; the CMIM's existence changes the behavior of other institutions such as the IMF in the global financial system; the ASEAN+3 institutions serve as a foundation on which to build, and ASEAN+3 could well activate the CMIM at some point in the future.

[5] See https://www.amro-asia.org/joint-statement-of-the-24th-asean3-finance-ministers-and-central-bank-governors-meeting-may-3-2021-virtual/.

crisis could be further expanded to provide longer maturity financing support for members hit by external shocks, such as the GFC, taper tantrum and COVID-19, and financial assistance to resolve a banking sector crisis.

Table 30.2: Classification of the IMF and RFAs Instruments

Organization	Crisis Resolution					Crisis Prevention		Other
	Liquidity Provision for Short-/Medium-Term Needs	Liquidity Provision Medium-/Long-Term Needs	Urgent Liquidity Provision	Sectoral Assistance	Concessional Support	Credit Lines with Ex-Ante Conditionality	Other Types of Credit Lines	
IMF	O	O	O		O¹	O		Signaling
Arab Monetary Fund	O	O	O	O	O			Guarantees
BRICS Contingency Reserve Arrangement (CRA)	O		O				O	
CMIM	O		O			O		
Eurasian Fund for Stabilia tion and Development (EFSD)	O	O			O			Investment loans grants
European Stability Mechanism (ESM)	O	O		O		O		Sovereign securities purchases
EU Facilities²	O						O	Grants
FLAR	O						O	

BRICS = Brazil, Russia, India, China, and South Africa, CMIM = Chiang Mai Initiative Multilateralisation, EU = European Union, FLAR = Fondo Latinoamericano de Reservas (Latin American Reserve Fund), IMF = International Monetary Fund, RFA = regional financing arrangement.

Notes:

[1] The IMF's Flexible Credit Line (FCL) and Precautionary and Liquidity Line (PLL) are designed to deal with actual, prospective, and potential balance of payments needs. As such, these can serve as both financing and precautionary tools. In comparison, RFAs' precautionary credit lines are all designed to address only potential financing needs.

[2] EU facilities include the EU balance of payments facility, the European Financial Stabilisation Mechanism, and the EU Macro-Financial Assistance.

Source: Cheng et al. (2020)

In addition, the CMIM's financing terms may need further reforms to enhance its effectiveness. The legal modality of the CMIM arrangement remains relatively weak. As the CMIM consists of a series of formal contractual agreements among participating central banks and finance ministries,

ASEAN+3 Regional Financial Cooperation in Retrospect 873

it has a lower degree of commitment than comparable RFAs that operate on paid-in capital. Despite the total size being doubled to USD 240 billion, the CMIM's fixed borrowing quota for each member could be viewed as too restrictive if several large members are hit by large shocks, as the assigned swap quota assumes that not all members would request assistance simultaneously. In this regard, it would be worth considering the introduction of flexible multiples of swap quota for small economies. Furthermore, the ASEAN+3 members may need to explore possible collaboration between the CMIM and BSAs (Kawai 2015), as the total size of the latter's swap arrangements amounted to USD 331 billion. Strong collaboration may be necessary to enhance market confidence in the sufficiency of available financing. On the terms of lending, the CMIM may consider lengthening the current maturity period of 180 days and the supporting period of up to 2 years, to provide a more reasonable period for addressing even temporary liquidity needs of member economies.[6] Furthermore, the CMIM's IMF-linked portion needs to be reduced further over time, eventually to zero. At the same time, the adequate size of the CMIM facility and swap quota should be reviewed periodically to take into account changes in the global economy and financial landscape.

Enhancing AMRO's Capacity for Surveillance and Program Design

To become a full-fledged and fully trusted "regional family doctor," AMRO's surveillance function should be further strengthened in three areas: (i) enhancing functional/sectoral surveillance capacity; (ii) expanding the scope of surveillance toward longer-term, structural issues; and (iii) building up expertise on program design for various types of crisis.

- First, functional and sectoral surveillance capacity needs to be enhanced through the creation of dedicated teams. Thus far, due to understaffing, most AMRO economists have had to work on several countries at the same time, or work in a country team and also in a functional team that deals with fiscal and financial issues. Gaining in-depth knowledge of country-specific institutional frameworks and market functions is essential in formulating customized policy recommendations during

---

[6] The IMF's financing facilities have longer durations than the CMIM. As precautionary measures, FCL and PLL have a maturity of 1–2 years. Meanwhile, the length of a Stand-By Arrangement (SBA) is flexible, and typically covers a period of 12–24 months, but no more than 36 months.

peacetime surveillance. A dedicated fiscal team would help AMRO focus on developing its own fiscal database, fiscal assessment framework, and tools. For financial surveillance, AMRO needs to further strengthen financial analysis, design new models, and evolve new tools to cover the main areas of relevance for surveillance, including capital flows, financial spillovers, reserve adequacy, and early warning systems. To fulfill AMRO's mandate, risk-focused, forward-looking analysis should be enhanced by fiscal and financial surveillance teams.

- Second, the scope of AMRO's surveillance can be further expanded to cover members' longer-term, structural challenges such as demographic evolution, global supply chains, digital technology, and climate change. AMRO's in-depth analysis of structural challenges in the region will help to formulate policy advice customized to the members concerned, and help them overcome the challenges or take mitigating measures to avoid falling into structural problems. In this aspect, regional research collaborations between AMRO and the ADB, EMEAP, and ASEAN+3 Finance Ministries' and Central Banks' members would help identify key structural challenges facing members and policies to build resilient economic systems in the post-pandemic world.

- Third, AMRO should continue to strengthen its ability to design, monitor, and implement financial programs from the beginning to the termination of the program for various types of crises. Since 2013, the CMIM/AMRO has conducted 11 test runs under various scenarios involving the two types of facilities. In particular, the 2016–2018 test runs were conducted with the IMF's participation.[7] Leveraging on these experiences, AMRO country teams should continue to build their own capacity to make timely assessments of members in difficulties, design policy programs to address problems, and monitor compliance and assess performance of the members. In this context, AMRO's newly created "Policy and Review Group" is expected to enhance the consistency and coherence of policy advice for ASEAN+3 member economies. The ERPD Matrix Framework (Ong

---

[7] Choi et al. (2020) document key lessons learned from the joint test runs, mainly revealing several key differences between CMIM and IMF facilities, which could potentially delay the coordination process between the two arrangements during an actual activation. Issues include burden sharing between the CMIM and the IMF, financing assurance from the CMIM to the IMF, CMIM financing terms and conditions, and the need for early information sharing.

and Gabriella 2020), a set of newly adopted eligibility criteria framework for assessing members' access to the IMF de-linked portion under the CMIM-SF and the CMIM-PL, should be integrated into AMRO's country surveillance work and used to operationalize the CMIM facility.

In view of the various tasks, AMRO has undertaken the role of the de facto secretariat of the CMIM, such as communicating with the IMF and other RFAs on ways of effective coordination to reinforce the global financial safety net, and working with ASEAN+3 members to enhance the operational readiness of the CMIM. It is thus timely for ASEAN+3 members to consider a new governance structure under which AMRO takes on a broader role in support of the CMIM, or serves as the CMIM's formal secretariat. Not only has AMRO accumulated a decade of experience, but it has also provided intellectual leadership and contributed to the achievement of several CMIM milestones. Given that ASEAN+3 members participate in various international forums with overlapping memberships, AMRO can be the focal point to lead the region's policy dialogue with other regional groupings or IOs to strengthen regional safety nets, with firm support from ASEAN+3 members.

Seeking Complementarities with the IMF

As a newly created regional safety net, the CMIM/AMRO should seek complementarities and collaborations with the IMF as the center of the global financial safety net. The IMF's bilateral and multilateral surveillance reports constitute one of the most useful references for AMRO, along with its other publications. Moreover, AMRO's policy assessments frequently complement and sometimes diverge from the IMF's assessments (Khor 2019). Thus, AMRO's surveillance provides an essential independent assessment and helps to bring diverse perspectives to bear on policy issues that may differ from the IMF's. It is noteworthy that IMF policies are formulated with a global perspective in mind. Thus, these may sometimes lack regional perspectives and contextual adaptability, and therefore may not be appropriate for addressing regional issues. As an IO with regional constituency, AMRO plays an essential complementary role to the IMF in providing an independent regional perspective and in helping to shape IMF views on policy issues so that they are more even handed.

In this regard, ASEAN+3 members would benefit from AMRO establishing its own institutional views on key policy issues, such as the CFMs and MPMs, that reflect country-specific factors and regional perspectives. It would help assist ASEAN+3 members in the timely formulation of policies to mitigate relevant risks and vulnerabilities while contributing to the policy discussions of global and regional safety nets.

Beyond the CMIM: Coping with Longer-Term Financing Needs

The COVID-19 pandemic highlights the ASEAN+3 region's needs for not only immediate, short-term but also longer-term financing arrangements for development, structural reforms, and budget support. The region entered the pandemic crisis in relatively good shape, with ample foreign exchange reserves and significant policy space. These factors have helped ASEAN+3 countries to navigate the pandemic with little or no reliance on external emergency financing from the IMF. While more than 80 countries have received financial assistance from the IMF since the onset of the pandemic, only one ASEAN+3 member — Myanmar — has received IMF emergency assistance of USD 729 million for medium- or long-term financing of development and budget support under the concessional Rapid Credit Facility (RCF) and Rapid Financing Instrument (RFI).[8] Other than these, financing has come from multilateral development banks such as the World Bank, the ADB, and the Asian Infrastructure Investment Bank (AIIB) to assist ASEAN+3 members in development, structural reform, and budget support in response to the COVID-19 pandemic, as shown in Table 30.3. This suggests that the current mandate of the CMIM may be too narrow to cover the needs for longer-term financing, which addresses structural challenges in the ASEAN+3 region, particularly for low-income economies.

Low-income countries with structural current account deficits tend to be highly vulnerable to external shocks, particularly when structural issues — such as a poor debt management capacity and under-developed financial markets — exacerbate liquidity problems. In terms of the scope of liquidity support, the current CMIM arrangement is most suitable for short-term balance of payments or temporary liquidity shocks such as the GFC and the

---

[8] The RCF was introduced in 2009 as a unified instrument for concessional emergency financing, replacing the Exogenous Shock Facility-Rapid Access Component, and the subsidized use of Emergency Natural Disaster Assistance and Emergency Post Conflict Assistance. The RFI was established in 2011 as part of a package of reforms to the General Resources Account lending toolkit. Financing assistance provided under the RFI is subject to the same financing terms as the FCL, the PLL, and SBA, and should be repaid within 3 ¼ to 5 years.

Table 30.3: Financial Assistance from the IMF and Multilateral Development Banks to ASEAN+3 Members During the COVID-19 Pandemic (USD million)

Member	IMF	World Bank	ADB	AIIB
China	...	...	20[1]	...
Cambodia	...	36	250	...
Indonesia	...	1,250	2,003	1,000
Lao PDR	...	58	20	...
Myanmar	729	250	185	...
Philippines	...	600	2,333	750
Thailand	...	...	1,500	500[2]
Vietnam	...	10	...	100
Total	729	2,204	6,311	2,350

... = not available, ADB = Asian Development Bank, AIIB = Asian Infrastructure Investment Bank, ASEAN = Association of Southeast Asian Nations, COVID-19 = coronavirus disease, IMF = International Monetary Fund, Lao PDR = Lao People's Democratic Republic, USD = United States dollar.
Notes:
[1] US dollar equivalent. This loan is denominated in the Chinese yuan.
[2] Based on the proposed amount, pending final approval.
Source: IMF, World Bank, ADB, and AIIB websites; AMRO staff calculations (as of September 9, 2020, except for Myanmar as of May 6, 2021; as the calculation method is different in each institution, the validity of the quoted amounts is subject to further change).

2013 taper tantrum. Hence, the CMIM appears to be inadequate to meet the potential needs of low-income countries for financial assistance to mitigate underlying economic, fiscal, and structural weaknesses.

Given the narrow focus of the current CMIM arrangements on short-term balance of payments problems, ASEAN+3 members need to find alternative ways to support medium- to long-term financing needs to cope with post-pandemic policy challenges — formulating an exit strategy, managing sovereign debt and financial risks, and rebuilding a more resilient economy — particularly for low-income economies. In this context, AMRO can increase its capacity to provide more technical assistance for low-income countries to overcome various types of structural problems that can give rise to balance of payments and/or short-term liquidity difficulties. Closer cooperation between the CMIM/AMRO and the ADB will help to accommodate members' growing needs for development, structural reform, and budgetary support in the post-pandemic period. Moreover, ASEAN+3 members may consider ramping up the current framework of regional financial cooperation toward strengthening long-term financing support. In this regard, the ongoing discussion on ASEAN+3 future initiatives may contribute to the development of a new macro-structural framework with new financing instruments to address structural challenges facing members in the post-pandemic era.

Conclusion

The past two decades have witnessed ASEAN+3 economies overcoming severe economic losses and damage from the AFC, skillfully managing the impacts of the GFC and other shocks, and emerging as the largest and most dynamic economic bloc in the world. Global trends and developments such as the increasing globalization of the world economy, the expansion of GVCs, and greater integration of the regional economies have contributed to the region's rapid economic growth. Moreover, ASEAN+3 policymakers have made great efforts to strengthen external buffers and enhance their macro-financial policy frameworks at the individual economy level. Over the past two decades, ASEAN+3 economies have made substantial progress in regional financial cooperation by upgrading the CMIM facility to the level of a regional safety net; launching AMRO as a full-fledged, regional surveillance organization; and helping develop local-currency bond markets.

The outbreak of the COVID-19 pandemic highlights the need for ASEAN+3 economies to strengthen regional financial cooperation not only to mitigate the effects of an unprecedented global health crisis but also to build more resilient economic systems in the post-pandemic era. In this regard, the usefulness of the CMIM facility has to be further enhanced with greater flexibility to better accommodate ASEAN+3 members' needs to manage various types of crises, for instance, by providing extended maturity liquidity support for members hit by external shocks, and financial assistance to resolve a banking sector crisis. In addition, AMRO should further strengthen its capacity to fully support the operational readiness of the CMIM by enhancing its peacetime surveillance capacity and, more importantly, stepping up its program design expertise and its implementation capability. AMRO should also seek to play an essential complementary role to the IMF in providing an independent regional perspective, based on its deeper understanding of the regional economy and financial markets. Furthermore, the ASEAN+3 region needs to respond to long-term policy challenges in the post-pandemic era, which would require longer-term financing for infrastructure development and structural reforms. Given the narrow remit of the CMIM arrangements, ASEAN+3 members may consider ramping up the existing framework of regional financial cooperation to provide long-term financing support, particularly for low-income economies.

ASEAN+3 members are highly diverse in terms of economic, social, and cultural aspects. From the perspective of economic development, the region is unique. Its members range from developing to developed economies. They include resource-rich economies, manufacturing industrial economies, and global financial centers. This diversity can contribute to sustained resiliency of the entire region. At the same time, the regional economies share many common interests such as maintaining open trade and investment regimes, achieving equitable and sustainable economic growth, and preserving financial stability. They can leverage on such common interests and synergize on their complementarities in order to drive regional financial cooperation to an even higher level of development. The lessons learned from the AFC and the GFC have led to a strengthening of ASEAN+3 region's economic fundamentals and financial cooperation, and the emergence of a dynamic and resilient regional economy that is highly integrated with the rest of the world, and a key growth engine of the world economy.

References

ASEAN+3 Macroeconomic Research Office. 2017a. "ASEAN+3 Regional Economic Outlook (AREO) 2017." https://amro-asia.org/wp-content/uploads/2017/05/AREO2017_Full-Text.pdf.

ASEAN+3 Macroeconomic Research Office. 2017b. "AMRO, ADB Sign MOU to Support Increased Regional Economic Growth, Stability." Press Release on May 3, 2017. https://www.amro-asia.org/amro-adb-sign-mou-to-support-increased-regional-economic-growth-stability/.

ASEAN+3 Macroeconomic Research Office. 2017c. "AMRO, IMF Enhance Cooperation to Support Regional and Global Financial Stability." Press Release on October 11, 2017. https://www.amro-asia.org/amro-imf-enhance-cooperation-to-support-regional-and-global-financial-stability/.

ASEAN+3 Macroeconomic Research Office. 2017d. "AMRO and ESM Sign Memorandum of Understanding." Press Release on October 11, 2017. https://www.amro-asia.org/amro-and-esm-sign-memorandum-of-understanding/.

ASEAN+3 Macroeconomic Research Office. 2020a. "ASEAN+3 Regional Economic Outlook (AREO) 2020." April 2020. https://www.amro-asia.org/wp-content/uploads/2020/04/AMRO-AREO-2020_23Apr.pdf.

ASEAN+3 Macroeconomic Research Office. 2021. "ASEAN+3 Regional Economic Outlook (AREO) 2021." March 2021. https://www.amro-asia.org/asean3-regional-economic-outlook-2021-full-report/.

Cheng, Gong, Dominika Miernik, Yisr Barnieh, Beomhee Han, Ika Mustika Sari, Faith Qiying Pang, Tigran Kostanyan, Alexander Efimov, Marie Houdart, Alexandra de Carvalho, Carlos Giraldo, and Viviana Monroy. October 31, 2018. "IMF–RFA Collaboration: Motives, State of Play, and Way Forward." European Stability Mechanism Discussion Paper No. 4. https://www.esm.europa.eu/publications/imf%E2%80%93rfa-collaboration-motives-state-play-and-way-forward.

Cheng, Gong, Dominika Miernik, and Teuta Turani. 2020. "Finding Complementarities in IMF and RFA Toolkits." European Stability Mechanism Discussion Paper No. 8, August 7. https://www.esm.europa.eu/publications/finding-complementarities-imf-and-rfa-toolkits.

Choi, Jinho, Jae Young Lee, Ika Mustika Sari, and Beomhee Han. 2020. "Macroeconomic Surveillance Frameworks and Practices in Non-Crisis Time." *AMRO Policy Perspectives Paper PP/20-02*, August. https://www.amro-asia.org/macroeconomic-surveillance-frameworks-and-practices-in-non-crisis-time/.

Executives' Meeting of East Asia-Pacific Central Banks 1998. Press Release — Third EMEAP Governors' Meeting on July 14, 1998, Tokyo, Japan. http://www.emeap.org/wp-content/uploads/2015/04/14jul98.pdf.

Giraldo, Carlos and Camilo Contreras. 2020. "Training and Institutional Capacity Development–Enhancing Collaboration among RFAs and between RFAs and the IMF." *FLAR Discussion Papers*, Latin American Reserve Fund, Fondo Latinoamericano de Reservas, FLAR, July. https://www.flar.net/sites/default/files/2021-03/Training%20and%20Institutional%20Capacity%20Development-%20Documento%20de%20discusi%C3%B3n..pdf.

Griffith-Jones, Stephany, and José Antonio Ocampo, with Jacques Cailloux. 1999. *The Poorest Countries and the Emerging International Financial Architecture*. Stockholm: Expert Group on Development Issues (EGDI).

Grimes, William W., and William N. Kring. 2020, "Institutionalizing Financial Cooperation in East Asia." *Global Governance* 26 (3): 428-448.

Hamanaka, Shintaro. 2011. "Asian Financial Cooperation in the 1990: The Politics of Membership." *Journal of East Asian Studies* 11 (1): 75-103.

Henning, C. Randall. 2020. "Regional Financial Arrangements and the International Monetary Fund: Sustaining Coherence in Global Financial Governance." Special Report, Centre for International Governance Innovation (CIGI), January 9. https://www.cigionline.org/publications/regional-financial-arrangements-and-international-monetary-fund-sustaining-coherence/.

International Monetary Fund. 2009. "Review of Fund Facilities — Analytical Basis for Fund Lending and Reform Options." *IMF Policy Papers*, February 6. https://www.imf.org/external/np/pp/eng/2009/020609A.pdf.

International Monetary Fund. 2017. "Collaboration between Regional Financing Arrangements and the IMF." *IMF Policy Papers*, July 31. https://www.imf.org/en/Publications/Policy-Papers/Issues/2017/07/31/pp073117-collaboration-between-regional-financing-arrangements-and-the-imf.

Jung, Jee-young. 2008. "Regional Financial Cooperation in Asia: Challenges and Path to Development." In *Regional Financial Integration in Asia: Present and Future*, BIS Papers No 42, 120-135, October. https://www.bis.org/publ/bppdf/bispap42d.pdf.

Kawai, Masahiro. 2000. "The Resolution of the East Asian Crisis: Financial and Corporate Sector Restructuring." *Journal of Asian Economics* 11 (2): 133-168.

Kawai, Masahiro. 2015. "From the Chiang Mai Initiative to an Asian Monetary Fund." ADBI Working Paper No. 527, Tokyo: Asian Development Bank Institute. http://www.adbi.org/working-paper/2015/05/20/6612.chiang.mai.asian.monetary.fund/.

Kawai, Masahiro. 2019. "Asian Bond Market Development." In *Financial Cooperation in East Asia*, edited by Tomoo Kikuchi and Masaya Sakuragawa, RSIS Monograph No. 35, March 2019. https://www.rsis.edu.sg/rsis-publication/cms/mn35-financial-cooperation-in-east-asia/#.YK4AlqgzaUk.

Kawai, Masahiro, and Cindy Houser. 2008. "Evolving ASEAN+3 ERPD: Toward Peer Reviews or Due Diligence?" In *Shaping Policy Reform and Peer Review in Southeast Asia: Integrating Economies amid Diversity*, edited by the OECD. Paris: Organisation for Economic Co-operation and Development.

Kawai, Masahiro, and Peter J. Morgan. 2014. "Regional Financial Regulation in Asia." In *New Global Economic Architecture: The Asian Perspective*, edited by Masahiro Kawai, Peter J. Morgan, and Pradumna B. Rana, 112–147. Cheltenham: Edward Elgar.

Khor, Hoe Ee. 2019. "Overview of AMRO and Policy Challenges." In *Financial Cooperation in East Asia*, edited by Tomoo Kikuchi and Masaya Sakuragawa. RSIS Monograph No. 35, March 2019. https://www.rsis.edu.sg/rsis-publication/cms/mn35-financial-cooperation-in-east-asia/#.YK4AlqgzaUk.

Mistry, Percy S. 1999. "Coping with Financial Crises: Are Regional Arrangements the Missing Link?." In *International Monetary and Financial Issues for the 1990s*, Vol. 10. Geneva: United Nations Conference on Trade and Development (UNCTAD).

Morgan, Peter J. 2018. "Regional Financial Regulation in Asia." In *Global Shocks and the New Global and Regional Financial Architecture*, edited by Naoyuki Yoshino, Peter J. Morgan, and Pradumna B. Rana. Asian Development Bank Institute and S. Rajaratnam School of International Studies (RSIS), May 2018. https://www.adb.org/publications/global-shocks-and-new-global-and-regional-financial-architecture-asian-perspectives.

Ocampo, José Antonio. 2002. "Recasting the International Financial Agenda." In *International Capital Markets: Systems in Transition*, edited by John Eatwell and Lance Taylor. Oxford University Press.

Ocampo, José Antonio, ed. 2006. *Regional Financial Cooperation*. Washington D.C.: Brookings Institution and Economic Commission for Latin America and the Caribbean (ECLAC).

Ong, Li Lian, and Laura Grace Gabriella. 2020. "The ERPD Matrix 'Scorecard': Quantifying the Macro-Financial Performance of the ASEAN+3 Economies." *AMRO Working Paper WP/20-01*, April. https://www.amro-asia.org/the-erpd-matrix-scorecard-quantifying-the-macro-financial-performance-of-the-asean3-economies/.

Sakakibara, Eisuke. 2003. "Asian Cooperation and the End of Pax Americana." In *Financial Stability and Growth in Emerging Economies*, edited by Jan Joost Teunissen and Mark Teunissen, 227-240. The Hague: Forum on Debt and Development (FONDAD).

List of Editors

Hoe Ee Khor is the Chief Economist of AMRO responsible for overseeing and developing the work on macroeconomic and financial market surveillance on East and Southeast Asian economies. He is also a member of the senior management team responsible for setting the strategic direction and management of AMRO. Prior to joining AMRO, he was a Deputy Director of the Asia and Pacific Department (APD) at the International Monetary Fund (IMF), responsible for overseeing the surveillance work on six ASEAN and 12 Pacific Island countries. Dr. Khor started his career as an economist at the IMF in 1981 and had worked on a wide range of economies in the Western Hemisphere and Asia and Pacific departments. He was the IMF Deputy Resident Representative in China from 1991–1993. From 2009–2010, he was Head of Economic Development and Chief Economist at the Abu Dhabi Council for Economic Development (ADCED). He joined the Monetary Authority of Singapore (MAS) in July 1996 and was Assistant Managing Director from 2001–2009 where he was responsible for economic research, monetary policy, macro-financial surveillance, and international relations. He obtained his Bachelor's Degree in Economics/Mathematics from the University of Rochester and a Ph.D. in Economics from Princeton University.

Diwa C. Guinigundo is former Deputy Governor of the Bangko Sentral ng Pilipinas (BSP). Mr. Guinigundo served the BSP for 41 years, handling monetary policy and operations, and other various aspects of central banking. A former alternate executive director at the International Monetary Fund (IMF) in Washington, D.C. from 2001–2003, he was also research head at the South

East Asian Central Banks (SEACEN) Centre in Kuala Lumpur from 1992–1994. Mr. Guinigundo graduated *cum laude* at the University of the Philippines School of Economics. He earned a M.Sc. in Economics at the London School of Economics as a scholar of the Central Bank of the Philippines. He holds an honorary Doctor of Divinity (DD) degree from Promise Christian University in Los Angeles, California. He is the senior pastor of the Fullness of Christ International Ministries. He writes weekly columns for the Manila Bulletin and BusinessWorld. He is a member of the Advisory Panel of the Institute for Financial Economics of Singapore Management University. He is also a member of the Board of Advisers of the International Care Ministries, Philippines. An independent director of Philam Investment Management Corporation since October 2020, he is also an external advisor to Bain & Company with headquarters in Boston, Massachusetts, USA.

 **Masahiro Kawai** is the Representative Director of the Economic Research Institute for Northeast Asia (ERINA) located in Niigata, Japan. He also teaches international finance focusing on Asia at the University of Tokyo as Professor Emeritus while serving as a Councilor of the Bank of Japan and a Senior Fellow of the Policy Research Institute of Japan's Finance Ministry. He began his professional career as a Research Fellow at the Brookings Institution and then taught economics at the Johns Hopkins University and the University of Tokyo. Dr. Kawai also served as Chief Economist for the World Bank's East Asia and the Pacific Region, Deputy Vice Minister of Finance for International Affairs and President of the Policy Research Institute of Japan's Ministry of Finance, and Dean and CEO of the Asian Development Bank Institute (ADBI). He has published extensively on international trade and finance, Asian economic integration and cooperation, and global economic governance. He holds a BA in economics from the University of Tokyo, and an MS in statistics and a PhD in economics from Stanford University.

List of Interviewees

Undersecretary **Gil S. Beltran** has been an Undersecretary of the Department of Finance (DOF), Republic of the Philippines, since 2005 and as the Department's Chief Economist since 2013. Usec. Beltran works on a variety of areas including fiscal policy, human resource and operations management, economic policy and research, and financial inclusion policies and strategies. He has been the Executive Director of the National Credit Council since 1998 and designated as Chairman of the ASEAN Single Window Steering Committee (ASWSC) in January 2017. Usec. Beltran graduated with a Master of Arts degree in Development Economics in 1982 as class valedictorian from Williams College Massachusetts and a bachelor's degree in AB Economics, cum laude, in 1977 from the University of the Philippines. He has more than 10 years of teaching experience at the Development Academy of the Philippines. He held various posts at the World Bank as Alternate Executive Director from January 2003 to January 2005 and advisor to the Executive Director from February to May 1995 and August to November 1990.

Thanong Bidaya is Chairman of the Board of Directors of TTW Public Company Limited and Chairman of the Board of Directors of CK Power Public Company Limited. His distinguished management, business, and public administration career has spanned the globe and involved numerous leading positions in both the public and private sectors. Dr. Bidaya was Chairman of National Economic and Social Development Board (NESDB). As voluntary service to his country, Dr. Bidaya was appointed Minister in the Royal Thai Government three times: first as Minister of Finance in 1997, Minister of

Commerce in 2005, and Minister of Finance for a second term from 2005 to 2006. In addition, he was Thai Trade Representative from 2001 to 2002. Dr. Bidaya studied Economics at Yokohama National University under a Japanese Government scholarship and was awarded a bachelor's degree in 1970. He then continued his graduate studies in the United States under the Ford Foundation Fellowship from 1971 to 1974 and completed his M.S. in Economics from Northwestern University in 1971, and Ph.D. in Management from Northwestern University in 1978.

Yang-ho Byeon is a Senior Advisor at VIG Partners, a private equity firm. He was a senior official at Korea's finance ministry, having served with the ministry in various positions, and made his mark during Korea's 1997 financial crisis. As the head of the ministry's International Financial Division (1997–1999), he was the key man negotiating with foreign creditors to roll over billions of dollars of Korea's external debt and newly selling US dollar-denominated bonds worth 4 billion to international investors. In addition, as Director General of Financial Policy Bureau (2001–2004), he played a pivotal role in restructuring the countries' ailing banking and corporate sectors, including facilitating M&As of Seoul Bank, Chohung Bank and LG Card, as well bailing out Korea Exchange Bank and Hynix, a chip maker. Dr Byeon also worked as a Senior Economist at the Southeast Asia and Pacific Department of the International Monetary Fund (1993–1994). His last official position was Commissioner of Korea Financial Intelligence Unit (2004–2005). After resigning from the government, he found VOGO FUND in 2005, a local private equity firm, where he has been a Managing Partner until 2019. He obtained his Bachelor's Degree from Seoul National University, and a Ph.D. in Economics from Northern Illinois University.

Norman T. L. Chan was the Chief Executive of the Hong Kong Monetary Authority (HKMA) from 2009–2019. In 1976, Mr. Chan graduated from the Chinese University of Hong Kong and joined the Hong Kong Government as an Administrative Officer. He became Deputy Director (Monetary Management) of the Office of the Exchange Fund in 1991. He was appointed as Executive Director of the HKMA when it was established in 1993. From 1996 to 2005, Mr. Chan served as Deputy Chief Executive of the HKMA. From December 2005 to June 2007, Mr. Chan was Vice Chairman, Asia of Standard Chartered Bank. Mr. Chan was Director of the Chief Executive's Office of the Hong Kong SAR Government from July 2007 to July 2009. Mr Chan is the Chairman of the Board of Trustees of Chung chi College, CUHK, from August 2021. He is the Founding Chairman of RD Wallet Technologies Ltd and RD ezLink Limited.

Joong-Kyung Choi is the Chairman of Korea-America Association. He was a career senior government official in various capacity in Korea, including Vice Minister of Strategy and Finance, Senior Advisor to the President, and Minister of Knowledge Economy. He was also the Executive Director at the World Bank and Ambassador of the Republic of Korea to the Philippines. He is considered as one of the key technocrats who shaped and strengthened Korea's international macroeconomic policy. At the height of the Asian financial crisis in the 1990s, he contributed to steering Korea out of the crisis by successfully leading the negotiation with the IMF as the head of Financial Cooperation Division at the finance ministry. Post-crisis, in various positions, he has launched series of initiatives to strengthen external stability, including doubling foreign reserves, enhancing capital flow management and macro-prudential measures (CFM and MPM), and stabilizing exchange rates, which has helped provide external buffers for Korean economy to remain resilient to external shocks during the global and the Eurozone Crises. After retirement, he taught courses on the Korean economy at Dongguk University and Korea University. He was also the President of the Korea Institute of Certified Public Accountants and the Chairman of the Korean Federation of Service Industry. He has published several books, including *Upside-Down Success Story of Korea's Economic Development* (2013), *Korea Is Not Seen in Washington D.C.* (2016, Korean), and *History Makes You Stronger* (2020, Korean). He obtained his Bachelor's and Master's Degrees in business administration from Seoul National University, and a Ph.D. in Economics from the University of Hawaii.

Duck-koo Chung is an East Asian expert leading the North-East Asia Research (NEAR) Foundation, Korea's most representative independent think tank, as a founder and chairman. He received his MBA from the University of Wisconsin-Madison and his BA from Korea University. Chung began his career as a government official in 1971 at Ministry of Finance and Economy. During the early stages of the Korea financial crisis, he became a deputy minister for international finance. He was a reformer and trouble-shooter during the crisis, and his words had a strong influence on the market. He gained a strong creditworthiness in the turbulent Asian financial market. After Chung came back from the New York old debt resolution negotiation, the Korean financial crisis was at a very critical turning point. Becoming a Vice-Minister of Finance later on, he successfully implemented a full-scaled economic and financial restructuring program which was a big cornerstone for the Korean economy. In 1999, Chung was appointed Minister of the Ministry of Commerce, Industry and Energy (MOCIE). Chung devoted his full efforts to transform the main industry from assembly-based to intermediate goods-based. He promoted multiple national projects to contribute to the export industrialization, which forms the basis of today's Korean industry. After retirement from the cabinet, Chung established the NEAR Foundation in 2007. He is the author of globally-renowned publications on the Korean economy and China relations including *Korea's Strategy & Attitudes toward China's Expansion, Korean Economic Growth & Distribution: Its Policy Implications during the 1960s – 2000s, Legacy Asset & Legacy Debt of Korean Financial Crisis, The Korean Economy Beyond the Crisis*, etc.

Roberto F. de Ocampo, former Secretary of Finance of the Philippines, was Euromoney "Global Finance Minister of the Year" in 1995 and Asian Finance Minister of the Year in 1996 and 1997. He was Chairman of the APEC and ASEAN Finance Ministers (at the onset of the Asian financial crisis whose meetings he chaired) and a member of the Boards of Governors of the World Bank, IMF, and the ADB. He also served as Chairman and CEO of the Development

Bank of the Philippines and of the Land Bank of the Philippines, was the past president of the Asian Institute of Management, and presently is the Chairman of the Philippine Veterans Bank, and the Board of Advisers of the RFO Center for Public Finance & Regional Economic Cooperation, as well as director or Chairman of 30 entities in the Philippines and abroad. Dr. de Ocampo is a recipient of many international awards: Most Excellent Order of the British Empire (OBE), Chevalier, the Ordre National de la Legion d' Honneur by the Republic of France, and KNIGHT of the Equestrian Order of the Holy Sepulchre of Jerusalem. He has also been awarded the Philippine Legion of Honor, is one of the first ASEAN members of the Trilateral Commission, the first recipient of the Man of the Year Award from the Association of Development Finance Institutions of Asia Pacific (ADFIAP), the Asian Human Resources Development Award by the Asia HRD Congress, a founding Partner of a Global Advisory Group (Centennial Group) based in Washington D.C., and a Founding Director of a recently established Global Economic Forum: The Emerging Markets Forum. Dr. de Ocampo was the 1975 Ten Outstanding Young Men (TOYM) awardee in the field of National Economic Development for pioneering the Philippine rural electrification program and was elected to the Boards of the Conference Board (based in New York), and the Global Reporting Initiative.

Dennis de Tray joined the World Bank's Research Department in 1983. He was appointed the Bank's Research Administrator in 1987 and moved to the Bank's Latin American operations complex in 1992. His last assignments at the Bank were as Country Director for Indonesia, 1994–1999, and then Central Asia, 2001–2006. For the past nine years, he has been Adviser to the President, and member of the Board of Trustees of Nazarbayev University, a new English language university in Astana, Kazakhstan. In Astana, he has spent the past 10 years building a world-class university from scratch. He is also a principal with the Results for Development Institute and a non-resident fellow at the Center for Strategic and International Studies (CSIS) both in Washington D.C. Dr. de Tray and his wife Mary have lived in many parts of Asia: Pakistan (1977–1979), Indonesia (1994–1999), Vietnam (1990–2001), and Kazakhstan (2002–2018).

Joseph Soedradjad Djiwandono, an economist by training, was Governor of Bank Indonesia, the nation's central bank, from 1993 to 1998. Prior to his tenure at Bank Indonesia, Professor Djiwandono had helmed public office in different capacities, including as Bureau Head in the National Development Planning Agency, and State Minister of Trade. Among other current appointments, he is also a Professor at the S. Rajaratnam School of International Studies, a Graduate School of Nanyang Technological University, Singapore and Emeritus Professor of Economics, the University of Indonesia. Over the course of his illustrious career, Professor Djiwandono has authored various publications that are well received within academia and policy circles. He continues to contribute to public policy debate by writing op-ed pieces on current economic issues, particularly regional monetary policy and financial governance.

Kyung-wook Hur has been a career technocrat in the Ministry of Finance & Economy of Korea for over 34 years. He also worked as Senior Economist at both the IMF and the World Bank. He served as Secretary of National Agenda of the Office of President (Blue House), and First Vice Minister of the Ministry of Finance & Economy. Later he served as the Korean ambassador to the OECD (Paris) for three years. After retiring from Korean government, he worked as Visiting Professor at Policy Graduate School of KDI and Graduate School of International Studies in Seoul National University, while serving as Advisor at AMRO Advisory committee. Currently, he is a Senior Advisor at the law firm, BKL LLC and a Board member of Samsung Life Insurance Corp. He is also a chairman of the Brettonwoods Club, Korea. He has MBA from Stanford Graduate School of Business and a CFA.

Ginandjar Kartasasmita was an Indonesian policymaker and politician, having been Minister overseeing various portfolios under the Suharto and Habibie presidencies. He served as Minister of Mines and Energy (1988–1993), Minister of State for National Development Planning (1993–1998), and Coordinating Minister of the Economy, Finance, and Industry (1998–1999). During the 2000s, Professor Ginandjar ran for political office and became a member of the newly established Indonesian Senate (House of Regional

Representatives). He was also elected its first Chairman (2004–2009). Widely sought for his expertise, Professor Ginandjar continues to serve the public interest. He holds various appointments, including as Visiting Professor at National Graduate Institute for Policy Studies (GRIPS) and a member of the Japan International Cooperation Agency (JICA) International Advisory Board.

Haruhiko Kuroda was appointed Governor of the Bank of Japan in March 2013 after serving for eight years as President of the Asian Development Bank. Prior to his position at ADB, Mr. Kuroda was Special Adviser to the Cabinet of Prime Minister Koizumi, and was Professor at Hitotsubashi University in Tokyo from 2003 to 2005. During his career at Japan's Ministry of Finance from 1967 to 2003, Mr. Kuroda's responsibilities encompassed fields including international finance and tax policies. From 1999 to 2003, he represented the Ministry as Vice Minister of Finance for International Affairs at numerous international monetary conferences such as the G7 and G20 meetings. Mr. Kuroda holds a Bachelor of Arts in Law from The University of Tokyo, and a Master of Philosophy in Economics from University of Oxford.

Chang-yuel Lim is the President and CEO of KINTEX, Korea's largest convention and exhibition center. He has held several high-level official positions, including Vice Minister of the Economic Planning Board, Minister of Trade and Industry, Minister of Finance and Economy, and Deputy Prime Minister. Before assuming these positions, he also served on the Board of Directors of the IMF and World Bank for five years. During the Asian financial crisis back in 1997, when Korea was subsequently forced into an IMF bail-out program, as Finance Minister and Deputy Primer, he played a crucial role in steering the country out of the crisis by launching effective economic policies and measures, including allowing the foreign exchange and interest rates to fluctuate in line with market conditions and implementing strong banking, corporate, labour market restructurings. He was later elected governor of Gyeonggi Province, Korea's most populous province with 13 million residents. During his tenure, Gyeonggi Province recorded remarkable economic growth of more than 20% for two consecutive years and succeeded in attracting more than US$10.5 billion in foreign direct investment. Under his leadership, KINTEX was awarded the 2019 UFI Marketing Award, the tradeshow and exhibition industry's highest honor, making Korea the first Asian country recipient in the award's history. He obtained his bachelor's degree in Business Administration from Seoul National University, a master's degree in Economics from Williams College, and a Ph.D. in Business Administration from Myongji University.

Lin See-Yan is currently an independent strategic and financial consultant. Dr. Lin has a long and distinguished history of service with the Government of Malaysia and the private sector. He was Chairman/President and Chief Executive Officer of the Pacific Bank Group and for 14 years previously, the Deputy Governor of Bank Negara Malaysia. Among his current appointments are Member of the Prime Minister's Economic Council Working Group; Director, Monash University Malaysia Sdn Bhd; Chairman Emeritus, Harvard Graduate School Alumni Council at Harvard University in Cambridge (USA); President of Harvard Club of Malaysia and Economic Advisor to the Associated Chinese Chambers of Commerce & Industry Malaysia. After his undergraduate studies at the University of Malaya in Singapore, Dr Lin graduated with three advanced degrees from Harvard University, including a PhD in economics. He is also Malaysia's first UK Chartered Statistician.

A veteran diplomat, student of philosophy, and author of nine books, **Kishore Mahbubani** is currently a Distinguished Fellow at the Asia Research Institute, National University of Singapore. Mahbubani has dedicated five decades of his life to the public service. Mahbubani is also a former President of the UN Security Council (January 2001, May 2002) and the Founding Dean of the Lee Kuan Yew School of Public Policy (2004–2017). Mahbubani writes and speaks prolifically on the rise of Asia, geopolitics, and global governance. His books and articles in *The New York Times*, *The Washington Post*, *Financial Times*, and *Foreign Affairs* have earned him global recognition as "the muse of the Asian century." He was inducted into the American Academy of Arts and Sciences in October 2019. His latest books, *Has China Won?* and *The Asian 21st Century*, were released on March 31, 2020 and 2022. More information can be found on www.mahbubani.net.

Hubert Neiss was Director of Central Asia Department and Director of Asia and Pacific Department at the IMF from 1991–1997 and 1997–2000, respectively. He also assumed the posts of Division Chief, Assistant Director, Deputy Director of Asian Department, Resident Representative in Indonesia, and Economist, Senior Economist, Assistant Division Chief of European Department at the IMF. He was part-time Lecturer in Economics at the University of Maryland from 1968–1971. He was Economic Analyst at the Austrian Institute for Economic Research, Vienna, Austria from 1961–1966. He was Chairman of Asia and Senior Advisor of Asia at the Deutsche Bank from 2000–2003 and 2003–2009, respectively. He obtained a M.A. in Economics from the University of Kansas, USA and his doctor's degree in Economics and Business from Hochschule für Welthandel, Vienna, Austria. His decorations include Great Silver Order with Star to the Republic of Austria in 1999 and Order of Industrial Service Merit Silver Tower to the Republic of Korea in 2002.

Bandid Nijathaworn is presently Visiting Professor at the Hitotsubashi University, Tokyo, Japan. He is also member of the Council of trustees and the board of directors of Thailand Development Research Institute, one of the most prominent think tanks in Thailand. Dr. Bandid is a well-known economist with a long working experience in macroeconomic and financial issues, including at the IMF where he joined as a young professional in the IMF Economist program. His insights are frequently sought after, both within Thailand and the region. Dr. Bandid left the Bank of Thailand in November 2010, where he joined in 1990 and had held the positions of Deputy Governor for monetary stability and for financial stability since 2004, to work on improving Thailand's corporate governance and manage the country's private sector anti-corruption initiative under the capacity of President and CEO of the Thai Institute of Directors. From 2015 to 2019, he served on the AMRO Advisory Panel. He writes regularly for leading Thai business journals and newspapers on economic and governance issues. He frequently lectures and chairs high-level policy and investors meetings throughout Asia.

Ooi Sang Kuang is Chairman of the Board of Oversea-Chinese Banking Corporation Limited. Mr. Ooi was first appointed to the Board in February 2012 and last re-elected as a Director in May 2020. He assumed the role of Board Chairman in September 2014. He was Special Advisor in Bank Negara Malaysia until he retired on December 31, 2011. Prior to this, he was Deputy Governor and Member of the Board of Directors of Bank Negara Malaysia, from 2002 to 2010. He obtained Bachelor of Economics (Honors) from the University of Malaysia and Master of Arts (Development Finance) from Boston University, USA. He is both a Fellow Member of the Asian Institute of Chartered Bankers and a Fellow of the Singapore Institute of Directors.

Supavud Saicheua is currently advisor to Kiatnakin Phatra Financial Group following his retirement as Managing Director and Head of Research at Phatra Securities Plc. He joined Phatra Finance and Securities Plc (as it was then known) in 1994. It was during these 25 years at Phatra that he and his team lived through many tumultuous economic events including being on ground zero during Thailand's financial crisis in 1997. Prior to his work at Phatra, he worked at the Ministry of Foreign Affairs where he was posted to Washington D.C. as the Thai Embassy's Economic Officer from 1986–1990. In his varied positions at Thailand's Ministry of Foreign affairs from 1978–1994, he participated in bilateral and multilateral talks including the Uruguay Round of Multilateral Trade Negotiations. He earned his Ph.D. from the University of Hawaii at Manoa in 1984.

 **Eisuke Sakakibara** has been a President of Institute for Indian Economic Studies since April 2020. From 1997–1999, he was Japan's Vice Minister of Finance for International Affairs. Prior to that, he held many government positions including that of Director General of the International Finance Bureau; President of the Institute of Fiscal and Monetary Policy; Director of the Treasury Division, Financial Bureau, Ministry of Finance; and Special Advisor to the President, Japan Center for International Finance. He has also served as Associate Professor of Economics, Institute for Policy Science, at Saitama University and Visiting Associate Professor of Economics, Economics Department, at Harvard University. Mr. Sakakibara is the recipient of numerous awards, including the Taylor's Award from the University of Michigan, the Bintang Mahaputra Utama from the Government of The Republic of Indonesia and The Order of the Sacred Treasure, Gold and Silver Star, Government of Japan, April 2011. He holds a BA in Economics from Tokyo University and a PhD in Economics from the University of Michigan.

 **Nor Shamsiah** is the 9th Governor of Bank Negara Malaysia (BNM), assuming office on July 1, 2018. She chairs the Monetary Policy Committee, the Financial Stability Committee, and BNM's Board of Directors. She joined BNM in 1987 and has served in various areas including prudential regulations, financial intelligence and enforcement, talent management, finance, and supervision. She was involved in the financial sector resolution initiatives during the Asian financial crisis. As Deputy Governor, she also represented BNM in the Basel Committee on Banking Supervision and the Financial Action Task Force. Prior to her appointment as Governor, she also served as Assistant Director of the Monetary and Capital Markets Division of the IMF. Ms. Nor Shamsiah graduated from the University of South Australia with a Bachelor of Arts in Accountancy and is a Certified Practising Accountant.

Andrew Sheng is Distinguished Fellow of Asia Global Institute, The University of Hong Kong. He is Chief Adviser to China Banking and Insurance Regulatory Commission, and a member of the international advisory councils of China Investment Corporation, China Development Bank, China Securities Regulatory Commission, and Bank of Indonesia Institute. He also chairs the International Advisory Council of the George Town Institute of Open and Advanced Studies in Wawasan Open University, Penang, Malaysia. He was appointed Pro-Chancellor of Bristol University on January 1, 2020. He writes regularly on international finance and monetary economics, financial regulation, and global governance for Project Syndicate, AsiaNewsNet, and leading economic magazines and newspaper in China and Asia. His latest book is *Shadow Banking in China: An Opportunity for Financial Reform*" with Ng Chow Soon (2016, John Wiley).

Anoop Singh has been a member of the 15th Finance Commission of India, a constitutional body to recommend tax sharing between the Union and the States for the period 2021–2026. He is Distinguished Fellow at the Centre for Social and Economic Progress (CSEP, the Brookings India successor), and has recently been adjunct Professor at Georgetown University, Washington DC. Before that, at the International Monetary Fund, he was Director of the Asia and Pacific Department, Director of the Western Hemisphere Department, and Director of Special Operations. His additional work experience includes being Special Advisor to the Governor of the Reserve Bank of India. He has also been Managing Director and Head of Regulatory Affairs, Asia Pacific, for JP Morgan. Mr. Singh, an Indian national, holds degrees from the universities of Bombay, Cambridge, and the London School of Economics.

M.R.Chatu Mongol Sonakul completed degrees in Mechanical Sciences Tripos part I and Economics Tripos part II at Cambridge University. Upon returning to Thailand, he was recruited by the then Central Bank Governor, Dr. Puey Ungphakorn. He served as Director-General of the Fiscal Policy Office of the Ministry of Finance and tried to build a team for country development. After the position of the Permanent Secretary of Ministry of Finance and upon the Asian financial crisis, M.R.Chatu Mongol was transferred to become the Bank of Thailand Governor. M.R.Chatu Mongol introduced Inflation Targeting and restructured the Central Bank into three separate functions, Monetary Policy, Banking Supervision, and Payment Systems, each headed by the Central Bank Governor. He then left for the private sector and later on became Minister of Labour, where he arranged for a minimum wage increase.

Teh Kok Peng retired from GIC at the end of June 2011 and stayed on as Adviser for two years. Before his retirement, he was President of GIC Special Investments from April 1999 to June 2011. Prior to this, he was concurrently Deputy Managing Director of Monetary Authority of Singapore (MAS) and Deputy Managing Director of GIC. He began his career with the World Bank under the Young Professionals Program in Washington D.C. In 2015, Dr. Teh stepped down as Chairman of Ascendas Pte Ltd and as board member of the China International Capital Corporation, but has been appointed Senior Adviser at the latter. He was a board member of Overseas Chinese Banking Corporation, SembCorp Industries, and Taikang Life Insurance Co, Ltd. He also has served on the boards of the National University of Singapore and the S. Rajaratnam Endowment, and chaired the Advisory Board of the Asia Private Equity Institute at the Singapore Management University. Dr. Teh is Chairman of Azalea Asset Management and is a board member of Hollysys, Aviva- Singlife board, and Fullerton Health Corporation. He chairs the East Asian Institute, National University of Singapore. He is also a member of the International Advisory Board of CMC Corporation. He has joined CDPQ's Global Economic and Financial Advisory Council. He is a member of the Trilateral Commission.

Dr. Teh obtained First Class Honors in Economics at La Trobe University, Melbourne, and a Doctorate in Economics at Nuffield College, Oxford University, England. He attended the Advanced Management Program at the Harvard Business School in the fall of 1989.

Amando M. Tetangco, Jr. was the Governor of the Bangko Sentral ng Pilipinas (BSP) and Chairman of the Monetary Board for two six-year terms covering July 4, 2005 to July 2, 2017. He is credited with strengthening the country's ability to promote growth and a stable environment after the 2008 global financial crisis (GFC). Through BSP's monetary and banking policies, the Philippines achieved the convergence of high economic growth and low inflation, a banking system that earned global competitive ratings, and a strong external position from ample international reserves. He also institutionalized financial inclusion, literacy, and consumer protection in the BSP's policy agenda. A career central banker, he was Deputy Governor of the Banking Services Sector, Economic Research, and Treasury immediately prior to his appointment. He also served as Alternate Executive Director of the International Monetary Fund from 1992 to 1994. He currently serves as director in major Philippine corporations engaged in property development, telecommunications, energy, auto, healthcare, and credit information, and as trustee in foundations involved in education, environmental projects, and social services. He has an economics degree from the Ateneo de Manila University, cum laude, and earned his Master's in Public Policy and Administration (Development Economics) from the University of Wisconsin-Madison, Wisconsin, USA as a Central Bank Scholar.

Jim Walker is chief economist at Aletheia Capital Limited, an independent research platform. Before that he was the founder and chief economist at Asianomics Group. Between 1991 and 2007, he was the chief economist at CLSA Asia-Pacific Markets. From 1994 to 2004 (11 years), Dr. Walker achieved the 'best economist' ranking in the Asiamoney poll. In 1995, he wrote about the prospect of Asia being forced off its de facto dollar peg "within the next two-three years." The Asian crisis began in July 1997. In recent years, he is best known for forecasting the US 2007 downturn and financial sector meltdown in his series of 'Apocalypse' reports. He remains deeply skeptical of the prevailing wisdom in central banks' approach to monetary policy and the consequent emergence of zombie companies resulting from ultra-easy monetary policies. He holds a BA Honors degree and a PhD in economics from the University of Strathclyde, Glasgow.

After graduating from the University of Tokyo, **Hiroshi Watanabe** joined the Ministry of Finance (MOF) in 1972. Before he was appointed to Vice Minister of Finance for International Affairs in 2004, he occupied various senior positions including Director-General of International Bureau, Personal Secretary to the Minister of Finance, and Director positions of Secretarial Division, Property Tax Policy Division and Indirect Tax Policy Division at the Ministry of Finance. He also served for the JCIF on lease. After his retirement in 2007, he was a professor at the Graduate School of Commerce and Management of Hitotsubashi University. From 2008 to 2016, he served as CEO of Japan Bank for International Cooperation. Since October 2016, he has been the President of the Institute for International Monetary Affairs (IIMA).

Wei Benhua is a member of the Academic Committee of International Monetary Institute at the Renmin University of China. Mr. Wei is a veteran in international department of the People's Bank of China (PBC), successively serving as deputy director, director, deputy director-general, and director-general. From August 2003 to January 2008, he assumed the posts of Deputy Administrator of the State Administration of Foreign Exchange of China and Chairman of the periodical *China Forex*. From February 2008 to January 2010, he served as counsellor of the PBC. Mr. Wei has rich experience in the field of financial and economic policymaking, including serving as the Alternate Executive Director for China at the ADB, the Executive Director for China at the IMF, and the first Director of AMRO. Mr. Wei obtained his Bachelor's Degree in English Language from Inner Mongolia Normal University and a Master's Degree in International Finance from the Graduate School of PBC.

 **Zhu Guangyao** serves as Counsellor of the State Council of China since July 2018. From May 2010 to June 2018, he was Vice Minister of the Ministry of Finance (MOF) of China. From 2007 to 2010, he was Assistant Minister of MOF. From 2005 to 2007, he was Director General of International Affairs Department, MOF. From 2001 to 2004, he was Executive Director for China at the World Bank Group. From 1998 to 2001, he was Director General of International Affairs Department, MOF. From 1997 to 1998, he was Deputy Director General of Treasury Bond and Finance Department, MOF. From 1994 to 1996, he was Alternative Executive Director for China at the World Bank Group. From 1992 to 1994, he was Deputy Director and then Director in Department of the World Bank, MOF. From 1988 to 1992, he was Secretary of the Secretariat (at Deputy Director level) at the Research Institute for Fiscal Science, MOF. He obtained Master of Economics from the Research Institute for Fiscal Science and Bachelor of Economics from the Beijing Technology and Business University.

List of Contributors

Iwan J. Azis is Professor of Emerging Markets in the Dyson School of Applied Economics and Management, Cornell University, and was the Director of Graduate Studies, Regional Science program (2005–2010). He is also Visiting Professor at the University of Indonesia. Awarded "Distinguished Scholar in Regional Science, Financial Economics, and Economic Modeling," his research focuses on the interlink between macro-financial economics, social-institutional issues, and spatial inequalities in emerging markets. He has been advising the Indonesian Central Bank and the Deposit Insurance Corporation on their research, and is a member of the International Advisory Panel of the Asian Infrastructure Investment Bank. He has published several books, including *Crisis, Complexity and Conflict* (Emerald, 2009), *Managing Elevated Risk* (Springer, 2015), *Mathematical Modeling For Economic Analysis* (UIP, 2018), *Regional Economics: Fundamental Concepts, Policies, and Institutions* (World Scientific, 2020), and *Periphery and Small Ones Matter: Interplay of Policy and Social Capital* (Springer, 2021). Among his recent articles is "Coping With the Dangerous Component of Capital Flows" in *Critical Junctures in Mobile Capital* (Cambridge University Press, 2018).

Jinho Choi is Deputy Group Head and Senior Economist at ASEAN+3 Macroeconomic Research Office (AMRO) in Singapore. Prior to joining AMRO, Dr. Choi worked for the Bank of Korea from December 1999 to March 2016 as economist and senior economist in the Research Department, Monetary Policy Department, and International Department. At the Bank, Dr. Choi conducted a wide range of policy-oriented research. His research articles have been published in several international journals, such as *Quantitative Economics*, *Economic Modelling*, and *Journal of Applied Econometrics*. He holds a Ph.D. in Economics from Indiana University at Bloomington, USA, and a Master in Applied Economics from the University of Michigan at Ann Arbor, USA. Dr. Choi graduated with M.B.A. in Finance and B.A. in Economics from Seoul National University.

Haihong Gao is Professor and Director of the Research Center for International Finance, Institute of World Economics and Politics, Chinese Academy of Social Sciences (CASS). She is the lead fellow of CASS' project "China and International Financial System." She serves as standing council director of China Society of World Economy and of China Society for Finance and Banking. She joined CASS in 1989. Before taking on the present post, she was visiting scholar at University of California at Davis, United States, and later visiting research fellow at Institute of Southeast Asian Studies, Singapore. She has been appointed as chief economist of Network of East Asian Think-Tanks China Working Group, and has led numerous projects sponsored by China's Ministry of Finance, People's Bank of China, and China's National Social Science Fund. Her authored books include: *A Changing International Monetary System: Theory and Chinese Practice* (2021), *G20 and Global Economic Governance* (2016), and *The Renminbi Exchange Rate: Policy Options and Risk Prevention from Global Perspective* (2008).

Hans Genberg is Professor of Economics and Senior Director of Central Banking and Finance Programs at the Asia School of Business (ASB) in Kuala Lumpur, Malaysia. He joined ASB on July 1, 2019, after having served as the Executive Director of the South East Asian Central Banks (SEACEN) Centre, also in Kuala Lumpur, since July 1, 2015. Prior to that, he had been an Adviser to the Centre since March 3, 2014. Prior to joining the SEACEN Centre, Dr. Genberg was Assistant Director at the Independent Evaluation Office of the International Monetary Fund after having been Executive Director, Research at the Hong Kong Monetary Authority (HKMA).

Before joining the HKMA, he was Professor of International Economics at the Graduate Institute of International Studies in Geneva, Switzerland. A Swedish national, Dr. Genberg holds a Ph.D. degree in Economics from the University of Chicago.

Joon-Ho Hahm is Professor of International Economics and Finance at the Graduate School of International Studies, Yonsei University. During 2014–2018, he was a Member of the Monetary Policy Board of the Bank of Korea. Dr. Hahm began his academic career as an Assistant Professor of Economics at the University of California, Santa Barbara, and was later a Research Fellow at the Korea Development Institute before joining the Yonsei faculty. He has been a Specialist Member of the Republic of Korea's Presidential Commission for Financial Reform, a Listing Committee Member for the Korea Exchange, and a Non-Executive Board of Director Member of the Korea Deposit Insurance Corporation, Woori Bank, Prudential Asset Management, and NH Life Insurance. He has served in a variety of advisory and consultative roles for the Korean government, and for international organizations including the World Bank and the Asian Development Bank. Dr. Hahm received his MBA and Ph.D. from Columbia University's Graduate School of Business. He has written extensively in the fields of economics and finance, with his academic articles having appeared in numerous internationally renowned journals including the *Journal of Economic Dynamics and Control, The Review of Economics and Statistics*, and the *Journal of Money, Credit and Banking*.

Han Beomhee has been serving as Group Head of CMIM Support Team at AMRO since October 1, 2016. His expertise include the issues of Chiang Mai Initiative Multilateralisation (CMIM), ASEAN+3 financial cooperation, regional and global financial safety net, treaty, and international and administrative law. His main job is to provide technical support to ASEAN+3 members in stepping up the CMIM as an effective and reliable regional financial safety net in the region. Before taking up the current position, he served as a legal advisor at AMRO since 2012. Before joining AMRO, he had worked for the Bank of Korea since 1999.

Hyeon-Wook Kim is Professor at Korea Development Institute (KDI) School of Public Policy and Management. Before he joined KDI in 2000, Dr. Kim served as an economist and an advisor to the Monetary Policy Committee and a secretary to the governor of the Bank of Korea from 1989. In 2011, he moved to the private sector and served as a Senior Director and Vice President at SK Group. Thereafter, he returned to KDI in 2017 and served as the Director of Macroeconomic Research, Director of Financial Policy Research, and Director of Macroeconomic Analysis and Forecasting. His areas of specialization and research interests include macroeconomics, international finance and trade, financial regulation, and foreign exchange market analysis. He has written numerous papers on the Korean banking industry, bank capital adequacy, monetary policy, and so on. As a graduate of Seoul National University, Dr. Kim earned a bachelor's degree in economics. Subsequently, he was awarded an M.A. and a Ph.D. in economics from Columbia University.

Hyungji Kim is Economist at the Bank of Korea. She received a Bachelor's and a Master's degree in economics from Seoul National University. She is currently studying at the PhD program in the Department of Economics at Seoul National University. She is interested in monetary policies, international capital flows, and the housing market.

Soyoung Kim is Professor at the Department of Economics, Seoul National University. He holds a PhD from Yale University. He was involved with various institutions like the IMF, BIS, ADB, ADBI, Bank of Spain, HKIMR, National Economic Advisory Council, Bank of Korea, CEPR, the Korea Chamber of Commerce and Industry, the Korean Ministry of Strategy and Finance, the Korean Ministry of Health and Welfare, Financial Services Commission in Korea, Statistics Korea, HKUST, Princeton University, University of Illinois, and USC under various designations. He received the Arnould O. Beckman Research Award, Tae Sung Kim Research Award, Chung Ram Research Award, NEAR Research Award, Maeil Business Newspaper

Economist Award, and Korean Economy Research Award. He was listed as one of the 100 most promising talents of Korea by Donga-Daily Newspaper. He is the president of Korea KAEA and Korea IEFS.

Lam San Ling is currently Adjunct Professor at the Singapore Management University (School of Economics). Formerly an Executive Director at the Monetary Authority of Singapore (MAS), she headed various departments including Macroprudential Surveillance and Capital Markets Intermediaries Supervision. Her central bank experience spanned the Asian financial crisis to the global financial crisis and beyond. She has also consulted for the International Monetary Fund (IMF) and the ASEAN+3 Macroeconomic Research Office (AMRO). She obtained her Bachelor of Social Science (First Class Honours) from the National University of Singapore and PhD in Economics from Harvard University.

Guanie Lim is Assistant Professor at the National Graduate Institute for Policy Studies (GRIPS), Japan. His main research interests are comparative political economy, production network analysis, and international capital flows. He is also interested in broader development issues within Asia, especially those of China, Vietnam, and Malaysia. His latest monograph — *The Political Economy of Growth in Vietnam: Between States and Markets* (published by Routledge) — details the catching-up experience of Vietnam since its 1986 *doi moi* (renovation) reforms.

Wilhelmina C. Mañalac was the Assistant Governor of the International Monetary Affairs and Surveillance Sub-Sector of the Bangko Sentral ng Pilipinas. She also worked as Assistant to the Executive Director and Alternate Executive Director of the International Monetary Fund (IMF) in Washington D.C. from January 1999–June 2001 and November 2006–November 2008, respectively. Ms. Mañalac has conducted lectures and seminars as well as published papers on various topics. She has also significantly contributed to the attainment of capital account liberalization in the region by serving as Chair of the Association of Southeast Asian Nations Working Committee on Capital Account Liberalization. Ms. Mañalac graduated cum laude with a Bachelor of Science degree in Statistics from the University of the Philippines and Master of Arts in Economics from the Ateneo de Manila University.

Jayant Menon is Visiting Senior Fellow at ISEAS-Yusof Ishak Institute. Dr. Menon's work focuses on trade and development in the Asian region. His last post was at the Asian Development Bank (ADB) as Lead Economist in the Office of the Chief Economist. He was also at the ADB Institute in Tokyo from 2005 to 2008. He started work as an academic in Australia, spending almost a decade at the Centre of Policy Studies at Monash University at its original campus in Clayton, Melbourne. He has also worked at the University of Melbourne, Victoria University, and the American University in Washington, D.C. He holds adjunct appointments with the Australian National University, University of Nottingham, United Kingdom, and IDEAS, Malaysia. He has authored/edited 15 books, 40 book chapters, and 80 articles in peer-reviewed journals.

Yoichi Nemoto is Professor of the Asian Public Policy Program, School of International and Public Policy at Hitotsubashi University. Dr. Nemoto was Director of the ASEAN+3 Macroeconomic Research Office (AMRO) between 2012 and 2016, where he contributed to the work of establishing the ASEAN+3 region's macroeconomic surveillance office, building up AMRO's surveillance capacity, and transforming it into an international organization. Dr. Nemoto was Counsellor to AMRO between 2011 and 2012. Prior to AMRO, Dr. Nemoto held other senior positions within Japan's Ministry of Finance, including Deputy Vice-Minister of Finance, Director of Regional Finance Co-operation, and Director of Foreign Exchange Markets. Between 2002 and 2004, Dr. Nemoto was a Visiting Fellow at Princeton University's Centre of International Studies and was requested to give a speech on the ASEAN+3 Chiang Mai Initiative that was about to take shape. Dr. Nemoto graduated with a Bachelor of Laws (LL.B.) degree from the University of Tokyo and holds a Ph.D. in Public Policy from Harvard University.

Freddy Orchard has been Director of economics at the Monetary Authority of Singapore (1995–1997) and GIC (1989–1999). He is the author of *Bold Vision: The Untold Story of Singapore's Reserves and its Sovereign Wealth Fund.*

Sukudhew (Sukhdave) Singh is former Deputy Governor of the Central Bank of Malaysia and a former independent director of Khazanah Nasional Berhad, a sovereign wealth fund of the Government of Malaysia. He spent over 30 years at the Central Bank, rising through the ranks, and was appointed deputy governor in 2013, a position he held until 2017. As deputy governor, he was a member of the bank's Monetary Policy Committee, Financial Stability Committee, and Board of Directors. Other positions he has held include being a director of the South East Asian Central Banks (SEACEN), a member of the Investment Panel of the Employees Provident Fund, and the Chairman of the Board of Payments Network Malaysia Sdn Bhd (PayNet).

Faith Pang Qiying currently holds the position of Senior Strategy & Coordination Officer at AMRO. Her responsibilities include strategy and policy planning, internal coordination, stakeholder engagement, and institutional relations and strategic partnerships. Ms. Pang has spent a decade working to promote ASEAN+3 financial collaboration. Before joining AMRO, Ms. Pang worked in the Singapore Ministry of Finance (International Relations Department) from 2011–2014. While in the Ministry of Finance, Ms. Pang travelled extensively in the ASEAN+3 region to promote greater regional financial cooperation. Ms. Pang studied in the University of Toronto where she obtained her Bachelor's degree in International Relations (Honours with Distinction), with the help of a Shaw Foundation Scholarship (2005-2009). She also minored in cinema studies and classical civilizations as an undergraduate. In 2010, she graduated with a Masters of Arts in Political Science under the Collaborative Master's Program in Asia-Pacific Studies from the Munk Centre at the University of Toronto.

Chalongphob Sussangkarn is currently Distinguished Fellow of the Thailand Development Research Institute (TDRI), a private non-profit policy research institute based in Bangkok. He obtained his Bachelor's degree through Ph.D. in economics from Cambridge University, UK. After obtaining his Ph.D., he taught in the department of economics of the University of California, Berkeley for 2 years (1977–79), then worked at the research department of the World Bank in Washington D.C. for 6 years (1979–1985). He returned to Thailand to join TDRI in 1985. Dr. Chalongphob was appointed President of TDRI in 1996, a post he held until he was appointed Thailand's Minister of Finance in March 2007. After ending his duties as Minister of Finance in February 2008, he rejoined TDRI. Dr. Chalongphob was a member of the Advisory Panel of AMRO for 4 years between 2011 and 2015, and chaired the Panel for 2 years during that period. In 2004, Dr. Chalongphob was awarded the National Outstanding Researcher Award for Economics from the National Research Council of Thailand.

Shinji Takagi is Distinguished Research Professor at the Asian Growth Research Institute, Kitakyushu, Japan and Professor Emeritus of Economics at Osaka University. After obtaining his PhD in economics from the University of Rochester, he worked as an economist at the International Monetary Fund from 1983 to 1990, when he joined the economics faculty at Osaka University. He is a specialist in international monetary economics and the author or coauthor of nearly 200 publications, including *Conquering the Fear of Freedom: Japanese Exchange Rate Policy since 1945* (Oxford: Oxford University Press, 2015). His professional experience has spanned more than 60 countries and territories, covering Asia-Pacific, Africa, Latin America, the Middle East, and Europe. Professor Takagi served as Advisor (2002–2006) and Assistant Director (2013–2018) at the IMF's Independent Evaluation Office, where he managed projects to evaluate, among other things, the IMF's engagement in the Asian, Brazilian, Argentine, and euro area crises.

Kimi Xu Jiang is Economist in the Surveillance Group at the ASEAN+3 Macroeconomic Research Office (AMRO). Before joining AMRO, he worked at the European Stability Mechanism (ESM), mainly focusing on monitoring and analysis of emerging risks to euro area sovereign debt markets, including analysis of sovereign market access, the European Central Bank's monetary policy, and market data. He started his career as a policy advisor at the financial market division of the Dutch Central Bank, working in the areas of monetary operations and financial market intelligence. He holds a Research Master and Bachelor in Economics from Tilburg University, the Netherlands, and is currently pursuing a part-time Ph.D. in Economics at Vrije Universiteit Amsterdam, the Netherlands.

Satoru Yamadera is Advisor at the Economic Research and Regional Cooperation Department at the Asian Development Bank (ADB). Mr. Yamadera has been serving as the Secretariat of the Asian Bond Markets Initiative (ABMI) of ASEAN+3 since 2014. He has vast experiences in capital market development, payment systems, fintech, cybersecurity, and regional financial cooperation. Currently, he leads the ASEAN+3 Bond Market Forum (ABMF), a common platform to foster standardization and harmonization of the bond markets. He also leads the Cross-Border Settlement Infrastructure Forum (CSIF) to create cross-border linkages among the central banks and central securities depositories. Mr. Yamadera has over 25 years of professional experience in central banking including research, banking supervision, and financial cooperation at the Bank of Japan. Mr. Yamadera obtained his BA in Law, Keio University, Japan; M.Sc in Public Administration and Public Policy from the London School of Economics and Political Science, United Kingdom; and M.Sc in Systems Management from Tsukuba University, Japan.

Index

CPSIA information can be obtained
at www.ICGtesting.com
Printed in the USA
JSHW042158110622
26918JS00002B/7

9 789811 253256